THE LAW OF CIVIL PROCEDURE

CASES AND MATERIALS

Fifth Edition

■ ■ ■

Joel Wm. Friedman

Jack M. Gordon Professor of Procedural Law and Jurisdiction
Tulane University School of Law

Michael G. Collins

Joseph M. Hartfield Professor
University of Virginia School of Law

AMERICAN CASEBOOK SERIES®

WEST
ACADEMIC
PUBLISHING

American Casebook Series is a trademark registered in the U.S. Patent and Trademark Office.

© West, a Thomson business, 2002, 2006
© 2010 Thomson Reuters
© 2013 LEG, Inc. d/b/a West Academic Publishing
© 2017 LEG, Inc. d/b/a West Academic
  444 Cedar Street, Suite 700
  St. Paul, MN 55101
  1-877-888-1330

Printed in the United States of America

ISBN: 978-1-68328-209-9

TO

VIVIANE SHELI, ALEXA, CHLOE & MAX
JWF

ANNIE
MGC

PREFACE TO THE FIFTH EDITION

Most professors who teach the basic course in civil procedure would agree that first year students often find it to be the most difficult and/or unapproachable course in the first-year curriculum. This is to be expected. Unlike the material covered in such first year courses as torts, contracts, property, criminal law, and constitutional law, the subjects addressed in the first year civil procedure course are foreign to their previous experience and are, for the most part, issues of concern only to lawyers. But they eventually recognize that the issues presented in the civil procedure course have a dramatic and profound impact on a wide range of contemporary transactions and events.

The first edition of this casebook was drafted expressly with the first year student in mind and was not intended to serve as both a casebook and hornbook. We continue that philosophy in this fifth edition. While this new edition keeps pace with recent developments — particularly in the areas of venue and subject matter jurisdiction, pleading, personal jurisdiction, and class actions, we have tried to avoid the temptation to provide the sort of encyclopedic presentation of issues that would appeal to the scholarly bent of law professors. Instead, we have tried to organize the material in a way that is approachable and helpful to students. To that end, we begin each chapter and subsidiary section with a textual explanation to provide the context in which the relevant issues arise and to highlight what those issues are. We also believe it is helpful to the pedagogic experience to offer case opinions that raise these issues in the context of contemporary problems. Consequently, aside from the expected assortment of foundational Supreme Court opinions, we have carefully chosen more modern cases that pose the relevant questions in a contemporary setting. We have also provided a rich collection of hypothetical problems to accompany each set of materials to give students with the opportunity to test their understanding of the cases, statutes, and rules of procedure that they encounter.

While we have tried to make the materials as approachable as possible, we were alert to the need to avoid oversimplification. In that regard, while we have edited all of the principal cases, we have chosen not to attempt to reduce each opinion to a few conclusory paragraphs. Part of the journey for first year students is to learn how to appreciate the context in which statements of law are made so that they can gain a deeper and more refined understanding of the court's decision.

We appreciate the reality that law schools differ in the number of semesters and number of credit hours they devote to the subject of civil procedure. With that in mind, this book was designed to cover the waterfront so that it could be used by those who, like the two of us, teach a single semester four credit hour course, or by others who teach a five or six hour course over an entire academic year. And by careful editing and, we hope, judicious use of explanatory material, we have been able to limit the length of the book to a manageable size. We hope you agree. Finally, this Edition has taken account of cases decided before May 29, 2017. Relevant cases decided thereafter will be included in an annual on-line Teachers' Update.

J.W.F.
New Orleans, La.

M.G.C.
Charlottesville, Va.

June 1, 2017

ACKNOWLEDGMENTS

We wish to thank the following authors and copyright holders for permitting the inclusion of portions of their publications in this book.

Edwards, Harry T., "Alternative Dispute Resolution: Panacea or Anathema?", Harvard Law Review, Vol. 99, pp. 676-82 (1986). Reprinted with permission of Judge Edwards and the Harvard Law Review Association.

Gauvey, Susan K., "ADR's Integration in the Federal Court System," Maryland Bar Journal, Vol. 34-APR, pp. 39-43 (2001). Reprinted with permission of Judge Gauvey and the Maryland Bar Journal.

Perritt, Jr., Henry H., "Dispute Resolution in Cyberspace: Demand for New Forms of ADR," Ohio State Journal on Dispute Resolution, Vol. 15, pp. 676,684-92,694,702 (2000). Reprinted with permission of Dean Perritt and the Ohio State Journal on Dispute Resolution.

"Developments in the Law, 'The Paths of Civil Litigation,'" Harvard Law Review, Vol. 113, pp. 1851-62 (2000). Reprinted with permission of the Harvard Law Review.

Leiberman, Jethro K. & Henry, James F., "Lessons from the Alternative Dispute Resolution Movement," University of Chicago Law Review, Vol. 53, pp. 425-35 (1986). Reprinted with permission of the University of Chicago Law Review.

We would also like to acknowledge Jonathan Landers for his contributions to the first edition of this book.

SUMMARY OF CONTENTS

TABLE OF CONTENTS

TABLE OF CASES

Principal cases are in italic type. Non-principal cases are in roman type. References are to pages.

THE LAW OF CIVIL PROCEDURE

CASES AND MATERIALS

Fifth Edition

CHAPTER 1

An Introduction to the Procedural System

Many students find Civil Procedure to be their most daunting first year course. The concepts are new and unfamiliar, and it is hard to get a mental picture of what is happening, where it is happening, who is doing what, and what the various pieces of paper look like. Even the terminology is strange. But take heart: Prior generations of law students have felt the same way and somehow they made it through. And you will too.

But be patient. The learning process is slow and plodding, and all the subjects are interrelated and overlapping. You won't see real results until the end.

Some tips along the way: Like it or not, this course involves statutes and rules. You have to read them — more than once. Try to get used to using the terminology by talking with other students or, heaven forbid, the professor.

Finally, try to think tactically. A lawsuit is an adversary process, and the quality of lawyering does make a difference (if it didn't, you wouldn't have to take this course). From beginning to end, a lawsuit will involve choices — whom to sue, where to sue, what claims to make, how to get information, whether to enforce procedural rights in the court, what issues to press at trial, and what to do if it's not going well. Also, at many junctures, there will be other types of choices for resolving the dispute — nonjudicial decisionmaking, settlement, or dismissal. Although theoretically, all of these decisions are those of the client, the client is usually ill equipped to make them and will look to you for advice. Once decisions are made, it may be difficult or impossible to reverse course and start down another route.

This chapter takes you through the basic procedural stages of a lawsuit. As you will see, the tactical choices arise before you even file your case.

SECTION A. WHERE CAN THE CASE BE BROUGHT?

Consider this situation: Henry and Wanda, husband and wife, had planned a "second honeymoon" in Las Vegas. They read various travel brochures and, being modern folks, checked the Internet and booked a room at the Carnival Hotel. While at the hotel, Wanda suffered serious injuries when the "Gambling Monster," a new video/gambling game, fell down on top of her. Wanda is now back home in New Jersey and consults you about obtaining legal redress.

Initially, you face tactical issues of whom to sue and where. Potential defendants include Carnival Hotel, Inc., a Nevada corporation with its principal place of business in Nevada, and GM, Inc., manufacturer of the Gambling Monster, an Iowa corporation with its principal place of business in Iowa.

To decide where to sue, you must identify the various possibilities. What state *can* you file in? What state *should* you file in? Should you file in a state or a federal court?

1. STRUCTURE OF THE JUDICIAL SYSTEM

Both the states and the federal government operate court systems. Each state operates its own court system, and the federal government operates a "national" system with one or more branches in each state. We call each branch of the federal system a "district," and each state is divided into one to four federal districts. For example, Nevada and New Jersey each constitute a single district; there are two districts in Iowa; and there are four districts in California.

To decide the possibilities for Wanda's action, we must determine which courts have subject matter jurisdiction, personal jurisdiction, and venue.

Subject matter jurisdiction relates to the power of the court to hear a particular matter. State courts are courts of "general jurisdiction," which means they can presumptively hear all cases unless state law precludes a particular category of cases. Federal courts are courts of limited jurisdiction — they can hear only cases that they are authorized to hear. That authorization is found in two places: Article III, section 2 of the Constitution states the outer limits of jurisdiction. If a case is not within Article III, section 2, it can't be heard in the federal courts. However, not all cases within Article III, section 2 can be heard in the federal courts. Instead, federal courts can only hear cases that they are also authorized to hear by statute, so one must find a federal statute authorizing jurisdiction. Two of the most common bases of subject matter jurisdiction are 28 U.S.C. §§1331 and 1332 — cases arising under the Constitution, laws and treaties of the United States, and cases between citizens of different states.

Personal jurisdiction requires that a state have a sufficient connection with or power over the defendant to exercise jurisdiction. In former times, a state could only exercise personal jurisdiction over a defendant who could be physically seized, and later, physically served with process, within the state. More modern cases have expanded this concept to allow for personal jurisdiction over defendants when there is a sufficient connection between the defendant, the underlying lawsuit, and the state. If the sufficient connection exists, then both state courts of that state and federal courts within that state have personal jurisdiction. Note that the state is not required to have personal jurisdiction over the plaintiff as opposed to the defendant. By filing suit in a state court (or a federal court in a state), the plaintiff effectively agrees (submits) to the jurisdiction of that court.

Venue means place of trial. It is an attempt to allocate judicial business to courts that have some connection with the parties and the dispute. Both federal courts and state courts have rules of venue. In recent years, however, concepts of proper personal jurisdiction have begun to overlap with venue statutes. 28 U.S.C. §1391 generally sets forth the venue requirements in the federal courts.

2. APPLYING THE CONCEPTS

In Wanda's case, let us assume that she cannot file the case in a state that has no connection with any of the parties or the matters in dispute. This assumption is generally, but not always, true, but it helps winnow down our choices from 50 states to 3: Nevada, Iowa and New Jersey (remember, of course, that even this assumption may change if there is another potential defendant — e.g., Indo Co., a New York corporation, that designed and tested the Gambling Monster, or Saylor Co., an Illinois corporation, that sold it to the Carnival Hotel). In addition, we may assume that a state always has jurisdiction over a party who is a citizen of that state — here, Nevada would have jurisdiction over Carnival; Iowa over GM Inc. Even so, other states might have jurisdiction over them as well.

One tactical decision is whether to sue both Carnival and GM. Even at this early stage of your career, you should be able to identify some considerations. If Wanda decides to sue only Carnival, where can she sue? Presumably, in either New Jersey or Nevada. Where do you think she would prefer to sue and why? Assuming you picked New Jersey, *can* she sue there? That question is addressed by the case that follows. If she cannot, and if she must sue in Nevada, may she invoke the jurisdiction of a federal court in that state, as opposed to a state court? What difference should it make? That question is addressed in Mas v. Perry, which you can read after the decision below.

Decker v. Circus Circus Hotel

United States District Court, District of New Jersey, 1999.
49 F. Supp. 2d 743.

WALLS, DISTRICT JUDGE.

This matter comes before the Court on the motion of the defendant, Circus Circus Hotel, to dismiss the complaint of Janice and Robert Decker for lack of personal jurisdiction and for improper venue pursuant to Federal Rules of Civil Procedure 12(b)(2), 12(b)(3), and to quash service of process, or, in the alternative, to transfer this action to the United States District Court for the District of Nevada pursuant to 28 U.S.C. §1404(a). The Court decides this motion without oral argument pursuant to Rule 78 of the Federal Rules of Civil Procedure. This action will be transferred to the District of Nevada pursuant to 28 U.S.C. §1406(a).

BACKGROUND

The plaintiffs, Janice and Robert Decker, are New Jersey residents who have brought a personal injury action against the defendant Circus Circus Hotel, a Nevada corporation with its only place of business in Las Vegas, Nevada, for injuries arising from an alleged negligent condition on the defendant's premises.

This complaint was originally filed in the Superior Court of New Jersey, Law Division, Morris County alleging negligence and seeking recovery for personal injuries. However, the defendant removed the action to this Court. In lieu of answering the complaint the defendant filed a motion to dismiss the complaint for lack of personal jurisdiction, pursuant to Federal Rules of Civil Procedure 12(b)(2) and 12(b)(3), and to quash or, in the alternative, to transfer venue to the United States District Court for the District of Nevada.

DISCUSSION

A. Applicable Law

Pursuant to Federal Rule of Civil Procedure 4(e), federal "district courts have personal jurisdiction over non-resident defendants to the extent authorized under the law of the forum state in which the district court sits." See Sunbelt Corp. v. Noble, Denton & Associates, Inc., 5 F.3d 28, 31 (3d Cir. 1993). New Jersey's long arm statute provides for personal jurisdiction as far as is permitted by the Fourteenth Amendment to the United States Constitution. See N.J. Ct. R. 4:4-4; Carteret Savings Bank, FA v. Shushan, 746 F.2d 141, 145 (3d Cir. 1992); DeJames v. Magnificence Carriers, Inc., 654 F.2d 280, 284 (3d Cir. 1981). Therefore, the question of whether this Court has jurisdiction over the defendant is determined by federal constitutional law. See Mesalic v. Fiberfloat Corp., 897 F.2d 696, 698 (3d Cir. 1990).

The Fourteenth Amendment permits a state to exercise jurisdiction over an out-of-state defendant only where "the defendant purposefully avails itself of the privilege of conducting activities within the forum State, thus invoking the benefits and protections of its laws." Burger King Corp. v. Rudzewicz, 471 U.S. 462, 475, 105 S.Ct. 2174, 2184, 85 L.Ed.2d 528 (1985) (quoting Hanson v. Denckla, 357 U.S. 235, 253, 78 S.Ct. 1228, 1239, 2 L.Ed.2d 1283 (1958)). It is the burden of the plaintiff to prove that the defendant has purposefully availed himself of the forum state.

To prove that the defendant has purposefully availed himself of that state, a plaintiff may rely upon a defendant's specific contacts with the forum state. Personal jurisdiction pursuant to such contacts is known as specific jurisdiction. Specific jurisdiction is invoked when a claim is related to or arises out of the defendant's contacts with the forum. See, Helicopteros Nacionales de Colombia, S.A. v. Hall, 466 U.S. 408, 416, 104 S.Ct. 1868, 1873, 80 L.Ed.2d 404 (1984); Dollar Sav. Bank v. First Security Bank of Utah, 746 F.2d 208, 211 (3d Cir. 1984). A court must first determine whether the defendant had the minimum contacts with the forum necessary for the defendant to have "reasonably anticipate[d] being haled into court there." World-Wide Volkswagen Corporation v. Woodson, 444 U.S. 286, 297, 100 S.Ct. 559, 62 L.Ed.2d 490 (1980) (citations omitted). What constitutes minimum contacts varies with the "quality and nature of defendant's activity." Hanson, 357 U.S. at 253, 78 S.Ct. at 1240. In assessing the sufficiency of minimum contacts for personal jurisdiction, the court must focus on the "relationship among the defendant, the forum and the litigation." Keeton v. Hustler, 465 U.S. 770, 104 S.Ct. 1473, 79 L.Ed.2d 790 (1984). Otherwise stated, there must be at least "a single deliberate contact" with the forum state that relates to the cause of action.

United States Golf Ass'n v. United States Amateur Golf Ass'n, 690 F. Supp. 317, 320 (D.N.J. 1988). The unilateral acts of the plaintiff, however, will not amount to minimum contacts. *Helicopteros*, 466 U.S. at 414, 104 S.Ct. 1868; *Hanson*, 357 U.S. at 253, 78 S.Ct. at 1240.

Second, assuming minimum contacts have been established, a court may inquire whether "the assertion of personal jurisdiction would comport with 'fair play and substantial justice.'" Burger King Corporation v. Rudzewicz, 471 U.S. 462, 476, 105 S.Ct. 2174, 85 L.Ed.2d 528 (1985) (quoting International Shoe Company v. Washington, 326 U.S. 310, 320, 66 S.Ct. 154, 90 L.Ed. 95 (1945)); Pennzoil Products Co. v. Colelli & Assoc., Inc., 149 F.3d 197, 201 (3d Cir. 1998). For personal jurisdiction to comport with "fair play and substantial justice," it must be reasonable to require the defendant to defend the suit in the forum state. See World-Wide Volkswagen, Corp. v. Woodson, 444 U.S. 286, 292, 100 S.Ct. 559, 564, 62 L.Ed.2d 490 (1980). To determine reasonableness, a court considers the following factors: the burden on the defendant, the forum state's interest in adjudicating the dispute, the plaintiff's interest in obtaining convenient and effective relief, the interstate judicial system's interest in obtaining the most efficient resolution of controversies, and the shared interest of the several States in furthering substantive social policies. Id. Only in "rare cases [do the] minimum requirements inherent in the concept of fair play and substantial justice . . . defeat the reasonableness of jurisdiction even [though] the defendant has purposefully engaged in forum activities." Asahi Metal Industry Co., Ltd. v. Superior Court of Cal., Solano County, 480 U.S. 102, 116, 107 S.Ct. 1026, 1034, 94 L.Ed.2d 92 (1987) (internal quotation marks omitted).

If the plaintiff cannot establish specific jurisdiction, a court may exercise general jurisdiction over the defendant if the defendant has maintained "continuous and systematic contacts" with the forum state. *Helicopteros*, 466 U.S. at 416, 104 S.Ct. at 1873. To establish general jurisdiction the plaintiff must show significantly more than mere minimum contacts with the forum state. Provident Nat'l Bank v. California Fed. Sav. & Loan Ass'n, 819 F.2d 434, 437 (3d Cir. 1987). Moreover, the facts required to establish general jurisdiction must be "extensive and [pervasive]." Reliance Steel Prods. v. Watson, Ess, Marshall & Enggas, 675 F.2d 587, 589 (3d Cir. 1982) [(quoting Compagnie des Bauxites de Guinea v. Ins. Co. of North America, 651 F.2d 877, 890 (3d Cir. 1981) (Gibbons, J., dissenting).]

B. Personal Jurisdiction

Plaintiffs allege that the defendant Circus Circus Hotel has sufficient contacts with New Jersey to allow this Court to exercise in personam jurisdiction over the defendant and points to the following facts: (1) the defendant has had one television advertisement which consisted of a single spot that aired on a national cable network in the New York-New Jersey metropolitan area; (2) the defendant advertises in national magazines and newspapers such as USA Today, People Magazine, and various other travel magazines which are distributed nationwide; (3) the defendant mails promotional material to former guests in New Jersey and those New Jersey citizens who directly request information from it; (4) the defendant has an Internet site where customers can make reservations; (5) the defendant's sister corporation, Circus Circus New Jersey, Inc. has filed for a gaming license with the New Jersey Casino Control Commission; and (6) the defendant's parent corporation, Circus Circus Enterprises, Inc., has filed a breach of contract suit in New Jersey. The defendant claims that these contacts are too tenuous for this Court to exercise specific or general personal jurisdiction over the defendant. The defendant further argues that specific jurisdiction over it is unwarranted because this cause of action did not arise out of nor is it related to any of the defendant's tenuous contacts to New Jersey. General jurisdiction is also unwarranted, the defendant contends, because the actions of the defendant's parent or subsidiary are wholly irrelevant, and because a national media campaign, an Internet site, and informational mailings to former customers do not amount to systematic and continuous contacts.

1. General Jurisdiction

Initially, this Court rejects the plaintiffs' contention that the actions of the defendant's parent or sister corporation could be the basis for personal jurisdiction in this matter. It is irrelevant that Circus Circus Enterprises, Inc. has engaged in litigation in New Jersey. It is also irrelevant to our analysis that Circus Circus New Jersey, Inc. has applied for a gaming license from the New Jersey Casino Control Commission. This Court will not disregard the existence of separate corporate entities save some evidence that the defendant subsidiary is dominated or controlled by the parent corporation — no such evidence exists in the record. The Third Circuit has advised that "a rule which imposes liability on a corporation which never exercised its general authority over its subsidiary . . . may unduly penalize the corporation . . . ." Lansford-Coaldale Joint Water Authority v. Tonolli Corp., 4 F.3d 1209, 1221 (3d Cir. 1993); see also, Culbreth v. Amosa (Pty) Ltd., 898 F.2d 13, 14 (3d Cir. 1990) (holding that party seeking to pierce corporate veil must establish that controlling corporation wholly ignored separate status of controlled corporation and so dominated and controlled its affairs that separate existence was a mere sham). [Note that the Supreme Court has since indicated that for a corporation to be subject to "general jurisdiction" in a state, it would have to essentially be "at home" in that state, such as (but perhaps not limited to) its state of incorporation or its principal place of business. Daimler AG v. Bauman, 571 U.S. ___, 134 S.Ct. 746, 187 L.Ed.2d 624 (2014)—Eds. Daimler is discussed in Chapter 2.)

Personal jurisdiction can be exercised over a defendant which maintains an Internet site where customers can transact business. See, CompuServe, Inc. v. Patterson, 89 F.3d 1257 (6th Cir. 1996); Weber v. Jolly Hotels, 977 F.Supp. 327 (D.N.J. 1997); Zippo Mfg. Co. v. Zippo Dot Com, Inc. 952 F.Supp. 1119 (W.D.Pa. 1997). A court may exercise personal jurisdiction over a defendant based on the existence of an Internet site in two situations: (1) where the site is used to actively transact business; and (2) where a user can exchange information with the host computer. In the first situation, the court will exercise personal jurisdiction because the defendants are "enter[ing] into contracts with residents of a foreign jurisdiction that involve the knowing and repeated transmission of computer files over the Internet." CompuServe, 89 F.3d at 1264, quoted in Zippo, 952 F.Supp. at 1124. In the second circumstance, the exercise of personal jurisdiction is determined by "examining the level of interactivity and commercial nature of the exchange of information that occurs on the Web site." *Zippo*, 952 F.Supp. at 1124 (citing Maritz, Inc. v. Cybergold, Inc., 947 F.Supp. 1328 (E.D.Mo. 1996)).

With regard to the defendant's Internet site, the plaintiffs' attorney attached a copy of printed pages from that site to his affidavit in this matter. From those pages it is clear that any customer can reserve a room through the Web site. This activity is certainly commercial in nature. Moreover, by making reservations available on the Internet, the defendants have effectively placed their hotel and its services into an endless stream of commerce. Under the "stream of commerce" theory, a forum state may exercise jurisdiction over a non-resident corporation "that delivers its product into the stream of commerce with expectation that they will be purchased by consumers in the forum state." *World-Wide Volkswagen*, 444 U.S. at 298, 100 S.Ct. 559.

However, the defendant's Internet site contains a forum selection clause requiring that by making a reservation over the Internet, customers agree to have their disputes settled in Nevada state and federal courts. This forum selection clause ought to be enforced. See Carnival Cruise Lines v. Shute, 499 U.S. 585, 111 S.Ct. 1522, 113 L.Ed.2d 622 (1991). "A clause establishing ex ante the forum for dispute resolution has the salutary effect of dispelling any confusion about where suits arising from the contract must be brought and defended, sparing litigants the time and expense of pretrial motions to determine the correct forum and conserving judicial resources that otherwise would be devoted to deciding those motions." *Carnival*, 499 U.S. at 593-94, 111 S.Ct. 1522 (citing Stewart Organization, Inc. v. Ricoh Corp., 487 U.S. 22, 33, 108 S.Ct. 2239, 2246, 101 L.Ed.2d 22 [1988] (concurring opinion)). This Court will not exercise personal jurisdiction over the defendant based on the maintenance of its Internet site.

What remains to establish the requisite contacts to the forum state are (1) a television advertisement which consisted of a single spot that aired on a national cable network in the tri-state area, (2) advertisements in national magazines and newspapers such as USA Today, People Magazine, and other travel magazines, and (3) the mailing of promotional material to former guests in New Jersey and New Jersey citizens who directly request information from the defendant.

National advertising and the mailing of information to former guests and those who request it, without more, is not enough to establish minimum contacts to the forum state. See Gehling v. St. George's School of Medicine Ltd., 773 F.2d 539, 542 (3d Cir. 1985); Scheidt v. Young, 389 F.2d 58, 60 (3d Cir. 1968); cf. Giangola v. Walt Disney World Co. 753 F.Supp. 148, 156 (D.N.J. 1990) (denying personal jurisdiction even where defendant placed advertisements in local newspapers and plaintiff relied on those ads); Rutherford v. Sherburne Corp., 616 F.Supp. 1456 (D.N.J. 1985) (finding personal jurisdiction where defendant advertised in four forum newspapers and where a "substantial number" of patrons haled from the forum state). In the instant case, the record does not reflect that the defendant ever specifically targeted New Jersey for its advertisements. The defendant maintains no offices in New Jersey, does not own any property in New Jersey, has no phone book or yellow page listings in

New Jersey, and has no bank accounts in New Jersey. Nor does it incur or pay taxes in New Jersey. Additionally, defendant does not have any agents in New Jersey authorized to receive service of process on its behalf. Defendant does not, and is not authorized to, conduct business in New Jersey — defendant has no plans to obtain such authorization; defendant has never advertised in any local New Jersey newspaper or publication. Defendant has never advertised on local television stations in New Jersey.

Our Third Circuit has refused to find personal jurisdiction even when the contacts to the forum state are much stronger than those here. In *Gehling*, the Third Circuit refused to exercise personal jurisdiction over a West Indies medical school for a negligence and breach of contract claim even when the defendant college had placed advertisements in non-Pennsylvania newspapers circulated throughout Pennsylvania, six percent of the college's students came from Pennsylvania, Pennsylvania residents annually paid several hundreds of thousands of dollars in tuition, and even where the college directly sent a letter of acceptance to a prospective student. Furthermore, it has been clearly held by this Circuit that advertising in national or international newspapers or magazines does not constitute "continuous and substantial" contacts with the forum state. See Reliance Steel Products v. Watson, Ess, Marshall & Enggas, 675 F.2d 587, 589 (3d Cir. 1982).

As said, a party must have purposefully availed itself of the laws of the forum state. See *Burger King Corp.*, 471 U.S. at 475, 105 S.Ct. 2174; Keeton, 465 U.S. at 774, 104 S.Ct. 1473; *World-Wide Volkswagen Corp.*, 444 U.S. at 299, 100 S.Ct. 559. Also, the plaintiffs must show with reasonable particularity, the nature and extent of the defendant's contacts with the forum state so as to permit this Court to exercise its in personam jurisdiction over the defendant. *Gehling*, 773 F.2d at 542. The plaintiffs have not met their burden. The facts here do not meet this constitutionally required standard for a finding of in personam jurisdiction. From the present record, it appears as though plaintiffs assert that their unilateral act of going to Nevada is enough to invoke jurisdiction: the unilateral acts of the plaintiffs will not amount to minimum contacts. *Helicopteros*, 466 U.S. at 414, 104 S.Ct. 1868; *Hanson*, 357 U.S. at 253, 78 S.Ct. at 1240. This Court constitutionally cannot exercise general personal jurisdiction over the defendant in this matter because the plaintiffs have not shown that the defendant has the requisite contacts with New Jersey.

2. Specific Jurisdiction

To establish specific jurisdiction, we must, initially, determine if this cause of action arose out of or is related to the defendant's above contacts with New Jersey. The record does not reflect precisely how the plaintiffs came to know of the Circus Circus Hotel in Las Vegas or how they came to make their vacation reservations. Plaintiffs have not alleged that they received promotional mailings from defendant, that they viewed defendant's television, newspaper, or magazine advertisements, or that they communicated to defendant through its Internet site. However, assuming that this litigation is related to one of the defendant's aforementioned contacts to the forum state, this Court cannot exercise its in personam jurisdiction because the defendant lacks the requisite minimum contacts with New Jersey.

Plaintiffs have failed to demonstrate facts sufficient for this Court to exercise personal jurisdiction. The burden to produce actual evidence of the defendant's contacts with the forum state rests on the plaintiffs. Time Share Vacation Club v. Atlantic Resorts, Ltd., 735 F.2d 61, 67 (3d Cir. 1984); see also Stranahan Gear Co., Inc. v. NL Industries, Inc., 800 F.2d 53, 58 (3d Cir. 1986) (cursory allegation reiterated in a sworn affidavit is insufficient to satisfy the plaintiff's burden of proof). The plaintiffs have not met this burden.

Plaintiffs have not established that defendant has the minimum contacts with New Jersey necessary for specific personal jurisdiction. As stated, defendant's national advertising was not purposefully directed at New Jersey. The forum selection clause in defendant's Web site demonstrates that it could not reasonably anticipate being haled into court in New Jersey. Moreover, plaintiffs have not alleged that their action arises out of any of defendant's tenuous contacts with this state. This Court has neither general nor specific jurisdiction over the defendant.

C. Transfer of Venue to the District of Nevada

Finding a lack of personal jurisdiction, this matter will be transferred to the District of Nevada pursuant to 28 U.S.C. §1406(a). Dismissal would be burdensome and worthless in light of the inevitable re-filing of this action in Nevada where jurisdiction and venue clearly lie. Even without personal jurisdiction over the defendant, this Court transfers this action to the Federal District Court for the District of Nevada. See Goldlawr, Inc. v. Heiman, 369 U.S. 463, 465, 82 S.Ct. 913, 8 L.Ed.2d 39 (1962); Gehling v. St. George's School of Medicine, 773 F.2d 539, 542, 544 (3d Cir. 1985).

CONCLUSION

The Court finds that it may not exercise personal jurisdiction over the defendant in this matter. This matter is hereby transferred to the District of Nevada pursuant to 28 U.S.C. §1406(a).

NOTES AND PROBLEMS FOR DISCUSSION

1. Consider whether the result in *Decker* would have been different if (a) the Deckers booked their room through a New Jersey travel agent who had been supplied with brochures by the hotel, (b) there was no "consent to jurisdiction" provision on the Internet site, or (c) the hotel advertised on a New Jersey television station.

2. Wanda now faces a tactical decision. The law seems to be against filing in New Jersey, but maybe it's close. Should Wanda file in New Jersey anyway? Read Rule 11.

3. Question 2 talks about Wanda making a decision. But in reality, she probably will rely almost completely on you as her counsel. What will you tell her?

4. Why does the place of filing make a difference? Even at this stage, you should be able to suggest some reasons why Wanda would be better off by suing in New Jersey rather than Nevada.

5. Suppose that Wanda realizes that because personal jurisdiction would be a sure thing against Carnival Hotel. May she go forward in a federal court in Nevada as opposed to a state court? If she may choose one or the other, what difference should it make to her?

Mas v. Perry

United States Court of Appeals, Fifth Circuit, 1974.
489 F.2d 1396.

AINSWORTH, CIRCUIT JUDGE.

This case presents questions pertaining to federal diversity jurisdiction under 28 U.S.C. § 1332, which, pursuant to article III, section II of the Constitution, provides for original jurisdiction in federal district courts of all civil actions that are between, inter alia, citizens of different States or citizens of a State and citizens of foreign states and in which the amount in controversy [requirement is satisfied.[*]]

Appellees Jean Paul Mas, a citizen of France, and Judy Mas were married at her home in Jackson, Mississippi. Prior to their marriage, Mr. and Mrs. Mas were graduate assistants, pursuing coursework as well as performing teaching duties, for approximately nine months and one year, respectively, at Louisiana State University in Baton Rouge, Louisiana. Shortly after their marriage, they returned to Baton Rouge to resume their duties as graduate assistants at LSU. They remained in Baton Rouge for approximately two more years, after which they moved to Park Ridge, Illinois. At the time of the trial in this case, it was their intention to return to Baton Rouge while Mr. Mas finished his studies for the degree of Doctor of Philosophy. Mr. and Mrs. Mas were undecided as to where they would reside after that.

Upon their return to Baton Rouge after their marriage, appellees rented an apartment from appellant Oliver H. Perry, a citizen of Louisiana. This appeal arises from a final judgment entered on a jury verdict awarding $5,000 to Mr. Mas and $15,000 to Mrs. Mas for damages incurred by them as a result of the discovery that their bedroom and bathroom contained "two-way" mirrors and that they had been watched through them by the appellant during three of the first four months of their marriage.

At the close of the appellees' case at trial, appellant made an oral motion to dismiss for lack of jurisdiction. The motion was denied by the district court. Before this Court, appellant challenges the final judgment below solely on jurisdictional grounds, contending that appellees failed to prove diversity of

---

[*] [When Mas v. Perry was decided the amount in controversy requirement called for by the diversity statute, 28 U.S.C. §1332, was an amount in excess of $10,000; now, it is an amount in excess of $75,000 — eds.]

citizenship among the parties * * *. Finding no merit to these contentions, we affirm. Under section 1332(a)(2), the federal judicial power extends to the claim of Mr. Mas, a citizen of France, against the appellant, a citizen of Louisiana. Since we conclude that Mrs. Mas is a citizen of Mississippi for diversity purposes, the district court also properly had jurisdiction under section 1332(a)(1) of her claim.

It has long been the general rule that complete diversity of parties is required in order that diversity jurisdiction obtain; that is, no party on one side may be a citizen of the same State as any party on the other side. Strawbridge v. Curtiss, 7 U.S. 267 (1806). This determination of one's State citizenship for diversity purposes is controlled by federal law, not by the law of any State. As is the case in other areas of federal jurisdiction, the diverse citizenship among adverse parties must be present at the time the complaint is filed. Jurisdiction is unaffected by subsequent changes in the citizenship of the parties. The burden of pleading the diverse citizenship is upon the party invoking federal jurisdiction and if the diversity jurisdiction is properly challenged, that party also bears the burden of proof. To be a citizen of a State within the meaning of section 1332, a natural person must be both a citizen of the United States and a domiciliary of that State. For diversity purposes, citizenship means domicile; mere residence in the State is not sufficient.

A person's domicile is the place of "his true, fixed, and permanent home and principal establishment, and to which he has the intention of returning whenever he is absent therefrom. . . ." A change of domicile may be effected only by a combination of two elements: (a) taking up residence in a different domicile with (b) the intention to remain there.

It is clear that at the time of her marriage, Mrs. Mas was a domiciliary of the State of Mississippi. * * * [W]e [also] find no precedent for extending [the older notion that a wife ordinarily takes the domicile of her husband] to the situation here, in which the husband is a citizen of a foreign state but resides in the United States. Indeed, such a fiction would work absurd results on the facts before us. If Mr. Mas were considered a domicilary of France — as he would be since he had lived in Louisiana as a student-teaching assistant prior to filing the suit — then Mrs. Mas would also be deemed a domiciliary [of France] and thus * * * would not be a citizen of any State and could not sue in a federal court on that basis; nor could she invoke the alienage jurisdiction to bring her claim in federal court, since she is not an alien. On the other hand, if Mrs. Mas's domicile were Louisiana, she would become a Louisiana citizen for diversity purposes and could not bring suit with her husband against appellant, also a Louisiana citizen, on the basis of diversity jurisdiction. These are curious results under a rule arising from the theoretical identity of person and interest of the married couple.

An American woman is not deemed to have lost her United States citizenship solely by reason of her marriage to an alien. 8 U.S.C. § 1489. Similarly, we conclude that for diversity purposes a woman does not have her domicile or State citizenship changed solely by reason of her marriage to an alien.

Mrs. Mas's Mississippi domicile was disturbed neither by her year in Louisiana prior to her marriage nor as a result of the time she and her husband spent at LSU after their marriage, since for both periods she was a graduate assistant at LSU. Though she testified that after her marriage she had no intention of returning to her parents' home in Mississippi, Mrs. Mas did not effect a change of domicile since she and Mr. Mas were in Louisiana only as students and lacked the requisite intention to remain there. Until she acquires a new domicile, she remains a domiciliary, and thus a citizen, of Mississippi.[2] . . . [Affirmed.]

NOTES AND PROBLEMS FOR DISCUSSION

1. Mr. Mas, as an alien, is diverse from Mr. Perry. Why does Mrs. Mas also have to be diverse from Perry in order to sue in federal court along with her spouse? See 28 U.S.C. §1332(a)(2) and (3).

2. Note that at the time of this decision, the provision denying diversity jurisdiction between a citizen of a state and a permanent resident alien who is domiciled in the same state (§1332(a)(2)) did not exist. Today, if Mr. Mas had been lawfully admitted to permanent resident alien status, would it change the outcome of the case?

3. Note that diversity cases (and most cases arising under federal law) may also be heard in state courts which have "concurrent" jurisdiction over them. Given the choice, why do you suppose that Mr. and Mrs. Mas wanted to pursue their suit in a federal court as opposed to a state court?

4. The court states that one's domicile is the place of one's true home, to which one always intends to return. Is it not clear that Mississippi (or at least the family home) may be the one place to which Mrs. Mas did *not* wish to return? If so, why is she a domiciliary of Mississippi?

5. Suppose that the appellate court had concluded that Mrs. Mas was a citizen of Louisiana, not Mississippi, at the time of the filing of the lawsuit against Mr. Perry. What would have been the consequence of such a finding? See Rule 21, Fed. R. Civ. P. What choices would that present the two plaintiffs?

6. *Mas v. Perry* discussed the domicile of individuals. Corporations are considered citizens of their state(s) of incorporation and their (one) principal place of business. See 28 U.S.C. §1332(c)(1). Consider Wanda's lawsuit noted ed above. Will Wanda be diverse from the defendants she might wish to sue?

---

[2] The original complaint in this case was filed within several days of Mr. and Mrs. Mas's realization that they had been watched through mirrors, quite some time before they moved to Park Ridge, Illinois. Because the district court's jurisdiction is not affected by actions of the parties subsequent to the commencement of the suit, the testimony concerning Mr. and Mrs. Mas's moves after that time is not determinative of the issue of diverse citizenship, though it is of interest so far as it supports their lack of intent to remain permanently in Louisiana.

Section B.   Getting the Case Started

Assume Wanda (or you) decides to file the case in United States District Court for the District of Nevada. What do you do to get it started?

Even the most rudimentary systems for resolving adversary disputes — such as those of schools or clubs — generally have two requirements for asserting a grievance: some form of notice to the other party which sets the adversary process in motion, and some form of statement describing what the dispute is about. In the federal courts, it is the "summons" which provides the notice and brings the defendant within the jurisdiction of the court, and the "complaint" that describes the grievance. See Rules 4 and 8, Form 1.

1.   The Complaint

The plaintiff's description of the dispute is called a "complaint." What must Wanda include in this document? Does she have to describe the events before and after her injury in great detail? Does she have to cite legal authorities — past decisions or statutes — which say that the defendant must compensate her for her injuries? Consider the following case:

Lewis v. U.S. Slicing Machine Co.

United States District Court, Western District of Pennsylvania, 1970.

311 F. Supp. 139.

GOURLEY, SENIOR DISTRICT JUDGE.

This is a diversity action based on ordinary negligence, implied warranties of merchantability and fitness.

On or about June 30, 1967, the minor plaintiff is alleged to have injured himself while cleaning a meat slicer alleged to have been manufactured by the defendant. It is further stated that the minor plaintiff was employed by the Isaly Company and in the course of his employment at the time of the accident.

It is alleged that the defendant was negligent, careless and reckless in manufacturing and/or designing said meat slicer. There is also a cause of action claimed for injuries under a breach of implied warranty of merchantability and/or fitness for purpose.

The Court has considered and reviewed all pleadings, briefs of counsel, and reviewed the authorities cited therein. No useful purpose could be gained through oral argument since the questions presented are so thoroughly reviewed, discussed and presented in the briefs of counsel.

The matter before the Court is a Motion to Dismiss under Rule 12 of the Federal Rules of Civil Procedure in which it is claimed that the Complaint does not comply or has not been drawn consistent with Rule 8(a)(2) and the forms suggested for pleadings in matters of this nature. In other words, assuming all facts as alleged to be true, does the complaint set forth a cause of action?

Under Federal Rule of Civil Procedure 8(a)(2), it is required that all claims for relief shall contain "a short and plain statement of the claim showing that the pleader is entitled to relief."

> The courts have recognized that the function of pleading under the Federal Rules is to give fair notice of the claim asserted so as to enable the adverse party to answer and prepare for trial, to allow for the application of the doctrine of res judicata and to show the type of case brought, so it may be assigned to the proper form of trial. Moore's Federal Practice 2nd ed., 8.13 p. 1695.

The function of a complaint under the Federal Rules of Civil Procedure, is to afford fair notice to the adversary of the nature and basis of the claim asserted and a general indication of the type of litigation involved.

I believe that it does so comply and states a cause of action under the law and decisions in the Commonwealth of Pennsylvania. A pleading in the federal jurisdiction is to be solely "notice pleading." If there are any additional facts needed, the discovery processes are available either by interrogatories or depositions. Motions for a More Definite Statement and/or Motion to Dismiss are improper.

In addition to the facts as alleged prima facie setting forth a cause of action based on ordinary negligence and breach of warranties, it well could be, a right to recover might or could be sustained on the theory of strict liability which has been extended to any person injured if a chattel is defectively designed and manufactured, and injury results to any person injured in the use thereof.

Rule 84 of the Federal Rules of Civil Procedure states that the forms contained in the Appendix of Forms are sufficient under the rules and are intended to indicate the simplicity and brevity of statement which the rules contemplate. Form 9 [the Forms have since been eliminated — eds.] does not suggest what the nature of the defendant's alleged negligence may have been. It may have consisted, e.g., in driving too fast, driving while drunk, driving with bad brakes or an otherwise defective car, or keeping an inadequate lookout. Appellant's complaint in the present case is similar. Like Form 9, it pleads no evidence.

One reason that the Courts can afford to be so liberal on the matter of pleading is, of course, the broad scope which the Rules give to the various pretrial devices for discovery of facts and formulation of issues. Under the old practice the pleadings not only served the function of giving notice of the claim asserted, but they also carried the burden of formulating the issues and to a large extent of advising the adverse party of the facts involved. Now the deposition and discovery procedure under Rules 26-37 and the pretrial conference under Rule 16 afford a much more efficient method of getting at the facts than pleadings ever offered, so that the only real office which the pleadings continue to serve is that of giving notice.

I, therefore, conclude that the allegations in plaintiffs' causes of action are not so indefinite and unclear as to deny the defendant notice of the nature of the claim filed against it, and the plaintiffs are entitled to maintain a cause of action for breach of any implied warranty and also on the theory of strict liability against the defendant manufacturer of the meat slicer.

NOTES AND PROBLEMS FOR DISCUSSION

1. What did the U.S. Slicing Machine Company want there to be in the complaint that was not there?

2. On the motion to dismiss a complaint for failure to state a claim for relief, the court "assume[es] all facts as alleged to be true." Why should that be? Recently the Supreme Court indicated that "conclusory" allegations will not be taken as true, and that the non-conclusory factual allegations (taken as true) must be sufficient to show that they "plausibly" give rise to a claim for relief. See Chapter 7 (discussing *Bell Atlantic v. Twombly*, 550 U.S. 544, 125 S.Ct. 1955, 167 L.Ed.2d 929 (2007), and *Ashcroft v. Iqbal,* 556 U.S. 652, 129 S.Ct. 1937, 173 L.Ed.2d 868 (2009)). Does the complaint in *Slicing Machine* satisfy that more demanding standard? Is it a standard that is consistent with Rule 8(a)(2)?

3. Explain how this case might help you in drafting Wanda's complaint. Notwithstanding this case, do you still have a problem under Rule 11?

4. Assume Wanda's complaint follows the plaintiff's in the *Slicing Machine* case. Will Wanda be able to win her case at trial with the information she has? When and how is she going to get more?

5. We have put aside the question of whom Wanda should sue. The Rules have quite elaborate rules regarding parties. Rule 20 governs whom the plaintiff can join. Under that Rule, could Wanda join both Carnival and GM as defendants?

6. We briefly alert students to three other concepts relating to litigation parties. Under Rule 19, a plaintiff can be compelled to join certain persons, even if she doesn't want to — these are sometimes called necessary and indispensable parties. Rule 24 allows some persons not in the lawsuit to intervene, even if the existing parties don't want them. Finally, a defendant has a right to bring in additional persons who are liable to the defendant for plaintiff's claim under Rule 14(a). We save these concepts for later.

2. THE ANSWER AND PRE-ANSWER MOTIONS

Once the plaintiff files and serves her complaint, attention shifts to the defendant. Here, procedural systems diverge. In a simple system, such as that in small claims courts, the defendant needn't do anything — it is simply assumed that the defendant will contest the plaintiff's allegations at trial. But in most judicial systems, the defendant is required to respond to the complaint. In the federal courts, this response is called an "answer." See Rule 8(b), (c), (d).

A defendant's answer may contain three types of responses. First, the defendant is asked to admit or deny what the plaintiff has said. Those matters which are denied will be in dispute; those admitted will not be. See Rule 8(b)(6). Second, the defendant may allege additional reasons why even if the plaintiff's story is true, she cannot recover. We call these affirmative defenses. See Rule 8(c). For example, what parts of Rule 8(c) would apply if the defendant believed that the plaintiff herself had been careless by kicking the machine, or that the plaintiff had waited too long to sue? Finally, the defendant may have claims against the plaintiff, which are called counterclaims. See Rule 13. All of these will be in the answer.

Zielinski v. Philadelphia Piers, Inc.

United States District Court, Eastern District of Pennsylvania, 1956.

139 F. Supp. 408.

DUSEN, DISTRICT JUDGE.

Plaintiff requests a ruling that, for the purposes of this case, the motordriven fork lift operated by Sandy Johnson on February 9, 1953, was owned by defendant and that Sandy Johnson was its agent acting in the course of his employment on that date. The following facts are established by the pleadings, interrogatories, depositions and uncontradicted portions of affidavits:

1. Plaintiff filed his complaint on April 28, 1953, for personal injuries received on February 9, 1953, while working on Pier 96, Philadelphia, for J. A. McCarthy, as a result of a collision of two motor-driven fork lifts.

2. Paragraph 5 of this complaint stated that "a motor-driven vehicle known as a fork lift or chisel, owned, operated and controlled by the defendant, its agents, servants and employees, was so negligently and carelessly managed * * * that the same * * * did come into contact with the plaintiff causing him to sustain the injuries more fully hereinafter set forth."

3. The "First Defense" of the Answer stated "Defendant * * * denies the averments of paragraph 5 * * *."

4. The motor-driven vehicle known as a fork lift or chisel, which collided with the McCarthy fork lift on which plaintiff was riding, had on it the initials "P.P.I."

5. On February 10, 1953, Carload Contractors, Inc. made a report of this accident to its insurance company, whose policy No. CL 3964 insured Carload Contractors, Inc. against potential liability for the negligence of its employees contributing to a collision of the type described in paragraph 2 above.

6. By letter of April 29, 1953, the complaint served on defendant was forwarded to the above-mentioned insurance company. This letter read as follows:

> Gentlemen:
>
> As per telephone conversation today with your office, we attach hereto "Complaint in Trespass" as brought against Philadelphia Piers, Inc. by one Frank Zielinski for supposed injuries sustained by him on February 9, 1953.
>
> We find that a fork lift truck operated by an employee of Carload Contractors, Inc. also insured by yourselves was involved in an accident with another chisel truck, which, was alleged, did cause injury to Frank

Zielinski, and same was reported to you by Carload Contractors, Inc. at the time, and you assigned Claim Number OL 0153-94 to this claim.

Should not this Complaint in Trespass be issued against Carload Contractors, Inc. and not Philadelphia Piers, Inc.?

We forward for your handling.

7. Interrogatories 1-5 and the answers thereto, which were sworn to by defendant's General Manager on June 12, 1953 * * * read as follows:

1. State whether you have received any information of an injury sustained by the plaintiff on February 9, 1953, South Wharves. If so, state when and from whom you first received notice of such injury. Answer: We were first notified of this accident on or about February 9, 1953 by Thomas Wilson.

2. State whether you caused an investigation to be made of the circumstances of said injury and if so, state who made such investigation and when it was made. Answer: We made a very brief investigation on February 9, 1953 and turned the matter over to (our insurance company) for further investigation. * * *

8. At a deposition taken August 18, 1953, Sandy Johnson testified that he was the employee of defendant on February 9, 1953, and had been their employee for approximately fifteen years.

9. At a pre-trial conference held on September 27, 1955,[3] plaintiff first learned that over a year before February 9, 1953, the business of moving freight on piers in Philadelphia, formerly conducted by defendant, had been sold by it to Carload Contractors, Inc. and Sandy Johnson had been transferred to the payroll of this corporation without apparently realizing it, since the nature or location of his work had not changed.

10. As a result of the following answers to Supplementary Interrogatories 16 to 19, filed October 21, 1955, plaintiff learned the facts stated in paragraphs 5 and 6 above in the fall of 1955[.]

     * * *

11. Defendant now admits that on February 9, 1953, it owned the fork lift in the custody of Sandy Johnson and that this fork lift was leased to Carload Contractors, Inc. It is also admitted that the pier on which the accident occurred was leased by defendant.

12. There is no indication of action by either party in bad faith and there is no proof of inaccurate statements being made with intent to deceive. Because defendant made a prompt investigation of the accident (see answers to Interrogatories 1, 2, 16 and 17), its insurance company has been representing the

---

[3] The applicable statute of limitations prevented any suit against Carload Contractors, Inc. after February 9, 1955.

defendant since suit was brought, and this company insures Carload Contractors, Inc. also, requiring defendant to defend this suit, will not prejudice it.

Under these circumstances, and for the purposes of this action, it is ordered that the following shall be stated to the jury at the trial:

> *It is admitted that, on February 9, 1953, the towmotor or fork lift bearing the initials "P.P.I." was owned by defendant and that Sandy Johnson was a servant in the employ of defendant and doing its work on that date.*

This ruling is based on the following principles:

Under the circumstances of this case, the answer contains an ineffective denial of that part of paragraph 5 of the complaint which alleges that "a motor driven vehicle known as a fork lift or chisel (was) owned, operated and controlled by the defendant, its agents, servants and employees."

F.R.Civ.P. 8(b), 28 U.S.C. provides:

> A party shall state in short and plain terms his defenses to each claim asserted and shall admit or deny the averments upon which the adverse party relies. * * * Denials shall fairly meet the substance of the averments denied. When a pleader intends in good faith to deny only a part or a qualification of an averment, he shall specify so much of it as is true and material and shall deny only the remainder.

For example, it is quite clear that defendant does not deny the averment in paragraph 5 that the fork lift came into contact with plaintiff, since it admits, in the answers to interrogatories, that an investigation of an occurrence of the accident had been made and that a report dated February 10, 1953, was sent to its insurance company stating "While Frank Zielinski was riding on bumper of chisel and holding rope to secure cargo, the chisel truck collided with another chisel truck operated by Sandy Johnson causing injuries to Frank Zielinski's legs and hurt head of Sandy Johnson." Compliance with the above-mentioned rule required that defendant file a more specific answer than a general denial. A specific denial of parts of this paragraph and specific admission of other parts would have warned plaintiff that he had sued the wrong defendant.

Paragraph 8.23 of Moore's Federal Practice (2d Edition) Vol. II, p. 1680, says: "In such a case, the defendant should make clear just what he is denying and what he is admitting." See, Kirby v. Turner-Day & Woolworth Handle Co., 50 F.Supp. 469 (E.D. Tenn. 1943). This answer to paragraph 5 does not make clear to plaintiff the defenses he must be prepared to meet. * * *

If Interrogatory 2 had been answered accurately[10] by saying that employees of Carload Contractors, Inc. had turned the matter over to the insurance

---

[10] At least one federal district court case has suggested that a contempt proceeding under 18 U.S.C. § 401 is the proper procedure to compensate the attorneys for one party who had been misled to their pecuniary damage by inaccurate answers to interrogatories. It suggested the imposition of a fine to be paid as civil liability to the attorneys for the complaining party, * * *

company,[11] it seems clear that plaintiff would have realized his mistake. The fact that if Sandy Johnson had testified accurately, the plaintiff could have brought its action against the proper party defendant within the statutory period of limitations is also a factor to be considered, since defendant was represented at the deposition and received knowledge of the inaccurate testimony.

At least one appellate court has stated that the doctrine of equitable estoppel will be applied to prevent a party from taking advantage of the statute of limitations where the plaintiff has been misled by conduct of such party. See Peters v. Public Service Corporation, 29 A.2d 189, 195 (1942). In that case, the court said "Of course, defendants were under no duty to advise complainants' attorney of his error, other than by appropriate pleadings, but neither did defendants have a right, knowing of the mistake, to foster it by its acts of omission."

This doctrine has been held to estop a party from taking advantage of a document of record where the misleading conduct occurred after the recording, so that application of this doctrine would not necessarily be precluded in a case such as this where the misleading answers to interrogatories and depositions were subsequent to the filing of the answer, even if the denial in the answer had been sufficient.

Since this is a pre-trial order, it may be modified at the trial if the trial judge determines from the facts which then appear that justice so requires.

NOTES AND PROBLEMS FOR DISCUSSION

1. Was the defendant's denial of the plaintiff's allegations inaccurate? How does the court suggest the defendant should have answered the complaint?

2. In pre-trial discovery (see below at Section C), the plaintiff asked if defendant had made an investigation, but never asked what the result of that investigation was. Should the defendant have to volunteer such information?

3. Ordinarily, a defendant who believes that the plaintiff has sued the wrong person or entity would have every incentive to bring that fact to the attention of the plaintiff. Why didn't that happen here?

4. Note the possible consequence of the court's ruling: The jury will be instructed that Sandy Johnson was an employee of Philadelphia Piers — i.e., it will be instructed in a falsehood. Is this an acceptable result, even if one assumes that the defendant was somehow responsible for the plaintiff's continued error?

5. Look at current Rule 15(c)(1)(C), which was not in place at the time of the *Zielinski* decision. Given the facts of *Zielinski*, would this Rule take care of the

---

[11] Pages 73 and 85 of the depositions of October 14, 1955, indicate that the answer to Interrogatory 2 was also inaccurate in saying that defendant made the investigation of the accident; but actually the employees of Carload Contractors, Inc. made the investigation.

problem presented in the case, by permitting the plaintiff to amend his complaint to name the correct party?

6. Finally, note that the defendant has another procedural option as an alternative to answering the Complaint. Consider Wanda's lawsuit discussed above. Assume that Wanda had sued in New Jersey rather than Nevada, and the defendant believed that New Jersey did not have personal jurisdiction for the reasons stated in the *Decker* case. The defendant could, of course, raise this matter in its Answer, if no pre-Answer motion is filed. Look at Rule 12(b), which sets forth a group of defenses that receive somewhat special treatment. Rule 12 also permits these matters to be made by a pre-Answer motion.

(a)   If Wanda sued Carnival in New Jersey, what Rule 12(b) defense might be available to Carnival?

(b)   Assume Carnival makes a motion to dismiss. Does it still have to answer the complaint before the motion is decided? See Rule 12(a)(4).

(c)   Note that the effect of a pre-Answer motion is to delay the progress of the case. For this reason, the defendant generally is entitled to only one pre-Answer motion; if that one motion is denied, it must answer. The provisions limiting a defendant to one pre-Answer motion, however, are complicated and will be discussed in detail later. See Rule 12(g), (h).

SECTION C.   OBTAINING INFORMATION ABOUT THE CASE

Normally, the parties know something about their case before they even seek legal assistance. For example, Wanda probably has a notion that large gambling machines don't fall down unless there is some problem, and she certainly knows what she was doing at the time and the nature and extent of her injuries. Carnival Hotel knows the manufacturer of the machine, and something about its installation. It may know about prior problems and it may have made an inspection or done some tests after the accident. There may have been a police report which provides further information, or a public report to a regulatory authority.

However, the parties will surely need more information to prove and defend their cases. Students tend to overlook the most obvious source — private investigation by each party. Discussions with persons who saw the accident, and consultation with persons who are knowledgeable about the installation of machines of this type may provide important information. Reference to industry sources may provide some information on similar accidents. And now, the Internet may provide a fertile source of information about the product itself and each of the parties.

Prior to the Federal Rules, the pleadings, knowledge of the parties, and information based on the parties' own investigation was about all that would be available to the parties prior to trial. The Federal Rules changed all that by containing broad provisions for pre-trial discovery — i.e. the ability of one party to a lawsuit to compel both other parties and nonparty witnesses to provide information about the case, whether they want to or not. See Rules 26-37. The discovery provisions are probably the most innovative aspect of the Rules, as well as the most controversial. On the plus side, access to full information may lead to a more just outcome, and compulsory access may somewhat offset inequalities in wealth. On the negative side, discovery can be extremely burdensome and expensive, can be used to oppress or harass, and may increase the level of adversariness.

The major discovery devices are as follow:

> • *Depositions* — these are oral questions by a lawyer and answers by the witness (sort of a trial without the judge). See Rules 30, 45.

> • *Interrogatories* — these are written questions to a party answered in writing. See Rule 33.

> • *Documents and inspection of land* — these are requests to produce documents, or permit inspection or testing of products and land. See Rules 34, 45.

> • *Physical and mental examinations* — these are available only as against a party, and only with court permission. See Rule 35.

One of the most significant aspects of discovery is that it generally operates without court involvement or supervision. Instead, the court tends to get involved only when there are problems. The problems may be anything from a witness not answering a question or a dispute about the scope or location of a deposition, to a refusal to permit discovery at all, or extremely disagreeable behavior. The court has the power both to compel answers, to limit discovery, to correct abuses, and to impose sanctions. See Rules 26(c), 37.

The next case will give you a flavor of the process in an extremely difficult setting.

Coleman v. American Red Cross

United States Court of Appeals, Sixth Circuit, 1994.
23 F.3d 1091.

GUY, CIRCUIT JUDGE.

Plaintiffs, Cheryl and Gerry Coleman, appeal the district court's dismissal of their negligence action under Federal Rule of Civil Procedure 41(b). The court dismissed their claim against the American Red Cross because it found that they had violated a discovery protective order. The plaintiffs also contend on appeal that the district court erred: (1) in applying the wrong standard to preclude the discovery of relevant information; and (2) in prohibiting the plaintiffs from obtaining discovery of documents located at the Red Cross' national headquarters. For the reasons discussed below, we affirm in part, reverse in part, and remand.

I

This case is now before us for a third time. See Coleman v. American Red Cross, 979 F.2d 1135 (6th Cir. 1992); Coleman v. American Red Cross, No. 91-1421 (6th Cir. Aug. 12, 1991). The issues raised on appeal involve substantially the same events that were outlined in *Coleman*, 979 F.2d at 1135. Thus, for purposes of this analysis, we only need to briefly summarize the facts.

On August 15, 1984, Cheryl Coleman received a blood transfusion at the University of Michigan Hospital. The blood Mrs. Coleman received had been donated to the Red Cross six days earlier. That blood apparently contained the Human Immunodeficiency Virus (HIV), the virus that causes Acquired Immune Deficiency Syndrome (AIDS). Mrs. Coleman's blood tested positive for HIV antibodies in September 1988.

The Colemans then filed an action, claiming that the Red Cross was negligent in failing to screen out the infected donor and in failing to test the donor's blood after collecting it. During discovery, the Colemans requested the donor's name and address, but the Red Cross refused to provide this information. Eventually, the district court ordered the Red Cross to furnish the donor's records to the Colemans but with all information that would identify the donor redacted. Coleman v. American Red Cross, 130 F.R.D. 360, 363 (E.D. Mich. 1990).

The Red Cross subsequently delivered several donor information cards to the Colemans. On one of the cards, the Red Cross inadvertently failed to redact the donor's social security number. The Coleman's attorney immediately hired a private investigator who was able to determine the donor's name and address from information he obtained as a result of having the social security number.

When the Red Cross learned of this, it moved for a protective order to prevent the Colemans and their attorney from using this information. The district court ordered the Colemans and their attorney to turn over any documents containing the donor's name and enjoined them from using the information for any purpose, including using the name to bring an action against the donor.

The Colemans appealed this order, arguing that the district court erred by enjoining them from suing the donor. We agreed, finding that the district court had abused its discretion by prohibiting the Colemans from bringing a separate proceeding against the donor. *Coleman*, 979 F.2d at 1141. We remanded to the district court for further proceedings.

When the case returned to the district court, the Red Cross filed a motion to dismiss pursuant to Rule 41(b). In support of its motion, the Red Cross claimed that it was substantially prejudiced by the Colemans' intentional violation of the protective order. The district court found that the facts supported this assertion and entered an order to dismiss the complaint. The Colemans then filed this appeal.

II

Under Rule 41(b) of the Federal Rules of Civil Procedure, when a plaintiff fails to comply with any order of the court, the defendant may move for dismissal of the action.[1] Court orders imposing sanctions under this rule are reviewable only for abuse of discretion. Carter v. City of Memphis, Tenn., 636 F.2d 159, 161 (6th Cir. 1980).

In the past, we have upheld the use of "dismissals as a sanction for failing to comply with discovery orders because it accomplishes the dual purposes of punishing the offending party and deterring similar misconduct by future litigants." Taylor v. Medtronics, Inc., 861 F.2d 980, 986 (6th Cir. 1988) (citations omitted). In response to the argument that a party should not be required to suffer harm for an attorney's derelictions, the Supreme Court stated:

> There is certainly no merit to the contention that dismissal of petitioner's claim because of his counsel's unexcused conduct imposes an unjust penalty on the client. Petitioner voluntarily chose this attorney as his representative in the action, and he cannot now avoid the consequences of the acts or omissions of this freely selected agent. Any other notion would be wholly inconsistent with our system of representative litigation, in which each party is deemed bound by the acts of his lawyer-agent and is considered to have "notice of all facts, notice of which can be charged upon the attorney."

Link v. Wabash R.R. Co., 370 U.S. 626, 633-34, 82 S.Ct. 1386, 1390, 8 L.Ed.2d 734 (1962) (citation omitted).

Despite the Supreme Court's unequivocal language, this court, like many others, has been extremely reluctant to uphold the dismissal of a case merely to discipline an attorney. In *Carter* we stated that the "dismissal of an action for an attorney's failure to comply is a harsh sanction which the court should order only in extreme situations showing 'a clear record of delay or contumacious conduct by the plaintiff.'" We also noted in *Carter* that "[d]ismissal is usually inappropriate where the neglect is solely the fault of the attorney."

In Patterson v. Township of Grand Blanc, 760 F.2d 686, 688 (6th Cir. 1985), we reversed a dismissal, adjudging that sanction to be "extremely harsh in that it deprives a plaintiff of his day in court due to the inept actions of his counsel[.]" *Patterson* relied upon *Carter*, which reversed a dismissal under Rule 41(b) because, while plaintiff's counsel had been inept, the plaintiff was blameless. We implicitly found that a potential claim against the plaintiff's attorney did not overcome the harm that the plaintiff would suffer from dismissing the action. See also Lolatchy v. Arthur Murray, Inc., 816 F.2d 951 (4th Cir. 1987) (reversing a default judgment, over a strong dissent, because the defendants did not contribute to their attorney's dilatory conduct); Carter v. Albert Einstein Medical Cent., 804 F.2d 805 (3d Cir. 1986) (reversing a dismissal because the plaintiff did not contribute to the attorney's negligent conduct). Thus, although

---

[1] The dissent would decide this case based upon an inherent power analysis and takes issue with our analysis under Rules 41(b) and 37(b). We do not dispute a court's inherent power to dismiss a case; however, we note that the factors considered when reviewing a dismissal under Rule 41(b), Rule 37(b), or a court's inherent power are largely the same. Therefore, even if we were to make an inherent power analysis, our holding would not change.

the *Link* principle remains valid, we have increasingly emphasized directly sanctioning the delinquent lawyer rather than an innocent client.

Here, all of the wrongful conduct must be attributed to counsel; the Colemans did not engage in any culpable conduct themselves. Even the district court itself noted that the "[d]efendants do not claim that plaintiffs participated directly in the investigation which culminated in discovering the identity of the purported donor." Admittedly, the attorney's actions in this case were more egregious than in the cases previously discussed; however, this does not mandate that the attorney's conduct be imputed to the Colemans.

The Red Cross argues that it was substantially prejudiced by the violation of the protective order. Previously, in reversing the district court's order that prohibited the Colemans from suing the donor, we noted that "the district court did not commit error in concluding that donor disclosure could imperil the safety and adequacy of the national blood supply." The genesis of this observation, however, was whether or not the court could consider the impact on the blood supply in fashioning its order. In no way did we endorse any substantive finding as to whether donor disclosure would imperil the blood supply. Thus, we now look for the first time to see if the defendants actually were prejudiced when the Colemans learned of the donor's identity.

There is no evidence that the Colemans have used, or could use, the donor's identity to directly prejudice the Red Cross insofar as this litigation is concerned. As proof of its having been prejudiced, the Red Cross points to a drop in blood donations, which it attributes to the publicity surrounding our previous decision.[2] This publicity, it claims, spawned fear among the public; fewer people are donating blood because now they fear possible liability. In response, the Colemans noted that even prior to the publication of the supposedly damaging article, Red Cross donations in the Detroit area were reportedly down 11 percent. Even the district court questioned the Red Cross' claim, stating that the Colemans' "argument that further study is needed to ascertain the exact cause or causes for the drop in blood donations has merit." Similarly, we find that the evidence presented by the Red Cross does not establish a causal connection between the violation of the court's protective order and a decrease in the number of people donating blood.

Nevertheless, the district court found that the Red Cross was prejudiced in other ways. The court noted that the original protective order was based upon specific findings that there could be harm to the blood supply if the donor's identity became known to the public. The court also found that the defendants were prejudiced because they complied with the court's order to produce the donor registration cards and did so relying on the court's order to protect documents that they had objected to producing in the first place. Finally, the

---

[2] In August 27, 1992, following our previous decision, which held that the district court had abused its discretion by enjoining the Colemans from bringing a second action against the donor, the Detroit Free Press published an article describing the case and the opinion of this court under the headline "Pair Can Sue Donor of AIDS Blood."

court noted that any party who complies with a court order to produce necessarily is prejudiced when another party abuses the judicial process to discover protected information.

In our opinion, these findings do not establish the type of prejudice that permits the dismissal of this case. There is no disputing that the Colemans' attorney intentionally violated the district court's protective order. Such behavior undermines the authority of the court and the attorney may be sanctioned accordingly; however, unless the Red Cross can articulate how it was prejudiced in this litigation, it was an abuse of discretion to dismiss this case.

We note in this regard that the defendants did not seek dismissal as a sanction when plaintiffs' counsel's misconduct was first discovered. Nor did the court, sua sponte, consider such a sanction. The only significant event that occurred in the interim was our decision to reverse the earlier ruling of the district court. It was our decision that generated the news coverage about which the defendant complained to the district court. We do not think the individual plaintiffs should be held accountable for whatever flowed from such coverage, if anything.

We previously stated:

> The donor's privacy interests are substantial, as is the public interest in maintaining a safe and adequate blood supply. However, we believe that the Colemans' right to litigate their claims against the donor substantially outweighs the competing interests, especially since there is significant evidence to suggest that the donor's conduct was suspect. Accordingly, we conclude that the district court abused its discretion by enjoining the Colemans from bringing a separate action against the donor.

Coleman, 979 F.2d at 1141. Similarly, we find that the Coleman's right to sue the Red Cross outweighs any harm demonstrated by the Red Cross.[3]

III

The Colemans also raise two issues pertaining to the district court's orders regarding discovery. The Red Cross asserts that this court lacks jurisdiction to review this claim because discovery orders are nonfinal decisions not subject to appeal. The law is well settled that an appeal from a final judgment draws into question all prior non-final rulings and orders. Rule 41(b) of the Federal Rules of Civil Procedure specifically provides: "Unless the court in its order for dismissal otherwise specifies, a dismissal under this subdivision . . . operates as an adjudication upon the merits."[*] Moreover, the defendants concede that "the order of dismissal presently on appeal is final because it ends the litigation on the merits[.]" Thus, we have jurisdiction to resolve the issues concerning the prior discovery orders.

---

[3] The donor involved in this case is now deceased.

[*] [The current version of the rule is slightly reworded, but is similar in its substance. — eds.]

"[I]t is well established that the scope of discovery is within the sound discretion of the trial court." United States v. Guy, 978 F.2d 934, 938 (6th Cir. 1992) (citations omitted). Accordingly, we review discovery matters under an abuse of discretion standard.

In their first contention of error, the Colemans argue that the district court improperly applied an "admissibility" standard rather than a "relevance" standard in precluding the discovery of certain information. The information sought to be discovered relates to one of the claims of negligence against the Red Cross: The Red Cross failed to use the hepatitis B core antibody test in screening the blood of the implicated donor.

The Colemans note that in a meeting held at the Center For Disease Control on January 4, 1983, it was reported that 90 percent of known AIDS cases were positive for the antibody to the core antigen of the hepatitis B virus (anti-HBc) and would be excluded as blood donors if the presence of hepatitis B core antibody was used as a laboratory surrogate screening test. The anti-HBc test was so successful because hepatitis B is prevalent in the same populations that are at high risk for AIDS.

Approximately one year later, the Red Cross' San Jose Region advised headquarters that its Medical Advisory Committee had approved the implementation of hepatitis B core antibody testing. In response, headquarters indicated that the test would not be performed in other regions as there was no evidence that such testing would reduce the number of cases of transfusion-associated AIDS.

On June 11, 1984, the Red Cross implemented the test at its San Jose, California, based region. The test, or other surrogate tests, were also being used at other non-Red Cross blood banks. The test was used until the spring of 1985, when a test identifying HIV became available.

The Colemans sought data on the number of transfusions associated with AIDS/HIV infections that had been reported in blood recipients that received blood from the San Jose region during the time the hepatitis B core antibody test was being used. The Colemans also inquired into the number of transfusion-associated AIDS/HIV infections from blood products produced by the Southeastern Michigan Region during the same period.

The Colemans contend that this information was readily available, as the Red Cross' "Look Back" program was used to identify units of blood that were contaminated with the AIDS virus and had been transfused prior to the implementation of the AIDS testing.

The Red Cross objected to this motion on the grounds that it was unduly burdensome and expensive. Counsel for the Red Cross argued that they already had responded to over 300 interrogatories and over 140 separate document requests, and had produced over 1,500 documents. But rather than denying the Colemans' motion on the grounds that it was overly burdensome, the district court stated:

> I'm going to at this time deny the motion finding on this record that what is sought is really information relative to a procedure that has been identified as a test procedure being used on a relatively short-time based

on counsel's statement on this record. I'm relying on that and finding that if it were [to] be introduced into this record it would be speculative at best based on what I presently have before me. It is a matter that could be brought back if deemed appropriate. From what I have now it's a different situation, a different setting, really a different population.

Thus, we must restrict our examination to this rationale in determining whether it was an abuse of discretion to deny the Colemans' discovery motion.

It is axiomatic that the "discovery of evidence, whether hearsay or not, is permitted if it is at all possible that it will lead to the discovery of admissible evidence." 4 James Wm. Moore, Moore's Federal Practice §26.56 [4]. Further, as we have previously noted, "[t]he scope of discovery is not limited to admissible evidence, but encompasses 'any matter, not privileged, which is relevant to the subject matter involved in the pending action.'" Marshall v. Bramer, 828 F.2d 355, 357-58 (6th Cir. 1987) (quoting Fed.R.Civ.P. 26(b)(1)).* A court is not permitted to preclude the discovery of arguably relevant information solely because, if the information were introduced at trial, it would be "speculative" at best. Accordingly, we find that it was an abuse of the district court's discretion to deny the Colemans' motion.

As to their second claim, the Colemans argue that the district court committed reversible error when it failed to consider and balance the elements enumerated in Federal Rule of Civil Procedure 26(b)(1) in ruling that they were precluded from obtaining discovery of documents located at the Red Cross' national headquarters.[5] The Red Cross objected to this request on the basis of it being overly burdensome, since the request would have required the Red Cross to search every file that exists at National Headquarters for any documents that might be of any relevance to any matter in the case. The Red Cross also argued that the hundreds of interrogatory responses, numerous depositions, and thousands of pages of documents that already had been produced were sufficient. The district court agreed with the Red Cross, and denied the motion because it found it overly burdensome. We find nothing in the record that indicates that the district court abused its discretion in refusing to grant this request.

For the reasons stated, we AFFIRM in part, REVERSE in part, and REMAND.

---

* [The discovery provisions have since been modified; see Chapter 8. — eds.]
[5] The Colemans sought information by way of interrogatories and document requests that included the following: (1) identification and production of documents relating to the decision to implement and relating to the use of the hepatitis B core antibody test in Central Region; (2) identification and production of documents relating to a December 1983 meeting which discussed the use of the hepatitis B core antibody test to screen blood; (3) documents relating to the use of a screening procedure whereby donors could designate their blood for non-transfusion or laboratory use; (4) documents which discussed the plasma industry's decision to exclude homosexuals from the donor pool; and (5) documents relating to donors sexual orientation as part of donor screening.

RYAN, CIRCUIT JUDGE (dissenting).

The only issue in this case is whether the district court abused its discretion in dismissing Cheryl Coleman's lawsuit as a sanction for her counsel's intentional disobedience of the court's protective order or, stated differently, whether dismissal was within the range of sanction options available to the district court. Plainly it was, and therefore, I respectfully dissent.

I

The district court offered three legal bases for its action: 1) Fed.R.Civ.P. 41(b); 2) the court's inherent power; and 3) Fed.R.Civ.P. 37(b). In its extensive written opinion, the district court provided a reasoned analysis and cited case authority to support its action on each of these grounds. The majority opinion, in holding that the district court abused its discretion in dismissing the plaintiff's case, analyzes the defendants' appeal under Rules 41(b) and 37(b) only. Although Rule 37(b) is nowhere cited in the majority opinion, a number of cases interpreting Rule 37(b) are cited, and the court's opinion seems to turn on a perceived absence of prejudice to the defendants, a factor derived from Rule 37(b) jurisprudence.

In my judgment, the majority's apparent conclusion that neither Rule 41(b) nor Rule 37(b) authorize the dismissal sanction the district court imposed misses the point, because neither Rule 41(b) nor Rule 37(b) are the proper bases for resolving this case. This is a case about the sanctions that are available to a district court for the violation of its protective order. Rules 41(b) and 37(b) have nothing to do with protective orders. It is understandable, however, that the majority relies upon Rule 41(b) and Rule 37(b) to analyze the case, because the district court itself relied, in part, upon those rules for its decision. But it also explicitly relied upon its inherent power, and cited Marrocco v. General Motors Corp., 966 F.2d 220 (7th Cir. 1992), in which the Seventh Circuit affirmed a district court's dismissal of a plaintiff's case as a sanction for violation of a protective order.

II

Rule 41(b) deals primarily with motions to dismiss for want of prosecution. Société Internationale Pour Participations Industrielles v. Rogers, 357 U.S. 197, 206-07, 78 S.Ct. 1087, 1092-93, 2 L.Ed.2d 1255 (1958). There was no want of prosecution in this case; to the contrary, the problem is that the plaintiff's counsel prosecuted too zealously, indeed contumaciously.

Rule 37(b) is primarily concerned with sanctions for failure to conduct or to cooperate in discovery. The text of Rule 37(b) refers to the situations in which it applies, and they include discovery orders pursuant to Rule 26(f). Nowhere does the rule mention protective orders or Rule 26(c), which is concerned with protective orders. Thus, neither Rule 41(b) nor Rule 37(b) are the proper bases for resolving this case.

Rule 37(b), upon which the district court relied, in part, and upon which the majority appears to have heavily relied, judging from its "prejudice" analysis, is singularly inappropriate authority for determining whether dismissal was an option available to the district court as a sanction for the violation of its protective order. For example, the four-factor test, and particularly the prejudice factor adopted by a number of courts including the district court in this case, for testing whether dismissal was a proper sanction under Rule 37(b), simply does not fit protective orders.

In analyzing the prejudice factor of the test, a few courts have held that whatever sanction under Rule 37(b) a district court selects must relate directly to the prejudice suffered. The rationale, of course, is that because discovery orders usually apply to the moving party's attempt to procure discovery with respect to a particular claim or defense, it is fairly easy to relate the misconduct to a narrowly tailored sanction. If the disobedient party has refused to cooperate in discovery relating to a particular claim, a proper and adequate sanction might include striking that claim. The majority opinion has relied heavily on this analysis, apparently failing to recognize that misconduct and sanction do not coincide so neatly when a protective order is violated. That is because a protective order rarely relates directly to a single claim or defense. Protective orders more often deal with such amorphous concerns as "embarrassment [or] oppression," Fed.R.Civ.P. 26(c), or broader considerations of public policy such as not discouraging blood donations.

III

The proper approach to determining whether dismissal was within the range of sanctions available to the district court in this case is an analysis of the district court's inherent power. Although the district court relied, mistakenly in my view, upon Rule 41(b) and Rule 37(b) for its authority to act, it also explicitly relied upon its own inherent power. As the Supreme Court has recognized, "[t]he inherent powers of federal courts are those which 'are necessary to the exercise of all others.'" Roadway Express, Inc. v. Piper, 447 U.S. 752, 764, 100 S.Ct. 2455, 2463, 65 L.Ed.2d 488 (1980) (quoting United States v. Hudson, 7 Cranch 32, 34, 11 U.S. 32, 3 L.Ed. 259, (1812)). The exercise of such powers is paramount to the court's ability to "'protect [ ] the due and orderly administration of justice and . . . maintain [ ] the authority and dignity of the court.'" Id. (quoting Cooke v. United States, 267 U.S. 517, 539, 45 S.Ct. 390, 395-96, 69 L.Ed. 767 (1925)). Federal procedural rules do not displace the power, because such enactments, taken alone or together, are not substitutes for the inherent power, for that power is both broader and narrower than other means of imposing sanctions. * * * [W]hereas each of the other mechanisms reaches only certain individuals or conduct, the inherent power extends to a full range of litigation abuses. Chambers v. NASCO, Inc., 501 U.S. 32, 33, 111 S.Ct. 2123, 2134, 115 L.Ed.2d 27 (1991). However, "[b]ecause inherent powers are shielded from direct democratic controls, they must be exercised with restraint and discretion." Roadway Express, 447 U.S. at 764, 100 S.Ct. at 2463.

This court has held that dismissal pursuant to the court's inherent power must be reserved to cases involving "'contumacious conduct'" or other flagrant abuses. Consolidation Coal Co. v. Gooding, 703 F.2d 230, 233 (6th Cir. 1983) (citation omitted). And, we recognized long ago that a trial court's inherent power includes a remedy of dismissal in cases such as this. Reid v. Prentice-Hall, Inc., 261 F.2d 700, 701 (6th Cir. 1958). As the Seventh Circuit opined in Marrocco, whose facts parallel the facts here, "wilful and unexcused violations of the protective order here certainly qualify as 'contumacious conduct.'" 966 F.2d at 224. To hold litigants to a lesser standard places the authority and dignity of the court at peril. Of all this, the majority opinion makes no mention whatever.

IV

Part of the majority's rationale for concluding that the district court abused its discretion in dismissing the plaintiff's case, is the majority's view that the sins of plaintiff's counsel may not be visited upon the plaintiff. Although the majority opinion cites cases from this and other courts for the view that "this court, like many others, has been extremely reluctant to uphold the dismissal of a case merely to discipline an attorney," none of the cited cases involve violation of a protective order. Moreover, dismissal was not ordered here "merely to discipline an attorney." It was ordered primarily to vindicate the authority of the federal judiciary by demonstrating that severe consequences flow to a party whose counsel deliberately and intentionally flaunts a court's protective order for the purpose of gaining advantage in the litigation through a means explicitly prohibited by the court.

But whatever the "reluctan[ce]" of a panel of this and other courts to uphold dismissal as a sanction for violation of a court's order, the Supreme Court has decided unequivocally that dismissal is a proper sanction for the misconduct of counsel without regard to the asserted innocence of the client:

> There is certainly no merit to the contention that dismissal of petitioner's claim because of his counsel's unexcused conduct imposes an unjust penalty on the client. Petitioner voluntarily chose this attorney as his representative in the action, and he cannot now avoid the consequences of the acts or omissions of this freely selected agent. Any other notion would be wholly inconsistent with our system of representative litigation, in which each party is deemed bound by the acts of his lawyer-agent and is considered to have "notice of all facts, notice of which can be charged upon the attorney."

Link v. Wabash R.R. Co., 370 U.S. 626, 633-34, 82 S.Ct. 1386, 1390, 8 L.Ed.2d 734 (1962) (citation omitted). Undoubtedly, there are cases, although they ought to be few, in which the contumacious conduct of the lawyer should not be attributed to the client. Such cases might include instances where the lawyer's misconduct was personal and independent of, or even contrary to, the client's interest; as, for example, where counsel's deportment in the courtroom is seriously intemperate or insolent toward the court, the jury, or fellow counsel; or where through culpable neglect, and contrary to the client's interest, counsel fails to advance the client's cause through discovery and pretrial procedures; and other such circumstances where counsel's misconduct is entirely personal and in no significant way advantages his client's cause.

But this is not such a case. Here, for purposes of enhancing Cheryl Coleman's prospects for recovering substantial money damages against the blood donor — and undoubtedly to apply further leverage against the collectible Red Cross — her lawyer deliberately disobeyed the court's order not to reveal the identity of the donor. To say that counsel's misconduct may not, as things are turning out, benefit Cheryl Coleman because the donor has expired, is irrelevant. Counsel's purpose was to benefit his client by increasing her prospects for a financially advantageous settlement or judgment, and, not incidentally, to benefit himself as well. And therein lies a disquieting reality demonstrating that counsel's deliberate disobedience of the court's order was not at all attenuated from his client's interest.

It is safe to assume that counsel's representation of Cheryl Coleman is on a contingent fee basis, the virtually universal arrangement in this country according to which plaintiff's counsel accept the representation of clients in negligence actions. Assuming the usual arrangement here, Cheryl Coleman and her attorney are joint business venturers in the prosecution of Cheryl Coleman's negligence action. Counsel brings to their joint enterprise his professional expertise, and Cheryl Coleman brings a cause of action for negligence — one conceivably worth a great deal of money, given the tragic consequences Coleman has suffered. Cheryl Coleman and her counsel share a financial incentive for counsel to disregard the court's order not to seek or to reveal, to an investigator for example, the identity of the blood donor. Plaintiff and her counsel will share, according to the terms of their contingent fee arrangement, whatever settlement or judgment may be realized against the Red Cross and the donor. Such judgment or settlement may very well be substantially enhanced by the public disclosure of the donor's identity, given the Red Cross's obvious interest in avoiding a jury's potential wrath on learning that the Red Cross has revealed a donor's identity.

Quite aside from the financial advantage Cheryl Coleman's attorney intended would result to his client and to himself as a result of counsel's misconduct, there is a failure of logic in the majority's argument that all of the professionally proper actions taken by counsel to advance Coleman's cause should redound to her benefit, but counsel's misconduct directed to the same purpose is attributable to him alone and not to his client. It is not surprising that the Supreme Court flatly rejected this reasoning in *Link*.

V

As I have said, I think the majority opinion mistakenly follows the district court's error in analyzing this case under Rule 41(b) and Rule 37(b). But the district court also relied upon its inherent power, a basis the majority ignores. There is a compelling, indeed binding, legal authority, see *Link*, to say nothing of judicial common sense, to support the conclusion that dismissal of the plaintiff's case was within the range of options available to the district court for dealing with counsel's misconduct.

It may be that the judges of this panel would have elected a different sanction, one directed exclusively at counsel. But we are not empowered to second-guess the district court's discretion. We owe the district court deference to its discretionary call unless we are able to conclude that it had no authority to act as it did; that, as a matter of law, dismissal was not an option available to the court. This the court cannot do since, plainly, the law is to the contrary. Id. But even if the Rule 41(b) and Rule 37(b) approach were correct, the majority opinion cites no authority for its conclusion that unless the Red Cross can articulate how it was prejudiced in this litigation, it was an abuse of discretion to dismiss the case; and understandably so, for until today, there was none.

I would affirm the judgment of dismissal.

NOTES AND PROBLEMS FOR DISCUSSION

1. State concisely on what point (or points) the majority and dissent disagree. In the dissent's view, why does the probable existence of a "contingent fee" arrangement make a difference? How do you think the majority would respond?

2. Consider the standard applied by the appeals court in deciding whether to grant discovery and also why the district court had denied discovery. Why did the appeals court reverse?

3. The Colemans wanted the information described in note 5. Didn't this information meet the standard for discovery? See Rule 26(b)(1). If so, why did the district court deny discovery and why did the court of appeals affirm? See Rule 26(c).

4. Now consider the original ruling that denied discovery of the name of the donor. Didn't the information meet the applicable standard for discovery? Was the ruling correct?

5. Depositions may be taken of a party or nonparty witness. Would you expect a lawyer in the ordinary case to take the deposition of her own client or a "friendly" witness?

6. Assume the plaintiff retains attorney Smith to represent him in an accident case. Smith negligently lets the statute of limitations run. Plaintiff then sues and, when the defendant seeks a dismissal of the case on the basis of the statute of limitations, argues that he should not suffer for the incompetence of his lawyer and cites the *Coleman* case. What result?

SECTION D. PRETRIAL PROCEDURES

One can divide the litigation process roughly into four stages: pleading (during which issues of jurisdiction, pleadings, and parties will be resolved), discovery, pretrial, and trial. While cases are not required to proceed strictly in this sequence, they often do and, to some extent, the rules assume that they will. The pretrial stage generally occurs when discovery is either substantially far along or complete. Sequentially, then, the pretrial phase comes after discovery and, by definition, before the trial begins.

Two important things may, and often do, take place during the pretrial phase. First, there is a pretrial conference. See Rule 16. Conceptually, the purpose of a pretrial conference is to plan, and hopefully simplify, the trial (the process is not dissimilar from planning a big meeting or event). Counsel for the parties meet with the judge to discuss such matters as (1) the length of trial, (2) the identification of the issues to be tried and, hopefully, what issues are uncontested, (3) the number of witnesses and any special witness issues (e.g., a witness's unavailability for part of the trial and therefore a need to take his testimony "out of sequence"), (4) the evidence to be introduced, special issues relating to the evidence (and possible motions in limine — before the trial begins) and stipulations on admissibility (e.g., the parties agree that copies of all documents will be admissible or stipulate in advance that certain documents will be admissible), any special needs (e.g., to take the jury to view the premises involved or for video equipment), the submission of trial briefs, and many others. The pretrial conference also gives the judge a chance to explore the prospects of settlement, without requiring either party to take the initiative (this supposedly being a sign of insecurity with one's case).

It is difficult to "study" the pretrial conference in the classroom since there are as many variations as there are judges. At the extremes, some judges require extensive planning and detail, and that attorneys' spend substantial time in preparation for the trial; others may conduct a perfunctory conference and leave it to the parties to "work it out." The pretrial conference culminates in a final pretrial order, which will supersede the pleadings and govern the course of trial. See Rule 16(f). As with the conference itself, pretrial orders differ substantially in coverage and detail.

The second thing that may occur during the pretrial phase is a motion for summary judgment. See Rule 56. It is a basic principle of a system of legal rules that the decisionmaker will apply the legal rules in reaching decisions. For example, if the substantive law requires Wanda to prove that Carnival Hotel was negligent, the legal system has various devices to assure that Wanda makes a plausible case that the Hotel was in fact negligent. If she can't, then she will not be permitted to recover.

One way to handle this situation would be simply to wait for the trial and see what she comes up with. Then, if she doesn't make a plausible case, there will be a mechanism to see that she loses. But it may be that, once Wanda has had time to investigate and to conduct discovery, it will be clear that Wanda simply does not have a plausible case. In such a situation, there isn't much point in gearing up the whole trial mechanism if Wanda will lose anyway. The motion for summary judgment is adapted to identifying cases where a trial would be a waste of time. But human affairs being what they are, it is not always possible to be so clairvoyant.

As you might expect, the Federal Rules have a more legalistic sounding test for cases that would be a "waste of time." Read Rule 56 which governs motions for summary judgment. Rule 56(c) provides that summary judgment should be granted "if the pleadings, the discovery and disclosure materials on file, and any affidavits show that there is no genuine issue as to any material fact and that the movant is entitled to judgment as a matter of law." In other words, a party moving for summary judgment must first show what the law requires the nonmovant factually to establish, and then must show that there is no genuine issue as to such fact. If you were a judge (and, although you may doubt this now, some of you will be), do you think a trial would be a waste of time in the following case?

Pryor v. Seyfarth, Shaw, Fairweather & Geraldson

United States Court of Appeals, Seventh Circuit, 2000.
212 F.3d 976.

POSNER, CHIEF JUDGE.

The plaintiff appeals from the dismissal of her suit, on motion for summary judgment, for sexual harassment, and for retaliation for complaining about it, all in violation of Title VII. She was a secretary at a large Chicago law firm and claims that in 1994 a partner named Woodford for whom she was working harassed her on account of her gender. She bases the claim on five incidents, which for purposes of this appeal we assume happened exactly as she claims they did, spread over the last half of the year:

1. Woodford asked to see a "Frederick's of Hollywood" catalog that was on the plaintiff's desk and asked her whether she had ever bought anything from Frederick's. When she said yes, Woodford responded: "Well, can I see some pictures of you in some of the outfits that you have bought from Frederick's of Hollywood?" She said she had bought only shoes from Frederick's, and so there were no pictures of her wearing outfits from that store. He said, "Well, when you get some pictures can I see them?"

2. He said her shoes were "unusual" and that he "prefer[red] to see you in shoes with your toes out as opposed to those type of shoes."

3. He asked her "What's the color for next week?" and when she replied that she didn't know he said, "Do all your clothes correspond?"

4. Working on a case the documents in which included a book that had pictures of women in bondage or black leather, Woodford asked Pryor to "look at this." When she inquired whether it was relevant to a case, he replied, "No, I just wanted you to see it."

5. Noticing an outfit in a shopping bag behind Pryor's desk, Woodford said, "Oh, a new outfit?" And when she said yes, he said, "Is that something you got from Frederick's of Hollywood?"

Neither singly nor in combination do these incidents rise to the level at which alleged sexual harassment becomes actionable under federal law. Incidents 3 and 5 seem entirely innocuous, 1 and 2 mildly flirtatious, and 4 possibly suggestive or even offensive, but not so offensive as to constitute actionable harassment. For Title VII does not forbid sexual harassment as such. The harassment must be sufficiently severe that a rational trier of fact could find that it had actually changed the conditions of the plaintiff's workplace, * * * for only sexual discrimination that changes those conditions is (so far as bears on sexual harassment at any rate) actionable under that statute. The harassment alleged here falls short of the harassment held in Baskerville v. Culligan Int'l Co., 50 F.3d 428 (7th Cir. 1995), and other cases, * * * to be beyond the reach of Title VII because insufficiently severe to change the conditions of employment as they would be perceived by a reasonable person, not hypersensitive.

Pryor seeks to distinguish these cases by means of two affidavits filed after her deposition, at which she testified about the five incidents summarized above. One affidavit is hers and asserts that Woodford had been harassing her for years. The other affidavit is by another former employee of the Seyfarth firm and alleges that she was harassed by Woodford too. As far as Pryor's affidavit is concerned, she gives us no reason to depart from the presumption that an affidavit which seeks to bolster a party's prior deposition is not entitled to consideration, * * * while the other affidavit shows only that Pryor's lawyer is confused about the rule that sexual harassment is actionable under Title VII only when it changes the plaintiff's conditions of employment. Insofar as Woodford harassed other employees, and did so without (so far as appears) Pryor's knowledge, it could not have altered *her* conditions of employment, and so she could not complain about that harassment under Title VII. At argument her lawyer told us that Woodford had leered at her without her knowing it, and he adduced this as evidence that Woodford's harassment was "pervasive." It was actually irrelevant.

So the claim of sexual harassment fails. But Seyfarth does not argue that the claim was so frivolous that the making of it showed that Pryor was unfit to remain at the firm — that *she* was the harasser. See McDonnell v. Cisneros, 84 F.3d 256, 259 (7th Cir. 1996). And so her claim of retaliation is unaffected by the failure of her claim of harassment.

Three months after she filed that claim she was fired by Seyfarth's personnel manager after being discovered glueing an artificial fingernail on the finger of a friend in the ladies' bathroom at the Seyfarth firm. Seyfarth points out that even if the offense seems a trivial one not meriting the discharge of a long-term employee, still, so long as the discharge was not motivated by the fact that Pryor had filed a claim against the firm the disproportionate character of the manager's action could not establish liability under Title VII. That is true, because Title VII is not a "good cause" statute; it creates a remedy against invidious discrimination (or, as here, retaliation), not against caprice. The circumstances leading up to the discharge, however, cast enough suspicion on the motive for firing Pryor to entitle her to a trial.

To begin with, if the facts are taken as they should be in the light most favorable to Pryor, there was no "offense." She was on her break when she applied the nail; she had been "doing" nails for her coworkers for years; there was no rule against having a visitor and doing the visitor's nail; and the procedure took only 30 seconds. We repeat that it is not our business whether the firm had good cause to fire Pryor; but it would be odd if the firm had delegated to its personnel manager the authority to fire a long-term employee for entirely capricious reasons — sufficiently odd to make one wonder whether retaliation rather than whim may have been the real cause of the firm's action.

Against this Seyfarth argues that the incident with the nail was merely the straw that broke the camel's back — Pryor's secretarial work was unsatisfactory and her attire "inappropriate." Yet she had been working for the firm for nine years when she was fired in May 1995, and, so far as the documentary record, at least, is concerned, her work had been entirely satisfactory throughout. As recently as the summer of 1994, her annual performance reviews (the last before she was fired) by the three lawyers she was working for then had been highly positive, especially the review by an associate named Dalinka for whom she worked. Dalinka in his deposition testified that Pryor's work had actually been unsatisfactory when he filled out the performance-review form and that he had given her a glowing report in order not to make her feel bad. Yet the form requires only that the reviewer check boxes (needs improvement, satisfactory, etc.) beside each task category. There are spaces for optional comments under the boxes, and Dalinka went out of his way to make positive comments in each space, though he could just have checked the boxes without hurting Pryor's feelings. His going the extra mile, as it were, casts doubt on his testimony that he was making a merely pro forma positive report, and by undermining his credibility also casts doubt on his further and more fundamental testimony that Pryor's work had deteriorated.

It is common for supervisors to overrate their subordinates for purposes of building morale, avoiding conflict, and deflecting criticisms that the supervisor isn't doing a good job (or that he shouldn't have hired this subordinate in the first place). Not much weight can be given to positive reviews. But not much does not equal zero. And by going out of his way to say nice things about the plaintiff Dalinka made it possible for a reasonable trier of fact to infer that his later denigration of her performance was invented for purposes of the litigation. Disbelieving a witness's testimony about one of the material facts in a case can justify the trier of fact in disbelieving the witness's contested testimony on other material facts. An affidavit from another lawyer for whom Pryor worked denied that she had any performance problems; and Dalinka never documented any of his concerns about her performance.   One doesn't want to encourage bureaucracy in the workplace; but of all employers, lawyers can be expected to be most sensitive to charges of employment discrimination and most assiduous about documenting actions calculated to rebut such charges. Especially a law firm like Seyfarth that specializes in employment law!

Dalinka testified that Pryor refused to learn the computer program Excel. He says that all secretaries were required to learn it, but Seyfarth cannot locate a document saying this. Pryor testified that, far from refusing to learn Excel (which however she testified was optional rather than mandatory), she was scheduled for an Excel lesson the very day she was fired.

Finally, the personnel manager criticized Pryor for "inappropriate attire" (apparently, wearing stretch pants and a sweater top). The manager testified that Pryor persisted in wearing such attire; Pryor testified that she immediately switched to wearing suits. Such a conflict cannot be resolved on summary judgment.

Not only may the grounds on which Pryor was fired have been pretextual, but she presented evidence that Seyfarth had a policy of progressive discipline which would have precluded the firing of Pryor for such trivial offenses without prior warnings which it is conceded she did not receive. Seyfarth denies the existence of such a policy, but this is another issue of fact that cannot be resolved on summary judgment. Its argument that an employee is incompetent to testify to the existence of an employment policy is absurd.

The personnel manager testified that she didn't know that Pryor had filed a claim against the firm when she fired her, but this was another bit of contested evidence that a jury would not be required to believe. The snitch who turned Pryor in to the personnel manager for the nail misdemeanor knew about the claim, and the manager spoke to other people at the firm before firing her, including Dalinka, whose complaints about Pryor's performance may have been fabricated as part of a retaliatory scheme. Dalinka, incidentally, worked in the same department of the firm as Woodford.

A reasonable jury could find that after and because Pryor filed a claim, the firm was "laying" for her, biding its time to create a space between the date of the claim and the date of the discharge, and in the interval gathering pretextual evidence of misconduct to provide a fig leaf for its retaliatory action. Of course we do not hold that this is the correct interpretation of the events, only that the matter is sufficiently in doubt to require a trial.

The dismissal of the harassment count is affirmed, but the dismissal of the retaliation count is reversed and the case remanded for further proceedings consistent with this opinion.

Affirmed in Part, Reversed in Part, and Remanded.

NOTES AND PROBLEMS FOR DISCUSSION

1. As noted earlier, the first step in a summary judgment motion is to identify what the plaintiff must establish to win. In this case, what must the plaintiff establish?

2. The defendant essentially says that the plaintiff hasn't established what she must. But the plaintiff says that she did, and sets forth various items of evidence to support her claim.

(a) How did the evidence get before the court?

(b) How does the court decide whether the evidence is true or not and why does the *Pryor* court seem to believe the defendant?

(c) Given your answer to (b), why does the court grant summary judgment on one claim and not on the other?

(d) As to the claim on which summary judgment was granted, why doesn't the plaintiff get a chance to prove her case to the jury?

3. If you represented Pryor, what additional evidence or arguments would you have offered in opposition to summary judgment?

4. Be sure you understand that the stakes are enormous on summary judgment. At first blush, it looks like a tie. But which side do you think will be celebrating?

5. Perhaps the most famous summary judgment case is ARNSTEIN v. PORTER, 154 F.2d 464 (2d Cir. 1994). Buddy Arnstein sued the famous composer Cole Porter, alleging that Porter had plagiarized various copyrighted and uncopyrighted songs of Arnstein. The court held that Arnstein had to show either similarities which supported an inference of copying or access, and that while there were small similarities (3 or 4 sequential notes), these were not adequate.   Although Arnstein alleged that his songs had been widely disseminated and also alleged break-ins to his apartment by "stooges," Porter vehemently denied copying, hearing the songs, and access.   The court denied summary judgment saying, in part, that (a) even if Arnstein's story seemed fantastic, justice should not be denied because plaintiff's story is improbable since "sometimes truth is stranger than fiction," (b) even though Porter had testified at his deposition, the court "cannot very well overestimate the importance of having the witness examined and cross-examined in presence of the court and jury," and (c) at trial, the jury would be able to listen to the various pieces of music in question and the testimony of experts about them.   A sharp dissent by Judge Clark, a major author of the Federal Rules, first argued that the works were so musically dissimilar as to negate plagiarism; second, that plagiarism issues were primarily for the court and not the jury; and third, that the decision seriously undermined the summary judgment procedure.   Do you think the *Pryor* court would agree and, if not, for which of reasons (a), (b) and/or (c)? At the actual trial, Arnstein did lose, and the verdict was summarily affirmed on appeal.

SECTION E.   THE TRIAL

Most of you have read, watched enough TV, or seen enough movies to have a general sense of what happens at a trial.   Briefly, the jury is selected (after questioning — called "voir dire"), the parties make opening statements (the plaintiff goes first), the parties introduce evidence (the plaintiff first, then the defendant, then the plaintiff, etc.), the parties make closing arguments (the defendant usually goes first; sometimes, it is the plaintiff, then the defendant, then the plaintiff again with a brief reply), the judge charges the jury, the jury deliberates, the jury delivers a verdict, and the judge enters judgment on the verdict.

In the discussion of summary judgment, we considered the notion of evidentiary sufficiency — that the plaintiff must make out a plausible case.   In the course of the trial, it is up to the trial judge to assure that she does.   See Rule 50.   Briefly, after the close of the plaintiff's evidence and after the close of all the evidence, the defendant can make a motion for judgment as a matter of law (formerly called a "directed verdict").   Under Rule 50(a)(1), a judgment as a matter of law should be granted if "a reasonable jury would not have a legally sufficient evidentiary basis to find for the [non-moving] party."

The standard is easy to say but not so easy to apply.   Since all cases are different, one can only get a feel for this standard by reading a number of cases, and observing the arguments and reasoning of the courts.   The following is one of the most famous decisions on sufficiency of the evidence.   But as you read it, keep in mind that the plaintiff is not required to prove what happened with absolute certainty or anything close to it, but instead, must provide a rational basis for a factfinder to accept her story as being more likely than not.

Lavender v. Kurn

Supreme Court of the United States, 1946.
327 U.S. 645, 66 S.Ct. 740, 90 L.Ed. 916.

MR. JUSTICE MURPHY delivered the opinion of the Court.

The Federal Employers' Liability Act permits recovery for personal injuries to an employee of a railroad engaged in interstate commerce if such injuries result "in whole or in part from the negligence of any of the officers, agents, or employees of such carrier, or by reason of any defect or insufficiency, due to its negligence, in its cars, engines, appliances, machinery, track, roadbed, works, boats, wharves, or other equipment." 45 U.S.C. §51.

Petitioner, the administrator of the estate of L. E. Haney, brought this suit under the Act against the respondent trustees of the St. Louis-San Francisco Railway Company (Frisco) and the respondent Illinois Central Railroad Company. It was charged that Haney, while employed as a switchtender by the respondents in the switchyard of the Grand Central Station in Memphis, Tennessee, was killed as a result of respondents' negligence. Following a trial in the Circuit Court of the City of St. Louis, Missouri, the jury returned a verdict in favor of petitioner and awarded damages in the amount of $30,000. Judgment was entered accordingly. On appeal, however, the Supreme Court of Missouri reversed the judgment, holding that there was no substantial evidence of negligence to support the submission of the case to the jury. We granted certiorari, to review the propriety of the Supreme Court's action under the circumstances of this case.

It was admitted that Haney was employed by the Illinois Central, or a subsidiary corporation thereof, as a switchtender in the railroad yards near the Grand Central Station, which was owned by the Illinois Central. His duties included the throwing of switches for the Illinois Central as well as for the Frisco and other railroads using that station. For these services, the trustees of Frisco paid the Illinois Central two-twelfths of Haney's wages; they also paid two-twelfths of the wages of two other switch-tenders who worked at the same switches. In addition, the trustees paid Illinois Central $1.87½ for each passenger car switched into Grand Central Station, which included all the cars in the Frisco train being switched into the station at the time Haney was killed.

The Illinois Central tracks run north and south directly past and into the Grand Central Station. About 2700 feet south of the station the Frisco tracks cross at right angles to the Illinois Central tracks. A westbound Frisco train wishing to use the station must stop some 250 feet or more west of this crossing and back into the station over a switch line curving east and north. The events in issue center about the switch several feet north of the main Frisco tracks at the point where the switch line branches off. This switch controls the tracks at this point.

It was very dark on the evening of December 21, 1939. At about 7:30 p.m. a westbound interstate Frisco passenger train stopped on the Frisco main line, its rear some 20 or 30 feet west of the switch. Haney, in the performance of his duties, threw or opened the switch to permit the train to back into the station. The respondents claimed that Haney was then required to cross to the south side of the track before the train passed the switch; and the conductor of the train testified that he saw Haney so cross. But there was also evidence that Haney's duties required him to wait at the switch north of the track until the train had cleared, close the switch, return to his shanty near the crossing and change the signals from red to green to permit trains on the Illinois Central tracks to use the crossing. The Frisco train cleared the switch, backing at the rate of 8 or 10 miles per hour. But the switch remained open and the signals still were red. Upon investigation Haney was found north of the track near the switch lying face down on the ground, unconscious. An ambulance was called, but he was dead upon arrival at the hospital.

Haney had been struck in the back of the head, causing a fractured skull from which he died. There were no known eye-witnesses to the fatal blow. Although it is not clear there is evidence that his body was extended north and south, the head to the south. Apparently he had fallen forward to the south; his face was bruised on the left side from hitting the ground and there were marks indicating that his toes had dragged a few inches southward as he fell. His head was about 5½ feet north of the Frisco tracks. Estimates ranged from 2 feet to 14 feet as to how far west of the switch he lay.

The injury to Haney's head was evidenced by a gash about two inches long from which blood flowed. The back of Haney's white cap had a corresponding black mark about an inch and a half long and an inch wide, running at an angle downward to the right of the center of the back of the head. A spot of blood was later found at a point 3 or 4 feet north of the tracks. The conclusion following an autopsy was that Haney's skull was fractured by "some fast moving small round object." One of the examining doctors testified that such an object might have been attached to a train backing at the rate of 8 or 10 miles per hour. But he also admitted that the fracture might have resulted from a blow from a pipe or club or some similar round object in the hands of an individual.

Petitioner's theory is that Haney was struck by the curled end or tip of a mail hook hanging down loosely on the outside of the mail car of the backing train. This curled end was 73 inches above the top of the rail, which was 7 inches high. The overhang of the mail car in relation to the rails was about 2 to 2½ feet. The evidence indicated that when the mail car swayed or moved around a curve the mail hook might pivot, its curled end swinging out as much as 12 to 14 inches. The curled end could thus be swung out to a point 3 to 3½ feet from the rail and about 73 inches above the top of the rail. Both east and west of the switch, however, was an uneven mound of cinders and dirt rising at its highest points 18 to 24 inches above the top of the rails. Witnesses differed as to how close the mound approached the rails, the estimates varying from 3 to 15 feet. But taking the figures most favorable to the petitioner, the mound extended to a point 6 to 12 inches north of the overhanging side of the mail car. If the mail hook end swung out 12 to 14 inches it would be 49 to 55 inches above the highest parts of the mound. Haney was 67½ inches tall. If he had been standing on the mound about a foot from the side of the mail car he could have been hit by the end of the mail hook, the exact point of contact depending upon the height of the mound at the particular point. His wound was about 4 inches below the top of his head, or 63½ inches above the point where he stood on the mound-well within the possible range of the mail hook end.

Respondents' theory is that Haney was murdered. They point to the estimates that the mound was 10 to 15 feet north of the rail, making it impossible for the mail hook end to reach a point of contact with Haney's head. Photographs were placed in the record to support the claim that the ground was level north of the rail for at least 10 feet. Moreover, it appears that the area immediately surrounding the switch was quite dark. Witnesses stated that it was so dark that it was impossible to see a 3-inch pipe 25 feet away. It also appears that many hoboes and tramps frequented the area at night in order to get rides on freight trains. Haney carried a pistol to protect himself. This pistol was found loose under his body by those who came to his rescue. It was testified, however, that the pistol had apparently slipped out of his pocket or scabbard as he fell. Haney's clothes were not disarranged and there was no evidence of a struggle or fight. No rods, pipes or weapons of any kind, except Haney's own pistol, were found near the scene. Moreover, his gold watch and diamond ring were still on him after he was struck. Six days later his unsoiled billfold was found on a high board fence about a block from the place where Haney was struck and near the point where he had been placed in an ambulance. It contained his social security card and other effects, but no money. His wife testified that he "never carried much money, not very much more than $10." Such were the facts in relation to respondents' theory of murder.

Finally, one of the Frisco foremen testified that he arrived at the scene shortly after Haney was found injured. He later examined the fireman's side of the train very carefully and found nothing sticking out or in disorder. In explaining why he examined this side of the train so carefully he stated that while he was at the scene of the accident "someone said they thought that train No. 106 backing in to Grand Central Station is what struck this man" and that Haney "was supposed to have been struck by something protruding on the side of the train." The foreman testified that these statements were made by an unknown Illinois Central switchman standing near the fallen body of Haney. The foreman admitted that the switchman "didn't see the accident." This testimony was admitted by the trial court over the strenuous objections of respondents' counsel that it was mere hearsay. . . . .

The jury was instructed that Frisco's trustees were liable if it was found that they negligently permitted a rod or other object to extend out from the side of the train as it backed past Haney and that Haney was killed as the direct result of such negligence, if any. The jury was further told that Illinois Central was liable if it was found that the company negligently maintained an unsafe and dangerous place for Haney to work, in that the ground was high and uneven and the light insufficient and inadequate, and that Haney was injured and killed as a direct result of the said place being unsafe and dangerous. This latter instruction as to Illinois Central did not require the jury to find that Haney was killed by something protruding from the train.

The Supreme Court, in upsetting the jury's verdict against both the Frisco trustees and the Illinois Central, admitted that "It could be inferred from the facts that Haney could have been struck by the mail hook knob if he were standing on the south side of the mound and the mail hook extended out as far as 12 or 14 inches." But it held that "all reasonable minds would agree that it would be mere speculation and conjecture to say that Haney was struck by the mail hook" and that "plaintiff failed to make a submissible case on that question." It also ruled that there "was no substantial evidence that the uneven ground and insufficient light were cause or contributing causes of the death of Haney." Finally, the Supreme Court held that the testimony of the foreman as to the statement made to him by the unknown switchmen was inadmissible under the res gestae rule since the switchman spoke from what he had heard rather than from his own knowledge.

We hold, however, that there was sufficient evidence of negligence on the part of both the Frisco trustee and the Illinois Central to justify the submission of the case to the jury and to require appellate courts to abide by the verdict rendered by the jury.

The evidence we have already detailed demonstrates that there was evidence from which it might be inferred that the end of the mail hook struck Haney in the back of the head, an inference that the Supreme Court admitted could be drawn. That inference is not rendered unreasonable by the fact that Haney apparently fell forward toward the main Frisco track so that his head was 5½ feet north of the rail. He may well have been struck and then wandered in a daze to the point where he fell forward. The testimony as to blood marks some distance away from his head lends credence to that possibility, indicating that he did not fall immediately upon being hit. When that is added to the evidence most favorable to the petitioner as to the height and swing-out of the hook, the height and location of the mound and the nature of Haney's duties, the inference that Haney was killed by the hook cannot be said to be unsupported by probative facts or to be so unreasonable as to warrant taking the case from the jury.

It is true that there is evidence tending to show that it was physically and mathematically impossible for the hook to strike Haney. And there are facts from which it might reasonably be inferred that Haney was murdered. But such evidence has become irrelevant upon appeal, there being a reasonable basis in the record for inferring that the hook struck Haney. The jury having made that inference, the respondents were not free to relitigate the factual dispute in a reviewing court. Under these circumstances it would be an undue invasion of the jury's historic function for an appellate court to weigh the conflicting evidence, judge the credibility of witnesses and arrive at a conclusion opposite from the one reached by the jury.

It is no answer to say that the jury's verdict involved speculation and conjecture. Whenever facts are in dispute or the evidence is such that fair-minded men may draw different inferences, a measure of speculation and conjecture is required on the part of those whose duty it is to settle the dispute by choosing what seems to them to be the most reasonable inference. Only when there is a complete absence of probative facts to support the conclusion reached does a reversible error appear. But where, as here, there is an evidentiary basis for the jury's verdict, the jury is free to discard or disbelieve whatever facts are inconsistent with its conclusion. And the appellate court's function is exhausted when that evidentiary basis becomes apparent, it being immaterial that the court might draw a contrary inference or feel that another conclusion is more reasonable.

We are unable, therefore, to sanction a reversal of the jury's verdict against Frisco's trustees. Nor can we approve any disturbance in the verdict as to Illinois Central. The evidence was uncontradicted that it was very dark at the place where Haney was working and the surrounding ground was high and uneven. The evidence also showed that this area was entirely within the domination and control of Illinois Central despite the fact that the area was technically located in a public street of the City of Memphis. It was not unreasonable to conclude that these conditions constituted an unsafe and dangerous working place and that such conditions contributed in part to Haney's death, assuming that it resulted primarily from the mail hook striking his head.

In view of the foregoing disposition of the case, it is unnecessary to decide whether the allegedly hearsay testimony was admissible under [an exception to the] rule. Rulings on the admissibility of evidence must normally be left to the sound discretion of the trial judge in actions under the Federal Employers' Liability Act. But inasmuch as there is adequate support in the record for the jury's verdict apart from the hearsay testimony, we need not determine whether that discretion was abused in this instance.

The judgment of the Supreme Court of Missouri is reversed and the case is remanded for whatever further proceedings may be necessary not inconsistent with this opinion. Reversed.

[THE CHIEF JUSTICE and MR. JUSTICE FRANKFURTER concur in the result.]

[MR. JUSTICE REED dissents.]

[MR. JUSTICE JACKSON took no part in the consideration or decision of this case.]

NOTES AND PROBLEMS FOR DISCUSSION

1. Given the case put on by the plaintiff and the defendants, how would you have decided the case if you were a juror? Would you make a distinction between Frisco and Illinois Central, the two defendants?

2. Consider whether the Supreme Court would have upheld a directed verdict for the defendant Frisco if (a) a witness testified that he saw someone hit Haney over the head with a blunt instrument, or (b) there were several robberies in the area the same night?

3. After the verdict is rendered and judgment entered for the winner, the loser in federal court can make a motion for a new trial. See Rule 59(a). The motion may be on the ground that the trial court made an error at the trial (e.g., in admitting or excluding evidence, by giving an erroneous charge to the jury), or that the verdict "is against the weight of the evidence." As trial judge in *Lavender*, if the jury came in with a verdict for the plaintiff, would you have granted the defendants' motion for a new trial on the latter ground?

4. For students who think *Lavender* is a relic of a bygone era, consider the more recent case of Sphere Drake Insurance PLC v. Trisko, 226 F.3d 951 (8th Cir. 2000). There, plaintiff's employees had displayed various unique pieces of jewelry at a show and, afterwards, put two suitcases containing the jewelry in the trunk of their car and sat in the car and talked and played the radio while waiting to be joined by other employees. After about half an hour, they were joined by other employees and, when the trunk was opened, the suitcases were gone. Plaintiff sued on an insurance policy alleging theft, and the defendant (insurance company) alleged it was an unexplained loss or mysterious disappearance outside of the coverage of the policy. At trial, the plaintiff relied largely on the expert testimony of a detective who testified (a) he thought it was a theft, (b) he had been told by an informant that two individuals were paid $20,000 to steal the jewelry, (c) sophisticated thieves could steal the suitcases without being noticed and without damage to the trunk, and (d) there was evidence of similar crimes in the Miami area. In addition, the plaintiff's employees testified that they were not paying attention and there was no evidence of damage or tampering with the car, and some of the stolen items showed up a few months later at a Miami jewelry store. The court cited the statement in *Lavender* to the effect that the drawing of inferences from disputed facts requires a measure of speculation and conjecture, and it affirmed a jury verdict for plaintiff. If you represented the insurance company, how would you seek to distinguish *Lavender*?

SECTION F. REPOSE (CLAIM AND ISSUE PRECLUSION)

Assume that Wanda's case proceeds to trial and that Wanda recovers $200,000. She thinks it is not enough, and her damages were $1 million. Or, suppose Wanda's lawyer decides that he should have called a witness who was available, and that failure to call the witness was a big mistake. Can she try again? Alternatively, suppose that Wanda had recovered $1.5 million, and Carnival Casino thinks this is highway robbery or that the courts made an error of law or fact. Can it bring a second action to undo the first decision?

The law generally says no — a party is only entitled to one try (win or lose). The rationale is based on notions of fairness, a social interest in ending the fight (called "repose"), and the importance of stability and respect for the judicial system. The questions posed above are easy applications of these principles — both Wanda and Carnival Casino each had an opportunity to try their case and should not have a second chance. If there was something wrong with the pretrial or trial process, the loser's remedy is to appeal — it is not to start over.

The principle is often called claim preclusion (the older term is "res judicata") — that the parties should have only one opportunity to try a claim and all defenses to that claim. This, too, is easily said, but not so easily applied. What does it mean for matters in a second lawsuit to be part of the "same claim" as in the first? For example, assume there has been a car accident, and that the plaintiff sues first for personal injuries and recovers damages. Can the plaintiff now sue for damage to her car?

Pavon v. Swift Transportation Co., Inc.

United States Court of Appeals, Ninth Circuit, 1999.
192 F.3d 902.

FLETCHER, CIRCUIT JUDGE.

Swift Transportation Company, Inc., ("Swift") appeals the district court's judgment, following a jury trial, in favor of Fernando Pavon in Pavon's wrongful discharge action, pursuant to 42 U.S.C. §1981, Title VII of the Civil Rights Act of 1964 (42 U.S.C. §2000e), and O.R.S. 659.030, arising when Pavon was terminated after complaining about ongoing racial harassment in his job as a diesel mechanic at Swift. Swift also appeals the district court's denial of its motion for a new trial. We have jurisdiction pursuant to 28 U.S.C. §1291, and we affirm.

FACTS AND PROCEDURAL BACKGROUND

Pavon was hired by Swift in November, 1994. Pavon is a United States citizen of Hispanic origin, born in Honduras. While working at his post in February, 1995, Pavon was subjected to racial slurs and harassment by his co-worker, Kevin Sterle. Sterle's harassment of Pavon included calling him "beaner," "fucking Mexican," "wet back," "spic," "illiterate," and "stupid." Sterle also taunted Pavon with comments like "go home," and "go back to Columbia," and threatening to turn him in to immigration.

Pavon complained several times to his shop foreman and supervisor, Ted Staley, about Sterle's remarks. Staley reported Pavon's complaints to his superior, Mark Janszen. The harassment continued on a near-daily basis. Pavon complained directly to Janszen, who issued Pavon a disciplinary warning. After meeting with Pavon and Sterle, Janszen decided to transfer Pavon to a separate workstation, the Fuel Shop. The transfer was not accompanied by a loss of pay or benefits, but Pavon saw it as a demotion and disciplinary action, because the Fuel Shop was a station to which new and inexperienced employees were normally assigned.

After Pavon's transfer, Sterle continued to search out Pavon and to taunt him with racial slurs. Plaintiff again complained to his supervisors. Janszen prepared disciplinary notices relating to Pavon. Larry Sampson, a colleague of Pavon's at Swift, advised Pavon to contact the company recruiter, Don Diggins, and Ron Rodriguez at company headquarters in Phoenix. Pavon could not reach Diggins, but did contact Rodriguez. Pavon followed the latter's advice to start keeping a notebook of what was going on. Despite having been told of Pavon's complaints by Sampson, Diggins took no action to interview Pavon or to investigate the allegations.

On July 5, 1995, Pavon was called into a meeting with Janszen and Diggins. Pavon continued to object to the company's discipline of him and its refusal to remedy the ongoing racial harassment. Diggins asked Pavon, "Do you know who Martin Luther King was? Remember what happened to him?" Pavon returned to work after the meeting. Later that day, he was terminated.

Following his termination, Pavon lost $1,218 in wages in a two week period before he secured comparable employment. On September 18, 1995, Pavon filed a complaint in Multnomah County District Court seeking unpaid wages. That action was dismissed following settlement by the parties. On October 2, 1995, Pavon filed this action in federal district court under Title VII of the Civil Rights Act of 1991, 42 U.S.C. §1981, and O.R.S. 659.030, as well as for common law wrongful discharge. Defendant's motion for summary judgment, based on the ground that the action was claim-precluded because it involved issues that could have been raised in the state court action, was denied. Following a three-day jury trial, judgment was entered in favor of Pavon. As total economic damages for all four of his claims, he was awarded $1,218. In addition, on his §1981, Title VII, and wrongful discharge claims, he was awarded $250,000 in noneconomic damages and $300,000 in punitive damages The Special Verdict form did not specify separate amounts for each claim. Defendant's motion for a new trial was denied, and Swift appealed.

DISCUSSION

Claim Preclusion

Swift's first argument is that all of Pavon's employment-related claims form a single transaction for purposes of claim preclusion. We review res judicata-claim preclusion-claims de novo. Because the underlying judgment was rendered in an Oregon state court, we must apply Oregon's rules of claim preclusion. 28 U.S.C. §1738; *Russell*, 76 F.3d at 244.

* * *

Upon review of Oregon law, we find that Pavon's federal suit was not barred by his state wage penalty action. Oregon law focuses on the transaction at issue in the state and federal cases and gives preclusive effect to all claims against the defendant that were available to the plaintiff arising from that transaction. Lee v. Mitchell, 152 Or.App. 159, 953 P.2d 414 (1998). "The expression 'trans-action, or series of connected transactions,' is not capable of a mathematically precise definition; it invokes a pragmatic standard to be applied with attention to the facts of the cases." Troutman v. Erlandson, 287 Or. 187, 598 P.2d 1211 (1979) (en banc), quoting Restatement (Second) of the Law of Judgments, §61, Comment B (1978). The court in *Troutman* listed the following criteria as relevant to the transaction inquiry: time, space, origin of the harm, subjective or objective motivation, convenience, and similar acts. We agree with the district court that there is not enough similarity of facts or claims underlying the federal and state claims for claim preclusion to apply. As the district court explained, Pavon's state court action was a wage penalty claim which required proof of unpaid wages and failure to pay within thirty days, and a payroll penalty claim involving the absence of authorization for a payroll deduction. His federal court action, in contrast, involves proof of an allegedly hostile work environment, plaintiff's complaints to management, defendant's alleged failure to take effective remedial action and retaliation against plaintiff for his complaints, defendant's termination of plaintiff, and the connection between the termination and plaintiff's membership in a protected class.

Showing discriminatory intent was an essential element of the federal claims, but not of the state claims. Pavon did need to show in his state court action that Swift's failure to pay him his final wages was "wilful" in order to recover. O.R.S. 652.150. However, under the statute, "wilful" means "merely that the thing done or omitted to be done was done or omitted intentionally." Sabin v. Willamette-Western Corp., 276 Or. 1083, 1094, 557 P.2d 1344 (1976). Showing "wilfulness" in the state proceedings required different witnesses, and different evidence than what was required to show discriminatory intent in federal court. While the events that gave rise to the federal claims were connected to those that gave rise to the wage claims, we find that aspects of the state and federal claims did not "necessarily overlap any complete litigation of another," Whitaker v. Bank of Newport, 313 Or. 450, 458, 836 P.2d 695 (1992) (emphasis added), and that therefore, under Oregon law, Swift's defense of claim preclusion would fail. *Affirmed.*

NOTES AND PROBLEMS FOR DISCUSSION

1.   All questions of claim preclusion involve two lawsuits — a claim is asserted in the second lawsuit, and one party in the second lawsuit argues that what happened in the first lawsuit should affect the second lawsuit. In *Pavon*, be sure you understand what the first lawsuit was for, and what the second lawsuit was for. How did Swift claim that the first lawsuit affected the second?

2.   What test does the Court apply to decide whether the claim in the second lawsuit was the same as the claim in the first lawsuit? Did Swift disagree with that test, and if not, what did it argue?

3.   Would Swift's argument have been stronger if it had won the first lawsuit?

4.   Since the Court held that Pavon's discrimination claim was not part of the same claim as the wage claim, a second doctrine called "issue preclusion" (also known as "collateral estoppel") applies. In brief, this doctrine provides that any issue decided against a party in the first case is binding against him in the second case and cannot be retried. As applied to Pavon's case, this means that the first court's decision that Pavon was not paid the full amount due, if relevant, would be binding on Swift and could not be retried in the second case.

5.   In a typical case, the Court will render decisions on various matters prior to the trial — e.g., Rule 12(b) motions, motions to amend pleadings, and discovery motions. These are called "interlocutory" orders. In the federal courts, interlocutory orders are not appealable; instead, at the end of the case (i.e., after a "final" order), the loser can appeal not only issues arising from a trial, but all interlocutory orders as well. See 28 U.S.C. §1291. That is, of course, what happened in *Pavon*, in which the denial of Swift's summary judgment motion arguing for claim preclusion was appealable only after the trial was over.

This is very significant procedurally, because it means that unless an order entered before a verdict and judgment after trial ends the case (and becomes a final order), the order during the pendency of the case is not immediately appealable. While the loser can appeal such an order after the case is over, the loser may be required to show not only that the order was wrong, but that she was prejudiced and/or that the issue raised and decided in the order was not superseded by later developments in the case. Consider whether each of the following may be immediately appealed:

(a) An order granting a motion under Rule 12(b)(2).

(b) An order denying such a motion.

(c) An order granting a motion to amend a complaint to add new claims.

(d) An order denying such a motion.

(e) An order granting defendant's discovery request, and requiring plaintiff to produce very harmful documents.

(f) An order denying such request.

CHAPTER 2

Adjudicative Power: Personal Jurisdiction

Imagine that you were whiling away some free time one Saturday afternoon this semester surfing the Internet on your home computer. During your cyberspace travels, you happened upon an interesting web site that offered you the opportunity to obtain a free, fully functional version of a well known financial planning and check writing program. You were not required to fill out any annoying application form or in any way to identify yourself or your location in order to obtain the file. You simply had to click an icon on the screen and the sponsor of the web site would automatically deliver a file to your computer containing this financial program. You decided to take advantage of the offer and downloaded the program onto the hard drive of your computer. For several days thereafter, you utilized the program without incident until you discovered that the program contained a "virus" that wiped out all of the data contained on the hard drive of your computer, including all of your confidential financial information, irretrievable personal and business correspondence, as well as the class notes, case briefs, and outlines from all of your current law school classes.

Assume further that you decided to file suit against both the web site sponsor and the software manufacturer instead of seeking redress through some non-litigative mechanism such as arbitration or mediation. Where would you like to file the suit? Do you have any reason to believe that there is or should be any limit on the courts in which you could pursue this action? For example, could you bring suit in a federal and/or a state court? And within either of these judicial systems, would any court be at your disposal or would (should) there be additional limits on forum availability? Intuitively, you sense that you are not likely to be able to proceed with this action in a traffic court, a bankruptcy court, or a juvenile court. But why is that intuition correct? What does this suggest about the extent of a court's adjudicative power other than that it is limited in some way?

The answer to these questions lies in the meaning of a fundamental concept called judicial jurisdiction. Judicial jurisdiction, sometimes referred to as adjudicative jurisdiction, is the demarcation of the authority or power of a court to adjudicate a particular dispute. Moreover, judicial jurisdiction is further divided into two constituent parts. A court must possess personal jurisdiction, i.e., the authority to issue a binding judgment over the parties to the action through its power either over these persons or their property. Additionally, the chosen tribunal must possess subject matter jurisdiction, i.e, the authority to adjudicate the type of controversy that has been placed before the court.

In this chapter we shall concentrate on personal jurisdiction, the power of a court to issue an enforceable judgment over persons and/or property. As you read through the several judicial opinions contained in this chapter, do so with these four related questions in mind: (1) what limits, if any, are imposed on a court's personal jurisdiction?; (2) what is the source or origin of these limitations?; (3) what interests or policies are these limits intended to promote?; and (4) are these interests or policies served by the purported source of the limitation?

We begin our investigation into the limits of personal jurisdiction with a judicial chestnut; a decision that has served as the analytical springboard for the succeeding one hundred and thirty-five years' worth of jurisdiction jurisprudence. And although this opinion has befuddled and bemused generations of law students, it provides the careful reader with a wonderful opportunity to critically analyze the structure, conclusions, and reasoning of a landmark judicial opinion.

SECTION A. THE HISTORICAL FOUNDATION

Pennoyer v. Neff

Supreme Court of the United States, 1877.
95 U.S. 714, 5 Otto 714, 24 L.Ed.2d 565.

ERROR to the Circuit Court of the United States for the District of Oregon.

MR. JUSTICE FIELD delivered the opinion of the court.

This is an action to recover the possession of a tract of land, of the alleged value of $15,000, situated in the State of Oregon. The plaintiff asserts title to the premises by a patent of the United States issued to him * * * [on March 19,] 1866 under the act of Congress of Sept. 27, 1850, usually known as the Donation Law of Oregon. The defendant claims to have acquired the premises under a sheriff's deed, made upon a sale of the property on execution issued upon a judgment recovered against the plaintiff in one of the circuit courts of the State. The case turns upon the validity of this judgment.

It appears from the record that the judgment was rendered in February, 1866, in favor of J. H. Mitchell, for less than $300, including costs, in an action brought by him upon a demand for services as an attorney; that, at the time the action was commenced and the judgment rendered, the defendant therein, the plaintiff here, was a non-resident of the State that he was not personally served with process, and did not appear therein; and that the judgment was entered upon his default in not answering the complaint, upon a constructive service of summons by publication.

The Code of Oregon provides for such service when an action is brought against a non-resident and absent defendant, who has property within the State. It also provides, where the action is for the recovery of money or damages, for the attachment of the property of the non-resident. And it also declares that no natural person is subject to the jurisdiction of a court of the State, "unless he appear in the court, or be found within the State, or be a resident thereof, or have property therein; and, in the last case, only to the extent of such property at the time the jurisdiction attached." Construing this latter provision to mean, that, in an action for money or damages where a defendant does not appear in the court, and is not found within the State, and is not a resident thereof, but has property therein, the jurisdiction of the court extends only over such property, the declaration expresses a principle of general, if not universal, law. The authority of every tribunal is necessarily restricted by the territorial limits of the State in which it is established. Any attempt to exercise authority beyond those limits would be deemed in every other forum, as has been said by this court, an illegitimate assumption of power, and be resisted as mere abuse. In the case against the plaintiff, the property here in controversy sold under the judgment rendered was not attached, nor in any way brought under the jurisdiction of the court. Its first connection with the case was caused by a levy of the execution. It was not, therefore, disposed of pursuant to any adjudication, but only in enforcement of a personal judgment, having no relation to the property, rendered against a non-resident without service of process upon him in the action, or his appearance therein. The court below did not consider that an attachment of the property was essential to its jurisdiction or to the validity of the sale, but held that the judgment was invalid from defects in the affidavit upon which the order of publication was obtained, and in the affidavit by which the publication was proved.

There is some difference of opinion among the members of this court as to the rulings upon these alleged defects. The majority are of opinion that inasmuch as the statute requires, for an order of publication, that certain facts shall appear by affidavit to the satisfaction of the court or judge, defects in such affidavit can only be taken advantage of on appeal, or by some other direct proceeding, and cannot be urged to impeach the judgment collaterally. The majority of the court are also of opinion that the provision of the statute requiring proof of the publication in a newspaper to be made by the "affidavit of the printer, or his foreman, or his principal clerk," is satisfied when the affidavit is made by the editor of the paper. * * *

If, therefore, we were confined to the rulings of the court below upon the defects in the affidavits mentioned, we should be unable to uphold its decision. But it was also contended in that court, and is insisted upon here, that the judgment in the State court against the plaintiff was void for want of personal service of process on him, or of his appearance in the action in which it was rendered and that the premises in controversy could not be subjected to the payment of the demand of a resident creditor except by a proceeding in rem; that is, by a direct proceeding against the property for that purpose. If these positions are sound, the ruling of the Circuit Court as to the invalidity of that judgment must be sustained, notwithstanding our dissent from the reasons upon which it was made. And that they are sound would seem to follow from two well-established principles of public law respecting the jurisdiction of an independent State over persons and property. The several States of the Union are not, it is true, in every respect independent, many of the rights and powers which originally belonged to them being now vested in the government created by the Constitution. But, except as restrained and limited by that instrument, they possess and exercise the authority of independent States, and the principles of public law to which we have referred are applicable to them. One of these principles is, that every State possesses exclusive jurisdiction and sovereignty over persons and property within its territory. As a consequence, every State has the power to determine for itself the civil status and capacities of its inhabitants; to prescribe the subjects upon which they may contract, the forms and solemnities with which their contracts shall be executed, the rights and obligations arising from them, and the mode in which their validity shall be determined and their obligations enforced; and also to regulate the manner and conditions upon which property situated within such territory, both personal and real, may be acquired, enjoyed, and transferred. The other principle of public law referred to follows from the one mentioned; that is, that no State can exercise direct jurisdiction and authority over persons or property without its territory. The several States are of equal dignity and authority, and the independence of one implies the exclusion of power from all others. * * *

But as * * * property may be held by non-residents, the exercise of the jurisdiction which every State is admitted to possess over persons and property within its own territory will often affect persons and property without it. To any influence exerted in this way by a State affecting persons resident or property situated elsewhere, no objection can be justly taken; whilst any direct exertion of authority upon them, in an attempt to give ex-territorial operation to its laws, or to enforce an ex-territorial jurisdiction by its tribunals, would be deemed an encroachment upon the independence of the State in which the persons are domiciled or the property is situated, and be resisted as usurpation.

* * *

So the State, through its tribunals, may subject property situated within its limits owned by non-residents to the payment of the demand of its own citizens against them; and the exercise of this jurisdiction in no respect infringes upon the sovereignty of the State where the owners are domiciled. Every State owes protection to its own citizens; and, when non-residents deal with them, it is a legitimate and just exercise of authority to hold and appropriate any property owned by such non-residents to satisfy the claims of its citizens. It is in virtue of the State's jurisdiction over the property of the non-resident situated within its limits that its tribunals can inquire into that non- resident's obligations to its own citizens, and the inquiry can then be carried only to the extent necessary to control the disposition of the property. If the non-resident have no property in the State, there is nothing upon which the tribunals can adjudicate.

* * *

* * * If, without personal service, judgments in personam, obtained ex parte against non-residents and absent parties, upon mere publication of process, which, in the great majority of cases, would never be seen by the parties interested, could be upheld and enforced, they would be the constant instruments of fraud and oppression. Judgments for all sorts of claims upon contracts and for torts, real or pretended, would be thus obtained, under which property would

be seized, when the evidence of the transactions upon which they were founded, if they ever had any existence, had perished.

Substituted service by publication, or in any other authorized form, may be sufficient to inform parties of the object of proceedings taken where property is once brought under the control of the court by seizure or some equivalent act. The law assumes that property is always in the possession of its owner, in person or by agent; and it proceeds upon the theory that its seizure will inform him, not only that it is taken into the custody of the court, but that he must look to any proceedings authorized by law upon such seizure for its condemnation and sale. * * * In other words, such service may answer in all actions which are substantially proceedings in rem. But where the entire object of the action is to determine the personal rights and obligations of the defendants, that is, where the suit is merely in personam, constructive service in this form upon a non-resident is ineffectual for any purpose. Process from the tribunals of one State cannot run into another State, and summon parties there domiciled to leave its territory and respond to proceedings against them. Publication of process or notice within the State where the tribunal sits cannot create any greater obligation upon the non-resident to appear. Process sent to him out of the State, and process published within it, are equally unavailing in proceedings to establish his personal liability.

The want of authority of the tribunals of a State to adjudicate upon the obligations of non-residents, where they have no property within its limits, is not denied by the court below: but the position is assumed, that, where they have property within the State, it is immaterial whether the property is in the first instance brought under the control of the court by attachment or some other equivalent act, and afterwards applied by its judgment to the satisfaction of demands against its owner; or such demands be first established in a personal action, and the property of the non-resident be afterwards seized and sold on execution. But the answer to this position has already been given in the statement, that the jurisdiction of the court to inquire into and determine his obligations at all is only incidental to its jurisdiction over the property. Its jurisdiction in that respect cannot be made to depend upon facts to be ascertained after it has tried the cause and rendered the judgment. If the judgment be previously void, it will not become valid by the subsequent discovery of property of the defendant, or by his subsequent acquisition of it. The judgment, if void when rendered, will always remain void: it cannot occupy the doubtful position of being valid if property be found, and void if there be none. Even if the position assumed were confined to cases where the non-resident defendant possessed property in the State at the commencement of the action, it would still make the validity of the proceedings and judgment depend upon the question whether, before the levy of the execution, the defendant had or had not disposed of the property. If before the levy the property should be sold, then, according to this position, the judgment would not be binding. This doctrine would introduce a new element of uncertainty in judicial proceedings. The contrary is the law: the validity of every judgment depends upon the jurisdiction of the court before it is rendered, not upon what may occur subsequently. * * *

The force and effect of judgments rendered against non-residents without personal service of process upon them, or their voluntary appearance, have been the subject of frequent consideration in the courts of the United States and of the several States, as attempts have been made to enforce such judgments in States other than those in which they were rendered, under the provision of the Constitution requiring that "full faith and credit shall be given in each State to the public acts, records, and judicial proceedings of every other State;" and the act of Congress providing for the mode of authenticating such acts, records, and proceedings, and declaring that, when thus authenticated, "they shall have such faith and credit given to them in every court within the United States as they have by law or usage in the courts of the State from which they are or shall be taken." In the earlier cases, it was supposed that the act gave to all judgments the same effect in other States which they had by law in the State where rendered. But this view was afterwards qualified so as to make the act applicable only when the court rendering the judgment had jurisdiction of the parties and of the subject-matter, and not to preclude an inquiry into the jurisdiction of the court in which the judgment was rendered, or the right of the State itself to exercise authority over the person or the subject-matter. * * *

* * *

* * * [T]he courts of the United States[,] * * * [w]hilst * * * not foreign tribunals in their relations to the State courts, they are tribunals of a different sovereignty, exercising a distinct and independent jurisdiction, and are bound to give to the judgments of the State courts only the same faith and credit which the courts of another State are bound to give to them.

Since the adoption of the Fourteenth Amendment to the Federal Constitution, the validity of such judgments may be directly questioned, and their enforcement in the State resisted, on the ground that proceedings in a court of justice to determine the personal rights and obligations of parties over whom that court has no jurisdiction do not constitute due process of law. Whatever difficulty may be experienced in giving to those terms a definition which will embrace every permissible exertion of power affecting private rights, and exclude such as is forbidden, there can be no doubt of their meaning when applied to judicial proceedings. They then mean a course of legal proceedings according to those rules and principles which have been established in our systems of jurisprudence for the protection and enforcement of private rights. To give such proceedings any validity, there must be a tribunal competent by its constitution — that is, by the law of its creation — to pass upon the subject-matter of the suit; and, if that involves merely a determination of the personal liability of the defendant, he must be brought within its jurisdiction by service of process within the State, or his voluntary appearance.

Except in cases affecting the personal status of the plaintiff, and cases in which that mode of service may be considered to have been assented to in advance, * * * the substituted service of process by publication, allowed by the law of Oregon * * *, where actions are brought against non-residents, is effectual only where, in connection with process against the person for commencing the action, property in the State is brought under the control of the court, and subjected to its disposition by process adapted to that purpose, or where the judgment is sought as a means of reaching such property or affecting some interest therein; in other words, where the action is in the nature of a proceeding in rem. As stated by Cooley in his Treatise on Constitutional Limitations, for any other purpose than to subject the property of a non-resident to valid claims against him in the State, "due process of law would require appearance or personal service before the defendant could be personally bound by any judgment rendered."

It is true that, in a strict sense, a proceeding in rem is one taken directly against property, and has for its object the disposition of the property, without reference to the title of individual claimants; but, in a larger and more general sense, the terms are applied to actions between parties, where the direct object is to reach and dispose of property owned by them, or of some interest therein. * * *

* * *

It follows from the views expressed that the personal judgment recovered in the State court of Oregon against the plaintiff herein, then a non-resident of the State, was without any validity, and did not authorize a sale of the property in controversy.

* * * [W]e do not mean to assert, by any thing we have said, that a State may not authorize proceedings to determine the status of one of its citizens towards a non-resident, which would be binding within the State, though made without service of process or personal notice to the non-resident. The jurisdiction which every State possesses to determine the civil status and capacities of all its inhabitants involves authority to prescribe the conditions on which proceedings affecting them may be commenced and carried on within its territory. The State, for example, has absolute right to prescribe the conditions upon which the marriage relation between its own citizens shall be created, and the causes for which it may be dissolved. One of the parties guilty of acts for which, by the law of the State, a dissolution may be granted, may have removed to a State where no dissolution is permitted. The complaining party would, therefore, fail if a divorce were sought in the State of the defendant; and if application could not be made to the tribunals of the complainant's domicile in such case, and proceedings be there instituted without personal service of process or personal notice to the offending party, the injured citizen would be without redress.

Neither do we mean to assert that a State may not require a non-resident entering into a partnership or association within its limits, or making contracts enforceable there, to appoint an agent or representative in the State to receive service of process and notice in legal proceedings instituted with respect to such partnership, association, or contracts, or to designate a place where such service may be made and notice given, and provide, upon their failure, to make such appointment or to designate such place that service may be made upon a public officer designated for that purpose, or in some other prescribed way, and that judgments rendered upon such service may not be binding upon the non-residents both within and without the State. * * * Nor do we doubt that a State, on creating corporations or other institutions for pecuniary or charitable purposes, may provide a mode in which their conduct may be investigated, their obligations enforced, or their charters revoked, which shall require other than personal service upon their officers or members. * * *

In the present case, there is no feature of this kind, and, consequently, no consideration of what would be the effect of such legislation in enforcing the contract of a non-resident can arise. * * *

Judgment affirmed.

MR. JUSTICE HUNT, dissenting.

* * *

To say that a sovereign State has the power to ordain that the property of non-residents within its territory may be subjected to the payment of debts due to its citizens, if the property is levied upon at the commencement of a suit, but that it has not such power if the property is levied upon at the end of the suit, is a refinement and a depreciation of a great general principle that, in my judgment, cannot be sustained.

* * *

It is undoubtedly true, that, in many cases where the question respecting due process of law has arisen, the case in hand was that of a proceeding in rem. It is true, also, as is asserted, that the process of a State cannot be supposed to run beyond its own territory. It is equally true, however, that, in every instance where the question has been presented, the validity of substituted service, which is used to subject property within the State belonging to a non-resident to a judgment obtained by means thereof, has been sustained. I have found no case in which it is adjudged that a statute must require a preliminary seizure of such property as necessary to the validity of the proceeding against it, or that there must have been a previous specific lien upon it; that is, I have found no case where such has been the judgment of the court upon facts making necessary the decision of the point. On the contrary, in the case of the attachment laws of New York and of New Jersey, which distribute all of the non-resident's property, not merely that levied on by the attachment * * * neither of these preliminary facts existed.

* * *

I am not willing to declare that a sovereign State cannot subject the land within its limits to the payment of debts due to its citizens, or that the power to do so depends upon the fact whether its statute shall authorize the property to be levied upon at the commencement of the suit or at its termination. This is a matter of detail, and I am of opinion, that if reasonable notice be given, with an opportunity to defend when appearance is made, the question of power will be fully satisfied.

NOTES AND PROBLEMS FOR DISCUSSION

1. The frequently obscure and archaic language of Justice Field's opinion, as well as its disorganized intermingling of analytically separate, though functionally related, doctrines of jurisdiction and notice, makes this a difficult opinion to fully comprehend. Nevertheless, a close reading of the opinion will unearth the important procedural history of the case, as well as the most significant facts. To discern and evaluate accurately the substance of the Court's decision, you should be able to answer the following questions:

(a) How many separate lawsuits were involved in the saga that culminated in the Supreme Court's opinion in *Pennoyer* and how do they relate to one another?

(b) How did the trial courts dispose of each of these actions?

The collateral facts involving the three participants in this legal drama are both amusing and sordid. For an entertaining discussion of this fascinating trio of characters and an equally thoughtful analysis of the Court's decision, see WENDY COLLINS PERDUE, *Sin, Scandal and Substantive Due Process: Personal Jurisdiction and Pennoyer Reconsidered*, 62 WASH.L.REV 479 (1987). An excellent paragraph-by-paragraph analysis of Justice Field's opinion can be found at JOHN B. OAKLEY, *The Pitfalls of "Hit and Run" History: A Critique of Professor Borchers's "Limited View" of* Pennoyer v. Neff, 28 U.C. DAVIS L.REV. 591, 601-616 (1995).

2. As an initial matter, personal jurisdiction is a creature of statute.

(a) What subjects are addressed by the Oregon Code and what does it say about each of them?

(b) What is the difference between the related, but distinct, concepts of jurisdiction and notice?

(c) What part of the Oregon Code provided the Oregon state court with a statutory basis for exercising personal jurisdiction over Neff?

3. (a) According to the Court, what is the limit on a state's exercise of personal jurisdiction and what authority does the Court rely on to create that particular limit?

(b) The Court refers to the obligation of courts to give "full faith and credit" to judgments rendered by other courts. What is the source of this doctrine and how is it relevant to the Court's jurisdictional analysis?

(c) Notice that the Court created an exception to its territorial limit on jurisdiction with respect to actions to determine the *status* of a forum resident towards a non-resident. Why should a different rule apply to domestic relations cases involving subjects such as marriage and divorce?

4. (a) What role does the Fourteenth Amendment play in the Court's analysis?

(b) To what extent should the facts that (1) this constitutional issue was not discussed by the lower court, and (2) the Fourteenth Amendment was not ratified until 1868 — after Mitchell sued Neff, obtained his default judgment, and arranged for the execution sale — affect the precedential value of the Court's reliance on the Fourteenth Amendment as a limitation on jurisdiction?

(c) If the source of the territorial limitation on personal jurisdiction is the need to preserve state sovereignty in a federalist system, how is the Due Process Clause, with its focus on protecting individuals' rights vis-à-vis actions by the state, relevant to this concern over interstate federalism?

5. An essential component of the opinion in *Pennoyer* is its discussion of the three varieties of personal jurisdiction, i.e., *in personam*, *in rem*, and *quasi in rem* jurisdiction. As the Court explains, each of these types of personal jurisdiction is characterized by two variables: (1) the objective of the proceeding, and (2) the source or "anchor" for the exercise of jurisdiction.

For example, an *in personam* action (a proceeding based on the exercise of the *in personam* form of personal jurisdiction) is an action whose object is the adjudication of the personal rights and obligations of the parties where the "anchor" for jurisdiction is the physical presence of the defendant within the territorial limits of the forum state.

In both *in rem* and *quasi in rem* proceedings, the "anchor" for jurisdiction is the presence of property within the forum state. Thus, each *in rem* action is seen as a proceeding against the property itself, with that property being brought within the court's physical control by attachment or other form of seizure. The impact of the *in rem* action on the interests of the claimants is merely a collateral result of the court's exercise of power over the *res*.

What distinguishes *in rem* from *quasi in rem* jurisdiction is the objective of the proceeding. A prototypical *in rem* proceeding is one in which the court adjudicates the claims of the entire world to the property (real or personal) that serves as the anchor for obtaining jurisdiction. *Quasi in rem* proceedings, however, can take one of two different forms. One version is where the court seeks to adjudicate the competing claims of a discrete, limited number of claimants to the property that is the anchor for jurisdiction. The other type combines the characteristics of both *in personam* and *in rem* proceedings. In this category of *quasi in rem* jurisdiction (Mitchell's suit for attorney fees is an example), the court is seeking to adjudicate a personal claim (the *in personam* trait) against the defendant that is totally unrelated to the property whose presence within the forum serves as the anchor (the *in rem* trait) for jurisdiction. Jurisdiction in these proceedings is typically asserted over the property because the defendant is beyond the territorial limits of the court's *in personam* jurisdiction.

The Court also indicated that the nature of service required to inform the defendant of the pendency of an action against her depends upon the type of jurisdiction invoked by the plaintiff. In an *in personam* action, personal service is the only acceptable form of service. On the other hand, substituted service such as publication will suffice in an *in rem* or *quasi in rem* proceeding if the service is accompanied by seizure of the property that serves as the anchor for exercising jurisdiction.

6. The Court declares in *Pennoyer* that *in personam* jurisdiction is available only if the defendant is (1) a resident of the forum, (2) found (i.e., personally served) within the forum, or (3) appears (either in person or via an agent) in the case and thereby consents to the exercise of jurisdiction. In either of these situations, the state possesses the *unlimited* power to issue an enforceable judgment affecting that defendant's rights and responsibilities.

(a) By enumerating these three bases for exercising *in personam* jurisdiction in the disjunctive, did the Court mean to imply that *in personam* jurisdiction would attach to a resident of the state who was temporarily absent during the pendency of the suit and who was not personally served within the forum's territory? In MILLIKEN v. MEYER, 311 U.S. 457, 61 S.Ct. 339, 85 L.Ed. 278 (1940), a Wyoming resident was sued in a Wyoming court but personally served in Colorado pursuant to a state statute that permitted extra-territorial personal service on forum residents. Four years after the plaintiff Milliken obtained a default judgment against him, Meyer filed an action in Colorado, asking the state court to enjoin Milliken from enforcing his default judgment and to issue a decree that the Wyoming judgment was unenforceable for lack of personal jurisdiction over Meyer. Milliken maintained that the Wyoming judgment was entitled to full faith and credit in Colorado. Although most of the opinion is devoted to an examination of whether substituted service was a constitutionally adequate form of notice, the Court also ruled on the jurisdictional issue, holding that the judgment was enforceable because Wyoming did have *in personam* jurisdiction over Meyer.

> "Domicile in the state is alone sufficient to bring an absent defendant within the reach of the state's jurisdiction for purposes of a personal judgment by means of appropriate substituted service. Substituted service in such cases has been quite uniformly upheld where the absent defendant was * * * personally served without the state. * * * The authority of a state over one of its citizens is not terminated by the mere fact of his absence from the state. The state which accords him privileges and affords protection to him and his property by virtue of his domicile may also exact reciprocal duties. * * * The attendant duties * * * are not dependent on continuous presence in the state. One such incidence of domicile is amenability to suit within the state during sojourns without the state, where the state has provided and employed a reasonable method for apprising such an absent party of the proceedings against him."

(b) At the opposite end of the extreme, does this disjunctive list mean that as long as the defendant is served while he is physically present within the forum territory, for even the briefest moment of time, he is subject to the court's *in personam* jurisdiction? The trial judge certainly thought so in GRACE v. McARTHUR, 170 F.Supp. 442 (E.D.Ark.1959). There the defendant was served while the airplane he was seated in was flying over Arkansas airspace. The court held that personal service upon a nonresident of Arkansas with no other apparent ties to that state was found to be sufficient to subject him to the *in personam* jurisdiction of an Arkansas court. Presumably, if the pilot of that flight had changed his flight plan and completely avoided Arkansas airspace, the service would have been unavailing. Should the existence of personal jurisdiction hinge on the fortuity of events, like these, that, among other things, are beyond the control of the parties to the lawsuit? See RESTATEMENT (SECOND) OF CONFLICT OF LAWS §28 (1971) ("A state has power to exercise judicial jurisdiction over an individual who is present within its territory, whether permanently or temporarily.").

7. A New York plaintiff sues (in New York) a New Jersey defendant who has never left his home state. The plaintiff telephones the defendant, pretending to be a radio announcer offering the defendant a chance to win $5000 by correctly answering a series of questions. The defendant answers the purported contest questions and is advised to pick up his winnings at the radio station office located only ten miles away, across the Hudson River in New York. When the defendant reaches the radio station office, he is met by a process server who presents him with his "prize" —a summons and complaint. Is he now subject to *in personam* jurisdiction in New York? What if the plaintiff had sent an armed guard across the border to the defendant's home and the guard had forcibly carried the defendant into the forum in order to serve him? See RESTATEMENT (2D) OF CONFLICT OF LAWS §82 (1969) ("A state will not exercise judicial jurisdiction, which has been obtained by fraud or unlawful force, over a defendant or his property.").

CREEPING PENNOYERISM: THE EVOLVING MEANING OF PRESENCE AND CONSENT

Towards the end of its opinion in *Pennoyer,* the Supreme Court suggested (in admitted dictum) that by participating in certain in-forum activities, a nonresident could be required to appoint an agent for service of process. Moreover, in the absence of such an express appointment, an agent would be appointed by the state, and service upon that agent would be an adequate substitute for personal service upon the defendant within the forum state. This language spawned two alternative explanations for the expansion of *in personam* jurisdiction — physical presence and consent. Under the first of these theories, the physical location of the agent within the forum was construed as the functional equivalent of the physical presence of the defendant herself. Thus, since serving the agent was tantamount to serving the defendant, the defendant could still be said to be physically present within the forum and therefore, subject to jurisdiction under strict *Pennoyer* doctrine. Alternatively, this language was interpreted to mean that by undertaking activities of these types, a nonresident (typically, corporate) defendant who had neither been served within the forum territory, nor who had explicitly authorized the appointment of an agent for service of process, had impliedly "consented" to the court's exercise of *in personam* jurisdiction.

Over the ensuing decades, through a continuously broadening interpretation of "presence" and "consent," the law governing personal jurisdiction slowly but unceasingly evolved to a point where the specific limitations on jurisdiction bore little resemblance to the territorial limits articulated in *Pennoyer*. During the twentieth century, the territorially-bound power premise that served as the limiting principle for jurisdiction in *Pennoyer* grew more and more unresponsive to the realities of a nation whose commercial and leisure activities became less locally bound and more multistate in scope. Even if it was not problematic in the latter half of the nineteenth century, it became apparent over the ensuing decades that there were pragmatic as well as analytical difficulties with the notions that a state possessed exclusive power over any person located within its territory, but was powerless as to persons who were party to activities that occurred or had effects within the forum state but who were physically absent from the forum. And the difficulty of assessing physical presence within the forum was compounded when the defendant was not a natural person but a creature of law such as a corporation — particularly where the corporation's activities touched more than one state. Which state, for example, could be said to have exclusive jurisdiction over a corporation that was incorporated under the laws of one state, had its headquarters located in a second state, a manufacturing plant located in a third state, a distribution warehouse situated in a fourth state, and that shipped thousands of its products to, and received millions of dollars in revenue from, the sale of its product in a fifth state? To accommodate more practically these evolving economic realities, the courts increasingly began to shoehorn modern factual patterns into the traditional *Pennoyer* framework by liberally interpreting the meaning of a defendant's physical "presence" within the forum state and/or its implied "consent" to the court's exercise of jurisdiction over it.

One well-known and striking example of the use of both the "presence" and "consent" justifications for the exercise of *in personam* jurisdiction over an individual is found in HESS v. PAWLOSKI, 274 U.S. 352, 47 S.Ct. 632, 71 L.Ed.2d 1091 (1927). There, a Pennsylvania resident (Hess) was sued in Massachusetts by a Massachusetts resident as the result of a car accident that occurred while both parties were driving on a Massachusetts highway. The Massachusetts legislature, relying on language in *Pennoyer*, had passed a statute providing that any nonresident who drove on the public highways in that state was deemed to have authorized a local official to be his agent for service of process in connection with any lawsuit arising out of the use of an automobile on the state's highways. The statute also required the plaintiff to mail a copy of the summons and complaint to the nonresident at the nonresident's home address. The Supreme Court upheld the constitutionality of the statute and rejected the defendant's claim that he was outside the court's *in personam* jurisdiction because he had not been served within the state's territory. With repeated references to the language in *Pennoyer* that both limited *in personam* jurisdiction to cases where the defendant or his agent is personally served within the state's territorial limits and provided for such jurisdiction in cases involving implied consent, the Court declared that since a State had legitimate interests in promoting care by those who use its public highways and providing a forum for its injured residents, the statutorily-implied consent, limited as it was to cases arising out of accidents on the state's highways, was fully in compliance with *Pennoyer* as long as the defendant actually received notice of the suit. "The difference between the formal and implied appointment," the Court opined, "is not substantial, so far as concerns the application of the due process clause of the Fourteenth Amendment."

NOTES AND PROBLEMS FOR DISCUSSION

1. Did Mr. Hess consent, in any meaningful way, to Massachusetts's appointment of the agent for service of process? Would the result in the case have changed if Hess had written to the Governor of Massachusetts announcing his impending visit to the Bay State, but explicitly disclaiming any intention to allow anyone to serve in this representative capacity? In a case decided a quarter of a century after *Hess*, the Supreme Court rejected the plaintiff's claim that a defendant had consented to be sued in the forum state. The consent argument was predicated upon the existence of a Kansas nonresident motorist statute that was identical to the Massachusetts statute examined in *Hess*. The Supreme Court subsequently offered this assessment of the theoretical foundation of *Hess*:

> "there has been some fictive talk to the effect that the reason why a non-resident can be subjected to a state's jurisdiction is that the nonresident has 'impliedly' consented to be sued there. In point of fact, however, jurisdiction in these cases does not rest on consent at all. The defendant may protest to high heaven his unwillingness to be sued and it avails him not. * * * But to conclude from [Hess v. Pawloski] * * * that the motorist, who never consented to anything and whose consent is altogether immaterial, has actually agreed to be sued * * * is surely to move in the world of Alice in Wonderland."

Olberding v. Illinois Cent. R.R., 346 U.S. 338, 341, 74 S.Ct. 83, 98 L.Ed. 39 (1953).

2. When it came to corporations, the courts increasingly focused on the nature of the entity's activities within the state as a manifestation of its "presence" in those instances where they did not rely on the implied "consent" generated by those activities as the basis for circumventing *Pennoyer's* territorial regime. But over time, the courts began to recognize that "presence" and "consent" had become no more than conclusory terms utilized simply to denote those set of circumstances which would suffice to subject the corporation to the forum's *in personam* jurisdiction. Eventually, the Supreme Court took the inevitable step of overtly shifting emphasis away from *Pennoyer's* formalistic insistence upon the artificial construct of physical presence as the mechanism for maintaining state sovereignty in a federalist system. In its place, the Court tendered a relatively less cumbersome appraisal of the extent to which the defendant had created some form of relationship or connection or "contacts" with the forum state. The unveiling of this more pragmatic approach occurred in the following landmark case.

SECTION B. THE MODERN APPROACH

International Shoe Co. v. State of Washington

Supreme Court of the United States, 1945.
326 U.S. 310, 66 S.Ct. 154, 90 L.Ed. 95.

MR. CHIEF JUSTICE STONE delivered the opinion of the Court.

[Under Washington law, employers were required to make contributions to the state's unemployment compensation program based on a percentage of the annual wages paid for their employees' services within the state. The statute also authorized the plaintiff state agency to collect delinquent contributions by personal service upon the employer if found within the state, or, if not, by registered mail to its last known address. The agency personally served a notice of assessment upon a salesperson employed by the defendant within Washington and also sent a copy by registered mail to the defendant's address in St. Louis, Missouri. The statute also provided for a series of administrative appeals from the initial agency decision followed by further appeal of issues of law to the Washington state courts.]

* * * Appellant appeared specially before the office of unemployment and moved to set aside the order and notice of assessment on the ground that the service upon appellant's salesman was not proper service upon appellant; that appellant was not a corporation of the State of Washington and was not doing business within the state; that it had no agent within the state upon whom service could be made; and that appellant is not an employer and does not furnish employment within the meaning of the statute.

The motion was heard * * * by the appeal tribunal which denied the motion and ruled that respondent Commissioner was entitled to recover the unpaid contributions. That action was affirmed by the Commissioner; both the [state] Superior Court and the Supreme Court affirmed. Appellant in each of these courts assailed the statute as applied, as a violation of the due process clause of the Fourteenth Amendment * * *. The cause comes here on appeal * * *.

The facts * * * are not in dispute. Appellant is a Delaware corporation, having its principal place of business in St. Louis, Missouri, and is engaged in the manufacture and sale of shoes and other footwear. It maintains places of business in several states, other than Washington, at which its manufacturing is carried on and from which its merchandise is distributed interstate through several sales units or branches located outside the State of Washington.

Appellant has no office in Washington and makes no contracts either for sale or purchase of merchandise there. It maintains no stock of merchandise in that state and makes there no deliveries of goods in intrastate commerce. During the years from 1937 to 1940, now in question, appellant employed eleven to thirteen salesmen under direct supervision and control of sales managers located in St. Louis. These salesmen resided in Washington; their principal activities were confined to that state; and they were compensated by commissions based upon the amount of their sales. The commissions for each year totaled more than $31,000. Appellant supplies its salesmen with a line of samples, each consisting of one shoe of a pair, which they display to prospective purchasers. On occasion they rent permanent sample rooms, for exhibiting samples, in business buildings, or rent rooms in hotels or business buildings temporarily for that purpose. The cost of such rentals is reimbursed by appellant.

The authority of the salesmen is limited to exhibiting their samples and soliciting orders from prospective buyers, at prices and on terms fixed by appellant. The salesmen transmit the orders to appellant's office in St. Louis for acceptance or rejection, and when accepted the merchandise for filling the orders is shipped f.o.b. from points outside Washington to the purchasers within the state. All the merchandise shipped into Washington is invoiced at the place of shipment from which collections are made. No salesman has authority to enter into contracts or to make collections.

* * *

Appellant * * * insists that its activities within the state were not sufficient to manifest its "presence" there and that in its absence the state courts were without jurisdiction, that consequently it was a denial of due process for the state to subject appellant to suit. It refers to those cases in which it was said that the mere solicitation of orders for the purchase of goods within a state, to be accepted without the state and filled by shipment of the purchased goods interstate, does not render the corporation seller amenable to suit within the state. * * *

Historically the jurisdiction of courts to render judgment in personam is grounded on their de facto power over the defendant's person. Hence his presence within the territorial jurisdiction of a court was prerequisite to its rendition of a judgment personally binding him. Pennoyer v. Neff. But now that the capias ad respondendum has given way to personal service of summons or other form of notice, due process requires only that in order to subject a defendant to a judgment in personam, if he be not present within the territory of the forum, he have certain minimum contacts with it such that the maintenance of the suit does not offend "traditional notions of fair play and substantial justice." Milliken v. Meyer.

Since the corporate personality is a fiction, * * * it is clear that unlike an individual its "presence" without, as well as within, the state of its origin can be manifested only by activities carried on in its behalf by those who are authorized to act for it. To say that the corporation is so far "present" there as to satisfy due process requirements, for purposes of taxation or the maintenance of suits against it in the courts of the state, is to beg the question to be decided. For the terms "present" or "presence" are used merely to symbolize those activities of the corporation's agent within the state which courts will deem to be sufficient to satisfy the demands of due process. Those demands may be met by such contacts of the corporation with the state of the forum as make it reasonable, in the context of our federal system of government, to require the corporation to defend the particular suit which is brought there. An "estimate of the inconveniences" which would result to the corporation from a trial away from its "home" or principal place of business is relevant in this connection.

"Presence" in the state in this sense has never been doubted when the activities of the corporation there have not only been continuous and systematic, but also give rise to the liabilities sued on, even though no consent to be sued or authorization to an agent to accept service of process has been given. Conversely it has been generally recognized that the casual presence of the corporate agent or even his conduct of single or isolated items of activities in a state in the corporation's behalf are not enough to subject it to suit on causes of action unconnected with the activities there. To require the corporation in such circumstances to defend the suit away from its home or other jurisdiction where it carries on more substantial activities has been thought to lay too great and unreasonable a burden on the corporation to comport with due process.

While it has been held in cases on which appellant relies that continuous activity of some sorts within a state is not enough to support the demand that the corporation be amenable to suits unrelated to that activity, there have been instances in which the continuous corporate operations within a state were thought so substantial and of such a nature as to justify suit against it on causes of action arising from dealings entirely distinct from those activities.

Finally, although the commission of some single or occasional acts of the corporate agent in a state sufficient to impose an obligation or liability on the corporation has not been thought to confer upon the state authority to enforce it, other such acts, because of their nature and quality and the circumstances of their commission, may be deemed sufficient to render the corporation liable to suit. Cf. Hess v. Pawloski. True, some of the decisions holding the corporation amenable to suit have been supported by resort to the legal fiction that it has given its consent to service and suit, consent being implied from its presence in the state through the acts of its authorized agents. But more realistically it may be said that those authorized acts were of such a nature as to justify the fiction.

It is evident that the criteria by which we mark the boundary line between those activities which justify the subjection of a corporation to suit, and those which do not, cannot be simply mechanical or quantitative. The test is not merely, as has sometimes been suggested, whether the activity, which the corporation has seen fit to procure through its agents in another state, is a little more or a little less. Whether due process is satisfied must depend rather upon the quality and nature of the activity in relation to the fair and orderly administration of the laws which it was the purpose of the due process clause to insure. That clause does not contemplate that a state may make binding a judgment in personam against an individual or corporate defendant with which the state has no contacts, ties, or relations. Cf. Pennoyer v. Neff.

But to the extent that a corporation exercises the privilege of conducting activities within a state, it enjoys the benefits and protection of the laws of that state. The exercise of that privilege may give rise to obligations; and, so far as those obligations arise out of or are connected with the activities within the state, a procedure which requires the corporation to respond to a suit brought to enforce them can, in most instances, hardly be said to be undue.

Applying these standards, the activities carried on in behalf of appellant in the State of Washington were neither irregular nor casual. They were systematic and continuous throughout the years in question. They resulted in a large volume of interstate business, in the course of which appellant received the benefits and protection of the laws of the state, including the right to resort to the courts for the enforcement of its rights. The obligation which is here sued upon arose out of those very activities. It is evident that these operations establish sufficient contacts or ties with the state of the forum to make it reasonable and just according to our traditional conception of fair play and substantial justice to permit the state to enforce the obligations which appellant has incurred there. Hence we cannot say that the maintenance of the present suit in the State of Washington involves an unreasonable or undue procedure.

We are likewise unable to conclude that the service of the process within the state upon an agent whose activities establish appellant's "presence" there was not sufficient notice of the suit, or that the suit was so unrelated to those activities as to make the agent an inappropriate vehicle for communicating the notice. It is enough that appellant has established such contacts with the state that the particular form of substituted service adopted there gives reasonable assurance that the notice will be actual. Nor can we say that the mailing of the notice of suit to appellant by registered mail at its home office was not reasonably calculated to apprise appellant of the suit.

* * *

Affirmed.

MR. JUSTICE JACKSON took no part in the consideration or decision of this case.

MR. JUSTICE BLACK delivered the following opinion.

* * *

Certainly appellant cannot in the light of our past decisions meritoriously claim that notice by registered mail and by personal service on its sales solicitors in Washington did not meet the requirements of procedural due process. And the due process clause is not brought in issue any more by appellant's further conceptualistic contention that Washington could not * * * bring suit against the corporation because it did not honor that State with its mystical "presence." For it is unthinkable that the vague due process clause was ever intended to prohibit a State from regulating * * * a business carried on within its boundaries simply because this is done by agents of a corporation organized and having its headquarters elsewhere. * * * The Court has * * * engaged in an unnecessary discussion in the course of which it has announced vague Constitutional criteria applied for the first time to the issue before us. It has thus introduced uncertain elements confusing the simple pattern and tending to curtail the exercise of State powers to an extent not justified by the Constitution.

It is true that this Court did use the terms "fair play" and "substantial justice" in explaining the philosophy underlying the holding that it could not be "due process of law" to render a personal judgment against a defendant without notice to and an opportunity to be heard by him. * * * And previous cases had indicated that the ancient rule against judgments without notice had stemmed from "natural justice" concepts. These cases, while giving additional reasons why notice under particular circumstances is inadequate, did not mean thereby that all legislative enactments which this Court might deem to be contrary to natural justice ought to be held invalid under the due process clause. None of the cases purport to support or could support a holding that a State can * * * sue corporations only if its action comports with this Court's notions of "natural justice." I should have thought the Tenth Amendment settled that.

I believe that the Federal Constitution leaves to each State, without any "ifs" or "buts", a power to * * * open the doors of its courts for its citizens to sue corporations whose agents do business in those States. Believing that the Constitution gave the States that power, I think it a judicial deprivation to condition its exercise upon this Court's notion of "fair play", however appealing that term may be. Nor can I stretch the meaning of due process so far as to authorize this Court to deprive a State of the right to afford judicial protection to its citizens on the ground that it would be more "convenient" for the corporation to be sued somewhere else.

There is a strong emotional appeal in the words "fair play", "justice", and "reasonableness." But they were not chosen by those who wrote the original Constitution or the Fourteenth Amendment as a measuring rod for this Court to use in invalidating State or Federal laws passed by elected legislative representatives. No one, not even those who most feared a democratic government, ever formally proposed that courts should be given power to invalidate legislation under any such elastic standards. Express prohibitions against certain types of legislation are found in the Constitution, and under the long settled practice, courts invalidate laws found to conflict with them. This requires interpretation, and interpretation, it is true, may result in extension of the Constitution's purpose. But that is no reason for reading the due process clause so as to restrict a State's power * * * to sue those whose activities affect persons and businesses within the State, provided proper service can be had. Superimposing the natural justice concept on the Constitution's specific prohibitions could operate as a drastic abridgment of democratic safeguards they embody, such as freedom of speech, press and religion, and the right to counsel. * * * For application of this natural law concept, whether under the terms "reasonableness", "justice", or "fair play", makes judges the supreme arbiters of the country's laws and practices. This result, I believe, alters the form of government our Constitution provides. I cannot agree.

* * *

NOTES AND PROBLEMS FOR DISCUSSION

1. (a) Compared to the ruling in *Pennoyer*, what is the source and nature of the limit on personal jurisdiction announced in *International Shoe*?

(b) Is there any difference in the interest sought to be protected by the jurisdictional limit announced in *Pennoyer* and *International Shoe*?

(c) What do you make of the Court's statement in *International Shoe* that the demands of due process can be satisfied by "such contacts of the corporation within the state of the forum as make it reasonable, *in the context of our federal system of government*, to require the corporation to defend the particular suit which is brought there." (emphasis added).

2. Describe the framework the Court provides in *International Shoe* to govern future evaluations of the constitutionality of exercising *in personam* jurisdiction over a nonresident defendant. How does the Court suggest that this analytical model will operate in the following factual contexts?:

(a) Bess Allen, a New York City resident who had never previously left the Empire State, drove briefly through West Virginia on Interstate 81 on her way to visit relatives in Virginia. At one point during her 30 minute drive through West Virginia, Bess ran her automobile into a car driven by Rick Ness, a West

Virginia citizen. Nevertheless, she was able to continue to Virginia after the accident. Is Bess *constitutionally* subject to *in personam* jurisdiction in an action for damages brought in a West Virginia state court by Rick? See generally, Burger King Corp. v. Rudzewicz, 471 U.S. 462, 105 S.Ct. 2174, 85 L.Ed.2d 528 (1985) (discussing "specific jurisdiction").

(b) A few days after her arrival in Virginia, Bess Allen got into another car accident, this time in front of her relative's home in Charlottesville. The victim, it turns out, was the aforesaid West Virginian, Rick Ness. Is Bess *constitutionally* subject to *in personam* jurisdiction in an action for damages associated solely with this second accident brought in a West Virginia state court by Rick?

(c) After recovering from all of his injuries, Rick Ness flew to New Orleans for a weekend vacation. While in that city's famous French Quarter, he consumed, to his great satisfaction, several bottles of Rajun Cajun Beer, a local potable brewed and bottled by a New Orleans microbrewery called Rajun Cajun Brewery. Upon his return to West Virginia, Rick logged onto Rajun Cajun's Internet web site and placed an order for a caseload of Rajun Cajun Beer. It turns out that hundreds of other West Virginians also have purchased thousands of bottles of Rajun Cajun Beer in the same manner over the past two years. Unfortunately for Rick, there was a small creature in one of the bottles that he purchased and he suffered serious internal injuries when he drank the bottle containing this unanticipated ingredient. Is the microbrewery *constitutionally* subject to *in personam* jurisdiction in an action by Rick for damages filed in a West Virginia state court? See generally Helicopteros Nacionales de Colombia v. Hall, 466 U.S. 408, 104 S.Ct. 1868, 80 L.Ed.2d 404 (1984).

(d) While visiting the restaurant at the same Rajun Cajun Brewery in New Orleans referred to in "(c)" above, Rick slipped and fell on a couple of empty crawfish shells that had been left on the floor. After returning home, Rick began to feel severe pain in his back. His physician diagnosed the condition as a consequence of the fall in the restaurant. Rick subsequently brought a tort action in West Virginia state court against Rajun Cajun. Does the court have the constitutional authority to exercise *in personam* jurisdiction over Rajun Cajun Brewery?

If John Mitchell had filed his claim for attorney fees against Marcus Neff in the post-*International Shoe* era, would the Oregon state court have been able to exercise *in personam* jurisdiction over Neff?

In assessing the constitutional sufficiency of contacts, should the court limit its scrutiny to those contacts that occurred at the time of the events that gave rise to the claim or also consider subsequent in-state contacts up to the time either of the filing of suit, the resolution of a jurisdictional motion, or rendering of judgment? For an interesting commentary on the limited jurisprudence addressing this issue and a proposal to address this timing question, *see* TODD DAVID PETERSON, *The Timing of Minimum Contacts*, 69 GEO.WASH.L.REV. 101 (2010).

3. (a) The Court in *International Shoe* reported that the defendant "appeared specially" before the state administrative agency to set aside its order and notice of assessment. What does this mean?

(b) Assume you represent an out-of-state defendant who believes that the forum does not have personal jurisdiction over her. What are your options upon receiving a copy of the plaintiff's complaint?

4. What is the nature of Justice Black's criticism of the majority opinion in *International Shoe*? For a thought-provoking reconception of the role to be played by the Due Process Clause in limiting state court adjudicatory power that proposes reasserting the primacy of state sovereignty and interstate federalism by replacing the Court's extant emphasis on burden and inconvenience to the defendant with an assessment of whether the forum state has a legitimate interest in resolving the dispute, see A. BENJAMIN SPENCER, *Jurisdiction to Adjudicate: A Revised Analysis*, 73 U.CHI.L.REV. 617 (2006).

CONSENT AND FORUM SELECTION CLAUSES

The disavowal in *International Shoe* of the Court's traditional reliance on implied consent as a justification for exercising *in personam* jurisdiction over nonresident defendants did not, however, mark the death knell for the utilization of consent as a jurisdictional predicate. As the *International Shoe* Court recognized, its prior decisions (such as *Hess*) were based upon the fiction that consent could be *implied* from actions by the defendant within or related to the forum state. It was not until *International Shoe* that the Court focused, instead, directly on these affiliating circumstances as the rationale for exercising jurisdiction.

But in certain circumstances, consent to jurisdiction can be *express*, such as when a defendant waives its objection to the court's exercise of jurisdiction or does an affirmative act that signals its agreement to subject itself to jurisdiction, such as making a general appearance. (Recall that in *Pennoyer*, the Supreme Court reaffirmed the traditional practice of exercising *in personam* jurisdiction solely on the basis of the defendant's voluntary appearance in the lawsuit.) This consent also, however, can be effected in advance of any specific litigation. In such an instance, should the parties' choice of forum be dispositive of all objections, constitutional or otherwise, to adjudicative jurisdiction? The enforceability of forum selection clauses has been examined by the Supreme Court in two different contexts.

In M/S BREMEN v. ZAPATA OFF-SHORE CO., 407 U.S. 1, 92 S.Ct. 1907, 32 L.Ed.2d 513 (1972), a German tug owner contracted to tow an American company's drilling rig from Louisiana to a location off the Italian coast in the Adriatic Sea. While the tug was carrying the rig in international waters in the Gulf of Mexico near Tampa, Florida, a storm arose and the rig was seriously damaged. The rig was then towed to Tampa for repairs. The towage contract contained, *inter alia*, a forum selection clause in which the parties agreed that any dispute arising under the contract "must be treated before the

London Court of Justice." The American rig owner sued the German tug owner in Tampa, alleging negligent towage and breach of contract. The defendant moved to dismiss the complaint for lack of jurisdiction on the basis of the forum selection clause. After acknowledging that forum selection clauses historically had been disfavored by American courts because they were viewed as contrary to public policy, the Court announced that such clauses "are prima facie valid and should be enforced unless enforcement is shown by the resisting party to be unreasonable under the circumstances." Enforcing these clauses, the Court reasoned, had the salutary effects of (a) promoting certainty, (b) forestalling the expense, use of judicial resources and inconvenience associated with litigating jurisdictional and related issues, and (c) avoiding the possibility of subjecting one of the parties to an inconvenient forum. To do otherwise, the Court continued, would discourage the continued expansion of American business in increasingly important international markets.

Accordingly, to meet its burden of showing that enforcement would be unreasonable, the opponent of the forum selection clause, the *Bremen* Court explained, must show either that (1) the forum clause was the result of overreaching or undue influence by one party to a non-arms-length transaction between inexperienced or unsophisticated businessmen who did not appreciate the significance of that contractual undertaking; (2) the contractually designated tribunal was neither neutral nor experienced in the type of case involved in the disputed matter; (3) enforcing the forum clause would contravene a strong public policy of the forum in which suit was brought; or (4) that trial in the contractually designated forum would be so gravely difficult in a way that was not foreseeable at the time of contracting that it would be tantamount to depriving that party of its day in court. The Court then remanded the case for an assessment of the instant forum clause pursuant to this standard.

Nearly twenty years later, the Court reexamined the enforceability of forum selection clauses in another admiralty case. This time, however, instead of a clause included within a commercial agreement negotiated by two sophisticated companies with significant experience in international commerce, the Court, in CARNIVAL CRUISE LINES, INC. v. SHUTE, 499 U.S. 585, 111 S.Ct. 1522, 113 L.Ed.2d 622 (1991), was asked to enforce a forum exclusivity clause contained in a standard cruise ticket purchased by a married couple from Washington State. While the defendant's ship was in international waters off the Mexican coast, the wife was injured when she slipped during a tour of the ship's galley. The couple filed a tort action in a federal district court in their home state of Washington. Their ticket contained language stating that all disputes arising under the contract shall be litigated in Florida. The defendant moved to dismiss the case on the ground that the forum clause required the plaintiff to file her action in a Florida court.

The Court began its analysis by noting that since this was an admiralty case, the enforceability of the forum selection clause was a matter to be resolved under federal, rather than state, common law principles. It then acknowledged that the plaintiffs in this case were not experienced business persons and had not, and could not have, negotiated the terms of the forum clause in this form contract. Nevertheless, "to account for the realities of form passage contracts," the majority announced that it was necessary to "refine the analysis of *The Bremen*" by removing the requirement that the clause be the knowing result of an arms-length transaction between sophisticated business parties. Enforcing forum clauses in form contracts, the Court explained, was justified because these clauses, like those that are the product of negotiation, provide both parties with a clear understanding of where suits involving that contract could be brought and defended. The Court also concluded that forum clauses promote the carrier's legitimate interest in limiting the number of jurisdictions in which it could be sued, a result that reduces costs that are then passed on to its passengers in the form of reduced fares. Thus, the Court determined, so long as the forum clause was not shown to be unreasonable — i.e., did not subject the consumer to an inexperienced, partisan, or remote alien forum and was not the result of a bad faith motive to designate a forum in order to discourage passengers from pursuing legitimate claims — it would not be set aside.

Applying this standard to the instant facts, the Court concluded that the contractually stipulated forum — Florida — wasn't a remote alien forum for these two American parties. It also found that Florida was not chosen by Carnival Cruise for malevolent purposes since the company's principal place of business was located there and many of its cruises either depart from or return to ports in that state. Finally, the Court determined that there was no evidence that the plaintiffs' agreement to the terms of the forum clause was the result of fraud or overreaching by the cruise company. Accordingly, it ruled that the clause was enforceable and ordered the Washington trial court to dismiss the complaint.

NOTES AND PROBLEMS FOR DISCUSSION

1. Do you agree with the Court's characterization of its ruling in *Carnival Cruise* as merely a "refinement" of the doctrine set forth in *The Bremen* or does this modification reflect a new and different justification for enforcing forum selection clauses?

2. The issue in *Carnival Cruise* was not whether the forum clause provided Florida with personal jurisdiction over the defendant. Florida undoubtedly would have had jurisdiction over the cruise line in the absence of this contractual provision. The objective of the clause was to immunize the defendant from jurisdiction anywhere but Florida. But suppose the forum clause had listed Iowa as the designated forum and that Carnival would not otherwise have been subject to *in personam* jurisdiction in that state. Would that have changed the result? Would it have rendered the contract so unreasonable as to be unenforceable?

3. If a defendant seeks to enforce a forum selection clause to challenge the plaintiff's choice of forum, what is the proper procedural mechanism? Neither *The Bremen* nor *Carnival Cruise* expressly addressed the question. The Supreme Court resolved a split among the circuits on the question when it rendered a unanimous opinion in ATLANTIC MARINE CONSTRUCTION CO. v. U.S. DISTRICT COURT FOR THE WESTERN DISTRICT OF TEXAS, 571 U.S. ___, 134 S.Ct. 568, 187 L.Ed.2d 487 (2013). In *Atlantic Marine,* the Court held that when the plaintiff files suit in a federal district court in which venue lies under the federal venue laws, and not in a federal district pointed to by a valid forum selection clause, the exclusive mechanism for dealing with this problem is not a motion to dismiss for lack of venue, but a motion to transfer under 28 U.S.C. §1404(a), the federal transfer of venue provision. And where a valid forum selection clause points only to court of a foreign country or to state courts, the proper course is for a defendant to file a motion to dismiss under the doctrine of *forum non conveniens*. Both §1404 and the doctrine of *forum non conveniens* are discussed in detail in Sections B and C of Chapter 4, *infra*.

THE LEGACY OF *INTERNATIONAL SHOE*:
THE EMERGENCE OF LONG ARM STATUTES AND THE
GENERAL/SPECIFIC JURISDICTION DICHOTOMY

The *International Shoe* Court's unequivocal signal that a state could expand the reach of its judicial jurisdiction beyond the territorial boundaries did not escape the attention of state legislators. Throughout the country, legislatures quickly passed jurisdictional statutes that extended the "long arm" of state judicial authority beyond its borders. Codifying the teaching of *International Shoe* — that jurisdiction could be predicated upon the existence of a varied array of relationships between a nonresident defendant who could not be physically served within the forum and the forum state — these "long arm statutes", as they came to be known, took a multitude of forms. Some enumerated a list of specific activities that would subject the actor to personal jurisdiction, such as the Massachusetts nonresident motorist statute applied in *Hess*. Others relied on broad categories of conduct, such as "transacting business within the state," or "ownership of real property within the state," or "committing a tortious act within the state," to accomplish this objective. Yet a third group, including those in California, Rhode Island and Louisiana, went so far as to assert jurisdiction "on any basis not inconsistent with the Constitution of the United States."

Naturally, the fact that state legislatures believed that their new jurisdictional regimes were consistent with the limitations on state authority imposed by the Fourteenth Amendment's Due Process Clause was not dispositive of that question. Rather, it meant that post-*International Shoe* jurisdictional challenges required the courts to undertake two separate inquiries. First, did the state long arm statute apply to the facts of the case? Then, if the statute could be applied, was the exercise of personal jurisdiction under those circumstances consistent with the requirements of constitutional due process?

The first of these two inquiries, i.e., the statutory analysis, generated interesting interpretive questions that often ended up being conflated with the constitutional query. For example, in WOODRING v. HALL, 200 Kan. 597, 438 P.2d 135 (1968), a Kansas resident sued her former son-in-law in Kansas state court for failing to repay a series of loans totaling $3,100 that she had made to him over a ten year period during his marriage to her daughter to cover the couple's living expenses and his medical school tuition. The defendant had been a resident of Kansas during this ten year period, but had moved to Texas two years before the plaintiff filed this action. He was personally served with process in Texas. Upon the defendant's failure to appear in the action, the plaintiff obtained a default judgment. About one year later, the defendant moved to set aside the default judgment and to dismiss the action for lack of personal jurisdiction.

The relevant portion of the Kansas long arm statute provided that any individual, "whether or not a citizen or resident of the state, who in person or through an agent * * * does any of the acts hereinafter enumerated, thereby submits said person * * * to the jurisdiction of the courts as to any cause of action arising from the doing of any of said acts: (1) the transaction of any business within this state * * *." The trial court granted the defendant's motion on the ground that this loan did not constitute the "transaction of any business." The Kansas Supreme Court reversed this ruling. The Court emphasized that rather than categorize "business" into components such as commercial, personal, corporate, or private, the legislature employed an "all encompassing" term "in its broadest legal sense and as intending to authorize [the exercise of jurisdiction] * * * to the full extent of the due process clause."

In contrast to the California or Rhode Island law, the Kansas legislature did not expressly incorporate the constitutional limits of authority as its jurisdictional standard. To the contrary, it set forth a list of specific activities that subjected a defendant to the jurisdiction of its courts. How, then, do you explain the Kansas Supreme Court's construction of the statute? For a thorough examination and critique of this widespread phenomcnon of state court construction of specific-act long arm statutes, see Douglas D. McFarland, *Dictum Run Wild: How Long-Arm Statutes Extended To the Limits of Due Process*, 84 B.U.L.REV. 491 (2004).

With respect to the constitutional inquiry, the Supreme Court's post-*International Shoe* opinions reflect the important role played by the second of the two variables articulated in *International Shoe* — whether or not the cause of action arose out of the defendant's activities within the forum state. As these cases demonstrate, characterizing a claim as being related or unrelated to the defendant's in-forum activities plays a crucial role in determining the scope of activities necessary to meet "traditional notions of fair play and substantial justice." Two decisions, reached in the same term, demonstrate this correlation.

In McGEE v. INTERNATIONAL LIFE INS. CO., 355 U.S. 220, 78 S.Ct. 199, 2 L.Ed.2d 223 (1957), the beneficiary (a California resident) on a life insurance policy brought suit in a California state court against the Texas-based insurer that failed to pay her upon the death of the California insured. The insurer had no office or agent in California and had never solicited or issued a single insurance policy in California other than the reinsurance agreement delivered to this California insured who mailed his premiums from California to the defendant in Texas. The insurer was served with process by registered mail at its Texas business address. After obtaining a default judgment in California, the plaintiff brought an enforcement action in a Texas state court, but the Texas courts refused to give full faith and credit to the California judgment on the ground that the California court lacked personal jurisdiction over the Texas insurer. Since the plaintiff's claim arose directly out of the one undisputed connection between the defendant and the forum state — an insurance contract that was delivered in the forum and that was paid for by premiums sent from the forum by an insured who was a resident of the forum — and because the forum state had a significant interest in providing a forum for its residents who are denied payment by a foreign insurer, the Supreme Court unanimously concluded that asserting jurisdiction did not amount to a denial of due process. The Court resolved that this single connection between the defendant and the forum satisfied the constitutional standard for the exercise of "specific" jurisdiction, i.e., jurisdiction in connection with a claim that arose out of the defendant's relationship (contacts) with the forum state.

Near the end of the same term in which it decided *McGee,* the Court also decided HANSON v. DENCKLA, 357 U.S. 235, 78 S.Ct. 1228, 2 L.Ed.2d 1283 (1958), an extremely complicated case which, boiled down to its essence, was a fight between three daughters over trust assets that were part of their mother's estate. The mother created the trust while she was living in Pennsylvania and named a Delaware trust company as trustee. Subsequently, she moved to Florida, where she executed a will naming two of the daughters as the primary beneficiaries. She also executed a power of appointment in Florida that provided the two children of the third daughter with $200,000 each from the trust assets. After the mother moved to Florida, the Delaware trustee sent the trust income to the mother and she periodically carried on some administrative tasks concerning the trust from her home. After the mother's death, the two daughters (the will legatees) sued in Florida to invalidate the appointment to the grandchildren in order to divert this portion of the trust to the will and, thereby, principally, to themselves. The question that ultimately reached the Supreme Court was whether the Florida court had personal jurisdiction over the Delaware trust company.

By a five to four margin, the Court concluded that Florida could not exercise personal jurisdiction over the Delaware trustee. With reference to *McGee*'s acknowledgement of the sustained expansion of jurisdiction over nonresidents, and with a glance back at *Pennoyer*, the majority in *Hanson* declared

> "it is a mistake to assume that this trend heralds the eventual demise of all restrictions on the personal jurisdiction of state courts. Those restrictions are more than a guarantee of immunity from inconvenient or distant litigation. They are a consequence of territorial limitations on the power of the respective States."

Then, despite the facts that the trust company had mailed income payments to the mother in Florida and had received certain of her administrative instructions from Florida, the Court found that the Delaware trust company did not have "minimum contacts" with Florida sufficient to subject it to personal jurisdiction. And even though the case turned on the validity of the power of appointment that had been executed by the mother in Florida and which instructed the Delaware trust company how to distribute the assets controlled by the trust agreement, the Court insisted that this connection with the forum state was undertaken by the settlor and not by the defendant trust company. Accordingly, in contrast with the "specific" jurisdiction it upheld in *McGee*, the Court characterized this as an inappropriate attempt to exercise "general" jurisdiction, i.e., jurisdiction in connection with a claim (to invalidate the trust agreement) unrelated to the defendant's in-forum conduct.

The opinion in *Hanson* also contains some now-familiar language that has become a benchmark for determining whether or not a defendant has conducted activities which yield constitutionally adequate "minimum contacts."

> "The unilateral activity of those who claim some relationship with a nonresident defendant cannot satisfy the requirement of contact with the forum State. The application of that rule will vary with the quality and nature of the defendant's activity, but it is essential in each case that there be some act by which the defendant purposefully avails itself of the privilege of conducting activities within the forum State, thus invoking the benefits and protections of its laws."

In contrast to the *Hanson* majority, Justice Black, in dissent, argued in favor of a "minimum contacts" test that assesses the relationship of *the underlying transaction* (the execution of the power of appointment) to the interests of the forum. Nevertheless, for the next twenty years, the essentially defendant-centered due process analysis set forth in *International Shoe* remained the jurisdictional gold standard. But after this extended period of quiescence, the Supreme Court again wrestled with the question of which, if any, considerations other than the defendant's contacts with the forum state and the relationship between the cause of action and those contacts were relevant to a constitutional challenge to the exercise of personal jurisdiction over nonresidents. The *ratio decidendi* of the next case demonstrates that the limiting language of *Hanson* and its associated resurrection of *Pennoyer*'s federalism underpinnings was more than just a passing fancy:

World-Wide Volkswagen Corporation v. Woodson

Supreme Court of the United States, 1980.

444 U.S. 286, 100 S.Ct. 559, 62 L.Ed.2d 490.

MR. JUSTICE WHITE delivered the opinion of the Court.

The issue before us is whether, consistently with the Due Process Clause of the Fourteenth Amendment, an Oklahoma court may exercise in personam jurisdiction over a nonresident automobile retailer and its wholesale distributor in a products-liability action, when the defendants' only connection with Oklahoma is the fact that an automobile sold in New York to New York residents became involved in an accident in Oklahoma.

I

Respondents Harry and Kay Robinson purchased a new Audi automobile from petitioner Seaway Volkswagen, Inc. (Seaway), in Massena, N. Y., in 1976. The following year the Robinson family, who resided in New York, left that State for a new home in Arizona. As they passed through the State of Oklahoma, another car struck their Audi in the rear, causing a fire which severely burned Kay Robinson and her two children.

The Robinsons subsequently brought a products-liability action in the District Court for Creek County, Okla., claiming that their injuries resulted from defective design and placement of the Audi's gas tank and fuel system. They joined as defendants the automobile's manufacturer, Audi * * *; its importer Volkswagen of America, Inc. (Volkswagen); its regional distributor, petitioner World-Wide Volkswagen Corp. (World-Wide); and its retail dealer, petitioner Seaway. Seaway and World-Wide entered special appearances,[1] claiming that Oklahoma's exercise of jurisdiction over them would offend the limitations on the State's jurisdiction imposed by the Due Process Clause of the Fourteenth Amendment.

* * * World-Wide is incorporated and has its business office in New York. It distributes vehicles, parts, and accessories, under contract with Volkswagen, to retail dealers in New York, New Jersey, and Connecticut. Seaway, one of these retail dealers, is incorporated and has its place of business in New York. Insofar as the record reveals, Seaway and World-Wide are fully independent corporations whose relations with each other and with Volkswagen and Audi are contractual only. Respondents adduced no evidence that either World-Wide or Seaway does any business in Oklahoma, ships or sells any products to or in that State, has an agent to receive process there, or purchases advertisements in any media calculated to reach Oklahoma. In fact, as respondents' counsel conceded at oral argument, there was no showing that any automobile sold by World-Wide or Seaway has ever entered Oklahoma with the single exception of the vehicle involved in the present case.

Despite the apparent paucity of contacts between petitioners and Oklahoma, the District Court rejected their constitutional claim * * *. Petitioners then sought a writ of prohibition in the Supreme Court of Oklahoma to restrain the District Judge, respondent Woodson, from exercising in personam jurisdiction over them. They renewed their contention that, because they had no "minimal contacts" with the State of Oklahoma, the actions of the District Judge were in violation of their rights under the Due Process Clause.

The Supreme Court of Oklahoma denied the writ, holding that personal jurisdiction over petitioners was authorized by Oklahoma's "long-arm" statute. Okla.Stat., Tit. 12, §1701.03(a)(4) (1971).[7] Although the court noted that the proper approach was to test jurisdiction against both statutory and constitutional standards, its analysis did not distinguish these questions, probably because §1701.03(a)(4) has been interpreted as conferring jurisdiction to the limits permitted by the United States Constitution. * * *

---

[1] Volkswagen also entered a special appearance in the District Court, but unlike World-Wide and Seaway, did not seek review in the Supreme Court of Oklahoma and is not a petitioner here. Both Volkswagen and Audi remain as defendants in the litigation pending before the District Court in Oklahoma.

[7] This subsection provides:

"A court may exercise personal jurisdiction over a person, who acts directly or by an agent, as to a cause of action or claim for relief arising from the person's * * * causing tortious injury in this state by an act or omission outside this state if he regularly does or solicits business or engages in any other persistent course of conduct, or derives substantial revenue from goods used or consumed or services rendered, in this state * * *."

The State Supreme Court rejected jurisdiction based on §1701.03(a)(3), which authorizes jurisdiction over any person "causing tortious injury in this state by an act or omission in this state." Something in addition to the infliction of tortious injury was required.

We granted certiorari to consider an important constitutional question with respect to state-court jurisdiction * * *. We reverse.

II

* * *

As has long been settled, and as we reaffirm today, a state court may exercise personal jurisdiction over a nonresident defendant only so long as there exist "minimum contacts" between the defendant and the forum State. International Shoe Co. The concept of minimum contacts, in turn, can be seen to perform two related, but distinguishable, functions. It protects the defendant against the burdens of litigating in a distant or inconvenient forum. And it acts to ensure that the States through their courts, do not reach out beyond the limits imposed on them by their status as coequal sovereigns in a federal system.

The protection against inconvenient litigation is typically described in terms of "reasonableness" or "fairness." We have said that the defendant's contacts with the forum State must be such that maintenance of the suit "does not offend 'traditional notions of fair play and substantial justice.'" International Shoe Co. v. Washington, quoting Milliken v. Meyer. The relationship between the defendant and the forum must be such that it is "reasonable . . . to require the corporation to defend the particular suit which is brought there." Implicit in this emphasis on reasonableness is the understanding that the burden on the defendant, while always a primary concern, will in an appropriate case be considered in light of other relevant factors, including the forum State's interest in adjudicating the dispute, see McGee v. International Life Ins. Co.; the plaintiff's interest in obtaining convenient and effective relief, at least when that interest is not adequately protected by the plaintiff's power to choose the forum; the interstate judicial system's interest in obtaining the most efficient resolution of controversies; and the shared interest of the several States in furthering fundamental substantive social policies.

The limits imposed on state jurisdiction by the Due Process Clause, in its role as a guarantor against inconvenient litigation, have been substantially relaxed over the years. As we noted in *McGee*, this trend is largely attributable to a fundamental transformation in the American economy. * * *

The historical developments noted in *McGee*, of course, have only accelerated in the generation since that case was decided.

Nevertheless, we have never accepted the proposition that state lines are irrelevant for jurisdictional purposes, nor could we, and remain faithful to the principles of interstate federalism embodied in the Constitution. The economic interdependence of the States was foreseen and desired by the Framers. * * * But the Framers also intended that the States retain many essential attributes of sovereignty, including, in particular, the sovereign power to try causes in their courts. The sovereignty of each State, in turn, implied a limitation on the sovereignty of all of its sister States—a limitation express or implicit in both the original scheme of the Constitution and the Fourteenth Amendment.

Hence, even while abandoning the shibboleth that "[t]he authority of every tribunal is necessarily restricted by the territorial limits of the State in which it is established," Pennoyer v. Neff, we emphasized that the reasonableness of asserting jurisdiction over the defendant must be assessed "in the context of our federal system of government," International Shoe Co., and stressed that the Due Process Clause ensures not only fairness, but also the "orderly administration of the laws." As we noted in Hanson v. Denckla:

> "* * * Those restrictions [on the personal jurisdiction of state courts] are more than a guarantee of immunity from inconvenient or distant litigation. They are a consequence of territorial limitations on the power of the respective States."

Thus, * * * [e]ven if the defendant would suffer minimal or no inconvenience from being forced to litigate before the tribunals of another State; even if the forum State has a strong interest in applying its law to the controversy; even if the forum State is the most convenient location for litigation, the Due Process Clause, acting as an instrument of interstate federalism, may sometimes act to divest the State of its power to render a valid judgment. Hanson v. Denckla.

III

Applying these principles to the case at hand, we find in the record before us a total absence of those affiliating circumstances that are a necessary predicate to any exercise of state-court jurisdiction. Petitioners carry on no activity whatsoever in Oklahoma. They close no sales and perform no services there. They avail themselves of none of the privileges and benefits of Oklahoma law. They solicit no business there either through salespersons or through advertising reasonably calculated to reach the State. Nor does the record show that they regularly sell cars at wholesale or retail to Oklahoma customers or residents or that they indirectly, through others, serve or seek to serve the Oklahoma market. In short, respondents seek to base jurisdiction on one, isolated occurrence and whatever inferences can be drawn therefrom: the fortuitous circumstance that a single Audi automobile, sold in New York to New York residents, happened to suffer an accident while passing through Oklahoma.

* * *

It is argued, however, that because an automobile is mobile by its very design and purpose it was "foreseeable" that the Robinsons' Audi would cause injury in Oklahoma. Yet "foreseeability" alone has never been a sufficient benchmark for personal jurisdiction under the Due Process Clause. * * *

* * *

This is not to say, of course, that foreseeability is wholly irrelevant. But the foreseeability that is critical to due process analysis is not the mere likelihood that a product will find its way into the forum State. Rather, it is that the defendant's conduct and connection with the forum State are such that he should reasonably anticipate being haled into court there. The Due Process Clause * * * gives a degree of predictability to the legal system that allows potential defendants to structure their primary conduct with some minimum assurance as to where that conduct will and will not render them liable to suit.

When a corporation "purposefully avails itself of the privilege of conducting activities within the forum State," Hanson v. Denckla, it has clear notice that it is subject to suit there, and can act to alleviate the risk of burdensome litigation by procuring insurance, passing the expected costs on to customers, or, if the risks are too great, severing its connection with the State. Hence if the sale of a product of a manufacturer or distributor such as Audi or Volkswagen is not simply an isolated occurrence, but arises from the efforts of the manufacturer or distributor to serve directly or indirectly, the market for its product in other States, it is not unreasonable to subject it to suit in one of those States if its allegedly defective merchandise has there been the source of injury to its owner or to others. The forum State does not exceed its powers under the Due Process Clause if it asserts personal jurisdiction over a corporation that delivers its products into the stream of commerce with the expectation that they will be purchased by consumers in the forum State. Cf. Gray v. American Radiator & Standard Sanitary Corp.

But there is no such or similar basis for Oklahoma jurisdiction over World-Wide or Seaway in this case. Seaway's sales are made in Massena, N. Y. World-Wide's market, although substantially larger, is limited to dealers in New York, New Jersey, and Connecticut. There is no evidence of record that any automobiles distributed by World-Wide are sold to retail customers outside this tristate area. It is foreseeable that the purchasers of automobiles sold by World-Wide and Seaway may take them to Oklahoma. But the mere "unilateral activity of those who claim some relationship with a nonresident defendant cannot satisfy the requirement of contact with the forum State." Hanson v. Denckla.

In a variant on the previous argument, it is contended that jurisdiction can be supported by the fact that petitioners earn substantial revenue from goods used in Oklahoma. The Oklahoma Supreme Court so found, drawing the inference that because one automobile sold by petitioners had been used in Oklahoma, others might have been used there also. While this inference seems less than compelling on the facts of the instant case, we need not question the court's factual findings in order to reject its reasoning.

This argument seems to make the point that the purchase of automobiles in New York, from which the petitioners earn substantial revenue, would not occur but for the fact that the automobiles are capable of use in distant States like Oklahoma. Respondents observe that the very purpose of an automobile is to travel, and that travel of automobiles sold by petitioners is facilitated by an extensive chain of Volkswagen service centers throughout the country, including some in Oklahoma.[12] * * * In our view, whatever marginal revenues petitioners may receive by virtue of the fact that their products are capable of use in Oklahoma is far too attenuated a contact to justify that State's exercise of in personam jurisdiction over them.

Because we find that petitioners have no "contacts, ties, or relations" with the State of Oklahoma, the judgment of the Supreme Court of Oklahoma is

Reversed.

---

[12] As we have noted, petitioners earn no direct revenues from these service centers.

MR. JUSTICE BRENNAN, dissenting.

* * * Because I believe that the Court reads *International Shoe* and its progeny too narrowly, and because I believe that the standards enunciated by those cases may already be obsolete as constitutional boundaries, I dissent.

I

The Court's opinions focus tightly on the existence of contacts between the forum and the defendant. In so doing, they accord too little weight to the strength of the forum State's interest in the case and fail to explore whether there would be any actual inconvenience to the defendant. The essential inquiry in locating the constitutional limits on state-court jurisdiction over absent defendants is whether the particular exercise of jurisdiction offends "'traditional notions of fair play and substantial justice.'" The clear focus in *International Shoe* was on fairness and reasonableness. * * *

The existence of contacts, so long as there were some, was merely one way of giving content to the determination of fairness and reasonableness.

Surely *International Shoe* contemplated that the significance of the contacts necessary to support jurisdiction would diminish if some other consideration helped establish that jurisdiction would be fair and reasonable. The interests of the State and other parties in proceeding with the case in a particular forum are such considerations. * * *

* * *

That considerations other than contacts between the forum and the defendant are relevant necessarily means that the Constitution does not require that trial be held in the State which has the "best contacts" with the defendant. The defendant has no constitutional entitlement to the best forum or, for that matter, to any particular forum. * * *

II

* * * I would find that the forum State has an interest in permitting the litigation to go forward, the litigation is connected to the forum, the defendant is linked to the forum, and the burden of defending is not unreasonable. Accordingly, I would hold that it is neither unfair nor unreasonable to require these defendants to defend in the forum State.

* * *

B

In [the instant case], the interest of the forum State and its connection to the litigation is strong. The automobile accident underlying the litigation occurred in Oklahoma. The plaintiffs were hospitalized in Oklahoma when they brought suit. Essential witnesses and evidence were in Oklahoma. The State has a legitimate interest in enforcing its laws designed to keep its highway system safe, and the trial can proceed at least as efficiently in Oklahoma as anywhere else.

The petitioners are not unconnected with the forum. Although both sell automobiles within limited sales territories, each sold the automobile which in fact was driven to Oklahoma where it was involved in an accident. It may be true, as the Court suggests, that each sincerely intended to limit its commercial impact to the limited territory, and that each intended to accept the benefits and protection of the laws only of those States within the territory. But obviously these were unrealistic hopes that cannot be treated as an automatic constitutional shield.

An automobile simply is not a stationary item or one designed to be used in one place. An automobile is intended to be moved around. Someone in the business of selling large numbers of automobiles can hardly plead ignorance of their mobility or pretend that the automobiles stay put after they are sold. * * * The sale of an automobile does purposefully inject the vehicle into the stream of interstate commerce so that it can travel to distant States.

* * *

The Court accepts that a State may exercise jurisdiction over a distributor which "serves" that State "indirectly" by "deliver[ing] its products into the stream of commerce with the expectation that they will be purchased by consumers in the forum State." It is difficult to see why the Constitution should distinguish between a case involving goods which reach a distant State through a chain of distribution and a case involving goods which reach the same State because a consumer, using them as the dealer knew the customer would, took them there. In each case the seller purposefully injects the goods into the stream of commerce and those goods predictably are used in the forum State.

Furthermore, an automobile seller derives substantial benefits from States other than its own. A large part of the value of automobiles is the extensive, nationwide network of highways. Significant portions of that network have been constructed by and are maintained by the individual States, including Oklahoma. The States, through their highway programs, contribute in a very direct and important way to the value of petitioners' businesses. Additionally, a network of other related dealerships with their service departments operates throughout the country under the protection of the laws of the various States, including Oklahoma, and enhances the value of petitioners' businesses by facilitating their customers' traveling.

Thus, the Court errs in its conclusion that "petitioners have no 'contacts, ties, or relations'" with Oklahoma. There obviously are contacts, and, given Oklahoma's connection to the litigation, the contacts are sufficiently significant to make it fair and reasonable for the petitioners to submit to Oklahoma's jurisdiction.

III

It may be that affirmance of the judgment [herein] * * * would approach the outer limits of *International Shoe*'s jurisdictional principle. But that principle, with its almost exclusive focus on the rights of defendants, may be outdated. * * *

International Shoe inherited its defendant focus from *Pennoyer*, and represented the last major step this Court has taken in the long process of liberalizing the doctrine of personal jurisdiction. Though its flexible approach represented a major advance, the structure of our society has changed in many significant ways since International Shoe was decided in 1945. * * *

* * *

* * * The model of society on which the *International Shoe* Court based its opinion is no longer accurate. Business people, no matter how local their businesses, cannot assume that goods remain in the business' locality.

* * *

The conclusion I draw is that constitutional concepts of fairness no longer require the extreme concern for defendants that was once necessary. Rather, * * * minimum contacts must exist "among the parties, the contested transaction, and the forum State."[15] * * * I do not think the Due Process Clause is offended merely because the defendant has to board a plane to get to the site of the trial.

The Court's opinion * * * suggests that the defendant ought to be subject to a State's jurisdiction only if he has contacts with the State "such that he should reasonably anticipate being haled into court there."[18] There is nothing unreasonable or unfair, however, about recognizing commercial reality. Given the tremendous mobility of goods and people, and the inability of businessmen to control where goods are taken by customers (or retailers), I do not think that the defendant should be in complete control of the geographical stretch of his amenability to suit. * * * When an action in fact causes injury in another State, the actor should be prepared to answer for it there unless defending in that State would be unfair for some reason other than that a state boundary must be crossed.[19]

* * *

The plaintiffs * * * brought suit in a forum with which they had significant contacts and which had significant contacts with the litigation. I am not convinced that the defendants would suffer any "heavy and disproportionate burden" in defending the suits. Accordingly, I would hold that the Constitution should not shield the defendants from appearing and defending in the plaintiffs' chosen fora.

MR. JUSTICE MARSHALL, with whom MR. JUSTICE BLACKMUN joins, dissenting.

This is a difficult case, and reasonable minds may differ as to whether respondents have alleged a sufficient relationship among the defendant[s], the forum, and the litigation to satisfy the requirements of *International Shoe*. I am concerned, however, that the majority has reached its result by taking an unnecessarily narrow view of petitioners' forum-related conduct. The majority

---

[15] In some cases, the inquiry will resemble the inquiry commonly undertaken in determining which State's law to apply. That it is fair to apply a State's law to a nonresident defendant is clearly relevant in determining whether it is fair to subject the defendant to jurisdiction in that State.

[18] The Court suggests that this is the critical foreseeability rather than the likelihood that the product will to to the forum State. But the reasoning begs the question. A defendant cannot know if his actions will subject him to jurisdiction in another State until we have declared what the law of jurisdiction is.

[19] One consideration that might create some unfairness would be if the choice of forum also imposed on the defendant an unfavorable substantive law which the defendant could justly have assumed would not apply.

asserts that "respondents seek to base jurisdiction on one, isolated occurrence and whatever inferences can be drawn therefrom: the fortuitous circumstance that a single Audi automobile, sold in New York to New York residents, happened to suffer an accident while passing through Oklahoma." If that were the case, I would readily agree that the minimum contacts necessary to sustain jurisdiction are not present. But the basis for the assertion of jurisdiction is not the happenstance that an individual over whom petitioner had no control made a unilateral decision to take a chattel with him to a distant State. Rather, jurisdiction is premised on the deliberate and purposeful actions of the defendants themselves in choosing to become part of a nationwide, indeed a global, network for marketing and servicing automobiles.

Petitioners are sellers of a product whose utility derives from its mobility. * * * Petitioners know that their customers buy cars not only to make short trips, but also to travel long distances. In fact, the nationwide service network with which they are affiliated was designed to facilitate and encourage such travel. Seaway would be unlikely to sell many cars if authorized service were available only in Massena, N. Y. Moreover, local dealers normally derive a substantial portion of their revenues from their service operations and thereby obtain a further economic benefit from the opportunity to service cars which were sold in other States. It is apparent that petitioners have not attempted to minimize the chance that their activities will have effects in other States; on the contrary, they have chosen to do business in a way that increases that chance, because it is to their economic advantage to do so.

To be sure, petitioners could not know in advance that this particular automobile would be driven to Oklahoma. They must have anticipated, however, that a substantial portion of the cars they sold would travel out of New York. Seaway, a local dealer in the second most populous State, and World-Wide, one of only seven regional Audi distributors in the entire country, would scarcely have been surprised to learn that a car sold by them had been driven in Oklahoma on Interstate 44, a heavily traveled transcontinental highway. In the case of the distributor, in particular, the probability that some of the cars it sells will be driven in every one of the contiguous States must amount to a virtual certainty. This knowledge should alert a reasonable businessman to the likelihood that a defect in the product might manifest itself in the forum State — not because of some unpredictable, aberrant, unilateral action by a single buyer, but in the normal course of the operation of the vehicles for their intended purpose.

It is misleading for the majority to characterize the argument in favor of jurisdiction as one of "'foreseeability' alone." As economic entities petitioners reach out from New York, knowingly causing effects in other States and receiving economic advantage both from the ability to cause such effects themselves and from the activities of dealers and distributors in other States. While they did not receive revenue from making direct sales in Oklahoma, they intentionally became part of an interstate economic network, which included dealerships in Oklahoma, for pecuniary gain. In light of this purposeful conduct I do not believe it can be said that petitioners had no reason to expect to be haled before a * * * court.

The majority apparently acknowledges that if a product is purchased in the forum State by a consumer, that State may assert jurisdiction over everyone in the chain of distribution. With this I agree. But I cannot agree that jurisdiction is necessarily lacking if the product enters the State not through the channels of distribution but in the course of its intended use by the consumer. We have recognized the role played by the automobile in the expansion of our notions of personal jurisdiction. See Hess v. Pawloski. Unlike most other chattels, which may find their way into States far from where they were purchased because their owner takes them there, the intended use of the automobile is precisely as a means of traveling from one place to another. In such a case, it is highly artificial to restrict the concept of the "stream of commerce" to the chain of distribution from the manufacturer to the ultimate consumer.

I sympathize with the majority's concern that the persons ought to be able to structure their conduct so as not to be subject to suit in distant forums. But that may not always be possible. Some activities by their very nature may foreclose the option of conducting them in such a way as to avoid subjecting oneself to jurisdiction in multiple forums. This is by no means to say that all sellers of automobiles should be subject to suit everywhere; but a distributor of automobiles to a multistate market and a local automobile dealer who makes himself part of a nationwide network of dealerships can fairly expect that the cars they sell may cause injury in distant States and that they may be called on to defend a resulting lawsuit there.

* * *

Of course, the Constitution forbids the exercise of jurisdiction if the defendant had no judicially cognizable contacts with the forum. But as the majority acknowledges, if such contacts are present the jurisdictional inquiry requires a balancing of various interests and policies. I believe such contacts are to be found here and that, considering all of the interests and policies at stake, requiring petitioners to defend this action in Oklahoma is not beyond the bounds of the Constitution. Accordingly, I dissent.

[The dissenting opinion of MR. JUSTICE BLACKMUN is omitted.]

NOTES AND PROBLEMS FOR DISCUSSION

1. Notice how federalism has been transformed from the single, stand-alone limit on state authority in *Pennoyer* to one of two coequal components of the due process constraint on judicial jurisdiction in *Volkswagen*. Do you agree with the *Volkswagen* Court that the "minimum contacts" benchmark was designed in *International Shoe* not only to protect defendants' due process rights but also to safeguard states from unwarranted exercises of power by other coequal sovereigns in the federal system?

Barely two years after issuing its decision in *Volkswagen*, however, the Court reasserted the primacy of individual liberty as the interest underlying the Due Process Clause's restriction on personal jurisdiction. In INSURANCE

CORP. OF IRELAND, LTD. v. COMPAGNIE DES BAUXITES, 456 U.S. 694, 102 S.Ct. 1099, 72 L.Ed.2d 492 (1982), the Court acknowledged that

> "The personal jurisdiction requirement recognizes and protects an individual liberty interest. It represents a restriction on judicial power not as a matter of sovereignty, but as a matter of individual liberty. It is true that we have stated that the requirement of personal jurisdiction, as applied to state courts, reflects an element of federalism and the character of state sovereignty vis-à-vis other States. * * * The restriction on state sovereign power described in World-Wide Volkswagen, however, must be seen as ultimately a function of the individual liberty interest preserved by the Due Process Clause. That Clause is the only source of the personal jurisdiction requirement and the Clause itself makes no mention of federalism concerns. Furthermore, if the federalism concept operated as an independent restriction on the sovereign power of the court, it would not be possible to waive the personal jurisdiction requirement. Individual actions cannot change the powers of sovereignty, although the individual can subject himself to powers from which he may otherwise be protected."

456 U.S. at 703 & n.10; 102 S.Ct. at 1105 & n.10. And three years later, in BURGER KING v. RUDZEWICZ, 471 U.S. 462, 105 S.Ct. 2174, 85 L.Ed.2d 528 (1985), the Court reiterated that the "minimum contacts" standard served only that single, individual-focused goal: to determine whether the defendant has "fair warning" that it could be haled before the forum's judiciary as a result of engaging in purposeful (as opposed to random, fortuitous, or attenuated) activity in the forum.

2. The majority in *Volkswagen* announced that "in an appropriate case" a court's assessment of the constitutionality of exercising personal jurisdiction should look beyond the *defendant's* forum contacts and consider

> "other relevant factors, including the forum State's interest in adjudicating the dispute; the plaintiff's interest in obtaining convenient and effective relief, at least when that interest is not adequately protected by the plaintiff's power to choose the forum; the interstate judicial system's interest in obtaining the most efficient resolution of controversies; and the shared interest of the several States in furthering fundamental substantive social policies."

What would constitute such "an appropriate case"? In *Burger King, supra*, a breach of contract case in which the forum sought to assert "specific" jurisdiction, the Court stated, in more definite and explicit terms than it had used in *Volkswagen*, that once the defendant is found to have purposefully established minimum contacts with the forum state, the trial court is to assess the extent of these contacts in light of the other "fair play and substantial justice" factors articulated in *Volkswagen*. And, the Court noted, the impact of these other factors could, under certain circumstances, trump the presence of minimum contacts to defeat jurisdiction.

3. There is often a lengthy distribution chain that separates a manufacturer (of either a finished product or a component part) or a distributor from the ultimate consumer. Consequently, it can be difficult to determine whether these actors have engaged in a "purposeful act" within the forum state.

(a) How did the majority in *Volkswagen* address this problem?

(b) What was the view espoused by dissenting Justices Brennan, Marshall and Blackmun?

(c) Which of these two perspectives is more consistent with the Court's prior statement in *Hanson* that "minimum contacts" must be the result of some purposeful act *by the defendant*?

(d) Does the purposefully availing criterion for "minimum contacts" serve the dual constitutional purposes articulated by the *Volkswagen* majority? For example, is state sovereignty less threatened when jurisdiction is exercised over a nonresident corporation that intentionally ships its products to the forum state than when it is exerted over a nonresident corporation whose product, through no fault of its own, lands in, and injures a resident of, the forum state? Alternatively, are a defendant's due process rights impaired more by the exercise of jurisdiction in the latter than in the former situation?

4. The "stream of commerce" metaphor initially developed in *Volkswagen* as a measure of the defendant's connection with the forum state reemerged shortly thereafter in two decisions, neither of which involved a traditional consumer products liability action. Rather, these two companion cases, KEETON v. HUSTLER MAGAZINE, 465 U.S. 770, 104 S.Ct. 1473, 79 L.Ed.2d 790 (1984) and CALDER v. JONES, 465 U.S. 783, 104 S.Ct. 1492, 79 L.Ed.2d 804 (1984), involved libel plaintiffs seeking jurisdiction against media defendants.

In *Keeton*, a New York resident sued Hustler Magazine (an Ohio Corporation with a California principal place of business) in New Hampshire. Between 10,000 and 15,000 copies of the magazine were sold each month in New Hampshire. The Court concluded that the defendant's targeted, purposeful circulation of its product in the forum satisfied the *Volkswagen* standard for minimum contacts. This otherwise unremarkable result, however, occurred in a unique context. Under the controlling substantive law, a single action seeking damages for injuries sustained in every part of the country could be filed by a defamation plaintiff in any state in which the publication caused injury. Thus, pursuant to this "single publication rule," this New York plaintiff sought to recover the damage to her reputation suffered throughout the United States by the actions of an Ohio/California publisher in a New Hampshire forum. (The plaintiff chose to bring her action in New Hampshire because of its unusually long statute of limitations.) The Court ruled that the sufficiency of the defendant's forum contacts should be appraised in light of that fact and not as if the plaintiff's claim was for damages sustained solely in the forum. It then concluded that the defendant's purposeful activity in the forum, combined with the forum's manifest interest in (1) redressing injuries suffered within the state (even by non-residents), and (2) providing a single forum for libel actions brought pursuant to the "single publication rule," was a sufficient justification for the exercise of jurisdiction despite the extremely limited connection between the plaintiff and the forum. The Court explicitly rejected the defendant's contention that the plaintiff's lack of connection with the forum should be a basis for denying jurisdiction.

Calder, on the other hand, involved a forum (California) plaintiff with a claim against individual employees — the reporter and the editor of an article about her that appeared in the *National Enquirer* — rather than against the corporate publisher. Consequently, the extent of the publication's circulation in the forum state could not serve as a basis for jurisdiction. Both of the defendants were residents of Florida who had limited contacts with California. But instead of focusing on the defendants' forum activities, or the forum state's interests in adjudicating this controversy, Chief Justice Rehnquist (who also authored the opinion in *Keeton*) declared that jurisdiction was constitutionally permissible because of *the effects* of the defendants' extra-territorial conduct within the forum state. Since both defendants knew that the plaintiff (television and screen star Shirley Jones) lived and worked in the forum state and that her reputation therefore would be most dramatically affected in California, jurisdiction was proper because the defendants' Florida conduct was "expressly aimed" at California.

The lower courts have had a lot of difficulty assessing the scope of this "effects" test. Some have construed it rather broadly to apply to any attempt to exercise specific jurisdiction in a case involving intentionally tortious conduct that occurred outside of the forum state but which is alleged to have caused injury to the plaintiff in the forum state. See e.g., Jamark, Inc v. Reidy, 132 F.3d 1200 (7th Cir.1997).

Other courts, however, construe *Calder* as demanding more than the fact that the plaintiff was located in the forum and therefore felt the effects of the intentionally tortious conduct there. They construe the "expressly aiming" language of *Calder* to require the plaintiff to establish that the defendant knew that the plaintiff would "suffer the brunt of the harm caused by the tortious conduct in the forum" by pointing to specific activity reflecting the defendant's intention to direct its tortious conduct at the forum.

For example, in GRIFFIS v. LUBAN, 646 N.W.2d 527 (Minn.S.Ct.2002), an Alabama resident brought a tort action against a Minnesota resident in Alabama state court alleging that the defendant distributed defamatory material on an Internet newsgroup. The Minnesota Supreme Court agreed that *Calder* required something more than defendant's knowledge that the plaintiff was a forum resident and would feel the effects of the intentionally tortious conduct in the forum. It did not believe that the *Calder* Court intended to create an intentional torts exception to traditional specific jurisdiction analysis so as to permit plaintiffs in such cases to always be able to sue in their home state. In the instant case, the court concluded, the record did not support the conclusion that the defendant's statements were "expressly aimed" at Alabama since the subject of the newsgroup — Egyptology — did not relate particularly to Alabama, nor was the universe of interested newsgroup participants primarily located in Alabama (unlike the close relationship between the plaintiff's profession and the forum state of California in *Calder*) since the newsgroup was available worldwide to anyone with an Internet connection. The fact that the defendant knew or should have known that the defamatory statements would affect the plaintiff in the forum state was not enough to demonstrate that Alabama was "the focal point" of the defendant's intentionally tortious conduct. See also Young v. New Haven Advocate, 315 F.3d 256 (4th Cir.2002) (no *Calder*-based *in personam* jurisdiction in Virginia over Internet posting of a Connecticut newspapers' article allegedly defaming warden of Virginia prison; since focus of the online article was the effect in Connecticut of transfer of Connecticut prisoners into the Virginia prison, defendants found not to have posted materials on Internet with manifest intent of targeting Virginia readers); Revell v. Lidov, 317 F.3d 467 (5th Cir.2002) (citing *Young* with approval and holding that the mere fact that the plaintiff in a defamation suit lives in the forum state and suffered harm in the forum state is not enough to establish *Calder*-based personal jurisdiction when defendant did not know of the forum in which the plaintiff would bear the brunt of the injury occasioned by his publication of an article on a web site); Pavlovich v. Superior Court of Santa Clara County, 29 Cal.4th 262, 58 P.3d 2, 127 Cal.Rptr.2d 329 (2002) (assertion that an individual with no direct contacts with California forum who posts, on his own Internet web site, the source code of a program that permits users to circumvent encryption technology on data contained on DVDs and thereby watch and/or copy movies contained on DVDs does not meet the *Calder* effects test; mere knowledge that posting of this program would harm the movie and computer industries in California is not enough to meet *Calder's* "expressly aimed" requirement).

On the other hand, a majority of the Ninth Circuit sitting *en banc* declared that the *Calder* effects test was not limited either to cases involving wrongful conduct or even to cases where the brunt of the harm was suffered by the plaintiff in the forum state. In YAHOO! INC. v. LA LIGUE CONTRE LE RACISM et L'ANTISEMITISME, 433 F.3d 1199 (9th Cir. 2006) (en banc), the Court upheld the exercise of personal jurisdiction by a federal district court in California over two French civil rights organizations based on the facts that these two groups had (1) sent the plaintiff Yahoo! a cease and desist letter to its California headquarters; (2) served Yahoo! with process in California in connection with a suit brought in a French court against Yahoo! by these two organizations; and (3) served the French court's two interim orders on Yahoo! in California. The French organizations had filed suit against Yahoo! in France seeking to require Yahoo! to block all access from French territory to Yahoo!'s web site's Nazi artifact auction service and to all other Yahoo! services depicting Nazi objects or symbols. After the French court issued an order requiring Yahoo! to do so, Yahoo! filed the instant suit in federal district court in California against the two French civil rights organizations seeking a declaratory judgment that the French court orders were not enforceable in the U.S. The trial court denied the defendants' motion to dismiss for lack of personal jurisdiction.

After a Ninth Circuit panel reversed the trial judge, 379 F.3d 1120 (9th Cir.2004), the court agreed to reconsider the case *en banc*, 399 F.3d 1010 (9th Cir.2005). A majority of the *en banc* court "clarified" its interpretation of *Calder*'s "expressly aiming" requirement by announcing that the "brunt" of the harm need not be suffered by the plaintiff in the forum state. Rather, as long as a "jurisdictionally sufficient" degree of harm was suffered in the forum state, it did not matter that a greater amount of harm was suffered in some other state. Moreover, the court declared that the *Calder* effects test was not limited to a situation where the defendant's actions expressly aimed at and causing injury in the forum were tortious or otherwise wrongful. Rather, it stated, *Calder* merely required an inquiry into all of the defendants' contacts with the forum to determine whether they constituted intentional acts that were expressly aimed at the forum state.

Applying that standard, the court found that the defendants intentionally had filed suit in a French court and that this suit was expressly aimed at California because it was designed to compel Yahoo! to modify the way it conducted business in that state. The French suit had been filed to stop Yahoo! from selling Nazi-related objects through its online services to anyone in France. And even though the effect sought by the French court would primarily be felt in France, since Yahoo!'s servers were located in California, the court reasoned, compliance with the French court decisions also would require Yahoo! to make changes to those servers. It further noted that as the French court orders included an imposition of financial penalties for noncompliance, the impact of any such penalties would be felt by Yahoo! at its corporate headquarters located in California. With respect to the final *Calder* criterion of whether the defendants knew that harm was likely to be suffered by the plaintiff in the forum state, the court admitted that the plaintiff had not demonstrated or even alleged that it actually had altered any of its behavior in response to the French court orders. Nor had the defendants sought enforcement of those orders in the U.S. In fact, the defendants had affirmed that they would not seek enforcement so long as Yahoo! continued its revised course of conduct. Nevertheless, the court determined, since the defendants had not sought to vacate the French court orders, it was possible that if Yahoo! reverted to its original course of conduct, they might seek enforcement. Consequently, while acknowledging that this was a close case, the court concluded that although the defendants' sending of the letter and the serving of process in the forum did not, by themselves, meet the *Calder* standard, the combination of all three of its contacts with California provided a sufficient basis for the exercise of personal jurisdiction.

The Supreme Court weighed in on this controversy in WALDEN v. FIORE, 571 U.S. ___, 134 S.Ct. 1115, 188 L.Ed.2d 12 (2014). There, two Nevada residents were stopped at the Atlanta airport by a local police officer working with the federal Drug Enforcement Agency who had a drug-sniffing dog perform a sniff test on their bags and then seized the large amount of cash contained in the bags. Ultimately, the money was returned. But the individuals filed suit against the police officer in federal court in Nevada seeking damages for various violations of their Fourth Amendment rights against unreasonable searches and seizures. The trial court dismissed the case for lack of personal jurisdiction over the Atlanta officer, but the Ninth Circuit reversed in part. A majority of the appellate panel ruled that the trial court could exercise personal jurisdiction over the defendant with respect to the claim that the officer had submitted a false affidavit to support the seizure because the complaint alleged that the officer had submitted the affidavit with knowledge that it would affect plaintiffs who resided in the forum state (Nevada). The Supreme Court unanimously reversed the Ninth Circuit and held, relying on its analysis in *Volkswagen*, that in a case asserting specific jurisdiction, the due process contacts standard required analysis of the *defendant's* forum-based conduct and not the defendant's connection to a plaintiff who had his or her own connection to the forum state. Moreover, in response to the plaintiff's contention that jurisdiction was proper in this intentional tort claim based on the *Calder* "effects" standard, the Court seemingly narrowed the impact of its *Calder* analysis. It construed *Calder* as focusing not primarily on the location of the impact of the defendant's tortious conduct on the plaintiff but on the fact that the intentional tort actually occurred in the forum state since the publication to third persons is an element of the tort of libel and the article was read (published) by third persons in the forum state of California. As the unanimous Court declared in *Walden*,

> *Calder* made clear that mere injury to a forum resident is not a sufficient connection [by the defendant] to the forum. Regardless of where a plaintiff lives or works, an injury is jurisdictionally relevant only insofar as it shows that the defendant has formed a contact with the forum state. The proper question is not where the plaintiff experienced a particular injury or effect but where the defendant's conduct connects him to the forum in a meaningful way.

As far as the Court was concerned, the fact that the defendant's conduct denied the plaintiffs access to their money for some time while they were in the forum state of Nevada was an insufficient basis for exercising jurisdiction. These plaintiffs, the Court reasoned, would have experienced that same lack of access in any state where they found themselves while awaiting the return of the funds, and the Court was not prepared to extend the existence of jurisdiction to all of those locations. This analysis suggests that the Court's previous defendant-focused assessment of contacts is also now equally applicable in intentional tort cases.

Is this "effects" test, however construed, consistent with the "stream of commerce" analysis discussed in *Volkswagen* or was the "stream of commerce" analysis intended to apply only to corporate defendants and not to employees who have no control over where the magazines containing the allegedly libelous article were marketed?

Since the Court in neither *Keeton* nor *Calder* formally applied the two-step "minimum contacts" test proffered in *Volkswagen*, these opinions did not help to resolve the division on the *Volkswagen* Court with respect to the precise meaning of the "stream of commerce" standard. The inability of a majority of the Court to coalesce around any particular formulation of this criterion became even more pronounced in the following case.

Asahi Metal Industry Co., Ltd. v. Superior Court of California

Supreme Court of the United States, 1987.

480 U.S. 102, 107 S.Ct. 1026, 94 L.Ed.2d 92.

JUSTICE O'CONNOR announced the judgment of the Court and delivered the unanimous opinion of the Court with respect to Part I, the opinion of the Court with respect to Part II-B, in which THE CHIEF JUSTICE, JUSTICE BRENNAN, JUSTICE WHITE, JUSTICE MARSHALL, JUSTICE BLACKMUN, JUSTICE POWELL, and JUSTICE STEVENS join, and an opinion with respect to Parts II-A and III, in which THE CHIEF JUSTICE, JUSTICE POWELL, and JUSTICE SCALIA join.

This case presents the question whether the mere awareness on the part of a foreign defendant that the components it manufactured, sold, and delivered outside the United States would reach the forum State in the stream of commerce constitutes "minimum contacts" between the defendant and the forum State such that the exercise of jurisdiction "does not offend 'traditional notions of fair play and substantial justice.'" International Shoe Co.

I

On September 23, 1978, on Interstate Highway 80 in Solano County, California, Gary Zurcher lost control of his Honda motorcycle and collided with a tractor. * * * In September 1979, Zurcher filed a product liability action in the Superior Court of the State of California in and for the County of Solano. Zurcher alleged that the 1978 accident was caused by a sudden loss of air and an explosion in the rear tire of the motorcycle, and alleged that the motorcycle tire, tube, and sealant were defective. Zurcher's complaint named, inter alia, Cheng Shin Rubber Industrial Co., Ltd. (Cheng Shin), the Taiwanese manufacturer of the tube. Cheng Shin in turn filed a cross-complaint seeking indemnification from its codefendants and from petitioner, Asahi Metal Industry Co., Ltd. (Asahi), the manufacturer of the tube's valve assembly. Zurcher's claims against Cheng Shin and the other defendants were eventually settled and dismissed, leaving only Cheng Shin's indemnity action against Asahi.

California's long-arm statute authorizes the exercise of jurisdiction "on any basis not inconsistent with the Constitution of this state or of the United States." Asahi moved to quash Cheng Shin's service of summons, arguing the State could not exert jurisdiction over it consistent with the Due Process Clause of the Fourteenth Amendment.

* * * Asahi is a Japanese corporation. It manufactures tire valve assemblies in Japan and sells the assemblies to Cheng Shin, and to several other tire manufacturers, for use as components in finished tire tubes. Asahi's sales to Cheng Shin took place in Taiwan. The shipments from Asahi to Cheng Shin were sent from Japan to Taiwan. Cheng Shin bought and incorporated into its tire tubes 150,000 Asahi valve assemblies in 1978; 500,000 in 1979; 500,000 in 1980; 100,000 in 1981; and 100,000 in 1982. Sales to Cheng Shin accounted for 1.24 percent of Asahi's income in 1981 and 0.44 percent in 1982. Cheng Shin alleged that approximately 20 percent of its sales in the United States are in

California. Cheng Shin purchases valve assemblies from other suppliers as well, and sells finished tubes throughout the world.

In 1983 an attorney for Cheng Shin conducted an informal examination of the valve stems of the tire tubes sold in one cycle store in Solano County. The attorney declared that of the approximately 115 tire tubes in the store, 97 were purportedly manufactured in Japan or Taiwan, and of those 97, 21 valve stems were marked with the circled letter "A", apparently Asahi's trademark. Of the 21 Asahi valve stems, 12 were incorporated into Cheng Shin tire tubes. The store contained 41 other Cheng Shin tubes that incorporated the valve assemblies of other manufacturers. An affidavit of a manager of Cheng Shin whose duties included the purchasing of component parts stated: "In discussions with Asahi regarding the purchase of valve stem assemblies the fact that my Company sells tubes throughout the world and specifically the United States has been discussed. I am informed and believe that Asahi was fully aware that valve stem assemblies sold to my Company and to others would end up throughout the United States and in California." An affidavit of the president of Asahi, on the other hand, declared that Asahi "has never contemplated that its limited sales of tire valves to Cheng Shin in Taiwan would subject it to lawsuits in California." The record does not include any contract between Cheng Shin and Asahi.

* * * [T]he Superior Court denied the motion to quash summons * * *.

The Court of Appeal of the State of California issued a peremptory writ of mandate commanding the Superior Court to quash service of summons. * * *

The Supreme Court of the State of California reversed and discharged the writ issued by the Court of Appeal. The court observed: "Asahi has no offices, property or agents in California. It solicits no business in California and has made no direct sales [in California]." Moreover, "Asahi did not design or control the system of distribution that carried its valve assemblies into California." Nevertheless, the court found the exercise of jurisdiction over Asahi to be consistent with the Due Process Clause. It concluded that Asahi knew that some of the valve assemblies sold to Cheng Shin would be incorporated into tire tubes sold in California, and that Asahi benefited indirectly from the sale in California of products incorporating its components. The court considered Asahi's intentional act of placing its components into the stream of commerce — that is, by delivering the components to Cheng Shin in Taiwan — coupled with Asahi's awareness that some of the components would eventually find their way into California, sufficient to form the basis for state court jurisdiction under the Due Process Clause.

We granted certiorari and now reverse.

II

A

The Due Process Clause of the Fourteenth Amendment limits the power of a state court to exert personal jurisdiction over a nonresident defendant. "[T]he constitutional touchstone" of the determination whether an exercise of personal jurisdiction comports with due process "remains whether the defendant purposefully established 'minimum contacts' in the forum State." Burger King Corp. v. Rudzewicz, quoting International Shoe. * * *

Applying the principle that minimum contacts must be based on an act of the defendant, the Court in World-Wide Volkswagen rejected the assertion that a consumer's unilateral act of bringing the defendant's product into the forum State was a sufficient constitutional basis for personal jurisdiction over the defendant. * * *

In World-Wide Volkswagen itself, the state court sought to base jurisdiction not on any act of the defendant, but on the foreseeable unilateral actions of the consumer. Since World-Wide Volkswagen, lower courts have been confronted with cases in which the defendant acted by placing a product in the stream of commerce, and the stream eventually swept defendant's product into the forum State, but the defendant did nothing else to purposefully avail itself of the market in the forum State. Some courts have understood the Due Process Clause, as interpreted in World-Wide Volkswagen, to allow an exercise of personal jurisdiction to be based on no more than the defendant's act of placing the product in the stream of commerce. Other courts have understood the Due Process Clause and the above-quoted language in World-Wide Volkswagen to require the action of the defendant to be more purposefully directed at the forum State than the mere act of placing a product in the stream of commerce.

The reasoning of the Supreme Court of California in the present case illustrates the former interpretation of World-Wide Volkswagen. The Supreme Court of California held that, because the stream of commerce eventually brought some valves Asahi sold Cheng Shin into California, Asahi's awareness that its valves would be sold in California was sufficient to permit California to exercise jurisdiction over Asahi consistent with the requirements of the Due Process Clause. The Supreme Court of California's position was consistent with those courts that have held that mere foreseeability or awareness was a constitutionally sufficient basis for personal jurisdiction if the defendant's product made its way into the forum State while still in the stream of commerce.

Other courts, however, have understood the Due Process Clause to require something more than that the defendant was aware of its product's entry into the forum State through the stream of commerce in order for the State to exert jurisdiction over the defendant. * * *

We now find this latter position to be consonant with the requirements of due process. The "substantial connection" between the defendant and the forum State necessary for a finding of minimum contacts must come about by an action of the defendant purposefully directed toward the forum State. The placement of a product into the stream of commerce, without more, is not an act of the defendant purposefully directed toward the forum State. Additional conduct of the defendant may indicate an intent or purpose to serve the market in the forum State, for example, designing the product for the market in the forum State, advertising in the forum State, establishing channels for providing regular advice to customers in the forum State, or marketing the product through a distributor who has agreed to serve as the sales agent in the forum State. But a defendant's awareness that the stream of commerce may or will sweep the product into the forum State does not convert the mere act of placing the product into the stream into an act purposefully directed toward the forum State.

Assuming, arguendo, that respondents have established Asahi's awareness that some of the valves sold to Cheng Shin would be incorporated into tire tubes sold in California, respondents have not demonstrated any action by Asahi to purposefully avail itself of the California market. Asahi does not do business in California. It has no office, agents, employees, or property in California. It does not advertise or otherwise solicit business in California. It did not create, control, or employ the distribution system that brought its valves to California. There is no evidence that Asahi designed its product in anticipation of sales in California. On the basis of these facts, the exertion of personal jurisdiction over Asahi by the Superior Court of California exceeds the limits of due process.

B

* * *

We have previously explained that the determination of the reasonableness of the exercise of jurisdiction in each case will depend on an evaluation of several factors. A court must consider the burden on the defendant, the interests of the forum State, and the plaintiff's interest in obtaining relief. It must also weigh in its determination "the interstate judicial system's interest in obtaining the most efficient resolution of controversies; and the shared interest of the several States in furthering fundamental substantive social policies."

A consideration of these factors in the present case clearly reveals the unreasonableness of the assertion of jurisdiction over Asahi, even apart from the question of the placement of goods in the stream of commerce.

Certainly the burden on the defendant in this case is severe. Asahi has been commanded by the Supreme Court of California not only to traverse the distance between Asahi's headquarters in Japan and the Superior Court of California * * *, but also to submit its dispute with Cheng Shin to a foreign nation's judicial system. The unique burdens placed upon one who must defend oneself in a foreign legal system should have significant weight in assessing the reasonableness of stretching the long arm of personal jurisdiction over national borders.

When minimum contacts have been established, often the interests of the plaintiff and the forum in the exercise of jurisdiction will justify even the serious burdens placed on the alien defendant. In the present case, however, the interests of the plaintiff and the forum in California's assertion of jurisdiction over Asahi are slight. All that remains is a claim for indemnification asserted by Cheng Shin, a Taiwanese corporation, against Asahi. The transaction on which the indemnification claim is based took place in Taiwan; Asahi's components were shipped from Japan to Taiwan. Cheng Shin has not demonstrated that it is more convenient for it to litigate its indemnification claim against Asahi in California rather than in Taiwan or Japan.

Because the plaintiff is not a California resident, California's legitimate interests in the dispute have considerably diminished. The Supreme Court of California argued that the State had an interest in "protecting its consumers by ensuring that foreign manufacturers comply with the state's safety standards." The State Supreme Court's definition of California's interest, however, was overly broad. The dispute between Cheng Shin and Asahi is primarily about indemnification rather than safety standards. Moreover, it is not at all clear at this point that California law should govern the question whether a Japanese corporation should indemnify a Taiwanese corporation on the basis of a sale made in Taiwan and a shipment of goods from Japan to Taiwan. The possibility of being haled into a California court as a result of an accident involving Asahi's components undoubtedly creates an additional deterrent to the manufacture of unsafe components; however, similar pressures will be placed on Asahi by the purchasers of its components as long as those who use Asahi components in their final products, and sell those products in California, are subject to the application of California tort law.

World-Wide Volkswagen also admonished courts to take into consideration the interests of the "several States," in addition to the forum State, in the efficient judicial resolution of the dispute and the advancement of substantive policies. In the present case, this advice calls for a court to consider the procedural and substantive policies of other nations whose interests are affected by the assertion of jurisdiction by the California court. The procedural and substantive interests of other nations in a state court's assertion of jurisdiction over an alien defendant will differ from case to case. In every case, however, those interests, as well as the Federal interest in Government's foreign relations policies, will be best served by a careful inquiry into the reasonableness of the assertion of jurisdiction in the particular case, and an unwillingness to find the serious burdens on an alien defendant outweighed by minimal interests on the part of the plaintiff or the forum State. * * *

Considering the international context, the heavy burden on the alien defendant, and the slight interests of the plaintiff and the forum State, the exercise of personal jurisdiction by a California court over Asahi in this instance would be unreasonable and unfair.

III

Because the facts of this case do not establish minimum contacts such that the exercise of personal jurisdiction is consistent with fair play and substantial justice, the judgment of the Supreme Court of California is reversed, and the case is remanded for further proceedings not inconsistent with this opinion.

It is so ordered.

JUSTICE BRENNAN, with whom JUSTICE WHITE, JUSTICE MARSHALL, and JUSTICE BLACKMUN join, concurring in part and concurring in the judgment.

I do not agree with the interpretation in Part II-A of the stream-of-commerce theory, nor with the conclusion that Asahi did not "purposely avail itself of the California market." I do agree, however, with the Court's conclusion in Part II-B that the exercise of personal jurisdiction over Asahi in this case would not comport with "fair play and substantial justice." This is one of those rare cases in which "minimum requirements inherent in the concept of 'fair play and substantial justice' . . . defeat the reasonableness of jurisdiction even [though] the defendant has purposefully engaged in forum activities." Burger King. I therefore join Parts I and II-B of the Court's opinion, and write separately to explain my disagreement with Part II-A.

Part II-A states that "a defendant's awareness that the stream of commerce may or will sweep the product into the forum State does not convert the mere act of placing the product into the stream into an act purposefully directed toward the forum State." Under this view, a plaintiff would be required to show "[a]dditional conduct" directed toward the forum before finding the exercise of jurisdiction over the defendant to be consistent with the Due Process Clause. I see no need for such a showing, however. The stream of commerce refers not to unpredictable currents or eddies, but to the regular and anticipated flow of products from manufacture to distribution to retail sale. As long as a participant in this process is aware that the final product is being marketed in the forum State, the possibility of a lawsuit there cannot come as a surprise. Nor will the litigation present a burden for which there is no corresponding benefit. A defendant who has placed goods in the stream of commerce benefits economically from the retail sale of the final product in the forum State, and indirectly benefits from the State's laws that regulate and facilitate commercial activity. These benefits accrue regardless of whether that participant directly conducts business in the forum State, or engages in additional conduct directed toward that State. Accordingly, most courts and commentators have found that jurisdiction premised on the placement of a product into the stream of commerce is consistent with the Due Process Clause, and have not required a showing of additional conduct.

* * * Part II-A * * * represents a marked retreat from the analysis in World-Wide Volkswagen. ***

* * *

The Court in World-Wide Volkswagen * * * took great care to distinguish "between a case involving goods which reach a distant State through a chain of distribution and a case involving goods which reach the same State because a consumer . . . took them there." The California Supreme Court took note of this distinction, and correctly concluded that our holding in World-Wide Volkswagen preserved the stream-of-commerce theory.

In this case, the facts found by the California Supreme Court support its finding of minimum contacts. The court found that "[a]lthough Asahi did not design or control the system of distribution that carried its valve assemblies into California, Asahi was aware of the distribution system's operation, and it knew that it would benefit economically from the sale in California of products incorporating its components." Accordingly, I cannot join the determination in Part II-A that Asahi's regular and extensive sales of component parts to a manufacturer it knew was making regular sales of the final product in California is insufficient to establish minimum contacts with California.

JUSTICE STEVENS, with whom JUSTICE WHITE and JUSTICE BLACKMUN join, concurring in part and concurring in the judgment.

The judgment of the Supreme Court of California should be reversed for the reasons stated in Part II-B of the Court's opinion. While I join Parts I and II-B, I do not join Part II-A for two reasons. First, it is not necessary to the Court's decision. An examination of minimum contacts is not always necessary to determine whether a state court's assertion of personal jurisdiction is constitutional. Part II-B establishes, after considering the factors set forth in World-Wide Volkswagen, that California's exercise of jurisdiction over Asahi in this case would be "unreasonable and unfair." This finding alone requires reversal * * *. Accordingly, I see no reason in this case for the plurality to articulate "purposeful direction" or any other test as the nexus between an act of a defendant and the forum State that is necessary to establish minimum contacts.

Second, even assuming that the test ought to be formulated here, Part II-A misapplies it to the facts of this case. The plurality seems to assume that an unwavering line can be drawn between "mere awareness" that a component will find its way into the forum State and "purposeful availment" of the forum's market. Over the course of its dealings with Cheng Shin, Asahi has arguably engaged in a higher quantum of conduct than "[t]he placement of a product into the stream of commerce, without more. . . ." Whether or not this conduct rises to the level of purposeful availment requires a constitutional determination that is affected by the volume, the value, and the hazardous character of the components. In most circumstances I would be inclined to conclude that a regular course of dealing that results in deliveries of over 100,000 units annually over a period of several years would constitute "purposeful availment" even though the item delivered to the forum State was a standard product marketed throughout the world.

NOTES AND PROBLEMS FOR DISCUSSION

1. To what extent, if at all, do you believe that the result in *Asahi* was a function of the fact that the sole remaining parties were foreign (i.e., non-American) corporations? Might the result have changed if Asahi had been a named defendant to the plaintiff's complaint rather than solely a third party defendant in Cheng Shin's claim for indemnity? If so, how does this fit in with the Court's statement in *Keeton* that "we have not to date required a plaintiff to have minimum contacts with the forum state?" For more on the issues explored in *Asahi*, and the decision's place in the galaxy of Supreme Court decisions concerning the limits of in personam jurisdiction, the following articles are quite useful: R. LAWRENCE DESSEM, *Personal Jurisdiction after Asahi: The Other (International) Shoe Drops*, 55 TENN. L. REV. 41 (1987); RUSSELL J. WEINTRAUB, *Asahi Sends Personal Jurisdiction Down the Tubes,* 23 TEXAS INT'L L.J. 55 (1988); CHRISTINE M. WISEMAN, *Reconstructing the Citadel: The Advent of Jurisdictional Privity*, 54 OHIO ST. L.J. 403 (1993).

2. The 4-4-1 split of opinions in *Asahi* left the lower courts in a quandary with respect to divining the proper formulation of the stream of commerce standard for determining the existence of "minimum contacts" between a foreign defendant and the forum state. They struggled to choose between or reconcile the O'Connor and Brennan-authored opinions. Yet for nearly a quarter of a century, the Court did not utter another word on whether the O'Connor quartet's "stream of commerce plus" or the Brennan group's foreseeability-based "stream of commerce lite" was the governing standard. And when the Court finally did speak, in the following opinion, it did nothing to reduce, let alone resolve, the ambiguity. This time, the Court split 4-2-3, with a four member plurality applying the O'Connor formula to reject the existence of specific jurisdiction, two Justices agreeing with the plurality that the state courts had erred in exercising jurisdiction but declining to choose between the two dueling *Asahi* formulations, and three dissenters upholding the exercise of jurisdiction by finding *Asahi* inapposite and ruling that Due Process was satisfied when a foreign manufacturer who used a nationwide distributor to attain its objective of selling its product anywhere and everywhere it could in the United States was subject to the specific jurisdiction of the courts of the State in which its product caused an injury.

J. McIntyre Machinery, Ltd. v. Nicastro

Supreme Court of the United States, 2011.

564 U.S. 873, 131 S.Ct. 2780, 180 L.Ed. 2d 765.

JUSTICE KENNEDY announced the judgment of the Court and delivered an opinion, in which THE CHIEF JUSTICE, JUSTICE SCALIA, and JUSTICE THOMAS join.

Whether a person or entity is subject to the jurisdiction of a state court despite not having been present in the State either at the time of suit or at the time of the alleged injury, and despite not having consented to the exercise of jurisdiction, is a question that arises with great frequency in the routine course of litigation. The rules and standards for determining when a State does or does not have jurisdiction over an absent party have been unclear because of decades-old questions left open in Asahi Metal Industry Co. v. Superior Court of Cal., 480 U.S. 102 (1987).

Here, the Supreme Court of New Jersey, relying in part on *Asahi,* held that New Jersey's courts can exercise jurisdiction over a foreign manufacturer of a product so long as the manufacturer "knows or reasonably should know that its products are distributed through a nationwide distribution system that might lead to those products being sold in any of the fifty states." Applying that test, the court concluded that a British manufacturer of scrap metal machines was subject to jurisdiction in New Jersey, even though at no time had it advertised in, sent goods to, or in any relevant sense targeted the State.

That decision cannot be sustained. Although the New Jersey Supreme Court issued an extensive opinion with careful attention to this Court's cases and to its own precedent, the "stream of commerce" metaphor carried the decision far afield. Due process protects the defendant's right not to be coerced except by lawful judicial power. As a general rule, the exercise of judicial power is not lawful unless the defendant "purposefully avails itself of the privilege of conducting activities within the forum State, thus invoking the benefits and protections of its laws." Hanson v. Denckla, 357 U.S. 235 (1958). There may be exceptions, say, for instance, in cases involving an intentional tort. But the general rule is applicable in this products-liability case, and the so-called "stream-of-commerce" doctrine cannot displace it.

I

This case arises from a products-liability suit filed in New Jersey state court. Robert Nicastro seriously injured his hand while using a metal-shearing machine manufactured by J. McIntyre Machinery, Ltd. (J. McIntyre). The accident occurred in New Jersey, but the machine was manufactured in England, where J. McIntyre is incorporated and operates. The question here is whether the New Jersey courts have jurisdiction over J. McIntyre, notwithstanding the fact that the company at no time either marketed goods in the State or shipped them there. Nicastro was a plaintiff in the New Jersey trial court and is the respondent here; J. McIntyre was a defendant and is now the petitioner.

At oral argument in this Court, Nicastro's counsel stressed three primary facts in defense of New Jersey's assertion of jurisdiction over J. McIntyre.

First, an independent company agreed to sell J. McIntyre's machines in the United States. J. McIntyre itself did not sell its machines to buyers in this country beyond the U.S. distributor, and there is no allegation that the distributor was under J. McIntyre's control.

Second, J. McIntyre officials attended annual conventions for the scrap recycling industry to advertise J. McIntyre's machines alongside the distributor. The conventions took place in various States, but never in New Jersey.

Third, no more than four machines (the record suggests only one), including the machine that caused the injuries that are the basis for this suit, ended up in New Jersey.

In addition to these facts emphasized by petitioner, the New Jersey Supreme Court noted that J. McIntyre held both United States and European patents on its recycling technology. It also noted that the U.S. distributor structured its advertising and sales efforts in accordance with J. McIntyre's direction and guidance whenever possible, and that at least some of the machines were sold on consignment to the distributor.

In light of these facts, the New Jersey Supreme Court concluded that New Jersey courts could exercise jurisdiction over petitioner without contravention of the Due Process Clause. Jurisdiction was proper, in that court's view, because the injury occurred in New Jersey; because petitioner knew or reasonably should have known "that its products are distributed through a nationwide distribution system that might lead to those products being sold in any of the fifty states"; and because petitioner failed to "take some reasonable step to prevent the distribution of its products in this State."

Both the New Jersey Supreme Court's holding and its account of what it called "the stream-of-commerce doctrine of jurisdiction," were incorrect, however. This Court's *Asahi* decision may be responsible in part for that court's error regarding the stream of commerce, and this case presents an opportunity to provide greater clarity.

II

The Due Process Clause protects an individual's right to be deprived of life, liberty, or property only by the exercise of lawful power. This is no less true with respect to the power of a sovereign to resolve disputes through judicial process than with respect to the power of a sovereign to prescribe rules of conduct for those within its sphere. * * *

A court may subject a defendant to judgment only when the defendant has sufficient contacts with the sovereign "such that the maintenance of the suit does not offend traditional notions of fair play and substantial justice." International Shoe Co. v. Washington. 326 U.S. 310 (1945). Freeform notions of fundamental fairness divorced from traditional practice cannot transform a judgment rendered in the absence of authority into law. As a general rule, the sovereign's exercise of power requires some act by which the defendant "purposefully avails itself of the privilege of conducting activities within the forum State, thus invoking the benefits and protections of its laws," *Hanson,* though in some cases, as with an intentional tort, the defendant might well fall within the State's authority by reason of his attempt to obstruct its laws. In products-liability cases like this one, it is the defendant's purposeful availment that makes jurisdiction consistent with "traditional notions of fair play and substantial justice."

A person may submit to a State's authority in a number of ways. There is, of course, explicit consent. E.g., Insurance Corp. of Ireland v. Compagnie des Bauxites de Guinee, 456 U.S. 694 (1982). Presence within a State at the time suit commences through service of process is another example. See Burnham v. Superior Court, 495 U.S. 604 (1990). Citizenship or domicile—or, by analogy, incorporation or principal place of business for corporation —also indicates general submission to a State's powers. Goodyear Dunlop Tires Operations, S.A. v. Brown [131 S.Ct. 2846 (2011)]. Each of these examples reveals circumstances, or a course of conduct, from which it is proper to infer an intention to benefit from and thus an intention to submit to the laws of the forum State. Cf. Burger King Corp. v. Rudzewicz, 471 U.S. 462 (1985). These examples support exercise of the general jurisdiction of the State's courts and allow the State to resolve both matters that originate within the State and those based on activities and events elsewhere. Helicopteros Nacionales de Colombia, S.A. v. Hall, 466 U.S. 408 (1984). By contrast, those who live or operate primarily outside a State have a due process right not to be subjected to judgment in its courts as a general matter.

There is also a more limited form of submission to a State's authority for disputes that "arise out of or are connected with the activities within the state." *International Shoe.* Where a defendant "purposefully avails itself of the privilege of conducting activities within the forum State, thus invoking the benefits and protections of its laws," *Hanson,* it submits to the judicial power of an otherwise foreign sovereign to the extent that power is exercised in connection with the defendant's activities touching on the State. In other words, submission through contact with and activity directed at a sovereign may justify specific jurisdiction "in a suit arising out of or related to the defendant's contacts with the forum." *Helicopteros*; see also *Goodyear.*

The imprecision arising from *Asahi,* for the most part, results from its statement of the relation between jurisdiction and the "stream of commerce." The stream of commerce, like other metaphors, has its deficiencies as well as its utility. It refers to the movement of goods from manufacturers through distributors to consumers, yet beyond that descriptive purpose its meaning is far from exact. This Court has stated that a defendant's placing goods into the stream of commerce "with the expectation that they will be purchased by consumers within the forum State" may indicate purposeful availment. World–Wide Volkswagen Corp. v. Woodson, 440 U.S. 286 (1980). But that statement does not amend the general rule of personal jurisdiction. It merely observes that a defendant may in an appropriate case be subject to jurisdiction without entering the forum — itself an unexceptional proposition — as where manufacturers or distributors "seek to serve" a given State's market. The principal inquiry in cases of this sort is whether the defendant's activities manifest an intention to submit to the power of a sovereign. In other words, the defendant must "purposefully avai[l] itself of the privilege of conducting activities within the forum State, thus invoking the benefits and protections of its laws." Sometimes a defendant does so by sending its goods rather than its agents. The defendant's transmission of goods permits the exercise of jurisdiction only where the defendant can be said to have targeted the forum; as a general rule, it is not enough that the defendant might have predicted that its goods will reach the forum State.

In *Asahi*, an opinion by Justice Brennan for four Justices outlined a different approach. It discarded the central concept of sovereign authority in favor of considerations of fairness and foreseeability. As that concurrence contended, "jurisdiction premised on the placement of a product into the stream of commerce [without more] is consistent with the Due Process Clause," for "[a]s long as a participant in this process is aware that the final product is being marketed in the forum State, the possibility of a lawsuit there cannot come as a surprise." It was the premise of the concurring opinion that the defendant's ability to anticipate suit renders the assertion of jurisdiction fair. In this way, the opinion made foreseeability the touchstone of jurisdiction.

The standard set forth in Justice Brennan's concurrence was rejected in an opinion written by Justice O'Connor; but the relevant part of that opinion, too, commanded the assent of only four Justices, not a majority of the Court. That opinion stated: "The 'substantial connection' between the defendant and the forum State necessary for a finding of minimum contacts must come about by an action of the defendant purposefully directed toward the forum State. The placement of a product into the stream of commerce, without more, is not an act of the defendant purposefully directed toward the forum State."

Since *Asahi* was decided, the courts have sought to reconcile the competing opinions. But Justice Brennan's concurrence, advocating a rule based on general notions of fairness and foreseeability, is inconsistent with the premises of lawful judicial power. This Court's precedents make clear that it is the defendant's actions, not his expectations, that empower a State's courts to subject him to judgment.

The conclusion that jurisdiction is in the first instance a question of authority rather than fairness explains, for example, why the principal opinion in *Burnham* "conducted no independent inquiry into the desirability or fairness" of the rule that service of process within a State suffices to establish jurisdiction over an otherwise foreign defendant. As that opinion explained, "[t]he view developed early that each State had the power to hale before its courts any individual who could be found within its borders." Furthermore, were general fairness considerations the touchstone of jurisdiction, a lack of purposeful availment might be excused where carefully crafted judicial procedures could otherwise protect the defendant's interests, or where the plaintiff would suffer substantial hardship if forced to litigate in a foreign forum. That such considerations have not been deemed controlling is instructive. See, e.g., *World–Wide Volkswagen.*

Two principles are implicit in the foregoing. First, personal jurisdiction requires a forum-by-forum, or sovereign-by-sovereign, analysis. The question is whether a defendant has followed a course of conduct directed at the society or economy existing within the jurisdiction of a given sovereign, so that the sovereign has the power to subject the defendant to judgment concerning that conduct. Personal jurisdiction, of course, restricts "judicial power not as a matter of sovereignty, but as a matter of individual liberty," for due process protects the individual's right to be subject only to lawful power. *Insurance Corp.* But whether a judicial judgment is lawful depends on whether the sovereign has authority to render it.

The second principle is a corollary of the first. Because the United States is a distinct sovereign, a defendant may in principle be subject to the jurisdiction of the courts of the United States but not of any particular State. This is consistent with the premises and unique genius of our Constitution. * * * For jurisdiction, a litigant may have the requisite relationship with the United States Government but not with the government of any individual State. That would be an exceptional case, however. If the defendant is a domestic domiciliary, the courts of its home State are available and can exercise general jurisdiction. And if another State were to assert jurisdiction in an inappropriate case, it would upset the federal balance, which posits that each State has a sovereignty that is not subject to unlawful intrusion by other States. Furthermore, foreign corporations will often target or concentrate on particular States, subjecting them to specific jurisdiction in those forums.

It must be remembered, however, that although this case and *Asahi* both involve foreign manufacturers, the undesirable consequences of Justice Brennan's approach are no less significant for domestic producers. The owner of a small Florida farm might sell crops to a large nearby distributor, for example, who might then distribute them to grocers across the country. If foreseeability were the controlling criterion, the farmer could be sued in Alaska or any number of other States' courts without ever leaving town. And the issue of foreseeability may itself be contested so that significant expenses are incurred just on the preliminary issue of jurisdiction. Jurisdictional rules should avoid these costs whenever possible.

The conclusion that the authority to subject a defendant to judgment depends on purposeful availment, consistent with Justice O'Connor's opinion in *Asahi,* does not by itself resolve many difficult questions of jurisdiction that will arise in particular cases. The defendant's conduct and the economic realities of the market the defendant seeks to serve will differ across cases, and judicial exposition will, in common-law fashion, clarify the contours of that principle.

III

In this case, petitioner directed marketing and sales efforts at the United States. It may be that, assuming it were otherwise empowered to legislate on the subject, the Congress could authorize the exercise of jurisdiction in appropriate courts. That circumstance is not presented in this case, however, and it is neither necessary nor appropriate to address here any constitutional concerns that might be attendant to that exercise of power. Nor is it necessary to determine what substantive law might apply were Congress to authorize jurisdiction in a federal court in New Jersey. A sovereign's legislative authority to regulate conduct may present considerations different from those presented by its authority to subject a defendant to judgment in its courts. Here the question concerns the authority of a New Jersey state court to exercise jurisdiction, so it is petitioner's purposeful contacts with New Jersey, not with the United States, that alone are relevant.

Respondent has not established that J. McIntyre engaged in conduct purposefully directed at New Jersey. Recall that respondent's claim of jurisdiction centers on three facts: The distributor agreed to sell J. McIntyre's machines in the United States; J. McIntyre officials attended trade shows in several States but not in New Jersey; and up to four machines ended up in New Jersey. The British manufacturer had no office in New Jersey; it neither paid taxes nor owned property there; and it neither advertised in, nor sent any employees to, the State. Indeed, after discovery the trial court found that the "defendant does not have a single contact with New Jersey short of the machine in question ending up in this state." These facts may reveal an intent to serve the U.S. market, but they do not show that J. McIntyre purposefully availed itself of the New Jersey market.

It is notable that the New Jersey Supreme Court appears to agree, for it could "not find that J. McIntyre had a presence or minimum contacts in this State — in any jurisprudential sense — that would justify a New Jersey court to exercise jurisdiction in this case." The court nonetheless held that petitioner could be sued in New Jersey based on a "stream-of-commerce theory of jurisdiction." As discussed, however, the stream-of-commerce metaphor cannot supersede either the mandate of the Due Process Clause or the limits on judicial authority that Clause ensures. The New Jersey Supreme Court also cited "significant policy reasons" to justify its holding, including the State's "strong interest in protecting its citizens from defective products." That interest is doubtless strong, but the Constitution commands restraint before discarding liberty in the name of expediency.

Due process protects petitioner's right to be subject only to lawful authority. At no time did petitioner engage in any activities in New Jersey that reveal an intent to invoke or benefit from the protection of its laws. New Jersey is without power to adjudge the rights and liabilities of J. McIntyre, and its exercise of jurisdiction would violate due process. The contrary judgment of the New Jersey Supreme Court is *Reversed.*

JUSTICE BREYER, with whom JUSTICE ALITO joins, concurring in the judgment.

The Supreme Court of New Jersey adopted a broad understanding of the scope of personal jurisdiction based on its view that "[t]he increasingly fast-paced globalization of the world economy has removed national borders as barriers to trade." I do not doubt that there have been many recent changes in commerce and communication, many of which are not anticipated by our precedents. But this case does not present any of those issues. So I think it unwise to announce a rule of broad applicability without full consideration of the modern-day consequences.

In my view, the outcome of this case is determined by our precedents. Based on the facts found by the New Jersey courts, respondent Robert Nicastro failed to meet his burden to demonstrate that it was constitutionally proper to exercise jurisdiction over petitioner J. McIntyre Machinery, Ltd. (British Manufacturer), a British firm that manufactures scrap-metal machines in Great Britain and sells them through an independent distributor in the United States (American Distributor). On that basis, I agree with the plurality that the contrary judgment of the Supreme Court of New Jersey should be reversed.

I

In asserting jurisdiction over the British Manufacturer, the Supreme Court of New Jersey relied most heavily on three primary facts as providing constitutionally sufficient "contacts" with New Jersey, thereby making it fundamentally fair to hale the British Manufacturer before its courts: (1) The American Distributor on one occasion sold and shipped one machine to a New Jersey customer, namely, Mr. Nicastro's employer, Mr. Curcio; (2) the British Manufacturer permitted, indeed wanted, its independent American Distributor to sell its machines to anyone in America willing to buy them; and (3) representatives of the British Manufacturer attended trade shows in "such cities as Chicago, Las Vegas, New Orleans, Orlando, San Diego, and San Francisco." In my view, these facts do not provide contacts between the British firm and the State of New Jersey constitutionally sufficient to support New Jersey's assertion of jurisdiction in this case.

None of our precedents finds that a single isolated sale, even if accompanied by the kind of sales effort indicated here, is sufficient. Rather, this Court's previous holdings suggest the contrary. The Court has held that a single sale to a customer who takes an accident-causing product to a different State (where the accident takes place) is not a sufficient basis for asserting jurisdiction. See *World–Wide Volkswagen*. And the Court, in separate opinions, has strongly suggested that a single sale of a product in a State does not constitute an adequate basis for asserting jurisdiction over an out-of-state defendant, even if that defendant places his goods in the stream of commerce, fully aware (and hoping) that such a sale will take place. See *Asahi* (opinion of O'Connor, J.) (requiring "something more" than simply placing "a product into the stream of commerce," even if defendant is "awar[e]" that the stream "may or will sweep the product into the forum State"); (Brennan, J., concurring in part and concurring in judgment) (jurisdiction should lie where a sale in a State is part of "the regular and anticipated flow" of commerce into the State, but not where that sale is only an "edd[y]," *i.e.,* an isolated occurrence); (Stevens, J., concurring in part and concurring in judgment) (indicating that "the volume, the value, and the hazardous character" of a good may affect the jurisdictional inquiry and emphasizing Asahi's "regular course of dealing").

Here, the relevant facts found by the New Jersey Supreme Court show no "regular . . . flow" or "regular course" of sales in New Jersey; and there is no "something more," such as special state-related design, advertising, advice, marketing, or anything else. Mr. Nicastro, who here bears the burden of proving jurisdiction, has shown no specific effort by the British Manufacturer to sell in New Jersey. He has introduced no list of potential New Jersey customers who might, for example, have regularly attended trade shows. And he has not otherwise shown that the British Manufacturer "purposefully avail[ed] itself of the privilege of conducting activities" within New Jersey, or that it delivered its goods in the stream of commerce "with the expectation that they will be purchased" by New Jersey users. *World–Wide Volkswagen.*

There may well have been other facts that Mr. Nicastro could have demonstrated in support of jurisdiction. And the dissent considers some of those facts (describing the size and scope of New Jersey's scrap-metal business). But the plaintiff bears the burden of establishing jurisdiction, and here I would take the facts precisely as the New Jersey Supreme Court stated them.

Accordingly, on the record present here, resolving this case requires no more than adhering to our precedents.

II

I would not go further. Because the incident at issue in this case does not implicate modern concerns, and because the factual record leaves many open questions, this is an unsuitable vehicle for making broad pronouncements that refashion basic jurisdictional rules.

A

The plurality seems to state strict rules that limit jurisdiction where a defendant does not "inten[d] to submit to the power of a sovereign" and cannot "be said to have targeted the forum." But what do those standards mean when a company targets the world by selling products from its Web site? And does it matter if, instead of shipping the products directly, a company consigns the products through an intermediary (say, Amazon.com) who then receives and fulfills the orders? And what if the company markets its products through popup advertisements that it knows will be viewed in a forum? Those issues have serious commercial consequences but are totally absent in this case.

B

But though I do not agree with the plurality's seemingly strict no-jurisdiction rule, I am not persuaded by the absolute approach adopted by the New Jersey Supreme Court and urged by respondent and his *amici.* Under that view, a producer is subject to jurisdiction for a products-liability action so long as it "knows or reasonably should know that its products are distributed through a nationwide distribution system that *might* lead to those products being sold in any of the fifty states." In the context of this case, I cannot agree.

For one thing, to adopt this view would abandon the heretofore accepted inquiry of whether, focusing upon the relationship between "the defendant, the *forum,* and the litigation," it is fair, in light of the defendant's contacts *with that forum,* to subject the defendant to suit there. *Shaffer v. Heitner.* It would ordinarily rest jurisdiction instead upon no more than the occurrence of a product-based accident in the forum State. But this Court has rejected the notion that a defendant's amenability to suit "travel[s] with the chattel." *World–Wide Volkswagen.*

For another, I cannot reconcile so automatic a rule with the constitutional demand for "minimum contacts" and "purposeful availment," each of which rest upon a particular notion of defendant-focused fairness. A rule like the New Jersey Supreme Court's would permit every State to assert jurisdiction in a products-liability suit against any domestic manufacturer who sells its products (made anywhere in the United States) to a national distributor, no matter how large or small the manufacturer, no matter how distant the forum, and no matter how few the number of items that end up in the particular forum at issue. What might appear fair in the case of a large manufacturer which specifically seeks, or expects, an equal-sized distributor to sell its product in a distant State might seem unfair in the case of a small manufacturer (say, an Appalachian potter) who sells his product (cups and saucers) exclusively to a large distributor, who resells a single item (a coffee mug) to a buyer from a distant State (Hawaii). I know too little about the range of these or in-between possibilities to abandon in favor of the more absolute rule what has previously been this Court's less absolute approach.

Further, the fact that the defendant is a foreign, rather than a domestic, manufacturer makes the basic fairness of an absolute rule yet more uncertain. I am again less certain than is the New Jersey Supreme Court that the nature of international commerce has changed so significantly as to require a new approach to personal jurisdiction.

It may be that a larger firm can readily "alleviate the risk of burdensome litigation by procuring insurance, passing the expected costs on to customers, or, if the risks are too great, severing its connection with the State." *World–Wide Volkswagen.* But manufacturers come in many shapes and sizes. It may be fundamentally unfair to require a small Egyptian shirt maker, a Brazilian manufacturing cooperative, or a Kenyan coffee farmer, selling its products through international distributors, to respond to products-liability tort suits in virtually every State in the United States, even those in respect to which the foreign firm has no connection at all but the sale of a single (allegedly defective) good. And a rule like the New Jersey Supreme Court suggests would require every product manufacturer, large or small, selling to American distributors to understand not only the tort law of every State, but also the wide variance in the way courts within different States apply that law.

C

At a minimum, I would not work such a change to the law in the way either the plurality or the New Jersey Supreme Court suggests without a better understanding of the relevant contemporary commercial circumstances. Insofar as such considerations are relevant to any change in present law, they might be presented in a case (unlike the present one) in which the Solicitor General participates.

This case presents no such occasion, and so I again reiterate that I would adhere strictly to our precedents and the limited facts found by the New Jersey Supreme Court. And on those grounds, I do not think we can find jurisdiction in this case. Accordingly, though I agree with the plurality as to the outcome of this case, I concur only in the judgment of that opinion and not its reasoning.

Justice Ginsburg, with whom Justice Sotomayor and Justice Kagan join, dissenting.

A foreign industrialist seeks to develop a market in the United States for machines it manufactures. It hopes to derive substantial revenue from sales it makes to United States purchasers. Where in the United States buyers reside does not matter to this manufacturer. Its goal is simply to sell as much as it can, wherever it can. It excludes no region or State from the market it wishes to reach. But, all things considered, it prefers to avoid products liability litigation in the United States. To that end, it engages a U.S. distributor to ship its machines stateside. Has it succeeded in escaping personal jurisdiction in a State where one of its products is sold and causes injury or even death to a local user?

Under this Court's pathmarking precedent in *International Shoe*, and subsequent decisions, one would expect the answer to be unequivocally, "No." But instead, six Justices of this Court, in divergent opinions, tell us that the manufacturer has avoided the jurisdiction of our state courts, except perhaps in States where its products arc sold in sizeable quantities. * * *

I

* * *

McIntyre UK representatives attended every ISRI [Institute of Scrap Recycling Industries] convention from 1990 through 2005. These annual expositions were held in diverse venues across the United States * * *. * * * UK exhibited its products at ISRI trade shows, the company acknowledged, hoping to reach anyone interested in the machine from anywhere in the United States.

* * *

From at least 1995 until 2001, McIntyre UK retained an Ohio-based company, McIntyre Machinery America, Ltd. (McIntyre America), as its exclusive distributor for the entire United States. Though similarly named, the two companies were separate and independent entities with no commonality of ownership or management. * * *

In a November 23, 1999 letter to McIntyre America, McIntyre UK's president spoke plainly about the manufacturer's objective in authorizing the exclusive distributorship: "All we wish to do is sell our products in the [United] States—and get paid!" * * * And in correspondence with McIntyre America, McIntyre UK noted that the manufacturer had products liability insurance coverage.

Over the years, McIntyre America distributed several McIntyre UK products to U.S. customers * * *. In promoting McIntyre UK's products at conventions and demonstration sites and in trade journal advertisements, McIntyre America looked to McIntyre UK for direction and guidance. To achieve McIntyre UK's objective, the two companies were acting closely in concert with each other. McIntyre UK never instructed its distributor to avoid certain States or regions of the country; rather, as just noted, the manufacturer engaged McIntyre America to attract customers from anywhere in the United States.

In sum, McIntyre UK's regular attendance and exhibitions at ISRI conventions was surely a purposeful step to reach customers for its products anywhere in the United States. At least as purposeful was McIntyre UK's engagement of McIntyre America as the conduit for sales of McIntyre UK's machines to buyers throughout the United States. Given McIntyre UK's endeavors to reach and profit from the United States market as a whole, Nicastro's suit, I would hold, has been brought in a forum entirely appropriate for the adjudication of his claim. He alleges that McIntyre UK's shear machine was defectively designed or manufactured and, as a result, caused injury to him at his workplace. The machine arrived in Nicastro's New Jersey workplace not randomly or fortuitously, but as a result of the U.S. connections and distribution system that McIntyre UK deliberately arranged. On what sensible view of the allocation of adjudicatory authority could the place of Nicastro's injury within the United States be deemed off limits for his products liability claim against a foreign manufacturer who targeted the United States (including all the States that constitute the Nation) as the territory it sought to develop?

II

A few points on which there should be no genuine debate bear statement at the outset. First, all agree, McIntyre UK surely is not subject to general (all-purpose) jurisdiction in New Jersey courts, for that foreign-country corporation is hardly "at home" in New Jersey. See *Goodyear Dunlop*. The question, rather, is one of specific jurisdiction, which turns on an "affiliatio[n] between the forum and the underlying controversy." [*Id.*]

Second, no issue of the fair and reasonable allocation of adjudicatory authority among States of the United States is present in this case. New Jersey's exercise of personal jurisdiction over a foreign manufacturer whose dangerous product caused a workplace injury in New Jersey does not tread on the domain, or diminish the sovereignty, of any sister State. Indeed, among States of the United States, the State in which the injury occurred would seem most suitable for litigation of a products liability tort claim. See *World–Wide Volkswagen* (if a manufacturer or distributor endeavors to develop a market for a product in several States, it is reasonable "to subject it to suit in one of those States if its allegedly defective [product] has there been the source of injury"); 28 U.S.C. §1391(a)-(b) (in federal-court suits, whether resting on diversity or federal-question jurisdiction, venue is proper in the judicial district "in which a substantial part of the events or omissions giving rise to the claim occurred").

Third, the constitutional limits on a state court's adjudicatory authority derive from considerations of due process, not state sovereignty. * * *

Finally, in *International Shoe* itself, and decisions thereafter, the Court has made plain that legal fictions, notably "presence" and "implied consent," should be discarded, for they conceal the actual bases on which jurisdiction rests. "[T]he relationship among the defendant, the forum, and the litigation" determines whether due process permits the exercise of personal jurisdiction over a defendant, *Shaffer*, and "fictions of implied consent" or "corporate presence" do not advance the proper inquiry.

Whatever the state of academic debate over the role of consent in modern jurisdictional doctrines, the plurality's notion that consent is the animating concept draws no support from controlling decisions of this Court. Quite the contrary, the Court has explained, a forum can exercise jurisdiction when its contacts with the controversy are sufficient; invocation of a fictitious consent, the Court has repeatedly said, is unnecessary and unhelpful. See, *e.g., Burger King Corp.* (Due Process Clause permits "forum . . . to assert specific jurisdiction over an out-of-state defendant who has not consented to suit there").[5]

III

This case is illustrative of marketing arrangements for sales in the United States common in today's commercial world.[6] A foreign-country manufacturer engages a U.S. company to promote and distribute the manufacturer's products, not in any particular State, but anywhere and everywhere in the United States the distributor can attract purchasers. The product proves defective and injures a user in the State where the user lives or works. Often, as here, the manufacturer will have liability insurance covering personal injuries caused by its products.

When industrial accidents happen, a long-arm statute in the State where the injury occurs generally permits assertion of jurisdiction, upon giving proper notice, over the foreign manufacturer. For example, the State's statute might provide, as does New York's long-arm statute, for the "exercise [of] personal jurisdiction over any non-domiciliary . . . who . . . "commits a tortious act without the state causing injury to person or property within the state, . . . if he . . . expects or should reasonably expect the act to have consequences in the state and derives substantial revenue from interstate or international commerce." Or, the State might simply provide, as New Jersey does, for the exercise of jurisdiction "consistent with due process of law."

The modern approach to jurisdiction over corporations and other legal entities, ushered in by *International Shoe,* gave prime place to reason and fairness. Is it not fair and reasonable, given the mode of trading of which this case is an example, to require the international seller to defend at the place its products cause injury?[9]   Do not litigational convenience and choice-of-law

---

[5] But see plurality opinion (maintaining that a forum may be fair and reasonable, based on its links to the episode in suit, yet off limits because the defendant has not submitted to the State's authority). The plurality's notion that jurisdiction over foreign corporations depends upon the defendant's "submission," seems scarcely different from the long-discredited fiction of implied consent. It bears emphasis that a majority of this Court's members do not share the plurality's view.

[6] New Jersey is the fourth-largest destination for manufactured commodities imported into the United States, after California, Texas, and New York.

[9] The plurality objects to a jurisdictional approach "divorced from traditional practice." But "the fundamental transformation of our national economy," this Court has recognized, warrants enlargement of "the permissible scope of state jurisdiction over foreign corporations and other nonresidents." McGee v. International Life Ins. Co., 355 U.S. 220 (1957).

considerations point in that direction? On what measure of reason and fairness can it be considered undue to require McIntyre UK to defend in New Jersey as an incident of its efforts to develop a market for its industrial machines anywhere and everywhere in the United States?[12] Is not the burden on McIntyre UK to defend in New Jersey fair, *i.e.,* a reasonable cost of transacting business internationally, in comparison to the burden on Nicastro to go to Nottingham, England to gain recompense for an injury he sustained using McIntyre's product at his workplace in Saddle Brook, New Jersey?

McIntyre UK dealt with the United States as a single market. Like most foreign manufacturers, it was concerned not with the prospect of suit in State X as opposed to State Y, but rather with its subjection to suit anywhere in the United States. * * * If McIntyre UK is answerable in the United States at all, is it not perfectly appropriate to permit the exercise of that jurisdiction at the place of injury?

In sum, McIntyre UK, by engaging McIntyre America to promote and sell its machines in the United States, "purposefully availed itself " of the United States market nationwide, not a market in a single State or a discrete collection of States. McIntyre UK thereby availed itself of the market of all States in which its products were sold by its exclusive distributor. "Th[e] 'purposeful availment' requirement," this Court has explained, simply "ensures that a defendant will not be haled into a jurisdiction solely as a result of 'random,' 'fortuitous,' or 'attenuated' contacts." *Burger King.* Adjudicatory authority is appropriately exercised where "actions by the defendant *himself* " give rise to the affiliation with the forum. *Ibid.* How could McIntyre UK not have intended, by its actions targeting a national market, to sell products in the fourth largest destination for imports among all States of the United States and the largest scrap metal market? * * *

IV

A

While this Court has not considered in any prior case the now-prevalent pattern presented here—a foreign-country manufacturer enlisting a U.S. distributor to develop a market in the United States for the manufacturer's products—none of the Court's decisions tug against the judgment made by the New Jersey Supreme Court. McIntyre contends otherwise, citing *World–Wide Volkswagen* and *Asahi.*

World–Wide Volkswagen concerned a New York car dealership that sold solely in the New York market, and a New York distributor who supplied retailers in three States only: New York, Connecticut, and New Jersey. New York residents had purchased an Audi from the New York dealer and were driving the new vehicle through Oklahoma en route to Arizona. On the road in

---

[12] The plurality suggests that the Due Process Clause might permit a federal district court in New Jersey, sitting in diversity and applying New Jersey law, to adjudicate McIntyre UK's liability to Nicastro. In other words, McIntyre UK might be compelled to bear the burden of traveling to New Jersey and defending itself there under New Jersey's products liability law, but would be entitled to federal adjudication of Nicastro's state-law claim. I see no basis in the Due Process Clause for such a curious limitation.

Oklahoma, another car struck the Audi in the rear, causing a fire which severely burned the Audi's occupants. Rejecting the Oklahoma courts' assertion of jurisdiction over the New York dealer and distributor, this Court observed that the defendants had done nothing to serve the market for cars in Oklahoma. Jurisdiction, the Court held, could not be based on the *customer's* unilateral act of driving the vehicle to Oklahoma.

Notably, the foreign manufacturer of the Audi in *World–Wide Volkswagen* did not object to the jurisdiction of the Oklahoma courts and the U.S. importer abandoned its initially stated objection. And most relevant here, the Court's opinion indicates that an objection to jurisdiction by the manufacturer or national distributor would have been unavailing. To reiterate, the Court said in *World–Wide Volkswagen* that, when a manufacturer or distributor aims to sell its product to customers in several States, it is reasonable "to subject it to suit in [any] one of those States if its allegedly defective [product] has there been the source of injury."

Asahi arose out of a motorcycle accident in California. Plaintiff, a California resident injured in the accident, sued the Taiwanese manufacturer of the motorcycle's tire tubes, claiming that defects in its product caused the accident. The tube manufacturer cross-claimed against Asahi, the Japanese maker of the valve assembly, and Asahi contested the California courts' jurisdiction. By the time the case reached this Court, the injured plaintiff had settled his case and only the indemnity claim by the Taiwanese company against the Japanese valve-assembly manufacturer remained.

The decision was not a close call. The Court had before it a foreign plaintiff, the Taiwanese manufacturer, and a foreign defendant, the Japanese valve-assembly maker, and the indemnification dispute concerned a transaction between those parties that occurred abroad. All agreed on the bottom line: The Japanese valve-assembly manufacturer was not reasonably brought into the California courts to litigate a dispute with another foreign party over a transaction that took place outside the United States.

Given the confines of the controversy, the dueling opinions of Justice Brennan and Justice O'Connor were hardly necessary. How the Court would have "estimate[d] . . . the inconveniences," see *International Shoe,* had the injured Californian originally sued Asahi is a debatable question. Would this Court have given the same weight to the burdens on the foreign defendant had those been counterbalanced by the burdens litigating in Japan imposed on the local California plaintiff?

In any event, Asahi, unlike McIntyre UK, did not itself seek out customers in the United States, it engaged no distributor to promote its wares here, it appeared at no tradeshows in the United States, and, of course, it had no Web site advertising its products to the world. Moreover, Asahi was a component-part manufacturer with little control over the final destination of its products once they were delivered into the stream of commerce. It was important to the Court in *Asahi* that "those who use Asahi components in their final products, and sell those products in California, [would be] subject to the application of California tort law." To hold that *Asahi* controls this case would, to put it bluntly, be dead wrong.[15]

B

The Court's judgment also puts United States plaintiffs at a disadvantage in comparison to similarly situated complainants elsewhere in the world. Of particular note, within the European Union, in which the United Kingdom is a participant, the jurisdiction New Jersey would have exercised is not at all exceptional. The European Regulation on Jurisdiction and the Recognition and Enforcement of Judgments provides for the exercise of specific jurisdiction "in matters relating to tort . . . in the courts for the place where the harmful event occurred." Council Reg. 44/2001, Art. 5, 2001 O.J. (L.12) 4. The European Court of Justice has interpreted this prescription to authorize jurisdiction either where the harmful act occurred or at the place of injury. See Handelskwekerij G.J. Bier B.V. v. Mines de Potasse d'Alsace S. A., 1976 E.C.R. 1735, 1748–1749.

* * *

For the reasons stated, I would hold McIntyre UK answerable in New Jersey for the harm Nicastro suffered at his workplace in that State using McIntyre UK's shearing machine. While I dissent from the Court's judgment, I take heart that the plurality opinion does not speak for the Court, for that opinion would take a giant step away from the "notions of fair play and substantial justice" underlying *International Shoe*.

NOTES AND PROBLEMS FOR DISCUSSION

1. What is the significance of the fact that only the four-member plurality relied extensively on *Asahi* in deciding the case? Does the fact that five Justices (the dissenters and the two concurring Justices) did not discuss either of the two dueling *Asahi* opinions suggest that neither formulation of the stream-of-commerce analysis has continuing force? Or does Justice Ginsburg's opinion implicitly take a position similar to the Brennan group in *Asahi*?

2. Justice Kennedy's plurality opinion, like Justice O'Connor's opinion in *Asahi*, demands something more than placement of a product in the stream of commerce with awareness of its ultimate destination. But consider his repeated references to sovereignty concerns and his suggestion that the jurisdictional focus should be on the defendant's "submission" to state power. Are these, as Justice Ginsberg suggests, a return to pre-*International Shoe* ways of thinking? Justice Ginsburg, by contrast, seems to focus on the contacts of McIntyre UK with the U.S. as a whole, rather than with a specific state, at least when it has dealt with a U.S. distributor and sells to any willing buyer in any of the states. Does her approach make more sense than the plurality's, at least when dealing with a foreign manufacturer like McIntyre UK?

---

[15] The plurality notes the low volume of sales in New Jersey. A $24,900 shearing machine, however, is unlikely to sell in bulk worldwide, much less in any given State. By dollar value, the price of a single machine represents a significant sale. Had a manufacturer sold in New Jersey $24,900 worth of flannel shirts, cigarette lighters, or wire-rope splices, the Court would presumably find the defendant amenable to suit in that State.

3. The opinion of Justices Breyer and Alito is the narrower of the two opinions upholding jurisdiction, and is therefore arguably controlling. How would you characterize their view?

4. For a sampling of early commentary on the decision in *McIntyre* — much of it critical—see the collection of essays by various authors in the symposium, *Personal Jurisdiction for the Twenty-First Century—The Implications of* McIntyre *and* Goodyear-Dunlop Tires, 62 S.C. L. REV. (Spring 2012).

5. As previously mentioned, in conducting the constitutional component of personal jurisdictional analysis, one must examine whether the trial court is being asked to exercise specific or general jurisdiction. That dichotomy turns upon whether or not the plaintiff's claim is deemed to "arise out of" the defendant's forum activities. The Supreme Court, however, has left it to the lower courts to fully articulate the meaning of this concept. And though the various circuits frame their specific jurisdiction analysis differently, the opinions largely fall into two camps. Some circuits require that the defendant's forum activities be the "proximate cause" of the plaintiff's injury, while others adhere more or less require that the defendant's forum activities constitute a "but for" cause of the plaintiff's injury. *Compare* Nowak v. Tak How Investments, Ltd., 94 F.3d 708 (1st Cir. 1996), cert. denied, 520 U.S. 1155, 117 S.Ct. 1333, 137 L.Ed.2d 493 (1997) (applying proximate cause standard) *with* Creech v. Roberts, 908 F.2d 75, 80 (6th Cir.1990) (relying on but-for standard of causation).

The next case is a rare unanimous opinion in which the Supreme Court proffered a new standard for the proper invocation of general jurisdiction over a foreign corporation.

Goodyear Dunlop Tires Operations, S.A. v. Brown

Supreme Court of the United States, 2011.

564 U.S. 915, 131 S.Ct. 2846, 180 L.Ed. 2d 796.

JUSTICE GINSBURG delivered the opinion of the Court.

This case concerns the jurisdiction of state courts over corporations organized and operating abroad. We address, in particular, this question: Are foreign subsidiaries of a United States parent corporation amenable to suit in state court on claims unrelated to any activity of the subsidiaries in the forum State?

A bus accident outside Paris that took the lives of two 13–year–old boys from North Carolina gave rise to the litigation we here consider. Attributing the accident to a defective tire manufactured in Turkey at the plant of a foreign subsidiary of The Goodyear Tire and Rubber Company (Goodyear USA), the boys' parents commenced an action for damages in a North Carolina state court; they named as defendants Goodyear USA, an Ohio corporation, and three of its subsidiaries, organized and operating, respectively, in Turkey, France, and Luxembourg. Goodyear USA, which had plants in North Carolina and regularly engaged in commercial activity there, did not contest the North Carolina court's jurisdiction over it; Goodyear USA's foreign subsidiaries, however, maintained that North Carolina lacked adjudicatory authority over them.

A state court's assertion of jurisdiction exposes defendants to the State's coercive power, and is therefore subject to review for compatibility with the Fourteenth Amendment's Due Process Clause. International Shoe Co. v. Washington, 326 U.S. 310 (1945) (assertion of jurisdiction over out-of-state corporation must comply with "traditional notions of fair play and substantial justice"). Opinions in the wake of the pathmarking *International Shoe* decision have differentiated between general or all-purpose jurisdiction, and specific or case-linked jurisdiction. Helicopteros Nacionales de Colombia, S.A. v. Hall, 466 U.S. 408, 414 nn. 8-9 (1984).

A court may assert general jurisdiction over foreign (sister-state or foreign-country) corporations to hear any and all claims against them when their affiliations with the State are so "continuous and systematic" as to render them essentially at home in the forum State. See *International Shoe*. Specific jurisdiction, on the other hand, depends on an affiliation between the forum and the underlying controversy, principally, activity or an occurrence that takes place in the forum State and is therefore subject to the State's regulation. In contrast to general, all-purpose jurisdiction, specific jurisdiction is confined to adjudication of issues deriving from, or connected with, the very controversy that establishes jurisdiction

Because the episode-in-suit, the bus accident, occurred in France, and the tire alleged to have caused the accident was manufactured and sold abroad, North Carolina courts lacked specific jurisdiction to adjudicate the controversy. The North Carolina Court of Appeals so acknowledged. Were the foreign subsidiaries nonetheless amenable to general jurisdiction in North Carolina courts? Confusing or blending general and specific jurisdictional inquiries, the North Carolina courts answered yes. Some of the tires made abroad by Goodyear's foreign subsidiaries, the North Carolina Court of Appeals stressed, had reached North Carolina through the stream of commerce; that connection, the Court of Appeals believed, gave North Carolina courts the handle needed for the exercise of general jurisdiction over the foreign corporations.

A connection so limited between the forum and the foreign corporation, we hold, is an inadequate basis for the exercise of general jurisdiction. Such a connection does not establish the "continuous and systematic" affiliation necessary to empower North Carolina courts to entertain claims unrelated to the foreign corporation's contacts with the State.

I

* * *

Goodyear Luxembourg Tires, SA (Goodyear Luxembourg), Goodyear Lastikleri T.A.S. (Goodyear Turkey), and Goodyear Dunlop Tires France, SA (Goodyear France), petitioners here, were named as defendants. Incorporated in Luxembourg, Turkey, and France, respectively, petitioners are indirect subsidiaries of Goodyear USA, an Ohio corporation also named as a defendant in the suit. Petitioners manufacture tires primarily for sale in European and Asian markets. Their tires differ in size and construction from tires ordinarily sold in the United States. They are designed to carry significantly heavier loads, and to serve under road conditions and speed limits in the manufacturers' primary markets.

In contrast to the parent company, Goodyear USA, which does not contest the North Carolina courts' personal jurisdiction over it, petitioners are not registered to do business in North Carolina. They have no place of business, employees, or bank accounts in North Carolina. They do not design, manufacture, or advertise their products in North Carolina. And they do not solicit business in North Carolina or themselves sell or ship tires to North Carolina customers. Even so, a small percentage of petitioners' tires (tens of thousands out of tens of millions manufactured between 2004 and 2007) were distributed within North Carolina by other Goodyear USA affiliates. These tires were typically custom ordered to equip specialized vehicles such as cement mixers, waste haulers, and boat and horse trailers. Petitioners state, and respondents do not here deny, that the type of tire involved in the accident, a Goodyear Regional RHS tire manufactured by Goodyear Turkey, was never distributed in North Carolina.

Petitioners moved to dismiss the claims against them for want of personal jurisdiction. The trial court denied the motion, and the North Carolina Court of Appeals affirmed. Acknowledging that the claims neither related to, nor arose from, petitioners' contacts with North Carolina, the Court of Appeals confined its analysis to "general rather than specific jurisdiction," which the court recognized required a "higher threshold" showing: A defendant must have "continuous and systematic contacts" with the forum. That threshold was crossed, the court determined, when petitioners placed their tires in the stream of interstate commerce without any limitation on the extent to which those tires could be sold in North Carolina.

Nothing in the record, the court observed, indicated that petitioners "took any affirmative action to cause tires which they had manufactured to be shipped into North Carolina." The court found, however, that tires made by petitioners reached North Carolina as a consequence of a "highly-organized distribution process" involving other Goodyear USA subsidiaries. Petitioners, the court noted, made no attempt to keep these tires from reaching the North Carolina market. Indeed, the very tire involved in the accident, the court observed, conformed to tire standards established by the U.S. Department of Transportation and bore markings required for sale in the United States.[2] As further support, the court invoked North Carolina's interest in providing a forum in which its citizens are able to seek redress for their injuries, and noted the hardship North Carolina plaintiffs would experience were they required to litigate their claims in France, a country to which they have no ties. The North Carolina Supreme Court denied discretionary review.

We granted certiorari to decide whether the general jurisdiction the North Carolina courts asserted over petitioners is consistent with the Due Process

---

[2]Such markings do not necessarily show that any of the tires were destined for sale in the United States. To facilitate trade, the Solicitor General explained, the United States encourages other countries to treat compliance with Department of Transportation standards, including through use of DOT markings, as evidence that the products are safely manufactured.

Clause of the Fourteenth Amendment.

II

A

The Due Process Clause of the Fourteenth Amendment sets the outer boundaries of a state tribunal's authority to proceed against a defendant. Shaffer v. Heitner, 433 U.S. 186, 207 (1977). The canonical opinion in this area remains *International Shoe*, in which we held that a State may authorize its courts to exercise personal jurisdiction over an out-of-state defendant if the defendant has "certain minimum contacts with [the State] such that the maintenance of the suit does not offend 'traditional notions of fair play and substantial justice.'"

Endeavoring to give specific content to the "fair play and substantial justice" concept, the Court in International Shoe classified cases involving out-of-state corporate defendants. First, as in *International Shoe* itself, jurisdiction unquestionably could be asserted where the corporation's in-state activity is continuous and systematic and that activity gave rise to the episode-in-suit. Further, the Court observed, the commission of certain "single or occasional acts" in a State may be sufficient to render a corporation answerable in that State with respect to those acts, though not with respect to matters unrelated to the forum connections. The heading courts today use to encompass these two International Shoe categories is "specific jurisdiction." Adjudicatory authority is "specific" when the suit "aris[es] out of or relate[s] to the defendant's contacts with the forum." *Helicopteros*.

International Shoe distinguished from cases that fit within the "specific jurisdiction" categories, "instances in which the continuous corporate operations within a state [are] so substantial and of such a nature as to justify suit against it on causes of action arising from dealings entirely distinct from those activities." Adjudicatory authority so grounded is today called "general jurisdiction." *Helicopteros*. For an individual, the paradigm forum for the exercise of general jurisdiction is the individual's domicile; for a corporation, it is an equivalent place, one in which the corporation is fairly regarded as at home.

Since *International Shoe*, this Court's decisions have elaborated primarily on circumstances that warrant the exercise of specific jurisdiction, particularly in cases involving "single or occasional acts" occurring or having their impact within the forum State. As a rule in these cases, this Court has inquired whether there was "some act by which the defendant purposefully avail[ed] itself of the privilege of conducting activities within the forum State, thus invoking the benefits and protections of its laws." Hanson v. Denckla, 357 U.S. 235, 253 (1958). See, e.g., World–Wide Volkswagen Corp. v. Woodson, 444 U.S. 286, 287 (1980) (Oklahoma court may not exercise personal jurisdiction "over a nonresident automobile retailer and its wholesale distributor in a products-liability action, when the defendants' only connection with Oklahoma is the fact that an automobile sold in New York to New York residents became involved in an accident in Oklahoma"); Burger King Corp. v. Rudzewicz, 471 U.S. 462, 474-75 (1985) (franchisor headquartered in Florida may maintain breach-of-contract action in Florida against Michigan franchisees, where agreement contemplated on-going interactions between franchisees and franchisor's headquarters); Asahi Metal Industry Co. v. Superior Court of Cal., 480 U.S. 102, 105 (1987) (Taiwanese tire manufacturer settled product liability action brought in California and sought indemnification there from Japanese valve assembly manufacturer; Japanese company's "mere awareness . . . that the components it manufactured, sold, and delivered outside the United States would reach the forum State in the stream of commerce" held insufficient to permit California court's adjudication of Taiwanese company's cross-complaint) (opinion of O'Connor, J.).

In only two decisions postdating *International Shoe*, has this Court considered whether an out-of-state corporate defendant's in-state contacts were sufficiently "continuous and systematic" to justify the exercise of general jurisdiction over claims unrelated to those contacts: Perkins v. Benguet Consol. Mining Co., 342 U.S. 437 (1952) (general jurisdiction appropriately exercised over Philippine corporation sued in Ohio, where the company's affairs were overseen during World War II); and *Helicopteros* (helicopter owned by Colombian corporation crashed in Peru; survivors of U.S. citizens who died in the crash, the Court held, could not maintain wrongful-death actions against the Colombian corporation in Texas, for the corporation's helicopter purchases and purchase-linked activity in Texas were insufficient to subject it to Texas court's general jurisdiction).

B

To justify the exercise of general jurisdiction over petitioners, the North Carolina courts relied on the petitioners' placement of their tires in the stream of commerce. The stream-of-commerce metaphor has been invoked frequently in lower court decisions permitting jurisdiction in products liability cases in which the product has traveled through an extensive chain of distribution before reaching the ultimate consumer. Typically, in such cases, a nonresident defendant, acting outside the forum, places in the stream of commerce a product that ultimately causes harm inside the forum.

Many States have enacted long-arm statutes authorizing courts to exercise specific jurisdiction over manufacturers when the events in suit, or some of them, occurred within the forum state. For example, the "Local Injury; Foreign Act" subsection of North Carolina's long-arm statute authorizes North Carolina courts to exercise personal jurisdiction in "any action claiming injury to person or property within this State arising out of [the defendant's] act or omission outside this State," if, "in addition, at or about the time of the injury, products manufactured by the defendant were used or consumed, within this State in the ordinary course of trade." As the North Carolina Court of Appeals recognized, this provision of the State's long-arm statute "does not apply to this case," for both the act alleged to have caused injury (the fabrication of the allegedly defective tire) and its impact (the accident) occurred outside the forum.[4]

---

[4] The court instead relied on N.C. Gen.Stat. Ann. § 1–75.4(1)(d), which provides for jurisdiction "whether the claim arises within or without [the] State," when the defendant "[i]s engaged in substantial activity within this State, whether such activity is wholly interstate, intrastate, or otherwise." This provision, the North Carolina Supreme Court has held, was "intended to make

The North Carolina court's stream-of-commerce analysis elided the essential difference between case-specific and all-purpose (general) jurisdiction. Flow of a manufacturer's products into the forum, we have explained, may bolster an affiliation germane to specific jurisdiction. See, e.g., *World–Wide Volkswagen* (where "the sale of a product . . . is not simply an isolated occurrence, but arises from the efforts of the manufacturer or distributor to serve . . . the market for its product in [several] States, it is not unreasonable to subject it to suit in one of those States if its allegedly defective merchandise *has there been the source of injury to its owner or to others*") (emphasis added). But ties serving to bolster the exercise of specific jurisdiction do not warrant a determination that, based on those ties, the forum has general jurisdiction over a defendant.

A corporation's "continuous activity of some sorts within a state," *International Shoe* instructed, "is not enough to support the demand that the corporation be amenable to suits unrelated to that activity." Our 1952 decision in *Perkins v. Benguet* remains the textbook case of general jurisdiction appropriately exercised over a foreign corporation that has not consented to suit in the forum.

Sued in Ohio, the defendant in Perkins was a Philippine mining corporation that had ceased activities in the Philippines during World War II. To the extent that the company was conducting any business during and immediately after the Japanese occupation of the Philippines, it was doing so in Ohio: the corporation's president maintained his office there, kept the company files in that office, and supervised from the Ohio office the necessarily limited wartime activities of the company. Although the claim-in-suit did not arise in Ohio, this Court ruled that it would not violate due process for Ohio to adjudicate the controversy.

We next addressed the exercise of general jurisdiction over an out-of-state corporation over three decades later, in *Helicopteros*. In that case, survivors of United States citizens who died in a helicopter crash in Peru instituted wrongful-death actions in a Texas state court against the owner and operator of the helicopter, a Colombian corporation. The Colombian corporation had no place of business in Texas and was not licensed to do business there. "Basically, [the company's] contacts with Texas consisted of sending its chief executive officer to Houston for a contract-negotiation session; accepting into its New York bank account checks drawn on a Houston bank; purchasing helicopters, equipment, and training services from [a Texas enterprise] for substantial sums; and sending personnel to [Texas] for training." [*Id.*] These links to Texas, we determined, did not "constitute the kind of continuous and systematic general business contacts ... found to exist in *Perkins*," and were insufficient to support the exercise of jurisdiction over a claim that neither "arose out of nor related to" the defendant's activities in Texas.

Helicopteros concluded that "mere purchases [made in the forum State], even if occurring at regular intervals, are not enough to warrant a State's

---

available to the North Carolina courts the full jurisdictional powers permissible under federal due process." Dillon v. Numismatic Funding Corp., 291 N.C. 674, 676, 231 S.E.2d 629, 630 (1977).

assertion of [general] jurisdiction over a nonresident corporation in a cause of action not related to those purchase transactions." We see no reason to differentiate from the ties to Texas held insufficient in *Helicopteros*, the sales of petitioners' tires sporadically made in North Carolina through intermediaries. Under the sprawling view of general jurisdiction urged by respondents and embraced by the North Carolina Court of Appeals, any substantial manufacturer or seller of goods would be amenable to suit, on any claim for relief, wherever its products are distributed. But cf. *World–Wide Volkswagen* (every seller of chattels does not, by virtue of the sale, "appoint the chattel his agent for service of process").

Measured against *Helicopteros* and *Perkins*, North Carolina is not a forum in which it would be permissible to subject petitioners to general jurisdiction. Unlike the defendant in *Perkins*, whose sole wartime business activity was conducted in Ohio, petitioners are in no sense at home in North Carolina. Their attenuated connections to the State fall far short of the "the continuous and systematic general business contacts" necessary to empower North Carolina to entertain suit against them on claims unrelated to anything that connects them to the State. *Helicopteros*.[5]

Respondents belatedly assert a "single enterprise" theory, asking us to consolidate petitioners' ties to North Carolina with those of Goodyear USA and other Goodyear entities. In effect, respondents would have us pierce Goodyear corporate veils, at least for jurisdictional purposes. Neither below nor in their brief in opposition to the petition for certiorari did respondents urge disregard of petitioners' discrete status as subsidiaries and treatment of all Goodyear entities as a "unitary business," so that jurisdiction over the parent would draw in the subsidiaries as well.[6] Respondents have therefore forfeited this contention, and we do not address it. [Reversed.]

NOTES AND PROBLEMS FOR DISCUSSION

1. Does the Court's repeated use of the "at home" metaphor as descriptive of the "paradigm" forum for the exercise of general jurisdiction over a foreign

---

[5] * * * [T]he North Carolina Court of Appeals invoked the State's "well-recognized interest in providing a forum in which its citizens are able to seek redress for injuries that they have sustained." But general jurisdiction to adjudicate has in United States practice never been based on the plaintiff's relationship to the forum. There is nothing in our law comparable to article 14 of the Civil Code of France (1804) under which the French nationality of the plaintiff is a sufficient ground for jurisdiction. When a defendant's act outside the forum causes injury in the forum, by contrast, a plaintiff's residence in the forum may strengthen the case for the exercise of specific jurisdiction. See Calder v. Jones, 465 U.S. 783 (1984).

[6] In the brief they filed in the North Carolina Court of Appeals, respondents stated that petitioners were part of an "integrated world-wide efforts to design, manufacture, market and sell their tires in the United States, including in North Carolina." Read in context, that assertion was offered in support of a narrower proposition: The distribution of petitioners' tires in North Carolina, respondents maintained, demonstrated petitioners' own "calculated and deliberate efforts to take advantage of the North Carolina market." As already explained, even regularly occurring sales of a product in a State do not justify the exercise of jurisdiction over a claim unrelated to those sales.

(sister state or foreign nation) corporate defendant, i.e., where that corporation's contacts with the forum state are so extensive that the forum is "fairly regarded as at home", denote a retrenchment on the availability of doing business-based claims of general jurisdiction?   Does the opinion suggest that only those corporations that are either incorporated or licensed to do business in the forum state will be sufficiently "at home" to be subject to general jurisdiction?   In answering that question, consider that in *J. McIntyre, Ltd. v. Nicastro, supra*, decided the same day as *Goodyear*, the Supreme Court cited *Goodyear* for the proposition that "incorporation or principal place of business for corporations * * * indicates general submission to a State's [adjudicate] powers."   The Court revisited this issue in the following case.

Daimler AG v. Bauman

Supreme Court of the United States, 2014.

571 U.S. ___, 134 S.Ct. 746, 187 L.Ed.2d 624.

JUSTICE GINSBURG delivered the opinion of the Court.

This case concerns the authority of a court in the United States to entertain a claim brought by foreign plaintiffs against a foreign defendant based on events occurring entirely outside the United States. The litigation commenced in 2004, when twenty-two Argentinian residents[1] filed a complaint in the United States District Court for the Northern District of California against DaimlerChrysler Aktiengesellschaft (Daimler),[2] a German public stock company, headquartered in Stuttgart, that manufactures Mercedes–Benz vehicles in Germany. The complaint alleged that during Argentina's 1976–1983 "Dirty War," Daimler's Argentinian subsidiary, Mercedes–Benz Argentina (MB Argentina) collaborated with state security forces to kidnap, detain, torture, and kill certain MB Argentina workers, among them, plaintiffs or persons closely related to plaintiffs. Damages for the alleged human-rights violations were sought from Daimler under the laws of the United States, California, and Argentina. Jurisdiction over the lawsuit was predicated on the California contacts of Mercedes–Benz USA, LLC (MBUSA), a subsidiary of Daimler incorporated in Delaware with its principal place of business in New Jersey. MBUSA distributes Daimler-manufactured vehicles to independent dealerships throughout the United States, including California.

The question presented is whether the Due Process Clause of the Fourteenth Amendment precludes the District Court from exercising jurisdiction over Daimler in this case, given the absence of any California connection to the atrocities, perpetrators, or victims described in the complaint. Plaintiffs invoked the court's general or all-purpose jurisdiction. California, they urge, is a place where Daimler may be sued on any and all claims against it, wherever in the world the claims may arise. For example, as plaintiffs' counsel affirmed, under

---

[1] One plaintiff is a resident of Argentina and a citizen of Chile; all other plaintiffs are residents and citizens of Argentina.

[2] Daimler was restructured in 2007 and is now known as Daimler AG. * * *

the proffered jurisdictional theory, if a Daimler-manufactured vehicle overturned in Poland, injuring a Polish driver and passenger, the injured parties could maintain a design defect suit in California. Exercises of personal jurisdiction so exorbitant, we hold, are barred by due process constraints on the assertion of adjudicatory authority.

In *Goodyear Dunlop Tires Operations, S.A. v. Brown,* 564 U.S. ——, 131 S.Ct. 2846, 180 L.Ed.2d 796 (2011), we addressed the distinction between general or all-purpose jurisdiction, and specific or conduct-linked jurisdiction. As to the former, we held that a court may assert jurisdiction over a foreign corporation "to hear any and all claims against [it]" only when the corporation's affiliations with the State in which suit is brought are so constant and pervasive "as to render [it] essentially at home in the forum State." Instructed by *Goodyear*, we conclude Daimler is not "at home" in California, and cannot be sued there for injuries plaintiffs attribute to MB Argentina's conduct in Argentina.

I

In 2004, plaintiffs (respondents here) filed suit in the United States District Court for the Northern District of California, alleging that MB Argentina collaborated with Argentinian state security forces to kidnap, detain, torture, and kill plaintiffs and their relatives during the military dictatorship in place there from 1976 through 1983, a period known as Argentina's "Dirty War." Based on those allegations, plaintiffs asserted claims under the Alien Tort Statute, 28 U.S.C. § 1350, and the Torture Victim Protection Act of 1991, as well as claims for wrongful death and intentional infliction of emotional distress under the laws of California and Argentina. The incidents recounted in the complaint center on MB Argentina's plant in Gonzalez Catan, Argentina; no part of MB Argentina's alleged collaboration with Argentinian authorities took place in California or anywhere else in the United States.

Plaintiffs' operative complaint names only one corporate defendant: Daimler, the petitioner here. Plaintiffs seek to hold Daimler vicariously liable for MB Argentina's alleged malfeasance. Daimler is a German *Aktiengesellschaft* (public stock company) that manufactures Mercedes–Benz vehicles in Germany and has its headquarters in Stuttgart. At times relevant to this case, MB Argentina was a subsidiary wholly owned by Daimler's predecessor in interest.

Daimler moved to dismiss the action for want of personal jurisdiction. Opposing the motion, plaintiffs submitted declarations and exhibits purporting to demonstrate the presence of Daimler itself in California. Alternatively, plaintiffs maintained that jurisdiction over Daimler could be founded on the California contacts of MBUSA, a distinct corporate entity that, according to plaintiffs, should be treated as Daimler's agent for jurisdictional purposes.

MBUSA, an indirect subsidiary of Daimler, is a Delaware limited liability corporation.[3] MBUSA serves as Daimler's exclusive importer and distributor in

---

[3] At times relevant to this suit, MBUSA was wholly owned by DaimlerChrysler North America Holding Corporation, a Daimler subsidiary.

the United States, purchasing Mercedes–Benz automobiles from Daimler in Germany, then importing those vehicles, and ultimately distributing them to independent dealerships located throughout the Nation. Although MBUSA's principal place of business is in New Jersey, MBUSA has multiple California-based facilities, including a regional office in Costa Mesa, a Vehicle Preparation Center in Carson, and a Classic Center in Irvine. According to the record developed below, MBUSA is the largest supplier of luxury vehicles to the California market. In particular, over 10% of all sales of new vehicles in the United States take place in California, and MBUSA's California sales account for 2.4% of Daimler's worldwide sales.

The relationship between Daimler and MBUSA is delineated in a General Distributor Agreement, which sets forth requirements for MBUSA's distribution of Mercedes–Benz vehicles in the United States. That agreement established MBUSA as an "independent contracto[r]" that "buy[s] and sell[s] [vehicles] ... as an independent business for [its] own account." The agreement "does not make [MBUSA] ... a general or special agent, partner, joint venturer or employee of DAIMLERCHRYSLER or any DaimlerChrysler Group Company"; MBUSA "ha[s] no authority to make binding obligations for or act on behalf of DAIMLERCHRYSLER or any DaimlerChrysler Group Company."

After allowing jurisdictional discovery on plaintiffs' agency allegations, the District Court granted Daimler's motion to dismiss. Daimler's own affiliations with California, the court first determined, were insufficient to support the exercise of all-purpose jurisdiction over the corporation. Next, the court declined to attribute MBUSA's California contacts to Daimler on an agency theory, concluding that plaintiffs failed to demonstrate that MBUSA acted as Daimler's agent.

The Ninth Circuit at first affirmed the District Court's judgment. Addressing solely the question of agency, the Court of Appeals held that plaintiffs had not shown the existence of an agency relationship of the kind that might warrant attribution of MBUSA's contacts to Daimler. Judge Reinhardt dissented. In his view, the agency test was satisfied and considerations of "reasonableness" did not bar the exercise of jurisdiction. Granting plaintiffs' petition for rehearing, the panel withdrew its initial opinion and replaced it with one authored by Judge Reinhardt, which elaborated on reasoning he initially expressed in dissent.

Daimler petitioned for rehearing and rehearing en banc, urging that the exercise of personal jurisdiction over Daimler could not be reconciled with this Court's decision in *Goodyear*. Over the dissent of eight judges, the Ninth Circuit denied Daimler's petition.

We granted certiorari to decide whether, consistent with the Due Process Clause of the Fourteenth Amendment, Daimler is amenable to suit in California courts for claims involving only foreign plaintiffs and conduct occurring entirely abroad.

II

Federal courts ordinarily follow state law in determining the bounds of their jurisdiction over persons. See Fed. Rule Civ. Proc. 4(k)(1)(A). Under California's long-arm statute, California state courts may exercise personal jurisdiction "on any basis not inconsistent with the Constitution of this state or of the United States." California's long-arm statute allows the exercise of personal jurisdiction to the full extent permissible under the U.S. Constitution. We therefore inquire whether the Ninth Circuit's holding comports with the limits imposed by federal due process. See, *e.g., Burger King Corp. v. Rudzewicz,* 471 U.S. 462, 464, 105 S.Ct. 2174, 85 L.Ed.2d 528 (1985).

III

In *Pennoyer v. Neff,* 95 U.S. 714, 24 L.Ed. 565 (1878), decided shortly after the enactment of the Fourteenth Amendment, the Court held that a tribunal's jurisdiction over persons reaches no farther than the geographic bounds of the forum. See also *Shaffer v. Heitner,* 433 U.S. 186, 197, 97 S.Ct. 2569, 53 L.Ed.2d 683 (1977) (Under *Pennoyer,* "any attempt 'directly' to assert extraterritorial jurisdiction over persons or property would offend sister States and exceed the inherent limits of the State's power."). In time, however, that strict territorial approach yielded to a less rigid understanding, spurred by "changes in the technology of transportation and communication, and the tremendous growth of interstate business activity." *Burnham v. Superior Court of Cal., County of Marin,* 495 U.S. 604, 617, 110 S.Ct. 2105, 109 L.Ed.2d 631 (1990) (opinion of SCALIA, J.).

"The canonical opinion in this area remains *International Shoe,* in which we held that a State may authorize its courts to exercise personal jurisdiction over an out-of-state defendant if the defendant has 'certain minimum contacts with [the State] such that the maintenance of the suit does not offend "traditional notions of fair play and substantial justice."' " *Goodyear* (quoting *International Shoe*). Following *International Shoe,* "the relationship among the defendant, the forum, and the litigation, rather than the mutually exclusive sovereignty of the States on which the rules of *Pennoyer* rest, became the central concern of the inquiry into personal jurisdiction." *Shaffer.*

International Shoe's conception of "fair play and substantial justice" presaged the development of two categories of personal jurisdiction. The first category is represented by *International Shoe* itself, a case in which the in-state activities of the corporate defendant "ha[d] not only been continuous and systematic, but also g[a]ve rise to the liabilities sued on." *International Shoe* recognized, as well, that "the commission of some single or occasional acts of the corporate agent in a state" may sometimes be enough to subject the corporation to jurisdiction in that State's tribunals with respect to suits relating to that in-state activity. Adjudicatory authority of this order, in which the suit "aris[es] out of or relate[s] to the defendant's contacts with the forum," *Helicopteros Nacionales de Colombia, S.A. v. Hall,* 466 U.S. 408, 414, n. 8, 104 S.Ct. 1868, 80 L.Ed.2d 404 (1984), is today called "specific jurisdiction." See *Goodyear* (citing von Mehren & Trautman, Jurisdiction to Adjudicate: A Suggested Analysis, 79 Harv. L.Rev. 1121, 1144–1163 (1966) (hereinafter von Mehren & Trautman)).

International Shoe distinguished between, on the one hand, exercises of specific jurisdiction, as just described, and on the other, situations where a foreign corporation's "continuous corporate operations within a state [are] so substantial and of such a nature as to justify suit against it on causes of action arising from dealings entirely distinct from those activities." As we have since explained, "[a] court may assert general jurisdiction over foreign (sister-state or foreign-country) corporations to hear any and all claims against them when their affiliations with the State are so 'continuous and systematic' as to render them essentially at home in the forum State." *Goodyear*; *Helicopteros*.[5]

Since *International Shoe,* "specific jurisdiction has become the centerpiece of modern jurisdiction theory, while general jurisdiction [has played] a reduced role." *Goodyear* (quoting Twitchell, The Myth of General Jurisdiction, 101 Harv. L.Rev. 610, 628 (1988)). *International Shoe*'s momentous departure from *Pennoyer*'s rigidly territorial focus, we have noted, unleashed a rapid expansion of tribunals' ability to hear claims against out-of-state defendants when the episode-in-suit occurred in the forum or the defendant purposefully availed itself of the forum.[6] Our subsequent decisions have continued to bear out the prediction that "specific jurisdiction will come into sharper relief and form a considerably more significant part of the scene." von Mehren & Trautman 1164.[7]

---

[5] Colloquy at oral argument illustrated the respective provinces of general and specific jurisdiction over persons. Two hypothetical scenarios were posed: *First,* if a California plaintiff, injured in a California accident involving a Daimler-manufactured vehicle, sued Daimler in California court alleging that the vehicle was defectively designed, that court's adjudicatory authority would be premised on specific jurisdiction. See Tr. of Oral Arg. 11 (Daimler's counsel acknowledged that specific jurisdiction "may well be ... available" in such a case, depending on whether Daimler purposefully availed itself of the forum). *Second,* if a similar accident took place in Poland and injured Polish plaintiffs sued Daimler in California court, the question would be one of general jurisdiction. See *id.,* at 29 (on plaintiffs' view, Daimler would be amenable to such a suit in California).

[6] See *Shaffer* ("The immediate effect of [*International Shoe*'s] departure from *Pennoyer*'s conceptual apparatus was to increase the ability of the state courts to obtain personal jurisdiction over nonresident defendants."); *McGee v. International Life Ins. Co.,* 355 U.S. 220, 222, 78 S.Ct. 199, 2 L.Ed.2d 223 (1957) ("[A] trend is clearly discernible toward expanding the permissible scope of state jurisdiction over foreign corporations and other nonresidents.").

[7] See, *e.g., Asahi Metal Industry Co. v. Superior Court of Cal., Solano Cty.,* 480 U.S. 102, 112, 107 S.Ct. 1026, 94 L.Ed.2d 92 (1987) (opinion of O'Connor, J.) (specific jurisdiction may lie over a foreign defendant that places a product into the "stream of commerce" while also "designing the product for the market in the forum State, advertising in the forum State, establishing channels for providing regular advice to customers in the forum State, or marketing the product through a distributor who has agreed to serve as the sales agent in the forum State"); *World–Wide Volkswagen Corp. v. Woodson,* 444 U.S. 286, 297, 100 S.Ct. 559, 62 L.Ed.2d 490 (1980) ("[I]f the sale of a product of a manufacturer or distributor such as Audi or Volkswagen is not simply an isolated occurrence, but arises from the efforts of the manufacturer or distributor to serve, directly or indirectly, the market for its product in other States, it is not unreasonable to subject it to suit in one of those States if its allegedly defective merchandise has there been the source of injury to its owner or to others."); *Calder v. Jones,* 465 U.S. 783, 789–790, 104 S.Ct. 1482, 79 L.Ed.2d 804 (1984) (California court had specific jurisdiction to hear suit brought by California plaintiff where Florida-based publisher of a newspaper having its largest circulation in California published an article allegedly defaming the complaining Californian; under those circumstances, defendants "must 'reasonably anticipate being haled into [a California] court' "); *Keeton v. Hustler Magazine, Inc.,* 465 U.S. 770, 780–781, 104 S.Ct. 1473, 79 L.Ed.2d 790 (1984) (New York resident may maintain suit for libel in New Hampshire state court against California-based magazine that sold 10,000 to 15,000 copies in New Hampshire each month; as long as the defendant "continuously

Our post-*International Shoe* opinions on general jurisdiction, by comparison, are few. "[The Court's] 1952 decision in *Perkins v. Benguet Consol. Mining Co.* remains the textbook case of general jurisdiction appropriately exercised over a foreign corporation that has not consented to suit in the forum." *Goodyear*. The defendant in *Perkins*, Benguet, was a company incorporated under the laws of the Philippines, where it operated gold and silver mines. Benguet ceased its mining operations during the Japanese occupation of the Philippines in World War II; its president moved to Ohio, where he kept an office, maintained the company's files, and oversaw the company's activities. The plaintiff, an Ohio resident, sued Benguet on a claim that neither arose in Ohio nor related to the corporation's activities in that State. We held that the Ohio courts could exercise general jurisdiction over Benguet without offending due process. That was so, we later noted, because "Ohio was the corporation's principal, if temporary, place of business." *Keeton*.[8]

The next case on point, *Helicopteros,* arose from a helicopter crash in Peru. Four U.S. citizens perished in that accident; their survivors and representatives brought suit in Texas state court against the helicopter's owner and operator, a Colombian corporation. That company's contacts with Texas were confined to sending its chief executive officer to Houston for a contract-negotiation session; accepting into its New York bank account checks drawn on a Houston bank;

---

and deliberately exploited the New Hampshire market," it could reasonably be expected to answer a libel suit there).

[8] Selectively referring to the trial court record in *Perkins* (as summarized in an opinion of the intermediate appellate court), Justice SOTOMAYOR posits that Benguet may have had extensive operations in places other than Ohio. See *post,* at n. 8 ("By the time the suit [in *Perkins*] was commenced, the company had resumed its considerable operations in the Philippines," "rebuilding its properties there" and "purchasing machinery, supplies and equipment." (internal quotation marks omitted)). See also *post,* at n. 5 (many of the corporation's "key management decisions" were made by the out-of-state purchasing agent and chief of staff). Justice SOTOMAYOR's account overlooks this Court's opinion in *Perkins* and the point on which that opinion turned: All of Benguet's activities were directed by the company's president from within Ohio. See *Perkins* (company's Philippine mining operations "were completely halted during the occupation ... by the Japanese"; and the company's president, from his Ohio office, "supervised policies dealing with the rehabilitation of the corporation's properties in the Philippines and ... dispatched funds to cover purchases of machinery for such rehabilitation"). On another day, Justice SOTOMAYOR joined a unanimous Court in recognizing: "To the extent that the company was conducting any business during and immediately after the Japanese occupation of the Philippines, it was doing so in Ohio...." *Goodyear*. Given the wartime circumstances, Ohio could be considered "a surrogate for the place of incorporation or head office." von Mehren & Trautman 1144. See also *ibid.* (*Perkins* "should be regarded as a decision on its exceptional facts, not as a significant reaffirmation of obsolescing notions of general jurisdiction" based on nothing more than a corporation's "doing business" in a forum).

Justice SOTOMAYOR emphasizes *Perkins* 'statement that Benguet's Ohio contacts, while "continuous and systematic," were but a "limited ... part of its general business.". Describing the company's "wartime activities" as "necessarily limited," however, this Court had in mind the diminution in operations resulting from the Japanese occupation and the ensuing shutdown of the company's Philippine mines. No fair reader of the full opinion in *Perkins* could conclude that the Court meant to convey anything other than that Ohio was the center of the corporation's wartime activities. But cf. *post,* at 768 ("If anything, [*Perkins*] intimated that the defendant's Ohio contacts were *not* substantial in comparison to its contacts elsewhere.").

purchasing helicopters, equipment, and training services from a Texas-based helicopter company for substantial sums; and sending personnel to Texas for training. Notably, those contacts bore no apparent relationship to the accident that gave rise to the suit. We held that the company's Texas connections did not resemble the "continuous and systematic general business contacts ... found to exist in *Perkins*." "[M]ere purchases, even if occurring at regular intervals," we clarified, "are not enough to warrant a State's assertion of *in personam* jurisdiction over a nonresident corporation in a cause of action not related to those purchase transactions."

Most recently, in *Goodyear*, we answered the question: "Are foreign subsidiaries of a United States parent corporation amenable to suit in state court on claims unrelated to any activity of the subsidiaries in the forum State?" That case arose from a bus accident outside Paris that killed two boys from North Carolina. The boys' parents brought a wrongful-death suit in North Carolina state court alleging that the bus's tire was defectively manufactured. The complaint named as defendants not only The Goodyear Tire and Rubber Company (Goodyear), an Ohio corporation, but also Goodyear's Turkish, French, and Luxembourgian subsidiaries. Those foreign subsidiaries, which manufactured tires for sale in Europe and Asia, lacked any affiliation with North Carolina. A small percentage of tires manufactured by the foreign subsidiaries were distributed in North Carolina, however, and on that ground, the North Carolina Court of Appeals held the subsidiaries amenable to the general jurisdiction of North Carolina courts.

We reversed, observing that the North Carolina court's analysis "elided the essential difference between case-specific and all-purpose (general) jurisdiction." Although the placement of a product into the stream of commerce "may bolster an affiliation germane to *specific* jurisdiction," we explained, such contacts "do not warrant a determination that, based on those ties, the forum has *general* jurisdiction over a defendant." As *International Shoe* itself teaches, a corporation's "continuous activity of some sorts within a state is not enough to support the demand that the corporation be amenable to suits unrelated to that activity." Because Goodyear's foreign subsidiaries were "in no sense at home in North Carolina," we held, those subsidiaries could not be required to submit to the general jurisdiction of that State's courts. See also *J. McIntyre Machinery, Ltd. v. Nicastro,* 564 U.S. ——, ——, 131 S.Ct. 2780, 2797–2798, 180 L.Ed.2d 765 (2011) (GINSBURG, J., dissenting) (noting unanimous agreement that a foreign manufacturer, which engaged an independent U.S.-based distributor to sell its machines throughout the United States, could not be exposed to all-purpose jurisdiction in New Jersey courts based on those contacts).

As is evident from *Perkins*, *Helicopteros,* and *Goodyear*, general and specific jurisdiction have followed markedly different trajectories post-*International Shoe*. Specific jurisdiction has been cut loose from *Pennoyer*'s sway, but we have declined to stretch general jurisdiction beyond limits traditionally recognized. As this Court has increasingly trained on the "relationship among the defendant, the forum, and the litigation," *Shaffer, i.e.,* specific jurisdiction,[10] general jurisdiction has come to occupy a less dominant place in the contemporary scheme.[11]

IV

With this background, we turn directly to the question whether Daimler's affiliations with California are sufficient to subject it to the general (all-purpose) personal jurisdiction of that State's courts. In the proceedings below, the parties agreed on, or failed to contest, certain points we now take as given. Plaintiffs have never attempted to fit this case into the *specific* jurisdiction category. Nor did plaintiffs challenge on appeal the District Court's holding that Daimler's own contacts with California were, by themselves, too sporadic to justify the exercise of general jurisdiction. While plaintiffs ultimately persuaded the Ninth Circuit to impute MBUSA's California contacts to Daimler on an agency theory, at no point have they maintained that MBUSA is an alter ego of Daimler.

Daimler, on the other hand, failed to object below to plaintiffs' assertion that the California courts could exercise all-purpose jurisdiction over MBUSA.[12] We will assume then, for purposes of this decision only, that MBUSA qualifies as at home in California.

A

In sustaining the exercise of general jurisdiction over Daimler, the Ninth Circuit relied on an agency theory, determining that MBUSA acted as Daimler's agent for jurisdictional purposes and then attributing MBUSA's California contacts to Daimler. The Ninth Circuit's agency analysis derived from Circuit precedent considering principally whether the subsidiary performs services that are sufficiently important to the foreign corporation that if it did not have a representative to perform them, the corporation's own officials would undertake to perform substantially similar services.

This Court has not yet addressed whether a foreign corporation may be subjected to a court's general jurisdiction based on the contacts of its in-state subsidiary. Daimler argues, and several Courts of Appeals have held, that a subsidiary's jurisdictional contacts can be imputed to its parent only when the former is so dominated by the latter as to be its alter ego. The Ninth Circuit

---

[10] Remarkably, Justice SOTOMAYOR treats specific jurisdiction as though it were barely there. Given the many decades in which specific jurisdiction has flourished, it would be hard to conjure up an example of the "deep injustice" Justice SOTOMAYOR predicts as a consequence of our holding that California is not an all-purpose forum for suits against Daimler. Justice SOTOMAYOR identifies "the concept of reciprocal fairness" as the "touchstone principle of due process in this field." (citing *International Shoe*). She overlooks, however, that in the very passage of *International Shoe* on which she relies, the Court left no doubt that it was addressing specific—not general—jurisdiction. ("The exercise of th[e] privilege [of conducting corporate activities within a State] may give rise to obligations, and, *so far as those obligations arise out of or are connected with the activities within the state,* a procedure which requires the corporation to respond to a suit brought to enforce them can, in most instances, hardly be said to be undue." (emphasis added)).

[11] As the Court made plain in *Goodyear* and repeats here, general jurisdiction requires affiliations "so 'continuous and systematic' as to render [the foreign corporation] essentially at home in the forum State", *i.e.,* comparable to a domestic enterprise in that State.

[12] MBUSA is not a defendant in this case.

adopted a less rigorous test based on what it described as an "agency" relationship. Agencies, we note, come in many sizes and shapes: "One may be an agent for some business purposes and not others so that the fact that one may be an agent for one purpose does not make him or her an agent for every purpose." 2A C. J. S., Agency § 43, p. 367 (2013) (footnote omitted).[13] A subsidiary, for example, might be its parent's agent for claims arising in the place where the subsidiary operates, yet not its agent regarding claims arising elsewhere. The Court of Appeals did not advert to that prospect. But we need not pass judgment on invocation of an agency theory in the context of general jurisdiction, for in no event can the appeals court's analysis be sustained.

The Ninth Circuit's agency finding rested primarily on its observation that MBUSA's services were "important" to Daimler, as gauged by Daimler's hypothetical readiness to perform those services itself if MBUSA did not exist. Formulated this way, the inquiry into importance stacks the deck, for it will always yield a pro-jurisdiction answer: "Anything a corporation does through an independent contractor, subsidiary, or distributor is presumably something that the corporation would do 'by other means' if the independent contractor, subsidiary, or distributor did not exist." 676 F.3d, at 777 (O'Scannlain, J., dissenting from denial of rehearing en banc).[14] The Ninth Circuit's agency theory thus appears to subject foreign corporations to general jurisdiction whenever they have an in-state subsidiary or affiliate, an outcome that would sweep beyond even the "sprawling view of general jurisdiction" we rejected in *Goodyear*.[15]

B

Even if we were to assume that MBUSA is at home in California, and further to assume MBUSA's contacts are imputable to Daimler, there would still be no basis to subject Daimler to general jurisdiction in California, for Daimler's slim contacts with the State hardly render it at home there.[16]

---

[13] Agency relationships, we have recognized, may be relevant to the existence of *specific* jurisdiction. "[T]he corporate personality," *International Shoe* observed, "is a fiction, although a fiction intended to be acted upon as though it were a fact." As such, a corporation can purposefully avail itself of a forum by directing its agents or distributors to take action there. See, *e.g., Asahi* (opinion of O'Connor, J.) (defendant's act of "marketing [a] product through a distributor who has agreed to serve as the sales agent in the forum State" may amount to purposeful availment); *International Shoe* ("the commission of some single or occasional acts of the corporate agent in a state" may sometimes "be deemed sufficient to render the corporation liable to suit" on related claims). It does not inevitably follow, however, that similar reasoning applies to *general* jurisdiction. Cf. *Goodyear* (faulting analysis that "elided the essential difference between case-specific and all-purpose (general) jurisdiction").

[14] Indeed, plaintiffs do not defend this aspect of the Ninth Circuit's analysis. See Brief for Respondents 39, n. 18 ("We do not believe that this gloss is particularly helpful.").

[15] The Ninth Circuit's agency analysis also looked to whether the parent enjoys the right to substantially control the subsidiary's activities. The Court of Appeals found the requisite "control" demonstrated by the General Distributor Agreement between Daimler and MBUSA, which gives Daimler the right to oversee certain of MBUSA's operations, even though that agreement expressly disavowed the creation of any agency relationship. Thus grounded, the separate inquiry into control hardly curtails the overbreadth of the Ninth Circuit's agency holding.

[16] By addressing this point, Justice SOTOMAYOR asserts, we have strayed from the question on which we granted certiorari to decide an issue not argued below. That assertion is doubly flawed.

Goodyear made clear that only a limited set of affiliations with a forum will render a defendant amenable to all-purpose jurisdiction there. "For an individual, the paradigm forum for the exercise of general jurisdiction is the individual's domicile; for a corporation, it is an equivalent place, one in which the corporation is fairly regarded as at home." With respect to a corporation, the place of incorporation and principal place of business are "paradig[m] ... bases for general jurisdiction." Those affiliations have the virtue of being unique — that is, each ordinarily indicates only one place — as well as easily ascertainable. Cf. *Hertz Corp. v. Friend,* 559 U.S. 77, 94, 130 S.Ct. 1181, 175 L.Ed.2d 1029 (2010) ("Simple jurisdictional rules . . . promote greater predictability."). These bases afford plaintiffs recourse to at least one clear and certain forum in which a corporate defendant may be sued on any and all claims.

Goodyear did not hold that a corporation may be subject to general jurisdiction *only* in a forum where it is incorporated or has its principal place of business; it simply typed those places paradigm all-purpose forums. Plaintiffs would have us look beyond the exemplar bases *Goodyear* identified, and approve the exercise of general jurisdiction in every State in which a corporation "engages in a substantial, continuous, and systematic course of business." Brief for Respondents. That formulation, we hold, is unacceptably grasping.

As noted, *supra,* the words "continuous and systematic" were used in *International Shoe* to describe instances in which the exercise of *specific* jurisdiction would be appropriate.[17] Turning to all-purpose jurisdiction, in contrast, *International Shoe* speaks of "instances in which the continuous corporate operations within a state [are] so substantial and of such a nature as to justify suit ... *on causes of action arising from dealings entirely distinct from those activities.*" (emphasis added). See also Twitchell, Why We Keep Doing Business With Doing–Business Jurisdiction, 2001 U. Chi. Legal Forum 171, 184 (*International Shoe* "is clearly not saying that dispute-blind jurisdiction exists whenever 'continuous and systematic' contacts are found.").[18] Accordingly, the

---

First, the question on which we granted certiorari, as stated in Daimler's petition, is "whether it violates due process for a court to exercise general personal jurisdiction over a foreign corporation based solely on the fact that an indirect corporate subsidiary performs services on behalf of the defendant in the forum State." That question fairly encompasses an inquiry into whether, in light of *Goodyear*, Daimler can be considered at home in California based on MBUSA's in-state activities. Moreover, both in the Ninth Circuit, and in this Court, *amici* in support of Daimler homed in on the insufficiency of Daimler's California contacts for general jurisdiction purposes. In short, and in light of our pathmarking opinion in *Goodyear*, we perceive no unfairness in deciding today that California is not an all-purpose forum for claims against Daimler.

[17] *International Shoe* also recognized, as noted above, that "some single or occasional acts of the corporate agent in a state ..., because of their nature and quality and the circumstances of their commission, may be deemed sufficient to render the corporation liable to suit."

[18] Plaintiffs emphasize two decisions, *Barrow S.S. Co. v. Kane,* 170 U.S. 100, 18 S.Ct. 526, 42 L.Ed. 964 (1898), and *Tauza v. Susquehanna Coal Co.,* 220 N.Y. 259, 115 N.E. 915 (1917) (Cardozo, J.), both cited in *Perkins v. Benguet Consol. Mining Co.,* 342 U.S. 437, 72 S.Ct. 413, 96 L.Ed. 485 (1952), just after the statement that a corporation's continuous operations in-state may suffice to establish general jurisdiction. *Barrow* and *Tauza* indeed upheld the exercise of general jurisdiction based on the presence of a local office, which signaled that the corporation was "doing business" in the forum. *Perkins'* unadorned citations to these cases, both decided in the era dominated by *Pennoyer's* territorial thinking, should not attract heavy reliance today. See

inquiry under *Goodyear* is not whether a foreign corporation's in-forum contacts can be said to be in some sense "continuous and systematic," it is whether that corporation's "affiliations with the State are so 'continuous and systematic' as to render [it] essentially at home in the forum State."[19]

Here, neither Daimler nor MBUSA is incorporated in California, nor does either entity have its principal place of business there. If Daimler's California activities sufficed to allow adjudication of this Argentina-rooted case in California, the same global reach would presumably be available in every other State in which MBUSA's sales are sizable. Such exorbitant exercises of all-purpose jurisdiction would scarcely permit out-of-state defendants "to structure their primary conduct with some minimum assurance as to where that conduct will and will not render them liable to suit." *Burger King.*

It was therefore error for the Ninth Circuit to conclude that Daimler, even with MBUSA's contacts attributed to it, was at home in California, and hence subject to suit there on claims by foreign plaintiffs having nothing to do with anything that occurred or had its principal impact in California.[20]

---

generally Feder, *Goodyear*, "Home," and the Uncertain Future of Doing Business Jurisdiction, 63 S.C. L. Rev. 671 (2012) (questioning whether "doing business" should persist as a basis for general jurisdiction).

[19] We do not foreclose the possibility that in an exceptional case, see, *e.g., Perkins*, a corporation's operations in a forum other than its formal place of incorporation or principal place of business may be so substantial and of such a nature as to render the corporation at home in that State. But this case presents no occasion to explore that question, because Daimler's activities in California plainly do not approach that level. It is one thing to hold a corporation answerable for operations in the forum State, quite another to expose it to suit on claims having no connection whatever to the forum State.

[20] To clarify in light of Justice SOTOMAYOR's opinion concurring in the judgment, the general jurisdiction inquiry does not "focu[s] solely on the magnitude of the defendant's in-state contacts." General jurisdiction instead calls for an appraisal of a corporation's activities in their entirety, nationwide and worldwide. A corporation that operates in many places can scarcely be deemed at home in all of them. Otherwise, "at home" would be synonymous with "doing business" tests framed before specific jurisdiction evolved in the United States. Nothing in *International Shoe* and its progeny suggests that "a particular quantum of local activity" should give a State authority over a far larger quantum of activity having no connection to any in-state activity.

Justice SOTOMAYOR would reach the same result, but for a different reason. Rather than concluding that Daimler is not at home in California, Justice SOTOMAYOR would hold that the exercise of general jurisdiction over Daimler would be unreasonable "in the unique circumstances of this case." In other words, she favors a resolution fit for this day and case only. True, a multipronged reasonableness check was articulated in *Asahi,* but not as a free-floating test. Instead, the check was to be essayed when *specific* jurisdiction is at issue. See also *Burger King*. First, a court is to determine whether the connection between the forum and the episode-in-suit could justify the exercise of specific jurisdiction. Then, in a second step, the court is to consider several additional factors to assess the reasonableness of entertaining the case. When a corporation is genuinely at home in the forum State, however, any second-step inquiry would be superfluous.

Justice SOTOMAYOR fears that our holding will "lead to greater unpredictability by radically expanding the scope of jurisdictional discovery." But it is hard to see why much in the way of discovery would be needed to determine where a corporation is at home. Justice SOTOMAYOR's proposal to import *Asahi*'s "reasonableness" check into the general jurisdiction determination, on the other hand, would indeed compound the jurisdictional inquiry. The reasonableness factors identified in *Asahi* include "the burden on the defendant," "the interests of the forum State," "the plaintiff's interest in obtaining relief," "the interstate judicial system's interest in obtaining the

C

Finally, the transnational context of this dispute bears attention. The Court of Appeals emphasized, as supportive of the exercise of general jurisdiction, plaintiffs' assertion of claims under the Alien Tort Statute (ATS) and the Torture Victim Protection Act of 1991 (TVPA). Recent decisions of this Court, however, have rendered plaintiffs' ATS and TVPA claims infirm. See *Kiobel v. Royal Dutch Petroleum Co.,* 133 S.Ct. 1659, 1669, 185 L.Ed.2d 671 (2013) (presumption against extraterritorial application controls claims under the ATS); *Mohamad v. Palestinian Authority,* 132 S.Ct. 1702, 1705, 182 L.Ed.2d 720 (2012) (only natural persons are subject to liability under the TVPA).

The Ninth Circuit, moreover, paid little heed to the risks to international comity its expansive view of general jurisdiction posed. Other nations do not share the uninhibited approach to personal jurisdiction advanced by the Court of Appeals in this case. In the European Union, for example, a corporation may generally be sued in the nation in which it is "domiciled," a term defined to refer only to the location of the corporation's "statutory seat," "central administration," or "principal place of business." European Parliament and Council Reg. 1215/2012, Arts. 4(1), and 63(1), 2012 O.J. (L. 351) 7, 18. See also *id.,* Art. 7(5), 2012 O.J. 7 (as to "a dispute *arising out of the operations of a branch, agency or other establishment,*" a corporation may be sued "in the courts for the place where the branch, agency or other establishment is situated" (emphasis added)). The Solicitor General informs us, in this regard, that "foreign governments' objections to some domestic courts' expansive views of general jurisdiction have in the past impeded negotiations of international agreements on the reciprocal recognition and enforcement of judgments." U.S. Brief 2. See also U.S. Brief 2 (expressing concern that unpredictable applications of general jurisdiction based on activities of U.S.-based subsidiaries could discourage foreign investor). Considerations of international rapport thus reinforce our determination that subjecting Daimler to the general jurisdiction of courts in California would not accord with the "fair play and substantial justice" due process demands. *International Shoe.*

For the reasons stated, the judgment of the United States Court of Appeals for the Ninth Circuit is

Reversed.

JUSTICE SOTOMAYOR, concurring in the judgment.

I agree with the Court's conclusion that the Due Process Clause prohibits the exercise of personal jurisdiction over Daimler in light of the unique circumstances of this case. I concur only in the judgment, however, because I cannot agree with the path the Court takes to arrive at that result.

The Court acknowledges that Mercedes–Benz USA, LLC (MBUSA),

---

most efficient resolution of controversies," "the shared interest of the several States in furthering fundamental substantive social policies," and, in the international context, "the procedural and substantive policies of other *nations* whose interests are affected by the assertion of jurisdiction." Imposing such a checklist in cases of general jurisdiction would hardly promote the efficient disposition of an issue that should be resolved expeditiously at the outset of litigation.

Daimler's wholly owned subsidiary, has considerable contacts with California. It has multiple facilities in the State, including a regional headquarters. Each year, it distributes in California tens of thousands of cars, the sale of which generated billions of dollars in the year this suit was brought. And it provides service and sales support to customers throughout the State. Daimler has conceded that California courts may exercise general jurisdiction over MBUSA on the basis of these contacts, and the Court assumes that MBUSA's contacts may be attributed to Daimler for the purpose of deciding whether Daimler is also subject to general jurisdiction.

Are these contacts sufficient to permit the exercise of general jurisdiction over Daimler? The Court holds that they are not, for a reason wholly foreign to our due process jurisprudence. The problem, the Court says, is not that Daimler's contacts with California are too few, but that its contacts with other forums are too many. In other words, the Court does not dispute that the presence of multiple offices, the direct distribution of thousands of products accounting for billions of dollars in sales, and continuous interaction with customers throughout a State would be enough to support the exercise of general jurisdiction over some businesses. Daimler is just not one of those businesses, the Court concludes, because its California contacts must be viewed in the context of its extensive "nationwide and worldwide" operations. *Ante,* at n. 20. In recent years, Americans have grown accustomed to the concept of multinational corporations that are supposedly "too big to fail"; today the Court deems Daimler "too big for general jurisdiction."

The Court's conclusion is wrong as a matter of both process and substance. As to process, the Court decides this case on a ground that was neither argued nor passed on below, and that Daimler raised for the first time in a footnote to its brief. As to substance, the Court's focus on Daimler's operations outside of California ignores the lodestar of our personal jurisdiction jurisprudence: A State may subject a defendant to the burden of suit if the defendant has sufficiently taken advantage of the State's laws and protections through its contacts in the State; whether the defendant has contacts elsewhere is immaterial.

Regrettably, these errors are unforced. The Court can and should decide this case on the far simpler ground that, no matter how extensive Daimler's contacts with California, that State's exercise of jurisdiction would be unreasonable given that the case involves foreign plaintiffs suing a foreign defendant based on foreign conduct, and given that a more appropriate forum is available. Because I would reverse the judgment below on this ground, I concur in the judgment only.I

I begin with the point on which the majority and I agree: The Ninth Circuit's decision should be reversed.

Our personal jurisdiction precedents call for a two-part analysis. The contacts prong asks whether the defendant has sufficient contacts with the forum State to support personal jurisdiction; the reasonableness prong asks whether the exercise of jurisdiction would be unreasonable under the circumstances. *Burger King*. As the majority points out, all of the cases in which we have applied the reasonableness prong have involved specific as opposed to general jurisdiction.

Whether the reasonableness prong should apply in the general jurisdiction context is therefore a question we have never decided,[1] and it is one on which I can appreciate the arguments on both sides. But it would be imprudent to decide that question in this case given that respondents have failed to argue against the application of the reasonableness prong during the entire 8–year history of this litigation. As a result, I would decide this case under the reasonableness prong without foreclosing future consideration of whether that prong should be limited to the specific jurisdiction context.[2]

We identified the factors that bear on reasonableness in *Asahi*: "the burden on the defendant, the interests of the forum State," "the plaintiff's interest in obtaining relief" in the forum State, and the interests of other sovereigns in resolving the dispute. We held in *Asahi* that it would be "unreasonable and unfair" for a California court to exercise jurisdiction over a claim between a Taiwanese plaintiff and a Japanese defendant that arose out of a transaction in Taiwan, particularly where the Taiwanese plaintiff had not shown that it would be more convenient to litigate in California than in Taiwan or Japan.

The same considerations resolve this case. It involves Argentine plaintiffs suing a German defendant for conduct that took place in Argentina. Like the plaintiffs in *Asahi,* respondents have failed to show that it would be more convenient to litigate in California than in Germany, a sovereign with a far greater interest in resolving the dispute. *Asahi* thus makes clear that it would be unreasonable for a court in California to subject Daimler to its jurisdiction.

II

The majority evidently agrees that, if the reasonableness prong were to apply, it would be unreasonable for California courts to exercise jurisdiction over Daimler in this case. See *ante* (noting that it would be "exorbitant" for California courts to exercise general jurisdiction over Daimler, a German defendant, in this "Argentina-rooted case" brought by "foreign plaintiffs"). But instead of resolving the case on this uncontroversial basis, the majority reaches out to decide it on a ground neither argued nor decided below.[3]

---

[1] The Courts of Appeals have uniformly held that the reasonableness prong does in fact apply in the general jurisdiction context. See *Metropolitan Life Ins. Co. v. Robertson–Ceco Corp.*, 84 F.3d 560, 573 (C.A.2 1996) ("[E]very circuit that has considered the question has held, implicitly or explicitly, that the reasonableness inquiry is applicable to *all* questions of personal jurisdiction, general or specific") * * *. Without the benefit of a single page of briefing on the issue, the majority casually adds each of these cases to the mounting list of decisions jettisoned as a consequence of today's ruling. See *ante,* at n. 8.

[2] While our decisions rejecting the exercise of personal jurisdiction have typically done so under the minimum-contacts prong, we have never required that prong to be decided first. See *Asahi* (Stevens, J., concurring in part and concurring in judgment) (rejecting personal jurisdiction under the reasonableness prong and declining to consider the minimum-contacts prong because doing so would not be "necessary"). And although the majority frets that deciding this case on the reasonableness ground would be "a resolution fit for this day and case only," I do not understand our constitutional duty to require otherwise.

[3] The majority appears to suggest that Daimler may have presented the argument in its petition for rehearing en banc before the Ninth Circuit. See *ante* (stating that Daimler "urg[ed] that the exercise of personal jurisdiction ... could not be reconciled with this Court's decision in *Goodyear*"). But Daimler's petition for rehearing did not argue what the Court holds today. The

We generally do not pass on arguments that lower courts have not addressed. After all, we are a court of review, not of first view. This principle carries even greater force where the argument at issue was never pressed below. Yet the majority disregards this principle, basing its decision on an argument raised for the first time in a footnote of Daimler's merits brief before this Court.

The majority's decision is troubling all the more because the parties were not asked to brief this issue. We granted certiorari on the question "whether it violates due process for a court to exercise general personal jurisdiction over a foreign corporation based solely on the fact that an indirect corporate subsidiary performs services on behalf of the defendant in the forum State." At no point in Daimler's petition for certiorari did the company contend that, even if this attribution question were decided against it, its contacts in California would still be insufficient to support general jurisdiction. The parties' merits briefs accordingly focused on the attribution-of-contacts question, addressing the reasonableness inquiry (which had been litigated and decided below) in most of the space that remained.

In bypassing the question on which we granted certiorari to decide an issue not litigated below, the Court leaves respondents without an unclouded opportunity to air the issue the Court today decides against them. Doing so does "not reflect well on the processes of the Court." Redrup v. New York, 386 U.S. 767, 772, 87 S.Ct. 1414, 18 L.Ed.2d 515 (1967) (Harlan, J., dissenting)). And by resolving a complex and fact-intensive question without the benefit of full briefing, the Court invites the error into which it has fallen.

The relevant facts are undeveloped because Daimler conceded at the start of this litigation that MBUSA is subject to general jurisdiction based on its California contacts. We therefore do not know the full extent of those contacts, though what little we do know suggests that Daimler was wise to concede what it did. MBUSA imports more than 200,000 vehicles into the United States and distributes many of them to independent dealerships in California, where they are sold. MBUSA's California sales account for 2.4% of Daimler's worldwide sales, which were $192 billion in 2004. And 2.4% of $192 billion is $4.6 billion, a considerable sum by any measure. MBUSA also has multiple offices and facilities in California, including a regional headquarters.

But the record does not answer a number of other important questions. Are any of Daimler's key files maintained in MBUSA's California offices? How many employees work in those offices? Do those employees make important strategic decisions or oversee in any manner Daimler's activities? These questions could well affect whether Daimler is subject to general jurisdiction. After all, this Court upheld the exercise of general jurisdiction in *Perkins* — which the majority refers to as a "textbook case" of general jurisdiction — on the basis that the foreign defendant maintained an office in Ohio, kept corporate

---

Court holds that Daimler's California contacts would be insufficient for general jurisdiction even assuming that MBUSA's contacts may be attributed to Daimler. Daimler's rehearing petition made a distinct argument — that attribution of MBUSA's contacts should not be permitted under an agency theory because doing so would raise significant constitutional concerns under *Goodyear*.

files there, and oversaw the company's activities from the State. California-based MBUSA employees may well have done similar things on Daimler's behalf.[5] But because the Court decides the issue without a developed record, we will never know.

III

While the majority's decisional process is problematic enough, I fear that process leads it to an even more troubling result.

A

Until today, our precedents had established a straightforward test for general jurisdiction: Does the defendant have "continuous corporate operations within a state" that are "so substantial and of such a nature as to justify suit against it on causes of action arising from dealings entirely distinct from those activities"? *International Shoe*; see also *Helicopteros* (asking whether defendant had "continuous and systematic general business contacts").[6] In every case where we have applied this test, we have focused solely on the magnitude of the defendant's in-state contacts, not the relative magnitude of those contacts in comparison to the defendant's contacts with other States.

In *Perkins*, for example, we found an Ohio court's exercise of general jurisdiction permissible where the president of the foreign defendant "maintained an office," "drew and distributed ... salary checks," used "two active bank accounts," "supervised ... the rehabilitation of the corporation's properties in the Philippines," and held "directors' meetings," in Ohio. At no point did we attempt to catalog the company's contacts in forums other than Ohio or to compare them with its Ohio contacts. If anything, we intimated that the defendant's Ohio contacts were *not* substantial in comparison to its contacts elsewhere (noting that the defendant's Ohio contacts, while "continuous and systematic," were but a "limited ... part of its general business").[7]

---

[5] To be sure, many of Daimler's key management decisions are undoubtedly made by employees outside California. But the same was true in *Perkins* (management decisions made by the company's chief of staff in Manila and a purchasing agent in California).

[6] While *Helicopteros* formulated the general jurisdiction inquiry as asking whether a foreign defendant possesses "continuous and systematic general business contacts," the majority correctly notes that International Shoe used the phrase "continuous and systematic" in the context of discussing specific jurisdiction. But the majority recognizes that *International Shoe* separately described the type of contacts needed for general jurisdiction as "continuous corporate operations" that are "so substantial" as to justify suit on unrelated causes of action. It is unclear why our precedents departed from *International Shoe*'s "continuous and substantial" formulation in favor of the "continuous and systematic" formulation, but the majority does not contend — nor do I perceive — that there is a material difference between the two.

[7] The majority suggests that I misinterpret language in *Perkins* that I do not even cite. Ante, at n. 8. The majority is quite correct that it has found a sentence in *Perkins* that does not address whether most of the Philippine corporation's activities took place outside of Ohio. See ante, at n. 8 (noting that *Perkins* described the company's "wartime activities" as "necessarily limited"). That is why I did not mention it. I instead rely on a sentence in *Perkins'* opening paragraph: "The [Philippine] corporation has been carrying on in Ohio a continuous and systematic, but limited, part of its general business." That sentence obviously does convey that most of the corporation's activities occurred in "places other than Ohio," ante, at n. 8. This is not surprising given that the company's Ohio contacts involved a single officer working from a home office, while its non-

We engaged in the same inquiry in *Helicopteros*. There, we held that a Colombian corporation was not subject to general jurisdiction in Texas simply because it occasionally sent its employees into the State, accepted checks drawn on a Texas bank, and purchased equipment and services from a Texas company. In no sense did our analysis turn on the extent of the company's operations beyond Texas.

Most recently, in *Goodyear*, our analysis again focused on the defendant's in-state contacts. *Goodyear* involved a suit against foreign tire manufacturers by North Carolina residents whose children had died in a bus accident in France. We held that North Carolina courts could not exercise general jurisdiction over the foreign defendants. Just as in *Perkins* and *Helicopteros,* our opinion in *Goodyear* did not identify the defendants' contacts outside of the forum State, but focused instead on the defendants' lack of offices, employees, direct sales, and business operations within the State.

This approach follows from the touchstone principle of due process in this field, the concept of reciprocal fairness. When a corporation chooses to invoke the benefits and protections of a State in which it operates, the State acquires the authority to subject the company to suit in its courts. See *International Shoe*. The majority's focus on the extent of a corporate defendant's out-of-forum contacts is untethered from this rationale. After all, the degree to which a company intentionally benefits from a forum State depends on its interactions with that State, not its interactions elsewhere. An article on which the majority relies (and on which *Goodyear* relied as well) expresses the point well: "We should not treat defendants as less amenable to suit merely because they carry on more substantial business in other states.... [T]he amount of activity elsewhere seems virtually irrelevant to ... the imposition of general jurisdiction over a defendant." Brilmayer et al., A General Look at General Jurisdiction, 66 Texas L.Rev. 721, 742 (1988).

Had the majority applied our settled approach, it would have had little trouble concluding that Daimler's California contacts rise to the requisite level, given the majority's assumption that MBUSA's contacts may be attributed to Daimler and given Daimler's concession that those contacts render MBUSA "at home" in California. Our cases have long stated the rule that a defendant's contacts with a forum State must be continuous, substantial, and systematic in order for the defendant to be subject to that State's general jurisdiction. We offered additional guidance in *Goodyear*, adding the phrase "essentially at home" to our prior formulation of the rule. We used the phrase "at home" to signify that in order for an out-of-state defendant to be subject to general jurisdiction, its continuous and substantial contacts with a forum State must be akin to those of a local enterprise that actually is "at home" in the State.[8]

Ohio contacts included significant mining properties and machinery operated throughout the Philippines, Philippine employees (including a chief of staff), a purchasing agent based in California, and board of directors meetings held in Washington, New York, and San Francisco.

[8] The majority views the phrase "at home" as serving a different purpose — that of requiring a comparison between a defendant's in-state and out-of-state contacts. That cannot be the correct understanding though, because among other things it would cast grave doubt on *Perkins* — a case

Under this standard, Daimler's concession that MBUSA is subject to general jurisdiction in California (a concession the Court accepts) should be dispositive. For if MBUSA's California contacts are so substantial and the resulting benefits to MBUSA so significant as to make MBUSA "at home" in California, the same must be true of Daimler when MBUSA's contacts and benefits are viewed as its own. Indeed, until a footnote in its brief before this Court, even Daimler did not dispute this conclusion for eight years of the litigation.

B

The majority today concludes otherwise. Referring to the "continuous and systematic" contacts inquiry that has been taught to generations of first-year law students as "unacceptably grasping," the majority announces the new rule that in order for a foreign defendant to be subject to general jurisdiction, it must not only possess continuous and systematic contacts with a forum State, but those contacts must also surpass some unspecified level when viewed in comparison to the company's "nationwide and worldwide" activities. *Ante*, at n. 20.[9]

Neither of the majority's two rationales for this proportionality requirement is persuasive. First, the majority suggests that its approach is necessary for the sake of predictability. Permitting general jurisdiction in every State where a corporation has continuous and substantial contacts, the majority asserts, would "scarcely permit out-of-state defendants 'to structure their primary conduct with some minimum assurance as to where that conduct will and will not render them liable to suit." (quoting *Burger King*). But there is nothing unpredictable about a

---

that *Goodyear* pointed to as an exemplar of general jurisdiction. For if *Perkins* had applied the majority's newly minted proportionality test, it would have come out the other way.

The majority apparently thinks that the Philippine corporate defendant in *Perkins* did not have meaningful operations in places other than Ohio. But one cannot get past the second sentence of *Perkins* before realizing that is wrong. That sentence reads: "The corporation has been carrying on in Ohio a continuous and systematic, but limited, part of its general business." Indeed, the facts of the case set forth by the Ohio Court of Appeals show just how "limited" the company's Ohio contacts — which included a single officer keeping files and managing affairs from his Ohio home office — were in comparison with its "general business" operations elsewhere. By the time the suit was commenced, the company had resumed its considerable mining operations in the Philippines, rebuilding its properties there and purchasing machinery, supplies and equipment. Moreover, the company employed key managers in other forums, including a purchasing agent in San Francisco and a chief of staff in the Philippines. The San Francisco purchasing agent negotiated the purchase of the company's machinery and supplies on the direction of the Company's Chief of Staff in Manila, a fact that squarely refutes the majority's assertion that "[a]ll of Benguet's activities were directed by the company's president from within Ohio." And the vast majority of the company's board of directors meetings took place outside Ohio, in locations such as Washington, New York, and San Francisco.

In light of these facts, it is all but impossible to reconcile the result in *Perkins* with the proportionality test the majority announces today. *Goodyear*'s use of the phrase "at home" is thus better understood to require the same general jurisdiction inquiry that *Perkins* required: An out-of-state business must have the kind of continuous and substantial in-state presence that a parallel local company would have.

[9] I accept at face value the majority's declaration that general jurisdiction is not limited to a corporation's place of incorporation and principal place of business * * *. Were that not so, our analysis of the defendants' in-state contacts in *Perkins*, *Helicopteros*, and *Goodyear* would have been irrelevant, as none of the defendants in those cases was sued in its place of incorporation or principal place of business.

rule that instructs multinational corporations that if they engage in continuous and substantial contacts with more than one State, they will be subject to general jurisdiction in each one. The majority may not favor that rule as a matter of policy, but such disagreement does not render an otherwise routine test unpredictable.

Nor is the majority's proportionality inquiry any more predictable than the approach it rejects. If anything, the majority's approach injects an additional layer of uncertainty because a corporate defendant must now try to foretell a court's analysis as to both the sufficiency of its contacts with the forum State itself, as well as the relative sufficiency of those contacts in light of the company's operations elsewhere. Moreover, the majority does not even try to explain just how extensive the company's in-state contacts must be in the context of its global operations in order for general jurisdiction to be proper.

The majority's approach will also lead to greater unpredictability by radically expanding the scope of jurisdictional discovery. Rather than ascertaining the extent of a corporate defendant's forum-state contacts alone, courts will now have to identify the extent of a company's contacts in every other forum where it does business in order to compare them against the company's in-state contacts. That considerable burden runs headlong into the majority's recitation of the familiar principle that "simple jurisdictional rules ... promote greater predictability." Hertz Corp. v. Friend, 559 U.S. 77, 94, 130 S.Ct. 1181, 175 L.Ed.2d 1029 (2010)).

Absent the predictability rationale, the majority's sole remaining justification for its proportionality approach is its unadorned concern for the consequences. "If Daimler's California activities sufficed to allow adjudication of this Argentina-rooted case in California," the majority laments, "the same global reach would presumably be available in every other State in which MBUSA's sales are sizable."

The majority characterizes this result as "exorbitant," but in reality it is an inevitable consequence of the rule of due process we set forth nearly 70 years ago, that there are "instances in which [a company's] continuous corporate operations within a state" are "so substantial and of such a nature as to justify suit against it on causes of action arising from dealings entirely distinct from those activities." *International Shoe*. In the era of *International Shoe,* it was rare for a corporation to have such substantial nationwide contacts that it would be subject to general jurisdiction in a large number of States. Today, that circumstance is less rare. But that is as it should be. What has changed since *International Shoe* is not the due process principle of fundamental fairness but rather the nature of the global economy. Just as it was fair to say in the 1940's that an out-of-state company could enjoy the benefits of a forum State enough to make it "essentially at home" in the State, it is fair to say today that a multinational conglomerate can enjoy such extensive benefits in multiple forum States that it is "essentially at home" in each one.

In any event, to the extent the majority is concerned with the modern-day consequences of *International Shoe*'s conception of personal jurisdiction, there remain other judicial doctrines available to mitigate any resulting unfairness to large corporate defendants. Here, for instance, the reasonableness prong may afford petitioner relief. In other cases, a defendant can assert the doctrine of *forum non conveniens* if a given State is a highly inconvenient place to litigate a dispute. See Gulf Oil Corp. v. Gilbert, 330 U.S. 501, 67 S.Ct. 839, 91 L.Ed. 1055 (1947). In still other cases, the federal change of venue statute can provide protection. See 28 U.S.C. § 1404(a). And to the degree that the majority worries these doctrines are not enough to protect the economic interests of multinational businesses (or that our longstanding approach to general jurisdiction poses "risks to international comity,"), the task of weighing those policy concerns belongs ultimately to legislators, who may amend state and federal long-arm statutes in accordance with the democratic process. Unfortunately, the majority short circuits that process by enshrining today's narrow rule of general jurisdiction as a matter of constitutional law.

C

The majority's concern for the consequences of its decision should have led it the other way, because the rule that it adopts will produce deep injustice in at least four respects.

First, the majority's approach unduly curtails the States' sovereign authority to adjudicate disputes against corporate defendants who have engaged in continuous and substantial business operations within their boundaries.[10] The majority docs not dispute that a State can exercise general jurisdiction where a corporate defendant has its corporate headquarters, and hence its principal place of business within the State. Yet it never explains why the State should lose that power when, as is increasingly common, a corporation divides its command and coordinating functions among officers who work at several different locations. Suppose a company divides its management functions equally among three offices in different States, with one office nominally deemed the company's corporate headquarters. If the State where the headquarters is located can exercise general jurisdiction, why should the other two States be constitutionally forbidden to do the same? Indeed, under the majority's approach, the result would be unchanged even if the company has substantial operations within the latter two States (and even if the company has no sales or other business operations in the first State). Put simply, the majority's rule defines the Due Process Clause so narrowly and arbitrarily as to contravene the States' sovereign prerogative to subject to judgment defendants who have manifested an unqualified "intention to benefit from and thus an intention to submit to the[ir] laws," *J. McIntyre,*(plurality opinion).

Second, the proportionality approach will treat small businesses unfairly in comparison to national and multinational conglomerates. Whereas a larger company will often be immunized from general jurisdiction in a State on

---

[10] States will of course continue to exercise specific jurisdiction in many cases, but we have never held that to be the outer limit of the States' authority under the Due Process Clause. That is because the two forms of jurisdiction address different concerns. Whereas specific jurisdiction focuses on the relationship between a defendant's challenged conduct and the forum State, general jurisdiction focuses on the defendant's substantial presence in the State irrespective of the location of the challenged conduct.

account of its extensive contacts outside the forum, a small business will not be. For instance, the majority holds today that Daimler is not subject to general jurisdiction in California despite its multiple offices, continuous operations, and billions of dollars' worth of sales there. But imagine a small business that manufactures luxury vehicles principally targeting the California market and that has substantially all of its sales and operations in the State — even though those sales and operations may amount to one-thousandth of Daimler's. Under the majority's rule, that small business will be subject to suit in California on any cause of action involving any of its activities anywhere in the world, while its far more pervasive competitor, Daimler, will not be. That will be so even if the small business incorporates and sets up its headquarters elsewhere (as Daimler does), since the small business' California sales and operations would still predominate when "apprais[ed]" in proportion to its minimal "nationwide and worldwide" operations.

Third, the majority's approach creates the incongruous result that an individual defendant whose only contact with a forum State is a one-time visit will be subject to general jurisdiction if served with process during that visit, *Burnham v. Superior Court of Cal., County of Marin,* 495 U.S. 604, 110 S.Ct. 2105, 109 L.Ed.2d 631 (1990), but a large corporation that owns property, employs workers, and does billions of dollars' worth of business in the State will not be, simply because the corporation has similar contacts elsewhere (though the visiting individual surely does as well).

Finally, it should be obvious that the ultimate effect of the majority's approach will be to shift the risk of loss from multinational corporations to the individuals harmed by their actions. Under the majority's rule, for example, a parent whose child is maimed due to the negligence of a foreign hotel owned by a multinational conglomerate will be unable to hold the hotel to account in a single U.S. court, even if the hotel company has a massive presence in multiple States. Similarly, a U.S. business that enters into a contract in a foreign country to sell its products to a multinational company there may be unable to seek relief in any U.S. court if the multinational company breaches the contract, even if that company has considerable operations in numerous U.S. forums.[12] Indeed, the majority's approach would preclude the plaintiffs in these examples from seeking recourse anywhere in the United States even if no other judicial system was available to provide relief. I cannot agree with the majority's conclusion that the Due Process Clause requires these results.

The Court rules against respondents today on a ground that no court has considered in the history of this case, that this Court did not grant certiorari to decide, and that Daimler raised only in a footnote of its brief. In doing so, the Court adopts a new rule of constitutional law that is unmoored from decades of precedent. Because I would reverse the Ninth Circuit's decision on the narrower

---

[12] The present case and the examples posited involve foreign corporate defendants, but the principle announced by the majority would apply equally to preclude general jurisdiction over a U.S. company that is incorporated and has its principal place of business in another U.S. State. Under the majority's rule, for example, a General Motors autoworker who retires to Florida would be unable to sue GM in that State for disabilities that develop from the retiree's labor at a Michigan parts plant, even though GM undertakes considerable business operations in Florida.

ground that the exercise of jurisdiction over Daimler would be unreasonable in any event, I respectfully concur in the judgment only.

NOTES AND PROBLEMS FOR DISCUSSION

1. After *assuming* that (1) the defendant's subsidiary's contacts with the forum state should be imputed to the defendant, and (2) that the subsidiary would be viewed as "at home" in the forum state, the majority (unlike Justice Sotomayor), nevertheless concluded that the defendant itself was not "at home" in the forum state and, therefore, could not be subject to general jurisdiction in that state. Justice Sotomayor, on the other hand, concluded that these two base assumptions led ineluctably to the conclusion that the defendant was "at home" in the forum state. Nevertheless, she agreed with the majority's bottom line that it was improper for California to exercise general jurisdiction over this foreign defendant with respect to claims brought by foreign plaintiffs arising out of events that occurred outside of the United States, by applying the "reasonableness" analysis initially articulated in *Volkswagen*.

(a) Who has the better of this argument?

(b) In making the assessment above, were you influenced by the differing positions taken by the majority and Justice Sotomayor as to whether or not this issue (whether general jurisdiction would exist over a defendant whose subsidiary was at home in the forum state and whose activities were attributed to it) was even properly before the Court in light of the proceedings below and the briefs filed with the Court?

2. One of the lynchpins of the Court's conclusion that the defendant was not "at home" in the forum state was its ruling that the "at home" calculation required a comparative assessment of the magnitude and importance of the defendant's forum-based contacts relative to the totality of its worldwide activities. Justice Sotomayor, on the other hand, insisted that all prior precedent focused solely on the extent of a defendant's relationship with the forum state and not any consideration of its out-of-forum activities. Who has the better of this one? And were you surprised that this most significant portion of the majority's opinion was relegated to (hidden in?) a footnote (i.e., footnote 8)?

3. The majority acknowledged in a footnote that the definition of "at home" was not necessarily limited, for a corporate defendant, to the state of its incorporation and principle place of business. But other than stating that this was available in "an exceptional case" (citing *Perkins* as an example thereof) and summarily concluding this defendant could not fit within this limited exception, the Court expressly declined to elaborate on the factors that would support such a limited exception. Does the citation to *Perkins*, in light of the majority's discussion of that case in its footnote 8, shed meaningful light on this question?

4. The majority and Justice Sotomayor also disagreed on the continued viability of the "reasonableness" component of Due Process-based jurisdictional analysis initially articulated in *Volkswagen*. The majority forcefully announced that it was abandoning this second component of due process analysis in cases involving general jurisdiction on the ground that all reasonableness concerns were necessarily resolved by a finding that the defendant was "at home" in the forum state. Justice Sotomayor, on the other hand, not only disagreed with this view, but based her ultimate judgment that the defendant (which she found had sufficient connection to the forum state to pass the *Shoe* "contacts" standard) could not be subjected to general jurisdiction based on her application of the reasonableness standard to the instant facts. Is the majority's renunciation of the reasonableness standard in general jurisdiction cases likely to have any meaningful impact on the way these cases are decided? Apparently Justice Sotomayor thought so. What do you think?

SECTION C. POWER OVER PROPERTY

As you will recall from the Supreme Court's decision in *Pennoyer*, the adjudicative authority enjoyed by a state court traditionally was predicated upon the presence of either the defendant or the defendant's property within that state's territory. The immediately preceding collection of cases, however, revealed how that notion evolved over the past century. The following materials address issues related particularly to the exercise of jurisdiction based on the presence of property within the forum.

Historically, such jurisdiction has been classified as either *in rem* or *quasi in rem*. To recapitulate what was previously discussed in Note 5 following *Pennoyer*, each of these concepts is an amalgam of two related components: (1) the objective of the underlying proceeding, and (2) the source or "anchor" for the exercise of jurisdiction. In instances where the court is exercising *in rem* or *quasi in rem* jurisdiction (commonly referred to as *in rem* or *quasi in rem* proceedings), the "anchor" for both forms of personal jurisdiction is the presence of property within the forum state. Consequently, opinions in such cases typically contain language indicating that the court proceeded against the property itself, and that the property was brought within the court's physical control by attachment or some other form of seizure.

What distinguishes *in rem* from *quasi in rem* jurisdiction, however, is the nature or objective of the underlying proceeding. In a prototypical (sometimes referred to as "pure") *in rem* proceeding, such as an eminent domain or admiralty proceeding, the court is said to adjudicate the claims of the entire world to the property (real or personal) that serves as the anchor for obtaining jurisdiction. This means that the court's adjudication is binding on everyone in the world, irrespective of whether they had actual notice of the action.

Quasi in rem jurisdiction, on the other hand, comes in two distinct flavors. One of these refers to those situations, such as a quiet title action, in which the court seeks to adjudicate the competing claims of a discrete, limited number of claimants to the property that is the anchor for jurisdiction. The other variety of *quasi in rem* proceeding combines the characteristics of both *in personam* and *in rem* proceedings. Here (as, for example, in John Mitchell's suit for attorney fees in the Pennoyer saga) the court is seeking to adjudicate a personal claim (the *in personam* trait) against a defendant that is totally unrelated to the property whose presence within the forum serves as the anchor (the *in rem* trait) for jurisdiction. Jurisdiction in these proceedings is typically asserted over the property because the defendant is beyond the territorial or other limits of the court's *in personam* jurisdiction. However, in light of the post-*Pennoyer* metamorphosis of the limits on *in personam* jurisdiction, and the *in personam*-like quality of this latter form of *quasi in rem* jurisdiction, should *Pennoyer's* now discarded territorial barrier still apply to these *quasi in rem* proceedings? After all, if the defendant's physical presence within the forum state is no longer required to invoke *in personam* jurisdiction, is there any reason to require the *res* to be located within the forum in order to exercise this type of *quasi in rem* jurisdiction? Alternatively, should either the transient or constructive presence of the defendant's property in the forum state continue to provide a sufficient basis *per se* for the exercise of jurisdiction over it?

Where the location of the *res* continues to play some role in determining the validity of exercising jurisdiction over property, the court naturally must determine the situs of that property. Although this issue is rarely troublesome when the case involves real property, it can become more vexing when, for example, *quasi in rem* jurisdiction is sought by attaching either movable or intangible forms of personal property. For example, what is the situs of a ship, or a bank account, or ten shares of Microsoft stock?

The difficulty in assigning a location to intangible property such as a debt, and the concomitant futility of continuing to rely on the fictive presence of such property as the predicate for exercising *quasi in rem* jurisdiction was amply demonstrated in the famous (though factually convoluted) turn-of-the-century case of HARRIS v. BALK, 198 U.S. 215, 25 S.Ct. 625, 49 L.Ed.2d 1023 (1905). Jacob Epstein an importer from Baltimore, regularly sold merchandise to one Balk, a retailer from North Carolina. Epstein filed an action against Balk in a Maryland court, alleging that Balk owed him $344 as the unpaid balance for four shipments of goods. Meanwhile, Isaac Harris, another dry goods merchant from Balk's home town in North Carolina, owed Balk $180, the result of several loans made to Harris by Balk. While Harris was in Baltimore on a business trip, the sheriff served him with a writ of garnishment pursuant to Epstein's request. Harris did not contest his debt to Balk and paid the $180 to Epstein's North Carolina attorney. Shortly after returning to North Carolina, Harris learned that he had been sued by Balk on the $180 debt. Naturally, Harris claimed that his payment of the debt to Epstein relieved him of his obligation to Balk. Balk, on the other hand, was equally emphatic in insisting that the North Carolina court not give full faith and credit to the Maryland proceeding because the Maryland court lacked jurisdiction over him to adjudicate his obligation to Epstein.

The Supreme Court, however, rejected Balk's argument, held that North Carolina was bound to enforce the Maryland judgment, and ruled, therefore, that Harris' payment to Epstein discharged Harris' debt to Balk. Although, the Court reasoned, it was certainly true that Balk could not fall within the Maryland court's *in personam* jurisdiction, since his property (the debt owed to him by Harris) was located in Maryland and had been properly and timely seized in that state, Balk was subject to Maryland's exercise of *quasi in rem* jurisdiction. Notwithstanding the fact that this debt had been created in North Carolina, the

Court explained, "[t]he obligation of the debtor to pay his debt clings to and accompanies him wherever he goes." Consequently, since Balk's debtor (Harris) was in Maryland, so was the debt. And even though the Court's conclusion was based on the premise that Balk could have sued Harris on the debt in Maryland, the effect of this statement was to significantly expand the concept of "presence" of property for *quasi in rem* jurisdiction purposes.

The ruling in *Harris*, while perhaps justifiable as an effort to avoid subjecting Harris to double payment of his debt to Balk, generated a significant amount of criticism and focused attention on the artificiality of basing jurisdiction over a defendant merely on the ephemeral situs of her intangible property. More than seventy years later, the Court revisited this issue in the following case.

Shaffer v. Heitner

Supreme Court of the United States, 1977.
433 U.S. 186, 97 S.Ct. 2569, 53 L.Ed.2d 683.

MR. JUSTICE MARSHALL delivered the opinion of the Court.

The controversy in this case concerns the constitutionality of a Delaware statute that allows a court of that State to take jurisdiction of a lawsuit by sequestering any property of the defendant that happens to be located in Delaware. Appellants contend that the sequestration statute as applied in this case violates the Due Process Clause of the Fourteenth Amendment * * * because it permits the state courts to exercise jurisdiction despite the absence of sufficient contacts among the defendants, the litigation, and the State of Delaware * * *.

I

Appellee Heitner, a nonresident of Delaware, is the owner of one share of stock in the Greyhound Corp., a business incorporated under the laws of Delaware with its principal place of business in Phoenix, Ariz. On May 22, 1974, he filed a shareholder's derivative suit[*] in the Court of Chancery for New Castle County, Del., in which he named as defendants Greyhound, its wholly owned subsidiary Greyhound Lines, Inc., and 28 present or former officers or directors of one or both of the corporations. In essence, Heitner alleged that the individual defendants had violated their duties to Greyhound by causing it and its subsidiary to engage in actions that resulted in the corporations being held liable for substantial damages in a private antitrust suit and a large fine in a criminal contempt action. The activities which led to these penalties took place in Oregon.

Simultaneously with his complaint, Heitner filed a motion for an order of sequestration of the Delaware property of the individual defendants pursuant to

---

[*][A stockholder's derivative action is a claim brought by a shareholder on the corporation's behalf that the corporation has failed to assert. Typically, as herein, the defendant is a corporate officer or director charged with wrongdoing in his or her official capacity. — eds.]

Del.Code Ann., Tit. 10, §366 (1975).[4] This motion was accompanied by a supporting affidavit of counsel which stated that the individual defendants were nonresidents of Delaware. The affidavit identified the property to be sequestered as "common stock * * * of the Defendant Greyhound Corporation, a Delaware corporation, as well as all options * * * to purchase stock issued to said individual Defendants * * *."

The requested sequestration order was signed the day the motion was filed. Pursuant to that order, the sequestrator "seized" approximately 82,000 shares of Greyhound common stock belonging to 19 of the defendants, and options belonging to another 2 defendants. These seizures were accomplished by placing "stop transfer" orders or their equivalents on the books of the Greyhound Corp. So far as the record shows, none of the certificates representing the seized property was physically present in Delaware. The stock was considered to be in Delaware, and so subject to seizure, by virtue of Del.Code Ann., Tit. 8, §169 (1975), which makes Delaware the situs of ownership of all stock in Delaware corporations.

All 28 defendants were notified of the initiation of the suit by certified mail directed to their last known addresses and by publication in a New Castle County newspaper. The 21 defendants whose property was seized (hereafter referred to as appellants) responded by entering a special appearance for the purpose of moving to quash service of process and to vacate the sequestration order. They contended that * * * under the rule of International Shoe, they did not have sufficient contacts with Delaware to sustain the jurisdiction of that State's courts.

The Court of Chancery rejected these arguments in a letter opinion * * *.

* * *

On appeal, the Delaware Supreme Court affirmed the judgment of the Court of Chancery.

---

[4] Section 366 provides:

"(a) If it appears in any complaint filed in the Court of Chancery that the defendant or any one or more of the defendants is a nonresident of the State, the Court may make an order directing such nonresident defendant or defendants to appear by a day certain to be designated. Such order shall be served on such nonresident defendant or defendants by mail or otherwise, if practicable * * *. The Court may compel the appearance of the defendant by the seizure of all or any part of his property, which property may be sold under the order of the Court to pay the demand of the plaintiff, if the defendant does not appear, or otherwise defaults. Any defendant whose property shall have been so seized and who shall have entered a general appearance in the cause may, upon notice to the plaintiff, petition the Court for an order releasing such property or any part thereof from the seizure. The Court shall release such property unless the plaintiff shall satisfy the Court that because of other circumstances there is a reasonable possibility that such release may render it substantially less likely that plaintiff will obtain satisfaction of any judgment secured. If such petition shall not be granted, or if no such petition shall be filed, such property shall remain subject to seizure and may be sold to satisfy any judgment entered in the cause. The Court may at any time release such property or any part thereof upon the giving of sufficient security.

"(b) The Court may * * * require the plaintiff to give approved security to abide any order of the Court respecting the property."

* * *.[12] We reverse.

II

The Delaware courts rejected appellants' jurisdictional challenge by noting that this suit was brought as a quasi in rem proceeding. Since quasi in rem jurisdiction is traditionally based on attachment or seizure of property present in the jurisdiction, not on contacts between the defendant and the State, the courts considered appellants' claimed lack of contacts with Delaware to be unimportant. This categorical analysis assumes the continued soundness of the conceptual structure founded on the century-old case of Pennoyer v. Neff.

* * *

* * * [U]nder Pennoyer, state authority to adjudicate was based on the jurisdiction's power over either persons or property. This fundamental concept is embodied in the very vocabulary which we use to describe judgments. If a court's jurisdiction is based on its authority over the defendant's person, the action and judgment are denominated "in personam" and can impose a personal obligation on the defendant in favor of the plaintiff. If jurisdiction is based on the court's power over property within its territory, the action is called "in rem" or "quasi in rem." The effect of a judgment in such a case is limited to the property that supports jurisdiction and does not impose a personal liability on the property owner, since he is not before the court.[17] * * *

* * * Pennoyer sharply limited the availability of in personam jurisdiction over defendants not resident in the forum State. If a nonresident defendant could not be found in a State, he could not be sued there. On the other hand, since the State in which property was located was considered to have exclusive sovereignty over that property, in rem actions could proceed regardless of the owner's location.

* * *

[Justice Marshall reviewed the post-*Pennoyer* expansion of in personam jurisdiction doctrine in *Hess v. Pawloski* and *International Shoe* and concluded with the following observation:]

Thus, the relationship among the defendant, the forum, and the litigation, rather than the mutually exclusive sovereignty of the States on which the rules of Pennoyer rest, became the central concern of the inquiry into personal jurisdiction.[20] * * *

---

[12] Under Delaware law, defendants whose property has been sequestered must enter a general appearance, thus subjecting themselves to in personam liability, before they can defend on the merits. * * *

[17] * * * [W]e will for convenience generally use the term "in rem" in place of "in rem and quasi in rem."

[20] Nothing in Hanson v. Denckla is to the contrary. The Hanson Court's statement that restrictions on state jurisdiction "are a consequence of territorial limitations on the power of the respective States" simply makes the point that the States are defined by their geographical territory. After making this point, the Court in Hanson determined that the defendant over which personal jurisdiction was claimed had not committed any acts sufficiently connected to the State to justify jurisdiction under the International Shoe standard.

No equally dramatic change has occurred in the law governing jurisdiction in rem. There have, however, been intimations that the collapse of the in personam wing of Pennoyer has not left that decision unweakened as a foundation for in rem jurisdiction. Well-reasoned lower court opinions have questioned the proposition that the presence of property in a State gives that State jurisdiction to adjudicate rights to the property regardless of the relationship of the underlying dispute and the property owner to the forum. The overwhelming majority of commentators have also rejected Pennoyer's premise that a proceeding "against" property is not a proceeding against the owners of that property. Accordingly, they urge that the "traditional notions of fair play and substantial justice" that govern a State's power to adjudicate in personam should also govern its power to adjudicate personal rights to property located in the State.

Although this Court has not addressed this argument directly, we have held that property cannot be subjected to a court's judgment unless reasonable and appropriate efforts have been made to give the property owners actual notice of the action. This conclusion recognizes, contrary to Pennoyer, that an adverse judgment in rem directly affects the property owner by divesting him of his rights in the property before the court. * * *

It is clear, therefore, that the law of state-court jurisdiction no longer stands securely on the foundation established in Pennoyer. We think that the time is ripe to consider whether the standard of fairness and substantial justice set forth in International Shoe should be held to govern actions in rem as well as in personam.

III

The case for applying to jurisdiction in rem the same test of "fair play and substantial justice" as governs assertions of jurisdiction in personam is simple and straightforward. It is premised on recognition that "(t)he phrase, 'judicial jurisdiction over a thing', is a customary elliptical way of referring to jurisdiction over the interests of persons in a thing." Restatement (Second) of Conflict of Laws §56, Introductory Note (1971). This recognition leads to the conclusion that in order to justify an exercise of jurisdiction in rem, the basis for jurisdiction must be sufficient to justify exercising "jurisdiction over the interests of persons in a thing."[23] The standard for determining whether an exercise of jurisdiction over the interests of persons is consistent with the Due Process Clause is the minimum-contacts standard elucidated in International Shoe.

This argument, of course, does not ignore the fact that the presence of property in a State may bear on the existence of jurisdiction by providing contacts among the forum State, the defendant, and the litigation. For example, when claims to the property itself are the source of the underlying controversy between the plaintiff and the defendant, it would be unusual for the State where the property is located not to have jurisdiction. In such cases, the defendant's

---

[23] It is true that the potential liability of a defendant in an in rem action is limited by the value of the property, but that limitation does not affect the argument. The fairness of subjecting a defendant to state-court jurisdiction does not depend on the size of the claim being litigated.

claim to property located in the State would normally indicate that he expected to benefit from the State's protection of his interest. The State's strong interests in assuring the marketability of property within its borders and in providing a procedure for peaceful resolution of disputes about the possession of that property would also support jurisdiction, as would the likelihood that important records and witnesses will be found in the State.[28] The presence of property may also favor jurisdiction in cases such as suits for injury suffered on the land of an absentee owner, where the defendant's ownership of the property is conceded but the cause of action is otherwise related to rights and duties growing out of that ownership.

It appears, therefore, that jurisdiction over many types of actions which now are or might be brought in rem would not be affected by a holding that any assertion of state-court jurisdiction must satisfy the International Shoe standard. For the type of quasi in rem action typified by Harris v. Balk and the present case, however, accepting the proposed analysis would result in significant change. These are cases where the property which now serves as the basis for state-court jurisdiction is completely unrelated to the plaintiff's cause of action. Thus, although the presence of the defendant's property in a State might suggest the existence of other ties among the defendant, the State, and the litigation, the presence of the property alone would not support the State's jurisdiction. If those other ties did not exist, cases over which the State is now thought to have jurisdiction could not be brought in that forum.

Since acceptance of the International Shoe test would most affect this class of cases, we examine the arguments against adopting that standard as they relate to this category of litigation.[31] Before doing so, however, we note that this type of case also presents the clearest illustration of the argument in favor of assessing assertions of jurisdiction by a single standard. For in cases such as Harris and this one, the only role played by the property is to provide the basis for bringing the defendant into court.[32] Indeed, the express purpose of the Delaware sequestration procedure is to compel the defendant to enter a personal appearance.[33] In such cases, if a direct assertion of personal jurisdiction over the defendant would violate the Constitution, it would seem that an indirect assertion of that jurisdiction should be equally impermissible.

The primary rationale for treating the presence of property as a sufficient basis for jurisdiction to adjudicate claims over which the State would not have jurisdiction if International Shoe applied is that a wrongdoer

---

[28] We do not suggest that these illustrations include all the factors that may affect the decision, nor that the factors we have mentioned are necessarily decisive.

[31] Concentrating on this category of cases is also appropriate because in the other categories, to the extent that presence of property in the State indicates the existence of sufficient contacts under International Shoe, there is no need to rely on the property as justifying jurisdiction regardless of the existence of those contacts.

[32] The value of the property seized does serve to limit the extent of possible liability, but that limitation does not provide support for the assertion of jurisdiction. See n.23, supra.

[33] This purpose is emphasized by Delaware's refusal to allow any defense on the merits unless the defendant enters a general appearance, thus submitting to full in personam liability. See n.12, supra.

"should not be able to avoid payment of his obligations by the expedient of removing his assets to a place where he is not subject to an in personam suit." Restatement §66, Comment a.

This justification, however, does not explain why jurisdiction should be recognized without regard to whether the property is present in the State because of an effort to avoid the owner's obligations. Nor does it support jurisdiction to adjudicate the underlying claim. At most, it suggests that a State in which property is located should have jurisdiction to attach that property, by use of proper procedures, as security for a judgment being sought in a forum where the litigation can be maintained consistently with International Shoe. Moreover, we know of nothing to justify the assumption that a debtor can avoid paying his obligations by removing his property to a State in which his creditor cannot obtain personal jurisdiction over him. The Full Faith and Credit Clause, after all, makes the valid in personam judgment of one State enforceable in all other States.[36]

It might also be suggested that allowing in rem jurisdiction avoids the uncertainty inherent in the International Shoe standard and assures a plaintiff of a forum.[37] We believe, however, that the fairness standard of International Shoe can be easily applied in the vast majority of cases. Moreover, when the existence of jurisdiction in a particular forum under International Shoe is unclear, the cost of simplifying the litigation by avoiding the jurisdictional question may be the sacrifice of "fair play and substantial justice." That cost is too high.

We are left, then, to consider the significance of the long history of jurisdiction based solely on the presence of property in a State. Although the theory that territorial power is both essential to and sufficient for jurisdiction has been undermined, we have never held that the presence of property in a State does not automatically confer jurisdiction over the owner's interest in that property. This history must be considered as supporting the proposition that jurisdiction based solely on the presence of property satisfies the demands of due process, but it is not decisive. * * * The fiction that an assertion of jurisdiction over property is anything but an assertion of jurisdiction over the owner of the property supports an ancient form without substantial modern justification. Its continued acceptance would serve only to allow state-court jurisdiction that is fundamentally unfair to the defendant.

We therefore conclude that all assertions of state-court jurisdiction must be evaluated according to the standards set forth in International Shoe and its progeny.[39]

---

[36] Once it has been determined by a court of competent jurisdiction that the defendant is a debtor of the plaintiff, there would seem to be no unfairness in allowing an action to realize on that debt in a State where the defendant has property, whether or not that State would have jurisdiction to determine the existence of the debt as an original matter.

[37] This case does not raise, and we therefore do not consider, the question whether the presence of a defendant's property in a State is a sufficient basis for jurisdiction when no other forum is available to the plaintiff.

[39] It would not be fruitful for us to re-examine the facts of cases decided on the rationales of Pennoyer and Harris to determine whether jurisdiction might have been sustained under the

IV

The Delaware courts based their assertion of jurisdiction in this case solely on the statutory presence of appellants' property in Delaware. Yet that property is not the subject matter of this litigation, nor is the underlying cause of action related to the property. Appellants' holdings in Greyhound do not, therefore, provide contacts with Delaware sufficient to support the jurisdiction of that State's courts over appellants. If it exists, that jurisdiction must have some other foundation.[40]

Appellee Heitner did not allege and does not now claim that appellants have ever set foot in Delaware. Nor does he identify any act related to his cause of action as having taken place in Delaware. Nevertheless, he contends that appellants' positions as directors and officers of a corporation chartered in Delaware provide sufficient "contacts, ties, or relations" with that State to give its courts jurisdiction over appellants in this stockholder's derivative action. This argument is based primarily on what Heitner asserts to be the strong interest of Delaware in supervising the management of a Delaware corporation. That interest is said to derive from the role of Delaware law in establishing the corporation and defining the obligations owed to it by its officers and directors. In order to protect this interest, appellee concludes, Delaware's courts must have jurisdiction over corporate fiduciaries such as appellants.

This argument is undercut by the failure of the Delaware Legislature to assert the state interest appellee finds so compelling. Delaware law bases jurisdiction, not on appellants' status as corporate fiduciaries, but rather on the presence of their property in the State. Although the sequestration procedure used here may be most frequently used in derivative suits against officers and directors, the authorizing statute evinces no specific concern with such actions. Sequestration can be used in any suit against a nonresident and reaches corporate fiduciaries only if they happen to own interests in a Delaware corporation, or other property in the State. But as Heitner's failure to secure jurisdiction over seven of the defendants named in his complaint demonstrates, there is no necessary relationship between holding a position as a corporate fiduciary and owning stock or other interests in the corporation.[43] If Delaware perceived its interest in securing jurisdiction over corporate fiduciaries to be as great as

---

standard we adopt today. To the extent that prior decisions are inconsistent with this standard, they are overruled.

[40] Appellants argue that our determination that the minimum-contacts standard of International Shoe governs jurisdiction here makes unnecessary any consideration of the existence of such contacts. They point out that they were never personally served with a summons, that Delaware has no long-arm statute which would authorize such service, and that the Delaware Supreme Court has authoritatively held that the existence of contacts is irrelevant to jurisdiction under Del.Code Ann., Tit. 10, §366. As part of its sequestration order, however, the Court of Chancery directed its clerk to send each appellant a copy of the summons and complaint by certified mail. The record indicates that those mailings were made and contains return receipts from at least 19 of the appellants. None of the appellants has suggested that he did not actually receive the summons which was directed to him in compliance with a Delaware statute designed to provide jurisdiction over nonresidents. In these circumstances, we will assume that the procedures followed would be sufficient to bring appellants before the Delaware courts, if minimum contacts existed.

[43] Delaware does not require directors to own stock.

Heitner suggests, we would expect it to have enacted a statute more clearly designed to protect that interest.

Moreover, even if Heitner's assessment of the importance of Delaware's interest is accepted, his argument * * * may support the application of Delaware law to resolve any controversy over appellants' actions in their capacities as officers and directors. But we have rejected the argument that if a State's law can properly be applied to a dispute, its courts necessarily have jurisdiction over the parties to that dispute.

> "(The State) does not acquire . . . jurisdiction by being the 'center of gravity' of the controversy, or the most convenient location for litigation. The issue is personal jurisdiction, not choice of law. It is resolved in this case by considering the acts of the (appellants)." Hanson v. Denckla.

Appellee suggests that by accepting positions as officers or directors of a Delaware corporation, appellants performed the acts required by Hanson v. Denckla. He notes that Delaware law provides substantial benefits to corporate officers and directors, and that these benefits were at least in part the incentive for appellants to assume their positions. It is, he says, "only fair and just" to require appellants, in return for these benefits, to respond in the State of Delaware when they are accused of misusing their power.

But like Heitner's first argument, this line of reasoning establishes only that it is appropriate for Delaware law to govern the obligations of appellants to Greyhound and its stockholders. It does not demonstrate that appellants have "purposefully avail(ed themselves) of the privilege of conducting activities within the forum State," Hanson v. Denckla, in a way that would justify bringing them before a Delaware tribunal. Appellants have simply had nothing to do with the State of Delaware. Moreover, appellants had no reason to expect to be haled before a Delaware court. Delaware, unlike some States, has not enacted a statute that treats acceptance of a directorship as consent to jurisdiction in the State. Appellants, who were not required to acquire interests in Greyhound in order to hold their positions, did not by acquiring those interests surrender their right to be brought to judgment only in States with which they had had "minimum contacts."

* * *

Delaware's assertion of jurisdiction over appellants in this case is inconsistent with that constitutional limitation on state power. The judgment of the Delaware Supreme Court must, therefore, be reversed.

MR. JUSTICE REHNQUIST took no part in the consideration or decision of this case.

MR. JUSTICE POWELL, concurring.

* * *.

I would explicitly reserve judgment * * * on whether the ownership of some forms of property whose situs is indisputably and permanently located within a

State may, without more, provide the contacts necessary to subject a defendant to jurisdiction within the State to the extent of the value of the property. In the case of real property, in particular, preservation of the common-law concept of quasi in rem jurisdiction arguably would avoid the uncertainty of the general International Shoe standard without significant cost to "traditional notions of fair play and substantial justice." Subject to the foregoing reservation, I join the opinion of the Court.

MR. JUSTICE STEVENS, concurring in the judgment.

The Due Process Clause affords protection against "judgments without notice." * * *.

The requirement of fair notice also, I believe, includes fair warning that a particular activity may subject a person to the jurisdiction of a foreign sovereign. ***

* * *

One who purchases shares of stock on the open market can hardly be expected to know that he has thereby become subject to suit in a forum remote from his residence and unrelated to the transaction. As a practical matter, the Delaware sequestration statute creates an unacceptable risk of judgment without notice. Unlike the 49 other States, Delaware treats the place of incorporation as the situs of the stock, even though both the owner and the custodian of the shares are elsewhere. Moreover, Delaware denies the defendant the opportunity to defend the merits of the suit unless he subjects himself to the unlimited jurisdiction of the court. Thus, it coerces a defendant either to submit to personal jurisdiction in a forum which could not otherwise obtain such jurisdiction or to lose the securities which have been attached. If its procedure were upheld, Delaware would, in effect, impose a duty of inquiry on every purchaser of securities in the national market. For unless the purchaser ascertains both the State of incorporation of the company whose shares he is buying, and also the idiosyncrasies of its law, he may be assuming an unknown risk of litigation. I therefore agree with the Court that on the record before us no adequate basis for jurisdiction exists and that the Delaware statute is unconstitutional on its face.

How the Court's opinion may be applied in other contexts is not entirely clear to me. I agree with Mr. Justice Powell that it should not be read to invalidate quasi in rem jurisdiction where real estate is involved. I would also not read it as invalidating other long-accepted methods of acquiring jurisdiction over persons with adequate notice of both the particular controversy and the fact that their local activities might subject them to suit. My uncertainty as to the reach of the opinion, and my fear that it purports to decide a great deal more than is necessary to dispose of this case, persuade me merely to concur in the judgment.

MR. JUSTICE BRENNAN, concurring in part and dissenting in part.

I join Parts I-III of the Court's opinion. I fully agree that the minimum-contacts analysis developed in International Shoe represents a far more sensible construct for the exercise of state-court jurisdiction than the patchwork of legal and factual fictions that has been generated from the decision in Pennoyer v. Neff. It is precisely because the inquiry into minimum contacts is now of such overriding importance, however, that I must respectfully dissent from Part IV of the Court's opinion.

I

* * *

[T]he issue of the existence of minimum contacts was never pleaded by appellee, made the subject of discovery, or ruled upon by the Delaware courts. These facts notwithstanding, the Court in Part IV reaches the minimum-contacts question and finds such contacts lacking as applied to appellants. Succinctly stated, once having properly and persuasively decided that the quasi in rem statute that Delaware admits to having enacted is invalid, the Court then proceeds to find that a minimum-contacts law that Delaware expressly denies having enacted also could not be constitutionally applied in this case.

In my view, a purer example of an advisory opinion is not to be found. True, appellants do not deny having received actual notice of the action in question. However, notice is but one ingredient of a proper assertion of state-court jurisdiction. The other is a statute authorizing the exercise of the State's judicial power along constitutionally permissible grounds which henceforth means minimum contacts. As of today, §366 is not such a law. Recognizing that today's decision fundamentally alters the relevant jurisdictional ground rules, I certainly would not want to rule out the possibility that Delaware's courts might decide that the legislature's overriding purpose of securing the personal appearance in state courts of defendants would best be served by reinterpreting its statute to permit state jurisdiction on the basis of constitutionally permissible contacts rather than stock ownership. Were the state courts to take this step, it would then become necessary to address the question of whether minimum contacts exist here. But in the present posture of this case, the Court's decision of this important issue is purely an abstract ruling.

* * * [A]n inquiry into minimum contacts inevitably is highly dependent on creating a proper factual foundation detailing the contacts between the forum State and the controversy in question. Because neither the plaintiff-appellee nor the state courts viewed such an inquiry as germane in this instance, the Court today is unable to draw upon a proper factual record in reaching its conclusion; moreover, its disposition denies appellee the normal opportunity to seek discovery on the contacts issue.

II

Nonetheless, because the Court rules on the minimum-contacts question, I feel impelled to express my view. While evidence derived through discovery might satisfy me that minimum contacts are lacking in a given case, I am convinced that as a general rule a state forum has jurisdiction to adjudicate a shareholder derivative action centering on the conduct and policies of the directors and officers of a corporation chartered by that State. Unlike the Court, I therefore would not foreclose Delaware from asserting jurisdiction over appellants were it persuaded to do so on the basis of minimum contacts.

* * *

* * * [T]he chartering State has an unusually powerful interest in insuring the availability of a convenient forum for litigating claims involving a possible multiplicity of defendant fiduciaries and for vindicating the State's substantive policies regarding the management of its domestic corporations. I believe that our cases fairly establish that the States's valid substantive interests are important considerations in assessing whether it constitutionally may claim jurisdiction over a given cause of action.

In this instance, Delaware can point to at least three interrelated public policies that are furthered by its assertion of jurisdiction. First, the State has a substantial interest in providing restitution for its local corporations that allegedly have been victimized by fiduciary misconduct, even if the managerial decisions occurred outside the State. * * * Second, state courts have legitimately read their jurisdiction expansively when a cause of action centers in an area in which the forum State possesses a manifest regulatory interest. * * * [T]he conduct of corporate fiduciaries is just such a matter in which the policies and interests of the domestic forum are ordinarily presumed to be paramount. Finally, a State like Delaware has a recognized interest in affording a convenient forum for supervising and overseeing the affairs of an entity that is purely the creation of that State's law. * * * I, of course, am not suggesting that Delaware's varied interests would justify its acceptance of jurisdiction over any transaction touching upon the affairs of its domestic corporations. But a derivative action which raises allegations of abuses of the basic management of an institution whose existence is created by the State and whose powers and duties are defined by state law fundamentally implicates the public policies of that forum.

To be sure, the Court is not blind to these considerations. It notes that the State's interests "may support the application of Delaware law to resolve any controversy over appellants' actions in their capacities as officers and directors." But this, the Court argues, pertains to choice of law, not jurisdiction. I recognize that the jurisdictional and choice-of-law inquiries are not identical. But I would not compartmentalize thinking in this area quite so rigidly as it seems to me the Court does today, for both inquiries are often closely related and to a substantial degree depend upon similar considerations. In either case an important linchpin is the extent of contacts between the controversy, the parties, and the forum State. At the minimum, the decision that it is fair to bind a defendant by a State's laws and rules should prove to be highly relevant to the fairness of permitting that same State to accept jurisdiction for adjudicating the controversy.

Furthermore, I believe that practical considerations argue in favor of seeking to bridge the distance between the choice-of-law and jurisdictional inquiries. Even when a court would apply the law of a different forum, as a general rule it will feel less knowledgeable and comfortable in interpretation, and less interested in fostering the policies of that foreign jurisdiction, than would the courts established by the State that provides the applicable law. * * * [W]hen a suitor seeks to lodge a suit in a State with a substantial interest in seeing its own law applied to the transaction in question, we could wisely act to minimize conflicts, confusion, and uncertainty by adopting a liberal view of jurisdiction, unless considerations of fairness or efficiency strongly point in the opposite direction.

This case is not one where, in my judgment, this preference for jurisdiction is adequately answered. Certainly nothing said by the Court persuades me that it would be unfair to subject appellants to suit in Delaware. The fact that the record does not reveal whether they "set foot" or committed "act(s) related to (the) cause of action" in Delaware is not decisive, for jurisdiction can be based strictly on out-of-state acts having foreseeable effects in the forum State. I have little difficulty in applying this principle to nonresident fiduciaries whose alleged breaches of trust are said to have substantial damaging effect on the financial posture of a resident corporation. Further, I cannot understand how the existence of minimum contacts in a constitutional sense is at all affected by Delaware's failure statutorily to express an interest in controlling corporate fiduciaries. To me this simply demonstrates that Delaware did not elect to assert jurisdiction to the extent the Constitution would allow.[5] * * *

I, therefore, would approach the minimum-contacts analysis differently than does the Court. Crucial to me is the fact that appellants voluntarily associated themselves with the State of Delaware, "invoking the benefits and protections of its laws" by entering into a long-term and fragile relationship with one of its domestic corporations. They thereby elected to assume powers and to undertake responsibilities wholly derived from that State's rules and regulations, and to become eligible for those benefits that Delaware law makes available to its corporations' officials. E.g., Del.Code Ann., Tit. 8, §143 (1975) (interest-free loans); §145 (1975 ed. and Supp.1976) (indemnification). While it is possible that countervailing issues of judicial efficiency and the like might clearly favor a different forum, they do not appear on the meager record before us;[8] and, of course, we are concerned solely with "minimum" contacts, not the "best" contacts. I thus do not believe that it is unfair to insist that appellants make themselves available to suit in a competent forum that Delaware might create for vindication of its important public policies directly pertaining to appellants' fiduciary associations with the State.

NOTES AND PROBLEMS FOR DISCUSSION

1. (a) When the Court announced in *Shaffer* that "all assertions of state-court jurisdiction must be evaluated according to the standards set forth in International Shoe and its progeny," did it intend merely to say that *some* evaluation of the factors associated with the minimum contacts test is now required, or that the *identical* constitutional inquiry is now mandated in all assessments of personal jurisdiction? In answering this question, consider footnote 23 of the majority opinion in *Shaffer*. If, as the text of that footnote

---

[5] In fact, it is quite plausible that the Delaware Legislature never felt the need to assert direct jurisdiction over corporate managers precisely because the sequestration statute heretofore has served as a somewhat awkward but effective basis for achieving such personal jurisdiction.

[8] And, of course, if a preferable forum exists elsewhere, a State that is constitutionally entitled to accept jurisdiction nonetheless remains free to arrange for the transfer of the litigation under the doctrine of forum non conveniens.

indicates, the jurisdictional stakes are lower in *quasi in rem* proceedings, i.e., the liability of defendants in these proceedings remains limited to the value of the property that served as the "anchor" for jurisdiction, does it make sense to require the plaintiff to make the same showing with respect to contacts and other fairness factors that would be required to sustain the exercise of potentially unlimited *in personam* jurisdiction?

(b) On the other hand, if an identical evidentiary obligation attaches to all forms of personal jurisdiction, what impact is *Shaffer* likely to have on the continued efficacy of *quasi in rem* jurisdiction? Realistically, if the constitutional hurdle that a plaintiff has to meet to obtain *quasi in rem* jurisdiction is identical to the one necessary to obtain *in personam* jurisdiction, why would anyone utilize the former when they could obtain the latter? Is footnote 37 of the majority opinion instructive on this point?

(c) Suppose, for example, that a state enacted a specific acts long arm statute and that the defendant's forum-related conduct, though sufficient to meet constitutional requirements, did not involve any act listed in the jurisdictional statute. If that defendant, however, owned property in the state, would or should *quasi in rem* jurisdiction be available? And if so, might it not make sense to restrict the defendant's liability to the value of that in-state property?

(d) To what extent, if any, may the information contained in footnotes 12 and 33 have influenced the Court's decision to extend *International Shoe*'s constitutional analysis to *quasi in rem* jurisdiction?

2. Why did the *Shaffer* Court rule that Delaware could not exercise *quasi in rem* jurisdiction over the defendants? Is it really because they did not have sufficient contacts to meet the due process requirement set forth in *International Shoe*? Suppose that prior to reading this opinion, you had been told that a plaintiff in a stockholder derivative suit sought to exercise *in personam* jurisdiction over the officers and directors of a forum corporation for malfeasance in office. Assume further that the state jurisdictional statute was either of the as-far-as-the-Constitution-permits persuasion, or provided for jurisdiction over nonresidents who commit a tortious act outside the state that causes an injury within the state. In resolving the remaining constitutional issue, would you conclude that the defendant's relationship with the forum was sufficient to pass constitutional muster or would you also examine other factors? Does that suggest anything with respect to the significance of the *Shaffer* majority's discussion of the interests served, and not served, by Delaware's sequestration/jurisdictional statute?

The Delaware legislature obviously took the hint from the *Shaffer* Court. Less than two weeks after the issuance of the Supreme Court's opinion, Delaware enacted a jurisdictional statute that paralleled the provisions of the Massachusetts nonresident motorist statute that the Supreme Court had approved of in *Hess* (see *supra*, at p. 61), but, interestingly, had derided as relying on an outdated, fictive theory of consent in *Shaffer*. Under the new Delaware law, any non-resident who accepted a position as a director of a Delaware corporation would be deemed to consent to the appointment of an in-state agent for service of process in any action alleging a violation of his or her corporate responsibilities. Although the Delaware Supreme Court subsequently upheld the constitutionality of the enactment, that did not end the matter, at least for Greyhound. In response to the legislative action, Greyhound terminated its existence in Delaware and reincorporated in Arizona to avoid subjecting its directors (many of whom lived in the western U.S.) to the possibility of being sued in Delaware.

3. The Court's ruling in *Shaffer* may be explained, in part, as a reaction to what was perceived to be an unacceptably expansive (and oppressive) interpretation of the limits of *quasi in rem* jurisdiction that it had prescribed in *Harris*. For example, an insurance policy contains a promise by the insurer to defend and indemnify the insured in connection with certain enumerated risks. The courts in New Hampshire, Minnesota and, most consistently, New York, held that this contingent contractual obligation on the insurer's part was a garnishable debt. Therefore, they reasoned, since *Harris* proclaimed that a debt is located wherever the debtor can be found, these creditor/policy holders were subject to *quasi in rem* jurisdiction wherever their insurer could be found. See e.g., Seider v. Roth, 17 N.Y.2d 111, 269 N.Y.S.2d 99, 216 N.E.2d 312 (1966). And in the case of the major insurance carriers, this meant that insured individuals were subject to virtually nationwide exposure. Any doubts as to whether or not *Shaffer* invalidated this utilization of *quasi in rem* jurisdiction were put to rest in RUSH v. SAVCHUK, 444 U.S. 320, 100 S.Ct. 571, 62 L.Ed.2d 516 (1980). There, the Court (in an opinion written by Justice Marshall, the author of *Shaffer*) ruled that the existence of contacts between the insurer and the forum state was no substitute for contacts between the defendant insured and the forum state (Minnesota). Accordingly, it held that in the absence of other contacts between the insured and the forum state, *quasi in rem* jurisdiction predicated solely on the attachment of the defendant's insurance policy with a company that was doing business in the forum state did not meet the constitutional requirements of *International Shoe*. This ruling, however, did not expressly preclude states from enacting "direct action" statutes, i.e., laws that permit injured plaintiffs to file suit directly against the alleged tortfeasor's insurance carrier. In fact, the opinion suggests only that states are precluded from seeking to accomplish that objective indirectly through the use of a *quasi in rem* jurisdictional provision.

4. In every personal jurisdiction opinion we have examined beginning with *International Shoe*, the Supreme Court has insisted that the Constitution demands that exercises of jurisdiction comport with "traditional notions of fair play and substantial justice." Presumably, the Court's use of "traditional" to modify "notions of fair play" was a calculated effort to impose some limit on each Justice's individual assessment of the meaning of "fair play and substantial justice." But if fairness is to be measured from an historical perspective, is it relevant to that calculation that the exercise of *quasi in rem* jurisdiction based solely on the defendant's ownership of property in the forum state had been an unquestioned part of the jurisdictional landscape in the U.S. for more than a century? How does the majority in *Shaffer* respond to that argument? This issue resurfaced thirteen years later, when, in the context of transient *in personam* jurisdiction, the Court addressed it and other questions raised anew by the ruling in *Shaffer*.

SECTION D.   TRANSIENT JURISDICTION: BACK TO THE FUTURE

Burnham v. Superior Court of California

Supreme Court of the United States, 1990.

495 U.S. 604, 110 S.Ct. 2105, 109 L.Ed.2d 631.

JUSTICE SCALIA announced the judgment of the Court and delivered an opinion in which THE CHIEF JUSTICE and JUSTICE KENNEDY join, and in which JUSTICE WHITE joins with respect to Parts I, II-A, II-B, and II-C.

The question presented is whether the Due Process Clause of the Fourteenth Amendment denies California courts jurisdiction over a nonresident, who was personally served with process while temporarily in that State, in a suit unrelated to his activities in the State.

I

Petitioner Dennis Burnham married Francie Burnham in 1976 in West Virginia. In 1977 the couple moved to New Jersey, where their two children were born. In July 1987 the Burnhams decided to separate. They agreed that Mrs. Burnham, who intended to move to California, would take custody of the children. * * *

* * * Mrs. Burnham * * * brought suit for divorce in California state court in early January 1988.

In late January, petitioner visited southern California on business, after which he went north to visit his children in the San Francisco Bay area, where his wife resided. He took the older child to San Francisco for the weekend. Upon returning the child to Mrs. Burnham's home on January 24, 1988, petitioner was served with a California court summons and a copy of Mrs. Burnham's divorce petition. He then returned to New Jersey.

* * *

[The defendant made a special appearance, contesting the exercise of personal jurisdiction, claiming that he did not have sufficient contacts with California. The state courts rejected his claim on the ground that being personally served while present within the forum state was a sufficient predicate for the exercise of *in personam* jurisdiction.]

II

A

* * *

* * *   [W]e said in International Shoe that a state court's assertion of personal jurisdiction satisfies the Due Process Clause if it does not violate "traditional notions of fair play and substantial justice." Since International

Shoe, we have only been called upon to decide whether these "traditional notions" permit States to exercise jurisdiction over absent defendants in a manner that deviates from the rules of jurisdiction applied in the 19th century. We have held such deviations permissible, but only with respect to suits arising out of the absent defendant's contacts with the State.[2] The question we must decide today is whether due process requires a similar connection between the litigation and the defendant's contacts with the State in cases where the defendant is physically present in the State at the time process is served upon him.

B

Among the most firmly established principles of personal jurisdiction in American tradition is that the courts of a State have jurisdiction over nonresidents who are physically present in the State. * * *

* * *

Decisions in the courts of many States in the 19th and early 20th centuries held that personal service upon a physically present defendant sufficed to confer jurisdiction, without regard to whether the defendant was only briefly in the State or whether the cause of action was related to his activities there. Although research has not revealed a case deciding the issue in every State's courts, that appears to be because the issue was so well settled that it went unlitigated. * * * Particularly striking is the fact that, as far as we have been able to determine, not one American case * * * until 1978 held, or even suggested, that in-state personal service on an individual was insufficient to confer personal jurisdiction.[3]

This American jurisdictional practice is, moreover, not merely old; it is continuing. It remains the practice of, not only a substantial number of the States, but as far as we are aware all the States and the Federal Government — if one disregards (as one must for this purpose) the few opinions since 1978 that have erroneously said, on grounds similar to those that petitioner presses here,

---

[2] We have said that "[e]ven when the cause of action does not arise out of or relate to the foreign corporation's activities in the forum State, due process is not offended by a State's subjecting the corporation to its in personam jurisdiction when there are sufficient contacts between the State and the foreign corporation." Helicopteros Nacionales de Colombia v. Hall. Our only holding supporting that statement, however, involved "regular service of summons upon [the corporation's] president while he was in [the forum State] acting in that capacity." See Perkins v. Benguet Consolidated Mining Co. It may be that whatever special rule exists permitting "continuous and systematic" contacts to support jurisdiction with respect to matters unrelated to activity in the forum applies only to corporations, which have never fitted comfortably in a jurisdictional regime based primarily upon "de facto power over the defendant's person." International Shoe Co. We express no views on these matters — and, for simplicity's sake, omit reference to this aspect of "contacts"-based jurisdiction in our discussion.

[3] Given this striking fact, and the unanimity of both cases and commentators in supporting the in-state service rule, one can only marvel at Justice Brennan's assertion that the rule * * * "did not receive wide currency until well after our decision in Pennoyer v. Neff." * * * Justice Brennan cites neither cases nor commentators from the relevant period to support his thesis (with exceptions I shall discuss presently), and instead relies upon modern secondary sources that do not mention, and were perhaps unaware of, many of the materials I have discussed. The cases cited by Justice Brennan do not remotely support his point. * * *

that this Court's due process decisions render the practice unconstitutional. We do not know of a single state or federal statute, or a single judicial decision resting upon state law, that has abandoned in-state service as a basis of jurisdiction. Many recent cases reaffirm it.

C

Despite this formidable body of precedent, petitioner contends, in reliance on our decisions applying the International Shoe standard, that in the absence of "continuous and systematic" contacts with the forum, a nonresident defendant can be subjected to judgment only as to matters that arise out of or relate to his contacts with the forum. This argument rests on a thorough misunderstanding of our cases.

The view of most courts in the 19th century was that a court simply could not exercise in personam jurisdiction over a nonresident who had not been personally served with process in the forum. Pennoyer v. Neff, while renowned for its statement of the principle that the Fourteenth Amendment prohibits such an exercise of jurisdiction, in fact set that forth only as dictum and decided the case (which involved a judgment rendered more than two years before the Fourteenth Amendment's ratification) under "well-established principles of public law." Those principles, embodied in the Due Process Clause, required (we said) that when proceedings "involv[e] merely a determination of the personal liability of the defendant, he must be brought within [the court's] jurisdiction by service of process within the State, or his voluntary appearance." * * *

Later years, however, saw the weakening of the Pennoyer rule. * * * States required, for example, * * * in-state "substituted service" for nonresident motorists who caused injury in the State and left before personal service could be accomplished, see, e.g., Hess v. Pawloski. We initially upheld these laws under the Due Process Clause on grounds that they complied with Pennoyer's rigid requirement of either "consent" or "presence." As many observed, however, the consent and presence were purely fictional. Our opinion in International Shoe cast those fictions aside and made explicit the underlying basis of these decisions: Due process does not necessarily require the States to adhere to the unbending territorial limits on jurisdiction set forth in Pennoyer. The validity of assertion of jurisdiction over a nonconsenting defendant who is not present in the forum depends upon whether "the quality and nature of [his] activity" in relation to the forum renders such jurisdiction consistent with "traditional notions of fair play and substantial justice." Subsequent cases have derived from the International Shoe standard the general rule that a State may dispense with in-forum personal service on nonresident defendants in suits arising out of their activities in the State. * * *

Nothing in International Shoe or the cases that have followed it, however, offers support for the very different proposition petitioner seeks to establish today: that a defendant's presence in the forum is not only unnecessary to validate novel, nontraditional assertions of jurisdiction, but is itself no longer sufficient to establish jurisdiction. That proposition is unfaithful to both elementary logic and the foundations of our due process jurisprudence. * * *

The short of the matter is that jurisdiction based on physical presence alone constitutes due process because it is one of the continuing traditions of our legal system that define the due process standard of "traditional notions of fair play and substantial justice." That standard was developed by analogy to "physical presence," and it would be perverse to say it could now be turned against that touchstone of jurisdiction.

D

Petitioner's strongest argument, though we ultimately reject it, relies upon our decision in Shaffer v. Heitner. In that case * * * we concluded that the normal rules we had developed under International Shoe for jurisdiction over suits against absent defendants should apply — viz., Delaware could not hear the suit because the defendants' sole contact with the State (ownership of property there) was unrelated to the lawsuit.

It goes too far to say, as petitioner contends, that Shaffer compels the conclusion that a State lacks jurisdiction over an individual unless the litigation arises out of his activities in the State. Shaffer, like International Shoe, involved jurisdiction over an absent defendant, and it stands for nothing more than the proposition that when the "minimum contact" that is a substitute for physical presence consists of property ownership it must, like other minimum contacts, be related to the litigation. Petitioner wrenches out of its context our statement in Shaffer that "all assertions of state-court jurisdiction must be evaluated according to the standards set forth in International Shoe and its progeny." * * *

Shaffer was saying, in other words, not that all bases for the assertion of in personam jurisdiction (including, presumably, in-state service) must be treated alike and subjected to the "minimum contacts" analysis of International Shoe; but rather that quasi in rem jurisdiction, that fictional "ancient form," and in personam jurisdiction, are really one and the same and must be treated alike — leading to the conclusion that quasi in rem jurisdiction, i.e., that form of in personam jurisdiction based upon a "property ownership" contact and by definition unaccompanied by personal, in-state service, must satisfy the litigation-relatedness requirement of International Shoe. The logic of Shaffer's holding — which places all suits against absent nonresidents on the same constitutional footing, regardless of whether a separate Latin label is attached to one particular basis of contact — does not compel the conclusion that physically present defendants must be treated identically to absent ones. As we have demonstrated at length, our tradition has treated the two classes of defendants quite differently, and it is unreasonable to read Shaffer as casually obliterating that distinction. International Shoe confined its "minimum contacts" requirement to situations in which the defendant "be not present within the territory of the forum," and nothing in Shaffer expands that requirement beyond that.

It is fair to say, however, that while our holding today does not contradict Shaffer, our basic approach to the due process question is different. We have conducted no independent inquiry into the desirability or fairness of the prevailing in-state service rule, leaving that judgment to the legislatures that are free to amend it; for our purposes, its validation is its pedigree, as the phrase "traditional notions of fair play and substantial justice" makes clear. Shaffer did conduct such an independent inquiry, asserting that "'traditional notions of fair play and substantial justice' can be as readily offended by the perpetuation of ancient forms that are no longer justified as by the adoption of new procedures that are inconsistent with the basic values of our constitutional heritage." Perhaps that assertion can be sustained when the "perpetuation of ancient forms" is engaged in by only a very small minority of the States. Where, however, as in the present case, a jurisdictional principle is both firmly approved by tradition and still favored, it is impossible to imagine what standard we could appeal to for the judgment that it is "no longer justified." While in no way receding from or casting doubt upon the holding of Shaffer or any other case, we reaffirm today our time-honored approach. For new procedures, hitherto unknown, the Due Process Clause requires analysis to determine whether "traditional notions of fair play and substantial justice" have been offended. But a doctrine of personal jurisdiction that dates back to the adoption of the Fourteenth Amendment and is still generally observed unquestionably meets that standard.

III

A few words in response to Justice Brennan's opinion concurring in the judgment: It insists that we apply "contemporary notions of due process" to determine the constitutionality of California's assertion of jurisdiction. But our analysis today comports with that prescription, at least if we give it the only sense allowed by our precedents. The "contemporary notions of due process" applicable to personal jurisdiction are the enduring "traditional notions of fair play and substantial justice" established as the test by International Shoe. By its very language, that test is satisfied if a state court adheres to jurisdictional rules that are generally applied and have always been applied in the United States.

But the concurrence's proposed standard of "contemporary notions of due process" requires more: It measures state-court jurisdiction not only against traditional doctrines in this country, including current state-court practice, but also against each Justice's subjective assessment of what is fair and just. Authority for that seductive standard is not to be found in any of our personal jurisdiction cases. It is, indeed, an outright break with the test of "traditional notions of fair play and substantial justice," which would have to be reformulated "our notions of fair play and substantial justice."

The subjectivity, and hence inadequacy, of this approach becomes apparent when the concurrence tries to explain why the assertion of jurisdiction in the present case meets its standard of continuing-American-tradition-plus-innate-fairness. Justice Brennan lists the "benefits" Mr. Burnham derived from the State of California — the fact that, during the few days he was there, "[h]is health and safety [were] guaranteed by the State's police, fire, and emergency medical services; he [was] free to travel on the State's roads and waterways; he likely enjoy[ed] the fruits of the State's economy." Three days' worth of these benefits strike us as powerfully inadequate to establish, as an abstract matter, that it is "fair" for California to decree the ownership of all Mr. Burnham's worldly goods acquired during the 10 years of his marriage, and the custody over his children. * * * Even less persuasive are the other "fairness" factors alluded to by Justice Brennan. It would create "an asymmetry," we are told, if

Burnham were permitted (as he is) to appear in California courts as a plaintiff, but were not compelled to appear in California courts as defendant; and travel being as easy as it is nowadays, and modern procedural devices being so convenient, it is no great hardship to appear in California courts. The problem with these assertions is that they justify the exercise of jurisdiction over everyone, whether or not he ever comes to California. The only "fairness" elements setting Mr. Burnham apart from the rest of the world are the three days' "benefits" referred to above — and even those, do not set him apart from many other people who have enjoyed three days in the Golden State (savoring the fruits of its economy, the availability of its roads and police services) but who were fortunate enough not to be served with process while they were there and thus are not (simply by reason of that savoring) subject to the general jurisdiction of California's courts. In other words, even if one agreed with Justice Brennan's conception of an equitable bargain, the "benefits" we have been discussing would explain why it is "fair" to assert general jurisdiction over Burnham-returned-to-New-Jersey-after-service only at the expense of proving that it is also "fair" to assert general jurisdiction over Burnham-returned-to-New-Jersey-without-service — which we know does not conform with "contemporary notions of due process."

There is, we must acknowledge, one factor mentioned by Justice Brennan that both relates distinctively to the assertion of jurisdiction on the basis of personal in-state service and is fully persuasive — namely, the fact that a defendant voluntarily present in a particular State has a "reasonable expectatio[n]" that he is subject to suit there. By formulating it as a "reasonable expectation" Justice Brennan makes that seem like a "fairness" factor; but in reality, of course, it is just tradition masquerading as "fairness." The only reason for charging Mr. Burnham with the reasonable expectation of being subject to suit is that the States of the Union assert adjudicatory jurisdiction over the person, and have always asserted adjudicatory jurisdiction over the person, by serving him with process during his temporary physical presence in their territory. That continuing tradition, which anyone entering California should have known about, renders it "fair" for Mr. Burnham, who voluntarily entered California, to be sued there for divorce — at least "fair" in the limited sense that he has no one but himself to blame. Justice Brennan's long journey is a circular one, leaving him, at the end of the day, in complete reliance upon the very factor he sought to avoid: The existence of a continuing tradition is not enough, fairness also must be considered; fairness exists here because there is a continuing tradition.

While Justice Brennan's concurrence is unwilling to confess that the Justices of this Court can possibly be bound by a continuing American tradition that a particular procedure is fair, neither is it willing to embrace the logical consequences of that refusal — or even to be clear about what consequences (logical or otherwise) it does embrace. Justice Brennan says that "[f]or these reasons [i.e., because of the reasonableness factors enumerated above], as a rule the exercise of personal jurisdiction over a defendant based on his voluntary presence in the forum will satisfy the requirements of due process." The use of the word "rule" conveys the reassuring feeling that he is establishing a principle of law one can rely upon — but of course he is not. Since Justice Brennan's only criterion of constitutionality is "fairness," the phrase "as a rule" represents nothing more than his estimation that, usually, all the elements of "fairness" he discusses in the present case will exist. But what if they do not? Suppose, for example, that a defendant in Mr. Burnham's situation enjoys not three days' worth of California's "benefits," but 15 minutes' worth. Or suppose we remove one of those "benefits" — "enjoy[ment of] the fruits of the State's economy" — by positing that Mr. Burnham had not come to California on business, but only to visit his children. Or suppose that Mr. Burnham were demonstrably so impecunious as to be unable to take advantage of the modern means of transportation and communication that Justice Brennan finds so relevant. Or suppose, finally, that the California courts lacked the "variety of procedural devices" that Justice Brennan says can reduce the burden upon out-of-state litigants. One may also make additional suppositions relating not to the absence of the factors that Justice Brennan discusses, but to the presence of additional factors bearing upon the ultimate criterion of "fairness." * * * Since, so far as one can tell, Justice Brennan's approval of applying the in-state service rule in the present case rests on the presence of all the factors he lists, and on the absence of any others, every different case will present a different litigable issue. Thus, despite the fact that he manages to work the word "rule" into his formulation, Justice Brennan's approach does not establish a rule of law at all, but only a "totality of the circumstances" test, guaranteeing what traditional territorial rules of jurisdiction were designed precisely to avoid: uncertainty and litigation over the preliminary issue of the forum's competence. It may be that those evils, necessarily accompanying a freestanding "reasonableness" inquiry, must be accepted at the margins, when we evaluate nontraditional forms of jurisdiction newly adopted by the State. But that is no reason for injecting them into the core of our American practice, exposing to such a "reasonableness" inquiry the ground of jurisdiction that has hitherto been considered the very baseline of reasonableness, physical presence.

The difference between us and Justice Brennan has * * * to do with whether changes are to be adopted as progressive by the American people or decreed as progressive by the Justices of this Court. Nothing we say today prevents individual States from limiting or entirely abandoning the in-state-service basis of jurisdiction. And nothing prevents an overwhelming majority of them from doing so, with the consequence that the "traditional notions of fairness" that this Court applies may change. But the States have overwhelmingly declined to adopt such limitation or abandonment, evidently not considering it to be progress.[5]   The question is whether, armed with no authority other than

---

[5] I find quite unacceptable as a basis for this Court's decisions Justice Brennan's view that "the raison d'etre of various constitutional doctrines designed to protect out-of-staters, such as the Art. IV Privileges and Immunities Clause and the Commerce Clause," entitled this Court to brand as "unfair," and hence unconstitutional, the refusal of all 50 States "to limit or abandon bases of jurisdiction that have become obsolete." "Due Process" (which is the constitutional text at issue here) does not mean that process which shifting majorities of this Court feel to be "due"; but that process which American society — self-interested American society, which expresses its judgments in the laws of self-interested States — has traditionally considered "due." The notion that the Constitution, through some penumbra emanating from the Privileges and Immunities

individual Justices' perceptions of fairness that conflict with both past and current practice, this Court can compel the States to make such a change on the ground that "due process" requires it. We hold that it cannot.

Because the Due Process Clause does not prohibit the California courts from exercising jurisdiction over petitioner based on the fact of in-state service of process, the judgment is

Affirmed.

JUSTICE WHITE, concurring in part and concurring in the judgment.

I join Parts I, II-A, II-B, and II-C of Justice Scalia's opinion and concur in the judgment of affirmance. The rule allowing jurisdiction to be obtained over a nonresident by personal service in the forum State, without more, has been and is so widely accepted throughout this country that I could not possibly strike it down, either on its face or as applied in this case, on the ground that it denies due process of law guaranteed by the Fourteenth Amendment. Although the Court has the authority under the Amendment to examine even traditionally accepted procedures and declare them invalid, e.g., Shaffer v. Heitner, there has been no showing here or elsewhere that as a general proposition the rule is so arbitrary and lacking in common sense in so many instances that it should be held violative of due process in every case. * * *

JUSTICE BRENNAN, with whom JUSTICE MARSHALL, JUSTICE BLACKMUN, and JUSTICE O'CONNOR join, concurring in the judgment.

I agree with Justice Scalia that the Due Process Clause of the Fourteenth Amendment generally permits a state court to exercise jurisdiction over a defendant if he is served with process while voluntarily present in the forum State.[1] I do not perceive the need, however, to decide that a jurisdictional rule that "has been immemorially the actual law of the land" automatically comports with due process simply by virtue of its "pedigree." Although I agree that history is an important factor in establishing whether a jurisdictional rule satisfies due process requirements, I cannot agree that it is the only factor such that all traditional rules of jurisdiction are, ipso facto, forever constitutional. Unlike Justice Scalia, I would undertake an "independent inquiry into the . . . fairness of the prevailing in-state service rule." I therefore concur only in the judgment.

I

I believe that the approach adopted by Justice Scalia's opinion today — reliance solely on historical pedigree — is foreclosed by our decisions in International Shoe and Shaffer.[2] * * * The critical insight of Shaffer is that all

---

Clause and the Commerce Clause, establishes this Court as a Platonic check upon the society's greedy adherence to its traditions can only be described as imperious.

[1] I use the term "transient jurisdiction" to refer to jurisdiction premised solely on the fact that a person is served with process while physically present in the forum State.

[2] Our reference in International Shoe to "traditional notions of fair play and substantial justice" meant simply that those concepts are indeed traditional ones, not that, as Justice Scalia's opinion

rules of jurisdiction, even ancient ones, must satisfy contemporary notions of due process. No longer were we content to limit our jurisdictional analysis to pronouncements that * * * "every State possesses exclusive jurisdiction and sovereignty over persons and property within its territory." Pennoyer. * * *

While our holding in Shaffer may have been limited to quasi in rem jurisdiction, our mode of analysis was not. Indeed, that we were willing in Shaffer to examine anew the appropriateness of the quasi in rem rule — until that time dutifully accepted by American courts for at least a century — demonstrates that we did not believe that the "pedigree" of a jurisdictional practice was dispositive in deciding whether it was consistent with due process. We later characterized Shaffer as "abandon[ing] the outworn rule of Harris v. Balk * * *." If we could discard an "ancient form without substantial modern justification" in Shaffer, we can do so again. * * *

II

Tradition, though alone not dispositive, is of course relevant to the question whether the rule of transient jurisdiction is consistent with due process.[7] Tradition is salient not in the sense that practices of the past are automatically reasonable today; indeed, under such a standard, the legitimacy of transient jurisdiction would be called into question because the rule's historical "pedigree" is a matter of intense debate. * * * For much of the 19th century, American courts did not uniformly recognize the concept of transient jurisdiction, and it appears that the transient rule did not receive wide currency until well after our decision in Pennoyer.

Rather, I find the historical background relevant because, however murky the jurisprudential origins of transient jurisdiction, the fact that American courts have announced the rule for perhaps a century (first in dicta, more recently in holdings) provides a defendant voluntarily present in a particular State today "clear notice that [he] is subject to suit" in the forum. * * * [O]ur common understanding now, fortified by a century of judicial practice, is that jurisdiction is often a function of geography. The transient rule is consistent with reasonable expectations and is entitled to a strong presumption that it comports with due process. * * *[11]

By visiting the forum State, a transient defendant actually "avail[s]" himself of significant benefits provided by the State. His health and safety are guaranteed by the State's police, fire, and emergency medical services; he is free

---

suggests, their specific content was to be determined by tradition alone. We recognized that contemporary societal norms must play a role in our analysis.

[7] I do not propose that the "contemporary notions of due process" to be applied are no more than "each Justice's subjective assessment of what is fair and just." Rather, the inquiry is guided by our decisions beginning with International Shoe and the specific factors that we have developed to ascertain whether a jurisdictional rule comports with "traditional notions of fair play and substantial justice." This analysis may not be "mechanical or quantitative," International Shoe, but neither is it "freestanding," or dependent on personal whim. Our experience with this approach demonstrates that it is well within our competence to employ.

[11] * * * [T]here may be cases in which a defendant's involuntary or unknowing presence in a State does not support the exercise of personal jurisdiction over him. The facts of the instant case do not require us to determine the outer limits of the transient jurisdiction rule.

to travel on the State's roads and waterways; he likely enjoys the fruits of the State's economy as well. Moreover, the Privileges and Immunities Clause of Article IV prevents a state government from discriminating against a transient defendant by denying him the protections of its law or the right of access to its courts.[12] Subject only to the doctrine of forum non conveniens, an out-of-state plaintiff may use state courts in all circumstances in which those courts would be available to state citizens. Without transient jurisdiction, an asymmetry would arise: A transient would have the full benefit of the power of the forum State's courts as a plaintiff while retaining immunity from their authority as a defendant.

The potential burdens on a transient defendant are slight. Modern transportation and communications have made it much less burdensome for a party sued to defend himself in a State outside his place of residence. That the defendant has already journeyed at least once before to the forum — as evidenced by the fact that he was served with process there — is an indication that suit in the forum likely would not be prohibitively inconvenient. Finally, any burdens that do arise can be ameliorated by a variety of procedural devices.[13] For these reasons, as a rule, the exercise of personal jurisdiction over a defendant based on his voluntary presence in the forum will satisfy the requirements of due process.[14]

In this case, it is undisputed that petitioner was served with process while voluntarily and knowingly in the State of California. I therefore concur in the judgment.

---

[12] That these privileges may independently be required by the Constitution does not mean that they must be ignored for purposes of determining the fairness of the transient jurisdiction rule. For example, in the context of specific jurisdiction, we consider whether a defendant "has availed himself of the privilege of conducting business" in the forum State, or has "invok[ed] the benefits and protections of its laws," even though the State could not deny the defendant the right to do so.

[13] For example, in the federal system, a transient defendant can avoid protracted litigation of a spurious suit through a motion to dismiss for failure to state a claim or through a motion for summary judgment. He can use relatively inexpensive methods of discovery, such as oral deposition by telephone, deposition upon written questions, interrogatories, and requests for admission, while * * * possibly obtaining costs and attorney's fees for some of the work involved. Moreover, a change of venue may be possible. In state court, many of the same procedural protections are available, as is the doctrine of forum non conveniens, under which the suit may be dismissed.

[14] I note * * * that the dual conclusions of Justice Scalia's opinion create a singularly unattractive result. Justice Scalia suggests that when and if a jurisdictional rule becomes substantively unfair or even "unconscionable," this Court is powerless to alter it. Instead, he is willing to rely on individual States to limit or abandon bases of jurisdiction that have become obsolete. This reliance is misplaced, for States have little incentive to limit rules such as transient jurisdiction that make it easier for their own citizens to sue out-of-state defendants. That States are more likely to expand their jurisdiction is illustrated by the adoption by many States of long-arm statutes extending the reach of personal jurisdiction to the limits established by the Federal Constitution. Out-of-staters do not vote in state elections or have a voice in state government. We should not assume, therefore, that States will be motivated by "notions of fairness" to curb jurisdictional rules like the one at issue here. The reasoning of Justice Scalia's opinion today is strikingly oblivious to the raison d'etre of various constitutional doctrines designed to protect out-of-staters, such as the Art. IV Privileges and Immunities Clause and the Commerce Clause.

JUSTICE STEVENS, concurring in the judgment.

As I explained in my separate writing, I did not join the Court's opinion in Shaffer because I was concerned by its unnecessarily broad reach. The same concern prevents me from joining either Justice Scalia's or Justice Brennan's opinion in this case. For me, it is sufficient to note that the historical evidence and consensus identified by Justice Scalia, the considerations of fairness identified by Justice Brennan, and the common sense displayed by Justice White, all combine to demonstrate that this is, indeed, a very easy case. Accordingly, I agree that the judgment should be affirmed.

NOTES AND PROBLEMS FOR DISCUSSION

1. (a) Although the Court unanimously voted to sustain the exercise of *in personam* jurisdiction over the defendant in *Burnham*, what can you glean from the four separate opinions about the future viability of transient jurisdiction?

(b) Does the sharp, and sharply worded, disagreement between Justice Scalia and Justice Brennan relate to a more fundamental divergence of opinion over the role of the Supreme Court in constitutional adjudication?

(c) Do you find Justice Scalia's bright line rule more persuasive than Justice Brennan's totality-of-circumstances approach?

2. Is it likely that the Supreme Court would have tackled the issue of transitory jurisdiction absent its prior ruling in *Shaffer*?

(a) Do you agree with Justice Brennan that the moral of *Shaffer* is "we did it once, we can do it again," or are you persuaded by Justice Scalia's efforts to distinguish *Shaffer* from *Burnham*?

(b) Alternatively, do you think that Justice Scalia may actually be suggesting that *Shaffer* is bad law and ought to be reversed?

3. (a) Recall the case of Grace v. McArthur, 70 F.Supp. 442 (E.D.Ark.1959), discussed in Note 6 after *Pennoyer, supra*, at 59. In that case, personal service upon a nonresident of Arkansas with no other apparent ties to that state was found to be sufficient to subject him to the *in personam* jurisdiction of an Arkansas court simply because he was served while seated in a plane flying over Arkansas airspace. Does that ruling survive *Burnham*?

(b) Does the other traditionally recognized exception to transient jurisdiction, discussed in Note 7 following *Pennoyer*, for cases where the defendant's presence (and service) within the forum state is obtained through fraud or force survive *Burnham*?

SECTION E.   A NEW JURISDICTIONAL FRONTIER: CYBERSPACE

One of the most interesting and increasingly active areas of development in modern jurisdiction law involves disputes arising out of commercial, communication, and other activities conducted in and related to cyberspace. The last few years have witnessed an explosion in the access to and utilization of ecommerce, email, and other digitally based methods of creating commercial and personal relationships. Not surprisingly, this exponentially expanding universe of activities is beginning to generate a corresponding increase in the amount of litigation, much of which has confronted the courts with the task of applying extant legal rules to contexts never imagined by the authors of the present jurisdictional regime.

For example, how should the reasoning set forth in cases like *International Shoe, Volkswagen*, and *Asahi* apply to the hypothetical we asked you to consider at the beginning of this chapter about a products liability claim against a software manufacturer and a web site sponsor who are alleged to have distributed a defective product to a consumer over the Internet? How would you go about determining whether these defendants have "contacts" with the plaintiff's home state? Once information is placed on the Internet, does that "stream of commerce" have any logical ending point or does it extend to every point in the globe? And once you have answered those questions, can you determine how a court should assess whether these entrepreneurs have purposefully availed themselves of the benefits and protections of forum law or have purposefully directed their activities towards the forum state? Consider the following:

Cybersell, Inc. v. Cybersell, Inc.

United States Court of Appeals, Ninth Circuit, 1997.
130 F.3d 414.

RYMER, CIRCUIT JUDGE.

We are asked to hold that the allegedly infringing use of a service mark in a home page on the World Wide Web suffices for personal jurisdiction in the state where the holder of the mark has its principal place of business. Cybersell, Inc., an Arizona corporation that advertises for commercial services over the Internet, claims that Cybersell, Inc., a Florida corporation that offers web page construction services over the Internet, infringed its federally registered mark and should be amenable to suit in Arizona because cyberspace is without borders and a web site which advertises a product or service is necessarily intended for use on a world wide basis. The district court disagreed, and so do we. Instead, applying our normal "minimum contacts" analysis, we conclude that it would not comport with "traditional notions of fair play and substantial justice" for Arizona to exercise personal jurisdiction over an allegedly infringing Florida web site advertiser who has no contacts with Arizona other than maintaining a home page that is accessible to Arizonans, and everyone else, over the Internet. We therefore affirm.

I

Cybersell, Inc. is an Arizona corporation, which we will refer to as Cybersell AZ. It was incorporated in May 1994 to provide Internet and web advertising and marketing services, including consulting. The principals of Cybersell AZ are Laurence Canter and Martha Siegel, known among web users for first "spamming" the Internet.[1] Mainstream print media carried the story of Canter and Siegel and their various efforts to commercialize the web.

On August 8, 1994, Cybersell AZ filed an application to register the name "Cybersell" as a service mark.[*] The application was approved and the grant was published on October 30, 1995. Cybersell AZ operated a web site using the mark from August 1994 through February 1995. The site was then taken down for reconstruction.

Meanwhile, in the summer of 1995, Matt Certo and his father, Dr. Samuel C. Certo, both Florida residents, formed Cybersell, Inc., a Florida corporation (Cybersell FL), with its principal place of business in Orlando. Matt was a business school student at Rollins College, where his father was a professor; Matt was particularly interested in the Internet, and their company was to provide business consulting services for strategic management and marketing on the web. At the time the Certos chose the name "Cybersell" for their venture, Cybersell AZ had no home page on the web nor had the PTO [U.S. Patent & Trademark Office] granted their application for the service mark.

As part of their marketing effort, the Certos created a web page at http:// www.cybsell.com/cybsell/index.htm. The home page has a logo at the top with "CyberSell" over a depiction of the planet earth, with the caption underneath "Professional Services for the World Wide Web" and a local (area code 407) phone number. It proclaims in large letters "Welcome to CyberSell!" A hypertext link[2] allows the browser to introduce himself, and invites a company not on the web — but interested in getting on the web — to "Email us to find out how!"

Canter found the Cybersell FL web page and sent an e-mail on November 27, 1995 notifying Dr. Certo that "Cybersell" is a service mark of Cybersell AZ. Trying to disassociate themselves from Canter and Siegel, the Certos changed the name of Cybersell FL to WebHorizons, Inc. on December 27 (later it was changed again to WebSolvers, Inc.) and by January 4, 1996, they had replaced the CyberSell logo at the top of their web page with WebHorizons, Inc. The WebHorizons page still said "Welcome to CyberSell!"

Cybersell AZ filed the complaint in this action * * * in the District of Arizona, alleging trademark infringement, unfair competition, fraud, and RICO violations.   * * *   Cybersell FL moved to dismiss for lack of personal jurisdiction. The district court * * * granted Cybersell FL's motion to dismiss for lack of personal jurisdiction.

II

The general principles that apply to the exercise of personal jurisdiction are

---

[1] Spamming refers to the posting indiscriminately of advertisements to news groups on the web. Unlike crossposting, spamming individually posts the advertisement to each news group, requiring the recipient to delete the message from each news group to which she has subscribed.

[*] [A "service mark" is a name, phrase, or symbol used to identify the services that the owner provides and to distinguish it from the services of others. It is analogous to a "trademark," which is a word, phrase, or symbol affixed to a tangible good or product. — eds.]

[2] A hypertext link allows a user to move directly from one web location to another by using the mouse to click twice on the colored link.

well known. As there is no federal statute governing personal jurisdiction in this case, the law of Arizona applies. Under Rule 4.2(a) of the Arizona Rules of Civil Procedure, an Arizona court

> may exercise personal jurisdiction over parties, whether found within or outside the state, to the maximum extent permitted by the Constitution of this state and the Constitution of the United States.

* * * Thus, Cybersell FL may be subject to personal jurisdiction in Arizona so long as doing so comports with due process.

A court may assert either specific or general jurisdiction over a defendant. Cybersell AZ concedes that general jurisdiction over Cybersell FL doesn't exist in Arizona, so the only issue in this case is whether specific jurisdiction is available.

We use a three-part test to determine whether a district court may exercise specific jurisdiction over a nonresident defendant: (1) the nonresident defendant must do some act or consummate some transaction with the forum or perform some act by which he purposefully avails himself of the privilege of conducting activities in the forum, thereby invoking the benefits and protections; (2) the claim must be one which arises out of or results from the defendant's forum-related activities; and (3) exercise of jurisdiction must be reasonable.

Cybersell AZ argues that the test is met because trademark infringement occurs when the passing off of the mark occurs, which in this case, it submits, happened when the name "Cybersell" was used on the Internet in connection with advertising. Cybersell FL, on the other hand, contends that a party should not be subject to nationwide, or perhaps worldwide, jurisdiction simply for using the Internet.

A

Since the jurisdictional facts are not in dispute, we turn to the first requirement, which is the most critical. As the Supreme Court emphasized in Hanson v. Denckla, "it is essential in each case that there be some act by which the defendant purposefully avails itself of the privilege of conducting activities within the forum State, thus invoking the benefits and protections of its laws." * * * [T]he "purposeful availment" requirement is satisfied if the defendant has taken deliberate action within the forum state or if he has created continuing obligations to forum residents. It is not required that a defendant be physically present within, or have physical contacts with, the forum, provided that his efforts are purposefully directed toward forum residents.

We have not yet considered when personal jurisdiction may be exercised in the context of cyberspace, but the Second and Sixth Circuits have had occasion to decide whether personal jurisdiction was properly exercised over defendants involved in transmissions over the Internet, see CompuServe, Inc. v. Patterson, 89 F.3d 1257 (6th Cir.1996); Bensusan Restaurant Corp. v. King, 937 F.Supp. 295 (S.D.N.Y.1996), aff'd, 126 F.3d 25 (2d Cir.1997), as have a number of district courts. Because this is a matter of first impression for us, we have looked to all of these cases for guidance. Not surprisingly, they reflect a broad spectrum of Internet use on the one hand, and contacts with the forum on the other. As CompuServe and Bensusan seem to represent opposite ends of the spectrum, we start with them.[4] CompuServe is a computer information service headquartered in Columbus, Ohio, that contracts with individual subscribers to provide access to computing and information services via the Internet. It also operates as an electronic conduit to provide computer software products to its subscribers. Computer software generated and distributed in this way is often referred to as "shareware." Patterson is a Texas resident who subscribed to CompuServe and placed items of "shareware" on the CompuServe system * * *. During the course of this relationship, Patterson electronically transmitted thirty-two master software files to CompuServe, which CompuServe stored and displayed to its subscribers. Sales were made in Ohio and elsewhere, and funds were transmitted through CompuServe in Ohio to Patterson in Texas. In effect, Patterson used CompuServe as a distribution center to market his software. When Patterson threatened litigation over allegedly infringing CompuServe software, CompuServe filed suit in Ohio seeking a declaratory judgment of noninfringement.   The court found that Patterson's relationship with CompuServe as a software provider and marketer was a crucial indicator that Patterson had knowingly reached out to CompuServe's Ohio home and benefited from CompuServe's handling of his software and fees. Because Patterson had chosen to transmit his product from Texas to CompuServe's system in Ohio, and that system provided access to his software to others to whom he advertised and sold his product, the court concluded that Patterson purposefully availed himself of the privilege of doing business in Ohio.

By contrast, the defendant in Bensusan owned a small jazz club known as "The Blue Note" in Columbia, Missouri. He created a general access[5] web page that contained information about the club in Missouri as well as a calendar of events and ticketing information. Tickets were not available through the web site, however. To order tickets, web browsers had to use the names and addresses of ticket outlets in Columbia or a telephone number for charge-by-phone ticket orders, which were available for pick-up on the night of the show at the Blue Note box office in Columbia. Bensusan was a New York corporation that owned "The Blue Note," a popular jazz club in the heart of Greenwich Village. Bensusan owned the rights to the "The Blue Note" mark. Bensusan sued King for trademark infringement in New York. The district court distinguished King's passive web page, which just posted information, from the defendant's use of the Internet in CompuServe by observing that whereas the Texas Internet user specifically targeted Ohio by subscribing to the service, entering into an agreement to sell his software over the Internet, advertising through the service, and sending his software to the service in Ohio,

> King has done nothing to purposefully avail himself of the benefits of New York. King, like numerous others, simply created a Web site and

---

[4] Since Bensusan was decided on the basis of New York's long-arm statute (which requires presence in the forum and is therefore more stringent than due process), its holding is not instructive, but the district court's analysis is. The district court dismissed for lack of personal jurisdiction under the long-arm statute as well as on due process grounds, while the Second Circuit affirmed on the statute and did not discuss the constitutional issue.

[5] A general access site requires no authentication or access code for entry. Thus, the site is accessible to anyone who has access to the Internet.

permitted anyone who could find it to access it. Creating a site, like placing a product into the stream of commerce, may be felt nationwide-or even worldwide-but, without more, it is not an act purposefully directed toward the forum state.

Bensusan (citing the plurality opinion in Asahi). Given these facts, the court reasoned that the argument that the defendant "should have foreseen that users could access the site in New York and be confused as to the relationship of the two Blue Note clubs is insufficient to satisfy due process."

"Interactive" web sites present somewhat different issues. Unlike passive sites such as the defendant's in Bensusan, users can exchange information with the host computer when the site is interactive. Courts that have addressed interactive sites have looked to the "level of interactivity and commercial nature of the exchange of information that occurs on the Web site" to determine if sufficient contacts exist to warrant the exercise of jurisdiction. See, e.g., Zippo Mfg. Co. v. Zippo Dot Com, Inc., 952 F.Supp. 1119, 1124 (W.D.Pa.1997) (finding purposeful availment based on Dot Com's interactive web site and contracts with 3000 individuals and seven Internet access providers in Pennsylvania allowing them to download the electronic messages that form the basis of the suit).

Cybersell AZ points to several district court decisions which it contends have held that the mere advertisement or solicitation for sale of goods and services on the Internet gives rise to specific jurisdiction in the plaintiff's forum. However, so far as we are aware, no court has ever held that an Internet advertisement alone is sufficient to subject the advertiser to jurisdiction in the plaintiff's home state. See, e.g., Smith v. Hobby Lobby Stores, 968 F.Supp. 1356 (W.D.Ark.1997) (no jurisdiction over Hong Kong defendant who advertised in trade journal posted on the Internet without sale of goods or services in Arkansas). Rather, in each, there has been "something more" to indicate that the defendant purposefully (albeit electronically) directed his activity in a substantial way to the forum state.

Inset Systems, Inc. v. Instruction Set, Inc., 937 F.Supp. 161 (D.Conn.1996), is the case most favorable to Cybersell AZ's position. Inset developed and marketed computer software throughout the world; Instruction Set, Inc. (ISI) provided computer technology and support. Inset owned the federal trademark "INSET"; but ISI obtained "INSET.COM" as its Internet domain address for advertising its goods and services. ISI also used the telephone number "1-800-US-INSET." Inset learned of ISI's domain address when it tried to get the same address, and filed suit for trademark infringement in Connecticut. The court reasoned that ISI had purposefully availed itself of doing business in Connecticut because it directed its advertising activities via the Internet and its toll-free number toward the state of Connecticut (and all states); Internet sites and toll-free numbers are designed to communicate with people and their businesses in every state; an Internet advertisement could reach as many as 10,000 Internet users within Connecticut alone; and once posted on the Internet, an advertisement is continuously available to any Internet user.

Cybersell AZ further points to the court's statement in EDIAS Software

International, L.L.C. v. BASIS International Ltd., 947 F.Supp. 413 (D.Ariz.1996), that a defendant "should not be permitted to take advantage of modern technology through an Internet Web page and forum and simultaneously escape traditional notions of jurisdiction." In that case, EDIAS (an Arizona company) alleged that BASIS (a New Mexico company) sent advertising and defamatory statements over the Internet through e-mail, its web page, and forums. However, the court did not rest its minimum contacts analysis on use of the Internet alone; in addition to the Internet, BASIS had a contract with EDIAS, it made sales to EDIAS and other Arizona customers, and its employees had visited Arizona during the course of the business relationship with EDIAS.

Some courts have also given weight to the number of "hits" received by a web page from residents in the forum state, and to other evidence that Internet activity was directed at, or bore fruit in, the forum state. See, e.g., Heroes, Inc. v. Heroes Found., 958 F.Supp. 1 (D.D.C.1996) (web page that solicited contributions and provided toll-free telephone number along with the defendant's use on the web page of the allegedly infringing trademark and logo, along with other contacts, provided sustained contact with the District).

In sum, the common thread, well stated by the district court in Zippo, is that "the likelihood that personal jurisdiction can be constitutionally exercised is directly proportionate to the nature and quality of commercial activity that an entity conducts over the Internet."

B

Here, Cybersell FL has conducted no commercial activity over the Internet in Arizona. All that it did was post an essentially passive home page on the web, using the name "CyberSell," which Cybersell AZ was in the process of registering as a federal service mark. While there is no question that anyone, anywhere could access that home page and thereby learn about the services offered, we cannot see how from that fact alone it can be inferred that Cybersell FL deliberately directed its merchandising efforts toward Arizona residents.

Cybersell FL did nothing to encourage people in Arizona to access its site, and there is no evidence that any part of its business (let alone a continuous part of its business) was sought or achieved in Arizona. To the contrary, it appears to be an operation where business was primarily generated by the personal contacts of one of its founders. While those contacts are not entirely local, they aren't in Arizona either. No Arizonan except for Cybersell AZ "hit" Cybersell FL's web site. There is no evidence that any Arizona resident signed up for Cybersell FL's web construction services. It entered into no contracts in Arizona, made no sales in Arizona, received no telephone calls from Arizona, earned no income from Arizona, and sent no messages over the Internet to Arizona. The only message it received over the Internet from Arizona was from Cybersell AZ. Cybersell FL did not have an "800" number, let alone a toll-free number that also used the "Cybersell" name. The interactivity of its web page is limited to receiving the browser's name and address and an indication of interest — signing up for the service is not an option, nor did anyone from Arizona do so. No money changed hands on the Internet from (or through) Arizona. In short, Cybersell FL has done no act and has consummated no transaction, nor has it performed any act by which it purposefully availed itself of the privilege of conducting activities, in Arizona, thereby invoking the benefits and protections of Arizona law.

We therefore hold that Cybersell FL's contacts are insufficient to establish "purposeful availment." Cybersell AZ has thus failed to satisfy the first prong of our three-part test for specific jurisdiction. We decline to go further solely on the footing that Cybersell AZ has alleged trademark infringement over the Internet by Cybersell FL's use of the registered name "Cybersell" on an essentially passive web page advertisement. Otherwise, every complaint arising out of alleged trademark infringement on the Internet would automatically result in personal jurisdiction wherever the plaintiff's principal place of business is located. That would not comport with traditional notions of what qualifies as purposeful activity invoking the benefits and protections of the forum state.

III

Cybersell AZ also invokes the "effects" test employed in Calder v. Jones with respect to intentional torts directed to the plaintiff, causing injury where the plaintiff lives. However, we don't see this as a Calder case. Because Shirley Jones was who she was (a famous entertainer who lived and worked in California) and was libeled by a story in the National Enquirer, which was published in Florida but had a nationwide circulation with a large audience in California, the Court could easily hold that California was the "focal point both of the story and of the harm suffered" and so jurisdiction in California based on the "effects" of the defendants' Florida conduct was proper. There is nothing comparable about Cybersell FL's web page. Nor does the "effects" test apply with the same force to Cybersell AZ as it would to an individual, because a corporation does not suffer harm in a particular geographic location in the same sense that an individual does. Cybersell FL's web page simply was not aimed intentionally at Arizona knowing that harm was likely to be caused there to Cybersell AZ.

IV

We conclude that the essentially passive nature of Cybersell FL's activity in posting a home page on the World Wide Web that allegedly used the service mark of Cybersell AZ does not qualify as purposeful activity invoking the benefits and protections of Arizona. As it engaged in no commercial activity and had no other contacts via the Internet or otherwise in Arizona, Cybersell FL lacks sufficient minimum contacts with Arizona for personal jurisdiction to be asserted over it there. Accordingly, its motion to dismiss for lack of personal jurisdiction was properly granted.

NOTES AND PROBLEMS FOR DISCUSSION

1. (a) How did the court in the principal case adapt traditional Due Process analysis to this newly developing context?

(b) Does the court's chosen analytical model square with either of the two "stream of commerce" formulations proffered in *Asahi*?

(c) By focusing on the level of interactivity of the defendant's site, is the court relying on the extent to which *third parties* have interacted with the defendant's site in the forum state? If so, is this consistent with the lesson of *Volkswagen* — that the appropriate subject of inquiry is the *defendant*'s activities within the forum rather than actions taken by others to bring the defendant's products or services into the forum?

(d) How did the court characterize the level of the Cybersell's contacts with the forum state? Do you agree with the court's finding?

2. Assuming that the states in each of the following problems enacted a long arm statute that provided jurisdiction to the extent permitted by the Constitution, would the court have personal jurisdiction in the following cases?

For a thoughtful analysis of the judicial approach to cyberspace jurisdiction and a suggestion that this analysis improperly ignores the availability of jurisdiction avoidance mechanisms, including technologies that enable a web site operator to limit access, see A. Benjamin Spencer, *Jurisdiction and the Internet: Returning To Traditional Principles to Analyze Network-Mediated Contacts,* 2006 U.ILL.L.REV. 71 (2006).

(a) A real estate agent living in Boston conducted much of her business through the use of an email address she obtained for free from Hotmail.com, a private company located in Chicago that offers free email service to the world. By visiting Hotmail's web site from her computer in Boston, she accessed the emails that were stored on Hotmail's servers in Chicago. Harvey, a Louisiana citizen, rented a summer home in Massachusetts through the agent and consummated the entire deal through an exchange of emails. He files a breach of contract claim against the agent in an Illinois state court, claiming that the home was not as represented in her various email messages.

(b) Same facts as in "(a)" except that Harvey moved to Chicago before suing the agent.

(c) Vivian, a Georgia citizen, purchased an electric knife at Cathy's Cutlery, a family owned business on Cape Cod that she patronized during a summer vacation. After Vivian returned home to Atlanta, the knife's electric cord caught on fire and injured her. She sued Cathy's Cutlery in Georgia state court. Cathy's Cutlery maintains a web site that contains pictures of the store, its complete inventory and invites visitors to place orders through the use of a credit card. Vivian has never visited this web site and no Georgia citizen has ever ordered anything from Cathy's through its web site or purchased anything directly from the Cape Cod store. *See* Gator.com Corp. v. L.L. Bean, Inc., 341 F.2d 1072 (9th Cir. 2002) (upholding exercise of general jurisdiction over the defendant retailer based on its extensive on-line marketing and sales in the forum state as well as its purchase of products from numerous forum-state vendors), 398 F.3d 1125 (9th Cir. 2005) (en banc) (dismissing appeal on grounds of mootness after case settled).

(d) James, an Oklahoma citizen, is addicted to Internet "chat rooms." He spends hours sending messages through the Internet to the scores and, occasionally, hundreds of folks participating in that "chat." Participants in chat rooms send messages from their computer to a central (host) server that then bounces the message to the individual computer of each person logged onto that chat room. In one of his messages, James vilified Ray, a former employer who now resides in Texas. Ray brings a defamation action against James in state court in Texas.

(e) Barbra, a Delaware citizen, is a "cyber pirate" who registers domain names on the Internet belonging to well known individuals and businesses. A domain name is the address of a web site that an Internet surfer uses to find and to access that site. In order for each domain name to have a unique address, each name must be registered. After Barbra registers these well-known domain names, she offers to sell them to the rightful owner of the trademark. Suppose that Pepsi, Inc. had not registered the "pepsi.com" domain name and that Barbra did. She then attempted to sell it to Pepsi for $1 million. Pepsi, Inc, a New York corporation with its headquarters in New York, files a trademark dilution action against Barbra in New York.

(f) Same facts as "(e)", above, except that Pepsi brought its suit in a federal district court in Virginia, the location of the company with which all ".com" domain names must be registered. This suit was brought under the terms of the Anticybersquatting Consumer Protection Act, 15 U.S.C. §1125(d) (1999) (ACPA), which allows the owner of a protected trademark to protect its rights under that mark by bringing an *in rem* action against the actual offending domain name, rather than the entity that registered the domain name, when the plaintiff cannot obtain personal jurisdiction over the allegedly cybersquatting registrant. The Act, which limits a plaintiff to the remedies of forfeiture, cancellation and transfer of the domain name, locates the situs of the domain name (and authorizes the bringing of such an *in rem* proceeding) in the district in which the register of domain names is located.

The enactment of the ACPA has not been without its critics. Some have suggested, for example, that the statute's *in rem* provisions were unnecessary because application of standard *International Shoe* doctrine would permit exercise of *in personam* jurisdiction over most cybersquatters. See Michael P. Allen, *In Rem Jurisdiction from Pennoyer to Shaffer to the Anticybersquatting Consumer Protection Act,* 11 Geo. Mason L.Rev. 243 (2002). Others have maintained that the creation of *in rem* jurisdiction where *in personam* jurisdiction is unavailable does not meet constitutional due process standards, see Catherine T. Struve & R. Polk Wagner, *Realspace Sovereigns In Cyberspace: Problems with the Anticybersquatting Consumer Protection Act,* 17 Berk.Tech.L.J. 990 (2002).

(g) Easy Access, a Georgia incorporated company, is an Internet Service Provider (ISP) that provides its customers with the bandwidth service needed to maintain their own websites. One of Easy Access' customers, Ripe Music, another Georgia corporation, has a website that sells bootleg versions of copyrighted songs. Johnny Dog, a nationally known rap artist, brought a copyright infringement action against both Ripe Music and Easy Access in his home state of Maryland. Easy Access' only office is located in Atlanta and it has no customers in Maryland. Since Ripe Music sold lots of pirated J. Dog recordings to Maryland customers, it did not contest the exercise of personal jurisdiction over it. See ALS Scan, Inc. v. Digital Service Consultants, Inc., 293 F.3d 707 (4th Cir.2002).

3. Unlike every other principal case that we have read to this point, the action in *Cybersell* was filed in a federal, rather than a state, trial court.

(a) Is there any reason why the scope of a federal court's jurisdictional authority should be different from that of a state court?

(b) Why did the court in *Cybersell* refer to the absence of a federal statute governing personal jurisdiction?

These two questions, and others, are the subject of the next section of this chapter.

SECTION F.   PERSONAL JURISDICTION OF THE FEDERAL COURTS

Each of the preceding sections of this chapter has dealt with the limitations on a *state* court's adjudicative authority. We began this chapter with the statement that every court must possess both personal and subject matter jurisdiction. We also noted, however, that the American judicial system is composed of both state and federal courts. And although this requirement for adjudicative authority applies to both sovereign judicial systems, one can well imagine that the scope of authority of both judicial systems over persons, property, and particular causes of action does not necessarily coincide if, for no other reason, than to avoid redundancy.

In this section of Chapter 2, we will briefly examine the limitations placed on the personal jurisdiction of federal courts. The more intricate topic of the subject matter jurisdiction of federal courts will occupy the entirety of Chapter 3.

The overarching analytical approach to federal court personal jurisdiction is identical to the one applied to state courts, i.e., a court must have a statutory basis for jurisdiction, and that statutory authorization must not exceed the due process constitutional limitations on the exercise of governmental authority. But within this common framework, the separate and distinct nature of the two systems suggests the possibility of different governing standards. For example, on the statutory side, would we expect Congress to have enacted national long-arm statutes? If so, would they focus on activities within a particular state, within a federal judicial district, or within the nation as a whole? Alternatively, in the absence of any applicable federal long-arm statute, what statutory rule should be invoked? Then, with respect to the constitutional inquiry, since federal governmental conduct is limited by the Fifth, rather than the Fourteenth Amendment, should the due process restraints on personal jurisdiction arising out of the Fifth Amendment necessarily replicate those associated with the due process clause of the Fourteenth Amendment? Would your answer to this latter question depend on the nature of the interest(s) served by each of these due process limitations?

1.   STATUTORY DELEGATION OF AUTHORITY

Read Rule 4(k) of the Federal Rules of Civil Procedure.

There are several sources of statutory authorization for federal court personal jurisdiction. On rare occasion, the federal statute providing the substantive rights that give rise to a cause of action contains a jurisdictional provision. In such instances, as in antitrust and securities legislation, these enactments provide for nationwide personal jurisdiction. Nationwide jurisdiction is also authorized over federal statutory interpleader actions, see 28 U.S.C. §2361, and in bankruptcy actions pursuant to the Federal Rules of Bankruptcy Procedure, see F.R.Bank.P. 7004(d). For the most part, however, substantive federal statutes are silent as to the enforcing court's personal jurisdiction. Additionally, as we will see in Chapter 3, federal courts, under certain circumstances, can hear (i.e., have subject matter jurisdiction over) cases arising under state law. Thus, in cases arising either under federal statutes lacking a personal jurisdictional provision or under state law (categories which together account for the overwhelming majority of federal court civil filings), a federal district court must look elsewhere for the standard governing its personal jurisdiction. Since Congress has not enacted any generally applicable long-arm statutes, this void in statutory authorization has been filled by a subsection of one of the Federal Rules of Civil Procedure.

Nearly all of the provisions of Rule 4 of the Federal Rules of Civil Procedure deal with a series of topics concerning the form by which, and manner in which, defendants can be served or have service of process waived. As you can see, however, Rule 4(k)(1) delimits the federal district courts' personal jurisdiction by providing that unless a federal statute or rule provides otherwise, a federal trial court's statutory grant of personal jurisdiction shall consist of the state jurisdictional statute of the state in which the federal court is located.

There are two exceptions to the general rule incorporating state law. One applies to cases involving either the joinder of additional parties needed for just adjudication under Rule 19 or third party defendants impleaded (i.e., sued for indemnity or contribution) under Rule 14. In these instances, pursuant to the so-called "bulge" provision, a federal district court has personal jurisdiction over any defendant joined under Rules 14 or 19 that is served within a radius of 100 miles from that trial court.

Secondly, with respect only to those claims arising under federal law, Rule 4(k)(2), added in 1993, authorizes the exercise of nationwide jurisdiction over any defendant who would not be subject to jurisdiction in any individual state when the exercise of nationwide jurisdiction is consistent with federal constitutional and statutory requirements. This provision, which functions as a sort of federal long-arm statute, was designed to fill the jurisdictional gap created in cases arising under federal statutes that do not provide for nationwide jurisdiction and which involve a foreign defendant who lacks sufficient contacts with any state to subject it to that state's jurisdiction (whether by reason of the paucity of contacts or because the type of contacts do not meet the requirements of that state's long-arm statute) but who has the requisite connection with the U.S. as a whole to make the exercise of jurisdiction by a federal court constitutional.

2. Constitutional Limitations

Where a federal trial court exercises jurisdiction pursuant to the long-arm statute of the state in which it sits, the constitutionality of that jurisdiction is evaluated according to the due process clause of the Fourteenth Amendment, since the delegation of jurisdiction flows from a state statute. But in the limited instances where a federal jurisdictional provision exists, or where nationwide jurisdiction is asserted under Rule 4(k)(2) (i.e., against a foreign defendant not subject to jurisdiction in any one state), the constitutionality of that jurisdiction is measured by the due process clause of the Fifth Amendment. According to the prevailing caselaw, this means that the "minimum contacts" inquiry is based on the extent of the defendant's aggregate contacts with the U.S. as a whole, rather than on the basis of contacts with any one particular state or federal judicial district.

This bifurcated analytical model can pose interesting problems. For example, which of the two standards applies when a plaintiff brings both state and federal law claims against one or more defendants and the federal statute creating the cause of action contains a nationwide jurisdictional provision? Similarly, which approach governs the personal jurisdictional inquiry when a claim against one defendant arises under a federal statute permitting nationwide service of process and another claim against that or a different defendant is based on a federal statute for which nationwide service of process is not available? These issues are confronted in the following case.

ESAB Group, Inc. v. Centricut, Inc.

United States Court of Appeals, Fourth Circuit, 1997.

126 F.3d 617, cert. denied, 523 U.S. 1048, 118 S.Ct. 1364, 140 L.Ed.2d 513 (1998).

NIEMEYER, CIRCUIT JUDGE:

In this case we must determine whether the district court in South Carolina obtained personal jurisdiction over New Hampshire defendants pursuant to a complaint alleging a civil RICO claim and related state law claims. * * *

* * *

I

The ESAB Group, Inc. is a Delaware corporation located in Florence, South Carolina, which engages in the business of developing and manufacturing welding and cutting systems. In its amended complaint against Centricut, Inc * * *, the ESAB Group alleged that Centricut * * * participated in a conspiracy to appropriate the ESAB Group's trade secrets and customer lists. * * * The complaint contains six counts based on state law, alleging conspiracy, intentional interference with economic relations, breach of contract accompanied by a fraudulent act, South Carolina Unfair Trade Practices Act violations, misappropriation of trade secrets, intentional interference with prospective contractual relations, and entitlement to equitable relief. It also contains a count for civil RICO based on 18 U.S.C. §1962.

Centricut is a New Hampshire limited liability company that manufactures and sells replacement parts for cutting machines, and arguably competes to some degree with the ESAB Group. Centricut conducts its business entirely through mail order. It has no offices or sales representatives in South Carolina; it has no property in South Carolina; it has no phone listings there; and it has never paid

South Carolina taxes. Moreover, it claims that no employee has ever traveled to South Carolina "for any purpose." As of 1995, Centricut did have 26 customers who resided in South Carolina, constituting 1% of all of its customers and representing .079% of its gross annual sales. It also purchased on one occasion between $10,000 and $20,000 worth of parts from a South Carolina supplier. Centricut stated that it had never targeted formal advertising at South Carolina, having only once published formal advertising in a trade journal of national circulation.

* * *

Centricut * * * filed several motions, one of which sought to dismiss the complaint under Federal Rule of Civil Procedure 12(b)(2), alleging that [its] contacts with South Carolina were insufficient to subject [it] to personal jurisdiction there. The ESAB Group responded that the defendant "purposefully directed * * * [its] activities toward the State of South Carolina and its corporate citizens, and this litigation arises from those activities." The ESAB Group claimed alternatively that the court had personal jurisdiction over the defendant by reason of the nationwide service of process in RICO actions permitted by 18 U.S.C. § 1965(b).

The district court denied the motion to dismiss, holding that it had personal jurisdiction over Centricut * * * based on "the effects test" drawn from Calder v. Jones. The district court said that because Centricut's actions "were designed to damage the [South Carolina] plaintiff . . . and did damage the plaintiff," it was fair to hale Centricut into a South Carolina court. The district court granted leave to the defendant to file an interlocutory appeal * * * and we did likewise.

II

Federal district courts may exercise in personam jurisdiction only to the degree authorized by Congress acting under its constitutional power to "ordain and establish" the lower federal courts. U.S. Const. art. III. The exercise of personal jurisdiction is also constrained by the Due Process Clause of the Fifth Amendment. As prerequisites to exercising personal jurisdiction over a defendant, a federal court must have * * * a constitutionally sufficient relationship between the defendant and the forum, and authorization for service of a summons on the person. Thus, a federal court's exercise of jurisdiction over a person is closely linked to effective service of process.

Federal Rule of Civil Procedure 4(k)(1) provides that "[s]ervice of a summons or filing a waiver of service is effective to establish [a federal court's] jurisdiction over the person of a defendant" if such service is accomplished on a defendant whom the law has made amenable to the court's process. Rule 4(k) enumerates five sources authorizing service to effect in personam jurisdiction: (1) state law; (2) Federal Rules of Civil Procedure 14 and 19 (relating to third party practice and joinder), provided service is effected "not more than 100 miles from the place from which the summons issues"; (3) the federal interpleader statute[*]; (4) federal statute; and (5) Federal Rule of Civil Procedure 4(k)(2) itself, to enforce claims "arising under federal law" on defendants who are not subject to the jurisdiction of any state.

In the district court, the ESAB Group argued that it had served the defendant in the manner specified by South Carolina's long-arm statute, and by RICO. Because the district court held that the ESAB Group had effectively served the defendant under South Carolina's long-arm statute, the court did not address whether service was effective under the RICO statute.

When authorized by Federal Rule of Civil Procedure 4(k)(1)(A), service of process sufficient to exercise jurisdiction over a defendant is limited by state law, so that any challenge to the personal jurisdiction requires us to assess the jurisdiction of the courts in the state where the district court is located. * * *

Since in personam jurisdiction of a state court is limited by that state's laws and by the Fourteenth Amendment, we first inquire whether the state long-arm statute authorizes the exercise of jurisdiction over the defendant. If it does, we must then determine whether the state court's exercise of such jurisdiction is consistent with the Due Process Clause of the Fourteenth Amendment. Because Rule 4(k)(1)(A) delimits the scope of effective federal service in terms of the limits on state court jurisdiction, our inquiry into the federal court's jurisdiction pursuant to Rule 4(k)(1)(A) incorporates the Fourteenth Amendment due process standard, even though that Amendment applies of its own force only to states.

[The court then explained that since South Carolina's long-arm statute had been interpreted to reach the outer bounds permitted by the Due Process Clause, it was appropriate to merge the statutory with the constitutional inquiry. The court then concluded that since the defendant had manifested no behavior intentionally targeted at or focused on the forum state, there was a constitutionally insufficient basis upon which to exercise either specific or general jurisdiction. Consequently, it held the federal trial court could not exercise *in personam* jurisdiction pursuant to service under Rule 4(k)(1)(A).]

* * *

III

Although we conclude that personal jurisdiction may not be exercised over Centricut * * * under Federal Rule of Civil Procedure 4(k)(1)(A) because a South Carolina court could not assert such jurisdiction, we must now address the ESAB Group's alternative basis for personal jurisdiction based on 18 U.S.C. § 1965(b).

One of the sources enumerated in Federal Rule of Civil Procedure 4(k) for service that effectively enables the exercise of personal jurisdiction over a defendant is "a statute of the United States." In this case, a federal statute does authorize such service.

In enacting the Organized Crime Control Act of 1970, Congress prohibited

---

[*] [The separate reference to interpleader in Rule 4(k)(1)(c) was eliminated by the 2007 amendments as redundant in light of the general provision recognizing personal jurisdiction authorized by a federal statute. — eds.]

various activities generally associated with organized crime. In addition to providing criminal penalties, Congress granted a private civil right of action to "[a]ny person injured in his business or property by reason of a violation of" the RICO provisions. The RICO statute authorizes * * * service of process "in any judicial district in which such person resides, is found, has an agent, or transacts his affairs," evidencing Congress' desire that "[p]rovision [be] made for nationwide * * * service of process." * * *

The due process constraint on service under Federal Rule of Civil Procedure 4(k)(1)(D) [now codified at 4(k)(1)(C) as a result of the 2007 amendments to the Federal Rules — eds.], is not, however, grounded in the Fourteenth Amendment, which circumscribes service under state process pursuant to Rule 4(k)(1)(A). Rather, it is the Due Process Clause of the Fifth Amendment which constrains the exercise of the federal government's sovereign powers. The Fifth Amendment's Due Process Clause not only limits the extraterritorial scope of federal sovereign power, but also protects the liberty interests of individuals against unfair burden and inconvenience. However, when the defendant is located within the United States, he must look primarily to federal venue requirements for protection from onerous litigation, because it is only in highly unusual cases that inconvenience will rise to a level of constitutional concern.

In this case, * * * Centricut has been served with process in a judicial district where [it] resides, [is] found, or transacts [its] affairs. Because * * * [it has] been validly served pursuant to RICO's nationwide service provision, in personam jurisdiction over [it] is established, provided that such jurisdiction comports with the Fifth Amendment. We believe that it does, discerning no evidence from the record in this case of such extreme inconvenience or unfairness as would outweigh the congressionally articulated policy of allowing the assertion of in personam jurisdiction in South Carolina. Nor do we believe the dictates of judicial efficiency counsel so strongly against a federal forum in South Carolina that constitutional due process is offended. While there is no doubt some inconvenience to the defendant in having to defend this action in South Carolina, it is not so extreme as to defeat the exercise of personal jurisdiction pursuant to valid service of process, although it may certainly factor into a transfer decision. Accordingly, we hold that the district court in South Carolina may constitutionally exercise in personam jurisdiction over * * * Centricut * * *.

In so holding, we do not decide any issues of venue raised by the defendants. The district court may ultimately have to decide whether venue is proper * * *. The question of in personam jurisdiction, however, depends on whether service of process has been authorized. Section 1965(d) authorizes service of process "in any judicial district in which such person . . . is found." Because service was accomplished on the defendants where they were found, personal jurisdiction was established.

IV

Even though the district court has personal jurisdiction over the defendant to adjudicate the RICO claim because of its authorization for nationwide service of process, the question remains whether that service authorizes the district court to assert personal jurisdiction over the defendant to adjudicate the state law claims against * * * [it].   If a defendant's conduct in the forum state provides insufficient contacts with the state to justify specific long-arm jurisdiction, two questions arise: First, whether the defendant has reasonable expectations not to be tried there on the state claims, which may not even arise under the laws of the forum state; and second, whether the defendant in these circumstances has a constitutional protection against adjudication of the state claims against him in a state which is not authorized to assert personal jurisdiction over him.   These questions have not been answered in this circuit.

The existence of these questions highlights the substantial variations in authorization provided by the sources enumerated in Federal Rule of Civil Procedure 4(k) for service of process.   Even for federal claims, the effective territorial authority of the federal court may differ significantly from case to case, depending on the federal statute involved.   For example, if the claim is based on a federal statute authorizing nationwide service of process, personal jurisdiction may be asserted over a defendant anywhere in the country, whereas if the statute creating the federal claim does not provide for nationwide service of process, process may extend only to the boundaries of the state in which the district lies.   This poses an infrequently presented question: If a case includes a claim brought under a federal statute authorizing a nationwide service of process and another claim under a statute or under state law for which nationwide service of process is not available, does the court have personal jurisdiction over the defendant to adjudicate the entire case?

A somewhat analogous problem arose in the context of subject matter jurisdiction, which, of course, is quite distinct in principle from personal jurisdiction.   Nevertheless, the analogy is useful.   To resolve the problem of whether a federal court which is presented with the resolution of a federal claim may also resolve state claims arising out of the same nucleus of operative fact, the Supreme Court developed the doctrine of pendent jurisdiction.   Under that doctrine, when a claim authorized by federal law and by Article III of the Constitution is properly in a federal court, and that claim is so related to a state claim not independently subject to federal jurisdiction that the two may be considered "one constitutional case," the federal court has pendent jurisdiction to adjudicate the state claim.   The Court articulated the necessary and proper relationship between the claims that they "must derive from a common nucleus of operative fact."   But even so, pendent jurisdiction is a discretionary power which is exercised in furtherance of "judicial economy, convenience and fairness to the litigants."   The doctrine has since been codified at 28 U.S.C. § 1367.

We believe that similar considerations urge that we recognize pendent personal jurisdiction of a district court which has obtained personal jurisdiction over a defendant by reason of a federal claim to adjudicate state claims properly within the court's subject matter jurisdiction, even though that state's long-arm statute could not authorize service over the defendants with respect to the state claims.

When a federal statute authorizes a federal district court to exercise personal jurisdiction over a defendant beyond the borders of the district and the defendant is effectively brought before the court, we can find little reason not to authorize the court to adjudicate a state claim properly within the court's subject matter jurisdiction so long as the facts of the federal and state claims arise from a common nucleus of operative fact. The defendant will have to adjudicate the facts of the federal claim, and it could impose only a minimal burden to require the defendant to provide a defense on the factually-related state claim. We agree with the observation that

> judicial economy and convenience of the parties is best facilitated by a consideration of all legal theories arising from a single set of operative facts. . . . Once that set of facts and defendants are legitimately before th[e] court . . . little would be gained by not requiring a defendant to defend against a certain type of theory superimposed upon those facts.

Sohns v. Dahl, 392 F.Supp. 1208, 1218 (W.D.Va.1975). Accordingly, we conclude that under the doctrine of pendent personal jurisdiction, the district court has authority over the defendants to decide both the federal and the state claims alleged against them. * * *

Our recognition of pendent personal jurisdiction should present no constitutional objection any more serious than did pendent jurisdiction involving the court's subject matter jurisdiction. Once a court has a constitutional case, in the Article III sense, properly before it, service by a court sufficient to assert personal jurisdiction over a defendant by any authorized mechanism consistent with due process may be held to apply to the entire constitutional case. In this case, the parties agree that the federal court has subject matter jurisdiction over the ESAB Group's claims and is thus competent to adjudicate them. They also agree that the factual nucleus for the state claims and the RICO claim is the same. Since the court has personal jurisdiction over the defendants under service of process authorized by the Federal Rule of Civil Procedure 4(k)(1)(D) and by the RICO statute, we can find no constitutional bar to requiring the defendants to defend the entire constitutional case, which includes both federal and state claims arising from the same nucleus of facts, so long as the federal claim is not wholly immaterial or insubstantial.

For the reasons provided in this opinion, we reverse the ruling of the district court that the defendants were properly served under South Carolina's long-arm statute but affirm its conclusion that the district court has personal jurisdiction over Centricut * * *. The case is remanded for further proceedings.

NOTES AND PROBLEMS FOR DISCUSSION

1. Nearly one year after the Fourth Circuit's decision in *ESAB Group*, the plaintiff filed another action against defendant Centricut, this time asserting an infringement claim under the federal patent statute. In response to the defendant's challenge to its exercise of personal jurisdiction, the court, without a word of explanation or reference to Rule 4(k)(1), looked to the forum state's long-arm statute and concluded that there was an insufficient basis for jurisdiction. ESAB Group, Inc. v. Centricut LLC, 34 F.Supp.2d 323 (D.S.C.1999). It turned out that Centricut, in addition to its mail order business, operated a web site on the Internet. Visitors to the web site could request literature about Centricut products, obtain product samples, and place orders for

Centricut products. To place an order, however, a consumer was required to call a toll free "800" number listed on the web site to establish an on-line ordering account. Only six individuals ever registered for on-line ordering and none of them were from the forum state. The trial judge characterized the web site as interactive, but concluded that as there was no evidence that any South Carolina resident had either visited the defendant's web page or purchased products through an on-line account, the possibility that someone from South Carolina *could* interact with the defendant's web site was insufficient to confer either general or specific jurisdiction over Centricut. The availability of on-line purchasing, the court reasoned, did not constitute either the sale of, or the offer to sell products in South Carolina since no one in South Carolina had been shown to have ever seen the web page. Is this decision consistent with the ruling in *Cybersell*?

2.   What was the statutory basis supporting the exercise of personal jurisdiction over the defendant with respect to each of the plaintiff's claims?

3.   Suppose that the plaintiff in *ESAB Group* had asserted only the state law claims against Centricut and that the civil RICO count had been asserted against a separate defendant. Would the result have changed?

4.   (a) What criteria did the court use in determining whether its exercise of personal jurisdiction under the civil RICO statute satisfied the due process requirements of the Fifth Amendment?

(b) Is this approach consistent with the standard developed by the Supreme Court in Fourteenth Amendment due process cases such as *International Shoe* and *Volkswagen*?

5.   When personal jurisdiction in a case arising under federal law is sought under Rule 4(k)(2), the plaintiff clearly bears the burden of establishing that the defendant's aggregate contacts with the U.S. meets Fifth Amendment due process requirements. But must the plaintiff also establish the absence of personal jurisdiction over the defendant in all fifty states or does the defendant have to show that it is subject to personal jurisdiction in at least one state? And irrespective of who bears the burden of persuasion on the question, does the requirement that the defendant not be subject to jurisdiction in any state encompass both personal and subject matter jurisdiction? See U.S. v. Swiss American Bank, Ltd., 191 F.3d 30 (1st Cir.1999).

SECTION G. SERVICE OF PROCESS: EXERCISING POWER AND PROVIDING NOTICE

1. INTRODUCTION

Implicit in the preceding discussion of the limits on a court's personal jurisdiction was the notion that procedures exist by which a court exercises its allotted adjudicative power over defendants. And just as the contours of the doctrine of personal jurisdiction have been transformed over time, the methods employed to exert power over defendants and to inform them of the pendency of civil actions also have evolved from their common law origins in response to advancements in communications and transportation modalities.

As the Supreme Court noted in *Pennoyer*, from the early days of the English common law, the presence of the defendants in actions at law was secured through the royal court's issuance of the common law writ of *capias ad respondendum*, which ordered the sheriff to seize the body of the defendant and hold it in custody until the defendant either posted sufficient security or appeared at the relevant proceeding. Similarly, in actions in equity, the defendant's appearance was obtained when the chancery (or equity) court issued a *subpoena ad respondendum* directly to the defendant, compelling him to appear. But, as the Court in *Pennoyer* also explained, these techniques, which were adopted by many colonial American courts, eventually gave way to less intrusive forms of what we now call *service of process*.

Although obtaining the defendant's appearance, or, as we now view it, exercising adjudicative authority over the defendant, is an essential function of service of process, it is not the only one. Any litigative system would lack legitimacy if it did not compel the moving party to provide the defendant(s) with some form of notice of the existence of the civil action and some information concerning the nature of the plaintiff's complaint. Affording defendants notice of pending litigation is the second function of service of process. And statutes and/or rules control the manner by which service, i.e., the transmission of process, is effectuated in both the state and federal judicial systems. These guidelines, for example, detail not only the manner of service (e.g., by hand, mail, publication, electronic mail, fax, etc.) but also the location of service, the contents of the process, and the identity of the recipient.

We already have seen how the constitutional right to due process of law became the benchmark for setting limits on a court's exercise of personal jurisdiction during the latter half of the twentieth century. This constitutional guarantee plays a similarly crucial role, and one of more longstanding duration, with respect to determining the fairness of the "notice" component of service of process. Due process, therefore, not only circumscribes the court's power to issue enforceable judgments; it also provides defendants with a right to be notified, at a minimum, in some objectively fair manner when actions are brought against them. In fact, as the limits of personal jurisdiction expand and an increasing number of defendants are required to defend in forums outside of their states of domicile, the method by which they are notified of these proceedings assumes increasing significance. You will recall, for example, that the Supreme Court in *Pennoyer* scrutinized the method used to bring the defendant Neff under the personal jurisdiction of the Oregon state court and, simultaneously, to notify him of the pendency of Mitchell's action. Moreover, as we discovered in the long arm statute context, the fact that a legislature has confected a particular service regime does not insulate that scheme from inquiry into whether or not it meets the constitutional standard of fairness embodied in the due process guarantees of the Fifth and Fourteenth Amendments to the U.S. Constitution. Conversely, however, the fact that a particular form of service might meet the constitutionally mandated threshold of fairness does not preclude a state from requiring service that is more demanding than this constitutional minimum. Consequently, just as we did in analyzing the existence of personal jurisdiction, to fully assess the adequacy of service of process, we must inquire both into whether the employed procedure comported with the applicable state or federal requirements as well as whether these requirements satisfy the constitutional due process measure of fairness.

Service of process refers to the mechanism by which *process* is transmitted to the defendant. *Process* typically consists of two documents; a summons and a complaint. A summons is an official court document notifying the defendant that a civil action has been filed against it and instructing it to appear in court upon penalty of default. A complaint sets forth the plaintiff's request for relief and some brief statement of the facts and legal theory underlying the claim. Since the different states vary in the extent to which they conform to this blueprint, we will, once again, turn to the uniform federal model to discern and evaluate the rules governing service of process.

2. SERVICE OF PROCESS UNDER THE FEDERAL RULES OF CIVIL PROCEDURE

In 1934, Congress passed the Rules Enabling Act, 28 U.S.C. §2072, which delegated to the U.S. Supreme Court the power to promulgate a set of unified rules governing the conduct of civil litigation in the federal courts. The Court, in turn, turned over this task to the Judicial Conference of the United States, which assigned responsibility for formulating and revising Federal Rules of Civil Procedure to its Standing Committee on Rules of Practice and Procedure. The actual drafting of new and amended rules, however, has been entrusted to a group of distinguished judges, attorneys and academics called the Advisory Committee to the Standing Committee on Rules of Practice and Procedure. Rules drafted by this Advisory Committee are sent to the Standing Committee for approval. (In resolving questions concerning the meaning and application of the Rules, courts frequently consult and rely upon the Advisory Committee Notes, a collection of annotations prepared by the Advisory Committee and attached to the textual provisions of the proposals.) Once approved, the proposed rules are published and interested parties are invited to attend public hearings to comment on them. The rules that emerge from these hearings, if approved by the Standing Committee and the Judicial Conference, are then sent to the Supreme Court for review. The Court rarely invokes this review authority and typically approves the proposals and submits them to Congress. The Rules then become effective unless rejected or altered by the legislature within a prescribed time frame. With rare exception, Congress does not reject the recommendations. But since these "Rules" are not the product of the traditional process governing administrative rulemaking, judicial adjudication, or legislative enactment, they are called "Rules" and not statutes, administrative regulations, or judicial opinions.

Read F.R.Civ.P. 4

The federal and state rules governing service of process all address certain basic questions. These include (a) how service is accomplished; (b) who is served (this is particularly important when the target of service is an entity such as a corporation, partnership, or governmental entity), (c) where service can or must take place; and (d) the time period within which service must occur.

Rule 4 of the Federal Rules of Civil Procedure sets forth the requirements for service in federally filed civil actions. This is not the first time we have encountered this Rule. You will recall that we examined it in the context of determining the limits on personal jurisdiction of federal district courts. We saw that Rule 4(k) provides for service to be an effective method of establishing personal jurisdiction only where the defendant would be subject to personal jurisdiction under the terms of the forum state's long-arm statute of the state, unless personal jurisdiction is otherwise authorized by a federal statute or rule. Rule 4(e) similarly incorporates state standards, by affording plaintiffs the option of effecting service pursuant to either (a) federal standards codified in Rule 4, or (b) the state law requirements of (1) the state where the district court is located or (2) the state where service is made. Moreover, these state law options are available in both diversity and federal question cases.

Prior to 1993, the extensive set of regulations contained in Rule 4 constituted the ground rules by which plaintiffs and their process servers played a not infrequent game of cat and mouse with those defendants who were less than eager to accept service. Stories became legion of process servers celebrated for the ingenious and often brazen tactics employed to lure reluctant targets out of hiding as they stalked and snared their prey. These efforts, however, also had a serious side. The time, effort, and resources spent in hunting down defendants put a strain on the judicial system.

In an attempt to reduce the time and cost of effecting service, Rule 4 was amended to impose an affirmative duty upon certain categories of defendants (i.e., competent adults, corporations, partnerships and unincorporated associations) located within the U.S. to avoid the unnecessary costs of service by agreeing to waive formal (i.e. personal) service of process in favor of service by mail or its equivalent. Under Rule 4(d)(1)(G), plaintiffs may transmit a copy of the request for waiver form to the defendants (other than incompetents, minors, and foreign, federal, state or local governments as to whom waiver is not available) by first class mail or other reliable means, including, according to the Advisory Committee Notes, private messenger services, fax or other electronic methods of communication. Defendants then have the option of agreeing or refusing to execute the waiver, and to influence this choice Rule 4(d) provides both a reward and a penalty. Those defendants who accept this notification in lieu of formal service by executing a waiver, are accorded additional time (60, rather than 21 days from the date notice is sent; 90 days if the defendant is outside of the U.S.) within which to file an answer. Moreover, Rule 4(d)(5) expressly guarantees that executing a waiver does not preclude a defendant from subsequently challenging either the court's personal jurisdiction or venue. (Although it does result in a waiver of any nonconstitutional objection to the sufficiency of service.)

On the other hand, if a defendant within the U.S. refuses to execute a waiver, Rule 4(d)(2) provides that the trial court "must" assess the defendant the plaintiff's costs sustained in effecting service, including reasonable attorney fees incurred in collecting these costs. This penalty can be avoided only if the defendant convinces the trial court that it had good cause for its failure to waive service. In ESTATE OF DARULIS v. GARATE, 401 F.3d 1060 (9th Cir.2005), a diversity plaintiff whose complaint had been dismissed as untimely filed under the applicable statute of limitations nevertheless sought an award of the costs it had incurred in effecting service on defendants who admittedly had refused to comply with his request for a waiver of service and had admitted an absence of good cause for failing to respond. Instead, the defendants maintained that because they were the prevailing party they were entitled to costs under F.R.Civ.P. 54(d)(1), including costs they otherwise would have to pay pursuant to 4(d)(2). At the time this case was decided, Rule 54(d)(1) stated that costs other than attorneys' fees "shall" be awarded as of course to the prevailing party except when another Federal Rule or a provision in a federal statute expressly applies. (The rule was amended to replace "shall" with "should" effective December 1, 2007). The trial court's denial of the plaintiff's motion for costs was reversed by the Ninth Circuit. The appellate court construed Rule 4(d)(2) as a "free-standing" cost provision that mandated an award of costs against a party who unreasonably failed to respond to a waiver request, even when that non-responding party had prevailed on the merits and was entitled to an award of *other* costs under 54(d)(1). The court read 4(d)(2) as reflecting a strong policy in favor of eliminating the costs of service and reasoned that adopting the defendant's position would contradict that policy by encouraging defendants to gamble on being able to sidestep 4(d)(2) by prevailing on the merits.

As an accommodation to the widespread availability of electronic transmission of documents, Rule 5(b)(2)(E) now permits electronic service of all pleadings and papers, other than the original complaint and summons (service of the complaint is governed by Rule 4), upon any party that provides written consent to such service. This Rule also states that such service is deemed completed upon transmission. And although there is a presumption of receipt arising from the completion of transmission, Rule 5(b)(2)(E) further provides that this presumption is defeated, i.e., electronic service is not effective, if the party making such service has actual knowledge that the attempted service did not reach the person to be served. (As the Advisory Committee Note acknowledges, however, the Rule does not provide any time frame within which such knowledge must occur). Additionally, this Rule authorizes the promulgation of local rules authorizing service through the court's electronic transmission facilities.

But since Rule 5(b)(2)(E) does not permit email service of the summons and complaint (service of the complaint is governed by the terms of Rule 4), this form of notice is unavailable for use by plaintiffs except in one limited context. Rule 4(f) provides plaintiffs with three options in addition to those otherwise provided by federal law when they are attempting to serve individuals outside of the United States from whom a waiver has not been obtained. (Rule 4(h)(2) extends the operation of the 4(f) alternatives to foreign business entities.). Among these alternatives is the option, codified at Rule 4(f)(3), for a federal trial court to order service by any means that is not prohibited by international agreement.

In RIO PROPERTIES, INC v. RIO INTERNATIONAL INTERLINK, 284 F.3d 1007 (9th Cir.2002), the Ninth Circuit issued the first appellate opinion analyzing the availability of email service under Rule 4(f)(3). The court began its opinion by declaring that Rule 4(f) did not erect a hierarchy of preferred service, i.e., that a court's exercise of its authority under Rule 4(f)(3) was not contingent upon an unsuccessful attempt to effect service by means listed under Rules 4(f)(1) and (2). The task of choosing the appropriate form of service in an individual case under Rule 4(f)(3), it determined, fell to the sound discretion of the trial court. The appellate court required only that the service be made by court order and that it not violate the terms of any applicable international agreement. Moreover, as long as the service was not violative of an applicable international treaty, it could be utilized even though it would be in contravention of the domestic laws of the country in which the defendant was served.

In the instant case, the trial court had granted the plaintiff's motion to order email to the company's email address after the plaintiff had attempted unsuccessfully to serve the defendant at its American address, at the address of its international courier, and through its American attorney. The Ninth Circuit held that under these circumstances, the court's order did not constitute an abuse of its discretion. The Court also declared that email service in this case met the constitutional due process requirement discussed in Section G.3. of this Chapter, *infra*, i.e., that it was reasonably calculated to apprise the defendant of the pendency of the action and afford it an opportunity to present its objections. Email, the court noted, had not only been "zealously embraced" within the business community generally, but this particular defendant, an Internet-based sports gambling operation, was an e-business that structured its business such that it could be contacted only via its email address. It had no easily discoverable street address and its website and print media designated its email address as its preferred contact information. Consequently, the court concluded, service via email was not only reasonably calculated to inform the defendant of the pendency of the action, it was the method of service most likely to actually reach the defendant. (The circuit court also upheld the trial judge's authorization of regular mail service upon the company's attorney and courier.)

Where a plaintiff is unsuccessful in obtaining a waiver, or where this alternative is unavailable, the plaintiff must effect service pursuant to the formal requirements of Rule 4. This Rule contains strict instructions with respect to who is served, as well as when, where and how service must take place. Briefly, under Rule 4(m), a plaintiff must serve a defendant located in the U.S. within 90 days after the complaint is filed or risk having the case dismissed without prejudice. Rule 4(h) prescribes who shall be served when the defendant is a corporation, partnership or unincorporated association. Similarly, Rule 4(i) governs service upon the federal government and its agencies, and Rule 4(j) sets forth the proper method for serving foreign, state, and local government defendants.

Rule 4(e) governs service upon individuals located within the U.S., and where there is not any applicable federal statutory provision concerning service, it permits service to be accomplished either by:

(1) following state law for serving a summons in an action brought in courts of general jurisdiction in the state where the district court is located or where service is made; or

(2) doing any of the following:

(A) delivering a copy of the summons and of the complaint to the to the defendant personally;

(B) leaving a copy of each at the individual's dwelling or usual place of abode with with someone of suitable age who resides there; or

(C) delivering a copy of each to an agent authorized by appointment or by the law to receive service; or

But while Rule 4(e) provides plaintiffs with a wide range of service options, remember that the mere fact that service is made in compliance with Rule 4(e) does not mean that personal jurisdiction over the defendant has been established. Rule 4(k), as previously mentioned, provides that service, or the filing of a waiver, establishes jurisdiction only if the defendant is constitutionally subject to personal jurisdiction under either the forum's state long-arm statute, a federal statute or, in the case of parties joined under Rule 14 or 19, where the defendant is served within a 100 mile radius of the trial court. Additionally, under Rule 4(k)(2), service establishes jurisdiction in claims arising under federal law against defendants who do not reside within the U.S., and who would not meet the requirements of any individual state's long-arm statute, but who have sufficient contacts with the nation as a whole to satisfy constitutional due process requirements.

Defendants located outside of the U.S. are served pursuant to the terms of Rule 4(f). And under Rule 4(c), service can be made by any non-party 18 years of age or older, as well as by a U.S. Marshal or other court appointed individual.

Defects in service can take one of two forms. Either the content of the process may not comply with the requirements of Rule 4(a) and (b) or the method by which the process was served may not satisfy the demands of Rule 4(c)-(j). A motion under Rule 12(b)(4) alleging insufficiency of process challenges the first type of defect. The latter form of challenge, such as where the defendant alleges that service was not left at his dwelling house or usual place of abode, or was left with an person not of suitable age and discretion, is made by a motion under Rule 12(b)(5) alleging insufficiency of service of process. Neither of these motions, however, is technically appropriate to challenge the trial court's exercise of personal jurisdiction. Nevertheless, although jurisdictional defects are properly raised in a Rule 12(b)(2) motion, because of the interconnection between service and the exercise of jurisdiction, trial courts typically permit objections to the exercise of personal jurisdiction to be asserted under both Rule 12(b)(2) and 12(b)(5) motions.

Since Rule 12(b)(4) motions are limited to defects in the content of the process, such as the failure to include a copy of the complaint, or a misnamed defendant, they are rarely asserted in comparison to Rule 12(b)(5) motions. Yet even though the Federal Rules are silent on this point, the jurisprudence is clear that the federal trial courts have the authority to issue one of two remedies when granting motions under either Rule. Where the trial court believes that it is reasonably likely that the plaintiff will be able to cure the defect in service, the court will issue an order quashing service of process. This means that the complaint remains on file and the plaintiff simply has to retry to serve the defendant. The alternative remedy is to dismiss the complaint without prejudice to the plaintiff's reinstitution of the action. And while the plaintiff in such situations will typically file an amended complaint, if the statute of limitations had expired after the filing of the original complaint, the practical consequence of the dismissal will be to extinguish the plaintiff's claim. On the other hand, where the court issues only a motion to quash service, the statute of limitations will not extinguish the plaintiff's claim unless the claim arose under the state law of a state whose limitations statute tolls on the date of effective service.

NOTES AND PROBLEMS FOR DISCUSSION

1. If, as is often the case, a plaintiff does not file her claim until just prior to the expiration of the governing statute of limitations, should she attempt to obtain a waiver of service or immediately proceed to effect personal service? Would your answer depend upon whether the plaintiff's claim arose under federal or state law? See Walker v. Armco Steel Corp., 446 U.S. 740, 100 S.Ct. 1978, 64 L.Ed.2d 659 (1980).

2. How should the court rule on the defendant's Rule 12(b)(5) motion in the following situations?

(a) Plaintiff's process server personally served the doorman of the luxury apartment building where the defendant resided. The doorman never gave the process to the defendant. See Churchill v. Barach, 863 F.Supp. 1266 (D.Nev.1994).

(b) Same facts as in "(a)", except that the doorman did transmit the process to the defendant.

(c) In a breach of contract case filed against a billionaire banker/financier from Switzerland who owned homes in six American cities, Paris, Monte Carlo, Rio de Janeiro, Hong Kong and Zurich, service is made by personally serving the live-in housekeeper at the defendant's ten-acre estate in Malibu, California. The defendant was in Monte Carlo on the day the housekeeper was served but did receive the process from his housekeeper. See National Development Company v. Triad Holding Corp., 930 F.2d 253 (2d Cir.1991).

(d) Same facts as in "(c)", except that the defendant was living in the Malibu estate when the housekeeper was served but she failed to transmit the process to him.

(e) After a messy divorce and child custody suit, the plaintiff sued her former husband for failure to pay child support. She effected service by having a copy of the process personally delivered to her former husband's attorney at the lawyer's office. See U.S. v. Ziegler Bolt and Parts Co., 111 F.3d 878 (Fed.Cir.1997).

(f) The form agreement signed by everyone who rents or leases a car from Tinkie Rent-A-Car provides that Mr. Talbot Po of Detroit Michigan is empowered to accept service of process in connection with any civil action that

Tinkie might file against the party renting or leasing one of its automobiles. Mr. Po is the secretary to Lori Lala, counsel for Tinkie. The contract does not require Mr. Po to forward a copy of the process to the named defendant. Tinkie sued Barbara Winky, a Chicago resident, for damage to a car she rented from Tinkie while vacationing in Hawaii. Process was served on Mr. Po, who forwarded the documents to Ms. Winky at her Chicago home. See National Equipment Rental, Ltd. v. Szukhent, 375 U.S. 311, 84 S.Ct. 411, 11 L.Ed.2d 354 (1964).

3. In our discussion of the role of consent in obtaining personal jurisdiction, see Note 7 following *Pennoyer*, we referred to the prevailing rule that personal service within the forum state will not provide the court with *in personam* jurisdiction where the defendant's presence was obtained through force or fraud unless the fraud or force is undertaken by a third party whose actions cannot be imputed to the plaintiff. Where the plaintiff cannot obtain a waiver of service, should the same anti-fraud rule apply to the tricks and other machinations used by process servers to flush resident defendants out from hiding?

3. THE CONSTITUTIONAL DIMENSION

As we mentioned in the introduction to this section, the constitutional guarantee of due process plays a crucial role in connection with each of the two distinct functions of service of process. Earlier in this chapter we examined how the due process clause operates to limit the use of service of process as the mechanism for exercising personal jurisdiction. We will now focus our attention on the impact of due process on the "notice" function of service of process.

Mullane v. Central Hanover Bank & Trust Co.

Supreme Court of the United States, 1950.

339 U.S. 306, 70 S.Ct. 652, 94 L.Ed. 865.

MR. JUSTICE JACKSON delivered the opinion of the Court.

This controversy questions the constitutional sufficiency of notice to beneficiaries on judicial settlement of accounts by the trustee of a common trust fund established under the New York Banking Law. * * *

[Banks created common trust funds to permit individuals with small and moderately sized trust funds to pool their resources into one fund for investment administration. This permitted small investors to take advantage of diversification of risk afforded by these larger investment funds and reduced the overhead costs incurred by the banks that managed such funds. New York banking law regulated New York banks' operation of such common trust funds and required periodic accountings to be made to a court to obtain a judicial settlement of accounts that was binding and conclusive as to any challenge to the management of the fund by anyone with an interest in the pooled fund or in any trust that participated in the fund.]

* * *

In January, 1946, Central Hanover Bank and Trust Company established a common trust fund * * * and * * * it petitioned the Surrogate's Court for settlement of its first account as common trustee. During the accounting period a total of 113 trusts * * * participated in the common trust fund, the gross capital of which was nearly three million dollars. The record does not show the number or residence of the beneficiaries, but they were many and it is clear that some of them were not residents of the State of New York.

The only notice given beneficiaries of this specific application was by publication in a local newspaper in strict compliance with the minimum requirements of N.Y. Banking Law §100-c(12): "After filing such petition (for judicial settlement of its account) the petitioner shall * * * publish not less than once in each week for four successive weeks in a newspaper to be designated by the court a notice or citation addressed generally without naming them to all parties interested in such common trust fund and in such estates, trusts or funds mentioned in the petition, all of which may be described * * * without setting forth the residence of any such decedent or donor of any such estate, trust or fund." Thus the only notice required, and the only one given, was by newspaper publication setting forth merely the name and address of the trust company, the name and the date of establishment of the common trust fund, and a list of all participating estates, trusts or funds.

At the time the first investment in the common fund was made on behalf of each participating estate, however, the trust company, pursuant to the requirements of §100-c(9), had notified by mail each person * * * whose name and address was then known to it and who was "entitled to share in the income therefrom * * * (or) * * * who would be entitled to share in the principal if the event upon which such estate, trust or fund will become distributable should have occurred at the time of sending such notice." Included in the notice was a copy of those provisions of the Act relating to the sending of the notice itself and to the judicial settlement of common trust fund accounts.

Upon the filing of the petition for the settlement of accounts, appellant was * * * appointed special guardian and attorney for all persons known or unknown not otherwise appearing who had or might thereafter have any interest in the income of the common trust fund; and appellee Vaughan was appointed to represent those similarly interested in the principal. There were no other appearances on behalf of any one interested in either interest or principal.

Appellant appeared specially, objecting that notice and the statutory provisions for notice to beneficiaries were inadequate to afford due process under the Fourteenth Amendment, and therefore that the court was without jurisdiction to render a final and binding decree. Appellant's objections were entertained and overruled, the Surrogate holding that the notice required and given was sufficient. A final decree accepting the accounts has been entered, affirmed by the Appellate Division of the Supreme Court and by the Court of Appeals of the State of New York.

The effect of this decree * * * is * * * that every right which beneficiaries would otherwise have against the trust company, either as trustee of the common fund or as trustee of any individual trust, for improper management of the common trust fund during the period covered by the accounting is sealed and wholly terminated by the decree.

* * *

Judicial proceedings to settle fiduciary accounts have been sometimes termed in rem, or more indefinitely quasi in rem, or more vaguely still, "in the nature of a proceeding in rem." It is not readily apparent how the courts of New York did or would classify the present proceeding, which has some characteristics and is wanting in some features of proceedings both in rem and in personam. But in any event we think that the requirements of the Fourteenth Amendment to the Federal Constitution do not depend upon a classification for which the standards are so elusive and confused generally and which, being primarily for state courts to define, may and do vary from state to state. Without disparaging the usefulness of distinctions between actions in rem and those in personam in many branches of law, or on other issues, or the reasoning which underlies them, we do not rest the power of the State to resort to constructive service in this proceeding upon how its courts or this Court may regard this historic antithesis. * * *

* * * Many controversies have raged about the cryptic and abstract words of the Due Process Clause but there can be no doubt that at a minimum they require that deprivation of life, liberty or property by adjudication be preceded by notice and opportunity for hearing appropriate to the nature of the case.

* * *

Personal service of written notice within the jurisdiction is the classic form of notice always adequate in any type of proceeding. But the vital interest of the State in bringing any issues as to its fiduciaries to a final settlement can be served only if interests or claims of individuals who are outside of the State can somehow be determined. A construction of the Due Process Clause which would place impossible or impractical obstacles in the way could not be justified.

Against this interest of the State we must balance the individual interest sought to be protected by the Fourteenth Amendment. * * * The fundamental requisite of due process of law is the opportunity to be heard. This right to be heard has little reality or worth unless one is informed that the matter is pending and can choose for himself whether to appear or default, acquiesce or contest.

* * *

An elementary and fundamental requirement of due process in any proceeding which is to be accorded finality is notice reasonably calculated, under all the circumstances, to apprise interested parties of the pendency of the action and afford them an opportunity to present their objections. * * * But if with due regard for the practicalities and peculiarities of the case these conditions are reasonably met the constitutional requirements are satisfied.

But when notice is a person's due, process which is a mere gesture is not due process. The means employed must be such as one desirous of actually informing the absentee might reasonably adopt to accomplish it. The reasonableness and hence the constitutional validity of any chosen method may be defended on the ground that it is in itself reasonably certain to inform those affected, compare Hess v. Pawloski with Wuchter v. Pizzutti, 276 U.S. 13, 48 S.Ct. 259, 72 L.Ed. 446, or, where conditions do not reasonably permit such notice, that the form chosen is not substantially less likely to bring home notice than other of the feasible and customary substitutes.

It would be idle to pretend that publication alone as prescribed here, is a reliable means of acquainting interested parties of the fact that their rights are before the courts. It is not an accident that the greater number of cases reaching this Court on the question of adequacy of notice have been concerned with actions founded on process constructively served through local newspapers. Chance alone brings to the attention of even a local resident an advertisement in small type inserted in the back pages of a newspaper, and if he makes his home outside the area of the newspaper's normal circulation the odds that the information will never reach him are large indeed. The chance of actual notice is further reduced when as here the notice required does not even name those whose attention it is supposed to attract, and does not inform acquaintances who might call it to attention. In weighing its sufficiency on the basis of equivalence with actual notice we are unable to regard this as more than a feint.

Nor is publication here reinforced by steps likely to attract the parties' attention to the proceeding. It is true that publication traditionally has been acceptable as notification supplemental to other action which in itself may reasonably be expected to convey a warning. The ways of an owner with tangible property are such that he usually arranges means to learn of any direct attack upon his possessory or proprietary rights. Hence, libel of a ship, attachment of a chattel or entry upon real estate in the name of law may reasonably be expected to come promptly to the owner's attention. When the state within which the owner has located such property seizes it for some reason, publication or posting affords an additional measure of notification. A state may indulge the assumption that one who has left tangible property in the state either has abandoned it, in which case proceedings against it deprive him of nothing, or that he has left some caretaker under a duty to let him know that it is being jeopardized. * * *

In the case before us there is, of course, no abandonment. On the other hand these beneficiaries do have a resident fiduciary as caretaker of their interest in this property. But it is their caretaker who in the accounting becomes their adversary. Their trustee is released from giving notice of jeopardy, and no one else is expected to do so. Not even the special guardian is required or apparently expected to communicate with his ward and client * * *.

This Court has not hesitated to approve of resort to publication as a customary substitute in another class of cases where it is not reasonably possible or practicable to give more adequate warning. Thus it has been recognized that, in the case of persons missing or unknown, employment of an indirect and even a probably futile means of notification is all that the situation permits and creates no constitutional bar to a final decree foreclosing their rights.

Those beneficiaries represented by appellant whose interests or where-abouts could not with due diligence be ascertained come clearly within this category. As to them the statutory notice is sufficient. However great the odds that publication will never reach the eyes of such unknown parties, it is not in the typical case much more likely to fail than any of the choices open to legislators endeavoring to prescribe the best notice practicable.

Nor do we consider it unreasonable for the State to dispense with more certain notice to those beneficiaries whose interests are either conjectural or future or, although they could be discovered upon investigation, do not in due course of business come to knowledge of the common trustee. Whatever searches might be required in another situation under ordinary standards of diligence, in view of the character of the proceedings and the nature of the interests here involved we think them unnecessary. We recognize the practical difficulties and costs that would be attendant on frequent investigations into the status of great numbers of beneficiaries, many of whose interests in the common fund are so remote as to be ephemeral; and we have no doubt that such impracticable and extended searches are not required in the name of due process. The expense of keeping informed from day to day of substitutions among even current income beneficiaries and presumptive remaindermen, to say nothing of the far greater number of contingent beneficiaries, would impose a severe burden on the plan, and would likely dissipate its advantages.   These are practical matters in which we should be reluctant to disturb the judgment of the state authorities.

Accordingly we overrule appellant's constitutional objections to published notice insofar as they are urged on behalf of any beneficiaries whose interests or addresses are unknown to the trustee.

As to known present beneficiaries of known place of residence, however, notice by publication stands on a different footing. Exceptions in the name of necessity do not sweep away the rule that within the limits of practicability notice must be such as is reasonably calculated to reach interested parties. Where the names and post office addresses of those affected by a proceeding are at hand, the reasons disappear for resort to means less likely than the mails to apprise them of its pendency.

The trustee has on its books the names and addresses of the income beneficiaries represented by appellant, and we find no tenable ground for dispensing with a serious effort to inform them personally of the accounting, at least by ordinary mail to the record addresses. * * * The trustee periodically remits their income to them, and we think that they might reasonably expect that with or apart from their remittances word might come to them personally that steps were being taken affecting their interests.

We need not weigh contentions that a requirement of personal service of citation on even the large number of known resident or nonresident beneficiaries would, by reasons of delay if not of expense, seriously interfere with the proper administration of the fund.   Of course personal service even without the jurisdiction of the issuing authority serves the end of actual and personal notice, whatever power of compulsion it might lack. However, no such service is required under the circumstances. This type of trust presupposes a large number of small interests. The individual interest does not stand alone but is identical with that of a class. The rights of each in the integrity of the fund and the fidelity of the trustee are shared by many other beneficiaries. Therefore notice reasonably certain to reach most of those interested in objecting is likely to safeguard the interests of all, since any objections sustained would inure to the benefit of all. We think that under such circumstances reasonable risks that notice might not actually reach every beneficiary are justifiable. * * *

The statutory notice to known beneficiaries is inadequate, not because in fact it fails to reach everyone, but because under the circumstances it is not reasonably calculated to reach those who could easily be informed by other means at hand. However it may have been in former times, the mails today are recognized as an efficient and inexpensive means of communication. Moreover, the fact that the trust company has been able to give mailed notice to known beneficiaries at the time the common trust fund was established is persuasive that postal notification at the time of accounting would not seriously burden the plan.

In some situations the law requires greater precautions in its proceedings than the business world accepts for its own purposes. In few, if any, will it be satisfied with less. Certainly it is instructive, in determining the reasonableness of the impersonal broadcast notification here used, to ask whether it would satisfy a prudent man of business, counting his pennies but finding it in his interest to convey information to many persons whose names and addresses are in his files. We are not satisfied that it would. Publication may theoretically be available for all the world to see, but it is too much in our day to suppose that each or any individual beneficiary does or could examine all that is published to see if something may be tucked away in it that affects his property interests. * * *

We hold the notice of judicial settlement of accounts required by the New York Banking Law §100-c(12) is incompatible with the requirements of the Fourteenth Amendment as a basis for adjudication depriving known persons whose whereabouts are also known of substantial property rights. Accordingly the judgment is reversed and the cause remanded for further proceedings not inconsistent with this opinion.

Reversed.

MR. JUSTICE DOUGLAS took no part in the consideration or decision of this case.

MR. JUSTICE BURTON, dissenting.

* * * Whether or not further notice to beneficiaries should supplement the notice and representation here provided is properly within the discretion of the State. The Federal Constitution does not require it here.

NOTES AND PROBLEMS FOR DISCUSSION

1. (a) Compare the Supreme Court's treatment of the constitutional requirements for notice in *Pennoyer* and *Mullane*.

(b) Does this vision of the constitutional demands of reasonable notice reflect the evolving view of the limits on personal jurisdiction announced in *International Shoe*?

2. The unusual factual setting of *Mullane* (including the existence of two classes of beneficiaries, many of whose members would undoubtedly never receive the notice required by the Court) led some observers to presume that the Court did not really intend to replace the traditional seizure-plus-publication rule of notice in true *in rem* proceedings. Similarly, after noting that the New York statute mandated only service by publication, the Court's rehashing of the rationale underlying the *Pennoyer* rule that publication coupled by attachment of property was sufficient (i.e., that owners could be expected to be monitoring the status of their property and would be alerted by its seizure) suggested that the *Mullane* Court was signaling more than a romantic attachment to the old notice regime.

But subsequent rulings by the Court in which it applied the *Mullane* formulation to classically *in rem* proceedings made it clear that this new standard would, indeed, be applied across the board. See Mennonite Bd. Of Missions v. Adams, 462 U.S. 791, 103 S.Ct. 2706, 77 L.Ed.2d 180 (1983) (requiring service by mail to a mortgagee's last known address in action to quiet title when mortgagee was identified in a publicly recorded mortgage); Walker v. City of Hutchinson, 352 U.S. 112, 77 S.Ct. 200, 1 L.Ed.2d 178 (1956) (requiring service by mail to property owners in state condemnation actions). In DUSENBERY v. U.S., 534 U.S. 161, 122 S.Ct. 694, 151 L.Ed.2d 597 (2002), for example, the Court found that the *Mullane* "reasonably calculated" standard was both applicable and satisfied in a case where the FBI sent notice by certified mail to the federal penitentiary where the plaintiff was incarcerated that cash seized during a warrant-based search of the residence where he was arrested was intended to be subjected to administrative forfeiture. The Court rejected his claim that the prison's procedures for delivering mail to inmates rendered the form of notice used by the FBI constitutionally deficient. Under its existing procedures, prison officials retrieved all mail from the local post office and signed for all certified mail. Once the mail was transported to the prison, certified mail was entered into a logbook and a staff employee signed for the mail to acknowledge its receipt before distributing it to the inmate during mail call. The plaintiff alleged that the notice was insufficient because Due Process required actual receipt of notice to interested parties prior to forfeiture. The Court rejected this claim, holding that the Due Process Clause did not require the state to provide actual notice, but rather, required it only to make a reasonable attempt to provide actual notice. Sending the notice via certified mail to the prison, the Court concluded, was reasonably calculated to apprise the plaintiff of the forfeiture action.

Suppose the state attempts to notify someone of the imminent deprivation of their property by a method that meets the *Mullane* standard. Assume also that the notice is not actually received and that the government is promptly informed that the notice has not been delivered. Does the government have a due process obligation to take additional steps to attempt to notify the property owner? The Supreme Court resolved a conflict in the circuits on this question in JONES v.

FLOWERS, 547 U.S. 220, 126 S.Ct. 1708, 164 L.Ed.2d 415 (2006). In *Jones,* after the defendant paid off the mortgage on his home, he discontinued paying property taxes. The property was certified as delinquent and the State attempted to notify the property owner of his tax delinquency by mailing a certified letter to him at that address. No one was home to sign for the certified letter and when nobody appeared at the post office to retrieve it, the post office returned the unopened packet to the State agency marked "unclaimed." Two years later, the State agency published a notice of public sale of the property in a local newspaper. After a bid was received, the State agency mailed another certified letter to the property owner at that same address informing him that the house would be sold if he did not pay his taxes. That second letter also was returned to the State agency marked "unclaimed." The property owner filed the instant action alleging that the State's failure to provide additional notice of the tax sale violated his Fourteenth Amendment due process rights.

Applying the *Mullane* standard, the majority concluded that the government's knowledge that its attempt at notice had failed was one of the circumstances to be considered in determining whether the notice used was reasonably calculated to reach its intended recipient. It reasoned that a person who actually desired to inform a property owner of an impending tax sale would do more than nothing when a certified letter had been returned unclaimed. When a letter is returned by the post office, the majority explained, a reasonable sender ordinarily will attempt to resend it, if it is practicable to do so, particularly when the letter concerned such an important and irreversible prospect as the loss of a house. The majority rejected the State's claim that the owner's failure to keep his address updated forfeited his right to constitutionally sufficient notice. It similarly rejected the claim that the government's notice obligation was eliminated by the property owner's knowledge that failure to pay taxes automatically renders the property subject to government seizure. Finally, the Court concluded that there were reasonable additional steps the government could have taken such that its failure to do anything rendered its notice effort constitutionally deficient. The majority suggested that the State could have resent notice by regular mail or posted a notice on the front door or addressed notice to occupant. Thus, without instructing the State on what specific additional step to take, the majority concluded that since reasonable additional steps were available, the government's decision to do nothing once it learned that its notice had been undelivered was insufficient under the *Mullane* standard.

3. In some cases, the issue before the Court is not whether the statutorily prescribed method of notice meets constitutional standards, but whether notice of any kind is required. For example, is the biological father of a two year old baby girl who was never married to nor lived with the mother, who never provided any financial support to the child, and who rarely saw the baby, entitled to any formal notice of the institution of an adoption proceeding by the baby's mother and her husband? In LEHR v. ROBERTSON, 463 U.S. 248, 103 S.Ct. 2985, 77 L.Ed.2d 614 (1983), the Supreme Court noted that New York law provided putative fathers with the right to notice of adoption proceedings if the father (1) had been adjudicated to be the father, (2) had been identified as the father on the child's birth certificate, (3) had lived openly with the mother and child, (4) had been identified as the father by the mother in a sworn statement, (5) was listed on a putative father registry, or (6) had been married to the mother before the child was six months old. The putative father admittedly did not fall within any of these six categories.

One month after the mother and the man she married several months after the child's birth instituted adoption proceedings, the putative father filed his own paternity petition (in a court located in a different county within New York State) asking for a determination of paternity and visitation privileges. After being served in the paternity proceeding, the mother informed the court hearing her adoption case of the putative father's paternity action. The court in the adoption case then issued an order staying the paternity action pending its ruling on a motion to change the venue of the paternity action. When the putative father received notice of the change of venue motion, he learned of the mother's adoption proceeding. Four days later, his attorney informed the judge presiding over the adoption proceeding that he intended to seek a stay of the adoption proceedings pending the resolution of the paternity action. The judge informed the attorney that he had already signed the adoption order earlier that day. The judge added that he was aware of the pending paternity action but had concluded that he was not required to give the putative father notice prior to issuing his adoption order. The New York State appellate courts affirmed this judgment. The Supreme Court ruled that since the putative father had never formed any relationship with the child, "the mere existence of a biological link" did not entitle him to the level of due process protection that would inure to someone with a demonstrated interest in maintaining personal contact with a child. Thus, notwithstanding the fact that the mother knew his name and address, the Court found that the putative father did not possess any due process right to additional notice. The statutory scheme for providing notice to putative fathers, the Court reasoned, was sufficient to protect his opportunity to form a relationship with the child.

At the outset of this Chapter, we stated that every judicial tribunal must possess both the authority to issue a judgment that will be binding upon the parties to the action as well as the power to adjudicate over the type of controversy involved in the case. In this Chapter we have examined the statutory and constitutional rules governing the exercise of the former element of adjudicative jurisdiction — personal jurisdiction. We now turn our attention to the other indispensable component of adjudicative power — subject matter jurisdiction.

CHAPTER 3

Adjudicative Power: Subject Matter Jurisdiction

As we know from the materials in the immediately preceding chapter, personal jurisdiction is one of two constituent elements of judicial, or adjudicative, jurisdiction. In order to effectively exercise adjudicative authority, courts must have power over the parties to the legal proceeding. But, as the Supreme Court affirmed in *Pennoyer*, every tribunal also must be "competent by its constitution — that is, by the law of its creation — to pass upon the subject-matter of the suit." Consequently, any systematic jurisdictional inquiry also must encompass an evaluation of whether the court has been empowered to adjudicate the particular type of dispute that has been placed before it.

The fact that all courts have been delegated — by the law of their creation — a circumscribed scope of subject matter jurisdiction accords with our intuition about the structure and functioning of our judicial system. We would not expect, that someone seeking a divorce or custody over a minor child would be able to institute such a proceeding in the same court used by someone who is defending herself against the issuance of a speeding ticket or seeking to probate a will. Nor would we anticipate that the loser in either of these proceedings would appeal that decision to the same court in which it was tried. And in a federal system with separate federal and state sovereignties, there needs to be some framework for distributing cases between the two systems. For reasons relating to both efficiency and expertise, among others, federal courts have a strictly limited jurisdiction; state courts by and large are not similarly limited, although their jurisdiction is defined by state constitutions and statutes.

As the Supreme Court noted in *Pennoyer*, subject matter jurisdiction is a creature of both constitutional and statutory authorization. In the federal system, Article III, §1 of the U.S. Constitution mandates the creation of a Supreme Court and authorizes the establishment of "such inferior Courts as the Congress may from time to time ordain and establish." Pursuant to that constitutional delegation of authority, the very first Congress immediately passed the Judiciary Act of 1789, which established a system of lower federal courts. Over time, a series of statutory amendments restructured the federal judiciary, ultimately resulting in its current three-tiered configuration.

Beyond authorizing the formation of a federal judiciary, Article III, in defining the "judicial power of the United States," sets forth the boundaries of the federal courts' subject matter jurisdiction and empowers Congress to assign jurisdiction over some or all of these types of disputes to the federal courts. In this chapter, we will examine the important, and often vexing problems associated with the allocation of limited subject matter jurisdiction to the federal courts. While it certainly would be worthwhile to explore the issues surrounding the assignment of subject matter jurisdiction to the courts of any particular state or group of states, choosing one or more specific state systems might not be representative of the problems faced by courts in all fifty jurisdictions. Instead, we have chosen to focus on the allocation of adjudicative authority between the federal and state judiciaries.

SECTION A. FEDERAL QUESTIONS

Among the types of controversies that Article III, §2 of the U.S. Constitution permits Congress to assign to the federal courts are all cases "arising under" the Constitution, laws and treaties of the United States. It was not until 1875, however, that Congress conferred on the lower federal courts the general power to hear cases arising under federal laws, treaties, and the Constitution — a power that they still retain. This was accomplished though the enactment of a statute empowering these federal courts to adjudicate cases "arising under" the federal constitution, laws and treaties. Suits falling within this category are referred to as "federal question" cases. The present version of this legislative award of federal question jurisdiction is found at 28 U.S.C. §1331.

Does or should "arising under" mean that federal courts can exercise jurisdiction over any case involving a question of federal law? For example, what if a retail computer supply store failed to pay for hundreds of copies of products that it had ordered and received from Microsoft, Inc. Microsoft files a complaint in federal district court, alleging that the supply store breached its contractual obligation to pay for the software, that this customer admitted ordering and receiving all of these products, but purported to justify its refusal to pay on the ground, which Microsoft vehemently denies, that Microsoft's pricing policy is one of many monopolistic practices that violate federal antitrust laws. Does this case fall within the court's "federal question" subject matter jurisdiction? Alternatively, suppose that the supply store got wind of Microsoft's intention to sue and decided, instead, to force the issue by filing its own action in federal court seeking a declaratory judgment that Microsoft's pricing policy violated the federal antitrust laws. Would this action fall within the court's "federal question" jurisdiction? These, and other, important questions are addressed in the following principal case and the subsequent Note material.

  Read 28 U.S.C. §1331.

Bracken v. Matgouranis

United States Court of Appeals, Third Circuit, 2002.
296 F.3d 160.

ROSENN, CIRCUIT JUDGE.

  This appeal presents an esoteric question of federal jurisdiction considered by the United States Supreme Court nearly a century ago in Louisville & Nashville Railroad Co. v. Mottley, 211 U.S. 149, 29 S.Ct. 42, 53 L.Ed. 126 (1908), and rarely reviewed since. The issue is whether the plaintiffs in a state-suit for defamation confer subject-matter jurisdiction on a federal court by raising a first amendment issue in response to an anticipatory defense.

The plaintiffs, Cheryl Ann Bracken and her attorney, H. David Rothman, brought suit in the Allegheny County, Pennsylvania, Court of Common Pleas, alleging that Panorea Matgouranis's attorney, defendant William J. Wyrick, defamed them during Bracken's December 8, 2000, deposition. The plaintiffs also filed a second cause of action based on the alleged defamation, seeking an accounting and the imposition of a constructive trust on the assets of Panorea Matgouranis and her husband, Martin.

The plaintiffs, in their Complaint, anticipated that the defendants would assert a defense of absolute privilege under Pennsylvania law. The plaintiffs, therefore, asserted that the exercise of such privilege would violate their first amendment rights under the United States Constitution. Based on this argument, as delineated in the plaintiffs' Complaint, the defendants successfully petitioned to have both cases removed to the United States District Court for the Western District of Pennsylvania.

The plaintiffs, asserting lack of federal jurisdiction, moved to remand the cases to the state court pursuant to 28 U.S.C. §1447. The District Court denied the motion, holding that the plaintiffs "have clearly raised federal constitutional issues in their complaint." The defendants moved to dismiss the cases, and, in due course, the District Court granted the motion. We hold that the District Court erred in assuming jurisdiction, and we will reverse.

I.

The plaintiffs allege that on November 6, 2000, Martin Matgouranis (Martin) gave Bracken, his employee and lover, a horrible beating that culminated in Martin shooting Bracken execution-style and leaving her for dead. Bracken survived and underwent facial surgery to reconstruct and repair her orbital area. Bracken was released from the hospital the same week she was admitted.

Rothman, on Bracken's behalf, wrote two letters to Martin's attorneys. Rothman requested that Martin advance Bracken money because she was disabled and unable to support herself during her convalescence. Rothman indicated that if and when Martin appeared for sentencing in any criminal proceeding arising out of the alleged assault on Bracken, Bracken would inform the sentencing judge of any "belated compassion shown" by Martin. Rothman further stated that any ex post facto lack of compassion would also be revealed at any sentencing proceeding arising out of the alleged assault.

On November 27, 2000, in the Court of Common Pleas of Allegheny County, Bracken filed an action to discover and freeze Martin's assets. On December 8, 2000, the defendants deposed Bracken. During the course of the deposition, Wyrick, attorney to Panorea Matgouranis, established that Bracken had approved Rothman's letters to Martin's attorneys. Wyrick then accused Bracken and Rothman of attempting to extort money from Martin. Thereupon, the plaintiffs filed the action for defamation and intentional infliction of emotional distress.

Title 28 U.S.C. §1447(d) provides "[a]n order remanding a case to the State Court from which it was removed is not reviewable on appeal or otherwise." Although §1447(d) narrows the circumstances under which this Court can review a District Court's order granting remand, appellate review of District Court orders denying remand is not prohibited. Irrespective of what §1447 provides, this Court has a continuing obligation to sua sponte raise the issue of subject matter jurisdiction if it is in question.

* * *   Removing state-court cases to federal court is proper only when federal courts would have had original jurisdiction over the case.[1]

The Complaint, alleging defamation and intentional infliction of emotional distress, sounds entirely in Pennsylvania law. The parties are not diverse, and thus the District Court's assumption of removal jurisdiction was predicated on original federal question jurisdiction pursuant to 28 U.S.C. §1331. Because the Complaint predicted that the defendants would assert a defense of absolute privilege under Pennsylvania law and in response asserted that such a defense would violate the United States Constitution, the District Court allowed the removal of the cases to federal court. The plaintiffs argued that the privilege defense was not an essential element of their state claims and moved to remand the cases to state court. The District Court denied the motion. Approximately a century of precedent compels us to reverse the District Court.

This appeal raises fundamental questions regarding federal jurisdiction, and this Court may not ignore applicable law. The plaintiffs argue that there is no federal subject matter jurisdiction, because their complaints sound in defamation and intentional infliction of emotional distress, and any reference to their rights of free speech was surplusage and not essential to their claims. *Mottley*, not cited by any of the parties, is the appropriate starting point for our analysis.

Mottley involved alleged injuries resulting from a collision of railroad trains that were owned by the defendant railroad company. The plaintiffs and the defendant there reached a settlement in which the plaintiffs released the defendant from liability for damages in return for free railroad passes. The defendant allegedly performed its duties for several years and then it refused to renew the plaintiffs' passes. The plaintiffs asserted that the defendant's refusal to comply with the agreement was a consequence of a federal law forbidding free passes. The plaintiffs argued that the federal law did not prohibit free passes under the circumstances of their case. Alternatively, the plaintiffs argued that if the federal law prohibited their free passes, the law was unconstitutional.

The District Court, based on the plaintiffs' anticipation of the defendant's defense, assumed jurisdiction. The United States Supreme Court reversed. Referring to the language of §1331's statutory predecessor, the Court stated:

It is the settled interpretation of these words, as used in this statute,

---

[1] The statute provides, in pertinent part: "[A]ny civil action brought in a State court of which the district courts of the United States have original jurisdiction, may be removed by the defendant ... to the district court of the United States." 28 U.S.C. §1441(a).

conferring jurisdiction, that a suit arises under the Constitution and laws of the United States only when the plaintiff's statement of his own cause of action shows that it is based upon those laws or that Constitution. It is not enough that the plaintiff alleges some anticipated defense to his cause of action and asserts that the defense is invalidated by some provision of the Constitution of the United States. Although such allegations show that very likely, in the course of the litigation, a question under the Constitution would arise, they do not show that the suit, that is, the plaintiff's original cause of action, arises under the Constitution.

211 U.S. at 152. Thus, the presence of federal question jurisdiction turns on the "well-pleaded complaint rule," which dictates that federal jurisdiction lies only when a federal question is presented on the face of the plaintiff's properly pleaded complaint.

The Supreme Court has labeled the "well-pleaded complaint rule" both reasonable and fair, Boston & Montana Consol. Copper & Silver Mining Co. v. Montana Ore Purchasing Co., 188 U.S. 632, 639, 23 S.Ct. 434, 47 L.Ed. 626 (1903), and has applied the rule consistently since its promulgation. E.g., Franchise Tax Bd. v. Constr. Laborers Vacation Trust, 463 U.S. 1, 9-11, 103 S.Ct. 2841, 77 L.Ed.2d 420 (1983). The Court stated that speculation on possible defenses and responding to such defenses in an attempt to demonstrate that a federal question would likely arise is not a necessary element of a plaintiff's cause of action, and thus does not create federal subject matter jurisdiction.

The plaintiffs' Complaint sounds entirely in State law. Indeed, in terms of federal proximity, this case is one degree further removed than was *Mottley*. In *Mottley*, the plaintiffs anticipated a federal defense and offered their reply to it. Here, on the other hand, the plaintiffs have anticipated a state defense (i.e., absolute privilege), and have developed a first amendment response to the defense in their Complaint (i.e., absolute privilege violates the United States Constitution). Speculation on a state defense and a constitutional answer to it just cannot be the basis for federal question jurisdiction.

Accordingly, the order of the District Court will be reversed and the proceedings remanded to the District Court with directions to vacate its order denying remand of the cases to the Allegheny County Court of Common Pleas. Upon remand, the District Court is instructed to enter an order granting plaintiffs' motion for remand to the state court * * *.

NOTES AND PROBLEMS FOR DISCUSSION

1. The plaintiffs filed their action in state court. How, then, did it end up in a federal district court and how does that maneuver relate to the nature of the Third Circuit's ultimate order in the case?

2. As mentioned in the introductory material to this Chapter, Article III, §2 of the U.S. Constitution empowered Congress to assign various categories of cases to the federal courts that it was authorized to establish under §1 of Article III. This authority, however, was not self-executing. In order to provide the federal courts with jurisdiction over any of the types of controversies that Article III of the Constitution placed within the federal judicial power, Congress had to take explicit action. One of these enumerated categories consists of "all cases, in law and equity, arising under this Constitution, the Laws of the United States, and Treaties made, or which shall be made, under their Authority." In 1875, Congress expressly exercised its constitutional authority by enacting a statute, now codified at 28 U.S.C. §1331, that provided the federal trial courts with original jurisdiction over "all civil actions arising under the Constitution, laws, or treaties of the United States." In fashioning the "well-pleaded complaint rule", was the Supreme Court in *Mottley* engaging in constitutional or statutory construction, i.e., was it interpreting the meaning of "arising under" found in Article III, §2 or in 28 U.S.C. §1331?

In OSBORN v. BANK OF THE UNITED STATES, 22 U.S. (9 Wheat.) 738, 6 L.Ed.204 (1824), a case that preceded *Mottley* by more than eighty years and predated Congress's enactment of the federal question jurisdictional statute by more than half a century, the Supreme Court was called upon to determine whether a federal statute chartering the Bank of the United States and authorizing it to "sue and be sued" in any federal Circuit Court fell within Congress' Article III authority to confer federal jurisdiction over cases "arising under" federal law. In his opinion for the Court, Chief Justice Marshall announced a broad *constitutional* standard. Congress, he wrote, was authorized by Article III to extend the federal judicial power to any cause of action as to which a federal question forms "an ingredient," regardless of (a) whether federal law was the source of that right of action, (b) how collateral that federal issue was to the resolution of the claim, or even (c) whether the federal matter was actually placed in issue at all. In several post-*Mottley* rulings, the Supreme Court consistently has held that notwithstanding the identity of the "arising under" language of §1331 and Article III, Congress chose not to confer jurisdiction over federal questions in §1331 to the full extent authorized by Article III, §2 of the Constitution. Consequently, it explained, the well-pleaded complaint rule articulated in *Mottley* was a permissible reading of §1331.

Although the Supreme Court has not fully resolved the precise contours of Article III "arising under" jurisdiction, it has frequently indicated that *Osborn* reflected the view that Article III contemplated a broader conception of "arising under" than §1331, i.e., that Congress could create federal question jurisdiction in all cases that might call for the application of federal law. *See e.g.*, Verlinden B.V. v. Central Bank of Nigeria, 461 U.S. 494, 103 S.Ct. 1962, 76 L.Ed.2d 81 (1983) (federal statute codifying doctrine of foreign sovereign immunity fell within Congress' authority under Article III "arising under" jurisdiction because all cases brought against foreign sovereign arose under federal law insofar as they required an interpretation of this statute to determine whether each case fell within limited exceptions to foreign sovereign immunity). For a detailed historical investigation of the origins of Article III's "arising under" clause that concludes that both the framers of the Constitution and the members of the *Osborn* Court actually intended for this provision to provide federal jurisdiction only where a plaintiff showed that an extant federal law was determinative of a right or title asserted therein and not in any case that *might* involve a question of federal law, see Anthony J. Bellia Jr., *The Origins of Article III "Arising Under" Jurisdiction*, 57 DUKE L.J. 263 (2007).

3. Why did the Third Circuit in *Bracken* conclude that the plaintiff's claims did not "arise under" federal law?

4. Does the "well-pleaded complaint" rule promote the objectives underlying Congress' delegation of authority over federal law matters to the federal courts?

5. In FRANCHISE TAX BOARD v. CONSTRUCTION LABORERS VACATION TRUST, 463 U.S. 1, 103 S.Ct. 2841, 77 L.Ed.2d 420 (1983), the Supreme Court announced that a case will meet the "well-pleaded complaint" test for federal jurisdiction if either (1) federal law creates the cause of action, or (2) the plaintiff's right to relief under a state law-created claim necessarily depends on resolution of a "substantial question of federal law."

(a) Determining whether federal law "creates" the cause of action is frequently not a simple matter of merely searching the relevant federal statutory or constitutional text for language expressly creating a cause of action to enforce the substantive rights created in that provision. While many statutes do contain such language, many others do not. And the latter scenario is typically the case when it comes to rights granted by the federal Constitution.

To deal with these situations, the Supreme Court has determined that both statutory and constitutional private rights of action can be created either expressly or by implication. In assessing whether or not the existence of a remedy should be implied from the creation of the substantive right, the courts undertake a complicated inquiry into whether or not Congress, in creating the substantive right, intended to provide the class of protected individuals with a remedy. A frequently invoked articulation of the standard used to determine whether a right of action should be implied from a federal statute can be found in CORT v. ASH, 422 U.S. 66, 95 S.Ct. 2080, 45 L.Ed.2d 26 (1975). There, the Court set forth four factors to consider in making this evaluation: (1) whether the plaintiff is a member of the protected class; (2) whether there is evidence of Congressional intention to create a remedy either explicitly or impliedly; (3) whether implying a remedy would be in accord with the underlying objectives of the statutory scheme; and (4) whether the cause of action is traditionally relegated to state law so that implication of a federal remedy would infringe on an area that is ordinarily left to State regulation. See also Davis v. Passman, 442 U.S. 228, 99 S.Ct. 2264, 60 L.Ed.2d 846 (1979) (a federal employee may assert an action for damages implied from her right to equal protection under the laws guaranteed by the Due Process Clause of the Fifth Amendment).

(b) Where the claim is not "created" by federal law, a claim may still be deemed to "arise under" federal law if the plaintiff's state law-created cause of action implicates a disputed and "substantial" question of federal law whose resolution by a federal court will not unduly disrupt the allocation of authority between the state and federal judicial systems. The Supreme Court's thinking on when an issue of federal law that is embedded in a state law-created claim meets this formulation of the "arising under" requirement of §1331 has evolved over a series of cases. Here is the one of the Court's more recent offerings:

Gunn v. Minton

Supreme Court of the United States, 2013.

568 U.S. ___, 133 S.Ct. 1059, 185 L.Ed.2d 72.

CHIEF JUSTICE ROBERTS delivered the opinion of the unanimous Court.

Federal courts have exclusive jurisdiction over cases "arising under any Act of Congress relating to patents." 28 U.S.C. §1338(a). The question presented is whether a state law claim alleging legal malpractice in the handling of a patent case must be brought in federal court.

I

In the early 1990s, respondent Vernon Minton developed a computer program and telecommunications network designed to facilitate securities trading. In March 1995, he leased the system — known as the Texas Computer Exchange Network, or TEXCEN — to R.M. Stark & Co., a securities brokerage. A little over a year later, he applied for a patent for an interactive securities trading system that was based substantially on TEXCEN. The U.S. Patent and Trademark Office issued the patent in January 2000.

Patent in hand, Minton filed a patent infringement suit in Federal District Court against the National Association of Securities Dealers, Inc. (NASD) and the NASDAQ Stock Market, Inc. He was represented by Jerry Gunn and the other petitioners. NASD and NASDAQ moved for summary judgment on the ground that Minton's patent was invalid under the "on sale" bar, 35 U.S.C. §102(b). That provision specifies that an inventor is not entitled to a patent if "the invention was ... on sale in [the United States], more than one year prior to the date of the application," and Minton had leased TEXCEN to Stark more than one year prior to filing his patent application. Rejecting Minton's argument that there were differences between TEXCEN and the patented system that precluded application of the on-sale bar, the District Court granted the summary judgment motion and declared Minton's patent invalid.

Minton then filed a motion for reconsideration in the District Court, arguing for the first time that the lease agreement with Stark was part of ongoing testing of TEXCEN and therefore fell within the "experimental use" exception to the on-sale bar. The District Court denied the motion. Minton appealed to the U.S. Court of Appeals for the Federal Circuit. That court affirmed, concluding that the District Court had appropriately held Minton's experimental-use argument waived.

Minton, convinced that his attorneys' failure to raise the experimental-use argument earlier had cost him the lawsuit and led to invalidation of his patent, brought this malpractice action in Texas state court. His former lawyers defended on the ground that the lease to Stark was not, in fact, for an experimental use, and that therefore Minton's patent infringement claims would have failed even if the experimental-use argument had been timely raised. The trial court agreed, holding that Minton had put forward "less than a scintilla of proof" that the lease had been for an experimental purpose. It accordingly granted summary judgment to Gunn and the other lawyer defendants.

On appeal, Minton raised a new argument: Because his legal malpractice claim was based on an alleged error in a patent case, it "arises under" federal patent law for purposes of 28 U.S.C. §1338(a). And because, under §1338(a), "no State court shall have jurisdiction over any claim for relief arising under any Act of Congress relating to patents," the Texas court — where Minton had originally brought his malpractice claim — lacked subject matter jurisdiction to decide the case. Accordingly, Minton argued, the trial court's order should be vacated and the case dismissed, leaving Minton free to start over in the Federal District Court.

A divided panel of the Court of Appeals of Texas rejected Minton's argument. Applying the test we articulated in Grable & Sons Metal Products, Inc. v. Darue Engineering & Mfg., 545 U.S. 308, 314, 125 S.Ct. 2363, 162 L.Ed.2d 257 (2005), it held that the federal interests implicated by Minton's state law claim were not sufficiently substantial to trigger §1338 "arising under" jurisdiction. It also held that finding exclusive federal jurisdiction over state legal malpractice actions would, contrary to Grable 's commands, disturb the balance of federal and state judicial responsibilities. Proceeding to the merits of Minton's malpractice claim, the Court of Appeals affirmed the trial court's determination that Minton had failed to establish experimental use and that arguments on that ground therefore would not have saved his infringement suit.

The Supreme Court of Texas reversed, relying heavily on a pair of cases from the U.S. Court of Appeals for the Federal Circuit. The Court concluded that Minton's claim involved "a substantial federal issue" within the meaning of *Grable* "because the success of Minton's malpractice claim is reliant upon the viability of the experimental use exception as a defense to the on-sale bar." Adjudication of Minton's claim in federal court was consistent with the appropriate balance between federal and state judicial responsibilities, it held, because "the federal government and patent litigants have an interest in the uniform application of patent law by courts well-versed in that subject matter." * * * We granted certiorari.

II

Federal courts are courts of limited jurisdiction, possessing only that power authorized by Constitution and statute. There is no dispute that the Constitution permits Congress to extend federal court jurisdiction to a case such as this one, see Osborn v. Bank of United States; the question is whether Congress has done so, see Powell v. McCormack.

As relevant here, Congress has authorized the federal district courts to exercise original jurisdiction in "all civil actions arising under the Constitution, laws, or treaties of the United States," 28 U.S.C. §1331, and, more particularly, over "any civil action arising under any Act of Congress relating to patents," §1338(a). Adhering to the demands of linguistic consistency, we have interpreted the phrase "arising under" in both sections identically, applying our §1331 and §1338(a) precedents interchangeably. See Christianson v. Colt Industries Operating Corp., 486 U.S. 800, 808–809, 108 S.Ct. 2166, 100 L.Ed.2d 811 (1988). For cases falling within the patent-specific arising under jurisdiction of §1338(a), however, Congress has not only provided for federal jurisdiction but also eliminated state jurisdiction, decreeing that "[n]o State court shall have jurisdiction over any claim for relief arising under any Act of Congress relating to patents." §1338(a). To determine whether jurisdiction was proper in the Texas courts, therefore, we must determine whether it would have been proper in a federal district court—whether, that is, the case "arises under any Act of Congress relating to patents."

For statutory purposes, a case can "arise under" federal law in two ways. Most directly, a case arises under federal law when federal law creates the cause of action asserted As a rule of inclusion, this "creation" test admits of only extremely rare exceptions and accounts for the vast bulk of suits that arise under federal law, see Franchise Tax Bd. of Cal. v. Construction Laborers Vacation Trust for Southern Cal., 463 U.S. 1, 9, 103 S.Ct. 2841, 77 L.Ed.2d 420 (1983). Minton's original patent infringement suit against NASD and NASDAQ, for example, arose under federal law in this manner because it was authorized by 35 U.S.C. §§271, 281.

But even where a claim finds its origins in state rather than federal law — as Minton's legal malpractice claim indisputably does — we have identified a "special and small category" of cases in which arising under jurisdiction still lies. Empire Healthchoice Assurance, Inc. v. McVeigh, 547 U.S. 677, 699, 126 S.Ct. 2121, 165 L.Ed.2d 131 (2006). In outlining the contours of this slim category, we do not paint on a blank canvas. Unfortunately, the canvas looks like one that Jackson Pollock got to first.

In an effort to bring some order to this unruly doctrine several Terms ago, we condensed our prior cases into the following inquiry: Does the "state-law claim necessarily raise a stated federal issue, actually disputed and substantial, which a federal forum may entertain without disturbing any congressionally approved balance of federal and state judicial responsibilities"? *Grable.* That is, federal jurisdiction over a state law claim will lie if a federal issue is: (1) necessarily raised, (2) actually disputed, (3) substantial, and (4) capable of resolution in federal court without disrupting the federal-state balance approved by Congress. Where all four of these requirements are met, we held, jurisdiction is proper because there is a "serious federal interest in claiming the advantages thought to be inherent in a federal forum," which can be vindicated without disrupting Congress's intended division of labor between state and federal courts. Id.

III

Applying *Grable* 's inquiry here, it is clear that Minton's legal malpractice claim does not arise under federal patent law. Indeed, for the reasons we discuss, we are comfortable concluding that state legal malpractice claims based on underlying patent matters will rarely, if ever, arise under federal patent law for purposes of §1338(a). Although such cases may necessarily raise disputed questions of patent law, those cases are by their nature unlikely to have the sort of significance for the federal system necessary to establish jurisdiction.

A

To begin, we acknowledge that resolution of a federal patent question is "necessary" to Minton's case. Under Texas law, a plaintiff alleging legal malpractice must establish four elements: (1) that the defendant attorney owed the plaintiff a duty; (2) that the attorney breached that duty; (3) that the breach was the proximate cause of the plaintiff's injury; and (4) that damages occurred. In cases like this one, in which the attorney's alleged error came in failing to make a particular argument, the causation element requires a "case within a case" analysis of whether, had the argument been made, the outcome of the earlier litigation would have been different. To prevail on his legal malpractice claim, therefore, Minton must show that he would have prevailed in his federal patent infringement case if only petitioners had timely made an experimental-use argument on his behalf. That will necessarily require application of patent law to the facts of Minton's case.

B

The federal issue is also "actually disputed" here — indeed, on the merits, it is the central point of dispute. Minton argues that the experimental-use exception properly applied to his lease to Stark, saving his patent from the on-sale bar; petitioners argue that it did not. This is just the sort of dispute respecting the effect of federal law that *Grable* envisioned.

C

Minton's argument founders on *Grable*'s next requirement, however, for the federal issue in this case is not substantial in the relevant sense. In reaching the opposite conclusion, the Supreme Court of Texas focused on the importance of the issue to the plaintiff's case and to the parties before it. As our past cases show, however, it is not enough that the federal issue be significant to the particular parties in the immediate suit; that will always be true when the state claim necessarily raises a disputed federal issue, as *Grable* separately requires. The substantiality inquiry under *Grable* looks instead to the importance of the issue to the federal system as a whole.

In *Grable* itself, for example, the Internal Revenue Service had seized property from the plaintiff and sold it to satisfy the plaintiff's federal tax delinquency. Five years later, the plaintiff filed a state law quiet title action against the third party that had purchased the property, alleging that the IRS had failed to comply with certain federally imposed notice requirements, so that the seizure and sale were invalid. In holding that the case arose under federal law, we primarily focused not on the interests of the litigants themselves, but rather on the broader significance of the notice question for the Federal Government. We emphasized the Government's "strong interest" in being able to recover delinquent taxes through seizure and sale of property, which in turn "required clear terms of notice to allow buyers to satisfy themselves that the Service has touched the bases necessary for good title. The Government's "direct interest in the availability of a federal forum to vindicate its own administrative action" made the question "an important issue of federal law that sensibly belong[ed] in a federal court." *Grable*.

A second illustration of the sort of substantiality we require comes from Smith v. Kansas City Title & Trust Co., 255 U.S. 180, 41 S.Ct. 243, 65 L.Ed. 577 (1921), which *Grable* described as "the classic example" of a state claim arising under federal law. In *Smith*, the plaintiff argued that the defendant bank could not purchase certain bonds issued by the Federal Government because the Government had acted unconstitutionally in issuing them. We held that the case arose under federal law, because the "decision depends upon the determination" of "the constitutional validity of an act of Congress which is directly drawn in question." Again, the relevant point was not the importance of the question to the parties alone but rather the importance more generally of a determination that the Government "securities were issued under an unconstitutional law, and hence of no validity." Ibid; see also Merrell Dow Pharmaceuticals Inc. v. Thompson, 478 U.S. 804, 814, n. 12, 106 S.Ct. 3229, 92 L.Ed.2d 650 (1986).

Here, the federal issue carries no such significance. Because of the backward-looking nature of a legal malpractice claim, the question is posed in a merely hypothetical sense: If Minton's lawyers had raised a timely experimental-use argument, would the result in the patent infringement proceeding have been different? No matter how the state courts resolve that hypothetical "case within a case," it will not change the real-world result of the prior federal patent litigation. Minton's patent will remain invalid.

Nor will allowing state courts to resolve these cases undermine "the development of a uniform body of [patent] law." Bonito Boats, Inc. v. Thunder Craft Boats, Inc., 489 U.S. 141, 162, 109 S.Ct. 971, 103 L.Ed.2d 118 (1989). Congress ensured such uniformity by vesting exclusive jurisdiction over actual patent cases in the federal district courts and exclusive appellate jurisdiction in the Federal Circuit. See 28 U.S.C. §§1338(a), 1295(a)(1). In resolving the nonhypothetical patent questions those cases present, the federal courts are of course not bound by state court case-within-a-case patent rulings. In any event, the state court case-within-a-case inquiry asks what would have happened in the prior federal proceeding if a particular argument had been made. In answering that question, state courts can be expected to hew closely to the pertinent federal precedents. It is those precedents, after all, that would have applied had the argument been made.

As for more novel questions of patent law that may arise for the first time in a state court "case within a case," they will at some point be decided by a federal court in the context of an actual patent case, with review in the Federal Circuit. If the question arises frequently, it will soon be resolved within the federal system, laying to rest any contrary state court precedent; if it does not arise frequently, it is unlikely to implicate substantial federal interests. The present case is "poles apart from Grable," in which a state court's resolution of the federal question "would be controlling in numerous other cases." Empire Healthchoice Assurance, Inc., 547 U.S., at 700, 126 S.Ct. 2121.

Minton also suggests that state courts' answers to hypothetical patent questions can sometimes have real-world effect on other patents through issue preclusion. Minton, for example, has filed what is known as a "continuation patent" application related to his original patent. He argues that, in evaluating this separate application, the patent examiner could be bound by the Texas trial court's interpretation of the scope of Minton's original patent. It is unclear whether this is true. The Patent and Trademark Office's Manual of Patent Examining Procedure provides that res judicata is a proper ground for rejecting a patent "only when the earlier decision was a decision of the Board of Appeals" or certain federal reviewing courts, giving no indication that state court decisions would have preclusive effect. In fact, Minton has not identified any case finding such preclusive effect based on a state court decision. But even assuming that a state court's case-within-a-case adjudication may be preclusive under some circumstances, the result would be limited to the parties and patents that had been before the state court. Such "fact-bound and situation-specific" effects are not sufficient to establish federal arising under jurisdiction. *Empire Healthchoice.*

Nor can we accept the suggestion that the federal courts' greater familiarity with patent law means that legal malpractice cases like this one belong in federal court. It is true that a similar interest was among those we considered in *Grable.* But the possibility that a state court will incorrectly resolve a state claim is not, by itself, enough to trigger the federal courts' exclusive patent jurisdiction, even if the potential error finds its root in a misunderstanding of patent law.

There is no doubt that resolution of a patent issue in the context of a state legal malpractice action can be vitally important to the particular parties in that case. But something more, demonstrating that the question is significant to the federal system as a whole, is needed. That is missing here.

D

It follows from the foregoing that *Grable* 's fourth requirement is also not met. That requirement is concerned with the appropriate "balance of federal and state judicial responsibilities." We have already explained the absence of a substantial federal issue within the meaning of *Grable.* The States, on the other hand, have "a special responsibility for maintaining standards among members of the licensed professions." Ohralik v. Ohio State Bar Assn., 436 U.S. 447, 460, 98 S.Ct. 1912, 56 L.Ed.2d 444 (1978). Their "interest ... in regulating lawyers is especially great since lawyers are essential to the primary governmental function of administering justice, and have historically been officers of the courts." Goldfarb v. Virginia State Bar, 421 U.S. 773, 792, 95 S.Ct. 2004, 44 L.Ed.2d 572 (1975). We have no reason to suppose that Congress — in establishing exclusive federal jurisdiction over patent cases — meant to bar from state courts state legal malpractice claims simply because they require resolution of a hypothetical patent issue.

* * *

As we recognized a century ago, "the Federal courts have exclusive jurisdiction of all cases arising under the patent laws, but not of all questions in which a patent may be the subject-matter of the controversy." New Marshall Engine Co. v. Marshall Engine Co., 223 U.S. 473, 478, 32 S.Ct. 238, 56 L.Ed. 513 (1912). In this case, although the state courts must answer a question of patent law to resolve Minton's legal malpractice claim, their answer will have no broader effects. It will not stand as binding precedent for any future patent claim; it will not even affect the validity of Minton's patent. Accordingly, there is no "serious federal interest in claiming the advantages thought to be inherent in a federal forum." *Grable.* Section 1338(a) does not deprive the state courts §27of subject matter jurisdiction. The judgment of the Supreme Court of Texas is reversed, and the case is remanded for further proceedings not inconsistent with this opinion. *It is so ordered.*

NOTES AND PROBLEMS FOR DISCUSSION

1. (a) For an historical analysis of the jurisprudence preceding the enactment in 1875 of §1331 that suggests that state law-created claims with embedded federal law issues might actually have been the paradigm of "arising under" cases that the nineteenth century Congress had in mind when it passed that general federal question jurisdiction provision, see Ann Woolhandler & Michael G. Collins, *Federal Question Jurisdiction and Justice Holmes*, 84 NOTRE DAME L.REV. 2151 (2009).

(b) Section 27 of the federal Securities Exchange Act of 1934 grants federal courts exclusive subject matter jurisdiction over all suits "brought to enforce any liability or duty created by" the substantive terms of that statute or regulations issued thereunder. When an investor believed that he had lost most of his stock investment because a stock broker and other financial institutions engaged in "naked short sale" trading that violated state racketeering, criminal, and common law, he filed suit in state court. The type of naked short sale that he alleged the defendants engaged in is also prohibited under SEC regulations issued under the Exchange Act. Never-theless, the plaintiff declined to file any claim under the federal securities laws or regulations (although the plaintiff mentioned violations of the regulations in his complaint). The defendants removed, asserting federal jurisdiction under §27 of the federal Exchange Act on the ground that this suit was brought to enforce duties created by regulations issued under the Exchange Act. The plaintiff moved to remand, challenging the existence of federal jurisdiction. In MERRILL LYNCH v. MANNING, 578 U.S. ___ , 136 S.Ct. 1562 (2016), the Supreme Court unanimously held (with two justices concurring in the judgment only), that the case was improperly removed and that the federal court lacked subject matter jurisdiction under §27. It announced that the test for determining the existence of federal jurisdiction under §27's "brought to enforce" language should be the same one that had been applied to the "arising under" language found in §1331. This meant, the Court explained, that when a complaint consists solely of state law-created claims, it was not sufficient (for federal jurisdiction purposes) for the complaint, either expressly or implicitly, to assert that the defendant breached a duty under the Exchange Act. And this was particularly true when, as here, the plaintiff could prevail on the state law claims without proving any violation of the federal statute or accompanying regulations. Nor did the fact that federal jurisdiction under §27 was exclusively federal argue for reading §27's jurisdictional provision more broadly than §1331. At the same time, however, the Court rejected the plaintiff's suggestion that federal jurisdiction was limited to cases where the suit is brought directly under the federal statute. Citing its ruling in *Grable*, the Court reiterated that federal jurisdiction can attach to a state law-created claim when that claim necessarily raises a substantial and disputed federal issue which a federal court can entertain "without disturbing any congressional approved balance" of federal and state power. But because the Third Circuit had ruled that the federal district court did not have jurisdiction under §1331 (because all the plaintiff's claims asserted sought relief under state law and none of them necessarily raised a federal issue), and since that particular ruling had not been challenged on appeal to the Supreme Court, that meant that the federal district court lacked subject matter jurisdiction and the case had to be remanded.

(c) The development and implementation of the well-pleaded complaint rule yielded two corollary principles, both of which are the product of the availability of removal jurisdiction. Since the defendant can trump the plaintiff's initial choice of forum by removing a case that the plaintiff could have filed in federal court, a plaintiff who, for tactical or other reasons, wants to avoid federal court (e.g., unfamiliarity with federal procedural rules, a belief that a state court judge and/or jury would be more sympathetic to her particular type of claim, a desire to retain tighter control over pace of litigation) might omit available federal claims from her complaint, choosing, instead, to plead only those claims that raise purely state law issues. According to one corollary to the well-pleaded complaint rule, the plaintiff is the "master of the complaint," and the defendant's protestations that the plaintiff is obstructing the federal court's legitimate exercise of jurisdiction over federal questions will not succeed and she will not be permitted to remove the case. In 2005, the Supreme Court reaffirmed its fidelity to the "master of the complaint" rule in the context of a removed case. See Lincoln Property Co. v. Roche, discussed *infra*, p. 240, Note 1(e).

However, the Supreme Court also has devised an exception to this principle, pursuant to which, under limited circumstances, courts are instructed to look beyond the face of the pleading to determine the availability of federal question jurisdiction. Under the "artful pleading" rule, where a plaintiff pleads only a state law claim, but federal law preempts any corresponding state law in the area covered by that claim, the state law claim will be viewed as an "essentially federal law claim" and jurisdiction will attach under §1331. And consequently, the plaintiff is not permitted to employ "artful pleading" to escape removal jurisdiction. A very helpful discussion of these doctrines can be found at Arthur R. Miller, *Artful Pleading: A Doctrine In Search of Definition*, 76 TEX.L.REV. 1781 (1998).

2. The original grant of federal question jurisdiction contained in the Act of 1875 included a provision restricting jurisdiction to cases in which the matter in dispute exceed the value of $500. Over the next century, in response to a concern that the continued expansion of federal statutory claims was congesting federal court dockets, Congress occasionally raised the jurisdictional ante. In 1887, the minimum amount of controversy requirement was augmented to $2000. This was increased to $3000 in 1911 and inflated again to $10,000 in 1958. In 1980, however, Congress reversed direction by abolishing the jurisdictional amount requirement for federal question cases altogether. One reason for the elimination of the jurisdictional amount in controversy was the fact that Congress had enacted a series of additional jurisdictional statutes that conferred subject matter jurisdiction over specialized types of federal claims, such as commerce, antitrust, civil rights, bankruptcy and maritime actions, and none of these statutes included a minimum amount in controversy requirement. See e.g., 28 U.S.C. §§1333, 1334, 1337, 1338 and 1343. Additionally, the elimination of the amount in controversy requirement in §1331 (sometimes referred to as the "general" federal question jurisdiction statute) was responsive to the frequently asserted concern that the presence of an amount in controversy requirement generated unnecessary and complicated litigation over the value of various statutory and constitutional rights in cases where the plaintiff was seeking equitable relief only.

3. The fact that both the framers of the Constitution and Congress provided federal courts with subject matter jurisdiction over questions of federal law does not mean that state courts are devoid of authority to entertain cases involving federal questions. Unless Congress has provided otherwise, state courts have inherent jurisdiction concurrent with that of the federal courts over claims arising under federal law. In a small minority of areas (including admiralty, antitrust, patent and copyright, and bankruptcy actions), Congress has provided the federal courts with exclusive jurisdiction. But the presumption is against vesting the federal courts with exclusive jurisdiction over federal questions, and the Supreme Court has declared that this presumption can be rebutted only by "an explicit statutory directive, by unmistakable implication from legislative history, or by a clear incompatibility between state-court jurisdiction and federal interests." Consequently, absent such evidence, the state courts will be deemed to possess concurrent jurisdiction over the federal claim. For an empirical analysis of the performance of state courts in federal question cases, see John F. Preis, *Reassessing the Purposes of Federal Question Jurisdiction,* 42 WAKE FOREST L.REV. 247 (2007).

Suppose, on the other hand, Congress passes a substantive statute that creates a private right of action and expressly states that such actions can be filed in state court. Does this mean that the plaintiff cannot bring suit in a federal court relying on §1331 as the jurisdictional predicate? For example, the federal Telephone Consumer Protection Act of 1991 (TCPA), 47 U.S.C. §227, prohibits the sending of unsolicited advertisements in a message from a fax machine, computer, or other device. Congress passed this statute largely to fill a gap in consumer protection caused by the states' lack of jurisdiction over telemarketers and others who use fax machines and computers to place interstate calls in a manner that is invasive of privacy. The statute authorizes States to bring civil actions to enjoin forbidden practices and also to seek damages on their residents' behalf. But the statute also provides that jurisdiction over such claims lies exclusively in the federal courts. However, another provision states that a private person or entity "may" bring suit for damages based on a violation of this law "in an appropriate court of [a] state."

In MIMS v. ARROW FINANCIAL SERVICES, LLC, 565 U.S. 368, 132 S.Ct. 740, 181 L.Ed. 2d 881 (2012), the Supreme Court examined whether this provision precluded a private individual from filing a civil action in federal court. Both the trial and circuit court read the jurisdictional provision as vesting state courts with exclusive jurisdiction and therefore dismissed the federal court complaint for lack of subject matter jurisdiction. The Supreme Court unanimously reversed these rulings. Since the TCPA created the right of action and provided the substantive rules of decision, the Court declared, the plaintiff's claim clearly arose under federal law within the meaning of §1331. And the fact that the statute expressly provided for state court jurisdiction did not rebut the presumption in favor of concurrent state and federal court subject matter jurisdiction. Typically, this presumption is used in response to a claim that Congress intended to oust the state court of jurisdiction and vest jurisdiction exclusively in the federal courts. In the instant case, however, the defense was arguing the converse, i.e., that by providing state courts with jurisdiction, Congress intended to oust the federal courts of their jurisdiction over federal statutory claims. The Court disagreed, and declared that the same presumption of concurrent jurisdiction would apply; i.e., only a determination that the federal statute that both creates the private right of action and furnishes the substantive rules of decision expressly "or by fair implication" excludes federal court jurisdiction would be sufficient to divest the federal courts of their §1331 jurisdiction over any suit brought under that statute. Applying that standard to the TCPA, the Court determined that the statutory grant of jurisdiction to state courts was permissive and could not be read to exclude federal court jurisdiction. In support of this conclusion, the Court noted, by way of contrast, that the jurisdictional provision governing suits by State Attorneys General did expressly vest jurisdiction exclusively in the federal courts. The natural inference of Congress' failure to use similar limiting language in the jurisdictional provision governing private rights of action, the Court added, was that it did not intend to confer exclusive state court jurisdiction in that section of the law. Finally, in response to the defense claim that the statutory language providing state courts with jurisdiction would be superfluous if construed to provide only concurrent jurisdiction (since state courts would have enjoyed concurrent jurisdiction if the statute had said nothing about state court jurisdiction), the Court opined that Congress may simply have intended to negate any claim that private actions, like those brought by State Attorneys General, must be filed in federal court.

4. Section 1331 provides that the federal trial courts shall have "original jurisdiction" over civil actions arising under federal law. What does "original" mean in this context? For example, is it to be distinguished from (a) appellate jurisdiction; (b) removal jurisdiction; and/or (c) supplemental jurisdiction? The answer to this question will be important when we examine the contours of the doctrines of supplemental and removal jurisdiction in Sections C and D, *infra*, of this chapter.

5. Would the court have §1331 jurisdiction in the following situations?

(a) The City of New Orleans sues a local landowner claiming that the landowner refused to abide by an agreement to sell her property to the city for $5,000 and that this sale price was not so unconscionably low as to constitute a taking without just compensation in violation of the Fourteenth Amendment to the U.S. Constitution.

(b) The landowner brings an action against the City of New Orleans under the federal Declaratory Judgment Act seeking a declaration that the City had violated the terms of the agreement by starting to bulldoze the land prior to receiving a deed of sale from the landowner. See Skelly Oil Co. v. Phillips Petroleum Co., 339 U.S. 667, 70 S.Ct. 876, 94 L.Ed. 1194 (1950).

6. Although it did not raise a question of federal subject matter jurisdiction, in JONES v. R.R. DONNELLEY & SONS COMPANY, 541 U.S. 369, 124 S.Ct. 1836, 158 L.Ed.2d 645 (2004), the Supreme Court had occasion to invoke its "arising under" doctrine. The plaintiffs had filed a class action alleging racial discrimination in a variety of employment decisions. They had filed their claim under a federal statute (42 U.S.C. §1981) that initially had been enacted in 1866 but that had been amended in 1991. It was undisputed that the plaintiffs' allegations could not have stated a claim under the original version of that statute. Moreover, this statute did not contain its own statute of limitations. In 1990, Congress had passed a catchall four-year limitations provision (28 U.S.C. §1658) to cover claims "arising under an Act of Congress" that had been enacted after December 1, 1990. Prior to the enactment of this catchall provision, the Supreme Court had ruled that where a federal statute did not contain its own limitations provision, a federal court was obliged to apply the most analogous state statute of limitations in actions brought under §1981. The question in *Jones* was whether the plaintiffs' claims were governed by §1658 or the shorter state law limitations provision.

The Court, in a unanimous opinion authored by Justice Stevens, concluded that its definition of "arising under" in neither the constitutional nor the statutory context led to an unambiguous resolution of this question. The "ingredient" test used for Article III purposes did not point to one clear result because both the amendment and the originally enacted statute could be said to form an ingredient of the plaintiffs' claims. Similarly, the Court explained, the statutorily-based well-pleaded complaint test failed to point unambiguously in one direction. For though the amendment clearly created a statutory right that did not previously exist, the original version contained the operative language setting forth the elements of discrimination claims. In the end, however, the Court held that §1658, and not state law, would be deemed to apply whenever the plaintiff's cause of action was not available until after 1990, i.e., whenever the post-1990 amendment created a new right of action. This ruling, the Court concluded, was faithful to the "common usage" of the word "arise" as defined in general and legal dictionaries. The Court also mentioned that this holding was consistent with its interpretation of "arising under" in federal subject matter jurisdictional provisions (such as §1331) since construing §1658 to apply only to claims based on post-1990 stand-alone enactments would be more akin to a "based solely upon" than an "arising under" standard.

SECTION B. DIVERSITY OF CITIZENSHIP AND ALIENAGE

As Article III, §2 reflects, the Framers of the Constitution intended for federal courts not to be limited to hearing only cases that arise under federal law. In addition to authorizing Congress to confer jurisdiction over disputes involving the United States, Ambassadors, Ministers and Consuls, and over admiralty and maritime cases, the Constitution contemplates that federal courts could adjudicate purely state law disputes *if* the adverse parties are either (a) citizens of different states within the Union, (b) a State and a citizen of another State, (c) two separate States, or (d) any State or a citizen of any State and any foreign sovereign or a citizen of any foreign sovereign. Congress subsequently exercised this constitutionally delegated authority to create such pockets of jurisdiction when it passed legislation, now found at 28 U.S.C. §1332, which provides for federal subject matter jurisdiction on the basis of diversity of citizenship and alienage.

In contrast to the justification for the creation of federal question jurisdiction, neither diversity nor alienage jurisdiction is grounded on either the purported comparative competence of federal judges or the need for uniformity of result. Rather, these two related bases of federal jurisdiction historically have been predicated on the notion that since out-of-staters (either from another State or another nation) could be victimized by the "home field advantage" enjoyed by forum citizens, they deserve the opportunity to bring their claims (or, in the case of removed actions, their defenses) before a federal judge whose appointment with life tenure renders her less amenable to local prejudices, pressures, and concerns than a state magistrate.

Read 28 U.S.C. §§1332(a)-(c) and 1359.

Coury v. Prot

United States Court of Appeals, Fifth Circuit, 1996.
85 F.3d 244.

Dennis, Circuit Judge.

In this case David Coury, a citizen of California, sued Alain Prot, a dual citizen of the United States and France, in a Texas state court to recover for damages resulting from breach of contract and fraud. Prot removed the action to the federal district court pleading that he was a dual citizen of France and the United States domiciled in France and therefore entitled to remove this action under the alienage provision of diversity jurisdiction, 28 U.S.C. §1332(a)(2). * * * [T]he jury * * * returned a verdict awarding Coury $164,500 * * *.

Prot appealed * * * contending * * * the district court lacked diversity jurisdiction under the alienage provision because * * * Prot was a dual citizen of the United States and France domiciled in France * * *.

* * *

Jurisdiction

The district court correctly determined that subject matter and diversity of citizenship jurisdiction exists. Prot was domiciled in Texas when the state court action was commenced and when he removed the case to federal court. Although * * * [when the action was filed and then removed to federal court] Prot had physically moved himself, his family and his business to France, he had not formed an intention to remain there.

* * *

What makes a person a citizen of a state? The fourteenth amendment to the Constitution provides that: "All persons born or naturalized in the United States, and subject to the jurisdiction thereof, are citizens of the United States and of the State wherein they reside." However, "reside" has been interpreted to mean more than to be temporarily living in the state; it means to be "domiciled" there. Thus, to be a citizen of a state within the meaning of the diversity provision, a natural person must be both (1) a citizen of the United States, and (2) a domiciliary of that state. Federal common law, not the law of any state, determines whether a person is a citizen of a particular state for purposes of diversity jurisdiction.

Consistent with general principles for determining federal jurisdiction, diversity of citizenship must exist at the time the action is commenced. In cases removed from state court, diversity of citizenship must exist both at the time of filing in state court and at the time of removal to federal court. If diversity is established at the commencement and removal of the suit, it will not be destroyed by subsequent changes in the citizenship of the extant parties.

The lack of subject matter jurisdiction may be raised at any time during pendency of the case by any party or by the court. Fed.R.Civ.P. 12(h)(3). Moreover, the Supreme Court has held that a party cannot waive the defense and cannot be estopped from raising it. Obviously, these principles can result in a tremendous waste of judicial and private resources. The general reaction is that this waste is simply a price that must be paid for federalism. Some cases cry out for an exception to the rules, for example, when a party who invokes federal jurisdiction recants his original jurisdictional allegations or "discovers" that there was no diversity after all after suffering a loss on the merits. So far, however, the traditional rule stands firm despite the urging of commentators for doctrines of estoppel or waiver to bar litigants from "playing fast and loose with the judicial machinery" and using the federal courts' limited subject matter jurisdiction in bad faith. * * *

* * *

In making a jurisdictional assessment, a federal court is not limited to the pleadings; it may look to any record evidence, and may receive affidavits, deposition testimony or live testimony concerning the facts underlying the citizenship of the parties. * * *

A person cannot be a "citizen" of a state unless she is also a citizen of the United States. A United States citizen who is domiciled in a state is a citizen of that state. Thus, with few exceptions, state citizenship for diversity purposes is regarded as synonymous with domicile. Accordingly, it has been held consistently that a diversity suit may not be maintained under 28 U.S.C. §1332(a)(1) by or against a United States citizen who is domiciled in a foreign country, for a resident of a foreign country is not necessarily a citizen thereof. Moreover, an American living abroad is not by virtue of that domicile a citizen or subject of the foreign state in which he resides so as to permit invocation of the alienage jurisdiction prescribed in 28 U.S.C. §1332(a)(2) * * *.

Furthermore, there is an emerging consensus among courts that, for a dual national citizen, only the American citizenship is relevant for purposes of diversity under 28 U.S.C. §1332. Consequently, diversity jurisdiction may be properly invoked only when a dual citizen's domicile, and thus his citizenship, is in a state diverse from that of adverse parties. Accordingly, the dual citizen should not be allowed to invoke alienage jurisdiction because this would give him an advantage not enjoyed by native-born American citizens. The latter conclusion is sound * * * because the major purpose of alienage jurisdiction is to promote international relations by assuring other countries that litigation involving their nationals will be treated at the national level, and alienage jurisdiction is also intended to allow foreign subjects to avoid real or perceived bias in the state courts — a justification that should not be available to the dual citizen who is an American.

A change in domicile typically requires only the concurrence of: (1) physical presence at the new location and (2) an intention to remain there indefinitely; or, as some courts articulate it, the absence of any intention to go elsewhere. Thus, a person who has the clear intent to change domicile does not accomplish the change until he is physically present in the new location with that intent. On the other hand, mere presence in a new location does not effect a change of domicile; it must be accompanied with the requisite intent. In most cases, the difficult issue is not presence but whether the intent to change domicile can be shown.

A person's domicile persists until a new one is acquired or it is clearly abandoned. There is a presumption in favor of the continuing domicile which requires the party seeking to show a change in domicile to come forward with * * * evidence to that effect * * *. While some opinions seem to imply that the burden of persuasion rests with the party attempting to show a change of domicile, this is an overstatement. The proper rule is that the party attempting to show a change assumes the burden of going forward on that issue. The ultimate burden on the issue of jurisdiction rests with the plaintiff or the party invoking federal jurisdiction.

In determining a litigant's domicile, the court must address a variety of factors. No single factor is determinative. The court should look to all evidence shedding light on the litigant's intention to establish domicile. The factors may include the places where the litigant exercises civil and political rights, pays taxes, owns real and personal property, has driver's and other licenses, maintains bank accounts, belongs to clubs and churches, has places of business or employment, and maintains a home for his family. A litigant's statement of intent is relevant to the determination of domicile, but it is entitled to little weight if it conflicts with the objective facts.

Most courts regard domicile as presenting a mixed question of law and fact. Nevertheless, in practice, the district court's determination of domicile is reviewed on appeal as a question of fact; it will be upheld unless "clearly erroneous."

* * *

Based on the evidence of record, much of which consisted of Prot's conflicting statements and actions, the district court found that Prot established a domicile in Texas in 1987, that he physically moved himself and his family to

France in 1991 * * * [to pursue a business opportunity located there], but that the evidence failed to show an essential requisite of a change in domicile, viz., that he formed an intention in 1991 or 1992, prior to the filing of the complaint and the removal of this case, to remain in France indefinitely. In view of Prot's repeated statements that he and his wife did not intend to stay in France indefinitely and that they always intended to return to Texas, we conclude that the district court's findings were not clearly erroneous.

Furthermore, the trial court applied the correct principles of law to these facts in concluding that diversity jurisdiction exists. Because Prot's domicile was determined to be Texas at the time the suit was filed and removed, while Coury's domicile was in California, diversity of citizenship existed between the two parties pursuant to 28 U.S.C. §1332(a)(1). The removal was improper, however, because a defendant may not remove a state action to federal court if a defendant is a citizen of the state in which the action is filed. 28 U.S.C. §1441(b). Coury waived this defect, however, by his failure to seek a remand of the action to state court within 30 days of removal. 28 U.S.C. §1447(c). Nevertheless, although removal may have been improper, subject matter jurisdiction is not lacking. Grubbs v. General Electric Credit Corp., 405 U.S. 699, 702, 92 S.Ct. 1344, 1347, 31 L.Ed.2d 612 (1972) (" * * * [W]here after removal a case is tried on the merits without objection and the federal court enters judgment, the issue in subsequent proceedings on appeal is not whether the case was properly removed, but whether the federal district court would have had original jurisdiction of the case had it been filed in that court.").

* * *

The judgment of the trial court is AFFIRMED * * *.

NOTES AND PROBLEMS FOR DISCUSSION

1. (a) Why did the appellate court in the principal case affirm the trial court's judgment? Did, or should it matter that the party challenging the existence of subject matter jurisdiction on appeal was the one who invoked it?

What happens when a party's domicile is changed involuntarily? Not surprisingly, the caselaw is clear that involuntary removal from the state of one's domicile, as when one is imprisoned, does not change the state of domicile for §1332 purposes. But should the same rule apply when the party is either a minor or incompetent? Although the courts generally agree that the domicile of a minor is determined by the parents since minors are legally incapable of forming the requisite intent to regard a place as a home, see RESTATEMENT (2D) OF CONFLICT OF LAWS §§11, 14, & 15 (1971), the courts are split on whether a guardian can change an incompetent's domicile. Compare Dakuras v. Edwards, 312 F.3d 256 (7th Cir.2002) (better view is that a guardian, like a parent, can change a ward or a child's domicile since responsibility for making essential life choices of children and wards is vested in them) with Long v. Sasser, 91 F.3d 645 (4th Cir.1996) (citizenship of an incompetent cannot be changed by decision of guardian; that citizenship can be deemed changed only if, after the adjudication of incompetency, the ward acquired sufficient understanding and mental capacity to make an intelligent choice of domicile).

(b) Suppose the court had determined that Mr. Prot had manifested his intention to shift his domicile permanently to France. How, if at all, would that have changed the court's ruling?

What if Helen Fredericks, a New York citizen filed a $100,000 breach of contract claim against a corporation that was incorporated under the laws of Delaware but which maintained its principal place of business in London, England. Would this case fit within a federal court's jurisdiction under §1332(a)? See §1332(c) (stating that "a corporation shall be deemed to be a citizen of every State and foreign state by which it has been incorporated and of the State or foreign state where it has its principal place of business"). Compare MAS Capital, Inc. v. Biodelivery Sciences Int'l, 524 F.3d 831 (7th Cir.2008) (concluding, based on an earlier version of the diversity statute, that the foreign principal place of business of a U.S. incorporated corporation is to be disregarded and the corporation is treated as a citizen only of the state of its incorporation).

(c) Assume that Coury's lawsuit had been filed in California rather than in Texas. If the federal district court had discovered that Mr. Coury had permanently shifted his domicile to Texas after filing his complaint in state court, but before Mr. Prot removed the case, would that have changed the court's decision?

Alternatively, assume that Coury, a California citizen, had filed his claim in the federal district court in Los Angeles. Also assume that Prot, a dual citizen of France and the U.S., was deemed to have permanently changed his domicile to Paris. Neither the defendant nor the federal trial judge raised the issue of lack of subject matter jurisdiction, the case went to trial and the jury rendered a verdict in favor of the plaintiff. A few days before trial, Prot and his family moved back to Texas with an express intention to resettle there on a permanent basis. After the jury rendered its verdict, Prot appealed on the ground that the trial court lacked subject matter jurisdiction. How should the court rule?

In GRUPO DATAFLUX v. ATLAS GLOBAL GROUP, L.P., 541 U.S. 567, 124 S.Ct. 1920, 158 L.Ed.2d 866 (2004), the Supreme Court reaffirmed its adherence to the time-of-filing rule, rejecting the plaintiff's request to recognize an exception to this doctrine. In *Grupo*, a partnership sued a Mexican corporation and asserted subject matter jurisdiction under §1332(a)(2). Under established doctrine, a partnership is deemed to be a citizen of each state and foreign country of which each of its partners is a citizen. Two of the plaintiff partnership's partners were Mexican citizens at the time the state-law complaint was filed in federal court. Despite the fact that this made the plaintiff, like the defendant, a citizen of Mexico, no one questioned the existence of diversity jurisdiction until after the jury rendered a verdict in favor of the plaintiff. One month before the trial began, the two Mexican partners left the partnership. After the verdict, but before entry of judgment by the trial judge, the defendant moved to dismiss the case for lack of subject matter jurisdiction on the ground that the parties were not diverse at the time of filing. Applying the time-of-filing rule, the trial judge granted the motion. The Fifth Circuit reversed on the ground that although citizenship generally is determined at the time of filing, an exception should be recognized when (1) the defect is not raised until after a jury verdict; and (2) that defect had been cured prior to the rendition of the verdict.

By a 5-4 vote, the Supreme Court reversed the Fifth Circuit and upheld the trial court's decision to dismiss the case. Noting that the time-of-filing rule was "hornbook law taught to first-year students in any basic course on federal civil procedure," the Court refused to recognize the exception proposed by the plaintiff and advanced by the Fifth Circuit. Regardless of the costs imposed, the Court declared, the interest in minimizing litigation over jurisdiction, as well as its 175 year adherence to the time-of-filing rule, argued against creation of this exception.

The Court acknowledged that it previously had recognized a limited exception to the time-of-filing rule when the jurisdictional defect was cured by the dismissal of a party that had destroyed diversity. But the majority rejected the dissenters' suggestion that this case fell within that exception. The departure of two partners from the plaintiff partnership did not, the majority explained, constitute a dismissal of a party. The partnership continued to be the party plaintiff; it merely changed its internal composition. Consequently, withdrawal of some of its partners did not change the fact that this entity remained the single party plaintiff.

Suppose, instead, that the plaintiff filed suit against a nondiverse defendant alleging only state law claims but that before any responsive pleading was filed by the defendant, the plaintiff filed an amended complaint that added a federal question claim and that forsook §1332 diversity as the basis of jurisdiction and premised jurisdiction on §1331 as to the federal question claim and §1367 (supplemental jurisdiction) over the state law claims. How should the trial court rule on the defendant's claim that the court lacks subject matter jurisdiction because the parties were not diverse at the time of filing? In CONNECTU LLC v. ZUCKERBERG, 522 F.3d 82 (1st Cir. 2008), under this set of facts, the trial judge, citing *Grupo Dataflux*, granted the defense motion to dismiss. It ruled that it was obliged to assess the existence of subject matter jurisdiction by reference only to the original complaint as it stood at the time of filing, that under the time-of-filing rule, an amended complaint could not cure *any* jurisdictional defect that might exist in the original complaint, and that at the time of original filing, diversity did not exist. The First Circuit reversed this ruling, construing *Grupo Dataflux* to apply the time-of-filing rule only to diversity cases since *Grupo Dataflux* arose solely in the diversity context. In declining to extend the ruling in *Grupo Dataflux* to federal question cases, the court noted that "no court has ever read the time-of-filing rule to bar a plaintiff from switching jurisdictional horses before any jurisdictional issue has been raised." Moreover, it ruled, since the plaintiff had an unqualified right to amend its complaint under Rule 15(a), the amended complaint superseded the original "lock, stock, and barrel" and the original no longer performed any function in the case. Additionally, the court declared that as the "master of the complaint," the plaintiff possessed the power to decide what jurisdictional argument to press. The time-of-filing rule, the court advised, was designed for diversity cases to minimize the risk of forum shopping and "unwholesome strategic behavior arising from the temptation to manufacture diversity through manipulation of the applicable constitutional and statutory requirements." As these policy concerns are largely absent in federal question cases, the court saw no reason to transplant the application of the time-of-filing rule to suits invoking federal question subject matter jurisdiction. Finally, the court rejected the defense claim that an amended complaint could not relate back to an earlier pleading over which the court had no subject matter jurisdiction. It held that Rule 15(c)'s language about the relation back of amendments was irrelevant in this context. Rule 15(c), the court explained, was designed to permit a plaintiff to avoid the preclusive effect of a statute of limitations under certain circumstances; it had nothing to do with the curing of jurisdictional defects in an antecedent pleading when the trial court's jurisdiction had not yet been questioned at the time of the amended filing.

(d) A citizen of Massachusetts is injured in an automobile accident with another citizen of that state. Because the injured party is in need of immediate cash, he assigns his cause of action against the driver of the other car to a citizen of New Jersey for $80,000. The assignee then brings the $200,000 tort claim in federal district court in Boston. Will the court have subject matter jurisdiction? See 28 U.S.C. §1359.

(e) Would it make a difference if the injured party mentioned directly above merely assigned the claim to the New Jersey citizen on the understanding that the latter would transfer all proceeds recovered at trial back to the injured party, less a fee for expenses and services provided?

(f) Suppose the parties to the automobile accident were citizens of different states and that the injured party assigned his cause of action to a citizen of the same state as the defendant in exchange for $5 and the assignee's right to 5% of the judgment, the rest going back to the injured party. After the assignee filed the tort claim for $200,000 in state court, the defendant removed the case. Does the federal court have diversity-based jurisdiction?

(g) Note that the grant of alienage jurisdiction in §§1332(a)(2) and (3) is limited to actions involving citizens or subjects of a foreign state. Neither of these provisions accords federal courts the authority to hear suits against a foreign state itself. For more than one hundred and ninety years, the U.S. Supreme Court consistently has accorded foreign sovereigns complete immunity from suits in American courts as a matter of grace and comity on the part of the United States, although not as a restriction imposed by the Constitution. See The Schooner Exchange v. McFaddon, 7 Cranch 116, 11 U.S. 116, 3 L.Ed. 287 (1812). Since the doctrine was not constitutionally mandated, the federal courts typically deferred to requests by the State Department to make exceptions to the general grant of immunity in specific cases. To free the government from this ad hoc approach to exertions of diplomatic pressure by foreign states seeking immunity, Congress, in 1976, passed the Foreign Sovereign Immunities Act, 28 U.S.C. §1330, which sets forth a list of discrete exceptions to this doctrine of foreign sovereign immunity. The exceptions include actions involving, *inter alia*, commercial activity within the U.S., property taken in violation of international law, or tortious acts occurring within the U.S. This statute further provides for the exercise of personal jurisdiction over a foreign state whenever subject matter jurisdiction exists and where proper service has been made. Finally, since the FSIA permits suits to be brought in either federal or state court where one of the specified exceptions to sovereign immunity applies, it also guarantees foreign states the right to remove such civil actions from state to federal court.

2. In STRAWBRIDGE v. CURTISS, 7 U.S. 267, 3 Cranch 267, 2 L.Ed. 435 (1806), Chief Justice Marshall announced what is now referred to as the rule of "complete diversity." Under this doctrine, diversity of citizenship requires that no party be a citizen of the same state as any adverse party. For over a century and one half, however, since the diversity language of §1332 parallels that found in Article III, §2, it was unclear whether Marshall had declared a rule of constitutional or statutory interpretation. Finally, in STATE FARM FIRE & CASUALTY CO. v. TASHIRE, 386 U.S. 523, 87 S.Ct. 1199, 18 L.Ed.2d 270 (1967), the Court resolved the controversy when it determined that *Strawbridge* involved a construction solely of the statutory predecessor to §1332, and not of the Constitution. Consequently, the Court ruled in *State Farm*, Article III, §2 does not prevent Congress from enacting a federal interpleader statute that provides federal jurisdiction in cases involving only "minimal" diversity, viz., where at least two adverse parties are not co-citizens, irrespective of whether other adverse claimants are citizens of the same state.

In 1958, Congress amended §1332 to include a definition of corporate citizenship for diversity purposes. Section 1332(c) provides that a corporation is deemed to be a citizen for diversity purposes of both the state of its incorporation and the state of its "principal place of business". For more than fifty years thereafter, the circuit courts could not agree on a uniform interpretation of this "principal place of business" language. Some circuits focused on a corporation's "nerve center", i.e., the location of its corporate headquarters where its business was directed and controlled. Others focused on the state in which the largest portion of the company's business activities was conducted. The Supreme Court resolved this controversy in HERTZ CORPORATION v. FRIEND, 559 U.S. 77, 130 S.Ct. 1181, 175 L.Ed.2d 1029 (2010). There, the Court unanimously adopted the "nerve center" test, holding that a corporation's "principal place of business" refers to "the place where the corporation's high level officers direct, control, and coordinate the corporation's activities." It added that this "nerve center" would "typically be found at a corporation's headquarters". The Court acknowledged that its primary motivation was to confect a standard that would be as simple to apply as possible. In rejecting the "business operations" test, the Court noted that this approach "had proved unusually difficult to apply" as evidenced by the fact that those circuits that had adopted this general approach had applied a variety of versions of highly general multifactor tests (including consideration of, *inter alia*, plant location, sales, servicing centers, payrolls) in different ways. And this was true, the Court explained, both in cases involving corporations with "far-flung" business activities as well as cases involving corporations that did business in only a few states. While acknowledging that the "nerve center" test might not be a "perfect test that satisfies all administrative and purposive criteria" and that it would, on occasion, generate hard cases, the Court determined that this standard would better promote the substantial interests in avoiding the diversion of scarce judicial and other litigative resources into jurisdictional challenges and promoting predictability for both plaintiffs and corporate defendants. Finally, the Court cautioned parties that if the record revealed an attempt to manipulate the existence or absence of diversity, such as by relying on a "nerve center" that was only a mail box drop or location of an annual meeting of the board of directors, the lower courts should look to the actual place of control and coordination in determining the corporation's true "nerve center."

(a) Suppose that the plaintiff in the principal case had filed his suit in a federal district court in his hometown of Los Angeles and that he had brought a claim against Mr. Prot and a corporation that, Coury alleged, was also a party to the same breach of contract and fraud. The complaint alleged that the company is incorporated under the laws of Delaware, that its corporate headquarters were situated in San Francisco, that its factory was located in Boston, and that it owned and operated several retail outlets in New York City. Finally, Mr. Coury sought $500,000 in damages against each of the two defendants. Would the court have subject matter jurisdiction under §1332?

(b) Would your answer to the above hypothetical change if the company's headquarters, factory and outlets were all located in Texas?

Banks can be chartered either by a State or by the federal government. Since a state-chartered bank's citizenship for diversity purposes would be governed by §1332(c), it would be deemed to be a citizen of the State in which it was chartered and the State in which it maintains its principal place of business. But Congress enacted a separate statute, 28 U.S.C. §1348, to govern the citizenship of federally chartered banks. Under this provision, federally chartered national banks are deemed citizens "of the States in which they are respectively located." In WACHOVIA BANK, NATIONAL ASS'N v. SCHMIDT, 546 U.S. 303, 126 S.Ct. 941, 163 L.Ed.2d 797 (2006), the Court was asked to construe whether the meaning of "located" — i.e., whether a federally chartered bank was deemed, for diversity purposes, to be a citizen only of the state in which its main office was located or whether it was a citizen of every State in which it maintained a branch. The Court chose the former, more restrictive interpretation. The Court's decision was based primarily on its determination that Congress meant to ensure that access to federal courts through diversity jurisdiction in suits involving federally chartered banks would be as expansive as that available in suits against state-chartered banks. Since a state-chartered bank is deemed a citizen only of the state in which it is incorporated and where it maintains its principal place of business, the Court concluded that in enacting §1348, Congress did not intend to curtail the availability of diversity in suits involving federally-chartered banks by making such national banks citizens of every state in which they maintained branches. The Court did acknowledge that its construction of "locate" did not put federal and state-charted banks in absolute parity since state banks are also deemed citizens of the state in which they maintain their principal place of business and §1348 does not contain comparable language. Nevertheless, it maintained, the absence of that option for national banks "may be of scant practical significance" because in almost every case, the location of a national bank's main office and its principal place of business coincide.

(c) What if all the company's facilities were in the District of Columbia? See §1332(e).

Notice that while §1332(c) defines citizenship for corporations, it does not make any mention of unincorporated entities, unions, partnerships, trusts, or any other non-corporate entity. The Supreme Court has defined citizenship of such non-corporate entities as the citizenship of each of their "members." Carden v. Arkoma Associates, 494 U.S. 185 (1990). So, a partnership consists of the citizenship of each of the partners; a joint-stock company has the citizenship of each of its shareholders; and a labor union has the citizenship of each of its members. Recently, an issue arose about the definition of citizenship for a real estate investment trust. In AMERICOLD REALTY TRUST v. CONAGRA FOODS, INC., 577 U.S. ___, 136 S.Ct. 1012, 194 L.Ed.2d 71 (2016), the Court noted that traditionally, legal proceedings involving a trust were brought by or against the trustees in their own name. Accordingly, diversity was assessed based on the citizenship of the trustees. But as real estate investment trusts are deemed by some states' law to be separate legal entities that can sue or be sued, the Court declined to limit the citizenship of such trusts to the citizenship of their trustees. Rather, it held that like any other non-corporate entity sued in its institutional name, the citizenship of a real estate investment trust is defined as the citizenship of each of its members, which means the citizenship of each of its stockholders.

In 2002, Congress took advantage of the ruling in *Tashire* to enact a statute that *does* provide for federal jurisdiction in a limited range of cases involving minimal (i.e., less-than-complete) diversity. The Multiparty, Multiforum Trial Jurisdiction Act of 2002, 28 U.S.C. §1369, provides federal courts with original jurisdiction over a case involving minimal diversity between adverse parties that arises out of a single accident where at least 75 persons died at a discrete location. But this jurisdiction is further limited to cases where one of the following three conditions are met: (1) at least one defendant resides in a state different from the state where a substantial part of the accident occurred; or (2) any two defendants reside in different states; or (3) substantial parts of the accident occurred in different states. Moreover, this enactment requires the federal district court to abstain from hearing a qualifying lawsuit if (1) a substantial majority of the plaintiffs are citizens of the same state as the primary defendants *and* (2) the claims will be governed primarily by the law of that state. Similarly, the Class Action Fairness Act (CAFA), 28 U.S.C. §1332(d)(2) (2006), enacted for the purpose of allowing federal district courts to hear large multistate state-law class actions, obliterates the complete diversity rule. It permits the federal courts to exercise subject matter jurisdiction over state-law class actions in which any single class member or representative is diverse from any named defendant and the *aggregate* matter in controversy exceeds $5 million and involves at least 100 class members. CAFA is discussed in greater detail in Chapter 10, § I.5, below.

(d) A French citizen and a citizen of California jointly bring suit against a citizen of Ohio and another French citizen. Does §1332(a)(3) provide a basis for federal jurisdiction over this case? See Tango Music, LLC v. Deadquick Music, Inc., 348 F.3d 244 (7th Cir.2003).

3. The court in *Coury* stated that "to be a citizen of a state within the meaning of the diversity provision, a natural person must be both (1) a citizen of the United States, and (2) a domiciliary of that state."

(a) If Mr. Prot had been a citizen only of France, but was lawfully admitted to reside permanently in the United States and had decided to live in Texas for the rest of his life, would a federal court have had subject matter jurisdiction over Coury's $500,000 breach of contract and fraud claims against Prot?

(b) Assume that Mr. Prot, a resident alien domiciled in Texas, filed a suit in a federal district court in Texas asserting a $100,000 breach of contact action against his French employer and a $100,000 breach of contract claim against an American citizen domiciled in Arkansas. Would the court have subject matter jurisdiction? Would your answer change if Prot had sued only his employer? Note that in the Federal Courts Jurisdiction and Venue Clarification Act of 2011, an Alien lawfully admitted for permanent residence is treated as an Alien for diversity purposes, "except when" such an alien is domiciled in the same state as a citizen of a state who is his adversary. 28 U.S.C. §1332(a)(2). Prior to the 2011 changes, courts had taken divergent approaches to the problem of permanent resident alien citizenship under the prior version of §1332. *Compare* Saadeh v. Farouki, 107 F.3d 52 (D.C.Cir.1997) *and* Intec USA v. Engle, 467 F.3d 1038 (7th Cir.2006) *with* Singh v. Daimler-Benz AG, 9 F.3d 303 (3d Cir.1993).

4. When it exercised its Article III, §2 jurisdiction-creating authority, Congress chose not to provide federal courts with the full range of authority over state law claims that the Constitution permitted. Instead, from the initial implementation of this authority in the Judiciary Act of 1789, Congress has required that the matter in controversy exceed some prescribed minimum dollar amount, primarily to impose some check on diversity filings. And as was true with the analogous provision in §1331, the federal question jurisdiction statute, this jurisdictional amount in controversy requirement has steadily increased over the succeeding two centuries. From its initial setting at in excess of $500 in 1789, the threshold was increased to in excess of: $2000 in 1887, $3000 in 1911, $10,000 in 1958, and $50,000 in 1988, eight years after this requirement was removed from §1331. The final increase occurred in 1997, when Congress set the limit at in excess of $75,000.

The availability of federal courts as forums for resolving purely state law claims has been a subject of longstanding controversy. Critics complain about congesting federal dockets with cases that are better and more efficiently resolved by state court judges, that the traditional concern over prejudice against non-forum citizens (if it was ever justifiable) does not comport with the modern reality of an increasingly mobile nation and world (and is totally inapposite in cases between American citizens where the suit is filed in a state of which neither party is a citizen, or where it is invoked by a forum citizen plaintiff), and that the exercise of diversity jurisdiction unnecessarily intrudes upon state autonomy. Eliminating or, at least, curtailing diversity jurisdiction, they add, would also relieve federal courts of the frequently time-consuming task of adjudicating threshold disputes concerning the existence of diversity and/or the minimum amount in controversy. Supporters of diversity, on the other hand, insist that access to both systems improves the quality of substantive and procedural rules employed by each as a result of the competitive environment created by concurrent jurisdiction as well as by the cross-pollination occasioned by the movement of practitioners back and forth between the two forums. They also maintain that diverting all state law cases to state courts will merely transfer the congestion from the federal to the state level and not improve litigants' access to a speedy resolution of their conflicts. There is also a lingering sentiment that state court juries manifest bias against foreign defendants — particularly corporations — and that such prejudice is less likely to occur in cases controlled by Article III judges. Finally, it has been suggested that federal judges are more adept at, or willing to, screen out cases that ought not to go trial than their state court counterparts.

According to statistics as of March, 2009, of the nearly quarter million civil cases either originally filed in or removed to the federal district courts, approximately one third were diversity of citizenship actions. In addition, those same data show that a substantial and growing percentage of those diversity cases were the result of removal from state to federal court. Does this data argue in support of or in opposition to retaining the status quo?

The reality of the situation is that only Congress can effect a change to the status quo and, so far, the highly organized and politically powerful lobbies that support retention of diversity jurisdiction had been able to forestall any meaningful change, other than token increases in the jurisdictional amount in controversy requirement.

In light of the existence of the present standard, can a federal court exercise subject matter jurisdiction in the following situations:

(a) A plaintiff brings a tort claim for $35,000 and a separate breach of contract claim for $55,000 against a single defendant. The parties are citizens of different States.

(b) A victim of an automobile accident sues both the owner and the driver of the car that caused the accident. He brings a negligence claim seeking $40,000 in damages against each of them. He is a citizen of Louisiana and they are both citizens of Texas.

(c) The same facts as above but the plaintiff seeks $75,000 in damages against each defendant. *See* Freeland v. Liberty Mutual Co. 632 F.3d 250 (6th Cir.2011) (heralding the significance of one penny where the amount in controversy is precisely $75,000).

(d) The driver and passenger of one car join in one lawsuit in which each asserts a negligence claim seeking $40,000 in damages against the driver of the other car. The driver and passenger are both Louisiana citizens, the other driver is a citizen of Mississippi.

(e) A Colorado plaintiff brings an $85,000 tort claim against a Delaware defendant in federal district. After trial, the jury awards the plaintiff $70,000.

(f) The plaintiff, a citizen of New Mexico, brought a tort claim for medical malpractice in federal court against her Utah-based physician alleging that an operation performed on January 1, 2001 was botched. Her complaint sought $1 million in damages. The jury rendered a verdict in favor of the defendant physician, finding her non-negligent. One year later, the plaintiff files another malpractice claim against the same doctor, alleging that the botched operation has caused additional, minor injuries to her that manifested only after the completion of the first trial. In this action, the plaintiff seeks $1 million for her prior injuries and $50,000 for the additional injuries. See Scherer v. Equitable Life Assurance Society of the U.S., 347 F.3d 394 (2d Cir.2003).

(g) As required by the arbitration clause contained in his employment agreement, a discharged employee was compelled to bring his claim of disability-based discrimination to an arbitrator. After the arbitrator ruled in favor of the employer, the employee filed an action in federal district court to vacate the arbitration award on the ground that the arbitration agreement constituted an unenforceable contract of adhesion. Although the case does not present a federal question, the parties are diverse. The employee's claim before the arbitrator included a request for $150,000 in lost wages. See Theis Research Inc. v. Brown & Bain, 386 F.3d 1180 (9th Cir.2004).

5. (a) When Elian Gonzalez was rescued at sea off the coast of Florida in 1999 and brought to the United States, an international incident erupted over the fight for custody between his father and his relatives in Miami. Suppose that Lazaro Gonzalez, the boy's uncle, an American citizen domiciled in Miami, brought an action in federal district court in Miami against the father, Juan Miguel Gonzalez, a citizen of Cuba, seeking permanent custody. Would the court have subject matter jurisdiction? See Ankenbrandt v. Richards, 504 U.S. 689, 112 S.Ct. 2206, 119 L.Ed.2d 468 (1992) (limiting traditional, judicially-created exception from diversity jurisdiction for domestic relations cases to suits involving the issuance of divorce, alimony, or child custody decrees).

(b) Suppose that instead of seeking child custody, a divorced mother domiciled in Arizona brought an action against her former husband, a citizen of New Jersey, for $1 million in damages alleging that he had physically and sexually abused their children. Would the federal district court in Arizona have subject matter jurisdiction?

(c) Can Mary Worth, a New York citizen, bring an action against her two siblings, both of whom are New Jersey citizens, in federal court to challenge the probate of their late father's $3 million estate? In MARSHALL v. MARSHALL, 547 U.S. 293, 126 S.Ct. 1735, 164 L.Ed.2d 480 (2006), the Supreme Court explained that it previously had recognized a probate exception akin to the domestic relations exception to federal jurisdiction that reserves the probate or annulment of a will and the administration of a decedent's estate exclusively to state probate courts. The circuit courts have split, however, on the question of whether the probate exception is limited to diversity cases. See Jones v. Brennan, 465 F.3d 304 (7th Cir.2006) (extending probate exception to federal question claims involving administration of decedent's estate because probate, like domestic relations exception to federal jurisdiction, is of statutory origin and similar "civil action" language setting forth parameters of both diversity and federal question jurisdiction in §§1331 and 1332 suggests that Congress intended for exceptions to be construed consistently in both jurisdictional contexts).

6. Does alienage jurisdiction extend over a corporation organized under the laws of the British Virgin Islands (BVI) in light of the fact that the BVI is a British Overseas Territory, unrecognized by the U.S. government as an independent foreign state? In JPMORGAN CHASE BANK v. TRAFFIC STREAM (BVI) INFRASTRUCTURE LTD., 536 U.S. 88, 122 S.Ct. 2054, 153 L.Ed.2d 95 (2002), the Supreme Court held that the fact that the BVI was not an independent foreign state did not preclude a corporation organized under BVI law from being deemed a "citizen or subject" of a foreign state for §1332(a) purposes. After evaluating the relationship between the BVI and the United Kingdom, the Court unanimously concluded that distinguishing between a formally recognized state and such a state's legal dependency did not promote the purposes of §1332(a). The fact that the U.K. retained and exercised ultimate authority over the BVI's statutory law (including its corporate law) and acted on its behalf in the international arena rendered BCI citizens, both natural and juridic (e.g., corporations) "citizens or subjects" of the United Kingdom under §1332(a).

7. For a thorough historical analysis of the origins of diversity jurisdiction that concludes that the Framers' decision to create lower federal courts and assign them diversity jurisdiction was primarily motivated by a desire to channel cases away from state court juries and direct them to juries picked by federal officials rather than to circumvent state court judges, see Robert L. Jones, *Finishing A Friendly Argument: the Jury and the Historical Origins of Diversity Jurisdiction*, 82 N.Y.U.L.REV. 997 (2007).

SECTION C. SUPPLEMENTAL JURISDICTION

We already have seen, in the case of the statutory requirements of complete diversity (as interpreted by the Supreme Court) and a minimum amount in controversy (as expressly provided by Congress) for diversity actions, that Congress has not exercised the full measure of its constitutionally delegated authority to confer subject matter jurisdiction on the federal courts. Where Congress has chosen not to occupy the entire constitutionally sanctioned jurisdictional field, does or should this prevent the courts themselves from expanding upon their statutory jurisdiction? For example, suppose an employee who believes she has been the victim of sexual harassment brings a claim against her employer under the federal Civil Rights Act. Assuming that she and the employer are citizens of the same State, should she, nevertheless, be able, in that same lawsuit, to add a tort claim against the company for assault or intentional infliction of emotional distress? And what if she also wants to sue the supervisor who allegedly harassed her? To avoid filing two separate suits, can she add a tort claim against that supervisor in the action against the employer when she and the supervisor are not of diverse citizenship? Alternatively, if the employee is diverse from the company but not from the supervisor, can she bring tort claims for infliction of emotional distress against both of them in the same federal action? Finally, what would happen, jurisdictionally, if the employee sues only the employer and the employer seeks, in that same suit, to bring a state law claim for indemnity against the nondiverse offending supervisor?

The issue of whether the a federal trial court can assume jurisdiction over claims that do not fall within its "original" jurisdiction (provided for in either the general federal question and diversity provisions of 28 U.S.C. §§1331 and 1332 or the various other subject or party-specific provisions of the Judicial Code) has been the subject of a significant amount of judicial and legislative attention.

United Mine Workers of America v. Gibbs

Supreme Court of the United States, 1966.

383 U.S. 715, 86 S.Ct. 1130, 16 L.Ed.2d 218.

MR. JUSTICE BRENNAN delivered the opinion of the Court.

[After a mining company closed one of its mines in southern Tennessee, its wholly owned subsidiary employed Mr. Gibbs as mine superintendent to open a new mine at a nearby location. The miners at the closed mine had been represented by a local union of the United Mine Workers International Union (UMW). Gibbs was instructed to use members of a rival union, the Southern Labor Union, to staff the new mine. The now-jobless members of the local UMW union threatened Gibbs and used physical violence to prevent the new mine from opening, claiming that they had been promised the jobs at the new site. When the leaders of the UMW were informed of the violence, they instructed the local union members to cease that activity and to engage solely in peaceful picketing, which they did. Nevertheless, Gibbs was discharged and alleged that he also lost other employment opportunities as a result of these events. He brought suit in federal district court against only the UMW, and not against either the local union or any of its members. The suit consisted of a secondary boycott claim under §303 of the federal Labor Management Relations Act and a state law cause of action claiming malicious interference with his employment contractual relations and seeking punitive damages that were unavailable under federal law.

The jury found in favor of Gibbs on both claims and awarded him compensatory and punitive damages. The trial court, however, set aside the verdict as to the federal claim on the ground that the challenged conduct did not constitute a secondary boycott as a matter of law. It sustained the award on the state claim. The Sixth Circuit affirmed both of these rulings.]

I.

A threshold question is whether the District Court properly entertained jurisdiction of the claim based on Tennessee law. * * *

* * *

* * * Pendent jurisdiction, in the sense of judicial power, exists whenever there is a claim "arising under (the) Constitution, the Laws of the United States, and Treaties made, or which shall be made, under their Authority * * *," U.S.Const., Art. III, §2, and the relationship between that claim and the state

claim permits the conclusion that the entire action before the court comprises but one constitutional "case." The federal claim must have substance sufficient to confer subject matter jurisdiction on the court. The state and federal claims must derive from a common nucleus of operative fact. But if, considered without regard to their federal or state character, a plaintiff's claims are such that he would ordinarily be expected to try them all in one judicial proceeding, then, assuming substantiality of the federal issues, there is power in federal courts to hear the whole.

That power need not be exercised in every case in which it is found to exist. It has consistently been recognized that pendent jurisdiction is a doctrine of discretion, not of plaintiff's right. Its justification lies in considerations of judicial economy, convenience and fairness to litigants; if these are not present a federal court should hesitate to exercise jurisdiction over state claims, even though bound to apply state law to them. Needless decisions of state law should be avoided both as a matter of comity and to promote justice between the parties, by procuring for them a surer-footed reading of applicable law. Certainly, if the federal claims are dismissed before trial, even though not insubstantial in a jurisdictional sense, the state claims should be dismissed as well. Similarly, if it appears that the state issues substantially predominate, whether in terms of proof, of the scope of the issues raised, or of the comprehensiveness of the remedy sought, the state claims may be dismissed without prejudice and left for resolution to state tribunals. There may, on the other hand, be situations in which the state claim is so closely tied to questions of federal policy that the argument for exercise of pendent jurisdiction is particularly strong.   * * * Finally, there may be reasons independent of jurisdictional considerations, such as the likelihood of jury confusion in treating divergent legal theories of relief, that would justify separating state and federal claims for trial, Fed.Rule Civ.Proc. 42(b). If so, jurisdiction should ordinarily be refused.

The question of power will ordinarily be resolved on the pleadings. But the issue whether pendent jurisdiction has been properly assumed is one which remains open throughout the litigation. Pretrial procedures or even the trial itself may reveal a substantial hegemony of state law claims, or likelihood of jury confusion, which could not have been anticipated at the pleading stage. Although it will of course be appropriate to take account in this circumstance of the already completed course of the litigation, dismissal of the state claim might even then be merited. For example, it may appear that the plaintiff was well aware of the nature of his proofs and the relative importance of his claims; recognition of a federal court's wide latitude to decide ancillary questions of state law does not imply that it must tolerate a litigant's effort to impose upon it what is in effect only a state law case. Once it appears that a state claim constitutes the real body of a case, to which the federal claim is only an appendage, the state claim may fairly be dismissed.

We are not prepared to say that in the present case the District Court exceeded its discretion in proceeding to judgment on the state claim.   * * * Although §303 limited recovery to compensatory damages based on secondary pressures, and state law allowed both compensatory and punitive damages, and allowed such damages as to both secondary and primary activity, the state and federal claims arose from the same nucleus of operative fact and reflected alternative remedies. * * *

It is true that the §303 claims ultimately failed and that the only recovery allowed respondent was on the state claim. We cannot confidently say, however, that the federal issues were so remote or played such a minor role at the trial that in effect the state claim only was tried. * * * [T]he court submitted the §303 claims * * * to the jury. The jury returned verdicts against petitioner on those §303 claims, and it was only on petitioner's motion for a directed verdict and a judgment n.o.v. that the verdicts on those claims were set aside. * * * Although there was some risk of confusing the jury in joining the state and federal claims — especially since, as will be developed, differing standards of proof of UMW involvement applied — the possibility of confusion could be lessened by employing a special verdict form, as the District Court did. * * * We thus conclude that although it may be that the District Court might, in its sound discretion, have dismissed the state claim, the circumstances show no error in refusing to do so.

* * *

THE CHIEF JUSTICE took no part in the decision of this case.

MR. JUSTICE HARLAN, whom MR. JUSTICE CLARK joins, concurring.

I agree with and join in Part I of the Court's opinion relating to pendent jurisdiction. * * *

NOTES AND PROBLEMS FOR DISCUSSION

1.   What is the constitutional authority for the Court's exercise of subject matter jurisdiction over the plaintiff's non-diverse state law claim? Is there any policy justification for providing this extra-original jurisdiction?

2.   Could a federal court exert pendent jurisdiction in the following situations:

(a) A New York plaintiff asserts a federal civil rights claim alleging sexual harassment and a tort claim seeking compensatory and punitive damages for negligent infliction of emotional distress against a New York incorporated employer where the issue of recovery of punitive damages in negligent infliction of emotional distress claims has not previously been addressed under (governing) New York law.

(b) A Connecticut corporation files a claim alleging that the Hartford Insurance Co. (whose principal place of business is in Connecticut) has engaged in anticompetitive pricing practices in violation of the federal antitrust laws and a separate breach of contract claim in which it asserts that Hartford refused to pay off on a covered claim.

(c) A California plaintiff files a $100,000 tort claim and a $40,000 breach of contract claim against a New Mexico defendant.

3. Repeating the mantra that the federal district courts are courts of limited subject matter jurisdiction, the Supreme Court repeatedly has declared that the federal judicial power is a creature of both constitutional and statutory law. Thus, even if exercising jurisdiction over a particular claim would not exceed the limits on federal judicial power set forth in Article III, a federal court could not exercise jurisdiction over that claim unless it also possessed statutory authorization to do so. Nevertheless, and without coming to grips with this doctrine, the Supreme Court in *Gibbs* decided to extend federal jurisdiction to claims that did not fall within the federal courts' original jurisdiction. Instead, the *Gibbs* Court focused only on a federal court's Article III authority to hear a a a "case" arising under federal law and broadly defined "case" to encompass all claims arising out of a common nucleus of operative facts. More than twenty years later, the Supreme Court finally addressed the statutory problem and rationalized its ruling in *Gibbs* as having rested on its determination that Congress must have intended for §1331 to be construed to its constitutionally permissible maximum, i.e., to extend federal jurisdiction to the entire "case" of which the federal question claim was but a part.

As a result of its ruling in *Gibbs*, the Supreme Court was confronted with other situations in which a federal court was asked to exercise jurisdiction over claims that lacked a statutory basis for jurisdiction. These cases fell into one of two broad categories:

(a) Cases involving a plaintiff with a federal question or diverse state law claim against one defendant who also sought to assert a state law claim against another, nondiverse defendant. This situation differed from the pendent claim context of *Gibbs* because here the nonfederal claim was being brought against a defendant against whom the plaintiff did *not* have a federal claim. Such a claim, if filed separately, would not have qualified for federal jurisdiction. Consequently, hearing it as part of a case containing a federal claim against a separate defendant would bring both an extra claim and an additional party to the case. This attempt at creating "pendent party" jurisdiction was the focus of attention in three other important decisions rendered by the U.S. Supreme Court.

The obvious question in all three of these cases was whether the recognition of pendent claim jurisdiction in *Gibbs* should extend to the pendent party context. In ALDINGER v. HOWARD, 427 U.S. 1, 96 S.Ct. 2413, 49 L.Ed.2d 276 (1976), the first of this trio, the plaintiff brought a federal question claim against several defendants and a state law claim against a nondiverse defendant. After acknowledging that the availability of pendent party jurisdiction depended upon an examination of both the constitutional and statutory authority for exercising that judicial power, the Court ignored the constitutional question and focused solely on whether or not Congress, through the jurisdictional predicate for the federal claim, expressly or by implication negated the existence of pendent party jurisdiction. It concluded that Congress, through the governing jurisdictional statute in the instant case, had impliedly declined to extend federal jurisdiction over this claim.

Similarly, in OWEN EQUIPMENT AND ERECTION CO. v. KROGER, 437 U.S. 365, 98 S.Ct. 2396, 57 L.Ed.2d 274 (1978), the Court again eschewed the constitutional question. Here, in contrast to *Aldinger*, federal jurisdiction was premised on diversity of citizenship—i.e., a state law cause of action rather than a federal question claim. After the plaintiff filed his tort action, the defendant, in that same lawsuit, brought an action for indemnity against a third party. The plaintiff subsequently amended his complaint to add a state law claim against that third party. Since the third party was not diverse from the plaintiff, this claim did not have an independent basis of subject matter jurisdiction and so the plaintiff asked the court to exercise pendent party jurisdiction over it. With respect to the constitutionality of pendent party jurisdiction in a diversity action, the Court merely cited *Aldinger* for the proposition that the *Gibbs* "common nucleus of operative fact" test *was* the constitutional minimum for the exercise of jurisdiction over a nonfederal claim. The remainder of the analysis was limited to determining whether the statute providing federal jurisdiction (here, §1332) could be construed as evincing Congress' intention to permit or negate the exercise of pendent party jurisdiction. The Court concluded that in light of the statutory requirement of complete diversity, Congress had evinced its intention not to permit the use of pendent party jurisdiction over a nondiverse state law claim.

Finally, in FINLEY v. U.S., 490 U.S. 545, 109 S.Ct. 2003, 104 L.Ed.2d 593 (1989), the plaintiff, as in *Aldinger*, sought to append a nondiverse state law claim against one defendant to a federal claim against another party; here, the federal government. The Court assumed, without deciding, that the *Gibbs* "common nucleus of operative fact" constitutional criterion for pendent claim jurisdiction was equally applicable to pendent party cases. Then, as in *Aldinger* and *Owen*, the Court concluded that the terms of the jurisdictional statute in the instant case (the Federal Tort Claims Act) did not support the exercise of pendent party jurisdiction. The language of the case also suggests that the Court would presume that Congress did not intend to permit the exercise of pendent party jurisdiction in the absence of an affirmative statement to the contrary in the applicable jurisdictional statute. This appears to conflict with language in *Aldinger* indicating that the statutory presumption was in favor of pendent party jurisdiction absent any evidence that Congress explicitly or impliedly meant to negate the existence of pendent party jurisdiction. Most significantly, however, after acknowledging that it had denied pendent party jurisdiction in both *Aldinger* and the instant case on statutory grounds, the Court noted that "[w]hatever we say regarding the scope of jurisdiction conferred by a particular statute can of course be changed by Congress." Congress accepted the Court's invitation to change the jurisdictional landscape in part by enacting §1367, the supplemental jurisdiction statute.

(b) Cases where a federal court was asked to exert subject matter jurisdiction over claims raised outside of the plaintiff's complaint that did not fall within the federal courts' original jurisdiction. Such "ancillary jurisdiction" was sought, for example, over a defendant's nondiverse state law counterclaim raised in response to the plaintiff's federal question claim against it. Or over a defendant's nondiverse, state law-based third party claim in a case where the plaintiff had asserted either a federal question or diverse state law claim against that defendant. Or over one defendant's nondiverse, state law cross-claim against a co-defendant in a case where the plaintiff had asserted either federal question or diverse state law claims against both defendants. Or even over a state law cross-claim filed by one plaintiff against a nondiverse co-plaintiff.

Ancillary jurisdiction also could arise in connection with a nondiverse state claim by the third party defendant against the plaintiff. The courts uniformly determined that they had the discretion to exercise ancillary jurisdiction as long as the ancillary claims satisfied the constitutional requirement set forth in *Gibbs*, i.e., where they could be viewed as part of the same "case" as the plaintiff's federal claim or claims.

4. Prior to the enactment of §1367, then, the Supreme Court had sanctioned the exercise of pendent claim jurisdiction but refused to permit the exercise of pendent party jurisdiction. But as mentioned at the end of Note 3(a), *supra*, Congress followed through on the Supreme Court's suggestion in *Finley* and enacted §1367. By creating a new term, "supplemental jurisdiction" Congress signaled its intent to merge the related doctrines of pendent and ancillary jurisdiction into a unified concept.

(a) How are cases like *Aldinger, Owen*, and *Finley* now resolved under the terms of §1367?

(b) Why do the exceptions to supplemental jurisdiction established in §1367(b) apply only to cases where the basis for federal jurisdiction is diversity and alienage but not to cases containing federal question or admiralty claims or where the U.S. is a party?

(c) The language employed by Congress in §1367(b) to describe those circumstances in which supplemental jurisdiction was unavailable in diversity-based cases led to a multitude of interpretive problems. Suppose, for example, that a state law-based class action is brought against a defendant. Further suppose that all of the members of the class certified under Rule 23 are diverse from the defendant but that the claims of only some of the members satisfy §1332(a)'s amount in controversy requirement. Can the court exercise supplemental jurisdiction over the claims that do not meet the jurisdictional amount requirement? Or what if the suit was not a class action but merely one involving several plaintiffs who voluntarily sought to join under Rule 20, only some, but not all, of whom asserted claims meeting the amount in controversy requirement? Or what if some of these plaintiffs in either the class or non-class action were diverse from the defendant but others were not? What is the effect of the language in §1367(b) barring the exercise of supplemental jurisdiction in diversity cases over claims by plaintiffs who are sought to be joined under Rule 19 or who seek to intervene under Rule 24? The Supreme Court addressed these, and related questions in the following case.

Exxon Mobil Corp. v. Allapattah Services, Inc.

Supreme Court of the United States, 2005.
545 U.S. 546, 125 S.Ct. 2611, 162 L.Ed.2d 502.

JUSTICE KENNEDY delivered the opinion of the Court.

These consolidated cases present the question whether a federal court in a diversity action may exercise supplemental jurisdiction over additional plaintiffs whose claims do not satisfy the minimum amount-in-controversy requirement, provided the claims are part of the same case or controversy as the claims of plaintiffs who do allege a sufficient amount in controversy. Our decision turns on the correct interpretation of 28 U.S.C. §1367. The question has divided the Courts of Appeals, and we granted certiorari to resolve the conflict.

We hold that, where the other elements of jurisdiction are present and at least one named plaintiff in the action satisfies the amount-in-controversy requirement, §1367 does authorize supplemental jurisdiction over the claims of other plaintiffs in the same Article III case or controversy, even if those claims are for less than the jurisdictional amount specified in the statute setting forth the requirements for diversity jurisdiction. We affirm the judgment of the Court of Appeals for the Eleventh Circuit [in Exxon], and we reverse the judgment of the Court of Appeals for the First Circuit [in Ortega].

I

In 1991, about 10,000 Exxon dealers filed a class-action suit against the Exxon Corporation in the United States District Court for the Northern District of Florida. The dealers alleged an intentional and systematic scheme by Exxon under which they were overcharged for fuel purchased from Exxon. The plaintiffs invoked the District Court's §1332(a) diversity jurisdiction. After a unanimous jury verdict in favor of the plaintiffs, the District Court certified the case for interlocutory review, asking whether it had properly exercised §1367 supplemental jurisdiction over the claims of class members who did not meet the jurisdictional minimum amount in controversy.

The Court of Appeals for the Eleventh Circuit upheld the District Court's extension of supplemental jurisdiction to these class members. *Allapattah Services, Inc. v. Exxon Corp.*, 333 F. 3d 1248 (2003). "[W]e find," the court held, "that §1367 clearly and unambiguously provides district courts with the authority in diversity class actions to exercise supplemental jurisdiction over the claims of class members who do not meet the minimum amount in controversy as long as the district court has original jurisdiction over the claims of at least one of the class representatives." This decision accords with the views of the Courts of Appeals for the Fourth, Sixth, and Seventh Circuits. The Courts of Appeals for the Fifth and Ninth Circuits, adopting a similar analysis of the statute, have held that in a diversity class action the unnamed class members need not meet the amount-in-controversy requirement, provided the named class members do. These decisions, however, are unclear on whether all the named plaintiffs must satisfy this requirement.

In the other case now before us [Ortega v. Star-Kist], the Court of Appeals for the First Circuit took a different position on the meaning of §1367(a). In that case, a 9-year-old girl sued Star-Kist in a diversity action in the United States District Court for the District of Puerto Rico, seeking damages for unusually severe injuries she received when she sliced her finger on a tuna can. Her family joined in the suit, seeking damages for emotional distress and certain medical expenses. The District Court granted summary judgment to Star-Kist, finding that none of the plaintiffs met the minimum amount-in-controversy requirement. The Court of Appeals for the First Circuit, however, ruled that the injured girl, but not her family members, had made allegations of damages in the requisite amount.

The Court of Appeals then addressed whether, in light of the fact that one plaintiff met the requirements for original jurisdiction, supplemental jurisdiction over the remaining plaintiffs' claims was proper under §1367. The court held that §1367 authorizes supplemental jurisdiction only when the district court has original jurisdiction over the action, and that in a diversity case original jurisdiction is lacking if one plaintiff fails to satisfy the amount-in-controversy requirement. Although the Court of Appeals claimed to "express no view" on whether the result would be the same in a class action, its analysis is inconsistent with that of the Court of Appeals for the Eleventh Circuit. The Court of Appeals for the First Circuit's view of §1367 is, however, shared by the Courts of Appeal for the Third, Eighth, and Tenth Circuits, and the latter two Courts of Appeals have expressly applied this rule to class actions.

II

A

The district courts of the United States, as we have said many times, are "courts of limited jurisdiction. They possess only that power authorized by Constitution and statute," *Kokkonen v. Guardian Life Ins. Co. of America,* 511 U.S. 375, 377 (1994). In order to provide a federal forum for plaintiffs who seek to vindicate federal rights, Congress has conferred on the district courts original jurisdiction in federal-question cases — civil actions that arise under the Constitution, laws, or treaties of the United States. 28 U S.C. §1331. In order to provide a neutral forum for what have come to be known as diversity cases, Congress also has granted district courts original jurisdiction in civil actions between citizens of different States, between U. S. citizens and foreign citizens, or by foreign states against U. S. citizens. §1332. To ensure that diversity jurisdiction does not flood the federal courts with minor disputes, §1332(a) requires that the matter in controversy in a diversity case exceed a specified amount, currently $75,000.

Although the district courts may not exercise jurisdiction absent a statutory basis, it is well established — in certain classes of cases — that, once a court has original jurisdiction over some claims in the action, it may exercise supplemental jurisdiction over additional claims that are part of the same case or controversy. The leading modern case for this principle is *Mine Workers v. Gibbs.* In *Gibbs,* the plaintiff alleged the defendant's conduct violated both federal and state law. The District Court, *Gibbs* held, had original jurisdiction over the action based on the federal claims. *Gibbs* confirmed that the District Court had the additional power (though not the obligation) to exercise supplemental jurisdiction over related state claims that arose from the same Article III case or controversy.

As we later noted, the decision allowing jurisdiction over pendent state claims in *Gibbs* did not mention, let alone come to grips with, the text of the jurisdictional statutes and the bedrock principle that federal courts have no jurisdiction without statutory authorization. *Finley v. United States,* 490 U. S. 545, 548 (1989). In *Finley,* we nonetheless reaffirmed and rationalized *Gibbs* and its progeny by inferring from it the interpretive principle that, in cases involving supplemental jurisdiction over additional claims between parties properly in federal court, the jurisdictional statutes should be read broadly, on the assumption that in this context Congress intended to authorize courts to exercise their full Article III power to dispose of an entire action before the court which comprises but one constitutional "case."

We have not, however, applied *Gibbs'* expansive interpretive approach to other aspects of the jurisdictional statutes. For instance, we have consistently interpreted §1332 as requiring complete diversity: In a case with multiple plaintiffs and multiple defendants, the presence in the action of a single plaintiff from the same State as a single defendant deprives the district court of original diversity jurisdiction over the entire action. *Strawbridge v. Curtiss,* 3 Cranch 267 (1806); *Owen Equipment & Erection Co. v. Kroger,* 437 U.S. 65, 375 (1978). The complete diversity requirement is not mandated by the Constitution, *State Farm Fire & Casualty Co. v. Tashire,* 386 U.S. 523 (1967), or by the plain text of §1332(a). The Court, nonetheless, has adhered to the complete diversity rule in light of the purpose of the diversity requirement, which is to provide a federal forum for important disputes where state courts might favor, or be perceived as favoring, home-state litigants. The presence of parties from the same State on both sides of a case dispels this concern, eliminating a principal reason for conferring §1332 jurisdiction over any of the claims in the action. The specific purpose of the complete diversity rule explains both why we have not adopted *Gibbs'* expansive interpretive approach to this aspect of the jurisdictional statute and why *Gibbs* does not undermine the complete diversity rule. In order for a federal court to invoke supplemental jurisdiction under *Gibbs*, it must first have original jurisdiction over at least one claim in the action. Incomplete diversity destroys original jurisdiction with respect to all claims, so there is nothing to which supplemental jurisdiction can adhere.

In contrast to the diversity requirement, most of the other statutory prerequisites for federal jurisdiction, including the federal-question and amount-in-controversy requirements, can be analyzed claim by claim. True, it does not follow by necessity from this that a district court has authority to exercise supplemental jurisdiction over all claims provided there is original jurisdiction over just one. Before the enactment of §1367, the Court declined in contexts other than the pendent-claim instance to follow *Gibbs'* expansive approach to interpretation of the jurisdictional statutes. The Court took a more restrictive view of the proper interpretation of these statutes in so-called pendent-party cases involving supplemental jurisdiction over claims involving additional parties — plaintiffs or defendants — where the district courts would lack original jurisdiction over claims by each of the parties standing alone.

Thus, with respect to plaintiff-specific jurisdictional requirements, the Court held in *Clark v. Paul Gray, Inc.,* 306 U.S. 583 (1939), that every plaintiff must separately satisfy the amount-in-controversy requirement. Though *Clark* was a federal-question case, at that time federal-question jurisdiction had an amount-in-controversy requirement analogous to the amount-in-controversy requirement for diversity cases. * * * The Court reaffirmed this rule, in the context of a class action brought invoking §1332(a) diversity jurisdiction, in *Zahn v.*

International Paper Co., 414 U.S. 291 (1973). It follows "inescapably" from *Clark*, the Court held in *Zahn*, that "any plaintiff without the jurisdictional amount must be dismissed from the case, even though others allege jurisdictionally sufficient claims."

The Court took a similar approach with respect to supplemental jurisdiction over claims against additional defendants that fall outside the district courts' original jurisdiction. In *Aldinger v. Howard,* 427 U.S. 1 (1976), the plaintiff brought a 42 U.S.C. §1983 action against county officials in district court pursuant to the statutory grant of jurisdiction in 28 U.S.C. §1343(3). The plaintiff further alleged the court had supplemental jurisdiction over her related state-law claims against the county, even though the county was not suable under §1983 and so was not subject to §1343(3)'s original jurisdiction. The Court held that supplemental jurisdiction could not be exercised because Congress, in enacting §1343(3), had declined (albeit implicitly) to extend federal jurisdiction over any party who could not be sued under the federal civil rights statutes. "Before it can be concluded that [supplemental] jurisdiction [over additional parties] exists," *Aldinger* held, "a federal court must satisfy itself not only that Art [icle] III permits it, but that Congress in the statutes conferring jurisdiction has not expressly or by implication negated its existence."

In *Finley v. United States,* 490 U.S. 545 (1989), we confronted a similar issue in a different statutory context. The plaintiff in *Finley* brought a Federal Tort Claims Act negligence suit against the Federal Aviation Administration in District Court, which had original jurisdiction under §1346(b). The plaintiff tried to add related claims against other defendants, invoking the District Court's supplemental jurisdiction over so-called pendent parties. We held that the District Court lacked a sufficient statutory basis for exercising supplemental jurisdiction over these claims. Relying primarily on *Zahn*, *Aldinger*, and *Kroger*, we held in *Finley* that "a grant of jurisdiction over claims involving particular parties does not itself confer jurisdiction over additional claims by or against different parties." While *Finley* did not limit or impair *Gibbs'* liberal approach to interpreting the jurisdictional statutes in the context of supplemental jurisdiction over additional claims involving the same parties, *Finley* nevertheless declined to extend that interpretive assumption to claims involving additional parties. *Finley* held that in the context of parties, in contrast to claims, "we will not assume that the full constitutional power has been congressionally authorized, and will not read jurisdictional statutes broadly."

As the jurisdictional statutes existed in 1989, then, here is how matters stood: First, the diversity requirement in §1332(a) required complete diversity; absent complete diversity, the district court lacked original jurisdiction over all of the claims in the action. *Strawbridge*; *Kroger*. Second, if the district court had original jurisdiction over at least one claim, the jurisdictional statutes implicitly authorized supplemental jurisdiction over all other claims between the same parties arising out of the same Article III case or controversy. *Gibbs*. Third, even when the district court had original jurisdiction over one or more claims between particular parties, the jurisdictional statutes did not authorize supplemental jurisdiction over additional claims involving other parties. *Clark*; *Zahn*; *Finley*.

B

In *Finley* we emphasized that "[w]hatever we say regarding the scope of jurisdiction conferred by a particular statute can of course be changed by Congress." In 1990, Congress accepted the invitation. It passed the Judicial Improvements Act, 104 Stat. 5089, which enacted §1367, the provision which controls these cases.

* * *

All parties to this litigation and all courts to consider the question agree that §1367 overturned the result in *Finley*. There is no warrant, however, for assuming that §1367 did no more than to overrule *Finley* and otherwise to codify the existing state of the law of supplemental jurisdiction. We must not give jurisdictional statutes a more expansive interpretation than their text warrants, but it is just as important not to adopt an artificial construction that is narrower than what the text provides. No sound canon of interpretation requires Congress to speak with extraordinary clarity in order to modify the rules of federal jurisdiction within appropriate constitutional bounds. Ordinary principles of statutory construction apply. In order to determine the scope of supplemental jurisdiction authorized by §1367, then, we must examine the statute's text in light of context, structure, and related statutory provisions.

Section 1367(a) is a broad grant of supplemental jurisdiction over other claims within the same case or controversy, as long as the action is one in which the district courts would have original jurisdiction. The last sentence of §1367(a) makes it clear that the grant of supplemental jurisdiction extends to claims involving joinder or intervention of additional parties. The single question before us, therefore, is whether a diversity case in which the claims of some plaintiffs satisfy the amount-in-controversy requirement, but the claims of others plaintiffs do not, presents a "civil action of which the district courts have original jurisdiction." If the answer is yes, §1367(a) confers supplemental jurisdiction over all claims, including those that do not independently satisfy the amount-in-controversy requirement, if the claims are part of the same Article III case or controversy. If the answer is no, §1367(a) is inapplicable and, in light of our holdings in *Clark* and *Zahn*, the district court has no statutory basis for exercising supplemental jurisdiction over the additional claims.

We now conclude the answer must be yes. When the well-pleaded complaint contains at least one claim that satisfies the amount-in-controversy requirement, and there are no other relevant jurisdictional defects, the district court, beyond all question, has original jurisdiction over that claim. The presence of other claims in the complaint, over which the district court may lack original jurisdiction, is of no moment. If the court has original jurisdiction over a single claim in the complaint, it has original jurisdiction over a "civil action" within the meaning of §1367(a), even if the civil action over which it has jurisdiction comprises fewer claims than were included in the complaint. Once the court determines it has original jurisdiction over the civil action, it can turn to the question whether it has a constitutional and statutory basis for exercising supplemental jurisdiction over the other claims in the action.

Section 1367(a) commences with the direction that §§1367(b) and (c), or other relevant statutes, may provide specific exceptions, but otherwise §1367(a) is a broad jurisdictional grant, with no distinction drawn between pendent-claim and pendent-party cases. In fact, the last sentence of §1367(a) makes clear that the provision grants supplemental jurisdiction over claims involving joinder or intervention of additional parties. The terms of §1367 do not acknowledge any distinction between pendent jurisdiction and the doctrine of so-called ancillary jurisdiction. Though the doctrines of pendent and ancillary jurisdiction developed separately as a historical matter, the Court has recognized that the doctrines are "two species of the same generic problem," *Kroger.* Nothing in §1367 indicates a congressional intent to recognize, preserve, or create some meaningful, substantive distinction between the jurisdictional categories we have historically labeled pendent and ancillary.

If §1367(a) were the sum total of the relevant statutory language, our holding would rest on that language alone. The statute, of course, instructs us to examine §1367(b) to determine if any of its exceptions apply, so we proceed to that section. While §1367(b) qualifies the broad rule of §1367(a), it does not withdraw supplemental jurisdiction over the claims of the additional parties at issue here. The specific exceptions to §1367(a) contained in §1367(b), moreover, provide additional support for our conclusion that §1367(a) confers supplemental jurisdiction over these claims. Section 1367(b), which applies only to diversity cases, withholds supplemental jurisdiction over the claims of plaintiffs proposed to be joined as indispensable parties under Federal Rule of Civil Procedure 19, or who seek to intervene pursuant to Rule 24. Nothing in the text of §1367(b), however, withholds supplemental jurisdiction over the claims of plaintiffs permissively joined under Rule 20 (like the additional plaintiffs in Ortega) or certified as class-action members pursuant to Rule 23 (like the additional plaintiffs in Exxon). The natural, indeed the necessary, inference is that §1367 confers supplemental jurisdiction over claims by Rule 20 and Rule 23 plaintiffs. This inference, at least with respect to Rule 20 plaintiffs, is strengthened by the fact that §1367(b) explicitly excludes supplemental jurisdiction over claims against defendants joined under Rule 20.

We cannot accept the view, urged by some of the parties, commentators, and Courts of Appeals, that a district court lacks original jurisdiction over a civil action unless the court has original jurisdiction over every claim in the complaint. As we understand this position, it requires assuming either that all claims in the complaint must stand or fall as a single, indivisible "civil action" as a matter of definitional necessity — what we will refer to as the "indivisibility theory" — or else that the inclusion of a claim or party falling outside the district court's original jurisdiction somehow contaminates every other claim in the complaint, depriving the court of original jurisdiction over any of these claims — what we will refer to as the "contamination theory."

The indivisibility theory is easily dismissed, as it is inconsistent with the whole notion of supplemental jurisdiction. If a district court must have original jurisdiction over every claim in the complaint in order to have "original jurisdiction" over a "civil action," then in *Gibbs* there was no civil action of which the district court could assume original jurisdiction under §1331, and so no basis for exercising supplemental jurisdiction over any of the claims. The indivisibility theory is further belied by our practice — in both federal-question and diversity cases — of allowing federal courts to cure jurisdictional defects by dismissing the offending parties rather than dismissing the entire action. *Clark*, for example, makes clear that claims that are jurisdictionally defective as to amount in controversy do not destroy original jurisdiction over other claims. If the presence of jurisdictionally problematic claims in the complaint meant the district court was without original jurisdiction over the single, indivisible civil action before it, then the district court would have to dismiss the whole action rather than particular parties.

We also find it unconvincing to say that the definitional indivisibility theory applies in the context of diversity cases but not in the context of federal-question cases. The broad and general language of the statute does not permit this result. The contention is premised on the notion that the phrase "original jurisdiction of all civil actions" means different things in §1331 and §1332. It is implausible, however, to say that the identical phrase means one thing (original jurisdiction in all actions where at least one claim in the complaint meets the following requirements) in §1331 and something else (original jurisdiction in all actions where every claim in the complaint meets the following requirements) in §1332.

The contamination theory, as we have noted, can make some sense in the special context of the complete diversity requirement because the presence of nondiverse parties on both sides of a lawsuit eliminates the justification for providing a federal forum. The theory, however, makes little sense with respect to the amount-in-controversy requirement, which is meant to ensure that a dispute is sufficiently important to warrant federal-court attention. The presence of a single nondiverse party may eliminate the fear of bias with respect to all claims, but the presence of a claim that falls short of the minimum amount in controversy does nothing to reduce the importance of the claims that do meet this requirement.

It is fallacious to suppose, simply from the proposition that §1332 imposes both the diversity requirement and the amount-in-controversy requirement, that the contamination theory germane to the former is also relevant to the latter. There is no inherent logical connection between the amount-in-controversy requirement and §1332 diversity jurisdiction. After all, federal-question jurisdiction once had an amount-in-controversy requirement as well. If such a requirement were revived under §1331, it is clear beyond peradventure that §1367(a) provides supplemental jurisdiction over federal-question cases where some, but not all, of the federal-law claims involve a sufficient amount in controversy. In other words, §1367(a) unambiguously overrules the holding and the result in *Clark*. If that is so, however, it would be quite extraordinary to say that §1367 did not also overrule *Zahn*, a case that was premised in substantial part on the holding in *Clark*.

In addition to the theoretical difficulties with the argument that a district court has original jurisdiction over a civil action only if it has original jurisdiction over each individual claim in the complaint, we have already considered and rejected a virtually identical argument in the closely analogous context of removal jurisdiction. In *Chicago v. International College of Surgeons,* 522 U.S. 156 (1997), the plaintiff brought federal and state law claims in state court. The defendant removed to federal court. The plaintiff objected to removal, citing the text of the removal statute, §1441(a). That statutory provision, which bears a striking similarity to the relevant portion of §1367, authorizes removal of "any civil action . . . of which the district courts of the United States have original jurisdiction . . . ." The *College of Surgeons* plaintiff urged that, because its state-law claims were not within the District Court's original jurisdiction, §1441(a) did not authorize removal. We disagreed. The federal law claims, we held, "suffice to make the actions 'civil actions' within the 'original jurisdiction' of the district courts . . . . Nothing in the jurisdictional statutes suggests that the presence of related state law claims somehow alters the fact that [the plaintiff's] complaints, by virtue of their federal claims, were 'civil actions' within the federal courts' 'original jurisdiction'." Once the case was removed, the District Court had original jurisdiction over the federal law claims and supplemental jurisdiction under §1367(a) over the state-law claims.

The dissent in *College of Surgeons* argued that because the plaintiff sought on-the-record review of a local administrative agency decision, the review it sought was outside the scope of the District Court's jurisdiction. (opinion of GINSBURG, J.). We rejected both the suggestion that state-law claims involving administrative appeals are beyond the scope of §1367 supplemental jurisdiction and the claim that the administrative review posture of the case deprived the District Court of original jurisdiction over the federal-law claims in the case. More importantly for present purposes, *College of Surgeons* stressed that a district court has original jurisdiction of a civil action for purposes of §1441(a) as long as it has original jurisdiction over a subset of the claims constituting the action. Even the *College of Surgeons* dissent, which took issue with the Court's interpretation of §1367, did not appear to contest this view of §1441(a).

Although *College of Surgeons* involved additional claims between the same parties, its interpretation of §1441(a) applies equally to cases involving additional parties whose claims fall short of the jurisdictional amount. If we were to adopt the contrary view that the presence of additional parties means there is no "civil action . . . of which the district courts . . . have original jurisdiction," those cases simply would not be removable. To our knowledge, no court has issued a reasoned opinion adopting this view of the removal statute. It is settled, of course, that absent complete diversity a case is not removable because the district court would lack original jurisdiction. *Caterpillar Inc. v. Lewis,* 519 U.S. 61, 73 (1996). This, however, is altogether consistent with our view of §1441(a). A failure of complete diversity, unlike the failure of some claims to meet the requisite amount in controversy, contaminates every claim in the action.

We also reject the argument, similar to the attempted distinction of *College of Surgeons* discussed above, that while the presence of additional claims over which the district court lacks jurisdiction does not mean the civil action is outside the purview of §1367(a), the presence of additional parties does. The basis for this distinction is not altogether clear, and it is in considerable tension with statutory text. Section 1367(a) applies by its terms to any civil action of which the district courts have original jurisdiction, and the last sentence of

§1367(a) expressly contemplates that the court may have supplemental jurisdiction over additional parties. So it cannot be the case that the presence of those parties destroys the court's original jurisdiction, within the meaning of §1367(a), over a civil action otherwise properly before it. Also, §1367(b) expressly withholds supplemental jurisdiction in diversity cases over claims by plaintiffs joined as indispensable parties under Rule 19. If joinder of such parties were sufficient to deprive the district court of original jurisdiction over the civil action within the meaning of §1367(a), this specific limitation on supplemental jurisdiction in §1367(b) would be superfluous. The argument that the presence of additional parties removes the civil action from the scope of §1367(a) also would mean that §1367 left the *Finley* result undisturbed. *Finley*, after all, involved a Federal Tort Claims Act suit against a federal defendant and state-law claims against additional defendants not otherwise subject to federal jurisdiction. Yet all concede that one purpose of §1367 was to change the result reached in *Finley*.

Finally, it is suggested that our interpretation of §1367(a) creates an anomaly regarding the exceptions listed in §1367(b): It is not immediately obvious why Congress would withhold supplemental jurisdiction over plaintiffs joined as parties "needed for just adjudication" under Rule 19 but would allow supplemental jurisdiction over plaintiffs permissively joined under Rule 20. The omission of Rule 20 plaintiffs from the list of exceptions in §1367(b) may have been an unintentional drafting gap. If that is the case, it is up to Congress rather than the courts to fix it. The omission may seem odd, but it is not absurd. An alternative explanation for the different treatment of Rule 19 and Rule 20 is that Congress was concerned that extending supplemental jurisdiction to Rule 19 plaintiffs would allow circumvention of the complete diversity rule: A nondiverse plaintiff might be omitted intentionally from the original action, but joined later under Rule 19 as a necessary party. The contamination theory described above, if applicable, means this ruse would fail, but Congress may have wanted to make assurance double sure. More generally, Congress may have concluded that federal jurisdiction is only appropriate if the district court would have original jurisdiction over the claims of all those plaintiffs who are so essential to the action that they could be joined under Rule 19.

To the extent that the omission of Rule 20 plaintiffs from the list of §1367(b) exceptions is anomalous, moreover, it is no more anomalous than the inclusion of Rule 19 plaintiffs in that list would be if the alternative view of §1367(a) were to prevail. If the district court lacks original jurisdiction over a civil diversity action where any plaintiff's claims fail to comply with all the requirements of §1332, there is no need for a special §1367(b) exception for Rule 19 plaintiffs who do not meet these requirements. Though the omission of Rule 20 plaintiffs from §1367(b) presents something of a puzzle on our view of the statute, the inclusion of Rule 19 plaintiffs in this section is at least as difficult to explain under the alternative view.

And so we circle back to the original question. When the well-pleaded complaint in district court includes multiple claims, all part of the same case or controversy, and some, but not all, of the claims are within the court's original jurisdiction, does the court have before it "any civil action of which the district courts have original jurisdiction"? It does. Under §1367, the court has original jurisdiction over the civil action comprising the claims for which there is no jurisdictional defect. No other reading of §1367 is plausible in light of the text and structure of the jurisdictional statute. Though the special nature and purpose of the diversity requirement mean that a single nondiverse party can contaminate every other claim in the lawsuit, the contamination does not occur with respect to jurisdictional defects that go only to the substantive importance of individual claims.

It follows from this conclusion that the threshold requirement of §1367(a) is satisfied in cases, like those now before us, where some, but not all, of the plaintiffs in a diversity action allege a sufficient amount in controversy. We hold that §1367 by its plain text overruled *Clark* and *Zahn* and authorized supplemental jurisdiction over all claims by diverse parties arising out of the same Article III case or controversy, subject only to enumerated exceptions not applicable in the cases now before us.

C

The proponents of the alternative view of §1367 insist that the statute is at least ambiguous and that we should look to other interpretive tools, including the legislative history of §1367, which supposedly demonstrate Congress did not intend §1367 to overrule *Zahn*. We can reject this argument at the very outset simply because §1367 is not ambiguous. For the reasons elaborated above, interpreting §1367 to foreclose supplemental jurisdiction over plaintiffs in diversity cases who do not meet the minimum amount in controversy is inconsistent with the text, read in light of other statutory provisions and our established jurisprudence. Even if we were to stipulate, however, that the reading these proponents urge upon us is textually plausible, the legislative history cited to support it would not alter our view as to the best interpretation of §1367.

Those who urge that the legislative history refutes our interpretation rely primarily on the House Judiciary Committee Report on the Judicial Improvements Act. This Report explained that §1367 would "authorize jurisdiction in a case like *Finley*, as well as essentially restore the pre-*Finley* understandings of the authorization for and limits on other forms of supplemental jurisdiction." The Report stated that §1367(a) "generally authorizes the district court to exercise jurisdiction over a supplemental claim whenever it forms part of the same constitutional case or controversy as the claim or claims that provide the basis of the district court's original jurisdiction," and in so doing codifies *Gibbs* and fills the statutory gap recognized in *Finley*. The Report then remarked that §1367(b) "is not intended to affect the jurisdictional requirements of [§1332] in diversity-only class actions, as those requirements were interpreted prior to *Finley*," citing, without further elaboration, *Zahn* * * *. The Report noted that the "net effect" of §1367(b) was to implement the "principal rationale" of *Kroger*, effecting only "one small change" in pre-*Finley* practice with respect to diversity actions: §1367(b) would exclude "Rule 23(a) plaintiff-intervenors to the same extent as those sought to be joined as plaintiffs under Rule 19." (It is evident that the report here meant to refer to Rule 24, not Rule 23.)

As we have repeatedly held, the authoritative statement is the statutory text, not the legislative history or any other extrinsic material. Extrinsic materials have a role in statutory interpretation only to the extent they shed a reliable light on the enacting Legislature's understanding of otherwise ambiguous terms. Not all extrinsic materials are reliable sources of insight into legislative understandings, however, and legislative history in particular is vulnerable to two serious criticisms. First, legislative history is itself often murky, ambiguous, and contradictory. Judicial investigation of legislative history has a tendency to become, to borrow Judge Leventhal's memorable phrase, an exercise in "looking over a crowd and picking out your friends." Second, judicial reliance on legislative materials like committee reports, which are not themselves subject to the requirements of Article I, may give unrepresentative committee members — or, worse yet, unelected staffers and lobbyists — both the power and the incentive to attempt strategic manipulations of legislative history to secure results they were unable to achieve through the statutory text. We need not comment here on whether these problems are sufficiently prevalent to render legislative history inherently unreliable in all circumstances, a point on which Members of this Court have disagreed. It is clear, however, that in this instance both criticisms are right on the mark.

First of all, the legislative history of §1367 is far murkier than selective quotation from the House Report would suggest. The text of §1367 is based substantially on a draft proposal contained in a Federal Court Study Committee working paper, which was drafted by a Subcommittee chaired by Judge Posner. While the Subcommittee explained, in language echoed by the House Report, that its proposal "basically restores the law as it existed prior to *Finley*," it observed in a footnote that its proposal would overrule *Zahn* and that this would be a good idea. Although the Federal Courts Study Committee did not expressly adopt the Subcommittee's specific reference to *Zahn*, it neither explicitly disagreed with the Subcommittee's conclusion that this was the best reading of the proposed text nor substantially modified the proposal to avoid this result. Therefore, even if the House Report could fairly be read to reflect an understanding that the text of §1367 did not overrule *Zahn*, the Subcommittee Working Paper on which §1367 was based reflected the opposite understanding. The House Report is no more authoritative than the Subcommittee Working Paper. The utility of either can extend no further than the light it sheds on how the enacting Legislature understood the statutory text. Trying to figure out how to square the Subcommittee Working Paper's understanding with the House Report's understanding, or which is more reflective of the understanding of the enacting legislators, is a hopeless task.

Second, the worst fears of critics who argue legislative history will be used to circumvent the Article I process were realized in this case. The telltale evidence is the statement, by three law professors who participated in drafting §1367 that §1367 "on its face" permits "supplemental jurisdiction over claims of class members that do not satisfy section 1332's jurisdictional amount requirement, which would overrule *[Zahn]*. [There is] a disclaimer of intent to accomplish this result in the legislative history . . . . It would have been better had the statute dealt explicitly with this problem, and the legislative history was an attempt to correct the oversight." Rowe, Burbank, & Mengler, Compounding or Creating Confusion About Supplemental Jurisdiction? A Reply to Professor Freer, 40 Emory L.J. 943, 960, n.90 (1991). The professors were frank to concede that if one refuses to consider the legislative history, one has no choice but to "conclude that section 1367 has wiped *Zahn* off the books." *Ibid.* So there exists an acknowledgment, by parties who have detailed, specific knowledge of the statute and the drafting process, both that the plain text of §1367 overruled *Zahn* and that language to the contrary in the House Report was a *post hoc* attempt to alter that result. One need not subscribe to the wholesale condemnation of legislative history to refuse to give any effect to such a deliberate effort to amend a statute through a committee report.

In sum, even if we believed resort to legislative history were appropriate in these cases — a point we do not concede — we would not give significant weight to the House Report. The distinguished jurists who drafted the Subcommittee Working Paper, along with three of the participants in the drafting of §1367, agree that this provision, on its face, overrules *Zahn*. This accords with the best reading of the statute's text, and nothing in the legislative history indicates directly and explicitly that Congress understood the phrase "civil action of which the district courts have original jurisdiction" to exclude cases in which some but not all of the diversity plaintiffs meet the amount in controversy requirement.

No credence, moreover, can be given to the claim that, if Congress understood §1367 to overrule *Zahn*, the proposal would have been more controversial. We have little sense whether any Member of Congress would have been particularly upset by this result. This is not a case where one can plausibly say that concerned legislators might not have realized the possible effect of the text they were adopting. Certainly, any competent legislative aide who studied the matter would have flagged this issue if it were a matter of importance to his or her boss, especially in light of the Subcommittee Working Paper. There are any number of reasons why legislators did not spend more time arguing over §1367, none of which are relevant to our interpretation of what the words of the statute mean.

D

Finally, we note that the Class Action Fairness Act (CAFA), enacted this year, has no bearing on our analysis of these cases. Subject to certain limitations, the CAFA confers federal diversity jurisdiction over class actions where the aggregate amount in controversy exceeds $5 million. It abrogates the rule against aggregating claims, a rule this Court * * * reaffirmed in *Zahn*. The CAFA, however, is not retroactive, and the views of the 2005 Congress are not relevant to our interpretation of a text enacted by Congress in 1990. The CAFA, moreover, does not moot the significance of our interpretation of §1367, as many proposed exercises of supplemental jurisdiction, even in the class-action context, might not fall within the CAFA's ambit. The CAFA, then, has no impact, one way or the other, on our interpretation of §1367.

The judgment of the Court of Appeals for the Eleventh Circuit is affirmed. The judgment of the Court of Appeals for the First Circuit is reversed, and the case is remanded for proceedings consistent with this opinion. It is so ordered.

JUSTICE STEVENS, with whom JUSTICE BREYER joins, dissenting.

JUSTICE GINSBURG's carefully reasoned opinion demonstrates the error in the Court's rather ambitious reading of this opaque jurisdictional statute. She also has demonstrated that "ambiguity" is a term that may have different meanings for different judges, for the Court has made the remarkable declaration that its reading of the statute is so obviously correct — and JUSTICE GINSBURG's so obviously wrong — that the text does not even qualify as "ambiguous." Because ambiguity is apparently in the eye of the beholder, I remain convinced that it is unwise to treat the ambiguity *vel non* of a statute as determinative of whether legislative history is consulted. Indeed, I believe that we as judges are more, rather than less, constrained when we make ourselves accountable to *all* reliable evidence of legislative intent.

The legislative history of §1367 provides powerful confirmation of JUSTICE GINSBURG's interpretation of that statute. It is helpful to consider in full the relevant portion of the House Report, which was also adopted by the Senate:

> "This section would authorize jurisdiction in a case like *Finley* as well as essentially restore the pre-*Finley* understandings of the authorization for and limits on other forms of supplemental jurisdiction. In federal question cases, it broadly authorizes the district courts to exercise supplemental jurisdiction over additional claims, including claims involving the joinder of additional parties. In diversity cases, the district courts may exercise supplemental jurisdiction, except when doing so would be inconsistent with the jurisdictional requirements of the diversity statute.

* * *

Not only does the House Report specifically say that §1367 was not intended to upset *Zahn*, but its entire explanation of the statute demonstrates that Congress had in mind a very specific and relatively modest task — undoing this Court's 5-to-4 decision in *Finley*. In addition to overturning that unfortunate and much-criticized decision,[2] the statute, according to the Report, codifies and preserves "the pre-*Finley* understandings of the authorization for and limits on other forms of supplemental jurisdiction," with the exception of making "one small change in pre-*Finley* practice," which is not relevant here.

The sweeping purpose that the Court's decision imputes to Congress bears no resemblance to the House Report's description of the statute. But this does not seem to trouble the Court, for its decision today treats statutory interpretation as a pedantic exercise, divorced from any serious attempt at ascertaining congressional intent. Of course, there are situations in which we do not honor Congress' apparent intent unless that intent is made clear in the text of a statute — in this way, we can be certain that Congress considered the issue and intended a disfavored outcome. But that principle provides no basis for

---

[2] As I pointed out in my dissent in *Finley*, the majority's decision was "not faithful to our precedents," and casually dismissed the accumulated wisdom of judges such as Henry Friendly, who had "special learning and expertise in matters of federal jurisdiction."

discounting the House Report, given that our cases have never recognized a presumption in *favor* of expansive diversity jurisdiction.

The Court's reasons for ignoring this virtual billboard of congressional intent are unpersuasive. That a subcommittee of the Federal Courts Study Committee believed that an earlier, substantially similar version of the statute overruled *Zahn,* only highlights the fact that the statute is ambiguous. What is determinative is that the House Report explicitly rejected that broad reading of the statutory text. Such a report has special significance as an indicator of legislative intent. In Congress, committee reports are normally considered the authoritative explication of a statute's text and purposes, and busy legislators and their assistants rely on that explication in casting their votes.

The Court's second reason — its comment on the three law professors who participated in drafting §1367, — is similarly off the mark. In the law review article that the Court refers to, the professors were merely saying that the text of the statute was susceptible to an overly broad (and simplistic) reading, and that clarification in the House Report was therefore appropriate. Significantly, the reference to *Zahn* in the House Report does not at all appear to be tacked-on or out of place; indeed, it is wholly consistent with the Report's broader explanation of Congress' goal of overruling *Finley* and preserving pre-*Finley* law. To suggest that these professors participated in a "deliberate effort to amend a statute through a committee report," reveals an unrealistic view of the legislative process, not to mention disrespect for three law professors who acted in the role of public servants. To be sure, legislative history can be manipulated. But, in the situation before us, there is little reason to fear that an unholy conspiracy of "unrepresentative committee members," law professors, and "unelected staffers and lobbyists," endeavored to torpedo Congress' attempt to overrule (without discussion) two longstanding features of this Court's diversity jurisprudence.

After nearly 20 pages of complicated analysis, which explores subtle doctrinal nuances and coins various neologisms, the Court announces that §1367 could not reasonably be read another way. That conclusion is difficult to accept. Given JUSTICE GINSBURG's persuasive account of the statutory text and its jurisprudential backdrop, and given the uncommonly clear legislative history, I am confident that the majority's interpretation of §1367 is mistaken. I respectfully dissent.

JUSTICE GINSBURG, with whom JUSTICE STEVENS, JUSTICE O'CONNOR, and JUSTICE BREYER join, dissenting.

* * *

Section 1367, all agree, was designed to overturn this Court's decision in *Finley.* * * *

What more §1367 wrought is an issue on which courts of appeals have sharply divided. * * *

The Court adopts a plausibly broad reading of §1367, a measure that is hardly a model of the careful drafter's art. There is another plausible reading, however, one less disruptive of our jurisprudence regarding supplemental jurisdiction. If one reads §1367(a) to instruct, as the statute's text suggests, that the district court must first have "original jurisdiction" over a "civil action" before supplemental jurisdiction can attach, then *Clark* and *Zahn* are preserved, and supplemental jurisdiction does not open the way for joinder of plaintiffs, or inclusion of class members, who do not independently meet the amount-in-controversy requirement. For the reasons that follow, I conclude that this narrower construction is the better reading of §1367.

I

A

Section 1367, captioned "Supplemental jurisdiction," codifies court-recognized doctrines formerly labeled "pendent" and "ancillary" jurisdiction. Pendent jurisdiction involved the enlargement of federal-question litigation to include related state-law claims. Ancillary jurisdiction evolved primarily to protect defending parties, or others whose rights might be adversely affected if they could not air their claims in an ongoing federal-court action. Given jurisdiction over the principal action, federal courts entertained certain matters deemed ancillary regardless of the citizenship of the parties or the amount in controversy.

* * *

In sum, in federal-question cases before §1367's enactment, the Court recognized pendent-claim jurisdiction, *Gibbs*, but not pendent-party jurisdiction, *Finley*. As to ancillary jurisdiction, the Court adhered to the limitation that in diversity cases, throughout the litigation, all plaintiffs must remain diverse from all defendants. See *Kroger*.

Although pendent jurisdiction and ancillary jurisdiction evolved discretely, the Court has recognized that they are "two species of the same generic problem: Under what circumstances may a federal court hear and decide a state-law claim arising between citizens of the same State?" *Kroger*. *Finley* regarded that question as one properly addressed to Congress.

B

Shortly before the Court decided *Finley,* Congress had established the Federal Courts Study Committee to take up issues relating to the federal courts' congestion, delay, expense, and expansion. * * *

Among recommendations, the Committee urged Congress to "authorize federal courts to assert pendent jurisdiction over parties without an independent federal jurisdictional base." If adopted, this recommendation would overrule *Finley*. Earlier, a subcommittee had recommended that Congress overrule both *Finley* and *Zahn*. In the subcommittee's view, "[f]rom a policy standpoint," *Zahn* "ma[de] little sense." The full Committee, however, urged only the overruling of *Finley* and did not adopt the recommendation to overrule *Zahn*.

* * *

Congress responded by adopting, as part of the Judicial Improvements Act of 1990, recommendations of the Federal Courts Study Committee ranked by the House Committee on the Judiciary as "modest" and "noncontroversial". Congress did not take up the Study Committee's immodest proposal to curtail diversity jurisdiction. It did, however, enact a supplemental jurisdiction statute, codified as 28 U.S.C. §1367.

II

A

Section 1367, by its terms, operates only in civil actions "of which the district courts have original jurisdiction." The "original jurisdiction" relevant here is diversity-of-citizenship jurisdiction, conferred by §1332. The character of that jurisdiction is the essential backdrop for comprehension of §1367.

The Constitution broadly provides for federal-court jurisdiction in controversies "between Citizens of different States." Art. III, § 2, cl. 1. This Court has read that provision to demand no more than "minimal diversity," *i.e.*, so long as one party on the plaintiffs' side and one party on the defendants' side are of diverse citizenship, Congress may authorize federal courts to exercise diversity jurisdiction. See *State Farm. v. Tashire.* Further, the Constitution includes no amount-in-controversy limitation on the exercise of federal jurisdiction. But from the start, Congress, as its measures have been construed by this Court, has limited federal court exercise of diversity jurisdiction in two principal ways. First, unless Congress specifies otherwise, diversity must be "complete," *i.e.*, all parties on plaintiffs' side must be diverse from all parties on defendants' side. *Strawbridge.* Second, each plaintiff's stake must independently meet the amount-in-controversy specification: When two or more plaintiffs, having separate and distinct demands, unite for convenience and economy in a single suit, it is essential that the demand of each be of the requisite jurisdictional amount.

The statute today governing federal court exercise of diversity jurisdiction in the generality of cases, §1332, like all its predecessors, incorporates both a diverse-citizenship requirement and an amount-in-controversy specification.[5] * * * This Court has long held that, in determining whether the amount-in-controversy requirement has been satisfied, a single plaintiff may aggregate two or more claims against a single defendant, even if the claims are unrelated. But in multiparty cases, including class actions, we have unyieldingly adhered to the nonaggregation rule stated in *Troy Bank.* See *Clark* (reaffirming the "familiar rule that when several plaintiffs assert separate and distinct demands in a single

---

[5] Endeavoring to preserve the "complete diversity" rule first stated in *Strawbridge*, the Court's opinion drives a wedge between the two components of §1332, treating the diversity-of-citizenship requirement as essential, the amount-in-controversy requirement as more readily disposable. Section 1332 itself, however, does not rank order the two requirements. What ordinary principle of statutory construction or sound canon of interpretation allows the Court to slice up §1332 this way? In partial explanation, the Court asserts that amount in controversy can be analyzed claim-by-claim, but the diversity requirement cannot. It is not altogether clear why that should be so. The cure for improper joinder of a nondiverse party is the same as the cure for improper joinder of a plaintiff who does not satisfy the jurisdictional amount. In both cases, original jurisdiction can be preserved by dismissing the nonqualifying party. See *Caterpillar Inc. v. Lewis,* 519 U.S. 61, 64 (1996) (diversity); *Newman-Green, Inc. v. Alfonzo-Larrain,* 490 U.S. 826, 836-838 (1989) (same); *Zahn,* 414 U.S., at 295, 300 (amount in controversy); *Clark v. Paul Gray, Inc.,* 306 U.S. 583, 590 (1939) (same).

suit, the amount involved in each separate controversy must be of the requisite amount to be within the jurisdiction of the district court, and that those amounts cannot be added together to satisfy jurisdictional requirements"); *Snyder v. Harris,* 394 U.S. 332, 339-340 (1969) (abandonment of the nonaggregation rule in class actions would undercut the congressional "purpose . . . to check, to some degree, the rising caseload of the federal courts").

* * *

The rule that each plaintiff must independently satisfy the amount-in-controversy requirement, unless Congress expressly orders otherwise, was thus the solidly established reading of §1332 when Congress enacted the Judicial Improvements Act of 1990, which added §1367 to Title 28.

B

These cases present the question whether Congress abrogated the nonaggregation rule long tied to §1332 when it enacted §1367. In answering that question, context should provide a crucial guide. The Court should assume, as it ordinarily does, that Congress legislated against a background of law already in place and the historical development of that law. Here, that background is the statutory grant of diversity jurisdiction, the amount-in-controversy condition that Congress, from the start, has tied to the grant, and the nonaggregation rule this Court has long applied to the determination of the "matter in controversy."

* * *

The Court is unanimous in reading §1367(a) to permit pendent-party jurisdiction in federal-question cases, and thus, to overrule *Finley.* * * * Since 1980, §1331 has contained no amount-in-controversy requirement. Once there is a civil action presenting a qualifying claim arising under federal law, §1331's sole requirement is met. District courts, we have held, may then adjudicate, additionally, state-law claims deriving from a common nucleus of operative fact. *Gibbs.* Section 1367(a) enlarges that category to include not only state-law claims against the defendant named in the federal claim, but also "[state-law] claims that involve the joinder or intervention of additional parties."[6]

The Court divides, however, on the impact of §1367(a) on diversity cases controlled by §1332. Under the majority's reading, §1367(a) permits the joinder of related claims cut loose from the nonaggregation rule that has long attended actions under §1332. Only the claims specified in §1367(b) would be excluded from §1367(a)'s expansion of §1332's grant of diversity jurisdiction. And because §1367(b) contains no exception for joinder of plaintiffs under Rule 20 or class actions under Rule 23, the Court concludes, *Clark* and *Zahn* have been

---

[6] The Court noted in *Zahn,* that when the exercise of §1331 federal-question jurisdiction and §1332 diversity jurisdiction were conditioned on the same jurisdictional-amount limitation, the same nonaggregation rule applied under both heads of federal jurisdiction. The Court added, however, that "Congress ha[d] exempted major areas of federal-question jurisdiction from any jurisdictional-amount requirements," thus diminishing the impact of §1331's "matter in controversy" specification in cases arising under federal law.

overruled.[8]

The Court's reading is surely plausible, especially if one detaches §1367(a) from its context and attempts no reconciliation with prior interpretations of §1332's amount-in-controversy requirement. But §1367(a)'s text, as the First Circuit held, can be read another way, one that would involve no rejection of *Clark* and *Zahn*.

As explained by the First Circuit in *Ortega*, and applied to class actions by the Tenth Circuit in *Leonhardt v. Western Sugar Co.*, 160 F.3d 631 (CA10 1998), §1367(a) addresses "civil action[s] of which the district courts have original jurisdiction," a formulation that, in diversity cases, is sensibly read to incorporate the rules on joinder and aggregation tightly tied to §1332 at the time of §1367's enactment. On this reading, a complaint must first meet that "original jurisdiction" measurement. If it does not, no supplemental jurisdiction is authorized. If it does, §1367(a) authorizes "supplemental jurisdiction" over related claims. In other words, §1367(a) would preserve undiminished, as part and parcel of §1332 "original jurisdiction" determinations, both the "complete diversity" rule and the decisions restricting aggregation to arrive at the amount in controversy.[9] Section 1367(b)'s office, then, would be to prevent the erosion of the complete diversity and amount-in-controversy requirements that might otherwise result from an expansive application of what was once termed the doctrine of ancillary jurisdiction. In contrast to the Court's construction of §1367, which draws a sharp line between the diversity and amount-in-controversy components of §1332, the interpretation presented here does not sever the two jurisdictional requirements.

The more restrained reading of §1367 just outlined would yield affirmance of the First Circuit's judgment in *Ortega*, and reversal of the Eleventh Circuit's judgment in *Exxon*. It would not discard entirely, as the Court does, the judicially developed doctrines of pendent and ancillary jurisdiction as they existed when *Finley* was decided.[10] Instead, it would recognize §1367 essentially as a codification of those doctrines, placing them under a single heading, but largely retaining their substance, with overriding *Finley* the only basic change: Supplemental jurisdiction, once the district court has original jurisdiction, would now include "claims that involve the joinder or intervention

---

[8] Under the Court's construction of §1367, Beatriz Ortega's family members can remain in the action because their joinder is merely permissive, see Rule 20. If, however, their presence was "needed for just adjudication," Rule 19, their dismissal would be required. The inclusion of those who may join, and exclusion of those who should or must join, defies rational explanation, and others adopting the interpretation the Court embraces have so acknowledged, see Stromberg Metal Works, Inc. v. Press Mechanical, Inc., 77 F.3d 928, 932 (CA7 1996) (recognizing the anomaly and inquiring: "What sense can this make?"); cf. 14B Wright & Miller §3704, p. 168 (3d ed. 1998) (distinction between Rule 19 and Rule 20 "seems incongruous, and serves no apparent public policy purpose").

[9] On this reading of §1367(a), it is immaterial that §1367(b) does not withdraw supplemental jurisdiction over the claims of the additional parties at issue here. Because those claims would not come within §1367(a) in the first place, Congress would have had no reason to list them in §1367(b).

[10] The Court's opinion blends the two doctrines, according no significance to their discrete development.

of additional parties." §1367(a).

Pendent jurisdiction applied only in federal-question cases and allowed plaintiffs to attach nonfederal claims to their jurisdiction-qualifying claims. Ancillary jurisdiction applied primarily, although not exclusively, in diversity cases and "typically involve[d] claims *by a defending party* haled into court against his will." *Kroger*. As the First Circuit observed, neither doctrine permitted a plaintiff to circumvent the dual requirements of §1332 (diversity of citizenship and amount in controversy) "simply by joining her [jurisdictionally inadequate] claim in an action brought by [a] jurisdictionally competent diversity plaintiff." *Ortega*, 370 F.3d, at 138.

Not only would the reading I find persuasive align statutory supplemental jurisdiction with the judicially developed doctrines of pendent and ancillary jurisdiction, it would also synchronize §1367 with the removal statute, §1441. As the First Circuit carefully explained:

"Section 1441, like §1367, applies only if the 'civil action' in question is one 'of which the district courts ... have original jurisdiction.' Relying on that language, the Supreme Court has interpreted §1441 to prohibit removal unless the entire action, as it stands at the time of removal, could have been filed in federal court in the first instance. *See, e.g., Syngenta Crop Protection, Inc. v. Henson*, 537 U.S. 28, 33 (2002); *Okla. Tax Comm'n v. Graham*, 489 U.S. 838, 840 (1989) (per curiam). Section 1441 has thus been held to incorporate the well-pleaded complaint rule, *see College of Surgeons*;[11] the complete diversity rule, *see Caterpillar, Inc. v. Lewis*, 519 U.S. 61,73 (1996); and rules for calculating the amount in controversy, *see St. Paul Mercury Indem. Co. v. Red Cab Co.*, 303 U.S. 283, 291-292 (1938)." *Ortega*, 370 F. 3d, at 138 (footnote added).

The less disruptive view I take of §1367 also accounts for the omission of Rule 20 plaintiffs and Rule 23 class actions in §1367(b)'s text. If one reads §1367(a) as a plenary grant of supplemental jurisdiction to federal courts sitting in diversity, one would indeed look for exceptions in §1367(b). Finding none for permissive joinder of parties or class actions, one would conclude that Congress effectively, even if unintentionally, overruled *Clark* and *Zahn*. But if one recognizes that the nonaggregation rule delineated in *Clark* and *Zahn* forms part of the determination whether "original jurisdiction" exists in a diversity case, then plaintiffs who do not meet the amount-in-controversy requirement would fail at the §1367(a) threshold. Congress would have no reason to resort to a §1367(b) exception to turn such plaintiffs away from federal court, given that their claims, from the start, would fall outside the court's §1332 jurisdiction.

Nor does the more moderate reading assign different meanings to "original jurisdiction" in diversity and federal-question cases. As the First Circuit stated:

"'[O]riginal jurisdiction' in §1367(a) has the same meaning in every case:

---

[11] The point of the Court's extended discussion of *College of Surgeons* in the instant cases slips from my grasp. There was no disagreement in that case, and there is none now, that §1367(a) is properly read to authorize the exercise of supplemental jurisdiction in removed cases.

[An] underlying statutory grant of original jurisdiction must be satisfied. What differs between federal question and diversity cases is not the meaning of 'original jurisdiction' but rather the [discrete] requirements of sections 1331 and 1332. Under §1331, the sole issue is whether a federal question appears on the face of the plaintiff's well-pleaded complaint; the [citizenship] of the parties and the amounts they stand to recover [do not bear on that determination]. Section 1332, by contrast, predicates original jurisdiction on the identity of the parties (*i.e.*, [their] complete diversity) and their [satisfaction of the amount-in-controversy specification]. [In short,] the 'original jurisdiction' language in §1367 operates differently in federal-question and diversity cases not because the meaning of that term varies, but because the [jurisdiction-granting] statutes are different." *Ortega*, 370 F. 3d, at 139-140.

What is the utility of §1367(b) under my reading of §1367(a)? Section 1367(a) allows parties other than the plaintiff to assert *reactive* claims once entertained under the heading ancillary jurisdiction. * * * [Section] 1367(b) stops plaintiffs from circumventing §1332's jurisdictional requirements by using another's claim as a hook to add a claim that the plaintiff could not have brought in the first instance. *Kroger* is the paradigm case. There, the Court held that ancillary jurisdiction did not extend to a plaintiff's claim against a nondiverse party who had been impleaded by the defendant under Rule 14. Section 1367(b), then, is corroborative of §1367(a)'s coverage of claims formerly called ancillary, but provides exceptions to assure that accommodation of added claims would not fundamentally alter the jurisdictional requirements of section 1332.

While §1367's enigmatic text[12] defies flawless interpretation,[13] the precedent-preservative reading, I am persuaded, better accords with the historical and legal context of Congress' enactment of the supplemental jurisdiction statute and the established limits on pendent and ancillary jurisdiction. It does not attribute to Congress a jurisdictional enlargement broader than the one to which the legislators adverted.[14]

For the reasons stated, I would hold that §1367 does not overrule *Clark* and *Zahn*. I would therefore affirm the judgment of the Court of Appeals for the

---

[12] The Court notes the passage this year of the Class Action Fairness Act (CAFA). * * * Significant here, CAFA's enlargement of federal-court diversity jurisdiction was accomplished, clearly and conspicuously, by amending §1332.

[13] If §1367(a) itself renders unnecessary the listing of Rule 20 plaintiffs and Rule 23 class actions in §1367(b), then it is similarly unnecessary to refer, as §1367(b) does, to "persons proposed to be joined as plaintiffs under Rule 19." On one account, Congress bracketed such persons with persons "seeking to intervene as plaintiffs under Rule 24" to modify pre-§1367 practice. Before enactment of §1367, courts entertained, under the heading ancillary jurisdiction, claims of Rule 24(a) intervenors "of right," see *Kroger*, but denied ancillary jurisdiction over claims of "necessary" Rule 19 plaintiffs. Congress may have sought simply to underscore that those seeking to join as plaintiffs, whether under Rule 19 or Rule 24, should be treated alike, *i.e.*, denied joinder when "inconsistent with the jurisdictional requirements of section 1332."

[14] While the interpretation of §1367 described in this opinion does not rely on the measure's legislative history, that history, as JUSTICE STEVENS has shown, is corroborative of the statutory reading set out above.

First Circuit and reverse the judgment of the Court of Appeals for the Eleventh Circuit.

NOTES AND PROBLEMS FOR DISCUSSION

1. Clearly, the point of divergence between the majority and the minority in *Exxon Mobil* was whether §1367(a)'s requirement of "original jurisdiction" in a diversity-based case (i.e., one without a single federal question claim), required adherence to *both* the complete diversity and nonaggregation requirements that the Court traditionally had attached to §1332. The majority insisted that a federal court could have original jurisdiction over a state law-based civil action as long as all adverse parties to the complaint were of diverse citizenship and at least one claim in the complaint independently satisfied the statutory amount in controversy requirement. The dissenters, on the other hand, construed §1367(a)'s requirement of "original jurisdiction" to demand that *every* claim satisfy *both* of §1332's requirements. They demanded adherence to both the complete diversity and nonaggregation rules, i.e., that all adverse parties to the complaint were of diverse citizenship *and* that each and every state law claim therein met §1332's jurisdictional amount in controversy requirement. Who has the better of this argument?

2. Both sides also had a lot of trouble making sense out of §1367(b)'s seemingly incomplete list of the joinder rules, i.e., specifically excluding supplemental jurisdiction over claims in diversity cases by plaintiffs joined under Rule 19 or intervening under Rule 24 but making no mention of plaintiffs joining under Rules 20 or 23. Does either side offer a more convincing construction of this "enigmatic text"?

3. *Exxon Mobil* comprised two consolidated cases. One was a class action involving the joinder of plaintiffs under Rule 23 and the other a non-class action involving the joinder of several plaintiffs under Rule 20 of the Federal Rules of Civil Procedure. But both of these cases also involved only a single defendant. This meant that the Court was required to construe only the second of the two exceptions codified in §1367(b), the one precluding the exercise of supplemental jurisdiction in diversity cases over claims by plaintiffs who are either proposed to be joined under Rule 19 or seeking to intervene under Rule 24. And in that context, the majority gave controlling importance to the omission of Rules 20 and 23 from that exclusionary language. But the first exception set forth in §1367(b) proscribes the assumption of supplemental jurisdiction in diversity cases over claims by plaintiffs *against persons* joined under Rules 14 and 20 as well as under Rules 19 and 24. So where this exception applies, the inclusion of Rule 20 in the list of covered joinder rules clearly would prohibit the exercise of supplemental jurisdiction and avoid the interpretive issue that tormented the Court in *Exxon Mobil*. Suppose, then, one plaintiff asserted claims against two diverse defendants, each of which met the amount requirement. Suppose further that a second plaintiff in that same case also asserted a state law claim against each of those two diverse defendants, but that neither of this plaintiff's claims satisfied the jurisdictional amount requirement. Which of the two exceptions in §1367(b) would apply? Does the literalist approach to statutory interpretation taken by the majority in *Exxon Mobil* offer any insight into the resolution of this problem?

4. (a) Does §1367(c) modify the nature of the court's discretionary inquiry from that set forth in *Gibbs*? In EXECUTIVE SOFTWARE NORTH AMERICA, INC. v. UNITED STATES DISTRICT COURT, 24 F.3d 1545, 1556-59 (9th Cir.1994), the court noted that although Congress expanded the number of factors available for consideration in making the discretionary inquiry, it also mandated a more focused and restrictive analysis than was prescribed in *Gibbs*:

* * *

A consequence of the statutory structure chosen by Congress is that §1367(c) somewhat changes the nature of the Gibbs discretionary inquiry. Although * * * Gibbs * * * identified a number of concrete instances in which declining pendent jurisdiction normally would be appropriate, the ultimate inquiry for the courts remained whether the assertion of pendent jurisdiction best accommodate[s] the values of economy convenience, fairness and comity. * * *

The statute, however, channels the application of the underlying values to a greater degree than the Gibbs regime, although §1367(c) continues to recognize the doctrine's dynamic aspects. Subsections (c)(1)-(c)(3) appear to codify concrete applications of the underlying Gibbs values recognized in preexisting case law. Subsection (c)(2) (state law claim "substantially predominates") and (c)(3) (district court has dismissed all claims over which it had original jurisdiction), are derived directly from Gibbs itself, while subsection (c)(1), permitting a remand when "the claim raises a novel or complex issue of State law," implicates the subsequently developed line of cases * * *.

By codifying preexisting applications of Gibbs in subsections (c)(1)-(3), however, it is clear that Congress intended the exercise of discretion to be triggered by the court's identification of a factual predicate that corresponds to one of the §1367(c) categories. Once that factual predicate is identified, the exercise of discretion, of course, still is informed by whether remanding the pendent state claims comports with the underlying objective of most sensibly accommodating the values of economy, convenience, fairness, and comity.

We believe that the "catchall" provided by subsection (c)(4) should be interpreted in a similar manner. Subsection (c)(4) permits a discretionary remand of pendent claims when "in exceptional circumstances, there are other compelling reasons for declining jurisdiction." Congress's use of the word "other" to modify "compelling reasons" indicates that what ought to qualify as "compelling reasons" for declining jurisdiction under subsection (c)(4) should be of the same nature as the reasons that gave rise to the categories listed in subsections (c)(1)-(3). Because, as discussed above, the subsection (c)(1)-(3) fact patterns constitute situations in which the underlying Gibbs values ordinarily will "point toward" declining jurisdiction, we believe that "compelling reasons" for the purposes of subsection (c)(4) similarly should be those that lead a court to conclude that declining jurisdiction best accommodate[s] the values of economy, convenience, fairness, and comity.[9]

[9]We therefore reject the interpretation, suggested by some courts and commentators, that "compelling" in §1367(c)(4) should be read back into §1367(c)(1)-(3) in the sense that an exercise of discretion under those categories should be made only in narrower circumstances than permitted under their Gibbs counterparts. The §1367(c)(1)-(3) categories are instead best characterized as describing circumstances that ordinarily present "compelling" reasons in and of themselves for remanding pendent claims.

* * * By providing that an exercise of discretion under subsection 1367(c)(4) ought to be made only in "exceptional circumstances" Congress has sounded a note of caution that the bases for declining jurisdiction should be extended beyond the circumstances identified in subsections (c)(1)-(3) only if the circumstances are quite unusual. In short, although we find that "other compelling reasons" clearly refers the district court back to the subsection (c)(1)-(3) categories, and thus requires the court to balance the underlying values that they embody, we think "exceptional circumstances" requires an additional inquiry.

Of course, when the balance of the Gibbs values indicates that there are "compelling reasons" to decline jurisdiction, the underlying circumstances that inform this calculus usually will demonstrate how the circumstances confronted are "exceptional." We do not believe, however, this always will be the case. Even when a court's balancing of the Gibbs values provides, in its judgment, "compelling reasons" for declining jurisdiction, it might still be the case that the differences between the case it is confronting and the case in which supplemental jurisdiction is appropriate are not sufficient to justify the conclusion that the court would, in fact, be applying subsection (c)(4) properly. We think that it clear from the language chosen by Congress, however, that declining jurisdiction outside of subsection (c)(1)-(3) should be the exception, rather than the rule. Courts therefore must ensure that the reasons identified as "compelling" are not deployed in circumstances that threaten this principle. The inquiry is not particularly burdensome. A court simply must articulate why the circumstances of the case are exceptional in addition to inquiring whether the balance of the Gibbs values provide compelling reasons for declining jurisdiction in such circumstances.

* * * As discussed above, the subsection (c)(1)-(3) categories require both the presence of a factual predicate that triggers the exercise of discretion and a case-specific analysis of whether the Gibbs values would be best served by declining jurisdiction. Our interpretation of subsection (c)(4) carries forward this structure into that subsection: the court must identify the predicate that triggers the applicability of the category (the exceptional circumstances), and then determine whether, in its judgment, the underlying Gibbs values are best served by declining jurisdiction in the particular case (the compelling reasons).

* * *

Therefore, to the extent that Gibbs * * * [was] interpreted as permitting courts to extend the doctrine's underlying values beyond previously recognized applications whenever doing so was consistent with those values, we believe that §1367(c)(4) more carefully channels courts' discretion by requiring the court to identify how the circumstances that it confronts, and in which it believes the balance of the Gibbs values provides "compelling reasons" for declining jurisdiction, are "exceptional."

Not every circuit court, however, agrees with the Ninth Circuit that §1367(c) narrows the range of discretionary factors previously made available to district courts by *Gibbs*. See e.g., Brazinski v. Amoco Petroleum Additives Co., 6 F.3d 1176 (7th Cir.1993) (§1367(c) codifies *Gibbs* factors).

(b) Section 1367(c)(3) provides that a district court "may decline" to exercise supplemental jurisdiction if "the district court has dismissed all claims over which it has original jurisdiction." Suppose the plaintiff's original complaint, filed in federal district court, asserted a federal statutory claim and a non-diverse state law claim, that both claims arose out of a common nucleus of operative fact, and that the complaint alleged the existence of supplemental jurisdiction over the state law claim. Further assume that the plaintiff subsequently amended the complaint to omit the federal statutory claim, leaving only the state law claim. Could the trial court continue to exercise supplemental jurisdiction over the remaining state law claim? In PINTANDO v. MIAMI-DADE HOUSING AGENCY, 501 F.3d 1241 (11th Cir.2007), the Eleventh Circuit joined several other circuits in holding that in an action originally filed in federal court, the existence of subject matter jurisdiction must be based on the contents of the amended and not the original complaint. Consequently, it ruled, since the amended complaint did not contain any federal law claim, there was no basis upon which to exercise supplemental jurisdiction over the plaintiff's state law claim. In an aside, the court noted that cases removed to federal court were treated differently in that the removal court was required to assess the existence of federal subject matter jurisdiction at the time of removal and that subsequent changes in the pleadings did not impact the court's exercise of supplemental jurisdiction.

5. Assume that a plaintiff's nondiverse state law claim was dismissed by the federal district court either because it did not meet the requirements for supplemental jurisdiction set forth in §1367(a), was precluded by the terms of §1367(b), or for any of the discretionary reasons listed in §1367(c). The plaintiff, who wished to preserve the dismissed claim, refiled it in state court. Further assume, however, that the governing state limitations period had expired by the time of the state court filing. Alternatively, suppose that after that supplemental claim was dismissed, the plaintiff voluntarily dismissed the remaining diversity state law claim that fell within the court's original jurisdiction and then refiled that latter claim in state court after the expiration of

the relevant state limitations period. Is the plaintiff in either or both of these contexts out of luck in state court or is there some basis for tolling the state limitations period?

Congress chose to protect plaintiffs in this situation by providing in §1367(d) that if a supplemental claim is dismissed, or if another claim is voluntarily dismissed after dismissal of a supplemental claim, any state limitations period governing those dismissed claims must be tolled for thirty days after the dismissal of the supplemental claim, unless the state law provides for a longer tolling period.

Suppose, however, that the supplemental claim was filed against a state government defendant and that the federal court dismissed this claim on the grounds that the State enjoyed sovereign immunity against such a claim under the Eleventh Amendment of the U.S. Constitution. Should §1367(d) apply when that state law claim is refiled in state court? In RAYGOR v. REGENTS OF THE UNIVERSITY OF MINNESOTA, 534 U.S. 533, 122 S.Ct. 999, 152 L.Ed.2d 27 (2002), the Court held that §1367(d) did *not* permit the tolling of a state limitations provision for state law claims against nonconsenting States that had been dismissed by a federal court on Eleventh Amendment grounds. In *Raygor*, the plaintiff filed an action in federal district court containing employment discrimination claims under both the federal Age Discrimination in Employment Act and the Minnesota Human Rights Act. The trial court dismissed all of the claims on sovereign immunity grounds. Three weeks after the dismissal, the plaintiff refiled the state law claim in state court. The defendant then moved for summary judgment on the ground that the state law claim was barred by the applicable state limitations period. The plaintiff maintained that the state limitations period had been tolled for thirty days from the date of the dismissal by §1367(d). In Pennhurst State School and Hospital v. Halderman, 465 U.S. 89, 104 S.Ct. 900, 79 L.Ed. 2d 67 (1984), a case decided prior to the enactment of §1367, the Court had held that the Eleventh Amendment precluded a federal court from exercising pendent jurisdiction over a state law claim against a nonconsenting state defendant. On the basis of that precedent the *Raygor* Court declared that for §1367 to be construed to provide jurisdiction over such state law claims, its intention to abrogate this constitutional impediment to federal jurisdiction would have to have to be manifested in "unmistakably clear" language. And since §1367(a), the Court continued, did not contain a clear statement of any intent to abrogate state sovereign immunity, it should not be read to authorize the exercise of supplemental jurisdiction over a state law claim against a nonconsenting state defendant. Consequently, it held that the state law claim was properly dismissed by the federal trial court on Eleventh Amendment grounds.

The Court then turned to the question of whether the tolling provision of §1367(d) applied to such a claim when it was refiled in a state court. After noting that §1367(d) purported to apply to dismissal of all claims under §1367(a), regardless of the reason for that dismissal, the Court nevertheless concluded that applying the tolling provision in this context would extend the state limitations period beyond that which would ordinarily apply to this state law claim had it never been filed in federal court. And since a limitations period is an important limitation or condition on the State's waiver of sovereign immunity, such an interpretation of §1367(d) would constitute a federal expansion of the scope of the State's waiver of immunity. Moreover, while federal tolling provisions are rebuttably presumed to affect the waiver of federal sovereign immunity in suits against the United States, the Court was not prepared to extend this doctrine to the effect of federal tolling provisions on a State's waiver of sovereign immunity. It did state, however, that the possibility that federal tolling of a state limitations period could affect the scope of a State's sovereign immunity raised a "serious constitutional doubt."

Under these circumstances, the Court reasoned, if a federal statute was to be construed to have an affect on a matter affecting the "constitutional balance between the States and the Federal Government" such as the scope of State sovereign immunity, even if this did not amount to an "abrogation" of state sovereign immunity, Congress would have make its intention to do so "unmistakably clear in the language of the statute." Section 1367(d), the Court explained, did not contain any clear expression of Congressional intent to toll the limitations period for claims dismissed against nonconsenting States on Eleventh Amendment grounds. According to the majority opinion, the fact that §1367(d) refers to all claims dismissed under §1367(a) was not good enough since it did not expressly refer to claims against nonconsenting States. Similarly, while §1367(d) could be read "in isolation" to authorize tolling regardless of the reason for dismissal of the state law claim, the Court decided that when read in the context of a statute that lists only a few reasons for dismissal — failure to form part of the same case as the federal claim; when exercising jurisdiction over the supplemental claim would be inconsistent with the grant of diversity jurisdiction; and the four specific situations set forth in §1367(c) — it was unclear whether the tolling provision was intended to apply to claims dismissed for some other reason, such as sovereign immunity. Thus, while §1367(d) did not explicitly *exclude* sovereign immunity from the list of grounds for dismissal that would invoke the tolling provision, since it did not explicitly *include* sovereign immunity as a basis for dismissal that would lend itself to tolling, it failed the "clear statement" test. Accordingly, the Court held, §1367(d) would not be construed to permit tolling of the state limitations period for claims against nonconsenting States dismissed on Eleventh Amendment grounds. By offering this narrow construction of the statute, however, the Court avoided ruling directly on the constitutional question.

Now assume that the supplemental claim asserted against a State or one of its instrumentalities was dismissed for a reason unrelated to sovereign immunity and that the plaintiff refiled that claim in state court within the thirty day period permitted by §1367(d) but after the expiration of the otherwise governing state limitations period. Does the Court's ruling in *Raygor* help answer the question of whether this federally imposed extension of time within which the State could be sued (beyond the period set by the state limitations statute) infringes on the State's right of sovereign immunity and thereby runs afoul of the Tenth Amendment to the U.S. Constitution?

In JINKS v. RICHLAND COUNTY, 538 U.S. 456, 123 S.Ct. 1667, 155 L.Ed. 2d 631 (2003), the Court unanimously upheld the constitutionality of

§1367(d), rejecting the State's dual contentions that (a) this provision was facially invalid because it exceeded the enumerated powers of Congress; and (b) with respect to cases involving claims against a State's political subdivisions the statute constituted an impermissible abrogation of sovereign immunity by interfering with the State's power to control the scope of its sovereign immunity.

With respect to the first claim of facial unconstitutionality, the Court ruled that §1367(d) fell within Congress' constitutional authority under the Necessary and Proper Clause of Article I. Section 1367(d), the Court determined, was necessary and proper for carrying into execution the judicial power of the United States. The "necessity" element, the Court explained, did not require that the statute be absolutely necessary, but only conducive to and plainly adapted to the fair and efficient operation of the federal courts. And §1367(d) promoted that end, the Court concluded, by (1) providing federal courts with an efficient alternative to the unsatisfactory options otherwise available when a federal court declined to exercise jurisdiction over supplemental state law claims; and (2) protecting plaintiffs with transactionally related federal and state law claims against the risk that their state law claims would be time barred in state court if the federal court declines to retain jurisdiction over them. The Court also found §1367(d) "plainly adapted" to Congress' power to provide for the fair and efficient exercise of the federal judicial power in that it could adduce no evidence that Congress enacted the statute for any other purpose. Finally, the Court rejected the claim that §1367(d) violated the Tenth Amendment right of state sovereignty by regulating state court procedure in cases involving purely state law claims. Assuming, without deciding, the usefulness of a procedure vs. substance dichotomy in this context, the Court concluded, consistent with its ruling in *Guaranty Trust*, that a state statute of limitations should be treated as substantive and, therefore, not as a procedural rule immune from congressional regulation.

As to the sovereign immunity challenge, the Court declared that while Congress could not interfere with a *State's* immunity from suit in its own courts, it could subject a *municipality* to suit in state court if that was accomplished pursuant to a valid exercise of its enumerated powers. Since municipalities, unlike States, do not enjoy a constitutionally protected right of sovereign immunity from suit, the Court concluded that Congress could, in the exercise of its enumerated powers, affect a municipality's state-law-based immunity from suit regardless of whether that suit was brought under state or federal law. The fact that this claim was against a State's political subdivision, rather than the State itself, the Court ruled, also served to distinguish the instant case from *Raygor*.

SECTION D. REMOVAL

As the party who initiates litigation, the plaintiff enjoys the privilege of choosing the forum that will adjudicate the dispute. But this right, as we saw in *Bracken* and *Mikulski*, is not absolute. Congress has provided defendants in civil actions with a mechanism, called removal, to trump the plaintiff's choice of a state court when the defendant prefers to have the case heard by a federal judge. Although unmentioned in the Constitution, removal has existed as a statutory phenomenon since the initial Judiciary Act of 1789.

Briefly put, a case that falls within the federal courts' original jurisdiction, i.e., one that the plaintiff originally could have filed in federal court, can be removed there by the defendant(s). This general rule, however, is subject to a series of statutorily designated exceptions, some of which expand upon, and others of which restrict, the limits of original jurisdiction. Moreover, this procedure operates in only one direction. A defendant cannot remove a case from federal to state court. Neither can a defendant transfer a case from one state court to a court of a different state. The specific requirements for removal are set forth at 28 U.S.C. §1441 and the procedural requirements governing this process are detailed at 28 U.S.C. §§1446 and 1447. We shall now explore several of the issues addressed and generated by these provisions.

Read 28 U.S.C. §§1441, 1446 and 1447.

Brown v. K–MAC Enterprises

United States District Court, Northern District of Oklahoma, 2012.
897 F. Supp. 2d 1098.

KERN, DISTRICT JUDGE.

Before the Court are Plaintiff's Motion to Remand * * *.

    * * *

I. Background

On January 17, 2012, Plaintiff filed [a complaint] against K–MAC and Taco Bell, LLC ("Taco Bell, LLC") alleging the following causes of action: (1) disability discrimination, in violation of the Americans with Disabilities Act ("ADA claim"); (2) race and gender discrimination in violation of Title VII ("Title VII claim"); (3) age discrimination in violation of the Age Discrimination in Employment Act ("ADEA claim"); (4) termination in violation of the public policy of Oklahoma ("*Burk* claim"), (5) denial and interference with the right to exercise Family and Medical Leave Act benefits ("FMLA claim"); (6) retaliation for filing a workers' compensation claim, in violation of title 85, section 341 of the Oklahoma Statutes ("workers' compensation retaliation claim"); and (7) intentional infliction of emotional distress ("IIED claim"). On February 9, 2012, Defendants removed the action, asserting that this Court has subject matter jurisdiction pursuant to 28 U.S.C. §1331, based upon the claims arising under federal law.

Plaintiff filed a motion to remand all claims based on the presence of the statutorily non-removable workers' compensation retaliation claim, *see* 28 U.S.C. §1445(c), and this Court's decision in *Pulley v. Bartlett–Collins Co.,* 2006 WL 3386909, at *3 (N.D.Okla. Nov.21, 2006) (concluding that all claims joined with non-removable workers' compensation retaliation claim must be remanded). In response to the motion to remand, Defendant argues that * * *

Pulley has been overruled by the Federal Courts Jurisdiction and Venue Clarification Act of 2011 ("FCJVCA") * * *.

II. Motion to Remand

This Court's decision in *Pulley* has been overruled by statute. *See Bivins v. Glanz*, No. 12–CV–103, 2012 WL 3136115, at * 2 (N.D.Okla. Aug. 1, 2012). As this Court recently explained:

> Under the amended 28 U.S.C. §1441(c)(2), the Court has no discretion to remand federal claims that are joined with a statutorily nonremovable claim, such as a workers' compensation retaliation claim. Instead, the Court must sever and remand the nonremovable claim and retain all other removed claims that are within the Court's original or supplemental jurisdiction.

* * *.

* * * Therefore, the Court will (1) sever and remand the workers' compensation retaliation claim; (2) retain the Title VII, ADA claim, ADEA claim, and FMLA claim because they are within the Court's original jurisdiction; and (3) retain the *Burk* claim and IIED claim because they form part of the same case or controversy as the federal claims and are within the Court's supplemental jurisdiction.

III. Conclusion

Plaintiff's Motion for Remand is GRANTED in part and DENIED in part. The workers' compensation retaliation claim is hereby SEVERED and REMANDED to the District Court for Tulsa County, State of Oklahoma. The motion to remand is denied as to all federal claims, the *Burk* claim, and the IIED claim.

NOTES AND PROBLEMS FOR DISCUSSION

1. Are the following actions removable?

(a) A complaint filed by a Nevada citizen alleging that the defendant, also a Nevada citizen, was part of a price fixing scheme in violation of Nevada Fair Trade Laws and that the application of this state statute to the defendant's pricing policies does not deprive the defendant of its property without due process of law in violation of the Fourteenth Amendment to the U.S. Constitution.

(b) Same facts as above but now the defendant bases removal not on the presence of a federal constitutional question, but on the assertion that since price-fixing is prohibited by the federal antitrust laws, the plaintiff's failure to assert this claim cannot operate to deprive the federal court of its original jurisdiction over this federal statutory question.

(c) Same facts as in "(a)" but this time the defendant bases removal on the presence of a federal question generated by a previous ruling by a federal district judge in an earlier case between the same parties in which that federal court ruled that this defendant's conduct did not violate the federal antitrust laws. See

Rivet v. Regions Bank of Louisiana, 522 U.S. 470, 118 S.Ct. 921, 139 L.Ed.2d 912 (1998).

(d) A Massachusetts tenant files an action for wrongful eviction against her Pennsylvania landlord in Massachusetts state court. The plaintiff seeks reinstatement of the lease plus $15,000 in damages.

Suppose that this Massachusetts plaintiff affirmatively wants to avoid having the case removed. So, in her state court complaint, she seeks only damages and, as permitted by state law, states only that she is seeking "an amount in excess of $10,000." Or suppose, as is permitted by the rules of procedure in many states, the plaintiff refrains from alleging any particular sum in the complaint's prayer for damages. When the defendant removes the case on the basis of diversity jurisdiction and the plaintiff then moves to remand on the ground that the federal court lacks subject matter jurisdiction because the case does not meet the jurisdictional amount in controversy requirement, how should the court rule? This, as the courts have acknowledged, reveals an oddity in diversity jurisdiction. If the plaintiff wished to secure federal jurisdiction, all it has to do is allege an amount in excess of $75,000 in its complaint. That will be enough to support removal unless the defendant can convince the trial court "to a legal certainty" that the plaintiff's claim cannot recover the jurisdictional minimum. But when it is the defendant who wishes to secure federal jurisdiction (and the burden of establishing jurisdiction is on the party seeking to invoke it), because the defendant has no control over the complaint, it cannot simply allege that the required amount of money is in controversy. So how, if at all, can the courts prevent plaintiffs from being able to avoid removal (and thereby frustrate Congress' intent to allow defendants in appropriate cases to invoke a federal forum) by declining to allege the jurisdictional amount? This problem was resolved by Congress as part of the amendments contained in the Federal Courts Jurisdiction & Venue Clarification Act of 2011. Sections 1446(c)(2)(A) and (B) provide that where the complaint's prayer for relief does not meet the statutory requirement because (a) the complaint seeks nonmonetary relief, or (2) State practice either does not permit the complaint to include a demand for a specific sum or permits recovery in excess of the amount sought in the complaint, the defendant can assert the amount in controversy in its notice of removal and the trial judge must determine, by a preponderance of the evidence standard, that the amount in controversy exceeds the statutory amount set forth in §1332(a).

(e) A breach of contract claim for $100,000 filed in New Jersey state court by a New York plaintiff against a New Jersey defendant.

The prohibition against removal when one of the defendants in a diversity case is a forum citizen was the backdrop for an interesting question that found its way to the Supreme Court. A pair of Virginia citizens who had discovered evidence of toxic mold in their apartment filed suit in Virginia state court seeking damages from their injuries occasioned by the presence of the mold. They sued the owner of the complex, an investment management group, and the developer of the complex. The three defendants, citizens of Texas, Wisconsin, and Georgia, removed the action on the basis of diversity. After the federal district court granted the defendants' motion for summary judgment, but before final judgment was entered, the plaintiffs moved to remand the case on the ground that the Texas owner was actually a Virginia citizen and, therefore, was not diverse from the plaintiffs. The trial judge denied the remand motion, finding that the owner was indeed a Texas citizen and, therefore, that all defendants were diverse from the plaintiffs and that no defendant was a forum citizen. But in a quirky opinion, the Fourth Circuit reversed. It concluded that although the owner was truly a Texas citizen, it was possible that the housing complex really was controlled by one of the owner's subsidiaries — a Virginia corporation or partnership. And it reasoned that since this Texas defendant had not negated the possibility that this real defendant in interest was a nondiverse party, the removing parties had not sustained their burden of establishing that joinder of that party would not destroy diversity.

In LINCOLN PROPERTY CO. v. ROCHE, 546 U.S. 81, 126 S.Ct. 606, 163 L.Ed.2d 415 (2005), the Supreme Court reversed the Fourth Circuit's ruling. Invoking the "master of the complaint" doctrine, Justice Ginsburg, writing for a unanimous Court, declared that since the named Texas defendant had admitted its control over the premises and accepted responsibility in the event the plaintiffs prevailed on the merits of their claims, that defendant was not, as the Fourth Circuit had suggested, merely a "nominal party" whose presence had to be supplemented by a missing party pursuant to the terms of Rule 19. To the contrary, the Court concluded, no absent party was needed for a just adjudication of the controversy. Consequently, in the absence of a missing party whose joinder was required under Rule 19, "the Fourth Circuit had no warrant to inquire whether some other person might have been joined as an additional or substitute defendant." It was up to the plaintiffs to decide who to join as defendants and all of their named defendants met all the jurisdictional requirements for removal.

(f) Same facts as in "(e)" but the claim is brought under a federal statute.

(g) An Ohio plaintiff brings a $250,000 tort claim against his next-door neighbor. The day after the defendant receives a copy of the complaint, he moves to Michigan and then seeks to remove the case.

(h) A New Jersey plaintiff files an $80,000 tort claim against a New York defendant in New Jersey state court. After the defendant removes the case, the plaintiff amends her complaint to seek only $75,000 in damages and then files a motion to remand. See St. Paul Mercury Indemnity Co. v. Red Cab Co., 303 U.S. 283, 58 S.Ct. 586, 82 L.Ed. 845 (1938). Alternatively, what if the plaintiff, in the original complaint, also included a $100 breach of contract claim against her live-in mother-in-law in addition to the $80,000 claim against the New York defendant?

Suppose that this New Jersey plaintiff had filed the action in an Ohio state court against the same New York defendant. After the defendant removed the case, the plaintiff amended her complaint by adding a $150,000 claim against an Ohio defendant. The plaintiff then filed a motion to remand. How should the court rule? See Spencer v. U.S. District Court for Northern District of California, 393 F.3d 867 (9th Cir.2004) (forum defendant rule applies only at time of notice of removal; post-removal joinder of a diverse, forum defendant does not negate removal jurisdiction because as long as removal was proper at time case is removed, subsequent events, at least those not destroying original subject matter jurisdiction, do not require remand).

Now suppose that all the previously stated facts remain the same except that the post-removal amendment added a claim against a citizen of New Jersey instead of a citizen of Ohio. How should the federal trial court handle this situation? In BORDEN v. ALLSTATE INSURANCE CO., 589 F.3d 168 (5th Cir.2009), the plaintiff sued a diverse insurer in state court after the defendant denied coverage for Hurricane Katrina flood loss. After the defendant removed based on diversity jurisdiction, the plaintiff sought to amend his complaint to add a claim against a non-diverse insurance agent. The defendant did not oppose the motion to amend, and the trial court granted the motion. The trial court thereafter granted the insurer's motion for summary judgment and dismissed the claim against the agent. The Fifth Circuit rejected the contention that the non-diverse defendant had been fraudulently joined, ruling that the fraudulent joinder doctrine was invocable only as to parties on the record in the state court action at the time of removal. Instead, it focused on 42 U.S.C. §1447(e), and construed this provision to mean that where a plaintiff seeks to join additional defendants *after* removal whose joinder would destroy subject matter jurisdiction, the court must either deny such joinder or permit that joinder but then remand for lack of subject matter jurisdiction. In the instant case, since the trial court had granted the plaintiff's motion to join the claim against the non-diverse defendant, that decision divested the trial court of diversity jurisdiction and ordinarily would have required a remand per §1447(e). As it turned out, however, the court also held that an insurance denial claim brought under a flood insurance policy issued pursuant to the National Flood Insurance Program invoked the court's §1331 federal question jurisdiction. Accordingly, the Fifth Circuit ruled that the trial court retained federal question jurisdiction over the NFIP claim against the insurer. It also upheld the trial court's ruling dismissing the claim against the agent as time-barred.

(i) A state law claim for $300,000 is filed in Maryland state court by a North Carolina plaintiff against a South Carolina defendant and a North Carolina defendant. Two months later, the plaintiff voluntarily dismisses the claim against the North Carolina defendant. Can the defendant now remove the case? Would the result be different if the state court dismissed the North Carolina defendant for lack of personal jurisdiction and the remaining defendant then removed the case?

Suppose, instead, that Ellen Reynolds, a Texas plaintiff, had filed a multi-million dollar tort action against two North Carolina tobacco manufacturers and a Texas convenience store. After the defendants removed the case, the plaintiff moved to remand on the ground that the presence of the convenience store defendant destroyed complete diversity. The defendants argued that the Federal Cigarette Labeling and Advertising Act precluded all state law claims against cigarette retailers, and therefore, that diversity-based removal against the other defendants was proper. The trial court granted the plaintiff's motion on the ground that the federal statute did not preempt state law and, therefore, that complete diversity was not present. Shortly after the remand decision, the U.S.

Supreme Court, in a separate case brought by a different plaintiff against the same tobacco manufacturers and convenience store, ruled that the Federal Cigarette Labeling and Advertising Act did, in fact, preclude all state law claims against cigarette retailers. Two days after the Supreme Court issued that decision, the defendants removed Ellen Reynolds' suit a second time. She again moved for remand. How should the court rule on her motion? In formulating your answer, consider the fact that §1446(b) allows removals to be filed within thirty days after receipt by the defendant of a copy of a pleading, motion, order or other paper from which it may first be ascertained that the case has become removable. See Green v. R.J. Reynolds Tobacco Co., 274 F.3d 263 (5th Cir.2001) (a judicial opinion in an unrelated case can constitute an "order" for §1446(b) purposes at least where the same party was a defendant in both cases and where both cases involve similar factual situations).

Or suppose that a plaintiff who was beaten by some police officers filed a claim alleging a tortious assault and battery. All parties are diverse, but the defendants chose not to remove. Subsequently, the plaintiff amended her complaint to allege a claim under 42 U.S.C. §1983, alleging that the police officers' conduct deprived her of her constitutional rights. The defendants then filed a notice of removal alleging §1331 jurisdiction. How should the federal court ruled on the plaintiff's motion to remand? See Wilson v. Intercollegiate (Big Ten) Conference Athletic Ass'n, 668 F.2d 962 (7th Cir.1982).

Suppose a tort plaintiff files a claim in state court and under governing state practice, the plaintiff is not permitted to seek damages in a sum certain. The parties are of diverse citizenship. Can the defendant, who is not a citizen of the forum state, remove the case?

What if the plaintiff filed a state law claim in state court as to which it sought only nonmonetary relief in against a diverse defendant who is not a citizen of the forum state? Is the case removable?

Suppose a plaintiff's original complaint asserts a $100,000 state law claim against a diverse defendant. Forty days after that defendant is served, the plaintiff amends her complaint to assert $100,000 claims against two additional defendants, both of whom are diverse from the plaintiff. These two additional defendants file a notice to remove ten days after they are served. The plaintiff then files a motion to remand. How should the federal district court rule on that motion? Note that this problem involves two removal-related rules: (a) the requirement for filing a notice of removal within thirty days from date of service; and (b) the requirement that all defendants join in the removal.

Prior to the enactment of the Federal Courts Jurisdiction and Venue Clarification Act of 2011, 12 Stat. 758, Pub.L. 112-63, the removal statute did not expressly require all defendants to join in removal. And though all the circuit courts read this requirement into the language of §1441(a), they did not agree as to how the unanimity must be manifested. But Congress addressed this issue in §1446(b)(2)(A), which now requires that all defendants either join in the notice of removal or otherwise "consent" to removal. Additionally, §1446(b)(2)(C) provides that where defendants are served at different times, as long as any later-served defendant has filed a timely notice of removal (i.e., within thirty days of being served), any earlier-served defendant who had not initiated or consented to removal may then *consent* to the removal even if more than thirty days has passed since the date on which that earlier-served defendant was served. Thus, such an earlier-served defendant does not ever have to file its own notice or even expressly join in the later-served defendant's notice of removal. It is sufficient if the later-served defendants state in their notice that the earlier-served defendant consents to the removal.

(j)   A New Mexico plaintiff files a $60,000 breach of contract claim in New Mexico state court against an Arizona corporation. The defendant files a counterclaim alleging defamation and seeking $1 million in damages. The plaintiff wants to remove the case. See Shamrock Oil & Gas Corp. v. Sheets, 313 U.S. 100, 61 S.Ct. 868, 85 L.Ed. 1214 (1941).

Would your analysis of this problem change if the defendant, instead, filed a counterclaim alleging a violation of the federal antitrust statute? In HOLMES GROUP, INC. v. VORNADO AIR CIRCULATION SYSTEMS, INC., 535 U.S. 826 122 S.Ct. 1889, 153 L.Ed. 2d 13 (2002), the Court reaffirmed the well-pleaded complaint rule and indicated that a federal counterclaim to a state law claim can no more create federal question jurisdiction than can a federal defense. *Holmes Group* involved the appellate jurisdiction of the Court of Appeals for the Federal Circuit over cases "arising under" the patent laws. The Supreme Court stated that under the well-pleaded complaint rule, a patent-infringement counterclaim in the district court couldn't serve as the basis for the Federal Circuit's specialized "arising under" jurisdiction. Given the similar "arising under" language of the general federal question statute, any contrary holding would "radically expand" the universe of removable cases, and contravene the longstanding rule that the plaintiff is the master of the complaint, because it would allow a removing defendant to defeat the plaintiff's choice of forum, simply by asserting a federal counterclaim. Consequently, the Court declined the transform the well-pleaded complaint rule into the well-pleaded complaint or counterclaim rule.

The Court reinforced this principle in VADEN v. DISCOVER BANK, 556 U.S. 49, 129 S.Ct. 1262, 173 L.Ed.2d 206 (2009). In *Vaden,* the plaintiff credit card issuer had filed a garden-variety breach of contract suit in state court against one of its customers to collect unpaid charges. The customer replied by filing a counterclaim alleging that Discover's demands violated state law. Discover then filed a separate petition with a federal court in the forum state seeking, pursuant to §4 of the Federal Arbitration Act, an order to compel arbitration of the claims raised by the state court counterclaim. Although the counterclaim consisted solely of state law claims, Discover insisted that such claims were completely preempted by federal banking law and, therefore, fell within the federal court's federal question jurisdiction. Under §4 of the Federal Arbitration Act, a federal court can entertain a petition to compel arbitration of a dispute not pending before it if the court would have jurisdiction over the dispute "save for the arbitration agreement." The Supreme Court construed this to mean that if the basis for federal jurisdiction enabling the invocation of §4 was the presence of a federal question, that assessment was governed by the well-pleaded complaint rule and, therefore, the corollary (citing *Holmes Group*) that federal question jurisdiction cannot be predicated upon the existence of a federal issue only in a counterclaim. According to the Court, whether or not federal law completely preempted the state law claims asserted in the state court counterclaim was therefore irrelevant. And in the absence of federal question jurisdiction, the federal court had no authority to issue an arbitration order.

What if the defendant filed a federal question third party complaint and the third party defendant sought to remove the entire case? See First National Bank of Pulaski v. Curry, 301 F.3d 456 (6th Cir.2002).

(k) Bill Whipple, a Montana citizen, filed an employment discrimination claim against his employer, a Pennsylvania corporation, with the Montana Fair Employment Bureau, a state administrative agency with jurisdiction over claims under the Montana antidiscrimination statute. After investigating the complaint, the Bureau served the employer with administrative charges alleging unlawful employment discrimination and scheduled a hearing before a state administrative law judge. The company removed the proceedings to the district court for the District of Montana. How should the trial court rule on the agency's motion to remand? Compare Oregon Bureau of Labor and Industries v. U.S. West Communications, Inc., 288 F.3d 414 (9th Cir.2002) with Floeter v. C.W. Transport, Inc., 597 F.2d 1100 (7th Cir.1979).

(l) After purchasing a defective appliance, the consumer, a citizen of Minnesota files an action in a Minnesota state court, asserting a $90,000 tort claim against the local Minnesota retailer and a $90,000 tort claim against the Wisconsin manufacturer.

(m) Same facts as in "(l)", except that instead of filing a tort claim against the Wisconsin manufacturer, the consumer brings a claim under the federal Consumer Protection Act.

(n) A landowner domiciled on the Mississippi side of the border with Alabama brings an action in an Alabama state court under the federal Clean Water Act against a factory in her hometown for discharging waste products into a nearby stream and a $100,000 tort claim against a neighbor on the Alabama side of the line who had dumped his sewerage onto her property.

Recall that under §1369, Congress provided federal district courts with original jurisdiction over certain multi-party, multi-forum cases predicated on minimal diversity. Consistent with the fundamental premise of the removal statute, i.e., that, with minor exception, a defendant should be able to remove any case that the plaintiff could have brought in federal court, Congress amended §1441(e) to provide that a defendant can remove any action that could have been brought in federal court under §1369 which would otherwise not be removable.

(o) On rare occasion, Congress has enacted a statute providing for the removal of a particular category of case. Such is the case with the Securities Litigation Uniform Standards Act of 1998 (SLUSA), 14 U.S.C. §78bb. This law provides for the removability of state-law based class actions, regardless of the citizenship of the adverse parties, alleging a misrepresentation or omission of a material fact in connection with the purchase or sale of any nationally traded security in which damages are sought on behalf of more than fifty persons. The statute also includes a federal preclusion defense that mandates the dismissal of such suits once removed. This statute, therefore, permits removal of a claim that does not fall within the federal court's original jurisdiction under either §§1331 or 1332. And while the statute does contain a federal preclusion defense, that federal issue would not be part of the plaintiff's well pleaded complaint. Has Congress overstepped its constitutional authority in enacting this provision? In PROCTOR v. VISHAY INTERTECHNOLOGY INC., 584 F.3d 1208 (9th Cir. 2009), the Ninth Circuit upheld the constitutionality of this removal provision. The court noted that Congress can provide for removal jurisdiction as long as the jurisdiction does not exceed the bounds of Article III. And the boundaries of "arising under" jurisdiction under Article III are broader than the well pleaded complaint limitation read into §1331. Consequently, the court held, the presence of the statutory federal preclusion *defense* "creates a federal question hook on which removal can hang."

2.   The specific procedure governing the removal process is codified at 28 U.S.C. §1446. Pursuant to its terms, removal is a self-executing act. Instead of requesting permission from either the state or federal district court to grant removal, the defendant simply files a notice of removal with the federal district court, and then gives written notice of the removal to all adverse parties and to the clerk of the state court from whence the case is removed. Once this is accomplished, the case is considered removed and the state court cannot undertake further proceedings in the matter. If the plaintiff wishes to challenge the removal, on either jurisdictional or procedural grounds, the mechanism for doing so is the filing of a motion to remand with the federal district court pursuant to 28 U.S.C. §1447. And even though the plaintiff is the moving party on the motion to remand, it is the defendant — the party seeking to invoke federal jurisdiction — that shoulders the burden of persuading the court of those facts supporting removal.

(a)   A Tennessee citizen is injured in a car accident in St. Louis when a truck driven by a Missouri citizen and owned by another Missouri citizen rams his car. The plaintiff files suit in a Tennessee state court seeking $400,000 in damages against each defendant. The driver, but not the car owner, preferred to have the case heard in federal court and so he alone filed a timely notice of removal. The plaintiff wants the case heard in state court. What must he do to accomplish this result?

(b)   An Illinois citizen brings a sexual harassment claim in Illinois state court against his Indiana employer under Title VII of the Civil Rights Act of 1964, 42 U.S.C. §2000(e), and a claim seeking $250,000 in damages for tortious assault and battery against the alleged harasser — his supervisor — who is a citizen of Indiana. The employer files a timely notice of removal. Can the federal court exercise jurisdiction over the entire case?

(c)   Same facts as in "(b)", except that both defendants join in filing the notice of removal and that case originally was filed in a state court in Indiana. Can the federal court exercise jurisdiction over the entire case?

Now suppose that the Illinois plaintiff filed only a $100,000 breach of contract claim against the Indiana defendant in Illinois state court. The defendant removed, in a timely fashion, on the basis of diversity. Five months after the defendant filed the timely notice of removal the plaintiff filed a motion to remand on the basis of a forum selection clause that required all actions brought under the contract to be filed in state court. How should the court rule? *See* Kamm v. ITEX Corp., 568 F.3d 752 (9th Cir. 2009).

(d) A novelist who is a citizen of New York files an action in New York state court alleging that a bookstore (New York citizen) has violated the federal copyright laws by selling pirated editions of his novel. In this suit he also brings a $1 million breach of contract claim against the publisher (a N.Y. citizen) for failure to honor its obligation to use its best efforts to promote the sale of his book. The bookstore files a notice of removal. Can a federal court exercise jurisdiction over the entire case?

(e) On January 1, 2002, Lane, a Colorado citizen filed a tort claim against Ron, a North Dakota citizen, and Sue, a Colorado citizen, seeking damages of $200,000 against each defendant. After extensive discovery, Lane determined that he had no claim against Sue and so dismissed the claim against her on December 18, 2002. On January 10, 2003, Ron removed the case on diversity grounds. Lane filed a motion to remand on October 1, 2003. How should the court rule on the remand motion? See Music v. Arrowood Indemnity Co., 632 F.3d 284 (6th Cir. 2011).

(f) Section 1447(c) also provides that when a federal court grants a motion to remand, it "may" require the removing defendant(s) to pay the opposing party's costs and attorney fees incurred as a result of the removal. But the statute offers no standard governing the awarding of attorney's fees. In MARTIN v. FRANKLIN CAPITAL CORPORATION, 546 U.S. 132, 126 S.Ct. 704, 163 L.Ed.2d 547 (2005), the Supreme Court resolved a circuit conflict by unanimously ruling that absent unusual circumstances, the trial court should not award attorney's fees unless the court finds that the removing party lacked an objectively reasonable basis for removal. The Court read §1447(c) to reflect Congress' desire to discourage only those removals sought solely for the improper purpose of prolonging litigation or imposing costs on the opposing party. Congress did not want, in the Court's assessment, for attorney fee awards in remanded cases to chill the exercise of this statutory right to the extent that defendants would be unprepared to remove except in cases where the presence of federal jurisdiction was obvious. Consequently, it ruled that absent unusual circumstances, attorney's fee awards should be issued under §1447(c) only where the removing defendant(s) lacked an objectively reasonable basis for seeking removal. Such unusual circumstances, the Court added, might occur where, for example, the plaintiff had unreasonably delayed in seeking remand or otherwise contributed to the defendant's inability to accurately determine whether or not jurisdiction existed. Since the plaintiffs in the instant case did not dispute the reasonableness of the defendants' removal arguments, the Supreme Court affirmed the Tenth Circuit's decision upholding the trial judge's denial of the plaintiffs' request for attorney fees.

(g) Section 1447(d) provides that "[a]n order remanding a case to the State Court from which it was removed is not reviewable on appeal or otherwise" except for civil rights cases remanded pursuant to §1443. Nevertheless, the Supreme Court has acknowledged on more than one occasion that the limitation on reviewability contained in §1447(d) covers "less than its words alone suggest." Most recently, in POWEREX CORP. v. RELIANT ENERGY SERVICES, INC., 551 U.S. 224, 127 S.Ct. 2411, 168 L.Ed.2d 112 (2007), the Court noted that this language in §1447(d) only limited the reviewability of cases remanded on the grounds specified in §1447(c). This, in turn, the Court explained, meant that §1447(d) only barred appellate review of remand orders based on lack of subject matter jurisdiction or for defects in removal procedure. And with respect to jurisdictional defect-based remand orders, the *Powerex* Court declared, a case could be deemed to have been remanded for lack of subject matter jurisdiction (and thus subject to §1447(d)'s ban on appellate review) even if it was properly removed in the first instance.

Suppose that a federal district judge, in a removed case, declined to exercise supplemental jurisdiction over nondiverse state law claims pursuant to the discretionary provisions of §1367(c) and, therefore, remanded the case. Is this decision reviewable on appeal or is review precluded by §1447(d)? In *Powerex*, the Court opined that it was "far from clear" that "when discretionary supplemental jurisdiction is declined the remand is not based on lack of subject-matter jurisdiction" for §1447(c) & (d) purposes. Subsequently, in CARLSBAD TECHNOLOGY, INC. v. HIF BIO, INC., 556 U.S. 635, 129 S.Ct. 1862, 173 L.Ed.2d 843 (2009), the Court answered the question when it unanimously ruled that a federal district court's remand order, based on a decision to decline to exercise supplemental jurisdiction over state law claims (in the instant case, because the federal question claim had been dismissed for failure to state a claim under Rule 12(b)(6)) was *not* a remand based on lack of subject matter jurisdiction within the meaning of §§1447(c), and, therefore, the remand order was not subject to §1447(d)'s ban on appellate review. The Court distinguished between the existence of subject matter jurisdiction and the decision whether or not to exercise it. Pursuant to the statutory grant of supplemental jurisdiction found at §1367(a), a federal court has subject matter jurisdiction over specified nondiverse state law claims. A court's choice whether to exercise that jurisdiction pursuant to factors set forth at §1367(c) is a matter of discretion, not a matter of the existence *vel non* of subject matter jurisdiction. Because the exercise of discretion under §1367(c), the Court ruled, is not a jurisdictional determination, a remand based thereon is not barred from appellate review by §1447(d). In the instant case, the trial court had §1331-based original jurisdiction over the plaintiff's federal RICO claim. It also possessed supplemental jurisdiction over the state law claims because they satisfied the relatedness standard of §1367(a). When the original jurisdiction (RICO) claim was dismissed, the court retained supplemental jurisdiction over the state law claims and the decision to decline to exercise that power was based on the court's discretionary choice and was not a subject matter jurisdiction defect.

3. (a) How does the removal statute deal with the removability of claims that would fall within the federal court's supplemental jurisdiction? See City of

Chicago v. Int'l College of Surgeons, 522 U.S. 156, 118 S.Ct. 523, 139 L.Ed.2d 525 (1997) and Syngenta Crop Protection, Inc. v. Henson, 537 U.S. 28, 123 S.Ct. 366, 154 L.Ed.2d 368 (2002).

(b) A plaintiff files an action consisting of one federal question and one transactionally related state law claim against a nondiverse defendant. After the defendant removed the case, the plaintiff did not file a motion to remand. Months later, the trial court granted the defendant's motion for summary judgment, dismissing the federal question claim on the merits. In light of the language of §1447(c), can the court retain jurisdiction over the state law claim, or must it either dismiss this claim or remand it to state court? *Compare* Albingia Verischerungs A.G. v. Schenker International Inc., 344 F.3d 931 (9th Cir.2003) and Anderson v. AON Corp., 2010 WL 2891098 (7th Cir.2010) *with* Mills v. Harmon Law Offices, P.C., 344 F.3d 42 (1st Cir.2003).

4. A Texas manufacturer of expensive cologne brings a claim in a Texas state court alleging that the defendant is marketing a cheap "knock-off" product that infringes the plaintiff's patented scent in violation of federal patent laws. The defendant removes the case. Assume that federal courts have exclusive subject matter jurisdiction over claims brought under the federal patent laws. The plaintiff files a motion to remand the case. What result?

5. Suppose a Montana rare book dealer was on vacation in Atlanta when he saw an interesting book at a yard sale. The book's owner informed this dealer that it was an authentic first edition copy of Jonathan Swift's *Gulliver's Travels*. The dealer paid $45,000 for it and, upon returning to Montana, took it to an expert who called it a fraud. The book dealer filed a $70,000 breach of contract action against the Georgia seller in Montana state court. The defendant removed and now wants to file a Rule 12(b)(2) motion to dismiss for lack of personal jurisdiction, claiming he has no connections of any kind with Montana, having never been in or conducted any business transactions, in that state. Can the court rule on that motion? See Ruhrgas AG v. Marathon Oil Co., 526 U.S. 574, 119 S.Ct. 1563, 143 L.Ed.2d 760 (1999).

Alternatively, suppose a Mexican tourist in Atlanta had gone to the yard sale an hour before the Montana dealer and bought that book. The tourist subsequently filed suit against the seller in federal court in Atlanta, claiming damages in the amount of $70,000. The defendant filed a motion to dismiss on the ground of forum non conveniens. How should the court rule on that motion? Compare In the Matter of Arbitration between Monegasque De Reassurances S.A.M. v. Nak Naftogaz of Ukraine, 311 F.3d 488 (2d Cir.2002) (federal court can decide any non-merits question, including forum non conveniens, before ruling on subject matter jurisdiction) with Dominguez-Cota v. Cooper Tire & Rubber Co., 396 F.3d 650 (5th Cir.2005) (expressly disavowing *Monagesque De Reassurances S.A.M.* and declining to read *Ruhrgas* broadly to encompass non-merits issues other than personal jurisdiction. The court also notes that even if it could "stretch" *Ruhrgas* to encompass non-jurisdictional types of non-merits issues, it was satisfied that forum non conveniens was *not* a non-merits issue since the analysis of public and private factors that goes into any forum non conveniens assessment requires the court to examine the particular facts of the case and, therefore, to become entangled in the merits of the underlying dispute.).

6. You will recall that parties to commercial agreements frequently include forum selection clauses within their contractual arrangements. Sometimes these clauses designate either state or federal courts within a particular state as the forum to adjudicate disputes arising under the contract; sometimes they designate a state court as the exclusive forum for the resolution of covered disputes. Where the forum selection clause designates a state court as the exclusive forum, and the plaintiff files either a federal question or diverse state law claim against the defendant, can the defendant remove that action to federal court or has the defendant, by agreeing to the forum selection clause, waived its §1441 right of removal? Although the Supreme Court has not directly resolved this issue, the majority of federal circuit courts have held that since the right to remove is waivable (when either the defendant chooses not to file a notice of removal or files one in an untimely fashion), when a defendant files a removal petition in contravention of the terms of an enforceable forum selection clause that clearly demonstrates the parties' intention to vest exclusive jurisdiction in a state court, the case is nonremovable and must be remanded to state court.

7. The Eleventh Amendment to the U.S. Constitution provides that the federal judicial power shall not "extend to any suit in law or equity" filed against a State by a citizen of another State or of a foreign country. Although not expressly provide in its text, the Eleventh Amendment has been construed to provide States with immunity from suits in federal court brought by their own citizens as well. Suppose a citizen brings a state law-based claim for money damages against her State in a state court. If the defendant State removes the case, does that act of removal constitute a waiver of its Eleventh Amendment right of sovereign immunity?

In LAPIDES v. BOARD OF REGENTS OF THE UNIVERSITY SYSTEM OF GEORGIA, 535 U.S. 613, 122 S.Ct. 1640, 152 L.Ed.2d 806 (2002), the Supreme Court unanimously held that the State of Georgia's voluntary invocation of federal court jurisdiction through removal of a state tort claim for damages constituted a waiver of its Eleventh Amendment defense of sovereign immunity. The Court reasoned that not only would it be "anomalous or inconsistent" for a State to invoke federal jurisdiction through removal and then to deny the existence of federal jurisdiction under the Eleventh Amendment, but that permitting such inconsistent action "could generate seriously unfair results." The Court found no special circumstances in this case that warranted deviating from the well established general principle that a State's *voluntary* decision to participate in federal court litigation amounts to a waiver of its Eleventh Amendment immunity. And although the State in the instant case was brought involuntarily into state court as a defendant, it voluntarily chose to remove the case to federal court, thereby voluntarily invoking federal jurisdiction.

The Court also declared that whether any particular conduct by a State or its officials constitutes a waiver of Eleventh Amendment immunity is a question of federal law. Consequently, the Court rejected the State of Georgia's contention that Georgia law did not authorize the Georgia Attorney General (who chose to remove the case) to waive the State's Eleventh Amendment immunity from suit in federal court. In so ruling, the Court explicitly overruled its previous ruling in Ford Motor Co. v. Dep't of Treasury of Ind., 323 U.S. 459, 65 S.Ct. 347, 89 L.Ed. 389 (1945), that a State could reassert a claim of Eleventh Amendment immunity after litigating, and losing, a claim brought against it in federal court on the ground that state law was, at least, unclear as to whether that State's attorney general was authorized to waive the State's Eleventh Amendment immunity.

The Supreme Court also rejected the State's claim that previous decisions permitting the federal government to assert sovereign immunity after voluntarily participating in litigation should be extended to action by a State. It distinguished the two situations on the ground that the cases involving the federal government did not arise under the Eleventh Amendment, which focuses on the State's sovereignty vis-à-vis the federal government.

Finally, the Court noted that since the plaintiff's federal claim (under 42 U.S.C. §1983) against the defendant State was not viable, the district court "might well" remand the plaintiff's only remaining claim — a nondiverse state law claim — to state court per §1367(c)(3).

CHAPTER 4

Non-Constitutional Limitations on the Exercise of Adjudicative Power

In the preceding two chapters, we examined the dual foundational requirements for the exercise of adjudicative power. As we now know, the rules governing both personal and subject matter jurisdiction derive from constitutional principles. The ultimate arbiters of the outer limits of either a federal or state tribunal's power to issue judgments binding on the parties are the due process guarantees found in the Fifth and Fourteenth Amendments to the U.S. Constitution. Similarly, federal and state constitutions delegate to their constituent courts authority or competence to adjudicate particular types of disputes. But the increasing nationalization (and globalization) of the modern economy, together with dramatic advances in modes of transportation and communication, has effectively shrunk the size of our nation (and world) and exposed commercial entities to personal jurisdiction in multiple states. Moreover, since subject matter jurisdiction requirements do not impose any independent geographic restraint on courts, it is not unusual for plaintiffs to be able to choose from a variety of forums, all of which meet the requirements for personal and subject matter jurisdiction.

For example, suppose a woman visiting New York City from Lake Placid, a village in northeastern New York State about 300 miles north of New York City, is involved in an automobile accident in New York City with a driver from New Jersey. Should she be able to file the suit in her hometown? If this defendant was also the absentee landlord of investment property in San Francisco, should the plaintiff be able to file her tort claim in Los Angeles or San Diego? Finally, what would happen if this plaintiff had been involved in an automobile accident on the Canadian side of the border with a driver from Quebec who frequently patronized restaurants in New York State?

Although the burdens of litigating in a distant or inconvenient forum play a key role in determining the existence of personal jurisdiction, the evolving jurisprudence reflects a distinctly relaxed application of that standard in the jurisdiction context. Consequently, to further restrict the plaintiff's ability to choose an inconvenient forum, Congress and all fifty state legislatures have enacted venue statutes. These laws are designed to channel lawsuits to courts within that sovereignty that are convenient to the parties and witnesses and that can efficiently handle the litigation. Thus, they address only litigative convenience and not adjudicative power. Moreover, they are not of constitutional dimension.

Nevertheless, venue requirements must be met (separate and apart from the subject matter and personal jurisdiction requirements) in every civil action. But as the role of the venue is to select from among the place or places with jurisdiction (personal and subject matter) those that are convenient to the parties and witnesses and that can efficiently dispose of the lawsuit, determining whether the plaintiff has laid venue in an appropriate court is undertaken only *after* the presence of jurisdiction has been established. Furthermore, where the plaintiff's choice of forum does not comply with the governing venue rules, it is the defendant's obligation to object. Here the rule mirrors the treatment of challenges to personal jurisdiction. That is, where the defendant does not assert a timely challenge to venue, the defect is waived and the court can hear the case.

While the specific factors used to determine venue vary from state to state, some generalizations can be made. As the principal objective of the venue requirement is to promote convenience to the parties and judicial efficiency, most state statutory schemes rely on one or more of the following factors: (a) residence of the plaintiff(s); (b) residence and/or business location of the defendant(s); (c) location of the events giving rise to the cause of action; and (d) situs of the object of the claim.

This chapter begins with an analysis of issues arising out of the venue rules. Here, as we did in connection with our discussion of subject matter jurisdiction, we have chosen to address these questions from the perspective of the comprehensive federal regime.

The latter two sections of the chapter concentrate on two responses to one particular venue-related phenomenon. Suppose the plaintiff lays venue in an appropriate forum. If either the defendant or the court itself believes that another tribunal, equally possessing of personal and subject matter jurisdiction, would be a more convenient forum, what, if anything, can be done? This will lead us to an examination of the statutory provision for transfer of venue and the related common law doctrine of *forum non conveniens*.

SECTION A. VENUE

Read 28 U.S.C. §§ 1390 & 1391, plus §§ 1404 & 1406.

The enactment of the Federal Courts Jurisdiction and Venue Clarification Act of 2011, 12 Stat. 758, Pub. L. 112-63, produced several important changes to the preexisting general venue statutes. It added, for the first time, at 28 U.S.C. §1390, a provision defining the meaning and scope of venue. Specifically, §1390(a) announces that venue serves only to specify the proper geographic location(s) in which to bring a suit when the case falls within the federal courts' subject matter jurisdiction. This provision also recognizes that venue requirements do not affect other statutory provisions that link subject matter jurisdiction to specific district or division. Section1390(c) makes clear that the general venue statute has no application to removed cases, whose venue is set forth in §1441(a) as the district in which the state court from which the case was removed is located. However, it also notes that the venue rules set forth in §1391 do apply to any venue assessments made as part of a decision concerning whether a removed case subsequently can be transferred under §§1404 or 1406.

Most importantly, however, the 2011 statute did away with the separate venue provisions for federal question and diversity-based actions that had been set forth in §§1391(a) and (b). Section 1391(a)(1) now states that all venue assessments are to be made under §1391(b), and, per §1391(a)(2), without any consideration of whether the action is local or transitory in nature. Section §1391(b) contains a single set of venue rules applicable to all federal actions "except as otherwise provided by law." This quoted language refers to the fact that many substantive federal statutes, including antitrust, bankruptcy, employment discrimination, labor, and patent laws, contain their own, specific venue provision. Civil actions brought under these enactments are subject to these special venue rules.

The substantive content of the venue rules, however, remains largely (though not entirely, as we will see in cases involving multiple defendants) intact. Section 1391(b) retains the two major options and the "fall-back" option for cases in which venue would not lie under either of the first two alternatives. Finally, newly worded §1391(d) retains the same definition of corporate residence for venue purposes that previously had been codified at §1391(c) with respect to corporations subject to personal jurisdiction in multi-district states. However, it eliminated the opening phrase of §1391(c) that had deemed a corporation a resident of any district in which it is subject to personal jurisdiction at the time the suit was filed.

Suppose, as is frequently the case, the plaintiff asserts several claims against one or more defendants in an action filed in federal district court. Some of these claims may arise under state law and some under federal law. The factors contained in the governing state law venue provisions may differ from those set forth in §1391(b). A complaint may also, or alternatively, contain some claims brought under the relatively small group of federal statutes that contain their own special venue provisions, which often differ from the terms of §1391(b). In these contexts, how is the court supposed to determine whether the plaintiff has laid venue in the proper district? Examine how the trial court in the following case handled this problem:

Coltrane v. Lappin

United States District Court, District of Columbia, 2012.

885 F. Supp. 2d 228.

WALTON, DISTRICT JUDGE.

Plaintiff Mary L. Coltrane, proceeding *pro se,* brings this action on behalf of herself and her deceased son, Carlton Coltrane, who was allegedly murdered on January 18, 2010, while under the care, custody, and control of the defendants at the United States Penitentiary, Pollock, Louisiana ("USP Pollock"). Currently before the Court is the defendants' motion to dismiss Counts 1 through 3 of the amended complaint or, in the alternative, to transfer this case to the United States District Court for the Western District of Louisiana. Upon careful consideration of the parties' submissions, the Court concludes for the following reasons that the defendants' alternative motion to transfer must be granted.

I. BACKGROUND

The amended complaint contains the following pertinent allegations. The plaintiff is a resident of the District of Columbia and the mother of the decedent, Carlton Coltrane, who was a federal prisoner detained at USP Pollock. On various occasions before January 18, 2010, Mr. Coltrane had informed USP Pollock staff, verbally and in writing, that he should be separated from the assailant or assailants involved in his murder, but they ignored these notices and generally failed to comply with Federal Bureau of Prisons' ("BOP") policies in handling his complaints. Then, on January 18, 2010, Coltrane was stabbed and murdered by one or more assailants at USP Pollock. The plaintiff was notified of her son's death on January 20, 2010.

The plaintiff instituted this action on January 18, 2011, and subsequently amended her complaint on December 16, 2011. The amended complaint names ten individual defendants, including Harley G. Lappin, former Director of the BOP, and Gerardo Maldonado, Jr., the Regional Director of the BOP charged with overseeing USP Pollock. The remaining eight individual defendants were employees of USP Pollock at the time of Mr. Coltrane's death. They are Joe Keffer; Newton E. Kendig, M.D.; Joel Alexander; John Doe or Jane Doe Operations Lieutenant; Willis Steortz, R.N.; Andre Molina Ossers, M.D.; Willie Vasquez, P.A.; and Dalynn Lentz, R.N. All of these defendants are sued in their personal and individual capacities. The United States is also named as a defendant.

The amended complaint sets forth three counts against the individual defendants: Count 1 asserts that the individual defendants engaged in a cover-up and conspiracy and continue to cover up the true facts of the murder of Carlton Coltrane in violation of the plaintiff's right to due process pursuant to the Fifth Amendment to the United States Constitution and the laws of the District of Columbia; Count 2 asserts that defendants Lappin, Maldonado, Keffer, John Doe or Jane Doe Operations Lieutenant, and Alexander maliciously deprived Carlton Coltrane of his life through their purposeful and deliberate failure to separate and protect him from the assailant or assailants that they knew or should have known were intent on doing him grievous bodily harm in violation of the Eighth Amendment to the United States Constitution and the laws of the District of Columbia; and Count 3 asserts that defendants Kendig, Alexander, Steortz, Molina Ossers, Vasquez, and Lentz maliciously deprived Carlton Coltrane of his life through their purposeful and deliberate failure to provide adequate medical care and transportation in a timely manner to the proper medical facilities in violation of the Eighth Amendment to the United States Constitution and the laws of the District of Columbia. Count 4 of the amended complaint asserts a tort claim against the United States for Mr. Coltrane's personal injury and death pursuant to the Federal Tort Claims Act ("FTCA").

The defendants have now moved to dismiss Counts 1 through 3 of the amended complaint for lack of subject matter jurisdiction under Federal Rule of Civil Procedure 12(b)(1), lack of personal jurisdiction under Rule 12(b)(2), improper venue under 12(b)(3), improper service of process under Rule 12(b)(5), and failure to state a claim upon which relief can be granted under Rule 12(b)(6). In the alternative, the defendants request that the Court transfer this case to the Western District of Louisiana.[3]

II. STANDARD OF REVIEW

Federal Rule of Civil Procedure 12(b)(3) authorizes a party to move for dismissal of a complaint for "improper venue." In considering a Rule 12(b)(3) motion, the court accepts the plaintiff's well-pled factual allegations regarding venue as true, draws all reasonable inferences from those allegations in the plaintiff's favor, and resolves any factual conflicts in the plaintiff's favor. Nevertheless, a plaintiff bears the burden of establishing that venue is proper. If a district court determines that venue is improper, it may either dismiss the case, "or if it be in the interest of justice, transfer such case to any district or division in which it could have been brought." 28 U.S.C. §1406(a).

III. ANALYSIS

A. The Plaintiff's Claims Against the Individual Defendants

1. Venue

Counts 1 through 3 of the amended complaint assert constitutional claims under the Fifth and Eighth Amendments against the individual defendants. The defendants move to dismiss these claims on the ground of improper venue.

The parties initially dispute which venue provision applies here. The defendants contend that the general venue provision, 28 U.S.C. §1391(b), applies because Counts 1 through 3 of the amended complaint seek money damages from the defendants in their individual capacities pursuant to *Bivens v. Six Unknown Named Agents of Federal Bureau of Narcotics,* 403 U.S. 388 (1971), and because venue in a *Bivens* case is governed by 28 U.S.C. §1391(b). The plaintiff, on the other hand, argues that the venue provision of 28 U.S.C. §1391(e) applies because she is suing the individual defendants in their official capacities.[5]

Even giving her the benefit of her *pro se* status, the Court finds the plaintiff's position meritless. First, her amended complaint premises venue in this Court solely on §1391(b); it does not mention §1391(e). Second, although

---

[3] The Court will only address the defendants' arguments regarding improper venue because it presents the most straightforward ground upon which to resolve the defendants' motion.

[5] 28 U.S.C. §1391(e)(1) provides as follows:

> A civil action in which a defendant is an officer or employee of the United States or any agency thereof acting in his official capacity or under color of legal authority, or an agency of the United States, or the United States, may, except as otherwise provided by law, be brought in any judicial district in which (A) a defendant in the action resides, (B) a substantial part of the events or omissions giving rise to the claim occurred, or a substantial part of property that is the subject of the action is situated, or (C) the plaintiff resides if no real property is involved in the action. * * *

the plaintiff now argues that she is suing the individual defendants in their official capacities and apparently is not advancing *Bivens* claims, her amended complaint asserts constitutional claims against the defendants only in their individual capacities, and requests compensatory damages from each individual defendant.[6] These are quintessential *Bivens* claims. Because §1391(e) applies only to suits against government officers in their official capacities, and not to *Bivens* actions, the controlling venue provision here is §1391(b).[7]

Having determined the applicable venue provision, the question now becomes whether venue properly lies in this District under §1391(b) with respect to the plaintiff's *Bivens* claims. Section 1391(b) provides that a civil action may be brought in any judicial district (1) "in which any defendant resides, if all defendants are residents of the State in which the district is located"; (2) "in which a substantial part of the events or omissions giving rise to the claim occurred, or a substantial part of property that is the subject of the action is situated"; or (3) "if there is no district in which an action may otherwise be brought as provided in this section, any judicial district in which any defendant is subject to the court's personal jurisdiction with respect to such action." As the defendants argue and the plaintiff does not contest, none of the provisions of §1391(b) authorize venue in this District because: (1) all of the individual defendants do not reside in the District of Columbia; (2) a substantial part of the events or omissions giving rise to the plaintiff's claims (all of which relate to the treatment and murder of her son at USP Pollock) did not occur in the District of Columbia; and (3) there *is* a judicial district in which venue would be proper under §1391(b)(2) — the Western District of Louisiana.

While not disputing the impropriety of venue in this District under §1391(b), the plaintiff asserts, without elaboration, that this Court should entertain her *Bivens* claims against the individual defendants pursuant to the doctrine of "pendent venue." Generally, a plaintiff must demonstrate proper venue with respect to each cause of action and each defendant. But when venue lies for *some* of a plaintiff's claims, the doctrine of pendent venue may allow the court to entertain other claims that are not properly venued in the court. Pursuant to pendent venue, federal courts may exercise their discretion to hear claims as to which venue is lacking if those claims arise out of a common nucleus of operative facts as the claims that are appropriately venued *and* the interests of judicial economy are furthered by hearing the claims together. The judicial efficiency rationale for pendent venue makes it clear that a district court has wide discretion to refuse to hear a pendent claim.

---

[6] Even assuming the plaintiff had asserted claims for money damages against the individual defendants in their official capacities, the Court would lack subject matter jurisdiction over those claims due to sovereign immunity.

[7] In addition to seeking money damages, the amended complaint requests a declaratory judgment that the practices, acts, and omissions complained of herein violated the plaintiff's rights. Assuming that this request for declaratory relief could be construed as a non-monetary claim against the individual defendants in their official capacities, §1391(e) would indeed be the controlling venue provision for this claim. Nevertheless, the Court would lack subject matter jurisdiction over the claim because an official capacity suit against a federal employee is deemed a suit against the United States, and the Declaratory Judgment Act does not waive the federal government's sovereign immunity.

Here, the Court declines to exercise pendent venue over the plaintiff's *Bivens* claims against the individual defendants. To be sure, venue is proper in this Court as to the plaintiff's FTCA claim against the United States because the plaintiff resides in the District of Columbia. *See* 28 U.S.C. §1402(b) ("Any civil action on a tort claim against the United States under subsection (b) of section 1346 of this title may be prosecuted only *in the judicial district where the plaintiff resides* or wherein the act or omission complained of occurred." The plaintiff's FTCA claim could, therefore, serve as the requisite "hook" for the Court to exercise pendent venue over the plaintiffs' *Bivens* claims. The Court finds for the following reasons, however, that exercising pendent venue here would not further the goals of judicial economy, convenience, and fairness to the litigants. First, considerations of convenience, such as proximity to witnesses and evidence, indicate that the Western District of Louisiana would be a more suitable forum for this case, given that the events that form the basis for the plaintiff's claims occurred at USP Pollock in Louisiana. Second, it would be inefficient to retain venue over the plaintiffs' *Bivens* claims because, without reaching the merits of the issue, this Court deems it highly unlikely that it has personal jurisdiction over at least seven of the individual defendants due to their lack of contacts with the District of Columbia. Needless to say, it would be futile to exercise pendent venue with respect to claims asserted against defendants over which this Court lacks personal jurisdiction. These considerations caution against invoking pendent venue in this case.

2. Transfer or Dismissal

Having determined that venue is improper as to the plaintiff's *Bivens* claims and that pendent venue is inappropriate, the Court may either dismiss the case, "or if it be in the interest of justice, transfer [the] case to any district or division in which it could have been brought." 28 U.S.C. §1406(a). Before transferring a case pursuant to §1406(a), a district court must decide as a preliminary matter that venue and jurisdiction would be proper as to all defendants in the transferee court. Once these prerequisites are satisfied, the decision whether a transfer or a dismissal is in the interest of justice rests within the sound discretion of the district court. The District of Columbia Circuit favors transfer under §1406(a) "when procedural obstacles" — such as "lack of personal jurisdiction, improper venue and statute of limitations bars — impede an expeditious and orderly adjudication on the merits." *Sinclair v. Kleindienst,*711 F.2d 291 (D.C.Cir.1983). And transfer is particularly favored over dismissal when the plaintiff is proceeding *pro se.*

The defendants argue that if the Court decides not to dismiss the plaintiff's *Bivens* claims, the claims should be transferred to the Western District of Louisiana. In evaluating whether this case is even *eligible* for transfer under §1406(a), the Court must first determine that the transferee court would possess both venue and personal jurisdiction. The Court finds that both conditions are satisfied here. To begin with, venue for the plaintiff's *Bivens* claims is proper in the Western District of Louisiana because that is the "judicial district in which a substantial part of the events or omissions giving rise to the claim[s] occurred." 28 U.S.C. §1391(b)(2); *see also* Defs.' Reply at 14 (conceding that "venue for this entire case is proper in the Western District of Louisiana"). In addition, the allegations in the amended complaint indicate that the Western District of Louisiana could exercise personal jurisdiction over the individual defendants based on the injuries they allegedly caused in Louisiana and their minimum contacts with that state. *See* La.Rev.Stat.Ann. §13:3201(A)(3) (Louisiana Long–Arm Statute) ("A court may exercise personal jurisdiction over a nonresident, who acts directly or by an agent, as to a cause of action arising from any . . . activity performed by the nonresident . . . causing injury or damage by an offense or quasi offense committed through an act or omission in this state."); *see also* §13:3201(B) ("[A] court of this state may exercise personal jurisdiction over a nonresident on any basis consistent with the constitution of this state and of the Constitution of the United States."). The defendants appear to concede this point. *See* Defs.' Mem. at 37 (The "plaintiff alleges that the individual defendants caused injuries within Louisiana either through an act or omission in that state or outside of it. Therefore, the U.S. District Court for the Western District of Louisiana would have personal jurisdiction over these defendants.").

With the prerequisites of venue and personal jurisdiction in the transferee court being satisfied, the Court has discretion to transfer this case to the Western District of Louisiana if it is "in the interest of justice." 28 U.S.C. §1406(a). Upon consideration of the relevant factors, the Court finds that transferring this case would indeed be in the interest of justice for the following reasons. First, procedural obstacles such as improper venue and lack of personal jurisdiction will impede an expeditious and orderly adjudication on the merits in this District, but not in the Western District of Louisiana. Second, the plaintiff is proceeding *pro* se and transfer is therefore favored over dismissal. Third, the Western District of Louisiana is the appropriate forum for this case because, as already noted, the plaintiff's claims arise principally out of events that occurred at USP Pollock in Louisiana, and convenience factors consequently weigh in favor of litigating this case in that District. Fourth, this lawsuit has no discernible connection to the District of Columbia. Accordingly, the Court will transfer the plaintiff's *Bivens* claims to the Western District of Louisiana pursuant to 28 U.S.C. §1406(a).

B. The Plaintiff's FTCA Claim against the United States

The plaintiff's FTCA claim is properly venued in this Court because the plaintiff resides in the District of Columbia. 28 U.S.C. §1402(b). But venue for her FTCA claim would also be proper in the Western District of Louisiana under §1402(b) because that was the "judicial district . . . wherein the act or omission complained of occurred." Thus, rather than bifurcating the litigation of the case by transferring only the plaintiff's *Bivens* claims, the Court will transfer the *entire* case to the Western District of Louisiana. Such an approach is common in this Circuit. *See, e.g., Sierra Club,* 623 F.Supp.2d at 38 n. 4 ("Although two of Plaintiff's claim are otherwise subject to proper venue in the District of Columbia, courts in this district have consistently transferred an entire case to another judicial district, rather than bifurcate the litigation."). As in *Sierra Club,* this Court finds that transferring all of the claims to the same forum assures that they will be heard together, preventing the unnecessary expenditure of judicial and party resources that would otherwise occur if the claims were heard in multiple judicial districts.

IV. CONCLUSION

For the foregoing reasons, the defendants' alternative motion to transfer is granted.

NOTES AND PROBLEMS FOR DISCUSSION

1. Does venue lie in the chosen forum in the following situations?

(a) Joe, a Houston domiciliary, was on vacation in New Orleans when his automobile collided with a truck owned by Jane, a New Orleanian, and driven by her friend Paul, a domiciliary of Baton Rouge. Joe brings a tort action seeking $150,000 in damages against both Jane and Paul in the Eastern District of Louisiana, which is located in New Orleans.

(b) Same facts as in "(a)" except that Joe files his action in the Middle District of Louisiana, located in Baton Rouge.

(c) Same facts as in "(a)" except that Joe files his action in the Southern District of Texas, located in Houston. Assume also that both defendants are subject to personal jurisdiction in Texas.

Suppose the owner of the truck had been United Van Lines, rather than Jane and that United Van Lines, a national shipping company that is incorporated under Delaware law and headquartered in Chicago, did lots of business in New Orleans. Joe chooses to file his suit in Chicago.

(d) While on a vacation cruise, Roy, a resident of New York City, disembarked to tour Cancun, Mexico. He was one of several vacationers who rented cars in Cancun. Unfortunately, two other rental cars driven by fellow vacationers sideswiped his car. One of those drivers was a resident of Los Angeles and the other came from Detroit. Roy brings a $200,000 tort action against both drivers in the Southern District of New York, located in his hometown.

(e) Same facts as in "(d)" except that Roy brings his action in the Eastern District of Michigan and names as defendants the driver from Detroit and the cruise line company, Carnival Cruise Lines, a corporation that is incorporated under Delaware law and has its principal place of business in San Francisco.

(f) Jane, a croupier from Boston who spent the summer of 2000 working in the casino of a Carnival Cruise Lines ship, claimed that while the ship was docked at Cancun, her supervisor, Bill, the pit boss, subjected her to sexual harassment by making unwelcomed sexual advances towards her. She brought an action under Title VII of the federal Civil Rights Act against both Bill and Carnival Cruise Lines in the District of Massachusetts. Bill resides in Greenville, South Carolina, but worked during the past ten summers at various hotels on Cape Cod, Massachusetts. Assume that Carnival would not be subject to personal jurisdiction in South Carolina and that the Civil Rights Act does not contain its own venue provision.

(g) Same facts as "(f)" except that Jane asserted her Title VII claim against only Carnival and brought a $100,000 tort claim for intentional infliction of emotional distress against Bill.

(h) Same facts as "(g)" except that Bill is a French national.

(i) Henri, a French national living in Philadelphia, brings an action in federal court in Philadelphia against Jane, a Boston resident, for defamation and seeks $250,000 in damages.

(j) Pat, a Denver resident, bought what he thought was an original Georgia O'Keefe painting at an art gallery in Santa Fe, New Mexico. When Pat discovered it was a fake, Pat brought an $850,000 breach of contract claim against Leslie, the owner of the art gallery, in state court in Denver. Colorado's venue statute provides for venue in the city where the plaintiff resides. Leslie subsequently removed the case in a timely fashion. Pat filed a motion to remand for lack of venue.

(k) Sue, an author residing in Atlanta, brings an action under a federal statute against Laura, a resident of Seattle. Since she cannot obtain personal jurisdiction over Laura anywhere but in the state of Washington, Sue files this action in the federal district court in Seattle. Assume that this federal statute provides that all actions brought to enforce the rights guaranteed therein must be filed in the federal district court for the district in which the plaintiff resides.

(l) Bob, a Milwaukee client of a Chicago law firm, brings a $250,000 negligence action against the entire firm in the federal district court in Milwaukee. The law firm is organized as a partnership.

2. Although the principal case, and several of the hypotheticals in Note 1, raised the question of how venue is determined in a multi-party, multi-claim civil action, in all of these instances the claims were filed only by the plaintiff. An examination of the application of federal venue rules to other types of claims, such as counter-claims, cross-claims, and third party claims, as well as the application of the venue rules to class actions, can be found in the materials in Chapter 10 that deal directly with those subjects. But does the language in both §§1391(a) and (b) stating that a civil action "may be brought" suggest anything about the application of these rules to such claims?

3. Is the treatment of aliens for venue purposes consistent with the manner in which aliens are treated for subject matter jurisdiction purposes?

4. What is the impact on venue requirements of contractual forum selection clauses that designate a specific federal district court as the exclusive forum?

Suppose a forum selection clause stated that "exclusive venue for any litigation related hereto shall occur in Jones County, Alabama." If the plaintiff files suit in federal district court located in Jones County, how should the trial judge rule on the defense motion to dismiss for improper venue? In ALLIANCE HEALTH GROUP LLC v. BRIDGING HEALTH OPTIONS LLC, 553 F.3d 397 (5th Cir. 2008), the Fifth Circuit affirmed the trial judge's denial of a motion to dismiss under these precise circumstances. Distinguishing the instant case from a situation where the plaintiff filed suit in a federal district court that encompassed, but was not physically located within the contractually designated

County, the court construed the selection clause to permit filings in a state or federal court that was located within the designated county. The court also emphasized that since the clause made reference only to courts "in" and not "of" the county, it should not be construed to preclude suit in a federal court since a federal court could be "in" a state but could not be "of" a state.

5. The court in *Coltrane* noted that §1406 provides two alternative remedies for improper venue. Does §1406 suggest a hierarchy of preferred remedies?

SECTION B. TRANSFER OF VENUE

Notwithstanding the fact that venue rules are rooted in convenience and efficiency concerns, the liberal provisions of the federal venue statute have not operated to restrict significantly a plaintiff's choice of forums. When combined with the relaxed application of the constitutional requirements for exercising personal jurisdiction, these broad venue provisions still permit plaintiffs to choose a forum that provides, in their views, tactical or other advantages. To respond to the opportunity for wide-ranging "forum shopping," Congress passed a statute providing either party with the option of transferring the case from a federal district possessing jurisdiction and venue to another, more convenient district with jurisdiction and venue. And while comparable statutory or common law rules exist under state law permitting transfers between courts within the same state, we will focus our attention on the federal transfer of venue provision.

Read 28 U.S.C. §§1404 & 1406.

Manley v. Navmar Applied Sciences Corp.

United States District Court, Eastern District of Pennsylvania, 2012.
2012 WL 5588757.

SANCHEZ, DISTRICT JUDGE.

Pro se Plaintiffs Eric Manley, Skylier Smith, and George Cook bring this unlawful termination action against Defendant Navmar Applied Sciences Corp. (Navmar) and nine individual defendants. Navmar and individual Defendant Thomas Fenerty[1] ask this Court to transfer this action to the United States District Court for the District of Arizona because, although Navmar has its principal place of business in Pennsylvania, all of the underlying events giving rise to this action occurred at its operations in Arizona, and only two of the individual defendants reside in Pennsylvania. Plaintiffs concede all of the events at issue occurred in Arizona, but argue their choice of forum should not be disturbed because Navmar is based in Pennsylvania and it would be too costly for them to litigate this case in Arizona, as they reside in Georgia and Texas.

---

[1] Individual Defendant Thomas Fenerty joined in Navmar's motion to transfer.

* * *

For the following reasons, Navmar's motion to transfer will be denied, and Navmar's motion to dismiss will be granted.

FACTS

This lawsuit centers around a six-week training program instituted by Navmar in 2011 at its Yuma, Arizona operations. Plaintiffs were hired by Navmar to attend the Yuma program, but were discharged prior to graduating from the program. Plaintiffs assert a myriad of claims against Navmar and nine individual Defendants, only one of whom has been served to date. This Defendant, Fenerty, resides in Pennsylvania. Seven of the remaining eight individual Defendants are either current or former employees of Navmar. According to Navmar's employment records containing the last-known addresses of its current and former employees, one of these Defendants resides in Pennsylvania, three reside in Arizona, one resides in Maryland, one resides in Virginia, and one resides in Texas. The final individual Defendant is a government employee who worked together with Navmar at its Yuma operations. Navmar is uncertain of this Defendant's current residence, though suspects he still resides in Arizona. It does not appear that any of these eight Defendants has been served to date. Moreover, although the pleadings are unclear, from what this Court can discern after hearing oral argument on Navmar's pending motions, Plaintiffs allege they were treated unfairly during the training program, and ultimately wrongfully terminated because of their race. In their Complaint, Plaintiffs allege an array of federal claims, including claims pursuant to, *inter alia,* 42 U.S.C. §1981, 42 U.S.C. §2000e, and 29 U.S.C. §621, as well as a host of state law claims, including, *inter alia,* breach of contract, negligent hiring, negligent supervision, negligent training, and tortious interference with contractual relations.

DISCUSSION

In support of their argument to transfer this case to Arizona, Defendants rely on the general venue statute, 28 U.S.C. §1391(b). * * *

In federal court, questions concerning proper venue are governed by 28 U.S.C. §§1404(a) or 1406. Section 1404(a) governs disputes where both the original and requested venue are proper, while §1406 applies where the original venue is improper, and provides for either transfer or dismissal of the case. In their motion, Navmar and Fenerty seek transfer for improper venue under §1406(a) and, in the alternative, for the convenience of the parties and in the interest of justice under §1404(a). Under §1391, venue is not proper in this district because all Defendants do not reside in Pennsylvania, the events giving rise to Plaintiffs' claims did not occur in this district, and there is another district in which this action may be brought. Thus, if §1391 were applicable to this case as Defendants argue, §1406(a) would require either transfer to the proper venue (Arizona) or dismissal of the case. 28 U.S.C. §1406(a). However, §1391 does not apply here because Navmar removed this case from state court. Thus, the removal statute governs the question of venue and provides for removal "to the district court of the United States for the district and division embracing the place where [the state action] is pending." 28 U.S.C. §1441(a). This action was originally filed in the Court of Common Pleas in Bucks County and could only have been removed to this federal district. *See* 28 U.S.C. §118(a) (providing that Eastern District includes Bucks County). By removing the case, Navmar effectively waived its objection to venue. Because venue in this district is proper, transfer pursuant to §1406(a) is inapplicable.

Even though venue is proper in this district, the case may still be transferred to Arizona pursuant to §1404(a). It is well settled that a court may transfer any civil action to any other district or division where it might have been brought "[f]or the convenience of parties and witnesses, in the interest of justice." 28 U.S.C. §1404(a). The purpose of the transfer provision is to prevent the waste of time, energy, and money and to protect litigants, witnesses and the public against unnecessary inconvenience and expense. Although a court has broad discretion to decide whether to order a transfer, a motion to transfer is not to be liberally granted. Indeed, a plaintiff's choice of venue should not be lightly disturbed. The burden of establishing the need for transfer rests with the moving party. The movant must prove with particularity the reasons why it is inconvenienced by the plaintiff's choice of forum.

In deciding whether to transfer a case to another district, a court should consider the following private and public interests: (1) the plaintiff's choice of forum; (2) the defendant's preference; (3) where the claim arose; (4) the convenience of the parties; (5) the convenience of the witnesses, but only to the extent the witnesses may actually be unavailable for trial in one of the fora; (6) the location of books and records, similarly limited to the extent the files could not be produced in the alternative forum; (7) the enforceability of the judgment; (8) practical considerations that could make the trial easy, expeditious, or inexpensive; (9) relative court congestion in the competing courts; (10) the local interest in deciding local controversies at home; (11) public policies of the fora; and (12) the familiarity of the trial judge with the applicable state law.

A plaintiff's choice of forum typically receives paramount consideration. Nevertheless, a court's analysis should focus on whether the requested forum is more convenient than the plaintiff's chosen forum and promotes considerations of justice. Where the plaintiff chooses a forum other than his state of residence, his choice is given considerably less weight. The plaintiff's choice is also given less deference when none of the operative facts underlying the claim occurred there. However, unless the balance of convenience of the parties is *strongly* in favor of defendant, the plaintiff's choice of forum should prevail.

Here, the only connection Pennsylvania has to this case is that two of the individual defendants reside in this Commonwealth, and Navmar has its principal place of business here. Consequently, Defendants argue Pennsylvania has no interest in adjudicating this dispute and this case should be transferred.

Indeed, several factors favor transfer: all of the operative facts giving rise to Plaintiffs' claims arose in Yuma, Arizona; Navmar's operations relevant to these claims are located in Yuma, Arizona; employment records relevant to the claims are presumably located in Yuma, given the nature of the allegations; Arizona's local interest in resolving its local controversies at home; Arizona's interest in resolving disputes involving its own law (to the extent Arizona law will apply to Plaintiffs' claims); the fact that a trial judge in the Eastern District of Pennsylvania has less familiarity with Arizona law than does a trial judge in the District of Arizona; Arizona is a more convenient forum for the three or four of the nine individual Defendants who reside there and for Navmar, which has its relevant operations there; and Arizona is a more convenient forum for any non-party witnesses, particularly if those witnesses still work for Navmar's Yuma operations and thus, presumably reside in Arizona. While these last factors concerning convenience of parties and witnesses normally weigh heavily in favor of transfer, the current posture of this case indicates these factors should be given less deference: none of the individual Defendants living in Arizona have been served to date, and the Court is unaware of any non-party witnesses. Courts consider the convenience of witnesses, but only to the extent that the witnesses may actually be unavailable for trial in one of the fora. Thus, at this time, trying this case in this district is more convenient for Fenerty, the one individual Defendant who has been served and who resides here.

By contrast, only a select number of factors weigh against transfer: the Plaintiffs' choice of forum; the convenience to Plaintiffs of trying this case here rather than in Arizona; the practical concerns of ease and expense of trial; and the proximity of the two fora, which is a greater issue when the two fora are not geographically close, as here. Though fewer in number, these factors carry significant weight given that Plaintiffs, pro se litigants, filed suit here on the basis of cost. Plaintiffs argue if this case were transferred to Arizona, they would face a much greater financial burden. For its part, Navmar does not argue that Pennsylvania is inconvenient to any current employee, named or not named in this lawsuit. In fact, Navmar has not identified any witnesses who will be inconvenienced by a denial of its motion, other than the individual Defendants who reside in Arizona. However, as set forth above, those Defendants have not yet been served in this action. Similarly, Navmar has not indicated whether transfer of this action would facilitate ease of access to sources of proof. While the nature of the allegations suggests that all relevant books and records would likely be maintained in Arizona, Navmar fails to demonstrate the extent or nature of such materials or whether there is any hardship in producing them here. Thus, although Navmar may incur costs in transporting materials or witnesses relevant to trial to this district, as a corporation, it is more capable of shouldering the financial burden of trial than the individual Plaintiffs. Accordingly, ordering transfer at this stage in the litigation would simply shift the expense to the parties less able to bear it. This weighs against transferring the case. Navmar argues only that the facts of this case bear no relation to the Eastern District of Pennsylvania and the case should therefore be transferred. While this may be true, Plaintiffs have chosen to litigate their claims in this forum, to which Navmar, by removing this case, waived any objection. Accordingly, to protect Plaintiffs' rights as pro se litigants - even if Plaintiffs' plea to keep this case in this district is fatal to some of their claims (based on jurisdictional issues that may arise)—this Court denies Navmar's motion to transfer without prejudice.

NOTES AND PROBLEMS FOR DISCUSSION

1. Compare §§1404 and 1406 with respect to:
    (a) the contexts in which they apply,
    (b) the standards governing the decision to transfer an action,
    (c) the consequence of declining to transfer the case, and
    (d) the impact of forum selection clauses on the court's power to transfer.

See Stewart Organization, Inc. v. Ricoh Corp., 487 U.S. 22, 108 S.Ct. 2239, 101 L.Ed.2d 22 (1988).

2. The transfer of a case from one federal district to another district raises an important choice of laws question. In VAN DUSEN v. BARRACK, 376 U.S. 612, 84 S.Ct. 805, 11 L.Ed.2d (1964), the Supreme Court held that when a diversity case is transferred under §1404, the transferee court must apply the same law, including the choice of law rules, which would have governed the transferor court. The rationale for this rule is that while a defendant is provided with an opportunity to overturn the plaintiff's choice of forum, §1404 was not designed to displace the state law advantages that the plaintiff might accrue from choosing among available forums. The Court rejected the "rather startling conclusion that one might get a change of law as a bonus for a change of venue." Instead, it emphasized that the sole purpose of §1404 was to authorize only a change of courtrooms on the basis of convenience and fairness.

Although this result clearly does nothing to discourage plaintiffs from shopping for a forum with advantageous law, that die was already cast by the enactment of liberal venue provisions which anticipate not only that a plaintiff will be able to choose among a multitude of available forums, but that this choice will be predicated upon a variety of factors, including choice of law considerations. On the other hand, when a case is transferred pursuant to §1406 — i.e., as a remedy for improper venue — the transferee court is to be treated as the court of initial filing, i.e., it must apply the substantive and choice of law rules that it would have applied had the plaintiff originally brought suit there. How do you explain this different result?

Once a case has been transferred under §1406, in determining whether the action is time barred by the limitations statute of the transferee forum, should the transferee court calculate the date of filing from the date of the filing in the (venue-defective) transferor forum or from the date of transfer? See Lafferty v. St. Riel, 495 F.3d 72 (3d Cir. 2007) (concluding that, at least where the limitations periods in the transferee and transferor forums are identical, the date of initial filing in the transferor forum counts as the date of filing for limitations analysis by the transferee court).

Alternatively, suppose the plaintiff's suit is based on a violation of a federal statute and the issue in dispute is one as to which the Supreme Court has not spoken. After the case is transferred under §1404, should the transferee court apply the teachings of its circuit on this question or should it be bound by the interpretation provided by the transferor circuit?

3. How should the following problems be resolved?

(a) A New Mexico plaintiff brings a $250,000 breach of contract claim against an Arizona defendant in federal court in New Mexico. Most of the events giving rise to the claim arose in New Mexico. The defendant, who is subject to personal jurisdiction in New Mexico, moves to transfer the case to the federal District of Colorado and in his motion states that although it has no contacts with the state of Colorado, he will waive all objections to personal jurisdiction and venue in that state.

(b) Same facts as "(a)", except that the defendant moved to Denver after the plaintiff filed her complaint but before he filed his motion to transfer.

(c) A North Dakota plaintiff brings $300,000 tort claims in a North Dakota federal court against two defendants, one an Idaho citizen and the other a citizen of Massachusetts. All of the events giving rise to the claim occurred in North Dakota, which is also the location of all witnesses to the accident that generated the action. After the complaint was filed, the plaintiff reached a settlement with the Massachusetts defendant and dismissed her from the suit. Thereafter, the Idaho defendant moved to transfer the case to the District of Idaho.

In IN RE VOLKSWAGEN OF AMERICA, INC., 545 F.3d 304 (5th Cir. 2008) (en banc), the Fifth Circuit, in an *en banc* opinion, ruled that a writ of mandamus was an appropriate means to test, on appeal, a trial court's ruling on a §1404(a) motion to transfer. The court declared, however, that it would only replace the district's court's judgment when it found that the trial court had committed a "clear" abuse of discretion that produced a "patently erroneous result." In applying that standard to the instant case, the Fifth Circuit found that the trial judge, in denying the defense motion to transfer, had given inordinate weight to the plaintiff's choice of venue. The court noted that the plaintiff's chosen forum had no connection to the parties, the witnesses, or the facts of the case, and that transfers can be granted upon a lesser showing of inconvenience than dismissals based on the doctrine of *forum non conveniens*. It stated that the trial court had erred in applying the more stringent standard applicable to a *forum non conveniens* motion for dismissal to a §1404(a) motion to transfer. By requiring the movants to show that the §1404(a) convenience factors "substantially outweighed" the plaintiff's choice of venue, the Fifth Circuit held, the trial court had applied the wrong legal standard. A plaintiff's choice of venue should be respected, the Fifth Circuit continued, *only* "when the transferee venue is not clearly more convenient than the venue chosen by the plaintiff." Thus, assuming the transferee venue is one in which the action might have been brought, where the movants demonstrates that the transferee venue is "clearly" more convenient than the plaintiff's chosen venue, the court should grant the transfer.

(d) A plaintiff from Maine filed a breach of contract claim in the federal district court for the District of Maine against a rare stamp dealer when he discovered that several stamps that he purchased at the dealer's store in Honolulu, Hawaii, were not what they were represented to be. The defendant, who has no contacts of any kind with Maine, filed a motion to transfer the case to the District of Hawaii. See Goldlawr v. Heiman, 369 U.S. 463, 82 S.Ct. 913, 8 L.Ed.2d 39 (1962).

(e) While visiting his brother in Cleveland, Ohio, a librarian from San Diego, California visited a local bakery. Upon returning home, the librarian discovered that he had contracted food poisoning and filed a tort claim seeking $200,000 in damages against the bakery in state court in San Diego. The defendant, who maintains an interactive web site, a toll free telephone number, and ships hundreds of its specialty cakes to customers in all fifty states, wants the case to be heard in the federal district court in Cleveland. Can he accomplish this objective?

(f) A Florida citizen brings an action under state law seeking an injunction and $25 million in damages against an Indiana development company to stop its construction of a hotel in the Florida Everglades. Believing that California law was most hospitable to such a claim, the attorney filed the action in a federal court in Los Angeles. Although none of the events underlying the claim are connected to California, because it does business all over the country, the defendant is subject to jurisdiction in that state. The plaintiff subsequently moves to transfer the case to the district court in Miami. See Ferens v. John Deere Co., 494 U.S. 516, 110 S.Ct. 1274, 108 L.Ed.2d 443 (1990).

(g) A New Hampshire citizen injured in an automobile accident in New York involving the drivers of two other cars, one a citizen of Connecticut and the other a Minnesota citizen, brought a $430,000 tort claim in federal court in New Hampshire. Both defendants had sufficient contacts with New Hampshire to be subject to personal jurisdiction there. But while all of the events relevant to the claim, including the plaintiff's hospitalization, occurred in New York, the defendants failed to file a timely motion challenging the New Hampshire district court's venue. Nevertheless, they subsequently filed a motion to transfer the case to the federal district court in New York where the accident occurred. How should the court rule on this motion?

(h) The federal Securities and Exchange Commission sued Apex, Inc. in federal court in Chicago alleging various violations of the federal securities laws. The defendant is a Wisconsin corporation that has a few clients in Illinois but does most of its business in Wisconsin. Accordingly, the defendant filed a §1404 motion to transfer the case to Wisconsin. How should the court rule? See In re National Presto Industries, Inc., 347 F.3d 662 (7th Cir.2003).

4. A separate provision, 28 U.S.C. §1407, provides the federal Judicial Panel on Multidistrict Litigation with the authority to transfer cases filed in a variety of districts into one district court, for pretrial purposes only, where these separate actions involve at least one common question of fact and where consolidation of the cases will serve the convenience of the parties and witnesses and promote the just and efficient prosecution of the cases. In such instances, the chosen district need not be one in which venue would lie for each of the consolidated cases. And although §1407 provides only for consolidation for pretrial purposes, it had become increasingly common for the district court to which the cases have been transferred to decline to remand the cases, as provided in §1407, when pretrial proceedings have been concluded. Instead, the court typically retained the cases for trial by transferring them to itself under §1404. However, in LEXECON INC. v. MILBERG WEISS BERSHAD HYNES & LERACH, 523 U.S. 26, 118 S.Ct. 956, 140 L.Ed.2d 62 (1998), the Supreme Court forbad this practice by ruling that it was prohibited by the terms of §1407. Section 1407 is most commonly used in airplane crash and other mass tort cases.

5. Suppose two parties enter into a contract that contains a contractually valid forum selection clause which designates a particular federal district as the situs for any litigation arising under the contract. Further assume, however, that the plaintiff chooses to file suit in a different federal district, but one in which venue would lie under §1391. If the defendant wants to object, is that objection properly made under §1404 or §1406 or Rule 12(b)(3)? In ATLANTIC MARINE CONSTRUCTION CO., INC. v. UNITED STATES DISTRICT COURT FOR THE WESTERN DISTRICT OF TEXAS, 571 U.S. ___, 134 S.Ct. 568, 187 L.Ed.2d 487 (2013), the Supreme Court unanimously ruled that where (1) venue lies in the plaintiff's chosen forum pursuant to the federal venue laws, and (2) a valid forum selection clause points to a different *federal* forum, then §1404(a) is the proper mechanism for enforcing that forum selection clause. The Court explained that §1406(a) (providing transfer when venue is bad because brought in the "wrong" district) and Rule 12(b)(3) (providing for dismissal for "improper" venue) apply only to cases where venue does *not* lie in the plaintiff's chosen forum and that the determination of whether venue was appropriate depends exclusively on the terms of the federal venue laws and not on the provisions of the forum selection clause. Consequently, it explained, where venue *does* lie under §1391 or any other applicable federal venue statutory provision, neither §1406(a) nor Rule 12(b)(3) is a proper vehicle for a motion to transfer or dismiss the case based on the presence of a forum selection clause. The terms of a forum selection clause are irrelevant to a determination of whether venue lies in a federally filed suit, the Court reasoned, because Congress contemplated the availability of federal venue (per §1391) when either the defendant's residence or substantial part of the underlying events was located in a federal district, or, as a fallback, where at least one defendant was subject to the personal jurisdiction of a federal court. Instead, §1404(a) is the proper mechanism for enforcing a valid forum selection clause because it permits transfer from a district where venue does lie to another district to which the parties have agreed by contract. (Although an *amicus* before the Court asserted that a defendant should be able to seek dismissal pursuant to the terms of a valid forum selection clause by filing a Rule 12(b)(6) motion for failure to state a claim, since the defendant had not filed such a motion in the instant case and since the parties had not briefed the issue, the Court declined to rule on it. It noted however, that if it were to rule that a defendant could use Rule 12(b)(6) to enforce a forum selection clause, it was unlikely that defendants would choose that route over §1404(a) (or *forum non conveniens*) because such a motion "might lead to a jury trial on venue if issues of material fact relating to the validity of the forum selection clause arise.")

Having concluded that forum selection clauses are to be enforced in this context by a motion to transfer under §1404(a), the Court in *Atlantic Marine* then addressed the method by which district courts should assess the balance of fairness and convenience interests required by that provision. The Court ruled that the balance of interests calculation normally undertaken in connection with a motion to transfer under §1404(a) must be "adjusted" in three ways given the presence of a contractually valid forum selection clause. First, the Court announced, the plaintiff's choice of forum is to be accorded no weight. Second, the trial court must not consider arguments about the parties' private interests. Having agreed to the chosen forum, the plaintiff already had exercised its privilege to choose the venue and all parties to the agreement had waived the right to challenge the preselected forum as inconvenient for themselves or their witnesses. And while this still permits the trial court to consider arguments concerning public interest factors, the Court opined, this will rarely defeat transfer. Third, and perhaps most significantly, the *Van Dusen* choice of law doctrine will not apply when transfer is made under §1404(a) to enforce a forum selection clause. This means that the law will not follow the case, but, rather, the transferee court in a diversity action will apply the law and choice of law rules of the State in which it is located, rather than the law and choice of law rules of the transferor court as in *Van Dusen*. The Court justified this departure from *Van Dusen* on the ground that by filing suit in contravention of the terms of a forum selection clause to which it had agreed, the plaintiff had forfeited its privilege of choosing the venue and the governing law. Therefore, the Court declared, in making the balance of interests calculation required under §1404(a), the terms of the forum selection clause must be given "controlling weight" in all but the most exceptional circumstances. Accordingly, it ruled, the §1404(a) motion to transfer should ordinarily be granted and the trial judge should transfer the case to the contractually specified forum except under extraordinary circumstances unrelated to the convenience of the parties.

Finally, the Court discussed the proper approach towards dealing with cases where the plaintiff's chosen forum meets the requirements of the governing federal venue statute but the forum selection clause points to only a nonfederal (i.e., foreign country or state) court. Once again, it stated, whether venue exists is governed exclusively by the federal venue laws, and because venue would be appropriate in this scenario, §1406(a) and Rule 12(b)(3) would be inapplicable. However, since §1404(a) does not provide for transfer to a nonfederal court, it could not be used to enforce such a forum selection clause. Instead, the Court opined, the appropriate way to enforce such a clause would be through a motion to dismiss based on the doctrine of *forum non conveniens*. And in applying that doctrine, the Court added, the court should give the same virtually dispositive weight to the terms of the forum selection clause that now applies to a §1404(a) motion to transfer.

SECTION C.   FORUM NON CONVENIENS

Although §1404 provides defendants in federal actions with the opportunity to override the plaintiff's choice of a highly inconvenient forum, this statute only provides relief when an alternative forum exists within the United States. In certain cases, however, such as those involving parties from a foreign country, no federal district other than the plaintiff's chosen forum will be an appropriate venue with personal jurisdiction over the defendants. For these cases, §1404 is wholly inapposite.

Prior to the passage of §1404 in 1948, the common law doctrine of *forum non conveniens* was devised to respond to those limited instances where the plaintiff's chosen forum was extraordinarily inconvenient to either the defendant or the chosen forum, and another court, within or without the forum country, was available. But with the passage of §1404, the appropriate response to the plaintiff's choice of a highly inconvenient federal district court when an alternative federal district court is an available forum is to transfer that case to the more convenient federal district in which the action could have been brought.

Consequently, the viability of *forum non conveniens* in federal actions is limited to those situations in which the available alternative to the plaintiff's choice of a highly inconvenient forum is a foreign (i.e., non-U.S.) court. However, since there is no statutory mechanism for transferring a civil action from a state court in one state to a state court in a different state (state statutes permitting intra-state changes of venue do exist), *forum non conveniens* enjoys a wider currency in actions filed in state courts.

In the following case, the Supreme Court expanded upon the doctrine of *forum non conveniens* in the context of a federal diversity action.

Piper Aircraft Company v. Reyno

Supreme Court of the United States, 1981.

454 U.S. 235, 102 S.Ct. 252, 70 L.Ed.2d 419.

JUSTICE MARSHALL delivered the opinion of the Court. * * *

I

A

In July 1976, a small commercial aircraft crashed in the Scottish highlands during * * * a charter flight from Blackpool to Perth. The pilot and five passengers were killed instantly. The decedents were all Scottish subjects and residents, as are their heirs and next of kin. There were no eyewitnesses to the accident. At the time of the crash the plane was subject to Scottish air traffic control.

The aircraft, a twin-engine Piper Aztec, was manufactured in Pennsylvania by petitioner Piper Aircraft Co. (Piper). The propellers were manufactured in Ohio by petitioner Hartzell Propeller, Inc. (Hartzell). At the time of the crash the aircraft was registered in Great Britain and was owned and maintained by Air Navigation and Trading Co., Ltd. (Air Navigation). It was operated by McDonald Aviation, Ltd. (McDonald), a Scottish air taxi service. Both Air Navigation and McDonald were organized in the United Kingdom. The wreckage of the plane is now in a hangar in Farnsborough, England.

* * *

* * * [A] California probate court appointed respondent Gaynell Reyno administratrix of the estates of the five passengers. Reyno is not related to and does not know any of the decedents or their survivors; she was a legal secretary to the attorney who filed this lawsuit. Several days after her appointment, Reyno commenced separate wrongful-death actions against Piper and Hartzell in the Superior Court of California, claiming negligence and strict liability. Air Navigation, McDonald, and the estate of the pilot are not parties to this litigation. The survivors of the five passengers whose estates are represented by Reyno filed a separate action in the United Kingdom against Air Navigation, McDonald, and the pilot's estate. Reyno candidly admits that the action against Piper and Hartzell was filed in the United States because its laws regarding liability, capacity to sue, and damages are more favorable to her position than are those of Scotland. Scottish law does not recognize strict liability in tort. Moreover, it permits wrongful-death actions only when brought by a decedent's relatives. The relatives may sue only for "loss of support and society."

On petitioners' motion, the suit was removed to the United States District Court for the Central District of California. Piper then moved for transfer to the United States District Court for the Middle District of Pennsylvania, pursuant to §1404(a). Hartzell moved to dismiss for lack of personal jurisdiction, or in the alternative, to transfer.[5] * * * [T]he District Court transferred the case to the Middle District of Pennsylvania. * * *

B

* * * [A]fter the suit had been transferred, both Hartzell and Piper moved to dismiss the action on the ground of forum non conveniens. The District Court granted these motions * * * and relied on the balancing test set forth by this Court in Gulf Oil Corp. v. Gilbert, 330 U.S. 501, 67 S.Ct. 839, 91 L.Ed. 1055 (1947), and its companion case, Koster v. Lumbermens Mut. Cas. Co., 330 U.S. 518, 67 S.Ct. 828, 91 L.Ed. 1067 (1947). In those decisions, the Court stated

---

[5] The District Court concluded that it could not assert personal jurisdiction over Hartzell consistent with due process. However, it decided not to dismiss Hartzell because the corporation would be amenable to process in Pennsylvania.

that a plaintiff's choice of forum should rarely be disturbed. However, when an alternative forum has jurisdiction to hear the case, and when trial in the chosen forum would "establish . . . oppressiveness and vexation to a defendant . . . out of all proportion to plaintiff's convenience," or when the "chosen forum [is] inappropriate because of considerations affecting the court's own administrative and legal problems," the court may, in the exercise of its sound discretion, dismiss the case. Koster. To guide trial court discretion, the Court provided a list of "private interest factors" affecting the convenience of the litigants, and a list of "public interest factors" affecting the convenience of the forum. Gilbert.[6]

* * * [T]he District Court * * * began by observing that an alternative forum existed in Scotland; Piper and Hartzell had agreed to submit to the jurisdiction of the Scottish courts and to waive any statute of limitations defense that might be available. It then stated that plaintiff's choice of forum was entitled to little weight. The court recognized that a plaintiff's choice ordinarily deserves substantial deference. It noted, however, that Reyno "is a representative of foreign citizens and residents seeking a forum in the United States because of the more liberal rules concerning products liability law," and that "the courts have been less solicitous when the plaintiff is not an American citizen or resident, and particularly when the foreign citizens seek to benefit from the more liberal tort rules provided for the protection of citizens and residents of the United States."

The District Court next examined several factors relating to the private interests of the litigants, and determined that these factors strongly pointed towards Scotland as the appropriate forum. Although evidence concerning the design, manufacture, and testing of the plane and propeller is located in the United States, the connections with Scotland are otherwise "overwhelming." The real parties in interest are citizens of Scotland, as were all the decedents. Witnesses who could testify regarding the maintenance of the aircraft, the training of the pilot, and the investigation of the accident — all essential to the defense — are in Great Britain. Moreover, all witnesses to damages are located in Scotland. Trial would be aided by familiarity with Scottish topography, and by easy access to the wreckage.

The District Court reasoned that because crucial witnesses and evidence were beyond the reach of compulsory process, and because the defendants would not be able to implead potential Scottish third-party defendants, it would

---

[6] The factors pertaining to the private interests of the litigants included the "relative ease of access to sources of proof; availability of compulsory process for attendance of unwilling, and the cost of obtaining attendance of willing, witnesses; possibility of view of premises, if view would be appropriate to the action; and all other practical problems that make trial of a case easy, expeditious and inexpensive." The public factors bearing on the question included the administrative difficulties flowing from court congestion; the "local interest in having localized controversies decided at home"; the interest in having the trial of a diversity case in a forum that is at home with the law that must govern the action; the avoidance of unnecessary problems in conflict of laws, or in the application of foreign law; and the unfairness of burdening citizens in an unrelated forum with jury duty.

be "unfair to make Piper and Hartzell proceed to trial in this forum." The survivors had brought separate actions in Scotland against the pilot, McDonald, and Air Navigation. "[I]t would be fairer to all parties and less costly if the entire case was presented to one jury with available testimony from all relevant witnesses." Although the court recognized that if trial were held in the United States, Piper and Hartzell could file indemnity or contribution actions against the Scottish defendants, it believed that there was a significant risk of inconsistent verdicts.[7]

The District Court concluded that the relevant public interests also pointed strongly towards dismissal. The court determined that Pennsylvania law would apply to Piper and Scottish law to Hartzell if the case were tried in the Middle District of Pennsylvania.[8] As a result, "trial in this forum would be hopelessly complex and confusing for a jury." In addition, the court noted that it was unfamiliar with Scottish law and thus would have to rely upon experts from that country. The court also found that the trial would be enormously costly and time-consuming; that it would be unfair to burden citizens with jury duty when the Middle District of Pennsylvania has little connection with the controversy; and that Scotland has a substantial interest in the outcome of the litigation.

In opposing the motions to dismiss, respondent contended that dismissal would be unfair because Scottish law was less favorable. The District Court explicitly rejected this claim. It reasoned that the possibility that dismissal might lead to an unfavorable change in the law did not deserve significant weight; any deficiency in the foreign law was a "matter to be dealt with in the foreign forum."

C

On appeal, the * * * Third Circuit reversed and remanded for trial. * * *

* * *

The Court of Appeals * * * rejected the District Court's balancing of the private * * * [and] public interest factors. * * *

* * * [Moreover, it] appears that the Court of Appeals would have reversed even if the District Court had properly balanced the public and private interests. The court * * * decided that dismissal is automatically barred if it would lead to

---

[7] The District Court explained that inconsistent verdicts might result if petitioners were held liable on the basis of strict liability here, and then required to prove negligence in an indemnity action in Scotland. Moreover, even if the same standard of liability applied, there was a danger that different juries would find different facts and produce inconsistent results

[8] Under Klaxon, a court ordinarily must apply the choice-of-law rules of the State in which it sits. However, where a case is transferred pursuant to §1404(a), it must apply the choice-of-law rules of the State from which the case was transferred. Van Dusen v. Barrack. Relying on these two cases, the District Court concluded that California choice-of-law rules would apply to Piper, and Pennsylvania choice-of-law rules would apply to Hartzell. It further concluded that California applied a "governmental interests" analysis in resolving choice-of-law problems, and that Pennsylvania employed a "significant contacts" analysis. The court used the "governmental interests" analysis to determine that Pennsylvania liability rules would apply to Piper, and the "significant contacts" analysis to determine that Scottish liability rules would apply to Hartzell.

a change in the applicable law unfavorable to the plaintiff.

We granted certiorari in these cases to consider the questions they raise concerning the proper application of the doctrine of forum non conveniens.

II

The Court of Appeals erred in holding that plaintiffs may defeat a motion to dismiss on the ground of forum non conveniens merely by showing that the substantive law that would be applied in the alternative forum is less favorable to the plaintiffs than that of the present forum. The possibility of a change in substantive law should ordinarily not be given conclusive or even substantial weight in the forum non conveniens inquiry.

* * *

* * *[13]   [B]y holding that the central focus of the forum non conveniens inquiry is convenience, Gilbert implicitly recognized that dismissal may not be barred solely because of the possibility of an unfavorable change in law. Under Gilbert, dismissal will ordinarily be appropriate where trial in the plaintiff's chosen forum imposes a heavy burden on the defendant or the court, and where the plaintiff is unable to offer any specific reasons of convenience supporting his choice.[15]   If substantial weight were given to the possibility of an unfavorable change in law, however, dismissal might be barred even where trial in the chosen forum was plainly inconvenient.

The Court of Appeals' decision is inconsistent with this Court's earlier forum non conveniens decisions in another respect. Those decisions have repeatedly emphasized the need to retain flexibility. In Gilbert, the Court refused to identify specific circumstances which will justify or require either grant or denial of remedy. * * * If central emphasis were placed on any one factor, the forum non conveniens doctrine would lose much of the very flexibility that makes it so valuable.

In fact, if conclusive or substantial weight were given to the possibility of a change in law, the forum non conveniens doctrine would become virtually

---

[13] The doctrine of forum non conveniens has a long history. It originated in Scotland and became part of the common law of many States. * * * In Williams v. Green Bay & Western R. Co., 326 U.S. 549, 66 S.Ct. 284, 90 L.Ed. 311 (1946), the Court first indicated that motions to dismiss on grounds of forum non conveniens could be made in federal diversity actions. The doctrine became firmly established when Gilbert and Koster were decided one year later.

In previous forum non conveniens decisions, the Court has left unresolved the question whether under Erie R. Co. v. Tompkins, 304 U.S. 64, 58 S.Ct. 817, 82 L.Ed. 1188 (1938), state or federal law of forum non conveniens applies in a diversity case. The Court did not decide this issue because the same result would have been reached in each case under federal or state law. The lower courts * * * [herein] reached the same conclusion: Pennsylvania and California law on forum non conveniens dismissals are virtually identical to federal law. Thus, here also, we need not resolve the Erie question.

[15] In other words, Gilbert held that dismissal may be warranted where a plaintiff chooses a particular forum, not because it is convenient, but solely in order to harass the defendant or take advantage of favorable law. This is precisely the situation in which the Court of Appeals' rule would bar dismissal.

useless. Jurisdiction and venue requirements are often easily satisfied. As a result, many plaintiffs are able to choose from among several forums. Ordinarily, these plaintiffs will select that forum whose choice-of-law rules are most advantageous. Thus, if the possibility of an unfavorable change in substantive law is given substantial weight in the forum non conveniens inquiry, dismissal would rarely be proper.

Except for the court below, every Federal Court of Appeals that has considered this question after Gilbert has held that dismissal on grounds of forum non conveniens may be granted even though the law applicable in the alternative forum is less favorable to the plaintiff's chance of recovery. * * *

The Court of Appeals' approach is not only inconsistent with the purpose of the forum non conveniens doctrine, but also poses substantial practical problems. If the possibility of a change in law were given substantial weight, deciding motions to dismiss on the ground of forum non conveniens would become quite difficult. Choice-of-law analysis would become extremely important, and the courts would frequently be required to interpret the law of foreign jurisdictions. First, the trial court would have to determine what law would apply if the case were tried in the chosen forum, and what law would apply if the case were tried in the alternative forum. It would then have to compare the rights, remedies, and procedures available under the law that would be applied in each forum. Dismissal would be appropriate only if the court concluded that the law applied by the alternative forum is as favorable to the plaintiff as that of the chosen forum. The doctrine of forum non conveniens, however, is designed in part to help courts avoid conducting complex exercises in comparative law. * * *

Upholding the decision of the Court of Appeals would result in other practical problems. At least where the foreign plaintiff named an American manufacturer as defendant,[17] a court could not dismiss the case on grounds of forum non conveniens where dismissal might lead to an unfavorable change in law. The American courts, which are already extremely attractive to foreign plaintiffs,[18] would become even more attractive. The flow of litigation into the

---

[17] In fact, the defendant might not even have to be American. A foreign plaintiff seeking damages for an accident that occurred abroad might be able to obtain service of process on a foreign defendant who does business in the United States. Under the Court of Appeals' holding, dismissal would be barred if the law in the alternative forum were less favorable to the plaintiff — even though none of the parties are American, and even though there is absolutely no nexus between the subject matter of the litigation and the United States.

[18] First, * * * strict liability remains primarily an American innovation. Second, the tort plaintiff may choose, at least potentially, from among 50 jurisdictions if he decides to file suit in the United States. Each of these jurisdictions applies its own set of malleable choice-of-law rules. Third, jury trials are almost always available in the United States, while they are never provided in civil law jurisdictions. Fourth, unlike most foreign jurisdictions, American courts allow contingent attorney's fees, and do not tax losing parties with their opponents' attorney's fees. Fifth, discovery is more extensive in American than in foreign courts.

United States would increase and further congest already crowded courts.[19]

The Court of Appeals based its decision, at least in part, on an analogy between dismissals on grounds of forum non conveniens and transfers between federal courts pursuant to §1404(a). In Van Dusen v. Barrack, this Court ruled that a §1404(a) transfer should not result in a change in the applicable law. * * * [T]he court below held that that principle is also applicable to a dismissal on forum non conveniens grounds. Congress enacted §1404(a) to permit change of venue between federal courts. Although the statute was drafted in accordance with the doctrine of forum non conveniens, it was intended to be a revision rather than a codification of the common law. District courts were given more discretion to transfer under §1404(a) than they had to dismiss on grounds of forum non conveniens. The reasoning employed in Van Dusen v. Barrack is simply inapplicable to dismissals on grounds of forum non conveniens. That case did not discuss the common-law doctrine. Rather, it focused on the construction and application of §1404(a). Emphasizing the remedial purpose of the statute, Barrack concluded that Congress could not have intended a transfer to be accompanied by a change in law. The statute was designed as a "federal housekeeping measure," allowing easy change of venue within a unified federal system. The Court feared that if a change in venue were accompanied by a change in law, forum-shopping parties would take unfair advantage of the relaxed standards for transfer. The rule was necessary to ensure the just and efficient operation of the statute.

We do not hold that the possibility of an unfavorable change in law should never be a relevant consideration in a forum non conveniens inquiry. Of course, if the remedy provided by the alternative forum is so clearly inadequate or unsatisfactory that it is no remedy at all, the unfavorable change in law may be given substantial weight; the district court may conclude that dismissal would not be in the interests of justice.[22] In these cases, however, the remedies that would be provided by the Scottish courts do not fall within this category.

---

[19] In holding that the possibility of a change in law unfavorable to the plaintiff should not be given substantial weight, we also necessarily hold that the possibility of a change in law favorable to defendant should not be considered. Respondent suggests that Piper and Hartzell filed the motion to dismiss, not simply because trial in the United States would be inconvenient, but also because they believe the laws of Scotland are more favorable. She argues that this should be taken into account in the analysis of the private interests. We recognize, of course, that Piper and Hartzell may be engaged in reverse forum-shopping. However, this possibility ordinarily should not enter into a trial court's analysis of the private interests. If the defendant is able to overcome the presumption in favor of plaintiff by showing that trial in the chosen forum would be unnecessarily burdensome, dismissal is appropriate — regardless of the fact that defendant may also be motivated by a desire to obtain a more favorable forum.

[22] At the outset of any forum non conveniens inquiry, the court must determine whether there exists an alternative forum. Ordinarily, this requirement will be satisfied when the defendant is "amenable to process" in the other jurisdiction. In rare circumstances, however, where the remedy offered by the other forum is clearly unsatisfactory, the other forum may not be an adequate alternative, and the initial requirement may not be satisfied. Thus, for example, dismissal would not be appropriate where the alternative forum does not permit litigation of the subject matter of the dispute.

Although the relatives of the decedents may not be able to rely on a strict liability theory, and although their potential damages award may be smaller, there is no danger that they will be deprived of any remedy or treated unfairly.

III

The Court of Appeals also erred in rejecting the District Court's *Gilbert* analysis. The Court of Appeals stated that more weight should have been given to the plaintiff's choice of forum, and criticized the District Court's analysis of the private and public interests. However, the District Court's decision regarding the deference due plaintiff's choice of forum was appropriate. Furthermore, we do not believe that the District Court abused its discretion in weighing the private and public interests.

A

The District Court acknowledged that there is ordinarily a strong presumption in favor of the plaintiff's choice of forum, which may be overcome only when the private and public interest factors clearly point towards trial in the alternative forum. It held, however, that the presumption applies with less force when the plaintiff or real parties in interest are foreign.

The District Court's distinction between resident or citizen plaintiffs and foreign plaintiffs is fully justified. In Koster, the Court indicated that a plaintiff's choice of forum is entitled to greater deference when the plaintiff has chosen the home forum.[23] When the home forum has been chosen, it is reasonable to assume that this choice is convenient. When the plaintiff is foreign, however, this assumption is much less reasonable. Because the central purpose of any forum non conveniens inquiry is to ensure that the trial is convenient, a foreign plaintiff's choice deserves less deference.

B

The forum non conveniens determination is committed to the sound discretion of the trial court. It may be reversed only when there has been a clear abuse of discretion; where the court has considered all relevant public and private interest factors, and where its balancing of these factors is reasonable, its decision deserves substantial deference. Here, the Court of Appeals expressly acknowledged that the standard of review was one of abuse of discretion. In examining the District Court's analysis of the public and private interests, however, the Court of Appeals seems to have lost sight of this rule, and substituted its own judgment for that of the District Court.

---

[23] In Koster, we stated that "[i]n any balancing of conveniences, a real showing of convenience by a plaintiff who has sued in his home forum will normally outweigh the inconvenience the defendant may have shown." As the District Court correctly noted in its opinion, the lower federal courts have routinely given less weight to a foreign plaintiff's choice of forum. A citizen's forum choice should not be given dispositive weight, however. Citizens or residents deserve somewhat more deference than foreign plaintiffs, but dismissal should not be automatically barred when a plaintiff has filed suit in his home forum. As always, if the balance of conveniences suggests that trial in the chosen forum would be unnecessarily burdensome for the defendant or the court, dismissal is proper.

(1)

In analyzing the private interest factors, the District Court stated that the connections with Scotland are "overwhelming." This characterization may be somewhat exaggerated. Particularly with respect to the question of relative ease of access to sources of proof, the private interests point in both directions. As respondent emphasizes, records concerning the design, manufacture, and testing of the propeller and plane are located in the United States. She would have greater access to sources of proof relevant to her strict liability and negligence theories if trial were held here. However, the District Court did not act unreasonably in concluding that fewer evidentiary problems would be posed if the trial were held in Scotland. A large proportion of the relevant evidence is located in Great Britain.

The Court of Appeals found that the problems of proof could not be given any weight because Piper and Hartzell failed to describe with specificity the evidence they would not be able to obtain if trial were held in the United States. It suggested that defendants seeking forum non conveniens dismissal must submit affidavits identifying the witnesses they would call and the testimony these witnesses would provide if the trial were held in the alternative forum. Such detail is not necessary. Piper and Hartzell have moved for dismissal precisely because many crucial witnesses are located beyond the reach of compulsory process, and thus are difficult to identify or interview. Requiring extensive investigation would defeat the purpose of their motion. Of course, defendants must provide enough information to enable the District Court to balance the parties' interests. Our examination of the record convinces us that sufficient information was provided here. Both Piper and Hartzell submitted affidavits describing the evidentiary problems they would face if the trial were held in the United States.

The District Court correctly concluded that the problems posed by the inability to implead potential third-party defendants clearly supported holding the trial in Scotland. Joinder of the pilot's estate, Air Navigation, and McDonald is crucial to the presentation of petitioners' defense. If Piper and Hartzell can show that the accident was caused not by a design defect, but rather by the negligence of the pilot, the plane's owners, or the charter company, they will be relieved of all liability. It is true, of course, that if Hartzell and Piper were found liable after a trial in the United States, they could institute an action for indemnity or contribution against these parties in Scotland. It would be far more convenient, however, to resolve all claims in one trial. The Court of Appeals rejected this argument. Forcing petitioners to rely on actions for indemnity or contributions would be "burdensome" but not "unfair." Finding that trial in the plaintiff's chosen forum would be burdensome, however, is sufficient to support dismissal on grounds of forum non conveniens.

(2)

The District Court's review of the factors relating to the public interest was also reasonable. On the basis of its choice-of-law analysis, it concluded that if the case were tried in the Middle District of Pennsylvania, Pennsylvania law would apply to Piper and Scottish law to Hartzell. It stated that a trial involving two sets of laws would be confusing to the jury. It also noted its own lack of familiarity with Scottish law. Consideration of these problems was clearly appropriate under Gilbert; in that case we explicitly held that the need to apply foreign law pointed towards dismissal. The Court of Appeals found that the District Court's choice-of-law analysis was incorrect, and that American law would apply to both Hartzell and Piper. Thus, lack of familiarity with foreign law would not be a problem. Even if the Court of Appeals' conclusion is correct, however, all other public interest factors favored trial in Scotland.

Scotland has a very strong interest in this litigation. The accident occurred in its airspace. All of the decedents were Scottish. Apart from Piper and Hartzell, all potential plaintiffs and defendants are either Scottish or English. As we stated in Gilbert, there is "a local interest in having localized controversies decided at home." Respondent argues that American citizens have an interest in ensuring that American manufacturers are deterred from producing defective products, and that additional deterrence might be obtained if Piper and Hartzell were tried in the United States, where they could be sued on the basis of both negligence and strict liability. However, the incremental deterrence that would be gained if this trial were held in an American court is likely to be insignificant. The American interest in this accident is simply not sufficient to justify the enormous commitment of judicial time and resources that would inevitably be required if the case were to be tried here.

IV

The Court of Appeals erred in holding that the possibility of an unfavorable change in law bars dismissal on the ground of forum non conveniens. It also erred in rejecting the District Court's Gilbert analysis. The District Court properly decided that the presumption in favor of the respondent's forum choice applied with less than maximum force because the real parties in interest are foreign. It did not act unreasonably in deciding that the private interests pointed towards trial in Scotland. Nor did it act unreasonably in deciding that the public interests favored trial in Scotland. Thus, the judgment of the Court of Appeals is Reversed.

JUSTICE POWELL took no part in the decision of these cases.

JUSTICE O'CONNOR took no part in the consideration or decision of these cases.

[The opinion of JUSTICE WHITE, concurring in part and dissenting in part, is omitted.]

[The dissenting opinion of JUSTICE STEVENS, with whom JUSTICE BRENNAN joined, is omitted.]

NOTES AND PROBLEMS FOR DISCUSSION

1. The complaint in this case was filed in a state court in California yet the motion to dismiss on the grounds of *forum non conveniens* was heard and resolved by a federal district court in Pennsylvania. How did that happen?

2. We previously noted that when a federal district court transfers a case under §1406 as a remedy for a defect in venue, the Supreme Court has ruled, in *Goldlawr*, that the transferor court can do so even when it does not have personal jurisdiction over the defendants. Can a federal court grant a motion to dismiss on *forum non conveniens* grounds prior to determining that the court has both subject matter and personal jurisdiction? The Supreme Court resolved a circuit split over this question in SINOCHEM INT'L CO. LTD. v. MALAYSIA INT'L SHIPPING CORP., 549 U.S. 442, 127 S.Ct. 1184, 167 L.Ed.2d 15 (2007). In an admiralty action brought by a Malaysian shipping company against a Chinese importer, the trial court determined that it possessed subject matter jurisdiction under 28 U.S.C. §1333 (admiralty or maritime jurisdiction), but that it lacked personal jurisdiction over the Chinese defendant under the forum state's long-arm statute. Nevertheless, the trial court also opined that permitting limited discovery might reveal the existence of national contacts sufficient to permit personal jurisdiction over the defendant under Rule 4(k)(2). Nevertheless, it did not permit such discovery because it determined that the case could be more conveniently and efficiently adjudicated in a Chinese court. Consequently, it granted the defendant's motion to dismiss under the doctrine of *forum non conveniens*. The Third Circuit agreed that the trial court had subject matter jurisdiction and that the question of personal jurisdiction could not be resolved without further discovery. But it ruled that the trial court could not dismiss the case under the *forum non conveniens* doctrine unless and until that court had determined that it had both subject matter and personal jurisdiction. So it reversed the order dismissing the case.

The Supreme Court unanimously vacated the Third Circuit's opinion. It ruled that a federal district court has discretion to dismiss on *forum non conveniens* grounds pursuant to the requirements of that doctrine, regardless of whether it has either subject matter or personal jurisdiction. Although a federal court cannot rule on the *merits* of a case without first determining that it has jurisdiction over both the subject matter and the parties, the Court pointed to its ruling in Ruhrgas AG v. Marathon Oil, 526 U.S. 574, 119 S.Ct. 1563, 143 L.Ed.2d 760 (1999) (that a court can dismiss for lack of personal jurisdiction without first establishing subject matter jurisdiction) as reflecting its judgment that there is no mandatory sequencing of jurisdictional issues, i.e., that one nonmerits threshold issue can be resolved without a prior resolution of another jurisdictional issue. The Court agreed with the Third Circuit that *forum non conveniens* is a nonmerits ground for dismissal. Accordingly, it concluded, the trial court could dispose of an action on *forum non conveniens* grounds without previously ruling on subject matter and personal jurisdictional issues.

In arriving at this conclusion, the Court also had to deal with its own language in *Gulf Oil* stating that "the doctrine of *forum non conveniens* can never apply if there is absence of jurisdiction" and that *forum non conveniens* "presupposes at least two forums in which the defendant is amenable to process." It offered two responses. First, that this language was "less than felicitously crafted." Second, that *Gulf Oil* was distinguishable from the case at bar because the trial court in *Gulf Oil* unquestionably had both subject matter and personal jurisdiction and so the issue raised in the instant case was not addressed by the Court in *Gulf Oil*. Thus, the Court reasoned, the first of the two statements in *Gulf Oil* meant only that once a court has *determined* that it does not possess jurisdiction, then it cannot dismiss under the *forum non conveniens* doctrine. But where it had not ruled on that nonmerits threshold question, the court has discretion to consider the *forum non conveniens* motion. And the second statement in *Gulf Oil* was inapplicable to the instant case because it was made in the context of a situation where the trial court did possess jurisdiction over the parties and subject matter.

Noting that trial courts often condition a *forum non conveniens* dismissal on the defendant's wavier of jurisdictional or other defense in the foreign forum, the Court sidestepped the question of whether a court that had not determined whether it possessed jurisdiction over the case and parties could issue such a conditional dismissal. It expressly reserved decision on that question because of its determination that the plaintiff in this case faced "no genuine risk" that the more convenient foreign forum would not take the case since the Chinese court had previously determined that it had jurisdiction over this matter and these parties in a prior proceeding. With respect to the standard that should govern the trial court's exercise of discretion in deciding whether to resolve the *forum non conveniens* issue ahead of the jurisdictional issue, the Court turned to the question of sequencing in *Ruhrgas*. Where resolution of the jurisdictional issues would not involve an arduous inquiry, then judicial economy and the solicitude traditionally accorded the plaintiff's choice of forum ordinarily should impel the trial court to resolve the jurisdictional issues before addressing the *forum non conveniens* motion. But where, as here, the jurisdictional issues would be arduous, expensive, or time consuming (because of the necessity for engaging in discovery to resolve the personal jurisdiction issue), and where the *forum non conveniens* factors weighed heavily in favor of dismissal, the trial court properly could take the "less burdensome" route of dealing immediately with the *forum non conveniens* motion.

3. What did the Supreme Court mean in *Piper* when it stated that "district courts were given more discretion to transfer under §1404(a) than they had to dismiss on grounds of forum non conveniens"? Consider this prior declaration by the Court in NORWOOD v. KIRKPATRICK, 349 U.S. 29, 75 S.Ct. 544, 99 L.Ed. 789 (1955):

> When Congress adopted §1404(a), it intended to do more than just codify the existing law on forum non conveniens. * * * Congress, in writing §1404(a) * * * was revising as well as codifying. The harshest

result of the application of the old doctrine of forum non conveniens, dismissal of the action, was eliminated by the provision in §1404 for transfer. When the harshest part of the doctrine is excised by statute, it can hardly be called mere codification. As a consequence, we believe that Congress, by the terms "for the convenience of parties and witnesses, in the interest of justice," intended to permit courts to grant transfers upon a lesser showing of inconvenience. This is not to say that the relevant factors have changed or that the plaintiff's choice of forum is not to be considered, but only that the discretion to be exercised is broader.

(a) Compare the results when a court grants a motion to transfer under §1404 versus a motion alleging *forum non conveniens*.

(b) Is there anything a trial court can do to soften the blow to the plaintiff when it decides to grant a motion based on *forum non conveniens*?

4. Note that in footnote 13 of *Piper*, the Court reserved decision on whether *forum non conveniens* motions should be resolved under federal or state common law in a diversity action. The prevailing view among the appellate courts is that, under the *Erie* doctrine (see Chapter 5, *infra*), federal law governs because even when failure to apply state law in federal court would lead to different outcomes in state and federal courts (i.e., the issue is outcome determinative), the interest in uniformity between federal and state courts within a single state is overwhelmed by the federal judiciary's interest in self-regulation and administrative independence. See e.g., Esfeld v. Costa Crociere, S.P.A., 289 F.3d 1300 (11th Cir.2002); Ravel Monegro v. Rosa, 211 F.3d 509 (9th Cir.2000), cert. denied, 531 U.S. 1112, 121 S.Ct. 857, 148 L.Ed.2d 771 (2001). Also notice that the defendants' decisions in *Piper* to remove the case to federal court and then to transfer it to a different federal district did not preclude them from subsequently making a *forum non conveniens* dismissal motion.

5. Presumably, defendants rarely will invoke the doctrine of *forum non conveniens* unless the more "convenient" forum also will apply more advantageous substantive law than the forum chosen by the plaintiff.

(a) If so, do you agree with the *Piper* Court's reasons for concluding that a plaintiff who has chosen a forum that meets all applicable venue and jurisdiction rules is, nevertheless, not entitled to the benefits of the substantive law that the chosen forum would have applied?

(b) Why is that plaintiff treated less favorably than the plaintiff whose forum choice is trumped by the defendant's successful §1404 motion?

(c) Other than providing defendants with an opportunity for forum shopping by overturning the plaintiff's choice of forum and applicable substantive law, is there any real justification for the doctrine of *forum non conveniens* that is not already served by the requirements associated with obtaining personal jurisdiction?

6. Should the trial court dismiss the action on the ground of *forum non conveniens* in the following situations?

(a) A New York citizen went to Paris for two years to work for a French investment banking firm. After one year, he was discharged. Upon his return to the U.S., he filed a claim in a federal district court in New York under Title VII of the 1964 Civil Rights Act alleging that his termination was the product of unlawful sex-based discrimination. The plaintiff opposed the defendant's motion to dismiss on the ground that a French court would apply French law to this dispute and that under French discrimination law he would have to establish malicious conduct beyond a reasonable doubt, whereas under Title VII he would only have to prove negligent conduct by a preponderance of the evidence.

(b) Same facts as in "(a)" except that French antidiscrimination law only prohibits discrimination on the basis of race, age and citizenship.

(c) While on business in Houston, a Mexican citizen rented a Chrysler automobile. He was so impressed, that upon his return home to Mexico City he purchased a new Chrysler from a local Chrysler dealership. He subsequently was injured and his young son was killed when the air bag in the new car unexpectedly and improperly deployed. He brought suit in federal district court in Arizona against the New Jersey company that manufactured the air bag. In response to the defense motion to dismiss on the ground of *forum non conveniens*, the plaintiff argued that since Mexican law caps the maximum award for the loss of child's life at approximately $2500, Mexico is an inadequate forum for resolving this tort suit. See Gonzalez v. Chrysler Corp., 301 F.3d 377 (5th Cir.2002).

This issue of the adequacy of the alternative forum that was examined in *Gonzalez* arose in an interesting context in a case involving a claim resulting from the war between Ethiopia and Eritrea. As part of the peace agreement that formally ended that conflict, the two nations created the Ethiopia/Eritrea Claims Commission. This Commission was authorized to decide through arbitration, *inter alia*, all claims for loss by nationals of one country against the government of the other country. The treaty also provided, however that (a) the countries were the only parties permitted to file claims, although they could do so on behalf of their nationals; (b) the Commission could only make damage awards to the petitioning country; and (c) the countries could settle any outstanding claim through direct negotiation. After some Eritrean nationals filed suit against the Republic of Ethiopia seeking recovery for property damage suffered during the war in federal district court for the District of Columbia, the trial court dismissed the action on the grounds of *forum non conveniens*, finding that the Claims Commission was a more appropriate forum for the plaintiffs' claims. The D.C. Circuit reversed, finding that while it was a close call, the trial court had abused its discretion in dismissing the case. Nemariam v. The Federal Democratic Republic of Ethiopia, 315 F.3d 390 (D.C.Cir.2003). The panel unanimously concluded that the Commission's inability to make an award directly to the individual claimants (regardless of the fact that Eritrea had asserted that it would voluntarily distribute awards to individual claims as a general matter) and Eritrea's ability to set off any individual Eritrean's claim (or any amount awarded to Eritrea on the basis of such a claim) against claims made by or an award in favor of Ethiopia, rendered the remedy provided by this alternative forum so clearly inadequate or unsatisfactory that it constituted no remedy at all. The court distinguished this case from *Gonzalez* by noting that while it was true that the availability of only a more limited recovery in the alternative forum than was available in the plaintiff's chosen forum does not *automatically* render the alternative forum inadequate, the alternative forum in this case was one in which the plaintiff could recover nothing for a valid claim. Having thus found the Commission an inadequate alternative forum, the appellate court reversed the trial court's dismissal of the claim on *forum non conveniens* grounds.

7. In Part IIIA of the majority opinion in *Piper*, the Court agreed with the trial judge's conclusion that that the strong presumption that attaches to the plaintiff's choice of forum applies with less force when the plaintiff is "foreign." As the Court explained, when the plaintiff has chosen her home forum, it is reasonable to assume that this choice is based on convenience. Conversely, when the plaintiff is "foreign" that assumption is less apt. Consequently, the Court concluded, "a foreign plaintiff's choice deserves less deference." If a U.S. citizen domiciled in California is injured in Mexico and sues the defendants in Connecticut, is her choice of forum entitled to less deference when the defendants move to dismiss the action on the ground of *forum non conveniens*? Would your answer depend upon whether the defendants were amenable to personal jurisdiction in Connecticut but not in California? In IRAGORRI v. UNITED TECHNOLGIES CORP., 274 F.3d 65 (2d Cir.2001) (en banc), the Second Circuit unanimously ruled that this level of deference to a U.S. citizen's forum choice is not limited to suits filed in the plaintiff's home state. Rather, the court explained, deference should be accorded whenever it appears that the plaintiff's choice was dictated by legitimate, rather than forum-shopping reasons. Such legitimate reasons, it continued, include the amenability of the defendant to suit because a plaintiff should not be expected to file suit in her home state where she is unlikely to perfect jurisdiction over the defendant. Accordingly, it reversed the trial court's dismissal of the complaint on *forum non conveniens* grounds because, it ruled, the trial judge did not accord appropriate deference to a Florida plaintiff's choice of a Connecticut forum in a case seeking damages against Connecticut defendants for an injury that occurred in Cali, Colombia.

Suppose the facts were reversed and a Mexican national was injured in Mexico by a U.S. citizen domiciled in California. If the Mexican plaintiff files suit in California, how should the court rule on the defendant's motion to dismiss based on *forum non conveniens*? In POLLUX HOLDING LTD. v. CHASE MANHATTAN BANK, 329 F.3d 64 (2d Cir.2003), two Liberian investment companies that handled the accounts of Greek citizens brought suit against the defendant New York banking company in New York. The court noted that Greece had entered into a treaty with the U.S. providing that Greek citizens be accorded the same right of access to U.S. courts as that accorded American citizens. But since the plaintiffs were the Liberian corporations, rather than their Greek customers, the treaty was inapposite. The court noted, however, that even when such treaties are applicable, foreign nationals of the signatory country are only entitled to the (lesser) deference to their choice of a U.S. forum that is afforded a U.S. citizen living abroad than that accorded American citizens living within the U.S.

The court then rejected the plaintiffs' suggestion that it adopt a *per se* rule favoring litigation in a defendant's home forum. Instead, the court applied the sliding scale deference standard it had set forth in *Iragorri*, i.e., the deference paid to a plaintiff's choice of forum depends upon whether that choice can be said to have been predicated on legitimate, rather than strategic considerations. It then offered this assessment of that calculation:

> "[A foreign plaintiff's choice of a forum based on the ability] to obtain jurisdiction over defendant is an instance where substantial deference would still be generally appropriate. But it is an untenable leap of logic to jump from that holding to the blanket assertion that a plaintiff's choice of forum deserves presumptive deference simply because the chosen forum is defendant's home forum. It is reasonable for a court to assume that a plaintiff's choice of her own home forum is motivated by convenience. The plaintiff's choice of the defendant's home forum provides a much less reliable proxy for convenience. Bearing in mind that litigants rarely are concerned with promoting their adversary's convenience at their own expense, a plaintiff's choice of the defendant's home forum over other fora where defendant is amenable to suit and to which the plaintiff and the circumstances of the case are much more closely connected suggests the possibility that plaintiff's choice was made for reasons of trial strategy. Accordingly, a plaintiff's choice to initiate suit in the defendant's home forum — as opposed to any other where the defendant is also amenable to suit — only merits heightened deference to the extent that the plaintiff and the case possess *bona fide* connections to, and convenience factors favor, that forum."

329 F.3d at 74. Since the plaintiffs offered no proof that they had connections to the United States and failed to demonstrate that New York was convenient for them (nearly all of their interactions with the bank occurred at its London branch), the court held that their choice of the defendant's home forum did not merit the same substantial deference afforded to a suit initiated in a plaintiff's home forum. Upon finding that the trial court had properly determined England to be an adequate alternative forum and had properly weighed the prescribed private and public interest factors, the circuit court upheld its decision to dismiss the complaint.

Note also that in *Atlantic Marine*, discussed in Section B, *supra*, the Supreme Court unanimously ruled that where a defendant files a motion to dismiss on the grounds of *forum non conveniens* in order to enforce the terms of a valid forum selection agreement, the trial court is to grant the motion except under extraordinary circumstances unrelated to the convenience of the parties.

CHAPTER 5

Choosing and Ascertaining the Applicable Law

SECTION A. CHOICE OF LAW — THE *ERIE* DOCTRINE

Once a court determines that it possesses adjudicative authority over both the parties to, and subject matter of a civil action, the chosen tribunal frequently must confront the nettlesome question of which law to apply to the issues raised in that case. This "choice of law" inquiry can take one of two forms. When, in the exercise of either its diversity or supplemental jurisdiction, a federal district court asserts jurisdiction over a claim that does not arise under a federal statutory, constitutional, or treaty provision, should the issues in that case be resolved by the application of federal or state law? Conversely, where a state court possesses concurrent jurisdiction over a federal question claim, should that court apply federal or state law to the issues in the case? This is frequently referred to as the "vertical choice of law" question. If this choice of law analysis leads the court in either of these contexts to conclude that state law applies, this raises the second, or "horizontal choice of law" question, i.e., which state's law should govern? This horizontal choice of law determination often involves an exceedingly complex series of mind-numbing calculations. This subject, however, is more appropriately left for detailed consideration in an advanced course such as Conflict of Laws. Here, we will examine only the issues relating to vertical choice of laws assessments. Included among them is the matter of how a federal court determines the content of a particular state's law once it has resolved the vertical and horizontal choice of law question in favor of the application of the law of a specific state.

The Supreme Court's opinion in the following case created a framework for allocating judicial power between the federal and state governments. Consequently, it is a crucial component of the Court's federalism jurisprudence. Moreover, it occupies such a central place in the resolution of vertical choice of law problems that the entire body of jurisprudence introduced in this case and refined in several subsequent opinions by the Court is collectively referred to as the "Erie doctrine." Here is where and how "the Erie doctrine" started:

Erie Railroad Co. v. Tompkins

Supreme Court of the United States, 1938.
304 U.S. 64, 58 S.Ct. 817, 82 L.Ed. 1188.

MR. JUSTICE BRANDEIS delivered the opinion of the Court.

The question for decision is whether the oft-challenged doctrine of Swift v. Tyson [41 U.S. 1, 10 L. Ed. 865(1842)] shall now be disapproved.

Tompkins, a citizen of Pennsylvania, was injured on a dark night by a passing freight train of the Erie Railroad Company while walking along its right of way at Hughestown in that state. He claimed that the accident occurred through negligence in the operation, or maintenance, of the train; that he was rightfully on the premises as licensee because on a commonly used beaten footpath which ran for a short distance alongside the tracks; and that he was struck by something which looked like a door projecting from one of the moving cars. To enforce that claim he brought an action in the federal court for Southern New York, which had jurisdiction because the company is a corporation of that state. * * *

The Erie insisted that its duty to Tompkins was no greater than that owed to a trespasser. It contended, among other things, that its duty to Tompkins, and hence its liability, should be determined in accordance with the Pennsylvania law; that under the law of Pennsylvania, as declared by its highest court, persons who use pathways along the railroad right of way — that is, a longitudinal pathway as distinguished from a crossing — are to be deemed trespassers; and that the railroad is not liable for injuries to undiscovered trespassers resulting from its negligence, unless it be wanton or willful. Tompkins denied that any such rule had been established by the decisions of the Pennsylvania courts; and contended that, since there was no statute of the state on the subject, the railroad's duty and liability is to be determined in federal courts as a matter of general law.

* * *

The Erie had contended that application of the Pennsylvania rule was required, among other things, by section 34 of the Federal Judiciary Act of September 24, 1789 [also known as the Rules of Decision Act] which provides: "The laws of the several States, except where the Constitution, treaties, or statutes of the United States otherwise require or provide, shall be regarded as rules of decision in trials at common law, in the courts of the United States, in cases where they apply." [The Act is currently codified, as amended, at 28 U.S.C. §1652],

Because of the importance of the question whether the federal court was free to disregard the alleged rule of the Pennsylvania common law, we granted certiorari.

* * * Swift v. Tyson held that federal courts exercising jurisdiction on the ground of diversity of citizenship need not, in matters of general jurisprudence,

apply the unwritten law of the state as declared by its highest court; that they are free to exercise an independent judgment as to what the common law of the state is — or should be; and that, as there stated by Mr. Justice Story, "the true interpretation of the 34th section limited its application to state laws, strictly local, that is to say, to the positive statutes of the state, and the construction thereof adopted by the local tribunals * * *."

The * * * federal courts assumed, in the broad field of "general law," the power to declare rules of decision which Congress was confessedly without power to enact as statutes. Doubt was repeatedly expressed as to the correctness of the construction given section 34, and as to the soundness of the rule which it introduced. But it was the more recent research of a competent scholar, who examined the original document, which established that the construction given to it by the Court was erroneous; and that the purpose of the section was merely to make certain that, in all matters except those in which some federal law is controlling, the federal courts exercising jurisdiction in diversity of citizenship cases would apply as their rules of decision the law of the state, unwritten as well as written.[5]

* * *

* * * Experience in applying the doctrine of Swift v. Tyson had revealed its defects, political and social; and the benefits expected to flow from the rule did not accrue. Persistence of state courts in their own opinions on questions of common law prevented uniformity; and the impossibility of discovering a satisfactory line of demarcation between the province of general law and that of local law developed a new well of uncertainties.

On the other hand, the mischievous results of the doctrine had become apparent. Diversity of citizenship jurisdiction was conferred in order to prevent apprehended discrimination in state courts against those not citizens of the state. Swift v. Tyson introduced grave discrimination by noncitizens against citizens. It made rights enjoyed under the unwritten "general law" vary according to whether enforcement was sought in the state or in the federal court; and the privilege of selecting the court in which the right should be determined was conferred upon the noncitizen. Thus, the doctrine rendered impossible equal protection of the law. In attempting to promote uniformity of law throughout the United States, the doctrine had prevented uniformity in the administration of the law of the state.

* * *

In part the discrimination resulted from the wide range of persons held entitled to avail themselves of the federal rule by resort to the diversity of citizenship jurisdiction. Through this jurisdiction individual citizens willing to remove from their own state and become citizens of another might avail themselves of the federal rule. And, without even change of residence, a corporate citizen of the state could avail itself of the federal rule by reincorporating under the laws of another state * * *.

---

[5] Charles Warren, New Light on the History of the Federal Judiciary Act of 1789 (1923) 37 Harv.L.Rev. 49, 51-52, 81-88, 108.

The injustice and confusion incident to the doctrine of Swift v. Tyson have been repeatedly urged as reasons for abolishing or limiting diversity of citizenship jurisdiction. Other legislative relief has been proposed.[21] If only a question of statutory construction were involved, we should not be prepared to abandon a doctrine so widely applied throughout nearly a century. But the unconstitutionality of the course pursued has now been made clear, and compels us to do so.

* * * Except in matters governed by the Federal Constitution or by acts of Congress, the law to be applied in any case is the law of the state. And whether the law of the state shall be declared by its Legislature in a statute or by its highest court in a decision is not a matter of federal concern. There is no federal general common law. Congress has no power to declare substantive rules of common law applicable in a state whether they be local in their nature or "general," be they commercial law or a part of the law of torts. And no clause in the Constitution purports to confer such a power upon the federal courts. * * *

The fallacy underlying the rule declared in Swift v. Tyson is made clear by Mr. Justice Holmes * * *:

> "* * * [L]aw in the sense in which courts speak of it today does not exist without some definite authority behind it. The common law so far as it is enforced in a State, whether called common law or not, is not the common law generally but the law of that State existing by the authority of that State without regard to what it may have been in England or anywhere else. * * *
>
> The authority and only authority is the State, and if that be so, the voice adopted by the State as its own (whether it be of its Legislature or of its Supreme Court) should utter the last word."

Thus the doctrine of Swift v. Tyson is, as Mr. Justice Holmes said, "an unconstitutional assumption of powers by the Courts of the United States which no lapse of time or respectable array of opinion should make us hesitate to correct." In disapproving that doctrine we do not hold unconstitutional section 34 of the Federal Judiciary Act of 1789 or any other act of Congress. We merely declare that in applying the doctrine this Court and the lower courts have invaded rights which in our opinion are reserved by the Constitution to the several states.

* * * The defendant contended that by the common law of Pennsylvania as declared by its highest court * * *, the only duty owed to the plaintiff was to refrain from willful or wanton injury. The plaintiff denied that such is the Pennsylvania law. * * * The Circuit Court of Appeals ruled that the question of liability is one of general law; and on that ground declined to decide the issue of state law. As we hold this was error, the judgment is reversed and the case remanded to it for further proceedings in conformity with our opinion.

Reversed.

---

[21] Thus, bills which would abrogate the doctrine of Swift v. Tyson have been introduced. State statutes on conflicting questions of "general law" have also been suggested.

MR. JUSTICE CARDOZO took no part in the consideration or decision of this case. [Due to illness — eds.]

MR. JUSTICE BUTLER (dissenting).

* * *

Defendant's petition for writ of certiorari presented two questions: Whether its duty toward plaintiff should have been determined in accordance with the law as found by the highest court of Pennsylvania, and whether the evidence conclusively showed plaintiff guilty of contributory negligence. Plaintiff contends that * * * the issues of negligence and contributory negligence are to be determined by general law against which local decisions may not be held conclusive; that defendant relies on a solitary Pennsylvania case of doubtful applicability, and that, even if the decisions of the courts of that state were deemed controlling, the same result would have to be reached.

No constitutional question was suggested or argued below or here. And as a general rule, this Court will not consider any question not raised below and presented by the petition. * * *

* * *

While amendments to section 34 have from time to time been suggested, the section stands as originally enacted. Evidently Congress has intended throughout the years that the rule of decision as construed should continue to govern fedcral courts in trials at common law. * * *

* * *

The course pursued by the Court in this case is repugnant to the Act of Congress of August 24, 1937. It declares that: "Whenever the constitutionality of any Act of Congress affecting the public interest is drawn in question in any court of the United States in any suit or proceeding to which the United States * * * is not a party, the court having jurisdiction of the suit or proceeding shall certify such fact to the Attorney General. In any such case the court shall permit the United States to intervene and become a party for presentation of evidence * * * and argument upon the question of the constitutionality of such Act. * * * That provision extends to this Court. If defendant had applied for and obtained the writ of certiorari upon the claim that, as now held, Congress has no power to prescribe the rule of decision, section 34 as construed, it would have been the duty of this Court to issue the prescribed certificate to the Attorney General in order that the United States might intervene and be heard on the constitutional question. Within the purpose of the statute and its true intent and meaning, the constitutionality of that measure has been "drawn in question." Congress intended to give the United States the right to be heard in every case involving constitutionality of an act affecting the public interest. In view of the rule that, in the absence of challenge of constitutionality, statutes will not here be invalidated on that ground, the Act of August 24, 1937 extends to cases where constitutionality is first "drawn in question" by the Court. No extraordinary or unusual action by the Court after submission of the cause should be permitted to frustrate the wholesome purpose of that act. The duty it imposes ought here to be willingly assumed. If it were doubtful whether this case is within the scope of the act, the Court should give the United States opportunity to intervene and, if so advised, to present argument on the constitutional question, for undoubtedly it is one of great public importance. That would be to construe the act according to its meaning.

The Court's opinion * * * states that it does not hold section 34 unconstitutional, but merely that, in applying the doctrine of Swift v. Tyson construing it, this Court and the lower courts have invaded rights which are reserved by the Constitution to the several states. But, plainly through the form of words employed, the substance of the decision appears; it strikes down as unconstitutional section 34 as construed by our decisions; it divests the Congress of power to prescribe rules to be followed by federal courts when deciding questions of general law. In that broad field it compels this and the lower federal courts to follow decisions of the courts of a particular state.

* * *

MR. JUSTICE MCREYNOLDS, concurs in this opinion.

MR. JUSTICE REED (concurring in part).

I concur in the conclusion reached in this case, in the disapproval of the doctrine of Swift v. Tyson, and in the reasoning of the majority opinion, except in so far as it relies upon the unconstitutionality of the 'course pursued' by the federal courts.

The "doctrine of Swift v. Tyson," as I understand it, is that the words "the laws," as used in section 34, line 1, of the Federal Judiciary Act of September 24, 1789, do not include in their meaning "the decisions of the local tribunals."

To decide the case now before us and to "disapprove" the doctrine of Swift v. Tyson requires only that we say that the words 'the laws' include in their meaning the decisions of the local tribunals. As the majority opinion shows, by its reference to Mr. Warren's researches and the first quotation from Mr. Justice Holmes, that this Court is now of the view that "laws" includes "decisions," it is unnecessary to go further and declare that the "course pursued" was "unconstitutional," instead of merely erroneous.

The "unconstitutional" course referred to in the majority opinion is apparently the ruling in Swift v. Tyson that the supposed omission of Congress to legislate as to the effect of decisions leaves federal courts free to interpret general law for themselves. I am not at all sure whether, in the absence of federal statutory direction, federal courts would be compelled to follow state decisions. There was sufficient doubt about the matter in 1789 to induce the first Congress to legislate. No former opinions of this Court have passed upon it. * * * If the opinion commits this Court to the position that the Congress is without power to declare what rules of substantive law shall govern the federal courts, that conclusion also seems questionable. The line between procedural and substantive law is hazy, but no one doubts federal power over procedure. The Judiciary Article, 3, and the "necessary and proper" clause of article 1, s 8, may fully authorize legislation, such as this section of the Judiciary Act.

In this Court, stare decisis, in statutory construction, is a useful rule, not an inexorable command. It seems preferable to overturn an established construction of an act of Congress, rather than, in the circumstances of this case, to interpret the Constitution. * * *

NOTES AND PROBLEMS FOR DISCUSSION

1. What choice of law regime governed federal courts in diversity cases under the Court's decision in *Swift*?

2. With respect to the stark question posed at the outset of the Justice Brandeis' opinion for the Court in *Erie*:

(a) What answer does the Court provide?

(b) What reasons does the Court offer for its answer to that question?

(c) What significance, if any, should attach to the fact, mentioned by Justice Butler, that Congress never amended the Rules of Decision Act during the 96-year period between the Court's rulings in *Swift* and *Erie*?

(d) When Justice Brandeis stated that implementation of the *Swift* doctrine had led to an equal protection violation by favoring noncitizens over citizens with respect to the opportunity for forum shopping, did he forget that forum citizen plaintiffs can also invoke diversity jurisdiction?

3. (a) What particular provision within the Constitution was the Court referring to when it declared the "unconstitutionality of the course pursued" under the doctrine of Swift v. Tyson?

(b) Couldn't Congress, pursuant to its Article 1, §8 authority to regulate commerce among the several states, enact a statute expressly providing that railroads owe a high duty of care to all individuals using the pathways along the railroads' right of way? If so, how do you explain the Justice Brandeis' declaration that a federal judge is constitutionally barred from fashioning an identical common law rule?

(c) What do you make of Justice Butler's insistence that couching the result in constitutional terms was inappropriate and Justice Reed's assertion that doing so was unnecessary?

4. For more than two centuries, American courts have recognized an "act of state" doctrine that dates back to the English common law of 1674. Under this principle, courts of one country abstain from judging the acts of another sovereign nation undertaken within its own borders. When an American plaintiff seeks redress for actions taken by either a foreign government or an instrumentality of that foreign government within that nation's territory and invokes the federal court's diversity jurisdiction under §1332(a)(4), should the scope of the act of state doctrine be determined by state or federal common law? In BANCO NATIONAL de CUBA v. SABBATINO, 376 U.S. 398, 84 S.Ct. 923, 11 L.Ed.2d 804 (1964), the Supreme Court held that this subject should be controlled exclusively by federal law. It stated that federal courts should fashion a single, uniform standard to avoid the possibility that rules affecting international law could be left to "divergent and perhaps parochial state interpretations." While acknowledging that the U.S. Constitution does not mandate application of the act of state doctrine, and, therefore, that American courts are not constitutionally incapacitated from reviewing the validity of acts of foreign states, the Court nevertheless reasoned that including this doctrine within the "enclaves of federal judge-made law which bind the States" was consistent with the constitutional delegation to the federal government of exclusive authority over the management of foreign affairs.

5. Did the majority in *Erie* suggest any limit to its conclusion that federal courts sitting in diversity should apply state "law" in the absence of an applicable federal statute?

(a) Is the line drawn by the majority in *Erie* either (1) supported by the language of the Rules of Decision Act; or (2) a workable standard for determining when state or federal law should govern the issue in question?

(b) Does Justice Reed's concurring opinion shed light on either of these questions?

The *Erie* Court's substance/procedure dichotomy generated a host of interpretive questions. For example, is a state statute of limitations merely a "procedural" matter that only affects the manner in which rights are enforced and which, under *Erie*, the federal court can disregard in favor of a federal rule? Or is it a "substantive" right, which, therefore, is binding upon the federal court? Seven years after its decision in *Erie*, the Court addressed this specific problem in the following case, which resulted in a reformulation of the Court's vertical choice of law analysis.

Guaranty Trust Co. of New York v. York

Supreme Court of the United States, 1945.

326 U.S. 99, 65 S.Ct. 1464, 89 L.Ed. 2079.

MR. JUSTICE FRANKFURTER delivered the opinion of the Court.

* * *

In May, 1930, Van Sweringen Corporation issued notes * * *. * * * Guaranty Trust Co. was named trustee with power and obligations to enforce the rights of the noteholders in the assets of the Corporation * * *. In October, 1930, petitioner, with other banks, made large advances to companies affiliated with the Corporation * * *. In October, 1931, when it was apparent that the Corporation could not meet its obligations, Guaranty co-operated in a plan for the purchase of the outstanding notes * * *.

* * * [This] suit, instituted as a class action on behalf of non-accepting noteholders and brought in a federal court solely because of diversity of citizenship, is based on an alleged breach of trust by Guaranty in that it failed to protect the interests of the noteholders in assenting to the exchange offer and failed to disclose its self-interest when sponsoring the offer. Petitioner moved for summary judgment, which was granted * * *. On appeal, the Circuit Court of Appeals * * * held that * * * a federal district court * * * is not required to apply the State statute of limitations that would govern like suits in the courts of a State where the federal court is sitting even though the exclusive basis of federal jurisdiction is diversity of citizenship. * * *

* * *

* * * [T]his case reduces itself to the narrow question whether, when no recovery could be had in a State court because the action is barred by the statute of limitations, a federal court * * * can take cognizance of the suit because there is diversity of citizenship between the parties. Is the outlawry, according to State law, of a claim created by the States a matter of "substantive rights" to be respected by a federal court * * * when that court's jurisdiction is dependent on the fact that there is a State-created right, or is such statute of "a mere remedial character," which a federal court may disregard?

Matters of "substance" and matters of "procedure" are much talked about in the books as though they defined a great divide cutting across the whole domain of law. But, of course, "substance" and "procedure" are the same key-words to very different problems. Neither "substance" nor "procedure" represents the same invariants. Each implies different variables depending upon the particular problem for which it is used. * * *

Here we are dealing with a right to recover derived not from the United States but from one of the States. When, because the plaintiff happens to be a nonresident, such a right is enforceable in a federal as well as in a State court, the forms and mode of enforcing the right may at times, naturally enough, vary because the two judicial systems are not identic. But since a federal court adjudicating a state-created right solely because of the diversity of citizenship of the parties is for that purpose, in effect, only another court of the State, it cannot afford recovery if the right to recover is made unavailable by the State nor can it substantially affect the enforcement of the right as given by the State.

And so the question is not whether a statute of limitations is deemed a matter of "procedure" in some sense. The question is whether such a statute concerns merely the manner and the means by which a right to recover, as recognized by the State, is enforced, or whether such statutory limitation is a matter of substance in the aspect that alone is relevant to our problem, namely, does it significantly affect the result of a litigation for a federal court to disregard a law of a State that would be controlling in an action upon the same claim by the same parties in a State court?

It is therefore immaterial whether statutes of limitation are characterized either as "substantive" or "procedural" in State court opinions in any use of those terms unrelated to the specific issue before us. Erie R. Co. v. Tompkins was not an endeavor to formulate scientific legal terminology. It expressed a policy that touches vitally the proper distribution of judicial power between State and federal courts. In essence, the intent of that decision was to insure that, in all cases where a federal court is exercising jurisdiction solely because of the diversity of citizenship of the parties, the outcome of the litigation in the federal court should be substantially the same, so far as legal rules determine the outcome of a litigation, as it would be if tried in a State court. The nub of the policy that underlies Erie R. Co. v. Tompkins is that for the same transaction the accident of a suit by a non-resident litigant in a federal court instead of in a State court a block away, should not lead to a substantially different result. And so, putting to one side abstractions regarding "substance" and "procedure," we have held that in diversity cases the federal courts must follow the law of the State as to burden of proof, as to conflict of laws, and as to contributory negligence. Erie R. Co. v. Tompkins has been applied with an eye alert to essentials in avoiding disregard of State law in diversity cases in the federal courts. A policy so important to our federalism must be kept free from entanglements with analytical or terminological niceties.

Plainly enough, a statute that would completely bar recovery in a suit if brought in a State court bears on a State-created right vitally and not merely formally or negligibly. As to consequences that so intimately affect recovery or non-recovery a federal court in a diversity case should follow State law. The fact that under New York law a statute of limitations might be lengthened or shortened, that a security may be foreclosed though the debt be barred, that a barred debt may be used as a set-off, are all matters of local law properly to be respected by federal courts sitting in New York when their incidence comes into play there. Such particular rules of local law, however, do not in the slightest change the crucial consideration that if a plea of the statute of limitations would bar recovery in a State court, a federal court ought not to afford recovery.

* * *

* * * The source of substantive rights enforced by a federal court under diversity jurisdiction, it cannot be said too often, is the law of the States. Whenever that law is authoritatively declared by a State, whether its voice be the legislature or its highest court, such law ought to govern in litigation founded on that law, whether the forum of application is a State or a federal court * * *.

* * *

The judgment is reversed and the case is remanded for proceedings not inconsistent with this opinion.

So ordered.

MR. JUSTICE ROBERTS and MR. JUSTICE DOUGLAS took no part in the consideration or decision of this case.

[The dissenting opinion of MR. JUSTICE RUTLEDGE is omitted.]

NOTES AND PROBLEMS FOR DISCUSSION

1. How did the Court in *Guaranty Trust* reformulate *Erie*'s substance/procedure distinction?

2. Did the Court in *Guaranty Trust* intend to do more than merely revise the *Erie* test for determining whether a federal diversity court should apply state or federal law to a particular issue? Specifically, by referring on three occasions to the *Erie* "policy" as opposed to "constitutional principle," did the Court intend to distance itself from the constitutional underpinnings of that doctrine?

3. Does the *Guaranty York* variation on the *Erie* formula provide federal courts with a brighter line standard than was offered by the original?

Byrd v. Blue Ridge Rural Electric Cooperative, Inc.

Supreme Court of the United States, 1958.

356 U.S. 525, 78 S.Ct. 893, 2 L.Ed.2d 953.

MR. JUSTICE BRENNAN delivered the opinion of the Court.

This case was brought in the District Court for the Western District of South Carolina. Jurisdiction was based on diversity of citizenship. The petitioner, a resident of North Carolina, sued respondent, a South Carolina corporation, for damages for injuries allegedly caused by the respondent's negligence. * * * The petitioner was injured while connecting power lines to one of the new substations.

One of respondent's affirmative defenses was that under the South Carolina Workmen's Compensation Act, the petitioner — because the work contracted to be done by his employer was work of the kind also done by the respondent's own construction and maintenance crews — had the status of a statutory employee of the respondent and was therefore barred from suing the respondent * * * because obliged to accept statutory compensation benefits as the exclusive remedy for his injuries. Two questions concerning this defense are before us: * * * (2) whether petitioner, state practice notwithstanding, is entitled to a jury determination of the factual issues raised by this defense.

* * *

[In the first section of its opinion, the Supreme Court determined that the Court of Appeals had erred in not remanding the case for a new trial on the question of whether the defendant was the plaintiff's statutory employer.]

II.

A question is also presented as to whether on remand the factual issue is to be decided by the judge or by the jury. The respondent argues on the basis of the decision of the Supreme Court of South Carolina in Adams v. Davison-Paxon Co., 230 S.C. 532, 96 S.E.2d 566, that the issue of immunity should be decided by the judge and not by the jury. * * *

The respondent argues that this state-court decision governs the present diversity case and divests the jury of its normal function to decide the disputed fact question of the respondent's immunity [as a statutory employer] under §72-111 [of the South Carolina Workmen's Compensation Act]. This is to contend that the federal court is bound under Erie R. Co. v. Tompkins to follow the state court's holding to secure uniform enforcement of the immunity created by the State.

First. It was decided in Erie R. Co. v. Tompkins that the federal courts in diversity cases must respect the definition of state-created rights and obligations by the state courts. We must, therefore, first examine the rule in Adams v. Davison-Paxon Co. to determine whether it is bound up with these rights and obligations in such a way that its application in the federal court is required.

The Workmen's Compensation Act is administered in South Carolina by its Industrial Commission. The South Carolina courts hold that, on judicial review of actions of the Commission under §72-111, the question whether the claim of an injured workman is within the Commission's jurisdiction is a matter of law for decision by the court, which makes its own findings of fact relating to that jurisdiction. The South Carolina Supreme Court states no reasons in Adams v. Davison-Paxon Co. why, although the jury decides all other factual issues raised by the cause of action and defenses, the jury is displaced as to the factual issue raised by the affirmative defense under §72-111. * * * A State may, of course, distribute the functions of its judicial machinery as it sees fit. The decisions relied upon, however, furnish no reason for selecting the judge rather than the jury to decide this single affirmative defense in the negligence action. They simply reflect a policy that administrative determination of "jurisdictional facts" should not be final but subject to judicial review. The conclusion is inescapable that the Adams holding is grounded in the practical consideration that the question had theretofore come before the South Carolina courts from the Industrial Commission and the courts had become accustomed to deciding the factual issue of immunity without the aid of juries. We find nothing to suggest that this rule was announced as an integral part of the special relationship created by the statute. Thus the requirement appears to be merely a form and mode of enforcing the immunity, Guaranty Trust Co. of New York v. York, and not a rule intended to be bound up with the definition of the rights and obligations of the parties. The situation is therefore not analogous to that in Dice v. Akron, C. & Y.R. Co., 342 U.S. 359, 72 S.Ct. 312, 96 L.Ed. 398, where this Court held that the right to trial by jury is so substantial a part of the cause of action created by the Federal Employers' Liability Act, that the Ohio courts could not apply, in an action under that statute, the Ohio rule that the question of fraudulent release was for determination by a judge rather than by a jury.

Second. But cases following Erie have evinced a broader policy to the effect that the federal courts should conform as near as may be — in the absence of other considerations — to state rules even of form and mode where the state rules may bear substantially on the question whether the litigation would come out one way in the federal court and another way in the state court if the federal court failed to apply a particular local rule. E.g., Guaranty Trust Co. of New York v. York. Concededly the nature of the tribunal which tries issues may be important in the enforcement of the parcel of rights making up a cause of action or defense, and bear significantly upon achievement of uniform enforcement of the right. It may well be that in the instant personal-injury case the outcome would be substantially affected by whether the issue of immunity is decided by a judge or a jury. Therefore, were "outcome" the only consideration, a strong case might appear for saying that the federal court should follow the state practice.

But there are affirmative countervailing considerations at work here. The federal system is an independent system for administering justice to litigants who properly invoke its jurisdiction. An essential characteristic of that system is the manner in which, in civil common-law actions, it distributes trial functions between judge and jury and, under the influence — if not the command[10] — of the Seventh Amendment, assigns the decisions of disputed questions of fact to the jury. The policy of uniform enforcement of state-created rights and obligations cannot in every case exact compliance with a state rule — not bound up with rights and obligations — which disrupts the federal system of allocating functions between judge and jury. Thus the inquiry here is whether the federal policy favoring jury decisions of disputed fact questions should yield to the state rule in the interest of furthering the objective that the litigation should not come out one way in the federal court and another way in the state court.

We think that in the circumstances of this case the federal court should not follow the state rule. It cannot be gainsaid that there is a strong federal policy against allowing state rules to disrupt the judge-jury relationship in the federal courts. * * * Perhaps even more clearly in light of the influence of the Seventh Amendment, the function assigned to the jury is an essential factor in the process for which the Federal Constitution provides. * * *

Third. We have discussed the problem upon the assumption that the outcome of the litigation may be substantially affected by whether the issue of immunity is decided by a judge or a jury. But clearly there is not present here the certainty that a different result would follow, or even the strong possibility that this would be the case. There are factors present here which might reduce that possibility. The trial judge in the federal system has powers denied the judges of many States to comment on the weight of evidence and credibility of witnesses, and discretion to grant a new trial if the verdict appears to him to be against the weight of the evidence. We do not think the likelihood of a different result is so strong as to require the federal practice of jury determination of disputed factual issues to yield to the state rule in the interest of uniformity of outcome.

* * * We accordingly remand the case to the Court of Appeals * * * with instructions that * * * the Court of Appeals shall remand the case to the District Court for a new trial of such issues as the Court of Appeals may direct.

Reversed and remanded.

[The opinion of MR. JUSTICE WHITTAKER concurring in part and dissenting in part is omitted.]

[The dissenting opinions of MR. JUSTICE FRANKFURTER and MR. JUSTICE HARLAN are omitted.]

NOTES AND PROBLEMS FOR DISCUSSION

1. What does this decision add to the *Guaranty Trust* formulation of the *Erie* rule on vertical choice of law?

---

[10] Our conclusion makes unnecessary the consideration of — and we intimate no view upon — the question whether the right of jury trial protected in federal courts by the Seventh Amendment embraces the factual issue of statutory immunity when asserted, as here, as an affirmative defense in a common-law negligence action.

2. Does the Court explain whether its balancing test is to apply in all, or just some circumstances?

(a) For example, would the Court have engaged in this balancing act if it had concluded that the state common law rule assigning the resolution of the statutory employer defense to judges was "bound up" with state-created rights and obligations?

(b) How does one tell when a state rule is sufficiently "bound up" with state-created rights?

3. (a) What is the federal policy that was so important that it trumped both the outcome-impacting nature of the state's fact-finding allocation principle and the *Erie* policies of promoting decisional uniformity and discouraging forum shopping?

(b) What did the Court mean by its reference to "the influence — if not the command — of the Seventh Amendment"?

4. The federal Conformity Act of 1872, 17 Stat. 196 (1872), provided that proceedings in non-equity and non-admiralty cases (i.e., actions at law) in federal courts "shall conform, as near as may be" to the procedures employed in state courts of the state in which that federal court was located. While this meant that cases filed in federal and state courts within the same state were subject, more or less, to the same procedural guidelines, the procedures followed by federal trial courts in one state would often differ from those governing the trial of a case filed in federal courts in another state. In 1934, through the passage of the Rules Enabling Act, Congress empowered the Supreme Court to develop and implement a uniform set procedural rules for civil actions filed in federal courts. As we discussed in Chapter 2, §G-2 in connection with the rules governing service of process, this statutory directive led, in 1938 (the same year in which the Supreme Court issued its ruling in *Erie*) to the promulgation of the Federal Rules of Civil Procedure. It was not long before the federal courts had to face the thorny question of whether these rules governing "procedure" would apply in diversity cases or whether, pursuant to the modified *Erie* doctrine, the courts were required to rely instead on comparable state rules, thereby thwarting the goal of providing a uniform system for processing all civil cases in the federal courts. The Supreme Court confronted and resolved this question in the following case:

Hanna v. Plumer

Supreme Court of the United States, 1965.

380 U.S. 460, 85 S.Ct. 1136, 14 L.Ed.2d 8.

Mr. Chief Justice Warren delivered the opinion of the Court.

The question to be decided is whether, in a civil action where the jurisdiction of the United States district court is based upon diversity of citizenship between the parties, service of process shall be made in the manner prescribed by state law or that set forth in Rule 4(d)(1) of the Federal Rules of Civil Procedure.

* * * [P]etitioner, a citizen of Ohio, filed her complaint in the District Court for the District of Massachusetts, claiming damages in excess of $10,000 for personal injuries resulting from an automobile accident in South Carolina, allegedly caused by the negligence of one Louise Plumer Osgood, a Massachusetts citizen deceased at the time of the filing of the complaint. Respondent, Mrs. Osgood's executor and also a Massachusetts citizen, was named as defendant. * * * [S]ervice was made by leaving copies of the summons and the complaint with respondent's wife at his residence, concededly in compliance with Rule 4(d)(1), which provides:

"* * * Service shall be made as follows:

(1) Upon an individual * * *, by delivering a copy of the summons and of the complaint to him personally or by leaving copies thereof at his dwelling house or usual place of abode with some person of suitable age and discretion then residing therein * * *."[*]

Respondent filed his answer * * * alleging, inter alia, that the action could not be maintained because it had been brought contrary to and in violation of the provisions of Massachusetts General Laws §9. That section provides:

"Except as provided in this chapter, an executor * * * shall not be held to answer to an action by a creditor of the deceased * * * unless before the expiration [of one year from the time of his giving bond for the performance of his trust] the writ in such action has been served by delivery in hand upon such executor * * * or service thereof accepted by him or a notice stating the name of the estate, the name and address of the creditor, the amount of the claim and the court in which the action has been brought has been filed in the proper registry of probate. * * *"

* * * [T]he District Court granted respondent's motion for summary judgment, citing Guaranty Trust Co. v. York, in support of its conclusion that the adequacy of the service was to be measured by §9, with which, the court held, petitioner had not complied. On appeal, petitioner admitted noncompliance with §9, but argued that Rule 4(d)(1) defines the method by which service of process is to be effected in diversity actions. The Court of Appeals for the First Circuit, finding that "(r)elatively recent amendments (to §9) evince a clear legislative purpose to require personal notification within the year,"[1] concluded

---

[*] [As a result of subsequent amendments to the Federal Rules, this provision is now found at Rule 4(e)(2).—eds.]

[1] Section 9 is in part a statute of limitations, providing that an executor need not "answer to an action * * * which is not commenced within one year from the time of his giving bond * * *." This part of the statute, the purpose of which is to speed the settlement of estates, is not involved in this case, since the action clearly was timely commenced. (Respondent filed bond on March 1, 1962; the complaint was filed February 6, 1963; and the service—the propriety of which is in dispute—was made on February 8, 1963.) Section 9 also provides for the manner of service. Generally, service of process must be made by "delivery in hand," although there are two alternatives: acceptance of service by the executor, or filing of a notice of claim, the components of which are set out in the statute, in the appropriate probate court. The purpose of this part of the statute, which is involved here, is, as the court below noted, to insure that executors will receive actual notice of claims. Actual notice is of course also the goal of Rule 4(d)(1); however, the Federal Rule reflects a determination that this goal can be achieved by a method less cumbersome than that prescribed in §9. In this case the goal seems to have been achieved; although the

that the conflict of state and federal rules was over "a substantive rather than a procedural matter," and unanimously affirmed. Because of the threat to the goal of uniformity of federal procedure posed by the decision below, we granted certiorari.

We conclude that the adoption of Rule 4(d)(1), designed to control service of process in diversity actions, neither exceeded the congressional mandate embodied in the Rules Enabling Act [28 U.S.C. §2072] nor transgressed constitutional bounds, and that the Rule is therefore the standard against which the District Court should have measured the adequacy of the service. Accordingly, we reverse the decision of the Court of Appeals.

The Rules Enabling Act provides, in pertinent part:

> "The Supreme Court shall have the power to prescribe, by general rules, the forms of process, writs, pleadings, and motions, and the practice and procedure of the district courts of the United States in civil actions.

> Such rules shall not abridge, enlarge or modify any substantive right and shall preserve the right of trial by jury * * *."

Under the cases construing the scope of the Enabling Act, Rule 4(d)(1) clearly passes muster. Prescribing the manner in which a defendant is to be notified that a suit has been instituted against him, it relates to the "practice and procedure of the district courts."

* * *

In Mississippi Pub. Corp. v. Murphree, 326 U.S. 438, 66 S.Ct. 242, 90 L.Ed. 185, this Court upheld Rule 4(f) [see current Rule 4(h)], which permits service of a summons anywhere within the State (and not merely the district) in which a district court sits:

> "We think that Rule 4(f) is in harmony with the Enabling Act * * *. Undoubtedly most alterations of the rules of practice and procedure may and often do affect the rights of litigants. Congress' prohibition of any alteration of substantive rights of litigants was obviously not addressed to such incidental effects as necessarily attend the adoption of the prescribed new rules of procedure upon the rights of litigants who, agreeably to rules of practice and procedure, have been brought before a court authorized to determine their rights. The fact that the application of Rule 4(f) will operate to subject petitioner's rights to adjudication by the district court for northern Mississippi will undoubtedly affect those rights. But it does not operate to abridge, enlarge or modify the rules of decision by which that court will adjudicate its rights."

Thus were there no conflicting state procedure, Rule 4(d)(1) would clearly control. However, respondent, focusing on the contrary Massachusetts rule, calls to the Court's attention another line of cases, a line which — like the Federal Rules — had its birth in 1938. Erie R. Co. v. Tompkins held that federal courts sitting in diversity cases, when deciding questions of "substantive" law,

---

affidavit filed by respondent in the District Court asserts that he had not been served in hand nor had he accepted service, it does not allege lack of actual notice.

are bound by state court decisions as well as state statutes. The broad command of Erie was therefore identical to that of the Enabling Act: federal courts are to apply state substantive law and federal procedural law. However, as subsequent cases sharpened the distinction between substance and procedure, the line of cases following Erie diverged markedly from the line construing the Enabling Act. Guaranty Trust Co. v. York made it clear that Erie-type problems were not to be solved by reference to any traditional or common-sense substance-procedure distinction:

> "And so the question is * * * does it significantly affect the result of a litigation for a federal court to disregard a law of a State that would be controlling in an action upon the same claim by the same parties in a State court?"

Respondent, by placing primary reliance on York * * *, suggests that the Erie doctrine acts as a check on the Federal Rules of Civil Procedure, that despite the clear command of Rule 4(d)(1), Erie and its progeny demand the application of the Massachusetts rule. Reduced to essentials, the argument is: (1) Erie, as refined in York, demands that federal courts apply state law whenever application of federal law in its stead will alter the outcome of the case. (2) In this case, a determination that the Massachusetts service requirements obtain will result in immediate victory for respondent. If, on the other hand, it should be held that Rule 4(d)(1) is applicable, the litigation will continue, with possible victory for petitioner. (3) Therefore, Erie demands application of the Massachusetts rule. The syllogism possesses an appealing simplicity, but is for several reasons invalid.

In the first place, it is doubtful that, even if there were no Federal Rule making it clear that in-hand service is not required in diversity actions, the Erie rule would have obligated the District Court to follow the Massachusetts procedure. "Outcome-determination" analysis was never intended to serve as a talisman. Byrd v. Blue Ridge. Indeed, the message of York itself is that choices between state and federal law are to be made not by application of any automatic, "litmus paper" criterion, but rather by reference to the policies underlying the Erie rule.

The Erie rule is rooted in part in a realization that it would be unfair for the character of result of a litigation materially to differ because the suit had been brought in a federal court.

* * *

The decision was also in part a reaction to the practice of "forum-shopping" which had grown up in response to the rule of Swift v. Tyson. That the York test was an attempt to effectuate these policies is demonstrated by the fact that the opinion framed the inquiry in terms of "substantial" variations between state and federal litigation. Not only are nonsubstantial, or trivial, variations not likely to raise the sort of equal protection problems which troubled the Court in Erie; they are also unlikely to influence the choice of a forum. The "outcome-determination" test therefore cannot be read without reference to the twin aims of the Erie rule: discouragement of forum-shopping and avoidance of inequitable administration of the laws.[9]

The difference between the conclusion that the Massachusetts rule is applicable, and the conclusion that it is not, is of course at this point "outcome-determinative" in the sense that if we hold the state rule to apply, respondent prevails, whereas if we hold that Rule 4(d)(1) governs, the litigation will continue.   But in this sense every procedural variation is "outcome-determinative." For example, having brought suit in a federal court, a plaintiff cannot then insist on the right to file subsequent pleadings in accord with the time limits applicable in state courts, even though enforcement of the federal timetable will, if he continues to insist that he must meet only the state time limit, result in determination of the controversy against him. So it is here. Though choice of the federal or state rule will at this point have a marked effect upon the outcome of the litigation, the difference between the two rules would be of scant, if any, relevance to the choice of a forum. Petitioner, in choosing her forum, was not presented with a situation where application of the state rule would wholly bar recovery; rather, adherence to the state rule would have resulted only in altering the way in which process was served.[11] Moreover, it is difficult to argue that permitting service of defendant's wife to take the place of inhand service of defendant himself alters the mode of enforcement of state-created rights in a fashion sufficiently "substantial" to raise the sort of equal protection problems to which the Erie opinion alluded.

There is, however, a more fundamental flaw in respondent's syllogism: the incorrect assumption that the rule of Erie constitutes the appropriate test of the validity and therefore the applicability of a Federal Rule of Civil Procedure. The Erie rule has never been invoked to void a Federal Rule. It is true that there have been cases where this Court has held applicable a state rule in the face of an argument that the situation was governed by one of the Federal Rules. But the holding of each such case was not that Erie commanded displacement of a Federal Rule by an inconsistent state rule, but rather that the scope of the Federal Rule was not as broad as the losing party urged, and therefore, there being no Federal Rule which covered the point in dispute, Erie commanded the

---

[9] The Court of Appeals seemed to frame the inquiry in terms of how "important" §9 is to the State. In support of its suggestion that §9 serves some interest the State regards as vital to its citizens, the court noted that something like §9 has been on the books in Massachusetts a long time, that §9 has been amended a number of times and that §9 is designed to make sure that executors receive actual notice. The apparent lack of relation among these three observations is not surprising, because it is not clear to what sort of question the Court of Appeals was addressing itself. One cannot meaningfully ask how important something is without first asking "important for what purpose?" Erie and its progeny make clear that when a federal court sitting in a diversity case is faced with a question of whether or not to apply state law, the importance of a state rule is indeed relevant, but only in the context of asking whether application of the rule would make so important a difference to the character or result of the litigation that failure to enforce it would unfairly discriminate against citizens of the forum State, or whether application of the rule would have so important an effect upon the fortunes of one or both of the litigants that failure to enforce it would be likely to cause a plaintiff to choose the federal court.

[11] We cannot seriously entertain the thought that one suing an estate would be led to choose the federal court because of a belief that adherence to Rule 4(d)(1) is less likely to give the executor actual notice than §9, and therefore more likely to produce a default judgment. Rule 4(d)(1) is well designed to give actual notice, as it did in this case.

enforcement of state law.

(Here, of course, the clash is unavoidable; Rule 4(d)(1) says — implicitly, but with unmistakable clarity — that inhand service is not required in federal courts.) At the same time, in cases adjudicating the validity of Federal Rules, we have not applied the York rule or other refinements of Erie, but have to this day continued to decide questions concerning the scope of the Enabling Act and the constitutionality of specific Federal Rules * * *.

Nor has the development of two separate lines of cases been inadvertent. The line between "substance" and "procedure" shifts as the legal context changes. "Each implies different variables depending upon the particular problem for which it is used." Guaranty Trust Co. v. York. It is true that both the Enabling Act and the Erie rule say, roughly, that federal courts are to apply state "substantive" law and federal "procedural" law, but from that it need not follow that the tests are identical. For they were designed to control very different sorts of decisions. When a situation is covered by one of the Federal Rules, the question facing the court is a far cry from the typical, relatively unguided Erie Choice: the court has been instructed to apply the Federal Rule, and can refuse to do so only if the Advisory Committee, this Court, and Congress erred in their prima facie judgment that the Rule in question transgresses neither the terms of the Enabling Act nor constitutional restrictions.

We are reminded by the Erie opinion that neither Congress nor the federal courts can, under the guise of formulating rules of decision for federal courts, fashion rules which are not supported by a grant of federal authority contained in Article I or some other section of the Constitution; in such areas state law must govern because there can be no other law. But the opinion in Erie, which involved no Federal Rule and dealt with a question which was "substantive" in every traditional sense (whether the railroad owed a duty of care to Tompkins as a trespasser or a licensee), surely neither said nor implied that measures like Rule 4(d)(1) are unconstitutional. For the constitutional provision for a federal court system (augmented by the Necessary and Proper Clause) carries with it congressional power to make rules governing the practice and pleading in those courts, which in turn includes a power to regulate matters which, though falling within the uncertain area between substance and procedure, are rationally capable of classification as either. Neither York nor the cases following it ever suggested that the rule there laid down for coping with situations where no Federal Rule applies is coextensive with the limitation on Congress to which Erie had adverted. Although this Court has never before been confronted with a case where the applicable Federal Rule is in direct collision with the law of the relevant State, courts of appeals faced with such clashes have rightly discerned the implications of our decisions.

> "One of the shaping purposes of the Federal Rules is to bring about uniformity in the federal courts by getting away from local rules. This is especially true of matters which relate to the administration of legal proceedings, an area in which federal courts have traditionally exerted strong inherent power, completely aside from the powers Congress expressly conferred in the Rules. The purpose of the Erie doctrine, even as extended in York * * *, was never to bottle up federal courts with

'outcome-determinative' and 'integral-relations' stoppers — when there are 'affirmative countervailing (federal) considerations' and when there is a Congressional mandate (the Rules) supported by constitutional authority." Lumbermen's Mutual Casualty Co. v. Wright, 322 F.2d 759, 764 (C.A.5th Cir. 1963).

Erie and its offspring cast no doubt on the long-recognized power of Congress to prescribe housekeeping rules for federal courts even though some of those rules will inevitably differ from comparable state rules. * * * Thus, though a court, in measuring a Federal Rule against the standards contained in the Enabling Act and the Constitution, need not wholly blind itself to the degree to which the Rule makes the character and result of the federal litigation stray from the course it would follow in state courts, it cannot be forgotten that the Erie rule, and the guidelines suggested in York, were created to serve another purpose altogether. To hold that a Federal Rule of Civil Procedure must cease to function whenever it alters the mode of enforcing state-created rights would be to disembowel either the Constitution's grant of power over federal procedure or Congress' attempt to exercise that power in the Enabling Act. Rule 4(d)(1) is valid and controls the instant case.

Reversed.

MR. JUSTICE BLACK concurs in the result.

MR. JUSTICE HARLAN, concurring.

It is unquestionably true that up to now Erie and the cases following it have not succeeded in articulating a workable doctrine governing choice of law in diversity actions. I respect the Court's effort to clarify the situation in today's opinion. However, in doing so I think it has misconceived the constitutional premises of Erie and has failed to deal adequately with those past decisions upon which the courts below relied.

Erie was something more than an opinion which worried about forum-shopping and avoidance of inequitable administration of the laws, although to be sure these were important elements of the decision. I have always regarded that decision as one of the modern cornerstones of our federalism, expressing policies that profoundly touch the allocation of judicial power between the state and federal systems. Erie recognized that there should not be two conflicting systems of law controlling the primary activity of citizens, for such alternative governing authority must necessarily give rise to a debilitating uncertainty in the planning of everyday affairs.[1] And it recognized that the scheme of our Constitution envisions an allocation of law-making functions between state and federal legislative processes which is undercut if the federal judiciary can make substantive law affecting state affairs beyond the bounds of congressional legislative powers in this regard. Thus, in diversity cases Erie commands that it be the state law governing primary private activity which prevails.

---

[1] Since the rules involved in the present case are parallel rather than conflicting, this first rationale does not come into play here.

The shorthand formulations which have appeared in some past decisions are prone to carry untoward results that frequently arise from oversimplification. The Court is quite right in stating that the "outcome-determinative" test of Guaranty Trust Co. v. York, if taken literally, proves too much, for any rule, no matter how clearly "procedural," can affect the outcome of litigation if it is not obeyed. In turning from the "outcome" test of York back to the unadorned forum-shopping rationale of Erie, however, the Court falls prey to like oversimplification, for a simple forum-shopping rule also proves too much; litigants often choose a federal forum merely to obtain what they consider the advantages of the Federal Rules of Civil Procedure or to try their cases before a supposedly more favorable judge. To my mind the proper line of approach in determining whether to apply a state or a federal rule, whether "substantive" or "procedural," is to stay close to basic principles by inquiring if the choice of rule would substantially affect those primary decisions respecting human conduct which our constitutional system leaves to state regulation.[2] If so, Erie and the Constitution require that the state rule prevail, even in the face of a conflicting federal rule.

The Court weakens, if indeed it does not submerge, this basic principle by finding, in effect, a grant of substantive legislative power in the constitutional provision for a federal court system (compare Swift v. Tyson), and through it, setting up the Federal Rules as a body of law inviolate.

* * *

So long as a reasonable man could characterize any duly adopted federal rule as "procedural," the Court, unless I misapprehend what is said, would have it apply no matter how seriously it frustrated a State's substantive regulation of the primary conduct and affairs of its citizens. Since the members of the Advisory Committee, the Judicial Conference, and this Court who formulated the Federal Rules are presumably reasonable men, it follows that the integrity of the Federal Rules is absolute. Whereas the unadulterated outcome and forum-shopping tests may err too far toward honoring state rules, I submit that the Court's "arguably procedural, ergo constitutional" test moves too fast and far in the other direction.

* * *

It remains to apply what has been said to the present case. The Massachusetts rule provides that an executor need not answer suits unless in-hand service was made upon him or notice of the action was filed in the proper registry of probate within one year of his giving bond. The evident intent of this statute is to permit an executor to distribute the estate which he is administering without fear that further liabilities may be outstanding for which he could be held personally liable. If the Federal District Court in Massachusetts applies Rule 4(d)(1) of the Federal Rules of Civil Procedure instead of the Massachusetts service rule, what effect would that have on the speed and assurance with which estates are distributed? As I see it, the effect would not be

---

[2] Byrd v. Blue Ridge indicated that state procedures would apply if the State had manifested a particularly strong interest in their employment.

substantial. It would mean simply that an executor would have to check at his own house or the federal courthouse as well as the registry of probate before he could distribute the estate with impunity. As this does not seem enough to give rise to any real impingement on the vitality of the state policy which the Massachusetts rule is intended to serve, I concur in the judgment of the Court.

NOTES AND PROBLEMS FOR DISCUSSION

1. (a) To what extent, if any, does the decision in *Hanna* represent a departure from the *Erie-York-Byrd* model for analyzing vertical choice of law problems?

(b) Why did Justice Harlan issue a separate concurring opinion?

2. (a) Under *Hanna*, in addition to determining the validity of the relevant Federal Rule, the court must determine whether that Rule applies to the matter in dispute. This inquiry has provided the Court with a measure of breathing room against the otherwise inevitable conclusion that the court should apply the Federal Rule rather than a competing state law or rule. For example, in RAGAN v. MERCHANTS TRANSFER & WAREHOUSE CO., 337 U.S. 530, 69 S.Ct. 1233, 93 L.Ed. 1520 (1949), a pre-*Hanna* case, the plaintiff's action was filed within the period prescribed by the relevant state statute of limitations, but the defendant was not served until after that statute had expired. Under state law, the statute of limitations was tolled by proper service, not the filing of the complaint. But Federal Rule of Civil Procedure 3 provides that an action is deemed to have commenced with the filing of the complaint. Consequently, the choice of whether the federal rule or state law should apply to the tolling question was critical to the maintenance of the plaintiff's action. The Supreme Court, by a divided vote, held that the state rule applied and, therefore, that the plaintiff's claim was barred by the expiration of the state limitations period. The Court revisited this same issue thirty years later in WALKER v. ARMCO STEEL CORPORATION, 446 U.S. 740, 100 S.Ct. 1978, 64 L.Ed.2d 659 (1980). There, in a post-*Hanna* case, the Court, this time unanimously, reaffirmed its ruling in *Ragan* that state law governed the issue of when an action was commenced for purposes of tolling the statute of limitations. After noting that the doctrine of *stare decisis* compels the Court to use caution whenever it is urged to break with established caselaw, the Court rested its decision on a more explicit statement than offered in *Ragan* to the effect that while Federal Rule 3 governed various timing requirements contained within the Federal Rules, it was not intended to affect state statutes of limitations. Thus, the Court reasoned, since the Federal Rule was not clearly applicable to the tolling issue, the *Hanna* exception to the *Erie* doctrine was inapposite and the decision was governed by traditional *Erie* analysis.

(b) If the Court in *Walker* had construed Rule 3 to apply in the statute of limitations context, is it clear that, under *Hanna*, it would have ruled that the Federal Rule, rather than state law, governed the tolling issue?

(c) In footnote 1 of *Hanna*, the majority notes that §9 — the Massachusetts statutory provision containing the state's in-hand service rule — also operated as a one year statute of limitations in probate cases. Is the Court's determination in *Hanna* that the service provision of Federal Rule 4 should be construed broadly to apply in the statute of limitations context (thereby creating a "direct collision" with state law) consistent with its treatment, in *Ragan* and *Walker*, of the scope of the commencement of litigation rule of Federal Rule 3?

(d) In both *Ragan* and *Walker*, the limited issue before the Court was whether Federal Rule 3 governing the tolling of a limitations period governing a state-law created cause of action. In a footnote to its decision in *Walker*, the Court expressly reserved decision on whether Rule 3 would apply to the tolling of a statute of limitations for a claim arising under federal law. The Court eventually resolved this issue in WEST v. CONRAIL, 481 U.S. 35, 107 S.Ct. 1538, 95 L.Ed.2d 32 (1987). There, it held that Federal Rule 3 did apply to the tolling of a statute of limitations that governed a federal cause of action. However, unlike either *Ragan* or *Walker*, this case did not involve the tolling of a *state* statute of limitations. The plaintiff in *West* brought a breach of duty of fair representation claim against his union, a claim that is authorized by §301 of the Labor Management Relations Act (LRMA). But since the LMRA did not contain a statute of limitations expressly applicable to fair representation claims, the Court had to "borrow" an analogous limitations statute from another federal statute — the National Labor Relations Act. Consequently, it was in the context of a statute of limitations borrowed from a federal statute different from the one creating the cause of action that the Court ruled that Rule 3 was the governing rule for tolling that limitations period. This case, then, did not involve the application of Rule 3 to a federal cause of action that was subject to the terms of a state statute of limitations.

(e) In order to discourage the filing of meritless medical malpractice lawsuits, the New Jersey legislature passed a law requiring the plaintiff in a medical malpractice case to submit, within sixty days after the filing of the defendant's answer, an affidavit from a licensed physician that a "reasonable probability" exists that the defendant's care failed to meet acceptable professional standards. The statute further provides that failure to timely file that affidavit results in dismissal of the complaint for failure to state a claim. Federal Rules of Civil Procedure 8 and 9 govern the content and specificity of pleadings. Rule 8 requires only that a pleading contain a "short and plain statement of the claim showing that the pleader is entitled to relief." Rule 9 sets forth more detailed pleading rules, but only in a prescribed list of claims, none of which includes medical malpractice actions. In deciding whether or not to require the plaintiff in a diversity-based malpractice action to comply with the New Jersey statute, should the federal district court apply *Hanna* or traditional *Erie* doctrine? See Chamberlain v. Giampapa, 210 F.3d 154 (3d Cir.2000).

3. (a) Suppose that a diversity action filed in federal district court contains an admittedly procedural issue that is addressed by a federal statute rather than by the Federal Rules of Civil Procedure. Was the ruling in *Hanna* intended to apply to this situation? In STEWART ORGANIZATION, INC. v. RICOH CORPORATION, 487 U.S. 22, 108 S.Ct. 2239, 101 L.Ed.2d 22 (1988), the defendant filed a motion to transfer venue under 28 U.S.C. §1404 or, alternatively, to dismiss the action for improper venue under §1406. The basis for these motions was a provision in a commercial agreement between the parties that requiring that all disputes arising out of that agreement be adjudicated in a state or federal court located in New York City. The plaintiff, however, filed this action, alleging breach of contract, fraud, breach of warranty and federal antitrust violations, in the federal district court for the Northern District of Alabama. The federal trial court determined that Alabama law should govern the resolution of these motions. Since the enforcement of forum selection clauses was disfavored under Alabama jurisprudence, the court denied both parts of the defendant's motion. This decision was reversed by the Eleventh Circuit, which held that questions of venue and the enforceability of forum selection clauses were to be governed by federal law. The Supreme Court affirmed that result, declaring that *Hanna* analysis extended to cases involving the application of federal procedural statutes.

> "Our cases indicate that when the federal law sought to be applied is a congressional statute, the first and chief question for the district court's determination is whether the statute is sufficiently broad to control the issue before the Court. This question involves a straightforward exercise in statutory interpretation to determine if the statute covers the point in dispute.
>
> If the district court determines that a federal statute covers the point in dispute, it proceeds to inquire whether the statute represents a valid exercise of Congress authority under the Constitution. See Hanna v. Plumer. If Congress intended to reach the issue before the District Court, and if it enacted its intention into law in a manner that abides with the Constitution, that is the end of the matter."

487 U.S. at 26-27, 108 S.Ct. at 2242-43. The Court further noted that since the federal law in the instant case was already codified in a statute, the additional *Hanna* requirement of determining whether the subject Federal Rule was authorized by the terms of the Rules Enabling Act was inapposite.

Applying *Hanna* analysis, the Court stated that the fact that §1404 and Alabama's common law policy against enforcing forum selection clauses were not "perfectly coextensive" was not fatal to a decision to apply federal law. The references in some of its earlier opinions to a "direct collision" between the competing laws was not intended, the Court explained, to "mandate that federal law and state law be perfectly coextensive and equally applicable to the issue at hand * * *." Rather, in order for the ruling in *Hanna* to apply, all that was required was that the federal statute "be sufficiently broad to cover the point in dispute." Having concluded that §1404 met that standard, the Court then ruled that since §1404 was a procedural rule, it fell within Congress' constitutional authority under Article III as augmented by the Necessary and Proper Clause. Consequently, the Court concluded that §1404 properly governed the venue dispute. (The parties did not appeal the trial court's ruling denying the §1406 motion to dismiss for lack of venue since the corporate defendant was subject to venue in the Northern District of Alabama. Additionally, the Court stated that in light of its ruling that federal, rather than state law, governed transfer of the state law claims, the presence of federal antitrust claims was of no consequence.).

Although the Supreme Court affirmed the Eleventh Circuit ruling that federal law applied and that the case should be transferred, it did not agree with the lower court's reasoning that transfer was mandated because under the federal common law standards for enforcing forum selection clauses set forth in *The Bremen* the instant forum selection clause was enforceable as a matter of (federal) law. But the Court sidestepped the hard question of whether the standards set forth in *the Bremen* (as subsequently "refined" in *Carnival Cruise*, see Chapter 2, §B, *supra*, at 70) should trump competing state law doctrine in this nonadmiralty case. Instead, the majority opinion simply stated that §1404 required a case-by-case evaluation of convenience and fairness, and that the presence of a forum selection clause was a significant factor to be considered in making these assessments. On the other hand, however, in a dissenting opinion, Justice Scalia concluded that the twin objectives of the *Erie* doctrine compelled the conclusion that state law should control the issue of the validity of a forum selection clause. To do otherwise, he explained, would encourage forum shopping and produce inequitable administration of the laws by discriminating between citizens and noncitizens of the forum state.

Post-*Ricoh*, the federal circuits have been unable to agree on whether federal or state law should govern the enforcement of forum selection clauses in diversity cases. Some circuits continue to avoid the issue on the ground that state and federal forum non conveniens principles coincide, while those that have taken a position are in conflict. Compare Evolution Online Systems, Inc. v. Koninklijke PTT Nederland N.V., 145 F.3d 505 (2d Cir. 1998) (enforcement of forum selection clauses are essentially procedural, rather than substantive, in nature and so federal law should govern their enforcement); Royal Bed and Spring Co., Inc. v. Famossul Industria E Comercio De Moveis LTDA., 906 F.2d 45 (1st Cir. 1990) (federal law controls the enforceability of a forum selection clause in a diversity case on the ground that this issue is a procedural issue and relying on federal law promotes a policy of uniformity within the federal system); and Manetti-Farrow, Inc. v. Gucci America, Inc., 858 F.2d 509 (9th Cir. 1988) (the federal procedural issues raised by forum selection clauses significantly outweigh the state interests, and so federal law controls enforcement of forum clauses in diversity cases) with Farmland Industries, Inc. v. Frazier-Parrott Commodities, Inc., 806 F.2d 848, 852 (8th Cir. 1986) (pre-*Ricoh*) ("Whether a contractual forum selection clause is substantive or procedural is a difficult question. On the one hand the clause determines venue and can be considered procedural, but on the other, choice of forum is an important contractual right of the parties. Because of the close relationship between substance and procedure in this case we believe that consideration should have been given to the public policy of Missouri [forbidding the enforcement of forum selection clauses]."); and General Engineering Corp. v. Martin Marietta Alumina, Inc., 783 F.2d 352 (3d Cir. 1986) (a pre-*Ricoh* case holding that a forum selection clause should be interpreted according to state law because the interpretation of forum selection clauses in commercial contracts is not an area of law that implicates a strong federal interest or policy sufficient to displace state law).

(b) When a defendant in a diversity case moves to dismiss the plaintiff's action under *forum non conveniens*, rather than to transfer it under §1404, should the ruling in *Hanna* apply or does this problem fall under the aegis of traditional

Erie principles since *forum non conveniens* is a federal common law doctrine that is not embodied in a Federal Rule of Civil Procedure or statute?

In footnote 13 of its seminal *forum non conveniens* ruling in *Piper*, see *supra,* at 247, the Supreme Court expressly reserved decision on whether state or federal law of *forum non conveniens* applies in a diversity case because it concluded that the same result would have obtained under either body of law. Ever since then, however, the federal appellate courts have failed to adhere to a uniform position on whether federal or state *forum non conveniens* principles govern when the two sources of law are in conflict. In RAVEL MONEGRO v. ROSA, 211 F.3d 506 (9th Cir.2000), a diversity (alienage) case brought in federal district court in San Francisco by baseball players from the Dominican Republic alleging, *inter alia*, that the San Francisco Giants scout who signed them to minor league contracts conditioned their continued employment upon submitting to his sexual advances, the defendants (the Giants and the scout) moved to dismiss the case on *forum non conveniens* ground in light of the availability of a forum in the Dominican Republic. The Ninth Circuit, reflecting the prevailing view, applying the traditional *Erie* doctrine (as modified by *Byrd*), ruled that federal law should be applied to a *forum non conveniens* motion because the federal judiciary's interest "in self-regulation, in administrative independence, and in self-management are more important than any interest in uniformity between the federal an state forums in a single state." 211 F.3d at 512. (Interestingly, after announcing that the Supreme Court's conclusion in *Piper* that California and federal *forum non conveniens* law were virtually identical was "almost certainly untrue when made" the court found that "it appears to have become true since then." Yet having said that, the court nevertheless chose to face the choice of law issue head-on despite its belief the result would "likely be the same" under federal and California *forum non conveniens* law.)

4. Once a federal court determines, under any of the formulations of the *Erie* doctrine, that state law is to govern a particular issue, the court must then resolve the horizontal choice of law question — i.e., which state's law is to apply. Notice that the Rules of Decision Act, which calls for the federal court to apply "the laws of the several states," does not help the court resolve this matter. In KLAXON CO. v. STENTOR ELECTRIC MFG. CO., 313 U.S. 487, 61 S.Ct. 1020, 85 L.Ed. 1477 (1941), however, the Supreme Court ruled that pursuant to its ruling in *Erie*, a federal court in a diversity case had to apply the choice of law doctrines of the state in which the court sat. *Klaxon* has remained a decidedly controversial decision. Some have suggested that creating a uniform federal choice of law jurisprudence would significantly promote the objective of rationality and predictability in the law. Others have noted that while *Klaxon* removes any incentive for forum shopping between a federal and state court within the same state, it does nothing to discourage forum shopping among those states with jurisdiction over the parties. And nearly two decades after *Klaxon* was decided, Circuit Judge Henry Friendly, in NOLAN v. TRANSOCEAN AIR LINES, 276 F.2d 280,281 (2d. Cir.1960), was prompted to remark that as a result of the *Klaxon* rule, a federal district judge sitting in New York could be required "to determine what New York Courts would think California Courts would think on an issue about which neither has thought." (A discussion of how a federal court goes about the frequently perplexing task of determining the content of state law is found in Section C, *infra*.)

In addition, the rule in *Klaxon* combines with *Erie* to add a further level of complexity to choice of law analysis. Many state choice of law rules employ a procedure/substance dichotomy to determine which state's law should apply to a particular issue. That is, where a state would perceive an issue as procedural, it typically will apply its own law. But where the matter in question is characterized as substantive, state choice of law rules might direct the forum to apply its own law or that of another state. At the same time, however, this substance/procedure standard is also used to make the vertical choice of law assessment under *Erie*. This poses an intriguing problem of chronology for a federal court in a diversity case. Should the court initially undertake the *Erie* inquiry and decide whether or not the issue in question is substantive or procedural for vertical choice of law questions and then, if necessary, per *Klaxon*, adopt the mindset of a state judge from that state to determine whether the issue is procedural or substantive under that state's choice of law rules? Or should it begin by making the substance/procedure choice for *Klaxon*'s horizontal choice of law purposes and then characterize it for *Erie*'s vertical choice of law determination. Since the denomination of an issue as either procedural or substantive does, in fact, sometimes differ under *Erie* and state choice of law rules, this is a real problem. At first blush, it would appear that a federal court should make the *Erie* assessment first, since a finding that the issue is procedural and that federal law governs would obviate the need for a horizontal choice of law determination. However, how can the federal court know whether the competing state rule is procedural or substantive until it knows the content of that state law? And how can it know that before it resolves which state's rule would be applied under the forum state's choice of law rules? This would suggest that the court should commence its choice of law analysis with *Klaxon*.

5. In footnote 9 of its opinion, the *Hanna* Court criticized, nearly to the point of derision, the circuit court's evaluation of the significance of the policy underlying the state's service rule. Although this discussion can be dismissed as *dicta* in light of the Court's ultimate conclusion that traditional *Erie* analysis does not apply where a Federal Rule of Civil Procedure is both applicable and valid, does it forecast the abandonment of the balancing-of-interests exercise undertaken in *Byrd*? While several lower courts read such a message into this text, the Court appears to have breathed new life into *Byrd* in GASPERINI v. CENTER FOR HUMANITIES, INC., 518 U.S. 415, 116 S.Ct. 2211, 135 L.Ed.2d 659 (1996). There, the Court confronted a potential conflict between a New York statute and a provision of the U.S. Constitution with respect to judicial scrutiny of jury damage awards. The state statute empowered state appellate courts to review the amount of jury verdicts and to order new trials when the award "materially deviates from what is reasonable compensation." This statute was enacted in 1986 to impose a greater level of judicial control over jury damage awards by replacing the state common law rule under which state courts would only disturb a jury award if the amount was so exorbitant that it "shocked the conscience of the court." Subsequently, state courts construed this statute to apply to state trial as well as appellate judges.

The plaintiff, a photojournalist, agreed to sell some of his color slides to the defendant for inclusion in a videotape it intended to produce. Although the defendant agreed to return the originals after completing the project, it could not find them. The plaintiff brought suit alleging breach of contract, negligence and conversion in federal court based on diversity jurisdiction. The defendant admitted liability and the case went to trial before a jury solely on the issue of damages. The jury awarded $450,000 in compensatory damages. The trial court denied the defendant's motion for a new trial based on, *inter alia*, the excessiveness of the jury verdict. On appeal, the Second Circuit applied the New York statute and, guided by its review of New York state appellate court decisions that reviewed jury awards in cases involving lost transparencies, concluded that the verdict "materially deviated" from reasonable compensation, and vacated the judgment that the trial court had entered upon the jury verdict.

The Supreme Court was asked to determine whether the circuit court had erred in applying the state law to its review of the jury verdicts in light of language in the Seventh Amendment to the U.S. Constitution stating that to preserve the right to a jury trial in actions at law brought in federal courts, no fact tried by a jury shall be "reexamined" in any federal court other than as permitted under "the rules of the common law." The Court began its analysis by asserting that the New York statute was both substantive and procedural in that it controlled the amount a plaintiff could be awarded (substantive) and assigned decision making authority over jury excessiveness claims to the state's appellate courts (procedural). It then invoked the *York* outcome determinative test. After noting that the parties had conceded that a statutory cap on damages would meet the "substance" standard of *Erie* that compelled the application of state law, the Court acknowledged that the New York scheme differed from a standard statutory cap in that instead of setting forth the maximum amount recoverable within the terms of the statute, that authority was assigned to the state courts. Nevertheless, the Court concluded, the New York statute was designed to achieve that same substantive objective of controlling damage awards and that failure to apply the state law would be expected to produce substantial variations between state and federal damage awards within New York since federal district judges in New York applied a "shock the conscience" standard test for jury awards as dictated by the Second Circuit.

Having said that, however, the Court then cited *Byrd* for the proposition that *York*'s outcome determination test "was an insufficient guide in cases presenting countervailing federal interests." After concluding that neither application of the statutory standard by federal trial judges nor appellate review of trial court decisions denying a new trial under an abuse of discretion standard was precluded by the Reexamination Clause of the Seventh Amendment, the Court fashioned a bipartite regime that would accommodate both the important federal interest in maintaining its allocation of responsibility between trial and appellate courts and the jury control/tort reform interests underlying the state statute. The Court ruled that federal trial courts should be assigned the task of performing the primary jury checking function by applying the state statutory "materially deviates" standard. Appellate review, in turn, would be limited to the federal abuse of discretion standard. Consequently, since the federal trial court in the instant case had not assessed the jury verdict in light of relevant state court decisions interpreting the New York statute, the Supreme Court vacated the Second Circuit's order and instructed it to remand the case to the trial court to test the jury verdict under the state statutory standard rather than under the federal "shock the conscience" test utilized in the Second Circuit.

Three dissenting Justices, in an opinion authored by Justice Scalia, characterized the case as presenting a conflict between the New York State and Rule 59 of the Federal Rules of Civil Procedure. Rule 59, they maintained, provided a federal standard for resolving motions for a new trial that covered this case and was in direct collision with the state standard. Accordingly, they concluded, since *Hanna*, rather than *Erie*, was the relevant case governing the choice of law issue, the federal district court should have been directed to apply the Federal Rule rather than the New York statute. The dissenters also rejected the majority's Seventh Amendment analysis, maintaining that it nullified a longstanding line of precedent holding that the Seventh Amendment prohibited appellate reexamination of civil jury awards as contrary to the weight of the evidence. Justice Stevens also dissented separately. (We include *Gasperini* in full in Chapter 11 in connection with the materials on New Trials.)

But fourteen years after deciding *Gasperini*, in SHADY GROVE ORTHOPEDIC ASSOCIATES, P.A. v. ALLSTATE INSURANCE CO., 559 U.S. 393, 130 S.Ct. 1431, 176 L.Ed. 2d 311 (2010), five Justices joined in that portion of the opinion of the Court that signaled at least a partial return to the Court's *Hanna*-based disinclination to engage in interest balancing. In *Shady Grove*, a medical care facility filed a diversity-based class action in federal district court in New York against an insurer, alleging that the defendant routinely refused to pay statutory interest that accrued under state law on overdue benefits. To shield defendants from excessive damage awards, New York state law precluded the bringing of any class action seeking the recovery of a "penalty" such as statutory interest. The issue in *Shady Grove* was whether the federal district court, sitting in diversity, should apply the New York law or Rule 23, Fed. R. Civ. P., in determining whether this class action could be brought. The district and circuit courts agreed that state law should apply and, therefore, that the complaint should be dismissed for lack of jurisdiction. In an opinion by Justice Scalia, five Members of the Court invoked *Hanna* to reverse the rulings below. The majority reasoned that the state statute and Rule 23 were in conflict on the same issue — the prerequisites to class certification. The majority read Rule 23 as mandating certification of any class that met the criteria set forth in Rule 23(a) and fit within one of the three categories set out in Rule 23(b). They also construed the New York statute as disqualifying any class action in which the plaintiffs sought penalties such as statutory interest. Consequently, in the majority's view, if Rule 23 fell within the authorization of the Rules Enabling Act, it, and not the state law, governed resolution of whether the class action could be maintained in federal court. And since five Justices, albeit for different reasons, concluded that Rule 23 was not *ultra vires*, the Court reversed the rulings below and remanded for a Rule 23 certification determination. The four dissenting Justices, relying principally on *Gasperini*, chided the majority for not interpreting the Federal rules with sensitivity to important state interests codified in the New York statute. The dissenters argued that Rule 23 did not reach the question whether a class action for a penalty could be maintained in federal court if barred by state law, and under *Erie*, they would have applied New York law and disallowed the class action.

SECTION B.   FEDERAL LAW IN STATE COURTS: THE "REVERSE-*ERIE*" PROBLEM

Throughout the first section of this chapter we have examined choice of law issues that confront a federal court when it is adjudicating a claim that was created by state statutory or common law. Should a comparable analysis apply to the converse situation, i.e., where the plaintiff files a federal statutory claim in state court? Since state courts enjoy concurrent subject matter jurisdiction over claims arising under the U.S. Constitution and the overwhelming percentage of federal statutes, this issue arises in those instances when the plaintiff chooses to exercise the state court option and the defendant declines to (or, as in the case of the Federal Employers' Liability Act, is not permitted to) remove the action to federal court.

As an initial matter, Article VI, §2 of the U.S. Constitution, the Supremacy Clause, requires state courts to apply and abide by federal law. But does this command also preclude the state court from applying its own rules of procedure in cases containing federal statutory claims? In DICE v. AKRON, CANTON & YOUNGSTOWN R. CO., 342 U.S. 359, 72 S.Ct. 312, 96 L.Ed. 398 (1951), a railroad fireman brought an action in Ohio state court seeking damages for injuries suffered when the engine in which he was riding jumped tracks. He filed his claim under the Federal Employers' Liability Act, a federal statute providing railroad employees with a right of action against their employer for negligently inflicted damages. The defendant railroad denied its negligence and maintained that the plaintiff had signed a release of claims in exchange for payment. The plaintiff challenged the validity of the release, claiming that he had signed it in reliance upon the railroad's deliberately false statement that the document was only a receipt for wages. The trial judge entered a judgment notwithstanding the jury's verdict in favor of the plaintiff. Under Ohio law, while issues of negligence are decided by the jury, where a release is alleged to have been fraudulently obtained, the trial judge determines the existence of fraud. On the other hand, federal practice makes no such distinction; the jury determines all such factual questions. The Supreme Court held that since the right to a jury trial was an essential part of the remedy provided to railroad workers under the FELA, it could not be classified as a "mere local rule of procedure" governed by state law. It therefore reversed the trial court and reinstated the jury verdict.

Similarly, in FELDER v. CASEY, 487 U.S. 131, 108 S.Ct. 2302, 101 L.Ed.2d 123 (1988), the Court held that a state statute requiring individuals with damage claims against state or local government defendants to provide notice of their intent to sue (including a description of the nature and amount of the claim) within 120 days of the injury and at least 120 days prior to filing the action in state court did *not* apply to federal civil rights action brought under 42 U.S.C. §1983, a statute providing individuals with a right of action for damages against state and local government agents who deprive the plaintiff of her federal civil rights. Where federal statutory claims are pursued in state court, the Supreme Court declared, "the federal right cannot be defeated by the forms of local practice." The Court concluded that because application of the state's "notice of claim" law would (1) conflict with the remedial objectives of §1983 by subjecting §1983 plaintiffs to a procedural obstacle in state court that they need not hurdle in federal court; and (2) have a predictable impact on the outcome of the litigation (failure to file the requisite notice constituted grounds for dismissing the action in state court), this state law must yield to the federal interest.

However, in JOHNSON v. FANKELL, 520 U.S. 911, 117 S.Ct. 1800, 138 L.Ed.2d 108 (1997), another §1983 case, the Court ruled that a state rule of appellate procedure that prohibited interlocutory appeals from denials of summary judgment on defense claims of qualified immunity did not have to yield to a federal statutory provision that permitted interlocutory appeals in these circumstances in federal court. In contrast to the right to jury trial involved in *Dice*, the Court explained, the instant state procedural rule did not significantly interfere with federal interests and did not affect the ultimate disposition of the case because applying the state procedural rule merely postponed, rather than affected the result of, appellate review of the trial court's ruling on the qualified immunity defense.

The combination of these three cases suggests that where a state procedural rule neither burdens nor frustrates the attainment of the federal statute's policies and objectives, and is not outcome determinative, the plaintiff who chooses to enforce her federal claim in state court takes the state courts as she finds them. She is subject to the same rules of procedure that would apply to actions arising under state law.

ERIE AND THE FEDERAL GENERAL
COMMON LAW: A POSTSCRIPT

Under the Rules of Decision Act, state law must provide the rule of decision unless the matter is otherwise governed by the federal constitution, treaties or statutes. The Act says nothing about rules created by federal judges. But when the Supreme Court in *Erie* declared that "[t]here is no federal general common law" did it mean that federal judges could never formulate binding substantive law doctrines through adjudication? If so, why did it insert "general" as a modifier for "common law"? Clearly, Justice Brandeis was concerned about the post-*Swift* practice of federal courts creating common law doctrines to govern a broad expanse of commercial activities. On the other hand, if the federal courts are not empowered to "create" common law doctrines to either fill in the gaps in constitutional and/or federal statutory provisions, or to provide rules of decision in cases involving important federal interests that have not been specifically targeted by any constitutional or federal statutory provision, who is left to perform this task in a manner that will yield a nationally uniform body of jurisprudence (albeit at the expense of intrastate uniformity)?

Both after and on the very day it issued its decision in *Erie*, the Supreme Court acknowledged the power of federal judges to confect substantive principles of common law. In HINDERLIDER v. LA PLATA RIVER & CHERRY CREEK DITCH CO., 304 U.S. 92,110 58 S.Ct. 803,811 82 L.Ed. 1202 (1938), decided on the same day as *Erie*, the Court (majority opinion written by none other than Justice Brandeis, the author of *Erie*!) was presented with a water dispute between Colorado and New Mexico. Clearly, it would have been awkward to resolve the controversy according to the law of either state. Accordingly, the Court announced that "whether the water of an interstate stream must be apportioned between the two States [into which it flows] is a question of federal common law upon which neither the statutes nor the decisions of either State can be conclusive."

The Court has expressly authorized the creation of federal common law in other areas involving important national interests. For example, in CLEARFIELD TRUST CO. v. UNITED STATES, 318 U.S. 363, 63 S.Ct. 573, 87 L.Ed. 838 (1943), the Court sanctioned the development of federal common law principles to govern the conduct of commercial activities by the U.S. Government when it ruled that in the absence of any applicable federal statute, it was up to the federal courts to "fashion the governing rule of law [concerning the rights and obligations of the federal government on federally issued commercial paper] according to their own standards." In DICE v. AKRON, CANTON & YOUNGSTOWN R. CO., 342 U.S. 359, 72 S.Ct. 312, 96 L.Ed. 398 (1951), described in Section B., *supra*, the Court ruled that the validity of releases in FELA cases was to be determined by federal law. And in TEXTILE WORKERS UNION v. LINCOLN MILLS OF ALABAMA, 353 U.S. 448, 77 S.Ct. 912, 1 L.Ed.2d 972 (1957), the Court directed the federal district courts to develop a federal common law of contracts to be applied in actions brought under §301 of the federal Labor Management Relations Act, a provision that supplied the federal courts with subject matter jurisdiction over claims to enforce collectively bargained agreements. In each of these situations, the Court was motivated, in significant part, by the desire, if not the need, to develop a nationally uniform set of rules to govern matters of uniquely federal concern.

Once it is determined that a particular issue is to be governed by the application of federal common law, where does the federal court look to determine its content? Is the federal common law intended to be an independent, uniform set of rules created afresh by federal judges or should the rules of decision be derived from existing state law principles? The Court has articulated a general balancing test to be applied to this inquiry. In U.S. v. KIMBELL FOODS, INC., 440 U.S. 715, 99 S.Ct. 1448, 59 L.Ed.2d 711 (1979), the Court was asked to determine whether liens held by the federal government arising from federal loan programs should take precedence over private liens when the borrower defaults on federal loans and the federal statutes creating these lending programs do not establish any lien priority schedule. Relying on its ruling in *Clearfield*, the Court first held that federal law governed this question since it concerned the rights of the federal government in connection with federal programs. It then noted that controversies affecting the operations of federal programs "do not inevitably require resort to uniform federal rules." Rather, it explained, the choice between absorbing state law or creating federal rules of decision depended upon a balancing of several factors:

> "Undoubtedly, federal programs that by their nature are and must be uniform in character throughout the Nation necessitate formulation of controlling federal rules. Conversely, when there is little need for a nationally uniform body of law, state law may be incorporated as the federal rule of decision. Apart from considerations of uniformity, we must also determine whether application of state law would frustrate specific objectives of the federal programs. If so, we must fashion special rules solicitous of those federal interests. Finally, our choice-of-law inquiry must consider the extent to which application of a federal rule would disrupt commercial relationships predicated on state law."

440 U.S. at 728-729, 99 S.Ct. at 1458-1459. Thus, according to this set of guidelines, the courts should gauge the need for uniformity and protection of federal interests against the dislocation of settled expectations generated by the replacement of state law with newly created federal doctrines.

The implementation of this blueprint, as expected, led the federal courts on some occasions to create their own doctrines and, in other instances, to "borrow" principles from state law. For example, many federal statutes do not contain a limitations provision governing the time limit within which claims can be filed. The Supreme Court, on several occasions, has instructed the lower federal courts to apply an existing state statute of limitations rather than create an independent federal limitations period. See e.g., Wilson v. Garcia, 471 U.S. 261, 105 S.Ct. 1983, 85 L.Ed.2d 254 (1985) (state limitations provision governing personal injury actions applies to all §1983 claims); and Goodman v. Lukens Steel Co., 482 U.S. 656, 107 S.Ct. 2617, 96 L.Ed.2d 572 (1987) (extending *Wilson* rule to actions brought under 42 U.S.C. §1981). But see DelCostello v. Teamsters, 462 U.S. 151, 103 S.Ct. 2281, 76 L.Ed.2d 476 (1983) (applying limitations provision of analogous federal statute where incorporating a very short state limitations period would frustrate the implementation of the policies underlying the federal substantive law). Conversely, to promote the creation and enforcement of a uniform national labor policy, the Court in *Lincoln Mills* charged the federal courts with the task of fashioning their own set of common law contract principles to govern actions to enforce collectively bargained agreements under the federal Labor Management Relations Act.

One of the more controversial manifestations of federal common law-making authority involves the judicial recognition or (depending upon your point of view) creation of "implied" constitutional and statutory rights of action. This occurs when a provision in either the U.S. Constitution or a federal statute creates a category of rights but does not expressly provide members of the protected class with a private right of action to enforce those rights. In fact, there is a significant debate about whether the decision to recognize an implied right of action even constitutes common lawmaking, or whether it is merely an exercise in statutory or constitutional interpretation.

For example, the Fourth Amendment to the U.S. Constitution protects individuals from unreasonable searches and seizures of their person and property. But nowhere in the text of that Amendment is an individual authorized to file a suit for damages against anyone who engages in constitutionally proscribed conduct. And although Congress has enacted a statute — 42 U.S.C. §1983 — that provides individuals with a right of action for money damages for invasions of their constitutional rights by persons acting under color of state law, this statute does not provide relief when the perpetrator is a federal agent. The Court filled this gap in BIVENS v. SIX UNKNOWN NAMED AGENTS OF FEDERAL BUREAU OF NARCOTICS, 403 U.S. 388, 91 S.Ct. 1999, 29 L.Ed.2d 619 (1971), when it ruled that an individual could assert a claim for money damages against a federal agent who, while acting under the color of his authority, violated the plaintiff's Fourth Amendment rights. Since monetary damages was historically regarded "as the ordinary remedy for an invasion of personal interests in liberty," where an invasion of rights has occurred and Congress has enacted a statute providing for a "general right to sue" for invasions of that right (although not with respect to the class of defendants in the instant case), the Court reasoned, "federal courts may use any available remedy to make good the wrong done." The Court subsequently recognized a similar private damages remedy for a violation of a federal employee's right to equal protection guaranteed by the due process clause of the Fifth Amendment, Davis v. Passman, 442 U.S. 228, 99 S.Ct. 2264, 60 L.Ed.2d 846 (1979) and for violation of a federal prisoner's rights under the Eighth Amendment, Carlson v. Green, 446 U.S. 14, 100 S.Ct. 1468, 64 L.Ed.2d 15 (1980).

In BUSH v. LUCAS, 462 U.S. 367, 103 S.Ct. 2404, 76 L.Ed.2d 648 (1983), however, the Court recognized and imposed a limitation upon a federal court's remedy-conferring authority. There, it refused to recognize a damage remedy for a federal employee who alleged a violation of the First Amendment by his supervisors. Unlike *Bivens* and *Davis*, where Congress had not provided a remedy against unconstitutional conduct by federal officials, federal employees were protected by "an elaborate, comprehensive scheme" that provides "meaningful" remedies for precisely the type of First Amendment claim asserted by the instant plaintiff. And even though (1) the plaintiff could not receive complete relief (he could obtain reinstatement plus back pay and retroactive seniority but not damages) under the extant regime; and (2) Congress had not expressly precluded the creation of such a remedy, the Court concluded that it should defer to Congress' determination that the public interest was best served by this type of remedial mechanism. And although the Court did not use this terminology, its reasoning reflects a concern over a potential separation of powers problem when unelected federal judges are seen as usurping the lawmaking powers of the politically accountable branch of government.

The judicial creation of damage remedies has not been limited to the universe of constitutional violations. In CORT v. ASH, 422 U.S. 66, 95 S.Ct. 2080, 45 L.Ed.2d 26 (1975), the Court formulated a four factor test to determine when it will recognize the existence of an "implied" cause of action. Under this standard, the Court examines whether (1) the plaintiff is a member of the statute's protected class; (2) there is evidence of Congressional intent either to preclude or create such a remedy; (3) implying such a remedy would be consistent with the statutory objectives; and (4) there would be a federalism problem in inferring a remedy under federal law because this cause of action is traditionally a matter of state concern relegated to state law. The application of this test has led the Court on most occasions to reject a request to imply a private right of action, although as with most generalizations, there are exceptions to the rule. For example, the Court authorized a private right of action under Title IX of the Educational Amendments of 1972 (prohibiting sex discrimination in federally funded educational programs), see Cannon v. University of Chicago, 441 U.S. 677, 99 S.Ct. 1946, 60 L.Ed.2d 560 (1979) and under the Commodities Future Trading Commission Act, see Merrill Lynch, Pierce, Fenner & Smith, Inc. v. Curran, 456 U.S. 353, 102 S.Ct. 1825, 72 L.Ed.2d 182 (1982). But the general pattern is reflected in NORTHWEST AIRLINES, INC. v. TRANSPORT WORKERS UNION OF AMERICA, AFL-CIO, 451 U.S. 77, 91, 101 S.Ct. 1571, 1580, 67 L.Ed.2d 750 (1981), where the Court unanimously held that there was no implied right of action for contribution in favor of an employer against a union under either Title VII or the Equal Pay Act. Moreover, in so ruling, the Court in *Northwest Airlines* declared that the task of resolving that question was not a matter of creating federal common law, but, rather, "one of statutory construction. The ultimate question in cases such as this is whether Congress intended to create the private remedy * * *." Yet immediately after concluding that the statute should not be interpreted to provide employers with a right of contribution, the Court undertook an independent examination of whether this same remedy should be created as a matter of federal common law. This separate analysis was required, the Court maintained, because "the authority to construe a statute is fundamentally different from the authority to fashion a new rule or to provide a new remedy which Congress has decided not to adopt." 451 U.S. at 97, 101 S.Ct. at 1583. Since both Title VII and the Equal Pay Act contained comprehensive remedial and enforcement schemes, the Court concluded that it was appropriate to act upon the presumption that the omission of an express right of contribution was a deliberate decision on Congress' part that the federal courts were not empowered to overturn through the creation of federal common law.

SECTION C. ASCERTAINING THE CONTENT OF STATE LAW

Once a federal court exercising diversity jurisdiction determines both (a) that state law provides the rule of decision over an issue; and (b) which state's law it will apply, the court obviously must determine the content of that law. As we know from the *Erie* doctrine, the preeminent reason for requiring the federal court to apply state law is to enhance the chance that the resolution of that issue will not depend upon the accident of diversity of citizenship, i.e., that the federal court will provide the same result that would obtain in a state court within that state. Therefore, the federal judge is under an obligation to put herself in the shoes of a state judge of the state whose law has been chosen and to determine how that judge would resolve the controversy at hand. But it often is not quite as simple as that. Regardless of whether the governing law is a state statute or state common law, there are inevitably interpretive questions that must be resolved. And while a federal judge would clearly be required to conform to a clear and distinct ruling by the relevant state's highest court, how does the federal court divine, or, indeed, predict the content of state law as to an issue (1) that is one of first impression, or (2) that was addressed by the state's highest court so long ago that its continued viability is questionable, or (3) that the state's judiciary has only addressed at the trial or intermediate appellate levels? Furthermore, once the trial judge has determined the content of unsettled state law, to what extent should her decision be reviewable by the federal court of appeals?

The Supreme Court's most frequently cited articulation of the analytical process that should guide a federal district judge in ascertaining the content of unsettled state law is found in a non-diversity case. In COMMISSIONER OF INTERNAL REVENUE v. ESTATE OF BOSCH, 387 U.S. 456, 87 S.Ct. 1776, 18 L.Ed.2d 886 (1967), the U.S. Tax Court concluded that it was bound by a determination of state law by a state trial court in a related case that, unlike the matter before the Tax Court, did not involve the U.S. as a party. After the Tax Court's ruling was appealed to a federal district and circuit court, it arrived at the Supreme Court. Upon concluding that the policy expressed in the Rules of Decision Act was properly applied in the instant context, the Court offered the following flexible approach to how federal trial courts should follow the *Erie* command of determining state law in diversity cases:

> "[W]hile decrees of lower state court should be attributed some weight, the decision is not controlling where the highest court of the State has not spoken on the point. * * * [A]n intermediate appellate state court is a datum for ascertaining state law which is not to be disregarded by a federal court unless it is convinced by other persuasive data that the highest court of the state would decide otherwise. Thus, under some conditions, federal authority may not be bound even by an intermediate state appellate court ruling. It follows here, then, that when the application of a federal statute is involved, the decision of a state trial court as to an underlying issue of state law should a fortiori not be controlling. This is but an application of the rule of Erie R. Co. v. Tompkins * * * [that] the underlying substantive rule involved is based on state law and the State's highest court is the best authority on its own law. If there be no decision by that court then federal authorities must apply what they find to be the state law after giving proper regard to relevant rulings of other courts of the state. In this respect, it may be said to be, in effect, sitting as a state court."

387 U.S. at 465, 87 S.Ct. at 1782-83.

This approach clearly gives federal judges more than a bit of wiggle room, since it has been interpreted to instruct them to look to all relevant data that a judge of the state's highest court would consider in attempting to resolve an unsettled issue of state law. And while the elasticity of this standard might lead some to wonder whether it creates the potential for a return to the *Swift* era of federal court-created general common law, a contrary rule compelling federal district judges to be conclusively bound by any decision of a trial or appellate state court could well lead to the sort of forum shopping (by parties favoring the retention of the jurisprudential status quo) that *Erie* sought to avoid.

Two independent mechanisms, however, have the potential for aiding the federal judges in their search for the meaning of state law: *certification* and *abstention*. More than thirty states, by statute or rule, provide federal courts (frequently only appellate and not trial courts) with the opportunity to certify a question of state law for resolution by the state's highest court. Where it exists, *certification* provides federal courts with the discretion to submit a question of unsettled state law to the state's highest court for determination. But once submitted for certification, the state court's resolution of the issue is binding upon the federal court. Despite its apparent attractions, certification is not, however, a painless solution to the guessing game that federal courts sometimes must otherwise undertake. It typically takes a significant amount of time, often more than a year, to get an answer from the state court, during which time the federal case remains unresolved. Additionally, the certified question is asked and answered in a vacuum in the sense that the state court does not engage in any fact finding or other pursuit to put the legal question into a specific context.

Abstention involves the willing suspension of a court's otherwise acknowledged authority to adjudicate a case. In this scenario, the federal case is either dismissed or stayed pending the filing of an action in state trial court. This means that the presence of an issue that convinced the federal court to abstain will not be authoritatively resolved until it reaches the state's highest tribunal, with the possibility of review by the U.S. Supreme Court. Abstention is not invoked, however, merely to avoid construing an unsettled question of state law. This extraordinary action is only undertaken in the presence of a discrete list of special circumstances. One of the most common examples of abstention occurs when the federal court believes that the resolution of the state law issue by the state courts would avoid the necessity of resolving a federal constitutional question. Another example is where the state law in question is part of an extensively regulated area of law that would be seriously impaired by a federal court's erroneous interpretation of state law. Any detailed examination of these and other circumstances warranting invocation of the abstention doctrine is best reserved to an advanced course in federal jurisdiction.

Assuming the federal trial court cannot or does not certify the question to the state court, once it construes the state law issue at hand, the only avenue for appeal is to go to another federal court — the circuit court of appeals. As you know, each federal circuit encompasses several states and since each appellate case is resolved, at least initially, by a panel of three circuit judges, it is likely that the panel sitting on a particular case will include no judge who is from the state whose law is being applied. Should the fact that the entire panel may be composed of judges whose prior career experiences did not include exposure to the governing state law be relevant to the level of deference the appellate court should accord the federal trial judge's ruling on the state law issue? Prior to 1991, the overwhelming majority of federal circuit courts subjected trial court rulings on state law issues to the very limited "clearly erroneous" standard of review. In effect, they treated these rulings of law like findings of fact, reversing the trial court only when they found the decision below to be clearly erroneous. That all changed, however, after the Court joined hands with the two dissenting circuit courts in the following case:

Salve Regina College v. Russell

Supreme Court of the United States, 1991.

499 U.S. 225, 111 S.Ct. 1217, 113 L.Ed.2d 190.

MR. JUSTICE BLACKMUN delivered the opinion of the Court.

The concept of a federal general common law, lurking (to use Justice Holmes' phrase) as a "brooding omnipresence in the sky," was questioned for some time before being firmly rejected in Erie R. Co. v. Tompkins. Erie mandates that a federal court sitting in diversity apply the substantive law of the forum State, absent a federal statutory or constitutional directive to the contrary. In decisions after Erie, this Court made clear that state law is to be determined in the same manner as a federal court resolves an evolving issue of federal law: with the aid of such light as [is] afforded by the materials for decision at hand, and in accordance with the applicable principles for determining state law.

In this case, we must decide specifically whether a federal court of appeals may review a district court's determination of state law under a standard less probing than that applied to a determination of federal law.

I

The issue presented arises out of a contract dispute between a college and one of its students. Petitioner Salve Regina College is an institution of higher education located in Newport, R.I. Respondent Sharon L. Russell was admitted to the college and began her studies as a freshman in 1982. The following year, respondent sought admission to the college's nursing department in order to pursue a bachelor of science degree in nursing. She was accepted by the department and began her nursing studies in the fall of 1983.

Respondent, who was 5'6" tall, weighed in excess of 300 pounds when she was accepted in the nursing program. Immediately after the 1983 school year began, respondent's weight became a topic of commentary and concern by officials of the nursing program. Respondent's first year in the program was marked by a series of confrontations and negotiations concerning her obesity and its effect upon her ability to complete the clinical requirements safely and satisfactorily. During her junior year, respondent signed a document that was designated as a "contract" and conditioned her further participation in the nursing program upon weekly attendance at a weight-loss seminar and a realized average loss of two pounds per week. When respondent failed to meet these commitments, she was asked to withdraw from the program and did so. She transferred to a nursing program at another college * * *. * * *

Soon after leaving Salve Regina College, respondent filed this civil action in the United States District Court for the District of Rhode Island. She asserted, among others, claims based on * * * nonperformance by the college of its implied agreement to educate respondent. Subject-matter jurisdiction in the District Court was based on diversity of citizenship. The parties agree that the law of Rhode Island applies to all substantive aspects of the action.

At the close of plaintiff-respondent's case in chief, the District Court * * * denied the college's motion for a directed verdict on the breach-of-contract claim, reasoning that "a legitimate factual issue" remained concerning whether "there was substantial performance by the plaintiff in her overall contractual relationship at Salve Regina."

At the close of all the evidence, the college renewed its motion for a directed verdict. It argued that under Rhode Island law the strict commercial doctrine of substantial performance did not apply in the general academic context. Therefore, according to petitioner, because respondent admitted she had not fulfilled the terms of the contract, the college was entitled to judgment as a matter of law.

The District Court denied petitioner's motion. Acknowledging that the Supreme Court of Rhode Island, to that point, had limited the application of the substantial-performance doctrine to construction contracts, the District Court nonetheless concluded, as a matter of law, that the Supreme Court of Rhode Island would apply that doctrine to the facts of respondent's case. The Federal District Judge based this conclusion, in part, on his observation that "I was a state trial judge for 18 and 1/2 years, and I have a feel for what the Rhode Island Supreme Court will do or won't do." Accordingly, the District Court submitted the breach-of-contract claim to the jury. The court instructed the jury:

> "The law provides that substantial and not exact performance accompanied by good faith is what is required in a case of a contract of this type. It is not necessary that the plaintiff have fully and completely performed every item specified in the contract between the parties. It is sufficient if there has been substantial performance, not necessarily full performance, so long as the substantial performance was in good faith and in compliance with the contract, except for some minor and relatively unimportant deviation or omission."

The jury returned a verdict for respondent, and determined that the damages were $30,513.40. Judgment was entered. Both respondent and petitioner appealed.

The United States Court of Appeals for the First Circuit affirmed. * * * Rejecting petitioner's argument that, under Rhode Island law, the doctrine of substantial performance does not apply in the college-student context, the court stated:

> "In this case of first impression, the district court held that the Rhode Island Supreme Court would apply the substantial performance standard to the contract in question. In view of the customary appellate deference accorded to interpretations of state law made by federal judges of that state, we hold that the district court's determination that the Rhode Island Supreme Court would apply standard contract principles is not reversible error."

Petitioner * * * alleged that the Court of Appeals erred in deferring to the District Court's determination of state law. A majority of the Courts of Appeals, although varying in their phraseology, embrace a rule of deference similar to that articulated by the Court of Appeals in this case. Two Courts of Appeals, however, have broken ranks recently with their sister Circuits. They have concluded that a district-court determination of state law is subject to plenary review by the appellate court. We granted certiorari to resolve the conflict.

II

We conclude that a court of appeals should review de novo a district court's determination of state law. As a general matter, of course, the courts of appeals are vested with plenary appellate authority over final decisions of district courts. The obligation of responsible appellate jurisdiction implies the requisite authority to review independently a lower court's determinations.

Independent appellate review of legal issues best serves the dual goals of doctrinal coherence and economy of judicial administration. District judges preside alone over fast-paced trials: Of necessity they devote much of their energy and resources to hearing witnesses and reviewing evidence. Similarly, the logistical burdens of trial advocacy limit the extent to which trial counsel is able to supplement the district judge's legal research with memoranda and briefs. Thus, trial judges often must resolve complicated legal questions without benefit of extended reflection or extensive information.

Courts of appeals, on the other hand, are structurally suited to the collaborative juridical process that promotes decisional accuracy. With the record having been constructed below and settled for purposes of the appeal, appellate judges are able to devote their primary attention to legal issues. As questions of law become the focus of appellate review, it can be expected that the parties' briefs will be refined to bring to bear on the legal issues more information and more comprehensive analysis than was provided for the district judge. Perhaps most important, courts of appeals employ multijudge panels, that permit reflective dialogue and collective judgment. * * *

Independent appellate review necessarily entails a careful consideration of the district court's legal analysis, and an efficient and sensitive appellate court at least will naturally consider this analysis in undertaking its review. Petitioner readily acknowledges the importance of a district court's reasoning to the appellate court's review. Any expertise possessed by the district court will inform the structure and content of its conclusions of law and thereby become evident to the reviewing court. If the court of appeals finds that the district court's analytical sophistication and research have exhausted the state-law inquiry, little more need be said in the appellate opinion. Independent review, however, does not admit of unreflective reliance on a lower court's inarticulable intuitions. Thus, an appropriately respectful application of de novo review should encourage a district court to explicate with care the basis for its legal conclusions.

Those circumstances in which Congress or this Court has articulated a standard of deference for appellate review of district-court determinations reflect an accommodation of the respective institutional advantages of trial and appellate courts. In deference to the unchallenged superiority of the district court's factfinding ability, Rule 52(a) commands that a trial court's findings of fact "shall not be set aside unless clearly erroneous, and due regard shall be given to the opportunity of the trial court to judge of the credibility of the witnesses." In addition, it is "especially common" for issues involving supervision of litigation to be reviewed for abuse of discretion. Finally, we have held that deferential review of mixed questions of law and fact is warranted when it appears that the district court is "better positioned" than the appellate court to decide the issue in question or that probing appellate scrutiny will not contribute to the clarity of legal doctrine.

Nothing about the exercise of diversity jurisdiction alters these functional components of decisionmaking or otherwise warrants departure from a rule of independent appellate review. Actually, appellate deference to the district court's determination of state law is inconsistent with the principles underlying this Court's decision in Erie. The twin aims of the Erie doctrine — discouragement of forum-shopping and avoidance of inequitable administration of the laws — are components of the goal of doctrinal coherence advanced by independent appellate review. As respondent has conceded, deferential appellate review invites divergent development of state law among the federal trial courts even within a single State. Moreover, by denying a litigant access to meaningful review of state-law claims, appellate courts that defer to the district courts' state-law determinations create a dual system of enforcement of state-created rights, in which the substantive rule applied to a dispute may depend on the choice of forum. Neither of these results, unavoidable in the absence of independent appellate review, can be reconciled with the commands of Erie.

* * *

III

In urging this Court to adopt the deferential standard embraced by the majority of the Courts of Appeals, respondent offers two arguments. First, respondent suggests that the appellate courts professing adherence to the rule of deference actually are reviewing de novo the district-court determinations of state law. Second, respondent presses the familiar contention that district judges are better arbiters of unsettled state law because they have exposure to the judicial system of the State in which they sit. We reject each of these arguments.

A

Respondent primarily contends that the Courts of Appeals that claim to accord special consideration to the District Court's state-law expertise actually undertake plenary review of a determination of state law. According to respondent, this is simply de novo review clothed in "deferential" robes. In support of this contention, respondent refers to several decisions in which the appellate court has announced that it is bound to review deferentially a district court's determination of state law, yet nonetheless has found that determination to constitute reversible error. Respondent also relies on cases in which the Courts of Appeals, while articulating a rule of deference, acknowledge their obligation to scrutinize closely the District Court's legal conclusions.

We decline the invitation to assume that courts of appeals craft their opinions disingenuously. The fact that an appellate court overturns an erroneous determination of state law in no way indicates that the appellate court is not applying the rule of deference articulated in the opinion. * * *

Nor does it suffice to recognize that little substantive difference may separate the form of deference articulated and applied by the several Courts of Appeals and the independent appellate review urged by petitioner. Respondent argues that the subtle differences between these standards are insufficient to warrant intrusion into the manner in which appellate courts review state-law determinations. * * *

As a practical matter, respondent * * * frequently may be correct. We do not doubt that in many cases the application of a rule of deference in lieu of independent review will not affect the outcome of an appeal. In many diversity cases the controlling issues of state law will have been squarely resolved by the state courts, and a district court's adherence to the settled rule will be indisputably correct. In a case where the controlling question of state law remains unsettled, it is not unreasonable to assume that the considered judgment of the court of appeals frequently will coincide with the reasoned determination of the district court. Where the state-law determinations of the two courts diverge, the choice between these standards of review is of no significance if the appellate court concludes that the district court was clearly wrong.[4]

Thus, the mandate of independent review will alter the appellate outcome only in those few cases where the appellate court would resolve an unsettled issue of state law differently from the district court's resolution, but cannot conclude that the district court's determination constitutes clear error. These few instances, however, make firm our conviction that the difference between a rule of deference and the duty to exercise independent review is "much more than a mere matter of degree." When de novo review is compelled, no form of appellate deference is acceptable.

B

Respondent also argues that de novo review is inappropriate because, as a general matter, a district judge is better positioned to determine an issue of state law than are the judges on the court of appeals. This superior capacity derives, it is said, from the regularity with which a district judge tries a diversity case governed by the law of the forum State, and from the extensive experience that the district judge generally has had as practitioner or judge in the forum State.

We are unpersuaded. As an initial matter, this argument seems to us to be founded fatally on overbroad generalizations. Moreover, and more important,

---

[4] Of course, a question of state law usually can be resolved definitively if the litigation is instituted in state court and is not finally removed to federal court, or if a certification procedure is available and is successfully utilized. Rhode Island provides a certification procedure. See, however, Lehman Brothers v. Schein, 416 U.S. 386, 390-391, 94 S.Ct. 1741, 1743-1744, 40 L.Ed.2d 215 (1974) ("We do not suggest that where there is doubt as to local law and where the certification procedure is available, resort to it is obligatory. It does, of course, in the long run save time, energy, and resources and helps build a cooperative judicial federalism. Its use in a given case rests in the sound discretion of the federal court.").

the proposition that a district judge is better able to "intuit" the answer to an unsettled question of state law is foreclosed by our holding in Erie. The very essence of the Erie doctrine is that the bases of state law are presumed to be communicable by the parties to a federal judge no less than to a state judge. * * * Similarly, the bases of state law are as equally communicable to the appellate judges as they are to the district judge. To the extent that the available state law on a controlling issue is so unsettled as to admit of no reasoned divination, we can see no sense in which a district judge's prior exposure or nonexposure to the state judiciary can be said to facilitate the rule of reason.

IV

The obligation of responsible appellate review and the principles of a cooperative judicial federalism underlying Erie require that courts of appeals review the state-law determinations of district courts de novo. The Court of Appeals in this case therefore erred in deferring to the local expertise of the District Court.

The judgment of the Court of Appeals is reversed, and the case is remanded for further proceedings consistent with this opinion.

[The dissenting opinion of CHIEF JUSTICE REHNQUIST, joined in by JUSTICES WHITE and STEVENS, is omitted.]

NOTES AND PROBLEMS FOR DISCUSSION

1. Do you agree with the majority that *Erie* mandates a de novo review standard?

2. (a) Suppose a diversity case was filed in the federal district court in New Orleans and it was undisputed that Florida state law applied to a particular issue. Further, assume that the Florida Supreme Court had not resolved this issue, but that it had been the subject of an opinion by the Eleventh Circuit Court of Appeals, which encompasses Florida. In conducting its de novo review of the state law issue, should the Eleventh Circuit's decision be conclusive on the Fifth Circuit or should it merely be viewed as a relevant factor to consider? See Factors Etc., Inc. v. Pro Arts, Inc., 652 F.2d 278 (2d Cir.1982), cert. denied, 456 U.S. 927, 102 S.Ct. 1973, 72 L.Ed.2d 442 (1982).

(b) Does the Supreme Court's ruling in *Salve Regina College* help answer this question?

3. To what extent should an intervening authoritative decision on state law by the state's highest court be relevant in a diversity case in the following circumstances?

(a) The state court decision is issued while the federal trial judge's ruling is on appeal before the circuit court. See Vandenbark v. Owen-Illinois Glass Co., 311 U.S. 538, 61 S.Ct. 347, 85 L.Ed. 327 (1941).

(b) The state court decision is issued after the federal circuit court has ruled and while the case is pending before the U.S. Supreme Court. See D.L. Thomas

v. American Home Products, Inc., 519 U.S. 913, 117 S.Ct. 282, 136 L.Ed.2d 201 (1996).

(c) The state court decision is issued after all federal appeals have been exhausted. See De Weerth v. Baldinger, 38 F.3d 1266 (2d Cir.1994), cert. denied, 513 U.S. 1001, 115 S.Ct. 512, 130 L.Ed.2d 419 (1994).

CHAPTER 6

Judicial Remedies

Those who contemplate bringing a lawsuit generally want something. Some may simply wish to see "justice" done, or to have the defendant punished somehow for his acts, or simply to make the defendant apologize. Others may want the psychological benefit of having their day in court, while still others may have something more specific in mind, such as changing the defendant's behavior or seeking compensation for injury. Of course, no relief of any kind is possible unless the plaintiff's claim, if proved, is one for which the law permits relief. We address in the next chapter the basic requirement that the plaintiff be able to state a valid claim. We treat the problem of remedies first, however, because no informed decision whether to file a lawsuit can be made without knowing what the available judicial remedies might be.

Despite the varied reasons that may initially lead a person to contemplate bringing a lawsuit, the kinds of relief that a court can award in civil litigation are relatively few in kind, and not all remedies may be available in all litigation. In the proper case, courts can award monetary damages, issue orders that compel a party to do something or to cease doing something, or, in some settings, they can simply declare the rights of the parties. The nature of available relief is significant because a would-be litigant must determine whether it is financially and emotionally worth it to pursue whatever it is that litigation can offer.

As discussed in greater detail in the next chapter, the availability of monetary relief as opposed to injunctive relief roughly correlates with the ancient division between courts of law and courts of equity. In the former, damages were the usual remedy, while in the latter, injunctive relief was the usual remedy. (Of course, exceptions to this rule of thumb existed in both systems.) The relationship between courts of law and courts of equity is brought out by the requirement that a court of equity not act unless the remedy at law — i.e., the remedy that would be available in a common law court — was somehow "inadequate." For example, because the common law courts would not recognize fraud as a defense to a contract under seal, equity would provide relief in the form of rescission of the contract if fraud were proved, and an injunction against further proceedings for breach of contract in the courts of law. Today most states have rid themselves of separate courts of law and equity (as have the federal courts), and equitable and legal remedies may now be available in the same lawsuit. But the law-equity distinction and the historical origins of particular remedies still affect the terms on which different remedies will be awarded.

Despite the modern-day merger of law and equity, the remedy of damages or injunctive relief will be available only if the underlying substantive legal theory permits the particular remedy. For example, in a suit for wrongful death, the proper remedy would be damages — not an injunction that tells the defendant to change his behavior in the future, even if such a change would be desirable or would make the decedent's relatives feel better. On the other hand, in a breach of contract action involving the sale of land, the plaintiff might be able to sue for damages for the breach (a "legal" remedy), or, alternatively, he might sue for specific performance — an injunction ordering the defendant to carry out the contract and convey the land to the plaintiff (an "equitable" remedy).

In this chapter, we provide a brief survey of the types of remedies that courts may grant and the significance of each as a possible incentive to the parties to litigate. We also discuss the role of lawyers in securing relief, and the incentives that litigation creates for them to bring suit, including contingent fee arrangements and rules respecting fee-shifting — i.e., loser-pays rules. The latter topic is significant because, under the "American Rule" each side ordinarily pays its own legal fees, win or lose. Consequently, many claims that could only result in small monetary awards, or which involve only injunctive or declaratory relief, may have a tough time in the legal market place, unless the expected remedy is sufficient to justify the cost of hiring an attorney. We also briefly discuss incentives for settlement within the framework of litigation.

SECTION A. MONETARY RELIEF

1. COMPENSATORY DAMAGES

An award of damages is perhaps the most common form of relief that a court may order. The main goal of compensatory relief is to compensate the plaintiff for the harm she has suffered because of the defendant's actions. As the court put it in United States v. Hatahley, 257 F.2d 920, 923 (10th Cir. 1958), "The fundamental principle of damages is to restore the injured party, as nearly as possible, to the position he would have been in had it not been for the wrong of the other party."

Of course, a damages award cannot turn back the clock and thus cannot really return the plaintiff to her former position. Thus, monetary remedies are sometimes referred to as a "substitutionary" remedy — money is substituted for the loss that must be quantified by the factfinder. In the grander scheme of things, monetary damages serve as a form of corrective justice — making the defendant pay for the harm he has inflicted and not forcing the plaintiff to bear the loss. Also, making those who cause harm pay for it arguably forces them to confront the true costs of their activities.

Not everyone will agree in every case how to formulate what it would take to put the plaintiff in the position she would have been in absent the defendant's wrong. Contract law, for example, has proved a fertile field for debates over the proper focus of damages for breach (e.g., reliance versus expectation interests). In tort cases, even when the interest to be compensated is clear, the calculation of damages can be uncertain. Emotional pain and suffering may be a traditional element of recovery in a modern personal injury case, but they are notoriously subjective. Of course, not putting a price tag on an item of injury because it may be hard to assess what the price tag should be would result in a windfall to the wrongdoing defendant, so some speculation may be called for. Sometimes however, the loss may appear to defy all quantification, such as a loss of constitutional rights. Consider the Supreme Court's treatment of the problem in the following decision.

Memphis Community School District v. Stachura

Supreme Court of the United States, 1986.
477 U.S. 299, 106 S.Ct. 2537, 91 L.Ed.2d 249.

JUSTICE POWELL delivered the Opinion of the Court.

[The plaintiff, Edward Stachura, was a public school teacher who had been suspended from his job, allegedly in violation of his first amendment rights. In connection with a chapter on human reproduction in a school-board-approved textbook, Stachura had shown his seventh-grade Life Science class two films on "human growth and sexuality" provided by the county health department, and photographs of Stachura's wife that had been taken while she was pregnant. Stachura was suspended after school officials received complaints from parents, although the complaints were apparently "based largely on inaccurate rumors about the allegedly sexually explicit nature of the pictures and films." Stachura was eventually reinstated, but he sued the school district and various individuals under §1983 for damages caused by his unconstitutional suspension. At the close of the trial, the district judge instructed the jury, if it found in favor of the plaintiff, it should award an amount sufficient to compensate him for the injuries caused by the defendants' unlawful actions, and to consider "lost earnings[,] loss of earning capacity[, and] out-of-pocket expenses," as well as damages for the "mental anguish or emotional distress" the plaintiff suffered as a consequence of the violation of his rights. The district judge also provided an instruction on punitive damages and, over the defendants' objection, offered the following instruction as well:

> If you find that the Plaintiff has been deprived of a Constitutional right, you may award damages to compensate him for the deprivation. Damages for this type of injury are more difficult to measure than damages for a physical injury or injury to one's property. There are no medical bills or other expenses by which you can judge how much compensation is appropriate. In one sense, no monetary value we place upon Constitutional rights can measure their importance in our society or compensate a citizen adequately for their deprivation. However, just because these rights are not capable of precise evaluation does not mean that an appropriate monetary amount should not be awarded.

> The precise value you place upon any Constitutional right which you find was denied to Plaintiff is within your discretion. You may wish to consider the importance of the right in our system of government, the role which this right has played in the history of our

republic, [and] the significance of the right in the context of the activities which the Plaintiff was engaged in at the time of the violation of the right.

Stachura was ultimately awarded $266,750 in compensatory damages and $36,000 in punitive damages.]

When §1983 plaintiffs seek damages for violations of constitutional rights, the level of damages is ordinarily determined according to principles derived from the common law of torts. * * * Punitive damages aside, damages in tort cases are designed to provide *"compensation* for the injury caused to plaintiff by defendant's breach of duty." 2 F. Harper, F. James & O. Gray, Law of Torts §25.1, p. 490 (2d ed. 1986) (emphasis in original). To that end, compensatory damages may include not only out-of-pocket loss and other monetary harms, but also such injuries as "impairment of reputation . . ., personal humiliation, and mental anguish and suffering." Gertz v. Robert Welch, Inc., 418 U.S. 323, 350 (1974). Deterrence is also an important purpose of this system, but it operates through the mechanism of damages that are *compensatory* — damages grounded in determinations of plaintiffs' actual losses. Congress adopted this common-law system of recovery when it established liability for "constitutional torts." Consequently, "the basic purpose" of §1983 damages is "to *compensate persons for injuries* that are caused by the deprivation of constitutional rights" [Carey v. Piphus, 435 U.S. 247, 254 (1978).]

* * *

The instructions at issue here cannot be squared with *Carey,* or with the principles of tort damages on which *Carey* and §1983 are grounded. The jurors in this case were told that, in determining how much was necessary to "compensate [respondent] for the deprivation" of his constitutional rights, they should place a money value on the "rights" themselves by considering such factors as the particular right's "importance . . . in our system of government," its role in American history, and its "significance . . . in the context of the activities" in which respondent was engaged. These factors focus, not on compensation for provable injury, but on the jury's subjective perception of the importance of constitutional rights as an abstract matter. *Carey* establishes that such an approach is impermissible. The constitutional right transgressed in *Carey* — the right to due process of law — is central to our system of ordered liberty. We nevertheless held that *no* compensatory damages could be awarded for violation of that right absent proof of actual injury. *Carey* thus makes clear that the abstract value of a constitutional right may not form the basis for §1983 damages.

Respondent nevertheless argues that *Carey* does not control here, because in this case a *substantive* constitutional right — respondent's First Amendment right to academic freedom — was infringed. The argument misperceives our analysis in *Carey.* That case does not establish a two-tiered system of constitutional rights, with substantive rights afforded greater protection than "mere" procedural safeguards. We did acknowledge in *Carey* that "the elements and prerequisites for recovery of damages" might vary depending on the interests protected by the constitutional right at issue. But we emphasized that, whatever the constitutional basis for §1983 liability, such damages must always be designed "to *compensate injuries* caused by the [constitutional] deprivation." (emphasis added). That conclusion simply leaves no room for noncompensatory damages measured by the jury's perception of the abstract "importance" of a constitutional right.

Nor do we find such damages necessary to vindicate the constitutional rights that §1983 protects. Section 1983 presupposes that damages that compensate for actual harm ordinarily suffice to deter constitutional violations. * * * Moreover, damages based on the "value" of constitutional rights are an unwieldy tool for ensuring compliance with the Constitution. History and tradition do not afford any sound guidance concerning the precise value that juries should place on constitutional protections. Accordingly, were such damages available, juries would be free to award arbitrary amounts without any evidentiary basis, or to use their unbounded discretion to punish unpopular defendants. Such damages would be too uncertain to be of any great value to plaintiffs, and would inject caprice into determinations of damages in §1983 cases. We therefore hold that damages based on the abstract "value" or "importance" of constitutional rights are not a permissible element of compensatory damages in such cases.

Respondent further argues that the challenged instructions authorized a form of "presumed" damages — a remedy that is both compensatory in nature and traditionally part of the range of tort law remedies. * * * Presumed damages are a *substitute* for ordinary compensatory damages, not a *supplement* for an award that fully compensates the alleged injury. When a plaintiff seeks compensation for an injury that is likely to have occurred but difficult to establish, some form of presumed damages may possibly be appropriate. * * * In those circumstances, presumed damages may roughly approximate the harm that the plaintiff suffered and thereby compensate for harms that may be impossible to measure. As we earlier explained, the instructions at issue in this case did not serve this purpose, but instead called on the jury to measure damages based on a subjective evaluation of the importance of particular constitutional values. Since such damages are wholly divorced from any compensatory purpose, they cannot be justified as presumed damages. Moreover, no rough substitute for compensatory damages was required in this case, since the jury was fully authorized to compensate respondent for both monetary and nonmonetary harms caused by petitioners' conduct. * * *

[Reversed and remanded.]

JUSTICE BRENNAN and JUSTICE STEVENS join the opinion of the Court and also join JUSTICE MARSHALL's opinion concurring in the judgment.

JUSTICE MARSHALL, with whom JUSTICE BRENNAN, JUSTICE BLACKMUN, and JUSTICE STEVENS join, concurring in the judgment.

I agree with the Court that this case must be remanded for a new trial on damages. Certain portions of the Court's opinion, however, can be read to suggest that damages in §1983 cases are necessarily limited to "out-of-pocket loss," "other monetary harms," and "such injuries as 'impairment of reputation

..., personal humiliation, and mental anguish and suffering.'" I do not understand the Court so to hold, and I write separately to emphasize that the violation of a constitutional right, in proper cases, may itself constitute a compensable injury.

* * * In *Carey*, we recognized that "the basic purpose of a §1983 damages award should be to compensate persons for injuries caused by the deprivation of constitutional rights." We explained, however, that application of that principle to concrete cases was not a simple matter. "It is not clear," we stated, "that common-law tort rules of damages will provide a complete solution to the damages issue in every §1983 case." Rather, "the rules governing compensation for injuries caused by the deprivation of constitutional rights should be tailored to the interests protected by the particular right in question — just as the common-law rules of damages themselves were defined by the interests protected in various branches of tort law."

* * * "[T]he elements and prerequisites for recovery of damages appropriate to compensate injuries caused by the deprivation of one constitutional right are not necessarily appropriate to compensate injuries caused by the deprivation of another." We referred to cases that support the award of substantial damages simply upon a showing that a plaintiff was wrongfully deprived of the right to vote, without requiring any further demonstration of damages.

Following *Carey*, the Courts of Appeals have recognized that invasions of constitutional rights sometimes cause injuries that cannot be redressed by a wooden application of common-law damages rules. In Hobson v. Wilson, 737 F.2d 1, 57-63 (D.C. Cir. 1984) * * * plaintiffs claimed that defendant [FBI] agents had invaded their First Amendment rights to assemble for peaceable political protest, to associate with others to engage in political expression, and to speak on public issues free of unreasonable government interference. The District Court found that the defendants had succeeded in diverting plaintiffs from, and impeding them in, their protest activities. The Court of Appeals for the District of Columbia Circuit held that that injury to a First Amendment-protected interest could itself constitute compensable injury wholly apart from any "emotional distress, humiliation and personal indignity, emotional pain, embarrassment, fear, anxiety and anguish" suffered by plaintiffs. The court warned, however, that that injury could be compensated with substantial damages only to the extent that it was "reasonably quantifiable"; damages should not be based on "the so-called inherent value of the rights violated." Ibid.

I believe that the *Hobson* court correctly stated the law. When a plaintiff is deprived, for example, of the opportunity to engage in a demonstration to express his political views, "[i]t is facile to suggest that no damage is done." * * * There is no reason why such an injury should not be compensable in damages. At the same time, however, the award must be proportional to the actual loss sustained.

The instructions given the jury in this case were improper because they did not require the jury to focus on the loss actually sustained by respondent. Rather, they invited the jury to base its award on speculation about "the importance of the right in our system of government" and "the role which this right has played in the history of our republic," guided only by the admonition that "[i]n one sense, no monetary value we place on Constitutional rights can measure their importance in our society or compensate a citizen adequately for their deprivation." These instructions invited the jury to speculate on matters wholly detached from the real injury occasioned respondent by the deprivation of the right. Further, the instructions might have led the jury to grant respondent damages based on the "abstract value" of the right to procedural due process — a course directly barred by our decision in *Carey*.

The Court therefore properly remands for a new trial on damages. I do not understand the Court, however, to hold that deprivations of constitutional rights can never themselves constitute compensable injuries. Such a rule would be inconsistent with the logic of *Carey*, and would defeat the purpose of §1983 by denying compensation for genuine injuries caused by the deprivation of constitutional rights.

NOTES AND PROBLEMS FOR DISCUSSION

1. The Court says that it is improper to compensate the plaintiff for the "abstract value" of the rights in question, even though it assumes that those rights have been violated. What is the problem with a jury awarding such compensation?

2. Some elements of compensatory damages may be easier to prove than others. Lost wages and benefits, medical expenses, and out of pocket costs may be susceptible to ready calculation. In the case of wrongful death or serious personal injury, the plaintiff's lost earning capacity over the remainder of his life might be susceptible to a mathematical formula. But consider how one measures "personal humiliation, mental anguish and suffering" — elements that the *Stachura* Court says are familiar to the common law; or the loss of emotional support of a spouse. Are these losses any easier to quantify than the abstract value of a constitutional right?

3. In a run-of-the-mine personal injury case, the plaintiff himself might testify as to his own pain and suffering caused by the defendant's illegal behavior. In addition, experts might be able to testify as to the magnitude and duration of the plaintiff's injury. Given the Court's discussion, how would an attorney seek to establish compensable injury arising from the denial of First Amendment free speech rights in a context such as that described by the concurrence in *Stachura*?

4. Why does the Court find the analogy to "presumed" damages unpersuasive in a case involving the loss of constitutional rights? The purpose of presumed damages is said to be to compensate for "certain" injury that happens to be difficult to establish (such as, said the Court in a footnote, the right to vote — "a nonmonetary harm that cannot be easily quantified"). If so, why don't free speech violations qualify for an award of presumed damages?

5. The Constitution protects interests that the common law might not. Yet the Court indicates that the injury to interests protected by the Constitution that lie beyond those protected at common law should be reducible to familiar common-law elements of harm. *Must* they be in order for a jury to be able to make a rational award of damages?

6. Difficulties of proof to one side, it is often unclear how courts ought to measure compensation in the first place. In UNITED STATES v. HATAHLEY, 257 F.2d 920 (10th Cir. 1958), members of the Navajo tribe filed suit against the U.S. seeking compensation for the government's 1952 taking and destruction of their horses and burros, as well as damages for the loss of other livestock that the horses and burros had been used to herd. The district court made a substantial award for the taking of property and the consequential harms that it produced, but the award was reversed on appeal. The Tenth Circuit held that the district court should have used market-based replacement costs for valuing the lost horses and burros, as opposed to estimating their value based on other items for which they might be traded, or their subjective value to the tribe to which the district court may have looked. In addition, the appeals court took issue with the lower court's assessment of the lost "use value" of these animals as it impacted tribe members' herds.

> Likewise, we think the court applied an erroneous rule, wholly unsupported by the evidence, in arriving at the amount of loss of use damage. There was testimony by the plaintiffs that because of the loss of their horses and burros they were not able to maintain and look after as much livestock as they had been able to before the unlawful taking, consequently the size of their herds was reduced. If the unlawful taking of the animals was the proximate cause of the herd reductions, the measure of damages would be the loss of profits occasioned thereby. * * *

> Applying the same formula to all plaintiffs, the court, without giving consideration to the condition, age or sex of the animals, found the value of the sheep and goats * * * to be $15 per head, and cattle to be $150 per head. The number of sheep, goats and cattle which each plaintiff had in 1952, as well as the number which each had at the date of the last hearing was established. This difference was multiplied by [$15 dollars and $150 respectively] and the judgment was entered for one-half of the amount of the result [one-half "represent[ing] damages * * * proximately caused by deprivation of the use of [the] horses."] The result, insofar as it related to use damage, was arbitrary, pure speculation, and clearly erroneous. [As the Fifth Circuit stated in a similar decision:]

> > [T]here has been no sufficient showing of how much of the damage from the loss of the sheep and goats was proximately caused by the Government * * * and how much of the damage resulted from other causes. There is no testimony whatever as to the specific dates of the loss of the sheep and goats, or as to their age, weight, condition and fair market value at the time of the alleged losses. It therefore becomes patent that the evidence as to the loss of these animals fails to rise above mere speculation and guess.

> Plaintiffs' evidence indicated that the loss of their animals made

it difficult and burdensome for them to obtain and transport needed water, food, and game, and curtailed their travel for medical care and to tribal council meetings and ceremonies. Plaintiffs also testified that because of the loss of their animals they were not able to grow crops and gardens as extensively as before. These were factors upon which damages for loss of use could have been based. This does not exclude the right to damages for loss of profits which may have resulted from reduction of the number of livestock, or actual loss of the animals, if the unlawful acts of the defendant agents were the proximate cause of the loss and were proved to a reasonable degree of certainty. * * * But the right to such damages does not extend forever, and it is limited to the time in which a prudent person would replace the destroyed horses and burros. The law requires only that the United States make full reparation for the pecuniary loss which their agents inflicted * * * .

257 F.2d at 923-24. On remand in *Hatahley*, what will the tribe members' lawyer have do to recover damages for the lost animals and other items?

7. The focus of compensatory damages is harm to the plaintiff. By contrast, "restitution" focuses on the unjust gain of the defendant, not the loss to the plaintiff. Restitution can take the form of an award of money damages to the plaintiff, although, if a specific thing has been taken from him, restitution may call for return of the thing (plus any profits from its use). One example of restitutionary damages is the recovery that a patent holder may obtain for unlawful infringement. A patent infringer may have profited from unlawful use of a patentholder's patent, but some of the profit may be profit that the patentholder never would have earned because, for example, the infringer made better use of the patent than the plaintiff would have. Even though some of the infringer's profits may not have represented a "loss" to the patentholder to the extent that the patentholder never would have earned them, the plaintiff may still recover all profits made by the infringer for his wrongful use of the plaintiff's patent. The remedy is restitutionary in nature, and arguably restores the defendant to the position the defendant would have been in had he not acted wrongfully (while compensatory damages restores the plaintiff to the position he would have been in but for the defendant's wrong). Of course, the damages paid by the infringer may tend to approximate the "loss" suffered by the plaintiff who might have profited had he sold the infringer a license. But the damages calculation here still focuses on the defendant's ill-gotten gain.

The remedy for patent infringement is one provided by federal statute. But restitution is often a remedy that a litigant proceeding under state law might choose in preference to a claim that could only produce compensatory damages. For example, if the defendant absconded with the plaintiff's machine and used it for profit, the plaintiff might sue in tort for conversion (with the measure of damages focusing on the harm to the plaintiff), or the plaintiff might forego suing in tort, and seek to recover on another legal theory that would provide a restitutionary remedy. Be sure you see why a party might choose restitution as a remedy over compensatory damages. As the above example shows, sometimes the defendant's gain exceeds the loss to the plaintiff; other times, the defendant obtains little or no gain when he causes the plaintiff injury (as in a car wreck);

and still other times, the defendant's gain and the plaintiff's loss may be commensurate. Obviously, in the car wreck setting, compensatory damages would be preferable to the plaintiff; in the stolen-machine example, restitution.

2. PUNITIVE DAMAGES

Punitive damages are designed to punish the defendant. Thus, they are an example of a quasi-criminal remedy intruding into civil litigation. But unlike most criminal sanctions, punitive damages have traditionally been awardable to the successful plaintiff rather than to the state, over and above any proved damages. In that respect, they are something of a windfall, although the deterrent and punitive function served by such damages may suggest that the plaintiff has served a public function as well, much like a prosecutor, and therefore deserves the bonus. (Today, there are some jurisdictions which provide that some part of the punitive damages obtained by the plaintiff will be payable to the state itself.) But punitive damages continue to spark debate, in large measure because they are perceived to be too freely awarded by juries and too little controlled by judges. Some states have outlawed them altogether, and a few have made them available only through specific statutory authorization. But most states allow them in some form or another. See generally Exxon Shipping v. Baker, 554 U.S. 461, 128 S.Ct. 2605, 171 L.Ed.2d 579 (2008).

As described in the decision below, punitive damages are ordinarily available only when the defendant's behavior is so outrageous or malicious that it fairly warrants a criminal-like sanction. Yet even when an award of punitive damages would be justified, a jury still has the discretion to deny them. In addition, while the question whether there is sufficient evidence to justify an award of punitive damages is a question of law for a court to decide, the *amount* of any award of punitive damages was once considered to be within the largely unfettered discretion of the jury. At common law, there was no judicial review of the amount of a punitive damages award, other than through the cumbersome mechanism of a new trial. See Chapter 12. In recent years, however, the Supreme Court has subjected the amount of punitive damages awards to scrutiny under the Due Process Clauses of the Fifth and Fourteenth Amendments. Those decisions are discussed in the opinion that follows. The inquiry has proceeded at two levels: First, what kind of procedures must be in place to insure that the amount of any award rests on a sufficient evidentiary basis? And second, should courts strike down an award that is not substantively "reasonable" by some definition of the term. The particular case that follows arose from one of the most famous (or infamous) environmental disasters in modern history. Although it was subject to later appeals and eventually went to the Supreme Court (see *Exxon Shipping v. Baker, supra*), its analysis remains instructive, and it provides a good window on how lower courts have had to wrestle with the Court's precedents in this area.

In re: The EXXON VALDEZ

United States Court of Appeals, Ninth Circuit, 2001.
270 F.3d 1215.

KLEINFELD, CIRCUIT JUDGE:

This is an appeal of a $5 billion punitive damages award arising out of the Exxon Valdez oil spill. This is not a case about befouling the environment. This is a case about commercial fishing. The jury was specifically instructed that it could not award damages for environmental harm. The reason is that under a stipulation with the United States and Alaska, Exxon had already been punished for environmental harm. The verdict in this case was for damage to economic expectations for commercial fishermen.

The plaintiffs here were almost entirely compensated for their damages years ago. The punitive damages at issue were awarded to punish Exxon, not to pay back the plaintiffs. Among the issues are whether punitive damages should have been barred as a matter of law and whether the award was excessive. * * *

Facts

[Shortly after midnight on March 24, 1989, the tanker Exxon Valdez ran onto Bligh Reef, located in Alaska's Prince William Sound, tearing the hull open and polluting Prince William Sound with eleven million gallons of oil. Bligh Island and Bligh Reef, named after Captain William Bligh — made infamous in Fletcher Christian's *Mutiny on the Bounty* — have been known to navigators since their discovery in 1794. The accident occurred on the bicentennial of the Bounty mutiny.

The vessel had left the port of Valdez at night. Because of heavy ice concentrations, the ship's Captain, Joseph Hazelwood, charted a path east of the established sea-lane, bringing its course directly toward Bligh Reef, unless it made a sharp turn to the west. Despite the prevailing conditions and the difficulty of turning the behemoth Valdez, Hazelwood decided not to remain on deck and went to his cabin two minutes before the turn was to be made. According to the testimony at trial, that was something that captains do not ordinarily do during such maneuvers. He left charge of the ship to an exhausted third mate, breaking protocol that two officers be on the bridge at all times. Hazelwood complicated the turn further by placing the vessel on autopilot, increasing the vessel's speed.

Captain Hazelwood's departure from the bridge was not inexplicable. The explanation put before the jury was that his judgment was impaired by alcohol and there was strong evidence that Hazelwood was an alcoholic; in fact, his condition was known to executives of Exxon shipping. Testimony established that prior to boarding his ship, hc had been drinking heavily at waterfront bars in Valdez.

Exxon spent over $3 billion to remove oil from the surrounding water and habitat, and for voluntary settlements with individuals, with the State of Alaska and with the United States. Hundreds of civil actions were also filed, and numerous appeals arose out of the litigation.

The district court certified the case into four class actions: three classes for compensatory damages (a "Commercial Fishing Class, a Native Class, and a Landowner Class"), and one, a "mandatory" punitive damages class action — i.e., all the plaintiffs were required to be parties to it, in order to prevent duplicate punitive awards. Exxon stipulated that its negligence caused the oil spill. In the first phase of the trial, the district court found that Hazelwood and Exxon had acted recklessly. In later stages of the trial, the court entered compensatory awards to the three classes in the hundreds of millions of dollars. The jury award of $287 million was reduced by released claims, settlements, and prior payments, to a net of almost $20 million. In addition, the jury awarded, in what was then the largest punitive damages award in American history, $5 billion in punitive damages against Exxon, as well as insignificant damages against Hazelwood. Exxon and Hazelwood appealed following various post-trial motions.]

Analysis

To assure that we respond to all the points raised in the very lengthy briefs, we treat the issues in the order that the appellants and cross appellants raise them.

I. PUNITIVE DAMAGES PERMISSIBILITY

Exxon argues that punitive damages ought to have been barred as a matter of law because as a matter of policy they are inappropriate in the circumstances, and because other principles of law bar them.

A. Policy

Exxon argues that as a matter of due process, no punitive damages can be awarded in this case because the criminal and civil sanctions, cleanup expenses and other consequences of the spill have already so thoroughly punished and deterred any similar conduct in the future that no public purpose is served by the award. Exxon was sanctioned with a fine and restitution award of $125 million for environmental crimes. The prosecutors and the district court, in approving the plea agreement and sentence, emphasized its sufficiency. Exxon also spent $2.1 billion cleaning up the spill, a massive deterrent to repeating the conduct that led to it. The expenses associated with the spill hurt Exxon's profits, even though the punitive damages award has not yet been paid pending resolution of this appeal.

As plaintiffs correctly point out, a prior criminal sanction does not generally, as a matter of law, bar punitive damages. Exxon's argument has some force as logic and policy. But it has no force, in the absence of precedent, to establish that the law, or the Constitution, bars punitive damages in these circumstances. Because we have not been made aware of a principle of law pursuant to which we should strike a punitive damages award on the ground that the conduct had already been sufficiently punished and deterred, we reject the argument.

* * *

IV. AMOUNT OF THE PUNITIVE DAMAGES AWARD

The jury awarded $5 billion in punitive damages against Exxon (as well as $5,000 in punitive damages against Captain Hazelwood). At the time, it was the largest punitive damages award in American history, so far as the litigants were able to determine. Exxon challenges the $5 billion award as excessive.

Ordinarily appellate courts must defer to juries. If a reasonable mind could reach the result the jury reached on the evidence before them, that is ordinarily the end of it. If there were no constitutional issue here, that might be the end of this discussion. This was a very bad oil spill. Captain Hazelwood's conduct, interpreting the evidence most strongly against him, was extremely reckless considering the difficulty and potential risk of his task, and Exxon was reckless to allow him to perform this task despite its knowledge that he was drinking again. The punitive damages amount, $5 billion, is about one year's net profits for the entire world-wide operations of Exxon, and the jury may well have decided that for such egregious conduct the company responsible ought to have a year without profit.

But a unique body of law governs punitive damages. In particular, under the Supreme Court's decision in Honda Motor Co. v. Oberg, 512 U.S. 415 (1994), a hands-off appellate deference to juries, typical of other kinds of cases and issues, is unconstitutional for punitive damages awards. In *Oberg*, the Oregon Constitution prohibited judicial reduction of punitive damages awards "unless the court can affirmatively say that there is no evidence to support the verdict." The Court held that the state constitutional denial of judicial review of the size of the award violated the due process clause of the Fourteenth Amendment. Review limited to a "no substantial evidence" test "provides no assurance that those whose conduct is sanctionable by punitive damages are not subjected to punitive damages of arbitrary amounts." The Court, explaining the importance of appellate review of punitive damages awards, noted that "more than half of those [punitive damages awards] appealed resulted in reductions or reversals of the punitive damages," and that this understated the importance of review, because so many awards are reduced by the trial court or settled for less pending appeal.

Before *Oberg*, we would not disturb punitive damage awards unless it appeared that the jury was influenced by passion or prejudice. However, * * * under *Oberg*, we must consider whether a punitive damages award passes "muster under federal due process analysis" in addition to reviewing whether the evidence is sufficient as a matter of law to support the award. The test of whether a punitive damages award survives review cannot be merely whether there is any evidence to support it, under *Oberg*.

Two critical Supreme Court opinions, decided after the district court's decision in this case, have expanded the way courts review constitutional challenges to large punitive damage awards. In 1996, the Court decided BMW of North America, Inc. v. Gore, 517 U.S. 559 (1996), and articulated, for the first time, factors that courts must consider when conducting a substantive review of a jury's punitive damages award. In *BMW*, a jury awarded the plaintiff $4,000 in compensatory damages and $4 million in punitive damages for the defendant's fraudulent conduct. The Court held that the amount of the punitive damage award was unconstitutional because the defendant lacked fair notice that such a severe award would be imposed. In concluding the award violated the Due Process Clause, the Court established three "guideposts" for courts to use in determining whether a punitive damage award is grossly excessive: (1) the reprehensibility of the defendant's conduct; (2) the ratio of the award to the harm inflicted on the plaintiff; and (3) the difference between the award and the civil or criminal penalties in comparable cases.

The Court reaffirmed the importance of the *BMW* guideposts several months ago in Cooper Industries, Inc. v. Leatherman Tool Group, Inc., 121 S. Ct. 1678 (2001). Following a large punitive damages jury verdict, the defendant in that case challenged the amount of the award in the district court. Relying on *BMW*, the district court considered and rejected the argument that the award was grossly excessive. On appeal, we reviewed the district court's determination for an abuse of discretion and affirmed. The Supreme Court reversed.

Cooper Industries examined the *BMW* factors to determine whether trial courts or appellate courts are in a better position to rule on the constitutionality of punitive damages awards, and ultimately concluded that "considerations of institutional competence" weigh in favor of independent appellate review. Specifically, the Court held that "courts of appeal should apply a de novo standard of review when passing on district courts' determinations of the constitutionality of punitive damages awards." * * * *Cooper Industries* said "unlike the measure of actual damages suffered, which presents a question of historical or predictive fact, the level of punitive damages is not really a 'fact' 'tried' by the jury." Thus, reduction of a punitive damages award does not implicate the Seventh Amendment. The Court in *BMW* and in *Cooper Industries* set out criteria for judicial review of jury awards for punitive damages.

In *BMW*, the Supreme Court held that a punitive damage award violated the Due Process Clause of the Fourteenth Amendment because it was so grossly excessive that the defendant lacked fair notice that it would be imposed. Dr. Gore's car was damaged in transit, and BMW repainted it but did not tell Dr. Gore about the repainting when it sold him the car. The jury found that to be fraudulent, and awarded $4,000 in compensatory damages for reduced value of the car and $4 million in punitive damages. The Alabama Supreme Court cut the award to $2 million, but the Court held that it was still so high as to deny BMW due process of law for lack of notice, because the award exceeded the amounts justified under three "guideposts." The *BMW* guideposts are: (1) the degree of reprehensibility of the person's conduct; (2) the disparity between the harm or potential harm suffered by the victim and his punitive damage award; and (3) the difference between the punitive damage award and the civil penalties authorized or imposed in comparable cases. We apply these three guideposts to evaluate whether "a defendant lacked 'fair notice' of the severity of a punitive damages award," and to stabilize the law by assuring the uniform treatment of similarly situated persons.

In this case, the district court has not reviewed the award under the standards announced in *BMW* and *Cooper Industries*. This is because neither case had been decided at the time the jury returned its verdict, and, equally important, Exxon raised no direct constitutional challenges to the amount of the award until after the judgment. We therefore have no constitutional analysis by the district court over which to exercise any de novo review. Because we believe the district court should, in the first instance, apply the appropriate standards, we remand for the district court to consider the constitutionality of the amount of the award in light of the guideposts established in *BMW*. We think on these facts, this is the better approach, and we provide the following analysis to aid their consideration.

A. Reprehensibility

Punitive damages "are not compensation for injury. Instead, they are private fines levied by civil juries to punish reprehensible conduct and to deter its future occurrence." The Supreme Court explained that "[p]erhaps the most important indicium of the reasonableness of a punitive damages award is the degree of reprehensibility of the defendant's conduct." "[E]xemplary damages should reflect the enormity of [the defendant's] offense," and "punitive damages may not be grossly out of proportion to the severity of the offense."

Degree of reprehensibility did not justify a $2 million punitive damages award in the *BMW* case for two reasons. First, the harm inflicted on Dr. Gore was "purely economic." BMW's recklessness was toward a person's economic interest in getting a car that had never been damaged, not toward his health or safety. The court drew an analogy to criminal cases, noting that for purposes of reprehensibility, "'nonviolent crimes are less serious than crimes marked by violence.'" Second, though fraudulent, BMW's conduct did not include active "trickery or deceit," just silence where there should have been disclosure. Likewise in the case at bar, there was no violence, no intentional spilling of oil (as in a "midnight dumping" case), and no executive trickery to hide or facilitate the spill. Although the huge oil spill obviously caused harm beyond the "purely economic," the punitive damages award was expressly limited by the instructions to exclude environmental harm[.]* The district court instructed the jury that in determining punitive damages "you should not consider any damage to natural resources or to the environment generally." It explained that "any liability for punitive damages relating to these harms has been fully resolved in proceedings involving the Exxon defendants and the Natural Resource Trustees." No party has challenged this instruction on appeal. The $5 billion punishment in this case was for injury to private economic interests — claims of commercial fishermen that they made less money from fishing on account of the spill, claims of land owners that their shores were polluted with spilled oil, and claims of Alaska Natives that their subsistence fishing was impaired by the spill.

Plaintiffs correctly argue that Exxon's conduct was reprehensible because it knew of the risk of an oil spill in the transportation of huge quantities of oil through the icy waters of Prince William Sound. And it knew Hazelwood was an alcoholic who was drinking. But this goes more to justify punitive damages than to justify punitive damages at so high a level.

Also, the $5 billion punitive damages award at issue was against Exxon, which had some direct responsibility because it did not fire or transfer Hazelwood after learning that he was drinking and taking command despite his

---

* [Such damages would have been barred by res judicata given prior resolution of other aspects of the case. — eds.]

alcohol treatment, as well as vicarious responsibility. However, the difference between the $5,000 awarded as punitive damages against the man who directly caused the oil spill, and the $5 billion awarded as punitive damages against his employer gives rise to concern about jury evaluation of their relative reprehensibility.[129]

Some factors reduce reprehensibility here compared to some other punitive damages cases. Exxon spent millions of dollars to compensate many people after the oil spill, thereby mitigating the harm to them and the reprehensibility of its conduct. Reprehensibility should be discounted if defendants act promptly and comprehensively to ameliorate any harm they cause in order to encourage such socially beneficial behavior.

Also, as bad as the oil spill was, *Exxon* did not spill the oil on purpose, and did not kill anyone. By contrast, in Protectus Alpha, 767 F.3d 1379 (9th Cir. 1985), a man was foreseeably killed by a deliberate act. And in Hilao v. Estate of Marcos, 103 F.3d 767 (9th Cir. 1996), a $1.2 billion punitive damages award, the defendant intentionally caused thousands of people to be tortured and killed.

B. Ratio

"The second and perhaps most commonly cited indicium of an unreasonable or excessive punitive damages award is its ratio to the actual harm inflicted on the plaintiff." *BMW*, 517 U.S. at 580. This analysis is based upon the "principle that exemplary damages must bear a 'reasonable relationship' to compensatory damages." The harm to be considered includes both the actual harm to the victim and the harm that was likely to occur.[134]

The "reasonable relationship" ratio is intrinsically somewhat indeterminate. The numerator is "the harm likely to result from the defendant's conduct." *BMW*, 517 U.S. at 581 (quoting TXO Production Corp. v. Alliance Resources Corp., 509 U.S. 443, 460 (1993)). The denominator is the amount of punitive damages. Because the numerator is ordinarily arguable, applying a mathematical bright line as though that were an objective measure of how high the punitive damages can go would give a false suggestion of precision. That is one reason why the Supreme Court has emphasized that it is not possible to "draw a mathematical bright line between the constitutionally acceptable and the constitutionally unacceptable that would fit every case." Nevertheless, a "general concern of reasonableness * * * properly enters into the constitutional calculus." Part of why the Court held that the punitive damages were excessive in *BMW* was a "breathtaking 500 to 1" ratio between the harm to the plaintiff himself and the award.

---

[129] Cf. Honda Motor Co. v. Oberg, 512 U.S. 415, 432 (1994) ("Punitive damages pose an acute danger of arbitrary deprivation of property, since jury instructions typically leave the jury with wide discretion in choosing amounts and since evidence of a defendant's net worth creates the potential that juries will use their verdicts to express biases against big businesses.").

[134] See *BMW*, 517 U.S. at 581. ("*TXO*, following dicta in *Haslip*, refined this analysis by confirming that the proper inquiry is 'whether there is a reasonable relationship between the punitive damages award and the harm likely to result from the defendant's conduct as well as the harm that actually has occurred.'") (quoting TXO Production Corp. v. Alliance Resources Corp., 509 U.S. 443, 460 (1993)).

Although it is difficult to determine the value of the harm from the oil spill in the case at bar, the jury awarded $287 million in compensatory damages, and the ratio of $5 billion punitive damages to $287 million in compensatory damages is 17.42 to 1. The district court determined that "total harm could range from $288.7 million to $418.7 million," which produces a ratio between 12 to 1 and 17 to 1. This ratio greatly exceeds the 4 to 1 ratio that the Supreme Court called "close to the line" in Pacific Mutual Life Ins. Co. v. Haslip, 499 U.S. 1 (1991).

The amount that a defendant voluntarily pays before judgment should generally not be used as part of the numerator, because that would deter settlements prior to judgment. "The general policy of federal courts to promote settlement before trial is even stronger in the context of large-scale class actions," such as this one.

The cleanup expenses Exxon paid should be considered as part of the deterrent already imposed. Depending on the circumstances, a firm might reasonably, were there no punishment, be deterred, in some cases but not all, by its actual expenses. For example, a person painting his trim may not carefully mask window glass, because it is cheaper and easier to scrape the paint off the glass than to mask it carefully. But if a person ruined a $10,000 rug by spilling a $5 bottle of ink, he would be exceedingly careful never to spill ink on the rug again, even if it cost him "only" $10,005 and he was not otherwise punished.

Exxon's casualty losses for the vessel and cargo (approximately $46 million), the costs of clean up (approximately $2.1 billion), the fine and restitution (approximately $125 million), settlement with the government entities (approximately $900 million), settlements with private parties (approximately $300 million), and the net compensatory damages (approximately $19.6 million) totaled over $3.4 billion. Whether cost of cleanup and compensatory damages, damage to the vessel, and lost oil deters bad future acts depends on whether it greatly exceeds the expense of avoiding such accidents, not whether the amounts are compensatory or punitive. A company hauling a cargo worth around $25.7 million has a large incentive to avoid a $3.4 billion expense for the trip. This case is like the ink on the rug example, not the paint on the window example. Just the expense, without any punishment, is too large for a prudent transporter to take much of a chance, given the low cost of making sure alcoholics do not command their oil tankers. Because the costs and settlements in this case are so large, a lesser amount is necessary to deter future acts.

Ratio analysis as required by *BMW* helps avoid overdeterrence. Justice Breyer's concurrence in *BMW* notes that "smaller damages would not sufficiently discourage firms from engaging in the harmful conduct, while larger damages would overdeter by leading potential defendants to spend more to prevent the activity that causes the economic harm, say, through employee training, than the cost of the harm itself." *BMW*, 517 U.S. at 593 (Breyer, J., concurring). It is hard to deter bad conduct without also deterring some good conduct that risks being misunderstood as bad, or that will look bad in retrospect. Every large company knows that it cannot exercise absolute control over all its employees, so if there is too much risk in performing some activity, the entire activity may be avoided as a preferable alternative to bearing potentially infinite costs of avoiding the harm, and society would lose the benefit of the productive activity. As bad as the oil spill is, fuel for the United States at moderate expense has great social value and that value as well as the value of avoiding horrendous oil spills can be reconciled by ratio analysis.

C. Comparable penalties

The third *BMW* "indicium of excessiveness" is the penalties, civil or criminal, "that could be imposed for comparable misconduct." The purpose of this particular indicium is to "accord 'substantial deference' to legislative judgments concerning appropriate sanctions for the conduct at issue." One reason the Court held that the $2 million punitive damages award was so excessive as to deny BMW due process of law, even though the corporation could easily pay it, was that the statutory sanctions were much lower than the punitive damages award.

This case is unusually rich in comparables. Both the state and federal governments pursued sanctions and obtained judicial approval for the amounts. Thus, we know the state and federal legislative and executive judgments, both in general and as applied to this case, about what sanctions were appropriate.

Criminal fines are particularly informative because punitive damages are quasi-criminal. The parties agree that 18 U.S.C. §3571 is the federal measure for fines in this case. It provides for up to a $500,000 fine for a felony, or for a misdemeanor resulting in death, or $200,000 for a class A misdemeanor not resulting in death. If $200,000 is the relevant legislative comparable judgment, then the punitive damages were twenty-five thousand times the legislative judgment, an excessiveness problem like *BMW*. Plaintiffs argue that we should use subsection (d) instead. That subsection provides an alternative fine where a "person derives pecuniary gain from the offense," or the offense "results in pecuniary loss" to another person, "not more than the greater of twice the gross gain or twice the gross loss." The district court calculated damages to others as $386.7 million to $516.7 million. Doubling the highest number suggests an exposure to a criminal fine of $1.03 billion. The plaintiffs would double various additional figures, most importantly the $2.1 billion Exxon spent cleaning up the spill, but that would not be included in the §3571(d) fine, because it is damage to Exxon itself, and the fine doubles only "loss to a person other than the defendant."

Ceilings on civil liability are also instructive. Congress provided in the Trans-Alaska Pipeline Act that "if oil that has been transported through the Trans-Alaska pipeline is loaded on a vessel at the terminal facilities of the pipeline, the owner and operator of the vessel . . . shall be strictly liable . . . for all damages, including clean-up costs, sustained by any person or entity, public, or private, including residents of Canada, as the result of discharges of oil from such vessel." 43 U.S.C. §1653(c)(1). However, "strict liability for all claims arising out of any one incident shall not exceed $100,000,000." Id. at (c)(3). That $100 million sanction is only 1/50 of the punitive damages award.

In addition to the legislative judgment, we have an actual penal evaluation made in this case by the attorneys general of the United States and the State of Alaska. Exxon and the United States entered a plea agreement for $150 million, which was subsequently reduced to a $25 million fine plus $100 million in restitution. This plea agreement was approved by the district court. At Exxon's sentencing hearing, the U.S. Attorney explained that "as a result [of the money Exxon agreed to pay under the Consent Decree], the total amount of the penalties, compensatory payments, and other voluntary expenditures will exceed 3.5 billion dollars" and that it was "hard to imagine a more adequate deterrence for negligence, [sic] but unintentional conduct." The Alaska Attorney General expressed similar views, indicating that the $150 million fine was "a number which the State can hold up to whether [sic] polluters that this is the fine which you face, 150 million dollars, and that certainly should be sufficient, the State believes, to give pause to those who do not show the proper regard for the Alaska environment." In approving the consent decree, the district judge indicated that "it contained an appropriate amount of punishment."

The district judge subsequently explained why the $150 million was not, after all, the appropriate amount of punishment, when he denied the motion for new trial on punitive damages, by noting that "the criminal payment was made before the harm to plaintiffs was quantified." While not a limit, the fine is nevertheless a significant datum, because the massiveness of the spill was apparent immediately, and the $150 million represents an adversarial judgment by the executive officers of the state and federal governments who had the public responsibility for seeking the appropriate level of punishment.

* * *

D. Summary

The $5 billion punitive damages award is too high to withstand the review we are required to give it under *BMW* and *Cooper Industries*. It must be reduced. Because these Supreme Court decisions came down after the district court ruled, it could not apply them. We therefore vacate the award and remand so that the district court can set a lower amount in light of the *BMW* and *Cooper Industries* standards. * * *

NOTES AND PROBLEMS FOR DISCUSSION

1. After a number of trips back and forth between the district court and the court of appeals, the question of punitive damages in *Exxon Valdez* eventually made it to the Supreme Court. In EXXON SHIPPING CO. v. BAKER, 554 U.S. 461, 128 S.Ct. 2605, 171 L.Ed.2d 570 (2008), the Court concluded that a ratio of punitive damages to compensatory damages in excess of 1:1 would be excessive as a matter of federal judge-made admiralty law. It thus effectively capped the punitive damages award at the level of compensatory damages (ultimately calculated at around $500 million). In the course of its opinion, the Court provided an extensive history of punitive damages and the purposes that they are designed to serve. Prior to *Exxon Shipping*, and subsequent to *Exxon Valdez*, the Supreme Court in STATE FARM MUTUAL AUTOMOBILE INS. CO. v. CAMPBELL, 538 U.S. 408, 123 S.Ct. 1513, 155 L.Ed.2d 585 (2003), had suggested that any ratio of punitive to compensatory damages above single digits was not likely to pass muster, as a matter of due process. *State Farm* is discussed further in Note 7, below.

2.   The *Exxon Valdez* court focuses greatly on the problem of deterrence in connection with the punitive damages award. Specifically, it focuses on the risk of too much deterrence arising from a large punitive award on top of an already substantial compensatory award, plus $2 billion already expended in clean up costs — all of which carry their own deterrent force. Although punitive damages are calculated to deter, they are also designed to punish and thereby to reflect society's condemnation of the defendant's acts. Did the court neglect the punishment aspect of the award?

3.   Since the plaintiffs seek to visit punishment on the defendant for the same acts that the government has already punished, isn't that a kind of double jeopardy from the defendant's perspective? Note that the "mandatory" class action for the assessment of punitive damages was itself designed to prevent multiple punishments of the defendant in multiple forums (and to permit all plaintiffs to share in any award).

4.   The court concludes that past criminal penalties obtained by the government do not foreclose punitive damage awards against the same defendant in private litigation. Yet it also suggests that the imposition of such penalties should loom large in the calculation of any such award. How are those past penalties both relevant and irrelevant at the same time?

5.   The court of appeals goes through the *BMW* analysis even though it acknowledges that the district court should engage in that analysis in the first instance on remand. Since the court of appeals will have de novo (i.e., plenary) review of the amount of the punitive damages award set by the district judge under *Cooper Industries*, why did it not just enter judgment based on its own assessment of the proper amount of a punitive award?

6.   *Exxon Valdez* was decided in a federal court in an admiralty case. But the due process requirements regarding the reasonableness of jury awards of punitive damages apply to state courts as well; indeed, most of the Supreme Court's precedents in the area (such as *BMW*) involved state court jury awards. Thus, a purely state law claim between two co-citizens litigated in a state court may be subject to review in the Supreme Court if the losing party claims that the punitive damages award is unreasonably high. And the fact that there may be sufficient evidence to support *some* award of punitive damages will not be a defense to a challenge to the amount of the award. Should a similar due process-based approach be taken to judicial review of the amount of an award of compensatory damages? Cf. Chapter 11 (discussing availability of new trials for excessive damages awards).

7.   In *State Farm, supra,* the Supreme Court reached a number of conclusions suggesting that it will be more difficult for large punitive damages awards to survive searching judicial scrutiny. The case involved a suit against an insurance company for its bad faith refusal to settle automobile accident claims brought against its insured by a third party, after a judgment had been entered against the insured well in excess of the policy limits. In the insured's suit against State Farm, the jury awarded him $2.6 million in compensatory damages (largely for emotional pain and distress), and $145 million in punitive damages. The punitive damages award was based on a showing at trial that State Farm had implemented a written policy of using the "claims adjustment process as a profit center" by systematically and arbitrarily lowering payouts on policies, and that this particular incident of failure to settle with a third-party was part of that policy — a policy that was said to be evidenced in part by other similar acts by State Farm around the country consistent with that policy.

The Supreme Court did not question the propriety of an award of punitive damages in the case, but stated that "a more modest punishment for this reprehensible conduct could have satisfied the State's legitimate objectives." The Court reaffirmed the tripartite inquiry of *BMW* (followed in *Exxon Valdez*) and elaborated on its requirements. First, the Court reemphasized the territorial limits on the "reprehensibility" inquiry, and indicated that any punishment must be for harm to the plaintiff. It concluded that the punitive damages in the instant case had been awarded based on out-of-state conduct of State Farm's that "bore no relation to the plaintiff's claims" — i.e., the other conduct involved failure to pay persons insured by State Farm as opposed to refusals to settle third-party lawsuits. Second, the Court provided greater specificity to the inquiry into the relationship between punitive and compensatory awards by suggesting that single digit ratios would ordinarily be all that due process would allow. And if there were a substantial compensatory award, a punitive award that equaled that amount might be all that the Constitution would permit.

8. In PHILIP MORRIS USA v. WILLIAMS, 549 U.S. 376, 127 S.Ct. 1057, 166 L.Ed.2d 940 (2007), the Court held that a punitive damages award, based in part on jury instructions that may have permitted the jury to punish a defendant for having harmed nonparties to the litigation, amounted to a taking of property without due process. In a state court action for negligence and deceit, the plaintiff alleged that her husband's death had been caused by smoking the defendant's cigarette products, and that the defendant had knowingly and falsely led the husband to believe that smoking them was safe. After a trial, a jury awarded the plaintiff $821,000 in compensatory damages, along with $79.5 million in punitive damages. Some of the proof on the question of punitive damages concerned harm that others had suffered when smoking the same cigarettes as had plaintiff's husband. In reversing the Oregon Supreme Court, which upheld the award, the U.S. Supreme Court stated that proof of harm to others could be relevant to show that the product that harmed the plaintiff's husband posed a substantial risk to others and was therefore "reprehensible" and thus deserving of an award of punitive damages. But the Court distinguished that permissible use of such evidence from what it perceived to have been the impermissible use in the particular case: namely, to punish defendant for harm that had been suffered by others. It therefore concluded that state courts must set up procedures to insure against unnecessary risks that such evidence, if introduced, will be impermissibly used. Given its disposition of the case, the Court did not consider whether the particular award was excessive. Following remand, the Oregon Supreme Court again upheld the punitive damages award. The Supreme Court granted certiorari in the case in June, 2008, but the writ was later dismissed as improvidently granted.

3. ENFORCING MONEY JUDGMENTS

Once a litigant obtains a money judgment from the court, what happens next? Perhaps the losing party will pay it off, and that will be the end of it. But the losing party may wish to file various post-trial motions that could have the effect of undoing the judgment, or he may wish to appeal. In theory, a judgment could be executed upon even before the resolution of these post-judgment procedures are concluded. But under the Federal Rules, there is an automatic 10-day stay of execution of a judgment (the same amount of time for filing post-trial motions), and the trial court has the discretion to stay a judgment's execution until the resolution of any post-trial motions that are filed. See Rule 62(b), Fed. R. Civ. P. In addition, when an appeal is taken, the appellant may defeat immediate enforcement of the judgment by posting an appropriate "supersedeas bond." Rule 62(d). State courts may provide similar procedures, although, as a practical matter, if the appeal bond is substantial (because the underlying judgment is substantial), a losing party may not be able to afford to forestall immediate execution on the judgment. See, e.g., Pennzoil Co. v. Texaco, Inc., 477 U.S. 903, 106 S.Ct. 3270, 91 L.Ed.2d 561 (1986) (denying injunction against state court's insistence on $11 billion appeal bond to stay execution of $11 billion judgment).

Eventually, however, once appeals are exhausted or the time for filing them has run, there will be a final and enforceable judgment. If the defendant does not pay the money judgment at this point, the party with the judgment (the judgment creditor) will have to enforce it against the losing party (the judgment debtor). And to do that, the courts' assistance will have to be enlisted once again.

Under Rule 69(a), Fed. R. Civ. P., a money judgment against a private party is ordinarily enforced by a "writ of execution" obtained from the court. The Rule also provides that execution and related matters shall be undertaken "in accordance with the practice and procedure of the state in which the district court is held," unless a federal statute directly addresses the particular kind of judgment. The states, whose practices are thus adopted as the default rules for the federal courts, employ various mechanisms for insuring that judgments will be enforced, so the form and mode of enforcement is not uniform throughout the country. And as you will discover, some states' laws for enforcement of judgments are far more expeditious than others. But most states have adopted one version or another of the model act called the Revised Uniform Enforcement of Foreign Judgments Act ("foreign" meaning domestic judgments from other courts in the U.S.). 13 Uniform Laws Annot. 261

A classic method of judgment enforcement under state law when the defendant is in possession of real or personal property is to have the appropriate public official (such as the sheriff) levy upon property sufficient to satisfy the judgment, and, if necessary, have it sold following notice and advertisement. The proceeds will go to the judgment creditor minus the official's expenses and fees, with any leftover to go to the defendant. Of course, when that practice is carried over to federal court, it is the federal marshal or other official of the district court who will do the seizure and sale.

Different states may make different exemptions from the types of real and personal property that can be executed upon — the most familiar being the homestead exemption. But states ordinarily limit the amount of any homestead exemption to a fixed dollar-amount, such that not all of a home's value can be shielded from enforcement efforts by judgment creditors. But some states (such as Florida, the adopted home of O.J. Simpson), have set the exemption at quite a high level. See Fla. Const. art. X.

Another tried and true method of enforcement of judgments under state law is the garnishment of wages of the judgment debtor. Here too there may be widely varying limits under state law. And federal consumer protection law (with some exceptions) limits garnishment to one quarter of the worker's disposable income. See 15 U.S.C. §1673(a). In addition, special provision is made in Rule 69(a) that discovery in any federal court proceedings relating to the judgment's execution may be had according to federal discovery rules *or* state rules, such as discovery to ascertain the location of the judgment debtor's assets. Depending on the state, discovery proceedings may occur in the execution proceedings themselves, or in other supplemental proceedings that might later become necessary to enforce the judgment. In addition, if assets are discovered to be in a federal judicial district other than that in which a federal court's judgment was entered, the original judgment, once it has become final, may be "registered" in the other district "by filing a certified copy of the judgment" and enforced there just as if it had been entered there. See 28 U.S.C. §1963. Of course, if the initial judgment is entered by a state court rather than a federal court and assets are located in another state, then the judgment creditor must arrange to have the judgment recognized and enforced in a court in that state pursuant to their procedure for recognition and enforcement of foreign judgments, and consistent with the Full Faith and Credit Act, 28 U.S.C. §1738. And whether recognition and enforcement of a state court judgment takes place in a federal or a state court, there will be only limited grounds by which to collaterally attack the validity of the earlier judgment. See generally Chapter 2.

Finally, note that if a money judgment is taken against a *foreign* party who does not have sufficient assets in the U.S. to satisfy the judgment, enforcement will have to occur in another country — perhaps the defendant's home country — where it has assets. At that point, enforcement will depend on the law of the foreign country or any treaty that the country might have entered into with the U.S. regarding the recognition and enforcement of judgments. Similarly, money judgments rendered in foreign courts may be enforced in U.S. courts as well, either pursuant to the strictures of a treaty (if there is one), or pursuant to notions of "comity" — i.e., a general respect for the acts of foreign sovereigns — a looser standard than full faith and credit and one that may allow for somewhat less respect for the judgments of foreign countries than those of sister states. See Ackermann v. Levine, 788 F.2d 830 (2d Cir. 1986) (recognizing that U.S. courts may assert "public policy" grounds for nonenforcement of foreign judgments). Here too a number of states have adopted a version of a 2005 model act called The Uniform Foreign-Country Money Judgments Recognition Act, or its predecessor. 13 Uniform Laws Annot. 149. But variations among the states are still considerable.

SECTION B.   PROVISIONAL REMEDIES

1.   PRE-JUDGMENT SEIZURE

Suppose that a party who is contemplating filing a lawsuit believes that, by the time she secures a money judgment from the court, the would-be defendant will no longer have assets sufficient to satisfy the judgment. Perhaps it is anticipated that the defendant will remove his assets from the jurisdiction or simply deplete or dispose of them in the interim. Without some mechanism immediately to lay hold of sufficient assets of the defendant pending the litigation, recovery on valid claims could easily become problematic. Historically, various forms of provisional remedies were available by statute from courts of law — interim remedies designed to ensure the availability of assets to satisfy a judgment — most of which involved the arrest or seizure of defendant's property pending the outcome of litigation. Rule 64, Fed. R. Civ. P., provides that prejudgment mechanisms for securing payment of judgment in a federal court are the same ones that would be available in a state court in the state in which the federal court sits. "The remedies thus available include arrest, attachment, garnishment, replevin, sequestration, and other corresponding or equivalent remedies, however designated." Id. Consequently, post-judgment enforcement procedures as well as pre-judgment mechanisms are largely governed by state practice in federal court.

Of course, the plaintiff's say-so will hardly suffice to freeze a defendant's assets. First of all, states will have regulations that limit the type of property that may be seized or the circumstances in which their courts will be permitted to intervene prior to judgment. In addition, as discussed in the following case, the Due Process Clause of the Fourteenth Amendment will impose limits on how a state may go about seizing a defendant's assets, since any seizure will necessarily implicate a deprivation of property (even if only temporarily). Consequently, the type of notice and hearing rights owed to the defendant are constitutional questions that must also be considered. And, depending on the setting, advance notice and an adversarial hearing at which the defendant is present may turn out to be counterproductive, if there is some special risk that assets will be depleted promptly upon the defendant's even learning of the lawsuit. On the other hand, an erroneous seizure — i.e., one that is later undone because the defendant prevails — may itself cause harm to the defendant, perhaps harm that the plaintiff will be unable to pay for. To protect against such a possibility the defendant may also need some security "up front," and before the litigation proceeds. Consider how those separate concerns ought to be resolved.

Connecticut v. Doehr

Supreme Court of the United States, 1991.

501 U.S. 1, 111 S. Ct. 2105, 115 L.Ed.2d 1.

Justice White delivered an opinion, Parts I, II, and III of which are the opinion of the Court.

This case requires us to determine whether a state statute that authorizes prejudgment attachment of real estate without prior notice or hearing, without a showing of extraordinary circumstances, and without a requirement that the person seeking the attachment post a bond, satisfies the Due Process Clause of the Fourteenth Amendment. We hold that, as applied to this case, it does not.

I

[DiGiovanni brought a civil action for damages against Doehr for assault and battery. At the time of bringing suit, petitioner also submitted to the court an application for a $75,000 prejudgment attachment on respondent's home. Connecticut law authorized prejudgment attachment of real property in civil actions, even when the lawsuit did not involve the property itself. The statute did not require any notice to the owner or opportunity to be heard before, as opposed to after, the attachment. The statute in question simply required a motion by the plaintiff that there exist "probable cause to sustain the validity of the plaintiff's claims" and that the property over which attachment is sought be real property. There was no requirement that the plaintiff post a bond for the payment of damages arising from the attachment if the plaintiff should lose, or to pay off a successful wrongful attachment lawsuit brought later by the defendant. DiGiovanni's five sentence affidavit set out the allegations of his claim, concluding with a statement that these allegations were sufficient to show probable cause that judgment would be rendered in his favor. The court agreed with DiGiovanni and issued a prejudgment attachment order.

Following the order of attachment, DiGiovanni was required to give notice to Doehr advising him of his right to a hearing to (1) object to the attachment order for lack of probable cause, (2) request the order be modified, vacated, dismissed, or that a bond be substituted in lieu of the lien, or (3) object to a portion of the property claimed to be exempt from the prejudgment order.

Doehr filed suit in Federal District Court, claiming the statute violated the Due Process Clause of the Fourteenth Amendment. The District Court upheld the constitutionality of Connecticut's statute and granted summary judgment to DiGiovanni. Upon appeal to the Second Circuit, a split panel reversed.]

II

With this case we return to the question of what process must be afforded by a state statute enabling an individual to enlist the aid of the State to deprive another of his or her property by means of the prejudgment attachment or similar procedure. Our cases reflect the numerous variations this type of remedy can entail. In Sniadach v. Family Finance Corp. of Bay View, 395 U.S. 337 (1969), the Court struck down a Wisconsin statute that permitted a creditor to effect prejudgment garnishment of wages without notice and prior hearing to the wage earner. In Fuentes v. Shevin, 407 U.S. 67 (1972), the Court likewise found a due process violation in state replevin provisions that permitted vendors to have goods seized through an ex parte application to a court clerk and the posting of a bond. Conversely, the Court upheld a Louisiana ex parte procedure allowing a lienholder to have disputed goods sequestered in Mitchell v. W. T. Grant Co., [416 U.S. 600 (1974)]. *Mitchell*, however, carefully noted that *Fuentes* was decided against "a factual and legal background sufficiently different . . . that it does not require the invalidation of the Louisiana sequestration statute." *Mitchell, at 615.* Those differences included Louisiana's provision of an immediate post-deprivation hearing along with the option of damages; the requirement that a judge rather than a clerk determine that there is a clear showing of entitlement to the writ; the necessity for a detailed affidavit; and an emphasis on the lien-holder's interest in preventing waste or alienation of the encumbered property. In North Georgia Finishing, Inc. v. Di-Chem, Inc., 419 U.S. 601 (1975), the Court again invalidated an ex parte garnishment statute that not only failed to provide for notice and prior hearing but also failed to require a bond, a detailed affidavit setting out the claim, the determination of a neutral magistrate, or a prompt postdeprivation hearing.

These cases "underscore the truism that '"due process," unlike some legal rules, is not a technical conception with a fixed content unrelated to time, place and circumstances.'" Mathews v. Eldridge, [424 U.S. 319, 334 (1976)]. In *Mathews*, we drew upon our prejudgment remedy decisions to determine what process is due when the government itself seeks to effect a deprivation on its own initiative. That analysis resulted in the now familiar threefold inquiry requiring consideration of "the private interest that will be affected by the official action"; "the risk of an erroneous deprivation of such interest through the procedures used, and the probable value, if any, of additional or substitute safeguards"; and lastly "the Government's interest, including the function involved and the fiscal and administrative burdens that the additional or substitute procedural requirement would entail." *Mathews*, at 335.

Here the inquiry is similar, but the focus is different. Prejudgment remedy statutes ordinarily apply to disputes between private parties rather than between an individual and the government. Such enactments are designed to enable one of the parties to "make use of state procedures with the overt, significant assistance of state officials," and they undoubtedly involve state action "substantial enough to implicate the Due Process Clause." Tulsa Professional Collection Services, Inc. v. Pope, 485 U.S. 478, 486 (1988). Nonetheless, any burden that increasing procedural safeguards entails primarily affects not the government, but the party seeking control of the other's property. For this type of case, therefore, the relevant inquiry requires, as in *Mathews*, first, consideration of the private interest that will be affected by the prejudgment measure; second, an examination of the risk of erroneous deprivation through the procedures under attack and the probable value of additional or alternative safeguards; and third, in contrast to *Mathews*, principal attention to the interest of the party seeking the prejudgment remedy, with, nonetheless, due regard for any ancillary interest the government may have in providing the procedure or forgoing the added burden of providing greater protections.

We now consider the *Mathews* factors in determining the adequacy of the procedures before us, first with regard to the safeguards of notice and a prior hearing, and then in relation to the protection of a bond.

III

We agree with the Court of Appeals that the property interests that attachment affects are significant. For a property owner like Doehr, attachment ordinarily clouds title; impairs the ability to sell or otherwise alienate the property; taints any credit rating; reduces the chance of obtaining a home equity loan or additional mortgage; and can even place an existing mortgage in technical default where there is an insecurity clause. Nor does Connecticut deny that any of these consequences occurs.

Instead, the State correctly points out that these effects do not amount to a complete, physical, or permanent deprivation of real property; their impact is less than the perhaps temporary total deprivation of household goods or wages. But the Court has never held that only such extreme deprivations trigger due process concerns. To the contrary, our cases show that even the temporary or partial impairments to property rights that attachments, liens, and similar encumbrances entail are sufficient to merit due process protection. Without doubt, state procedures for creating and enforcing attachments, as with liens, "are subject to the strictures of due process." Peralta v. Heights Medical Center, Inc., 485 U.S. 80, 85 (1988).

We also agree with the Court of Appeals that the risk of erroneous deprivation that the State permits here is substantial. By definition, attachment statutes premise a deprivation of property on one ultimate factual contingency — the award of damages to the plaintiff which the defendant may not be able to satisfy. For attachments before judgment, Connecticut mandates that this determination be made by means of a procedural inquiry that asks whether "there is probable cause to sustain the validity of the plaintiff's claim." Conn. Gen. Stat. §52-278e(a) (1991). The statute elsewhere defines the validity of the claim in terms of the likelihood "that judgment will be rendered in the matter in favor of the plaintiff." What probable cause means in this context, however, remains obscure. * * *

* * * [T]he statute presents too great a risk of erroneous deprivation under any of [the interpretations offered]. If the statute demands inquiry into the sufficiency of the complaint, or, still less, the plaintiff's good-faith belief that the complaint is sufficient, requirement of a complaint and a factual affidavit would permit a court to make these minimal determinations. But neither inquiry adequately reduces the risk of erroneous deprivation. Permitting a court to authorize attachment merely because the plaintiff believes the defendant is liable, or because the plaintiff can make out a facially valid complaint, would permit the deprivation of the defendant's property when the claim would fail to convince a jury, when it rested on factual allegations that were sufficient to state a cause of action but which the defendant would dispute, or in the case of a mere good-faith standard, even when the complaint failed to state a claim upon which relief could be granted. The potential for unwarranted attachment in these

situations is self-evident and too great to satisfy the requirements of due process absent any countervailing consideration.

Even if the provision requires the plaintiff to demonstrate, and the judge to find, probable cause to believe that judgment will be rendered in favor of the plaintiff, the risk of error was substantial in this case. As the record shows, and as the State concedes, only a skeletal affidavit need be, and was, filed. * * * It is self-evident that the judge could make no realistic assessment concerning the likelihood of an action's success based upon these one-sided, self-serving, and conclusory submissions. And * * * in a case like this involving an alleged assault, even a detailed affidavit would give only the plaintiff's version of the confrontation. Unlike determining the existence of a debt or delinquent payments, the issue does not concern "ordinarily uncomplicated matters that lend themselves to documentary proof." *Mitchell,* 416 U.S. at 609. The likelihood of error that results illustrates that "fairness can rarely be obtained by secret, one-sided determination of facts decisive of rights . . . . [And n]o better instrument has been devised for arriving at truth than to give a person in jeopardy of serious loss notice of the case against him and opportunity to meet it." Joint Anti-Fascist Refugee Comm. v. McGrath, 341 U.S. 123, 170-172 (1951) (Frankfurter, J., concurring).

What safeguards the State does afford do not adequately reduce this risk. Connecticut points out that the statute also provides an "expeditiou[s]" postattachment adversary hearing; notice for such a hearing; judicial review of an adverse decision; and a double damages action if the original suit is commenced without probable cause. Similar considerations were present in *Mitchell.* * * * [But n]one of [the *Mitchell*] factors diminishing the need for a predeprivation hearing is present in this case. It is true that a later hearing might negate the presence of probable cause, but this would not cure the temporary deprivation that an earlier hearing might have prevented. * * *

Finally, we conclude that the interests in favor of an *ex parte* attachment, particularly the interests of the plaintiff, are too minimal to supply such a consideration here. The plaintiff had no existing interest in Doehr's real estate when he sought the attachment. His only interest in attaching the property was to ensure the availability of assets to satisfy his judgment if he prevailed on the merits of his action. Yet there was no allegation that Doehr was about to transfer or encumber his real estate or take any other action during the pendency of the action that would render his real estate unavailable to satisfy a judgment. Our cases have recognized such a properly supported claim would be an exigent circumstance permitting postponing any notice or hearing until after the attachment is effected. Absent such allegations, however, the plaintiff's interest in attaching the property does not justify the burdening of Doehr's ownership rights without a hearing to determine the likelihood of recovery.

No interest the government may have affects the analysis. The State's substantive interest in protecting any rights of the plaintiff cannot be any more weighty than those rights themselves. Here the plaintiff's interest is *de minimis.* Moreover, the State cannot seriously plead additional financial or administrative burdens involving predeprivation hearings when it already claims to provide an immediate post-deprivation hearing.

Historical and contemporary practices support our analysis. Prejudgment attachment is a remedy unknown at common law. * * * Generally speaking, attachment measures in both England and this country had several limitations that reduced the risk of erroneous deprivation which Connecticut permits. Although attachments ordinarily did not require prior notice or a hearing, they were usually authorized only where the defendant had taken or threatened to take some action that would place the satisfaction of the plaintiff's potential award in jeopardy. Attachments, moreover, were generally confined to claims by creditors. As we * * * have noted, disputes between debtors and creditors more readily lend themselves to accurate ex parte assessments of the merits. Tort actions, like the assault and battery claim at issue here, do not. Finally, as we will discuss below, attachment statutes historically required that the plaintiff post a bond.

Connecticut's statute appears even more suspect in light of current practice. A survey of state attachment provisions reveals that nearly every State requires either a preattachment hearing, a showing of some exigent circumstance, or both, before permitting an attachment to take place. * * * Only Washington, Connecticut, and Rhode Island authorize attachments without a prior hearing in situations that do not involve any purportedly heightened threat to the plaintiff's interests. * * * [T]he States for the most part no longer confine attachments to creditor claims. This development, however, only increases the importance of the other limitations.

We do not mean to imply that any given exigency requirement protects an attachment from constitutional attack. * * * We do believe, however, that the procedures of almost all the States confirm our view that the Connecticut provision before us, by failing to provide a preattachment hearing without at least requiring a showing of some exigent circumstance, clearly falls short of the demands of due process.

IV

[A plurality of four Justices (JUSTICE WHITE, joined by JUSTICES MARSHALL, STEVENS and O'CONNOR) addressed whether due process ordinarily requires a plaintiff to post a bond or similar security in addition to a preattachment hearing, and concluded that it did. Of particular concern to them was the risk of severe detriment the defendant may suffer by the encumbrance of his property through mistaken attachment.

Relying on *Di-Chem*, JUSTICE WHITE concluded that the requirement of posting a bond to protect property rights of individuals in these circumstances was a principle the Court had already recognized. He argued that when extraordinary circumstances otherwise allow for ex parte prejudgment attachment, the posting of a bond protected defendants from interim harms arising from erroneous deprivations that the plaintiff might not be able to repay. And, when prejudgment attachment is not ex parte, but follows an adversarial hearing, he argued that due process still called for the posting of a bond, given the presence of highly contentious claims where judicial predictions of the outcome is not easily assessed.

JUSTICE WHITE concluded that the presence of a bond did not render moot the requirements for a preattachment hearing or other safeguards called for in the majority opinion. Rather, the posting of a bond is designed to enhance these safeguards, he stated, not replace them.]

V

Because Connecticut's prejudgment remedy provision, Conn. Gen. Stat. §52-278e(a)(1), violates the requirements of due process by authorizing prejudgment attachment without prior notice or a hearing, the judgment of the Court of Appeals is affirmed, and the case is remanded to that court for further proceedings consistent with this opinion.

It is so ordered.

[The concurring opinion of CHIEF JUSTICE REHNQUIST in which JUSTICE BLACKMUN joined, and the separate concurring opinion of JUSTICE SCALIA, are omitted.]

NOTES AND PROBLEMS FOR DISCUSSION

1. First, put yourself in the position of the plaintiff in the state court tort proceeding and consider the reasons why you would want the defendant's property seized at the outset of litigation. Since notice must eventually be given and a hearing held, what difference does it make to the plaintiff whether the notice and hearing precede or follow the attachment in this case?

2. Now, put yourself in the position of the defendant (Doehr). What difference does the timing of the notice and hearing make to him in this case?

3. The *Doehr* Court canvasses its earlier precedents in the area beginning with Sniadach v. Family Finance Corp., 395 U.S. 337, 89 S.Ct. 1820, 23 L.Ed.2d 349 (1969). In most of those decisions, the prejudgment seizure would have temporarily prevented the defendant from the use of the property (e.g., through garnishment of wages, or the seizure of specific property). Should it matter that the prejudgment attachment in *Doehr* would leave the defendant in possession of his property, and that only a lien on the property would have been created?

4. A majority in *Doehr* did not resolve the question whether a plaintiff would be required to post a bond as a constitutional prerequisite to obtaining prejudgment attachment from a court. Should it have? Note that the defendant's need for security in the event of a wrongful attachment is not altogether unlike the plaintiff's need for security to prevent potentially irrecoverable loss. For example, the plaintiff might win an order of attachment, but lose the case on the merits; yet the plaintiff might not be able to afford to pay the defendant the damages arising from the attachment (which might be lifted only at the conclusion of the trial). For the same reason, a post-judgment double-damages lawsuit for a wrongful attachment may also be inadequate for someone in the position of Doehr.

5. Try to imagine a setting in which a plaintiff would need the intervention of a court *even before* notice to the defendant and an opportunity to be heard. What kind of a showing should the plaintiff be required to make in order to obtain prejudgment attachment on such an ex parte basis (i.e., without the presence of the other side)?

6. Given the above, what change or combination of changes would make the Connecticut statute constitutional? In MITCHELL v. W.T. GRANT CO., 416 U.S. 600, 94 S.Ct. 1895, 40 L.Ed.2d 406 (1974), the Court upheld a Louisiana prejudgment attachment statute that did not provide for preseizure notice or hearing. Nevertheless, the statute allowed property to be seized (on a "writ of sequestration") only upon a detailed, sworn showing made to a judge that the defendant would dispose of or alienate the property during the pendency of proceedings. The procedure could only be invoked by a mortgage or lien holder in the property seized, it required the posting of a bond, and it provided for a prompt post-seizure hearing in which the plaintiff had the burden of proof to justify continued prejudgment attachment.

7. Sometimes the goal of prejudgment attachment is to make sure that assets will be available to pay off any potential money judgment. Other times, the goal may be to take possession of specific property in the defendant's hands to which the plaintiff claims to be entitled. For example, a party might seek a court's help in recovering household appliances that he sold to the defendant under a conditional sales contract (in which the seller retains an interest in the property until paid for), and the defendant has failed to make monthly installment payments. Traditionally, and pursuant to statute, the seller's interest might be vindicated by the writ of replevin. But the Supreme Court made clear in FUENTES v. SHEVIN, 407 U.S. 67, 92 S.Ct. 1983, 32 L.Ed.2d 556 (1972), discussed in *Doehr*, that state replevin provisions would be subject to the requirements of due process, no less than prejudgment writs of attachment of property in which the plaintiff claimed no preexisting property interest (such as garnishment of wages — see *Sniadach, supra*). As the Court in *Fuentes* put it, the household goods sought to be replevied were in the "possession" of the defendants although "most if not all of the [defendants] lacked full title to the chattels; and their claim even to continue possession was a matter in dispute." "Nonetheless," added the Court summarily, "it is clear that the [defendants] were deprived of a possessory interest in those chattels that were within the protection of the Fourteenth Amendment." How, if at all, should the plaintiff's claimed ownership interest in the defendant's property affect the *Mathews v. Eldridge* calculus described in *Doehr*?

8. Note that a party seeking to repossess property in the hands of another may still be able to engage in self-help, assuming self-help is possible in the relevant jurisdiction. The Supreme Court concluded that due process is not implicated when private parties — acting without the direct aid of state judicial or law enforcement officials — seize property, because the Fourteenth Amendment only addresses "state" action. Flagg Bros., Inc. v. Brooks, 436 U.S. 149, 98 S.Ct. 1729, 56 L.Ed.2d 185 (1978). Thus, a private party, acting without the aid of local officials, could conduct a seizure in a manner that might not comport with due process.

9. Finally, contrast the availability of the "legal" remedy of prejudgment attachment with the equitable remedy of preliminary injunctive relief to prevent a party's disposing of property that lies outside the court's jurisdiction. See

Grupo Mexicano de Desarrollo, S.A. v. Alliance Fund, Inc., 527 U.S. 308, 119 S.Ct. 1961, 144 L.Ed.2d 319 (1999) (discussed below).

2. INTERIM INJUNCTIVE RELIEF

The remedy of attachment or replevin is generally a remedy that is available in the courts of law, as distinguished from the courts of equity. As further discussed in Chapter 7, the distinctive traditions of those two systems that we inherited from England continue to play a large role in the administration of remedies, even though most states and the federal courts administer legal and equitable remedies in a single (i.e., merged) court system. Equitable remedies — by and large consisting of orders to a person to do something or to refrain from doing something — were ones initially administered by an official known as the Chancellor, and they were typically available only when the remedy in the courts of law were somehow "inadequate." In addition, the Chancellor would not grant relief without balancing the relevant equities, including the harm to the plaintiff if equity did not intervene, as well as the harm which the requested relief might do to the wrongdoer or to others, if granted. And typically, the party seeking the intervention of the Chancellor had to show that without it, the party would suffer "irreparable harm." This contrasts with decisions regarding liability in actions at law which typically are limited to determining whether the plaintiff has fit herself into one of the pigeonholes created by the common law or statutes entitling her to relief. Although, in most states, the courts of equity are long gone, modern judges continue to follow a process similar to that of the Chancellor's when deciding whether to grant equitable relief.

Thus, in addition to or alternative to seeking the remedy of damages, a plaintiff might seek injunctive relief to compel the defendant under the applicable law to do something or to refrain from doing something. Of course, a final order of injunctive relief will be awarded only after disposition of the merits of the case, perhaps only after a lengthy trial. But here, too, a party may need injunctive relief sooner rather than later, to prevent an imminent threat of harm (or to prevent ongoing harm) that may be irreparable — i.e., unable to be made good afterwards. For example, city employees show up on your property unannounced with a work order to cut down the pair of 150 year-old oaks in your front yard to make way for street widening. You are pretty sure that the work order has the wrong street. Maybe you are wrong, but finding out that you are right only after the trees are felled may be too little, too late.

There are two kinds of injunctive relief that may be granted prior to a final decision on a request for permanent injunctive relief. One is the temporary restraining order (TRO), and the other is a preliminary injunction. Both remedies are extraordinary in that they ask the court to grant the requested injunctive relief before the trial is complete. A preliminary injunction, when issued, generally comes early in the litigation, but it can only be issued after notice to the opposing party and after a full adversarial hearing; a TRO by contrast, has no such requirement, and may issue ex parte (without notice to or the presence of the other side) and immediately — often with the filing of the complaint. A preliminary injunction is an injunction pending the resolution of the merits of the litigation; a TRO is an injunction pending the determination of a preliminary injunction — i.e., where a party can't even wait for the time it would take to have a hearing on a request for a preliminary injunction.

Under Rule 65, Fed. R. Civ. P., a TRO requires a showing by affidavit that "immediate and irreparable injury loss or damage will result to the movant before the adverse party can be heard in opposition." The oak-tree hypothetical above would likely fit this category. If a TRO is granted, it will ordinarily be dissolved after 14 days under current Rule 65(b)(2), although it can be extended during that period for another 14 days. The grant or denial of a TRO (unlike a preliminary injunction) is not immediately appealable.

A motion for a preliminary injunction argues that the party seeking permanent injunctive relief should enjoy the benefits of the injunction throughout the trial. Traditionally, courts have looked to a number of considerations, including the plaintiff's likelihood of success and the respective risks of harm to the parties and others should the relief be granted or denied. A plaintiff will ordinarily not be granted a preliminary injunction unless she can show a probability of success on the merits (i.e., success at trial), that her remedies at law are inadequate, and that she will face irreparable harm if relief is not granted now. Note that these considerations parallel the due process issues discussed in the context of prejudgment attachment where litigants are also seeking an order from the court to preserve the status quo. The decision below offers an example of how courts approach the problem of preliminary injunctive relief, although in a setting involving Beanie Babies, not ancient oaks.

Ty, Inc. v. The Jones Group, Inc.

United States Court of Appeals, Seventh Circuit, 2001.
237 F.3d 891.

FLAUM, CHIEF JUDGE.

The Jones Group, Inc. ("Jones") manufactures and sells "Beanie Racers," which are plush toys shaped like race cars. Ty, which sells plush toys under the name "Beanie Babies," obtained a preliminary injunction against Jones, forcing it to stop producing and selling Beanie Racers. Jones asks us to reverse the magistrate judge's grant of a preliminary injunction in favor of Ty on several grounds. For the reasons stated herein, we affirm.

I. BACKGROUND

Ty in 1993 began selling plush toys throughout the United States under the name "Beanie Babies" and has sold over a billion Beanie Babies since the product's inception. Dozens of newspaper and magazine articles, television news stories, web sites, books, and magazines have emerged concerning Ty's Beanie Babies, apparently making the product a national sales phenomenon. Ty has obtained U.S. Federal Trademark Registrations for the marks "Beanie Babies" and "The Beanie Babies Collection." Beanie Babies are small, plush animals filled with plastic pellets. Generally, they are eight to nine inches long and typically are made from a velboa-type fabric. A red, heart-shaped hang tag with Ty's logo on it is attached to each Beanie Babies product.

Jones is a licensee of NASCAR and began in 1998 manufacturing and selling Beanie Racers, which are bean-filled replicas of NASCAR racing cars. Attached to each Beanie Racer is a white and rectangular shaped hang tag with the following information on it: (1) the Beanie Racers mark; (2) the multi-colored NASCAR mark; (3) the signature of the driver of each NASCAR race car, including a disclosure which recognizes the individual or entity who owns the rights to such signature; and (4) the corporate sponsor of each NASCAR race car. Beanie Racers are approximately eight inches long, are filled with plastic pellets, and are made of velboa-type plush fabric.

Ty sent Jones a cease and desist letter dated July 17, 1997 informing Jones that its Beanie Racers infringed upon Ty's trademark rights. Jones proceeded forward with the production of its Beanie Racers and Ty responded by pursuing legal action against Jones. In its suit, Ty alleges that Jones engaged in trademark infringement, unfair competition, and dilution in violation of federal and state laws. On November 17, 1999, Ty requested a preliminary injunction against Jones prohibiting Jones from selling plush toys under the name Beanie Racers pending the outcome of the suit. The magistrate judge granted Ty's motion for a preliminary injunction in an Opinion and Order dated June 5, 2000. Jones requested a reconsideration of the magistrate judge's opinion, but the magistrate judge decided not to alter his original opinion. On July 7, 2000, the magistrate judge entered the preliminary injunction against Jones and set a bond in the amount of $500,000. Jones is appealing the grant of the preliminary injunction pursuant to an interlocutory appeal, 28 U.S.C. §1292(a)(1).

II. DISCUSSION

A. Sliding Scale Analysis

A party seeking to obtain a preliminary injunction must demonstrate: (1) its case has some likelihood of success on the merits; (2) that no adequate remedy at law exists; and (3) it will suffer irreparable harm if the injunction is not granted. See Abbott Labs. v. Mead Johnson & Co., 971 F.2d 6, 11 (7th Cir. 1992). If the court is satisfied that these three conditions have been met, then it must consider the irreparable harm that the nonmoving party will suffer if preliminary relief is granted, balancing such harm against the irreparable harm the moving party will suffer if relief is denied. See Storck USA, L.P. v. Farley Candy Co., 14 F.3d 311, 314 (7th Cir. 1994). Finally, the court must consider the public interest (non-parties) in denying or granting the injunction. Id. The court then weighs all of these factors, "sitting as would a chancellor in equity," when it decides whether to grant the injunction. *Abbott Labs.*, 971 F.2d at 12. This process involves engaging in what we term the sliding scale approach; the more likely the plaintiff will succeed on the merits, the less the balance of irreparable harms need favor the plaintiff's position. Id. The sliding scale approach is not mathematical in nature, rather "it is more properly characterized as subjective and intuitive, one which permits district courts to weigh the competing considerations and mold appropriate relief." Id. (internal citations and quotation marks omitted).

We review a district court's decision to grant or deny a preliminary injunction under the abuse of discretion standard. A district court when analyzing the relevant factors abuses it discretion when it commits a clear error of fact or an error of law. We accord, absent any clear error of fact or an error of law, "great deference" to the district court's weighing of the relevant factors. "While our review is more searching than an examination of whether the district court weighed those factors irrationally or fancifully, we may not substitute our judgment for that of the district court." Id. (internal citations and quotation marks omitted).

* * *

B. *Likelihood of Success on the Merits*

Ty's trademark infringement case against Jones claims that Jones' use of the name Beanie Racers violates §43(a) of the Lanham Act, 15 U.S.C. §1125(a). In order to prevail in an action under §43(a) of the Lanham Act, Ty must establish: "(1) that it has a protectible trademark, and (2) a likelihood of confusion as to the origin of the defendant's product." * * * Ty need only demonstrate at the preliminary injunction stage that it has a "better than negligible" chance of succeeding on the merits so that injunctive relief would be justified. Id. Jones did not contest the magistrate judge's conclusion that Ty has a protectible interest in the term "Beanie" because it has a better than negligible chance of proving that the mark has acquired secondary meaning. We will therefore accept the magistrate judge's determination regarding Ty's protectible interest in the term "Beanie."

Next, we turn to whether Ty has a valid likelihood of consumer confusion claim regarding the origin of Jones' product. We employ the following factors to evaluate whether a likelihood of confusion exists in a trademark case: (1) the similarity of the marks in appearance and suggestion; (2) the similarity of the products; (3) the area and manner of concurrent use; (4) the degree of care likely to be used by consumers; (5) the strength of the plaintiff's mark; (6) whether any actual confusion exists; and (7) the defendant's intent to palm off its goods as those of the plaintiffs. * * * The magistrate judge recognized that "none of these factors by itself is dispositive of the likelihood of confusion question, and different factors will weigh more heavily from case to case depending on the particular facts and circumstances involved." * * * As a consequence, the "weight and totality of the most important factors in each case will ultimately be determinative of the likelihood of confusion, not whether the majority of the factors tilt the scale in favor of one side or the other." Schwinn Bicycle Co. v. Ross Bicycles, Inc., 870 F.2d 1176, 1187 (7th Cir. 1989). Even though no one factor is decisive, the similarity of the marks, the intent of the defendant, and evidence of actual confusion are the "most important factors" in a likelihood of confusion case. * * * The magistrate judge's findings with regard to likelihood of confusion are findings of fact and are subject to a clearly erroneous standard of review.

[The magistrate judge determined that Ty had both a protectible interest in the "Beanie" mark and that there was a likelihood of confusion as to the origin of the Beanie Racers product. He concluded Ty had about a 50-50 chance of likelihood of success on the merits. The court of appeals stated that it could "detect no clear error in the magistrate judge's analysis of the facts" and therefore affirmed the magistrate judge's decision to find that Ty had some likelihood of succeeding on the merits.]

* * *

C. Balancing of the Harms

Jones challenges the manner in which the magistrate judge balanced the respective irreparable harms that may result to each party if an injunction is granted or denied. We review a court's balancing of the preliminary injunction factors for an abuse of discretion. * * * A court when weighing the interests of the private parties and the public interest should try to "minimize the costs of being mistaken." *Abbott Labs.*, 971 F.2d at 12. The costs in this case could run high considering the possible practical harms that may flow from the grant of a preliminary injunction in favor of Ty. Jones notes that even if one were to assume that Ty had about a 50-50 chance of succeeding on the merits, Ty had to show that it would suffer more harm from the denial of an injunction than Jones would suffer from an entry of an injunction. Jones argues that by granting an injunction, the magistrate judge effectively ended the parties' dispute and allowed Ty to seek the relief it desired without undergoing a trial on the merits. If Jones desires to continue selling its product, it could decide to rename the product, which would involve changing the hang tags, displays, promotional materials, and the NASCAR license agreement. Alternatively, Jones could refrain from selling Beanie Racers all together. Either option is burdensome and a change in name will most likely result in a loss of goodwill because consumers since 1998 have known the product as Beanie Racers. There is also the possibility that it would be difficult for Jones to change the name of its product back to Beanie Racers if it were to prevail in a later litigation. Therefore, Jones contends if it were not forced to go out of business, "at the very least [Jones] would face the Hobson's choice of designing and producing still another new package or taking its product off the market until a decision on the merits might be had." * * *. Additionally, according to Jones, the possibility exists that the injunction would actually cause Jones to go out of business, whereas Ty's irreparable harm must have been less compelling considering it waited almost eight months to move for a preliminary injunction. For all of these reasons, Jones advances that the harm in granting an injunction would be more burdensome on its business than denying Ty the right to a preliminary injunction.

The magistrate judge determined that the harm to Ty would be more significant if a preliminary injunction was not granted. Initially, the magistrate judge acknowledged that there is no way to measure Ty's remedy at law since "damages occasioned by trademark infringement are by their very nature irreparable." * * * These type of injuries are presumed to be irreparable because "it is virtually impossible to ascertain the precise economic consequences of intangible harms, such as damage to reputation and loss of goodwill, caused by such violations." *Abbott Labs.*, 971 F.2d at 16. In considering Jones' argument that the eight month delay on Ty's part in pursuing the preliminary injunction shows that it did not face a threat of irreparable injury, the magistrate judge conceded that Ty may have delayed in bringing its motion for a preliminary injunction, but he stated that "it cannot be said that this minimal delay lulled Defendant into a false sense of security, nor that the delay was unreasonable." Delay in pursuing a preliminary injunction may raise questions regarding the plaintiff's claim that he or she will face irreparable harm if a preliminary injunction is not entered. See Ideal Indus., Inc. v. Gardner Bender, Inc., 612 F.2d 1018, 1025 (7th Cir. 1979). Whether the defendant has been "lulled into a false sense of security or had acted in reliance on the plaintiff's delay" influences whether we will find that a plaintiff's decision to delay in moving for a preliminary injunction is acceptable or not. Id. Jones has not presented any affirmative evidence that Ty's delay in seeking a preliminary injunction caused Jones to be lulled into a false sense of security or that Jones in any way relied on Ty's delay. The magistrate judge therefore properly decided that the evidence of mere delay alone, without any explanation on Jones' part of why such a delay negatively affected them, would not lessen Ty's claim of irreparable injury.

What appears to drive the magistrate judge to find that the balance of the harms favors Ty is Jones' knowledge of Ty's trademarks prior to adopting its Beanie Racers mark. Jones has posited several economic burdens it will face if an injunction is granted; however, Jones' position, according to the magistrate judge, is less than convincing in light of the fact that the "Defendant conceded that it had full knowledge of Plaintiff's trademarks prior to adopting its mark. In assessing Defendant's irreparable harm, the court excludes the burden it voluntarily assumed by proceeding in the face of a known risk." Jones argues that it consulted extensively with legal counsel to establish intellectual property rights, marks, and agreements prior to selling or manufacturing its Beanie Racers product, but these actions do not lessen the fact that it had knowledge of Ty's product and the possible confusion that could be created between Beanie Racers and Beanie Babies. "One entering a field already occupied by another has a duty to select a trademark that will avoid confusion." Ideal Indus., 612 F.2d at 1026. After all, both products use the same salient term — that is, "Beanie." Jones was forewarned of the possibility that Ty would sue considering Ty sent Jones a cease and desist letter. Jones went ahead with its production of the Beanie Racers, despite such a warning, knowing full well it may face legal challenges to its product and in turn negative financial consequences. Jones "having adopted its course . . . cannot now complain that having to mend its ways will be too expensive." Id. The magistrate judge acknowledged with respect to Jones' concern that it might be driven out of business because of the preliminary injunction that "I have seen no evidence in the case . . . that this [injunction] would . . . put them out of business . . . . I certainly would not want to put anybody . . . out of business, but I have not seen anything that would indicate that this [action] is . . . unjust." Jones' claim of irreparable harm rings hollow considering when it decided to produce the Beanie Racers it had knowledge of the potential consequences. In contrast, Ty, according to the magistrate judge, "stands to suffer significantly if a preliminary injunction is not entered, as Plaintiff could lose control of its reputation and goodwill. Plaintiff would risk losing years of nurturing its business."

The magistrate judge was careful not to leave Jones in a totally vulnerable position before a hearing on the merits. He provided for a bond of $500,000, which he believed would adequately compensate Jones for any harm that may result from the preliminary injunction. As we have previously noted, the magistrate judge found Ty's likelihood of success on the merits was not slight and accordingly there was no need for Ty to make a proportionately stronger showing that the balance of the harms was in its favor. See *Farley Candy Co.,* 14 F.3d at 315 ("Once the district court determined that Storck's likelihood of success on the merits of its claim was slight, it required Storck to make a proportionately stronger showing that the balance of harms was in its favor. Accord *Abbott Labs.,* 971 F.2d at 12."). Based upon the magistrate judge's balancing of the harms, we find that he did not abuse his discretion when he found the harms facing Jones if a preliminary injunction was granted did not outweigh the harms facing Ty if such an injunction was not granted.

III. CONCLUSION

The magistrate judge assessed the various relevant factors when considering Ty's request for a preliminary injunction against Jones and we conclude that the magistrate judge did not abuse his discretion when he granted said injunction in favor of Ty. Therefore, we *Affirm* the magistrate judge's decision.

NOTES AND PROBLEMS FOR DISCUSSION

1. As the opinion suggests, a party seeking a preliminary injunction must ordinarily show "some likelihood" of success. Should that require something *more* than a showing that the odds of eventual success will be 50-50?

2. If it appears near the outset of litigation that it is somewhat more likely that *the defendant* would prevail (or it is a coin flip as to who will win), why should an extraordinary remedy like a preliminary injunction be granted to the plaintiff, absent a clear showing that the respective balance of harms strongly favors the plaintiff?

3. For an attempt at a somewhat more mathematical spin on the calculus for entering a preliminary injunction, consider Lawson Prods, Inc. v. Avnet, Inc., 782 F.2d 1429, 1434 (7th Cir. 1986). There, Judge Posner stated that "the magnitude of erroneously denying the injunction, arrived at by multiplying the probability that the plaintiff will prevail at trial by the harm to the plaintiff caused by the denial of the injunction" must be greater than "the magnitude of an erroneously granted injunction measured by multiplying the probability that the defendant will prevail at trial . . . by the harm to the defendant caused by the granting of the motion." Does the formula help? Judge Posner elaborated on the point further in American Hospital Supply v. Hospital Prods., 780 F.2d 589 (7th Cir. 1986), in which he called the formula "a procedural counterpart to Judge Learned Hand's famous negligence formula[.]"

4. In what respect would the possible harm to Ty be "irreparable" if the preliminary injunction was not granted? If it turns out that the order was entered in error, and judgment is ultimately rendered for Jones (a 50-50 possibility according to the lower court), the harm *to Jones* has presumably been calculated to be reparable if it is within the limits of the bond. Is the nature of the possible interim harm to Ty any *less* calculable?

5. In Samuel v. Herrick Memorial Hosp., 201 F.3d 830 (6th Cir. 2000), an African-American doctor sought a preliminary injunction to restrain a hospital from temporarily suspending his staff privileges, claiming that the hospital had acted in a racially discriminatory manner in violation of federal law and had otherwise conspired to harm him in violation of state law. The hospital argued that the doctor's privileges had been suspended because of poor medical practices and that he needed further training. The trial court granted the injunction and reinstated the doctor's hospital privileges, finding that the plaintiff would be irreparably harmed by suspension of privileges, even though his likelihood of success was not especially strong.

The Sixth Circuit reversed, concluding that the district court had abused its discretion. Like the lower court, the appeals court found that the likelihood of the plaintiff's ultimately prevailing on either his federal or state law claims was not particularly strong, although the district court had permitted certain of the claims to go to trial. And while it seemed to agree that the doctor would be irreparably harmed by the temporary suspension of privileges should he ultimately prevail, it concluded that the potential harm to the hospital and to the public if the doctor were allowed to continue to practice without further medical training clearly outweighed the possible harm to the doctor. Is *Samuel* consistent with *Ty*?

6. In GRUPO MEXICANO DE DESARROLLO, S.A. v. ALLIANCE FUND, INC., 527 U.S. 308, 119 S.Ct. 1961, 144 L.Ed.2d 319 (1999), a divided Supreme Court concluded that a federal trial court lacked equitable power to issue a preliminary injunction preventing a Mexican construction company from transferring its assets in Mexico, pending the outcome of litigation against it in a New York federal court. Alliance sued Grupo Mexicano for damages in federal court after its Mexican highway project failed, leaving the Alliance and other American creditors financially unsatisfied. The New York federal court issued a preliminary injunction against Grupo Mexicano under Rule 65, Fed. R. Civ. P., preventing the liquidation of any of the failing company's Mexican assets, and the Second Circuit affirmed. The Supreme Court reversed. It held that the Rule did not alter the availability of equitable remedies in the federal courts, and that, as a historical matter, equity ordinarily required a prior judgment in an action at law before an injunction could issue to freeze property that was not the subject of the prior litigation.

An obvious question in the wake of the *Alliance* case is why the plaintiffs did not simply seek prejudgment attachment under Rule 64 (rather than an equitable remedy under Rule 65), if such was permitted by state law. The answer is not altogether clear, but it is doubtful whether state attachment statutes speak to anything other than property within the state in which the attachment is sought. It might have been possible, therefore, for Alliance to attach the property of Grupo Mexicano in New York, or even in California (by seeking such relief from a federal district court there, in aid of the New York proceeding — see Carolina Power & Light Co. v. Uranex, 451 F. Supp. 1044 (N.D. Cal. 1977)). Consequently, the decision in *Alliance* may have its primary, if not exclusive impact in litigation involving a defendant with property that is outside the United States and which cannot readily be reached through any state's attachment laws. The *Alliance* Court also refused to consider whether, if the law of New York would have permitted an injunction against a party in the position of Grupo Mexicano, the federal courts would have been able or obliged to follow New York law. The reason, said the Court, was that no one had raised the issue.

SECTION C. INJUNCTIONS AND DECLARATORY RELIEF

1. PERMANENT INJUNCTIVE RELIEF

A final order of injunctive relief commanding the defendant to do something or to refrain from doing something was the classic remedy of courts of equity, and its award is said to be committed to the discretion of the court. Whereas damages are a substitute for the harm arising from a defendant's acts, an injunction decrees a specific act. Take the case of *Memphis Community School District v. Stachura, supra.* The plaintiff might have sought the specific remedy of reinstatement as well as the substitutionary remedy of damages for the harm from having been unconstitutionally fired.

As noted above, permanent injunctive relief, like equitable relief more generally, requires that remedies at law be inadequate, and that the balance of equities and the public interest favor such relief. Consequently, in private litigation, the remedy of an injunction is more extraordinary than a damages award, which will often prove adequate. In addition, it is often stated that a permanent injunction will be granted only to avoid irreparable harm — often referred to as harm for which damages may not fully or readily compensate. Nevertheless, the notion of irreparable harm tends to be a far less demanding requirement when the injunction is to be awarded after trial than when it is interlocutory — i.e., pending litigation on the merits. See Section B.2, *supra*. Some courts have gone even further in minimizing the role of irreparable harm in deciding on permanent injunctive relief:

> The plaintiff who seeks an injunction has the burden of persuasion — damages are the norm, so the plaintiff must show why his case is abnormal. But when, as in this case, the issue is whether to grant a permanent injunction, not whether to grant a temporary one, the burden is to show that damages are inadequate, not that the denial of the injunction will work irreparable harm. "Irreparable" in the injunction context means not rectifiable by the entry of a final judgment. It has nothing to do with whether to grant a permanent injunction, which, in the usual case anyway, is the final judgment. The use of "irreparable harm" or "irreparable injury" as synonyms for inadequate remedy at law is a confusing usage. It should be avoided.

Walgreen Co. v. Sara Creek Property Co., 966 F.2d 273, 275 (7th Cir. 1992) (noting that a court should consider how an injunction might obviate the cost and difficulties of calculation of damages, and balance that against the costs of the court's having to supervise an injunction's enforcement). Also, unlike a preliminary injunction, there is no "likelihood of success" issue to worry about, for the simple reason that no permanent injunction can issue until the plaintiff has prevailed.

In addition, injunctions might range from a relatively simple order, such as an order of reinstatement to a job, to complex orders of injunctive relief that may require a governmental defendant to restructure one of its institutions, such as desegregating its public schools or reforming its prison system. When federal courts issue and supervise a "structural" injunction, special concerns of federalism may arise to the extent that federal courts may find themselves in the position of ongoing supervision of a particular state institution, if not running it outright. Consequently, the Supreme Court has insisted that the scope of any remedy not exceed the scope of the harm to be cured, and that the court take into account the public's interest in running its own local institutions. See *Missouri v. Jenkins*, 515 U.S. 70, 115 S.Ct. 2038, 132 L.Ed.2d 63 (1995). On the other hand, injunctions in the context of constitutional or public law litigation probably tend to be far more ordinary than extraordinary, thus inverting the usual preference for damages over equitable relief.

2. ENFORCEMENT OF INJUNCTIONS

The standard mechanism for enforcing compliance with a court's order of injunctive relief (whether of the permanent or interim variety) is the sanction of contempt. Depending on the setting, contempt may result in either jail time and/or the payment of money, and much turns on whether the contempt is labeled civil as opposed to criminal. Criminal contempt is designed to punish the party who has disobeyed the court's order and to remedy the insult to the court's authority. Consequently, a criminal contempt sanction is "backwards-looking" and will either be a one-shot fine payable to the court, or a jail sentence for a fixed period of time. Criminal contempts are also attended by heightened procedures and a burden of proof associated with criminal trials.

Civil contempt, by contrast, is designed to aid the party who is the beneficiary of the court's order of injunctive relief, and it is often designed to bring the defendant into future compliance with the court's order. Consequently, civil contempt can often be more "forward looking," and may consist of an ongoing fine or an indefinite confinement in jail, until such time as the defendant complies with the injunction. For example, when the City of Yonkers, New York, failed to undertake certain actions pursuant to a consent decree (i.e., an agreement between the parties entered by the court as a judgment), it was ordered to pay a fine of $100 for the first day, to be doubled every day until it complied with the decree (you can do the math). See *Spallone v. United States*, 493 U.S. 265, 110 S.Ct. 625, 107 L.Ed.2d 644 (1990) (upholding lower court's limiting of maximum fine to $1 million per day). Such contempt is often referred to as coercive or "conditional" insofar as the party in contempt has it within his power to fulfill the condition placed on him by the court (i.e. by complying with the order). Civil contempt may also be backward looking and simply consist of a one-shot payment from the enjoined party to the prevailing party for injury to the party arising from noncompliance (referred to as "civil compensatory contempt").

As is true of money judgments, Rule 62(a) mandates an automatic 10-day stay of execution of a final judgment ordering injunctive relief, and Rule 62(b) gives district courts discretion to stay execution pending resolution of post-trial motions. Injunctive orders are also subject to being suspended or modified pending appeal in the discretion of the district judge, with or without the posting of a bond or other security. See Rule 62(c). But an erroneously entered order of injunctive relief by a court of competent jurisdiction must continue to be obeyed until such time as it is overturned, and criminal contempt can attach to noncompliance. And even a jurisdictionally incompetent court can insist on compliance with its orders until such time as the question of its jurisdiction is resolved. See United States v. United Mine Workers, 330 U.S. 258, 67 S.Ct. 677, 91 L.Ed. 884 (1947).

Finally, note that in connection with an order of permanent injunctive relief, a court may be required to maintain continuing jurisdiction over the case for purposes of enforcement and possible modification. One of the distinctions between damages and injunctions is that orders of injunctive relief can be modified when conditions change, or even dissolved altogether when they are no longer needed, as when the defendant has brought itself into compliance with the law. See, e.g., Rufo v. Inmates of Suffolk Cty. Jail, 502 U.S. 367, 112 S.Ct. 748, 116 L.Ed.2d 867 (1992); see also Rule 60(b) (discussed in Chapter 12).

3. DECLARATORY JUDGMENTS

Suits for damages or injunctions are suits for coercive relief — they seek to force the defendant to do something: pay money or to act in a certain way. A suit for a declaratory judgment seeks only to have the court declare the respective rights of the parties who present their dispute to the court, nothing more. As such, it is noncoercive because it does not tell anyone to do anything (although as a result of a declaratory judgment the parties may be well-advised as to how to proceed in order to avoid a suit for damages or injunctive relief.)

Why would parties ever want this sort of kinder, gentler remedy? Imagine a company on the verge of expending great money and effort toward the building of a bridge across a river. Persons engaged in shipping along the river inform the builder that, as planned, the completed bridge will unlawfully interfere with river traffic, and they threaten to bring suit. Ideally, they would sue to enjoin construction of the bridge before construction began so the parties' rights could be resolved then and there. But the builder cannot know when, if ever, they may be sued for such relief. If the builder had to wait until after construction were commenced (or substantially completed) to be sued, the work might prove to have been wasted effort. In such a setting, the builder itself has no suit for damages or injunctive relief of its own that it might bring. Consequently, the builder would like to be able to go to court and obtain a judgment declaring whether the bridge, if completed as planned, will pose an unlawful interference with river traffic.

For some time, there was serious question whether courts, especially federal courts, could properly issue declaratory judgments. In one sense they are "advisory," and if uncontrolled, would enable friendly (i.e., nonadversarial) parties to go to court — not to resolve a genuine dispute — but to get legal preclearance regarding a whole range of potential actions. Such a possibility would present a serious problem of "justiciability" insofar as the federal courts are concerned, because they are limited to resolving "cases or controversies" — i.e., matters appropriate for the resolution of a court. See U.S. Const. art. III. Feigned or hypothetical cases are not appropriate grist for courts whose task is to resolve disputes and to declare the law only as a byproduct of that task. Consequently, in the federal courts at least, a declaratory judgment must involve "a case of actual controversy." 28 U.S.C. §2201. That would appear to mean that the dispute between the parties must be sufficiently ripe (if not on the verge of a suit for coercive relief), and that there otherwise be a justiciable controversy between parties with a genuine stake in the outcome.

A request for a declaratory judgment is sometimes made in tandem with a request for injunctive or other coercive relief, especially in litigation challenging the constitutionality of legislation or other governmental action. And sometimes a declaratory judgment might be sought in lieu of a suit for injunctive relief if some of the traditional equitable prerequisites for an injunction are missing. But a declaratory judgment is not enforceable in the sense that money judgments or injunctions can be, simply because no one will have been ordered to do anything. Nevertheless, a declaratory judgment can be the basis of a later injunction based on the findings made therein. See 28 U.S.C. §2202.

SECTION D. FEE SHIFTING, COSTS, AND SETTLEMENT INCENTIVES

Under the "American Rule," parties to civil litigation ordinarily must absorb the expense of hiring their own attorney, win or lose. This particular "cost" of civil litigation is therefore generally noncompensable — at least if the litigation is brought and maintained in good faith. Also, unlike the constitutional guarantee to criminal defendants under the Sixth Amendment, there is no right to counsel paid for by the state if the litigant cannot afford one. Nevertheless, legal services organizations funded by government can provide some help to the indigent, and advocacy groups (as well as law school clinics) may provide other free or low cost legal assistance to those who cannot afford it.

In addition, the contingent-fee contract has traditionally provided some measure of court access to injured parties who cannot afford to hire counsel. Under such arrangements, an attorney takes her payment out of any recovery by the plaintiff. But ordinarily such agreements are entered into only when victory is likely, and when the expected award (from which fees will be paid) will be substantial. The risk of nonrecovery, as well as the lost time-value of money — i.e., the free loan of legal services — is accounted for by a contract through which the lawyer takes a sometimes hefty percentage of the plaintiff's ultimate recovery.

406

City of Riverside v. Rivera

Supreme Court of the United States, 1986.

477 U.S. 561, 106 S.Ct. 2686, 91 L.Ed.2d 466.

JUSTICE BRENNAN announced the judgment of the Court and delivered an opinion in which JUSTICE MARSHALL, JUSTICE BLACKMUN and JUSTICE STEVENS joined.

The issue presented in this case is whether an award of attorney's fees under 42 U.S.C. §1988 is per se "unreasonable" within the meaning of the statute if it exceeds the amount of damages recovered by the plaintiff in the underlying civil rights action.

I

Respondents, eight Chicano individuals, attended a party on the evening of August 1, 1975, at the Riverside, California, home of respondents Santos and Jennie Rivera. A large number of unidentified police officers, acting without a warrant, broke up the party using tear gas and, as found by the District Court, "unnecessary physical force." Many of the guests, including four of the respondents, were arrested. The District Court later found that "[t]he party was not creating a disturbance in the community at the time of the break-in." Criminal charges against the arrestees were ultimately dismissed for lack of probable cause.

On June 4, 1976, respondents sued the city of Riverside, its Chief of Police, and 30 individual police officers under 42 U.S.C. §§1981, 1983, 1985(3), and 1986 for allegedly violating their First, Fourth, and Fourteenth Amendment rights. The complaint, which also alleged numerous state-law claims, sought damages and declaratory and injunctive relief. On August 5, 1977, 23 of the individual police officers moved for summary judgment; the District Court granted summary judgment in favor of 17 of these officers. The case against the remaining defendants proceeded to trial in September 1980. The jury returned a total of 37 individual verdicts in favor of the respondents and against the city and five individual officers, finding 11 violations of §1983, 4 instances of false arrest and imprisonment, and 22 instances of negligence. Respondents were awarded $33,350 in compensatory and punitive damages: $13,300 for their federal claims, and $20,050 for their state-law claims.

Respondents also sought attorney's fees and costs under §1988. They requested compensation for 1,946.75 hours expended by their two attorneys at a rate of $125 per hour, and for 84.5 hours expended by law clerks at a rate of $25 per hour, a total of $245,456.25. The District Court found both the hours and rates reasonable, and awarded respondents $245,456.25 in attorney's fees. * * * [The appellate court affirmed.]

Petitioners * * * sought a writ of certiorari from this Court, alleging that the District Court's fee award was not "reasonable" within the meaning of §1988, because it was disproportionate to the amount of damages recovered by respondents. [We affirm.]

II

In Alyeska Pipeline Service Co. v. Wilderness Society, 421 U.S. 240 (1975), the Court reaffirmed the "American Rule" that, at least absent express statutory authorization to the contrary, each party to a lawsuit ordinarily shall bear its own attorney's fees. In response to *Alyeska*, Congress enacted the Civil Rights Attorney's Fees Awards Act of 1976, 42 U.S.C. §1988, which authorized the district courts to award reasonable attorney's fees to prevailing parties in specified civil rights litigation. While the statute itself does not explain what constitutes a reasonable fee, both the House and Senate Reports accompanying §1988 expressly endorse the analysis set forth in Johnson v. Georgia Highway Express, Inc., 488 F.2d 714 (CA5 1974). See S. Rep. No. 94-1011, p. 6 (1976) (hereafter Senate Report); H.R.Rep. No. 94-1558, p. 8 (1976) (hereafter House Report). *Johnson* identifies 12 factors to be considered in calculating a reasonable attorney's fee.[3]

Hensley v. Eckerhart, 461 U.S. 424 (1983) announced certain guidelines for calculating a reasonable attorney's fee under §1988. *Hensley* stated that "[t]he most useful starting point for determining the amount of a reasonable fee is the number of hours reasonably expended on the litigation multiplied by a reasonable hourly rate." This figure, commonly referred to as the "lodestar," is presumed to be the reasonable fee contemplated by §1988. The opinion cautioned that "[t]he district court ... should exclude from this initial fee calculation hours that were not 'reasonably expended'" on the litigation. ([Q]uoting Senate Report, at 6).

[The plurality opinion then noted that *Hensley* had also suggested that the lodestar might be revised upward or downward depending on other considerations, including the "results obtained," while cautioning that the fee award "should not be reduced simply because the plaintiff [who has obtained excellent results] failed to prevail on every contention raised in the lawsuit." The plurality concluded that *Hensley* had been faithfully followed by the district court insofar as it made specific findings that the hours spent by counsel were reasonable. It also approved the district court's refusal to reduce the award because of claims on which plaintiffs did not prevail, since the winning and losing claims were "closely related" and "based on a common core of facts."]

The District Court also considered the amount of damages recovered, and determined that the size of the damages award did not imply that respondents' success was limited:

> "[T]he size of the jury award resulted from (a) the general reluctance of jurors to make large awards against police officers, and (b) the dignified restraint which the plaintiffs exercised in describing their injuries to the

---

[3] These factors are: (1) the time and labor required; (2) the novelty and difficulty of the questions; (3) the skill requisite to perform the legal service properly; (4) the preclusion of employment by the attorney due to acceptance of the case; (5) the customary fee; (6) whether the fee is fixed or contingent; (7) time limitations imposed by the client or the circumstances; (8) the amount involved and the results obtained; (9) the experience, reputation, and ability of the attorneys; (10) the "undesirability" of the case; (11) the nature and length of the professional relationship with the client; and (12) awards in similar cases.

jury. For example, although some of the actions of the police would clearly have been insulting and humiliating to even the most insensitive person and were, in the opinion of the Court, intentionally so, plaintiffs did not attempt to play up this aspect of the case."

The court paid particular attention to the fact that the case "presented complex and interrelated issues of fact and law," and that "[a] fee award in this civil rights action will * * * advance the public interest":

> "Counsel for plaintiffs . . . served the public interest by vindicating important constitutional rights. Defendants had engaged in lawless, unconstitutional conduct, and the litigation of plaintiffs' case was necessary to remedy defendants' misconduct. Indeed, the Court was shocked at some of the acts of the police officers in this case and was convinced from the testimony that these acts were motivated by a general hostility to the Chicano community in the area where the incident occurred. The amount of time expended by plaintiffs' counsel in conducting this litigation was clearly reasonable and necessary to serve the public interest as well as the interests of plaintiffs in the vindication of their constitutional rights."

Finally, the District Court "focus[ed] on the significance of the overall relief obtained by [plaintiffs] in relation to the hours reasonably expended on the litigation." *Hensley,* at 435. The court concluded that respondents had "achieved a level of success in this case that makes the total number of hours expended by counsel a proper basis for making the fee award[.]" * * *

Based on our review of the record, we agree with the Court of Appeals that the District Court's findings were not clearly erroneous. We conclude that the District Court correctly applied the factors announced in *Hensley* in calculating respondents' fee award, and that the court did not abuse its discretion in awarding attorney's fees for all time reasonably spent litigating the case.

III

Petitioners, joined by the United States as amicus curiae, maintain that *Hensley's* lodestar approach is inappropriate in civil rights cases where a plaintiff recovers only monetary damages. * * * Likening such cases to private tort actions, petitioners and the United States submit that attorney's fees in such cases should be proportionate to the amount of damages a plaintiff recovers. Specifically, they suggest that fee awards in damages cases should be modeled upon the contingent-fee arrangements commonly used in personal injury litigation. * * *

* * *

As an initial matter, we reject the notion that a civil rights action for damages constitutes nothing more than a private tort suit benefiting only the individual plaintiffs whose rights were violated. Unlike most private tort litigants, a civil rights plaintiff seeks to vindicate important civil and constitutional rights that cannot be valued solely in monetary terms. See Carey v. Piphus, 435 U.S. 247, 266 (1978). And, Congress has determined that "the public as a whole has an interest in the vindication of the rights conferred by the statutes enumerated in §1988, over and above the value of a civil rights remedy to a particular plaintiff . . . ." *Hensley*, 461 U.S., at 444, n. 4 (BRENNAN, J., concurring in part and dissenting in part). Regardless of the form of relief he actually obtains, a successful civil rights plaintiff often secures important social benefits that are not reflected in nominal or relatively small damages awards. * * * In addition, the damages a plaintiff recovers contributes significantly to the deterrence of civil rights violations in the future. * * * This deterrent effect is particularly evident in the area of individual police misconduct, where injunctive relief generally is unavailable.

Congress expressly recognized that a plaintiff who obtains relief in a civil rights lawsuit "'does so not for himself alone but also as a 'private attorney general,' vindicating a policy that Congress considered of the highest importance.'" House Report, at 2 (quoting Newman v. Piggie Park Enterprises, Inc., 390 U.S. 400, 402 (1968)). "If the citizen does not have the resources, his day in court is denied him; the congressional policy which he seeks to assert and vindicate goes unvindicated; and the entire Nation, not just the individual citizen, suffers." 122 Cong. Rec. 33313 (1976) (remarks of Sen. Tunney).

Because damages awards do not reflect fully the public benefit advanced by civil rights litigation, Congress did not intend for fees in civil rights cases, unlike most private law cases, to depend on obtaining substantial monetary relief. Rather, Congress made clear that it "intended that the amount of fees awarded under [§1988] be governed by the same standards which prevail in other types of equally complex Federal litigation, such as antitrust cases and not be reduced because the rights involved may be nonpecuniary in nature." * * * "[C]ounsel for prevailing parties should be paid, as is traditional with attorneys compensated by a fee-paying client, 'for all time reasonably expended on a matter.'" * * * Thus, Congress recognized that reasonable attorney's fees under §1988 are not conditioned upon and need not be proportionate to an award of money damages. * * *

A rule that limits attorney's fees in civil rights cases to a proportion of the damages awarded would seriously undermine Congress' purpose in enacting §1988. Congress enacted §1988 specifically because it found that the private market for legal services failed to provide many victims of civil rights violations with effective access to the judicial process. These victims ordinarily cannot afford to purchase legal services at the rates set by the private market. * * * Moreover, the contingent fee arrangements that make legal services available to many victims of personal injuries would often not encourage lawyers to accept civil rights cases, which frequently involve substantial expenditures of time and effort but produce only small monetary recoveries. * * * Congress enacted §1988 specifically to enable plaintiffs to enforce the civil rights laws even where the amount of damages at stake would not otherwise make it feasible for them to do so[.] * * *

A rule of proportionality would make it difficult, if not impossible, for individuals with meritorious civil rights claims but relatively small potential damages to obtain redress from the courts. This is totally inconsistent with Congress' purpose in enacting §1988. Congress recognized that private-sector fee arrangements were inadequate to ensure sufficiently vigorous enforcement of civil rights. In order to ensure that lawyers would be willing to represent persons with legitimate civil rights grievances, Congress determined that it would be necessary to compensate lawyers for all time reasonably expended on a case.

This case illustrates why the enforcement of civil rights laws cannot be entrusted to private-sector fee arrangements. * * * In light of the difficult nature of the issues presented by this lawsuit and the low pecuniary value of many of the rights respondents sought to vindicate, it is highly unlikely that the prospect of a fee equal to a fraction of the damages respondents might recover would have been sufficient to attract competent counsel.[10] Moreover, since counsel might not have found it economically feasible to expend the amount of time respondents' counsel found necessary to litigate the case properly, it is even less likely that counsel would have achieved the excellent results that respondents' counsel obtained here. Thus, had respondents had to rely on private-sector fee arrangements, they might well have been unable to obtain redress for their grievances. It is precisely for this reason that Congress enacted §1988.

IV

We agree with petitioners that Congress intended that statutory fee awards be "adequate to attract competent counsel, but . . . not produce windfalls to attorneys." However, we find no evidence that Congress intended that, in order to avoid "windfalls to attorneys," attorney's fees be proportionate to the amount of damages a civil rights plaintiff might recover. Rather, there already exists a wide range of safeguards designed to protect civil rights defendants against the possibility of excessive fee awards. * * * The district court has the discretion to deny fees to prevailing plaintiffs under special circumstances, * * * and to award attorney's fees against plaintiffs who litigate frivolous or vexatious claims. See Christiansburg Garment Co. v. EEOC, 434 U.S. 412, 416-417 (1978); * * * Furthermore, we have held that a civil rights defendant is not liable for attorney's fees incurred after a pretrial settlement offer, where the judgment recovered by the plaintiff is less than the offer. Marek v. Chesny, 473 U.S. 1 (1985). We believe that these safeguards adequately protect against the possibility that §1988 might produce a "windfall" to civil rights attorneys. [Affirmed.]

JUSTICE POWELL, concurring in the judgment.

I join only the Court's judgment. * * * For me affirmance — quite simply — is required by the District Court's detailed findings of fact, which were approved by the Court of Appeals. On its face, the fee award seems unreasonable. But I find no basis for this Court to reject the findings made and approved by the courts below. [See Rule 52(a), Fed. R. Civ. P.]

---

[10] The United States suggests that "[t]he prospect of recovering $11,000 for representing [respondents] in a damages suit (assuming a contingency rate of 33%) is likely to attract a substantial number of attorneys." However, the District Court found that the 1,946.75 hours respondents' counsel spent litigating the case were reasonable and that "[t]here was not any possible way that you could have avoided putting in that amount of time . . . ." We reject the United States' suggestion that the prospect of working nearly 2,000 hours at a rate of $ 5.65 an hour, to be paid more than 10 years after the work began, is "likely to attract a substantial number of attorneys."

* * *

[The dissenting Opinion of CHIEF JUSTICE BURGER is omitted.]

JUSTICE REHNQUIST, with whom THE CHIEF JUSTICE, JUSTICE WHITE, and JUSTICE O'CONNOR join, dissenting.

* * *

The analysis of whether the extraordinary number of hours put in by respondents' attorneys in this case was "reasonable" must be made in light of both the traditional billing practices in the profession, and the fundamental principle that the award of a "reasonable" attorney's fee under §1988 means a fee that would have been deemed reasonable if billed to affluent plaintiffs by their own attorneys. * * *

Suppose that A offers to sell Blackacre to B for $10,000. It is commonly known and accepted that Blackacre has a fair market value of $10,000. B consults an attorney and requests a determination whether A can convey good title to Blackacre. The attorney writes an elaborate memorandum concluding that A's title to Blackacre is defective, and submits a bill to B for $25,000. B refuses to pay the bill, the attorney sues, and the parties stipulate that the attorney spent 200 hours researching the title issue because of an extraordinarily complex legal and factual situation, and that the prevailing rate at which the attorney billed, which was also a "reasonable" rate, was $125. Does anyone seriously think that a court should award the attorney the full $25,000 which he claims? Surely a court would start from the proposition that, unless special arrangements were made between the client and the attorney, a "reasonable" attorney's fee for researching the title to a piece of property worth $10,000 could not exceed the value of the property. Otherwise the client would have been far better off never going to an attorney in the first place, and simply giving A $10,000 for a worthless deed. The client thereby would have saved himself $15,000.

Obviously the billing situation in a typical litigated case is more complex than in this bedrock example of a defective title claim, but some of the same principles are surely applicable. If A has a claim for contract damages in the amount of $10,000 against B, and retains an attorney to prosecute the claim, it would be both extraordinary and unjustifiable, in the absence of any special arrangement, for the attorney to put in 200 hours on the case and send the client a bill for $25,000. Such a bill would be "unreasonable," regardless of whether A obtained a judgment against B for $10,000 or obtained a take-nothing judgment. And in such a case, where the prospective recovery is limited, it is exactly this "billing judgment" which enables the parties to achieve a settlement; any competent attorney, whether prosecuting or defending a contract action for $10,000, would realize that the case simply cannot justify a fee in excess of the potential recovery on the part of either the plaintiff's or the defendant's attorney. * * *

The amount of damages which a jury is likely to award in a tort case is of course more difficult to predict than the amount it is likely to award in a contract case. But even in a tort case some measure of the kind of "billing judgment" previously described must be brought to bear in computing a "reasonable" attorney's fee. * * * If, at the time respondents filed their lawsuit in 1976, there had been in the Central District of California a widely publicized survey of jury verdicts in this type of civil rights action which showed that successful plaintiffs recovered between $10,000 and $75,000 in damages, could it possibly be said that it would have been "reasonable" for respondents' attorneys to put in on the case hours which, when multiplied by the attorneys' prevailing hourly rate, would result in an attorney's fee of over $245,000? * * *

* * * I agree with the plurality that the importation of the contingent-fee model to govern fee awards under §1988 is not warranted by the terms and legislative history of the statute. But I do not agree with the plurality if it means to reject the kind of "proportionality" that I have previously described. * * *

NOTES AND PROBLEMS FOR DISCUSSION

1. Understand the bottom line in *City of Riverside*: The plaintiffs' lawyers recovered a quarter of a million dollars, while eight plaintiffs divided $33,350. Since success in litigation is never assured, would a court uphold *any* amount of time spent on vindicating constitutional rights as "reasonable"?

2. The Court states that the possibility of a fully compensatory fee award may be necessary to give plaintiff's counsel incentive to take a difficult case having only a modest dollar value. Is the benefit to society from the vindication of rights and the deterrence of similar illegal action, when added to any dollar recovery by the plaintiff, enough to account for the fee in a case such as *City of Riverside*?

3. Consider the decision in *City of Riverside* in light of another decision under §1983 in this chapter — *Memphis Community School District v. Stachura, supra*. Does the availability of an award *to counsel* make up for the fact that monetary relief for the plaintiff may be hard to come by? In Farrar v. Hobby, 506 U.S. 103, 113 S.Ct. 566, 121 L.Ed.2d 494 (1992), the Court held that a party who recovers only nominal damages (because of a failure to prove actual injury) will be a "prevailing party," and thus is entitled to a reasonable fee. But it undercut the force of that holding by concluding that when only nominal damages are awarded, "the only reasonable fee is usually no fee at all."

4. The dissent in *City of Riverside* is concerned that counsel might ignore "billing judgment" in cases in which there exists a statutory provision for fee-shifting. Are those concerns realistic? The dissent is clearly bothered that it may cost more to litigate certain rights than they are worth in the market. But the premise of a fee-shifting statute is that some rights cannot pay their way in the market and would not be financially worth litigating (absent an additional financial incentive to bring them). Is it likely that the decision in *City of Riverside* will give a green light to plaintiff's counsel to run up hours in excess of what any fee-paying client would pay for?

5. Hensley v. Eckerhart, 461 U.S. 424, 103 S.Ct. 1933, 76 L.Ed.2d 40 (1983), provides that the starting point for calculating a reasonable fee should be the prevailing rate in the community for similarly complex litigation. Note that an attorney who could not be paid when she does her work, but only in the event of success and only after years of litigation, would presumably not charge the same hourly rate that she would charge a client who paid his bills on a regular basis. Should the "reasonable" rate therefore take account of the risk of not prevailing (or the delay in payment)?

6.   After some false starts, the Supreme Court in CITY OF BURLINGTON v. DAGUE, 505 U.S. 557, 112 S.Ct. 2638, 120 L.Ed.2d 449 (1992), concluded that there could be no enhancement beyond the reasonable noncontingent hourly rate to take account of the risk of nonrecovery. The Court in *Burlington* — a suit under federal environmental laws — was struck by a number of concerns. First, it suggested that the "lodestar" figure — i.e., reasonable hours multiplied by a reasonable rate — would itself reflect the difficulty of establishing the claim. Second, it suggested that there would be an incentive to bring "relatively meritless" cases as often as good ones if such an enhancement were available. In addition, the Court was concerned that any payment for the risk of not prevailing was a kind of subsidy to plaintiff's counsel for other equally risky cases that counsel might bring and lose. Thus, to the extent that such an enhancement would compensate plaintiff's counsel for cases in which she had not prevailed, it ran counter to the express provision of the fee statute that recovery could only be had by prevailing parties. Justices Blackmun and Stevens dissented, arguing that a premium for contingency compensated both for the risk of not prevailing and for the delay in payment. Foreclosing additional compensation for the risk of not prevailing would, they said, reduce statutory fees below the market rate and frustrate the vindication of federal rights.

7.   Despite the neutral, loser-pays language of §1988 and other federal fee-shifting provisions, successful plaintiffs customarily recover fees under these statutes absent extraordinary circumstances, but successful defendants generally recover fees only when the plaintiff has brought or maintained an objectively unreasonable lawsuit. Is such "one-way" fee-shifting fair, or a fair reading of the language of a statute like §1988?

8.   Note also that a party's "subjective" bad faith in pursuing litigation has long permitted a shifting of fees against that party as a sanction, at least as to those fees incurred as a result of the bad faith. See Chambers v. NASCO, 501 U.S. 32, 111 S.Ct. 2123, 115 L.Ed.2d 27 (1991); Goodyear Tire & Rubber Co. v. Haeger, 581 U.S. ___, 137 S.Ct. 1178 (2017). And tort law has long recognized that having to defend against a malicious lawsuit brought without probable cause can be a compensable harm. In addition, there are various provisions of the Federal Rules respecting pleadings and discovery (see Chapters 7 and 8) that may provide for fee shifting in some cases of unreasonable behavior, although not necessarily involving subjective bad faith or intentional wrongdoing.[*] In addition, states have begun to experiment with various sorts of loser-pays rules, ostensibly as a disincentive to the bringing of frivolous or marginal lawsuits.

---

[*]   Also, if an *attorney* "unreasonably and vexatiously" exacerbates the proceedings, he may be personally liable for the fees incurred by opposing counsel as a consequence of his misbehavior. 28 U.S.C. §1927.

9. The prospect of having to pay an award of fees — an award that may far outstrip any eventual award of damages — creates an incentive for defendants to settle early on, as Justice Brennan suggests in *City of Riverside*. Does it also mean that injuries that are perhaps undeserving of compensation will be compensated, so that the defendant may avoid a substantial fee award? Under Rule 68, Fed. R. Civ. P., the defendant may make an offer of judgment and, if the plaintiff's ultimate recovery does not exceed that offer, the plaintiff will have to pay "costs" incurred after the making of the offer. The following decision considers Rule 68 as it intersects with fee-shifting statutes such as the one at issue in *City of Riverside*. Note that Rule 68 has been slightly reworded since the decision below, but not in a way that affects its meaning.

Marek v. Chesny

Supreme Court of the United States, 1985.

473 U.S. 1, 105 S.Ct. 3012, 87 L.Ed.2d 1.

CHIEF JUSTICE BURGER delivered the opinion of the Court.

We granted certiorari to decide whether attorney's fees incurred by a plaintiff subsequent to an offer of settlement under Federal Rule of Civil Procedure 68 must be paid by the defendant under 42 U.S.C. §1988, when the plaintiff recovers a judgment less than the offer.

I

Petitioners, three police officers, in answering a call on a domestic disturbance, shot and killed respondent's adult son. Respondent, in his own behalf and as administrator of his son's estate, filed suit against the officers in the United States District Court under 42 U.S.C. §1983 and state tort law.

Prior to trial, petitioners made a timely offer of settlement "for a sum, including costs now accrued and attorney's fees, of ONE HUNDRED THOUSAND ($100,000) DOLLARS." Respondent did not accept the offer. The case went to trial and respondent was awarded $5,000 on the state-law "wrongful death" claim, $52,000 for the §1983 violation, and $3,000 in punitive damages.

Respondent filed a request for $171,692.47 in costs, including attorney's fees. This amount included costs incurred after the settlement offer. Petitioners opposed the claim for post-offer costs, relying on Federal Rule of Civil Procedure 68, which shifts to the plaintiff all "costs" incurred subsequent to an offer of judgment not exceeded by the ultimate recovery at trial. Petitioners argued that attorney's fees are part of the "costs" covered by Rule 68. The District Court agreed with petitioners and declined to award respondent "costs, including attorney's fees, incurred after the offer of judgment." The parties subsequently agreed that $32,000 fairly represented the allowable costs, including attorney's fees, accrued prior to petitioner's offer of settlement. Respondent appealed the denial of post-offer costs.

The Court of Appeals reversed. * * *

We granted certiorari. We reverse.

II

Rule 68 provides that if a timely pretrial offer of settlement is not accepted and "the judgment finally obtained by the offeree is not more favorable than the offer, the offeree must pay *the costs incurred after the making of the offer*." (emphasis added). The plain purpose of Rule 68 is to encourage settlement and avoid litigation. Delta Air Lines, Inc. v. August, 450 U.S. 346, 352 (1981). The Rule prompts both parties to a suit to evaluate the risks and costs of litigation, and to balance them against the likelihood of success upon trial on the merits. This case requires us to decide whether the offer in this case was a proper one under Rule 68, and whether the term "costs" as used in Rule 68 includes attorney's fees awardable under 42 U.S.C. §1988.

A

The first question we address is whether petitioners' offer was valid under Rule 68. Respondent contends that the offer was invalid because it lumped petitioners' proposal for damages with their proposal for costs. Respondent argues that Rule 68 requires that an offer must separately recite the amount that the defendant is offering in settlement of the substantive claim and the amount he is offering to cover accrued costs. Only if the offer is bifurcated, he contends, so that it is clear how much the defendant is offering for the substantive claim, can a plaintiff possibly assess whether it would be wise to accept the offer. * * *

* * * If defendants are not allowed to make lump sum offers that would, if accepted, represent their total liability, they would understandably be reluctant to make settlement offers. As the Court of Appeals observed, "many a defendant would be unwilling to make a binding settlement offer on terms that left it exposed to liability for attorney's fees in whatever amount the court might fix on motion of the plaintiff." 720 F.2d, at 477.

Contrary to respondent's suggestion, reading the Rule in this way does not frustrate plaintiffs' efforts to determine whether defendants' offers are adequate. At the time an offer is made, the plaintiff knows the amount in damages caused by the challenged conduct. The plaintiff also knows, or can ascertain, the costs then accrued. A reasonable determination whether to accept the offer can be made by simply adding these two figures and comparing the sum to the amount offered. Respondent is troubled that a plaintiff will not know whether the offer on the substantive claim would be exceeded at trial, but this is so whenever an offer of settlement is made. In any event, requiring itemization of damages separate from costs would not in any way help plaintiffs know in advance whether the judgment at trial will exceed a defendant's offer.

* * *

B

The second question we address is whether the term "costs" in Rule 68 includes attorney's fees awardable under 42 U.S.C. §1988. By the time the Federal Rules of Civil Procedure were adopted in 1938, federal statutes had authorized and defined awards of costs to prevailing parties for more than 85 years. See generally Alyeska Pipeline Service Co. v. Wilderness Society, 421

U.S. 240 (1975). Unlike in England, such "costs" generally had not included attorney's fees; under the "American Rule," each party had been required to bear its own attorney's fees. The "American Rule" as applied in federal courts, however, had become subject to certain exceptions by the late 1930's. Some of these exceptions had evolved as a product of the "inherent power in the courts to allow attorney's fees in particular situations." But most of the exceptions were found in federal statutes that directed courts to award attorney's fees as part of costs in particular cases.

* * *

The authors of Federal Rule of Civil Procedure 68 were fully aware of these exceptions to the American Rule. The Advisory Committee's Note to Rule 54(d) contains an extensive list of the federal statutes which allowed for costs in particular cases; of the 35 "statutes as to costs" set forth in the final paragraph of the Note, no fewer than 11 allowed for attorney's fees as part of costs. Against this background of varying definitions of "costs," the drafters of Rule 68 did not define the term; nor is there any explanation whatever as to its intended meaning in the history of the Rule.

In this setting, given the importance of "costs" to the Rule, it is very unlikely that this omission was mere oversight; on the contrary, the most reasonable inference is that the term "costs" in Rule 68 was intended to refer to all costs properly awardable under the relevant substantive statute or other authority. In other words, all costs properly awardable in an action are to be considered within the scope of Rule 68 "costs." Thus, absent Congressional expressions to the contrary, where the underlying statute defines "costs" to include attorney's fees, we are satisfied such fees are to be included as costs for purposes of Rule 68.

Here, respondent sued under 42 U.S.C. §1983. Pursuant to the Civil Rights Attorney's Fees Awards Act of 1976, 42 U.S.C. §1988, a prevailing party in a §1983 action may be awarded attorney's fees "as part of the costs." Since Congress expressly included attorney's fees as "costs" available to a plaintiff in a §1983 suit, such fees are subject to the cost-shifting provision of Rule 68. This "plain meaning" interpretation of the interplay between Rule 68 and §1988 is the only construction that gives meaning to each word in both Rule 68 and §1988.[2]

Unlike the Court of Appeals, we do not believe that this "plain meaning" construction of the statute and the Rule will frustrate Congress' objective in §1988 of ensuring that civil rights plaintiffs obtain "effective access to the judicial process." Hensley v. Eckerhart, 461 U.S. 424 (1983), quoting H.R. Rep.No. 94-1558, p.1 (1976). Merely subjecting civil rights plaintiffs to the settlement provision of Rule 68 does not curtail their access to the courts, or

---

[2] Respondent suggests that Roadway Express, Inc. v. Piper, 447 U.S. 752 (1980), requires a different result. *Roadway Express,* however, is not relevant to our decision today. In *Roadway,* attorney's fees were sought as part of costs under 28 U.S.C. §1927, which allows the imposition of costs as a penalty on attorneys for vexatiously multiplying litigation. We held in *Roadway Express* that §1927 came with its own statutory definition of costs, and that this definition did not include attorney's fees. The critical distinction here is that Rule 68 does not come with a definition of costs; rather, it incorporates the definition of costs that otherwise applies to the case.

significantly deter them from bringing suit. Application of Rule 68 will serve as a disincentive for the plaintiff's attorney to continue litigation after the defendant makes a settlement offer. There is no evidence, however, that Congress, in considering §1988, had any thought that civil rights claims were to be on any different footing from other civil claims insofar as settlement is concerned. Indeed, Congress made clear its concern that civil rights plaintiffs not be penalized for "helping to lessen docket congestion" by settling their cases out of court. See H.R.Rep.No. 94-1588, *supra*, at 7.

Moreover, Rule 68's policy of encouraging settlements is neutral, favoring neither plaintiffs nor defendants; it expresses a clear policy of favoring settlement of all lawsuits. Civil rights plaintiffs — along with other plaintiffs — who reject an offer more favorable than what is thereafter recovered at trial will not recover attorney's fees for services performed after the offer is rejected. But, since the Rule is neutral, many civil rights plaintiffs will benefit from the offers of settlement encouraged by Rule 68. Some plaintiffs will receive compensation in settlement where, on trial, they might not have recovered, or would have recovered less than what was offered. And, even for those who would prevail at trial, settlement will provide them with compensation at an earlier date without the burdens, stress, and time of litigation. In short, settlements rather than litigation will serve the interests of plaintiffs as well as defendants.

To be sure, application of Rule 68 will require plaintiffs to "think very hard" about whether continued litigation is worthwhile; that is precisely what Rule 68 contemplates. This effect of Rule 68, however, is in no sense inconsistent with the congressional policies underlying §1983 and §1988. Section 1988 authorizes courts to award only "reasonable" attorney's fees to prevailing parties. In *Hensley v. Eckerhart, supra*, we held that "the most critical factor" in determining a reasonable fee "is the degree of success obtained." We specifically noted that prevailing at trial "may say little about whether the expenditure of counsel's time was reasonable in relation to the success achieved." In a case where a rejected settlement offer exceeds the ultimate recovery, the plaintiff — although technically the prevailing party — has not received any monetary benefits from the post-offer services of his attorney. This case presents a good example: the $139,692 in post-offer legal services resulted in a recovery $8,000 less than petitioner's settlement offer. Given Congress' focus on the success achieved, we are not persuaded that shifting the post-offer costs to respondent in these circumstances would in any sense thwart its intent under §1988.

Rather than "cutting against the grain" of §1988, as the Court of Appeals held, we are convinced that applying Rule 68 in the context of a §1983 action is consistent with the policies and objectives of §1988. Section 1988 encourages plaintiffs to bring meritorious civil rights suits; Rule 68 simply encourages settlements. There is nothing incompatible in these two objectives. The judgment of the Court of Appeals is *Reversed*.

* * *

[JUSTICES POWELL's and JUSTICE REHNQUIST's separate concurring opinions are omitted.]

JUSTICE BRENNAN, with whom JUSTICES MARSHALL and BLACKMUN join, dissenting.

The question presented by this case is whether the term "costs" as it is used in Rule 68 of the Federal Rules of Civil Procedure and elsewhere throughout the Rules refers simply to those taxable costs defined in 28 U.S.C. §1920 and traditionally understood as "costs" — court fees, printing expenses, and the like — or instead includes attorney's fees when an underlying fees-award statute happens to refer to fees "as part of" the awardable costs. Relying on what it recurrently emphasizes is the "plain language" of one such statute, 42 U.S.C. §1988, the Court today holds that a prevailing civil-rights litigant entitled to fees under that statute is per se barred by Rule 68 from recovering any fees for work performed after rejecting a settlement offer where he ultimately recovers less than the proffered amount in settlement.

I dissent. The Court's reasoning is wholly inconsistent with the history and structure of the Federal Rules, and its application to the over 100 attorney's fees statutes enacted by Congress will produce absurd variations in Rule 68's operation based on nothing more than picayune differences in statutory phraseology. Neither Congress nor the drafters of the Rules could possibly have intended such inexplicable variations in settlement incentives. Moreover, the Court's interpretation will seriously undermine the purposes behind the attorney's fees provisions of the civil-rights laws, * * * — provisions imposed by Congress pursuant to §5 of the Fourteenth Amendment. * * *

* * *

I

The Court's "plain language" analysis goes as follows: Section 1988 provides that a "prevailing party" may recover "a reasonable attorney's fee as part of the costs." Rule 68 in turn provides that, where an offeree obtains a judgment for less than the amount of a previous settlement offer, "the offeree must pay the costs incurred after the making of the offer." Because "attorney's fees" are "costs," the Court concludes, the "plain meaning" of Rule 68 per se prohibits a prevailing civil-rights plaintiff from recovering fees incurred after he rejected the proposed out-of-court settlement.

The Court's "plain language" approach is, as Judge Posner's opinion for the court below noted, "in a sense logical." However, while the starting point in interpreting statutes and rules is always the plain words themselves, "[t]he particular inquiry is not what is the abstract force of the words or what they may comprehend, but in what sense were they intended to be understood or what understanding they convey when used in the particular act." * * * We previously have been confronted with "superficially appealing argument[s]" strikingly similar to those adopted by the Court today, and we have found that they "cannot survive careful consideration." Roadway Express, Inc. v. Piper, 447 U.S. 752, 758 (1980). So it is here.

In *Roadway Express,* the petitioner argued that under 28 U.S.C. §1927,[6] "costs" should be interpreted to include attorney's fees when the underlying fees-award statute provided for fees "as part of the costs." We rejected that argument, concluding that "costs" as it was used in §1927 had a well-settled meaning limited to the traditional taxable items of costs set forth in 28 U.S.C. §1920. * * *

The Court today restricts its discussion of *Roadway* to a single footnote, urging that that case "is not relevant to our decision" because "section 1927 came with its own statutory definition of costs" whereas "Rule 68 does not come with a definition of costs." But this purported "distinction" merely begs the question. As in *Roadway,* the question we face is whether a cost-shifting provision "come[s] with a definition of costs" — that set forth in §1920 in an effort "to standardize the treatment of costs in federal courts," — or instead may vary wildly in meaning depending on the phraseology of the underlying fees-award statute. The parties' arguments in this case and in *Roadway* are virtually interchangeable, and our analysis is not much advanced simply by the conclusory statement that the cases are different.

For a number of reasons, "costs" as that term is used in the Federal Rules should be interpreted uniformly in accordance with the definition of costs set forth in §1920:

First. The limited history of the costs provisions in the Federal Rules suggests that the drafters intended "costs" to mean only taxable costs traditionally allowed under the common law or pursuant to the statutory predecessor of §1920. Nowhere was it suggested that the meaning of taxable "costs" might vary from case to case depending on the language of the substantive statute involved — a practice that would have cut against the drafters' intent to create uniform procedures applicable to "every action" in federal court. Fed. Rule Civ. Proc. 1.

Second. The Rules provide that "costs" may automatically be taxed by the clerk of the court on one day's notice, Fed. Rule Civ. Proc. 54(d) — strongly suggesting that "costs" were intended to refer only to those routine, readily determinable charges that could appropriately be left to a clerk, and as to which a single day's notice of settlement would be appropriate. Attorney's fees, which are awardable only by the *court* and which frequently entail lengthy disputes and hearings, obviously do not fall within that category.

Third. When particular provisions of the Federal Rules are *intended* to encompass attorney's fees, they do so *explicitly.* Eleven different provisions of the Rules authorize a court to award attorney's fees as "expenses" in particular circumstances, demonstrating that the drafters knew the difference, and intended a difference, between "costs," "expenses," and "attorney's fees."[11]

---

[6] That section provided that any attorney "who so multiplies the proceedings in any case as to increase costs unreasonably and vexatiously may be required by the court to satisfy personally such excess costs." The section was amended after *Roadway Express* to require the payment of "excess costs, expenses, and attorneys' fees reasonably incurred because of such conduct."

[11] See Fed. Rules Civ. Proc. 11 (signing of pleadings, motions, or other papers in violation of the Rule), 16(f) (noncompliance with rules respecting pretrial conferences), 26(g) (certification of

Fourth. With the exception of one recent Court of Appeals opinion and two recent District Court opinions, the Court can point to no authority suggesting that courts or attorneys have ever viewed the cost-shifting provisions of Rule 68 as including attorney's fees. Yet Rule 68 has been in effect for 47 years, and potentially could have been applied to numerous fee statutes during this time. "The fact that the defense bar did not develop a practice of seeking" to shift or reduce fees under Rule 68 "is persuasive evidence that trial lawyers have interpreted the Rule in accordance with" the definition of costs in §1920. *Delta Air Lines, Inc. v. August*, 450 U.S., at 360.

Fifth. We previously have held that words and phrases in the Federal Rules must be given a consistent usage and be read *in pari materia,* reasoning that to do otherwise would "attribute a schizophrenic intent to the drafters." Applying the Court's "plain language" approach consistently throughout the Rules, however, would produce absurd results that would turn statutes like §1988 on their heads. * * * For example, Rule 54(d) provides that "costs shall be allowed as of course to the prevailing party unless the court otherwise directs." Similarly, the *plain* language of Rule 68 provides that a plaintiff covered by the Rule "must pay the costs incurred after the making of the offer" — language requiring the plaintiff to bear both his post-offer costs and the defendant's post-offer costs. If "costs" as used in these provisions were interpreted to include attorney's fees by virtue of the wording of §1988, losing civil-rights plaintiffs would be required by the "plain language" of Rule 54(d) to pay the defendant's attorney's fees, and prevailing plaintiffs falling within Rule 68 would be required to bear the defendant's post-offer attorney's fees.[*]

Had it addressed this troubling consequence of its "plain language" approach, perhaps the Court would have acknowledged that such a reading would conflict directly with §1988, which allows an award of attorney's fees to a prevailing defendant *only* where "the suit was vexatious, frivolous, or brought to harass or embarrass the defendant," and that the substantive standard set forth in §1988 therefore overrides the otherwise "plain meaning" of Rules 54(d) and 68. But that is precisely the point, and the Court cannot have it both ways. Unless we are to engage in "schizophrenic" construction, *Delta Air Lines, Inc. v. August,* 450 U.S., at 360, the word "costs" as it is used in the Federal Rules either does or does not allow the inclusion of attorney's fees. If the word "costs" does subsume attorney's fees, this "would alter fundamentally the nature of" civil-rights attorney's fee legislation. *Roadway Express, Inc. v. Piper*, 447 U.S., at 762. To avoid this extreme result while still interpreting Rule 68 to include fees in *some* circumstances, however, the Court would have to "select on an ad

---

discovery requests, responses, or objections made in violation of Rule), 30(g)(1) (failure of party giving notice of a deposition to attend), 30(g)(2) (failure of party giving notice of a deposition to serve subpoena on witness), 37(a)(4) (conduct necessitating motion to compel discovery), 37(b) (failure to obey discovery orders), 37(c) (expenses on failure to admit), 37(d) (failure of party to attend at own deposition, serve answers to interrogatories, or respond to request for inspection), 37(g) (failure to participate in good faith in framing of a discovery plan), 56(g) (summary-judgment affidavits made in bad faith).

[*] [The defendant had requested such fees, but they were denied by the trial court. Defendant did not appeal the issue. — eds.]

hoc basis those features of §1988 * * * that should be read into" Rule 68 — a process of construction that would constitute nothing short of "standardless judicial lawmaking."[16]

Sixth. As with all of the Federal Rules, the drafters intended Rule 68 to have a uniform, consistent application in *all* proceedings in federal court. In accordance with this intent, Rule 68 should be interpreted to provide uniform, consistent incentives "to encourage the settlement of litigation." *Delta Air Lines, Inc. v. August, supra*, 450 U.S., at 352. Yet today's decision will lead to dramatically different settlement incentives depending on minor variations in the phraseology of the underlying fees-award statutes — distinctions that would appear to be nothing short of irrational and for which the Court has no plausible explanation.

Congress has enacted well over 100 attorney's fees statutes, many of which would appear to be affected by today's decision. * * * Congress has employed a variety of slightly different wordings in these statutes. It sometimes has referred to the awarding of "attorney's fees *as part of* the costs," to "costs *including* attorney's fees," and to "attorney's fees and other litigation costs." Under the "plain language" approach of today's decision, Rule 68 will operate to *include* the potential loss of otherwise-recoverable attorney's fees as an incentive to settlement in litigation under these statutes. But Congress frequently has referred in other statutes to the awarding of "costs *and* a reasonable attorney's fee," of "costs *together* with a reasonable attorney's fee," or simply of "attorney's fees" without reference to costs. Under the Court's "plain language" analysis, Rule 68 obviously will *not* include the potential loss of otherwise recoverable attorney's fees as a settlement incentive in litigation under these statutes because they do not refer to fees "as" costs.

* * *

II

Although the Court's opinion fails to discuss any of the problems reviewed above, it does devote some space to arguing that its interpretation of Rule 68 "is in no sense inconsistent with the Congressional policies underlying §1983 and §1988." The Court goes so far as to assert that its interpretation fits in smoothly with §1988 as interpreted by Hensley v. Eckerhart, 461 U.S. 424 (1983).

The Court is wrong. Congress has instructed that attorney's fee entitlement under §1988 be governed by a *reasonableness* standard. * * * Although the starting point is always "the number of hours *reasonably* expended on the litigation," this "does not end the inquiry": a number of considerations set forth in the legislative history of §1988 "may lead the district court to adjust the fee

---

[16] It also might be argued that a defendant may not recover post-offer attorney's fees under the "plain language" of Rule 68 because he is not the "prevailing party" within the meaning of §1988. We have made clear, however, that a party may "prevail" under §1988 on some elements of the litigation but not on others. Thus while the plaintiff would prevail for purposes of preoffer fees, the defendant could be viewed as the prevailing party for purposes of the postoffer fees. Shifting fees to the defendant in such circumstances would plainly violate §1988 for the reasons set forth above in text, and the substantive standards of §1988 must therefore override the otherwise "plain language" approach taken by the Court.

upward or downward." We also have emphasized that the district court "necessarily has discretion in making this equitable judgment" because of its "superior understanding of the litigation." Section 1988's reasonableness standard is, in sum, "acutely sensitive to the merits of an action and to antidiscrimination policy." *Roadway Express, Inc. v. Piper*, 447 U.S., at 762.

Rule 68, on the other hand, is not "sensitive" at all to the merits of an action and to antidiscrimination policy. It is a mechanical *per se* provision automatically shifting "costs" incurred after an offer is rejected, and it deprives a district court of *all* discretion with respect to the matter by using "the strongest verb of its type known to the English language — 'must.'" *Delta Air Lines, Inc. v. August*, 450 U.S., at 369. The potential for conflict between §1988 and Rule 68 could not be more apparent.[40]

Of course, a civil-rights plaintiff who *unreasonably* fails to accept a settlement offer, and who thereafter recovers less than the proffered amount in settlement, is barred under §1988 itself from recovering fees for unproductive work performed in the wake of the rejection. This is because "the extent of a plaintiffs success is *a* crucial factor in determining the proper amount of an award of attorney's fees," hours that are "excessive, redundant, or otherwise unnecessary" must be excluded from that calculus. 461 U.S., at 440. To this extent, the results might sometimes be the same under either §1988's reasonableness inquiry or the Court's wooden application of Rule 68. * * *

But the results under §1988 and Rule 68 will *not* always be congruent, because §1988 mandates the careful consideration of a broad range of other factors and accords appropriate leeway to the district court's informed discretion. Contrary to the Court's protestations, it is not at all clear that "[t]his case presents a good example" of the smooth interplay of §1988 and Rule 68, because there has never been an evidentiary consideration of the reasonableness or unreasonableness of the respondent's fee request. It *is* clear, however, that under the Court's interpretation of Rule 68 a plaintiff who ultimately recovers only slightly less than the proffered amount in settlement will *per se* be barred from recovering trial fees even if he otherwise "has obtained excellent results" in litigation that will have far-reaching benefit to the public interest. Today's decision necessarily will require the disallowance of some fees that otherwise would have passed muster under §1988's reasonableness standard, and there is *nothing* in §1988's legislative history even vaguely suggesting that Congress intended such a result.

* * * The Court's decision inevitably will encourage defendants who know they have violated the law to make "low-ball" offers immediately after suit is filed and before plaintiffs have been able to obtain the information they are entitled to by way of discovery to assess the strength of their claims and the reasonableness of the offers. The result will put severe pressure on plaintiffs to settle on the basis of inadequate information in order to avoid the risk of bearing

---

[40] It might be argued that Rule 68's offer-of-judgment provisions merely serve to define one aspect of "reasonableness" within the meaning of *Hensley v. Eckerhart, supra.* This argument is foreclosed by Congress' rejection of *per se* "mathematical approach[es]" that would "end the inquiry" without allowing consideration of "all the relevant factors."

all of their fees even if reasonable discovery might reveal that the defendants were subject to far greater liability. Indeed, because Rule 68 offers may be made recurrently without limitation, defendants will be well advised to make ever-slightly larger offers throughout the discovery process and before plaintiffs have conducted all reasonably necessary discovery.

This sort of so-called "incentive" is fundamentally incompatible with Congress' goals. Congress intended for "private citizens * * * to be able to assert their civil rights" and for "those who violate the Nation's fundamental laws" not to be able "to proceed with impunity." Accordingly, civil rights plaintiffs "'appear before the court cloaked in a mantle of public interest'"; to promote the "*vigorous* enforcement of modern civil rights legislation," Congress has directed that such "private attorneys general" shall not "be deterred from bringing good faith actions to vindicate the fundamental rights here involved." Yet requiring plaintiffs to make wholly uninformed decisions on settlement offers, at the risk of *automatically* losing all of their post-offer fees no matter what the circumstances and notwithstanding the "excellent" results they might achieve after the full picture emerges, will work just such a deterrent effect.

Other difficulties will follow from the Court's decision. For example, if a plaintiff recovers less money than was offered before trial but obtains potentially far-reaching injunctive or declaratory relief, it is altogether unclear how the Court intends judges to go about quantifying the "value" of the plaintiffs success. * * * These are difficult policy questions, and I do not mean to suggest that stronger settlement incentives would necessarily conflict with the effective enforcement of the civil-rights laws. But contrary to the Court's 4-paragraph discussion, the policy considerations do not all point in one direction, and the question of whether and to what extent attorney's fees should be included within Rule 68 has provoked sharp debate in Congress, in the Advisory Committee on the Federal Rules, and among commentators. The Court has offered some interesting arguments based on an economic analysis of settlement incentives and aggregate results. But I believe Judge Posner had the better of this argument in concluding that the incentives created by interpreting Rule 68 in its current form to include attorney's fees would "cu[t] against the grain of section 1988," and that in any event a modification of Rule 68 to encompass fees is for Congress, not the courts. * * *

NOTES AND PROBLEMS FOR DISCUSSION

1. If you are a defendant, when will you make an offer such as that provided for in Rule 68? Note that the "benefit" of Rule 68 (in the form of having the plaintiff pay costs) only attaches if the plaintiff later wins, but wins less than what she was offered.

2. Consider the goals of Rule 68 outside of the fee-shifting setting. How serious a penalty does it visit on the prevailing party in a damages action who happens to recover less than what they were offered? Note also that in such a setting the predominant figures to be taken account of are the plaintiff's estimated recovery at trial and the offer of judgment itself.

3. Now, factor in a fee-shifting statute. How have the stakes been raised if an offer is rejected? Notice that in cases such as *City of Riverside, supra,* the plaintiff's ultimate monetary recovery may be almost secondary in the calculation. Does that put the plaintiff's counsel in a potentially adversarial relationship with his client when there is a lump-sum offer that purports to include fees as well as compensatory damages?

4. The Court in *Marek* purports to apply a plain meaning approach to Rule 68 by reading "costs" to include attorneys fees, at least when the fee shifting statute refers to an award of fees as "part of costs." Does the majority respond to the dissent's suggestion that a plain meaning approach to Rule 68 would also require the offeree who prevailed but recovered less than what she was offered, to pay the loser's attorney's fees, as part of costs?

5. Requiring the successful plaintiff to pay the defendants attorney's fees incurred after a more favorable offer of judgment would appear to run afoul of the fee-shifting statute which is read as saying that defendants can recover fees only if they prevail and only if the plaintiff has litigated in bad faith. Why doesn't that same reasoning apply to the refusal to award the prevailing plaintiff his attorney fees incurred after a good faith rejection of the offer of judgment as occurred in *Marek*?

6. Finally, consider what would happen if an attorney brought suit for injunctive relief only, had put substantial time and effort into the case, and was offered a settlement on the eve of trial that gave the client essentially all that he had asked for, but specifically conditioned the offer on the nonrecovery of attorney's fees. Could the lawyer ethically refuse the offer?

In EVANS v. JEFF D., 475 U.S. 717, 106 S.Ct. 1531, 89 L.Ed.2d 747 (1986), the Supreme Court said it was an offer that the plaintiffs' counsel couldn't refuse. *Jeff D.* was a class action, filed on behalf of emotionally and mentally handicapped children, and it sought to correct deficiencies in health care and other services provided to the children by Idaho officials. Plaintiffs were represented by an attorney from the state legal aid society. After suit was filed, the parties entered into settlement negotiations on certain issues, while other issues were prepared for trial. The parties came to agreement on some aspects of the suit quickly, but agreed on others only much later and nearer to trial. The defendants ultimately offered the plaintiff class virtually all of the injunctive relief that it had requested. In fact, the injunctive relief that was offered appeared to exceed even what the district court had been prepared to grant. The offer, however, was conditioned on plaintiffs' counsel waiving any request for fees. Plaintiffs' counsel accepted the offer because he felt ethically compelled to do so — despite the fact that the legal aid society found the fee waiver unacceptable. After accepting the offer, however, the attorney asked the trial court to approve the settlement under Rule 23(e), Fed. R. Civ. P., but to reject the fee waiver. The district court approved the entire settlement, including the fee waiver. On appeal, the Ninth Circuit affirmed the settlement, but threw out the fee waiver.

The Supreme Court, in an opinion by Justice Stevens, reversed, and upheld the entire settlement, including the fee waiver. The Court found that the plaintiffs' attorney had not been in an ethical dilemma at all and that he had no ethical choice but to accept the settlement. The opinion also concluded that the Fees Act could be read neither as proscribing simultaneous negotiation of fees and the merits, nor as proscribing settlement offers conditioned on waiver of fees. If defense counsel could not settle fees and the merits simultaneously, said the Court, settlements would be discouraged because total liability would remain uncertain. It found unassailable the district court's conclusion that the extensive structural relief offered was an adequate quid pro quo for the waiver, and it rejected the Court of Appeals' attempt to sever the judgment and retain only the favorable aspects of the settlement. In a concluding footnote the Court stated:

> We are cognizant of the possibility that decisions by individual clients to bargain away fee awards may, in the aggregate and in the long run, diminish lawyers' expectations of statutory fees in civil rights cases. If this occurred, the pool of lawyers willing to represent plaintiffs in such cases might shrink, constricting the "effective access to the judicial process" for persons with civil rights grievances, which the Fees Act was intended to provide. * * * That the "tyranny of small decisions" may operate in this fashion is not to say that there is any reason or documentation to support such a concern at the present time. Comment on this issue is therefore premature at this juncture. We believe, however, that as a practical matter the likelihood of this circumstance arising is remote. * * *

Id. at 741-42 n.34.

Justice Brennan wrote a dissent for himself and two others. He objected to the majority's view of fees as "merely . . . another remedy to vindicate the rights of individual plaintiffs" that could be negotiated away as a quid pro quo for providing substantial relief to a particular plaintiff. Rather, because "Congress determined [in the Fees Act] that the public as a whole has an interest in the vindication of the rights conferred by the civil rights statutes over and above the value of a civil rights remedy to a particular plaintiff," the correct question to ask was "whether permitting negotiated fee waivers is consistent with Congress's goal of attracting competent counsel" in civil rights cases generally. The dissent concluded that the two were not consistent. It first noted that it was obvious (and that the Court itself had all but conceded) that allowing defendants to condition settlement of the merits on a waiver of statutory fees would decrease the willingness of lawyers to accept civil rights cases in the long run. It then addressed the Court's concern that not allowing such waivers would reduce the likelihood of settlements (id. at 760-61):

> I agree with the Court that encouraging settlements is a desirable policy. But it is a *judicially* created policy, applicable to litigation of any kind and having no special force in the context of civil rights cases. The *congressional* policy underlying the Fees Act is * * * to create incentives for lawyers to devote time to civil rights cases by making it economically feasible for them to do so. * * * [P]ermitting fee waivers significantly undercuts this policy. Thus, even if prohibiting fee waivers does discourage some settlements, a *judicial* policy favoring settlement cannot possibly take precedence over this express *congressional* policy.

* * *

    * * * The fact that fee waivers may produce some settlement offers that are beneficial to a few individual plaintiffs is hardly consistent with the purposes of the Fees Act, if permitting fee waivers fundamentally undermines what Congress sought to achieve. Each individual plaintiff who waives his right to statutory fees in order to obtain additional relief for himself makes it that much more difficult for the next victim of a civil rights violation to find a lawyer willing or able to bring *his* case. * * *

7.   Some have argued that the goals of settlement may not be equally valuable in public law as opposed to private law litigation. Do the goals of settlement outweigh the threat to effective enforcement of federal rights that may result from a decision such as *Jeff D.*?

8.   Suppose, in a suit for injunctive relief, that the defendant changes his behavior as requested in the complaint, and urges the court to dismiss the case as moot (i.e., there is no longer any dispute for the court to resolve). Should plaintiff's counsel be able to recover fees under a fee-shifting statute if bringing the lawsuit served as the catalyst for the settlement? "Yes," if the settlement is entered as a judgment by the court; but "no," if the settlement is voluntary, and without any order from the court. See Buckhannon, Bd. & Care Home, Inc. v. West Virginia Dept. of Health and Human Resources, 532 U.S. 998, 121 S.Ct. 1835, 149 L.Ed.2d 855 (2001). What incentives does this give to defendants who might be inclined to settle (if sued), especially in tandem with *Jeff D.*? Note that state courts are free to go their own way, at least when adjudicating state-law claims for relief. See, e.g., Graham v. DaimlerChrysler Corp., 101 P.3d 140, 148 (Cal. 2005) (upholding catalyst theory in state court public interest litigation, post-*Buckhannon*).

CHAPTER 7

Pleading

A typical civil case occurs in a fairly orderly sequence — getting the case started (pleading and joinder), fleshing it out (discovery), getting ready for trial (summary judgment and other pretrial proceedings), trial and appeal. There are also post-trial mechanisms for reopening judgments in very limited circumstances. Although there is some overlap, one phase generally does not begin until the prior phase has ended or is far along. The first step in the process is pleading — what the plaintiff and defendant must say to start the case.

What the parties must say to start the case depends on what role pleading plays in the litigation process. Historically, pleadings served objectives now largely served by a combination of modern-day mechanisms, including pretrial motions, discovery, summary judgment, the pretrial conference and order, as well as the pleadings. Those objectives were to provide detailed information about the case and the legal and factual issues, to separate meritorious cases from nonmeritorious cases, and to provide some indication of the evidence in support of the position of each party. Once the pleadings were completed, there was either a decision by the court or a trial. Present day mechanisms for discovery and pretrial procedure were all but nonexistent in common law courts.

Modern procedure starts from the premise that pleadings inadequately performed their multiple roles. Over time, the role played by pleadings became limited to accomplishing certain introductory functions, while discovery and pretrial procedures such as summary judgment, became the preeminent vehicles for providing information about a case, for identifying cases that are not meritorious, and for otherwise preparing the case for trial. Indeed, the availability of broad discovery implicitly assumes that most cases will not be resolved at the pleading stage.

Although pleadings may be less important today than they once were, that hardly means that they are unimportant, and the Supreme Court has recently elevated their importance (as noted below). Pleadings play multiple roles. In addition to providing notice of what the case is about, they are the first opportunity each side has to state its position as to certain issues (with the risk that any change may have to be explained and/or subject to court approval); they are likely to be read by the judge (for example, in connection with a motion or pretrial conference) and may provide her first impression of the case; and they offer both sides the opportunity for procedural maneuvering and tactical advantage. Thus, in framing pleadings, lawyers must ask not only what is the minimum the law requires, but how the pleadings will be used throughout the case and whether they will be adequate for those purposes. After a brief historical introduction, we will focus primarily on the federal courts, largely because they offer a representative example of modern pleading conventions. Be aware, however, that some state courts still accord a role to pleading that is more reflective of older practices.

SECTION A. AN INTRODUCTORY NOTE ON SUBSTANTIVE LAW

A client comes into your office with a grievance. Normally, the client does not think of her grievance in terms of legal categories, but in terms of righting some perceived wrong. She may tell of a business deal gone sour, of being fired from her job, of an accident and injury, of a competitor who is stealing her secrets, or of a dispute with a neighbor over the proper property line. The client wants to remedy the grievance.

The first step is to determine whether the client has a legal right to relief — i.e., is the other person's conduct actionable. Only if it is, can your client sue. To determine whether your client has a right to sue, you must look to the substantive principles of law — rules of tort, contract, property, unfair competition, discrimination, and so on. The sources of substantive principles of law can include the Constitution, statutes and ordinances, and the "common law" (which consists of judge-developed principles of substantive law). Until comparatively recently, most substantive principles were based on the common law, but the changing legal landscape over the past century has witnessed a furious enactment of statutes that have both codified and expanded (or sometimes contracted) common law substantive principles, and which recognized new substantive principles. For example, most of the substantive law governing employment discrimination is based on statutes enacted in the past fifty years.

When consulting the substantive law, you are likely to find that it says that your client has a right to relief only if she can establish several different factual matters (sometimes called elements of a claim). For example, the client with a sour business deal may have to show that (1) she had an agreement with another person, (2) the agreement was supported by "consideration," (3) she performed her part of the agreement, (4) the other party didn't perform his part of the agreement, and (5) she suffered damages as a result. The accident-injury client may have to show (1) he was involved in an accident with the defendant, (2) the defendant owed a duty of care and was negligent, (3) the defendant's negligence was the proximate cause of the accident, and (4) he was injured and suffered damages as a result.

Pleadings then are an implicit contention about substantive law — that the plaintiff (the client) has a right to recover on one or more substantive theories, and that she will be able to establish a basis for each element of her case. (We put aside for now questions which arise from the fact that each side may be responsible for one or more of the elements involved in a substantive claim.) As you go through the section on pleading, keep in mind that a plaintiff must plead, and a defendant must defend against, a claim under the substantive law. As you will see, if what the plaintiff has pleaded — even if she could prove all of it at trial — is not something that the law would allow her to recover for, the case can (and should) be stopped in its tracks. Also, keep in mind that pleadings are not proof of anything; they are only allegations. Proof comes later. Pleadings merely get the case going.

Section B. A Brief History of Pleading

1. Common Law

(a) The Origins. The history of modern procedure can be traced to developments in England beginning early in the last Millennium. The origin and much of the early development are shrouded in the mists of history. But what we now call common law procedure was not static; rather, it was a constantly evolving system that continued to develop for hundreds of years.

For present purposes, only a few aspects of this development are noteworthy. First, the "common law" — both substantive law and procedural law — was initially elaborated and developed by judges. (The common law thus contrasts with many other legal systems, such as Roman Law or Civil Law, where "law" was contained primarily in written codes or statutes.) As time went on, statutes were passed governing certain aspects of procedure, but most procedure remained part of the common law for a very long time. A consequence of this history was that procedure tended to be law for the lawyer, to be highly specialized, and to be free of the kinds of political compromises inherent in legislation. Second, the development of Royal courts (and in turn, common law procedure) went hand in hand with the centralization of power in England. Previously, "justice" was in the hands of various courts run by local lords, barons, and landlords. Gradually, the King's courts assumed the power to hear more and more cases previously heard only in local courts. But initially, since Royal jurisdiction was "special," a litigant had to establish the reason why his case properly belonged in the Royal courts. Not surprisingly, the earliest cases were criminal and quasi-criminal — a breach of the King's peace — although, over time, this notion of a special Royal interest became attenuated. For pleading purposes, the key point is that the facts of the plaintiff's grievance had to establish both a right to relief and a right to be in the Royal courts. Third, common law procedure initially used oral pleadings. As a consequence, pleadings tended to be specific in identifying the matters at issue. Also, a very dialectical approach was followed — the plaintiff would plead matters in his complaint, the defendant would answer, the plaintiff would rebut, the defendant would surrebut, and so on. Fourth, pleadings played a key role in the lawsuit in (a) establishing jurisdiction, (b) identifying the factual basis for the lawsuit, (c) separating meritorious from nonmeritorious cases, (d) determining which cases required a trial and which cases could be decided without a trial, and (e) if there was a trial, determining what issues would be decided.

(b) The Forms of Action. As suggested above, common law procedure was very "theory" minded. Substantive law — the right to recover damages — was reflected in the various forms of action. Terms such as "trespass," "trespass on the case" (or simply "case"), "trover," "covenant," "debt," "special assumpsit," "general assumpsit," and "replevin" are some of the more common of these

forms of action. Each form of action provided a substantive basis for recovery, the elements the plaintiff had to prove to obtain such a recovery, and a set of procedural requirements (which were different among the different forms of action) to guide the determination. The plaintiff started the case by preparing and having the sheriff serve a writ setting out the case — actually, setting out the case twice since the first set of allegations established the jurisdiction of the court, and they were largely repeated to allege the substantive claim. If the plaintiff brought an action on one form of action and could not establish all the elements, his case was dismissed (nonsuited), but he was free to start over on another form of action if time permitted. This appears to have happened frequently, especially as the common law developed, because the requirements of different forms of action were themselves in a process of evolution. For example, in the famous case of Scott v. Shepherd, 96 Eng. Rep. 525 (K.B. 1773), defendant threw a lighted squib (firecracker) in a marketplace, and it landed on A's stall; A threw it on B's stall, and B threw it on plaintiff's stall where it exploded putting out his eye. It was argued, although unsuccessfully, that the plaintiff's action in trespass should be nonsuited because the action should have been trespass on the case (because the injury to plaintiff was merely indirect). But the Court essentially expanded the scope of trespass in ruling for the plaintiff. If the plaintiff's grievance was not included in any form of action, however, the plaintiff was largely out of luck.

(c) The Dialectical Nature of Pleading. Pleading at common law was a highly structured affair. The objective was to produce a single issue of law or fact for decision — not because cases just had a single issue, but rather because of the developments described above. Pleading continued until that one issue was identified and joined by both parties.

(i) Plaintiff. The Plaintiff started with a declaration. The declaration was set out in the writ and incorporated jurisdictional allegations, as well as the factual basis for the form of action which served as the basis for the writ.

(ii) Defendant. The Defendant had a choice. He could demur or plead. A demurrer presented the legal question of whether plaintiff's declaration set out a valid claim for relief within the form of action used (and it made no difference that the declaration might set out a valid claim for relief under some other form of action). There were two types of pleas. A "dilatory" plea raised various matters relating to the jurisdiction of the court (i.e., was the action brought in the proper place), and matters relating to joinder of parties or claims. As is implicit in the name, a dilatory plea did not go to the merits of the action. Conversely, the other type of plea — a "plea in bar" — went to the merits. A plea in bar could be one of two types: a "traverse" which essentially denied the operative facts; and a plea in "confession and avoidance" which admitted the operative facts (confession), but set forth some new matter which would deny the plaintiff a right to relief (avoidance). However, since the plea in confession and avoidance required a confession, the defendant could not traverse as well — it was either a traverse, *or* confession and avoidance.

(iii) Plaintiff. If the defendant had demurred or entered a dilatory plea, this would raise an issue for the court to decide. If the defendant had

pleaded a traverse, this generally created an issue for the jury to decide. In either case, the pleadings were essentially over at this point. But if the defendant had pleaded in confession and avoidance, there was another round of pleading — plaintiff could demur (which would raise the legal question whether the defense was adequate), or plead in replication. A replication again could contain a traverse or a plea of confession and avoidance.

(iv) Defendant and later pleadings. If the defendant demurred, the pleadings were over, and there would be an issue for the court to decide. The defendant could plead a rebutter — again a traverse, or confession and avoidance. And so the process went through the plaintiff's surrebutter, and later pleadings until an issue was finally joined.

An example may help: Assume the plaintiff declares in trespass that the defendant entered the plaintiff's land ("the close"), and that the plaintiff was damaged as a result. The defendant could demur, although this is not likely since the declaration appears to state a claim in trespass. The defendant could enter a dilatory plea, or a plea in bar. A plea in bar might be a traverse (denial of the trespass), which would then leave an issue for the jury. Or, the defendant might plead in confession and avoidance — admitting that he went on the plaintiff's land, but alleging that it was for an emergency to rescue a stray calf. The plaintiff then could demur (which raises the legal issue whether going on the plaintiff's land to rescue a stray calf is a legal defense), or plead by traverse (deny that the defendant went on the land to rescue a stray calf) or confession and avoidance (admit that the defendant originally went on the land to rescue a stray calf, but allege that defendant unnecessarily entered plaintiff's house). Your imagination should suggest later pleadings.

Initially, the common law pleading system was fairly flexible. Parties could try out various declarations and pleas, and, as described below, a plaintiff who made a pleading mistake could start over. By the Eighteenth Century, however, the system became more rigid with an increasing number of cases being decided on what we would now call "legal technicalities." There were at least two exceptions to these developments. In actions of general assumpsit, a type of very loose pleading was permitted which included almost no information about the case. These were called the "common counts" and included such matters as goods sold and delivered, money had and received, and labor performed and services rendered. The other exception — which appears to be at least partially a response to the common counts — was the plea of the "general issue." As described above, a defendant had a choice to demur or plead, and a plea could be either a traverse or confession and avoidance. But the plea of the general issue in certain actions of assumpsit included both a denial as well as certain affirmative defenses.

(d) Code Pleading. Common law procedure, with its forms of action, generally took root in the United States, and was followed for many years after American independence. As in England, however, the system became rigid, and there were demands for reform. The most significant reform occurred in New York in 1848, when a Code of Civil Procedure was adopted by the New York legislature. The Code was largely the work of David Dudley Field, and thus frequently is referred to as the "Field Code"; pleading under the Field Code is

called "Code Pleading." The Field Code was soon adopted in whole or substantial part in many other states. Today, although many states have adopted or adapted the Federal Rules of Civil Procedure as state law, both New York and California still follow updated versions of the Field Code.

There were a number of pleading innovations in the Field Code. First, the forms of action were abolished — there was to be one kind of action, a civil action, for all cases. Second, the special forms of pleading and many other arcane requirements were eliminated. Instead, the pleading was required to contain only "facts constituting the cause of action." Finally, there was an attempt to restrict use of the plea of the "general issue," because this plea was thought to hide the real issues in the case.

Many years ago, the distinguished scholar William Maitland observed that although the common law writ system was dead, it ruled us from its grave. Remember that the Field Code purported to change procedural law but not substantive law as reflected in the forms. Also, the common law system was premised on the notion that courts ordinarily would follow precedent in new cases. Given the precedential nature of the system and the conservative bent of many judges, it is not surprising that they looked to common law precedent to resolve "new" issues arising under the Codes.

The Code led to several unhappy results. For one, although courts were told that there was only one kind of action, the substantive law actually provided different bases for recovery. Some courts adopted a so-called "theory of pleadings" — they read the complaint to adopt one substantive theory to the exclusion of others (even though the allegations of the complaint might support others). More important was the direction to plead "facts constituting the cause of action." Courts required pleadings to state so-called ultimate facts, rather than conclusions (too general) or evidentiary facts (too specific). It was never clear whether there was a conceptual or analytical distinction between these categories. What was clear, was that courts could not figure out what the difference might be so that it could be followed by lawyers drafting pleadings, and reports became cluttered with decisions attempting to articulate the difference and apply it to a specific complaint. In many cases, courts dismissed cases because the plaintiff could not get it right. And in many more, the result was one or more trips back to the courthouse with the court saying that the pleading didn't say it right and telling plaintiff to do it over (sometimes with guidance on what would be acceptable, and sometimes, without a clue). Ultimately, dissatisfaction with this and other aspects of procedure under the Codes, led to the Federal Rules of Civil Procedure, adopted in 1938.

2. EQUITY

So far, we have discussed procedure in the common law courts. But as the common law system was developing there was a somewhat parallel development of a system of equity, including courts of equity.

Although the origins of equity are, as with the common law, somewhat obscure, the rough outline seems to be as follows. As noted above, the common law courts had become quite rigid both in the law they applied and in their procedures. For example, the substantive law did not permit a defendant to prove fraud as a defense to a sealed instrument and provided no relief when the parties had made a mistake in writing their agreement. The only remedy provided was money damages (the main exceptions being ejectment from land, and replevin of goods). The common law did not permit interested parties to be witnesses, even though they might be the only available witnesses. The common law had no provision for obtaining information from third parties who would not cooperate. In addition, the common law only recognized legal titles and ownership interests, and it had difficulty with trust relationships where one person had legal title for the benefit of another person. It also had difficulty with cases of faithless trustees who sold the property they ostensibly owned — i.e., breaches of fiduciary duty. Common law procedure (with its focused pleadings for isolating a single issue), and trial by jury were ill-suited for dealing with such matters as administration of estates and trusts, matters involving examination of numerous accounts and transactions (as, for example, in determining rights of partners), and situations where it might be necessary to appoint a court officer to oversee a business (as in an insolvency or liquidation of a business).

The common law could not deal with these matters, even though a person might have a legitimate grievance. Over time, persons with a grievance began going directly to the King — the idea being that the King had a "reservoir of justice," and was being asked to dip into that reservoir to handle the petitioner's grievance which could not be resolved in the ordinary law courts. Procedures evolved by which these petitions were referred to the King's secretary — the Chancellor — and a more formal mechanism developed for dealing with them. And this, in turn, led to what was called a "court of equity." As might be expected, the courts of law (and those who found themselves subject to procedures in equity) were not happy, and the clash between equity and law produced the famous Coke-Ellesmere dispute. Lord Coke was what we would now call chief justice of the common-law courts, and Lord Ellesmere the chief justice of the equity courts. Ultimately, the King was asked to preserve the integrity of the common-law courts by terminating equity's procedures, but he declined to do so; the work of the court of equity was preserved, side by side with the courts of law.

Why does this history and the law-equity rivalry matter today? There are several reasons. For one, the existence of a right to jury trial in civil actions under the Seventh Amendment can still depend on an historical test, asking whether the case would have been tried in a court of law or a court of equity in 1791 when the Amendment was ratified. For another, these events reveal a key feature of the law of remedies — that equitable remedies such as an injunction and specific performance are considered extraordinary, and cannot be granted unless one's remedy at law is "inadequate." Finally, modern procedure has borrowed important components from equity procedure, such as discovery (although it is much different now) and broad joinder of parties and claims.

SECTION C. PLEADING UNDER THE FEDERAL RULES

Common law pleadings and, to a lesser extent, Code Pleading, served a number of different functions. First, pleadings provided the parties with general notice of what the case was about. Second, pleadings provided the only pre-trial information regarding the factual and legal issues. Remember, there was no pretrial discovery and no pretrial conference, so the parties went from pleadings to trial with very little in between. Third, pleadings served to identify various jurisdictional and technical problems, and to provide a mechanism for their resolution. Fourth, pleadings served as a screening device to identify cases that were substantively deficient (no right to recover under the substantive law), factually deficient (inadequate evidence), or just plain frivolous (this covers a lot of sins).

Modern pleading is less ambitious. It is the first step in a long process, rather than the first of two steps. Courts generally are reluctant to dismiss cases at the pleading stage, and there is a strong element of not only giving the plaintiff the benefit of the doubt but of giving him a second (and sometimes a third and fourth) chance. It is not clear how often pleading motions are made, although some evidence suggests that only a small percentage of cases are dismissed on such motions.

The modern approach to pleading has not gone without criticism. Critics note that the failure to decide cases at an early stage imposes significant costs on the litigants and the public, and that these costs provide a significant economic incentive to settle regardless of merit. Critics also believe that many cases are unmeritorious, and that litigants and the public generally would benefit from a process that looked more into the merits before the litigation gets into full gear. As we shall see, these views have been in the ascendancy in recent years.

Our goals for this section are modest, and we do not intend to teach how to "write" good pleadings. Instead, we want to focus on certain questions. What allegations must be in a pleading? Must the plaintiff plead a legal theory and all the factual elements necessary to establish that legal theory? How much detail is required? How does one identify the difference between a pleading problem which a plaintiff can correct and a substantive problem which she can't? If there are situations where more detail or information is required, why is it required, and how much is enough?

1. THE TRADITIONAL APPROACH

Federal Rules of Civil Procedure 8, 9, and 10 tell plaintiffs what must be in the complaint. Rule 8(a)(2) requires "a short and plain statement of the claim showing that the pleader is entitled to relief." Rule 8(d)(1) states that each averment shall be "simple, concise, and direct" and that no "technical forms of pleading" are required, and Rule 10(b) adds that averments "shall be made in numbered paragraphs, the contents of each of which shall be limited as far as practicable to a statement of a single set of circumstances." These may convey a "gestalt" of brevity, generality, and simplicity, but they don't provide much guidance to pleaders or courts.

For many years, the obligatory citation in any pleading case had been to CONLEY v. GIBSON, 355 U.S. 41, 78 S.Ct. 99, 2 L.Ed.2d 80 (1957). There, in an action by railroad employees generally alleging racial discrimination by their union, the Supreme Court explained its approach to pleadings:

> In appraising the sufficiency of the complaint we follow, of course, the accepted rule that a complaint should not be dismissed for failure to state a claim unless it appears beyond doubt that the plaintiff can prove no set of facts in support of his claim which would entitle him to relief. Here, the complaint alleged, in part, that petitioners were discharged wrongfully by the Railroad and that the Union, acting according to plan, refused to protect their jobs as it did those of white employees or to help them with their grievances all because they were Negroes. If these allegations are proven there has been a manifest breach of the Union's statutory duty to represent fairly and without hostile discrimination all of the employees in the bargaining unit. * * *

> The respondents also argue that the complaint failed to set forth specific facts to support its general allegations of discrimination and that its dismissal is therefore proper. The decisive answer to this is that the Federal Rules of Civil Procedure do not require a claimant to set out in detail the facts upon which he bases his claim. To the contrary, all the Rules require is "a short and plain statement of the claim" that will give the defendant fair notice of what the plaintiff's claim is and the grounds upon which it rests. The illustrative forms appended to the Rules plainly demonstrate this. Such simplified "notice pleading" is made possible by the liberal opportunity for discovery and the other pretrial procedures established by the Rules to disclose more precisely the basis of both claim and defense and to define more narrowly the disputed facts and issues. Following the simple guide of Rule 8(f) that "all pleadings shall be so construed as to do substantial justice," we have no doubt that petitioners' complaint adequately set forth a claim and gave the respondents fair notice of its basis. The Federal Rules reject the approach that pleading is a game of skill in which one misstep by counsel may be decisive to the outcome and accept the principle that the purpose of pleading is to facilitate a proper decision on the merits.

Id. at 45-47. Was this liberal approach to pleading the right way to go? In Bell Atlantic Corp. v. Twombly, 550 U.S. 544, 127 S.Ct. 1955, 167 L.Ed.2d 929 (2007), the Supreme Court purported to "retire" much of *Conley*, particularly its "no set of facts" language. See also Ashcroft v. Iqbal, 556 U.S. 652, 129 S.Ct. 1937, 173 L.Ed.2d 868 (2009). Once you have read *Twombly* (set out in the materials that follow), consider whether the Court's newer approach is to be preferred. The two decisions that follow were decided in the reign of *Conley v. Gibson*. Would anything in the Court's more recent decisions suggest that the outcome would be different as a pleading matter?

The Dartmouth Review v. Dartmouth College

United States Court of Appeals, First Circuit, 1989.
889 F.2d 13.

SELYA, CIRCUIT JUDGE.

This suit was brought in consequence of a riptide of unpleasantness which flooded the Dartmouth College campus during the second semester of the 1987-88 academic year.[1] The district court ordered dismissal for failure to state a claim. We affirm.

As needs must, we start by summarizing the factbound allegations of plaintiffs' two-count complaint insofar as material to our inquiry. In so doing, we do not purport to divine the truth of a conflicted situation, but describe only what plaintiffs claim the facts to have been, parroting the complaint's well-pled averments. It is in reliance on these facts — albeit much embroidered in 39 pages laced with rhetoric and invective — that plaintiffs sued in New Hampshire's federal district court charging violations of 42 U.S.C. §1981 (1982) and 42 U.S.C. §2000d et seq. (1982) (Title VI). And it is on these facts that the district court determined that no federal-law claim was presented.

I

Dartmouth is a private college. Christopher Baldwin, John Quilhot, and John Sutter (collectively, the Students), all white men enrolled at Dartmouth, were staff members of the Review, an off-campus, non-profit newspaper. In February 1988, the Review published features strongly critical of two Dartmouth professors. One target was William Cole,[2] a black music professor said to have used improper language and taught "irrelevant" material. The Students hoped Cole would respond in the Review's next issue. Telephone calls having proved unavailing, they approached Cole in his classroom moments after class ended on February 25. The Students (armed with camera and tape recorder) told the professor why they had come, but he screamed profanities at them. Baldwin attempted to hand Cole a letter inviting a response to the article. Cole became violent, breaking the camera's flash attachment and "poking his fingers at Mr. Baldwin's eyes." The Students departed.

These events precipitated what the complaint terms an "anti-Review hysteria." Cole lost little time in contacting the Committee on Standards (COS), which preferred charges of harassment and disorderly conduct against the Students. The Students, in turn, filed charges against Cole (who was found not guilty). Posters appeared alleging, without foundation, that Sutter was guilty of racial slurs. Threats of violence were communicated to Review members.

---

[1] Plaintiffs (appellants before us) comprise the Dartmouth Review (Review); its publisher, Hanover Review, Inc.; and three collegians active in the Review's affairs. Defendants (appellees) are the College; its Committee on Standards (a joint administration/faculty/student board responsible for enforcing standards of conduct on campus); and various officials of the College (including its president and trustees).

[2] There is apparently documented antagonism between Cole and the Review dating back to 1983. The complaint gives plaintiffs' version of that history.

Dartmouth's president, speaking at an anti-Review rally sponsored by the school's Afro-American Society, declared "that racism, sexism and other forms of ignorance and disrespect have no place at Dartmouth." He told the *Boston Globe*:

> I feel dreadful about the attack on Professor Cole . . . . I do not want one minority or woman student to decline to come to Dartmouth because of the perception that this incident is representative of the true Dartmouth. It is not. The timing of this is dreadfully suspicious, coming five weeks before acceptances [of new students] go out.

The president refused to grant the Students an audience, but met freely with anti-Review undergraduates (most of whom were black). The College's dean, who chaired the COS, refused to give the Students assistance or guidance, despite explicit provisions in the College's student handbook promising such help. According to the complaint, such actions show that the administration had "publicly prejudge[d]" the February 25 incident and harbored an anti-Review bias, ascribing "a racial and anti-Dartmouth animus" to plaintiffs.

The COS hearing took place in March. The Students allege that the hearing afforded them "no fundamental fairness and sacrificed numerous procedural safeguards;" for example, they were not allowed representation by counsel, effective cross-examination, or an unbiased hearing panel. They were found guilty of all charges. Quilhot was suspended until the fall of 1988; Sutter and Baldwin for a year longer. The suspensions were upheld on appeal to the dean. Betimes, the president continued his verbal assault, accusing the Review of "bullying tactics . . . designed to have the effect of discouraging women and members of minority groups from joining our faculty or enrolling as students. . . ."

As previously recounted, the district court ruled that the complaint was insufficient to state an actionable claim. This proceeding ensued.

II

The standard of review is not in doubt. Like the district court, we are governed by the familiar constraints of Fed.R.Civ.P. 12(b)(6). Accordingly, we must accept all well-pled factual averments as true, and draw all reasonable inferences therefrom in appellants' favor. In so doing, however, we "eschew any reliance on bald assertions, unsupportable conclusions, and 'opprobrious epithets.'" Chongris v. Board of Appeals, 811 F.2d 36 37 (1st Cir.), cert. denied, 483 U.S. 1021, 97 L.Ed. 2d 765, 107 S.Ct. 3266 (1987) (quoting Snowden v. Hughes, 321 U.S. 1, 10, 88 L.Ed. 497, 64 S.Ct. 397 (1944)). It is only if the complaint, so viewed, presents no set of facts justifying recovery that we may affirm the dismissal. Conley v. Gibson, 355 U.S. 41, 45-48, 2 L.Ed. 2d 80, 78 S.Ct. 99 (1957).

We have repeatedly cautioned that, notice pleading notwithstanding, Rule 12(b)(6) is not entirely a toothless tiger. "Minimal requirements are not tantamount to nonexistent requirements. The threshold [for stating a claim] may be low, but it is real . . . ." Thus, plaintiffs are obliged to set forth in their complaint "factual allegations, either direct or inferential, regarding each material element necessary to sustain recovery under some actionable legal theory." The need is perhaps greater where allegations of civil rights violations lie at the suit's core[*]:

> Dismissal of a claim requires the most close analysis by an appellate court, balancing the overall liberal thrust of the simplified civil rules on the one hand, against the repeated demands by our and other courts that there be more than conclusory allegations, even in civil rights cases.

Dewey v. University of New Hampshire, 694 F.2d 1, 3 (1st Cir. 1982) (citation omitted), cert. denied, 461 U.S. 944, 77 L.Ed. 2d 1301, 103 S.Ct. 2121 (1983). Gauzy generalities, unsupported conclusions, subjective characterizations, and problematic suppositions can sprout as easily as crabgrass in an imaginative litigant's (or lawyer's) word processor. Therefore, to avoid tarring defendants' reputations unfairly and to prevent potential abuses, we have consistently required plaintiffs to outline facts sufficient to convey specific instances of unlawful discrimination. As we have said in the summary judgment context, plaintiffs must point, if not to fire, at least to some still-warm embers; "smoke alone is not enough to force the defendants to a trial to prove that their actions were not [racially] discriminatory."

We are cognizant that the line between "facts" and "conclusions" is often blurred. But, there are some general parameters. Most often, facts are susceptible to objective verification. Conclusions, on the other hand, are empirically unverifiable in the usual case. They represent the pleader's reactions to, sometimes called "inferences from," the underlying facts. It is only when such conclusions are logically compelled, or at least supported, by the stated facts, that is, when the suggested inference rises to what experience indicates is an acceptable level of probability, that "conclusions" become "facts" for pleading purposes.

With these precepts in mind, we turn to the business at hand.

III

Appellants contend that the facts alleged in Count I make out a cognizable claim under a statute which provides:

> All persons within the jurisdiction of the United States shall have the same right in every State and Territory to make and enforce contracts, to sue, be parties, give evidence, and to the full and equal benefit of all laws and proceedings for the security of persons and property as is enjoyed by white citizens, and shall be subject to like punishment, pains, penalties, taxes, licenses, and exactions of every kind, and to no other.

42 U.S.C. §1981. The statute extends to private conduct as well as state action. Independent academic institutions are within the law's prohibitory reach. Nevertheless, section 1981 does not forbid all discrimination in contractual matters, but only certain contract-related acts, and then, only if the discrimination in question is both purposeful and based on race. If any of these elements is missing, a section 1981 claim cannot flower.

---

[*] [Arguably, the Supreme Court has since thrown some cold water on whether a heightened pleading requirement can legitimately be applied to civil rights cases as suggested by the First (and, at times, other) Circuit(s). We take up the issue below in Section E. — eds.]

In Patterson [v. McLean Credit Union, 491 U.S. 164 (1989)], an opinion handed down after the district court dismissed the instant complaint, the Supreme Court narrowed the list of activities proscribed by 42 U.S.C. §1981, stating that "Section 1981 cannot be construed as a general proscription of racial discrimination in all aspects of contract relations, for it expressly prohibits discrimination only in the making and enforcement of contracts." Once the existence of a contract is established, "the right to enforce [it] does not . . . extend beyond conduct by an employer which impairs an employee's ability to enforce through legal process his or her established contract rights." *Patterson* raises obvious questions as to whether the complaint in this case implicates only "postformation conduct," a type of activity not subject to the prohibitions of §1981. We leave those queries unanswered and abjure any attempt to chart more precisely the gulf which *Patterson* visualized between section 1981 and certain types of contract-related discrimination. Because we believe that insufficient facts are alleged to advance a cognizable claim of purposeful race-based discrimination, we need not explore the boundaries of section 1981 in these other respects.

A

The viability of appellants' statement of claim depends on whether, given the facts averred, *their* race can be said to have been an actual or decisive reason behind the alleged discrimination. Put another way, the key question is whether plaintiffs assembled specific facts adequate to show or raise a plausible inference that they were subjected to race-based discrimination.

The crux of the complaint is the charge that defendants, by pandering to the popular perception of the Cole confrontation as a racial incident and playing "racial politics," chilled expression and prevented plaintiffs from receiving a fair hearing. In that manner, defendants are alleged to have impermissibly "consider[ed] race as a factor in [the] discipline or discharge" of the Students. That is to say, by accusing plaintiffs of committing, and condemning them for, an allegedly racist act against a black professor, defendants are charged with having made the Students' white race a determining factor in the administration's handling of the matter and in a disproportionately severe punishment that followed. Had they been black or Professor Cole white, appellants' thesis runs, the sequelae would have been significantly less onerous. We find this to be a ketchup-bottle type of argument: it looks quite full, but it is remarkably difficult to get anything useful out of it.

Appellants' theory necessarily depends upon an unmitigated assumption: that, for the College to have branded appellants' behavior toward a black professor as "racist," it was necessary that they were white. The assumption is not only unproven, but unfounded, neither logically nor legally compelled. And, the reasoning associated with the assumption is sophistic. Racial difference is by no means a condition precedent to labeling an incident "racist;" nor are belligerent responses to perceived racial attacks, without more, presumed to be based on the *perpetrators'* race. Condemning acts as racist implies nothing about the actor's race, but signifies only that the *victim's* race was the cause of invidious harm. Persons of one race can discriminate against their fellows as easily as persons of a different race — and often, more cruelly. Simply put, racial polarity is not a prerequisite to the practice of racism.

Recognition of this homely truth undermines plaintiffs' position, no matter how purple the prose in which the complaint is couched. Discarding the flawed assumption, we are left with no more than conclusory statements and subjective characterizations of the type regularly found wanting in civil rights cases. Far from leading to a reasoned inference that the College was guilty of discrimination based on the Students' color, the administration's reaction (as plaintiffs described it) proves no more than that the College hierarchy perceived the Students' acts as racist and hence, deserving of harsher punishment than other infractions. That is short of the mark.[4] And the fact that the administration met with black undergraduates and tolerated — even abetted — a rally with an anti-racist theme directed at the Review, adds little to the mix. Neither general denunciations of racism nor refusals to meet with Review members — even white Review members — are enough to premise an inference of discrimination based on the Students' race. As one court has written:

> Disputes generally arise out of mutual misunderstanding, misinterpretation and overreaction, and without more, such disputes do not give rise to an inference of discrimination.

Johnson v. Legal Services of Arkansas, Inc., 813 F.2d 893, 896 (8th Cir. 1987).

Appellants' iteration of certain procedural defects in the disciplinary proceedings and their claim that some COS members harbored anti-Review biases fall equally flat. If true, such a litany may be indicative of prejudice toward plaintiffs, their ideology, and their journal. But it is far too long a leap to take these averments as evidence of race-based discrimination. Without more, allegations that perceived racist infractions were punished more harshly than other infractions do not tend to show racial discrimination against the persons accused. Weighting the scales heavily against those who are believed to practice race discrimination may seem to some inequitable, and unjustified; but fair or unfair, justified or not, differentials drawn along such an axis do not constitute the type of disparate treatment outlawed by section 1981. Unfairness alone does not invoke the statute. And merely juxtaposing the fact of one's race with an instance of discrimination is insufficient to state a claim. Absent some

---

[4]   Certainly, the caselaw lends no support to plaintiffs' argument that racial motivation can be shown merely by an accusation of racism. In their flagship case, Lincoln v. Board of Regents, 697 F.2d 928 (11th Cir.), cert. denied, 464 U.S. 826 (1983), the evidence established that school officials discharged a teacher, relying in part on accusations of racism contained in a student petition. But in *Lincoln*, there was considerable proof that the charge was pretextual and defendants bigoted. There was evidence that they did not believe plaintiff to be racist; that one defendant had referred to plaintiff as "this white lady [who] came down here thinking she was going to get some easy retirement;" and that another defendant had stated that he "hate[d] white people." It was in this larger context that the district court "may thus reasonably have inferred that a deeper significance rested in the allegations of [plaintiff's] racism." In the case at bar, there are no facts set forth to show that the allegations of racism were not reflective of defendants' sincere (if, perhaps, mistaken) belief. Above all, plaintiffs' complaint contains no specific allegation which, alone or in combination with other well-pled facts, is capable of supporting an inference that any defendant possessed an anti-white racial animus.

meaningful, fact-specific allegation of a causal link between defendants' conduct and plaintiffs' race, the complaint's first count cannot stand.

B

Plaintiffs have a second string to their section 1981 bow. They argue that they stated a claim by describing defendants' handling of other incidents involving blacks and showing that, in contrast, the Students were disciplined much more sternly. These details, appellants asseverate, sustain an inference that defendants were guilty of race-based discrimination on this occasion. We examine the law and the well-pled facts.

It is apodictic that evidence of past treatment toward others similarly situated can be used to demonstrate intent in a race discrimination suit. To put flesh upon the bare bones of this theory, appellants' obligation was to identify and relate specific instances where persons situated similarly "in all relevant aspects" were treated differently, instances which have the capacity to demonstrate that the Students were "singled . . . out for unlawful oppression." In general, this requires that the other incidents' circumstances be "reasonably comparable" to those surrounding appellants' suspensions, and that "the nature of the infraction and knowledge of the evidence by college officials [be] sufficiently similar to support a finding of facial inconsistency." The test is whether a prudent person, looking objectively at the incidents, would think them roughly equivalent and the protagonists similarly situated. Much as in the lawyer's art of distinguishing cases, the "relevant aspects" are those factual elements which determine whether reasoned analogy supports, or demands, a like result. Exact correlation is neither likely nor necessary, but the cases must be fair congeners. In other words, apples should be compared to apples.

Once again, appellants' burden is in the typical Rule 12(b)(6) mold: to allege particulars sufficient to sanction a factfinder in drawing a reasonable inference of intentional disparate treatment based on race. For this purpose, appellants rely on (1) the flip side of the February 25 coin, and (2) an unrelated set of on-campus incidents. We deal separately with each grouping.

1. *Cole's Treatment*. Appellants point to what they style as "incongruities" between the administration's responses to Cole and the Students, respectively, in the wake of the February 25 interlude. The allegation's gist is that Cole behaved far worse than the Students, yet was treated far more solicitously. Taking this as true, plaintiffs are not assisted: the parties cannot fairly be equated. We agree with the district court that "a tenured faculty member and a student are not similarly situated simply because they were both involved in the same incident."

Appellants argue that, though accurately stated, this distinction simply renders Dartmouth's discriminatory conduct all the more egregious; docents, after all, should be held to stricter standards than pupils. Such an argument succeeds simultaneously in proving too much and too little. It proves too much by conceding that Cole was to be treated according to a different behavioral standard while proving too little because the mere existence of disparate treatment — even widely disparate treatment — does not furnish adequate basis for an inference that the discrimination was racially motivated.

2. *The Apartheid Protest.* Appellants fare no better in attempting to show disparate treatment by comparing the Cole confrontation, and its aftermath, with a controversy which racked the Dartmouth campus in 1985. At that time, several Dartmouth students employed various means, some disruptive in nature, to protest Dartmouth's investment in the stock of companies doing business in South Africa.

The demonstrators were apparently from diverse backgrounds, although plaintiffs allege that "many" of them were minorities. Among other things, the disaffected group erected shanties on campus and staged sit-ins at college offices. A policeman was assaulted when the protesters resisted efforts to remove the shanties. According to appellants, these activities violated a myriad of student regulations, but no discipline was imposed and no criminal charges prosecuted.

But, this is no apple-to-apple match. Distinctions abound. Notwithstanding that undergraduates were involved in both controversies, we see no commonality sufficient to permit the close comparisons urged by plaintiffs. The participants in the 1985 protest movement were racially diverse. What is more, the complaint's detailed recital of the episode fails to adumbrate any direct, ongoing confrontation *between students and faculty* of a kind which would especially concern a college's administration; the faculty, after all, was not managing Dartmouth's endowment. Most importantly, the particularized, personal focus of plaintiffs' actions on February 25 sets the happening here at issue leagues apart from the mass protest activities.

Even bending backward as Rule 12(b)(6) suggests, neither series of events furnishes a viable, legally sufficient basis to animate appellants' disparate treatment theory. The delineated incidents, rather than meeting a "prudent person" test of comparability, wander far afield. We agree with the Second Circuit that, if we allow a complaint like this to proceed in the context of student discipline,

> every conclusory selective-enforcement claim would lead to discovery concerning the entire disciplinary history of a college and then to a confusing, unmanageable and ultimately incoherent retrial of every disciplinary decision, including decisions not to investigate.

We will not permit plaintiffs to embark on so wide-ranging a safari without some threshold demonstration that game of the desired type and kind has been seen lurking in the groves of academe.

C

We recapitulate briefly. The complaint, read in the light most flattering to appellants, portrays a scenario in which white students civilly approached a black professor who behaved badly in the face of what he mistakenly perceived as a racist attack. As word spread, the College community erupted in denunciation of what was widely thought to be a color-coded incident. In a highly charged atmosphere of racial tension, the College's president spoke out against the Review and its members, falsely implying that bigotry had played a part. The Review's "provocative" and "controversial" views were misinter-preted in some quarters — especially within the administration — as evidencing racial animus.

With so stacked a deck, the claim runs, appellants could not have received a fair hearing from the COS — and they did not receive one.

If the facts are as alleged, thoughtful persons might well deplore defendants' behavior. By accepting the popular perception of events at face value, it is possible that the administration unfairly and incorrectly branded the Review, the Students, and their tactics, as racist. The complaint can even be read as unmasking viewpoint-based discrimination; the accusation leveled against the Students, and the sanctions that followed, may arguably have been used as weapons to silence or mute the Review's criticism, thereby chilling freedom of expression. Yet, no matter how flamboyant the rhetorical trappings in which plaintiffs' allegations are dressed, they do not state a federal-law claim. Although the complaint mentions that appellants are white, and claims that they were victims of discrimination, no specific facts are alleged which, if proven, could plausibly lead to a supportable finding that *plaintiffs' race* was the reason for the unfairness.

At the bottom line, appellants insist that 42 U.S.C. §1981 reaches conduct stemming from the naked (mis)perception that certain persons harbor racist tendencies. They are wrong. The statute was designed to outlaw, and thereby to end, discrimination based on race. It has been interpreted liberally in some respects; but the Court has never lost sight of the "racial character" of the rights which the law presumes to protect. In our opinion, section 1981 is not so elastic as to accommodate plaintiffs' theory — and stretching it to fit would not only distort the statute's essential meaning, but would also hamstring its utility. After all, institutions must be reasonably free to investigate allegations of bias to ensure that racial discrimination is not being practiced on their turf. If every such investigation could be sidetracked by the accused's cries of racism, the cause of racial equality would unfairly be burdened. Section 1981 contemplates no such double agenda.

We neither minimize nor condone the evils inherent in the suppression of ideas. But, if expressive rights — rather than rights of a racial character — are genuinely at stake, appellants are not powerless to combat institutional overreaching or overly zealous academic disciplinarians. State-law anodynes exist for breach of contract, slander, malicious interference, and other torts. Furthermore, if discriminatory conduct is viewpoint-based or infrigidates first amendment freedoms, then remedies may exist as against state actors or in connection with federally funded programs. Be that as it may, absent a plausible allegation of race-based discrimination, section 1981 is not properly includable in the armamentarium available to victims of unfair treatment. We have neither reason nor warrant to stand the statute on its head, as appellants would like, and force the square peg of viewpoint-based discrimination into section 1981's circular maw. * * *

V

We have one more bridge to cross before arriving at a final destination. In a last-ditch effort to salvage the case, appellants ask, should we uphold the ruling below, that we "direct . . . the district court [to] grant leave to the Students to amend their Complaint." We decline the invitation.

To be sure, the Civil Rules provide that a "party may amend the party's pleading once as a matter of course at any time before a responsive pleading is served . . . ." Fed.R.Civ.P. 15(a). And, defendants filed no "responsive pleading" here. Yet, the thrust of Rule 15(a) is aimed at the pre-judgment phases of litigation. In this case, plaintiffs elected not to amend as of right before the district court spoke; and thereafter, they filed no motion below for leave to amend. In this Circuit, "it is a party's first obligation to seek any relief that might fairly have been thought available in the district court before seeking it on appeal." Beaulieu v. United States Internal Revenue Service, 865 F.2d 1351, 1352 (1st Cir. 1989). Thus, here — as in *Beaulieu* — the question of "whether it might have been error for the court to have denied leave to amend is not before us," because "plaintiff[s] never requested it."[9]

After judgment has entered and jurisdiction has been transferred to an appellate court, amendments are still possible — but, as the case passes through various litigatory stages, the pleader's burden grows progressively heavier. The instant request emerges fairly well along the continuum: judgment entered below; no motion was filed post-judgment asking the district court for leave to amend; during the appeal's pendency, no effort was made to secure a remand for the purpose of seeking permission to amend; and the case has now been fully briefed and argued. We have confronted such cases before, and a rule of thumb has evolved. "When, in the ordinary case, 'the pleader has stood upon his pleading and appealed from a judgment of dismissal, amendment will not ordinarily be permitted . . . if the order of dismissal is affirmed.'" Our approach is not totally inflexible; amendments will sometimes be allowed, but such instances comprise the long-odds exception, not the rule. The touchstone is equitable and case-specific: leave to amend will be granted sparingly and only if "justice . . . requires further proceedings."

This case presents us with nothing powerful enough to trigger the narrow exception to the general rule. There is no indication that appellants were laboring under any disability, or that the district court may have missed a plausible though ambiguously stated theory, or that some new concept has surfaced, making workable an action previously in the doldrums. To this day, appellants have given no meaningful indication that additional facts could be pleaded which would make a dispositive difference. From what little we have been told, the "new" facts are of the same genre as the "old" facts — sufficient, if believed, to show that the Students were treated unfairly, but insufficient, whether or not believed, to show that the unfairness stemmed from a preoccupation with plaintiffs' race. * * *

---

[9] Appellants seek to excuse this omission on the ground that, in light of the district court's opinion, requesting leave to amend would have been futile. That dog will not hunt. Nothing in the lower court's opinion or elsewhere in the record supports the idea. To the contrary, the district judge appears to have been meticulous in protecting the parties' rights and in holding the balance steady and true. There is no sign his heels were dug in. Furthermore, any uncertainty in this regard must be resolved against appellants. Parties who decide not to seek permissive relief in the trial court must clearly understand that they will have an uphill fight in this circuit to convince the court of appeals to consider a request for the relief as a matter of first impression.

In fine, no satisfactory reason appears why plaintiffs, if desirous of amending, should not have followed the usual course and asked the district court for permission. Given their default in that regard, the absence of special circumstances, and what appears to be an altogether unpromising prospect for amendment in any event, the interests of justice would be served poorly by an order allowing plaintiffs to amend at this late date. Finality is a critically important concept in our system of jurisprudence. At some point, battles must end.

VI

To sum up, we see neither smoke nor fire. Although plaintiffs may have been penalized for their speech and ideas — a matter which we do not address — the aggregate facts described in the complaint fail to sustain a reasonable inference that they were victims of race-based discrimination. Whether the defendants treated the Students fairly or unfairly is not the question in this case. Either way, the College's handling of the matter, as limned in the complaint, fell outside the purview of 42 U.S.C. §1981 and Title VI. It follows, then, that the complaint was properly dismissed. And, the record reflects no circumstances so exceptional as to warrant permitting plaintiffs to amend, bypassing the rule that requests for relief ought to be addressed first to the trial judge and, in the bargain, undermining the accustomed finality of judicial decisions.

We need go no further. The judgment below must be *Affirmed*.

NOTES AND PROBLEMS FOR DISCUSSION

1. Modern litigation often gives rise to strong emotions, but one must learn to be a bit dispassionate. Start with the plaintiffs.

(a) Recall the note above on substantive law. What claims are the plaintiffs making, and in order to win on these claims, what elements or facts will they ultimately have to establish at trial?

(b) Plaintiffs alleged that the College violated a number of their procedural rights in connection with the discipline meted out to them. Certainly, the plaintiffs alleged more detail than required under *Conley v. Gibson, supra*. Why did the court affirm the dismissal of their suit, and deny them the opportunity to prove their case to a jury?

(c) In many ways, this is a decision about substantive law. The court expresses a particular concern with recognizing that the plaintiffs have a claim. What is it?

2. The appeals court denied the plaintiffs leave to amend in part because the motion should have been made in the district court, but in part because of the merits. Given liberal pleading and the policy of Rule 15(a) on amendments, why not give the plaintiffs a chance to correct their pleading?

3. Now turn to the defendants. Recall where the plaintiffs brought this lawsuit and the basis of jurisdiction. Are the defendants out of the woods yet, or is there something else the plaintiffs can do? (If so, why didn't they do it at the outset?)

4. The Privacy Act, 5 U.S.C. §552a(b), provides that a federal agency may not disclose (with some exceptions) "any record which is contained in a system of records by any means of communication to any person . . . ." Case law establishes that this includes oral disclosure of the content of records. Brad had been an assistant U.S. Attorney who was recently fired from his position with a private firm. Brad brought an action against the United States under the Privacy Act and alleged that his former supervisor in the U.S. Attorney's office called the private firm and told the firm that his performance had been deficient, and that this reference was a wrongful disclosure of "records." The United States moved to dismiss the action on the ground that Brad had failed to "identify any 'records' that have been wrongfully disclosed." Defendant cites *Dartmouth Review*, and plaintiff *Conley v. Gibson*. What result? See Krieger v. Fadely, 211 F.3d 134 (D.C. Cir. 2000).

Langadinos v. American Airlines, Inc.

United States Court of Appeals, First Circuit, 2000.
199 F.3d 68.

LIPEZ, CIRCUIT JUDGE.

Gregory Langadinos appeals from the district court's order dismissing his amended complaint against American Airlines, Inc. ("American"). The amended complaint alleges that American violated the Warsaw Convention[1] by continuing to serve alcohol to an intoxicated passenger who then assaulted Langadinos. American filed a motion to dismiss for failure to state a cause of action, arguing, *inter alia*, that the Warsaw Convention count was based on unsubstantiated, conclusory allegations. The district court granted the motion to dismiss, pursuant to Fed. R. Civ. P. 12(b)(6). We vacate and remand.

I

"In the Rule 12(b)(6) milieu, an appellate court operates under the same constraints that bind the district court, that is, we may affirm a dismissal for failure to state a claim only if it clearly appears, according to the facts alleged, that the plaintiff cannot recover on any viable theory." Correa-Martinez v. Arrillaga-Belendez, 903 F.2d 49, 52 (1st Cir. 1990); see also Conley v. Gibson, 355 U.S. 41, 45-48, 2 L.Ed. 2d 80, 78 S.Ct. 99 (1957). In making this determination, we must accept the well-pled facts of Langadinos's amended complaint as true and indulge every reasonable inference in his favor. We state the facts, therefore, as Langadinos alleges them.

On June 13, 1996, Langadinos boarded an American Airlines flight in Boston, bound for Paris. A few hours after take-off, Langadinos approached a flight attendant for aspirin. The flight attendant ignored Langadinos, and continued with her current chore: spoon-feeding ice cream into the mouth of

---

[1] Convention for the Unification of Certain Rules Relating to International Transportation by Air, Oct. 12, 1929, 49 Stat. 3000, T.S. No. 876 (1934)), note following 49 U.S.C. §40105 [hereinafter Warsaw Convention or the Convention].

passenger Christopher Debord. As Langadinos waited, Debord "stared in a conspicuous and strange fashion" at him and whispered something into the flight attendant's ear.

Later in the flight, Langadinos went to the lavatory. While he waited in line, Debord forcefully grabbed Langadinos's testicles, causing "excruciating pain." Then, Debord grabbed Langadinos's hand and pulled it to his own groin. Although Langadinos reported the assault to the flight crew, he was unsatisfied with their response. The flight attendant who had fed Debord ice cream commented, "Chris is my friend; he is harmless." Despite the promise of a second crew member to have Debord arrested upon arrival in Paris, the alleged assailant was not detained.

Langadinos filed a two-count complaint against American in the district court for the District of Massachusetts, alleging a common law tort and a breach of the Warsaw Convention. Before American responded, Langadinos filed an amended complaint, identical to the original in every respect but one: it included the additional allegation, made on information and belief, that American served alcohol to Debord just prior to the assault, knowing that he was intoxicated and that his behavior was "erratic" and "aggressive."

Rather than answer the amended complaint, American filed a motion to dismiss for "failure of the pleading to state a claim upon which relief can be granted." Fed. R. Civ. P. 12(b)(6). The district court dismissed the complaint in a margin order, "based on the arguments in defendant's motion and memorandum." On appeal, Langadinos argues that the district court erred in dismissing count two of the amended complaint, which alleges a violation of the Warsaw Convention.[2] We agree.

II

A. Requisites of a Warsaw Convention Claim

Article 17 of the Warsaw Convention sets forth the circumstances under which an international air carrier may be liable for injuries to passengers. It provides:

> The carrier shall be liable for damage sustained in the event of death or wounding of a passenger or any other bodily injury suffered by a passenger, if the accident which caused the damage so sustained took place on board the aircraft or in the course of any of the operations of embarking or disembarking.

(emphasis added). Although the Warsaw Convention does not define the term "accident," the Supreme Court shed light on its meaning in Air France v. Saks, 470 U.S. 392, 84 L.Ed. 2d 289, 105 S.Ct. 1338 (1985). The Court ruled that an injury to the plaintiff's ear caused by the normal operation of the cabin pressurization system was not an "accident" within the meaning of the Warsaw Convention. The Court held that "liability under Article 17 of the Warsaw

---

[2] Langadinos did not appeal the dismissal of count one of the complaint, which alleges a common law tort. "Recovery for a personal injury suffered on board an aircraft or in the course of any of the operations of embarking or disembarking, if not allowed under the Convention, is not available at all."

Convention arises only if a passenger's injury is caused by an unexpected or unusual event or happening that is external to the passenger." When the aircraft operates in a "usual, normal, and expected" manner, a passenger is unable to recover.

The Supreme Court's definition of "accident" is broad enough to permit recovery for torts committed by fellow passengers. Indeed, the *Saks* Court cited lower court decisions recognizing passenger-on-passenger torts as "accidents" for the proposition that the accident requirement must be "flexibly applied." Of course, not every tort committed by a fellow passenger is a Warsaw Convention accident. Where the airline personnel play no causal role in the commission of the tort, courts have found no Warsaw accident. See, e.g., Potter v. Delta Airlines [98 F.3d 881 (5th Cir. 1996)] (finding no "accident" where injury in passenger dispute over seat position took place without involvement of airline personnel); Stone v. Continental Airlines [905 F. Supp. 823 (D. Hawaii 1995)] (finding no "accident" where one passenger punched second passenger). On the flip side, courts have found Warsaw accidents where airline personnel play a causal role in a passenger-on-passenger tort. See, e.g., Schneider v. Swiss Air Transp. Co. [686 F. Supp. 15 (D. Me. 1988)] ("accident" when plaintiff injured by fellow passenger's refusal to put seat upright because plaintiff was denied assistance by flight attendant).

Langadinos's claim survives under these standards. He has alleged that (1) Debord appeared intoxicated, aggressive and erratic, (2) American was aware of this behavior and (3) despite this awareness, American continued to serve him alcohol. Serving alcohol to an intoxicated passenger may, in some instances, create a foreseeable risk that the passenger will cause injury to others. Indeed, the Supreme Court cited a case of this type as an example of the flexible operation of the accident requirement. See *Saks*, 470 U.S. at 405 (Warsaw accident liability where airline served alcohol to drunken passenger, who then fell and injured fellow passenger).

Of course, Langadinos cannot prevail simply by proving that American served Debord excessive alcohol. He will also have to establish that he suffered a compensable injury[3] and that American's service of alcohol to the assailant was a proximate cause of his injury. Recognizing that we can affirm the dismissal of the complaint only "if it is clear that no relief could be granted under any set of facts that could be proved consistent with the allegations," we are not able to say, at this stage in the proceedings, whether American bears causal responsibility for the alleged assault. * * * In this case, discovery will be required before such an assessment can be made.[4]

---

[3] American claims that Langadinos has alleged only "emotional injuries," which, standing alone, are not recoverable under Article 17 of the Warsaw Convention. Langadinos, however, has plainly alleged "excruciating pain" in the groin area following the assault. Although it is unclear whether he can claim damages for concurrent emotional injuries, we need not explore this issue as Langadinos's allegation of a physical injury takes him beyond a motion to dismiss.

[4] American also argues that the complaint should be dismissed inasmuch as it alleges "willful" misconduct on the part of American. This objection is misplaced. The distinction between mere Warsaw accidents and "willful" misconduct goes only to damages: if the plaintiff can prove willful misconduct, the $75,000 damage limit applicable to accidents taking place during this time

B.   Defects in the Pleading

American argues that even if serving excessive alcohol to a passenger can create a Warsaw accident, Langadinos pled this allegation with such generality that we should not credit it in reviewing the decision to dismiss his complaint. The allegation of over-serving is crucial, American contends, because Langadinos is unable to state a Warsaw Convention "accident" claim without it.

We agree with American that Langadinos's complaint could not survive without a properly pled allegation of over-serving.   Other than the service of alcohol to Debord, Langadinos has not alleged any action by American that even arguably led to his sexual assault.   Langadinos's claim that American flight attendants were rude to him and that they "spoon-fed" ice cream to Debord does not affix American with causal responsibility for an assault.   Likewise, Langadinos's claim that the American crew treated him poorly after the incident does not demonstrate that they played any role in its cause.   Without the allegation of over-serving, therefore, American could not bear any causal responsibility for Langadinos's injuries and there would be no Warsaw Convention accident.

We disagree with American, however, that the charge of over-serving was pled defectively.   Langadinos alleged the following in paragraph 17 of the amended complaint:

> On information and belief, just prior to the aforesaid Mr. Debord's above-described assault and battery upon Mr. Langadinos [American] served intoxicating liquors/intoxicants to said Mr. Debord and — not withstanding his aggressive and erratic behavior and his evident state of diminished cognitive and physical capacity — continued to serve Mr. Debord intoxicants, thereby foreseeably generating otherwise unnecessary risk of harm to all other passengers of Flight No. 146 . . . . Upon information and belief, [American] continued to serve Mr. Debord alcohol, knowing that he was intoxicated . . . .

American asks us to disregard this allegation because it relies on words and phrases like "erratic," "aggressive," and "diminished cognitive and physical capacity," which American argues are conclusory.   In particular, American says that Langadinos failed to describe precisely the conduct of Debord that was "erratic" or "aggressive" or that demonstrated his "diminished capacity."

American demands from Langadinos more detail in his complaint than the Federal Rules of Civil Procedure require.   The pleading rules

> do not require a claimant to set out in detail the facts upon which he bases his claim.   To the contrary, all the Rules require is 'a short and plain statement of the claim' that will give the defendant fair notice of what the plaintiff's claim is and the grounds upon which it rests.   The

---

period does not apply.   See Warsaw Convention, Art. 25.   Given that the complaint states facts sufficient to allege a Warsaw accident, Langadinos is entitled to seek damages above the cap by attempting to prove that the accident was caused by American's willful misconduct.

       illustrative forms appended to the Rules plainly demonstrate this.[5]

Conley v. Gibson, 355 U.S. 41, 47-48, 2 L.Ed.2d 80, 78 S.Ct. 99 (1957). While defendants may prefer highly detailed factual allegations, a generalized statement of facts is adequate so long as it gives the defendant sufficient notice to file a responsive pleading.[6]

       We have demanded greater factual detail in a complaint in a few specific categories of cases. For example, we have followed Rule 9(b)'s requirement that "in all averments of fraud or mistake, the circumstances constituting fraud or mistake shall be stated with particularity." * * * Apart from these "specialized areas not implicated here, it is enough for a plaintiff to sketch an actionable claim by means of 'a generalized statement of facts from which the defendant will be able to frame a responsive pleading.'" Langadinos has met this standard, putting American on notice that it is accused of serving alcohol to an aggressive, erratic, and incapacitated passenger, even though it knew he was intoxicated.

       American repeatedly reminds us that Langadinos only alleged the over-serving of alcohol in his amended complaint on the basis of information and belief. A plaintiff may rely, however, on an amended complaint, and, as American concedes, a plaintiff can make allegations either on the basis of personal knowledge or on "information and belief." Langadinos's attorney is entitled to include such "information and belief" allegations in the complaint as long as he had a good faith basis for doing so, based on the reasonable inquiry that Fed. R. Civ. P. 11(b) requires.[9]

---

[5] Indeed, a perusal of these forms nicely illustrates just how little factual detail is required. For example, Form 9 [later eliminated—eds.], the model form for negligence pleadings reads, in whole, as follows:

   1.   Allegation of jurisdiction.

   2.   On June 1, 1936, in a public highway called Boylston Street in Boston, Massachusetts, defendant negligently drove a motor vehicle against plaintiff who was then crossing said highway.

   3.   As a result plaintiff was thrown down and had his leg broken and was otherwise injured, was prevented from transacting his business, suffered great pain of body and mind, and incurred expenses for medical attention and hospitalization in the sum of one thousand dollars.

    Wheretofore plaintiff demands judgment against defendant in the sum of [blank] dollars and costs.

[6] If the complaint "is so vague or ambiguous that a party cannot reasonably be required to frame a responsive pleading, the party may move for a more definite statement before interposing a responsive pleading." Fed. R. Civ. P. 12(e). Perhaps tellingly, American made no such motion here.

[9] Fed. R. Civ. P. 11(b) states, in pertinent part:

    (b) Representations to Court. By presenting to the court (whether by signing, filing, submitting, or later advocating) a pleading, written motion, or other paper, an attorney or unrepresented party is certifying that to the best of the person's knowledge, information, and belief, formed after a reasonable inquiry under the circumstances, . . .

    (3) the allegations and other factual contentions have evidentiary support or, if specifically so identified, are likely to have evidentiary support after a reasonable opportunity for further investigation or discovery . . . .

III

For the reasons stated above, we conclude that Langadinos has stated a valid claim under the Warsaw Convention. We therefore vacate the district court order dismissing the claim and remand for further proceedings consistent with this opinion.

NOTES AND PROBLEMS FOR DISCUSSION

1. Make sure you understand why Part II-A of the opinion was necessary. What argument was American Airlines making? If the Court had agreed with American in Part II-A, would it have been necessary to write Part II-B?

2. Conversely, why didn't the Court simply omit Part II-A and say that as long as the pleading of intoxication was adequate, the Rule 12(b)(6) motion should be denied?

3. At common law, a common carrier owed a passenger a high duty of care, and failure to carry out such a duty is actionable. The plaintiff alleged such a claim, but then failed to pursue it on appeal. Why?

4. American argued that the plaintiff's pleading was inadequate. What more could the plaintiff have pleaded?

5. This is the same Court that decided *Dartmouth Review*. Are the cases consistent?

6. Many lawyers instinctively jump at an opportunity to make a Rule 12(b)(6) motion. If you represented American and were rendering advice whether to make such a motion, explain (a) what are the possible outcomes of such a motion, (b) which of these is a "win," and (c) whether there are any possible downsides of losing, other than time, effort, and expense.

7. The court suggests (at footnote 6) that American might have made a Rule 12(e) motion. Could American satisfy the requirements of that Rule? Before you answer, consider the background: Under the Codes, defendants could respond to a complaint lacking details with a motion for a bill of particulars (essentially, asking for more details). The original version of Rule 12(e) permitted a similar motion. Experience under the original rule was that there were more motions for a bill of particulars than any other motion under the Federal Rules, and in actual practice, the rule undermined the "notice pleading" philosophy and frequently was used as a discovery device. In 1948, the Rule was amended to its present form.

8. Note that plaintiff did not originally allege intoxication. Reconsider question 1 above, and see whether you understand what would have happened if plaintiff hadn't added it. Now, consider American's argument that it was an afterthought to "save the day." Although we will consider Rule 11 later, consider what the plaintiff's lawyer must do (if anything) to make an allegation of intoxication and not run afoul of Rule 11(b)(3).

9. After the decision in *Langadinos*, what issues remain for trial and what are the defendant's chances of winning?

10. As discussed at the outset of this chapter, a pleading is an implicit contention about substantive law. Must a plaintiff allege the "law" itself? The answer generally is "no" so long as, from the allegations, it is clear what substantive law is being invoked. Nevertheless, plaintiffs bringing actions under statutes generally refer to the statute in question. Of course, if the defendant makes a Rule 12(b)(6) motion, the plaintiff will have to be able to identify a substantive law basis for her claim.

11. Substantive law generally requires a plaintiff to establish several different elements to win — e.g., duty, negligence, proximate cause and damages in an accident case. Must the plaintiff allege each element? While courts differ on this question (and sometimes find one element implicitly alleged in others), they are understandably skeptical if the plaintiff cannot even allege an element she must later prove at trial. What might be the reason for a plaintiff to fail to allege each of the relevant elements of a particular cause of action?and how much is enough?

2. RETRENCHMENT

The *Dartmouth College* and *Langadinos* cases illustrate that the pleading requirements serve, in part, as "gatekeepers" to screen nonmeritorious actions before the defendant (and the court) must devote time and expense to the case. Once the plaintiff's pleading passes through the gate, the defendant must answer, other parties may be joined, and the discovery process will get under way. As a practical matter, the next opportunity for the court to review the merits will not come until a possible motion for summary judgment under Rule 56, Fed. R. Civ. P. Even though such a motion may be brought "at any time until 30 days after the close of all discovery," it ordinarily will not be considered until after there has been time for discovery. See Chapter 9. Courts have long struggled with the notion that there ought to be some mechanism to screen out nonmeritorious cases before the litigation proceeds to this next stage. Consider the following effort:

Bell Atlantic Corp. v. Twombly

Supreme Court of the United States, 2007.

550 U.S. 544, 125 S.Ct. 1955, 167 L.Ed.2d 929.

JUSTICE SOUTER delivered the opinion of the Court.

Liability under § 1 of the Sherman [Antitrust] Act, 15 U.S.C. § 1, requires a "contract, combination . . . , or conspiracy, in restraint of trade or commerce." The question in this putative class action is whether a § 1 complaint can survive a motion to dismiss when it alleges that major telecommunications providers engaged in certain parallel conduct unfavorable to competition, absent some factual context suggesting agreement, as distinct from identical, independent action. We hold that such a complaint should be dismissed.

I

The upshot of the 1984 divestiture of the American Telephone & Telegraph Company's (AT&T) local telephone business was a system of regional service monopolies (variously called "Regional Bell Operating Companies," "Baby Bells," or "Incumbent Local Exchange Carriers" (ILECs)), and a separate, competitive market for long-distance service from which the ILECs were excluded. More than a decade later, Congress withdrew approval of the ILECs' monopolies by enacting the Telecommunications Act of 1996 (1996 Act), which "fundamentally restructure[d] local telephone markets" and "subject[ed] [ILECs] to a host of duties intended to facilitate market entry." In recompense, the 1996 Act set conditions for authorizing ILECs to enter the long-distance market. * * *

Respondents William Twombly and Lawrence Marcus (hereinafter plaintiffs) represent a putative class consisting of all "subscribers of local telephone and/or high speed internet services . . . from February 8, 1996 to present." In this action against [defendant] petitioners, a group of ILECs,[1] plaintiffs * * * claimed violations of § 1 of the Sherman Act, 15 U.S.C. § 1, which prohibits "[e]very contract, combination in the form of trust or otherwise, or conspiracy, in restraint of trade or commerce among the several States, or with foreign nations." * * *

The complaint couches its ultimate allegations this way:

> "In the absence of any meaningful competition between the [ILECs] in one another's markets, and in light of the parallel course of conduct that each engaged in to prevent competition * * * within their respective local telephone and/or high speed internet services markets and the other facts and market circumstances alleged above, Plaintiffs allege upon information and belief that [the ILECs] have entered into a contract, combination or conspiracy to prevent competitive entry in their respective local telephone and/or high speed internet services markets and have agreed not to compete with one another and otherwise allocated customers and markets to one another."

The United States District Court for the Southern District of New York dismissed the complaint for failure to state a claim upon which relief can be granted. The District Court acknowledged that "plaintiffs may allege a conspiracy by citing instances of parallel business behavior that suggest an agreement," but emphasized that "while '[c]ircumstantial evidence of consciously parallel behavior may have made heavy inroads into the traditional judicial attitude toward conspiracy, . . . "conscious parallelism" has not yet read conspiracy out of the Sherman Act entirely.'" Thus, the District Court understood that allegations of parallel business conduct, taken alone, do not state a claim under § 1; plaintiffs must allege additional facts that "ten[d] to exclude independent self-interested conduct as an explanation for defendants' parallel

---

[1] The 1984 divestiture of AT&T's local telephone service created seven Regional Bell Operating Companies. Through a series of mergers and acquisitions, those seven companies were consolidated into the four ILECs named in this suit: BellSouth Corporation, Qwest Communications International, Inc., SBC Communications, Inc., and Verizon Communications, Inc. (successor-in-interest to Bell Atlantic Corporation). Together, these ILECs allegedly control 90 percent or more of the market for local telephone service in the 48 contiguous States.

behavior." The District Court found plaintiffs' allegations of parallel ILEC actions to discourage competition inadequate because "the behavior of each ILEC * * * is fully explained by the ILEC's own interests in defending its individual territory." As to the ILECs' supposed agreement against competing with each other, the District Court found that the complaint does not "alleg[e] facts . . . suggesting that refraining from competing in other territories * * * was contrary to [the ILECs'] apparent economic interests, and consequently [does] not rais[e] an inference that [the ILECs'] actions were the result of a conspiracy."

The Court of Appeals for the Second Circuit reversed, holding that the District Court tested the complaint by the wrong standard. [The Second Circuit] held that "plus factors are not *required* to be pleaded to permit an antitrust claim based on parallel conduct to survive dismissal." * * *

We granted certiorari to address the proper standard for pleading an antitrust conspiracy through allegations of parallel conduct, and now reverse.

II

A

Because § 1 of the Sherman Act "does not prohibit [all] unreasonable restraint of trade . . . but only restraints effectuated by contract, combination, or conspiracy, the crucial question" is whether the challenged anticompetitive conduct "stem[s] from independent decision or from an agreement, tacit or express." While a showing of parallel "business behavior is admissible circumstantial evidence from which the fact finder may infer agreement," it falls short of "conclusively establish[ing] agreement or . . . itself constitut[ing] a Sherman Act offense." Even "conscious parallelism," a common reaction of "firms in a concentrated market [that] recogniz[e] their shared economic interests and their interdependence with respect to price and output decisions" is "not in itself unlawful." * * *

B

This case presents the antecedent question of what a plaintiff must plead in order to state a claim under § 1 of the Sherman Act. Federal Rule of Civil Procedure 8(a)(2) requires only "a short and plain statement of the claim showing that the pleader is entitled to relief," in order to "give the defendant fair notice of what the . . . claim is and the grounds upon which it rests," Conley v. Gibson, 355 U.S. 41, 47 (1957). While a complaint attacked by a * * * motion to dismiss does not need detailed factual allegations, a plaintiff's obligation to provide the "grounds" of his "entitle[ment] to relief" requires more than labels and conclusions, and a formulaic recitation of the elements of a cause of action will not do, see Papasan v. Allain, 478 U.S. 265, 265 (1986) (on a motion to dismiss, courts "are not bound to accept as true a legal conclusion couched as a factual allegation"). Factual allegations must be enough to raise a right to relief above the speculative level. * * * ("The pleading must contain something more . . . than . . . a statement of facts that merely creates a suspicion [of] a legally cognizable right of action"),[3] on the assumption that all the allegations in the complaint are true (even if doubtful in fact)[.]

In applying these general standards to a § 1 claim, we hold that stating such a claim requires a complaint with enough factual matter (taken as true) to suggest that an agreement was made. Asking for plausible grounds to infer an agreement does not impose a probability requirement at the pleading stage; it simply calls for enough fact [sic] to raise a reasonable expectation that discovery will reveal evidence of illegal agreement.[4] And, of course, a well-pleaded complaint may proceed even if it strikes a savvy judge that actual proof of those facts is improbable, and "that a recovery is very remote and unlikely." * * * It makes sense to say, therefore, that an allegation of parallel conduct and a bare assertion of conspiracy will not suffice. Without more, parallel conduct does not suggest conspiracy, and a conclusory allegation of agreement at some unidentified point does not supply facts adequate to show illegality. Hence, when allegations of parallel conduct are set out in order to make a § 1 claim, they must be placed in a context that raises a suggestion of a preceding agreement, not merely parallel conduct that could just as well be independent action.

The need at the pleading stage for allegations plausibly suggesting (not merely consistent with) agreement reflects the threshold requirement of Rule 8(a)(2) that the "plain statement" possess enough heft to "sho[w] that the pleader is entitled to relief." A statement of parallel conduct, even conduct consciously undertaken, needs some setting suggesting the agreement necessary to make out a § 1 claim; without that further circumstance pointing toward a meeting of the minds, an account of a defendant's commercial efforts stays in neutral territory. An allegation of parallel conduct is thus much like a naked assertion of conspiracy in a § 1 complaint: it gets the complaint close to stating a claim, but without some further factual enhancement it stops short of the line between possibility and plausibility of "entitlement to relief." * * *

Thus, it is one thing to be cautious before dismissing an antitrust complaint in advance of discovery, * * * but quite another to forget that proceeding to antitrust discovery can be expensive. * * * That potential expense is obvious

---

[3] The dissent greatly oversimplifies matters by suggesting that the Federal Rules somehow dispensed with the pleading of facts altogether * * * . While, for most types of cases, the Federal Rules eliminated the cumbersome requirement that a claimant "set out *in detail* the facts upon which he bases his claim," *Conley v. Gibson* (emphasis added), Rule 8(a)(2) still requires a "showing," rather than a blanket assertion, of entitlement to relief. Without some factual allegation in the complaint, it is hard to see how a claimant could satisfy the requirement of providing not only "fair notice" of the nature of the claim, but also "grounds" on which the claim rests. (Rule 8(a) "contemplate[s] the statement of circumstances, occurrences, and events in support of the claim presented" and does not authorize a pleader's "bare averment that he wants relief and is entitled to it").

[4] Commentators have offered several examples of parallel conduct allegations that would state a § 1 claim under this standard * * * [including] * * * "parallel behavior that would probably not result from chance, coincidence, independent responses to common stimuli, or mere interdependence unaided by an advance understanding among the parties" [and] "conduct [that] indicates the sort of restricted freedom of action and sense of obligation that one generally associates with agreement." * * *

enough in the present cases: [plaintiffs represent] at least 90 percent of all subscribers to local telephone or high-speed internet service in the continental United States, in an action against America's largest telecommunications firms. * * *

Plaintiffs do not, of course, dispute the requirement of plausibility and the need for something more than merely parallel behavior * * * and their main argument against the plausibility standard at the pleading stage is its ostensible conflict with an early statement of ours construing Rule 8. Justice Black's opinion for the Court in *Conley v. Gibson* spoke not only of the need for fair notice of the grounds for entitlement to relief but of "the accepted rule that a complaint should not be dismissed for failure * * * to state a claim unless it appears beyond doubt that the plaintiff can prove no set of facts in support of his claim which would entitle him to relief." This "no set of facts" language can be read in isolation as saying that any statement revealing the theory of the claim will suffice unless its factual impossibility may be shown from the face of the pleadings; and the Court of Appeals appears to have read *Conley* in some such way when formulating its understanding of the proper pleading standard[.] * * *

On such a focused and literal reading of *Conley's* "no set of facts," a wholly conclusory statement of claim would survive a motion to dismiss whenever the pleadings left open the possibility that a plaintiff might later establish some "set of [undisclosed] facts" to support recovery. So here, the Court of Appeals specifically found the prospect of unearthing direct evidence of conspiracy sufficient to preclude dismissal, even though the complaint does not set forth a single fact in a context that suggests an agreement. * * *

We could go on, but there is no need to pile up further citations to show that *Conley's* "no set of facts" language has been questioned, criticized, and explained away long enough. * * * [A]fter puzzling the profession for 50 years, this famous observation has earned its retirement. The phrase is best forgotten as an incomplete, negative gloss on an accepted pleading standard: once a claim has been stated adequately, it may be supported by showing any set of facts consistent with the allegations in the complaint. * * * *Conley,* then, described the breadth of opportunity to prove what an adequate complaint claims, not the minimum standard of adequate pleading to govern a complaint's survival.

III

When we look for plausibility in this complaint, we agree with the District Court that plaintiffs' claim of conspiracy in restraint of trade comes up short. To begin with, the complaint leaves no doubt that plaintiffs rest their § 1 claim on descriptions of parallel conduct and not on any independent allegation of actual agreement among the ILECs. Although in form a few stray statements speak directly of agreement,[9] on fair reading these are merely legal conclusions resting on the prior allegations. Thus, the complaint first takes account of the alleged "absence of any meaningful competition between [the ILECs] in one another's markets," "the parallel course of conduct that each [ILEC] engaged in to prevent

---

[9] See Complaint ¶¶51, 64, App. 27, 30-31 (alleging that ILECs engaged in a "contract, combination or conspiracy" and agreed not to compete with one another).

competition from CLECs [competitive local exchange carriers]," "and the other facts and market circumstances alleged [earlier]"; "in light of" these, the complaint concludes "that [the ILECs] have entered into a contract, combination or conspiracy to prevent competitive entry into their . . . markets and have agreed not to compete with one another."[10] The nub of the complaint, then, is the ILECs' parallel behavior, consisting of steps to keep the CLECs out and manifest disinterest in becoming CLECs themselves, and its sufficiency turns on the suggestions raised by this conduct when viewed in light of common economic experience.[11]

We think that nothing contained in the complaint invests either the action or inaction alleged with a plausible suggestion of conspiracy. As to the ILECs' supposed agreement to disobey the 1996 Act and thwart the CLECs' attempts to compete, we agree with the District Court that nothing in the complaint intimates that the resistance to the upstarts was anything more than the natural, unilateral reaction of each ILEC intent on keeping its regional dominance. The 1996 Act did more than just subject the ILECs to competition; it obliged them to subsidize their competitors with their own equipment at wholesale rates. The economic incentive to resist was powerful, but resisting competition is routine market conduct, and even if the ILECs flouted the 1996 Act in all the ways the plaintiffs allege, * * * there is no reason to infer that the companies had agreed among themselves to do what was only natural anyway; so natural, in fact, that if alleging parallel decisions to resist competition were enough to imply an antitrust conspiracy, pleading a § 1 violation against almost any group of competing businesses would be a sure thing.

The complaint makes its closest pass at a predicate for conspiracy with the claim that collusion was necessary because success by even one CLEC in an ILEC's territory "would have revealed the degree to which competitive entry by CLECs would have been successful in the other territories." But, its logic aside, this general premise still fails to answer the point that there was just no need for joint encouragement to resist the 1996 Act; as the District Court said, "each

---

[10] If the complaint had not explained that the claim of agreement rested on the parallel conduct described, we doubt that the complaint's references to an agreement among the ILECs would have given the notice required by Rule 8. Apart from identifying a seven-year span in which the § 1 violations were supposed to have occurred (i.e., "beginning at least as early as February 6, 1996, and continuing to the present,"), the pleadings mentioned no specific time, place, or person involved in the alleged conspiracies. This lack of notice contrasts sharply with the model form for pleading negligence, Form 9 [since abrigated — eds.], which the dissent says exemplifies the kind of "bare allegation" that survives a motion to dismiss. Whereas the model form alleges that the defendant struck the plaintiff with his car while plaintiff was crossing a particular highway at a specified date and time, the complaint here furnishes no clue as to which of the four ILECs (much less which of their employees) supposedly agreed, or when and where the illicit agreement took place. A defendant wishing to prepare an answer in the simple fact pattern laid out in Form 9 would know what to answer; a defendant seeking to respond to plaintiffs' conclusory allegations in the § 1 context would have little idea where to begin.

[11] The dissent's quotations from the complaint leave the impression that plaintiffs directly allege illegal agreement; in fact, they proceed exclusively via allegations of parallel conduct, as both the District Court and Court of Appeals recognized.

ILEC has reason to want to avoid dealing with CLECs" and "each ILEC would attempt to keep CLECs out, regardless of the actions of the other ILECs." 313 F. Supp. 2d, at 184; cf. Kramer v. Pollock-Krasner Foundation, 890 F. Supp. 250, 256 (SDNY 1995) (while plaintiff "may believe the defendants conspired . . ., the defendants' allegedly conspiratorial actions could equally have been prompted by lawful, independent goals which do not constitute a conspiracy").

Plaintiffs' second conspiracy theory rests on the competitive reticence among the ILECs themselves in the wake of the 1996 Act, which was supposedly passed in the "'hope that the large incumbent local monopoly companies . . . might attack their neighbors' service areas, as they are the best situated to do so.'" Complaint ¶38 (quoting Consumer Federation of America, Lessons from 1996 Telecommunications Act: Deregulation Before Meaningful Competition Spells Consumer Disaster, p. 12 (Feb. 2000)). Contrary to hope, the ILECs declined "'to enter each other's service territories in any significant way,'" and the local telephone and high speed Internet market remains highly compartmentalized geographically, with minimal competition. Based on this state of affairs, and perceiving the ILECs to be blessed with "especially attractive business opportunities" in surrounding markets dominated by other ILECs, the plaintiffs assert that the ILECs' parallel conduct was "strongly suggestive of conspiracy."

But it was not suggestive of conspiracy, not if history teaches anything. In a traditionally unregulated industry with low barriers to entry, sparse competition among large firms dominating separate geographical segments of the market could very well signify illegal agreement, but here we have an obvious alternative explanation. In the decade preceding the 1996 Act and well before that, monopoly was the norm in telecommunications, not the exception. See Verizon Communs., Inc. v. FCC, 535 U.S. 467, 477-478 (2002) (describing telephone service providers as traditional public monopolies). The ILECs were born in that world, doubtless liked the world the way it was, and surely knew the adage about him who lives by the sword. Hence, a natural explanation for the noncompetition alleged is that the former Government-sanctioned monopolists were sitting tight, expecting their neighbors to do the same thing.

In fact, the complaint itself gives reasons to believe that the ILECs would see their best interests in keeping to their old turf. Although the complaint says generally that the ILECs passed up "especially attractive business opportunities" by declining to compete as CLECs against other ILECs, it does not allege that competition as CLECs was potentially any more lucrative than other opportunities being pursued by the ILECs during the same period,[13] and the

---

[13] The complaint quoted a reported statement of Qwest's CEO, Richard Notebaert, to suggest that the ILECs declined to compete against each other despite recognizing that it "'might be a good way to turn a quick dollar.'" * * * This was only part of what he reportedly said, however, and the District Court was entitled to take notice of the full contents of the published articles referenced in the complaint, from which the truncated quotations were drawn. See Fed. Rule Evid. 201.

Notebaert was also quoted as saying that entering new markets as a CLEC would not be "a sustainable economic model" because the CLEC pricing model is "just . . . nuts." * * * Another source cited in the complaint quotes Notebaert as saying he thought it "unwise" to "base a business

complaint is replete with indications that any CLEC faced nearly insurmountable barriers to profitability owing to the ILECs' flagrant resistance to the network sharing requirements of the 1996 Act[.] Not only that, but even without a monopolistic tradition and the peculiar difficulty of mandating shared networks, "firms do not expand without limit and none of them enters every market that an outside observer might regard as profitable, or even a small portion of such markets." P. Areeda & H. Hovenkamp, Antitrust Law (2d ed. 2003) ¶307d, at 155 (Supp. 2006) (commenting on the case at bar). The upshot is that Congress may have expected some ILECs to become CLECs in the legacy territories of other ILECs, but the disappointment does not make conspiracy plausible. We agree with the District Court's assessment that antitrust conspiracy was not suggested by the facts adduced under either theory of the complaint, which thus fails to state a valid § 1 claim.[14]

JUSTICE STEVENS, with whom JUSTICE GINSBURG joins except as to Part IV, dissenting.

In the first paragraph of its 24-page opinion the Court states that the question to be decided is whether allegations that "major telecommunications providers engaged in certain parallel conduct unfavorable to competition" suffice to state a violation of § 1 of the Sherman Act. The answer to that question has been settled for more than 50 years. If that were indeed the issue, a summary reversal citing Theatre Enterprises v. Paramount Film Distrib., 346 U.S. 537 (1954), would adequately resolve this case. As *Theatre Enterprises* held, parallel conduct is circumstantial evidence admissible on the issue of conspiracy, but it is not itself illegal.

Thus, this is a case in which there is no dispute about the substantive law. If the defendants acted independently, their conduct was perfectly lawful. If, however, that conduct is the product of a horizontal agreement among potential competitors, it was unlawful. Plaintiffs have alleged such an agreement and, because the complaint was dismissed in advance of answer, the allegation has not even been denied. Why, then, does the case not proceed? Does a judicial opinion that the charge is not "plausible" provide a legally acceptable reason for dismissing the complaint? I think not.

Respondents' amended complaint describes a variety of circumstantial evidence and makes the straightforward allegation that petitioners

---

plan" on the privileges accorded to CLECs under the 1996 Act because the regulatory environment was too unstable. * * *

[14] In reaching this conclusion, we do not apply any "heightened" pleading standard, nor do we seek to broaden the scope of Federal Rule of Civil Procedure 9, which can only be accomplished "'by the process of amending the Federal Rules, and not by judicial interpretation.'" Swierkiewicz v. Sorema N. A., 534 U.S. 506, 515 (2002) (quoting Leatherman v. Tarrant County Narcotics Intelligence and Coordination Unit, 507 U.S. 163, 168 (1993)). On certain subjects understood to raise a high risk of abusive litigation, a plaintiff must state factual allegations with greater particularity than Rule 8 requires. Fed. Rules Civ. Proc. 9(b)-(c). Here, our concern is not that the allegations in the complaint were insufficiently "particularized", ibid.; rather, the complaint warranted dismissal because it failed *in toto* to render plaintiffs' entitlement to relief plausible.

> "entered into a contract, combination or conspiracy to prevent competitive entry in their respective local telephone and/or high speed internet services markets and have agreed not to compete with one another and otherwise allocated customers and markets to one another."

The complaint explains that, contrary to Congress' expectation when it enacted the 1996 Telecommunications Act, and consistent with their own economic self-interests, petitioner Incumbent Local Exchange Carriers (ILECs) have assiduously avoided infringing upon each other's markets and have refused to permit nonincumbent competitors to access their networks. * * * In sum, respondents allege that petitioners entered into an agreement that has long been recognized as a classic *per se* violation of the Sherman Act. * * *

Under rules of procedure that have been well settled * * * a judge ruling on a defendant's motion to dismiss a complaint, "must accept as true all of the factual allegations contained in the complaint." But instead of requiring knowledgeable executives * * * to respond to these allegations by way of sworn depositions or other limited discovery — and indeed without so much as requiring petitioners to file an answer denying that they entered into any agreement — the majority permits immediate dismissal based on the assurances of company lawyers that nothing untoward was afoot. The Court embraces the argument of those lawyers that "there is no reason to infer that the companies had agreed among themselves to do what was only natural anyway," that "there was just no need for joint encouragement to resist the 1996 Act," and that the "natural explanation for the noncompetition alleged is that the former Government-sanctioned monopolists were sitting tight, expecting their neighbors to do the same thing."

The Court and petitioners' legal team are no doubt correct that the parallel conduct alleged is consistent with the absence of any contract, combination, or conspiracy. But that conduct is also entirely consistent with the *presence* of the illegal agreement alleged in the complaint. * * * As such, the Federal Rules of Civil Procedure, our longstanding precedent, and sound practice mandate that the District Court at least require some sort of response from petitioners before dismissing the case. * * *

I

Rule 8(a)(2) of the Federal Rules requires that a complaint contain "a short and plain statement of the claim showing that the pleader is entitled to relief." * * *

Under the relaxed pleading standards of the Federal Rules, the idea was not to keep litigants out of court but rather to keep them in. The merits of a claim would be sorted out during a flexible pretrial process and, as appropriate, through the crucible of trial. See *Swierkiewicz,* 534 U.S., at 514 ("The liberal notice pleading of Rule 8(a) is the starting point of a simplified pleading system, which was adopted to focus litigation on the merits of a claim"). Charles E. Clark, the "principal draftsman" of the Federal Rules, put it thus:

> "Experience has shown . . . that we cannot expect the proof of the case to be made through the pleadings, and that such proof is really not their function. We can expect a general statement distinguishing the case

from all others, so that the manner and form of trial and remedy expected are clear * * * ."

The pleading paradigm under the new Federal Rules was well illustrated by the inclusion in the appendix of Form 9, a complaint for negligence. As relevant, the Form 9 complaint states only: "On June 1, 1936, in a public highway called Boylston Street in Boston, Massachusetts, defendant negligently drove a motor vehicle against plaintiff who was then crossing said highway." [The current version is now Form 11, and it is worded slightly differently — eds.] The complaint then describes the plaintiff's injuries and demands judgment. The asserted ground for relief — namely, the defendant's negligent driving — would have been called a "'conclusion of law'" under the code pleading of old. But that bare allegation suffices under a system that "restrict[s] the pleadings to the task of general notice-giving and invest[s] the deposition-discovery process with a vital role in the preparation for trial."[3]

II

It is in the context of this history that Conley v. Gibson must be understood. The *Conley* plaintiffs were black railroad workers who alleged that their union local had refused to protect them against discriminatory discharges, in violation of the National Railway Labor Act. The union sought to dismiss the complaint on the ground that its general allegations of discriminatory treatment by the defendants lacked sufficient specificity. Writing for a unanimous Court, Justice Black rejected the union's claim as foreclosed by the language of Rule 8. In the course of doing so, he articulated the formulation the Court rejects today: "In appraising the sufficiency of the complaint we follow, of course, the accepted rule that a complaint should not be dismissed for failure to state a claim unless it appears beyond doubt that the plaintiff can prove no set of facts in support of his claim which would entitle him to relief."

Consistent with the design of the Federal Rules, *Conley's* "no set of facts" formulation permits outright dismissal only when proceeding to discovery or beyond would be futile. Once it is clear that a plaintiff has stated a claim that, if true, would entitle him to relief, matters of proof are appropriately relegated to other stages of the trial process. Today, however, in its explanation of a decision to dismiss a complaint that it regards as a fishing expedition, the Court scraps *Conley's* "no set of facts" language. Concluding that the phrase has been "questioned, criticized, and explained away long enough," the Court dismisses it as careless composition.

If *Conley's* "no set of facts" language is to be interred, let it not be without a eulogy. That exact language, which the majority says has "puzzl[ed] the profession for 50 years," has been cited as authority in a dozen opinions of this Court and four separate writings. In not one of those 16 opinions was the language "questioned," "criticized," or "explained away." Indeed, today's opinion is the first by any Member of this Court to express *any* doubt as to the adequacy of the *Conley* formulation. * * *

---

[3] The Federal Rules do impose a "particularity" requirement on "all averments of fraud or mistake," Fed. Rule Civ. Proc. 9(b), neither of which has been alleged in this case. We have recognized that the canon of *expresio unius est exclusio alterius* applies to Rule 9(b).

Petitioners have not requested that the *Conley* formulation be retired, nor have any of the six amici who filed briefs in support of petitioners. I would not rewrite the Nation's civil procedure textbooks and call into doubt the pleading rules of most of its States without far more informed deliberation as to the costs of doing so. Congress has established a process — a rulemaking process — for revisions of that order. See 28 U.S.C. §§ 2072-2074[.]

Today's majority calls *Conley's* "'no set of facts'" language "an incomplete, negative gloss on an accepted pleading standard: once a claim has been stated adequately, it may be supported by showing any set of facts consistent with the allegations in the complaint." This is not and cannot be what the *Conley* Court meant. First, as I have explained, and as the *Conley* Court well knew, the pleading standard the Federal Rules meant to codify does not require, or even invite, the pleading of facts.[6] The "pleading standard" label the majority gives to what it reads into the *Conley* opinion — a statement of the permissible factual support for an adequately pleaded complaint — would not, therefore, have impressed the *Conley* Court itself. Rather, that Court would have understood the majority's remodeling of its language to express an *evidentiary* standard, which the *Conley* Court had neither need nor want to explicate. Second, it is pellucidly clear that the *Conley* Court was interested in what a complaint *must* contain, not what it *may* contain. In fact, the Court said without qualification that it was "appraising the *sufficiency* of the complaint." It was, to paraphrase today's majority, describing "the minimum standard of adequate pleading to govern a complaint's survival." * * *

We have consistently reaffirmed that basic understanding of the Federal Rules in the half century since *Conley*. * * *

In this "Big Case," the Court succumbs to the temptation that previous Courts have steadfastly resisted. While the majority assures us that it is not applying any "heightened" pleading standard, I shall now explain why I have a difficult time understanding its opinion any other way. * * *

III

The Court does not suggest that an agreement to do what the plaintiffs allege would be permissible under the antitrust laws * * *. Nor does the Court hold that these plaintiffs have failed to allege an injury entitling them to sue for damages under those laws * * *. Rather, the theory on which the Court permits dismissal is that, so far as the Federal Rules are concerned, no agreement has been alleged at all. This is a mind-boggling conclusion.

---

[6] The majority is correct to say that what the Federal Rules require is a "showing" of entitlement to relief. Whether and to what extent that "showing" requires allegations of fact will depend on the particulars of the claim. For example, had the amended complaint in this case alleged *only* parallel conduct, it would not have made the required "showing." Similarly, had the pleadings contained *only* an allegation of agreement, without specifying the nature or object of that agreement, they would have been susceptible to the charge that they did not provide sufficient notice that the defendants may answer intelligently. Omissions of that sort instance the type of "bareness" with which the Federal Rules are concerned. A plaintiff's inability to persuade a district court that the allegations actually included in her complaint are "plausible" is an altogether different kind of failing, and one that should not be fatal at the pleading stage.

465

[The dissent suggested that the majority too easily dismissed the "few stray statements in the complaint" that "speak directly of agreement" as being merely "legal conclusions resting on the prior allegations" of parallel conduct. "The Court's dichotomy," said the dissent, "between factual allegations and 'legal conclusions' is the stuff of a byegone era[.]" And it suggested that the plaintiff's allegations about defendants entering into an agreement was no more a legal conclusion that "defendant negligently drove" in Form 9.]

Even if I were inclined to accept the Court's anachronistic dichotomy and ignore the complaint's actual allegations, I would dispute the Court's suggestion that any inference of agreement from petitioners' parallel conduct is "implausible." Many years ago a truly great economist perceptively observed that "people of the same trade seldom meet together, even for merriment and diversion, but the conversation ends in a conspiracy against the public, or in some contrivance to raise prices." Adam Smith, *An Inquiry Into the Nature and Causes of the Wealth of Nations*, in 39 Great Books of the Western World 55 (R. Hutchins & M. Adler eds. 1952). I am not so cynical as to accept that sentiment at face value, but I need not do so here. Respondents' complaint points not only to petitioners' numerous opportunities to meet with each other, but also to Notebaert's curious statement that encroaching on a fellow incumbent's territory "might be a good way to turn a quick dollar but that doesn't make it right[.]" What did he mean by that? One possible (indeed plausible) inference is that he meant that while it would be in his company's economic self-interest to compete with its brethren, he had agreed with his competitors not to do so. According to the complaint, that is how the Illinois Coalition for Competitive Telecom construed Notebaert's statement (calling the statement "evidence of potential collusion among regional Bell phone monopolies to not compete against one another and kill off potential competitors in local phone service"), and [according to the complaint] that is how Members of Congress construed his company's behavior (describing a letter to the Justice Department requesting an investigation into the possibility that the ILECs' "very apparent non-competition policy" was coordinated). * * *

IV

* * * The transparent policy concern that drives the decision is the interest in protecting antitrust defendants — who in this case are some of the wealthiest corporations in our economy — from the burdens of pretrial discovery. * * *

If the allegation of conspiracy happens to be true, today's decision obstructs the congressional policy favoring competition that undergirds both the Telecommunications Act of 1996 and the Sherman Act itself. More importantly, even if there is abundant evidence that the allegation is untrue, directing that the case be dismissed without even looking at any of that evidence marks a fundamental—pand unjustified—change in the character of pretrial practice. * * *

NOTES AND PROBLEMS FOR DISCUSSION

1. After *Twombly*, is notice pleading dead? Or is *Twombly* only a case about antitrust law, or conspiracy cases, or perhaps other "big" cases that present opportunities for plaintiffs to put financial pressure on defendants to settle claims that may have only marginal chances of ultimate success? In Ashcroft v. Iqbal, 556 U.S. 652, 129 S.Ct. 1937, 173 L.Ed.2d 868 (2009) (discussed in Note 7, below), the Court rejected an argument that *Twombly* "should be limited to pleadings made in the context of an antitrust dispute," concluding that "[o]ur decision in *Twombly* expounded the pleading standard for 'all civil actions,' . . . and it applies to antitrust and discrimination suits alike."

2. It may be difficult to appreciate the role that procedure is playing in *Twombly* without understanding what the underlying substantive law calls for. At trial, plaintiffs would have to adduce proof of an agreement or conspiracy to restrain trade. At the complaint stage, shouldn't it be sufficient to *allege* such an agreement or conspiracy? Much was made by the Court of the allegations of "parallel conduct." Parallel conduct between two would-be competitors is not itself illegal, and standing by itself, is insufficient to show an agreement or conspiracy to restrain trade. In the language of *Twombly*, such an inference would not be a "plausible" one. But parallel conduct may provide circumstantial evidence of a conspiracy or agreement to restrain trade. What more than an allegation of such conduct should it take to successfully allege a conspiracy? And what if plaintiffs are not in possession of facts that would allow them to bring the allegations up to the level of plausibility? Note that defendants, more often than plaintiffs, are likely to have information respecting the existence of a conspiracy. Should that information imbalance matter to pleading requirements?

3. If the purpose of notice pleading is to apprise the opposing party of the basis of one's claim, how wasn't that function served by the plaintiff's complaint in *Twombly*? Was the defendant really not in a position to be able to answer the allegations of the plaintiff? *Twombly* obviously makes life more difficult for plaintiffs; will *Twombly* apply equally to defenses raised by defendants?

4. In Swierkiewicz v. Sorema, N.A. 534 U.S. 506, 122 S.Ct. 922, 152 L.Ed.2d 1 (2002) — a pre-*Twombly* decision — the Court sustained the largely conclusory allegations of the plaintiff in a case under Title VII of the 1964 Civil Rights Act that he had been discriminated against on the basis of his age. The Court concluded that the plaintiff did not have to allege factual matters that would suggest that he had a prima facie case. Is *Swierkiewicz* still good law? Compare, e.g., E.E.O.C. v. Concentra Health Services, Inc., 496 F.3d 773 (7th Cir. 2007), in which the majority concluded it was "doubtful" whether *Twombly* "changed the level of detail required by notice pleading" and that its precedents — holding that a pleading which stated "[D]efendant discriminated against me on the basis of race" was sufficient — were still good law. Is that a fair assessment of *Twombly*?

5. A plaintiff alleging a claim of fraud must plead it with "particularity." Rule 9(b), Fed. R. Civ. P. But that is not true of most other claims. Is the *Twombly* Court's suggestion that it is not imposing a particularity requirement persuasive?

Ordinarily the Federal Rules are amended through the rulemaking process. In that process, there is the opportunity for public comment, and ultimately, congressional oversight. Did the Court short-circuit that process by its ruling?

6. Not long after the Court's decision in *Twombly*, the Court concluded that the largely conclusory allegations of a prisoner's complaint challenging cruel and unusual prison conditions had satisfied Rule 8's short, plain statement requirement. ERICKSON v. PARDUS, 551 U.S. 89, 127 S.Ct. 2197, 167 L.Ed.2d 1081 (2007) (per curiam). In a civil rights action under 42 U.S.C. § 1983, the prisoner alleged that the defendants had been indifferent to his medical condition in violation of the Eighth Amendment's prohibition on cruel and unusual punishment. The prisoner's complaint alleged that his removal from medical treatment for Hepatitis C "endanger[ed] his life," that he was "still in need of treatment for the disease," and that the defendants "refused to provide treatment." These allegations, said the Court, were sufficient to satisfy Rule 8(a). In so doing, the Court declared that allegations of "specific facts are not necessary; the statements necessarily give the defendant fair notice of what the claim is and the grounds on which it rests." It summarily reversed the court of appeals, which had concluded that the plaintiff's allegations were "too conclusory to establish that plaintiff had suffered a cognizable 'independent harm' as a result of his removal from the Hepatitis C treatment program." Finally, the Supreme Court noted:

> The Court of Appeals' departure from the liberal pleading standards set forth by Rule 8(a)(2) is even more pronounced in this particular case because petitioner has been proceeding, from the litigation's outset, without counsel. A document filed pro se is to be liberally construed, * * * and a pro se complaint, however inartfully pleaded, must be held to a less stringent standard than formal pleadings drafted by lawyers[.] Cf. Fed. Rule Civ. Proc. 8(f) ("All pleadings shall be so construed as to do substantial justice").

7. Two years after *Twombly*, the Court split badly on its meaning in the context of a civil rights action against federal officials arising out of the 9/11 terrorist attacks. ASHCROFT v. IQBAL, 556 U.S. 652, 129 S.Ct. 1937, 173 L.Ed.2d 868 (2009). The plaintiff was a Pakistani Muslim who was arrested in November 2001 for fraud regarding identification documents. He was held in a maximum security facility in New York as a person of "high interest" in connection with the 9/11 investigation. He eventually pled guilty to the criminal charges, served his term, and returned to Pakistan. He then filed a damages action in federal court against the U.S. Attorney General (Ashcroft), the head of the FBI (Mueller), and others, claiming that he was subjected to harsh treatment because of his race, religion or national origin, in violation of the Constitution. According to the Court:

> The complaint alleges that "the [FBI], under the direction of Defendant Mueller, arrested and detained thousands of Arab Muslim men . . . as part of its investigation of the events of September 11." It further alleges that "[t]he policy of holding post-September-11th detainees in highly restrictive conditions of confinement until they were 'cleared' by the FBI

was approved by Defendants Ashcroft and Mueller in discussions in the weeks after September 11, 2001." Lastly, the complaint posits that petitioners "each knew of, condoned, and willfully and maliciously agreed to subject" respondent to harsh conditions of confinement "as a matter of policy, solely on account of [his] religion, race, and/or national origin and for no legitimate penological interest." The pleading names Ashcroft as the "principal architect" of the policy, and identifies Mueller as "instrumental in [its] adoption, promulgation, and implementation."

In the sort of action brought by plaintiff, the Court declared that "to state a claim . . . respondent must plead sufficient factual matter to show that petitioners adopted and implemented the detention policies at issue not for a neutral, investigative reason but for the purpose of discriminating on account of race, religion, or national origin." Moreover, he would ultimately have to show that defendants acted with a discriminatory purpose; it would not be enough that they might have known of and acquiesced in discrimination by subordinates. The Court found that the complaint failed under *Twombly* to state a claim for relief against Ashcroft and Mueller.

Two working principles underlie our decision in *Twombly*. First, the tenet that a court must accept as true all of the allegations contained in a complaint is inapplicable to legal conclusions. Threadbare recitals of the elements of a cause of action, supported by mere conclusory statements, do not suffice. * * * Rule 8 marks a notable and generous departure from the hyper-technical, code-pleading regime of a prior era, but it does not unlock the doors of discovery for a plaintiff armed with nothing more than conclusions. Second, only a complaint that states a plausible claim for relief survives a motion to dismiss. Determining whether a complaint states a plausible claim for relief will, as the Court of Appeals observed, be a context-specific task that requires the reviewing court to draw on its judicial experience and common sense. But where the well-pleaded facts do not permit the court to infer more than the mere possibility of misconduct, the complaint has alleged — but it has not "show[n]" — "that the pleader is entitled to relief."

In keeping with these principles a court considering a motion to dismiss can choose to begin by identifying pleadings that, because they are no more than conclusions, are not entitled to the assumption of truth. While legal conclusions can provide the framework of a complaint, they must be supported by factual allegations. When there are well-pleaded factual allegations, a court should assume their veracity and then determine whether they plausibly give rise to an entitlement to relief.

Under *Twombly*'s construction of Rule 8, we conclude that respondent's complaint has not "nudged [his] claims" of invidious discrimination "across the line from conceivable to plausible." * * *

We begin our analysis by identifying the allegations in the complaint that are not entitled to the assumption of truth. Respondent pleads that petitioners "knew of, condoned, and willfully and maliciously agreed to subject [him]" to harsh conditions of confinement "as a matter of policy, solely on account of [his] religion, race, and/or national origin and for no legitimate penological interest." The complaint alleges that Ashcroft was the "principal architect" of this invidious policy, and that Mueller was "instrumental" in adopting and executing it. These bare assertions, much like the pleading of conspiracy in *Twombly,* amount to nothing more than a "formulaic recitation of the elements" of a constitutional discrimination claim, namely, that petitioners adopted a policy "'because of,' not merely 'in spite of,' its adverse effects upon an identifiable group." As such, the allegations are conclusory and not entitled to be assumed true. To be clear, we do not reject these bald allegations on the ground that they are unrealistic or nonsensical. We do not so characterize them any more than the Court in *Twombly* rejected the plaintiffs' express allegation of a "'contract, combination or conspiracy to prevent competitive entry,'" because it thought that claim too chimerical to be maintained. It is the conclusory nature of respondent's allegations, rather than their extravagantly fanciful nature, that disentitles them to the presumption of truth.

We next consider the factual allegations in respondent's complaint to determine if they plausibly suggest an entitlement to relief. The complaint alleges that "the [FBI], under the direction of Defendant Mueller, arrested and detained thousands of Arab Muslim men . . . as part of its investigation of the events of September 11." It further claims that "[t]he policy of holding post-September-11th detainees in highly restrictive conditions of confinement until they were 'cleared' by the FBI was approved by Defendants Ashcroft and Mueller in discussions in the weeks after September 11, 2001." Taken as true, these allegations are consistent with petitioners' purposefully designating detainees "of high interest" because of their race, religion, or national origin. But given more likely explanations, they do not plausibly establish this purpose.

The September 11 attacks were perpetrated by 19 Arab Muslim hijackers who counted themselves members in good standing of al Qaeda, an Islamic fundamentalist group. Al Qaeda was headed by another Arab Muslim — Osama bin Laden — and composed in large part of his Arab Muslim disciples. It should come as no surprise that a legitimate policy directing law enforcement to arrest and detain individuals because of their suspected link to the attacks would produce a disparate, incidental impact on Arab Muslims, even though the purpose of the policy was to target neither Arabs nor Muslims. On the facts respondent alleges the arrests Mueller oversaw were likely lawful and justified by his nondiscriminatory intent to detain aliens who were illegally present in the United States and who had potential connections to those who committed terrorist acts. As between that "obvious alternative explanation" for the arrests, and the purposeful, invidious discrimination respondent asks us to infer, discrimination is not a plausible conclusion.

But even if the complaint's well-pleaded facts give rise to a plausible inference that respondent's arrest was the result of unconstitutional discrimination, that inference alone would not entitle respondent to relief. It is important to recall that respondent's complaint challenges neither the constitutionality of his arrest nor his initial detention * * *. Respondent's constitutional claims against petitioners rest solely on their ostensible "policy of holding post-September-11th detainees" in the [maximum security facility] once they were categorized as "of high interest." To prevail on that theory, the complaint must contain facts plausibly showing that petitioners purposefully adopted a policy of classifying post-September-11 detainees as "of high interest" because of their race, religion, or national origin.

This the complaint fails to do. Though respondent alleges that various other defendants, who are not before us, may have labeled him a person of "of high interest" for impermissible reasons, his only factual allegation against petitioners accuses them of adopting a policy approving "restrictive conditions of confinement" for post-September-11 detainees until they were "'cleared' by the FBI." Accepting the truth of that allegation, the complaint does not show, or even intimate, that petitioners purposefully housed detainees in the [facility] due to their race, religion, or national origin. All it plausibly suggests is that the Nation's top law enforcement officers, in the aftermath of a devastating terrorist attack, sought to keep suspected terrorists in the most secure conditions available until the suspects could be cleared of terrorist activity. Respondent does not argue, nor can he, that such a motive would violate petitioners' constitutional obligations. He would need to allege more by way of factual content to "nudg[e]" his claim of purposeful discrimination "across the line from conceivable to plausible." * * *

It is important to note, however, that we express no opinion concerning the sufficiency of respondent's complaint against the defendants who are not before us. Respondent's account of his prison ordeal alleges serious official misconduct that we need not address here. Our decision is limited to the determination that respondent's complaint does not entitle him to relief from petitioners.

Justice Souter, who authored *Twombly*, dissented in an opinion for a four-Justice minority. He contended that the majority had "misundersood" *Twombly*'s command, and disagreed regarding its substantive assessment that there could be no supervisory liability in such cases.

Twombly does not require a court at the motion-to-dismiss stage to consider whether the factual allegations are probably true. We made it clear, on the contrary, that a court must take the allegations as true, no matter how skeptical the court may be. * * * The sole exception to this rule lies with allegations that are sufficiently fantastic to defy reality as we know it: claims about little green men, or the plaintiff's recent trip to Pluto, or experiences in time travel. That is not what we have here.

Under *Twombly,* the relevant question is whether, assuming the factual allegations are true, the plaintiff has stated a ground for relief that is plausible. That is, in *Twombly*'s words, a plaintiff must "allege facts" that, taken as true, are "suggestive of illegal conduct." * * * Here, by contrast, the allegations in the complaint are neither confined to naked legal conclusions nor consistent with legal conduct. The complaint alleges that FBI officials discriminated against Iqbal solely on account of his race, religion, and national origin, and it alleges the knowledge and deliberate indifference that, by Ashcroft and Mueller's own admission, are sufficient to make them liable for the illegal action. Iqbal's complaint therefore contains "enough facts to state a claim to relief that is plausible on its face."

8. Was the holding in *Iqbal* a step beyond *Twombly*, as the dissenters argued? One must still take the plaintiff's allegations as true in a motion under Rule 12(b)(6), but minus the "conclusory" allegations. At the pleading stage, are you sure you can spot a conclusory allegation from a nonconclusory one? How, for example, were the prisoner's allegations about cruel and unusual treatment in *Erickson v. Pardus, supra* (Note 6), *not* conclusory within the meaning of *Iqbal*? And what about the allegations of negligence in the automobile accident complaint set out in Federal Rules of Civil Procedure, Form 11?

9. In addition, as previously declared in *Twombly*, the claim inferred from the nonconclusory allegations must be a "plausible" one. What was implausible about the claim of discrimination alleged by the plaintiff in *Iqbal*?

10. In FIFTH THIRD BANCORP v. DUDENHOEFFER, 573 U.S. ___, 134 S.Ct. 2459, 189 L.Ed.2d 457 (2014), plaintiff employees brought suit against Fifth Third and certain of its officers for breach of fiduciary duty in managing an employee stock ownership plan (ESOP). They sued under federal retirement laws (ERISA) and alleged that defendants should have known—on the basis of public as well as inside information—that Fifth Third's stock was overpriced, that they should have sold it and ceased future purchases, or disclosed the negative inside information so that the stock price would be corrected downward. The district court dismissed the case for failure to state a claim, in part because it found that ESOP fiduciaries, unlike other ERISA fiduciaries, are entitled to a "presumption of prudence," which the plaintiffs' allegations could not overcome. The Sixth Circuit reversed. It found that although ESOP fiduciaries are entitled to a presumption of prudence at the trial stage, no such presumption was available at the pleading stage. Consequently, the court of appeals concluded that the plaintiffs had stated a claim for relief. The U.S. Supreme Court vacated and remanded, concluding that no such presumption was available at either stage, and—in Part IV of its opinion—the Court instructed the Sixth Circuit to reconsider whether plaintiff had stated a claim under the standards of *Twombly* and *Iqbal*.

The Court specifically asked that the appeals court to make its decision in light of the Court's following determinations: (1) An allegation that a fiduciary—on the basis of *publicly* available information—had acted imprudently in not recognizing that the market was mis-valuing the price of publicly traded stock, would be "implausible as a general rule," because fiduciaries, like individual investors, may ordinarily rely on the integrity of a stock's market price as reflecting the stock's underlying value; (2) To state a claim that defendants imprudently failed to act on the basis of *inside* information, the complaint must plausibly allege alternative, lawful actions that the fiduciary could have taken that could not be viewed as more likely to harm the fund that to help it. In determining the plausibility of the claim, the Court directed the lower courts to consider the extent to which insider trading prohibitions would constrain the fiduciary's decisions and the extent to which either cessation of purchases or public disclosure of inside information might do more harm than good by devaluing the stock already held in the fund.

11. Note that the language in the removal statute, 28 U.S.C. §1446(a), requires—as does Rule 8(a)(1)—a "short and plain statement" of the grounds for jurisdiction (for removal). Do the teachings of *Twombly* and *Iqbal* apply to the interpretation of §1446(a)? In DART CHEROKEE BASIC OPERATING CO. v. OWENS, 574 U.S. ___, 135 S.Ct. 574, 190 L.Ed.2d 495 (2014), the Court concluded that a removing defendant did not need to include, in his notice of removal of a class action, evidence showing that the requisite amount in controversy was met under the Class Action Fairness Act (see Chapter 10, sec. I). Rather, "[t]o assert the amount in controversy adequately in the removal notice," it would "suffice to allege the requisite amount plausibly," and the defendant need not "incorporate into the notice of removal evidence supporting the allegation. . . . A statement 'short and plain' need not contain evidentiary submissions." Cf. JOHNSON v. CITY OF SHELBY, 574 U.S. ___, 135 S.Ct. 346, 190 L.Ed.2d 309 (2014) (per curiam) (holding that complaint plausibly alleging constitutional violation actionable under 42 U.S.C. §1983 need not include a citation to §1983 itself.)

12. For a representative sampling of the considerable wave of scholarship (mostly negative) ushered in by *Twombly* and *Iqbal*, see the collection of articles in the symposium "Pondering *Iqbal*," at 14 LEWIS & CLARK L. REV. 1-309 (2010). For a somewhat less calamitous view, see Edward Hartnett, *Taming Twombly, Even After Iqbal*, 158 U. PA. L. REV. (2010).

3. FRAUD

Rule 9(b) requires that in all averments of fraud or mistake, "a party must state with particularity the circumstances constituting fraud or mistake." This clearly requires something more than under Rule 8 and *Conley*, but how much more? And, why are fraud and mistake singled out for special treatment? Reconsider these questions after the following case.

In Re Advanta Corp. Securities Litigation

United States Court of Appeals, Third Circuit, 1999.
180 F.3d 525.

SCIRICA, CIRCUIT JUDGE.

This is a securities class action lawsuit brought by shareholders of Advanta Corporation against the corporation and several of its officers. Plaintiffs allege the defendants made false and misleading statements and material omissions regarding the company's earnings potential and value of its stock, in violation of the Securities and Exchange Act of 1934. The District Court granted Advanta's motion to dismiss for failure to meet the pleading requirements of Fed. R. Civ. P. 9(b) and the Private Securities Litigation Reform Act of 1995, 15 U.S.C. §78u-4 et seq. (West Supp. 1999) (the "Reform Act"). We will affirm.

BACKGROUND

Plaintiffs are former shareholders of Advanta Corporation ("Advanta"), a leading issuer of MasterCard and VISA credit cards. Advanta forged its reputation in the credit card industry by innovating the practice of attracting new customers with unusually low introductory interest rates, known as "teaser rates," which remain in effect for a limited period of time, often six months. At the end of this period, the interest rate returns to a higher, permanent level. During the early and mid-1990s, Advanta used this practice to achieve rapid growth and earn large profits.

The focus of this litigation concerns a $20 million first-quarter loss that Advanta announced on March 17, 1997. According to plaintiffs' complaint, the loss was caused by Advanta's decision to implement aggressive techniques to attract new credit card customers. Specifically, plaintiffs allege Advanta began issuing cards with lower teaser rates and longer introductory periods than standard industry practice, resulting in riskier customers and, ultimately, a decrease in revenues as many of the new customers defaulted on their repayment obligations. The increased delinquency rates produced greater "charge-offs," which are the costs incurred by the credit card company when a card holder's balance becomes uncollectable.

Plaintiffs claim Advanta officers failed to disclose these practices despite knowledge of the risks involved, even after it became clear that losses were inevitable, and simultaneously made various statements that allegedly were false or materially misleading. Much of plaintiffs' complaint focuses on a statement made by Janet Point, Advanta's Vice President for Investor Relations, in a September 12, 1996 Dow Jones article. The article reads in part, "Over the next six months Advanta will experience a large increase in revenues as it converts more than $5 billion in accounts that are now at teaser rates of about 7% to its normal interest rate of about 17%, said Advanta spokeswoman Janet Point." This statement ("the Point statement") allegedly contradicts a subsequent statement by Dennis Alter, Advanta's chairman and former CEO ("the Alter statement"). In a June 1997 article entitled "House of Cards" that appeared in Philadelphia Magazine, Alter was quoted as saying: "What happened is when the introductory period ended, we were probably not as aggressive as we could have been [repricing our rates] . . . . Instead of repricing to 18 percent we repriced closer to 13 or 14 percent in order to retain our image and the luster of being a low-cost provider." Plaintiffs allege the Alter statement proves the Point statement was false and misleading, because the Point statement appears to indicate that Advanta was planning to reprice its teaser rates to 17 percent, yet the Alter statement apparently reveals that Advanta repriced to only 13 or 14 percent.

In addition, plaintiffs identify various statements portraying Advanta in what plaintiffs believe was an unduly positive light. These "positive portrayals" include the following statements, among others:

> (1) Advanta's 1996 third-quarter report states in part: "Our track record underscores our commitment to excel . . . [Advanta is] a rapidly growing customer financial services enterprise . . . . Despite challenging industry environment, we are pleased to report that Advanta produced continued, consistent earnings growth in the third quarter. . . . For the fifth consecutive year, return on equity has met or exceeded the 25% level achieved this quarter."

> (2) In a Form 10-Q filed on November 12, 1996, Advanta stated: "The changes in the delinquency and charge-off rates from year-to-year . . . reflect the trend in unsecured credit quality which is being experienced throughout the credit industry."

> (3) Announcing a shareholder dividend on November 13, 1996, Advanta released a statement reading in part, "This dividend increase reflects management's confidence in the company's earnings momentum and Advanta's continuing commitment to enhancing shareholder value."

> (4) On January 21, 1997, Advanta chairman Dennis Alter stated, "I am pleased to report that in 1996, Advanta maintained the growth of its current businesses and accelerated its expansion into new ventures."

According to plaintiffs, these statements were made with knowledge that they were false and misleading, and plaintiffs relied on them in deciding to buy (or not to sell) Advanta stock. Consequently, the complaint alleges that the positive portrayals constitute a violation of section 10(b) of the Securities Exchange Act of 1934 ("Exchange Act") and Rule 10b-5. * * *

On December 17, 1997, plaintiffs filed a complaint naming Advanta and seven of its present and former officers and directors as defendants. Count I of the complaint alleges the defendants are liable under Section 10(b) of the Exchange Act, 15 U.S.C.A. §78j(b) (West Supp. 1999), and Rule 10b-5 promulgated thereunder, 17 C.F.R. §240.10b-5 (1998), for the Point statement and the positive portrayals. Count II, based on the same factual allegations, asserts the liability of the individual defendants under section 20(a) of the Exchange Act. Count III asserts Weinberg's section 20(A) claim of contemporaneous trading against individual defendants Greenawalt and Marshall.

The District Court granted defendants' motions to dismiss all three counts. Specifically, the District Court held that Count I's claims based on the Point statement and the positive portrayals failed to meet the pleading requirements imposed by Fed. R. Civ. P. 9(b) and the Reform Act. The court dismissed these claims without prejudice and granted 30 days' leave for plaintiffs to amend their complaint. The court also dismissed without prejudice Counts II and III, holding that they were derivative of Count I. Rather than amend their complaint, plaintiffs elected to file a Notice of Intention to Stand on the Complaint, which the District Court construed as a request to dismiss the remaining claims with prejudice. By an order entered September 18, 1998, the District Court denied plaintiffs' request and this appeal followed.

ANALYSIS

A. Applicable Pleading Requirements

At the outset, we must determine the effect of the Reform Act on the pleading requirements governing securities fraud lawsuits, particularly with respect to pleading scienter. Plaintiffs argue the Reform Act codified the standard developed by the Court of Appeals for the Second Circuit. Under the Second Circuit standard, a plaintiff must plead facts supporting a "strong inference" that the defendant acted with the requisite scienter, by alleging either "facts establishing a motive to commit fraud and an opportunity to do so" or "facts constituting circumstantial evidence of either reckless or conscious behavior." Defendants argue the Reform Act establishes a pleading standard that is more stringent than all previously existing standards, including the Second Circuit's.

To date, two federal courts of appeals have concluded without analysis that the Reform Act codified the Second Circuit standard. Numerous district courts have considered the issue, with split results. A majority have held the Reform Act essentially codified the Second Circuit's approach. Others, including a district court of this circuit, have held the Act imposes an even more stringent pleading standard.

The Reform Act requires a plaintiff alleging a Rule 10b-5 violation to

> specify each statement alleged to have been misleading, the reason or reasons why the statement is misleading, and, if an allegation regarding the statement or omission is made on information and belief, the complaint shall state with particularity all facts on which that belief is formed.

15 U.S.C.A. §78u-4(b)(1) (West Supp. 1999). Regarding scienter, or knowledge, section 21D(b)(2) of the Reform Act provides:

> In any private action arising under this chapter in which the plaintiff may recover money damages only on proof that the defendant acted with a particular state of mind, the complaint shall, with respect to each act or omission alleged to violate this chapter, state with particularity facts giving rise to a strong inference that the defendant acted with the required state of mind.

Id. §78u-4(b)(2). Failure to meet these requirements will result in dismissal of the complaint. See id. §78u-4(b)(3)(A). Complaints alleging securities fraud must also comply with Rule 9(b), which provides: "In all averments of fraud or mistake, the circumstances constituting fraud or mistake shall be stated with particularity. Malice, intent, knowledge, and other condition of mind of a person may be averred generally." Fed. R. Civ. P. 9(b).[5]

Although the Reform Act's "strong inference" language mirrors the Second Circuit's, the precise extent to which Congress intended to adopt the Second Circuit standard is not clear. The Reform Act's legislative history on this point is ambiguous and even contradictory. The purpose of the Act was to restrict abuses in securities class-action litigation, including: (1) the practice of filing lawsuits against issuers of securities in response to any significant change in stock price, regardless of defendants' culpability; (2) the targeting of "deep pocket" defendants; (3) the abuse of the discovery process to coerce settlement; and (4) manipulation of clients by class action attorneys. * * *

President Clinton vetoed the Reform Act on the grounds that it imposed excessively stringent pleading requirements:

> I believe that the pleading requirements of the Conference Report with regard to a defendant's state of mind impose an unacceptable procedural hurdle to meritorious claims being heard in Federal courts. I am prepared to support the high pleading standards of the U.S. Court of Appeals for the Second Circuit — the highest pleading standard of any Federal circuit court. But the conferees make crystal clear in the Statement of Managers their intent to raise the standard even beyond that level. I am not prepared to accept that.

141 Cong. Rec. H15214 (daily ed. Dec. 20, 1995) (veto message of President Clinton). Subsequently, both houses of Congress overrode the President's veto and the Reform Act was enacted into law without changes to the pleading standard. * * *

Ultimately, we believe there is little to gain in attempting to reconcile the conflicting expressions of legislative intent, including the President's veto statement. The legislative history on this point is contradictory and inconclusive, and we are reluctant to accord it much weight. Accordingly, we direct our attention to the Reform Act's plain language, which is the customary starting point in statutory interpretation. The text of section 21D(b)(2) closely mirrors language employed by the Second Circuit, particularly as it requires the plaintiff to allege facts supporting a "strong inference" of scienter. * * * We believe Congress's use of the Second Circuit's language compels the conclusion that the Reform Act establishes a pleading standard approximately equal in stringency to that of the Second Circuit. Because the Second Circuit standard was regarded as the most restrictive prior the Reform Act, this interpretation is consistent with Congress's stated intent of strengthening pleading requirements and deterring

---

[5]	Rule 9(b)'s provision allowing state of mind to be averred generally conflicts with the Reform Act's requirement that plaintiffs "state with particularity facts giving rise to a strong inference" of scienter. In that sense, we believe the Reform Act supersedes Rule 9(b) as it relates to Rule 10b-5 actions.

frivolous securities litigation. Moreover, even in jurisdictions already employing the Second Circuit standard, the additional requirement that plaintiffs state facts "with particularity" represents a heightening of the standard. This language echoes precisely Fed. R. Civ. P. 9(b) and therefore requires plaintiffs to plead "the who, what, when, where, and how: the first paragraph of any newspaper story."

Although the Reform Act established a uniform pleading standard, it did not purport to alter the substantive contours of scienter. On this point, the legislative history is uncontradicted and reinforces the view that these provisions impose strictly procedural requirements. It also states that section 21D(b)(2) imposes a "heightened pleading standard" in response to disparate interpretations of Fed. R. Civ. P. 9(b), a procedural rule. Likewise, the floor debate and committee reports in both houses of Congress, as well as the President's veto statement, all describe the Reform Act as imposing new "pleading requirements." In view of the statutory language and supporting legislative history, we believe section 21D(b)(2) was intended to modify procedural requirements while leaving substantive law undisturbed.

Accordingly, we hold that it remains sufficient for plaintiffs plead scienter by alleging facts "establishing a motive and an opportunity to commit fraud, or by setting forth facts that constitute circumstantial evidence of either reckless or conscious behavior." Motive and opportunity, like all other allegations of scienter (intentional, conscious, or reckless behavior), must now be supported by facts stated "with particularity" and must give rise to a "strong inference" of scienter. These heightened pleading requirements address the previous ease of alleging motive and opportunity on the part of corporate officers to commit securities fraud. Permitting blanket assertions of motive and opportunity to serve as a basis for liability under the Exchange Act would undermine the more rigorous pleading standard Congress has established. After the Reform Act, catch-all allegations that defendants stood to benefit from wrongdoing and had the opportunity to implement a fraudulent scheme are no longer sufficient, because they do not state facts with particularity or give rise to a strong inference of scienter.

As for recklessness, we reiterate our previous holding that it remains a sufficient basis for liability. Retaining recklessness not only is consistent with the Reform Act's expressly procedural language, but also promotes the policy objectives of discouraging deliberate ignorance and preventing defendants from escaping liability solely because of the difficulty of proving conscious intent to commit fraud. A reckless statement is one "'involving not merely simple, or even inexcusable negligence, but an extreme departure from the standards of ordinary care, and which presents a danger of misleading buyers or sellers that is either known to the defendant or is so obvious that the actor must have been aware of it.'" We also note that scienter may be alleged by stating with particularity facts giving rise to a strong inference of conscious wrongdoing, such as intentional fraud or other deliberate illegal behavior.

We now turn to the particulars of plaintiffs' complaint.

B. The Point Statement

Plaintiffs contend the Point statement subjects Advanta to liability under section 10(b) of the Exchange Act, which makes it unlawful for any person to "use or employ, in connection with the purchase or sale of any security, . . . any manipulative or deceptive device or contrivance in contravention of such rules and regulations as the Commission may prescribe." Rule 10b-5, in turn, makes it unlawful to "make any untrue statement of a material fact or to omit to state a material fact necessary in order to make the statements made in the light of the circumstances under which they were made, not misleading . . . in connection with the purchase or sale of any security." These provisions create a private right of action for plaintiffs to recover damages for "false or misleading statements or omissions of material fact that affect trading on the secondary market."

The Reform Act establishes a safe harbor protecting certain "forward-looking" statements from Rule 10b-5 liability. Regarding statements made by natural persons (as opposed to business entities), the Act provides that a forward-looking statement is shielded by the safe-harbor provision unless the plaintiff proves it was made with "actual knowledge . . . that the statement was false or misleading." The District Court held the Point statement was forward-looking and qualified for protection under the Act because "plaintiffs' catch-all allegation that all speakers knew their statements were false when made is too broad and Alter's comments indicate nothing more than Advanta's failure to follow through exactly as planned on its proposed interest increase, rather than purposeful intent to fool the public." The Advanta shareholders contend that the Point statement was not forward-looking, and that even if it was, it was made with actual knowledge of its false and misleading nature and therefore does not qualify for protection.

Under the Reform Act, a statement is forward-looking if, inter alia, it is "a statement containing a projection of revenues, income (including income loss), earnings (including earnings loss) per share, capital expenditures, dividends, capital structure, or other financial items." The first portion of the Point statement reads, "Over the next six months Advanta will experience a large increase in revenues. . . ." In our view, this portion of the statement clearly qualifies as "a projection of revenues" and therefore is forward-looking. The remaining portion of the statement, "as [Advanta] converts more than $5 billion in accounts that are now at teaser rates of about 7% to its normal interest rate of about 17%," is a statement of Advanta's plan to reprice its teaser-rate accounts to a rate of about 17%. We believe this part of the statement is forward-looking as well, because it is "a statement of the plans and objectives of management for future operations, including plans or objectives relating to the products or services of the issuer." Consequently, we hold that the entire Point statement is "forward-looking" within the meaning of the Act.

Nonetheless, the safe harbor will not apply if the statement was made with "actual knowledge" that the statement was false or misleading. Plaintiffs argue the falsity of the Point statement is proved by Dennis Alter's subsequent comment that "we were probably not as aggressive as we could have been [repricing our rates] . . . Instead of repricing to 18 percent we repriced closer to

13 or 14 percent in order to retain our image and the luster of being a low-cost provider." Because Point was Advanta's spokesperson, plaintiffs argue, she must have possessed actual knowledge that Advanta was not repricing to 17 percent, but only 13 or 14 percent, at the time the statement was made. Plaintiffs further contend that even if Point did not possess actual knowledge, the failure of Advanta's executives to repudiate the statement constituted a ratification of it.

The complaint does not plead any specific facts to support an inference that Point, or anyone else at Advanta, had actual knowledge of her statement's falsity. The complaint's only specific factual allegation regarding the falsity of the Point statement is the existence of the Alter statement some nine months later. But the Point statement and the Alter statement are not inconsistent: Point stated in September 1996 that Advanta planned to reprice its teaser rates to 17%; nine months later, Alter expressed regret that Advanta did not reprice to that level. Even assuming the two statements referred to precisely the same accounts, it does not follow that Point's statement was false: Advanta may have intended to reprice the accounts to 17 percent at the time of the Point statement and subsequently changed its business strategy. As the defendants point out, Advanta owed no duty to update the Point statement. See 15 U.S.C.A. §78u-5(d) (West 1999) ("Nothing in this section shall impose upon any person a duty to update a forward-looking statement."); In re Burlington Coat Factory, 114 F.3d 1410 (3d Cir. 1977) ("The voluntary disclosure of an ordinary earnings forecast does not trigger any duty to update.").[9] At best, comparison of the Point and Alter statements suggests that Advanta made a series of unwise business decisions in its attempt to attract new customers. But section 10(b) does not "'regulate transactions which constitute no more than internal corporate mismanagement.'"

Plaintiffs' complaint fails to plead any other facts supporting an inference that the Point statement was made with "actual knowledge" of its falsity. Accordingly, we believe the statement was protected by the safe-harbor provision for forward-looking statements.

C. The "Positive Portrayals"

Next, we consider whether plaintiffs adequately pleaded a cause of action relating to the "positive portrayals" made by Advanta and its officers. To state a securities fraud claim under section 10(b) and rule 10b-5, a private plaintiff must plead the following elements: "(1) that the defendant made a misrepresentation or omission of (2) a material (3) fact; (4) that the defendant acted with knowledge or recklessness and (5) that the plaintiff reasonably relied on the misrepresentation or omission and (6) consequently suffered damage." In re Westinghouse Sec. Litig., 90 F.3d 696, 710 (3d Cir. 1996).

Plaintiffs' amended complaint identifies a number of representations alleged to satisfy these criteria. In addition to those set forth above (upon which the

---

[9] We also reject plaintiffs' argument that the Alter statement, along with proposed corrective measures announced by Advanta in the wake of the $20 million loss, constitute "admissions" of securities fraud liability. If this were so, all companies that suffer losses and then publicly discuss how they plan to improve earnings in the future would be guilty of admissions that they defrauded investors.

District Court focused its analysis), the complaint identifies the following statements:

(1) An April 1996 letter to shareholders, signed by defendants Hart, Alter, Greenawalt and Rosoff, stated:

Advanta's credit quality continues to be among the best in the industry. Our emphasis on gold cards — and targeting of high quality customer prospects with great potential for profitability — sets us apart from other credit card issuers.

The Company is among the most efficient producers in the credit card industry. Our superior cost structure for delivering and servicing financial products allows us to achieve outstanding returns with highly competitive pricing and flexibility.

The letter also touted Advanta's strengths, including "an experienced management team, technological expertise . . . and expanding distribution channels."

(2) Advanta's 1995 Annual Report included the following representations regarding the quality of its credit portfolio:

While we added substantially to our account base, our credit quality remained excellent.

. . .

Our emphasis on gold cards — and targeting of better quality customers — helps us maintain an enviable credit quality profile. Gold cards made up 82% of our credit card balances in 1995, nearly double the industry average.

The 1995 Annual Report also referred to Advanta's "risk-adjusted pricing strategy" in which "credit cards are issued with lower rates to customers whose credit quality is expected to result in a lower rate of credit losses."

(3) A July 18, 1996 letter to shareholders, again signed by defendants Alter, Hart, Greenawalt and Rosoff, stated that "despite industry-wide pressure on credit card asset quality, Advanta continued to produce better-than-industry credit measures, and achieved excellent growth and returns throughout our core businesses."

(4) A Form 8-K filed with the SEC on October 17, 1996 and signed by defendant Schneyer stated, "The Company's credit card asset quality statistics continue to be better than industry averages."

According to plaintiffs, these statements (as well as those set forth supra, Part I) were materially false and misleading because they failed to disclose the deterioration in credit quality allegedly caused by Advanta's aggressive efforts to attract new customers. The District Court held the statements do not prove Advanta intentionally misled or defrauded investors, but only that profits failed to live up to expectations. Consequently, the court rejected plaintiffs' arguments as "attempts to plead fraud by hindsight." Id.

Rule 10b-5 liability does not attach merely because "at one time the firm bathes itself in a favorable light" but "later the firm discloses that things are less rosy." Rather, the plaintiff must demonstrate that the loss was attributable to the defendant's fraudulent conduct. As noted, the Reform Act requires plaintiffs to "specify each statement alleged to have been misleading, the reason or reasons why the statement is misleading, and, if an allegation regarding the statement or omission is made on information and belief, the complaint shall state with particularity all facts on which that belief is formed." Furthermore, the complaint must "state with particularity facts giving rise to a strong inference that the defendant acted with the required state of mind."

The complaint here alleges that during the time period in which Advanta issued the positive portrayals, the company implemented policies relaxing its underwriting and monitoring procedures and "superior credit risk customers were switching to other credit card companies at rates that would have a materially negative impact on the Company's reported earnings." Elsewhere, it alleges that Advanta changed its methodology for computing bankruptcy charge-offs without promptly disclosing this change to the marketplace; that Advanta repriced its teaser rates to 13 or 14 percent rather than its normal rate of 17 percent, causing a substantial decline in revenues; and that Advanta lacked adequate collection capability to support the expansion in its customer base. According to plaintiffs, the juxtaposition of these alleged facts against the positive portrayals shows that the statements were materially misleading when made.

We disagree. Even assuming plaintiffs' allegations are true, the positive portrayals do not contradict any of defendants' other statements but merely report previous successes and express confidence in Advanta's prospects for future growth. Factual recitations of past earnings, so long as they are accurate, do not create liability under Section 10(b). Similarly, vague and general statements of optimism "constitute no more than 'puffery' and are understood by reasonable investors as such." Such statements, even if arguably misleading, do not give rise to a federal securities claim because they are not material: there is no "substantial likelihood that the disclosure of the omitted fact would have been viewed by the reasonable investor as having significantly altered the 'total mix' of information made available." The representations identified by plaintiffs fall entirely into these categories: accurate reports of past earnings, and non-actionable expressions of optimism for the future. We are skeptical that plaintiffs or any other reasonable investors would make investment decisions based on the positive portrayals.

Even if the positive portrayals were materially misleading, we believe the complaint suffers a more fundamental defect in that it fails to satisfy the Reform Act's requirements for pleading scienter. Rather than state with particularity facts supporting a strong inference that defendants possessed the requisite scienter, plaintiffs offer conclusory assertions that the defendants acted "knowingly," as well as blanket statements that defendants must have been aware of the impending losses by virtue of their positions within the company. It is well established that a pleading of scienter "may not rest on a bare inference that a defendant 'must have had' knowledge of the facts." Likewise, allegations that a securities-fraud defendant, because of his position within the company, "must have known" a statement was false or misleading are "precisely the types of inferences which [courts], on numerous occasions, have determined to be inadequate to withstand Rule 9(b) scrutiny." Generalized imputations of knowledge do not suffice, regardless of the defendants' positions within the company. In re Ancor Communications, Inc. Sec. Litig., 22 F. Supp. 2d 999 (D. Minn. 1998), relied upon by plaintiffs, does not suggest otherwise. There the court inferred that key officers were aware their product would likely prove incompatible with the products of another company with whom Ancor had entered into a supply contract. The court expressly based its holding on the facts that the contract "was undeniably the most significant contract in Ancor's history," thus supporting an unusually strong inference of scienter, and that plaintiffs' complaint also cited extrinsic evidence such as discussions among officers regarding product incompatibility and an escape clause in the supply agreement governing this contingency. Such considerations are not present here.

Plaintiffs also argue that even if defendants did not intentionally mislead investors, they recklessly disregarded negative trends in the credit card industry and in Advanta's customer base, and therefore possessed the requisite scienter. In particular, plaintiffs contend the positive portrayals were reckless in light of industry-wide increases in personal bankruptcies and charge-offs, especially as exacerbated by Advanta's alleged decisions to reprice introductory rates to only 13 or 14 percent and to relax underwriting and monitoring practices. We disagree. For purposes of the scienter requirement of Section 10(b) and Rule 10b-5, we have [chosen to adopt a] definition of a reckless statement as one "'involving not merely simple, or even inexcusable negligence, but an extreme departure from the standards of ordinary care, and which presents a danger of misleading buyers or sellers that is either known to the defendant or is so obvious that the actor must have been aware of it.'" Plaintiffs' allegations, even if true, would not demonstrate an "extreme departure" from the standards of ordinary care. At most, the complaint demonstrates that Advanta embarked on a business strategy of aggressively recruiting new customers without adequately accounting for the increased risk this endeavor posed. None of the facts in the complaint suggests this strategy represented an egregious departure from the range of reasonable business decisions, as opposed to simple mismanagement. But "claims essentially grounded on corporate mismanagement are not cognizable under federal law." Accordingly, we find that the positive portrayals do not support a strong inference of recklessness.

The complaint's remaining allegation regarding scienter is that several of the individual defendants — most prominently, Richard Greenawalt, Dennis Alter, Robert Marshall, and Gene Schneyer — sold large blocks of their Advanta stock during November and December 1996, approximately three months before the $20 million loss was announced to the marketplace. Plaintiffs allege these transactions suggest defendants knew of the impending first-quarter loss or at least had the motive and opportunity to commit fraud. The complaint sets forth the dates, numbers of shares, and proceeds of the sales.

We have held that "we will not infer fraudulent intent from the mere fact that some officers sold stock." But if the stock sales were unusual in scope or timing, they may support an inference of scienter. In *Burlington Coat Factory*, we found the stock sales did not permit an inference of scienter because only three of the five defendants sold stock, plaintiffs provided information on the total stock holdings of only one defendant who had traded only 0.5 percent of his holdings, and plaintiffs failed to plead facts indicating whether such trades were "normal and routine" for the defendants and whether the trading profits were substantial in comparison to their overall compensation.

Here, three of the individual defendants sold no stock at all during the class period, raising doubt whether the sales were motivated by an intent to profit from inflated stock prices before the upcoming losses were reported. In addition, although the complaint fails to provide information on the percentage of total holdings sold by the defendants, it appears the defendants who did trade stock during the class period sold only small percentages of their holdings. According to Form 45s that were filed with the SEC and attached to Advanta's motion to dismiss, Schneyer and Alter sold only 7 percent and 5 percent, respectively, of their total holdings. Alter, in particular, continued to hold a sizable percentage of Advanta's outstanding stock even after the 1996 sales. Far from supporting a "strong inference" that defendants had a motive to capitalize on artificially inflated stock prices, these facts suggest they had every incentive to keep Advanta profitable.

Nor were the sales at issue particularly large in comparison to the individual defendants' previous trading practices. The complaint alleges that Greenawalt, Alter, Marshall, and Schneyer sold a total of 1,023,766 shares during the eight-month class period, as compared to 580,814 during the previous 28 months. It makes no reference to the previous trading practices of the other individual defendants. Although the profits realized by the defendants were significant relative to their base salaries, these proceeds were the result of accumulated stock options and were an intended part of their overall compensation package. As we recognized in *Burlington Coat Factory*, "[a] large number of today's corporate executives are compensated in terms of stock and stock options. It follows then that these individuals will trade those securities in the normal course of events."

Thus, we hold that the allegations concerning defendants' stock transactions do not permit a strong inference of scienter, as required by the Reform Act.[11] Nor have plaintiffs alleged other specific facts supporting such an inference. Consequently, we believe the claims relating to positive portrayals fail to comply with statutory pleading requirements and were correctly dismissed. * * *

CONCLUSION

The District Court correctly dismissed plaintiffs' claim based upon the Point statement because the statement was protected by the Reform Act's safe-harbor provision. The remaining claims in Count I failed to comply with the pleading requirements of the Reform Act, and the section 20(A) claim is derivative of Count I. Accordingly, these claims were properly dismissed as well.

We will affirm the judgment of the District Court.

---

[11] Because the complaint fails to meet the pleading requirements of the Reform Act, we need not address whether it also fails to meet the requirements of Fed. R. Civ. P. 9(b).

NOTES AND PROBLEMS FOR DISCUSSION

1. The *Advanta Securities* case, as is true of most securities fraud cases, is complex. Start with a chart. Consider first the elements of the plaintiffs' claim and which of them were the subject of this pleading motion. Then, consider what the plaintiffs alleged with respect to each element. What was wrong with their allegations?

2. The Private Securities Reform Act is explicit about requiring the pleadings to serve a gatekeeping role. Under the Act, what are proper pleadings a gateway to?

3. Assume for the moment that Advanta engaged in serious wrongdoing, beyond what was alleged in the complaint. How will plaintiffs find out?

4. The *Advanta Securities* case was decided under the Reform Act. How would it have come out under Rule 9(b)? As noted in *Advanta Securities*, the Reform Act was vetoed by President Clinton. It is the only legislation passed over such a veto during his two terms in office.

5. In Dura Pharmaceuticals v. Broudo, 544 U.S. 336, 125 S.Ct. 1627, 161 L.Ed.2d 277 (2004), the Supreme Court found that a complaint in a securities fraud case fell below even the liberal standard of *Conley v. Gibson, supra*. The complaint alleged merely that the plaintiff had paid "artificially inflated" prices for the defendant's publicly traded stock, after defendant had made various fraudulent misrepresentations about the stock and that plaintiff had relied on the market fairly to reflect the price of the stock. The Court found that, as a matter of substantive law, merely paying an inflated price was not itself a compensable loss. The loss, if any, would only come at a point of sale. Also, under the substantive law, the plaintiff would eventually have to prove both loss as well as causation (i.e., that the loss was caused by the defendant's fraud). In addition to failing to allege and thereby apprise the defendant of what her losses were, plaintiff had failed to allege how defendant's acts had caused whatever that loss was.

6. In TELLABS v. MAKOR ISSUES & RIGHTS, LTD., 551 U.S. 308, 127 S.Ct. 2499, 168 L.Ed.2d 179 (2007), the Supreme Court fleshed out the precise meaning of section 21D(b)(2) of the 1995 Private Securities Litigation Reform Act that was at issue in *Advanta*, and which requires the pleader to state, with particularity, facts that give rise to a "strong inference" of scienter — i.e., the defendant's intention to deceive, misrepresent, or defraud. The Court concluded that this requirement meant that the facts alleged in the plaintiff's complaint must show more than that scienter is a plausible or reasonable inference. Instead, it meant that the complaint had to show that the inference of scienter was a "cogent" or "powerful" one, and at least as compelling as any other possible (innocent) inference that might be drawn from the alleged facts. This, in turn, requires courts to engage in a comparative assessment of the strength of other competing inferences.

> We establish the following prescriptions: *First*, faced with a Rule 12(b)(6) motion to dismiss a § 10(b) action [under the Securities Exchange Act of 1934], courts must, as with any motion to dismiss for failure to

plead a claim on which relief can be granted, accept all factual allegations in the complaint as true. * * *

Second, courts must consider the complaint in its entirety, as well as other sources courts ordinarily examine when ruling on Rule 12(b)(6) motions to dismiss, in particular, documents incorporated into the complaint by reference, and matters of which a court may take judicial notice. * * * The inquiry, as several Courts of Appeals have recognized, is whether *all* of the facts alleged, taken collectively, give rise to a strong inference of scienter, not whether any individual allegation, scrutinized in isolation, meets that standard. * * *

Third, in determining whether the pleaded facts give rise to a "strong" inference of scienter, the court must take into account plausible opposing inferences. The Seventh Circuit expressly declined to engage in such a comparative inquiry. A complaint could survive, that court said, as long as it "alleges facts from which, if true, a reasonable person could infer that the defendant acted with the required intent"; in other words, only "[i]f a reasonable person could not draw such an inference from the alleged facts" would the defendant prevail on a motion to dismiss. But in § 21D(b)(2), Congress did not merely require plaintiffs to "provide a factual basis for [their] scienter allegations," * * * *i.e.*, to allege facts from which an inference of scienter rationally *could* be drawn. Instead, Congress required plaintiffs to plead with particularity facts that give rise to a "strong" — *i.e.*, a powerful or cogent — inference. * * *

The strength of an inference cannot be decided in a vacuum. The inquiry is inherently comparative: How likely is it that one conclusion, as compared to others, follows from the underlying facts? To determine whether the plaintiff has alleged facts that give rise to the requisite "strong inference" of scienter, a court must consider plausible nonculpable explanations for the defendant's conduct, as well as inferences favoring the plaintiff. The inference that the defendant acted with scienter need not be irrefutable, *i.e.*, of the "smoking-gun" genre, or even the "most plausible of competing inferences," * * * Recall in this regard that § 21D(b)'s pleading requirements are but one constraint among many the PSLRA installed to screen out frivolous suits, while allowing meritorious actions to move forward. Yet the inference of scienter must be more than merely "reasonable" or "permissible" — it must be cogent and compelling, thus strong in light of other explanations. A complaint will survive, we hold, only if a reasonable person would deem the inference of scienter cogent and at least as compelling as any opposing inference one could draw from the facts alleged.

When one combines *Tellabs* (a strict pleading case) with *Twombly* (nominally not a strict pleading case*)* — both decided in the same Term — is the impression not irresistible that the Supreme Court was trying to say something about the direction that pleadings should take in the future? Did *Iqbal* confirm that impression?

4. RULE 11

Rule 11 attempts to deal comprehensively with the conduct of parties and lawyers in litigation. It raises numerous questions which are fundamental to the legal system, including the proper role of a lawyer, whether vigorous representation can be distinguished from overzealous advocacy, whether the lawyer has duties to the court that are separate from client representation, the rationale for and effectiveness of sanctions, and whether it is possible to make close calls on these issues in the heat of litigation.

Some version of Rule 11 has been in the Federal Rules from the start. The original version had little effect on the conduct of litigation since courts required proof of subjective bad faith to impose sanctions, an almost impossible showing. In 1983, the Rule was amended to change the standard (under the amended rule, the attorney was taken to certify that a pleading or other paper was well grounded in fact and warranted by existing law or a good faith argument for change, "after reasonable inquiry") and to make compensatory sanctions (i.e., attorneys' fees against the wrongdoer) virtually mandatory for a violation. The Supreme Court interpreted the new rule as requiring sanctions to be determined by an "objective" standard of reasonableness under all the circumstances. Business Guides, Inc. v. Chromatic Communications Enterprises, Inc., 498 U.S. 533, 111 S.Ct. 922, 112 L.Ed.2d 1140 (1991).

The amended Rule 11 dramatically changed the litigation landscape. As might be expected, not only did the number of sanctions motions increase dramatically, but the threatening of sanctions motions and the inclusion of sanctions motions in responses to motions filed by adversaries, became a standard litigation tactic. Moreover, the practical impact of a sanctions motion by one party was often a cross-motion for sanctions by her adversary. As applied to pleading issues, the amended rule was interpreted to require the plaintiff's attorney to conduct a reasonable prefiling investigation of the facts, and to conduct at least some legal research on the law.

The 1983 rule proved extremely controversial as motions and cross-motions for sanctions flooded the courts. As applied to pleading issues, and especially the filing of complaints, the requirement of a reasonable prefiling investigation seemed to prevent the filing of complaints solely on the basis of information supplied by the client, and it had particular bite when the facts were in the hands of others (especially the alleged wrongdoers). See, e.g., Judin v. United States, 110 F.3d 780 (Fed. Cir. 1997) (attorney filed a patent case involving optical scanners on the basis of information of the client who was "highly knowledgeable in the field of optical scanners"; court directed imposition of sanctions for inadequate investigation). The Rule increased the "front end" costs of litigation (by requiring up-front expenditures, and preventing primary reliance on post-complaint discovery), and thus partially undermined doctrines of notice pleading and permitting the case to develop by discovery. In addition, it also led to a potential Rule 11 issue every time a Rule 12(b)(6) or Rule 56 motion was granted. Consider whether, for example, under the 1983 rule, motions for sanctions should be granted on the facts of *Dartmouth College* or *Advanta Securities*.

In 1993, and later with the Dec. 1, 2007 stylistic revisions, Rule 11 was amended to its present form. The parties' obligations were more specifically defined and somewhat softened, the sanctions provisions were changed to emphasize deterrence rather than compensation, a "safe-harbor" provision was introduced, sanctions were made discretionary, and a separate motion was required to obtain sanctions. (Make sure you understand why a separate motion requirement has the effect of deterring Rule 11 motions.) As particularly applicable to pleadings, the "law" provision (Rule 11(b)(2)) was modified by adding a test of "nonfrivolous argument" for new legal theories, and the "fact" provision of 11(b)(3) was modified by permitting allegations that "are likely to have evidentiary support after a reasonable opportunity for further investigation or discovery."

Rule 11 is by no means limited to pleadings, but several parts of it specifically address pleading issues, and it has had major impact in the pleading area. One purpose of the earlier (1983) version of the Rule, of course, was to deter the filing of nonmeritorious claims and defenses. Of course, whether a claim or defense is sufficiently meritorious to be asserted, is often in the eye of the beholder — especially in a system that permits notice pleading and broad discovery. And despite the choppy subsequent history associated with the 1993 revisions, there have sometimes been rumblings in Congress portending a possible return to mandatory sanctions.

Read Rule 11(b) in light of what you have learned about pleadings thus far. Note that Rule 11(b)(1) deals with the purpose of the pleading, (b)(2) deals with legal contentions, and (b)(3) and (4) deal with factual allegations.

Seawright v. Charter Furniture Rental, Inc.

United States District Court, Northern District of Texas, 1999.

39 F. Supp. 2d 795.

KENDALL, DISTRICT JUDGE.

[Seawright was an account manager for Charter, a company engaged in the furniture leasing business. In 1985 Seawright began living with and having a homosexual relationship with John Hull, and Seawright made "every effort" to conceal the relationship from Charter and its employees. In 1993, Hull developed AIDS, and by early 1995, Hull was unable to work and had "numerous medical problems." Seawright was Hull's primary care giver.

On a number of occasions, Seawright lied about his relationship with Hull and about Hull's illness. Among other things, Seawright said Hull was his roommate and that he had a girlfriend, and that Hull had colon cancer. Later, Seawright said that Hull had died and requested a leave to attend the funeral (which was granted); in fact, Seawright went to visit Hull who had then moved to his parents' house.

During his employment Seawright received various warnings about his performance, which included inadequate sales, nondelivery of orders, failure to process leases for delivery, failure to fulfill commitments to employees, and failure to perform his duties respecting showroom shifts. (It appears, although the opinion is not clear, that these difficulties coincided with Hull's illness and the care being provided by Seawright). Ultimately, Seawright was fired.

Seawright brought an action against Charter for violation of the Americans With Disabilities Act (ADA). He claimed that he had a disability (AIDS or possible AIDS), or that Hull had a disability and that Seawright was thus a person associated with a person with a disability and that this gave him various rights under the ADA. In either event, Seawright had to establish either that Charter knew he had a disability or that Hull had a disability and Seawright was an "associate with a disability." Both of these determinations turned on whether Charter knew (1) of the relationship between Seawright and Hull, and (2) that Hull had AIDS.

The Court initially granted Charter summary judgment finding that Charter did not know either of these facts. Seawright alleged that Charter knew these facts because he had told two employees, but Charter established that these two employees had not communicated the facts to anyone else. Seawright also claimed that Charter knew because "it's a family-owned business where there's a lot of 'talk' about everything," but the Court found that this was "speculation and conjecture." Instead, the Court found that Seawright had lied about these matters.

The Court then granted Charter attorneys' fees as against Seawright pursuant to a specific statutory provision in the ADA. Specifically, the Court found Seawright knew that the claims were frivolous, lied to Charter about his relationship with Hull and Hull's illness ("spun a web of lies"), had no information that Charter knew the real facts, and knew that he had been consistently warned about his poor performance and told that he would be terminated if there was no improvement. The Court further found that Charter had warned Seawright that if he continued to pursue the action, it would seek to recover attorneys' fees.

The Court then turned to Charter's motion for sanctions against Seawright's counsel.]

* * *

MOTIONS FOR ATTORNEYS' FEES

Charter seeks its reasonable and necessary attorneys' fees and expenses from Seawright as the prevailing party under the ADA. Charter also seeks its reasonable and necessary attorneys' fees and expenses from Seawright's counsel, alleging that she failed to perform a proper pre-filing investigation as required by Rule 11 and that she continued to pursue a frivolous lawsuit.

Attorneys' Fees as to Seawright

The ADA provides that the Court, "in its discretion, may allow the prevailing party, other than the United States, a reasonable attorney's fee, including litigation expenses, and costs . . . ." 42 U.S.C. §12205. The standard for awarding fees to a prevailing defendant/employer is higher than for a prevailing plaintiff; a district court may in its discretion award attorneys' fees to a prevailing defendant only if the court finds that the plaintiff's claim was "frivolous, unreasonable, or groundless, or that the plaintiff continued to litigate after it clearly became so." Christiansburg Garment Co. v. EEOC, 434 U.S. 412, 421-22, 54 L.Ed. 2d 648, 98 S.Ct. 694 (1978); See also Adkins v. Briggs & Stratton Corp., 159 F.3d 306, 307 (7th Cir. 1998); Summers v. A. Teichert & Son, Inc., 127 F.3d 1150, 1154 (9th Cir. 1997). The Court need not find subjective bad faith on the plaintiff's part to award fees to the prevailing defendant, but if the plaintiff is found to have brought or continued his claim in bad faith, "there will be an even stronger basis for charging him with the attorney's fees incurred by the defense." *Christiansburg Garment Co.*, 434 U.S. at 422.

The Court concludes that Seawright knew at the time he filed his lawsuit that his claims were frivolous, unreasonable, and groundless, and also concludes that Seawright brought this suit in bad faith. Specifically, Seawright knew when he brought this lawsuit that he had lied to Charter about his true relationship with his roommate Hull, about Hull having HIV, about Hull dying of cancer and not AIDS, and about the date of Hull's death. Seawright also knew when he brought this lawsuit that he had no personal knowledge that anyone in Charter management knew the truth concerning any of the matters about which he had consistently lied. The summary judgment evidence demonstrated that Charter dealt with Seawright in good faith, while Seawright spun a web of lies and then filed suit contending that Charter couldn't have actually believed those lies.[21]

Finally, Seawright knew when he brought this lawsuit that he had had several disciplinary meetings with Charter management prior to being discharged. In the months just prior to Seawright's termination, his sales were down, his customers were not getting their furniture delivered on time, leases were sitting on his desk unprocessed, he was missing showroom shifts, and he was coming in late for the shifts he did work.[22] Seawright had been warned verbally and in writing about his performance problems and had been admonished that his employment would be terminated if the problems were not corrected.

Charter repeatedly cautioned Seawright that if he continued to pursue this action, Charter would seek its attorneys' fees. Charter is a small, family-owned business, and the defense costs it was forced to incur are substantial. Regardless of whether Seawright pursued this frivolous, groundless, and unreasonable lawsuit because of some vendetta against his former employer or as merely a shakedown to extract a settlement the Court concludes that he initiated and then

---

[21] Seawright denies any improper motive in bringing the lawsuit by arguing: "To maintain a lawsuit against Charter, Mr. Seawright was forced to reveal the extent of his relationship with his roommate. This revelation was extremely difficult for him and required a complete conviction to his belief that he had been discriminated against." Plaintiff's Response to Defendant's Rule 11 Motion at 7. Yet Seawright alleged in his lawsuit that everyone at Charter (a small office) already knew the truth about his relationship with Hull, which he claimed led to Charter's discrimination against him in violation of the ADA.

[22] In his response, Seawright acknowledges that his sales numbers were "slipping," but argues that they were still at or above the level of his co-workers. Seawright repeatedly attempts to persuade the Court to focus solely on sales numbers. This is not surprising, as Seawright apparently doesn't dispute these other serious performance deficiencies.

continued to pursue this lawsuit in bad faith.[23]   See Schutts v. Bently Nevada Corp., 966 F. Supp. 1549, 1557 (D. Nev. 1997). This determination was made according to the standard Seawright requested, that the Court "should not look at the results, but rather examine the reasonableness of the Plaintiff's claims going into the lawsuit." The Court hereby grants Charter's motion for attorneys' fees, and pursuant to 42 U.S.C. §12205, the Court orders Seawright to pay the sum of $29,809.00 to prevailing party Charter for the reasonable and necessary attorneys' fees Charter incurred in defending this case.

Attorneys' Fees as to Seawright's Counsel

Charter asserts that Seawright's counsel, Janette Johnson, failed to conduct a proper pre-filing investigation as required by Rule 11(b), which would have revealed that the allegations and other factual contentions Johnson set forth in Seawright's Complaint had no evidentiary support and were unlikely to have evidentiary support after a reasonable opportunity for further investigation and discovery. Charter contends that had Johnson conducted a proper pre-filing investigation, she would have realized the truth of what Charter management and counsel stressed at the Rule 26(f) meeting held shortly after she filed suit: that Charter had legitimate, nondiscriminatory reasons for discharging Seawright and that because of Seawright's lies to Charter, Charter had no knowledge of Seawright's true relationship with Hull or the real cause of Hull's death. Charter submits that after Johnson compelled Charter to incur more than $30,000 in attorney's fees and expenses in defending this lawsuit, she did not obtain any new evidence different from what was learned at the Rule 26(f) meeting and what she should have learned in a pre-filing investigation.

Rule 11(b) of the Federal Rules of Civil Procedure provides that by presenting to the court a pleading, motion, or other paper, an attorney is certifying that to the best of his knowledge, information, and belief, formed after an inquiry reasonable under the circumstances,

> (1) it is not being presented for any improper purpose, such as to harass or to cause unnecessary delay or needless increase in the cost of litigation;
>
> (2) the claims, defenses, and other legal contentions therein are warranted by existing law or by a nonfrivolous argument for the extension, modification, or reversal of existing law or the establishment of new law;
>
> (3) the allegations and other factual contentions have evidentiary support or, if specifically so identified, are likely to have evidentiary support after a reasonable opportunity for further investigation or discovery; and
>
> (4) the denials of factual contentions are warranted on the evidence or, if specifically so identified, are reasonably based on a lack of

---

[23] Under the heading of "no good deed goes unpunished," Seawright argues that because Charter didn't choose to fight Seawright's eligibility for unemployment benefits, "it was reasonable for [Seawright] to believe that reasons other than the stated reasons may have motivated his termination."

information or belief.

"The central purpose of Rule 11 is to deter baseless filings in district court and thus . . . streamline the administration and procedure of the federal courts." Cooter & Gell v. Hartmarx Corp., 496 U.S. 384, 393, 110 L.Ed. 2d 359, 110 S.Ct. 2447 (1990). To achieve this purpose, Rule 11 provides "a means by which litigants certify to the court, by signature, that any papers filed are well founded." Business Guides, Inc. v. Chromatic Communications Enterprises, Inc., 498 U.S. 533, 542, 112 L.Ed. 2d 1140, 111 S.Ct. 922 (1991). In the Fifth Circuit, a district court must apply the "snapshot" rule: sanctions under Rule 11 may not be imposed "merely for the eventual failure of a claim; rather, sanctions are to be applied only where, *at the time of the filing*, the position advocated is unwarranted." Matta v. May, 118 F.3d 410, 415 (5th Cir. 1997) (emphasis added).

In determining whether an attorney has made a reasonable inquiry into the law, the Court may consider: "the time available to the attorney to prepare the document; the plausibility of the legal view contained in the document; the pro se status of the litigant; and the complexity of the legal and factual issues raised." Thomas v. Capital Security Services, Inc., 836 F.2d 866, 875-76 (5th Cir. 1988) (en banc). The determination of whether an attorney has made a reasonable inquiry into the facts of the case depends, of course, on the particular facts, but the Court may consider such factors as:

> the time available to the signer for investigation; the extent of the attorney's reliance upon his client for the factual support for the document; the feasibility of a prefiling investigation; whether the signing attorney accepted the case from another member of the bar or a forwarding attorney; the complexity of the factual and legal issues; and the extent to which development of the factual circumstances underlying the claim requires discovery.

Thomas, 836 F.2d at 875. An attorney who has filed court papers with no basis in fact needs no more notice of her Rule 11 violation than the existence of Rule 11 itself. Merriman v. Security Ins. Co. of Hartford, 100 F.3d 1187, 1191 (5th Cir. 1996).

When Rule 11 has been violated, the Court must "carefully choose sanctions that foster the appropriate purpose of the rule, depending upon the parties, the violation, and the nature of the case." *Thomas*, 836 F.2d at 877. The sanction imposed should be the least severe sanction that would adequately deter an attorney from violating the rule. See id. at 878; *Merriman*, 100 F.3d at 1194. Appropriate sanctions might include monetary sanctions, admonishment or a reprimand, or requiring some form of legal education. *See Thomas*, 836 F.2d at 877-78. When warranted for effective deterrence, the sanctions imposed for violations of Rule 11 may include an order directing payment to the movant of some or all of the reasonable attorney's fees and other expenses incurred as a direct result of the violation. See *Merriman*, 100 F.3d at 1194-95; Fed. R. Civ. P. 11(c)(2).

The chronology of events in this case is as follows:

— 9/11/95 Seawright's employment with Charter is terminated.

— 7/4/96 Seawright's previous lawyer, Catherine Kneeland, sends a demand letter to Charter's lawyer.

— 7/15/96 Charter's lawyer responds — Kneeland is told Seawright was terminated for performance problems: "Your claim that Mr. Seawright was discharged because of a perception by Charter Furniture that he was HIV positive is wholly untrue, false, and groundless." Kneeland is invited to review Seawright's employment file. The letter also cautions, "Please be advised that you will be held to the standards of Rule 11 . . . Reasonable inquiry should clearly indicate that the allegations made by Mr. Seawright have absolutely no evidentiary support." Janette Johnson acknowledges she saw this letter before she filed suit.

— 6/26/97 Seawright receives his right-to-sue notice letter from the EEOC (90-day deadline to file suit).

— 9/12/97 With 12 days left to sue, Seawright contacts attorney Janette Johnson about representation.

9/24/97 Johnson files suit.

— 11/97 Rule 26(f) conference — Charter's lawyer and Charter's management tell Seawright and his counsel in no uncertain terms the lawsuit is groundless and they will seek attorney's fees and expenses from both Seawright and his counsel.

— 11/18/97 Parties file Joint Status Report — Charter reiterates its belief that the lawsuit is groundless, frivolous, and intended solely for harassment, and outlines Seawright's performance problems, stating, "Defendant invited Plaintiff's counsel to review the employment file prior to filing the lawsuit, but Plaintiff's counsel ignored such invitation and filed the Complaint. Accordingly, Defendant will be seeking recovery of its attorneys fees and expenses in this lawsuit."

— 5/7/98 Charter files its motion for summary judgment. Charter asks for its attorneys' fees, expenses and costs from Seawright and Johnson pursuant to the ADA section awarding attorneys' fees to the prevailing party and Rule 11.

— 7/9/98 The Court issues its Memorandum Opinion and Order dismissing the case.

— 7/17/98 Charter files a motion for award of attorneys' fees against Seawright and Johnson.

— 8/17/98 Seawright, proceeding *pro se*, files a notice of appeal.

— 9/1/98 Charter files a separate motion for attorneys' fees against Johnson.

— 10/6/98 The Fifth Circuit dismisses Seawright's appeal as untimely filed.

Johnson acknowledges that she did not review Seawright's employment file with Charter or contact Charter for its reasons for Seawright's termination before she filed suit. Seawright first contacted Johnson's firm on September 12, 1997, which was 12 days before his time limit to sue in federal court would have expired. A week later, Seawright came into Johnson's offices for further consultation with attorney Kurt Banowsky that lasted more than two hours. Seawright also met with Johnson that day.

Seawright presented Johnson and Banowsky with his sales figures; letters of commendation; various written versions of Seawright's claims; other documents not even tangentially relevant to the core issue of Charter's knowledge of the truth about Seawright and Hull; a tape recording of a conversation between Seawright and another Charter employee, "wherein the employee seems to indicate knowledge on the part of Charter of Mr. Seawright's roommate's AIDS status;" a tape recording of a disciplinary meeting Charter management had with Seawright; and the letter from Charter's counsel cautioning that Seawright's allegations had no evidentiary support. Although Seawright admits that he lied to Charter time after time after time about Hull, his illness, and their relationship, Johnson submits that "at no point prior to or after filing the lawsuit did the law firm have any reason to doubt that Mr. Seawright was not being truthful with the law firm or that he would not be truthful in the ensuing litigation."

Johnson argues that "at the outset, it was reasonable to believe that other issues, such at [sic] the Defendant's knowledge of Mr. Seawright's roommate's illness, would have been developed favorably to Plaintiff through discovery." This is simply not true. Charter's counsel notified Seawright's former counsel in July 1996, thirteen months before Johnson filed suit, that Seawright's perception that he was fired because Charter though he was HIV-positive was utterly groundless. Charter never wavered from that position, and Charter told Seawright and Johnson again and again and again that its management had no knowledge of Seawright's true relationship with Hull, had no knowledge that Hull died of AIDS, and had believed in good faith Seawright's elaborate deception about the situation. Cutting through Johnson's self-serving justification of her pre-filing "investigation," Johnson clearly filed this lawsuit based on nothing more than her client's speculation and their presumption that there is a lot of "talk" in a small office.

The Court must address four factors in its imposition of sanctions under Rule 11. First, the "court must announce the sanctionable conduct giving rise to its order." In this case, this Rule 11 sanction is imposed for the reasons articulated at length above. Johnson violated Rule 11(b)(3) by asserting allegations and other factual contentions (not pled on information and belief) that had absolutely no evidentiary support whatsoever. Seawright acknowledged in his deposition that he had no personal knowledge that anyone ever told Charter management that Hull was HIV-positive or had AIDS or had died from AIDS prior to his termination. The Court finds that Johnson's pre-filing factual investigation was wholly inadequate in this case. See Forbes v. Merrill Lynch, Fenner & Smith, Inc., 179 F.R.D. 107, 110 (S.D.N.Y. 1998) (Rule 11 sanctions imposed in ADA case where attorney did not reasonably investigate whether, when, and under what circumstances plaintiff informed his employer he had AIDS, which was a crucial admission given that the employer's notice was the "crux of the case").

The second factor to be addressed is the connection between the amount of monetary sanctions the Court imposes and Johnson's sanctionable conduct. As discussed above, Johnson filed and continued to prosecute a meritless lawsuit on the basis of nothing more substantial than her client Seawright's suspicions that Charter didn't believe his consistent lies. Every dollar of attorneys' fees expended by Defendant Charter was a dollar wasted.[32]

With the third factor, the Court must review whether the costs or expenses were "reasonable," as opposed to self-imposed, mitigable, or the result of delay in seeking court intervention. The Court's review of the affidavits in support of Charter's requests for attorneys' fees shows the fees to be eminently reasonable. Charter alerted Johnson in its very first contacts with her that she had filed unfounded, factually baseless claims, and it repeatedly put Johnson on notice that it would seek its attorneys' fees for having to defend this frivolous lawsuit. The amount of attorneys' fees incurred in this case increased due to Johnson's stubborn refusal to acknowledge the futility of the claims. The Court can perceive no actions taken unnecessarily by Charter in the defense of the lawsuit.

Considering the * * * "factors" that must be applied by district courts in the Fifth Circuit, lead counsel for Charter, Kelly Crawford, is an experienced, able practitioner who specializes in the area of commercial litigation, including employment disputes. Crawford was also assisted by associates Annabel Hoffman (a former law clerk to the Honorable Jorge Solis) and Rebecca Price. The Court found the quality of their written work product to be excellent. Their rates of $160 per hour for Crawford, $130 per hour for Hoffman and Price, and $80 per hour for paralegal time certainly comport with the going rate for attorneys in this district and division with their qualifications and experience. In fact, the hourly rates are on the low side. The Court also concludes that the amount of time Crawford and his colleagues expended in defending this lawsuit was reasonable and necessary. Crawford's efforts on his client's behalf were successful, as he obtained a victory on the merits. Johnson has not objected to opposing counsel's hourly rates or their calculations of the time they expended in defending this lawsuit.

Lastly, the Court must consider whether the sanction imposed is the least severe sanction adequate to achieve the purpose of Rule 11. Johnson filed and prosecuted a groundless lawsuit and forced the opposing party to needlessly incur a substantial sum in attorneys' fees to defend itself. Johnson had many opportunities throughout this case to retreat from her factually unsupported, groundless assertions. Instead of acknowledging the truth, she protracted the litigation until the Court granted summary judgment in favor of the Defendant. Johnson cannot claim that inexperience contributed to her conduct; she has been admitted to practice in the Northern District of Texas since 1989. Indeed, Johnson is board certified in labor and employment law, and she is a prominent member of the employment law bar in Dallas.

---

[32] Johnson's arguments as to why she shouldn't be sanctioned include "we're plaintiffs' lawyers, we're the good guys," and "I can't possibly afford to pay Charter's attorney's fees." Neither consideration is relevant in the determination of whether Johnson violated Rule 11. Furthermore, such arguments are not relevant as to what the appropriate sanction for a Rule 11 violation should be.

After carefully considering other available sanctions, the Court concludes that a monetary sanction that requires Johnson to "fix what she broke" would be fair and just. However, applying the binding law of this Circuit, the Court concludes that a monetary sanction is not the least severe sanction adequate to deter Janette Johnson from such conduct in the future.

To the Court's knowledge, Janette Johnson has not been sanctioned for a violation of Rule 11 before. Therefore, the Court concludes and holds that a published reprimand coupled with a strong admonishment and warning to not engage in the future in the conduct chronicled above is the least severe sanction that is likely to deter Ms. Johnson from such conduct in the future.

A court may not impose Rule 11 sanctions "merely for the eventual failure of factual and legal arguments after a trial; sanctions are to be applied only where, at the time of filing, such arguments were unwarranted." FDIC v. Calhoun, 34 F.3d 1291, 1300 (5th Cir. 1994). Such is the case here. The Court specifically finds that Johnson violated Rule 11 in the filing and prosecution of this frivolous lawsuit. Upon careful review of the documents filed in this case, the Court concludes that this lawsuit was frivolous, groundless, and filed in bad faith. The Court hereby publicly reprimands Janette Johnson for violation of Rule 11 in this case and admonishes her that any such conduct in the future will be more severely sanctioned.

CONCLUSION

For the reasons discussed above, Defendant's Motion for Award of Attorneys' Fees and Expenses is Granted as to plaintiff J. Scott Seawright, as set forth above. Defendant's Motion to Recover Attorneys' Fees and Expenses From Plaintiff's Counsel is Denied. Plaintiff's counsel, Janette Johnson, is publicly reprimanded and admonished as set forth above. Within 30 days of the date of this Order, Plaintiff J. Scott Seawright is Ordered to pay the sum of $29,809.00 to Defendant Charter Furniture Rental, Inc., as the reasonable and necessary attorneys' fees Charter incurred in defending this case.

NOTES AND PROBLEMS FOR DISCUSSION

1. *Seawright* is a difficult case. It is clear from the opinion (especially in parts omitted), that the court viewed the case as frivolous and unjustified. On the other hand, it is clear from the factual recitation that the plaintiff's attorney did carry out some prefiling investigation.

(a) What more could the plaintiff's lawyer have done? Clearly, she could have spoken to Charter, but that had apparently already been done and Charter's view was clear. As far as other employees of Charter are concerned, is it unreasonable to suppose that they will be less than forthcoming against their employer absent legal compulsion?

(b) What is the relevance of the court's statement that the factual contentions were "not pled on information and belief"?

(c) Is it relevant that the plaintiff's lawyer was retained just 12 days before the statute of limitations was to run?

2. Now turn to the actual result. Is it consistent with Rule 11 and the Rule's purpose, or does it turn Rule 11 into a paper tiger (or, to continue the animal metaphor, a "one free bite" rule)?

3. Reconsider this case in light of the earlier discussion of pleading. Is it likely that a Rule 12(b)(6) motion would have been granted? Probably not, because the plaintiff clearly has notified the defendant of the claims, and his allegations are presumed true. The next step is discovery, and here the plaintiff took several depositions. Then came the motion for summary judgment and sanctions. In this situation, can one say for sure that plaintiff's counsel did not conduct an adequate prefiling investigation because her suppositions were not borne out by discovery? To ask the question in another way: Could the court have sanctioned the plaintiff's attorney even if discovery had revealed information favorable to the plaintiff (after all, an inadequate investigation is inadequate even if one is proven correct)?

4. There is another issue lurking here, which we simply want to flag at this stage. Here, the ultimate issue is "What did the defendant know?" Should the plaintiff be permitted to take his case to a jury and argue that the defendant's denials are untrue, or at least be permitted to try to determine the truth in discovery without potential Rule 11 sanctions?

5. When a court imposes sanctions on its own — i.e., sua sponte — and denies a party an opportunity to take advantage of Rule 11's safe harbor provision that would allow for removal of, or amending, the offending pleading or paper, what should the relevant focus be? On the "objective" reasonableness of the attorney's actions (as is usually the case under Rule 11); or the attorney's "subjective" bad faith? Why? See In re Pennie & Edmunds, LLP, 323 F.3d 86 (2d Cir. 2003) (calling for focus on subjective bad faith).

6. Consider the reference in Rule 11(b)(1) to "improper purpose." Can a paper that otherwise satisfied the requirements of 11(b)(2) ever run afoul of Rule 11 simply because of an improper motive on the part of the filing lawyer? Consider Whitehead v. Food Max of Mississippi, 332 F.3d 796 (5th Cir. 2003). There, plaintiff's counsel secured a writ of execution to satisfy a money judgment that he had obtained against the defendant in a federal court. Plaintiff's counsel stated that he wished to "embarrass" the defendant by having the federal marshal enforce the writ by emptying the cash registers of the defendant's store. The appeals court assumed that nothing was improper in any of that except, apparently, the motive behind the defendant's application for the writ of attachment. The Fifth Circuit was unwilling to view the purpose of embarrassment as distinguishable from an improper motive to harass the defendant. It ruled that although the obtaining of the writ of execution may have been proper otherwise, Rule 11 had been violated.

7. How inventive a lawyer can be in making arguments that are "warranted by existing law?" If all courts have rejected the particular argument, is it no longer one that a reasonably competent attorney would think to raise? Desegregation of public schools did not become a federal constitutional imperative before the Supreme Court's landmark decision in Brown v. Board of Education, 347 U.S. 483, 74 S.Ct. 686, 98 L.Ed. 873 (1954). Before then (and assuming modern

Rule 11 existed) would a frontal assault on "separate but equal" — previously enshrined by the Court as the law of the land — have been subject to sanctions because not warranted by then-existing law? Note that failure to cite controlling authority can be sanctionable under Rule 11, and distortion of legal authority by selective quotation from precedents can be the equivalent of the failure to cite controlling authority. See Precision Specialty Metals, Inc. v. United States, 315 F.3d 1346 (Fed. Cir. 2003) (upholding sanction of reprimand against U.S. Attorney under the Court of International Trade's equivalent to Rule 11).

8. Rule 11 is not the only provision that deals with the problem of monetary sanctions for bad faith behavior. Rule 11 is expressly inapplicable to "disclosures and discovery requests, responses, objections, and motions under Rules 26 through 37." We discuss these provisions in the next chapter. In addition, under 28 U.S.C. §1927, a lawyer who "unreasonably and vexatiously" "multiplies the proceedings" can be personally liable for the additional fees incurred because of such conduct. Section 1927 also lacks the limitation to "pleading[s], motions[s] or other paper[s]" that appears in Rule 11. Under Rule 54(d), a limited number of "costs" (generally not including attorney's fees) may be shifted to the losing side in litigation. And federal courts have long been able to impose sanctions for conduct of litigants or lawyers that a court finds to be in "subjective" bad faith as part of their "inherent" authority to sanction abuses of the judicial process. See Chambers v. NASCO, Inc., 501 U.S. 32, 111 S.Ct. 2123, 115 L.Ed.2d 27 (1991) (noting that such power might permit sanctions when §1927 and Rule 11 would not).

SECTION D. THE DEFENDANT'S RESPONSE

In Chapter 2 we discussed the rules for starting a lawsuit, the location of the suit, and service of process. In this chapter, we have just discussed what the plaintiff must plead regarding his claim. But keep in mind that even if the plaintiff has filed suit in an improper location, and even if the plaintiff's pleading is inadequate, that will not automatically cause the lawsuit to be dismissed. Instead, the lawsuit will continue despite its infirmities unless the defendant somehow questions or attacks the location or pleading (although, if the mistake in location of the suit implicates the court's subject matter jurisdiction, the infirmity can be addressed by the court on its own). We have already seen those kinds of attacks in the materials, but we now turn specifically to the procedural options available to the defendant upon getting the complaint.

The defendant basically has two options. The defendant may file a "motion," such as a motion under one of the many rubrics of Rule 12. See Rule 7(c). Or, the defendant may file an answer. See Rules 7(a), 8(b), (c), (d). A motion requests the court to do something in regard to the complaint — either to dismiss it (throw plaintiff out of court), or to require plaintiff to do it over in some different way. An "answer" is a written response which states the defendant's version of the situation. It does not ask the court to do anything. Instead, the case goes forward.

There are essentially seven categories of responses.

1. This Lawsuit Does Not Belong in this Court. Here, the defendant alleges that the lawsuit has not been properly brought in the court where it was brought. The court may not have subject matter jurisdiction or personal jurisdiction, venue may be improper, or the plaintiff may not have brought the defendant before the court by proper service of process. See Rules 12(b)(1)-(5).

2. The Plaintiff Has No Right to Recover for What She Has Alleged. Here, the defendant says that even if everything the plaintiff says is true, the law gives her no right to recover. For example, a complaint that alleged that the defendant declined the plaintiff's dinner invitation, or that the defendant "made a face" would fail to state a claim for relief, even if the plaintiff also alleged injury caused by those events. Recall the discussion of substantive law and the notion that plaintiff must have some substantive right to recover. *Dartmouth College* held that a student newspaper could not recover damages for actions of the college which interfered with the paper's activities, and in *Langadinos*, the defendant said that the plaintiff's pleading failed to state a claim under the Warsaw Convention. In practice, a Rule 12(b)(6) motion is used both for cases where the question is clearly substantive inadequacy, as well as cases where plaintiff's complaint may be inadequate because it lacks sufficient detail and/or lacks elements of the substantive claim.

3. What the Plaintiff Says Isn't True. In legal terms, this is called a "denial." The truth of the plaintiff's allegations and the defendant's denial will generally be determined by the factfinder at trial. A variant of this is where the defendant doesn't know whether an allegation is true or not. Read how Rule 8(b) deals with this situation.

4. The Plaintiff Hasn't Told the Whole Story. Perhaps the plaintiff's allegations are sufficient to state a claim for relief, but there may be other matters which have not been alleged which would defeat the claim. For example, if the statute of limitations has run (i.e., the suit is filed too late), or the statute of frauds applies (e.g., the suit seeks recovery on an oral promise that must be in writing), or when there has been accord and satisfaction (i.e., the parties have already settled and resolved the issue), the defendant may assert such matters as "affirmative defenses." Rule 8(c) contains a list of such defenses, a test for determining what is an affirmative defense, and tells what the defendant must do with them. Affirmative defenses hark back to the common law plea of confession and avoidance, although the confession is no longer required.

5. There is a Missing Party. Assume the plaintiff sues on a promissory note signed jointly by X and Y, but she only sues X. X may claim that the plaintiff should not sue him alone, but should have to bring the suit against both X and Y. In procedural terms, it may be that Y is a necessary party (someone who should be joined if possible — possible meaning that Y can be joined without destroying subject matter jurisdiction and that Y is subject to personal jurisdiction). And if Y can't be joined, the whole lawsuit should be dismissed. Rule 12(b)(7) and Rule 19 deal with this concept.

6. A Response is not Possible. There may be cases where the complaint is such a jumble of facts and allegations that the defendant just can't figure out what the lawsuit is about. Rule 12(e) deals with this situation and permits the defendant to seek a "more definite statement." But, as already discussed, the rule has a lot of historical baggage. Originally, such a motion was called a motion for a "bill of particulars," and it was generally used to require more detail in the complaint. Subsequently. courts said that the defendant should obtain the detail by discovery. For this reason, this motion is more often granted today when the complaint is confused or is too long and detailed.

7. *Claims Against the Plaintiff.* It is not uncommon that when a plaintiff sues a defendant, the defendant may have grievances against the plaintiff. Indeed, this is quite common in accident cases. Rule 13 deals with such "counterclaims," and divides them into "compulsory" counterclaims (those that arise out of the same transaction or occurrence as outlined in the plaintiff's claim) and "permissive" ones.

The remainder of this section will explore these concepts in more detail although we provide a fuller treatment of counterclaims in Chapter 10.

1. RULE 12 PRACTICE

Read Rule 12(b). Keep in mind that the Rule concerns reasons why the court should not go forward and, perhaps, should never go forward. As you consider these reasons, you will see that: (a) they generally do not involve factual issues or, if they do, the factual issues are likely not to be disputed or to be relatively straightforward; (b) they are preemptive in the sense that if sustained, the plaintiff loses (even if her case on the merits happens to be strong); and (c) Rules 12(b)(1)-(5) all relate to whether the case belongs in the court where it was filed and provide good reasons for resolving these matters before the case gets going. If it is determined only later that the court was not proper, much time and effort will have been wasted.

Now read Rules 12(g) and (h) closely. These are designed to serve three objectives: first, to permit the Rule 12(b) matters to be raised by a pre-answer motion; second, to permit only one pre-answer motion; and third, to require certain defenses to be raised early in the case or be lost.

NOTES AND PROBLEMS FOR DISCUSSION

1. Paul sues Drake for injuries arising from an accident. Drake moves (i.e., makes a motion) to dismiss for improper service of process, and the motion is denied.

(a) Can Drake now move to dismiss for lack of personal jurisdiction?

(b) Can Drake include the defense of lack of personal jurisdiction in his answer?

(c) Can Drake now move to dismiss for failure to state a claim upon which relief can be granted?

(d) Can Drake include the defense of failure to state a claim upon which relief can be granted in his answer?

2. Paula sues Daisy for injuries arising from an accident. Daisy files an answer which denies various allegations in the complaint.

(a) Can Daisy now move to dismiss for lack of personal jurisdiction?

(b) If not, can Daisy amend her answer to allege lack of personal jurisdiction, assuming it is 40 days after her answer was served?

(c) Can Daisy make a motion under Rule 12(e) to require a more definite statement?

(d) Can Daisy make a motion for judgment on the pleadings on the ground that Paula improperly failed to join Tyrone as required by Rule 19?

(e) Can Daisy make a motion to dismiss for lack of subject matter jurisdiction?

3. Rule 12(f) provides for a motion to strike scandalous and impertinent material. Courts do not regard such motions favorably but they are, on occasion, granted. See, e.g., Foster v. Pfizer Inc., 2000 U.S. Dist. LEXIS 19814 (D. Kan. 2000) (granting defendant's motion to strike portions of plaintiff's pleadings because of their "scandalous and impertinent" character which implied an illegal or immoral conspiracy between the drug company Pfizer and the U.S. Food and Drug Administration). Of course, any defendant making such a motion must consider the cost and likely result of such a motion, and whether it is worth bringing it. For this reason, Rule 12(f) motions tend to be made by parties who are also making a Rule 12 motion on other grounds.

4. Assume the plaintiff files a complaint with two separate claims, and defendant believes that one claim states a valid claim and one doesn't. Can the defendant make a pre-answer motion? See Rules 12(b) and (f).

2. THE ANSWER

If the defendant has made a pre-answer motion that was denied, or if he did not make one at all, he must now file an answer. The answer will contain (a) admissions and denials of allegations, (b) affirmative defenses, and (c) counterclaims.

a. Denials. If the plaintiff makes a particular allegation, the defendant has essentially three possible responses — admit, deny, and don't know. Make sure you understand how Rule 8 deals with each of these responses:

(1) Assume that Paul files a complaint against Triangle Manufacturing Co. and alleges: (i) Paul is a citizen of California, and Triangle is a citizen of Oregon; (ii) At all times in question, Dillon was operating the vehicle described below in the scope of his employment for Triangle, and the vehicle operated by Dillon was owned, operated and controlled by Triangle; (iii) On February 1, 2012, Paul and Dillon were involved in a two-car collision at Bush and Kearny Streets in San Francisco, California; (iv) the collision resulted from the negligent driving of Dillon, and his negligence in driving with defective brakes; (v) Paul was seriously injured, and the injury resulted from the negligence of Dillon; and (vi) [here Paul describes his injuries and other

damages]. You represent Triangle, who tells you that this is outrageous and to "just deny everything." Do you see a problem with denying everything?

(2) At common law, a defendant could plead a "general denial" (denying each and every allegation of the complaint) or, in some cases, he could plead the "general issue" which denied all allegations and also included certain affirmative defenses. Is this an option under Rule 8?

(3) If the defendant purports to make a general denial, does the plaintiff have a remedy? See Rule 11(b)(4).

(4) Lawyers are creatures of habit, and old practices die hard. So defendants will sometimes generally deny the entire complaint, or the operative paragraphs (aside from the jurisdictional allegations), even when some of the allegations are ones they do not really contest. As a practical matter, this sort of sloppiness normally causes little harm, since the parties know what the case is about and what is really at issue, or will soon learn from discovery. But consider a problem based on a well-known case:

Assume that under applicable principles of tort law, an employer is liable for the negligence of its employees in driving a car that is operated and controlled by his employer. And assume in response to the complaint in paragraph (1), the defendant simply denies each and every allegation of the complaint. Now, assume it later turns out (after the statute of limitations has run), that the car driven by Dillon was owned by Triangle, but it was leased to Quadrangle Company, and Dillon was actually employed by Quadrangle. On these facts, (a) is *Triangle* liable for the injury based on the tort law described above? (b) If not, who is? (c) Can Paul now sue this party? (d) Does Paul have a legitimate objection to the way Triangle has answered the complaint? Before you answer, keep in mind that Triangle in fact denied that it operated and controlled the car.

b. Affirmative Defenses. Rule 8(c) sets forth specific examples of affirmative defenses, and then a general test — i.e., "any other matter constituting an avoidance or affirmative defense." These affirmative defenses must be set forth specifically in a pleading. Make sure you understand what happens if they are not.

(i) When is Rule 8(c) triggered? Consider the following decision reached under an earlier, but only slightly rephrased, version of the Rule:

LaFont v. Decker-Angel

United States Court of Appeals, Tenth Circuit, 1999.

1999 U.S. App. LEXIS 8336.

HENRY, CIRCUIT JUDGE.

* * *

Plaintiff Gerald LaFont sued defendant Judith M. Decker-Angel in federal court based on diversity of citizenship, alleging fraud, conversion, and constructive trust in relation to a check for $250,000 given to defendant by plaintiff. Defendant counter-claimed for collection on a promissory note for an additional $250,000. Following a bench trial, the district court found that the $250,000 check was a gift from plaintiff to defendant and entered judgment against plaintiff on his claims. It further found that plaintiff did not intend to make a gift to defendant of both the check and the note and entered judgment against defendant on her counter-claim. Plaintiff appeals, and we affirm.

In his complaint and at trial, plaintiff asserted that he issued the check to defendant for the purpose of satisfying his financial obligation toward a joint purchase of property. He alleged that instead of preserving the funds for the future purchase of property, defendant fraudulently converted the proceeds of the check for her own use. Defendant contended that plaintiff gave her the money in compensation for her services as plaintiff's companion, advisor, and lover, and in compensation for giving up her home and business in Arizona to move to Monument Valley, Utah, to work for plaintiff. Defendant denied all of plaintiff's allegations of fraud and conversion.

Plaintiff's only issue on appeal is whether the district court erred in ruling, over plaintiff's objection, that defendant's evidence and testimony that the check was a gift was not waived under Fed.R.Civ.P. 8(c). Rule 8(c) "requires a party pleading to a preceding pleading to set forth affirmatively all matters which the pleading party intends to use as an avoidance or affirmative defense." Failure to plead, move under Rule 12(b), or try by consent of both parties an affirmative defense or avoidance waives that defense and bars evidence on the point as a matter of law.

Here, defendant did not assert any affirmative defenses by way of answer or pretrial order, but initially raised her assertion of a gift during opening arguments at trial. Over plaintiff's objection, the court allowed the evidence, concluding that defendant's general denials of conversion and fraud adequately included the averment that she came by the check rightfully, and therefore, a gift did not need to be pled as an affirmative defense.

The giving of a gift is certainly not one of the nineteen affirmative defenses specifically enumerated in Rule 8(c). The question then becomes whether giving a gift falls into the catchall category of "any other matter constituting an avoidance or affirmative defense." Fed.R.Civ.P. 8(c). "Rule 8(c) does not elaborate this catchall statement and thus offers no assistance in defining what constitutes 'an avoidance or affirmative defense.'" 5 Charles A. Wright & Arthur R. Miller, Federal Practice and Procedure §1271, at 429-31 (2d ed. 1990). The Fifth Circuit has noted that although "the Federal Rules of Civil Procedure provide the manner and time in which defenses are raised and when waiver occurs," we look to state law for definition of the "nature of defenses." Here, Utah law provides us with some guidance in this matter.

Under Utah law, "a defense that merely controverts plaintiff's prima facie case is negative in character and should be pleaded in accordance with rule 8(b).[2]

---

[2]   Fed.R.Civ.P. 8(b) provides in part that: A party shall state in short and plain terms the party's defenses to each claim asserted and shall admit or deny the averments upon which the adverse

A rule 8(c) affirmative defense, in contrast, raises matter outside the plaintiff's prima facie case." Here, defendant's contention that the check from plaintiff was a gift does not raise a matter outside plaintiff's claims, but merely controverts plaintiff's claims by asserting that she came into possession of the funds rightfully and legally. This is in accord with this court's rationale in Marino v. Otis Engineering Corp., 839 F.2d 1404, 1408 (10th Cir. 1988), in which we drew a distinction between the introduction of evidence in support of an avoidance or affirmative defense and the introduction of evidence to refute the plaintiff's allegations in the complaint.

In sum, we agree with the district court's determination that defendant's averment that the check was a gift was not an avoidance or affirmative defense, but was introduced instead for the purpose of disproving plaintiff's claims.

Therefore, the judgment of the United States District Court is affirmed.

NOTES AND PROBLEMS FOR DISCUSSION

1. Note how the defendant raised the issue at trial that the check was a gift. If the trial court had ruled for the plaintiff, what procedural move might the defendant have made? See Rule 15(b).

2. How does one decide whether some matter not on the list in Rule 8(c) falls into the category of an affirmative defense?

(a) Is the test in *LaFont* — matters controverting plaintiff's claim — of much help?

(b) What about another test — matters constituting an "avoidance"?

(c) If you think either of these helps, assume a case where plaintiff sues to eject defendant from certain land, alleging that he owns the land and has a right to possession. Now, assume that the defendant denies the allegations. At trial, the plaintiff introduces a recorded deed and rests. The defendant now proposes to introduce evidence that he has lived "open and notoriously" on the land for 11 years and, under applicable law, has title by "adverse possession." At this point, consider what procedural move the plaintiff could make. Cf. Rule 15(b). What would the plaintiff argue with reference to the matter of title by adverse possession, and what would the defendant argue in response?

3. If you think #2 is easy, how would you deal with (a) the defendant's defense to a claim of negligence that the matter was caused by an "Act of God," (b) the defendant's defense to a claim of hit and run that he didn't do it, but the wrongdoer was someone else, or (c) the defendant's defense to an action for the rental price of a hotel suite during the anticipated visit of Tiger Woods for a celebrity golf tournament that Tiger cancelled and the tournament was cancelled because of rain (i.e., frustration of purpose).

4. Now, consider this more complex situation: Virginia Woodfield was involved in an accident with Scott Bowman and Lane Trucking Corp., and was seriously injured. Woodfield sued Bowman and Lane, and also sued her own

party relies. If a party is without knowledge or information sufficient to form a belief as to the truth of an averment, the party shall so state and this has the effect of a denial.

insurer, Nationwide Insurance Company. The suit against Nationwide was brought pursuant to so-called uninsured motorist coverage, which covers an insured if she is involved in an accident with an uninsured or underinsured defendant (here, Bowman had only $10,000 of coverage). Woodfield settled with Lane and, as part of the settlement, assigned all her rights under the Nationwide policy to Lane's insurer (Planet), so the lawsuit became essentially Lane's insurer against Nationwide. As one of it's defenses, Nationwide pleaded "The claims, demands and causes of action of Woodfield and Planet are barred, or alternatively reduced, by the doctrines of accord and satisfaction, transaction and compromise, waiver and/or release." At trial, Nationwide lost, and moved to set aside the judgment on the ground that its policy had a provision requiring it to consent to an assignment, and that it had not consented to the assignment to Planet. Planet responded by calling attention to Rule 8(c) and Nationwide, in turn, called attention to the defense noted above. What result? See Woodfield v. Bowman, 193 F.3d 354 (5th Cir. 1999).

5. In how much detail must the defendant plead an affirmative defense? For example, Meteor Manufacturing sold equipment to First Bank and, when the equipment didn't work properly, First Bank sued Meteor alleging breach of warranty. Meteor asserted, as affirmative defenses, that the plaintiff's action is barred by the defenses of "laches" (i.e., plaintiff waited an unreasonable time to sue) and "waiver." First Bank moves to strike the affirmative defenses. What result? See Fleet Business Credit Corp. v. National City Leasing Corp., 191 F.R.D. 568 (N.D. Ill. 1999).

(ii) The Burden of Pleading

A second issue surrounding affirmative defenses relates to the allocation of the responsibility for pleading various issues. Assume that a state passes a statute abrogating the common law dogbite rule (in which the first bite is "free"). The statute provides that (i) if a person is bitten by a dog, (ii) provided that the person bitten was not tormenting the dog or acting in a threatening manner toward the owner, (iii) such person may recover actual damages. Who must plead (ii) — tormenting/threatening or not tormenting/not threatening? Must the plaintiff plead that she was not tormenting the dog as part of her case, or may she say nothing, on the theory that it is the defendant who must plead that the plaintiff was tormenting the dog, as part of his defense? Consider whether the next case provides an answer.

Gomez v. Toledo

Supreme Court of the United States, 1980.
446 U.S. 635, 100 S.Ct. 1920, 64 L.Ed.2d 572.

MR. JUSTICE MARSHALL delivered the opinion of the Court.

The question presented is whether, in an action brought under 42 U.S.C. §1983 against a public official whose position might entitle him to qualified immunity, a plaintiff must allege that the official has acted in bad faith in order to state a claim for relief or, alternatively, whether the defendant must plead good faith as an affirmative defense.

I

Petitioner Carlos Rivera Gomez brought this action against respondent, the Superintendent of the Police of the Commonwealth of Puerto Rico, contending that respondent had violated his right to procedural due process by discharging him from employment with the Police Department's Bureau of Criminal Investigation. Basing jurisdiction on 28 U.S.C. §1343(3),[2] petitioner alleged the following facts in his complaint.[3] Petitioner had been employed as an agent with the Puerto Rican police since 1968. In April 1975, he submitted a sworn statement to his supervisor in which he asserted that two other agents had offered false evidence for use in a criminal case under their investigation. As a result of this statement, petitioner was immediately transferred from the Criminal Investigation Corps for the Southern Area to Police Headquarters in San Juan, and a few weeks later to the Police Academy in Gurabo, where he was given no investigative authority. In the meantime respondent ordered an investigation of petitioner's claims, and the Legal Division of the Police Department concluded that all of petitioner's factual allegations were true.

In April 1976, while still stationed at the Police Academy, petitioner was subpoenaed to give testimony in a criminal case arising out of the evidence that petitioner had alleged to be false. At the trial petitioner, appearing as a defense witness, testified that the evidence was in fact false. As a result of this testimony, criminal charges, filed on the basis of information furnished by respondent, were brought against petitioner for the allegedly unlawful wire-tapping of the agents' telephones. Respondent suspended petitioner in May 1976 and discharged him without a hearing in July. In October, the District Court of Puerto Rico found no probable cause to believe that petitioner was guilty of the allegedly unlawful wiretapping and, upon appeal by the prosecution, the Superior Court affirmed. Petitioner in turn sought review of his discharge before the Investigation, Prosecution, and Appeals Commission of Puerto Rico, which, after a hearing, revoked the discharge order rendered by respondent and ordered that petitioner be reinstated with backpay.

Based on the foregoing factual allegations, petitioner brought this suit for damages, contending that his discharge violated his right to procedural due process, and that it had caused him anxiety, embarrassment, and injury to his reputation in the community. In his answer, respondent denied a number of petitioner's allegations of fact and asserted several affirmative defenses. Respondent then moved to dismiss the complaint for failure to state a cause of action, see Fed. Rule Civ. Proc. 12(b)(6), and the District Court granted the motion. Observing that respondent was entitled to qualified immunity for acts

---

[2] That section grants the federal district courts jurisdiction "[to] redress the deprivation, under color of any State law, statute, ordinance, regulation, custom or usage, of any right, privilege or immunity secured by the Constitution of the United States or by any Act of Congress providing for equal rights of citizens or of all persons within the jurisdiction of the United States."

[3] At this stage of the proceedings, of course, all allegations of the complaint must be accepted as true.

done in good faith within the scope of his official duties, it concluded that petitioner was required to plead as part of his claim for relief that, in committing the actions alleged, respondent was motivated by bad faith. The absence of any such allegation, it held, required dismissal of the complaint. The United States Court of Appeals for the First Circuit affirmed.

We granted certiorari to resolve a conflict among the Courts of Appeals. We now reverse.

II

Section 1983 provides a cause of action for "the deprivation of any rights, privileges, or immunities secured by the Constitution and laws" by any person acting "under color of any statute, ordinance, regulation, custom, or usage, of any State or Territory." 42 U.S.C. §1983.[6] This statute, enacted to aid in "'the preservation of human liberty and human rights,'" Owen v. City of Independence, 445 U.S. 622, 636 (1980), reflects a congressional judgment that a "damages remedy against the offending party is a vital component of any scheme for vindicating cherished constitutional guarantees." As remedial legislation, §1983 is to be construed generously to further its primary purpose.

In certain limited circumstances, we have held that public officers are entitled to a qualified immunity from damages liability under §1983. This conclusion has been based on an unwillingness to infer from legislative silence a congressional intention to abrogate immunities that were both "well established at common law" and "compatible with the purposes of the Civil Rights Act." Findings of immunity have thus been "predicated upon a considered inquiry into the immunity historically accorded the relevant official at common law and the interests behind it." In Pierson v. Ray, 386 U.S. 547, 555 (1967), for example, we concluded that a police officer would be "[excused] from liability for acting under a statute that he reasonably believed to be valid but that was later held unconstitutional, on its face or as applied." And in other contexts we have held, on the basis of "[common law] tradition . . . and strong public-policy reasons," Wood v. Strickland, 420 U.S. 308, 318 (1975), that certain categories of executive officers should be allowed qualified immunity from liability for acts done on the basis of an objectively reasonable belief that those acts were lawful.

Nothing in the language or legislative history of §1983, however, suggests that in an action brought against a public official whose position might entitle him to immunity if he acted in good faith, a plaintiff must allege bad faith in order to state a claim for relief. By the plain terms of §1983, two — and only two — allegations are required in order to state a cause of action under that statute. First, the plaintiff must allege that some person has deprived him of a federal right. Second, he must allege that the person who has deprived him of that right acted under color of state or territorial law. See Monroe v. Pape, 365 U.S. 167, 171 (1961). Petitioner has made both of the required allegations. He

---

[6] Section 1983 provides in full: "Every person who, under color of any statute, ordinance, regulation, custom, or usage, of any State or Territory, subjects, or causes to be subjected, any citizen of the United States or other person within the jurisdiction thereof to the deprivation of any rights, privileges, or immunities secured by the Constitution and laws, shall be liable to the party injured in an action at law, suit in equity, or other proper proceeding for redress."

alleged that his discharge by respondent violated his right to procedural due process, and that respondent acted under color of Puerto Rican law.

Moreover, this Court has never indicated that qualified immunity is relevant to the existence of the plaintiff's cause of action; instead we have described it as a defense available to the official in question. Since qualified immunity is a defense, the burden of pleading it rests with the defendant. See Fed. Rule Civ. Proc. 8(c) (defendant must plead any "matter constituting an avoidance or affirmative defense"); 5 C. Wright & A. Miller, Federal Practice and Procedure §1271 (1969). It is for the official to claim that his conduct was justified by an objectively reasonable belief that it was lawful. We see no basis for imposing on the plaintiff an obligation to anticipate such a defense by stating in his complaint that the defendant acted in bad faith.

Our conclusion as to the allocation of the burden of pleading is supported by the nature of the qualified immunity defense. As our decisions make clear, whether such immunity has been established depends on facts peculiarly within the knowledge and control of the defendant. Thus we have stated that "[it] is the existence of reasonable grounds for the belief formed at the time and in light of all the circumstances, coupled with good-faith belief, that affords a basis for qualified immunity of executive officers for acts performed in the course of official conduct." The applicable test focuses not only on whether the official has an objectively reasonable basis for that belief, but also on whether "[the] official himself [is] acting sincerely and with a belief that he is doing right." There may be no way for a plaintiff to know in advance whether the official has such a belief or, indeed, whether he will even claim that he does. The existence of a subjective belief will frequently turn on factors which a plaintiff cannot reasonably be expected to know. For example, the official's belief may be based on state or local law, advice of counsel, administrative practice, or some other factor of which the official alone is aware. To impose the pleading burden on the plaintiff would ignore this elementary fact and be contrary to the established practice in analogous areas of the law.[8]

The decision of the Court of Appeals is reversed, and the case is remanded to that court for further proceedings consistent with this opinion.

It is so ordered.

MR. JUSTICE REHNQUIST joins the opinion of the Court, reading it as he does to leave open the issue of the burden of persuasion, as opposed to the burden of pleading, with respect to a defense of qualified immunity.

NOTES AND PROBLEMS FOR DISCUSSION

1. Traditional discussions regarding the allocation of the burdens of pleading describe three critical factors: (a) fairness, in terms of who has easier access to

---

[8] As then Dean Charles Clark stated over 40 years ago: "It seems to be considered only fair that certain types of things which in common law pleading were matters in confession and avoidance — *i.e.*, matters which seemed more or less to admit the general complaint and yet to suggest some other reason why there was no right — must be specifically pleaded in the answer, and that has been a general rule."

information and the ability to raise the issue; (b) policy, in terms of whether the particular claim should be encouraged or discouraged; and (c) probabilities, in terms of which party's situation is more likely to be the norm (with the party whose situation deviates from it having to allege the matter). Which of these is applicable in *Gomez*?

2. Consider the *Gomez* Court's reasoning for saying that fairness dictates allocating the issue of immunity to the defendant. Would the Court have reached the same result if the rule of law as to whether the officer was entitled to immunity was a wholly objective test — i.e., whether a reasonable officer would have known the action was not proper, without regard to his subjective good faith? In fact, the Court two years later in Harlow v. Fitzgerald, 457 U.S. 800, 818-19, 102 S.Ct. 2727, 73 L.Ed.2d 396 (1982), concluded that an officer's good faith is determined by the objective reasonableness of the official's conduct. This was defined as conduct that "does not violate clearly established statutory or constitutional rights of which a reasonable person should have known."

3. How would you argue the issue of who must plead tormenting/threatening in the dogbite hypothetical that prefaced *Gomez*?

4. Changes in allocation of pleading (and along with it, typically, the burden of proof) may reflect shifting attitudes of society toward particular claims. For example, most courts consider contributory negligence to be a defense to be pleaded and proved by the defendant, but some jurisdictions have required the plaintiff to plead and prove lack of contributory negligence as part of her case in chief. E.g., Hardware State Bank v. Cotner, 302 N.E.2d 257 (Ill. 1973). Other times, the change may be constitutionally inspired. At common law, for example, defendants in defamation cases had the burden of pleading and proving the "truth" of the challenged statements as a defense to liability. But the Supreme Court concluded that free speech principles embodied in the First Amendment required that the burden of establishing the falsity of the challenged statements be born by the party defamed — not the speaker. Philadelphia Newspapers, Inc. v. Hepps, 475 U.S. 767, 106 S.Ct. 1558, 89 L.Ed.2d 783 (1985).

3. COUNTERCLAIMS

A defense, if successful, merely operates to ward off liability. But the party sued may have an affirmative claim of his own against the party who has sued him. In the federal system, such proceedings are known as counterclaims, and are governed by Rule 13. We take up the issue of counterclaims in some detail in our discussion of joinder of claims and parties in Chapter 10. But you already have seen examples of both defenses and counterclaims. In *Gomez*, the defense of qualified immunity was just that — a defense; no claim was brought by the defendant against the plaintiff (for example, for abuse of process). By contrast, in *LaFont*, the defendant was sued for fraud and conversion in connection with the proceeds of a check written by the plaintiff. Not only did the defendant deny liability by alleging that the money was a gift, but the defendant brought an affirmative claim against the plaintiff for nonpayment of a promissory note. The critical distinction is that a counterclaim does not necessarily rise or fall on the success of the plaintiff's claim (although, as discussed in Chapter 10, older devices that antedated the counterclaim, such as a "set-off" did). Note also that while it is usually the case that the original defendant would bring a counterclaim against the original plaintiff, a counterclaim can be brought against anyone in the litigation who has had a claim brought against them (e.g., by a party impleaded as a third-party defendant on an indemnity and contribution claim against the defendant who impleaded them).

SECTION E.   AMENDMENTS

1. THE BASICS–RULE 15(a)

Beeck v. Aquaslide 'N' Dive Corp.

United States Court of Appeals, Eighth Circuit, 1977.
562 F.2d 537.

BENSON, DISTRICT JUDGE (sitting by designation).

This case is an appeal from the trial court's exercise of discretion on procedural matters in a diversity personal injury action.

Jerry A. Beeck was severely injured on July 15, 1972, while using a water slide. He and his wife, Judy A. Beeck, sued Aquaslide 'N' Dive Corporation (Aquaslide), a Texas corporation, alleging it manufactured the slide involved in the accident, and sought to recover substantial damages on theories of negligence, strict liability and breach of implied warranty.

Aquaslide initially admitted manufacture of the slide, but later moved to amend its answer to deny manufacture; the motion was resisted. The district court granted leave to amend. On motion of the defendant, a separate trial was held on the issue of "whether the defendant designed, manufactured or sold the slide in question." This motion was also resisted by the plaintiffs. The issue was tried to a jury, which returned a verdict for the defendant, after which the trial court entered summary judgment of dismissal of the case. Plaintiffs took this appeal, and stated the issues presented for review to be:

1. Where the manufacturer of the product, a water slide, admitted in its Answer and later in its Answer to Interrogatories both filed prior to the running of the statute of limitations that it designed, manufactured and sold the water slide in question, was it an abuse of the trial court's discretion to grant leave to amend to the manufacturer in order to deny these admissions after the running of the statute of limitations?

2. After granting the manufacturer's Motion for Leave to Amend in order to deny the prior admissions of design, manufacture and sale of the water slide in question, was it an abuse of the trial court's discretion to further grant the manufacturer's Motion for a Separate

Trial on the issue of manufacture?

I. FACTS

A brief review of the facts found by the trial court in its order granting leave to amend, and which do not appear to have been in dispute, is essential to a full understanding of appellants' claims.

In 1971 Kimberly Village Home Association of Davenport, Iowa, ordered an Aquaslide product from one George Boldt, who was a local distributor handling defendant's products. The order was forwarded by Boldt to Sentry Pool and Chemical Supply Co. in Rock Island, Illinois, and Sentry forwarded the order to Purity Swimming Pool Supply in Hammond, Indiana. A slide was delivered from a Purity warehouse to Kimberly Village, and was installed by Kimberly employees. On July 15, 1972, Jerry A. Beeck was injured while using the slide at a social gathering sponsored at Kimberly Village by his employer, Harker Wholesale Meats, Inc. Soon after the accident investigations were undertaken by representatives of the separate insurers of Harker and Kimberly Village. On October 31, 1972, Aquaslide first learned of the accident through a letter sent by a representative of Kimberly's insurer to Aquaslide, advising that "one of your Queen Model # Q-3D slides" was involved in the accident. Aquaslide forwarded this notification to its insurer. Aquaslide's insurance adjuster made an on-site investigation of the slide in May, 1973, and also interviewed persons connected with the ordering and assembly of the slide. An inter-office letter dated September 23, 1973, indicates that Aquaslide's insurer was of the opinion the "Aquaslide in question was definitely manufactured by our insured." The complaint was filed October 15, 1973.[3] Investigators for three different insurance companies, representing Harker, Kimberly and the defendant, had concluded that the slide had been manufactured by Aquaslide, and the defendant, with no information to the contrary, answered the complaint on December 12, 1973, and admitted that it "designed, manufactured, assembled and sold" the slide in question.[4]

The statute of limitations on plaintiff's personal injury claim expired on July 15, 1974. About six and one-half months later Carl Meyer, president and owner of Aquaslide, visited the site of the accident prior to the taking of his deposition by the plaintiff.[5] From his on-site inspection of the slide, he determined it was not a product of the defendant. Thereafter, Aquaslide moved the court for leave to amend its answer to deny manufacture of the slide.

II. LEAVE TO AMEND

Amendment of pleadings in civil actions is governed by Rule 15(a), which provides in part that once issue is joined in a lawsuit, a party may amend his pleading "only by leave of court or by written consent of the adverse party; and leave shall be freely given when justice so requires."

---

[3]   Aquaslide 'N' Dive Corporation was the sole defendant named in the complaint.

[4]   In answers to interrogatories filed on June 3, 1974, Aquaslide again admitted manufacture of the slide in question.

[5]   Plaintiffs apparently requested Meyer to inspect the slide prior to the taking of his deposition to determine whether it was defectively installed or assembled.

In Foman v. Davis, 371 U.S. 178, 9 L.Ed. 2d 222, 83 S.Ct. 227 (1962), the Supreme Court had occasion to construe that portion of Rule 15(a) set out above:

> Rule 15(a) declares that leave to amend "shall be freely given when justice so requires," this mandate is to be heeded . . . . If the underlying facts or circumstances relied upon by a plaintiff may be a proper subject of relief, he ought to be afforded an opportunity to test his claim on the merits. In the absence of any apparent or declared reason — such as undue delay, bad faith or dilatory motive on the part of the movant, repeated failure to cure deficiencies by amendments previously allowed, undue prejudice to the opposing party by virtue of allowance of the amendment, futility of amendment, etc. — the leave sought should, as the rules require, be "freely given." Of course, the grant or denial of an opportunity to amend is within the discretion of the District Court, ...

This Court in Hanson v. Hunt Oil Co., 398 F.2d 578, 582 (8th Cir. 1968), held that "prejudice *must be shown.*" The burden is on the party opposing the amendment to show such prejudice. In ruling on a motion for leave to amend, the trial court must inquire into the issue of prejudice to the opposing party, in light of the particular facts of the case.

Certain principles apply to appellate review of a trial court's grant or denial of a motion to amend pleadings. First, as noted in *Foman v. Davis,* allowance or denial of leave to amend lies within the sound discretion of the trial court, and is reviewable only for an abuse of discretion. The appellate court must view the case in the posture in which the trial court acted in ruling on the motion to amend.

It is evident from the order of the district court that in the exercise of its discretion in ruling on defendant's motion for leave to amend, it searched the record for evidence of bad faith, prejudice and undue delay which might be sufficient to overbalance the mandate of Rule 15(a), and *Foman v. Davis,* that leave to amend should be "freely given." Plaintiffs had not at any time conceded that the slide in question had not been manufactured by the defendant, and at the time the motion for leave to amend was at issue, the court had to decide whether the defendant should be permitted to litigate a material factual issue on its merits.

In inquiring into the issue of bad faith, the court noted the fact that the defendant, in initially concluding that it had manufactured the slide, relied upon the conclusions of three different insurance companies,[6] each of which had conducted an investigation into the circumstances surrounding the accident. This reliance upon investigations of three insurance companies, and the fact that "no contention has been made by anyone that the defendant influenced this possibly erroneous conclusion," persuaded the court that "defendant has not acted in such bad faith as to be precluded from contesting the issue of manufacture at trial." The court further found "to the extent that 'blame' is to be

---

[6] The insurer of Beeck's employer, the insurer of Kimberly Village, as well as the defendant's insurer had each concluded the slide in question was an Aquaslide.

spread regarding the original identification, the record indicates that it should be shared equally."

In considering the issue of prejudice that might result to the plaintiffs from the granting of the motion for leave to amend, the trial court held that the facts presented to it did not support plaintiffs' assertion that, because of the running of the two year Iowa statute of limitations on personal injury claims, the allowance of the amendment would sound the "death knell" of the litigation. In order to accept plaintiffs' argument, the court would have had to assume that the defendant would prevail at trial on the factual issue of manufacture of the slide, and further that plaintiffs would be foreclosed, should the amendment be allowed, from proceeding against other parties if they were unsuccessful in pressing their claim against Aquaslide. On the state of the record before it, the trial court was unwilling to make such assumptions,[7] and concluded "under these circumstances, the Court deems that the possible prejudice to the plaintiffs is an insufficient basis on which to deny the proposed amendment." The court reasoned that the amendment would merely allow the defendant to contest a disputed factual issue at trial, and further that it would be prejudicial to the defendant to deny the amendment.

The court also held that defendant and its insurance carrier, in investigating the circumstances surrounding the accident, had not been so lacking in diligence as to dictate a denial of the right to litigate the factual issue of manufacture of the slide.

On this record we hold that the trial court did not abuse its discretion in allowing the defendant to amend its answer.

III. SEPARATE TRIALS

After Aquaslide was granted leave to amend its answer, it moved pursuant to Rule 42(b),[8] for a separate trial on the issue of manufacture of the slide involved in the accident. The grounds upon which the motion was based were:

> (1) a separate trial solely on the issue of whether the slide was manufactured by Aquaslide would save considerable trial time and unnecessary expense and preparation for all parties and the court, and

---

[7] The district court noted in its order granting leave to amend that plaintiffs may be able to sue other parties as a result of the substituting of a "counterfeit" slide for the Aquaslide, if indeed this occurred. The court added:

> again, the Court is handicapped by an unclear record on this issue. If, in fact, the slide in question is not an Aquaslide, the replacement entered the picture somewhere along the Boldt to Sentry, Sentry to Purity, Purity to Kimberly Village chain of distribution. Depending upon the circumstances of its entry, a cause of action sounding in fraud or contract might lie. If so, the applicable statute of limitations period would not have run. Further, as defendant points out, the doctrine of equitable estoppel might possibly preclude another defendant from asserting the two-year statute as a defense.

[8] Rule 42(b), F.R.Civ.P., provides as follows:

> Separate Trials. The court, in furtherance of convenience or to avoid prejudice, or when separate trials will be conducive to expedition and economy, may order a separate trial of any claim, cross-claim, counterclaim, or third-party claim, or of any separate issue or of any number of claims, cross-claims, counterclaims, third-party claims, or issues, always preserving inviolate the right of trial by jury as declared by the Seventh Amendment to the Constitution or as given by a statute of the United States.

(2) a separate trial solely on the issue of manufacture would protect Aquaslide from substantial prejudice.

The court granted the motion for a separate trial on the issue of manufacture, and this grant of a separate trial is challenged by appellants as being an abuse of discretion.

A trial court's severance of trial will not be disturbed on appeal except for an abuse of discretion.

The record indicates that Carl Meyer, president and owner of Aquaslide, designs the slides sold by Aquaslide. The slide which plaintiff Jerry A. Beeck was using at the time of his accident was very similar in appearance to an Aquaslide product, and was without identifying marks. Kimberly Village had in fact ordered an Aquaslide for its swimming pool, and thought it had received one. After Meyer's inspection and Aquaslide's subsequent assertion that it was not an Aquaslide product, plaintiffs elected to stand on their contention that it was in fact an Aquaslide. This raised a substantial issue of material fact which, if resolved in defendant's favor, would exonerate defendant from liability.

Plaintiff Jerry A. Beeck had been severely injured, and he and his wife together were seeking damages arising out of those injuries in the sum of $2,225,000.00. Evidence of plaintiffs' injuries and damages would clearly have taken up several days of trial time, and because of the severity of the injuries, may have been prejudicial to the defendant's claim of non-manufacture. The jury, by special interrogatory, found that the slide had not been manufactured by Aquaslide. That finding has not been questioned on appeal. Judicial economy, beneficial to all the parties, was obviously served by the trial court's grant of a separate trial. We hold the Rule 42(b) separation was not an abuse of discretion.

The judgment of the district court is affirmed.

NOTES AND PROBLEMS FOR DISCUSSION

1. The *Beeck* court says that the test under Rule 15 is prejudice to the nonamending party. Wasn't Beeck prejudiced because the amendment gave the defendant a defense it wouldn't otherwise have had and, absent such a defense, Beeck had a good chance to win? If that isn't prejudice, then what is?

2. The Court states that any blame regarding the misidentification should be "shared equally." In light of the defendant's answer, was the plaintiff somehow at fault?

3. If you represented Beeck, what additional arguments might you make to show prejudice?

4. In the actual case, there was later litigation during which it was revealed that the defendant knew of at least three other incidents of counterfeit slides before filing its answer. Does this give Beeck a further argument?

5. It seems likely that the identification by the defendant's president was fairly convincing — it was probably one of those little things in the product that most wouldn't notice but which provides clear identification. If so, why did Beeck's lawyer still go to trial on the identification issue?

6. If the court had disallowed Aquaslide's amendment, the jury would have been instructed that Aquaslide had manufactured the slide in question. If you represented Aquaslide, how would you defend, for example, against evidence of negligence in the design or manufacture of some other manufacturer's product?

7. After this decision, Beeck (with new lawyers) sued Aquaslide 'N' Dive in an Iowa state court claiming that the defendant was negligent in admitting it manufactured the slide, and the plaintiff was damaged as a result. Beeck won on this somewhat unusual negligence claim, but the decision was reversed and remanded for still another trial in a lengthy opinion by the Iowa Supreme Court. It concluded that, to recover against Aquaslide on a negligent misrepresentation theory, Beeck would have to be able to show that he could have recovered (i.e., collected) a judgment against the real manufacturer. Beeck v. Aquaslide 'N' Dive Corp., 350 N.W.2d 149 (Iowa 1984).

8. Do not succumb to the misleading impression that amendments are always, or almost always granted. It isn't necessarily so. After all, the appeals court in *Beeck* did not hold that the motion to amend had to be granted, did it? A rough rule of thumb is that the court will be more reluctant to permit amendments as the case proceeds. Explain why this is especially true (a) after discovery is fully or largely completed; (b) after the filing of a motion for summary judgment; or (c) after the final pretrial conference.

2. RELATION BACK — RULES 15(b) AND 15(c)

Consider the relationship among Rules 15(a), (b), and (c) and when each applies. This presents a difficult set of issues because Rules 15(b) and 15(c) assume a familiarity with certain legal doctrines which are unfamiliar to most students. Rule 15(a) generally sets forth the standards for granting all amendments to pleadings. Rule 15(b) deals with amendments at trial. Rule 15(c) deals with amendments when the amendment gives rise to a statute of limitations issue.

In back of an understanding of Rule 15(b) is the doctrine of "variance" or "variance between pleading and proof." As noted earlier, at common law (and even under the Codes) there was virtually no discovery or pretrial procedure, and after the pleadings were completed came the trial. Under such a system, courts viewed the pleadings as a sort of detailed outline of the issues and matters to be raised at trial. If one party sought to introduce evidence or issues that were "outside" the pleadings, it was called a "variance" and such evidence would ordinarily not be admitted. To take a simple example, if a plaintiff sued a defendant and alleged that the defendant drove his car carelessly, evidence that the car itself was defective would be a variance and might not be admitted. Similarly, if the defendant pleaded contributory negligence, and the defendant sought to introduce evidence that the plaintiff had assumed the risk, such evidence would be a variance and might not be admitted.

The doctrine of variance has less significance today because of the liberality in allowing amendment to pleadings, the availability of discovery to identify issues, and pretrial procedures to pin down what is to be tried. Nevertheless, variance-related concerns sometimes do come up at trial, and Rule 15(b) deals with them in two alternative ways. One part of 15(b) covers the situation where one party fails to object when the evidence or issues outside the pleadings are raised. Another deals with the situation where one party does object at trial to evidence or issues on the ground of variance.

Rule 15(c) concerns amendments that seek to add a contest which, were it to be filed as an original pleading on its own, would be barred by the statute of limitations. Rule 15(c) provides that even if the new contest would now be barred by the applicable statute of limitations, the filing may "relate back" to the date of the original pleading, provided the amended pleading satisfies the conditions set forth in the Rule. Rule 15(c) deals with two such possible situations — one where the plaintiff wants to add new, different, or additional *claims* against the same defendant; the other where the plaintiff wants to add a new *party* as a defendant (either as an additional defendant, or as a substitute for the defendant already in the case).

With respect to the addition of a claim on which the statute of limitations has run in the interim (i.e., since the date of the filing of the Complaint), consider the following: An employee who has been discriminatorily discharged from his job might have two claims against his employer — one claim under federal statutes barring employment discrimination and one claim under state law for breach of contract. But suppose the employee brought only his federal claim in federal court. He later seeks to amend his complaint to add the state law claim. Had he brought the state law claim in the original complaint, it would have been timely. But in the interim, the statute of limitations on the contract claim has run.

Will Rule 15(c) help the plaintiff out, and if so, what is the reason for allowing the amendment? Note that the inquiry into whether the state law claim arises out of the same transaction or occurrence as the federal claim is the very same "nexus" inquiry that is repeated elsewhere in the rules. See, e.g., Rule 20 (party joinder); Rule 13(a) (compulsory counterclaims); Rule 13(g) (cross claims). And it bears at least a passing resemblance to the nexus requirement mentioned in the supplemental jurisdiction statute, 28 U.S.C. §1367(a). Does it matter if state law would expressly *forbid* the possibility of relation back? And if not, does Rule 15(c) thereby "abridge, enlarge, or modify [a] substantive right" in violation of the Rules Enabling Act, 28 U.S.C. §2072?

Now, consider the addition of a new party. One purpose of Rule 15(c) in connection with the addition or supplementation of parties is to deal with simple misidentification cases. For example, the defendant might be named as "Jonothan Nash," when the correct spelling is "Jonathan Nash." Another purpose deals with the corporate group company, where several companies operate under common ownership in common facilities but the plaintiff sues the wrong one — e.g., she alleges that the plaintiff was injured by a truck that says "West" on the side and sues West Development Co.; in fact, the truck is owned and operated by West Property Management Co. which occupies the same offices and is a subsidiary of West Development Co. Make sure you understand how Rule 15(c) deals with these "simple" situations. Finally, consider a more difficult problem:

Krupski v. Costa Crociere, S.p.A.

Supreme Court of the United States, 2010.
560 U.S. 538, 130 S.Ct. 2485, 177 L.Ed. 2d 48.

JUSTICE SOTOMAYOR delivered the opinion of the Court.

Rule 15(c) of the Federal Rules of Civil Procedure governs when an amended pleading "relates back" to the date of a timely filed original pleading and is thus itself timely even though it was filed outside an applicable statute of limitations. Where an amended pleading changes a party or a party's name, the Rule requires, among other things, that "the party to be brought in by amendment . . . knew or should have known that the action would have been brought against it, but for a mistake concerning the proper party's identity." Rule 15(c)(1)(C). In this case, the Court of Appeals held that Rule 15(c) was not satisfied because the plaintiff knew or should have known of the proper defendant before filing her original complaint. The court also held that relation back was not appropriate because the plaintiff had unduly delayed in seeking to amend. We hold that relation back under Rule 15(c)(1)(C) depends on what the party to be added knew or should have known, not on the amending party's knowledge or its timeliness in seeking to amend the pleading. Accordingly, we reverse the judgment of the Court of Appeals.

I

[Wanda Krupski slipped and fell on a cruise ship (the "Costa Magica") operated by the Italian carrier, "Costa Crociere," sailing from Florida. Krupski booked her ticket with a local (South Carolina) travel agent through "Costa Cruise" — the Florida-based North American sales and booking agent for the carrier, Costa Crociere. The ticket included a provision that any suit arising out of the cruise be filed within one year of the alleged injury, and it identified Costa Crociere as the carrier. Krupski was injured on Feb. 21, 2007, and Krupski's attorney timely filed suit on Feb. 1, 2008. But Krupski's complaint named Costa Cruise as the defendant, rather than the carrier, Costa Crociere. The defendant answered on Feb. 25, 2008, four days after the contractual limitations period expired. In its answer, Costa Cruise stated that it was only the sales and booking agent for the carrier, Costa Crociere. Then, on March 20, 2008, Costa Cruise listed Costa Corciere as an interested party in its corporate disclosure statement. And on May 6, 2008, Costa Cruise moved for summary judgment stating that Costa Crociere was the proper defendant. In response to the summary judgment motion, Krupski moved to amend her complaint to name Costa Crociere, and to dismiss Costa Cruise as a defendant. The district court granted both motions. Costa Cruise was served with an amended complaint on August 21, 2008. Shortly thereafter, Costa Crociere (represented by the same attorney as for Costa Cruise) moved to dismiss Krupski's amended complaint as untimely, arguing that it did not "relate back" to the time of the filing of the original complaint against Costa Cruise.]

The District Court agreed. * * * Rule 15(c), the court explained, imposes three requirements before an amended complaint against a newly named defendant can relate back to the original complaint. First, the claim against the newly named defendant must have arisen "out of the conduct, transaction, or occurrence set out—or attempted to be set out—in the original pleading." Fed. Rules Civ. Proc. 15(c)(1)(B),(C). Second, "within the period provided by Rule 4(m) for serving the summons and complaint" (which is ordinarily 120 days from when the complaint is filed, see Rule 4(m)—[now 90 days.—eds.]), the newly named defendant must have "received such notice of the action that it will not be prejudiced in defending on the merits." Rule 15(c)(1)(C)(i). Finally, the plaintiff must show that, within the Rule 4(m) period, the newly named defendant "knew or should have known that the action would have been brought against it, but for a mistake concerning the proper party's identity." Rule 15(c)(1)(C)(ii).

The first two conditions posed no problem, the court explained: The claim against Costa Crociere clearly involved the same occurrence as the original claim against Costa Cruise, and Costa Crociere had constructive notice of the action and had not shown that any unfair prejudice would result from relation back. But the court found the third condition fatal to Krupski's attempt to relate back, concluding that Krupski had not made a mistake concerning the identity of the proper party. Relying on Eleventh Circuit precedent, the court explained that the word "mistake" should not be construed to encompass a deliberate decision not to sue a party whose identity the plaintiff knew before the statute of limitations had run. Because Costa Cruise informed Krupski that Costa Crociere was the proper defendant in its answer, corporate disclosure statement, and motion for summary judgment, and yet Krupski delayed for months in moving to amend and then in filing an amended complaint, the court concluded that Krupski knew of the proper defendant and made no mistake.

The Eleventh Circuit affirmed in an unpublished per curiam opinion. Rather than relying on the information contained in Costa Cruise's filings, all of which were made after the statute of limitations had expired, as evidence that Krupski did not make a mistake, the Court of Appeals noted that the relevant information was located within Krupski's passenger ticket, which she had furnished to her counsel well before the end of the limitations period. Because the ticket clearly identified Costa Crociere as the carrier, the court stated, Krupski either knew or should have known of Costa Crociere's identity as a potential party. It was therefore appropriate to treat Krupski as having chosen to sue one potential party over another. Alternatively, even assuming that she first learned of Costa Crociere's identity as the correct party from Costa Cruise's answer, the Court of Appeals observed that Krupski waited 133 days from the time she filed her original complaint to seek leave to amend and did not file an amended complaint for another month after that. In light of this delay, the Court of Appeals concluded that the District Court did not abuse its discretion in denying relation back.

We granted certiorari to resolve tension among the Circuits over the breadth of Rule 15(c)(1)(C)(ii), and we now reverse.

II

Under the Federal Rules of Civil Procedure, an amendment to a pleading relates back to the date of the original pleading when:

> "(A) the law that provides the applicable statute of limitations allows relation back;

> "(B) the amendment asserts a claim or defense that arose out of the conduct, transaction, or occurrence set out—or attempted to be set out—in the original pleading; or

> "(C) the amendment changes the party or the naming of the party against whom a claim is asserted, if Rule 15(c)(1)(B) is satisfied and if, within the period provided by Rule 4(m) for serving the summons and complaint, the party to be brought in by amendment:

>> "(i) received such notice of the action that it will not be prejudiced in defending on the merits; and

>> "(ii) knew or should have known that the action would have been brought against it, but for a mistake concerning the proper party's identity." Rule 15(c)(1).

In our view, neither of the Court of Appeals' reasons for denying relation back under Rule 15(c)(1)(C)(ii) finds support in the text of the Rule. We consider each reason in turn.

A

The Court of Appeals first decided that Krupski either knew or should have known of the proper party's identity and thus determined that she had made a deliberate choice instead of a mistake in not naming Costa Crociere as a party in her original pleading. By focusing on Krupski's knowledge, the Court of Appeals chose the wrong starting point. The question under Rule 15(c)(1)(C)(ii) is not whether Krupski knew or should have known the identity of Costa Crociere as the proper defendant, but whether Costa Crociere knew or should have known that it would have been named as a defendant but for an error. Rule 15(c)(1)(C)(ii) asks what the prospective defendant knew or should have known during the Rule 4(m) period, not what the plaintiff knew or should have known at the time of filing her original complaint.[3]

Information in the plaintiff's possession is relevant only if it bears on the defendant's understanding of whether the plaintiff made a mistake regarding the

---

[3] Rule 15(c)(1)(C) speaks generally of an amendment to a "pleading" that changes "the party against whom a claim is asserted," and it therefore is not limited to the circumstance of a plaintiff filing an amended complaint seeking to bring in a new defendant. Nevertheless, because the latter is the "typical case" of Rule 15(c)(1)(C)'s applicability, * * * we use this circumstance as a shorthand throughout this opinion. * * *

proper party's identity. For purposes of that inquiry, it would be error to conflate knowledge of a party's existence with the absence of mistake. A mistake is "[a]n error, misconception, or misunderstanding; an erroneous belief." Black's Law Dictionary 1092 (9th ed. 2009); see also Webster's Third New International Dictionary 1446 (2002) (defining "mistake" as "a misunderstanding of the meaning or implication of something"; "a wrong action or statement proceeding from faulty judgment, inadequate knowledge, or inattention"; "an erroneous belief"; or "a state of mind not in accordance with the facts"). That a plaintiff knows of a party's existence does not preclude her from making a mistake with respect to that party's identity. A plaintiff may know that a prospective defendant—call him party A—exists, while erroneously believing him to have the status of party B. Similarly, a plaintiff may know generally what party A does while misunderstanding the roles that party A and party B played in the "conduct, transaction, or occurrence" giving rise to her claim. If the plaintiff sues party B instead of party A under these circumstances, she has made a "mistake concerning the proper party's identity" notwithstanding her knowledge of the existence of both parties. The only question under Rule 15(c)(1)(C)(ii), then, is whether party A knew or should have known that, absent some mistake, the action would have been brought against him.

Respondent urges that the key issue under Rule 15(c)(1)(C)(ii) is whether the plaintiff made a deliberate choice to sue one party over another. We agree that making a deliberate choice to sue one party instead of another while fully understanding the factual and legal differences between the two parties is the antithesis of making a mistake concerning the proper party's identity. We disagree, however, with respondent's position that any time a plaintiff is aware of the existence of two parties and chooses to sue the wrong one, the proper defendant could reasonably believe that the plaintiff made no mistake. The reasonableness of the mistake is not itself at issue. As noted, a plaintiff might know that the prospective defendant exists but nonetheless harbor a misunderstanding about his status or role in the events giving rise to the claim at issue, and she may mistakenly choose to sue a different defendant based on that misimpression. That kind of deliberate but mistaken choice does not foreclose a finding that Rule 15(c)(1)(C)(ii) has been satisfied.

This reading is consistent with the purpose of relation back: to balance the interests of the defendant protected by the statute of limitations with the preference expressed in the Federal Rules of Civil Procedure in general, and Rule 15 in particular, for resolving disputes on their merits. See, e.g., Advisory Committee's 1966 Notes 122; 3 Moore's Federal Practice §§ 15.02[1], 15.19[3][a] (3d ed. 2009). A prospective defendant who legitimately believed that the limitations period had passed without any attempt to sue him has a strong interest in repose. But repose would be a windfall for a prospective defendant who understood, or who should have understood, that he escaped suit during the limitations period only because the plaintiff misunderstood a crucial fact about his identity. Because a plaintiff's knowledge of the existence of a party does not foreclose the possibility that she has made a mistake of identity about which that party should have been aware, such knowledge does not support that party's interest in repose.

Our reading is also consistent with the history of Rule 15(c)(1)(C). That provision was added in 1966 to respond to a recurring problem in suits against the Federal Government, particularly in the Social Security context. * * * Individuals who had filed timely lawsuits challenging the administrative denial of benefits often failed to name the party identified in the statute as the proper defendant—the current Secretary of what was then the Department of Health, Education, and Welfare—and named instead the United States; the Department of Health, Education, and Welfare itself; the nonexistent "Federal Security Administration"; or a Secretary who had recently retired from office. *Ibid.* By the time the plaintiffs discovered their mistakes, the statute of limitations in many cases had expired, and the district courts denied the plaintiffs leave to amend on the ground that the amended complaints would not relate back. Rule 15(c) was therefore "amplified to provide a general solution" to this problem. *Ibid.* It is conceivable that the Social Security litigants knew or reasonably should have known the identity of the proper defendant either because of documents in their administrative cases or by dint of the statute setting forth the filing requirements. See 42 U.S.C. § 405(g) (1958 ed., Supp. III). Nonetheless, the Advisory Committee clearly meant their filings to qualify as mistakes under the Rule.

Respondent suggests that our decision in Nelson v. Adams USA, Inc., 529 U.S. 460 (2000), forecloses the reading of Rule 15(c)(1)(C)(ii) we adopt today. We disagree. In that case, Adams USA, Inc. (Adams), had obtained an award of attorney's fees against the corporation of which Donald Nelson was the president and sole shareholder. After Adams became concerned that the corporation did not have sufficient funds to pay the award, Adams sought to amend its pleading to add Nelson as a party and simultaneously moved to amend the judgment to hold Nelson responsible. The District Court granted both motions, and the Court of Appeals affirmed. We reversed, holding that the requirements of due process, as codified in Rules 12 and 15 of the Federal Rules of Civil Procedure, demand that an added party have the opportunity to respond before judgment is entered against him. *Id.*, at 465-467. In a footnote explaining that relation back does not deny the added party an opportunity to respond to the amended pleading, we noted that the case did not arise under the "mistake clause" of Rule 15(c): "Respondent Adams made no such mistake. It knew of Nelson's role and existence and, until it moved to amend its pleading, chose to assert its claim for costs and fees only against [Nelson's company]." *Id.*, at 467, n. 1.

Contrary to respondent's claim, *Nelson* does not suggest that Rule 15(c)(1)(C)(ii) cannot be satisfied if a plaintiff knew of the prospective defendant's existence at the time she filed her original complaint. In that case, there was nothing in the initial pleading suggesting that Nelson was an intended party, while there was evidence in the record (of which Nelson was aware) that Adams sought to add him only after learning that the company would not be able to satisfy the judgment. *Id.*, at 463-464. This evidence countered any implication that Adams had originally failed to name Nelson because of any "mistake concerning the proper party's identity," and instead suggested that Adams decided to name Nelson only after the fact in an attempt to ensure that the fee award would be paid. The footnote merely observes that Adams had originally been under no misimpression about the function Nelson played in the underlying dispute. We said, after all, that Adams knew of Nelson's "role" as well as his existence. *Id.,* at 467, n. 1. Read in context, the footnote in Nelson is entirely consistent with our understanding of the Rule: When the original complaint and the plaintiff's conduct compel the conclusion that the failure to name the prospective defendant in the original complaint was the result of a fully informed decision as opposed to a mistake concerning the proper defendant's identity, the requirements of Rule 15(c)(1)(C)(ii) are not met. This conclusion is in keeping with our rejection today of the Court of Appeals' reliance on the plaintiff's knowledge to deny relation back.

B

The Court of Appeals offered a second reason why Krupski's amended complaint did not relate back: Krupski had unduly delayed in seeking to file, and in eventually filing, an amended complaint. The Court of Appeals offered no support for its view that a plaintiff's dilatory conduct can justify the denial of relation back under Rule 15(c)(1)(C), and we find none. The Rule plainly sets forth an exclusive list of requirements for relation back, and the amending party's diligence is not among them. Moreover, the Rule mandates relation back once the Rule's requirements are satisfied; it does not leave the decision whether to grant relation back to the district court's equitable discretion. See Rule 15(c)(1) ("An amendment . . . relates back . . . when" the three listed requirements are met).

The mandatory nature of the inquiry for relation back under Rule 15(c) is particularly striking in contrast to the inquiry under Rule 15(a), which sets forth the circumstances in which a party may amend its pleading before trial. By its terms, Rule 15(a) gives discretion to the district court in deciding whether to grant a motion to amend a pleading to add a party or a claim. Following an initial period after filing a pleading during which a party may amend once "as a matter of course," "a party may amend its pleading only with the opposing party's written consent or the court's leave," which the court "should freely give . . . when justice so requires." Rules 15(a)(1)-(2). We have previously explained that a court may consider a movant's "undue delay" or "dilatory motive" in deciding whether to grant leave to amend under Rule 15(a). Foman v. Davis, 371 U.S. 178, 182 (1962). As the contrast between Rule 15(a) and Rule 15(c) makes clear, however, the speed with which a plaintiff moves to amend her complaint or files an amended complaint after obtaining leave to do so has no bearing on whether the amended complaint relates back. Cf. 6A C. Wright, A. Miller, & M. Kane, Federal Practice and Procedure § 1498, pp. 142-143, and nn. 49-50 (2d ed. 1990 and Supp. 2010).

Rule 15(c)(1)(C) does permit a court to examine a plaintiff's conduct during the Rule 4(m) period, but not in the way or for the purpose respondent or the

Court of Appeals suggests. As we have explained, the question under Rule 15(c)(1)(C)(ii) is what the prospective defendant reasonably should have understood about the plaintiff's intent in filing the original complaint against the first defendant. To the extent the plaintiff's postfiling conduct informs the prospective defendant's understanding of whether the plaintiff initially made a "mistake concerning the proper party's identity," a court may consider the conduct. Cf. Leonard v. Parry, 219 F.3d 25, 29 (CA1 2000) ("[P]ost-filing events occasionally can shed light on the plaintiff's state of mind at an earlier time" and "can inform a defendant's reasonable beliefs concerning whether her omission from the original complaint represented a mistake (as opposed to a conscious choice)"). The plaintiff's postfiling conduct is otherwise immaterial to the question whether an amended complaint relates back.[5]

C

Applying these principles to the facts of this case, we think it clear that the courts below erred in denying relation back under Rule 15(c)(1)(C)(ii). The District Court held that Costa Crociere had "constructive notice" of Krupski's complaint within the Rule 4(m) period. Costa Crociere has not challenged this finding. Because the complaint made clear that Krupski meant to sue the company that "owned, operated, managed, supervised and controlled" the ship on which she was injured, and also indicated (mistakenly) that Costa Cruise performed those roles, Costa Crociere should have known, within the Rule 4(m) period, that it was not named as a defendant in that complaint only because of Krupski's misunderstanding about which "Costa" entity was in charge of the ship—clearly a "mistake concerning the proper party's identity."

Respondent contends that because the original complaint referred to the ticket's forum requirement and pre-suit claims notification procedure, Krupski was clearly aware of the contents of the ticket, and because the ticket identified Costa Crociere as the carrier and proper party for a lawsuit, respondent was entitled to think that she made a deliberate choice to sue Costa Cruise instead of Costa Crociere. As we have explained, however, that Krupski may have known the contents of the ticket does not foreclose the possibility that she nonetheless misunderstood crucial facts regarding the two companies' identities. Especially because the face of the complaint plainly indicated such a misunderstanding, respondent's contention is not persuasive. Moreover, respondent has articulated no strategy that it could reasonably have thought Krupski was pursuing in suing a defendant that was legally unable to provide relief.

Respondent also argues that Krupski's failure to move to amend her complaint during the Rule 4(m) period shows that she made no mistake in that period. But as discussed, any delay on Krupski's part is relevant only to the

---

[5] Similarly, we reject respondent's suggestion that Rule 15(c) requires a plaintiff to move to amend her complaint or to file and serve an amended complaint within the Rule 4(m) period. Rule 15(c)(1)(C)(i) simply requires that the prospective defendant has received sufficient "notice of the action" within the Rule 4(m) period that he will not be prejudiced in defending the case on the merits. The Advisory Committee Notes to the 1966 Amendment clarify that "the notice need not be formal." Advisory Committee's 1966 Notes 122.

extent it may have informed Costa Crociere's understanding during the Rule 4(m) period of whether she made a mistake originally. Krupski's failure to add Costa Crociere during the Rule 4(m) period is not sufficient to make reasonable any belief that she had made a deliberate and informed decision not to sue Costa Crociere in the first instance.[6] Nothing in Krupski's conduct during the Rule 4(m) period suggests that she failed to name Costa Crociere because of anything other than a mistake.

It is also worth noting that Costa Cruise and Costa Crociere are related corporate entities with very similar names; "crociera" even means "cruise" in Italian. Cassell's Italian Dictionary 137, 670 (1967). This interrelationship and similarity heighten the expectation that Costa Crociere should suspect a mistake has been made when Costa Cruise is named in a complaint that actually describes Costa Crociere's activities. Cf. Morel v. Daimler-Chrysler AG, 565 F.3d 20, 27 (CA1 2009) (where complaint conveyed plaintiffs' attempt to sue automobile manufacturer and erroneously named the manufacturer as Daimler-Chrysler Corporation instead of the actual manufacturer, a legally distinct but related entity named DaimlerChrysler AG, the latter should have realized it had not been named because of plaintiffs' mistake); Goodman v. Praxair, Inc., 494 F.3d 458, 473-475 (CA4 2007) (en banc) (where complaint named parent company Praxair, Inc., but described status of subsidiary company Praxair Services, Inc., subsidiary company knew or should have known it had not been named because of plaintiff's mistake). In addition, Costa Crociere's own actions contributed to passenger confusion over "the proper party" for a lawsuit. The front of the ticket advertises that "Costa Cruises" has achieved a certification of quality, without clarifying whether "Costa Cruises" is Costa Cruise Lines, Costa Crociere, or some other related "Costa" company. Indeed, Costa Crociere is evidently aware that the difference between Costa Cruise and Costa Crociere can be confusing for cruise ship passengers. See, e.g., Suppa v. Costa Crociere, S.p.A., 2007 WL 4287508, *1, (SD Fla., Dec. 4, 2007) (denying Costa Crociere's motion to dismiss the amended complaint where the original complaint had named Costa Cruise as a defendant after "find[ing] it simply inconceivable that Defendant Costa Crociere was not on notice . . . that . . . but for the mistake in the original Complaint, Costa Crociere was the appropriate party to be named in the action").

In light of these facts, Costa Crociere should have known that Krupski's failure to name it as a defendant in her original complaint was due to a mistake concerning the proper party's identity. We therefore reverse the judgment of the Court of Appeals for the Eleventh Circuit and remand the case for further proceedings consistent with this opinion.

---

[6] The Court of Appeals concluded that Krupski was not diligent merely because she did not seek leave to add Costa Crociere until 133 days after she filed her original complaint and did not actually file an amended complaint for another a month after that. It is not clear why Krupski should have been found dilatory for not accepting at face value the unproven allegations in Costa Cruise's answer and corporate disclosure form. In fact, Krupski moved to amend her complaint to add Costa Crociere within the time period prescribed by the District Court's scheduling order. * * *

It is so ordered.

[JUSTICE SCALIA, concurring in part (omitted).]

NOTES AND PROBLEMS FOR DISCUSSION

1. Prior to *Krupski*, a number of courts had refused to allow relation back when the plaintiff's "mistake" was due to a lack of knowledge as to the proper defendant to sue, as opposed to a misnomer. See, e.g., Locklear v. Bergman & Beving AB, 457 F.3d 363 (4th Cir.), cert. den., 549 U.S. 1208 (2006). Do such cases survive *Krupski*?

2. Suppose Aston is in an altercation at a sports bar and he is badly injured when another patron clubbed him on the head with a baseball bat. Aston thinks that Martin was the person who hit him, but in fact it was Cooper. Aston was aware that Cooper was in the bar, but after a pre-suit investigation, Aston concluded that Martin was the one that hit him. Aston sues and serves Martin in a timely manner, all well within the statute of limitations; Cooper learns of the lawsuit when reading the newspaper, the day after suit was filed. After Aston deposed various witnesses, but more than a year after the limitations period had run, Aston realizes that he made a mistake. He then promptly moves to amend his complaint to dismiss Martin and to substitute Cooper. After *Krupski*, will the amendment relate back? Should it?

3. Consider a variation on the facts above: Suppose that both Cooper and Martin hit Aston, and that Aston is aware of this. Nevertheless, Aston sues only Cooper, believing that Cooper is rich (i.e., a deep-pocket) and that Martin is broke (i.e., judgment-proof). In fact, the opposite is true, as Aston finds out during discovery, well after the limitations period has run. Aston moves to amend his complaint to dismiss Cooper and to add Martin. Assume that the original complaint was timely filed and served, and that Martin was notified of it in a timely manner under Rule 15(c). After *Krupski*, will Aston's amended complaint relate back? Surely Aston has made a mistake, but is it a "mistake" concerning "the proper party's identity"?

4. The *Krupski* Court contrasts the discretion available to the district judge under Rule 15(a), with what it suggests is the mandatory nature of Rule 15(c) respecting relation back (assuming its three requirements are met). Does the Court mean to suggest that Rule 15(c) operates to the exclusion of Rule 15(a)? Or is it saying that Rule 15(c) allows no room for discretion in determining whether an amended pleading relates back, but that general considerations of Rule 15(a) are still relevant, as a separate matter, whenever there is an amendment? Assuming Rule 15(a) is indeed still relevant in such cases, what arguments could defendant, Costa Crociere, have made in support of denying Krupski's amendment?

5. *Krupski* relies on the fact that the current version of Rule 15(c) permits relation back of a party amendment only if (among other things) the "new" party received notice of the suit within 120 days from the filing of the complaint as allowed for by Rule 4(m) for service of process, and provided the suit was originally filed within the statute of limitations. As a consequence of this provision, the new party may end up receiving notice of the suit only after the statute of limitations has run (although this is often true under Rule 4(m) for properly named parties as well). Under the Court's reading of an earlier version of Rule 15(c), its prerequisites had to be satisfied within the limitations period, without the buffer period provided for service in Rule 4(m). See Schiavone v. Fortune, 477 U.S. 21, 106 S.Ct. 2379, 91 L.Ed.2d 18 (1986). If a state does not permit relation back unless the new party was notified within the statute of limitations, does current Rule 15(c) create a problem under the Rules Enabling Act, 28 U.S.C. § 2072?

6. Suppose a non-party to a suit has received notice of the suit and knows that it would have been filed against him, but for a mistake of the plaintiff concerning the proper defendant's identity. Suppose further that the non-party learned of it within the statute of limitations, but more than 120 days from filing as referenced under Rule 4(m). Will an amended complaint against the non-party relate back, within the language of the Rule? Should it?

CHAPTER 8

Discovery

Discovery is the most important, and controversial, innovation of modern procedure. On the positive side, it gives parties access to substantial information about the case and thereby should increase the chances of a fair result, and it encourages settlement by reducing the possibility of trial surprises. But there are negatives including the costs, delays, excesses, and difficulties in establishing effective judicial supervision and control. The discovery system in the United States is considered extreme by many other commercial nations; not surprisingly, foreign parties often are aghast and offended by the nature and scope of discovery when they become involved in litigation in our courts.

It is almost impossible to provide a "feel" for discovery in a classroom setting, and our objectives are more modest. We want students to understand the various discovery devices, the limitations on discovery, and some of the major policy issues. To do this, students must become especially familiar with the very specific provisions of the discovery rules. Much of this is not intuitive and, as we tell our students, being bright won't necessarily get you to the right place.

Our coverage begins with a very brief overview of the principal discovery devices, including their timing and enforcement. The chapter is then divided into three parts: The first describes the scope and limitations of discovery; the second examines the specific devices; and the third discusses discovery breakdowns — enforcement and sanctions.

There are five major forms of discovery: disclosure, depositions, interrogatories, documents, and physical and mental examinations. In addition, provisions regarding electronic discovery went into effect as of December 1, 2006.

1. Mandatory Disclosure. Rule 26(a) requires a party to produce certain information initially, at the outset of the case. For example, a party must identify key witnesses and documents that it may use to support its case, and information about damage calculations and insurance agreements. (But a party is no longer obligated to disclose witnesses or documents, whether favorable or unfavorable, that it does not intend to use.) The rule is based on the premise that an adversary would always want this basic information, and therefore, production should be mandatory without requiring some form of initial request. Note that simply the filing of the complaint and the passage of time will ordinarily trigger the obligation to respond. Certain specified categories of proceedings are exempted from the initial disclosure requirements under 26(a)(1)(B).

2. Depositions. Depositions involve oral questions posed by the attorney for one party to a party or witness under oath. The format is similar to that at a trial, except that there is no judge present. The questioner asks questions, the answers are recorded (by shorthand, video- or audio-taping), and the attorney for the deponent can raise objections (objections are simply noted although, in certain limited circumstances, the attorney also may direct the witness not to answer). Depositions are extremely useful in developing information, pinning down witnesses, following up lines of inquiry, and seeking explanations of documents and events. But they are expensive, can be time consuming (although presumptively limited to a single day), are often contentious, and sometimes bring out the worst in lawyers and clients alike. Read Rule 30(c)-(d) to get a flavor of the "reality" of depositions.

3. Interrogatories. Interrogatories are written questions addressed to a party, to be answered in writing and under oath. See Rule 33. They are inexpensive to prepare, but can be very expensive to answer. They are very useful for specific information — e.g., who works in the shipping department, what are their salaries, how long have they been employed at their jobs, and so on. But unfortunately, given the fact that the answering party must "construe" the question, and given the vagaries of the English language, interrogatories seeking explanations of "how" and "why" are often of limited value.

4. Documents/Inspection. Rule 34 permits a party to seek production of documents, electronically stored information and inspection/testing of land and tangible items. As with interrogatories, document requests are inexpensive to prepare, but responding may be time consuming and expensive. And again, language is a problem — if requests are too specific, important documents may be missed; if they are too general, the responding party may produce thousands of documents for review.

5. Physical and Mental Examinations. Rule 35 permits a party to seek the physical or mental examination of a party or person under the legal control of a party. But significantly, the party seeking the examination must show "good cause" and that the opposing party's condition is "in controversy." Examinations are routinely given when a plaintiff sues claiming physical injuries or mental impairment, thereby putting his condition at issue. But they raise significant privacy issues, and are difficult to get in some instances.

6. Electronic Discovery. Relatively recent Rules dealing with the discovery of information and data stored in electronic form, and which amended Rules 16, 26, 33, 34, 37 and 45, went into effect on December 1, 2006. The package of amendments came after long study and reflects a sense that electronic discovery merits separate mention because of its distinctive nature. "Electronically stored information" was specifically added to the items that are discoverable under Rule 34. Other changes included the adding of e-discovery to the parties' discovery conference (see below); provision for "two tiers" of electronically-stored information based on its accessibility; and provisions for the manner in which electronic data is to be produced.

In actual litigation, the use of the discovery devices can be divided into three phases. The first is the disclosure phase which concludes with the discovery conference and discovery order. This lasts for the first 90-120 days in the case.

Generally, no other discovery can take place during this first phase. See Rules 26(d) & (f); but cf. Rule 26(d)(2) (allowing early Rule 34 requests). The second is the formal discovery process — i.e., depositions, interrogatories, document requests, etc. — in which the parties can use any or all of the discovery devices. This phase may last anywhere from months to years, but ends as the case approaches the trial. In fact, in many cases, the court will set a specific discovery cutoff date. The third phase is a pretrial phase where discovery is addressed to the trial itself. During this phase, the parties will be required to disclose the expert information described in Rule 26(a)(2) and expert depositions may take place; the parties will be required to disclose lists of trial witnesses and documents as described in Rule 26(a)(3); and the parties may seek admissions on key issues under Rule 36.

Finally, a word about policing the system. The court's involvement in discovery is limited. The court may manage the process through a discovery conference (Rule 16) and a discovery order. Otherwise, the court will generally not be involved unless there is a problem. There are three primary ways the court may become involved. First, a party may seek to compel answers or responses to depositions, interrogatories, or document requests. See Rule 37(a). Second, a party may seek sanctions for allegedly improper responses or conduct during the discovery process. See Rules 26(g), 30(d)(2), and 37(b). Third, a party who wants to preclude, limit, change, or otherwise impose restrictions on discovery may seek a protective order. See Rule 26(c).

We are now ready for the plunge. The first section deals with general rules affecting all discovery.

SECTION A. THE SCOPE OF DISCOVERY

1. RELEVANCE

Rule 26(b)(1) currently permits discovery of any nonprivileged matter which is "relevant to any party's claim or defense." Relevant evidence need not be admissible at trial, however: "Information within this scope of discovery need not be admissible in evidence to be discoverable." The current language — "relevant to the claim or defense" — was a change from the former language of the Rule that had allowed discovery of any non-privileged matter that was "relevant to the subject matter involved in the pending action." (Now, it is only "for good cause" that the court may order the broader, relevant-to-the-subject-matter, discovery.) While the newer language was designed to effect a narrowing of discovery and to involve the judge in discovery more than before, it remains to be seen how great a change has been wrought.

In addition, Rule 26(b)(1) was substantially (and controversially) changed effective Dec. 1, 2015, by requiring that discovery must be "proportional to the needs of the case" in light of various considerations. The italicized language below was added to (b)(1):

> Parties may obtain discovery of any nonprivileged matter that is relevant to any party's claim or defense *and proportional to the needs of the case, considering the importance of the issues at stake in the action, the amount in controversy, the parties' relative access to relevant information, the parties' resources, the importance of discovery in resolving the issues, and whether the burden or expense of the proposed discovery outweighs its likely benefit.*

Somewhat similar proportionality provisions were in former Rule 26(b)(2)(C), but, as amended, were moved from there to the main provision regarding discovery's scope in (b)(1), along with some changes in language. In addition, amended Rule 26(b)(1) eliminated the language which had provided: "For good cause, the court may order discovery of any matter relevant to the subject matter involved in the action." It also eliminated the language that had provided that "Relevant information need not be admissible at the trial if the discovery appears reasonably calculated to lead to the discovery of admissible evidence." Instead the Rule now merely states (at the end of the italicized language above) that "Information within this scope of discovery need not be admissible in evidence to be discoverable."

Note that the Federal Rules do not themselves provide a definition of relevance, and most of the law on relevance has been developed in the trial context. Rule 401 of the Federal Rules of Evidence defines "relevant evidence" as "evidence having any tendency to make the existence of any fact that is of consequence to the determination of the action more probable or less probable than it would be without the evidence." Since the scope of discovery remains broader than trial relevance, this suggests that some information will be potentially relevant for discovery purposes even if it would be deemed irrelevant at trial.

There are two other important points in this regard. When a trial court considers whether evidence is relevant at trial, it will decide based on the specific evidence offered and its relation to the issues as framed for trial. By contrast, during discovery, the issues have not been completely framed and, as discussed earlier, the pleadings may not provide many details regarding the precise issues for trial. Moreover, since the discovery itself has not yet been completed, the court does not know much about the range of possible responses. Instead, the question of discovery must be based on possibilities, and the party seeking discovery may only have to hypothesize that certain responses could be relevant to her claim or defense. Conversely, a party cannot resist discovery by showing that the actual response will not be relevant at trial. Under the older formulation that allowed discovery of any matter relevant to the "subject matter" of the lawsuit, parties sometimes posed broad ranging discovery requests that went far beyond the parties' claims and defenses — sometimes with the hope of developing new claims or defenses. Now, only the court can order such broader discovery. The following case was decided under the old Rule which was in effect until December 1, 2000. When reading the decision, consider whether the amendments to Rule 26(b) would make any difference to the outcome.

Pacitti v. Macy's

United States Court of Appeals, Third Circuit, 1999.
193 F.3d 766.

ALITO, CIRCUIT JUDGE.

Stella and Joseph Pacitti, on behalf of their daughter, Joanna Pacitti ("plaintiffs"), appeal the District Court's grant of summary judgment in favor of Macy's East, Inc. ("Macy's") on their state-law contract and tort claims arising from Macy's role as promoter and host of "Macy's Search for Broadway's New 'Annie'" (the "Search"). Plaintiffs also appeal the District Court's order limiting the scope of discovery. For the reasons that follow, we reverse on both grounds and remand for further proceedings.

I

In May 1996, the producers of "Annie," the Classic Annie Production Limited Partnership (the "producers"), and Macy's, a retail department store chain, entered into an agreement under which Macy's agreed to sponsor the "Annie 20th Anniversary Talent Search." Specifically, Macy's agreed to promote the event and to host the auditions at its stores in the following locations: New York City, Boston, Atlanta, Miami, and King of Prussia, Pennsylvania. The producers agreed to select one finalist from each regional store to compete in a final audition at Macy's Herald Square store in New York City. The producers also agreed to offer the winner of the final audition "a contract for that role to appear in the 20th Anniversary Production of Annie * * * subject to good faith negotiations and in accordance with standard Actors' Equity Production Contract guidelines" (the "standard actors' equity contract").[1]

Macy's publicized the Search in newspapers and in its stores in the five regional locations. All of the promotional materials referred to the event as "Macy's Search for Broadway's New 'Annie.'" Plaintiffs learned of the Search from an advertisement in the Philadelphia Inquirer that stated, in pertinent part:

> If you are a girl between 7 and 12 years old and 4' 6" or under, the starring role in this 20th Anniversary Broadway production and national tour could be yours! Just get your hands on an application . . . and bring it to the audition at Macy's King of Prussia store. . . . Annie's

---

[1] The Actors' Equity Association requires producers to attach its standard "Agreement and Rules Governing Employment under the Production Contract" to "all contracts where production is bonded as a Bus and Truck Tour." As we discuss below, that contract provides, among other things, that the producer retains the authority to replace the actor at any time so long as the actor is compensated through the term of the contract.

director/lyricist . . . will pick the lucky actress for final callbacks . . . at Macy's Herald Square. Annie goes on the road this fall and opens on Broadway Spring 1997.

In June 1996, Joanna, then 11-years old, and her mother picked up an application at the King of Prussia store. The application form announced:

Annie, America's most beloved musical[,] and Macy's, the world's largest store, are conducting a talent search for a new "Annie" to star in the 20th Anniversary Broadway production and national Tour of Annie. . . .

The reverse side of the application form contained the "Official Rules [of] Macy's Search for Broadway's New 'Annie.'" In addition to explaining the two-part audition process, the official rules provided, in relevant part:

1. All participants must be accompanied by a parent or legal guardian and must bring completed application forms to one of the Macy's audition locations . . . and be prepared to audition. . . .

2. The "Annie" selected at the "Annie-Off-Final Callback" will be required to work with a trained dog. The tour commences in Fall 1996, with a Broadway opening tentatively scheduled for Spring 1997, [and] with a post-Broadway tour to follow.

. . . .

6. You and your parent or legal guardian are responsible for your own conduct, and hereby release Macy's . . . and the Producers . . . from any liability to or with regard to the participants and/or her parent or legal guardian with respect to the audition(s).

. . . .

8. All determinations made by the Producers or their designated judges are being made at their sole discretion and each such determination is final.

Unlike Macy's contract with the producers, neither the official rules[3] nor any of the promotional materials included a provision informing the participants that the winner of the Search would receive only the opportunity to enter into a standard actors' equity contract with the producers.

Joanna and her mother signed the official rules and proceeded to the initial audition at the King of Prussia store. Macy's publicized the event by placing balloons, signs, pins, and other promotional materials advertising "Macy's Search for Broadway's New 'Annie'" throughout the store. After auditioning hundreds of "Annie" hopefuls, the producers selected Joanna as the regional finalist. In a press release, Macy's announced Joanna's success to the public: "One in Ten She'll Be a Star!!! Macy's Brings Local Girl One Step Closer

---

[3] Throughout the remainder of this opinion, we refer to the official rules and the application form as the "official rules."

Towards 'Tomorrow' to Become Broadway's New 'Annie.'" The press release further provided:

> Philadelphia's own, twelve year-old Joanna Pacitti, will join nine other talented girls for a final audition to cast the title role in the 20th Anniversary production of the classic Tony Award-winning musical, Annie, coming to Broadway this season. . . . Ten finalists, most of whom were selected from over two thousand "Annie" hopefuls . . ., will vie for the chance to become Broadway's new "Annie."

At the producers' expense, Joanna and her mother traveled to New York City for Joanna to participate in the "Annie-Off-Final Call Back" at Macy's Herald Square store. After auditioning for two days, the producers selected Joanna to star as "Annie" in the 20th Anniversary Broadway production. Again, Macy's announced Joanna's success to the public, referring to her as "Broadway's New 'Annie.'"

Joanna and her mother met with the producers and signed an "Actors' Equity Association Standard Run-of-the-Play Production Contract." Consistent with the Actors' Equity Association's rules governing production contracts, the producers retained the right to replace Joanna with another actor at any time as long as they paid her salary through the term of her contract.

For nearly a four-month period, Joanna performed the role of "Annie" in the production's national tour. In so doing, Joanna appeared in over 100 performances and in six cities. In February 1997, approximately three weeks before the scheduled Broadway opening, the producers informed Joanna that her "services [would] no longer be needed," and she was replaced by her understudy.

On March 21, 1997, plaintiffs filed suit against Macy's in Pennsylvania state court, alleging breach of contract and the following tort claims: (1) fraudulent misrepresentation, (2) equitable estoppel, (3) public policy tort, (4) breach of implied covenant of good faith and fair dealing, and (5) punitive damages. In particular, plaintiffs alleged that Macy's failed to deliver the prize it had offered, *i.e.*, the starring role of "Annie" on Broadway, and that Macy's knew it could not award this prize but promoted its ability to do so nonetheless. Macy's subsequently removed the suit to federal district court based on diversity.

During discovery, plaintiffs sought to uncover information on the relationship between Macy's and the producers and on the pecuniary benefit Macy's received from sponsoring the Search. Macy's objected to their request, and the District Court limited discovery to "what promises, if any, were made by defendant prior to and at the final audition . . . in New York City that the person selected at that audition would appear in the role as Annie." Plaintiffs moved for reconsideration, and the District Court denied that motion on December 19, 1997.

Macy's then moved for summary judgment, contending that it did not deprive Joanna of any prize she had been promised and that her rights were limited by the terms of her contract with the producers. In support of its motion,

Macy's proffered, among other things, its contract with the producers, which, as explained above, specified that the successful contestant would receive only the opportunity to enter into a standard actors' equity contract with the producers.

The District Court granted summary judgment in favor of Macy's. Addressing plaintiffs' breach of contract claim, the District Court concluded that the contract was unambiguous and capable of only one reasonable interpretation — i.e., that Macy's offered only an audition for the opportunity to enter into a standard actors' equity contract with the producers for the title role in "Annie." Therefore, the Court rejected plaintiffs' contention that Macy's offered Joanna a guaranteed Broadway opening, and the Court concluded:

> Plaintiffs received the benefit of their bargain by being offered a contract with the Producers for the "Annie" role, in exchange for Ms. Pacitti participating in "Macy's Search for Broadway's New Annie." . . . When the Producers offered a contract to Plaintiffs consistent with the terms of the Official Rules[,] any possible obligation Macy's had to Plaintiffs was fully met.

After rejecting plaintiffs' breach of contract claim, the District Court turned to their tort claims. Reasoning that each cause of action was predicated upon the assertion that Macy's offered Joanna the role of "Annie" on Broadway, and concluding that Macy's made no such representation, the District Court granted Macy's motion for summary judgment on these claims as well.

Plaintiffs then took this appeal. In their notice of appeal, plaintiffs state only that they appeal from the District Court's order granting summary judgment for Macy's. See App. at 235a. In this appeal, however, plaintiffs also argue that the District Court abused its discretion in limiting the scope of discovery.

II

[The Court held that summary judgment should not have been granted.]

III

We now turn to plaintiffs' contention that the District Court abused its discretion by limiting the scope of discovery. Specifically, plaintiffs argue that the District Court's discovery order precluded them from uncovering facts relevant to their fraudulent misrepresentation claims. Macy's asserts that review of this issue is improper and, in the alternative, that the District Court's order was a proper exercise of discretion. We conclude that review is appropriate and that the District Court abused its discretion.

A

[The Court held it had jurisdiction to review the discovery order.]

B

Having found that we have jurisdiction to review this issue, we must next determine whether the District Court abused its discretion in limiting discovery to "what promises, if any, were made by defendant prior to and at the final audition . . . in New York City that the person selected at that audition would appear in the role as Annie." Plaintiffs contend that the District Court abused its discretion by unduly limiting discovery to preclude them from obtaining information relevant to their fraudulent misrepresentation claims. We review the District Court's discovery order for abuse of discretion.

The Federal Rules of Civil Procedure provide, in pertinent part:

> Parties may obtain discovery regarding any matter, not privileged, which is relevant to the subject matter involved in the pending action, whether it relates to the claim or defense of the party seeking discovery or to the claim or defense of any other party. . . . The information sought need not be admissible at the trial if the information sought appears reasonably calculated to lead to the discovery of admissible evidence.

Fed. R. Civ. P. 26(b)(1) [see current Rule 26(b)(1), which is differently worded — eds.]. It is well recognized that the federal rules allow broad and liberal discovery. See In re Madden, 151 F.3d 125, 128 (3d Cir. 1998) ("Pretrial discovery is . . . 'accorded a broad and liberal treatment.'") (citing Hickman v. Taylor, 329 U.S. 495, 507, 91 L.Ed. 451, 67 S.Ct. 385 (1947)); see also Wright, Miller & Marcus, Federal Practice & Procedure, Civil 2d §2007 ("The rule does allow broad scope to discovery and this has been well recognized by the courts.").

To succeed on a claim for fraudulent misrepresentation under Pennsylvania law, plaintiffs must establish the following elements: (1) a misrepresentation, (2) a fraudulent utterance, (3) an intention to induce action on the part of the recipient, (4) a justifiable reliance by the recipient upon the misrepresentation, and (5) damage to the recipient as a proximate result. To prove these elements, plaintiffs must demonstrate that Macy's fraudulently misrepresented that the successful participant would perform as "Annie" on Broadway, that it did so with the intent to induce participation in the Search, and that Joanna relied to her detriment upon the misrepresentation.

Plaintiffs seek production of the following: (1) Macy's communications with, and relationship to, the producers regarding the terms of the contract that the producers intended to offer the successful contestant and (2) the pecuniary benefit Macy's received as a result of the Search. This information could shed light on Macy's knowledge that it could not offer a Broadway opening and its motives for failing to limit the offer accordingly. Thus, we conclude that the discovery sought here is directly relevant to the subject matter of this dispute.

We also find it noteworthy that Macy's submitted its contract with the producers in support of summary judgment. As previously noted, the federal rules permit discovery of, among other things, "any matter, not privileged, which is relevant to the subject matter involved in the pending action, whether it relates to the claim or defense of the party seeking discovery *or to the claim or defense of any other party* . . . ." Fed. R. Civ. P. 26(b)(1) (emphasis added).

Macy's asserts that the only relevant representations are "those to which plaintiffs were . . . privy" and "upon which plaintiffs could have reasonably relied." This "what they don't know can't hurt them" argument is unconvincing. The fact that plaintiffs were not privy to the information that Macy's possessed when Joanna relied on its representations and participated in the Search forms the very basis of plaintiffs' fraudulent misrepresentation claims.

Accordingly, we conclude that the District Court erred in limiting discovery.

IV

For the reasons discussed above, we reverse the grant of summary judgment on all claims and remand for further proceedings in accordance with this opinion. We also reverse and remand for plaintiffs to conduct discovery consistent with this opinion.

[The dissenting opinion of JUDGE STAFFORD is omitted.]

NOTES AND PROBLEMS FOR DISCUSSION

1. The district court granted summary judgment to Macy's on the theory that the contract between Pacitti and Macy's was clear that Pacitti would only receive a standard actor's equity contract which provided for cancellation without penalty, and Macy's did not promise a Broadway opening. It dismissed the tort claims on the theory that all were premised on such a promise. Judge Alito for the court of appeals reversed on the ground that the contract and surrounding circumstances permitted a contrary interpretation promising a Broadway opening, and that dismissal of the tort claims had been based on the predicate that there had been no such promise.

2. What information does Pacitti want, and why does Pacitti argue that this information is within Rule 26(b)(1)?

3. Why does Macy's argue that this information is not within Rule 26(b)(1)? Insofar as Pacitti was arguing that the information was "relevant to [a] claim" of the plaintiffs' (as opposed to being merely "relevant to the subject matter" of the lawsuit), would the current language of Rule 26(b)(1) permit a similar result? See note 6, below.

4. What if Macy's opposed discovery of its communications with the producers on the ground that their contract with the producers provided for the standard actor's equity contract, and there was never any mention (one way or the other) of a Broadway opening?

5. The facts suggest that the producers had intended to use Pacitti on Broadway, but that something happened to cause them to turn to her understudy. Is Pacitti entitled to discovery relating to the reasons for this decision?

6. The Advisory Committee's Note on current Rule 26(b)(1) (prior to a modest stylistic revision), provides a glimpse of how it perceived the Rule would operate vis-à-vis the older, broader language:

> [A] variety of types of information not directly pertinent to the incident in suit could be relevant to the claims or defenses raised in a given action. For example, other incidents of the same type, or involving the same product, could be properly discoverable under the revised standard. Information about organizational arrangements or filing

systems of a party could be discoverable if likely to yield or lead to the discovery of admissible evidence. Similarly, information that could be used to impeach a likely witness, although not otherwise relevant to the claims or defenses might be discoverable. In each instance, the determination whether such information is discoverable because it is relevant to the claims or defenses depends on the circumstances of the pending action.

Commentary to Rule Changes, Court Rules, 192 F.R.D. 340, 389. The difficulty with the Note, however, is that while it gives examples of what is included in the new language, it gives no example of something that would be excluded by the new language, yet permitted by the old (and for which judicial approval must now be had). Consequently, one is left to speculate as to the difference the change makes. One court made the best it could out of the changes, and cautioned against "debating the difference between discovery relevant to the 'claims and defenses' as opposed to the 'subject matter of the pending action' — the judicial equivalent to debating the number of angels that can dance on the head of a pin":

> While the pleadings will be important, it would be a mistake to argue that no fact may be discovered unless it directly correlates with a factual allegation in the complaint or answer. Such a restrictive approach would run counter to the underlying purpose of the rule changes, as explained by the commentary, run afoul of Fed.R.Civ.P. 1, and undoubtedly do disservice to the requirement of notice pleading in Rule 8, as parties would be encouraged to plead evidentiary facts, unnecessary to a "short and plain statement of the claim showing that the pleader is entitled to relief," Rule 3, 8(a)(2), simply to increase the likelihood of getting broader discovery. It equally is clear, however, that the new rule represents a change from the old version, and that, unless expanded by the court for good cause shown, it is intended that the scope of discovery be narrower than it was, in some meaningful way.

Thompson v. Dep't of Housing and Urban Dev., 199 F.R.D. 168, 172 (D. Md. 2001).

7. Postscript: Joanna Pacitti later appeared on various T.V. shows, including *Rosie O'Donnell* and *Good Morning America*, to discuss her firing, reportedly declaring: "I just have to remember that . . . I'm the real Annie . . . and the sun will come out tomorrow." In 2001, she released a single "Watch Me Shine," which was on the soundtrack for the movie "Legally Blonde." More recently, after various stints on MTV and releasing her first album, she appeared as a contestant on the show "American Idol."

2. PRIVILEGES

Rule 26(b)(1) permits discovery of any appropriately relevant matter which is "nonprivileged." A privilege is a right of a witness, person, or entity not to give information or testify with regard to certain matters. In the federal courts, privileges are governed by (a) the Constitution, a statute, or rules prescribed by the Supreme Court, and (b) otherwise are governed by (i) "principles of the common law as they may be interpreted by the courts of the United States in light of reason and experience," or (ii) in matters governed by State law, "in accordance with State law." Fed. Rule of Evidence 501.

The best known privilege created by the Constitution or a statute is the privilege against self-incrimination found in the Fifth Amendment (no person "shall be compelled in any criminal case to be a witness against himself"). The privilege has been extended to testimony in civil cases when the witness can show a genuine threat of criminal prosecution, although in civil cases the consequences of exercising the privilege are different. For example, in a criminal case, the prosecution cannot comment on the failure of the accused to testify whereas such comment by counsel is permitted in civil cases.

Most privileges in the federal courts are based on the "principles of the common law." In matters governed by state law, if there is no constitutional, statutory or federal rules provision, privileges are governed by state law. Most states have statutes on such matters, and among the privileges widely recognized are attorney-client, doctor-patient, priest-penitent, and husband-wife. California has a constitutional right of privacy which effectively operates as a privilege. And New York's high court has recently held that communications at "AA" meetings are privileged. In many states, the question of privilege is politically sensitive and various professions and occupations often seek legislative sanction for privileges. Controversial areas have included accountants, psychologists and social workers, and financial advisors.

There are three critical things to keep in mind about the law of privileges. First, if information is privileged, disclosure typically cannot be compelled. It doesn't matter how relevant or necessary the information may be — indeed, privileged information often is highly relevant and may be critical. Second, information not covered by a specific privilege is not privileged simply because it was given in confidence, as there is no general limitation on the disclosure of confidential, secret, private, or even embarrassing information. Third, a privilege can be waived. For example, the attorney-client privilege may be lost as to information disclosed to a third party. Or, the privilege may be lost if matters covered by the privilege are at issue in the lawsuit. For example, if a client sues an attorney for malpractice, the attorney will be able to use privileged information as a defense. Similarly, if a defendant asserts a defense based on a good faith belief that its conduct was legally permitted and relied on advice of counsel (which may be a defense to certain claims as well as a defense to claims for punitive damages), many courts would hold the privilege has been waived.

Or, if a person sues for physical or mental damages, she may waive the doctor-patient privilege by putting her condition at issue.

Santelli v. Electro-Motive

United States District Court, Northern District of Illinois, 1999.
188 F.R.D. 306.

MATTHEW F. KENNELLY, DISTRICT JUDGE.

This matter is before the Court on the defendant Electro-Motive's objections to Magistrate Judge Rosemond's June 16, 1999 Order denying its motion to compel the production of plaintiff's medical records. Plaintiff Mary Santelli brought suit under Title VII for damages resulting from defendant's alleged sex discrimination and retaliation. Plaintiff claims she was unlawfully discriminated against on account of her sex when she was denied certain welding positions at defendant's factory. Her complaint includes an allegation that her damages included "mental distress." Plaintiff testified at her deposition that she was seeking compensation for emotional distress caused by the alleged discrimination and that she had seen a psychotherapist for treatment of this distress. This prompted Electro-Motive to move to compel production of plaintiff's medical records — specifically, records of psychotherapy, alcohol and drug treatment, and HIV testing — on the theory that these records are probative of whether her alleged emotional distress was caused by factors other than the sex discrimination she says she endured. Defendant argued that by making a claim of emotional distress, plaintiff had waived any privileges that might otherwise prevent production of these records.

In arguing this motion before Judge Rosemond, plaintiff's attorney represented that plaintiff would seek compensatory damages only for humiliation and embarrassment, not for emotional distress. Based on this representation, Judge Rosemond denied defendant's motion to compel, but he also precluded plaintiff from "testifying about any emotional distress that necessitated care or treatment by a physician," limiting her emotional distress damages to "humiliation, embarrassment, anger, disgust, frustration, and similar emotions."

I

The Supreme Court has recognized a federal psychotherapist-patient privilege. Jaffee v. Redmond, 518 U.S. 1, 15-16, 135 L.Ed.2d 337, 116 S.Ct. 1923 (1996). Confidential communications between a patient and a licensed psychotherapist (or the equivalent), during the course of diagnosis or treatment, are privileged and protected from discovery. The interest underlying the psychotherapist-patient privilege was clearly articulated by the Court: it facilitates the "provision of appropriate treatment for individuals suffering the effects of a mental or emotional problem." The psychotherapist-patient relationship depends on "an atmosphere of confidence and trust in which the patient is willing to make a frank and complete disclosure of facts, emotions, memories, and fears." "If the privilege were rejected, confidential conversations between psychotherapists and their patients would surely be chilled . . ."

In *Jaffee*, the Court recognized that like other privileges, the psychotherapist-patient privilege can be waived. The Court, however, did not define the contours of the privilege, such as when or how it can be waived. These issues were left to be worked out on a case-by-case basis.

Although communications between a psychotherapist and patient may be relevant to a particular issue in a case or significant to the party opposing the privilege, that alone is not enough to deprive a party of this privilege. By definition, privileges exclude from a case otherwise relevant information.

One way a privilege holder can waive the privilege is by affirmatively putting the privileged communications directly at issue in a lawsuit. Garcia v. Zenith Electronics Corp., 58 F.3d 1171, 1175 n.1 (7th Cir. 1995) ("The attorney-client privilege is generally waived when the client asserts claims or defenses that put his attorney's advice at issue in the litigation."). Illustrative of this principle are medical and legal malpractice cases. A person who brings such a case waives any applicable privileges: she cannot allege malpractice in her attorney's representation or psychotherapist's treatment but at the same time expect her communications with the person she has sued to remain privileged.

The issue here is whether a Title VII plaintiff puts privileged communications with her psychotherapist at issue, and thus waives her privilege, by seeking to recover damages for emotional distress. See 42 U.S.C. §1981a (b) (3) (damages for emotional pain, suffering, mental anguish, and loss of enjoyment of life are recoverable in cases of intentional employment discrimination). The lower federal courts are split as to when a party seeking such damages waives the privilege. One approach is that the privilege is deemed waived only when the plaintiff introduces privileged communications in evidence either directly or by calling the particular psychotherapist as a witness. See, e.g., Vanderbilt v. Town of Chilmark, 174 F.R.D. 225, 229 (D. Mass. 1997). The problem with this narrow waiver rule is that it would enable a party who had undergone psychotherapy to offer at trial only the testimony of a retained, non-treating expert and thereby prevent discovery of what she had told her treating psychotherapist. Among other things, this would allow the party to provide the expert with a selective "history," while preventing the veracity of that history from being tested by comparing it to what the party had reported to her treating psychotherapist. We find this result unacceptable, as it would allow the privilege holder to thwart the truth seeking process by using the privilege as both a shield and a sword. Predictability is one rationale used to support the narrower use-based waiver rule. As the court reasoned in *Vanderbilt*, patients need to know with certainty at the time of the communication whether and under what circumstances confidentiality will be maintained at a later date. We do not find this persuasive. One bright-line rule does not make the application of the privilege any more predictable than any other bright-line rule. In other words, if we were to hold that merely asserting a claim for emotional distress damages in a complaint waives the privilege, that would make for an equally predictable rule.

Parties would know for certain that if they want to maintain the privilege, they cannot seek emotional distress damages.

Some lower federal courts have adopted this very rule and have found implied waiver simply because a party makes a claim for emotional distress damages. In Lorenz v. Valley Forge, 815 F.2d 1095 (7th Cir. 1986), which concerned the attorney-client privilege (which *Jaffee* found to be analogous to the psychotherapist-patient privilege), the court indicated that a waiver of the privilege can occur "when a holder [of the privilege] relies on a legal claim or defense, the truthful resolution of which will require examining confidential communications." It would seem that under *Lorenz*, the plaintiff's insistence on a claim for emotional distress damages, depending on the scope of the claim, would be enough to cause a waiver of her psychotherapist-patient privilege. A party cannot inject his or her psychological treatment, conditions, or symptoms into a case and expect to be able to prevent discovery of information relevant to those issues.

In this case, however, Santelli has limited the scope of her emotional distress claim. As noted earlier, she represented to Judge Rosemond that her claim was limited to compensation for humiliation, embarrassment, and other similar emotions, and Judge Rosemond accordingly precluded her from introducing evidence about emotional distress that necessitated care or treatment by a physician. Put another way, plaintiff's emotional distress claim has been limited to the negative emotions that she experienced essentially as the intrinsic result of the defendant's alleged conduct, while she has been barred from introducing evidence of any resulting symptoms or conditions that she might have suffered. See generally Seaton v. Sky Realty Co., 491 F.2d 634, 637-38 (7th Cir. 1974) (holding that compensatory damages may be awarded for humiliation, either inferred from circumstances or established by testimony, and that medical evidence of mental or emotional impairment is not necessary to sustain such an award).

We conclude that as a result of plaintiff's self-imposed limitations, and those imposed by Judge Rosemond, plaintiff's claim has been narrowed to such an extent that she has successfully avoided waiver of her psychotherapist-patient privilege. In a sense, plaintiff's communications to her psychotherapist are no longer relevant, or if relevant are only barely so. She will be precluded at trial from introducing the fact or details of her treatment; she may not offer evidence through any witness about symptoms or conditions that she suffered (*e.g.,* sleeplessness, nervousness, depression); and she will not be permitted to offer any evidence regarding a medical or psychological diagnosis. Rather, she will be permitted to testify only that she felt humiliated, embarrassed, angry or upset because of the alleged discrimination. While we believe that a party waives her psychotherapist-patient privilege by electing to inject into a case either the fact of her treatment or any symptoms or conditions that she may have experienced, Santelli is doing neither.

This may be a meager victory for Santelli. Bare testimony of humiliation or disgust may prevent her from fully recovering for her alleged emotional distress.

She may be better off disclosing her psychological records, which would allow her to make a broader damage claim. The choice, however, is hers. She has made her choice, and as a result we conclude that defendant is not entitled to discover records of her treatment by psychotherapists, for those records remain privileged.

There are some limits to the privilege we uphold here. It does not prevent disclosure of the dates of Santelli's treatment or to the identity of her psychotherapists. Given the limitations placed on Santelli's damage claim, this information is of marginal relevance at most * * * We leave for another day whether defendant will be permitted to offer this evidence at trial.

II

The defendant also seeks discovery of plaintiff's HIV test results and drug and alcohol treatment records. Plaintiff argues that these records are privileged, but cites no case law in support of her argument. While we are skeptical of plaintiff's claims, we need not resolve them here. Plaintiff's HIV test results and drug and alcohol testing records are irrelevant and thus are not discoverable in view of the fact that her emotional distress claim has been limited to her emotional reaction to the alleged discrimination. The fact that a particular person may have had a drug or alcohol problem or a positive HIV test has no logical bearing on whether she felt humiliation or disgust as a result of unlawful discrimination. We uphold Judge Rosemond's order that defendant is not entitled to obtain these records.

Conclusion

We overrule the defendant's objections to Magistrate Judge Rosemond's June 16, 1999 Order denying the defendant's motion to compel the production of the plaintiff's psychological and medical records. The Order is affirmed, with the one modification we have made, namely that defendant is entitled to production of information showing the dates of any treatment of plaintiff by a psychotherapist and the identity of the psychotherapist.

NOTES AND PROBLEMS FOR DISCUSSION

1. This is a close case. What is Electro-Motive's argument as to why disclosure is required and what is the court's response?

2. Would the result have been different if Santelli sought damages for "continuing psychological damage"?

3. Make an argument that the court took back much of the protection it purported to offer.

4. Would the result be the same if Electro-Motive sought information about possible medical conditions of Santelli, and sought information regarding medical treatments? To answer this, consider what privilege question must first be answered.

5. The Court refers to the Supreme Court's decision in Jaffee v. Redmond, 518 U.S. 1, 116 S.Ct. 1923, 135 L.Ed.2d 337 (1996), recognizing a psychotherapist privilege. In fact, *Jaffe* involved consultations with a clinical social worker. It thus raises the question of how far the privilege extends beyond "traditional" psychotherapists. Query whether it extends to a school counselor or a close friend? Or a letter to Ann Landers?

3. WORK PRODUCT

The next case, *Hickman v. Taylor*, is one of the classics of modern procedure. Note that present Rule 26(b)(3) and (b)(4) were not part of the rules at the time this case was decided.

Hickman v. Taylor

Supreme Court of the United States, 1947.

329 U.S. 495, 67 S.Ct. 385, 91 L.Ed. 451.

MR. JUSTICE MURPHY delivered the opinion of the Court.

This case presents an important problem under the Federal Rules of Civil Procedure as to the extent to which a party may inquire into oral and written statements of witnesses, or other information, secured by an adverse party's counsel in the course of preparation for possible litigation after a claim has arisen. Examination into a person's files and records, including those resulting from the professional activities of an attorney, must be judged with care. It is not without reason that various safeguards have been established to preclude unwarranted excursions into the privacy of a man's work. At the same time, public policy supports reasonable and necessary inquiries. Properly to balance these competing interests is a delicate and difficult task.

On February 7, 1943, the tug "J. M. Taylor" sank while engaged in helping to tow a car float of the Baltimore & Ohio Railroad across the Delaware River at Philadelphia. The accident was apparently unusual in nature, the cause of it still being unknown. Five of the nine crew members were drowned. Three days later the tug owners and the underwriters employed a law firm, of which respondent Fortenbaugh is a member, to defend them against potential suits by representatives of the deceased crew members and to sue the railroad for damages to the tug.

A public hearing was held on March 4, 1943, before the United States Steamboat Inspectors, at which the four survivors were examined. This testimony was recorded and made available to all interested parties. Shortly thereafter, Fortenbaugh privately interviewed the survivors and took statements from them with an eye toward the anticipated litigation; the survivors signed these statements on March 29. Fortenbaugh also interviewed other persons believed to have some information relating to the accident and in some cases he made memoranda of what they told him. At the time when Fortenbaugh secured the statements of the survivors, representatives of two of the deceased crew members had been in communication with him. Ultimately claims were presented by representatives of all five of the deceased; four of the claims, however, were settled without litigation. The fifth claimant, petitioner herein, brought suit in a federal court under the Jones Act on November 26, 1943, naming as defendants the two tug owners, individually and as partners, and the railroad.

One year later, petitioner filed 39 interrogatories directed to the tug owners. The 38th interrogatory read: "State whether any statements of the members of the crews of the Tugs 'J. M. Taylor' and 'Philadelphia' or of any other vessel were taken in connection with the towing of the car float and the sinking of the Tug 'John M. Taylor.' Attach hereto exact copies of all such statements if in writing, and if oral, set forth in detail the exact provisions of any such oral statements or reports."

Supplemental interrogatories asked whether any oral or written statements, records, reports or other memoranda had been made concerning any matter relative to the towing operation, the sinking of the tug, the salvaging and repair of the tug, and the death of the deceased. If the answer was in the affirmative, the tug owners were then requested to set forth the nature of all such records, reports, statements or other memoranda.

The tug owners, through Fortenbaugh, answered all of the interrogatories except No. 38 and the supplemental ones just described. While admitting that statements of the survivors had been taken, they declined to summarize or set forth the contents. They did so on the ground that such requests called "for privileged matter obtained in preparation for litigation" and constituted "an attempt to obtain indirectly counsel's private files." It was claimed that answering these requests "would involve practically turning over not only the complete files, but also the telephone records and, almost, the thoughts of counsel."

In connection with the hearing on these objections, Fortenbaugh made a written statement and gave an informal oral deposition explaining the circumstances under which he had taken the statements. But he was not expressly asked in the deposition to produce the statements. The District Court for the Eastern District of Pennsylvania, sitting en banc, held that the requested matters were not privileged. The court then decreed that the tug owners and Fortenbaugh, as counsel and agent for the tug owners, forthwith "answer Plaintiff's 38th interrogatory and supplementary interrogatories; produce all written statements of witnesses obtained by Mr. Fortenbaugh, as counsel and agent for Defendants; state in substance any fact concerning this case which Defendants learned through oral statements made by witnesses to Mr. Fortenbaugh whether or not included in his private memoranda and produce Mr. Fortenbaugh's memoranda containing statements of fact by witnesses or to submit these memoranda to the Court for determination of those portions which should be revealed to Plaintiff." Upon their refusal, the court adjudged them in contempt and ordered them imprisoned until they complied.

The Third Circuit Court of Appeals, also sitting en banc, reversed the judgment of the District Court. It held that the information here sought was part of the "work product of the lawyer" and hence privileged from discovery under the Federal Rules of Civil Procedure. The importance of the problem, which has engendered a great divergence of views among district courts, led us to grant certiorari.

The pre-trial deposition-discovery mechanism established by Rules 26 to 37 is one of the most significant innovations of the Federal Rules of Civil Procedure. Under the prior federal practice, the pre-trial functions of notice-giving, issue-formulation and fact-revelation were performed primarily and inadequately by the pleadings. Inquiry into the issues and the facts before trial was narrowly confined and was often cumbersome in method. The new rules, however, restrict the pleadings to the task of general notice-giving and invest the deposition-discovery process with a vital role in the preparation for trial. The various instruments of discovery now serve (1) as a device, along with the pre-trial hearing under Rule 16, to narrow and clarify the basic issues between the parties, and (2) as a device for ascertaining the facts, or information as to the existence or whereabouts of facts, relative to those issues. Thus civil trials in the federal courts no longer need be carried on in the dark. The way is now clear, consistent with recognized privileges, for the parties to obtain the fullest possible knowledge of the issues and facts before trial.

[The Court held that petitioner ought to have proceeded under Rule 45 and sought documents in the context of a deposition of Fortenbaugh who was not a party but only a witness, rather than under Rule 33.]

But, under the circumstances, we deem it unnecessary and unwise to rest our decision upon this procedural irregularity, an irregularity which is not strongly urged upon us and which was disregarded in the two courts below. The deposition-discovery rules create integrated procedural devices. And the basic question at stake is whether any of those devices may be used to inquire into materials collected by an adverse party's counsel in the course of preparation for possible litigation. The fact that the petitioner may have used the wrong method does not destroy the main thrust of his attempt. Having noted the proper procedure, we may accordingly turn our attention to the substance of the underlying problem.

In urging that he has a right to inquire into the materials secured and prepared by Fortenbaugh, petitioner emphasizes that the deposition-discovery portions of the Federal Rules of Civil Procedure are designed to enable the parties to discover the true facts and to compel their disclosure wherever they may be found. It is said that inquiry may be made under these rules, epitomized by Rule 26, as to any relevant matter which is not privileged; and since the discovery provisions are to be applied as broadly and liberally as possible, the privilege limitation must be restricted to its narrowest bounds. On the premise that the attorney-client privilege is the one involved in this case, petitioner argues that it must be strictly confined to confidential communications made by a client to his attorney. And since the materials here in issue were secured by Fortenbaugh from third persons rather than from his clients, the tug owners, the conclusion is reached that these materials are proper subjects for discovery under Rule 26.

As additional support for this result, petitioner claims that to prohibit discovery under these circumstances would give a corporate defendant a tremendous advantage in a suit by an individual plaintiff. Thus in a suit by an injured employee against a railroad or in a suit by an insured person against an insurance company the corporate defendant could pull a dark veil of secrecy over all the pertinent facts it can collect after the claim arises merely on the assertion that such facts were gathered by its large staff of attorneys and claim agents. At the same time, the individual plaintiff, who often has direct knowledge of the matter in issue and has no counsel until some time after his claim arises could be compelled to disclose all the intimate details of his case. By endowing with immunity from disclosure all that a lawyer discovers in the course of his duties, it is said, the rights of individual litigants in such cases are drained of vitality and the lawsuit becomes more of a battle of deception than a search for truth.

But framing the problem in terms of assisting individual plaintiffs in their suits against corporate defendants is unsatisfactory. Discovery concededly may work to the disadvantage as well as to the advantage of individual plaintiffs. Discovery, in other words, is not a one-way proposition. It is available in all types of cases at the behest of any party, individual or corporate, plaintiff or defendant. The problem thus far transcends the situation confronting this petitioner. And we must view that problem in light of the limitless situations where the particular kind of discovery sought by petitioner might be used.

We agree, of course, that the deposition-discovery rules are to be accorded a broad and liberal treatment. No longer can the time-honored cry of "fishing expedition" serve to preclude a party from inquiring into the facts underlying his opponent's case. Mutual knowledge of all the relevant facts gathered by both parties is essential to proper litigation. To that end, either party may compel the other to disgorge whatever facts he has in his possession. The deposition-discovery procedure simply advances the stage at which the disclosure can be compelled from the time of trial to the period preceding it, thus reducing the possibility of surprise. But discovery, like all matters of procedure, has ultimate and necessary boundaries. As indicated by Rules 30(b) and (d) and 31(d), limitations inevitably arise when it can be shown that the examination is being conducted in bad faith or in such a manner as to annoy, embarrass or oppress the person subject to the inquiry. And as Rule 26(b) provides, further limitations come into existence when the inquiry touches upon the irrelevant or encroaches upon the recognized domains of privilege.

We also agree that the memoranda, statements and mental impressions in issue in this case fall outside the scope of the attorney-client privilege and hence are not protected from discovery on that basis. It is unnecessary here to delineate the content and scope of that privilege as recognized in the federal courts. For present purposes, it suffices to note that the protective cloak of this privilege does not extend to information which an attorney secures from a witness while acting for his client in anticipation of litigation. Nor does this privilege concern the memoranda, briefs, communications and other writings prepared by counsel for his own use in prosecuting his client's case; and it is equally unrelated to writings which reflect an attorney's mental impressions, conclusions, opinions or legal theories.

But the impropriety of invoking that privilege does not provide an answer to the problem before us. Petitioner has made more than an ordinary request for relevant, nonprivileged facts in the possession of his adversaries or their counsel. He has sought discovery as of right of oral and written statements of witnesses whose identity is well known and whose availability to petitioner appears unimpaired. He has sought production of these matters after making the most searching inquiries of his opponents as to the circumstances surrounding the fatal accident, which inquiries were sworn to have been answered to the best of their information and belief. Interrogatories were directed toward all the events prior to, during and subsequent to the sinking of the tug. Full and honest answers to such broad inquiries would necessarily have included all pertinent information gleaned by Fortenbaugh through his interviews with the witnesses. Petitioner makes no suggestion, and we cannot assume, that the tug owners or Fortenbaugh were incomplete or dishonest in the framing of their answers. In addition, petitioner was free to examine the public testimony of the witnesses taken before the United States Steamboat Inspectors. We are thus dealing with an attempt to secure the production of written statements and mental impressions contained in the files and the mind of the attorney Fortenbaugh without any showing of necessity or any indication or claim that denial of such production would unduly prejudice the preparation of petitioner's case or cause him any hardship or injustice. For aught that appears, the essence of what petitioner seeks either has been revealed to him already through the interrogatories or is readily available to him direct from the witnesses for the asking.

The District Court, after hearing objections to petitioner's request, commanded Fortenbaugh to produce all written statements of witnesses and to state in substance any facts learned through oral statements of witnesses to him. Fortenbaugh was to submit any memoranda he had made of the oral statements so that the court might determine what portions should be revealed to petitioner. All of this was ordered without any showing by petitioner, or any requirement that he make a proper showing, of the necessity for the production of any of this material or any demonstration that denial of production would cause hardship or injustice. The court simply ordered production on the theory that the facts sought were material and were not privileged as constituting attorney-client communications.

In our opinion, neither Rule 26 nor any other rule dealing with discovery contemplates production under such circumstances. That is not because the subject matter is privileged or irrelevant, as those concepts are used in these rules. Here is simply an attempt, without purported necessity or justification, to secure written statements, private memoranda and personal recollections prepared or formed by an adverse party's counsel in the course of his legal duties. As such, it falls outside the arena of discovery and contravenes the public policy underlying the orderly prosecution and defense of legal claims. Not even the most liberal of discovery theories can justify unwarranted inquiries into the files and the mental impressions of an attorney.

Historically, a lawyer is an officer of the court and is bound to work for the advancement of justice while faithfully protecting the rightful interests of his clients. In performing his various duties, however, it is essential that a lawyer work with a certain degree of privacy, free from unnecessary intrusion by opposing parties and their counsel. Proper preparation of a client's case demands that he assemble information, sift what he considers to be the relevant from the irrelevant facts, prepare his legal theories and plan his strategy without undue and needless interference. That is the historical and the necessary way in which lawyers act within the framework of our system of jurisprudence to promote justice and to protect their clients' interests. This work is reflected, of course, in interviews, statements, memoranda, correspondence, briefs, mental impressions, personal beliefs, and countless other tangible and intangible ways — aptly though roughly termed by the Circuit Court of Appeals in this case as the "work product of the lawyer." Were such materials open to opposing counsel on mere demand, much of what is now put down in writing would remain unwritten. An attorney's thoughts, heretofore inviolate, would not be his own. Inefficiency, unfairness and sharp practices would inevitably develop in the giving of legal advice and in the preparation of cases for trial. The effect on the legal profession would be demoralizing. And the interests of the clients and the cause of justice would be poorly served.

We do not mean to say that all written materials obtained or prepared by an adversary's counsel with an eye toward litigation are necessarily free from discovery in all cases. Where relevant and non-privileged facts remain hidden in an attorney's file and where production of those facts is essential to the preparation of one's case, discovery may properly be had. Such written statements and documents might, under certain circumstances, be admissible in evidence or give clues as to the existence or location of relevant facts. Or they might be useful for purposes of impeachment or corroboration. And production might be justified where the witnesses are no longer available or can be reached only with difficulty. Were production of written statements and documents to be precluded under such circumstances, the liberal ideals of the deposition-discovery portions of the Federal Rules of Civil Procedure would be stripped of much of their meaning. But the general policy against invading the privacy of an attorney's course of preparation is so well recognized and so essential to an orderly working of our system of legal procedure that a burden rests on the one who would invade that privacy to establish adequate reasons to justify production through a subpoena or court order. That burden, we believe, is necessarily implicit in the rules as now constituted.

Rule 30(b), as presently written, gives the trial judge the requisite discretion to make a judgment as to whether discovery should be allowed as to written statements secured from witnesses. But in the instant case there was no room for that discretion to operate in favor of the petitioner. No attempt was made to establish any reason why Fortenbaugh should be forced to produce the written statements. There was only a naked, general demand for these materials as of right and a finding by the District Court that no recognizable privilege was involved. That was insufficient to justify discovery under these circumstances and the court should have sustained the refusal of the tug owners and Fortenbaugh to produce.

But as to oral statements made by witnesses to Fortenbaugh, whether presently in the form of his mental impressions or memoranda, we do not believe that any showing of necessity can be made under the circumstances of this case so as to justify production. Under ordinary conditions, forcing an attorney to repeat or write out all that witnesses have told him and to deliver the account to his adversary gives rise to grave dangers of inaccuracy and untrustworthiness. No legitimate purpose is served by such production. The practice forces the attorney to testify as to what he remembers or what he saw fit to write down regarding witnesses' remarks. Such testimony could not qualify as evidence; and to use it for impeachment or corroborative purposes would make the attorney much less an officer of the court and much more an ordinary witness. The standards of the profession would thereby suffer.

Denial of production of this nature does not mean that any material, non-privileged facts can be hidden from the petitioner in this case. He need not be unduly hindered in the preparation of his case, in the discovery of facts or in his anticipation of his opponents' position. Searching interrogatories directed to Fortenbaugh and the tug owners, production of written documents and statements upon a proper showing and direct interviews with the witnesses themselves all serve to reveal the facts in Fortenbaugh's possession to the fullest possible extent consistent with public policy. Petitioner's counsel frankly admits that he wants the oral statements only to help prepare himself to examine witnesses and to make sure that he has overlooked nothing. That is insufficient under the circumstances to permit him an exception to the policy underlying the privacy of Fortenbaugh's professional activities. If there should be a rare situation justifying production of these matters, petitioner's case is not of that type.

We fully appreciate the wide-spread controversy among the members of the legal profession over the problem raised by this case. It is a problem that rests on what has been one of the most hazy frontiers of the discovery process. But until some rule or statute definitely prescribes otherwise, we are not justified in permitting discovery in a situation of this nature as a matter of unqualified right. When Rule 26 and the other discovery rules were adopted, this Court and the members of the bar in general certainly did not believe or contemplate that all the files and mental processes of lawyers were thereby opened to the free scrutiny of their adversaries. And we refuse to interpret the rules at this time so as to reach so harsh and unwarranted a result.

We therefore affirm the judgment of the Circuit Court of Appeals.

Affirmed.

MR. JUSTICE JACKSON, concurring.

The narrow question in this case concerns only one of thirty-nine interrogatories which defendants and their counsel refused to answer. As there was persistence in refusal after the court ordered them to answer it, counsel and clients were committed to jail by the district court until they should purge themselves of contempt.

The interrogatory asked whether statements were taken from the crews of the tugs involved in the accident, or of any other vessel, and demanded "Attach hereto exact copies of all such statements if in writing, and if oral, set forth in detail the exact provisions of any such oral statements or reports." The question is simply whether such a demand is authorized by the rules relating to various aspects of "discovery."

The primary effect of the practice advocated here would be on the legal profession itself. But it too often is overlooked that the lawyer and the law office are indispensable parts of our administration of justice. Law-abiding people can go nowhere else to learn the ever changing and constantly multiplying rules by which they must behave and to obtain redress for their wrongs. The welfare and tone of the legal profession is therefore of prime consequence to society, which would feel the consequences of such a practice as petitioner urges secondarily but certainly.

"Discovery" is one of the working tools of the legal profession. It traces back to the equity bill of discovery in English Chancery practice and seems to have had a forerunner in Continental practice. Since 1848 when the draftsmen of New York's Code of Procedure recognized the importance of a better system of discovery, the impetus to extend and expand discovery, as well as the opposition to it, has come from within the Bar itself. It happens in this case that it is the plaintiff's attorney who demands such unprecedented latitude of discovery and, strangely enough, amicus briefs in his support have been filed by several labor unions representing plaintiffs as a class. It is the history of the movement for broader discovery, however, that in actual experience the chief opposition to its extension has come from lawyers who specialize in representing plaintiffs, because defendants have made liberal use of it to force plaintiffs to disclose their cases in advance. Discovery is a two-edged sword and we cannot decide this problem on any doctrine of extending help to one class of litigants.

To consider first the most extreme aspect of the requirement in litigation here, we find it calls upon counsel, if he has had any conversations with any of the crews of the vessels in question or of any other, to "set forth in detail the exact provision of any such oral statements or reports." Thus the demand is not for the production of a transcript in existence but calls for the creation of a written statement not in being. But the statement by counsel of what a witness told him is not evidence when written. Plaintiff could not introduce it to prove his case. What, then, is the purpose sought to be served by demanding this of adverse counsel?

Counsel for the petitioner candidly said on argument that he wanted this information to help prepare himself to examine witnesses, to make sure he overlooked nothing. He bases his claim to it in his brief on the view that the Rules were to do away with the old situation where a law suit developed into "a battle of wits between counsel." But a common law trial is and always should be an adversary proceeding. Discovery was hardly intended to enable a learned profession to perform its functions either without wits or on wits borrowed from the adversary.

The real purpose and the probable effect of the practice ordered by the district court would be to put trials on a level even lower than a "battle of wits." I can conceive of no practice more demoralizing to the Bar than to require a lawyer to write out and deliver to his adversary an account of what witnesses have told him. Even if his recollection were perfect, the statement would be his language, permeated with his inferences. Every one who has tried it knows that it is almost impossible so fairly to record the expressions and emphasis of a witness that when he testifies in the environment of the court and under the influence of the leading question there will not be departures in some respects. Whenever the testimony of the witness would differ from the "exact" statement the lawyer had delivered, the lawyer's statement would be whipped out to impeach the witness. Counsel producing his adversary's "inexact" statement could lose nothing by saying, "Here is a contradiction, gentlemen of the jury. I do not know whether it is my adversary or his witness who is not telling the truth, but one is not." Of course, if this practice were adopted, that scene would be repeated over and over again. The lawyer who delivers such statements often would find himself branded a deceiver afraid to take the stand to support his own version of the witness's conversation with him, or else he will have to go on the stand to defend his own credibility — perhaps against that of his chief witness, or possibly even his client.

Every lawyer dislikes to take the witness stand and will do so only for grave reasons. This is partly because it is not his role; he is almost invariably a poor witness. But he steps out of professional character to do it. He regrets it; the profession discourages it. But the practice advocated here is one which would force him to be a witness, not as to what he has seen or done but as to other witnesses' stories, and not because he wants to do so but in self-defense.

And what is the lawyer to do who has interviewed one whom he believes to be a biased, lying or hostile witness to get his unfavorable statements and know what to meet? He must record and deliver such statements even though he would not vouch for the credibility of the witness by calling him. Perhaps the other side would not want to call him either, but the attorney is open to the charge of suppressing evidence at the trial if he fails to call such a hostile witness even though he never regarded him as reliable or truthful.

Having been supplied the names of the witnesses, petitioner's lawyer gives no reason why he cannot interview them himself. If an employee-witness refuses to tell his story, he, too, may be examined under the Rules. He may be compelled on discovery, as fully as on the trial, to disclose his version of the facts. But that is his own disclosure — it can be used to impeach him if he contradicts it and such a deposition is not useful to promote an unseemly disagreement between the witness and the counsel in the case.

It is true that the literal language of the Rules would admit of an interpretation that would sustain the district court's order. But all such procedural measures have a background of custom and practice which was assumed by those who wrote and should be by those who apply them. Certainly nothing in the tradition or practice of discovery up to the time of these Rules would have suggested that they would authorize such a practice as here proposed.

The question remains as to signed statements or those written by witnesses. Such statements are not evidence for the defendant. Nor should I think they ordinarily could be evidence for the plaintiff. But such a statement might be useful for impeachment of the witness who signed it, if he is called and if he departs from the statement. There might be circumstances, too, where impossibility or difficulty of access to the witness or his refusal to respond to requests for information or other facts would show that the interests of justice require that such statements be made available. Production of such statements are governed by Rule 34 and on "showing good cause therefor" the court may order their inspection, copying or photographing. No such application has here been made; the demand is made on the basis of right, not on showing of cause.

I agree to the affirmance of the judgment of the Circuit Court of Appeals which reversed the district court.

MR. JUSTICE FRANKFURTER joins in this opinion.

NOTES AND PROBLEMS FOR DISCUSSION

1. Be sure you understand the difference between documents and communications that are privileged, and those that are subject to the work product rule.

(a) Assume in *Hickman* that the owner of the tug spoke to Fortenbaugh about the merits of the case, trial strategy, and whether he should settle. Can the plaintiff take a deposition of the owner and ask him what Fortenbaugh said? If not, is this because it is not relevant, because it is work product, or because of some other reason?

(b) Assume that Mr. Hickman had survived and spoke to his wife about the case, including what "really happened" and whether he should settle. Can the defendant take a deposition of Mrs. Hickman and ask what Mr. Hickman said? If not, is this because it is not relevant, because it is work product, or because of some other reason?

(c) Does your answer to (a) or (b) change if we assume that the information is absolutely critical, and there is no other way to get it?

2. As noted, the work product doctrine has since been "codified" in Rule 26(b)(3). Apply the rule to the following variations of *Hickman*:

(a) John Jones, a dockworker, told Fortenbaugh that he saw the tug just before it left on the ill-fated voyage, and that he observed five loose plates just above the water line. Can plaintiff get this information and, if so, how?

(b) Wilma Waters, who was riding on the barge, was interviewed by Fortenbaugh, soon after the accident. She recently moved to the Kingdom of Bhutan (in southern Asia), and is unavailable. Can plaintiff get (a) a statement signed by Wilma, and (b) Fortenbaugh's notes of the interview?

(c) Shortly after the accident, the tug's owner made a report of the accident to the Coast Guard, describing the background and events in question. Can plaintiff get the report?

(d) Shortly after the accident, Sally Snoope, a claims adjuster for the tug's owner went to the scene and interviewed various persons on the dock as well as Eli Watson who was on a boat that rescued the four survivors. If the plaintiff takes Snoope's deposition, is she (Snoope) required (i) to testify regarding the content of her interviews, or (ii) to produce her interview notes?

(e) Eli Watson met with the plaintiff and "can't remember" whether he gave a statement to Snoope. Can the plaintiff (i) find out whether Eli gave a statement, and (ii) if so, get a copy of the statement?

3. Lily D'Illigente is an in-house attorney for Bolt Manufacturing Company. Recently, Bolt engaged in negotiations regarding an acquisition of Nutt & Co., numerous documents were exchanged, and a letter of intent was signed. Lily participated in all of the negotiations, and was copied-in on all internal memos and documents relating to the acquisition. Bolt decided not to go forward with the transaction, and Nutt sued claiming that the parties had a binding agreement which Bolt breached. On discovery, Bolt objected to (a) the production of all internal Bolt memos relating to the acquisition sent by or copied to Lily, and (b) any deposition questions relating to discussions among members of the Bolt negotiating team if Lily was a participant. How should the court rule on Nutt's motion to compel discovery? See Cavallaro v. United States, 284 F.3d 236 (1st Cir. 2002) (denying attorney-client protection to records disclosed to third-party accountant because disclosure to third party constituted waiver of privilege).

4. Expert Information

Experts play an ever increasing role in modern litigation. But the role is a somewhat hybrid one. An expert is part witness and part a member of the litigant's team. That is, she is a witness in that she may or will testify at trial. But she also may be a member of the litigant's team in that she may work with the attorney and other experts in developing facts and litigation strategy, in assisting in discovery (especially in formulating deposition questions, interrogatory questions, and document requests), and in preparing for trial. And, ultimately, if her testimony proves to be unhelpful (or even if another expert turns out to be a better witness, or to have better information), she may not testify at all; she may even participate actively in the decision whether or not to testify.[*]

Having dual roles of witness and advocate does not fit easily within an adversary system that sharply distinguishes the lawyer and her team (other lawyers, legal assistants, investigators) from witnesses. At the discovery level, expert discovery presented a stark conflict between two policies: the policy of open discovery of relevant information (and especially information from trial witnesses), versus the policy of attorney confidentiality of trial preparation and work product. Today, these issues are governed by Rule 26(b)(4) and 26(a)(2), although when enacted, the Federal Rules had no provisions on expert discovery, and original Rule 26(b)(4) had rather different provisions than at present.

NOTES AND PROBLEMS FOR DISCUSSION

1.   Suppose a case is filed on January 2, 2006, and is set for trial on June 1, 2007.

(a) About when is the expert's report due?

(b) When are any expert depositions likely to take place?

(c) Timewise, what is the likely relationship between the time for (a) and (b), and the time for other discovery and the date for the trial?

2.   What policies do your answers to the above questions reflect?

3.   Courts increasingly require an expert to disclose virtually all information she has considered and consulted in connection with her testimony. E.g., Johnson v. Gmeinder, 191 F.R.D. 638, 641 (D. Kan. 2000) ("considered" means read, even if not relied on in formulating opinion); Rule 26(a)(2)(B). Explain how this principle effectively limits the expert's ability to play the dual roles of expert witness and advisor.

4.   The most difficult questions under Rule 26(b)(4) have been who is an expert within the rule, and the availability of discovery from nontestifying experts. The next case deals with the former issue; the notes, the latter. For background, the case is brought in admiralty pursuant to a special admiralty procedure which permits the owner to limit liability to the value of his vessel.

---

[*]   Because of this problem, some litigants separate advisory from testifying experts, and use only the advisory experts for general advice and consultation on the case. This avoids some of the problems noted above, but increases the expense.

In Re Illusions Holdings, Inc.

United States District Court, Southern District of New York, 1999.

189 F.R.D. 316.

BERMAN, DISTRICT JUDGE.

Steven M. Wagner ("Wagner" or "Claimant") seeks damages resulting from injuries he allegedly sustained (to his shoulder) while scuba diving in the British Virgin Islands on December 23, 1994. Wagner alleges that the injury resulted from the negligence of Illusions Holdings, Inc. ("Illusions" or "Petitioner"), which is the owner of the boat named ILLUSIONS from which the dive was conducted. ILLUSIONS' Captain Tom Zurich ("Zurich") led the dive.

Wagner has moved, in limine, to preclude at the forthcoming trial of this case the testimony of Joe Giacinto ("Giacinto"), the President of BVI Dive Operators Association, and Michael Van Blaricum ("Van Blaricum"), the owner of Kibrides Sunchaser Scuba, two non-party witnesses who were deposed by Illusions, purportedly as "fact" or "lay" witnesses. Wagner asserts that the testimony of Giacinto and Van Blaricum was elicited as expert testimony by Illusions. Because Illusions did not comply with the requirements of Rule 26 of the Federal Rules of Civil Procedure ("Fed. R. Civ. P.") relating to disclosure of expert testimony, Wagner contends that the testimony of both witnesses should be precluded. Wagner also contends that he should be awarded the costs of the instant motion and the costs of attending the Giacinto and Van Blaricum depositions.

For the reasons set forth below, Wagner's motion is granted.

I. BACKGROUND

In November 1998, Illusions advised Wagner that it would be deposing Tom Zurich, who, as noted, was the captain of ILLUSIONS at the time of Wagner's diving accident in Tortola, British Virgin Islands. On December 2, 1998, counsel for Illusions wrote to counsel for Wagner, and advised that Zurich's deposition would be conducted on January 14, 1999. In the same letter, counsel for Illusions stated, for the first time, his intention to depose Giacinto and Van Blaricum, "both of whom are familiar with dive sights in the British Virgin Islands, the local current conditions, dive procedures and the suitability of the dive sight where Steven Wagner was injured for conducting recreational dives by a certified diver with Mr. Wagner's experience in open water diving." (Hornig Letter dated December 2, 1998).

On December 11, 1998, Wagner served a Demand for Report of Expert Witness on Illusions. Counsel for Wagner also telephoned counsel for Illusions and offered to reschedule the depositions of Giacinto and Van Blaricum to allow Illusions additional time to provide expert reports for the two witnesses. A letter confirming the telephone conversation and confirming Wagner's objection to the testimony of the two witnesses without prior disclosure of expert reports was sent to Illusions on December 11, 1998.

By letter dated December 15, 1998, counsel for Illusions rejected Wagner's request for expert disclosure stating that "it is our opinion that these witnesses are not experts, however, we note your contentions and arguments that their testimony may be interpreted to be expert testimony. In any event, the trial court will ultimately rule on the issue of whether their testimony is admissible at the trial of this action." (Hornig Letter dated December 15, 1998).

Accordingly, the depositions of Giacinto and Van Blaricum were conducted over the objections of Wagner on January 13, 1999 in Virgin Gorda, British Virgin Islands.

II. ANALYSIS

Fed. R. Civ. P. 26(a)(2)(B) provides as follows[*]:

> Except as otherwise stipulated or directed by the court, this disclosure shall, *with respect to a witness who is retained or specifically employed to provide expert testimony in the case or whose duties as an employee of the party regularly involve giving expert testimony, be accompanied by a written report prepared and signed by the witness.* The report shall contain a complete statement of all opinions to be expressed and the basis and reasons therefor; the data or other information considered by the witness in forming the opinions; any exhibits to be used as a summary of or support for the opinions; the qualifications of the witness, including a list of all publications authored by the witness within the preceding ten years; the compensation to be paid for the study and testimony; and a listing of any other cases in which the witness has testified as an expert at trial or by deposition within the preceding four years. (emphasis added).

Fed. R. Civ. P. 26(b)(4)(A) provides, in relevant part, that "if a report from the expert is required under subdivision (a)(2)(B), *the deposition shall not be conducted until after the report is provided.*" (emphasis added).

Fed. R. Civ. P. 37(c)(1) provides, in relevant part, as follows:

> *A party that without substantial justification fails to disclose information required by Rule 26(a) or 26(e)(1) shall not, unless such failure is harmless, be permitted to use as evidence at a trial, at a hearing, or on a motion any witness or information not so disclosed.* In addition to or in lieu of this sanction, the court, on motion, and after affording an opportunity to be heard, may impose other appropriate sanctions. . . . (emphasis added).

Testimony by expert witnesses is governed by Federal Rule of Evidence ("Fed. R. Evid." or "Rule") 702, which provides that:

> If scientific, technical, or other specialized knowledge will assist the trier of fact to understand the evidence or to determine a fact in issue, a

---

[*] [Note that the current version of Rule 26(a)(2) has been substantially restructured. — eds.]

witness qualified as an expert by knowledge, skill, experience, training, or education, may testify thereto in the form of an opinion or otherwise.

Opinion testimony by lay witnesses is governed by Fed. R. Evid. 701 which provides that:

> If the witness is not testifying as an expert, the witness' testimony in the form of opinions or inferences is limited to those opinions or inferences which are (a) rationally based on the perception of the witness and (b) helpful to a clear understanding of the witness' testimony or the determination of a fact in issue.

The distinction between lay and expert opinion testimony has been the topic of considerable discussion, if not debate. In fact, certain of the Fed. R. Evid. (e.g., Rules 701, 702 and 703) are currently the subject of (re)analysis and proposed revision by the Committee on Rules of Practice and Procedure of the Judicial Conference of the United States ("Standing Committee"). The proposed revisions must also be reviewed by the United States Supreme Court and Congress before they can take effect.

In Daubert v. Merrell Dow Pharmaceuticals, Inc., 509 U.S. 579, 125 L.Ed.2d 469, 113 S.Ct. 2786 (1993), the leading decision on expert testimony, the United States Supreme Court has held that the (earlier) *Frye* test [Frye v. United States, 293 F. 1013 (D.C. Cir. 1923)] has been superseded in Federal proceedings by the Fed. R. Evid.[3] Id. at 589 n.6. The Supreme Court contemplated "a gatekeeping role for the [Federal trial] judge," stating that the Rules "assign to the trial judge the task of ensuring that an expert's testimony both rests on a reliable foundation and is relevant to the task at hand." Id. at 597. The Supreme Court has recently elaborated on the holding in *Daubert*, stating "that *Daubert*'s . . . holding — setting forth the trial judge's general 'gatekeeping' obligation — applies not only to testimony based on 'scientific' knowledge, but also to testimony based on 'technical' and 'other specialized' knowledge." Kumho Tire Co., Ltd. v. Carmichael, 526 U.S. 137, 119 S.Ct. 1167, 1171, 143 L.Ed.2d 238 (1999) (citation omitted).

Since *Daubert*, the line between lay witness (opinion) testimony, governed by Rule 701, and expert witness (opinion) testimony, governed by Rule 702, has sometimes seemed blurred. For example, in Doddy v. Oxy USA, Inc., 101 F.3d 448 (5th Cir. 1996), the Court of Appeals for the Fifth Circuit held that "a person may testify as a lay witness only if his opinions or inferences do not require any specialized knowledge and could be reached by any ordinary person." Id. at 460 (citing Brady v. Chemical Construction Corp., 740 F.2d 195, 200 (2d Cir. 1984)).

---

[3] Some state courts have not embraced *Daubert*. See, e.g., Brim v. State of Florida, 695 So. 2d 268, 271-72 (Fla. 1997) ("[D]espite the federal adoption of a more lenient standard in *Daubert v. Merrell Dow Pharmaceuticals, Inc.* . . . we have maintained the higher standard of reliability as dictated by *Frye*.") (citation omitted).

On the other hand, in Asplundh Manufacturing Division v. Benton Harbor Engineering, 57 F.3d 1190 (3d Cir. 1995), the Court of Appeals for the Third Circuit held that:

> Though we agree . . . that the admission of lay opinion evidence in these technical areas (e.g., concerning the existence vel non of a product defect or whether an accident was caused by a certain condition) can result in an attenuated form of expert opinion evidence far removed from the consideration . . . animating the lay opinion rule, it is not for us to rewrite the rule or reinterpret Rule 701 across the board. *Accordingly, we refuse to hold, . . . that all lay witnesses offering opinions that require special knowledge or experience must qualify under Rule 702.*

Id. at 1200-01 (emphasis added). The Third Circuit went on explicitly to call for a "brightening" of the line between opinion testimony under Rules 701 and 702, observing that:

> We believe, however, that such distinctions can and might well be made by the drafters of the Federal Rules, in that, as our discussion suggests, a better formulation of the lay opinion rule would perhaps eliminate these matters from the ambit of Rule 701. Such an approach has been adopted by some states . . . We take the liberty of commending this issue to the attention of the Judicial Conference Advisory Committee on Rules of Evidence. . . .

Id. at 1201 n.14.

In the instant case, having reviewed the deposition transcripts of Giacinto and Van Blaricum, the Court is convinced that the testimony at issue involves expert, not lay, opinion(s). For example, Giacinto testified as follows:

> Q: Can you tell me generally what the currents are generally in this area or if they vary —
>
>   . . . .
>
> A: I would say currents in general are not a problem in the British Virgin Islands. However, some of the dive sites — and not all, certainly not all. Some of the dive sites can during certain tidal movements become less desirable to dive than others because of current situations.
>
> Q: What about visibility generally?
>
> A: Visibility is usually very good.
>
> Q: And what does that mean, just because you're depth scope might be read —
>
> A: Very good. I would say for us, I mean, average is more than 60 feet. And in the world, 60-foot visibility as an average would be extremely good. . . .
>
> Q: When rising — when using a BC [buoyancy control device] to rise from the bottom, is it necessary to inflate it slightly to get some positive buoyancy?

A: You don't, you don't as a rule use that to raise yourself from the bottom.

Q: You just swim up?

A: You can, but you swim up slowly so you can control your ascent.

Q: Okay.

A: Air in a BC can be a problem and cause too fast an ascent.

Q: Can a BC also be used as a flotation device on the surface?

A: Absolutely.

(Giacinto Deposition Transcript at 9-11, 16-17).

Similarly, Van Blaricum testified as follows:

Q: Okay. And what's the function of a BC?

A: Flotation at the surface, neutral buoyancy at depth.

Q: And what's the — a person's diving off an inflatable, what's the procedure for getting off your BC if there is one?

A: Well, it depends on the type of BC. Some of them you would have shoulder straps that you just unclip real quick and undo the waistband and the whole thing falls off of you basically.

Some you would have to work your arms out if it doesn't have the clips, you know. You could pull it off over your head or you could dive down underneath it or slide down underneath it and lift your arms and it floats off over the top of you.

Q: Is there any preferable practice when a diver's going to go into a dinghy to take his BC with his tank and octopus off before getting in the boat or does he get in with the equipment on or is it optional?

A: It would be optional, you know. It depends on the individual, you know. Most people probably would take it off though just to have less weight to carry into the boat.

Q: Now if the BC has been inflated so it acts as a lifevest, is it any more difficult to get it off than if it's not inflated?

A: It would be a little more restrictive, but if it had buckles on it, you just pop the buckles and the whole thing pops off, you know. If it doesn't have buckles — in over 90 percent of them now, they do. If it didn't have buckles, you'd want to let a little air out first. It would just be easier.

In addition, the two witnesses acknowledged that they were called upon to provide expert testimony. Giacinto testified as follows:

Q: And what was it that you understood you were going to be testifying about?

A: *Conditions and my opinion on conditions in the BVI [British Virgin Islands]*.

Similarly, Van Blaricum testified as follows:

> Q: Did you have any conversation with [counsel for Illusions] about this deposition before —
>
> A: *He called and asked if I knew of the area and if I could be of assistance in expertise of being here for 10 years.*

(emphasis added).

The advisory committee notes to Fed. R. Evid. 702 (concerning testimony by experts) explain that:

> *The rule is broadly phrased.* The fields of knowledge which may be drawn upon are not limited merely to the "scientific" or "technical" but extend to all "specialized" knowledge. Similarly, the expert is viewed, not in a narrow sense, but as a person qualified by "knowledge, skill, experience, training or education." Thus within the scope of the rule are not only experts in the strictest sense of the word, e.g., physicians, physicists, and architects, but also the large group sometimes called "skilled" witnesses, such as bankers or landowners testifying to land values. (emphasis added).

The testimony of Giacinto and Van Blaricum reflected in their depositions and concerning, among other things, scuba diving training methods, procedures for scuba diving, and their opinions about currents, water temperature, visibility, and certain dive sites in the British Virgin Islands "surely satisfy this broad [expert] definition." Queen v. Washington Metropolitan Area Transit Authority, 268 U.S. App. D.C. 480, 842 F.2d 476, 482 (D.C. Cir. 1988). Counsel for Wagner was disadvantaged (harmed) in deposition cross-examination by the absence of required disclosure under Fed. R. Civ. P. 26. Because Illusions did not comply with the disclosure requirements of Fed. R. Civ. P. 26, in the face of Wagner's request that it do so, the testimony of Giacinto and Van Blaricum may not be used at trial. See Fed. R. Civ. P. 37(c)(1).[7]

Not only is the preclusion of Giacinto and Van Blaricum's testimony required under current law, it is also consistent with the proposed amendment to Fed. R. Evid. 701:

> If the witness is not testifying as an expert, the witness' testimony in the form of opinions or inferences is limited to those opinions or inferences which are (a) rationally based on the perception of the witness, (b) helpful to a clear understanding of the witness' testimony or the determination of a fact in issue *and (c) not based on scientific, technical or other specialized knowledge within the scope of Rule 702.* (emphasis added).

---

[7] The testimony of Giacinto and Van Blaricum does not qualify as lay opinion testimony because it does not satisfy the requirements of Rule 701. Their testimony does not, for example, relate to the incident at bar or to the specific dive site where Wagner allegedly sustained his injury. The testimony of Giacinto and Van Blaricum would not, among other things, be "helpful to a clear understanding of the witness' testimony or the determination of a fact in issue." Fed. R. Evid. 701.

The advisory committee notes to the proposed amendment to Fed. R. Evid. 701 state that *"the amendment makes clear that any part of a witness' testimony that is based upon scientific, technical, or other specialized knowledge within the scope of Rule 702 is governed by the standards of Rule 702 and the corresponding disclosure requirements of the Civil and Criminal Rules."* (emphasis added). That is the case here. That is, the testimony of Giacinto and Van Blaricum is clearly based upon "specialized knowledge" (i.e., their diving expertise) within the scope of Rule 702 and is, therefore, subject to the disclosure requirements of Fed. R. Civ. P. 26. Since Illusions refused to make the disclosures required under Fed. R. Civ. P. 26, the testimony of Giacinto and Van Blaricum may not be used at trial.

III. Conclusion

For the foregoing reasons, Wagner's motion in limine is granted. At the close of trial, the Court will request additional written submissions from counsel concerning the costs incurred by Wagner for attending the depositions of Giacinto and Van Blaricum and for preparing the instant motion.

NOTES AND PROBLEMS FOR DISCUSSION

1. Why did Illusions Holdings argue that Giacinto and Van Blaricum were not experts within Rule 26(b)(4), and what is the Court's rationale for rejecting the argument?

2. Suppose that Giacinto and Van Blaricum were not professional divers but, instead, highly experienced recreational divers living in the same locale. Would it have made a difference?

3. As noted above, one of the most difficult issues has been when discovery can be obtained against a *non*testifying expert. Assume you are Judge Berman, and had to rule on the following variations of the facts in *Illusions Holdings* in the case of various nontestifying experts:

(a) Joe Diverman, who had been retained by Wagner as an expert on diving procedures. Although Diverman was not present when Wagner was injured, he was diving that day at about the same time in the same general area.

(b) Sally Skye, who was retained by Illusions Holdings to prepare a "working tidal model" of the currents and conditions at the site of the injury, at a cost of $75,000.

(c) Same as (b) except Wagner is impecunious and, even though seriously injured, has no funds to pay for a comparable model.

4. Consider what happens in *Illusions Holdings* now, and whether that will present the defendant with any problem. If you had been counsel for defendant, how would you have dealt with the uncertainty over whether Giacinto and Van Blaricum were experts?

5. The Supreme Court's decision in the *Daubert* case, referred to in *Illusions Holdings*, significantly changed the role of the Court in matters respecting expert witnesses. The case was a response to criticism of some expert testimony as involving essentially junk science, unworthy of consideration. The Supreme Court ruled that the trial court has a preliminary gatekeeping function to assure that the scientific testimony "rests on a reliable foundation." In the *Kumho Tire* case, also referred to in *Illusions Holdings*, the Court extended this principle to testimony on technical and other specialized matters (i.e., most expert testimony). While these cases primarily raise issues for trial, they raise discovery issues as well if the motion to disqualify an expert follows the Rule 26(a)(2) disclosures and the expert is disqualified either on the eve of trial or during the trial. Do you see what the problem is?

5. PROTECTIVE ORDERS

While the rules governing the scope of discovery (and the use of the various devices) provide some guidelines, they are necessarily general and do not deal with the almost limitless number of issues and problems that can arise during the actual discovery process. Although the rules have been amended a number of times, generally to deal more specifically with problem areas, those amendments barely scratch the surface of such issues and problems.

There are essentially two ways to deal with discovery disputes, and they are somewhat overlapping. First, as noted, discovery generally proceeds without court intervention unless there is a dispute over discovery. That is, the court neither approves or even reviews most discovery requests.* One way of dealing with a perceived problem with a discovery request is for the party responding to discovery to object to the request and to decline to respond. Even at this point, nothing happens unless and until the party seeking discovery seeks to compel a response. See Rule 37(a). If the discovering party never seeks to compel a response, the request essentially drops out of the case.

The other method is for the party resisting discovery to seek a "protective order" under Rule 26(c). The term "protective order" really is a misnomer, since it applies to matters that have little to do with "protection" or "abuse." A more proper name might be a "discovery order," or a "dispute resolution order." Courts have a very large amount of discretion in dealing with such matters. Read Rule 26(c) to get a flavor of some of the areas that commonly give rise to protective orders. In actuality, any dispute may give rise to a request for a protective order, especially if the matter or issue has application beyond one or two questions or requests. In this regard, note that Rule 37(a)(5)(B) and (C) specifically authorize the district court to enter a protective order in connection with a motion to compel discovery under Rule 37(a). Some examples of commonly raised issues are as follow:

(1) *Confidentiality of Information/Documents.* Here, one party requests that documents or information be kept confidential and, often, that there be limited

---

*   Under the original Federal Rules, discovery requests did have to be filed with the Court.

access. Such issues commonly arise in litigation regarding trade secrets, business torts, and employment cases.

(2) *Location of Depositions.* This tends to be an issue when there is litigation involving parties in different parts of the country (or world). The most frequently litigated issue has to do with when a party must travel to the location of its adversary for a deposition.

(3) *Scope of Document Discovery.* Even with the recent amendments to the scope of discovery, rules of relevance don't provide an effective limit on discovery since lawyers generally can hypothesize some reason why certain information might be relevant. In a large business case, it was, and likely still is possible to frame discovery requests which would require the production of perhaps millions of documents. Frequently, parties will seek a protective order to limit the production of documents of tangential relevance (and of course, they often do not agree on what is tangential).

(4) *Order of Discovery.* A plaintiff sues claiming a slip and fall and damage to his back. Assume that defendant has located a witness who is prepared to testify that he saw the plaintiff a month after the incident going bungee jumping. Or, assume that the plaintiff is about to be deposed and requests a statement he gave to defendant's lawyer under Rule 26(b)(3). What kind of protective order might defendant request in such cases and on what basis?

6. THE COSTS OF DISCOVERY

Before turning specifically to the discovery process, a word about the "costs" of the process. Here, we talk about legal expense related to the discovery process. But there are other costs as well: social costs in supervising the litigation process, the time and effort expended by parties and witnesses, and the frustration and dissatisfaction with the process itself, with the legal profession, and with the overall system for administering justice.

By any measure, the costs of the process may be considerable. As you think about these materials, try to imagine how many hours of lawyers' time will be spent to take and defend a one-day deposition, to draft and respond to a "reasonable" set of interrogatories, and to draft a "reasonable" document request and to produce the requested documents. Then multiply these numbers for additional depositions, factor in a degree of unpleasantness and unreasonableness, and multiply again if there are multiple parties. And finally, add lots of administrative time (because these things don't happen by magic), and lots of wasted motions, and you get a small sense of what is involved.

There has been a broad feeling that discovery costs are "too high" (whatever that means), but little agreement on responsibility or solutions. This feeling is reflected both in statutes, such as recent amendments to the Securities Act which seek to set up "gatekeeping" rules in an effort to prevent cases which may lack any substance from reaching discovery, and doctrines such as those recognized by the Supreme Court in civil rights actions against public officials who often have a right to a determination of the "qualified immunity" defense before discovery can begin. In recent years, numerous changes to the discovery rules have been proposed, and some have been enacted, to deal with discovery matters. Among rules enacted in the comparatively recent past are those (a) narrowing the scope of permissible discovery, (b) requiring certain disclosures at the outset of the case, (c) increasing court supervision of the discovery process, (d) limiting depositions to 10 and interrogatories to 25, (e) adopting new deposition procedures, and (f) adding attorney certification requirements and beefing up sanctions. The effectiveness of these remedies and their impact on the discovery process are sharply debated.

There are more fundamental questions as well. In litigation where there are different levels of resources, the "poorer" party may run the risk of being overwhelmed by the cost of discovery and being compelled to seek an unfavorable settlement as a result. Conversely, corporations and organizations often complain that the discovery process enables plaintiffs to impose millions of dollars of discovery expense, and complain that they settle nonmeritorious claims simply to avoid such costs. Of course, whether a case involves abusive discovery, hiding the facts, unmeritorious claims, fishing expeditions, and piling-on often depends on who is telling the story. We intimate no view on these issues, but a student is likely to hear and use the expressions sooner than she thinks.

7. ELECTRONIC DISCOVERY

Amendments to the Federal Rules went into effect in 2006 that deal with the phenomenon of electronically stored information ("ESI") and its discovery. Amendments were made to Rules 16, 26, 33, 34, 37, 45, and to Form 35. These "e-discovery rules" are treated here collectively, rather than separately, at the point where the particular rule is discussed in this Chapter. In the words of the Standing Committee Report:

> The proposed amendments to Rules 16, 26, 33, 34, 37, 45, and revisions to Form 35 are aimed at discovery of electronically stored information. The advisory committee first heard about problems with computer-based discovery at a discovery conference in 1996. In 1999, the then-chair laid out the advisory committee's daunting mission to devise "mechanisms for providing full disclosure in a context where potential access to information is virtually unlimited and in which full discovery could involve burdens far beyond anything justified by the interests of the parties to the litigation." The advisory committee began intensive work on this subject in 2000. Since then, bar organizations, attorneys, computer specialists, and members of the public have devoted much time and energy in helping the rules committees understand and address the serious problems arising from discovery of electronically stored information. The advisory committee's study included several mini-conferences and one major conference, bringing together lawyers,

academics, judges, and litigants with a variety of experiences and viewpoints. The advisory committee also heard from experts in information technology who provide technical electronic discovery services to lawyers and litigants.

The discovery of electronically stored information raises markedly different issues from conventional discovery of paper records. Electronically stored information is characterized by exponentially greater volume than hard-copy documents. Commonly cited current examples of such volume include the capacity of large organizations' computer networks to store information in terabytes, each of which represents the equivalent of 500 million typewritten pages of plain text, and to receive 250 to 300 million e-mail messages monthly. Computer information, unlike paper, is also dynamic; merely turning a computer on or off can change the information it stores. Computers operate by overwriting and deleting information, often without the operator's specific direction or knowledge. A third important difference is that electronically stored information, unlike words on paper, may be incomprehensible when separated from the system that created it. These and other differences are causing problems in discovery that rule amendments can helpfully address.

The advisory committee monitored the experiences of the bar and bench with these issues for several years. It found that the discovery of electronically stored information is becoming more time-consuming, burdensome, and costly. The current discovery rules, last amended in 1970 to take into account changes in information technology, provide inadequate guidance to litigants, judges, and lawyers in determining discovery rights and obligations in particular cases. Developing case law on discovery into electronically stored information under the current rules is not consistent and is necessarily limited by the specific facts involved. Disparate local rules have emerged to fill this gap between the existing discovery rules and practice, and more courts are considering local rules. Without national rules adequate to address the issues raised by electronic discovery, a patchwork of rules and requirements is likely to develop. While such inconsistencies are particularly confusing and debilitating to large public and private organizations, the uncertainty, expense, delays, and burdens of such discovery also affect small organizations and even individual litigants.

The costs of complying with unclear and at times vague discovery obligations, which vary from district to district in ways unwarranted by local variations in practice, are becoming increasingly problematic. Unless timely action is taken to make the federal discovery rules better able to accommodate the distinctive features of electronic discovery, those rules will become increasingly removed from practice, and similarly situated litigants will continue to be treated differently depending on the federal forum.

The proposed amendments were published in 2004, following which there was a public comment period with extensive feedback, which resulted in still further changes. There are six primary areas to which the amendments are addressed; we discuss each of them in greater detail, below:

- Acknowledging and defining "electronically stored information" (ESI);
- Early attention to, and "meet and confer" obligations respecting ESI;
- The manner of ESI production;
- ESI discovery from sources not reasonably accessible;
- Privilege assertion and review; and
- Sanctions and a "safe harbor" limit for the loss of ESI.

1. Acknowledging and Defining ESI

"Electronically stored information" is specifically made discoverable. The phrase is added to Rules 16(b)(3)(B)(iii), 26(a)(1)(A)(ii), 33(d), 34(a)-(b), 37(e), and Rule 45. Rule 34 recognizes that ESI makes up a category of items, in addition to "documents" and "things," that is subject to discovery. According to the Committee Notes, the phrase ESI is to be given a "broad meaning" and refers to "data or data compilations stored in any medium — from which information can be obtained." The rules also recognize that ESI may be stored in various forms.

2. Early Attention to, and Meet and Confer Obligations Respecting ESI

Because early attention to electronic discovery issues is important for controlling the scope and the costs of e-discovery, and discovery disputes generally, a number of amendments to the Rules require the parties to address such issues early on in the discovery process. Rule 26(f)(3) requires the parties to meet and confer regarding the preservation of discoverable ESI and the form in which it will be produced. Importantly, it also requires parties to discuss issues relating to possible claims of protection for privilege or work product. Rule 26(a)(1)(A)(ii) now requires parties to disclose any ESI that the party plans to use to support their claims or defenses, as part of their initial disclosures. And Rule 16(b)(3)(B)(iii) includes provisions "for [the] disclosure or discovery of ESI" as a matter that may be properly included in the court's scheduling order, as can "agreements the parties reach for asserting claims of privilege or of protection as trial-preparation material after production."

3. The Manner of ESI Production

Rule 34(b) addresses the form in which ESI will be produced. It permits the requesting party to designate the form in which it wants electronically stored information produced (e.g., paper versus electronic), but it does not require the requesting party to choose a form of production. Dispute resolution over the form of production, should the responding party objects to the requested format(s), is also addressed by the rule. Finally, the rule provides that "if no form" is specified in a request, or if the responding party objects to the requested form, the responding party must notify the requesting party of the form in which they intend to produce the electronically stored material — with the option of producing it either in a form in which the information is "ordinarily maintained," or in "a reasonably usable form or forms."

4. ESI Discovery from Sources not Reasonably Accessible

Amended Rule 26(b)(2) addresses the parties' obligations to produce requested ESI that is not reasonably accessible. The Rule creates two categories of ESI: reasonably accessible ESI and that which is not. A party need not produce "inaccessible" ESI — ESI from sources not reasonably accessible "because of undue burden or cost." But the party must identify and describe the information and show why its retrieval would be unduly burdensome or costly thus making it inaccessible within the meaning of the rule. If that showing is made, a court may nevertheless order discovery, if the requesting party shows good cause, and considering the remaining provisions of the rule.

5. Privilege Assertion and Review

Rule 26(b)(5) addresses the problems associated with the inadvertent disclosure of material that is "subject to a claim of privilege or of protection." It provides a process by which a party who has inadvertently produced such material to assert a protective claim as to that material. The party seeking to establish the privilege or work product claim may notify the receiving parties of their claim of privilege or protection and the basis for it, and the receiving parties must then "return, sequester, or destroy" the identified information. A receiving party "may promptly present the information to the court under seal for a determination of the claim" of privilege or protection. If the receiving party has already disclosed the information, the receiving party "must take reasonable steps to retrieve [it]." The Advisory Committee Note states that the rule "does not address whether the privilege or protection asserted after production was waived by the production." It merely prohibits the receiving party from using it or disclosing it to others.

6. Sanctions and Safe Harbor

Rule 37(e)(1)-(2) addresses the consequences of a failure to maintain "electronically stored information" (ESI). Initially, Rule 37(e) provided that good faith failures to preserve ESI should not ordinarily result in sanctions, but current Rule 37(e) deals with ESI that "should have been preserved" in the anticipation or conduct of litigation. It now states that "upon finding prejudice" to a party from loss of ESI, the district court "may order measures no greater than necessary to cure the prejudice." But if a court finds that a party acted with "intent to deprive" another party of the information's use, sanctions can include an instruction to the jury that it "may or must presume" that the lost ESI was "unfavorable to the party" who failed to preserve it, or even outright dismissal of the action or entry of a default judgment. Rule 37(e)(2).

NOTES AND PROBLEMS FOR DISCUSSION

1. If there is a dispute over discovery that cannot be resolved informally, it will be necessary to seek judicial relief. The most common situations are (a) a motion to compel an answer or response to discovery, (b) a motion for a protective order, and (c) a motion for sanctions. Students (and many law professors) frequently deal with discovery disputes by noting the availability of judicial relief as a panacea for problems. Before you jump at this "solution," consider the next question.

2. Take a simple discovery motion such as that involved in the *Santelli* case — i.e., defendant sought discovery of plaintiff's psychological records. How much lawyer time is involved? To figure it out, start with asking what the process will be for the moving and nonmoving party from beginning to end. Assume then that each lawyer charges by the hour, and then determine how much she charges in the area where your law school is located (or where you live or want to practice). Now do the math.

3. Problem #2 above asks you to estimate the costs of a relatively simple motion involving a relatively simple issue. As you go through the following materials, keep this number in mind and be prepared to multiply it (sometimes many times over) as the legal or factual issues become more complex.

SECTION B.   DISCOVERY IN ACTION

With the above background, we move to the specifics of discovery. We have eschewed using cases because most discovery issues are intensely factual, and the cases are simply illustrative of rulings in a concrete situation. Instead, we will discuss each of the major discovery devices, and follow up with detailed questions. It bears repeating that, like it or not, you must read the Rules to deal with these issues.

1. DISCLOSURE

Rule 26(a)(1) requires both of the parties to provide various pieces of information at the outset of the case. It is based on the premise that the required information is so basic that the parties would almost always want it, and thus, no purpose is served by a more formal request-and-respond process.

An earlier version of the Rule proved extremely controversial. Before December 1, 2000, it required parties to disclose certain information that would be relevant not only to the party's own claim or defense, but also information that would be relevant to the opposing party's claim or defense (and thus potentially harmful to the disclosing party). Perhaps because of its controversial nature, the old Rule also permitted district courts to opt out of the mandatory discovery provisions, and a great many did. Current Rule 26(a)(1) now generally requires a party to disclose only those witnesses and documents that the disclosing party may use to support its own claims and defenses. Being less controversial, it also eliminates the possibility of opt out. To focus the issues, we start with a hypothetical factual situation:

Facts: Paul, a citizen of Pennsylvania, was involved in a car accident with Doone, a citizen of Wyoming, in Jackson, Wyoming. Paul brought an action for damages in the United States District Court for the District of Wyoming. The complaint alleged (1) jurisdiction and the parties' citizenship; (2) that Paul was crossing Cache Street in front of the Silver Dollar saloon, when he was hit by a car driven by Doone; (3) that Doone was negligent in the operation of her car, and in maintaining the condition of the car including, but not limited to, failure to keep a proper lookout and having defective brakes; (4) that Doone's negligence was the proximate cause of the accident; and (5) that damages exceeded $75,000 for injuries and emotional distress (including post accident depression). Doone filed an answer which admitted that she was driving the car and that the car came in contact with Paul; she denied the other allegations of the complaint and pleaded Paul's contributory negligence. The complaint was filed February 1, 2006 and served February 10. The answer was served on March 10, 2006.

NOTES AND PROBLEMS FOR DISCUSSION

1. When do the parties have to provide disclosures under Rule 26(a)(1)? A hint: Before answering this question, you must first determine when the parties must hold the discovery meeting (see Rule 26(f)), and when they must hold the discovery conference (see Rule 16(b)).

2. Assume that it is now the deadline date you have determined in #1, and you represent Doone. You have heard nothing from Paul. Should you serve your responses, and what problem do you face if you do, and Paul doesn't?

3. Consider how the time limits for disclosures mesh with rules which delay discovery on substantive grounds. For example, under the amendments to the Securities Act, discovery may be delayed until an initial pleading motion is decided. Or, in cases involving qualified immunity, discovery may sometimes be delayed until the qualified immunity issue is resolved. Do these stay the time limits under Rule 26(a), and if so, for both parties, only the plaintiff, or only the defendant?

4. Can Doone serve a notice to take the deposition of Paul on April 1 (and does it depend on when the deposition is scheduled)?

5. Assume that at the outset of the case, your client Paul asks what the earliest possible time is for taking the deposition of Doone. How do you answer him?

6. Which of the following persons likely to have discoverable information must be identified under current Rule 26(a)(1)(A) (and does it depend on what use the party in question may make of them)?

(a) By Paul, (i) Bill Bystander, who was the first to reach Paul after he was hit, (ii) Mary, Paul's wife of 20 years, and (iii) the bartender at the Silver Dollar.

(b) By Doone, (i) the mechanic at her garage, (ii) Doone's teenage son who knows his mother has a hard time seeing, and (iii) the name of the person to whom she was talking on her cell phone at the time of the accident.

7. Which documents or other items must be identified under current Rule 26(a)(1)(B) (and does it depend on what use the party in question may make of them)?

(a) By Paul, (i) the report of his most recent physical exam, and (ii) a photograph of Doone talking on her cell phone moments before impact, taken by an amateur photographer.

(b) By Doone, (i) records from her garage, (ii) a report containing the results of her most recent eye exam, (iii) her cell phone, and (iv) a traffic citation she recently received for reckless driving.

8. How would your answers change if the parties were operating under the prior version of the Rule? Do your answers indicate why the Rule might have been so controversial?

9. Assume Paul makes no disclosures at all. One possibility is for Doone to make a motion to compel under Rule 37(a). A second possibility is for Doone to continue with the case and rely on Rule 37(c) at the trial. What are the disadvantages of each?

10. Assume that Doone never disclosed that she was using the cell phone during the accident, Paul does not learn of this information during discovery, and the information does not come out at trial (at which Doone prevails). Does Paul have any remedy?

2. DEPOSITIONS

Depositions are the most useful device for getting the story of a witness, or for dealing with contested or disputed information. As described earlier, a deposition is similar in format to a trial without the judge. The questioning lawyer asks the witness questions, his answers are transcribed (or recorded or videotaped), and the defending lawyer can object to questions. But unlike at a trial, there is no one to rule on objections, so we briefly explain how the process works.

A defending party may object to a question on essentially two grounds: One is that the question is somehow defective as a question (e.g., it is too long or complicated, it assumes a fact not in evidence, it fails to identify background facts, or it is unclear as to time or place). For these questions, the objecting party has no objection to answering a properly framed question. Moreover, under the rules governing use of a deposition at a trial, a party can't object to the admission of an otherwise admissible deposition answer on the ground that the form of the question was improper or imprecise; instead, the opposing party must object at the deposition so the deposing party can fix the problem.

A second category of objections involves questions that are not only objectionable but that the defending party does not want to be answered at all. Objections on the ground of privilege or confidentiality, for example, would fit into this category.

An objection based on relevance could conceivably fit into either of the categories. The objector may not care if certain questions are answered, and object simply to preserve the objection. But in other cases, the objector does not want an answer at all. Note, however, that Rule 30(c)(2) indicates that it is generally not proper to instruct a witness not to answer on grounds of relevance, insofar as it identifies only a handful of circumstances in which such an instruction is allowed, and relevance is not one of them. (An instruction not to answer to prevent bad faith questioning or harassment is permitted, however.)

When the objecting party does not want the question answered for some reason — e.g., for reasons of privilege, confidentiality, harassment, relevance, or perhaps some other ground — the attorney generally will direct the witness not to answer the question. The witness almost always complies. At this point, the burden is on the questioning party to do something further if it wants an answer, and it will have to decide whether it is worthwhile to ask the court to compel a response.

The legal issues involved in the taking of depositions are legion. They range from "procedural" issues such as location, length, order of witnesses, and who can attend, to more basic issues of scope, dealing with objections, nonresponsive witnesses, and abusive practices. Again, our treatment is based on a factual situation and a series of questions.

Facts: Herbert and Wilma Riche, residents of Berkeley, California, recently purchased a painting by the famous French artist Monet, entitled "University at Sunset," from Durango Galleries, located in New York. The Riches had a dinner party soon after the purchase, and one of the guests was Professor Anita Blanche of the University of Kansas in Lawrence, Kansas. When Prof. Blanche saw the picture, she quickly said "Oh, it's a fake. I hope you didn't pay very much for it." Needless to say this put a damper on the dinner. The Riches brought an action against Durango in the United States District Court for the Northern District of California and alleged claims based on (1) breach of express and implied warranty (the sales slip identified the painting as "University at Sunset by Claude Monet, painted 1898"), (2) intentional misrepresentation (i.e., Durango knew it was a fake), and (3) negligent misrepresentation (Durango negligently said it was a Monet, the Riches relied on this representation, and it was not true).

NOTES AND PROBLEMS FOR DISCUSSION

1. Your firm represents Durango. You serve a notice to take the deposition of Herbert Riche in New York City. Does Herbert have to show up?

2. Your firm represents Durango, and you want to take the deposition of Professor Blanche. Where can you take it, and what steps must you follow to take it?

3. Your firm represents the Riches. Durango is taking the deposition of Wilma, and she is asked about previous purchases of valuable antiques other than paintings. You do not believe the question is relevant on the ground that the case involves paintings; and anyway, the question is unduly intrusive. What steps should you take?

4. Your firm represents Durango, and you are taking the deposition of Herbert. Every time you ask a "hard" question, Herbert hesitates, and your opposing counsel whispers something in Herbert's ear. What steps should you take?

5. Your firm represents the Riches, and you want to take the deposition of the person at Durango who is most knowledgeable about (a) steps taken to authenticate its paintings, and (b) the authentication of the painting in question. How do you identify the proper person?

6. Your firm represents Durango, and you are defending the deposition of Jean Paul Durango, president of Durango. After a short time, opposing counsel begins to ask a series of questions about Durango's personal life, and the fact that his former wife accused him of child abuse. You object and ask opposing counsel to desist. Thereafter, opposing counsel asked "Isn't it a fact that you were arrested for child abuse in 2005?" If you want to stop this type of questioning what steps might you take?

7. Your firm represents the Riches and you are taking the deposition of Jean Paul Durango. You ask Jean Paul what person or entity sold Durango Galleries the painting in question, and counsel for Durango objected on the ground that the information was confidential and irrelevant, and directed Jean Paul not to answer. What happens now with respect to the remainder of the deposition, and what steps would you take to get an answer to the question?

8. Think about what happens if you represent the Riches, and Durango is a large firm with many employees. You want to take the deposition of a person with information about authenticity, but you don't know who is the right person. Read Rule 30(b)(6). Assume you follow Rule 30(b)(6), and Durango produces its curator, James Hogge. Hogge testified that he is in charge of authentication, and testified generally about authentication procedures. When asked about the painting in question, Hogge testified: "Don't know, haven't ever seen it, haven't looked at the records, out of the country at the time, real unfortunate." What now? See Quantachrome Corp. v. Micromeritics Inst. Corp., 189 F.R.D. 697 (S.D. Fla. 1999) (broad duty to produce persons with information and prepare witness).

3. INTERROGATORIES AND DOCUMENT REQUESTS

We treat these together because they have certain common characteristics and present certain overlapping issues. Indeed, Rule 33(d) gives parties responding to interrogatories the option, under certain circumstances, to produce documents for inspection.

Interrogatories are written questions addressed to a party that must be answered by a party. Often, lawyers draft the answers with review by clients. Document requests are requests to produce documents and tangible items, to permit inspection of premises, and to permit testing or sampling. Although Rule 34 is limited to parties, documents may be subpoenaed from nonparty witnesses pursuant to Rule 45(c)(2).

One of their common characteristics is that both interrogatories and document requests are relatively easy and inexpensive to formulate and yet may be very time consuming, burdensome and expensive to respond to. For example, in a complex business case, it is easy to formulate document requests relating to the defendant's business practices which may require the production of thousands (or millions) of documents. Thus, in a price fixing case, a plaintiff might demand every document relating to every sales transaction of the defendant as relevant to a claim of price fixing. Parties also have an incentive to frame broad requests because of a fear of leaving something out.

A second common characteristic is that both interrogatories and document requests demand precision and the absence of ambiguity — a precision which is often difficult to attain given the vagaries of language. Moreover, the inquiry or request will be "construed" by an adversary with the incentive to adopt the narrowest possible construction that can be rationally defended. One way for a party to protect against a "narrow construction" of her inquiry or requests is to make them broad enough that nothing slips through the cracks.

The Rules do have provisions which seek to control interrogatories and document requests and limit abuses, but these provisions tend to be somewhat general, and they raise issues themselves. They provide little guidance in concrete situations. For example:

- Rule 33(a) limits interrogatories to 25, absent agreement, unless the court orders otherwise.
- Rule 33(b)(1)(B) requires a corporation or organization to, in effect, search its records to respond to an interrogatory ("available to the party").
- Rule 33(b)(4) requires objections with specificity.
- Rule 33(d) provides an option to produce business records in lieu of answering an interrogatory.
- Rule 34(a) requires production of "designated" documents.
- Rule 34(b)(2) requires objections to be limited to only part of a request if the entire request is not objectionable.
- Rule 26(b)(2)(C)(iii) requires the limitation of requests when the proposed discovery is outside the scope permitted by Rule 26(b)(1).

NOTES AND PROBLEMS FOR DISCUSSION

Problem: Mark Monroe, an assistant professor in the history department at the University of Nebraska was denied tenure on the ground that he "lacked sufficient promise as a teacher and scholar." Monroe filed suit against the University claiming he was denied tenure on account of his race (African-American), and seeks tenure and money damages. Consider the following:

1. Monroe served an interrogatory asking: "State each and every reason that plaintiff was denied tenure." The University answered: "Plaintiff was denied tenure because he lacked sufficient promise as a teacher and scholar in that (1) he was not an effective teacher, (2) his publication record was anemic and his publications were shallow, and (3) he lacked an abiding interest in the academic life."

  (a) As counsel for Monroe, are you satisfied with this answer?

  (b) If not, what remedies do you have?

  (c) Upon reflection, how might you rephrase the question?

2. Monroe served the following document request: "All documents concerning or relating to the granting of tenure, the denial of tenure, standards for granting tenure, or other matters relating to tenure for the University from 1990 through the present."

  (a) As counsel for the University, what are the possible responses to (or actions that you might take with respect to) this request?

  (b) Counsel for the University has asked you, as counsel for Monroe, to narrow the request to "the documents you really want." What is your response and suggested redraft?

3. Monroe served 45 interrogatories upon the University. As counsel for the University, what response do you propose?

4. Monroe served the following interrogatory: "For each person who was granted tenure, denied tenure, or considered for tenure since 1995, state the person's qualifications, publications, teaching evaluations, peer reviews, recommendations and evaluations, summary of considerations, and reasons for decision." As counsel for the University, what issues does this raise? See Patt v. Family Health Systems, Inc., 189 F.R.D. 518 (E.D. Wis. 1999) (concluding, with limited discussion, that plaintiff surgeon suing for gender discrimination was entitled to peer review records concerning other surgeons in group).

5. Assume the University responded to the interrogatory in #4 as follows: "Since 1995, 716 individuals were granted tenure, denied tenure or considered for tenure. Subject to the execution of an appropriate confidentiality order, the University will make all files relating to each such individual available." As counsel for Monroe, is this acceptable and, if not, what response do you suggest?

6. You are counsel for the University. In considering how to respond to the interrogatory in #4, you learn that some departments generally do not consider

an individual for tenure unless the individual is likely to be granted tenure; individuals who are not likely to be granted tenure are "counseled" to delay seeking tenure (often with specific suggestions to improve the likelihood it will be granted in the future), or to think about moving elsewhere. Must your response to the interrogatory include information relating to such individuals?

4. MENTAL AND PHYSICAL EXAMINATIONS

Mental and physical examinations present difficult legal issues because they raise somewhat contradictory social and legal policies. On the one hand, there are strongly felt notions of privacy, the inviolability of the person, and the right of freedom from unwarranted government intrusion. On the other hand, mental and physical condition often is an issue in modern litigation, and a basic premise of modern procedure is that there is a strong social interest in pretrial discovery of matters relevant to the case.

For many years after the Rules were enacted, this issue did not prove terribly litigious. It generally arose only in cases involving physical injury and, in such cases, plaintiffs recognized (if only grudgingly) that they were unlikely to get a meaningful settlement unless the defendant could obtain information about the plaintiff's injuries. Recently, however, the issue has become more contentious as more plaintiffs seek damages for emotional or psychological distress, and as defendants raise issues involving psychological condition as defenses to employment discrimination and other types of litigation. We have already seen these issues arise in the *Santelli* case and its discussion of Jaffee v. Redmond, 518 U.S. 1, 116 S.Ct. 1923, 135 L.Ed.2d 337 (1996) (recognizing a psychotherapist privilege).

Nevertheless, there still is very little litigation at the appellate level and the next case, although more than thirty-five years old, is still very much the governing authority.

Schlagenhauf v. Holder

Supreme Court of the United States, 1964.
379 U.S. 104, 85 S.Ct. 234, 13 L.Ed.2d 152.

MR. JUSTICE GOLDBERG delivered the opinion of the Court.

This case involves the validity and construction of Rule 35(a) of the Federal Rules of Civil Procedure as applied to the examination of a defendant in a negligence action. Rule 35(a) provides:

"Physical and Mental Examination of Persons. (a) Order for examination. In an action in which the mental or physical condition of a party is in controversy, the court in which the action is pending may order him to submit to a physical or mental examination by a physician.

The order may be made only on motion for good cause shown and upon notice to the party to be examined and to all other parties and shall specify the time, place, manner, conditions, and scope of the examination and the person or persons by whom it is to be made."

I

An action based on diversity of citizenship was brought in the District Court seeking damages arising from personal injuries suffered by passengers of a bus which collided with the rear of a tractor-trailer. The named defendants were The Greyhound Corporation, owner of the bus; petitioner, Robert L. Schlagenhauf, the bus driver; Contract Carriers, Inc., owner of the tractor; Joseph L. McCorkhill, driver of the tractor;[1] and National Lead Company, owner of the trailer. Answers were filed by each of the defendants denying negligence.

Greyhound then cross-claimed against Contract Carriers and National Lead for damage to Greyhound's bus, alleging that the collision was due solely to their negligence in that the tractor-trailer was driven at an unreasonably low speed, had not remained in its lane, and was not equipped with proper rear lights. Contract Carriers filed an answer to this cross-claim denying its negligence and asserting "that the negligence of the driver of the ... bus [petitioner Schlagenhauf] proximately caused and contributed to ... Greyhound's damages."

Pursuant to a pretrial order, Contract Carriers filed a letter — which the trial court treated as, and we consider to be, part of the answer — alleging that Schlagenhauf was "not mentally or physically capable" of driving a bus at the time of the accident.

Contract Carriers and National Lead then petitioned the District Court for an order directing petitioner Schlagenhauf to submit to both mental and physical examinations by one specialist in each of the following fields: (1) Internal medicine; (2) Ophthalmology; (3) Neurology; and (4) Psychiatry.

For the purpose of offering a choice to the District Court of one specialist in each field, the petition recommended two specialists in internal medicine, ophthalmology, and psychiatry, respectively, and three specialists in neurology — a total of nine physicians. The petition alleged that the mental and physical condition of Schlagenhauf was "in controversy" as it had been raised by Contract Carriers' answer to Greyhound's cross-claim. This was supported by a brief of legal authorities and an affidavit of Contract Carriers' attorney stating that Schlagenhauf had seen red lights 10 to 15 seconds before the accident, that another witness had seen the rear lights of the trailer from a distance of three-quarters to one-half mile, and that Schlagenhauf had been involved in a prior accident.

The certified record indicates that petitioner's attorneys filed in the District Court a brief in opposition to this petition asserting, among other things, that

---

[1]   In all the pleadings McCorkhill was joined with Contract Carriers. For simplicity, both will be referred to as Contract Carriers.

"the physical and mental condition of the defendant Robert L. Schlagenhauf is not 'in controversy' herein in the sense that these words are used in Rule 35 of the Federal Rules of Civil Procedure; [and] that good cause has not been shown for the multiple examinations prayed for by the cross-defendant . . . ."

While disposition of this petition was pending, National Lead filed its answer to Greyhound's cross-claim and itself "cross-claimed" against Greyhound and Schlagenhauf for damage to its trailer. The answer asserted generally that Schlagenhauf's negligence proximately caused the accident. The cross-claim additionally alleged that Greyhound and Schlagenhauf were negligent "by permitting said bus to be operated over and upon said public highway by the said defendant, Robert L. Schlagenhauf, when both the said Greyhound Corporation and said Robert L. Schlagenhauf knew that the eyes and vision of the said Robert L. Schlagenhauf was [sic] impaired and deficient."

The District Court, on the basis of the petition filed by Contract Carriers, and without any hearing, ordered Schlagenhauf to submit to nine examinations — one by each of the recommended specialists — despite the fact that the petition clearly requested a total of only four examinations.[3]

Petitioner applied for a writ of mandamus in the Court of Appeals against the respondent, the District Court Judge, seeking to have set aside the order requiring his mental and physical examinations. The Court of Appeals denied mandamus, one judge dissenting.

We granted certiorari to review undecided questions concerning the validity and construction of Rule 35.

II

A threshold problem arises due to the fact that this case was in the Court of Appeals on a petition for a writ of mandamus. Although it is not disputed that we have jurisdiction to review the judgment of the Court of Appeals, 28 U.S.C. §1254(1) (1958 ed.), respondent urges that the judgment below dismissing the writ be affirmed on the ground that mandamus was not an appropriate remedy.

Here petitioner's basic allegation was lack of power in a district court to order a mental and physical examination of a defendant. That this issue was substantial is underscored by the fact that the challenged order requiring examination of a defendant appears to be the first of its kind in any reported decision in the federal courts under Rule 35, and we have found only one such modern case in the state courts. The Court of Appeals recognized that it had the power to review on a petition for mandamus the basic, undecided question of whether a district court could order the mental or physical examination of a

---

[3] After the Court of Appeals denied mandamus, the order was corrected by the District Court to reduce the number of examinations to the four requested. We agree with respondent that the issue of that error has become moot. However, the fact that the District Court ordered nine examinations is not irrelevant, together with all the other circumstances, in the consideration of whether the District Court gave to the petition for mental and physical examinations that discriminating application, which Rule 35 requires.

defendant. We agree that, under these unusual circumstances and in light of the authorities, the Court of Appeals had such power.

III

Rule 35 on its face applies to all "parties," which under any normal reading would include a defendant. Petitioner contends, however, that the application of the Rule to a defendant would be an unconstitutional invasion of his privacy, or, at the least, be a modification of substantive rights existing prior to the adoption of the Federal Rules of Civil Procedure and thus beyond the congressional mandate of the Rules Enabling Act.[9]

These same contentions were raised in Sibbach v. Wilson & Co., 312 U.S. 1, by a plaintiff in a negligence action who asserted a physical injury as a basis for recovery. The Court, by a closely divided vote, sustained the Rule as there applied. Both the majority and dissenting opinions, however, agreed that Rule 35 could not be assailed on constitutional grounds. The division in the Court was on the issue of whether the Rule was procedural or a modification of substantive rights. The majority held that the Rule was a regulation of procedure and thus within the scope of the Enabling Act — the dissenters deemed it substantive. Petitioner does not challenge the holding in *Sibbach* as applied to plaintiffs. He contends, however, that it should not be extended to defendants. We can see no basis under the *Sibbach* holding for such a distinction. Discovery "is not a one-way proposition." *Hickman v. Taylor*. Issues cannot be resolved by a doctrine of favoring one class of litigants over another.

We recognize that, insofar as reported cases show, this type of discovery in federal courts has been applied solely to plaintiffs, and that some early state cases seem to have proceeded on a theory that a plaintiff who seeks redress for injuries in a court of law thereby "waives" his right to claim the inviolability of his person.

However, it is clear that *Sibbach* was not decided on any "waiver" theory. As Mr. Justice Roberts, for the majority, stated, one of the rights of a person "is the right not to be injured in one's person by another's negligence, to redress infraction of which the present action was brought." For the dissenters, Mr. Justice Frankfurter pointed out that "of course the Rule is compulsive in that the doors of the federal courts otherwise open may be shut to litigants who do not submit to such a physical examination."

These statements demonstrate the invalidity of any waiver theory. The chain of events leading to an ultimate determination on the merits begins with the injury of the plaintiff, an involuntary act on his part. Seeking court redress is just one step in this chain. If the plaintiff is prevented or deterred from this redress, the loss is thereby forced on him to the same extent as if the defendant were prevented or deterred from defending against the action.

---

[9]   28 U.S.C. §2072 (1958 ed.), which provides that the Rules "shall not abridge, enlarge or modify any substantive right . . . ."

Moreover, the rationalization of *Sibbach* on a waiver theory would mean that a plaintiff has waived a right by exercising his right of access to the federal courts. Such a result might create constitutional problems. Also, if a waiver theory is espoused, problems would arise as to a plaintiff who originally brought his action in a state court (where there was no equivalent of Rule 35) and then has the case removed by the defendant to federal court.

We hold that Rule 35, as applied to either plaintiffs or defendants to an action, is free of constitutional difficulty and is within the scope of the Enabling Act. We therefore agree with the Court of Appeals that the District Court had power to apply Rule 35 to a party defendant in an appropriate case.

IV

There remains the issue of the construction of Rule 35. We enter upon determination of this construction with the basic premise "that the deposition-discovery rules are to be accorded a broad and liberal treatment," *Hickman* v. *Taylor,* to effectuate their purpose that "civil trials in the federal courts no longer need be carried on in the dark."

Petitioner contends that even if Rule 35 is to be applied to defendants, which we have determined it must, nevertheless it should not be applied to him as he was not a party in relation to Contract Carriers and National Lead — the movants for the mental and physical examinations — at the time the examinations were sought.[11] The Court of Appeals agreed with petitioner's general legal proposition, holding that the person sought to be examined must be an opposing party *vis-à-vis* the movant (or at least one of them). While it is clear that the person to be examined must be a party to the case,[12] we are of the view that the Court of Appeals gave an unduly restrictive interpretation to that term. Rule 35 only requires that the person to be examined be a party to the "action," not that he be an opposing party *vis-à-vis* the movant. There is no doubt that Schlagenhauf was a "party" to this "action" by virtue of the original complaint. Therefore, Rule 35 permitted examination of him (a party defendant) upon petition of Contract Carriers and National Lead (codefendants), provided, of course, that the other requirements of the Rule were met. Insistence that the movant have filed a pleading against the person to be examined would have the undesirable result of an unnecessary proliferation of cross-claims and counterclaims and would not be in keeping with the aims of a liberal, nontechnical application of the Federal Rules. See *Hickman* v. *Taylor, supra.*

---

[11] We have already pointed out, that at the time of the first petition, Schlagenhauf was a named defendant in the original complaint but was not a named cross-defendant in any pleadings filed by Contract Carriers or National Lead.

[12] Although petitioner was an agent of Greyhound, he was himself a party to the action. He is to be distinguished from one who is not a party but is, for example, merely the agent of a party. This is not only clear in the wording of the Rule, but is reinforced by the fact that this Court has never approved the Advisory Committee's proposed amendment to Rule 35 which would include within the scope of the Rule "an agent or a person in the custody or under the legal control of a party." [Rule 35(a) now includes such language. — eds.]

While the Court of Appeals held that petitioner was not a party *vis-à-vis* National Lead or Contract Carriers at the time the examinations were first sought, it went on to hold that he had become a party *vis-à-vis* National Lead by the time of a second order entered by the District Court and thus was a party within its rule. This second order, identical in all material respects with the first, was entered on the basis of supplementary petitions filed by National Lead and Contract Carriers. These petitions gave no new basis for the examinations, except for the allegation that petitioner's mental and physical condition had been additionally put in controversy by the National Lead answer and cross-claim, which had been filed subsequent to the first petition for examinations. Although the filing of the petition for mandamus intervened between these two orders, we accept, for purposes of this opinion, the determination of the Court of Appeals that this second order was the one before it and agree that petitioner was clearly a party at this juncture under any test.

Petitioner next contends that his mental or physical condition was not "in controversy" and "good cause" was not shown for the examinations, both as required by the express terms of Rule 35.

The discovery devices sanctioned by Part V of the Federal Rules include the taking of oral and written depositions (Rules 26-32), interrogatories to parties (Rule 33), production of documents (Rule 34), and physical and mental examinations of parties (Rule 35). The scope of discovery in each instance is limited by Rule 26(b)'s [then existing—eds.] provision that "the deponent may be examined regarding any matter, not privileged, which is *relevant to the subject matter involved* in the pending action" (emphasis added), and by the provisions of Rule 30(b) permitting the district court, upon motion, to limit, terminate, or otherwise control the use of discovery devices so as to prevent either their use in bad faith or undue "annoyance, embarrassment, or oppression."

It is notable, however, that in none of the other discovery provisions is there a restriction that the matter be "in controversy," and only in Rule 34 is there Rule 35's requirement that the movant affirmatively demonstrate "good cause."[*]

This additional requirement of "good cause" was reviewed by Chief Judge Soboloff in Guilford National Bank v. Southern R. Co., 297 F.2d 921, 924 (C. A. 4th Cir.), in the following words:

> "Subject to . . . [the restrictions of Rules 26 (b) and 30 (b) and (d)], a party may take depositions and serve interrogatories without prior sanction of the court or even its knowledge of what the party is doing. Only if a deponent refuses to answer in the belief that the question is irrelevant, can the moving party request under Rule 37 a court order requiring an answer.

> "Significantly, this freedom of action, afforded a party who resorts to depositions and interrogatories, is not granted to one proceeding under

---

[*] [This requirement is no longer contained in Rule 34. — eds.]

Rules 34 and 35. Instead, the court must decide as an initial matter, and in every case, whether the motion requesting production of documents or the making of a physical or mental examination adequately demonstrates good cause. The specific requirement of good cause would be meaningless if good cause could be sufficiently established by merely showing that the desired materials are relevant, for the relevancy standard has already been imposed by Rule 26 (b). Thus, by adding the words '. . . good cause . . . ,' the Rules indicate that there must be greater showing of need under Rules 34 and 35 than under the other discovery rules."

The courts of appeals in other cases have also recognized that Rule 34's good-cause requirement is not a mere formality, but is a plainly expressed limitation on the use of that Rule. This is obviously true as to the "in controversy" and " good cause" requirements of Rule 35. They are not met by mere conclusory allegations of the pleadings — by mere relevance to the case[*] — but require an affirmative showing by the movant that each condition as to which the examination is sought is really and genuinely in controversy and that good cause exists for ordering each particular examination. Obviously, what may be good cause for one type of examination may not be so for another. The ability of the movant to obtain the desired information by other means is also relevant.

Rule 35, therefore, requires discriminating application by the trial judge, who must decide, as an initial matter in every case, whether the party requesting a mental or physical examination or examinations has adequately demonstrated the existence of the Rule's requirements of "in controversy" and "good cause," which requirements, as the Court of Appeals in this case itself recognized, are necessarily related. This does not, of course, mean that the movant must prove his case on the merits in order to meet the requirements for a mental or physical examination. Nor does it mean that an evidentiary hearing is required in all cases. This may be necessary in some cases, but in other cases the showing could be made by affidavits or other usual methods short of a hearing. It does mean, though, that the movant must produce sufficient information, by whatever means, so that the district judge can fulfill his function mandated by the Rule.

Of course, there are situations where the pleadings alone are sufficient to meet these requirements. A plaintiff in a negligence action who asserts mental or physical injury, cf. *Sibbach* v. *Wilson & Co.,* places that mental or physical injury clearly in controversy and provides the defendant with good cause for an examination to determine the existence and extent of such asserted injury. This is not only true as to a plaintiff, but applies equally to a defendant who asserts his mental or physical condition as a defense to a claim, such as, for example, where insanity is asserted as a defense to a divorce action.

---

[*] [Note that the Rules have undergone substantial changes regarding the good-cause provision. See Section A.1., above— eds.]

Here, however, Schlagenhauf did not assert his mental or physical condition either in support of or in defense of a claim. His condition was sought to be placed in issue by other parties. Thus, under the principles discussed above, Rule 35 required that these parties make an affirmative showing that petitioner's mental or physical condition was in controversy and that there was good cause for the examinations requested. This, the record plainly shows, they failed to do.

The only allegations in the pleadings relating to this subject were the general conclusory statement in Contract Carriers' answer to the cross-claim that "Schlagenhauf was not mentally or physically capable of operating" the bus at the time of the accident and the limited allegation in National Lead's cross-claim that, at the time of the accident, "the eyes and vision of . . . Schlagenhauf was [sic] impaired and deficient."

The attorney's affidavit attached to the petition for the examinations provided:

> "That . . . Schlagenhauf, in his deposition . . . admitted that he saw red lights for 10 to 15 seconds prior to a collision with a semi-tractor trailer unit and yet drove his vehicle on without reducing speed and without altering the course thereof.
>
> "The only eye-witness to this accident known to this affiant . . . testified that immediately prior to the impact between the bus and truck that he had also been approaching the truck from the rear and that he had clearly seen the lights of the truck for a distance of three-quarters to one-half mile to the rear thereof.
>
> ". . . Schlagenhauf has admitted in his deposition . . . that he was involved in a [prior] similar type rear end collision . . . ."

This record cannot support even the corrected order which required one examination in each of the four specialties of internal medicine, ophthalmology, neurology, and psychiatry. Nothing in the pleadings or affidavit would afford a basis for a belief that Schlagenhauf was suffering from a mental or neurological illness warranting wide-ranging psychiatric or neurological examinations. Nor is there anything stated justifying the broad internal medicine examination.[16]

The only specific allegation made in support of the four examinations ordered was that the "eyes and vision" of Schlagenhauf were impaired. Considering this in conjunction with the affidavit, we would be hesitant to set aside a visual examination if it had been the only one ordered. However, as the case must be remanded to the District Court because of the other examinations ordered, it would be appropriate for the District Judge to reconsider also this order in light of the guidelines set forth in this opinion.

---

[16] Moreover, it seems clear that there was no compliance with Rule 35's requirement that the trial judge delineate the "conditions, and scope" of the examinations. Here the examinations were ordered in very broad, general areas. The internal medicine examination might for example, at the instance of the movant or its recommended physician extend to such things as blood tests, electrocardiograms, gastro-intestinal and other X-ray examinations. It is hard to conceive how some of these could be relevant under any possible theory of the case.

The Federal Rules of Civil Procedure should be liberally construed, but they should not be expanded by disregarding plainly expressed limitations. The "good cause" and "in controversy" requirements of Rule 35 make it very apparent that sweeping examinations of a party who has not affirmatively put into issue his own mental or physical condition are not to be automatically ordered merely because the person has been involved in an accident — or, as in this case, two accidents — and a general charge of negligence is lodged. Mental and physical examinations are only to be ordered upon a discriminating application by the district judge of the limitations prescribed by the Rule. To hold otherwise would mean that such examinations could be ordered routinely in automobile accident cases. The plain language of Rule 35 precludes such an untoward result.

Accordingly, the judgment of the Court of Appeals is vacated and the case remanded to the District Court to reconsider the examination order in light of the guidelines herein formulated and for further proceedings in conformity with this opinion.

Vacated and remanded.

MR. JUSTICE BLACK, with whom MR. JUSTICE CLARK joins, concurring in part and dissenting in part.

I agree with the Court that under Rule 35(a): (1) a plaintiff and a defendant have precisely the same right to obtain a court order for physical or mental examination of the other party or parties to a lawsuit; (2) before obtaining such an order it must be shown that physical or mental health is "in controversy" as to a relevant and material issue in the case; and (3) such an order "may be made only on motion for good cause shown" after "notice to the party to be examined and to all other parties." Unlike the Court, however, I think this record plainly shows that there *was* a controversy as to Schlagenhauf's mental and physical health and that "good cause" *was* shown for a physical and mental examination of him, unless failure to deny the allegations amounted to an admission that they were true. While the papers filed in connection with this motion were informal, there can be no doubt that other parties in the lawsuit specifically and unequivocally charged that Schlagenhauf was not mentally or physically capable of operating a motor bus at the time of the collision, and that his negligent operation of the bus caused the resulting injuries and damage. The other parties filed an affidavit based on depositions of Schlagenhauf and a witness stating that Schlagenhauf, driving the bus along a four-lane highway in what apparently was good weather, had come upon a tractor-trailer down the road in front of him. The tractor-trailer was displaying red lights visible for at least half a mile, and Schlagenhauf admitted seeing them. Yet after coming in sight of the vehicle Schlagenhauf continued driving the bus in a straight line, without slowing down, for a full 10 or 15 seconds until the bus struck the tractor-trailer. Schlagenhauf admitted also that he had been involved in the very same kind of accident once before. Schlagenhauf has never at any time in the proceedings denied and he does not even now deny the charges that his mental and physical health and his eyes and vision were impaired and deficient.

In a collision case like this one, evidence concerning very bad eyesight or impaired mental or physical health which may affect the ability to drive is obviously of the highest relevance. It is equally obvious, I think, that when a vehicle continues down an open road and smashes into a truck in front of it although the truck is in plain sight and there is ample time and room to avoid collision, the chances are good that the driver has some physical, mental or moral defect. When such a thing happens twice, one is even more likely to ask, "What is the matter with that driver? Is he blind or crazy?" Plainly the allegations of the other parties were relevant and put the question of Schlagenhauf's health and vision "in controversy." The Court nevertheless holds that these charges were not a sufficient basis on which to rest a court-ordered examination of Schlagenhauf. It says with reference to the charges of impaired physical or mental health that the charges are "conclusory." I had not thought there was anything strange about pleadings being "conclusory" — that is their function, at least since modern rules of procedure have attempted to substitute simple pleadings for the complicated and redundant ones which long kept the common-law courts in disrepute. I therefore cannot agree that the charges about Schlagenhauf's health and vision were not sufficient upon which to base an order under Rule 35(a), particularly since he was a party who raised every technical objection to being required to subject himself to an examination but never once denied that his health and vision were bad. In these circumstances the allegations here should be more than enough to show probable cause to justify a court order requiring some kind of physical and mental examination.

MR. JUSTICE DOUGLAS, dissenting in part.

While I join the Court in reversing this judgment, I would, on the remand, deny all relief asked under Rule 35.

I do not suppose there is any licensed driver of a car or a truck who does not suffer from some ailment, whether it be ulcers, bad eyesight, abnormal blood pressure, deafness, liver malfunction, bursitis, rheumatism, or what not. If he or she is turned over to the plaintiff's doctors and psychoanalysts to discover the cause of the mishap, the door will be opened for grave miscarriages of justice. When the defendant's doctors examine plaintiff, they are normally interested only in answering a single question: did plaintiff in fact sustain the specific injuries claimed? But plaintiff's doctors will naturally be inclined to go on a fishing expedition in search of *anything* which will tend to prove that the defendant was unfit to perform the acts which resulted in the plaintiff's injury. And a doctor for a fee can easily discover something wrong with any patient — a condition that in prejudiced medical eyes might have caused the accident. Once defendants are turned over to medical or psychiatric clinics for an analysis of their physical well-being and the condition of their psyche, the effective trial will be held there and not before the jury. There are no lawyers in those clinics to stop the doctor from probing this organ or that one, to halt a further inquiry, to object to a line of questioning. And there is no judge to sit as arbiter. The doctor or the psychiatrist has a holiday in the privacy of his office. The defendant is at the doctor's (or psychiatrist's) mercy; and his report may either overawe or confuse the jury and prevent a fair trial.

The Court in *Sibbach* v. *Wilson & Co.* was divided when it came to submission of a plaintiff to a compulsory medical examination. The division was not over the constitutional power to require it but only as to whether Congress had authorized a rule to that effect. I accept that point as one governed by *stare decisis*. But no decision that when a *plaintiff* claims damages his "mental or physical condition" is "in controversy," within the meaning of Rule 35, governs the present case. The *plaintiff* by suing puts those issues "in controversy." A plaintiff, by coming into court and asserting that he has suffered an injury at the hands of the defendant, has thereby put his physical or mental condition "in controversy." Thus it may be only fair to provide that he may not be permitted to recover his judgment unless he permits an inquiry into the true nature of his condition.

A defendant's physical and mental condition is not, however, immediately and directly "in controversy" in a negligence suit. The issue is whether he was negligent. His physical or mental condition may of course be relevant to that issue; and he may be questioned concerning it and various methods of discovery can be used. But I balk at saying those issues are "in controversy" within the meaning of Rule 35 in every negligence suit or that they may be put "in controversy" by the addition of a few words in the complaint. As I have said, *Sibbach* proceeded on the basis that a plaintiff who seeks a decree of a federal court for his damages may not conceal or make difficult the proof of the claim he makes. The defendant, however, is dragged there; and to find "waiver" of the "inviolability of the person" is beyond reality.

Neither the Court nor Congress up to today has determined that any person whose physical or mental condition is brought into question during some lawsuit must surrender his right to keep his person inviolate. Congress did, according to *Sibbach*, require a plaintiff to choose between his privacy and his purse; but before today it has not been thought that any other "party" had lost this historic immunity. Congress and this Court can authorize such a rule. But a rule suited to purposes of discovery against defendants must be carefully drawn in light of the great potential of blackmail.

Mr. Justice Harlan, dissenting. [Omitted.]

NOTES AND PROBLEMS FOR DISCUSSION

1. Rule 35 requires the movant to show that physical or mental condition is "in controversy" and that there is "good cause" for the examination. What is the difference between the two factors?

2. The majority opinion and Justice Douglas's partial dissent reflect discomfort with the entire notion of a physical examination of a defendant to prove negligence. But at the end of the day, the Court says that the Rules provide for such an examination. Having said that, it is hard to resist Justice Black's suggestion that this is about as clear a case for an examination as one can expect to see. If so, why did the Court not approve the eye examination?

3. Assume Peggy, an African-American woman, brings a lawsuit against her employer, the brokerage firm of Mary Lynch, and against Joe Smythe (head of the ML office where she worked) claiming that she was improperly fired from her job as a broker because of racial and sex discrimination. She seeks to take a mental examination of Joe, and attaches (a) an affidavit of Dr. Noe saying that he was a licensed psychologist and had spoken with Joe at a number of ML social gatherings, including situations where Joe was "inebriated and boisterous" and is convinced that "Joe had a deep seated neurosis arising from his relationship with his mother, which included a deep seated regression complex and extreme hostility toward females"; and (b) an affidavit of Stan, a former ML employee, who stated that Joe had trouble relating to women. Should the court order a mental examination?

4. A plaintiff suing for mental or psychological damages often will have to submit to a mental examination. But consider the ground rules. If you were the judge, how would you decide the following requests made by a plaintiff: (a) that the examination take place in her house, (b) that the examination be tape recorded, (c) that the examination be limited to 2 hours, (d) that plaintiff should be permitted to take breaks at any time she felt "stressed out," and (e) that the plaintiff's lawyer and her psychiatrist should be present?

5. As noted earlier, plaintiffs in personal injury cases will normally submit to a physical examination both because of settlement prospects and also because they know the court is likely to grant it. Rule 35(b) deals with the report of the examination. Consider the following:

(a) Hal sues XYZ Corporation for injuries suffered when he was hit by XYZ's truck. Hal agrees to submit to a physical examination by XYZ's doctor. The exam has been completed. What options does Hal have with respect to the doctor's report, and what are the consequences of each option on reports prepared by his doctor?

(b) What is the relationship between Rule 35(b)(1) and the required disclosures under Rule 26(a)(2)?

SECTION C.   COST SHIFTING AND SANCTIONS

The "American Rule" is that each party bears its own legal expenses, win or lose. Discovery rules have long had provisions for sanctions for improper conduct, however, and one sanction often has involved cost-shifting. And in recent years, the rules have included provisions that provide a kind of cost-shifting for losing (or for necessitating) a discovery motion even without necessarily requiring a finding of malevolence or some form of intentionally wrongful behavior.

When the Federal Rules were enacted in 1938, the only provisions for cost-shifting and sanctions were contained in Rule 37. Numerous amendments have added new provisions, as well as strengthened Rule 37. To some extent, they are overlapping. Thus, we first summarize the cost-shifting/sanctions provisions, then offer some problems of simple application, and then include a true sanctions case. At the outset, however, we note a basic distinction in the remedial provisions dealing with fees and costs. Analytically, a discovery dispute presents two overlapping but distinct costs. First, there are the costs incurred in connection with the conduct giving rise to the dispute or motion — e.g., the costs of attending a deposition at which opposing counsel has acted improperly, or the costs of responding to an improper discovery request. Second, there are the costs incurred in seeking judicial relief — e.g., the costs of making a motion to compel, or for a protective order. As you go through the specific provisions, consider which of these costs is covered.

The following rules deal with sanctions/cost-shifting in the described situations:

- Rule 26(c) (which cross-references Rule 37(a)(5)) provides for expenses in relation to a motion for a protective order.

- Rule 26(g) provides that disclosures, and discovery requests, responses, and objections shall be signed; and it further provides that the signature is a certification that they are or may be warranted by existing law, are not interposed for an improper purpose, and are not unduly burdensome or expensive given the nature of the case and previous discovery. Sanctions are provided for a violation.

- Rule 30(d) deals with various alleged abuses in oral depositions, and provides for an award of expenses in relation to the motion.

- Rule 30(g) provides for a party who fails to obtain the presence of a witness at a deposition to pay various expenses to other parties.

- Rule 37(a) provides for the making of motions to compel discovery in situations where a party has responded to a discovery request, but the response is unsatisfactory (e.g., a refusal to answer certain interrogatories or produce certain requested documents). Under various circumstances, the court shall award the costs of making or opposing the motion.

- Rule 37(d) deals with a complete failure to respond to discovery — e.g., the party doesn't show up at all for its deposition, or doesn't respond to interrogatories or document requests. In such cases, a more severe set of sanctions is available than for motions to compel.

- Rule 37(b)(2) generally provides for sanctions for failing to comply with court orders in the discovery setting.

- Rule 37(c)(1) provides sanctions for failing to make disclosures required under 26(a). The basic sanction is exclusion of evidence.

NOTES AND PROBLEMS FOR DISCUSSION

1. Marsha was denied a job as an accountant in the Chicago office of TMF & Co., an international accounting firm, and Marsha brought an action against TMF claiming sex discrimination. Marsha served a document request seeking discovery of all documents relating to the hiring and promotion of professionals for the two years prior to denying employment to Marsha. TMF filed a response saying "TMF will produce all documents relating to the hiring of professionals in the Chicago office. The remainder of the request is irrelevant and/or outside of discovery permitted by Rule 26(b)(1)." Marsha's counsel then wrote TMF a letter saying, "As you know, Courts have repeatedly held that discovery in employment cases may include firm-wide employment information, and is not limited to the office or the job in question." TMF did not respond but, during a telephone "meet and confer" call said that it thought its position was amply justified. What remedies does Marsha have and under what rules?

2. Marsha moved to compel the production of the withheld documents. The judge granted the motion saying: "While some early cases supported TMF's position, the overwhelming weight of recent authority — including several appellate decisions — is that discovery in discrimination cases is not limited to job and office, but instead, covers firm-wide employment practices." What cost shifting and/or sanctions should the Court consider, and in that regard, what further issues must it resolve?

3. TMF is taking the deposition of Marsha. Counsel for TMF asks "Isn't it a fact that in your last job you regularly consumed liquor at your desk?" Marsha said: "I will not dignify that question or your impertinent behavior by my further presence," and she walked out. What remedies does TMF have?

Chrysler Corp. v. Carey

United States Court of Appeals, Eighth Circuit, 1999.

186 F.3d 1016.

BEAM, CIRCUIT JUDGE.

Chrysler brought this action for breach of fiduciary duty against its former counsel. Chrysler alleged that its former counsel had shared or used its confidential information to aid attorneys prosecuting product liability claims against Chrysler. After four days of trial, the evidence established repeated discovery abuses by the defendants. As a sanction, the district court struck the pleadings of the defendants, entered judgment against the defendants on the issue of liability, and submitted the case to the jury to determine damages. Defendants appeal and we affirm.

I. BACKGROUND

The defendants, John Carey and Joseph Danis are both attorneys and former associates of the St. Louis law firm of Thompson & Mitchell (T&M). T&M represented Chrysler as lead counsel in most of Chrysler's product liability class action litigation. Carey and Danis worked on five Chrysler lawsuits: the Osley case, involving allegedly defective heater cores; and four others involving allegedly defective door latches. Carey, the more senior of the two attorneys, drafted motions and briefs, conducted discovery, and communicated frequently with Chrysler's in-house counsel. Specifically, he drafted a third-party complaint, identified potential expert witnesses and participated in discussions with Chrysler regarding class action defense issues and settlement strategy. In connection with the settlement of the Osley case, Carey redrafted the plaintiffs' amended complaint in order to make it as broad as possible to achieve the greatest possible res judicata effect. Most of Danis's Chrysler work consisted of research, writing briefs, and drafting discovery requests and responses. In 1993 and 1994, his last two years at T&M, Carey billed twenty-seven percent of his time to Chrysler litigation. In 1994, Danis billed twenty-three percent of his time to Chrysler. During the litigation of these cases, regular exchanges of confidential information took place between Chrysler and T&M. Carey and Danis had complete access to T&M's Chrysler files and T&M's computer network which contained drafts and final versions of pleadings, research, memoranda, and communications with Chrysler.

Carey and Danis left T&M in January 1995 and formed their own law firm, Carey & Danis, L.L.C. (Carey & Danis). They shared office space with the law firm of Danis's father, David Danis, Danis, Cooper, Cavanaugh & Hartweger, L.L.P. (Danis, Cooper). When they left T&M, Carey and Danis took 996 pages of Chrysler-related documents, including documents pertaining to cases they had never worked on and memoranda labeled "Confidential and Privileged."

Shortly after Carey and Danis started their firm, they became members of a small, informal group of attorneys who regularly worked together on class action lawsuits. This group included David Danis, Joseph Phebus of Illinois, John Deakle of Mississippi, Michael Campbell of Florida, and J.L. Chestnut of Alabama (the group). In 1995 and 1996, members of the group filed class actions against Chrysler in New Jersey, Mississippi, and Alabama. In August 1995, Cary & Danis became involved with Dennis Beam regarding a potential class action suit against Chrysler involving an anti-lock brake system (ABS). Carey & Danis arranged to have Beam represented by Danis, Cooper and another firm. However, the petition in the Beam case was modeled on the Osley amended complaint that Carey had drafted for Chrysler and taken from T&M. After it become aware that Chrysler was investigating a possible conflict of interest, the second firm withdrew and Carey & Danis joined Danis, Cooper as attorneys of record for Beam. In December 1995, T&M wrote Carey & Danis and demanded that they withdraw from the Beam case because their actions were "wholly inconsistent with their fiduciary obligations" to Chrysler. Meanwhile, Carey & Danis had already begun to explore the possibility of joining Beam with another class action ABS case against Chrysler that was already filed in New Jersey, Chin v. Chrysler. After receiving the letter from T&M, David Danis dismissed the Beam case in St. Louis without prejudice and joined Beam with the Chin case. The amended complaint listed only Danis, Cooper as co-counsel. Later, Danis, Cooper withdrew from the case after its involvement was challenged by Chrysler.

In October 1995, another member of the informal group, John Deakle, filed an ABS class action suit against Chrysler in Mississippi and sent Carey & Danis a letter discussing a potential division of fees. Portions of Deakle's complaint mirrored the Beam complaint. In June 1996, group member Chestnut filed an ABS class action suit against Chrysler in Alabama. Carey and Danis deny that they participated in any class action suit against Chrysler.

Chrysler filed this action against Carey, Danis, and their firm in March 1996 alleging, *inter alia,* breach of fiduciary duty. In an effort to determine the extent of the role Carey and Danis played in the ABS cases, Chrysler served interrogatories and requests for documents upon Carey and Danis, and upon the non-party members of the group as well. When asked to produce documents pertaining to any communication Carey & Danis had with anyone else regarding ABS class action litigation against Chrysler, Carey & Danis responded "No such documents exist." The discovery process was, to say the least, protracted and acrimonious. The non-party attorneys fought every effort to produce documents, forcing Chrysler to litigate the issue in several different jurisdictions. The pre-trial litigation lasted over two years.

At trial, Chrysler introduced forty-two letters and other pieces of correspondence which had been sent to or from Carey and Danis that involved class action litigation against Chrysler. On the morning of the fourth day of trial, defense counsel[3] shared with Chrysler's counsel some documents he intended to use in the cross-examination of a witness. Among those documents, was a letter dated December 13, 1995, written by Joseph Danis to Paul Grossman, the attorney representing the plaintiffs in the New Jersey ABS class action against Chrysler. The letter was a recap of a previous meeting between Danis, his father David Danis, and Grossman regarding the possibility of joining Beam as a plaintiff in the action filed by Grossman. The letter had never been disclosed to Chrysler. Shortly before the lunch break, Chrysler brought the letter to the court's attention and moved that the court strike the defendants' answer. After reviewing interrogatories and requests for production of documents and corresponding responses, and after hearing from counsel, the district court struck the defendants' answer, resulting in a default judgment for Chrysler on the issue of liability.

Carey and Danis appeal, arguing that the imposition of the sanction was an abuse of discretion, and that even if a sanction were warranted, the severity of the sanction was an abuse of discretion. They further argue that they did not receive a fair hearing before the court struck their pleadings.

---

[3]   The attorneys representing Carey and Danis in this appeal did not represent them at trial.

II. DISCUSSION

The district court imposed the sanction under Rule 37 of the Federal Rules of Civil Procedure and the inherent authority of the court. Our review is deferential, and we will not reverse a decision by the district court imposing sanctions absent an abuse of discretion. This review applies to the decision to impose a sanction, the nature of the sanction imposed, and the factual basis for the court's decision.

In order to impose sanctions under Rule 37, there must be an order compelling discovery, a willful violation of that order, and prejudice to the other party. Carey and Danis argue that Chrysler suffered no prejudice from the nondisclosure of the letter because Chrysler, through depositions, was already aware of all the information contained in the letter.[4] Carey and Danis also argue that the court could not have found the failure to produce the letter to be a willful violation of discovery.[5] We agree with the defendants, as far as their argument goes. The letter revealed little or nothing unknown to Chrysler. A year before trial, Chrysler knew of the meeting between David Danis, Danis and Grossman as well as the attempted joinder of the Beam case to the New Jersey case. In fact, much of the information contained in the letter was recited in the district court's May 1998 order denying summary judgment. Chrysler also knew of Deakle's Mississippi case, and had deposed Deakle. Had the letter been properly produced in discovery, as it should have been, it may have made Chrysler's later discovery more efficient, or at most may have led to further inquiry. However, that speculation does not translate into prejudice sufficient to sustain the drastic sanction of a stricken answer. Chrysler points to nothing that would have changed the nature of its case or its trial strategy had it known about the letter.

Unfortunately, our review of the record shows Carey and Danis mischaracterize the district court's ruling. While the production of the letter on the fourth day of trial may have been the catalyst for the investigation leading to the imposition of the sanction, a fair appraisal of the record reveals that the court was motivated in fact by a systematic pattern of abuse and "blatant disregard of the Court's orders and the discovery rules." After it was presented with the last-minute disclosure of the letter, the court reviewed interrogatories and document requests along with the corresponding responses by the defendants. The court soon concluded that, not only was the letter plainly responsive to multiple requests, but so too were many, if not all, of the forty-two documents obtained from the other members of the informal group which had been either sent to, or

---

[4] The essential facts contained in the letter are: (1) Danis and his father met with the two attorneys in New York the Sunday before the letter was written; (2) the New York attorneys represented plaintiffs in an ABS class action against Chrysler filed in New Jersey; (3) the conversation centered around joining the Beam case with the New Jersey litigation; (4) Carey and Danis were aware of a Brown case filed by Deakle in Mississippi; (5) Carey and Danis had lined up plaintiffs in other states; and (6) Danis suggested a basic agreement allocating attorney's fees at the beginning of the joint endeavor.

[5] The defendants do not dispute the existence of a court order.

written by, the defendants. Thus discovery responses by Carey and Danis denying the existence of communications and documents were clearly false in regards to at least those documents, and probably more.

Even if the court had accepted the explanation offered by the defendants as to why they failed to produce the letter to Grossman, it was faced with a large number of other documents that were clearly responsive to multiple interrogatories and document requests, yet had not been produced. The court concluded that the answers to the interrogatories and document requests were plainly perjurious and not credible, as was the defendants' deposition testimony. This alone is sufficient violation of discovery rules to warrant sanction by the district court.

Carey and Danis further argue that, even if the sanction were appropriate, the extreme sanction of striking their pleadings was not. As they correctly point out, our review of sanctions imposed by the district court is more focused when the drastic sanction of dismissal or default is imposed. We review such severe sanctions more closely because "in our system of justice the opportunity to be heard is a litigant's most precious right and should be sparingly denied." As this court recently noted, there is a strong policy in favor of deciding a case on its merits, and against depriving a party of his day in court. However, if a default judgment lies within the spectrum of appropriate sanctions, we will not substitute our own judgment for that of the district court even though we may have chosen a different sanction had we been standing in the shoes of the trial court. See National Hockey League v. Metropolitan Hockey Club, Inc., 427 U.S. 639, 642, 49 L.Ed.2d 747, 96 S.Ct. 2778 (1976).

In this case, the district court found that the defendants repeatedly lied during the discovery process, denying the existence of conversations and documents which had in fact occurred and did exist. This is far more egregious conduct than simple foot-dragging or even making unfounded challenges to discovery requests. The defendants' flat denials that conversations had occurred and that documents existed precluded any follow-up discovery and thus denied Chrysler the ability to conduct effective discovery. And, as these statements were made under oath, they are a direct affront to the court.

Several examples of the defendants' responses will suffice to show the egregiousness. In its initial interrogatories, Chrysler asked Carey and Danis if they had communicated with anyone regarding the class actions against Chrysler in St. Louis, Mississippi, New Jersey, or in the Brown case in Alabama. They responded that the only communication was a few casual conversations over lunch with Danis's father (of the Danis, Cooper firm), and only about the New Jersey case. However, the documents later received into evidence showed that, by the time the interrogatory was answered, at least eighteen documents relating to one or more of the listed cases had been sent to Carey & Danis, not to mention the letter Danis sent to Grossman. And though the correspondence continued, the interrogatories were never supplemented to reflect the communications and documents. It is obvious from the evidence that Carey and Danis were at the least being kept abreast of developments and strategy in these cases. In March 1997, in response to the court's order, Carey and Danis stated that the only agreement they had for another to pay their fees and expenses in defending the instant action was with CNA, their insurance carrier, and that they had no agreements to share in any fees generated from litigation against Chrysler. However, correspondence among members of the group (copies of which had been sent to Carey and Danis) makes it clear that not only had the group agreed to pay the expenses incurred in this action, but that they had agreed to pay the expenses out of awards received in the various cases they had pending against Chrysler.

The district court thus concluded that the letter to Grossman was just "the tip of the iceberg," when viewed in conjunction with the forty-two other documents. The court determined that the defendants had not only failed to follow the normal rules of discovery, but had probably withheld more material as well.[7] The court went on to state that "I no longer have faith in the adversary system being conducted according to the rules. . . . I have lost faith in the discovery rules being followed in this case. I have no faith that they have been followed, and I don't know what else has been concealed. That is why I am imposing the sanction."

Faced with evidence of widespread abuse of the discovery process, the prejudice to Chrysler goes far beyond merely the added time and resources expended to discover evidence. Chrysler went to trial lacking evidence it would have had but for the deceit of the defendants. The efforts by Carey and Danis to deny and conceal evidence, and to provide false and misleading testimony, seriously threatened the integrity of the trial as well as the judicial process in general. We have reviewed the record and find substantial evidence that the misleading statements by the defendants were willful and resulted in prejudice to Chrysler. Although the failure to recall seeing a document may be a plausible explanation in some circumstances, the same cannot be said when that excuse is used for forty-two documents, some of which were written by the defendants themselves.

We have previously noted that "when a litigant's conduct abuses the judicial process, . . . dismissal of a lawsuit [is] a remedy within the inherent power of the court." Similarly, Rule 37 "grants a district court the authority to enter a default judgment against a party who abuses the discovery process." Thus, striking a party's pleadings under Rule 37 is within the range of appropriate sanctions when a party demonstrates a "blatant disregard of the Court's orders and the discovery rules," engaging in a pattern of deceit by presenting false and misleading answers and testimony under oath in order to prevent their opponent from fairly presenting its case. We find that the district court did not abuse its discretion by striking the defendants' answer.

---

[7] Chrysler had been unable to compel all the members of the group to produce documents, and the court acknowledged that it had placed limits on the number of documents some of the non-party law firms had to produce.

Carey and Danis assert that the court should not have stricken the pleadings when the sanction of a monetary penalty was available. Sanctions are "not merely to penalize those whose conduct may be deemed to warrant such a sanction, but [also] to deter those who might be tempted to such conduct in the absence of such a deterrent." *National Hockey*, 427 U.S. at 643. The district court is not constrained to impose the least onerous sanction available, but may exercise its discretion to choose the most appropriate sanction under the circumstances. The sanction was imposed after four days of trial, near the close of Chrysler's evidence. Even if a monetary penalty could have achieved the desired punitive and deterrent effects, it could have done nothing to remedy the lack of integrity in the case being presented to the jury. The district court expressly considered less onerous sanctions and determined that under the circumstances a lesser sanction "would not remedy the wrong that has been done to the litigation process before us."

Carey and Danis next argue that the district court failed to give them a hearing before imposing the sanction. While there is no requirement for an evidentiary hearing prior to the imposition of sanctions, the power of the district court is limited by the due process clause of the Fifth Amendment. See Societe Internationale v. Rogers, 357 U.S. 197, 209, 78 S.Ct. 1087, 2 L.Ed.2d 1255 (1958). This court has previously held that no hearing is necessary before sanctions are imposed where the record demonstrates a willful and bad faith abuse of discovery and the non-cooperating party could not be unfairly surprised by the sanction. As noted, the record amply demonstrates such bad faith on the part of Carey and Danis. Since Carey and Danis are both attorneys, and were warned, along with Chrysler, that failure to comply in good faith with the Rules of Civil Procedure could result in sanctions "which could be dispositive of this case," we find no surprise, much less unfair surprise.

In any event, we find that Carey and Danis received a hearing adequate to satisfy the dictates of due process. The letter was brought to the court's attention shortly before the noon recess. Some discussion was had between counsel and the court as to the origin of the letter and why it had not been produced. The court then compared the letter to various interrogatories and document requests and determined that the responses to them were plainly false. The court also noted the connection between the letter and the forty-two documents introduced earlier. Counsel was then permitted to argue to the court on the issue of prejudice. After lunch, defense counsel was allowed to offer another explanation as to why the letter had not been produced, and there was a significant amount of discussion between counsel and the court. The court then recessed for about an hour to review interrogatories, document requests, the responses, and the record. After the recess, the court recapped the discovery in the case and presented its conclusion that sanctions were appropriate. The court then invited defense counsel to argue in support of a sanction less drastic than that asked for by Chrysler. Defense counsel did so at length in a soliloquy covering five pages of transcript. The court then struck the defendants' answer.

Contrary to the defendants' clear assertion, the district court did not decline to grant them a hearing "despite repeated requests" by the defendants. The record clearly shows no such requests were made prior to the imposition of the sanction. The following Monday morning, defense counsel was again allowed to argue against the sanction, and present segments of deposition testimony to bolster the claims made earlier that the letter had been innocently withheld. Defense counsel was also permitted to make an offer of proof on the testimony of Joseph Danis, if he were questioned about the creation and subsequent handling of the letter. However, we find nothing in the offer of proof that is different from the arguments that had already been presented by defense counsel. The proposed testimony involved only the letter and did not address the pattern of deceit that motivated the court to impose the sanction. The lack of any new argument shows that Carey and Danis had a full opportunity to argue their case before the district court. Due process is satisfied if the sanctioned party has a real and full opportunity to explain its questionable conduct before sanctions are imposed.

III. CONCLUSION

For the foregoing reasons, the judgment of the district court is *affirmed*.

NOTES AND PROBLEMS FOR DISCUSSION

1. State in one sentence what conduct was sanctioned.

2. The *Carey* case provides an excellent illustration of some of the problems faced in the discovery process. In many cases discovery is a long and complex affair, with hundreds of situations where parties must make judgment calls, and in which they can be less than cooperative or forthright. In this process, the line between aggressively protecting a client's rights and abusive conduct is not easy to draw. Moreover, motions for discovery sanctions and responses often show only a small part of an overall pattern, and sometimes resemble two small children fighting over a toy. It is no wonder that courts often tell lawyers "a pox on both your houses," or "go work it out." The problem may be exacerbated if a magistrate judge rules on discovery matters, thus minimizing the risk that a discovery dispute will somehow impact the trial judge's view of the case. But, as *Carey* indicates, there is a limit.

3. Now consider the actual sanction in *Carey*.

(a) Were there other possibly effective sanctions or was judgment on liability the only choice?

(b) Did defendants have a warning that Judge Perry was close to the line?

(c) Did they really get notice and an effective hearing and would it have mattered since Perry would have been the judge at trial?

4. Finally, would the *Carey* court have reached the same result if the defendants were not lawyers?

CHAPTER 9

Disposition Without Trial

Simply because a case is filed and pleadings are exchanged doesn't mean that there will be a trial. In fact, only a tiny percentage of civil cases filed in the federal courts are disposed of by trial — as of 2008, approximately 2% of the more than a quarter million civil cases filed. There are a number of ways in which a case can end without a trial. For example, we have already examined the possibility of pre-trial disposition in connection with various motions to dismiss under Rule 12. In this Chapter, we assume that the pleading phase of the case is complete, and consider a variety of other devices for terminating the case without a trial. The first section deals with motions to dismiss and default judgments; the second section discusses motions for summary judgment.

SECTION A. DEFAULT AND PRE-TRIAL DISMISSALS

Apart from motions to dismiss under Rule 12, a case can be dismissed before trial on various grounds including the following: First, the defendant can fail to answer and the court can grant a default judgment. See Rule 55. Second, the court can grant an involuntary dismissal on a variety of grounds. See Rule 41(b). These grounds generally relate to the failure to observe various procedural requirements such as appearing for hearings, complying with scheduling orders, filing documents, and the like. In addition, we have already considered the possibility of an involuntary dismissal for discovery abuses. See Rule 37(b)(2)(A). Finally, in certain situations plaintiff is permitted voluntarily to dismiss her lawsuit. See Rule 41(a).

1. DEFAULT

If, after service of process, a defendant fails to plead or otherwise defend the litigation, the court can enter a default judgment. Under Rule 55, Fed. R. Civ. P., the first step is for the clerk to enter the party's default on the record following the failure to plead or defend. This step is referred to as "entering a default." A "default judgment" is actually a second step in the proceedings. The clerk may enter such a judgment if the claim "is for a sum certain or a sum that can be made certain by computation." Otherwise, only the court may enter the judgment by default upon application by the party entitled to judgment. According to Rule 54(c), a plaintiff is limited in a default judgment to the relief demanded in the complaint.

If a default judgment is sought against a party who has "appeared" in the action — for example, by raising an unsuccessful motion under Rule 12, but who then fails to file an answer — the party is to be given written notice at least seven days prior to the hearing on the application for judgment by default. Rule 55(b)(2). If necessary, particularly for the assessment of damages, evidence may be taken at such a hearing. Relief from an entry of default may be had under Rule 55(c) for good cause, and a default judgment may be set aside in appropriate circumstances under Rule 60(b). Interestingly, attorney negligence can, but will usually will not amount to "excusable neglect" for purposes of Rule 60(b)(1). See Easley v. Krimsee, 382 F.3d 693, 698 (7th Cir. 2004) ("Although attorney carelessness can constitute "excusable neglect" under Rule 60(b)(1), . . . attorney inattentiveness to litigation is not excusable, no matter what the resulting consequences the attorney's somnolent behavior may have on a litigant.") Compare Community Dental Servs. v. Tani, 282 F.3d 1164 (9th Cir. 2002) (holding that an attorney's "gross" negligence was a ground for reopening a judgment under the more stringent standard of Rule 60(b)(6)).

But courts also say that default judgments are disfavored. See, e.g., Lacy v. Sitel Corp., 227 F.3d 290, 292 (5th Cir. 2000). And although a default judgment will be res judicata if entered by a court of competent jurisdiction, collateral estoppel will generally not attach to the extent that there was no actual litigation of any particular issue. Similar mechanisms existed at common law and in equity, although, prior to the Federal Rules and under the old Conformity Act, state law would be followed in federal court actions at common law.

2. INVOLUNTARY DISMISSAL

Under Rule 41(b), Fed. R. Civ. P., a defendant may move to have a case dismissed "if the plaintiff fails to prosecute or comply with these rules or a court order." See, e.g., Coleman v. American Red Cross, 23 F.3d 1091 (6th Cir. 1994), discussed in Chapter 1. Such dismissals — and most other dismissals *not* provided for under Rule 41(b) — are within the district court's discretion and ordinarily operate as an adjudication on the merits, unless otherwise specified by the court. Consequently, such involuntary dismissals would ordinarily have res judicata consequences. Rule 41(b), however, expressly states that dismissals on jurisdictional grounds, for lack of venue, or for failure to join a party under Rule 19, do not operate as an adjudication on the merits. Note also that in a diversity action, the preclusive effect that a state court would give to a particular involuntary dismissal (such as on statute-of-limitations grounds) may control. See Semtek Int'l, Inc. v. Lockheed Martin Corp., 531 U.S. 497, 121 S.Ct. 1021, 149 L.Ed.2d 42 (2001) (discussed in Chapter 13). In Link v. Wabash R.R. Co., 370 U.S. 626, 82 S.Ct. 1386, 8 L.Ed.2d 714 (1962), the Supreme Court upheld a district court's sua sponte dismissal as a permissible sanction for plaintiff's counsel's repeated failures to prosecute a case. Such a sanction, said the Court "has been expressly recognized in [Rule] 41(b)," and was a "power . . . of ancient origin, having its roots in judgments of nonsuit and non prosequitur entered at common law." States also have rules for involuntary dismissal for nonprosecution, some of them providing explicit timetables for plaintiff inaction as giving rise to mandatory dismissal. See, e.g., Cal. Code Civ. Pro. §§583.310, 583.420(a)(2)(A).

What constitutes a jurisdictional dismissal under Rule 41(b) versus a dismissal on the merits has been the bone of some contention. In SAYLOR v. LINDSLEY, 391 F.2d 965 (2d Cir. 1968), a shareholder derivative action was brought on behalf of a corporation and its shareholders against various of its officers for violations of securities laws and breach of fiduciary duty. The complaint was dismissed "with prejudice" when the class representative failed to post a bond as security for certain potential costs of the litigation. A later suit raising a similar claim was brought on behalf of a similar class by a different representative, Saylor. On appeal of the district court's dismissal of the second proceeding on res judicata grounds, the Second Circuit reversed. It assumed that the dismissal of the first action for failure to post a security bond would bring it "within the literal words of Rule 41(b)" as an involuntary dismissal warranting preclusive effect. Nevertheless, the court distinguished the failure to post a bond from the failure to prosecute. It stated that the purpose of Rule 41(b) was to spare the defendant of having to put on a defense more than once, and in the earlier proceedings, the defendant had not previously been put to the inconvenience of mounting a defense on the merits.

In so stating, the Second Circuit relied on language to similar effect from Costello v. United States, 365 U.S. 265, 81 S.Ct. 534, 5 L.Ed.2d 551 (1961). *Costello* was also invoked for the proposition that Rule 41(b) was not intended "to change the common-law principles of res judicata 'with respect to dismissals in which the merits could not be reached for failure of the plaintiff to satisfy a precondition'" to filing suit — in *Costello*, the failure of the U.S. to file an affidavit of good cause as a prerequisite to a denaturalization proceeding. In *Costello*, however, the Supreme Court held that the first dismissal had been on jurisdictional grounds and therefore could not have been "on the merits," unlike the express decision of the district court in the first round of *Saylor* that the dismissal was "with prejudice." Was the appeals court suggesting that the district court was in error in concluding that the first round was dismissed with prejudice? Or was the problem that the first suit should not have been held to bind the unnamed members of the shareholder class on whose behalf Saylor later sued, given the earlier neglect of class counsel?

3. VOLUNTARY DISMISSAL

After filing suit, the plaintiff may realize for one reason or another that she would like to dismiss and start over again, perhaps in another forum. In most non-class action litigation, the plaintiff may unilaterally terminate her lawsuit any time before service of an answer or a motion for summary judgment, whichever comes first, by filing a "notice of dismissal" under Rule 41(a)(1)(A)(i), Fed. R. Civ. P. Outside of those time limits, she may also voluntarily dismiss her case by filing a "stipulation of dismissal" signed by all parties who have appeared in the lawsuit. Rule 41(a)(1)(A)(ii). Such dismissals are generally without prejudice to the plaintiff's refiling the same suit over again (unless the dismissal follows an earlier voluntary dismissal of the same claim, in which case the second dismissal will be with prejudice, in order to spare the defendant from repeated use of the practice). This practice of voluntary dismissal has echoes in procedures at common law that were quite liberal in allowing a plaintiff voluntarily to dismiss her lawsuit — sometimes quite late in the game — without suffering adverse consequences.

Absent a notice of dismissal or a stipulation of dismissal consistent with Rule 41(a), court permission is required, even for the plaintiff voluntarily to dismiss her lawsuit. Under Rule 41(a)(2) "an action may be dismissed at the plaintiff's request only by court order, on terms that the court considers proper." And if the defendant has filed a counterclaim, the plaintiff's suit "shall not be dismissed" over the defendant's objection unless the counterclaim is allowed to go forward on its own.

Voluntary dismissals, if entered with prejudice, will ordinarily require the voluntarily dismissing party to pay costs under Rule 54(d) to the other party. In Mother and Father v. Cassidy, 338 F.3d 704 (7th Cir. 2003), the Court of Appeals overturned a district court's effort to leave to the state courts, the assessment of costs under Rule 54(d) against the plaintiffs following the voluntary dismissal under Rule 41 of their civil rights claims in federal court. After extensive discovery, the federal plaintiffs voluntarily dismissed their lawsuit in which they had raised both federal and state law claims. Their intent was to have the federal claims dismissed with prejudice and then to go forward with the state-law claims in state court where a related action had already been filed by similarly situated parties. The federal trial court had concluded that, despite the more than $100,000 in costs that had been incurred in the federal proceedings, the "Rule 54 costs would travel to the state courts," to be paid by whoever was the loser there. The appeals court concluded that the district court had exceeded its authority in refusing to rule on the award of costs itself, and remanded for a determination of such costs "unless one of the recognized situations warranting a denial of costs is present."

4. SETTLEMENT

The parties, of course, may simply choose to settle their litigation short of trial. In the non-class action setting, such settlement may take place without the intervention of the court. Settlement of private lawsuits is desirable insofar as it reduces the costs of litigation and allows the parties to resolve a dispute on terms that they find agreeable. Under Rule 23(e), however, settlement and voluntary dismissal of suits certified as class actions require a hearing and judicial approval, and "reasonable" notice must be given in order to safeguard the interests of the unnamed class members who will be bound by the disposition of the case. Cf. Matsushita Elec. Inc. v. Epstein, 516 U.S. 367, 116 S.Ct. 873, 134 L.Ed.2d 6 (1996) (holding that state law regarding binding nature of state court class action consent decree would govern in subsequently resolved, overlapping class-wide litigation in federal court, provided there was adequate representation).

Sometimes the settlement is made part of a consent judgment that is entered by the court. Such judgments, like default judgments, will generally have res judicata effects, but not issue preclusive effects, given the absence of actual litigation. But it is possible that the parties might stipulate, as a contractual matter, as to the issue preclusive consequences of a consent judgment as well. Violation of a consent judgment entered by the court may permit a party to return to that court to enforce the consent judgment; absent a settlement's being made part of a court-entered consent judgment, however, the only action that may be brought is one for breach of contract — i.e., breach of the settlement agreement itself. Whether jurisdiction exists in a federal court will then likely depend on whether the parties are of diverse citizenship, since such settlement agreements, if not entered by the court, are generally contracts governed by state law, even if the underlying suit that was the subject of settlement was itself a suit that arose under federal law. Kokkonen v. Guardian Life Ins. Co., 511 U.S. 375, 114 S.Ct. 1673, 128 L.Ed.2d 391 (1994). Thus, the surest way for a litigant settling a federal question case to guarantee a federal forum for any breach of the settlement agreement is to have it entered by the court as a consent judgment thereby allowing the court to retain jurisdiction over any claim of settlement violation.

The goals of settlement are also encouraged by Rule 68 which permits defendants to make an offer of judgment to the plaintiff and visits a kind of penalty on the plaintiff if she ultimately prevails but recovers less than what she was offered. If the judgment obtained by the plaintiff is not more favorable than the offer, the plaintiff must pay the "costs" of litigation incurred after the point of the offer of judgment. But Rule 68 will *not* apply if the plaintiff simply loses, as opposed to winning and recovering less than what was offered in the offer of judgment.

In connection with Rule 68, the Supreme Court has gone so far as to hold that a prevailing party in a civil rights action — who would ordinarily be entitled to recover reasonable attorney's fees "as part of costs" from the losing defendant pursuant to a fee-shifting statute, 42 U.S.C. §1988(b) — could not recover fees for the time spent after rejecting an offer of judgment that turned out to be more favorable than the judgment eventually recovered. Marek v. Chesny, 473 U.S. 1, 105 S.Ct. 3012, 87 L.Ed.2d 1 (1985). In doing so, the Court arguably permitted a Court-promulgated Rule to trump §1988 insofar as it reflected Congress's statutory goal of allowing recovery for all time reasonably spent in the successful prosecution of such cases (assuming the rejection of the offer of settlement was not unreasonable). We discuss *Marek* in Chapter 6.

SECTION B. SUMMARY JUDGMENT

Common law procedure had essentially two steps — elaborate pleading and then a trial. If the plaintiff's case was legally insufficient, or the defendant had a defense that was dispositive, the defendant could seek to have the case dismissed during the pleading stage sometimes by a demurrer or other device. But if not, the defendant's first chance to challenge the plaintiff's case came only at trial. At that time, the defendant could move for a nonsuit and allege that the plaintiff had no right to recover on the basis of the evidence presented.

Today, there are at least some cases, and some believe many cases, which do not warrant a trial. Plaintiff may have no substantive theory giving a right to recover. Or, the plaintiff may have a theory but does not have evidence to support the theory. Or the defendant may have a dispositive defense. Or the plaintiff's case is overwhelming and defendant has no response. Or the defendant may have admitted the plaintiff's case and asserted a defense which is legally invalid, or one for which the defendant has no evidentiary support. Theoretically, some of these cases might be decided at the pleading stage, but a combination of modern notice pleading and a reluctance to determine cases on pleading motions unless there is no possibility of recovery or defense, means that many will not. Moreover, a basic premise of pre-trial discovery is that parties ordinarily will have an opportunity for discovery before a final decision on the case.

The motion for summary judgment has been adapted as a screening device — to identify and end cases where there is no need for a trial. But what does it mean to say that there is "no need for a trial"? It means that given the law and the available evidence, one side would have to win and thus a trial would be a waste of time.

Rule 56(a) provides for summary judgment if "there is no genuine dispute as to any material fact and the movant is entitled to judgment as a matter of law." Courts also apply this rule to permit so-called partial summary judgment — for example, on one or more but not all claims, or on an affirmative defense, or on liability and not damages. See Rule 56(a) (summary judgment on claim or defense or on "part of" a claim a claim or defense).

Under Rule 56(b) motions for summary judgment can be made almost any time after the case begins. But this is somewhat misleading. Summary judgment requires that there be no genuine issue as to any material fact, and the absence of a genuine issue will typically have to be established on the basis of discovery and affidavits. Moreover, the provisions for discovery themselves would be somewhat illusory if a party could preempt discovery by moving for summary judgment at the outset of a case. For this reason, courts generally view summary judgment as a motion that comes after a reasonable time for discovery. Indeed, Rule 56(d)(2) contemplates that a motion for summary judgment may be denied or continued to permit discovery.

The two difficult issues surrounding the propriety of granting summary judgment have been (1) what showing the party moving for summary judgment must make, and (2) assuming the movant makes such a showing, what showing the nonmoving party must make to avoid summary judgment. See Rule 56(c)(1) ("Supporting Factual Positions"). Be warned, however, that there are literally thousands of cases discussing whether, in a given situation, summary judgment should be granted. In a sense, the issues are always sui generis. It is also clear that good lawyering makes a significant difference in winning and losing motions for summary judgment.

1. AN INTRODUCTORY NOTE ON BURDEN OF PROOF

Summary judgment cannot be understood without understanding the concept of burden of proof. Linguistically, courts use the term "burden of proof" to refer to two distinct concepts — burden of production and burden of persuasion.

a. Burden of Production. "Burden of production" refers to the concept that a party must produce sufficient evidence to permit a rational trier of fact to find in its favor. If a party must establish several issues to win its case, it may be said to have the burden of production on each issue. For example, in a negligence case, the plaintiff has the burden of production to show that the defendant owed a duty to the plaintiff, the defendant fell below the required standard of care (i.e., was negligent), the defendant's negligence was the proximate cause of plaintiff's damages, and that the plaintiff has suffered damages.

How much evidence is necessary to satisfy the burden of production? Here courts necessarily resort to generalities — for example: "Is there sufficient evidence which, if believed, would lead a fair minded or rational decisionmaker to find for the plaintiff?" or words to such effect. Not that the jury must find for the plaintiff if he satisfies his burden of production, but only that it could rationally do so. But these generalities don't really answer the question on specific facts of specific cases. Instead, one only gets a sense from cases and "experience" how much evidence is enough.

What is the purpose of such a concept? It is essentially a device to assure that the decisionmaker renders a rational verdict under the law. Put in a somewhat less grandiose manner, it is a device to control the rationality of the fact-finding process, and to assure that the jury hasn't done something "out of the blue" or "off the wall." Due process requires, at a minimum, that the state (through a jury verdict) have a rational basis for acting to deprive a person of his liberty or property.

For example, if a plaintiff sued a defendant for negligence as a result of a car accident and the plaintiff simply proved injury, a court would say that a verdict for plaintiff was irrational — either the jury was trying to change the law (by eliminating proof of negligence) or was acting improperly by finding negligence in the absence of evidentiary support for such a finding.

In most cases, once the party with the burden of production on an issue satisfies its burden, the question enters the province of the decisionmaker. Occasionally, however, the party with the burden will produce so much evidence, or evidence which appears incontestable, that we may say that the burden of production switches to its adversary. If the adversary doesn't produce any evidence at that point, judgment will be granted for the party with the initial burden of production. If the adversary does produce sufficient evidence so that reasonable persons can again differ, the question again becomes one for the trier of fact.

In determining whether a party has satisfied its burden of production, courts ordinarily do not determine credibility — i.e., who is telling the truth. Rather, courts will leave to the trier of fact the resolution of all credibility issues, and will permit the trier of fact to draw all reasonable favorable inferences from the evidence; the court will only ask whether (on those assumptions) a party has satisfied his burden of production. Of course, at a trial, the jury decides credibility and reasonable inferences; for this reason, a party can satisfy its burden of production and still lose.

b.   Burden of Persuasion.   The burden of persuasion is not a device to test the sufficiency of evidence.   Rather, it *presupposes* that there is sufficient evidence for the trier of fact to decide for either party.   Instead, the burden of persuasion tells the jury (or court) how to decide if it can't decide — it is thus a sort of "tie breaker" rule.

In most civil cases, the party with the burden of persuasion must convince the jury that its view is "more probable than not."   If the trier can't decide — some say when the evidence is "in equipoise" — then a verdict should be rendered against the party with the burden of persuasion.   But significantly, showing to the satisfaction of the factfinder that something is more probable than not is not a very significant burden.   Moreover, in most cases (where all burdens of production have been met), the trier can rationally decide one way or the other.   Thus, burden of persuasion probably doesn't "decide" many cases.[1]

In certain cases, we require the trier to be persuaded to a higher degree of assurance than "more probable than not."   In certain civil cases, including many actions for defamation and fraud, certain issues must be proven by "clear and convincing evidence."   And most students are familiar with the requirement in criminal cases that a defendant's guilt be established beyond a reasonable doubt.[2]   (And criminal juries may acquit for virtually any reason, and to that particular extent, their possible irrationality is unreviewable.)

c.   Application to Summary Judgment.   Assume a simple case where there is one issue, and the plaintiff has the burden of production on that issue.   If the case goes to trial and the plaintiff does not satisfy her burden of production, the court will grant a judgment as a matter of law for the defendant.   The judgment may come before the verdict (sometimes called a directed verdict), or after the verdict (sometimes called a judgment n.o.v.).   See Rule 50.   But one way or the other, the trial court's grant of such a motion is to assure rational decisionmaking.

These motions for judgment as a matter of law come after the trial has begun.   In a sense, they say that the case should never have been tried in the first place.   However, there are social and other costs involved in a trial, and especially an unnecessary trial.   Rule 56 is a device to enable a party to seek summary judgment before the start of what might be an unnecessary and wasteful trial.   It is a kind of pre-trial judgment as a matter of law.

In the typical case, and the one which has caused the most difficulty, the motion for summary judgment will be made by the party who does not have the burden of production.   By definition, such a party normally has little or no initial showing to make at an actual trial because the burden of production is on her

---

[1]   Notwithstanding this, burden of persuasion is significant in jury cases because the judge must charge who has the burden of persuasion on each material issue in the case, and if the judge gets it wrong in her charge to the jury, it is reversible error.   Also, sometimes jurors misunderstand the concept and require the party with the burden to make a stronger showing than the concept actually requires.

[2]   The difference in burdens suggests that it is not irrational, but perfectly consistent, for a defendant prosecuted for tax fraud, and sued civilly for unpaid taxes, to be held not guilty on the criminal charge but to be held liable to pay the taxes.

adversary. But what about on a motion for summary judgment? Consider what kind of showing the movant should have to make to establish a prima facie right to summary judgment. And if the movant makes this showing, consider what kind of showing the nonmoving party must make to defeat the motion. These issues are covered in the next two subsections.

2. THE MOVANT'S SHOWING

Rule 56(a) describes what the movant must establish to get summary judgment. Rule 56(c)(1)-(4) tells you what documents and information may be used. But no rule tells you exactly how much is enough. And keep in mind what summary judgment is — i.e., a preemptive termination of a case which prevents a party from going before the jury. Those who see the jury as a bulwark of liberty don't view the device with enthusiasm.

Because of its preemptive and final character, courts have had difficulty with summary judgment, including the Supreme Court. In ADICKES v. S.H. KRESS & CO., 398 U.S. 144, 90 S.Ct. 1598, 26 L.Ed.2d 142 (1970), plaintiff, a New York educator teaching at a Mississippi Freedom School in the 1960's, went into a Kress store with six of her African-American students to eat lunch; Kress refused to serve her, and when she left the store, she was arrested for vagrancy by two policemen. Adickes sued on the ground that Kress had violated her civil rights under color of state law; to recover under the law at time, she had to show "state action" (involvement of government — state or local — in the process).[3] Adickes sought to establish the necessary state action by asserting that the arrest outside the store by the officers was part of a conspiracy — that Kress's employee and the policemen "somehow reached an understanding . . . to cause her subsequent arrest because she was in the company of Negroes."

Kress moved for summary judgment alleging that Adickes had the burden of production to show a conspiracy, and that there was no evidence whatsoever of such a conspiracy. The lower courts granted summary judgment, but the Supreme Court reversed, stating:

> We think that on the basis of this record, it was error to grant summary judgment. As the moving party, [Kress] has the burden of showing the absence of a genuine issue as to any material fact, and for these purposes the material it lodged must be reviewed in the light most favorable to [Adickes]. [Kress] did not carry its burden because of its failure to foreclose the possibility that there was a policeman in the Kress store while [Adickes] was awaiting service, and that this policeman reached an understanding with some Kress employee that [she] not be served.

> It is true that Mr. Powell, the store manager, claimed in his deposition that he had not seen or communicated with a policeman prior to his tacit signal to Miss Baggett, the supervisor of the food counter.

---

[3] In 1964, after the events in question, Congress passed legislation which would have permitted an action against a private party such as Kress, without the need to show state action. 42 U.S.C. §2000a(b).

But [Kress] did not submit any affidavits from Miss Baggett, or from Miss Freeman, the waitress who actually refused [Adickes] service, either of whom might well have seen and communicated with a policeman in the store. Further, we find it particularly noteworthy that the two officers involved in the arrest each failed in his affidavit to foreclose the possibility (1) that he was in the store while [Adickes] was there; and (2) that, upon seeing [Adickes] with Negroes, he communicated his disapproval to a Kress employee, thereby influencing the decision not to serve petitioner.

Given these unexplained gaps in the material submitted by [Kress], we conclude that [Kress] failed to fulfill its initial burden of demonstrating what is a critical element in this aspect of the case — that there was no policeman in the store. If a policeman were present, we think it would be open to a jury, in light of the sequence that followed, to infer from the circumstances that the policeman and a Kress employee had a "meeting of the minds" and thus reached an understanding that [Adickes] should be refused service . . . [Kress's] failure to show there was no policeman in the store requires reversal.

Several things are noteworthy about *Adickes*:

- The Court never gets to the question of what kind of a showing Adickes must make to oppose summary judgment. Instead, the Court says Kress's showing was inadequate to get summary judgment, and Adickes didn't have to make any defensive showing at all.

- At a trial, Adickes, not Kress, would have the burden of production on the question of whether an officer was in the store. If she produced no evidence that an officer was present (and no other evidence of conspiracy), a judgment as a matter of law would be granted against her. Conversely, Kress would not have to offer any evidence from the employees or the officer.

- The Court thus appeared to require Kress to produce evidence to support summary judgment, which it would *not* have to produce to support a judgment as a matter of law at trial. This was interpreted to mean that, regardless of who had the burden of production at trial, the movant clearly had it on summary judgment.

After *Adickes*, how did a movant for summary judgment satisfy its burden such that the nonmoving party would be required to respond? Here, there was no agreement. Some courts said that the movant's evidence had to be overwhelming — the movant had to show that reasonable people could not differ as to the correctness of its view. Under this approach, which certainly finds some support in the above passages of the opinion in *Kress*, the movant had to establish both that (1) its version was clearly correct, and (2) that there was no alternative evidence or explanation that might undermine its correctness. Other courts held that the movant initially only had to come forward with evidence from which reasonable persons could find in its favor on the relevant issue (even though, at trial, this burden of production would have been on the plaintiff).

Regardless of which these interpretations of *Adickes* was correct, it is clear that either of them would make it difficult for parties to get summary judgment. The Supreme Court signaled a change in direction in the opinion that follows. Note, however, that the current version of Rule 56 includes changes that were made subsequent to the opinion.

Celotex Corp. v. Catrett

Supreme Court of the United States, 1986.
477 U.S. 317, 106 S.Ct. 2548, 91 L.Ed.2d 265.

JUSTICE REHNQUIST delivered the opinion of the Court.

The United States District Court for the District of Columbia granted the motion of petitioner Celotex Corporation for summary judgment against respondent Catrett because the latter was unable to produce evidence in support of her allegation in her wrongful-death complaint that the decedent had been exposed to petitioner's asbestos products. A divided panel of the Court of Appeals for the District of Columbia Circuit reversed, however, holding that petitioner's failure to support its motion with evidence tending to negate such exposure precluded the entry of summary judgment in its favor. Catrett v. Johns-Manville Sales Corp., 244 U.S. App. D.C. 160, 756 F.2d 181 (1985). This view conflicted with that of the Third Circuit in In re Japanese Electronic Products, 723 F.2d 238 (1983), *rev'd on other grounds sub nom.* Matsushita Electric Industrial Co. v. Zenith Radio Corp., 475 U.S. 574 (1986). We granted certiorari to resolve the conflict, 474 U.S. 944 (1985), and now reverse the decision of the District of Columbia Circuit.

Respondent commenced this lawsuit in September 1980, alleging that the death in 1979 of her husband, Louis H. Catrett, resulted from his exposure to products containing asbestos manufactured or distributed by 15 named corporations. Respondent's complaint sounded in negligence, breach of warranty, and strict liability. Two of the defendants filed motions challenging the District Court's in personam jurisdiction, and the remaining 13, including petitioner, filed motions for summary judgment. Petitioner's motion, which was first filed in September 1981, argued that summary judgment was proper because respondent had "failed to produce evidence that any [Celotex] product ... was the proximate cause of the injuries alleged within the jurisdictional limits of [the District] Court." In particular, petitioner noted that respondent had failed to identify, in answering interrogatories specifically requesting such information, any witnesses who could testify about the decedent's exposure to petitioner's asbestos products. In response to petitioner's summary judgment motion, respondent then produced three documents which she claimed "demonstrate that there is a genuine material factual dispute" as to whether the decedent had ever been exposed to petitioner's asbestos products. The three documents included a transcript of a deposition of the decedent, a letter from an official of one of the decedent's former employers whom petitioner planned to call as a trial witness, and a letter from an insurance company to respondent's attorney, all tending to establish that the decedent had been exposed to petitioner's asbestos products in Chicago during 1970-1971. Petitioner, in turn, argued that the three documents were inadmissible hearsay and thus could not be considered in opposition to the summary judgment motion.

In July 1982, almost two years after the commencement of the lawsuit, the District Court granted all of the motions filed by the various defendants. The court explained that it was granting petitioner's summary judgment motion because "there [was] no showing that the plaintiff was exposed to the defendant Celotex's product in the District of Columbia or elsewhere within the statutory period." Respondent appealed only the grant of summary judgment in favor of petitioner, and a divided panel of the District of Columbia Circuit reversed. The majority of the Court of Appeals held that petitioner's summary judgment motion was rendered "fatally defective" by the fact that petitioner "made no effort to adduce *any* evidence, in the form of affidavits or otherwise, to support its motion." 244 U.S. App. D.C., at 163, 756 F.2d, at 184 (emphasis in original). According to the majority, Rule 56(e) of the Federal Rules of Civil Procedure, and this Court's decision in Adickes v. S. H. Kress & Co., 398 U.S. 144, 159 (1970), establish that "the party opposing the motion for summary judgment bears the burden of responding *only after* the moving party has met its burden of coming forward with proof of the absence of any genuine issues of material fact." 244 U.S. App. D.C., at 163, 756 F.2d, at 184 (emphasis in original; footnote omitted). The majority therefore declined to consider petitioner's argument that none of the evidence produced by respondent in opposition to the motion for summary judgment would have been admissible at trial. Ibid. The dissenting judge argued that "[t]he majority errs in supposing that a party seeking summary judgment must always make an affirmative evidentiary showing, even in cases where there is not a triable, factual dispute." Id. at 167, 756 F.2d, at 188 (Bork, J., dissenting). According to the dissenting judge, the majority's decision "undermines the traditional authority of trial judges to grant summary judgment in meritless cases." Id. at 166, 756 F.2d at 187.

We think that the position taken by the majority of the Court of Appeals is inconsistent with the standard for summary judgment set forth in Rule 56(c) of the Federal Rules of Civil Procedure. [The basic standard for summary judgment is now set out at Rule 56(a), and is worded somewhat differently.–eds.] Under Rule 56(c), summary judgment is proper "if the pleadings, depositions, answers to interrogatories, and admissions on file, together with the affidavits, if any, show that there is no genuine issue as to any material fact and that the moving party is entitled to a judgment as a matter of law." In our view, the plain language of Rule 56(c) mandates the entry of summary judgment, after adequate time for discovery and upon motion, against a party who fails to make a showing sufficient to establish the existence of an element essential to that party's case, and on which that party will bear the burden of proof at trial. In such a situation, there can be "no genuine issue as to any material fact," since a complete failure of proof concerning an essential element of the nonmoving party's case necessarily renders all other facts immaterial. The moving party is "entitled to a judgment as a matter of law" because the nonmoving party has failed to make a sufficient showing on an essential element of her case with respect to which she has the burden of proof. "[The] standard [for granting summary judgment] mirrors the standard for a directed verdict under Federal Rule of Civil Procedure 50(a) . . . ." Anderson v. Liberty Lobby, Inc. [477 U.S. 242,] 250 [(1986)].

Of course, a party seeking summary judgment always bears the initial responsibility of informing the district court of the basis for its motion, and identifying those portions of "the pleadings, depositions, answers to interrogatories, and admissions on file, together with the affidavits, if any," which it believes demonstrate the absence of a genuine issue of material fact. But unlike the Court of Appeals, we find no express or implied requirement in Rule 56 that the moving party support its motion with affidavits or other similar materials negating the opponent's claim. On the contrary, Rule 56(c), which refers to "the affidavits, if any," suggests the absence of such a requirement. And if there were any doubt about the meaning of Rule 56(c) in this regard, such doubt is clearly removed by Rules 56(a) and (b), which provide that claimants and defendants, respectively, may move for summary judgment "with or without supporting affidavits". [The language "affidavits, if any" is no longer in Rule 56, but affidavits still do not appear to be required.—eds.] The import of these subsections is that, regardless of whether the moving party accompanies its summary judgment motion with affidavits, the motion may, and should, be granted so long as whatever is before the district court demonstrates that the standard for the entry of summary judgment, as set forth in Rule 56(c), is satisfied. One of the principal purposes of the summary judgment rule is to isolate and dispose of factually unsupported claims or defenses, and we think it should be interpreted in a way that allows it to accomplish this purpose.

Respondent argues, however, that Rule 56(e), by its terms, places on the nonmoving party the burden of coming forward with rebuttal affidavits, or other specified kinds of materials, only in response to a motion for summary judgment "made and supported as provided in this rule." According to respondent's argument, since petitioner did not "support" its motion with affidavits, summary judgment was improper in this case. But as we have already explained, a motion for summary judgment may be made pursuant to Rule 56 "with or without supporting affidavits." In cases like the instant one, where the nonmoving party will bear the burden of proof at trial on a dispositive issue, a summary judgment motion may properly be made in reliance solely on the "pleadings, depositions, answers to interrogatories, and admissions on file." Such a motion, whether or not accompanied by affidavits, will be "made and supported as provided in this rule," and Rule 56(e) therefore requires the nonmoving party to go beyond the pleadings and by her own affidavits, or by the "depositions, answers to interrogatories, and admissions on file," designate "specific facts showing that there is a genuine issue for trial."

We do not mean that the nonmoving party must produce evidence in a form that would be admissible at trial in order to avoid summary judgment. Obviously, Rule 56 does not require the nonmoving party to depose her own witnesses. Rule 56(e) permits a proper summary judgment motion to be opposed by any of the kinds of evidentiary materials listed in Rule 56(c), except the mere pleadings themselves, and it is from this list that one would normally expect the nonmoving party to make the showing to which we have referred.

The Court of Appeals in this case felt itself constrained, however, by language in our decision in Adickes v. S. H. Kress & Co., 398 U.S. 144 (1970). There we held that summary judgment had been improperly entered in favor of the defendant restaurant in an action brought under 42 U.S.C. §1983. In the course of its opinion, the *Adickes* Court said that "both the commentary on and the background of the 1963 amendment conclusively show that it was not intended to modify the burden of the moving party . . . to show initially the absence of a genuine issue concerning any material fact." Id. at 159. We think that this statement is accurate in a literal sense, since we fully agree with the *Adickes* Court that the 1963 amendment to Rule 56(e) was not designed to modify the burden of making the showing generally required by Rule 56(c). It also appears to us that, on the basis of the showing before the Court in *Adickes*, the motion for summary judgment in that case should have been denied. But we do not think the *Adickes* language quoted above should be construed to mean that the burden is on the party moving for summary judgment to produce evidence showing the absence of a genuine issue of material fact, even with respect to an issue on which the nonmoving party bears the burden of proof. Instead, as we have explained, the burden on the moving party may be discharged by "showing" — that is, pointing out to the district court — that there is an absence of evidence to support the nonmoving party's case.

The last two sentences of Rule 56(e) were added, as this Court indicated in *Adickes*, to disapprove a line of cases allowing a party opposing summary judgment to resist a properly made motion by reference only to its pleadings. While the *Adickes* Court was undoubtedly correct in concluding that these two sentences were not intended to reduce the burden of the moving party, it is also obvious that they were not adopted to add to that burden. Yet that is exactly the result which the reasoning of the Court of Appeals would produce; in effect, an amendment to Rule 56(e) designed to facilitate the granting of motions for summary judgment would be interpreted to make it more difficult to grant such motions. Nothing in the two sentences themselves requires this result, for the reasons we have previously indicated, and we now put to rest any inference that they do so.

Our conclusion is bolstered by the fact that district courts are widely acknowledged to possess the power to enter summary judgments sua sponte, so long as the losing party was on notice that she had to come forward with all of her evidence. It would surely defy common sense to hold that the District Court could have entered summary judgment sua sponte in favor of petitioner in the instant case, but that petitioner's filing of a motion requesting such a disposition precluded the District Court from ordering it.

Respondent commenced this action in September 1980, and petitioner's motion was filed in September 1981. The parties had conducted discovery, and no serious claim can be made that respondent was in any sense "railroaded" by a premature motion for summary judgment. Any potential problem with such premature motions can be adequately dealt with under Rule 56(f), which allows a summary judgment motion to be denied, or the hearing on the motion to be continued, if the nonmoving party has not had an opportunity to make full discovery.

In this Court, respondent's brief and oral argument have been devoted as much to the proposition that an adequate showing of exposure to petitioner's asbestos products was made as to the proposition that no such showing should have been required. But the Court of Appeals declined to address either the adequacy of the showing made by respondent in opposition to petitioner's motion for summary judgment, or the question whether such a showing, if reduced to admissible evidence, would be sufficient to carry respondent's burden of proof at trial. We think the Court of Appeals with its superior knowledge of local law is better suited than we are to make these determinations in the first instance.

The Federal Rules of Civil Procedure have for almost 50 years authorized motions for summary judgment upon proper showings of the lack of a genuine, triable issue of material fact. Summary judgment procedure is properly regarded not as a disfavored procedural shortcut, but rather as an integral part of the Federal Rules as a whole, which are designed "to secure the just, speedy and inexpensive determination of every action." Fed. Rule Civ. Proc. 1; see Schwarzer, Summary Judgment Under the Federal Rules: Defining Genuine Issues of Material Fact, 99 F.R.D. 465, 467 (1984). Before the shift to "notice pleading" accomplished by the Federal Rules, motions to dismiss a complaint or to strike a defense were the principal tools by which factually insufficient claims or defenses could be isolated and prevented from going to trial with the attendant unwarranted consumption of public and private resources. But with the advent of "notice pleading," the motion to dismiss seldom fulfills this function any more, and its place has been taken by the motion for summary judgment. Rule 56 must be construed with due regard not only for the rights of persons asserting claims and defenses that are adequately based in fact to have those claims and defenses tried to a jury, but also for the rights of persons opposing such claims and defenses to demonstrate in the manner provided by the Rule, prior to trial, that the claims and defenses have no factual basis.

The judgment of the Court of Appeals is accordingly reversed, and the case is remanded for further proceedings consistent with this opinion.

It is so ordered.

JUSTICE WHITE, concurring.

I agree that the Court of Appeals was wrong in holding that the moving defendant must always support his motion with evidence or affidavits showing the absence of a genuine dispute about a material fact. I also agree that the movant may rely on depositions, answers to interrogatories, and the like, to demonstrate that the plaintiff has no evidence to prove his case and hence that there can be no factual dispute. But the movant must discharge the burden the Rules place upon him: It is not enough to move for summary judgment without supporting the motion in any way or with a conclusory assertion that the plaintiff has no evidence to prove his case.

* * *

Petitioner Celotex does not dispute that if respondent has named a witness to support her claim, summary judgment should not be granted without Celotex somehow showing that the named witness' possible testimony raises no genuine issue of material fact. It asserts, however, that respondent has failed on request to produce any basis for her case. Respondent, on the other hand, does not contend that she was not obligated to reveal her witnesses and evidence but insists that she has revealed enough to defeat the motion for summary judgment. Because the Court of Appeals found it unnecessary to address this aspect of the case, I agree that the case should be remanded for further proceedings.

JUSTICE BRENNAN, with whom THE CHIEF JUSTICE and JUSTICE BLACKMUN, join, dissenting.

This case requires the Court to determine whether Celotex satisfied its initial burden of production in moving for summary judgment on the ground that the plaintiff lacked evidence to establish an essential element of her case at trial. I do not disagree with the Court's legal analysis. The Court clearly rejects the ruling of the Court of Appeals that the defendant must provide affirmative evidence disproving the plaintiff's case. Beyond this, however, the Court has not clearly explained what is required of a moving party seeking summary judgment on the ground that the nonmoving party cannot prove its case.[1] This lack of clarity is unfortunate: district courts must routinely decide summary judgment motions, and the Court's opinion will very likely create confusion. For this reason, even if I agreed with the Court's result, I would have written separately to explain more clearly the law in this area. However, because I believe that Celotex did not meet its burden of production under Federal Rule of Civil Procedure 56, I respectfully dissent from the Court's judgment.

I

Summary judgment is appropriate where the court is satisfied "that there is no genuine issue as to any material fact and that the moving party is entitled to a judgment as a matter of law." Fed. Rule Civ. Proc. 56(c). The burden of establishing the nonexistence of a "genuine issue" is on the party moving for summary judgment. This burden has two distinct components: an initial burden of production, which shifts to the nonmoving party if satisfied by the moving party; and an ultimate burden of persuasion, which always remains on the moving party. The court need not decide whether the moving party has satisfied its ultimate burden of persuasion[2] unless and until the court finds that the

---

[1] It is also unclear what the Court of Appeals is supposed to do in this case on remand. JUSTICE WHITE — who has provided the Court's fifth vote — plainly believes that the Court of Appeals should reevaluate whether the defendant met its initial burden of production. However, the decision to reverse rather than to vacate the judgment below implies that the Court of Appeals should assume that Celotex has met its initial burden of production and ask only whether the plaintiff responded adequately, and, if so, whether the defendant has met its ultimate burden of persuasion that no genuine issue exists for trial. Absent some clearer expression from the Court to the contrary, JUSTICE WHITE's understanding would seem to be controlling. Cf. Marks v. United States, 430 U.S. 188, 193 (1977).

[2] The burden of persuasion imposed on a moving party by Rule 56 is a stringent one. Summary judgment should not be granted unless it is clear that a trial is unnecessary, * * * and any doubt as to the existence of a genuine issue for trial should be resolved against the moving party, Adickes v. S.H. Kress & Co., 398 U.S. 144, 158-159 (1970). In determining whether a moving party has met its burden of persuasion, the court is obliged to take account of the entire setting of the case and

moving party has discharged its initial burden of production. Adickes v. S. H. Kress & Co., 398 U.S. 144, 157-161 (1970); 1963 Advisory Committee's Notes on Fed. Rule Civ. Proc. 56(e).

The burden of production imposed by Rule 56 requires the moving party to make a prima facie showing that it is entitled to summary judgment. The manner in which this showing can be made depends upon which party will bear the burden of persuasion on the challenged claim at trial. If the moving party will bear the burden of *persuasion* at trial, that party must support its motion with credible evidence using any of the materials specified in Rule 56(c) that would entitle it to a directed verdict if not controverted at trial. Ibid. Such an affirmative showing shifts the burden of production to the party opposing the motion and requires that party either to produce evidentiary materials that demonstrate the existence of a "genuine issue" for trial or to submit an affidavit requesting additional time for discovery. Fed. Rules Civ. Proc. 56(e), (f).

If the burden of persuasion at trial would be on the nonmoving party, the party moving for summary judgment may satisfy Rule 56's burden of production in either of two ways. First, the moving party may submit affirmative evidence that negates an essential element of the nonmoving party's claim. Second, the moving party may demonstrate to the court that the nonmoving party's evidence is insufficient to establish an essential element of the nonmoving party's claim. If the nonmoving party cannot muster sufficient evidence to make out its claim, a trial would be useless and the moving party is entitled to summary judgment as a matter of law.

Where the moving party adopts this second option and seeks summary judgment on the ground that the nonmoving party — who will bear the burden of persuasion at trial — has no evidence, the mechanics of discharging Rule 56's burden of production are somewhat trickier. Plainly, a conclusory assertion that the nonmoving party has no evidence is insufficient. See ante (WHITE, J., concurring). Such a "burden" of production is no burden at all and would simply permit summary judgment procedure to be converted into a tool for harassment. Rather, as the Court confirms, a party who moves for summary judgment on the ground that the nonmoving party has no evidence must affirmatively show the absence of evidence in the record. This may require the moving party to depose the nonmoving party's witnesses or to establish the inadequacy of documentary evidence. If there is literally no evidence in the record, the moving party may demonstrate this by reviewing for the court the admissions, interrogatories, and other exchanges between the parties that are in the record. Either way, however, the moving party must affirmatively demonstrate that there is no evidence in the record to support a judgment for the nonmoving party.

---

must consider all papers of record as well as any materials prepared for the motion. As explained by the Court of Appeals for the Third Circuit in In re Japanese Electronic Products Antitrust Litigation, 723 F.2d 238 (1983), rev'd on other grounds sub nom. Matsushita Electric Industrial Co. v. Zenith Radio Corp., 475 U.S. 574 (1986), "[i]f . . . there is any evidence in the record from any source from which a reasonable inference in the [nonmoving party's] favor may be drawn, the moving party simply cannot obtain a summary judgment . . . ." 723 F.2d, at 258.

If the moving party has not fully discharged this initial burden of production, its motion for summary judgment must be denied, and the court need not consider whether the moving party has met its ultimate burden of persuasion. Accordingly, the nonmoving party may defeat a motion for summary judgment that asserts that the nonmoving party has no evidence by calling the court's attention to supporting evidence already in the record that was overlooked or ignored by the moving party. In that event, the moving party must respond by making an attempt to demonstrate the inadequacy of this evidence, for it is only by attacking all the record evidence allegedly supporting the nonmoving party that a party seeking summary judgment satisfies Rule 56's burden of production.[3] Thus, if the record disclosed that the moving party had overlooked a witness who would provide relevant testimony for the nonmoving party at trial, the court could not find that the moving party had discharged its initial burden of production unless the moving party sought to demonstrate the inadequacy of this witness' testimony. Absent such a demonstration, summary judgment would have to be denied on the ground that the moving party had failed to meet its burden of production under Rule 56.

The result in *Adickes v. S. H. Kress & Co., supra,* is fully consistent with these principles. * * *

The opinion in *Adickes* has sometimes been read to hold that summary judgment was inappropriate because the respondent had not submitted affirmative evidence to negate the possibility that there was a policeman in the store. The Court of Appeals apparently read *Adickes* this way and therefore required Celotex to submit evidence establishing that plaintiff's decedent had not been exposed to Celotex asbestos. I agree with the Court that this reading of *Adickes* was erroneous and that Celotex could seek summary judgment on the ground that plaintiff could not prove exposure to Celotex asbestos at trial. However, Celotex was still required to satisfy its initial burden of production.

II

I do not read the Court's opinion to say anything inconsistent with or different than the preceding discussion. My disagreement with the Court concerns the application of these principles to the facts of this case.

Defendant Celotex sought summary judgment on the ground that plaintiff had "failed to produce" any evidence that her decedent had ever been exposed to Celotex asbestos. Celotex supported this motion with a two-page "Statement of Material Facts as to Which There is No Genuine Issue" and a three-page "Memorandum of Points and Authorities" which asserted that the plaintiff had failed to identify any evidence in responding to two sets of interrogatories

---

[3] Once the moving party has attacked whatever record evidence — if any — the nonmoving party purports to rely upon, the burden of production shifts to the nonmoving party, who must either (1) rehabilitate the evidence attacked in the moving party's papers, (2) produce additional evidence showing the existence of a genuine issue for trial as provided in Rule 56(e), or (3) submit an affidavit explaining why further discovery is necessary as provided in Rule 56(f). Summary judgment should be granted if the nonmoving party fails to respond in one or more of these ways, or if, after the nonmoving party responds, the court determines that the moving party has met its ultimate burden of persuading the court that there is no genuine issue of material fact for trial.

propounded by Celotex and that therefore the record was "totally devoid" of evidence to support plaintiff's claim.

Approximately three months earlier, Celotex had filed an essentially identical motion. Plaintiff responded to this earlier motion by producing three pieces of evidence which she claimed "[a]t the very least . . . demonstrate that there is a genuine factual dispute for trial,": (1) a letter from an insurance representative of another defendant describing asbestos products to which plaintiff's decedent had been exposed; (2) a letter from T. R. Hoff, a former supervisor of decedent, describing asbestos products to which decedent had been exposed; and (3) a copy of decedent's deposition from earlier workmen's compensation proceedings. Plaintiff also apparently indicated at that time that she intended to call Mr. Hoff as a witness at trial.

Celotex subsequently withdrew its first motion for summary judgment. However, as a result of this motion, when Celotex filed its second summary judgment motion, the record did contain evidence — including at least one witness — supporting plaintiff's claim. Indeed, counsel for Celotex admitted to this Court at oral argument that Celotex was aware of this evidence and of plaintiff's intention to call Mr. Hoff as a witness at trial when the second summary judgment motion was filed. Moreover, plaintiff's response to Celotex' second motion pointed to this evidence — noting that it had already been provided to counsel for Celotex in connection with the first motion — and argued that Celotex had failed to "meet its burden of proving that there is no genuine factual dispute for trial."

On these facts, there is simply no question that Celotex failed to discharge its initial burden of production. Having chosen to base its motion on the argument that there was no evidence in the record to support plaintiff's claim, Celotex was not free to ignore supporting evidence that the record clearly contained. Rather, Celotex was required, as an initial matter, to attack the adequacy of this evidence. Celotex' failure to fulfill this simple requirement constituted a failure to discharge its initial burden of production under Rule 56, and thereby rendered summary judgment improper.

This case is indistinguishable from *Adickes*. Here, as there, the defendant moved for summary judgment on the ground that the record contained no evidence to support an essential element of the plaintiff's claim. Here, as there, the plaintiff responded by drawing the court's attention to evidence that was already in the record and that had been ignored by the moving party. Consequently, here, as there, summary judgment should be denied on the ground that the moving party failed to satisfy its initial burden of production.

JUSTICE STEVENS, dissenting. [Omitted.]

NOTES AND PROBLEMS FOR DISCUSSION

1. State the factual issue involved in the summary judgment motions in *Adickes* and in *Celotex*. Who would have had the burden of production on those issues at trial in each of those cases?

2.   No purpose is served by trying to resolve here whether *Celotex* overruled or simply distinguished *Adickes*, but you should be able to make the argument one way or the other. Also, make sure you understand what the fight is about: (a) What showing would Celotex have had to make on the issue you identified above if the *Celotex* Court followed *Adickes* (and did it make such a showing); and (b) What showing would Kress have had to make on the issue you identified above if the *Adickes* Court followed *Celotex* (and did it make such a showing)? Does anything in the latest version of Rule 56 suggest there would be a different outcome in either *Adickes* or *Celotex*?

3.   In Nissan Fire & Marine Ins. Co. v. Fritz Companies, Inc., 210 F.3d 1099, 1103-04 (9th Cir. 1999), Judge (former Professor) Fletcher sought to reconcile *Celotex* and *Adickes* as follows:

> We believe that the perceived tension * * * may be explained by the fact that the cases focused on different questions. The central question in *Adickes* was whether the moving party had carried its initial burden of production by producing affirmative evidence negating an essential element of the non-moving party's claim. The central question in *Celotex* was whether the moving party had carried its initial burden of production by showing that the nonmoving party did not have enough evidence to carry its ultimate burden of persuasion at trial. In other words, *Adickes* and *Celotex* dealt with the two different methods by which a moving party can carry its initial burden of production.

Judge Fletcher then explained that the summary judgment issue in *Adickes* was whether there was state action in the form of some agreement or understanding between Kress and the local police. And Kress had not adequately negated this possibility because Kress did not submit an affidavit of the employees involved, and the affidavits of the police officers did not negate their presence in the store and possible communications of disapproval to a Kress employee. A possible response to Judge Fletcher is that Kress's papers (post-*Celotex*) could be read to suggest that Adickes did not have enough evidence as well, thus putting the burden on her to show that she had some.

4.   Suppose that Harrison Corp. contracted to ship a large machine through Fortier, a freight forwarder, on Titan Airlines. The machine was heavily damaged in shipment. Under applicable law, Harrison Corp. could not assert a claim against Fortier or Titan unless "written notice of the damage is dispatched within seven days of the receipt of the damaged goods." Fortier and Titan both moved for summary judgment on the ground of lack of timely notice. Fortier's motion included an affidavit of its export manager that "Fortier did not receive written notice of the loss within the seven day period." Titan produced affidavits of two employees that "The first notice of loss received by Titan was in a letter dated March 12, 2007, which was more than two years after the loss." What result?

5.   It is not clear how much support, if any, the movant for summary judgment who does not have the burden of production at trial must offer in order to satisfy the reduced "burden" under *Celotex*. For example, may it simply say that the other side has no evidence, or must it offer some evidence to support its version, or "summarize" the available evidence (e.g., from discovery)? See Rule 56(c)(1)(B) (as amended in 2010) (indicating that a party may support its assertion that a fact cannot be genuinely disputed by "showing that the materials [in the record] cited do not establish the . . . presence of a genuine dispute, or that an adverse party cannot produce admissible evidence to support the fact"). In the real world, it probably doesn't make that much difference — a movant for summary judgment doesn't try to figure out how *little* support it can get away with, but rather, tries to produce as much support for its position as possible (whether affirmatively in support of its own case, or negatively to defeat what appears to be the nonmovant's case).

6. Consider the sources of information which will be presented to the court on the motion for summary judgment. To start, make sure you understand that summary judgment does not involve live testimony at a live trial. Instead, both the movant and the nonmovant use various forms of information — affidavits, documents, depositions, answers to interrogatories, etc. However, to be a realistic predictor of the trial, the support for and opposition to summary judgment must reflect what will ultimately be admissible at trial. Rule 56(c)(1)-(4) deals with these issues.

7. On remand, the court of appeals read the *Celotex* decision to say that Celotex had satisfied whatever burden it had to show a basis for summary judgment, and that the burden shifted to Mrs. Catrett to show that there was a genuine issue for trial on the question of exposure to asbestos. Recall that she had tried to do so primarily on the basis of the deposition transcript, the insurance company letter, and the letter from a former supervisor of the decedent. The court of appeals ruled that the deposition transcript and insurance company letter were hearsay and would be inadmissable at trial.[*] Should this mean that they cannot be considered on summary judgment? As to the letter from the supervisor, there was a sharp split. Judge Kenneth Starr (later, an Independent Counsel) held that the letter was sufficient because it predicted testimony that would be available at trial. Judge Robert Bork (not, later, a Supreme Court Justice) dissented on the ground that the letter was inadmissible hearsay and did not establish exposure. Based on this letter and certain other items, the court of appeals held Mrs. Catrett was able to avoid summary judgment.

8. The Court in *Celotex* reinforces the notion that summary judgment normally will come after discovery. But, after how much? What about a party whose strategy is to wait until the last minute before doing discovery?

9. On the same day that *Celotex* was decided, the Court also decided ANDERSON v. LIBERTY LOBBY, INC., 477 U.S. 242, 91 L.Ed.2d 202, 106 S.Ct. 2505 (1986). There it concluded that in a summary judgment motion in a defamation case the district court was obliged to factor-in the relevant burden of persuasion in determining whether the case was trial worthy. Under the Supreme Court's First Amendment precedents involving public figure

---

[*] It might be supposed that, pursuant to Rule 32(a)(4)(A) Catrett's deposition should have been admissible since he was deceased. However, the deposition had been taken in a worker compensation proceeding, and Celotex had not been represented in that matter.

defamation, there would have to be clear and convincing evidence that the defaming party knew that its statements were false, or were made with reckless disregard of their truth or falsity. Therefore, only if no rational factfinder could find, by clear and convincing evidence (1) knowledge of falsity or (2) reckless disregard, would summary judgment be proper. An analogous standard exists in criminal cases, in which the prosecution's case will not be allowed to go to the jury (or a guilty verdict will be thrown out) when there is insufficient evidence for a factfinder to find guilt beyond a reasonable doubt. See Jackson v. Virginia, 443 U.S. 307, 318, 99 S.Ct. 2781, 2789, 61 L.Ed.2d 560 (1979). Of course, in the criminal setting, jury rationality is a one-way street, because even if there is no room for reasonable doubt as to defendant's guilt, a case will still go to the jury, and the jury may still acquit.

10. In SCOTT v. HARRIS, 550 U.S. 372, 127 S.Ct. 1769, 167 L.Ed.2d 686 (2007), the plaintiff brought a civil rights suit against a police officer for severe injuries that the plaintiff received as a consequence of a high speed chase. The chase ended when the defendant officer applied his front bumper to the rear of the plaintiff's car in an effort to end a 10-mile high speed chase on public highways. As a consequence of this maneuver, the plaintiff lost control of his car, ran off the road, down an embankment, and crashed. The plaintiff alleged that the officer used excessive force under the circumstances. Under the relevant law, force is considered excessive, and a violation of the Fourth Amendment of the Constitution, if it is "objectively unreasonable" — i.e., a reasonable officer under the circumstances would not have used such force. "Objective reasonableness" is a question of law. But the underlying facts that plug into the objective reasonableness inquiry are often in dispute, and they can ordinarily present a question for the factfinder. As part of his argument that the officer acted unreasonably, the plaintiff was prepared to testify that there was little if any actual threat to other motorists or pedestrians at the time the officer hit the plaintiff's car. But as the Supreme Court put it, a videotape of the chase told another story. And it was the events as depicted in the videotape, not as depicted in the plaintiff's version, that should be the touchstone for measuring whether the officer's actions were reasonable:

> The first step in assessing the constitutionality of [Deputy] Scott's actions is to determine the relevant facts. As this case was decided on summary judgment, there have not yet been factual findings by a judge or jury, and respondent's version of events (unsurprisingly) differs substantially from Scott's version. When things are in such a posture, courts are required to view the facts and draw reasonable inferences "in the light most favorable to the party opposing the [summary judgment] motion." United States v. Diebold, Inc., 369 U.S. 654, 655 (1962) (per curiam); * * * [T]his usually means adopting (as the Court of Appeals did here) the plaintiff's version of the facts.

> There is, however, an added wrinkle in this case: existence in the record of a videotape capturing the events in question. There are no allegations or indications that this videotape was doctored or altered in any way, nor any contention that what it depicts differs from what actually happened. The videotape quite clearly contradicts the version of the story

told by respondent and adopted by the Court of Appeals.[5] For example, the Court of Appeals adopted respondent's assertions that, during the chase, "there was little, if any, actual threat to pedestrians or other motorists, as the roads were mostly empty and [respondent] remained in control of his vehicle." Indeed, reading the lower court's opinion, one gets the impression that respondent, rather than fleeing from police, was attempting to pass his driving test: "Taking the facts from the non-movant's viewpoint, [respondent] remained in control of his vehicle, slowed for turns and intersections, and typically used his indicators for turns. He did not run any motorists off the road. Nor was he a threat to pedestrians in the shopping center parking lot, which was free from pedestrian and vehicular traffic as the center was closed. Significantly, by the time the parties were back on the highway and Scott rammed [respondent], the motorway had been cleared of motorists and pedestrians allegedly because of police blockades of the nearby intersections."

The videotape tells quite a different story. There we see respondent's vehicle racing down narrow, two-lane roads in the dead of night at speeds that are shockingly fast. We see it swerve around more than a dozen other cars, cross the double-yellow line, and force cars traveling in both directions to their respective shoulders to avoid being hit.[6] We see it run multiple red lights and travel for considerable periods of time in the occasional center left-turn-only lane, chased by numerous police cars forced to engage in the same hazardous maneuvers just to keep up. Far from being the cautious and controlled driver the lower court depicts, what we see on the video more closely resembles a Hollywood-style car chase of the most frightening sort, placing police officers and innocent bystanders alike at great risk of serious injury.[7]

At the summary judgment stage, facts must be viewed in the light most favorable to the nonmoving party only if there is a "genuine" dispute as to those facts. Fed. Rule Civ. Proc. 56(c). As we have emphasized,

---

[5] [The dissent] suggests that our reaction to the videotape is somehow idiosyncratic, and seems to believe we are misrepresenting its contents. * * * We are happy to allow the videotape to speak for itself. [To see the video, go to the URL at the end of this excerpt. — eds.]

[6] [The dissent] hypothesizes that these cars "had already pulled to the side of the road or were driving along the shoulder because they heard the police sirens or saw the flashing lights," so that "[a] jury could certainly conclude that those motorists were exposed to no greater risk than persons who take the same action in response to a speeding ambulance." It is not our experience that ambulances and fire engines careen down two-lane roads at 85-plus miles per hour, with an unmarked scout car out in front of them. The risk they pose to the public is vastly less than what respondent created here. But even if that were not so, it would in no way lead to the conclusion that it was unreasonable to eliminate the threat to life that respondent posed. Society accepts the risk of speeding ambulances and fire engines in order to save life and property; it need not (and assuredly does not) accept a similar risk posed by a reckless motorist fleeing the police.

[7] This is not to say that each and every factual statement made by the Court of Appeals is inaccurate. For example, the videotape validates the court's statement that when Scott rammed respondent's vehicle it was not threatening any other vehicles or pedestrians. (Undoubtedly Scott waited for the road to be clear before executing his maneuver.)

"when the moving party has carried its burden under Rule 56(c), its opponent must do more than simply show that there is some metaphysical doubt as to the material facts * * * . Where the record taken as a whole could not lead a rational trier of fact to find for the nonmoving party, there is no 'genuine issue for trial.'" Matsushita Elec. Industrial Co. v. Zenith Radio Corp., 475 U.S. 574, 586-587 (1986) (footnote omitted). "The mere existence of some alleged factual dispute between the parties will not defeat an otherwise properly supported motion for summary judgment; the requirement is that there be no genuine issue of material fact." Anderson v. Liberty Lobby, Inc., 477 U.S. 242, 247-248 (1986). When opposing parties tell two different stories, one of which is blatantly contradicted by the record, so that no reasonable jury could believe it, a court should not adopt that version of the facts for purposes of ruling on a motion for summary judgment.

That was the case here with regard to the factual issue whether respondent was driving in such fashion as to endanger human life. Respondent's version of events is so utterly discredited by the record that no reasonable jury could have believed him. The Court of Appeals should not have relied on such visible fiction; it should have viewed the facts in the light depicted by the videotape.

Judging the matter on that basis, we think it is quite clear that Deputy Scott did not violate the Fourth Amendment.[8] * * *

The car chase that respondent initiated in this case posed a substantial and immediate risk of serious physical injury to others; no reasonable jury could conclude otherwise. Scott's attempt to terminate the chase by forcing respondent off the road was reasonable, and Scott is entitled to summary judgment. The Court of Appeals' decision to the contrary is reversed.

Justice Stevens filed a dissent in which he suggested that those of his generation who learned to drive on two-lane roads (Justice Stevens was born in 1920) might have viewed the video with far less alarm than did the majority. See http://www.supremecourtus.gov/opinions/video/scott_v_harris.html .

Was the Court right that this case was an appropriate one for summary judgment? Note that although the case was decided as one for summary judgment, a similar analysis would have been appropriate on the question whether to withdraw the case from the jury if the case had somehow proceeded to trial.

11. With *Scott v. Harris*, compare TOLAN v. COTTON, 572 U.S. ___, 134 S. Ct. 1861, 188 L.Ed.2d. 895 (2014) (per curiam), in which the Supreme Court

---

[8] [The dissent] incorrectly declares this to be "a question of fact best reserved for a jury," and complains we are "usurping the jury's factfinding function." At the summary judgment stage, however, once we have determined the relevant set of facts and drawn all inferences in favor of the nonmoving party to the extent supportable by the record, see Part III-A, supra, the reasonableness of Scott's actions * * * is a pure question of law.

vacated an order affirming a grant of summary judgment in an excessive force case, because the court of appeals failed to properly view the evidence presented in the light most favorable to the plaintiff. Plaintiff (Tolan) and his cousin were stopped early one morning in front of plaintiff's home by a police officer (Edwards) on suspicion of possessing a stolen vehicle. Edwards suspected the vehicle had been stolen because a typographical error in his otherwise routine license-plate search returned a vehicle similar to Tolan's as stolen. After Tolan complied with the officer's request to lie face-down on the front porch, Tolan's mother appeared from inside the house and attempted to explain to Officer Edwards that the vehicle was indeed owned by the family. At that point, Sergeant Cotton arrived on the scene.

The parties dispute what happened next. Plaintiff's mother and cousin stated that Cotton grabbed her arm and slammed her into the garage, while Cotton claims that he was escorting her to the garage. The parties agree that Tolan responded "[G]et your [expletive] hands off of my mom." But the tone of the plaintiff's statement was disputed by the parties. At that point, the Sergeant Cotton fired three shots at Tolan, one of which entered Tolan's chest, collapsing his right lung and piercing his liver. It was disputed whether Cotton gave a warning before firing the shots. In his deposition, Cotton claimed that he thought that Tolan was in the process of standing up, causing him to fear for his safety, while Tolan stated that he was on his knees when he was shot.

Following discovery, the trial court granted Cotton's motion for summary judgment, holding that the use of force was not unreasonable under the circumstances and thus did not violate the Fourth Amendment. The Fifth Circuit affirmed on different grounds, holding that summary judgment was appropriate because, even if the Fourth Amendment was violated, the defendant was entitled to qualified immunity.

To adjudicate questions of qualified immunity at summary judgment, courts use a two-prong analysis. The first prong asks whether the facts, taken in the light most favorable to the plaintiff asserting the injury, show the officer's conduct violated a federal right. The second prong asks whether the right in question was clearly established at the time of the violation. The Fifth Circuit determined that summary judgment was appropriate because Sargent Cotton "did not violate a clearly established right." The court of appeals found that "it was clearly established that an officer had the right to use deadly force if the officer harbored an objective and reasonable belief that a suspect presented an immediate threat to his safety." It then held that summary judgment was appropriate because a reasonable officer could believe that the plaintiff presented an immediate threat to the officer's safety.

In drawing its conclusion, the Fifth Circuit relied on several inferences of fact, many of which were disputed by the plaintiff. It concluded that:

> [T]he front porch had been "dimly-lit"; Tolan's mother had "refused orders to remain quiet and calm"; and Tolan's words had amounted to a "verbal threat" to Officer Cotton. Further, [it] concluded that "Tolan was moving to intervene in" Cotton's handling of his mother and . . . that Cotton therefore could reasonably have feared for his life.

The Supreme Court, however, concluded that the Fifth Circuit failed to apply the facts in the manner most favorable to the plaintiff. At the summary judgment phase, said the Court, a "judge's function . . . is not to weight the evidence and determine the truth of the matter but to determine whether there is a genuine issue [of fact] for trial."

The Court went on to demonstrate that four of the factual findings used by the court of appeals in granting summary judgment were not made in the manner most favorable to the plaintiff. First, the lower court relied on the conclusion that the porch was "dimly-lit." While Sergeant Cotton did include in his statement that the porch was "fairly dark" and lit only by a "decorative" glass lamp, the plaintiff's father had testified that the light was not "more decorative than illuminating" and further testified that there were two floodlights on the driveway at the time of the incident. Second, the lower court wrongly concluded that the plaintiff's mother "refused orders to remain quiet and clam" despite her testimony that she was "neither aggravated nor agitated." Third, the lower court improperly drew the conclusion that Tolan was "shouting . . . and verbally threatening the officer" given that Tolan stated that he was not screaming. The Court further found that a reasonable jury could infer "that his words, in context, did not amount to a statement of intent to inflict harm" and that "[a] jury could conclude that a reasonable officer would have heard Tolan's words not as a threat, but as a son's plea not to continue any assault of his mother." Finally, the Court held that the Fifth Circuit's conclusion that the plaintiff was moving towards Cotton was directly contradicted by the plaintiff's testimony that he was shot while on his knees.

> Considered together, the facts lead to the inescapable conclusion that the court below credited the evidence of the party seeking summary judgment and failed to properly acknowledge key evidence offered by the party opposing that motion.
>
>   * * *
>
> [T]he opinion below reflects a clear misapprehension of summary judgment standards in light of our precedents. . . . The witnesses on both sides come to this case with their own perceptions, recollections, and even potential biases. It is in part for that reason that genuine disputes are generally resolved by juries in our adversarial system. By weighing the evidence and reaching factual inferences contrary to Tolan's competent evidence, the court below neglected to adhere to the fundamental principle that at the summary judgment stage, reasonable inferences should be drawn in favor of the nonmoving party.

On remand, the Fifth Circuit was instructed to determine whether summary judgment for the defendant was proper when evaluated using factual inferences construed most favorably for the plaintiff.

3. THE NONMOVANT'S RESPONSE

Assume that the movant has succeeded in its post-*Celotex* showing that there is no genuine issue of material fact. At this point, what must the nonmovant show to be entitled to a trial and to withstand summary judgment?

A substantial number of summary judgment motions arise in cases involving employment discrimination — usually motions made by the defendant-employer. To understand the summary judgment motion, it is helpful briefly to outline the substantive law in this area. Assume a plaintiff sues for job discrimination (which may involve any term or condition of employment) on the basis of some prohibited trait (such as race, age, or gender). At the trial of such a case (1) the plaintiff will first have to establish a prima facie case of discrimination (i.e., put on evidence that gives rise to a presumption of discrimination); (2) then, the defendant must come forward with evidence of a legitimate, nondiscriminatory reason for its action (e.g., reduction in staff, incompetence, etc.); and (3) then, the plaintiff must show that the asserted reason was a pretext for the real reason — discrimination. The case below (a state-law based employment discrimination suit) involves a motion for summary judgment on (3), which is usually the heart of the issue at trial.[*]

Nidds v. Schindler Elevator Corp.

United States Court of Appeals, Ninth Circuit, 1996.

113 F.3d 912, cert. denied, 522 U.S. 950, 118 S.Ct. 369, 139 L.Ed.2d 287.

SNEED, CIRCUIT JUDGE.

Raymond Vincent Nidds appeals the grant of summary judgment in favor of his former employer, Schindler Elevator Corp. ("Schindler"), on his California Fair Employment and Housing Act ("FEHA") discrimination and retaliation claims. Federal jurisdiction is based on the parties' diversity of citizenship. Nidds also contests the district court's refusal to continue discovery before ruling on Schindler's summary judgment motion. We have jurisdiction under 28 U.S.C. §1291, and we affirm.

I

BACKGROUND OF THE DISPUTE

Nidds was a highly experienced, 54-year-old elevator service mechanic when he was hired by Schindler on June 13, 1988, and assigned to a downtown San Francisco service route. He was well-liked by his customers and his employer. Sometime in 1989 or 1990, Schindler's District Service Supervisor, Darrel Graham, allegedly told another service mechanic that he intended to get rid of all the "old timers" because they would not "kiss my ass." On October 5, 1990, Nidds and two other service mechanics were laid off. Graham wrote a

---

[*] Note that the Supreme Court has focused on the sort of showing necessary under (3) in connection with an employee's effort to avoid judgment as a matter of law at trial in an age discrimination suit brought in federal court. Reeves v. Sanderson Plumbing Prods., Inc., 530 U.S. 133, 120 S.Ct. 2097, 147 L.Ed.2d 105 (2000), discussed in Chapter 11.

favorable letter of recommendation for Nidds, and assured him that he would be considered for reemployment should business pick up. Shortly thereafter, his route was assigned at least in substantial part to 25-year-old Greg Cardenas, a former "helper" (an apprentice) employed by Schindler since 1985, who had passed his mechanic's test only 30 days earlier.

When Nidds learned that his route had been assumed by Cardenas, he filed an age discrimination complaint with the California Department of Fair Employment and Housing ("DFEH") on December 7, 1990. The investigation by DFEH revealed that Schindler laid off a total of eleven employees during 1990 due to a purported downturn in business. Sixty-four percent of those employees were over 40 years old. Asked how it selected employees for layoff, Schindler initially responded that seniority was the basis, and later, that it looked at a combination of factors, including seniority, job performance, special expertise, and competence. Schindler explained that Nidds was overall a very good employee but that he was less proficient on the modern "Solid State" equipment than other mechanics. As to Nidds' claim that there was no downturn in work in the company's service arm, Schindler explained that the downturn was in the construction arm, and that its practice was to shift its best employees from construction to service to avoid losing them to competitors, and to lay off employees from service to compensate. In November 1991, the DFEH informed Nidds that it would not pursue his claim.

Earlier Schindler had made two offers to rehire Nidds, the first for a route in Fresno, the second for an Oakland route; Nidds rejected the first but accepted the latter in January 1991. Schindler soon began receiving complaints from the manager of 1800 Harrison, a building that accounted for 60% of the revenues on the Oakland route. Schindler also allegedly received complaints from its troubleshooters, who said that Nidds needed their help more than did other mechanics.

In March 1992, Nidds was purportedly asked by a supervisor whether he had dropped his DFEH complaint, to which he replied that he had not. Later that month, Nidds' attorney informed Schindler of Nidds' intention to sue the company for age discrimination. In April 1992, Schindler removed Nidds from the Oakland route and assigned him to the restoration department. Although his compensation was unaffected, Nidds characterizes this transfer as a demotion. In response, Nidds filed a second complaint, charging age discrimination and retaliation, with the DFEH on June 10, 1992.

Schindler transferred Nidds again in June 1992, from the restoration department to a service route that included the Geneva Towers, an allegedly high-crime housing complex in San Francisco. On June 26, Nidds left Geneva Towers in the middle of the day after learning of riots at nearby Woodrow Wilson High School. Although he returned later in the afternoon to repair two malfunctioning elevators, his behavior annoyed Geneva Towers' management. A subsequent cascade of meetings and correspondence between Geneva Towers and Schindler resulted in a decision to remove Nidds from the route. Nidds, who went on vacation from July 2 to July 22, learned of this decision on his return. Shortly thereafter, on July 28, he was laid off for the second and final time.

Nidds filed his employment discrimination and retaliation complaint in California Superior Court on May 5, 1992. In June, Schindler removed the action to federal court based on the parties' diversity of citizenship. Following extensive discovery by Nidds' attorney and several discovery disputes during 1992 and 1993, the magistrate set a discovery cutoff date of November 1, 1993. On July 23, however, Schindler proceeded to move for summary judgment. Nidds requested a continuance so that he could depose several of Schindler's declarants and obtain additional documents. The district court denied the continuance in August, but deferred ruling on the summary judgment motion to allow Nidds to take three more depositions and to allow time for supplemental briefing. The depositions were never taken, and on November 17, 1994, the district court granted Schindler's motion for summary judgment on all of Nidds' claims. Nidds timely appealed.

II

THE AGE DISCRIMINATION CLAIM

We review the district court's grant of summary judgment on both the age discrimination and retaliation claims de novo. We must decide whether there is a "genuine issue as to any material fact." Fed. R. Civ. P. 56(c). [Again, the basic summary judgment standard is now set out at Rule 56(a), and is worded somewhat differently. –eds.] The criteria of "genuineness" and "materiality" are distinct requirements. Anderson v. Liberty Lobby, Inc., 477 U.S. 242, 248, 91 L.Ed. 2d 202, 106 S.Ct. 2505 (1986). The requirement that an issue be "genuine" relates to the quantum of evidence the plaintiff must produce to defeat the defendant's motion for summary judgment. There must be sufficient evidence "that a reasonable jury could return a verdict for the nonmoving party." Id. at 248. "If the evidence is merely colorable, or is not significantly probative, summary judgment may be granted." Id. at 249-50.

"As to materiality, the substantive law will identify which facts are material." Id. at 248. Nidds' age discrimination claim, which relates to his October 1990 layoff, is based on the California Fair Employment and Housing Act ("FEHA"). FEHA reads in relevant part: "It is an unlawful employment practice for an employer to refuse to hire or employ, or to discharge, dismiss, reduce, suspend, or demote, any individual over the age of 40 on the ground of age, except in cases where the law compels or provides for such action." Cal. Gov't Code §12941. California courts interpreting FEHA often look to federal cases interpreting the Age Discrimination in Employment Act ("ADEA"), 29 U.S.C. §§621 et seq., and Title VII of the Civil Rights Act, 42 U.S.C. §§2000e et seq. See Stephens v. Coldwell Banker Commercial Group, Inc., 199 Cal. App. 3d 1394, 245 Cal. Rptr. 606, 609 (App. 1988). Therefore, we too rely on such cases where helpful.

An age discrimination case alleging disparate treatment, such as this one, involves shifting burdens of proof as follows:

> [A] plaintiff must first establish a prima facie case of discrimination. If the plaintiff establishes a prima facie case, the burden then shifts to the defendant to articulate a legitimate nondiscriminatory reason for its employment decision. Then, in order to prevail, the plaintiff must

demonstrate that the employer's alleged reason for the adverse employment decision is a pretext for another motive which is discriminatory.

Wallis v. J. R. Simplot Co., 26 F.3d 885, 889 (9th Cir. 1994). However, the burden of persuasion remains at all times with the plaintiff. *Washington v. Garrett*, 10 F.3d 1421, 1432 (9th Cir. 1994).

A. The Prima Facie Case Barrier

"In order to show a prima facie case of discrimination, 'a plaintiff must offer evidence that "give[s] rise to an inference of unlawful discrimination."'" That evidence may be either direct or circumstantial, and very little is required.

To establish a prima facie case of age discrimination through circumstantial evidence, the plaintiff must show that he was: (1) a member of a protected class [age 40-70]; (2) performing his job in a satisfactory manner; (3) discharged; and (4) replaced by a substantially younger employee with equal or inferior qualifications. *Wallis*, 26 F.2d at 891 (quoting Rose v. Wells Fargo & Co., 902 F.2d 1417, 1421 (9th Cir. 1990)).

The fourth element, however, has been treated with some flexibility: "We have held that the failure to prove replacement by a younger employee is 'not necessarily fatal' to an age discrimination claim where the discharge results from a general reduction in the work force due to business conditions." *Rose*, 902 F.2d at 1421. Rather, courts "require instead that the plaintiff show through circumstantial, statistical, or direct evidence that the discharge occurred under circumstances giving rise to an inference of age discrimination." This inference "can be established by showing the employer had a continuing need for his skills and services in that his various duties were still being performed," *Wallis*, 26 F.3d at 891 (internal quotation omitted), or by showing "that others not in her protected class were treated more favorably."

The district court ignored the flexibility these cases require and erred in concluding that to establish a prima facie case, Nidds was required to show that he was at least as qualified as his replacement. The court also erred by counting against Nidds the fact that he was not directly replaced by the younger employee, Cardenas. Under *Rose*, *Wallis*, and *Washington*, it is enough that Nidds' duties were substantially transferred to Cardenas.

In summary, Nidds has shown that he was discharged; that he was performing satisfactorily; and that his duties continued to be performed by a substantially younger individual. Nidds therefore cleared the prima facie case barrier and established "a presumption that the employer unlawfully discriminated against the employee." St. Mary's Honor Ctr. v. Hicks, 509 U.S. 502, 506, 125 L.Ed. 2d 407, 113 S.Ct. 2742 (1993) (internal quotation omitted).

B. Schindler's Burden

However, to rebut this presumption the employer must merely articulate a legitimate, nondiscriminatory reason for the action. Id. Once the employer meets this burden, the presumption of discrimination drops away. *St. Mary's*, 509 U.S. at 507.

Schindler met its burden by offering some evidence that a downturn in work required some layoffs, and that it used a combination of factors, including performance, technical qualifications, and seniority, in deciding whom to discharge. As a consequence, the burden returned to Nidds to show that Schindler's articulated reason was a pretext for discrimination.

C. Pretext

To satisfy that burden, and survive summary judgment, Nidds must produce enough evidence to allow a reasonable factfinder to conclude either: (a) that the alleged reason for Nidds' discharge was false, or (b) that the true reason for his discharge was a discriminatory one. *Warren*, 58 F.3d at 443 (stating that the plaintiff "must produce evidence of facts that either show a discriminatory motive or show that the [employer's] explanation for his rejection is not credible").[2]

Applying the law to the facts before us, we hold that Schindler was entitled to summary judgment, because the evidence Nidds has offered is not sufficiently probative that it would allow a reasonable factfinder to conclude either that the alleged reason for his discharge was false, or that the true reason for his discharge was a discriminatory one.

Nidds presents three distinct arguments that, he says, raise sufficient factual disputes that require his case to proceed to trial. First, he argues that Schindler's explanation for the initial layoff, a downturn in business, was false. Nidds asserts that there was no downturn in business. In support of this claim, Nidds adduces some evidence that Schindler's service business was doing quite well. But this evidence does not raise a genuine issue of material fact. Schindler explained that there was a downturn in construction business, not service business, and that it responded to the downturn in its construction business by moving employees from construction to service, and then laying off service employees. Nidds has failed to adduce any evidence that calls into question the veracity of Schindler's explanation.

Second, Nidds argues that summary judgment against his claims was improper because of Schindler's shifting explanations for the October 1990 layoff. These alone, he insists, are enough to raise a genuine issue as to its discriminatory motives. He cites *Washington*, 10 F.3d at 1434 ("We note that, in the ordinary case, such fundamentally different justifications for an employer's action would give rise to a genuine issue of fact with respect to pretext since they suggest the possibility that neither of the official reasons was the true reason"), and Lindahl v. Air France, 930 F.2d 1434, 1438-39 (9th Cir.

---

[2] At trial, Nidds must prove "*both* that the [employer's alleged] reason was false, *and* that discrimination was the real reason." *St. Mary's*, 509 U.S. at 515 (emphasis in original). However, if Nidds persuades the jury that the defendant's alleged reason is false, then "the factfinder's disbelief of the reasons put forward by the defendant . . . together with the elements of the prima facie case . . . will permit the trier of fact to infer the ultimate fact of intentional discrimination, and . . . no additional proof of discrimination is required." Id. at 511. Thus, to survive summary judgment, Nidds is not required to provide direct evidence of discriminatory intent as long as a reasonable factfinder could conclude — based on Nidds' prima facie case and the factfinder's disbelief of Schindler's reasons for discharge — that discrimination was the real reason for Nidds' discharge.

1991) (reasons for discharge not credible where they were vague, unsupported by the facts, and not articulated until the litigation commenced). However, the reasons given by Schindler are not incompatible, and therefore not properly described as "shifting reasons." "Lack of work" was the reason given for the layoffs in general, while Nidds' lack of seniority and poorer performance relative to other mechanics were the reasons given for his layoff specifically. Therefore, Nidds' evidence is insufficient to raise a genuine issue of fact as to whether Schindler's reasons for the layoff were pretextual.

Moreover, there is insufficient evidence to raise a genuine issue of fact as to whether the actual reason was a discriminatory one. Nidds cites the "old timers" comment allegedly made by Graham as evidence of a discriminatory motive. That comment, however, was very much like the comments in Nesbit v. Pepsico, Inc., 994 F.2d 703, 705 (9th Cir. 1993), which the court held did not support an inference of discriminatory motive. In *Nesbit*, the plaintiff's immediate supervisor commented to Nesbit that "we don't necessarily like gray hair." The court found that the "comment was uttered in an ambivalent manner and was not tied directly to Nesbit's termination," and upheld the grant of summary judgment in favor of the employer. Id.

Similarly, Graham's comment was ambiguous because it could refer as well to longtime employees or to employees who failed to follow directions as to employees over 40. Moreover, the comment was not tied directly to Nidds' layoff. Like the comment in *Nesbit*, therefore, it is weak evidence and not enough to create an inference of age discrimination.

Also distinguishable is Schnidrig v. Columbia Mach., Inc., 80 F.3d 1406, 1411 (9th Cir. 1996), cert. denied, 136 L.Ed. 2d 214, 117 S.Ct. 295 (1996), upon which Nidds relies. There, we reversed the grant of summary judgment in favor of the employer where the employee had alleged "that on three separate occasions, when he asked to be considered for president, he was told the Board wanted somebody younger for the job" and had submitted evidence to the same effect in the form of meeting notes and an affidavit of a coworker. Nidds' evidence, by contrast, is neither as direct nor as weighty. It is not enough to support an inference of age discrimination.

III

THE RETALIATION CLAIM

A. Prima Facie Case

In a retaliation case, the burden shifting scheme is much the same as that in an age discrimination case. A prima facie case requires the plaintiff to show "that he engaged in a protected activity, his employer subjected him to adverse employment action, and there is a causal link between the protected activity and the employer's action." Flait v. North Am. Watch Corp., 3 Cal. App. 4th 467, 4 Cal. Rptr. 2d 522, 528 (App. 1992).

Nidds' complaints to the DFEH were protected activity because California law specifically prohibits employers from taking adverse actions against employees as a result of their filing a complaint alleging FEHA violations. See Cal. Gov't Code §12940(f). Although we decline to view Nidds' transfer to the restoration department as an adverse employment action, his ultimate termination on July 28, 1992, certainly was.

Moreover, Nidds has submitted sufficient evidence to create an inference of a "causal link" between Nidds' complaints and his July 1992 layoff. The layoff occurred only four months after his supervisor allegedly asked him if he had dropped his first discrimination complaint (March 1992) and only one month after he filed his second complaint (June 10, 1992). The temporal proximity of events was sufficient to satisfy the third element of the prima facie case. See *Flait*, 4 Cal. Rptr. 2d at 529-30 (sufficient causal link where supervisor who terminated employee had made sexist comments to another employee and fired employee five months after a confrontation).

B. The Employer's Burden

Schindler, however, also met its burden of articulating a legitimate reason for the layoff. It was that the management of Geneva Towers requested that Nidds be removed from the route, and that Schindler had no other place for him. Thus, the deciding question again is whether Nidds has produced enough evidence from which a reasonable factfinder could conclude that Schindler's reason was a pretext for retaliatory termination. We hold that again Nidds has failed to make that showing.

C. Pretext

The crux of Nidds' argument is that Schindler encouraged the management of Geneva Towers to complain about Nidds so that Schindler would have a reason to terminate Nidds in retaliation for his filing his second age discrimination claim and intent to sue letter. For support, he cites the letter and testimony of Arthur Hutton, Geneva Towers' administrator, concerning an incident in which Nidds purportedly failed to respond to a service call.

In Hutton's letter to Ken Robinson of Schindler, dated July 21, 1992, he stated: "Pursuant to our conversation of today, we feel that it is in both our interest to relieve Mr. Ray Niddes [sic] from his duties at Geneva Towers Apartments. The environment seems to dictate whether he is able to perform his duties on a day-to-day basis." Hutton testified at his deposition that "I believe that I wrote that letter immediately — well, I believe that I spoke with Ken Robinson immediately after I became aware that the incident took place. Shortly after that, if my recollection serves me correctly, I proceeded to write the letter." Hutton testified further that "[Robinson] suggested that I write a letter expressing what we talked about over the phone."

Nidds argues that because he was on vacation from July 2 through July 21, this evidence shows that "another Schindler mechanic failed to respond to the Geneva Towers' service call. Then Robinson, seeking to find a pretext for Nidds' termination, asked Hutton to write a letter regarding Nidds' failure to service the route."

Nidds' proposed inference is not one that a reasonable factfinder could make. Hutton's own testimony indicates that he called Robinson and then wrote to him when he became aware of the incident, not when it actually happened. Moreover, the incident that prompted the call was clearly the June 26 incident when Nidds left Geneva Towers after hearing about a gang riot at the nearby high school: Hutton stated at deposition that "I do know that the information that I received indicated that Mr. Nidds didn't want to come out because he had heard that there had been violence, gang violence, during the course of that day." It is unlikely that the same incident recurred a month later with the same response from some other Schindler mechanic. Although the time lag between the June 26 incident and Hutton's phone call of about July 21 remains unexplained, the reasonable inference from Hutton's testimony is that he did not learn of the incident until the latter date.

Other evidence also supports Schindler's explanation that Geneva Towers was dissatisfied with Nidds' performance. Schindler employee Larry Scharfe stated in a declaration that "Mr. Gray [of Geneva Towers] expressed some concerns regarding Mr. Nidds leaving his job. He said that he and others in management at the apartment complex were not satisfied with the service or the attitude of the new service person, Mr. Nidds." Schindler employee Ken Robinson stated that "Mr. Gray said that he or someone else would set out their concerns regarding Mr. Nidds in writing and send them to Schindler." In a June 26, 1992, memo to Graham, Robinson explained that "At our June 25, 1992 meeting, Mr. Gray expressed his concern that Geneva Towers was merely a number on Mr. Nidds' route sheet. Mr. Gray told me that he was concerned that the level of service would decline now that Nidds had been assigned because Mr. Nidds did not care about Geneva Towers' problems."

In light of this evidence, neither Hutton's letter nor his testimony are sufficient to allow a reasonable factfinder to conclude that Schindler used Geneva Towers' concerns as a pretext to discharge Nidds. We therefore affirm summary judgment on this claim as well.

IV

THE RULE 56(f) MOTION

"We review a district court's denial of a [Fed. R. Civ. P. 56(f)] request for further discovery by a party opposing summary judgment for abuse of discretion." Conkle v. Jeong, 73 F.3d 909, 914 (9th Cir. 1995), cert. denied, 117 S.Ct. 56, 136 L.Ed.2d 19 (1996). [The relevant provision is now set out at Rule 56(e).—eds.] The burden is on the party seeking additional discovery to proffer sufficient facts to show that the evidence sought exists, id., and that it would prevent summary judgment. Qualls v. Blue Cross of California, Inc., 22 F.3d 839, 844 (9th Cir. 1994). "Moreover, the district court does not abuse its discretion by denying further discovery if the movant has failed diligently to pursue discovery in the past." Conkle, 73 F.3d at 914 (internal quotation omitted).

A problem might exist had the district court denied Nidds' motion for a continuance where Nidds had outstanding discovery requests and November, the cutoff date for discovery, was still several months away. Here, however, the court postponed ruling on the summary judgment motion for over a year to give Nidds time to take three depositions. Yet, Nidds never took the depositions. This lack of diligence precludes a finding that the district court abused its discretion. See, e.g., Hauser v. Farrell, 14 F.3d 1338, 1340-41 (9th Cir. 1994) (denial of Rule 56(f) motion proper in light of failure to depose witness within

27 months of filing suit); Mackey v. Pioneer Nat'l Bank, 867 F.2d 520, 524 (9th Cir. 1989) (failure to take advantage of additional month of discovery granted by district court showed lack of diligence).

V

CONCLUSION

Because Nidds' evidence of discrimination and retaliation is insufficient, we affirm the grant of summary judgment in favor of Schindler. We also hold that the district court did not abuse its discretion in denying Nidds' motion for a continuance of the summary judgment hearing.

Affirmed.

Noonan, Circuit Judge, dissenting.

We all agree that the district court erred in finding that Nidds had not made a prima facie case. He had, and the burden shifted to Schindler to produce a nonpretextual nondiscriminatory reason for his discharge. What we disagree about is whether Nidds produced enough evidence from which a reasonable juror could have inferred that Schindler's reason was pretextual and that in fact it laid him off because of his age.

Nidds had two witnesses (not one, as the court appears to assume) whose evidence was that Graham, the district superintendent, wanted to get rid of the "Old Timers." The court in its opinion suggests that Graham's comment was "ambiguous." There was not much ambiguity about it. That the Old Timers would not kowtow to Graham was connected by him to their length of service; and length of service in this industry meant being over forty. In his comment to Julia Stuart, Schindler's Assistant Field Supervisor, Graham said that he wanted to replace the Old Timers with "new blood" — another distinct reference to age. Even if I agreed with the court that the remark was ambiguous, a reasonable juror could resolve whatever ambiguity there is by an inference in Nidds' favor. We're operating under circuit law which is unequivocal in setting "a high standard for the granting of summary judgment in employment discrimination cases." Schnidrig v. Columbia Mach., Inc., 80 F.3d 1406, 1410 (9th Cir. 1996), cert. denied, 136 L.Ed. 2d 214, 117 S.Ct. 295 (1996). The standard should not unaccountedly be lowered.

Nidds' evidence of discriminatory intent is properly taken into account with Schindler's shifting explanation of why it laid him off. Schindler said, first, that it was seniority and stuck to that in a proceeding before the DFEH; finally, when pressed, a year after the layoff Schindler said Nidds was a poor performer on the newer Solid State equipment. Yet when Schindler took Nidds back only four months later, it assigned him to a service route in Oakland which had over twice as many units of Solid State equipment as his old route, and Graham said that Nidds was "the most qualified person at that time." A reasonable jury could easily infer that Schindler was cloaking the discrimination already expressed by Graham with these made-up stories of why the company laid off this old and experienced and efficient employee whom Graham had rated as "excellent."

As to retaliation, it is Nidds' evidence that assignment to Geneva Towers was the company's not very nice and not very subtle way of dumping employees it wanted to punish; and it was the convenient prelude to pushing him out altogether. Schindler put him there shortly after Schindler had pointedly inquired about his discrimination filing before the DFEH. Within two months, Nidds was fired from this route as a result of a letter which in so many words indicates that the request of Geneva Towers to remove Nidds was coordinated with Schindler management. The opinion of the court turns somersaults trying to explain why Nidds' evidence on this point should not be believed. The opinion includes a pure speculation as to whether two incidents of gang violence in a gang-infested neighborhood could occur within a month. It's good jury reasoning. It's highly inappropriate for an appellate body or for a district court that is supposed to respect the different functions of judge and jury.

We are dealing here not with some procedural rule or even with a statutory direction. We are under compulsion of a constitutional command entitling persons to trial by jury as it existed at common law. U.S. Const. amend. VII. * * *

It can happen that a judge distrustful of a jury's sympathy for the hard luck of a plaintiff, or a judge conscious that he is the master of the facts and can speed up the process by killing a case early, will enter summary judgment where there are facts open to different interpretation by the jury. However benevolent the judge's motive, the judge is denying the litigants their constitutional right to trial by their peers. We should be the last to give countenance or comfort to such a departure from the basic structure of our law. Therefore, I dissent.

NOTES AND PROBLEMS FOR DISCUSSION

1. How did Schindler satisfy its initial burden under *Celotex*?

2. Now, consider what Nidds had to show to escape summary judgment and the evidence that he offered. Why does the *Nidds* court think that his evidence is not enough, and why does Judge Noonan think that it is?

3. Why didn't Nidds produce more evidence to oppose summary judgment, or is this just a case of bad lawyering?

4. In Poller v. Columbia Broadcasting System, Inc., 368 U.S. 464, 82 S.Ct. 486, 7 L.Ed.2d 458 (1962), the Supreme Court said that summary procedures should be "used sparingly in complex antitrust litigation where motive and intent play leading roles, the proof is largely in the hands of the alleged conspirators, and hostile witnesses thicken the plot." Is this consistent with the decision in *Nidds*? With *Celotex*?

5. Isn't there some possibility in the *Nidds* case that Graham is lying, and if so, why didn't the court consider such a possibility?

6. Title VII of the 1964 Civil Rights Act forbids employment discrimination on a number of grounds, including race and gender. In WEINSTOCK v. COLUMBIA UNIVERSITY, 224 F.3d 33 (2d Cir. 2000), the court upheld a grant of summary judgment in favor of the employer against a professor's claim that she had been denied tenure because she was a woman. Shelley Weinstock was an assistant professor at Barnard College, an affiliate of Columbia

University. She was denied tenure when the Columbia Provost did not accept an ad hoc committee's recommendation of tenure. The Provost explained that:

> a favorable vote of 3-2 [by the ad hoc committee] was not a strong endorsement; the two Columbia members of the committee . . . felt that Weinstock's research was limited and below the quality expected of a candidate for tenure; candidates from Columbia and Barnard were to be judged for tenure by the same standards; . . . the outside member of the ad hoc committee had stated that [the plaintiff] would not receive tenure at a research university such as Columbia; and evaluations [from other professors] confirmed his assessment that Weinstock did not merit tenure.

Weinstock filed suit under Title VII, and after discovery, Columbia filed a motion for summary judgment that the district court granted. The court of appeals stated that in a Title VII sex discrimination case, a plaintiff must generally establish a prima facie case of discrimination to stave off a motion for summary judgment. To do so, the plaintiff must show that "she is a member of a protected class; she is qualified for her position; she suffered an adverse employment action; and the circumstances give rise to an inference of discrimination." Then, a defendant may only succeed on his motion for summary judgment if he can point to evidence of a legitimate, non-discriminatory reason for the employment action. The case will only continue thereafter if the plaintiff can point to evidence from which a rational factfinder could find that the non-discriminatory reason is a mere pretext for actual discrimination.

The district court found that Weinstock established her prima facie case, but that Columbia had articulated a legitimate, non-discriminatory reason for denying Weinstock tenure. Columbia's reason for denying tenure was that Weinstock's scholarship was not of a high enough quality to meet the university standards. Weinstock argued that this was a pretext for actual discrimination because there was evidence of gender stereotyping, procedural irregularities, and disparate treatment. The court found no gender stereotyping in the use of terms such as "nice" and "nurturing" in reference to Weinstock; it found no procedural irregularities that could reasonably be linked to Weinstock's sex; and no evidence of disparate treatment because the quality of research expected from Columbia and Barnard professors was identical. The appeals court concluded that the district court correctly granted the motion for summary judgment because Weinstock failed to show any evidence from which a factfinder could conclude that the legitimate, non-discriminatory reason for denying tenure was a pretext for discrimination.

7. Is *Weinstock* a harder case than *Nidds*? There was a strong dissent in *Weinstock* by Judge Cardamone who argued that the evidence of procedural irregularities in the plaintiff's tenure decision, plus the use of gender stereotypes, more than raised a genuine issue of fact as to the pretextual nature of Columbia's proffered reason for denying her tenure. Was he right?

8. Perhaps the two most famous summary judgment cases are Arnstein v. Porter, 154 F.2d 464 (2d Cir. 1946) (also noted in Chapter 1) and Dyer v.

MacDougall, 201 F.2d 265 (2d Cir. 1953). In *Arnstein*, the plaintiff sued Cole Porter for copyright infringement, claiming that Porter arranged to break into his house and steal his songs. The plaintiff also claimed that a million copies of one of his compositions were sold, smaller numbers of others, and that his works were occasionally played. In his deposition, Porter said that he had never heard Arnstein's songs and didn't break into his house. Porter moved for summary judgment on the ground that there was no evidence of access to the songs. What result? In *Dyer*, plaintiff sued for libel and slander based on statements that MacDougall and his wife allegedly made accusing Dyer of blackmail. The defendants all denied making the statements, and moved for summary judgment. What result?

9. In *Adickes*, Justice Black concurred on the ground that the existence or nonexistence of a conspiracy was essentially a factual issue for the jury, and "[t]he advantages of trial before a live jury with live witnesses, and all the possibilities of considering the human factors, should not be eliminated by substituting trial by affidavit and the sterile bareness of summary judgment." Would he have agreed with Judge Sneed or Judge Noonan in *Nidds*?

10. For a number of years, courts wrestled with two related issues. First, there was the so-called "slightest doubt" test — that summary judgment may not be rendered when there is the "slightest doubt" as to the facts. What, do you suppose, is the present status of this test? Second, there was a debate about whether the standards for summary judgment in big, tough, complicated cases were different — with some courts thinking that summary judgment ought to be more readily granted in such cases, and others, less readily. Can you make the arguments?

11. Can a court grant summary judgment in favor of the party with the burden of proof (both of production and persuasion)? Most courts would say yes, but rarely. In such a case, the movant must not only establish a prima facie case for summary judgment but also show that the evidence is so overwhelming that she would be entitled to a directed verdict at trial. Moreover, there is a question whether a movant ever can make such a showing in a case where the credibility of witnesses is involved since many courts would say that their credibility (if prerequisite to satisfying the burden of proof) is always for the jury. These issues came to the fore in a case similar to *Nidds* involving the Equal Pay Act, 29 U.S.C. §206(d), which essentially requires men and women to receive equal pay for equal work. In the case, Brinkley was fired from her job as general manager (GM) of a golf club and claimed sex discrimination and liability under the Equal Pay Act. On the latter claim, she alleged that her male successor received significantly higher pay for the same work. The Club asserted as an affirmative defense that the differential was justified by a factor other than sex, and the Club had the burden of proof on this issue. To satisfy its burden of proof, the Club alleged that Paschal (the new GM) was better qualified, had a higher salary history and more experience, and that Paschal's salary was typical in the industry. In rebuttal, Brinkley cited a history of gender hostility (various remarks about women as supervisors and about the physical attributes of a waitress) and alleged that Paschal had a checkered employment history (fired from prior positions) and that he had no college degree or formal business education. The district court granted summary judgment which the appeals court affirmed, over a sharp dissent from Judge Motz. How would you have argued on·her behalf to avoid summary judgment? Brinkley v. Harbour Recreation Club, 180 F.3d 598 (4th Cir. 1999).

12. The discussion in the text omits another use of summary judgment which is less controversial. This occurs when the facts are essentially undisputed, and the only issue is a legal one for the court to decide. For example, if the only issue is the meaning or application of a statute and the underlying facts are not in dispute, or the only issue is the interpretation of a written contract where the decision is allocated to the court, the issue will frequently be resolved on a motion for summary judgment (in fact, both sides will often cross-move for summary judgment). Of course, in contract litigation, it is not always clear whether a given issue, even of contract interpretation, will be factual or legal — a point that we consider in Chapter 11 in connection with jury trial rights.

CHAPTER 10

Joinder of Claims and Parties

In the chapter on pleadings, we addressed what the parties to a lawsuit had to say to begin the litigation process. But we assumed a simple case — one in which a single plaintiff sued a single defendant on a single claim. But unfortunately, human affairs are rarely so simple. This chapter addresses issues relating to joinder of claims and parties (i.e., those who can be and those who must be included in the lawsuit).

Try to understand why joinder matters from the perspective of the parties. Either the plaintiff or the defendant might wish to join additional claims or parties to the litigation. For example, plaintiffs may wish to bring more than one claim against a single defendant, or to sue additional defendants on the same claim(s) (or perhaps on a different claim). A plaintiff might also wish to have other plaintiffs join with them in litigation. Similarly, a defendant may have a claim of its own against the plaintiff, or a claim against another defendant along with whom he was sued. Alternatively, he might wish to bring someone else into the action whom the plaintiff has not sued.

Each of these (and other) permutations on the simple two-party, A v. B lawsuit implicate questions of joinder. Modern joinder provisions allow for the expansion of the lawsuit through devices that were once unfamiliar to courts of law. In your reading, consider what limits, if any, ought to be imposed on the parties' ability to expand the litigation. As indicated above, some joinder questions will involve the addition of claims against persons already parties, while other joinder questions will involve the addition of parties against whom claims will be made. These additional "contests" will have to clear a number of hurdles before they can be brought in any court system.

First of all, there ordinarily has to be a Federal Rule of Civil Procedure that allows the addition of the claim or party. Such Rules will be our primary but not exclusive focus in this chapter. As you will see, the Rules do not always allow for the joinder of all possible claims and parties, and those that do allow joinder may require some threshold to be met (such as the relationship between the additional contest and the existing suit). Furthermore, some examples of joinder are permissive, in the sense that it is the party's option to join or not join a particular claim or party. On the other hand, joinder is sometimes said to be mandatory, either by the relevant procedural rules, or because of the operation of principles of preclusion for failure to bring certain claims. In addition, when a new party is sought to be added, questions of personal jurisdiction must also be considered, even if the relevant rules would otherwise allow joinder. Also, in the federal court system, the addition of any new claim or party must also conform to limits on the federal courts' subject matter jurisdiction, as noted below. Thus, perhaps the best way to consider the question of joinder is to see it as involving a number of layers of inquiry, only the first of which is the relevant joinder rule.

We start with joinder of claims under Rule 18 in relatively simple settings, including the two-party lawsuit. We then turn to joinder of parties. It is helpful to think of party-joinder sequentially. Start with the plaintiff. Initially, even if there is only one plaintiff, it must be the right plaintiff — one with an interest in the subject matter and the right to bring the lawsuit. In legal terms, the plaintiff must be the real party in interest under Rule 17. Then, the plaintiff has the first crack at determining the lineup of parties, both as to plaintiffs (assuming they are willing to join) and defendants. Rule 20's permissive joinder provisions deal with such issues, and the case as filed reflects the lineup as determined by the plaintiff.

Next, turn to the defendant. The defendant can, of course, accept the choice of parties made by the plaintiff. But what if the defendant thinks that someone has been left out that it would like to have in the lawsuit? In certain cases, the defendant can join this third party under Rule 14(a), although as we shall see this power is limited. In other cases, the defendant may request the court to require the plaintiffs to add one or more parties under Rule 19.

Apart from the lineup of plaintiffs as determined by the plaintiff and as modified by the defendant, an additional party who remains outside the lawsuit may want to get in. It may be that the absent party has an interest in the lawsuit and is afraid that something that happens in the lawsuit will affect that interest. To use the precise term, the absentee wants to intervene under Rule 24.

Foreign lawyers who operate in a unitary (i.e., a non-federal) system have trouble understanding all the fuss about joinder of parties. In a unitary system, the only joinder issue is who may and should be in the lawsuit. In our federal system, the matter is not so simple because joinder is limited not only by personal jurisdiction (which is typically state-centered) but also by subject matter jurisdiction (which, insofar as the federal courts are concerned, is limited). Remember that federal subject matter jurisdiction requires (for example) that a case arise under federal law or that there be diversity of citizenship, and diversity has been interpreted to require complete diversity between all plaintiffs and all defendants. In addition, a defendant must have some connection with a state to be subject to personal jurisdiction in the state or federal courts of that state.

The following example may help to illustrate these concerns. Assume that A, a citizen of California, and B, a citizen of Nevada, want to bring a lawsuit arising under state law against C, another citizen of Nevada. They can't do so in a federal court because complete diversity is lacking. Similarly, if a party wants to bring suit in New York against two defendants but one of them has never had any connection whatsoever with New York, he can't sue both of them in New York, even if one of the defendants is a domiciliary of New York, because the other is not subject to personal jurisdiction there.

These same considerations apply to the defendant. Assume A, a California citizen sues C, a Texas citizen, in federal court, and C believes B should be required to be made a defendant as well. What happens if B is a California citizen, and would destroy diversity? Or what happens if B is not subject to personal jurisdiction in the forum selected by the plaintiff? Finally, what if a party wants to intervene as a plaintiff or defendant, and the party's joinder would destroy diversity? These are not easy questions. However, you will find it easier going if you separate the question of joinder under the Rules from whether the joinder would cause jurisdictional problems.

Joinder issues are governed by rather specific provisions of the Rules, and there is no substitute for reading them carefully as you proceed through the materials. An introduction to terminology, however, may prove helpful even if it may be a bit oversimplified.

- *Joinder of Claims.* Claim joinder deals with the ability of one party to join two or more separate claims against another party. It is generally governed by Rule 18.
- *Counterclaims.* These are claims by the defendant against the plaintiff, and are governed by Rule 13. However, when we say "defendant," the term can include any party against whom a claim has been brought.
- *Cross-claims.* These are claims by one defendant against a co-defendant, and are governed by Rule 13(g).
- *Third-party claims.* These are claims by a defendant against a new party not in the lawsuit, and are governed by Rule 14. In this situation, the defendant is also called the "third-party plaintiff" and the new party is called the "third-party defendant."
- *Necessary and indispensable parties.* These are parties not in the lawsuit whom the defendant says should be in the lawsuit. Their joinder is governed by Rule 19.
- *Intervenors.* These are parties not in the lawsuit who want to get in. Their joinder is governed by Rule 24.
- *Interpleader.* This is a form of involuntary joinder by which a party who faces claims by different persons to the same property or "res" can join those persons — e.g., two claimants to the same painting. It is governed by the Interpleader Act, 28 U.S.C. §1335, and/or Rule 22.

SECTION A. CLAIM JOINDER (IN A TWO-PARTY SETTING)

1. BY PLAINTIFF

Assume Verna had a contract with Linda to purchase Linda's set of antique silver, and Linda refused to go forward with the contract. Three months later, when Verna was driving her car, a car negligently driven by Linda struck her. Can Verna join her contract and negligence claims in a single lawsuit against Linda?

Note that Rule 18 imposes no barriers to claim joinder as far as the Rules are concerned; a party may join as many claims as she has against her adversary.

There is no requirement that the claims be related to each other, or indeed any other requirement except that the additional claim be against a party whom one has sued. In an important respect, therefore, Rule 18 is no rule at all, since it imposes no limits on joinder of claims. In this respect, Rule 18 is considerably different from joinder rules that preceded it.

Historically, at common law, it was possible to join unrelated claims against a defendant, but only if the claims were based on the same common law "writ" or "form of action." See Chapter 7. For example, a plaintiff could bring two claims alleging trespass by the defendant even if the acts of trespass involved entirely different conduct occurring at different times and places. But the same-form-of-action requirement also meant that even related claims could not be brought together if they involved different common-law writs. For example, if the defendant trespassed on the plaintiff's land and took his horse, the plaintiff could not, in the same suit, sue for trespass (for damages) and for replevin (to get the horse back). Trespass and replevin were different writs or forms of action. Suits in equity, however, were more accommodating to claim joinder, given the equity courts' traditional desire to try cases in as convenient a package as possible. But, as discussed in Chapter 11 (and with exceptions, such as the so-called "clean up doctrine") claims for monetary relief could ordinarily not be joined with equitable claims. The modern federal rule respecting liberal claim joinder, however, was itself adapted from rules that previously governed equitable proceedings in the federal courts.

Before concluding from the wide-open language of Rule 18, that a plaintiff can really bring any additional claim she has against a defendant she has sued in federal court, consider the role of subject matter jurisdiction. Suppose X, a citizen of Illinois has a suit against a non-diverse defendant Y (another citizen of Illinois) that arises under federal law; assume also that X wishes to add a completely unrelated claim against Y that arises under state law. Can she add the additional claim in federal court?

Rule 18 presents no problem. But the additional claim will still not be able to get into federal court. That is because the additional claim lacks an independent basis of subject matter jurisdiction — i.e., it could not get into federal court on its own (absent diversity). And supplemental jurisdiction will attach to the additional claim only if it is sufficiently related to the federal question claim that it can be said to form part of the same constitutional case under 28 U.S.C. §1367(a). See also UMW v. Gibbs, 383 U.S. 258, 86 S.Ct. 1130, 16 L.Ed.2d 218 (1966) (discussed in Chapter 3) (calling for a "common nucleus of operative fact" as a constitutional prerequisite to joinder of state law claims in federal question suit against non-diverse party). Thus, Rule 18 notwithstanding, the additional state law claim against a nondiverse defendant could only be brought into a federal court if it is sufficiently related to the underlying federal claim. Consequently, the lawsuit just described would not be a problem in a state court with general subject matter jurisdiction, assuming that the state had a provision like Rule 18.

Venue can also be a problem in connection with claim joinder under Rule 18. If, for example, substantial events giving rise to both claims did not occur in the single district in which suit is brought, and venue cannot be premised on the defendant's district of residence, venue may be proper only for the claim that arose in the district. Most claims that are sufficiently related for purposes of supplemental jurisdiction, however, will likely share a district in which substantial events giving rise to the related claims occurred (or be able to be brought in the district of the defendant's residence), thus avoiding the need for a notion of "supplemental venue" in most cases.

Finally, as written, Rule 18 is permissive. It does not purport to require that a party join any claim, even a related one. But applicable preclusion principles relating to claim-splitting may *require* a party to bring all transactionally related claims against a party whom she has sued, or else be unable to raise them later. So some claims, although merely permissive as far as Rule 18 is concerned, may nevertheless be considered compulsory. Don't be fooled by the Rule. Compulsory claim joinder is a reality, but there is no Federal Rule of Civil Procedure requiring it.

2. BY DEFENDANT (COUNTERCLAIMS)

A defendant who is sued may seek to avoid liability by raising a defense which, if established to the satisfaction of the factfinder, would operate to defeat the plaintiff's case. If the defendant prevailed in defense, the plaintiff would recover nothing. But the defendant may also wish to assert her own claim against the plaintiff, and she might wish to do it in the very lawsuit which the plaintiff has filed against her. Current Rule 13 governing counterclaims allows a party to do so, and similar but not entirely analogous devices existed more anciently.

For example, at common law, a defendant might seek a "set-off" from the plaintiff — e.g., where the plaintiff sued to recover a debt owed by the defendant, the defendant might seek a set-off based on another debt the plaintiff owed him. The matter that formed the basis for the set-off did *not* have to arise out of the same transaction that gave rise to the plaintiff's claim, yet the set-off did not provide the basis of an independent judgment against the plaintiff without regard to the plaintiff's recovery. In other words, the only effect of the set-off would be to lower any amount otherwise recovered by the plaintiff (or to nullify any net recovery altogether). If the plaintiff lost on her underlying claim, the set-off would not be resolved. A related procedural device at common law was "recoupment," in which the defendant's claim did have to arise out of the plaintiff's underlying claim. Procedural innovations such as those in the New York Field Code in the mid-nineteenth century allowed for true counterclaims in which a separate judgment could be entered against the plaintiff, without regard to the success of the plaintiff's claim.

Under the Federal Rules, counterclaims come in two packages: ones that are "compulsory," and ones that are "permissive." Different definitional requirements under Rule 13 attach to the two sorts of counterclaims. In addition, because one must always consider the subject matter jurisdiction consequences of adding a new contest that might not have an independent basis of federal subject matter jurisdiction, it is important to consider what difference it makes jurisdictionally if a counterclaim is permissive or compulsory. Consider that question in the following decision:

Iglesias v. Mutual Life Ins. Co.

United States Court of Appeals, First Circuit, 1998.
156 F.3d 237.

CAMPBELL, SENIOR CIRCUIT JUDGE.

Manuel A. Iglesias appeals from the district court's grant of summary judgment on his discrimination and contract claims against his former employer, Mutual Life Insurance Company of New York ("MONY"). MONY appeals from the court's dismissal of its counterclaim for restitution of money that Iglesias obtained by submitting admittedly overstated expense reports. We affirm the judgment for MONY against Iglesias. We vacate the order *dismissing* MONY's counterclaim and remand the counterclaim with directions to dismiss the counterclaim without prejudice for want of jurisdiction.

I

Iglesias's Claims. [The Court held the Iglesias' discrimination claim which was based on federal law was barred by the statute of limitations, and his pendent state-law contract claims against MONY were contradicted by the contract.]

II

MONY's Counterclaim. MONY reimbursed Iglesias for expenses that he incurred as a result of his professional activities. To supplement his income, Iglesias admits that he "padded" his expense reimbursement requests from 1981 to 1988. MONY first learned of Iglesias's practice of overstating his expenses in 1987. At that time, MONY took no legal action against Iglesias. Instead, after notifying him that his conduct conflicted with company policy, MONY requested that he submit accurate reports in the future. Subsequently, Iglesias brought the present action against MONY for discrimination and breach of contract. On November 7, 1991, in the course of a deposition, Iglesias admitted that he had continued submitting exaggerated expense reports even after MONY's 1987 warning.

MONY tried to use the information obtained at the 1991 deposition in three ways. First, MONY questioned Iglesias about his expense reports during trial in an effort to impeach his credibility. Second, MONY attempted to raise the falsified expense requests as an affirmative defense to Iglesias's discrimination claims, arguing that they provided MONY with a valid non-discriminatory reason to terminate Iglesias. The court did not allow MONY to pursue this strategy because MONY learned of these improprieties only after it had terminated Iglesias.

Third, and more importantly for our purposes, MONY sought leave to amend its answer to add a counterclaim for restitution. On March 17, 1992, the magistrate judge granted MONY's request. For four years, the parties conducted discovery on the counterclaim. On August 6, 1996, Iglesias moved for dismissal of MONY's counterclaim arguing, inter alia, that it was barred by laches. On August 14, 1996, the district court dismissed the counterclaim as untimely. MONY now appeals from that dismissal.

Although neither of the parties has raised the issue, we have an obligation to inquire into our subject matter jurisdiction over MONY's counterclaim. Since MONY's counterclaim sounds in state law, a federal court may not hear it unless it falls within the ambit of supplemental jurisdiction or is supported by an independent jurisdictional basis.

The parties appear to have assumed that MONY's counterclaim was within the court's supplemental jurisdiction. [MONY and Iglesias were diverse, but the counterclaim did not appear to be in excess of the then applicable amount in controversy, $50,000.] When considering supplemental jurisdiction, the nature of the counterclaim is crucial. Federal Rule of Civil Procedure 13 describes two types of counterclaims: compulsory and permissive. A compulsory counterclaim is one that "arises out of the transaction or occurrence that is the subject matter of the opposing party's claim." Fed. R. Civ. P. 13(a). All counterclaims that are not compulsory are permissive. See Fed. R. Civ. P. 13(b). Only compulsory counterclaims can rely upon supplemental jurisdiction; permissive counterclaims require their own jurisdictional basis.

There are at least four tests to determine whether a counterclaim is compulsory or permissive: (1) Are the issues of fact and law raised by the claim and counterclaim largely the same? (2) Would res judicata bar a subsequent suit on defendant's claim absent the compulsory counterclaim rule? (3) Will substantially the same evidence support or refute plaintiff's claim as well as defendant's counterclaim? (4) Is there any logical relation between the claim and the counterclaim?

Of these tests, only the fourth — the "logical relation" test — could possibly encompass MONY's counterclaim. In *McCaffrey*, we adopted the Fifth Circuit's treatment of the logical relation test. Under this approach, a claim qualifies as compulsory only if:

> it arises out of the same aggregate of operative facts as the original claim in two senses: (1) the same aggregate of operative facts serves as the basis of both claims; or (2) that the aggregate core of facts upon which the original claim rests activates additional legal rights in a party defendant that would otherwise remain dormant.

McCaffrey v. Rex Motor Transp., Inc., 672 F.2d at 246, 249 (1st Cir. 1982).

Applying this standard, MONY's counterclaim is permissive. First, the aggregate of operative facts giving rise to Iglesias's claims is entirely different from the facts supporting MONY's counterclaim. Iglesias alleges that MONY removed its disability insurance product from the Puerto Rico market in 1981 for discriminatory reasons. That change in policy, he claims, led to his eventual termination, which therefore was also discriminatory. The evidence relevant to these claims includes the terms of Iglesias's employment contract and documentary, testimonial or other evidence concerning MONY's actions in Puerto Rico. By contrast, MONY's counterclaim is for restitution of monies that

Iglesias wrongfully obtained from the company over the period from 1981 to 1988. The facts supporting the restitution claim include Iglesias's records and expense vouchers for travel and meals, his admissions during deposition, and documentary, testimonial or other evidence regarding MONY's reimbursement policies. Notwithstanding both claims arose during the same time period, they therefore rest on different sets of supporting facts.

Second, MONY's ability to recover restitution does not depend on the success or failure of Iglesias's claims. Iglesias has admitted that he overbilled his expenses to enhance his compensation. Although MONY discovered Iglesias's false reimbursement requests for 1988 in a deposition that was part of the present action, Iglesias's claims did not "activate" otherwise dormant claims. MONY could have sought reimbursement for its payments based on Iglesias's false expense reports prior to 1988 at any point. Even MONY's claim relating to 1988 expenses is not tied to the merits of the discrimination and contract claims. In other words, MONY's counterclaim bears no logical relation to the claims in the main action.

We conclude that MONY's counterclaim is permissive rather than compulsory, and is not supported by federal supplemental jurisdiction.

NOTES AND PROBLEMS FOR DISCUSSION

1. Would the result in *Iglesias* change if MONY had fired Iglesias because he had overstated his expenses, or if Iglesias sought reinstatement to his job?

2. Like many other Rules that make up the Federal Rules of Civil Procedure (and unlike Rule 18), the compulsory counterclaim provisions of Rule 13(a) require a certain degree of connection between the underlying contest and the contest to be added. In the language of the Rule 13(a), the needed nexus is the same "transaction or occurrence." The opinion in *Iglesias* tries to suggest a number of fairly typical considerations or "tests" that may help to answer the question of what constitutes the same "transaction or occurrence."

3. Are the different inquiries suggested by the court for determining what is or is not a compulsory counterclaim helpful?

(a) One suggestion of the court's is that if res judicata would bar the claim later if it is not brought now, it is compulsory. But there is a certain amount of circularity with this suggestion because it may be hard to know the answer to the res judicata question unless we know whether the claim is one that ought to have been brought in the first place.

(b) Another suggested inquiry involves whether the counterclaim would involve similar proof or evidence. But consider how much overlap is required. If it is enough that there is common evidence that will be relevant to the counterclaim as well as the claim to which it responds, will that not largely duplicate one of the court's other suggested inquiries — namely, whether issues of fact (and law) would overlap?

(c) The court's final suggested inquiry has to do with whether the counterclaim is "logically" related to the underlying claim. If logically related means that the claims are in an "if-then" relationship (e.g., *if* the plaintiff loses her claim, *then* the defendant wins on his claim, or vice versa), many counterclaims would not be considered compulsory, because they might not rise or fall with the success of the plaintiff's claim. By contrast, a defendant's claim against a third party for indemnity and contribution (discussed below), is in a strictly logical relationship with the main claim insofar as it asserts if the defendant is liable to the plaintiff, then the third party is liable to the defendant.

4. The First Circuit indicates that the logical relationship test will be met if the counterclaim arises out of "the same aggregate of operative facts" as the main claim. Cf. UMW v. Gibbs, Chapter 3. But if the Court wants to call counterclaims "compulsory" when they are transactionally related, why use the unhelpful (if not misleading) phrase "logically" related? On the other hand, if logical relationship is defined as "transactional relationship," it merely restates the Rule — namely that a compulsory counterclaim must arise out of the same transaction or occurrence as the plaintiff's claim. If so, we are back to square-one.

5. Consider what turns on whether a counterclaim is compulsory or not. To focus the question, assume that you represented MONY in the main case. When you learn about the overstatement of expenses, you attempt to determine whether it is a compulsory counterclaim or not. After research, you conclude that it probably isn't compulsory, but you are only 80% sure. What are your procedural options and which would you take (and why)?

6. Note that the Rule itself speaks of "compulsory" counterclaims that "must" be stated, but it does not expressly state the consequences of the failure to bring such a claim. Nevertheless, the language of compulsoriness in Rule 13(a) does not mean that the defendant will be forced to assert a claim that she doesn't wish to sue on (in the sense that she will be compelled to litigate it against her wishes). So it can only be referring to the preclusive consequences of the failure to bring such a claim. It may be unclear, however, whether the Rule would (or should) bar assertion of an omitted state-law counterclaim in a later state court proceeding, if the federal proceeding was grounded in diversity and the relevant state's law did not consider the counterclaim to be compulsory. Compare Hanna v. Plumer (discussed in Chapter 5), with Semtek Int'l Inc. v. Lockheed-Martin (discussed in Chapter 13).

7. Now that you've answered #5, you can see why there are few cases involving previously omitted counterclaims. Instead, the typical situation involves a plaintiff who sues under a federal statute; the defendant interposes a counterclaim and asserts that it is compulsory and within the supplemental jurisdiction of the court; and the plaintiff moves to dismiss the counterclaim on the ground it is permissive and not within the jurisdiction of the court.

8. Be sure you understand why, if a counterclaim is compulsory (i.e., it arises out of the same transaction or occurrence as the plaintiff's claim), it will qualify for supplemental jurisdiction (if needed): If the compulsory counterclaim has the requisite nexus with the plaintiff's claim for purposes of Rule 13(a), it will satisfy the "same constitutional case" nexus called for by the supplemental jurisdiction statute, 28 U.S.C. §1367(a). In a federal question case such as *Iglesias*, the exceptions to supplemental jurisdiction in §1367(b) would be inapplicable. But is the converse equally true (as *Iglesias* seems to assume)? In other words, will failure to satisfy Rule 13(a)'s requirements inevitably result in the absence of supplemental jurisdiction over a (permissive) counterclaim? See Note 12, below.

9. If, unlike in *Iglesias*, the plaintiff's ticket into federal court was based on diversity only, would anything in §1367(b) prevent supplemental jurisdiction over a compulsory counterclaim that lacked an independent basis of subject matter jurisdiction (e.g., if it were for less than the jurisdictional amount)? What about a permissive counterclaim (see Note 12, below.)

10. The compulsory counterclaim issue has arisen with some frequency in cases involving various federal consumer protection statutes. In generic form, the statutes give consumers a private remedy (that may be asserted in the federal courts) for a violation, even though the underlying transaction which gave rise to the violation often involves a dispute between a consumer and a business located in the same state. For example, assume Carl Consumer takes out a loan from Friendly Finance and brings an action in a federal court against Friendly claiming Friendly made improper disclosures of the cost of the loan as required in violation of the federal Truth in Lending Act (the statute that requires all those disclosures when you borrow money — e.g., your student loans). Carl and Friendly are citizens of the same state. Assuming that the federal court has jurisdiction if a counterclaim is compulsory, would Friendly's counterclaim to collect any money that Carl has failed to pay be compulsory or permissive? See Plant v. Blazer Financial Servs., 598 F.2d 1357 (5th Cir. 1979).

11. Note that when it comes to a defendant's counterclaim against the plaintiff, personal jurisdiction and venue do not present a serious question, insofar as the plaintiff has already chosen to sue in the particular forum. Only if the defendant wishes to add a new party to the counterclaim will personal jurisdiction and venue become an issue. See Rule 13(a), 13(h). Although there is some authority for the proposition that a defendant who brings a counterclaim may be waiving any objection that he may have to venue or personal jurisdiction in the underlying suit, it is less than clear whether Rule 12 would sanction such a waiver, especially if the asserted counterclaim is compulsory.

12. The above discussion, as did *Iglesias* itself, has assumed that compulsory counterclaims could get supplemental jurisdiction if they needed it, but that permissive counterclaims could not. Instead, a permissive counterclaim would need an independent basis of subject matter jurisdiction. Should that be true of every permissive counterclaim? Is it possible to imagine a counterclaim that simultaneously does *not* arise out of the same transaction or occurrence as the plaintiff's claim for purposes of Rule 13(a), yet still has a sufficient nexus to the plaintiff's claim to satisfy §1367(a)'s requirement that it be part of the same constitutional case? Some courts have so concluded. See, e.g., JONES v. FORD MOTOR CREDIT CO., 358 F.3d 205 (2d Cir. 2004).

Jones was a class action brought by African Americans alleging race discrimination in lending by Ford Motor Credit, in violation of the Equal Credit Opportunity Act, 15 U.S.C. §1691 et seq. Ford Credit's counterclaim was to recover on the underlying unpaid loans of many of the class members, including that of Jones — the class representative. The appeals court first found the counterclaim to be permissive:

> We agree with the District Court that the debt collection counterclaims were permissive rather than compulsory. The Plaintiffs' ECOA claim centers on Ford Credit's mark-up policy, based on subjective factors, which allegedly resulted in higher finance charges on their purchase contracts than on those of similarly situated White customers. Ford Credit's debt collection counterclaims are related to those purchase contracts, but not to any particular clause or rate. Rather, the debt collection counterclaims concern the individual Plaintiffs' non-payment after the contract price was set. Thus, the relationship between the counterclaims and the ECOA claim is "logical" only in the sense that the sale, allegedly on discriminatory credit terms, was the "but for" cause of the non-payment. That is not the sort of relationship contemplated by our case law on compulsory counterclaims. The essential facts for proving the counterclaims and the ECOA claim are not so closely related that resolving both sets of issues in one lawsuit would yield judicial efficiency.

After a lengthy analysis of the history of §1367 and its relationship to prior caselaw (such as United Mine Workers v. Gibbs, 383 U.S. 715, 86 S.Ct. 1130, 16 L.Ed.2d 218 (1966)), the appeals court concluded as follows:

> Whether or not the *Gibbs* "common nucleus" standard provides the outer limit of an Article III "case," and is therefore a requirement for entertaining a permissive counterclaim that otherwise lacks a jurisdictional basis, the facts of Ford Credit's counterclaims and those of the Plaintiffs' ECOA claims satisfy that standard, even though the relationship is not such as would make the counterclaims compulsory. * * * The counterclaims and the underlying claim bear a sufficient factual relationship (if one is necessary) to constitute the same "case" within the meaning of Article III and hence of section 1367. Both the ECOA claim and the debt collection claims originate from the Plaintiffs' decisions to purchase Ford cars.

13. Does it make sense to see daylight between the standard for a compulsory counterclaim (same transaction or occurrence) and the requirements for supplemental jurisdiction (same constitutional case)? Even if it does, did the court in *Ford Motor Credit* arguably interpret the former too narrowly or the latter too broadly?

Now, reconsider the decision in *Iglesias*. There, the First Circuit concluded that MONY's counterclaim did not arise out of the same transaction or occurrence as Iglesias's claim and therefore was not compulsory. The court recited the traditional rule that "permissive counterclaims require their own jurisdictional basis." After *Ford Motor Credit*, could any argument be made that the counterclaim in *Iglesias* was sufficiently related for purposes of §1367(a), even though *not* sufficiently related for purposes of Rule 13(a)?

3. CROSS-CLAIMS

A defendant may want to bring a claim against a co-defendant whom the plaintiff has also joined as a party. For example, if Betty was involved in a three-car collision, and she sued the drivers of the other two cars as defendants (Rob and Sally), one defendant (Rob) might seek to recover for his own injuries from his co-defendant (Sally), at least if he believes that Sally's negligence was in some degree the cause of injuries that he (Rob) suffered. Under Rule 13(g) of the Federal Rules, cross-claims may be filed between those *already named* as defendants on a claim, provided that the claim arises out of the same transaction or occurrence as the underlying claim. Thus, in the three-car collision lawsuit just noted, Rule 13 would permit a cross-claim between Rob and Sally for negligence arising out of the accident over which Betty sued, but it would not permit Rob to bring a cross-claim against Sally for her breach of a contract to purchase Rob's house.

Again, however, even when the joinder rule is satisfied, subject matter jurisdiction must be considered. A cross-claim will have an independent basis of jurisdiction if, for example, it arises under federal law, or if the parties to the cross-claim are diverse and the claim is in excess of $75,000. But if not, supplemental jurisdiction will attach only if the claims are sufficiently related to satisfy 28 U.S.C. §1367(a). Cross-claims by definition must "arise out of the transaction or occurrence that is the subject matter" of the underlying dispute — so the nexus requirement of §1367(a) will typically be satisfied. And even if the underlying suit is grounded solely on diversity (thus implicating §1367(b)), nothing in paragraph (b) denies supplemental jurisdiction over cross-claims. Note also that venue and personal jurisdiction are ordinarily nonissues in connection with cross-claims between co-parties, assuming they were satisfied in the initial lawsuit.

Finally, note that cross-claims between plaintiffs will be rare. Co-plaintiffs voluntarily join together when bringing suit, so they are not antagonistic to one another. However, it might happen that co-plaintiffs are jointly sued by the defendant on a counterclaim, at which point the plaintiffs might become antagonistic, and one of them might then seek to bring a cross-claim against the other, as defendants on the counterclaim.

SECTION B.   REAL PARTY IN INTEREST

Naghiu v. Inter-Continental Hotels Group, Inc.

United States District Court, District of Delaware, 1996.
165 F.R.D. 413.

MURRAY M. SCHWARTZ, SENIOR DISTRICT JUDGE.

Plaintiffs Leslie and Laverne Naghiu, citizens of Virginia, have filed suit in this diversity action against the Inter-Continental Hotels Group, Inc. ("Inter-

Continental" or "defendant"), a Delaware corporation. Plaintiffs aver that during Leslie Naghiu's ("Naghiu" or "plaintiff") stay as a guest of defendant's hotel in Zaire, Africa in March, 1993, he was attacked in his room, causing him to suffer personal bodily injury and a loss of $146,000 in property. Laverne Naghiu claims a loss of consortium flowing from her husband's injuries.

Inter-Continental has moved for dismissal under Rule 12(b)(6) of the Federal Rules of Civil Procedure, arguing that plaintiff is not the real party in interest in this case as to the loss of personal property. * * *

Jurisdiction is invoked pursuant to 28 U.S.C. §1332. For the reasons stated below, the Court will grant defendant's motion[].

* * *

II

The Court views the facts in this case, which are rich with intrigue, in the light most favorable to the plaintiffs. Naghiu, an employee of the Christian Broadcast Network, Inc. ("CBN"), serves as the director of executive protection for [Reverend] Pat Robertson ("Robertson"). In this capacity, Naghiu coordinates security arrangements for Robertson on his trips abroad. Naghiu is an employee of CBN but is not an officer or director of CBN; he has no ownership or voting control in the affairs of CBN. Naghiu's employment with CBN is based out of Virginia Beach, Virginia.

In March 1993, on behalf of Robertson, Naghiu traveled to Zaire to purchase diamonds and render humanitarian aid. To that end, Naghiu estimates that he carried on his person approximately $100,000 in cash, kept in an attaché case. He describes the "street" environment in Zaire as follows:

> There is very little street crime in Zaire. The crime in Zaire is perpetrated nine out of ten times by the military. But that doesn't keep CBN away from performing the humanitarian tasks and the businesses that [Robertson] is there for. As CBN likes to put it, if you don't like the heat in the kitchen you can leave.

Naghiu further delineated the risks of travel abroad to Zaire:

> It is a risk to anyone who is involved in the international arena from the standpoint of a security person. We are not talking about a security guard at the K-Mart. We are talking about someone that works the international arena and knows what the circumstances and consequences can be in a volatile continent. I am not trying to earmark Zaire. I happen to enjoy working in Zaire. What I am saying is that the continent itself today there are 23 countries in that continent that are under military strife.

From 1992-93, Naghiu traveled numerous times to Zaire on behalf of CBN. Out of concern for Robertson's safety and welfare, Naghiu twice recommended that Robertson not personally travel to Zaire when Naghiu perceived conditions as too dangerous. Robertson followed Naghiu's advice on those occasions.

As of the March, 1993 CBN expedition to Zaire, Robertson's corporation had rendered approximately two million dollars in humanitarian aid to that country. With this legacy of prior aid, CBN's March, 1993 return to Zaire was covered by the Zaire media, including television. During all of this, Naghiu was charged with the security of the attaché case containing the money. The Robertson entourage booked its stay at defendant's Inter-Continental Hotel Kinshasa ("hotel"), the only suitable lodging for business travelers in Kinshasa, Zaire. Inter-Continental admits that it routinely advised all paying guests to give their valuables, including cash, to the hotel staff for safe-keeping.

Upon arrival at the Inter-Continental Kinshasa, Naghiu asked the night personnel to procure a safe deposit box for the cash. The night clerk told Naghiu there were no accessible boxes available until the following morning. From his vantage point at the registration desk, Naghiu could see the boxes and perceived them to be in a state of "disarray."

Naghiu claims that the following morning he again approached Inter-Continental's front desk clerk and requested a safe deposit box, but was told to "come back later." Naghiu retained the attaché case containing the cash. A short time later in his stay, Naghiu complained to the hotel's General Manager that there were prostitutes roaming the hotel's elevators and corridors soliciting business from the hotel's guests. Although he had the opportunity, Naghiu did not mention to the General Manager about his inability to obtain a safe deposit box for his valuables. At some point during the CBN trip, $46,000 was added to the attaché as proceeds of a diamond transaction.

On the evening of March 23, 1993, Naghiu supped at a private residence that was ". . . 45 minutes outside of Kinshasa in an area where soldiers and military types have stopped vehicles, accosted foreigners and even Zairians, manhandled them. Shot them." Consequently, as Naghiu has testified, he left the attaché case and its contents in his hotel room while he left the premises. He did not consider making another effort at obtaining a hotel safe deposit box. Naghiu hid the attaché case behind a couch and set of heavy drapes in his hotel room on the 19th floor.

According to Naghiu, he returned from dinner to his hotel door and used his key to enter his room. He remembers now that the door appeared to have been unlocked, although it did not strike him at the time as out of the ordinary. Upon gaining entry, he attempted to turn on the overhead light, without success. Naghiu finally located a floor lamp that lit and then immediately witnessed a man going through his large suitcase, strewing clothing on the floor. Naghiu yelled at the man, who brandished a "long, very thin bladed Belgian sabre" and lunged at Naghiu. The man missed Naghiu and instead impaled the hotel room wall, leaving "a tremendous indentation." Naghiu then claims the man assaulted him with the knife, cutting him above the ear on the left side of his head and on the right forearm. Naghiu says he fought his assailant when another man approached from the bathroom; that is the last thing Naghiu remembers before being knocked unconscious.

Naghiu's companions found him unconscious in his room and brought him to another site for medical attention. Inter-Continental refused to allow Naghiu's fellow security officer into the room to perform an immediate investigation. According to plaintiff, within 24 hours of the attack, the holes in the wall made by the attacker's knife were filled in, the room had been painted and the carpet had been replaced. Naghiu subsequently filed criminal charges with the Zairian authorities. When he returned stateside, Naghiu claims that Robertson expected reimbursement of the stolen money. Robertson later told Naghiu, however, not "to worry about [the money], that [Naghiu] was bonded."

III

A

Inter-Continental has filed a Rule 12(b)(6) motion to dismiss plaintiff's claim for recovery of the $146,000 for failure to state a claim upon which relief can be granted. When making a determination under this rule, the Court looks only to the complaint and cannot consider matters outside the pleadings. Kulwicki v. Dawson, 969 F.2d 1454, 1462 (3d Cir. 1992). In support of its motion, however, defendant relied on exhibits and plaintiff's deposition testimony in addition to the complaint. In his answering brief as to this issue, plaintiff relied extensively on his deposition testimony as well. * * *

When both parties present extraneous materials as part of a Rule 12(b)(6) motion or in opposition thereto, the Court has discretion to accept the extraneous material and convert the motion to one for summary judgment pursuant to Fed. R. Civ. P. 56. Kulwicki, 969 F.2d at 1462 (citations omitted); 5A Wright & Miller Federal Practice and Procedure §1366 (2d ed. 1990). Because the Court has accepted the type of evidence usually considered under Rule 56(c) for summary judgment, the Court will convert defendant's motion to dismiss into a motion for summary judgment.

* * *

C

Defendants first argue that plaintiff may not recover for the alleged loss of the $146,000 because plaintiff is not the real party in interest as required by the Federal Rules of Civil Procedure. Fed. R. Civ. P. 17(a) requires that "every action shall be prosecuted in the name of the real party in interest." Unless a party is "an executor, administrator, guardian, bailee, trustee of an express trust, a party with whom or in whose name a contract has been made for the benefit of another, or a party authorized by statute," a litigant cannot sue in his "own name without joining the party for whose benefit the action is brought." Fed. R. Civ. P. 17(a). The underlying aim of the rule is to ensure fairness to the defendant by protecting the defendant against a subsequent action by the party actually entitled to relief, and by ensuring that the judgment will have proper res judicata effect. * * *

1. Choice of Law

Naghiu argues that he was a bailee of the money and as such, is a real party in interest as explicitly enumerated by Fed. R. Civ. P. 17. In analyzing plaintiff's status as bailee *vel non,* the Court looks to the substantive law creating the right being sued upon to ascertain whether plaintiff possesses a substantive right to relief. Gee v. CBS, Inc., 471 F. Supp. 600, 617 (E.D. Pa.) (quoting 6A Wright & Miller at §1544), aff'd without op., 612 F.2d 572 (3d Cir. 1979)[.] As a threshold matter, the Court must decide which jurisdiction's law controls the issue of whether plaintiff is to be considered a bailee of the $146,000.

Where, as here, the jurisdiction of a federal court is founded upon the diversity statute, 28 U.S.C. §1332, the Court applies the substantive law, including the choice of law provisions of the state in which the federal court sits. Carrick v. Zurich Am. Ins. Group, 14 F.3d 907, 909 (3d Cir. 1994) (citing Klaxon Co. v. Stentor Elec. Mfg. Co., 313 U.S. 487, 496, 85 L. Ed. 1477, 61 S. Ct. 1020 (1941)). This Court therefore will look to Delaware choice of law rules to determine the substantive law that governs the dispute between Naghiu and Inter-Continental.

For choice of law questions sounding in contract Delaware courts follow the "most significant relationship" approach of the Restatement (Second) of Conflict of Laws. Travelers Indem. Co. v. Lake, 594 A.2d 38, 41 (Del. 1991) (citing Oliver B. Cannon & Son, Inc. v. Dorr-Oliver, Inc., 394 A.2d 1160, 1166 (Del. 1978)). Under Restatement section 188, the rights and duties of the parties with respect to an issue in contract are determined by the local law of the state with the most significant relationship to the transaction and the parties by reference to the following principles: a) the place of contracting, b) the place of negotiation of the contract, c) the place of performance, d) the location of the subject matter of the contract, and e) the domicile, residence, or place of incorporation and place of business of the parties. Restatement (Second) of Conflicts §188 (1971). Considering plaintiff as a putative bailee of CBN based in Virginia, the Court finds that factors a, b, c, d and part of e of the Restatement approach point to Virginia. Accordingly, the Court holds that Virginia has the most significant relationship to the occurrence and the parties with respect to whether plaintiff was a bailee of the cash and thus satisfies Rule 17's real party in interest requirement. Thus, Virginia law shall control as to whether plaintiff was in fact a bailee.

The Supreme Court of Virginia has ruled that "[a] bailment has been broadly defined as 'the rightful possession of goods by one who is not the owner.'" K-B Corp. v. Gallagher, 218 Va. 381, 237 S.E.2d 183, 185 (Va. 1977) (quoting 9 S. Williston, Contracts §875 (3d ed. 1967)). In addition, to be considered a bailee, one must have both physical control of the goods and an intent to exercise that control. *K-B Corp.*, 237 S.E.2d at 185 (citation omitted).

Although there may be superficial similarity, a master and servant (or employer and employee) do not stand in the relationship of a bailor and bailee to one another. Unlike the employer's relationship with his employee, the bailor has no control over the bailee. The bailment relation is concerned only with personal property, and the bailee is not subject to direction in carrying out the purposes of the bailment, except as the bailment contract provides, but occupies rather the position of an independent contractor. On the other hand, employment imports control and direction of the employee's acts within the scope of the employment relationship. "Where an owner of a chattel delivers it to another to perform work in respect to or by means of it, the relationship of the parties is that of bailor and bailee where the owner parts with control over it and is that of master and servant where he retains control thereof." Payne v. Kinder, 147 W. Va. 352, 127 S.E.2d 726 (W.Va. 1962)[.]

As an employee of CBN, Naghiu was charged with safekeeping the cash as a duty of his master-servant relationship. In reality, Naghiu had only custodial possession of the money; others in the CBN party exercised control over how the money or diamonds were to be transacted. Thus, contrary to plaintiff's assertions, he could not be considered a bailee to satisfy Rule 17's real party in interest requirement. In sum, Naghiu has not demonstrated any legal interest in the cash allegedly stolen from his hotel room on March 23, 1993. He has testified under oath that he has no ownership interest in the money, and has no written authorization to seek its recovery. In addition, he has never claimed to be suing on Pat Robertson's or anyone else's behalf. Thus, as to defendant's liability for the stolen cash, plaintiff has proffered no theory supporting his status as a real party in interest to this action.

Rule 17(a) also provides that

> No action shall be dismissed on the ground that it is not prosecuted in the name of the real party in interest until a reasonable time has been allowed after objection for ratification of commencement of the action by, or joinder or substitution of, the real party in interest. . . .

A proper ratification under Rule 17(a) requires the ratifying party to: 1) authorize continuation of the action; and 2) agree to be bound by the lawsuit's result. Assuming arguendo that Pat Robertson or CBN would be the real party in interest to recover the cash in this action, there is no evidence that either have authorized continuation of this action and have agreed to be bound by the result in this suit. The evidentiary record contains a September, 1995 letter discussing Naghiu's plight sent by Zairean "Counsellors at Law" to Pat Robertson at his corporate address in Virginia Beach, Va. From this the Court necessarily concludes that Robertson had notice of this action as of that date that Naghiu had initiated suit for return of Robertson's (or his corporation's) money. In addition, defendant first objected to Naghiu's lack of status as a real party in interest as to the stolen cash well over a year ago. Consequently, the Court holds that plaintiff has had reasonable opportunity to locate and formally join, substitute, or seek ratification from Robertson or CBN, the real parties in interest. Because this has not occurred, the Court holds that Rule 17's real party in interest requirement has not been satisfied as to the loss of personal property in this case. As to this first issue, the Court will grant summary judgment in favor of defendant.

* * *

IV

For the above reasons, the Court holds that plaintiff is not a real party in interest for purposes of his claim for loss of $146,000, property in which he had no legal interest. [The Court also held that plaintiff Leslie Naghiu failed to establish the existence of the essential elements of his case with respect to his claim for negligence. The Court therefore granted summary judgment in favor of defendant.]

NOTES AND PROBLEMS FOR DISCUSSION

1. *Naghiu* clearly was an agent of the Christian Broadcast Network. Why didn't this give him sufficient authority to maintain the lawsuit?

2. The real party in interest issue frequently arises in insurance subrogation cases. Under insurance law, and under most liability policies, if an insurance company pays the claim of a policyholder arising from an accident with a third party, the insurance company is subrogated (steps into the shoes of) its insured. Assume that Victim is involved in a collision with Driver, and Victim has an insurance policy with Estate Farm. Consider the following questions:

(a) Victim's car is damaged, and Estate Farm pays $20,000 to Victim for the damage. Can Estate Farm bring an action in Victim's name against Driver?

(b) Same facts. Can Victim bring an action in his name against Driver for personal injuries?

(c) Same facts except assume that Victim's policy has a $1,000 deductible (which means Victim has to pay the first $1,000 of damage himself). Can Estate Farm bring an action in Victim's name against Driver for $20,000?

3. Levy's Jewelers was robbed, and suffered $300,000 of losses, of which $200,000 was covered by insurance. Levy's sued ADT Security Inc. claiming ADT's system failed and it was responsible for the loss. ADT moved to require Levy's insurance company to join as a plaintiff to prevent double recovery. If you represented the insurance company (a) would you recommend to your client that it join the action and, (b) if not, what might you suggest that the insurer do to avoid the problem raised by ADT's argument? See Levy Jewelers, Inc. v. ADT Security Systems, Inc., 187 F.R.D. 701 (S.D. Ga. 1999).

4.   Finally, note that Rule 17(a) directs that "an action must be *prosecuted* in the name of the real party in interest." (Emphasis supplied.) The Supreme Court has noted that it therefore "speaks to joinder of *plaintiffs*, not defendants." Lincoln Property Co. v. Roche, 546 U.S. 81, 90 (2005) (emphasis in original). Does this mean that there exists no notion of proper party defendants, outside of Rule 17? Or would such concerns be taken care of by Rule 12(b)(6) — failure to state a claim for relief?

SECTION C. JOINDER OF PARTIES

As described earlier, plaintiff has considerable choice of who will be in the lawsuit as plaintiffs and as defendants. These choices, however, are limited by Rule 20.

Puricelli v. CNA Insurance Company

United States District Court, Northern District of New York, 1999.
185 F.R.D. 139.

RALPH W. SMITH, JR., UNITED STATES MAGISTRATE JUDGE.

Plaintiffs, Diane Puricelli and Charles Hughes, jointly filed suit against their former employer, defendant CNA, seeking relief for alleged violations of the Age Discrimination in Employment Act of 1967 (ADEA), the New York State

Human Rights Law, and intentional infliction of emotional distress. Defendant now moves this court pursuant to Fed. R. Civ. P. 20(a) and 21 to sever the claims of plaintiffs Puricelli and Hughes on the ground that the claims are misjoined because they neither arise out of the same transaction or occurrence or present common questions of law or fact. In the alternative, defendant seeks relief under Fed. R. Civ. P. 42(b) in the form of separate trials. In order to determine whether plaintiffs' claims meet the permissive joinder requirements of Fed. R. Civ. P. 20(a), a complete factual review is necessary.

A. *Plaintiff Puricelli*

Plaintiff Puricelli was employed by Continental Insurance Company in Glens Falls, New York, from March 1986 through May 1995. Continental was taken over by defendant CNA in May 1995. Following the takeover, Puricelli continued her employment and held the position of litigation supervisor until July 1996, when she was allegedly demoted to bodily injury adjuster. Puricelli worked in that capacity until December 27, 1996, the date of her alleged termination. Puricelli then alleges that defendant embarked on a campaign to remove older employees from the claims department, involving disparaging remarks and harassment related to Puricelli's age, which culminated in her discharge on an allegedly pretextual ground and replacement by a younger employee.

Shortly after the takeover in June 1995, Puricelli was given a performance evaluation by Kevin Romer, to whom she reported, and received a rating of "3" (performance meets expectations). Following the review, Romer counseled Puricelli on the specific areas of her performance that needed improvement. In June 1996, Puricelli was placed on a 30-day probationary action plan designed to correct those performance problems. By the end of the third week of the 30-day period, Puricelli was given the option of taking a demotion to litigation adjuster, or to continue the plan and possibly face termination if her performance did not improve by the end of the period. Puricelli opted for the demotion, resulting in a $3,000 reduction in salary, and thereafter reported to Mark Romano. Romano evaluated Puricelli in September 1996 and rated her at a "3" (performance meets expectations). In light of the favorable recommendation, Romano recommended Puricelli for a "spot bonus". The bonus was approved by Romer, but before disbursement, Puricelli notified Romano in December 1996 that she had accepted a position with another insurance company.

B. *Plaintiff Hughes*

Plaintiff Hughes was employed by Continental Insurance Company from 1977 to May 1995, and then by CNA until his alleged termination on November 8, 1996. After the takeover, Hughes initially occupied the position of litigation adjuster until he was allegedly demoted to liability bodily injury adjuster in July 1996. Hughes similarly claims that defendant orchestrated a campaign to remove older employees from the claims department, and that his alleged discharge and replacement by a younger employee was pretextual.

The events preceding Hughes' termination are more involved. From the time of the takeover until August 1996, Hughes reported to Puricelli, who at that time was a claims supervisor. During the summer of 1996, defendant reorganized the claims department to reflect its "aggressive new philosophy of cost-effective management." As a result of the restructuring, Hughes was transferred from the litigation unit to the represented unit. The transfer did not affect his title or pay. Hughes was thereafter evaluated by Romano in September 1996 and was given a rating of "4" (performance does not meet the minimum requirements). The basis for the low rating was Hughes' inability to learn defendant's new computer system as well as his "worst case scenario" approach to claims. No disciplinary action was taken. In October 1996, Hughes notified Romano that he planned to retire and accept an offer with another insurance company.

In support of its motion, defendant asserts that the circumstances underlying plaintiffs' claims are so factually distinct that the requirements of permissive joinder have not been satisfied and alternatively that a joint trial would cause undue prejudice and confusion. In opposition to defendant's severance motion, plaintiffs concede that the individual circumstances surrounding their respective claims vary, but they contend that both were subject to a similar pattern of discriminatory action by the defendant, thus bringing their claims within the purview of Rule 20(a).

DISCUSSION

Rule 21 of the Fed. R. Civ. P. addresses the misjoinder of parties. The rule is silent with regard to the grounds for misjoinder, but it is well-settled that parties are misjoined when the preconditions of permissive joinder, set forth in Rule 20(a), have not been satisfied. * * * Pursuant to Rule 20(a), proper joinder of parties requires the satisfaction of two criteria: (1) the right to relief sought by all plaintiffs must arise out of the same transaction or occurrence, or series of transactions or occurrences; and (2) a common question of law or fact as to all plaintiffs must arise in the action. Fed. R. Civ. P. 20(a)[.] A determination on the question of joinder of parties lies within the discretion of the district court. Mosley v. General Motors Corp., 497 F.2d 1330, 1332 (8th Cir. 1974) (citing 7 C. Wright, *Federal Practice and Procedure*, §1653 at 270 (1972)).

The well-established policy underlying permissive joinder is to promote trial convenience and expedite the resolution of lawsuits. The Supreme Court has recognized this policy, stating that "the impulse [under the Rule] is toward entertaining the broadest possible scope of action consistent with fairness to the parties; joinder of claims, parties and remedies is strongly encouraged." United Mine Workers of America v. Gibbs, 383 U.S. 715, 724, 86 S. Ct. 1130, 1137, 16 L. Ed. 2d 218 (1966). As such, severance is appropriate only where the prerequisites of permissive joinder have not been satisfied.

A. Same Transaction or Occurrence

Courts have generally adopted a case-by-case approach in determining whether plaintiffs' claims constitute a "single transaction or occurrence" for purposes of Rule 20. *Mosley*, 497 F.2d at 1333. In attempting to affix a definition to "transaction or occurrence," courts have found Fed. R. Civ. P. 13(a) to be particularly instructive, and have concluded with reference to that Rule that the phrase encompasses "all logically related claims." *Mosley*, 497 F.2d at 1333[.]

The presence of material dissimilarities between the substantive allegations of the joined plaintiffs does not automatically bring such claims outside the "same transaction or occurrence" language. * * * Hohlbein v. Heritage Mutual Ins. Co., 106 F.R.D. 73, 77 (E.D. Wis. 1985). In [one decision] three plaintiffs joined in a discrimination suit brought against their employer. The plaintiffs were terminated under different circumstances, at different times, and by two different named defendants, approximately one year apart. The court denied defendants' motion for misjoinder because the plaintiffs alleged "actions by Defendants which subjected them to intense scrutiny and strict punishment." In [another decision] three female employees sued their employer for sex discrimination and sexual harassment. Defendant's motion for severance was denied because all three plaintiffs alleged injury by the same general policy of permitting discrimination against women. In *Hohlbein*, a motion for severance was denied where four plaintiffs, although employed at different times and in different positions, alleged a continuing pattern and practice with respect to defendant's employment of unrelated individuals.

In support of its motion, defendant contends that there is no logical relationship between plaintiffs' claims in light of the myriad differences which distinguish their respective claims. Plaintiffs, on the other hand, contend that their claims meet the "logically related" threshold given the similar pattern of discriminatory conduct to which they were both subjected. Both plaintiffs received poor or borderline performance evaluations, and the basis for those evaluations was the same; i.e., failure to meet the new and aggressive standards (albeit different ones) implemented by CNA after the takeover. Plaintiffs further assert that they both were demoted and replaced by younger employees. In short, plaintiffs claim that they were both "subjected to a similar method of removal from their pre-takeover positions through performance evaluations, performed by . . . Mr. Romer, during the same time period, and left the employ of CNA within one month of each other."

Plaintiffs have satisfied the "same transaction or occurrence" prong of the Rule 20(a) analysis. Despite the differences in the factual underpinnings of their respective claims, plaintiffs have alleged a pattern of conduct, commencing after the takeover of Continental, which discriminated against them on the basis of age. Both plaintiffs similarly allege that the basis for the adverse employment decisions was their failure to meet the demands of defendant's new and aggressive management style.

B. *Common Question of Law or Fact*

The second requirement of Rule 20(a) is that the action raises a question of law or fact common to all the parties. The Rule does not require the commonality of all questions of law and fact raised in the dispute, rather, the requirement is satisfied if there is any question of law or fact common to all parties. Plaintiffs have also satisfied the "common question of law or fact" prong of the Rule 20(a) analysis. Many of the same factors set forth above support a finding of commonality here as well. Initially, both plaintiffs have alleged claims under the ADEA, the New York State Human Rights Law, and intentional infliction of emotional distress. In addition, both plaintiffs allege actions, occurring after the takeover, that were selectively applied to them on the basis of age. Both plaintiffs also implicate Kevin Romer as a key player in the employment decisions set forth in the complaint.

C. *Separate Trials under Fed. R. Civ. P. 42(b)*

In the alternative, defendant asks this court to grant its motion pursuant to Fed. R. Civ. P. 42(b) for separate trials on the ground that a joint trial will cause prejudice to the defendant and lead to confusion. Pursuant to Rule 42(b), the court may order separate trials of any claims or issues in furtherance of convenience or to avoid prejudice, or when separate trials will be conducive to expedition and economy. Amato v. Saratoga Springs, 170 F.3d 311 (2d Cir. 1999); Smith v. Lightning Bolt Productions, Inc., 861 F.2d 363, 370 (2d Cir. 1988).

Defendant contends that both confusion and prejudice warrant an order of separate trials. Grayson v. K-Mart Corp., 849 F. Supp. 785 (N.D. Ga. 1994); Accord Henderson v. AT&T, 918 F. Supp. 1059, 1063 (S.D. Tex. 1996). According to defendant, confusion will result from the varying factual underpinnings of the plaintiffs' individual claims. In terms of prejudice, defendant asserts that although plaintiffs must each establish defendant's liability to them individually, a joint trial may bias the jury against defendant generally.

In support of its argument, defendant relies heavily upon *Grayson* and *Henderson*. A review of those cases instantly reveals, however, that the factors which motivated the courts to order separate trials are not present in the case at bar. In *Grayson*, eleven plaintiffs filed an age discrimination suit against their employer. *Grayson*, 849 F. Supp. at 791. A joint trial of plaintiffs' claims would have involved eleven different factual situations, eleven sets of work histories, eleven sets of witnesses and testimony, and the laws of four different states. Id. *Accord Henderson*, decided in the context of a Rule 21 motion, involved five plaintiffs asserting more than twenty different claims. Finding a joint trial in such a situation likely to be extraordinarily confusing, the court ordered severance of three of the plaintiffs' claims. It is also worthy of note that the *Accord Henderson* court permitted two of the plaintiffs to proceed jointly, despite differences in their claims, finding that the jury could easily keep the claims of two plaintiffs separate.

The case at bar stands in stark contrast to the factual situations before the *Grayson* and *Accord Henderson* courts. Here, there are two plaintiffs, and each plaintiff has alleged the very same claims; i.e., violations of the ADEA, the New York State Human Rights Law, and intentional infliction of emotional distress. As such, the prejudice and confusion contemplated by the defendant is not sufficient to warrant separate trials. At the very least, any prejudice or confusion can be remedied by a carefully drafted jury instruction.

On the basis of the foregoing, it is ordered that defendant's motion under Fed. R. Civ. P. 20(a) and 21, and alternatively under Fed. R. Civ. P. 42(b), is denied and the plaintiffs shall be allowed to proceed jointly.

NOTES AND PROBLEMS FOR DISCUSSION

1. Consider the result if the plaintiffs in *Puricelli* also sought to join as plaintiffs:

(a) Cynthia Chin, who claims she was fired because of discrimination against persons of Asian descent;

(b) Peter Young, who claims he was not hired because he was over 50 and was thus a victim of age discrimination;

(c) George Colgate, who has similar claims to Puricelli, but who worked in the Syracuse office of CNA.

2. Now consider tactics. Why do Puricelli and Hughes want to join as plaintiffs and why should the defendants care whether that happens?

3. You should distinguish between the joinder question and the separate-trials question, and the different Rules that govern each. Read Rules 21 and 42. What difference does it make between permitting joinder and requiring separate trials, as opposed to not permitting joinder at all?

4. As in other joinder settings, be sure to keep in mind the possible jurisdictional limitations on joinder. In *Puricelli*, there was subject matter jurisdiction by virtue of a federal claim for relief (actually, there were specific jurisdictional provisions in the federal antidiscrimination laws) and the defendant was subject to personal jurisdiction in New York. But all cases are not so easy. For example, even though Rule 20 might be satisfied because the plaintiff's claim against a second defendant arose out of the same transaction or occurrence with the plaintiff's claim against the first defendant, joinder of an additional defendant will not be possible in a diversity action if the additional defendant would destroy complete diversity. Indeed, the supplemental jurisdiction statute, 28 U.S.C. §1367(b), expressly precludes supplemental jurisdiction over claims by plaintiffs against parties joined under Rule 20. And venue, no less than personal or subject matter jurisdiction, may also preclude joinder of an additional defendant otherwise qualifying for joinder under Rule 20. The customary remedy for such "misjoinder" — assuming that the nondiverse party is not someone whose presence is required under Rule 19 (see Section F, below) — is simply to dismiss the nondiverse party, not the entire action. See Rule 21; see also note 6, below

5. Joinder of an additional *plaintiff* in a diversity case under Rule 20 presents special problems when the additional plaintiff's claim lacks an independent subject matter basis for being in federal court. Unlike with joinder of a nondiverse Rule 20 defendant, supplemental jurisdiction over Rule 20 parties joined as plaintiffs is *not* expressly precluded under §1367(b). Does this mean that a plaintiff who is not diverse from the defendant can join a plaintiff who is diverse from the defendant? Complete diversity has long been the traditional reading of the diversity statute 28 U.S.C. §1332, but it was arguable that §1367 had modified it. Nevertheless, the Supreme Court recently ruled that the complete diversity rule remained intact in such cases. EXXON MOBIL CORP. INC., v. ALLAPATTAH SERVICES, 125 S.Ct. 2621, 162 L.Ed.2d 502 (2005). Yet it simultaneously concluded that another traditional reading of §1332 — that

each plaintiff have the requisite amount in controversy with each defendant —
had been modified by §1367. Can the Court have it both ways?

6.   The practice regarding misjoinder (see note 4) had a long pedigree. See, e.g.,
Horn v. Lockhart, 84 U.S. (17 Wall.) 570, 579 (1873). Nevertheless, some of the
language in *Exxon Mobil, supra,* suggested that the presence of a nondiverse
Rule 20 plaintiff would somehow "contaminate" the other plaintiff's claim over
which there was good diversity jurisdiction, with the result that there would then
be no jurisdiction over either claim: "A failure of complete diversity, unlike the
failure of some claims to meet the requisite amount in controversy, contaminates
every claim in the action". Although the Court did not say so, this language, if
taken seriously, suggests that Rule 21 is inconsistent with §1332 insofar as the
Rule would allow for the dismissal of only the diversity-offending, dispensable
party, while allowing a federal court to keep the jurisdictionally valid claim.
Would there be any point in requiring dismissal of the jurisdictionally valid
claim in such circumstances when it could simply be refiled, and next time,
without the claim of the other (dispensable) party?

SECTION D. THIRD-PARTY PRACTICE

Imagine that there is a car accident. Ellen Ostrow was a passenger in a car
driven by Adele Hoffman. It collided with a truck owned by Bloomingdale's,
and driven by Joseph Parcelle. Ostrow sues Bloomingdale's, and
Bloomingdale's doesn't like it at all. It would like Hoffman to be a party
because it believes the accident was Hoffman's fault. It also would like to bring
in Parcelle as a defendant since the jury might be reluctant to find that Parcelle
was at fault (thereby foreclosing Bloomingdale's liability on a respondeat
superior — i.e., vicarious liability — theory). Can it do so? Read Rule 14.

Allstate Insurance Co. v. Hugh Cole Builder, Inc.

United States District Court, Middle District of Alabama, 1999.

187 F.R.D. 671.

W. HAROLD ALBRITTON, DISTRICT JUDGE.

I

This case is before the court on Third-Party Defendant Jenkins Brick
Company's Motion to Strike, or in the Alternative, Motion to Dismiss, or in the
Alternative, Motion for Judgment on the Pleadings as to Third-Party Complaint
and Amendment to Third-Party Complaint filed on June 16, 1999. Jenkins
contends that the Third-Party Complaint is improper under Federal Rule of Civil
Procedure 14(a). Also before the court is Third-Party Defendant Coston
Plumbing Company's Motion for Summary Judgment on the Amended Third-
Party Complaint, filed on June 18, 1999.

II

This action arises out of a December 22, 1996 fire which caused extensive damage to the home of Russell Davis. In 1996, the Davis family home was constructed at 7143 Wyngrove Drive, Montgomery, Alabama. Hugh Cole Builder, Inc. ("HCB") was the builder and general contractor for the construction. Coston Plumbing Company ("Coston"), as a subcontractor, agreed to install the gas fireplace starter in the fire box of the home. Jenkins Brick Company ("Jenkins"), another subcontractor, agreed to construct and install the fire box in which the gas fireplace starter was located. The Davis family moved into the home in early December of 1996. On December 22, 1996, a fire occurred in the home. The fireplace was the point of origin for the fire.

Pursuant to an insurance policy with Allstate Insurance Company ("Allstate"), Davis made a claim seeking indemnification and reimbursement for damages resulting from the fire. Allstate paid to Davis $718,107.48 for fire-related damage. On December 21, 1998, Allstate, as subrogee of Russell Davis, filed suit in this court against HCB and Hugh Cole, alleging negligence, breach of the implied warranty of habitability, and breach of contract. Allstate seeks to recover the amount paid to or on behalf of the Davis family for reconstruction of the home, replacement of the contents, and living expenses incurred by the Davis family during the reconstruction.

HCB and Cole subsequently filed a Third-Party Complaint, alleging that Coston and Jenkins (collectively the "Third-Party Defendants") were responsible for any negligent installation, testing, construction, or inspection of the fireplace and gas piping. Coston filed a Motion for Summary Judgment on April 2, 1999, asserting that HCB and Cole cannot pursue an action for contribution or indemnity under the facts of this case. In response to Coston's motion, HCB and Cole filed an Amendment to the Third-Party Complaint.

In their Amended Third-Party Complaint, HCB and Cole allege claims against the Third-Party Defendants for negligence (Count I), breach of implied warranty (Count II), breach of contract (Count III), violation of the Alabama Extended Manufacturers Liability Doctrine (Count IV), and breach of express warranty (Count V). The Amended Third-Party Complaint alleges that, as a result of the Third-Party Defendants' actions, the Defendants/Third-Party Plaintiffs have been damaged and have been sued for damages. On June 8, 1999, this court entered an Order denying Coston's summary judgment motion as moot because that motion was not directed to the Amended Complaint. The court ordered the Third-Party Defendants to respond to the Amended Complaint by June 18, 1999. In accordance with the court's order, the Third-Party Defendants filed the motions presently before the court.

III

Third-Party Defendant Jenkins moves to strike the Third-Party Complaint pursuant to Rule 14(a) of the Federal Rules of Civil Procedure. "In evaluating a motion to strike, the court must treat all well pleaded facts as admitted, and cannot consider matters beyond the pleadings." Carlson Corp./Southeast v. School Bd. of Seminole County, 778 F. Supp. 518, 519 (M.D. Fla. 1991).

Federal Rule of Civil Procedure 14(a) governs the impleader of third-party defendants. Rule 14(a) provides in part, "At any time after commencement of the action a defending party, as a third-party plaintiff, may cause a summons and complaint to be served upon a person not a party to the action who is or may be liable to the third-party plaintiff for all or part of the plaintiff's claim against the third-party plaintiff." Fed. R. Civ. P. 14(a). Jenkins contends that HCB and Cole are attempting to state separate and distinct causes of action against a Third-Party, a practice not allowed by Rule 14(a).

Addressing Rule 14(a), the Fifth Circuit held that impleader is permitted "only in cases where the Third Party's liability was in some way derivative of the outcome of the main claim." United States v. Joe Grasso & Son, Inc., 380 F.2d 749, 751 (1967). Thus, for impleader to be available, the Third Party must be "liable secondarily to the original defendant in the event that the latter is held liable to the plaintiff." Id. "An entirely separate and independent claim cannot be maintained against a Third Party under Rule 14, even though it does arise out of the same general set of facts as the main claim." Id. A leading treatise on federal practice states as follows:

> The test for joinder of a Third Party under the impleader rule is not transactional. Thus, it differs from the standards for compulsory counterclaims and cross-claims, which are appropriate only if they arise from the same "transaction or occurrence" as the underlying suit. Impleader, in contrast, is narrower. It must involve an attempt to pass on to the Third Party all or part of the liability asserted against the defendant. Thus, it must be an assertion of the third-party defendant's *derivative* liability to the third-party plaintiff. An impleader claim cannot be used to assert any and all rights to recovery arising from the same transaction or occurrence as the underlying action.

3 Moore's Federal Practice, P 14.04(3)(a) (3rd ed. 1999) (footnotes omitted) (emphasis in original); see also City of Orange Beach v. Scottsdale Ins. Co., 166 F.R.D. 506, 511 (S.D. Ala. 1996), *aff'd* 113 F.3d 1251 (11th Cir. 1997).

The Third-Party Plaintiffs contend that their claims against the subcontractors are proper under Rule 14(a) because the rule was intended to avoid duplicative litigation, which would result if the Third-Party Defendants were dismissed from this action. In support, they cite an Alabama Supreme Court opinion wherein the court stated:

> Third-party practice, as available under Rule 14, is particularly viable in cases such as this, where the alleged liability of a general contractor has its origin in the defective performance of one or more of the numerous subcontractors or suppliers. Without impleader, a contractor found in breach of the contract and liable for the resulting damages must then initiate one or more actions to determine the liability of the subcontractors and suppliers. The witnesses and evidence presented in these subsequent actions will be substantially identical to those in the first trial, as will the posture of the issues themselves, as well as the factual and legal questions to be resolved.

Ex Parte Duncan Construction Co., 460 So. 2d 852, 854 (Ala. 1984). That case, however, involved an order severing the third-party complaints for trial on the basis that "the case will be unduly complicated and very difficult for the jury to comprehend if any third-party defendants are allowed to remain in the case." Id. at 853. There was no contention that the third-party claims were inappropriate under Rule 14, as the third-party plaintiff was asserting indemnity claims. See id. Instead, the Alabama Supreme Court addressed whether the trial court abused its discretion by choosing to sever valid third-party claims under Rule 14.

Contending that impleader would avoid duplicative litigation does not relieve the Third-Party Plaintiffs of the essential requirements of Rule 14. HCB and Cole have not asserted any right to contribution or indemnification in their Amended Complaint. They do not assert derivative liability on the part of the Third-Party Defendants. In their Response in Opposition to Jenkins' Motion, the Third-Party Plaintiffs vigorously assert that they are not seeking contribution or indemnification. The Third-Party Plaintiffs state, "Cole has not sought contribution from Jenkins. Rather, Cole has asserted claims against Jenkins which arise out of the same transaction or circumstances giving rise to the Plaintiff's claim against Cole." As noted above, the transactional test does not apply to claims brought under Rule 14.

Because the Third-Party Plaintiffs attempt to assert separate and independent claims and do not assert derivative liability on the part of the Third-Party Defendants, they cannot bring their claims against the subcontractors in the present action under Rule 14(a). Accordingly, Jenkins' Motion to Strike the Third-Party Complaint is granted. For the same reason, the claims against Third-Party Defendant Coston are dismissed. * * *

NOTES AND PROBLEMS FOR DISCUSSION

1. Why is Allstate the plaintiff rather than Davis?

2. The parties seem to agree that the fireplace was the point of origin of the fire. And there are five possibilities with respect to responsibility for the fire. (1) HCB (and Cole) is liable; (2) Costin is liable; (3) Jenkins is liable; (4) some combination of HCB, Costin and Jenkins are liable; and (5) none of these parties has any liability. Couldn't Allstate join HCB, Costin and Jenkins as defendants under Rule 20?

3. Since it would make sense to have all of these relevant parties in the litigation, why does the Court dismiss the third-party claims against Costin and Jenkins?

4. The answer to the preceding question makes it clear that Rule 14(a) cannot be used simply because (a) the defendant wants to say "it's him and not me"; or (b) there is a transactional nexus between the underlying suit and the third-party's actions; or (c) the absent parties are important witnesses. Instead, Rule 14(a) is applicable only to situations where, if the defendant loses, it has a right to recover all or part of *its* loss from a third party. Such a right may arise by contract (e.g., an insurance or indemnity agreement), or state law may create such a right, such as the right to contribution among joint tortfeasors. For example, if a retailer can be held liable for selling a defective product under applicable law, it may also be able to obtain indemnity from the manufacturer. The seller's liability here often referred to as derivative or "secondary."

5. Another instance of derivative liability arises if an employee commits a tort in the scope of his employment — e.g., driving on the employer's business. Under tort law, the employer (master) is vicariously liable for the torts of its employee (servant), but the employer's liability is secondary to that of the employee. If X is injured and brings an action against Employer, can Employer implead Employee under Rule 14(a)? If X sued only Employee, could Employee implead Employer?

6. As noted above, under traditional doctrines of contribution among joint tortfeasors, one tortfeasor may obtain contribution from another for jointly caused torts. For example, A and B collide and injure P, a pedestrian. P sues A. Traditionally, under doctrines of joint and several liability, a plaintiff could look to any tortfeasor to collect 100% of her damages even if the tortfeasor was only partly responsible. A may therefore have the right to obtain contribution from B for all or some of the loss A has to pay P. And in such situations, provided state substantive law provides for contribution, then A could use Rule 14(a) to bring in B. In other words, a defendant must first determine whether there is a right of contribution (presumably, still covered in your Torts class) and, depending on the answer, such defendant may be able to use Rule 14(a). Where the common law rule of joint and several liability has been statutorily modified, however, matters become more difficult. For example, if a state allowed a defendant to be liable to the initial plaintiff only to the extent of his or her degree of fault, no right of contribution against co-tortfeasors would normally arise under state tort law.

7. As with all instances of joinder of an additional party, questions of personal jurisdiction crop up when a third-party is added under Rule 14(a), and perhaps questions of venue as well — a topic with which we deal briefly, at the end of the note material in Section E, Note 5, below.

SECTION E.   MORE COMPLEX PATTERNS

Each of the above sections dealt with a single joinder issue. But sometimes joinder issues occur together and require applications of two or more of the joinder rules. Let us start with some easy applications and move on to the more difficult.

1. Although we have previously discussed a counterclaim as being by defendant against plaintiff, it is not necessarily so limited. For example, assume a car accident in which cars driven by Acton and Barker collide and, as a result, Karen (a pedestrian), Acton and Barker are all injured. Karen sues Acton and Barker.

(a) Are Acton and Barker properly joined as defendants? See Rule 20.

(b) Can Acton assert a claim for his injuries against Barker? See Rule 13(g).

(c) If the answer to (b) is "yes," can Barker counterclaim against Acton? See Rule 13(a).

(d) If the answer to (b) is "yes," can Acton join Ford, manufacturer of Barker's car, on the theory that the car had defective brakes which may have caused the accident? See Rule 13(h).

2. Same facts as #1, except Karen sues only Ford, the manufacturer of Barker's car. Can Karen join an additional claim against Ford arising from her own purchase of a Ford which was defective? See Rule 18.

3. Same basic facts as #1, except Karen sues Acton, Barker, and Ford, and Acton cross-claims against Ford. Can Barker assert a claim against Ford arising from his purchase of another Ford, not involved in the accident, which was defective? If you said yes to #2 and no to #3, explain the different results.

4. The above questions arise in the cross-claim context, but note that you can have exactly the same kinds of issues arising in connection with third-party claims under Rule 14(a).

5. Venue and third-party joinder. Thus far, we have kept the jurisdictional issues associated with joinder to a minimum. But as we indicated earlier in this chapter, satisfaction of the joinder Rules is only a first step in resolving an issue of joinder. Personal jurisdiction is always a consideration when a third-party is brought in, as in *Asahi v. Superior Court*, discussed in Chapter 2. But venue is generally thought not to be affected by the joinder of a third-party if venue is already proper in the underlying action. See Gundle Lining Constr. Corp. v. Adams County Asphalt, 85 F.3d 201, 209 (5th Cir. 1996); One Beacon Ins. Co. v. JNB Storage Trailer Rental Corp., 312 F.Supp. 2d 824, 829 (E.D. Va. 2004) ("the statutory venue limitations have no application to Rule 14 claims") (quoting 6 Charles Alan Wright et al., Federal Practice & Procedure §1445, at 348 (2d ed. 1990)). Subject matter jurisdiction concerns in connection with third-party practice under Rule 14 (impleader) are more complex. Consider the following decision (decided before the advent of 28 U.S.C. §1367):

Owen Equipment & Erection Corp. v. Kroger

Supreme Court of the United States, 1978.

437 U.S. 365, 98 S.Ct. 2369, 57 L.Ed.2d 274.

Mr. Justice Stewart delivered the opinion of the Court.

In an action in which federal jurisdiction is based on diversity of citizenship, may the plaintiff assert a claim against a third-party defendant when there is no independent basis for federal jurisdiction over that claim? The Court of Appeals for the Eighth Circuit held in this case that such a claim is within the ancillary jurisdiction of the federal courts. We granted certiorari, because this decision conflicts with several recent decisions of other Courts of Appeals.

I

On January 18, 1972, James Kroger was electrocuted when the boom of a steel crane next to which he was walking came too close to a high-tension electric power line. The respondent (his widow, who is the administratrix of his estate) filed a wrongful-death action in the United States District Court for the District of Nebraska against the Omaha Public Power District (OPPD). Her complaint alleged that OPPD's negligent construction, maintenance, and operation of the power line had caused Kroger's death. Federal jurisdiction was based on diversity of citizenship, since the respondent was a citizen of Iowa and OPPD was a Nebraska corporation.

OPPD then filed a third-party complaint pursuant to Fed. Rule Civ. Proc. 14(a) against the petitioner, Owen Equipment and Erection Co. (Owen), alleging that the crane was owned and operated by Owen, and that Owen's negligence had been the proximate cause of Kroger's death.[3] OPPD later moved for summary judgment on the respondent's complaint against it. While this motion was pending, the respondent was granted leave to file an amended complaint naming Owen as an additional defendant. Thereafter, the District Court granted OPPD's motion for summary judgment in an unreported opinion. The case thus went to trial between the respondent and the petitioner alone.

The respondent's amended complaint alleged that Owen was "a Nebraska corporation with its principal place of business in Nebraska." Owen's answer admitted that it was "a corporation organized and existing under the laws of the State of Nebraska," and denied every other allegation of the complaint. On the third day of trial, however, it was disclosed that the petitioner's principal place of business was in Iowa, not Nebraska,[5] and that the petitioner and the respondent were thus both citizens of Iowa. The petitioner then moved to dismiss the complaint for lack of jurisdiction. The District Court reserved decision on the motion, and the jury thereafter returned a verdict in favor of the respondent. In an unreported opinion issued after the trial, the District Court denied the petitioner's motion to dismiss the complaint.

The judgment was affirmed on appeal. The Court of Appeals held that under this Court's decision in Mine Workers v. Gibbs, 383 U.S. 715, the District Court had jurisdictional power, in its discretion, to adjudicate the respondent's claim against the petitioner because that claim arose from the "core of 'operative facts' giving rise to both [respondent's] claim against OPPD and OPPD's claim

---

[3]   Under Rule 14 (a), a third-party defendant may not be impleaded merely because he may be liable to the plaintiff. See * * * Advisory Committee's Notes on 1946 Amendment to Fed. Rule Civ. Proc. 14, 28 U.S.C. App., pp. 7752-7753. While the third-party complaint in this case alleged merely that Owen's negligence caused Kroger's death, and the basis of Owen's alleged liability to OPPD is nowhere spelled out, OPPD evidently relied upon the state common-law right of contribution among joint tortfeasors. See Dairyland Ins. Co. v. Mumert, 212 N.W.2d 436, 438 (Iowa); Best v. Yerkes, 247 Iowa 800, 77 N.W.2d 23. The petitioner has never challenged the propriety of the third-party complaint as such.

[5]   The problem apparently was one of geography. Although the Missouri River generally marks the boundary between Iowa and Nebraska, Carter Lake, Iowa, where the accident occurred and where Owen had its main office, lies west of the river, adjacent to Omaha, Neb. Apparently the river once avulsed at one of its bends, cutting Carter Lake off from the rest of Iowa.

against Owen." It further held that the District Court had properly exercised its discretion in proceeding to decide the case even after summary judgment had been granted to OPPD, because the petitioner had concealed its Iowa citizenship from the respondent.

II

It is undisputed that there was no independent basis of federal jurisdiction over the respondent's state-law tort action against the petitioner, since both are citizens of Iowa. And although Fed. Rule Civ. Proc. 14(a) permits a plaintiff to assert a claim against a third-party defendant, it does not purport to say whether or not such a claim requires an independent basis of federal jurisdiction. Indeed, it could not determine that question, since it is axiomatic that the Federal Rules of Civil Procedure do not create or withdraw federal jurisdiction.

In affirming the District Court's judgment, the Court of Appeals relied upon the doctrine of ancillary jurisdiction, whose contours it believed were defined by this Court's holding in *Mine Workers v. Gibbs, supra.* The *Gibbs* case differed from this one in that it involved pendent jurisdiction, which concerns the resolution of a plaintiff's federal-and state-law claims against a single defendant in one action. By contrast, in this case there was no claim based upon substantive federal law, but rather state-law tort claims against two different defendants. Nonetheless, the Court of Appeals was correct in perceiving that *Gibbs* and this case are two species of the same generic problem: Under what circumstances may a federal court hear and decide a state-law claim arising between citizens of the same State? But we believe that the Court of Appeals failed to understand the scope of the doctrine of the *Gibbs* case.

The plaintiff in *Gibbs* alleged that the defendant union had violated the common law of Tennessee as well as the federal prohibition of secondary boycotts. This Court held that, although the parties were not of diverse citizenship, the District Court properly entertained the state-law claim as pendent to the federal claim. The crucial holding was stated as follows:

> "Pendent jurisdiction, in the sense of judicial *power*, exists whenever there is a claim 'arising under [the] Constitution, the Laws of the United States, and Treaties made, or which shall be made, under their Authority . . .,' U.S. Const., Art. III, 2, and the relationship between that claim and the state claim permits the conclusion that the entire action before the court comprises but one constitutional 'case.' . . . The state and federal claims must derive from a common nucleus of operative fact. But if, considered without regard to their federal or state character, a plaintiff's claims are such that he would ordinarily be expected to try them all in one judicial proceeding, then, assuming substantiality of the federal issues, there is power in federal courts to hear the whole." 383 U.S., at 725 (emphasis in original).[9]

---

[9] The Court further noted that even when such power exists, its exercise remains a matter of discretion based upon "considerations of judicial economy, convenience and fairness to litigants," 383 U.S., at 726, and held that the District Court had not abused its discretion in retaining jurisdiction of the state-law claim.

It is apparent that *Gibbs* delineated the constitutional limits of federal judicial power. But even if it be assumed that the District Court in the present case had constitutional power to decide the respondent's lawsuit against the petitioner, it does not follow that the decision of the Court of Appeals was correct. Constitutional power is merely the first hurdle that must be overcome in determining that a federal court has jurisdiction over a particular controversy. For the jurisdiction of the federal courts is limited not only by the provisions of Art. III of the Constitution, but also by Acts of Congress. Palmore v. United States, 411 U.S. 389, 401; Lockerty v. Phillips, 319 U.S. 182, 187; Kline v. Burke Constr. Co., 260 U.S. 226, 234; Cary v. Curtis, 3 How. 236, 245.

That statutory law as well as the Constitution may limit a federal court's jurisdiction over nonfederal claims[11] is well illustrated by two recent decisions of this Court, Aldinger v. Howard, 427 U.S. 1, and Zahn v. International Paper Co., 414 U.S. 291. In *Aldinger* the Court held that a Federal District Court lacked jurisdiction over a state-law claim against a county, even if that claim was alleged to be pendent to one against county officials under 42 U.S.C. §1983. In *Zahn* the Court held that in a diversity class action under Fed. Rule Civ. Proc. 23(b)(3), the claim of each member of the plaintiff class must independently satisfy the minimum jurisdictional amount set by 28 U.S.C. §1332(a), and rejected the argument that jurisdiction existed over those claims that involved $10,000 or less as ancillary to those that involved more. In each case, despite the fact that federal and nonfederal claims arose from a "common nucleus of operative fact," the Court held that the statute conferring jurisdiction over the federal claim did not allow the exercise of jurisdiction over the nonfederal claims.

The *Aldinger* and *Zahn* cases thus make clear that a finding that federal and nonfederal claims arise from a "common nucleus of operative fact," the test of *Gibbs*, does not end the inquiry into whether a federal court has power to hear the nonfederal claims along with the federal ones. Beyond this constitutional minimum, there must be an examination of the posture in which the nonfederal claim is asserted and of the specific statute that confers jurisdiction over the federal claim, in order to determine whether "Congress in [that statute] has . . . expressly or by implication negated" the exercise of jurisdiction over the particular nonfederal claim.

III

The relevant statute in this case, 28 U.S.C. §1332(a)(1), confers upon federal courts jurisdiction over "civil actions where the matter in controversy exceeds the sum or value of $10,000 . . . and is between . . . citizens of different States." This statute and its predecessors have consistently been held to require complete diversity of citizenship. That is, diversity jurisdiction does not exist unless each defendant is a citizen of a different State from each plaintiff. Over the years Congress has repeatedly re-enacted or amended the statute conferring diversity jurisdiction, leaving intact this rule of complete diversity. Whatever may have

---

[11] As used in this opinion, the term "nonfederal claim" means one as to which there is no independent basis for federal jurisdiction. Conversely, a "federal claim" means one as to which an independent basis for federal jurisdiction exists.

been the original purposes of diversity-of-citizenship jurisdiction, this subsequent history clearly demonstrates a congressional mandate that diversity jurisdiction is not to be available when any plaintiff is a citizen of the same State as any defendant. Cf. Snyder v. Harris, 394 U.S. 332, 338-339.

Thus it is clear that the respondent could not originally have brought suit in federal court naming Owen and OPPD as codefendants, since citizens of Iowa would have been on both sides of the litigation. Yet the identical lawsuit resulted when she amended her complaint. Complete diversity was destroyed just as surely as if she had sued Owen initially. In either situation, in the plain language of the statute, the "matter in controversy" could not be "between . . . citizens of different States."

It is a fundamental precept that federal courts are courts of limited jurisdiction. The limits upon federal jurisdiction, whether imposed by the Constitution or by Congress, must be neither disregarded nor evaded. Yet under the reasoning of the Court of Appeals in this case, a plaintiff could defeat the statutory requirement of complete diversity by the simple expedient of suing only those defendants who were of diverse citizenship and waiting for them to implead nondiverse defendants.[17] If, as the Court of Appeals thought, a "common nucleus of operative fact" were the only requirement for ancillary jurisdiction in a diversity case, there would be no principled reason why the respondent in this case could not have joined her cause of action against Owen in her original complaint as ancillary to her claim against OPPD. Congress' requirement of complete diversity would thus have been evaded completely.

It is true, as the Court of Appeals noted, that the exercise of ancillary jurisdiction over nonfederal claims has often been upheld in situations involving impleader, cross-claims or counterclaims. But in determining whether jurisdiction over a nonfederal claim exists, the context in which the nonfederal claim is asserted is crucial. See Aldinger v. Howard, 427 U.S., at 14. And the claim here arises in a setting quite different from the kinds of nonfederal claims that have been viewed in other cases as falling within the ancillary jurisdiction of the federal courts.

First, the nonfederal claim in this case was simply not ancillary to the federal one in the same sense that, for example, the impleader by a defendant of a third-party defendant always is. A third-party complaint depends at least in part upon the resolution of the primary lawsuit. See n. 3, supra. Its relation to the original complaint is thus not mere factual similarity but logical dependence. Cf. Moore v. New York Cotton Exchange, 270 U.S. 593, 610. The respondent's claim against the petitioner, however, was entirely separate from her original claim

---

[17] This is not an unlikely hypothesis, since a defendant in a tort suit such as this one would surely try to limit his liability by impleading any joint tortfeasors for indemnity or contribution. Some commentators have suggested that the possible abuse of third-party practice could be dealt with under 28 U.S.C. §1359, which forbids collusive attempts to create federal jurisdiction. * * * The dissenting opinion today also expresses this view. But there is nothing necessarily collusive about a plaintiff's selectively suing only those tortfeasors of diverse citizenship, or about the named defendants' desire to implead joint tortfeasors. Nonetheless, the requirement of complete diversity would be eviscerated by such a course of events.

against OPPD, since the petitioner's liability to her depended not at all upon whether or not OPPD was also liable. Far from being an ancillary and dependent claim, it was a new and independent one.

Second, the nonfederal claim here was asserted by the plaintiff, who voluntarily chose to bring suit upon a state-law claim in a federal court. By contrast, ancillary jurisdiction typically involves claims by a defending party haled into court against his will, or by another person whose rights might be irretrievably lost unless he could assert them in an ongoing action in a federal court. A plaintiff cannot complain if ancillary jurisdiction does not encompass all of his possible claims in a case such as this one, since it is he who has chosen the federal rather than the state forum and must thus accept its limitations. "[T]he efficiency plaintiff seeks so avidly is available without question in the state courts." Kenrose Mfg. Co. v. Fred Whitaker Co., 512 F.2d 890, 894 (CA4).[20]

It is not unreasonable to assume that, in generally requiring complete diversity, Congress did not intend to confine the jurisdiction of federal courts so inflexibly that they are unable to protect legal rights or effectively to resolve an entire, logically entwined lawsuit. Those practical needs are the basis of the doctrine of ancillary jurisdiction. But neither the convenience of litigants nor considerations of judicial economy can suffice to justify extension of the doctrine of ancillary jurisdiction to a plaintiff's cause of action against a citizen of the same State in a diversity case. Congress has established the basic rule that diversity jurisdiction exists under 28 U.S.C. §1332 only when there is complete diversity of citizenship. "The policy of the statute calls for its strict construction." Healy v. Ratta, 292 U.S. 263, 270; Indianapolis v. Chase Nat. Bank, 314 U.S. 63, 76; Thomson v. Gaskill, 315 U.S. 442, 446; Snyder v. Harris, 394 U.S., at 340. To allow the requirement of complete diversity to be circumvented as it was in this case would simply flout the congressional command.[21]

Accordingly, the judgment of the Court of Appeals is reversed.

It is so ordered.

MR. JUSTICE WHITE, with whom MR. JUSTICE BRENNAN joins, dissenting.

The Court today states that "[i]t is not unreasonable to assume that, in generally requiring complete diversity, Congress did not intend to confine the jurisdiction of federal courts so inflexibly that they are unable . . . effectively to resolve an entire, logically entwined lawsuit." In spite of this recognition, the majority goes on to hold that in diversity suits federal courts do not have the jurisdictional power to entertain a claim asserted by a plaintiff against a third-party defendant, no matter how entwined it is with the matter already before the

---

[20] Whether Iowa's statute of limitations would now bar an action by the respondent in an Iowa court is, of course, entirely a matter of state law. * * *

[21] Our holding is that the District Court lacked power to entertain the respondent's lawsuit against the petitioner. Thus, the asserted inequity in the respondent's alleged concealment of its citizenship is irrelevant. Federal judicial power does not depend upon "prior action or consent of the parties." American Fire & Cas. Co. v. Finn, 341 U.S., at 17-18.

court, unless there is an independent basis for jurisdiction over that claim. Because I find no support for such a requirement in either Art. III of the Constitution or in any statutory law, I dissent from the Court's "unnecessarily grudging" approach.

The plaintiff below, Mrs. Kroger, chose to bring her lawsuit against the Omaha Public Power District (OPPD) in Federal District Court. No one questions the power of the District Court to entertain this claim, for Mrs. Kroger at the time was a citizen of Iowa, OPPD was a citizen of Nebraska, and the amount in controversy was greater than $10,000; jurisdiction therefore existed under 28 U.S.C. §1332(a). As permitted by Fed. Rule Civ. Proc. 14(a), OPPD impleaded petitioner Owen Equipment & Erection Co. (Owen). Although OPPD's claim against Owen did not raise a federal question and although it was alleged that Owen was a citizen of the same State as OPPD, the parties and the court apparently believed that the District Court's ancillary jurisdiction encompassed this claim. Subsequently, Mrs. Kroger asserted a claim against Owen, everyone believing at the time that these two parties were citizens of different States. Because it later came to light that Mrs. Kroger and Owen were in fact both citizens of Iowa, the Court concludes that the District Court lacked jurisdiction over the claim.

In Mine Workers v. Gibbs, 383 U.S. 715, 725 (1966), we held that once a claim has been stated that is of sufficient substance to confer subject-matter jurisdiction on the federal district court, the court has judicial power to consider a nonfederal claim if it and the federal claim are derived from "a common nucleus of operative fact." Although the specific facts of that case concerned a state claim that was said to be pendent to a federal-question claim, the Court's language and reasoning were broad enough to cover the instant factual situation: "[I]f, considered without regard to their federal or state character, a plaintiff's claims are such that he would ordinarily be expected to try them all in one judicial proceeding, then, assuming substantiality of the federal issues, there is power in federal courts to hear the whole." Ibid. (footnote omitted). In the present case, Mrs. Kroger's claim against Owen and her claim against OPPD derived from a common nucleus of fact; this is necessarily so because in order for a plaintiff to assert a claim against a third-party defendant, Fed. Rule Civ. Proc. 14(a) requires that it "aris[e] out of the transaction or occurrence that is the subject matter of the plaintiff's claim against the third-party plaintiff ...." Furthermore, the substantiality of the claim Mrs. Kroger asserted against OPPD is unquestioned. Accordingly, as far as Art. III of the Constitution is concerned, the District Court had power to entertain Mrs. Kroger's claim against Owen.

The majority correctly points out, however, that the analysis cannot stop here. As Aldinger v. Howard, 427 U.S. 1 (1976), teaches, the jurisdictional power of the federal courts may be limited by Congress, as well as by the Constitution. In *Aldinger*, although the plaintiff's state claim against Spokane County was closely connected with her 42 U.S.C. §1983 claim against the county treasurer, the Court held that the District Court did not have pendent jurisdiction over the state claim, for, under the Court's precedents at that time, it was thought that Congress had specifically determined not to confer on the federal courts jurisdiction over civil rights claims against cities and counties.

That being so, the Court refused to allow "the federal courts to fashion a jurisdictional doctrine under the general language of Art. III enabling them to circumvent this exclusion . . . ." 427 U.S., at 16.

In the present case, the only indication of congressional intent that the Court can find is that contained in the diversity jurisdiction statute, 28 U.S.C. §1332(a), which states that "district courts shall have original jurisdiction of all civil actions where the matter in controversy exceeds the sum or value of $10,000 . . . and is between . . . citizens of different States . . . ." Because this statute has been interpreted as requiring complete diversity of citizenship between each plaintiff and each defendant, Strawbridge v. Curtiss, 3 Cranch 267 (1806), the Court holds that the District Court did not have ancillary jurisdiction over Mrs. Kroger's claim against Owen. In so holding, the Court unnecessarily expands the scope of the complete-diversity requirement while substantially limiting the doctrine of ancillary jurisdiction.

The complete-diversity requirement, of course, could be viewed as meaning that in a diversity case, a federal district court may adjudicate only those claims that are between parties of different States. Thus, in order for a defendant to implead a third-party defendant, there would have to be diversity of citizenship; the same would also be true for cross-claims between defendants and for a third-party defendant's claim against a plaintiff. Even the majority, however, refuses to read the complete-diversity requirement so broadly; it recognizes with seeming approval the exercise of ancillary jurisdiction over nonfederal claims in situations involving impleader, cross-claims, and counterclaims. Given the Court's willingness to recognize ancillary jurisdiction in these contexts, despite the requirements of 1332(a), I see no justification for the Court's refusal to approve the District Court's exercise of ancillary jurisdiction in the present case.

It is significant that a plaintiff who asserts a claim against a third-party defendant is not seeking to add a new party to the lawsuit. In the present case, for example, Owen had already been brought into the suit by OPPD, and, that having been done, Mrs. Kroger merely sought to assert against Owen a claim arising out of the same transaction that was already before the court. Thus the situation presented here is unlike that in *Aldinger, supra*, wherein the Court noted:

> "[I]t is one thing to authorize two parties, already present in federal court by virtue of a case over which the court has jurisdiction, to litigate in addition to their federal claim a state-law claim over which there is no independent basis of federal jurisdiction. But it is quite another thing to permit a plaintiff, who has asserted a claim against one defendant with respect to which there is federal jurisdiction, to join an entirely different defendant on the basis of a state-law claim over which there is no independent basis of federal jurisdiction, simply because his claim against the first defendant and his claim against the second defendant 'derive from a common nucleus of operative fact.' . . . True, the same considerations of judicial economy would be served insofar as plaintiff's claims 'are such that he would ordinarily be expected to try them all in one judicial proceeding . . . .' [*Gibbs*, 383 U.S., at 725.] But the addition of a completely new party would run counter to the well-established

principle that federal courts, as opposed to state trial courts of general jurisdiction, are courts of limited jurisdiction marked out by Congress." 427 U.S., at 14-15.

Because in the instant case Mrs. Kroger merely sought to assert a claim against someone already a party to the suit, considerations of judicial economy, convenience, and fairness to the litigants — the factors relied upon in Gibbs — support the recognition of ancillary jurisdiction here. Already before the court was the whole question of the cause of Mr. Kroger's death. Mrs. Kroger initially contended that OPPD was responsible; OPPD in turn contended that Owen's negligence had been the proximate cause of Mr. Kroger's death. In spite of the fact that the question of Owen's negligence was already before the District Court, the majority requires Mrs. Kroger to bring a separate action in state court in order to assert that very claim. Even if the Iowa statute of limitations will still permit such a suit, see ante n.20, considerations of judicial economy are certainly not served by requiring such duplicative litigation.[4]

The majority, however, brushes aside such considerations of convenience, judicial economy, and fairness because it concludes that recognizing ancillary jurisdiction over a plaintiff's claim against a third-party defendant would permit the plaintiff to circumvent the complete-diversity requirement and thereby "flout the congressional command." Since the plaintiff in such a case does not bring the third-party defendant into the suit, however, there is no occasion for deliberate circumvention of the diversity requirement, absent collusion, with the defendant. In the case of such collusion, of which there is absolutely no indication here, the court can dismiss the action under the authority of 28 U.S.C. §1359. In the absence of such collusion, there is no reason to adopt an absolute rule prohibiting the plaintiff from asserting those claims that he may properly assert against the third-party defendant pursuant to Fed. Rule Civ. Proc. 14(a). The plaintiff in such a situation brings suit against the defendant only, with absolutely no assurance that the defendant will decide or be able to implead a particular third-party defendant. Since the plaintiff has no control over the defendant's decision to implead a third party, the fact that he could not have originally sued that party in federal court should be irrelevant. Moreover, the fact that a plaintiff in some cases may be able to foresee the subsequent chain of events leading to the impleader does not seem to me to be a sufficient reason to declare that a district court does not have the power to exercise ancillary jurisdiction over the plaintiff's claims against the third-party defendant.[7]

---

[4] It is true that prior to trial OPPD was dismissed as a party to the suit and that, as we indicated in *Gibbs*, the dismissal prior to trial of the federal claim will generally require the dismissal of the nonfederal claim as well. See 383 U.S., at 726. Given the unusual facts of the present case, however — in particular, the fact that the actual location of Owen's principal place of business was not revealed until the third day of trial — fairness to the parties would lead me to conclude that the District Court did not abuse its discretion in retaining jurisdiction over Mrs. Kroger's claim against Owen. Under the Court's disposition, of course, it would not matter whether or not the federal claim is tried, for in either situation the court would have no jurisdiction over the plaintiff's nonfederal claim against the third-party defendant.

[7] Under the *Gibbs* analysis, recognition of the district court's power to hear a plaintiff's nonfederal claim against a third-party defendant in a diversity suit would not mean that the court

[I]t seems to me appropriate to view §1332 as requiring complete diversity only between the plaintiff and those parties he actually brings into the suit. Beyond that, I would hold that in a diversity case the District Court has power, both constitutional and statutory, to entertain all claims among the parties arising from the same nucleus of operative fact as the plaintiff's original, jurisdiction-conferring claim against the defendant. Accordingly, I dissent from the Court's disposition of the present case.

NOTES AND PROBLEMS FOR DISCUSSION

1. *Kroger* was decided before the advent of 28 U.S.C. §1367. Under the statute, would the result be the same? To answer the question, focus first on two aspects of joinder in the case: (a) impleader of the third-party defendant; and (b) Kroger's claim against the third-party defendant.

(a) *OPPD's impleading of Owen.* Omaha Public Power District (OPPD) brought in Owen Equipment as a third-party defendant. The majority finds this unproblematic from the perspective of Rule 14. See footnote 3 of the opinion. The majority, however, does not expressly discuss the jurisdictional issues in connection with OPPD's impleading of Owen. Clearly there was personal jurisdiction. And the Court appears to assume that subject matter jurisdiction was not a problem either. Why was that? OPPD was a citizen of Nebraska and Owen was ultimately determined to be a citizen of Iowa and Nebraska. Complete diversity was lacking as between them as well as between the plaintiff and Owen. In the course of the opinion, however, the Court observes that (pre-§1367) "ancillary" jurisdiction would attach to impleader.

Now consider what the result would be under §1367. Take your time here. First, determine whether paragraph (a)'s nexus requirement for supplemental jurisdiction is satisfied by the defendant's addition of a third-party. Next, because the case is one that is grounded solely on diversity, determine whether paragraph (b) lists impleader as an exception to the exercise of supplemental jurisdiction in diversity cases. Note that Rule 14 claims are mentioned in this paragraph, but only when a *plaintiff* seeks to add a claim against a Rule 14 party. What does this say about the availability of supplemental jurisdiction over impleader claims brought by defendants in the first instance?

(b) *Kroger's claim against Owen.* Now, turn to the possible basis in the federal rules for Kroger's claim against Owen (for which there was no independent subject matter jurisdictional basis). See Rule 14(a)(3). Consider (first) §1367(a); and (second) §1367(b). Do you see how the language referencing Rule 14 in §1367(b) begins to echo the pre-§1367 result in *Kroger* itself?

---

would be required to entertain such claims in all cases. The district court would have the discretion to dismiss the nonfederal claim if it concluded that the interests of judicial economy, convenience, and fairness would not be served by the retention of the claim in the federal lawsuit. See *Gibbs*, 383 U.S., at 726. Accordingly, the majority's concerns that lead it to conclude that ancillary jurisdiction should not be recognized in the present situation could be met on a case-by-case basis, rather than by the absolute rule it adopts.

2. At a more basic level, consider why federal courts (and now, Congress) proved more willing to allow a defendant to implead a third-party defendant who "busts" diversity than, for example, to allow a plaintiff in her original complaint to add a second defendant who busts diversity. Strictly speaking, neither may be consistent with the complete diversity rule, and yet one of the two joinders is tolerated. Is there an explanation?

3. The majority in *Kroger* (and Congress in §1367) refuses to distinguish between the plaintiff's effort to sue the third-party, Owen, from an initial decision to join two defendants, one diverse, and one not. Yet the defendant Owen is already "there" in a relevant sense by the time Kroger sues them. And, in the typical case, the possible fault of the third-party defendant vis-à-vis the plaintiff will likely be considered along with the defendant's possible fault, *whether or not* the plaintiff does or can assert a claim against the third party. Are the majority's (and now, perhaps, Congress's) fears of plaintiffs playing fast and loose with joinder rules realistic?

4. Consider the relevance of OPPD's having been dismissed from the action on summary judgment. If the Court had been willing to allow a plaintiff to add a claim against an otherwise properly impleaded (albeit nondiverse) third-party defendant (Owen), would the later disappearance of the original (diverse) defendant (OPPD) work a loss of power to hear the remainder of the case, in the jurisdictional sense? See also §1367(c) (allowing for discretionary (i.e., nonmandatory) dismissal of a supplemental claim when federal jurisdiction conferring elements drop out early on).

5. An endlessly entertaining question is a variant on *Kroger*: Suppose that, instead of Kroger adding a claim against Owen after it is brought-in as a third-party, Owen was able to assert some sort of claim against Kroger (e.g., the decedent's negligence was responsible for damage to Owen's crane). See Rule 14(a); §1367(a) & (b). Assuming that this is allowable, may Kroger *then* assert a claim against Owen, and secure supplemental jurisdiction over her claim, as a "defending party" in *Kroger*'s language? Can such a result be squared with the language of §1367(b)?

6. Finally, note that the *Kroger* problem arises today because of §1367(b), which, among other things, appears to codify the decision's result. But if, for example, a plaintiff seeks to add a claim against a third-party defendant in a case originally brought by the plaintiff on the basis of federal law, §1367(b) will not be an obstacle, even if the third-party is nondiverse from the plaintiff, and even if the plaintiff's claim against the third-party is premised on state law. Nor will it pose a problem when there is an independent subject matter jurisdictional basis for plaintiff's claim against the third-party defendant (e.g., because it arises under federal law, or because plaintiff and the third-party defendant are diverse and the claim is in excess of the amount in controversy).

SECTION F. MANDATORY JOINDER OF PARTIES

Under Rule 20, the plaintiff establishes the initial line up of parties — both as to plaintiffs (who must be willing to join) and defendants (whether or not they are willing to join). The defendant has the power to assert counterclaims against the plaintiff and cross-claims against co-defendants, and to bring in third parties who may be liable to the defendant for all or part of plaintiff's claims. If the counterclaims or cross-claims involve the addition of new parties, they too can be joined as far as the Rules are concerned. See Rule 13(h).

Here, we consider a different concept — that the defendant (and perhaps the court) can insist on the joinder of a party who satisfies none of these requirements. Rule 19 divides such parties into two categories: parties who meet the requirements of Rule 19(a), often called necessary parties, and those who meet the further tests of Rule 19(b), often called indispensable parties.

Consider the significance of an absent party being in one category or the other. If an absent party is determined to fall within Rule 19(a), that party must be joined "if feasible." This means that the existing plaintiff must seek to join that party and has lost a measure of control over the party lineup. The "if feasible" refers to personal and subject matter jurisdiction, and venue; it is not "feasible" to join a party if joinder would destroy subject matter jurisdiction, or involves a party who cannot be served, or whose joinder would destroy venue. If a party falls within Rule 19(a) and their joinder is not possible, the court must determine whether that party also falls within Rule 19(b). What do you think happens if the court's answer to that question is "yes"?

In short, Rule 19 carries a threat to the plaintiff — to undermine plaintiff's choice of parties and any strategy based on the original lineup, and worse, to require her to start over elsewhere (if she can).

Temple v. Synthes Corp.

Supreme Court of the United States, 1990.

498 U.S. 5, 111 S.Ct. 315, 112 L.Ed.2d 263.

PER CURIAM.

Petitioner Temple, a Mississippi resident, underwent surgery in October 1986 in which a "plate and screw device" was implanted in his lower spine. The device was manufactured by respondent Synthes, Ltd. (U.S.A.) (Synthes), a Pennsylvania corporation. Dr. S. Henry LaRocca performed the surgery at St. Charles General Hospital in New Orleans, Louisiana. Following surgery, the device's screws broke off inside Temple's back.

Temple filed suit against Synthes in the United States District Court for the Eastern District of Louisiana. The suit, which rested on diversity jurisdiction, alleged defective design and manufacture of the device. At the same time, Temple filed a state administrative proceeding against Dr. LaRocca and the hospital for malpractice and negligence. At the conclusion of the administrative proceeding, Temple filed suit against the doctor and the hospital in Louisiana state court.

Synthes did not attempt to bring the doctor and the hospital into the federal action by means of a third-party complaint, as provided in Federal Rule of Civil Procedure 14(a). Instead, Synthes filed a motion to dismiss Temple's federal suit for failure to join necessary parties pursuant to Federal Rule of Civil Procedure 19. Following a hearing, the District Court ordered Temple to join the doctor and the hospital as defendants within 20 days or risk dismissal of the lawsuit. According to the court, the most significant reason for requiring joinder was the interest of judicial economy. The court relied on this Court's decision in Provident Tradesmens Bank & Trust Co. v. Patterson, 390 U.S. 102 (1968), wherein we recognized that one focus of Rule 19 is "the interest of the courts and the public in complete, consistent, and efficient settlement of controversies." Id., at 111. When Temple failed to join the doctor and the hospital, the court dismissed the suit with prejudice.

Temple appealed, and the United States Court of Appeals for the Fifth Circuit affirmed. 898 F. 2d 152 (1990). The court deemed it "obviously prejudicial to the defendants to have the separate litigations being carried on," because Synthes' defense might be that the plate was not defective but that the doctor and the hospital were negligent, while the doctor and the hospital, on the other hand, might claim that they were not negligent but that the plate was defective. The Court of Appeals found that the claims overlapped and that the District Court therefore had not abused its discretion in ordering joinder under Rule 19. A petition for rehearing was denied.

In his petition for certiorari to this Court, Temple contends that it was error to label joint tortfeasors as indispensable parties under Rule 19(b) and to dismiss the lawsuit with prejudice for failure to join those parties. We agree. Synthes does not deny that it, the doctor, and the hospital are potential joint tortfeasors. It has long been the rule that it is not necessary for all joint tortfeasors to be named as defendants in a single lawsuit. See Lawlor v. National Screen Service Corp., 349 U.S. 322, 329-330 (1955); Bigelow v. Old Dominion Copper Mining & Smelting Co., 225 U.S. 111, 132 (1912). See also Nottingham v. General American Communications Corp., 811 F. 2d 873, 880 (CA5) (per curiam), cert. denied, 484 U.S. 854 (1987). Nothing in the 1966 revision of Rule 19 changed that principle. See *Provident Bank, supra,* at 116-117, n. 12. The Advisory Committee Notes to Rule 19(a) explicitly state that "a tortfeasor with the usual 'joint-and-several' liability is merely a permissive party to an action against another with like liability." 28 U.S.C. App., p. 595. There is nothing in Louisiana tort law to the contrary. See Mullin v. Skains, 252 La. 1009, 1014, 215 So. 2d 643, 645 (1968); La. Civ. Code Ann., Arts. 1794, 1795 (West 1987).

The opinion in *Provident Bank, supra,* does speak of the public interest in limiting multiple litigation, but that case is not controlling here. There, the estate of a tort victim brought a declaratory judgment action against an insurance company. We assumed that the policyholder was a person "who, under 19(a), should be 'joined if feasible.'" 390 U.S., at 108, and went on to discuss the appropriate analysis under Rule 19(b), because the policy holder could not be joined without destroying diversity. Id., at 109-116. After examining the factors set forth in Rule 19(b), we determined that the action could proceed without the policyholder; he therefore was not an indispensable party whose absence required dismissal of the suit. Id., at 116,119.

Here, no inquiry under Rule 19(b) is necessary, because the threshold requirements of Rule 19(a) have not been satisfied. As potential joint tortfeasors with Synthes, Dr. LaRocca and the hospital were merely permissive parties. The Court of Appeals erred by failing to hold that the District Court abused its discretion in ordering them joined as defendants and in dismissing the action when Temple failed to comply with the court's order. For these reasons, we grant the petition for certiorari, reverse the judgment of the Court of Appeals for the Fifth Circuit, and remand for further proceedings consistent with this opinion.

It is so ordered.

NOTES AND PROBLEMS FOR DISCUSSION

1. Consider what the main issues would be in the trial of Temple's case. Since the doctor and the hospital certainly could have been joined in the federal action (i.e., their joinder was feasible), wouldn't it make sense to have them as parties, both for purposes of efficiency and avoidance of multiple litigation, and possibly even inconsistent results?

2. The Court in *Temple* tersely points out that it has been the traditional practice not to consider joint tortfeasors as parties who must be joined if feasible under Rule 19(a), and that the Advisory Committee did not wish to change this practice when it amended Rule 19 to its present form. Work carefully through the language of Rule 19(a) and explain why the requirements for mandatory joinder are not met.

3. If the Doctor and the Hospital are not joined in the litigation in federal court, there is of course a risk of inconsistent judgments arising from multiple litigation over the same issues (e.g., the federal court might conclude that the medical device was not a cause of the plaintiff's injuries, while the state courts might conclude that the cause was neither the doctor nor the hospital, but the medical device). Does Rule 19(a) seek to guard against multiple litigation or inconsistent results? See Southern Co. Energy Marketing, L.P. v. Virginia Elec. & Power Co., 190 F.R.D. 182 (E.D. Va. 1999) (indicating that only "inconsistent obligations" not "inconsistent judgments" are the focus of Rule 19(a)); see also Field v. Volkswagenwerk AG, 626 F.2d 293 (3d Cir. 1980) (noting that the distinction between Rule 20 and Rule 19 would be obliterated if Rule 19's "complete relief" provision were read to require joinder of factually and legally similar claims arising out of the same incident).

4. *Temple*'s approach to Rule 19 notwithstanding, at least one state court experimented with a version of its own mandatory joinder rule requiring that the "entire controversy" be resolved in a single proceeding. See Cogdell v. Hospital Center at Orange, 116 N.J. 7, 26 (1989). The experiment was short lived, however, partly because the obligatory joinder of multiple claims and parties made litigation larger and more complicated than it had to be. Also, it was not always possible to know in advance what would be encompassed by the notion of the "entire controversy" (with preclusion as the penalty for nonjoinder). See Olds v. Donnelly, 150 N.J. 424 (1997).

5. As noted above in the discussion of third-party practice, some states have modified the common-law principles of joint and several liability. A state, for example, might only permit a defendant to be liable for his or her own share of fault, rather than be liable for the entire amount of the plaintiff's damages (with a right of contribution from any other tortfeasor(s)). Consider the plaintiff's incentives as far as joinder is concerned in such a state. If a suit based on state law is brought in a state with such a rule, will it affect the Rule 19 calculus as elaborated under *Temple*?

6. Some common applications of necessary party rules have been in cases where there are owners of jointly owned property, joint obligors or joint obligees, and, sometimes where there are trustees or other representatives and beneficiaries. In light of the language of Rule 19(a), how are these examples distinguishable from the joint tortfeasor context of *Temple*?

7. Note the consequence if a court determines (as did the lower federal courts in *Temple*) that the missing parties were indeed the type of parties to which Rule 19(a) refers. Their joinder is required, if it is feasible. And if joinder is then not made, the case is dismissed. On the other hand, if a party meets the requirements of Rule 19(a) and his joinder is not feasible for some reason, then and only then is it necessary to proceed to consider whether the missing party is "indispensable" to the litigation under Rule 19(b).

8. Rule 19 is a limitation on a party's ordinary freedom not to sue someone the party doesn't wish to sue and thereby initially to package the litigation as she sees fit. Because Rule 19 is not triggered in cases such as *Temple*, it reinforces the notion that the plaintiff is ordinarily the "master of the complaint." See Lincoln Property Co. v. Roche, 546 U.S. 81, 126 S.Ct. 606, 163 L.Ed.2d 415 (2005) (refusing to find in-state subsidiary of out-of-state corporation a Rule 19 party and concluding that plaintiff could choose not to sue the arguably more directly responsible subsidiary in favor of the parent corporation who was (also) in a position to be liable for the judgment).

9. Note the interplay between principles of claim preclusion and Rule 19. Claim preclusion consequences are not ordinarily presented by a decision of a party to litigation *not* to sue someone, even if such a suit arises out of the events that give rise to the litigation. Rather, even in jurisdictions with expansive views of preclusion, claim preclusion arises only when party A fails to include a transactionally related claim against party B, against whom A already has a claim. Thus, in terms of compelling joinder of parties, claim preclusion adds little to Rule 19. Compare Rule 18 (claim joinder).

10. The doctrine of indispensable parties has a long and tortured history, as witnessed by SHIELDS v. BARROW, 53 U.S. (17 How.) 130, 15 L.Ed. 158 (1854). In 1836, Robert Barrow, a Louisiana citizen, sold Thomas Shields, also a citizen of Louisiana, a Louisiana plantation for $227,000. The sale was made pursuant to a note, payable in full by 1844. After $107,000 of the note had been paid by late 1842, the Louisiana real estate market collapsed, eliminating the financial viability of the remainder. Barrow brought suit on the contract in state court and a compromise was reached under which Barrow agreed to the return of the property (from Shields) for the additional payment of $32,000 (from Shields) and the release of Shields from liability. The $32,000 promissory note was endorsed by six individuals in addition to Shields — four Louisiana citizens and two Mississippi citizens. When the note proved uncollectable, Barrow later filed an action in a Louisiana federal court against the two Mississippi endorsers (one of whom was named Victoire Shields) seeking restoration of the original contract, claiming the rescission note was procured under fraud. The court granted the relief Barrow sought, from which decision Victoire Shields appealed. The Supreme Court held that Thomas Shields and all six endorsers were indispensable parties to the action but the Louisiana citizens could not be made parties to the federal proceeding because they were not diverse from Barrow. As a result the court below lacked jurisdiction to issue its decree. *Shields* divided the universe of parties into:

> 1. Formal parties. 2. Persons having an interest in the controversy, and who ought to be made parties, in order that the court may act on that rule which requires it to decide on, and finally determine the entire controversy, and do complete justice, by adjusting all the rights involved in it. These persons are commonly termed necessary parties; but if their interests are separable from those of the parties before the court, so that the court can proceed to a decree, and do complete and final justice, without affecting other persons not before the court, the latter are not indispensable parties. 3. Persons who not only have an interest in the controversy, but an interest of such a nature that a final decree cannot be made without either affecting that interest, or leaving the controversy in such a condition that its final termination may be wholly inconsistent with equity and good conscience.

The endorsers fell into the latter category. "The contract of compromise was one entire subject, and from its nature could not be rescinded" as to some but not all (even though each of the six different endorsers was responsible only for a portion of the $32,000). Although the language of Rule 19 does not include the terms "necessary" and "indispensable," the terms continue to be used to describe parties who satisfy the provisions of modern Rule 19(a) and (b) respectively.

11. The doctrine of indispensable parties originally reflected notions that a court should not decide a case where it could not render effective relief, and that a court should not decide an issue if the decision would have a strong impact on a nonparty. While these premises might make sense if there was an alternative forum that could render effective relief or in which the absent party could be joined, they were applied to a system in which personal jurisdiction was very limited (and when there were no long arm statutes). The result would sometimes be that a case would be dismissed, although it was doubtful whether another forum was available.

Helzberg's Diamond Shops, Inc. v. Valley West Des Moines Shopping Center, Inc.

United States Court of Appeals, Eighth Circuit, 1977.
564 F.2d 816.

ALSOP, DISTRICT JUDGE [sitting by designation].

On February 3, 1975, Helzberg's Diamond Shops, Inc. (Helzberg), a Missouri corporation, and Valley West Des Moines Shopping Center, Inc. (Valley West), an Iowa corporation, executed a written Lease Agreement. The Lease Agreement granted Helzberg the right to operate a full line jewelry store at space 254 in the Valley West Mall in West Des Moines, Iowa. Section 6 of Article V of the Lease Agreement provides:

> [Valley West] agrees it will not lease premises in the shopping center for use as a catalog jewelry store nor lease premises for more than two full line jewelry stores in the shopping center in addition to the leased premises. This clause shall not prohibit other stores such as department stores from selling jewelry from catalogs or in any way restrict the shopping center department stores.

Subsequently, Helzberg commenced operation of a full line jewelry store in the Valley West Mall.

Between February 3, 1975 and November 2, 1976 Valley West and two other corporations entered into leases for spaces in the Valley West Mall for use as full line jewelry stores. Pursuant to those leases the two corporations also initiated actual operation of full line jewelry stores.

On November 2, 1976, Valley West and Kirk's Incorporated, Jewelers, an Iowa corporation, doing business as Lord's Jewelers (Lord's), entered into a written Lease Agreement. The Lease Agreement granted Lord's the right to occupy space 261 in the Valley West Mall. Section 1 of Article V of the Lease Agreement provides that Lord's will use space 261

> . . . only as a retail specialty jewelry store (and not as a catalogue or full line jewelry store) featuring watches, jewelry (and the repair of same) and incidental better gift items.

However, Lord's intended to open and operate what constituted a full line jewelry store at space 261.

In an attempt to avoid the opening of a fourth full line jewelry store in the Valley West Mall and the resulting breach of the Helzberg-Valley West Lease Agreement, Helzberg instituted suit seeking preliminary and permanent injunctive relief restraining Valley West's breach of the Lease Agreement. The suit was filed in the United States District Court for the Western District of Missouri. Subject matter jurisdiction was invoked pursuant to 28 U.S.C. §1332 based upon diversity of citizenship between the parties and an amount in controversy which exceeded $10,000. Personal jurisdiction was established by service of process on Valley West pursuant to the Missouri "long arm" statute, Rev. Stat. Mo. §506.500 et seq. (1977). Rule 4(e), Fed.R.Civ.P.

Valley West moved to dismiss pursuant to Rule 19 because Helzberg had failed to join Lord's as a party defendant.[1]   That motion was denied.   The District Court went on to order that

> pending the determination of [the] action on the merits, that [Valley West] be, and it is hereby, enjoined and restrained from allowing, and shall take all necessary steps to prevent, any other tenant in its Valley West Mall (including but not limited to Kirk's Incorporated, Jewelers, dba Lord's Jewelers) to open and operate on March 30, 1977, or at any other time, or to be operated during the term of [Helzberg's] present leasehold, a fourth full line jewelry store meaning a jewelry store offering for sale at retail a broad range of jewelry items at various prices such as diamonds and diamond jewelry, precious and semi-precious stones, watches, rings, gold jewelry, costume jewelry, gold chains, pendants, bracelets, belt buckles, tie tacs, tie slides and earrings, provided, however, nothing contained herein shall be construed to enjoin [Valley West] from allowing the opening in said Valley West Mall of a small store, known by [Valley West] as a boutique, which sells limited items such as only Indian jewelry, only watches, only earrings, or only pearls.

From this order Valley West appeals.

It is clear that Valley West is entitled to appeal from the order granting preliminary injunctive relief. 28 U.S.C. §1292(a)(1).   However, Valley West does not attack the propriety of the issuance of a preliminary injunction directly; instead, it challenges the District Court's denial of its motion to dismiss for failure to join an indispensable party and argues that the District Court's order fails for lack of specificity in describing the acts of Valley West to be restrained.

* * *

Because Helzberg was seeking and the District Court ordered injunctive relief which may prevent Lord's from operating its jewelry store in the Valley West Mall in the manner in which Lord's originally intended, the District Court correctly concluded that Lord's was a party to be joined if feasible. See Rule 19 (a)(2)(i), Fed.R.Civ.P. [See current Rule 19(a)(1)(B)(i) — eds.] Therefore, because Lord's was not and is not subject to personal jurisdiction in the Western District of Missouri, the District Court was required to determine whether or not Lord's should be regarded as indispensable. After considering the factors which Rule 19(b) mandates be considered, the District Court concluded that Lord's was not to be regarded as indispensable. We agree.

The determination of whether or not a person is an indispensable party is one which must be made on a case-by-case basis and is dependent upon the facts and circumstances of each case.   Provident Tradesmens Bank & Trust Co. v. Patterson, 390 U.S. 102, 19 L.Ed. 2d 936, 88 S.Ct. 733 (1968); 7 C. Wright & A. Miller, Federal Practice & Procedure §1607 (1972); 3A J. Moore, Federal Practice para. 19.07-2 [0] (1976).   An analysis of the facts and circumstances of the case before us lead us to conclude that Lord's was not an indispensable party

---

[1]   Lord's was not subject to the personal jurisdiction of the District Court.

and that, therefore, the District Court did not err in denying Valley West's motion to dismiss.

Rule 19(b) requires the court to look first to the extent to which a judgment rendered in Lord's absence might be prejudicial to Lord's or to Valley West. Valley West argues that the District Court's order granting preliminary injunctive relief does prejudice Lord's and may prejudice Valley West. We do not agree.

It seems axiomatic that none of Lord's rights or obligations will be ultimately determined in a suit to which it is not a party. * * * Even if, as a result of the District Court's granting of the preliminary injunction, Valley West should attempt to terminate Lord's leasehold interest in space 261 in the Valley West Mall, Lord's will retain all of its rights under its Lease Agreement with Valley West. None of its rights or obligations will have been adjudicated as a result of the present proceedings, proceedings to which it is not a party. Therefore, we conclude that Lord's will not be prejudiced in a way contemplated by Rule 19(b) as a result of this action.

Likewise, we think that Lord's absence will not prejudice Valley West in a way contemplated by Rule 19(b). Valley West contends that it may be subjected to inconsistent obligations as a result of a determination in this action and a determination in another forum that Valley West should proceed in a fashion contrary to what has been ordered in these proceedings.

It is true that the obligations of Valley West to Helzberg, as determined in these proceedings, may be inconsistent with Valley West's obligations to Lord's. However, we are of the opinion that any inconsistency in those obligations will result from Valley West's voluntary execution of two Lease Agreements which impose inconsistent obligations rather than from Lord's absence from the present proceedings.

Helzberg seeks only to restrain Valley West's breach of the Lease Agreement to which Helzberg and Valley West were the sole parties. Certainly, all of the rights and obligations arising under a lease can be adjudicated where all of the parties to the lease are before the court. See Lomayaktewa v. Hathaway, 520 F.2d 1324 (9th Cir. 1975), cert. denied, 425 U.S. 903, 96 S.Ct. 1492, 47 L.Ed.2d 752 (1976). Thus, in the context of these proceedings the District Court can determine all of the rights and obligations of both Helzberg and Valley West based upon the Lease Agreement between them, even though Lord's is not a party to the proceedings.

Valley West's contention that it may be subjected to inconsistent judgments if Lord's should choose to file suit elsewhere and be awarded judgment is speculative at best. In the first place, Lord's has not filed such a suit. Secondly, there is no showing that another court is likely to interpret the language of the two Lease Agreements differently from the way in which the District Court would. Therefore, we also conclude that Valley West will suffer no prejudice as a result of the District Court's proceeding in Lord's absence. Any prejudice which Valley West may suffer by way of inconsistent judgments would be the result of Valley West's execution of Lease Agreements which impose inconsistent obligations and not the result of the proceedings in the District Court.

Rule 19(b) also requires the court to consider ways in which prejudice to the absent party can be lessened or avoided. The District Court afforded Lord's an opportunity to intervene in order to protect any interest it might have in the outcome of this litigation. Lord's chose not to do so. In light of Lord's decision not to intervene we conclude that the District Court acted in such a way as to sufficiently protect Lord's interests. Cf. 7 C. Wright & A. Miller, Federal Practice & Procedure §1610, at 103 (1972).

Similarly, we also conclude that the District Court's determinations that a judgment rendered in Lord's absence would be adequate and that there is no controlling significance to the fact that Helzberg would have an adequate remedy in the Iowa courts were not erroneous. It follows that the District Court's conclusion that in equity and good conscience the action should be allowed to proceed was a correct one.

In sum, it is generally recognized that a person does not become indispensable to an action to determine rights under a contract simply because that person's rights or obligations under an entirely separate contract will be affected by the result of the action. 3A J. Moore, Federal Practice para. 19.10, at 2349-50 (1976); see also Division 525, Railway Conductors v. Gorman, 133 F.2d 273 (8th Cir. 1943); 7 C. Wright & A. Miller, Federal Practice & Procedure §1613, at 135 (1972). This principle applies to an action against a lessor who has entered into other leases which also may be affected by the result in the action in which the other lessees are argued to be indispensable parties. See Cherokee Nation v. Hitchcock, 187 U.S. 294, 47 L.Ed. 183, 23 S.Ct. 115 (1902). We conclude that the District Court properly denied the motion to dismiss for failure to join an indispensable party.

* * *

In view of the foregoing, it follows that the judgment of the District Court is affirmed.

NOTES AND PROBLEMS FOR DISCUSSION

1. As *Temple* and *Helzberg* both demonstrate, an issue of a nonjoined party's indispensability to the litigation under Rule 19(b) never arises unless it is first determined that the missing party is someone who ought to be joined in the first place under Rule 19(a) (i.e., that they are "necessary"). The *Helzberg* court briefly concludes that Lords *is* a necessary party and should be joined if feasible under Rule 19(a), but it supplies no analysis for its conclusion. What is the argument that would permit the court to distinguish a case like *Temple*?

2. Consider who faces the greatest risk of harm if Lord's is not brought into the litigation. Is it Helzberg, who filed the suit without joining Lord's; Lord's, whose rights will not be affected if he is a non-party to the Helzberg/Valley West lawsuit; or Valley West?

3. Although Lord's was a party who should be joined "if feasible," (step-1 in the court's analysis) joinder was not feasible because Lord's was beyond the personal jurisdiction of Missouri (step-2). Subject matter jurisdiction may also create a barrier when, for example, the party's joinder in a diversity action would destroy complete diversity. (Note that there is no supplemental jurisdiction over diversity-destroying Rule 19 parties, neither historically under judge-made doctrines of ancillary jurisdiction, nor today under §1367(b).) In addition, Rule 19(a) itself suggests that a proper objection to venue will prevent a party's joinder. Step–3 of the court's analysis under Rule 19(b) — whether the court can go on without Lord's in any event — is reached only if steps 1 and 2 have identified Lord's as a party who should be joined if joinder is possible, and yet joinder isn't possible.

4. The Supreme Court's first full-dress encounter with current Rule 19(b) occurred shortly after the Rule's revision in 1966 in PROVIDENT TRADESMENS BANK & TRUST CO. v. PATTERSON, 390 U.S. 102, 88 S.Ct. 733, 19 L.Ed. 2d 936 (1968). There, the driver (Cionci) of a car owned by another (Dutcher) was involved in a serious accident with a truck in which Cionci as well as one of his two passengers was killed. Dutcher had an insurance policy with Lumbermens Insurance, with a limit of $100,000 for all claims arising out of a single accident. The policy arguably covered Cionci (at least if he was driving the car with Dutcher's permission), as well as the potential vicarious liability of Dutcher as owner of the car. Various cases were filed in state court against Dutcher, Cionci, and the estate of Lynch, one of the passengers in the car. Provident Tradesmens Bank & Trust, as executor of Lynch's estate, sued Cionci's estate in a federal court diversity action and recovered a verdict of $50,000. Lumbermens refused to defend (believing that Cionci lacked Dutcher's permission and therefore was not covered by the policy) and a judgment was rendered against Cionci. Provident (along with two others who were plaintiffs in the state court proceedings), then brought a diversity action against Lumbermens seeking a declaration that Cionci's use of Dutcher's car had been with "permission," and that the policy could therefore be reached in any judgment against Cionci. Judgment was entered against Lumbermens by the district court.

On appeal, Lumbermens argued, for the first time, that Dutcher (who was nondiverse from Provident) was an indispensable party to the declaratory suit brought by Provident against Lumbermens; the Court of Appeals agreed and ordered that the action be dismissed. The Supreme Court reversed. It first concluded that Dutcher, at the time of trial, was someone to be joined if feasible under Rule 19(a) because, if the Lumbermens policy could be used to satisfy claims against Cionci, it might be unavailable or diminished for claims against Dutcher. It then discussed the application of Rule 19(b) as follows:

> Rule 19(b) suggests four "interests" that must be examined in each case to determine whether, in equity and good conscience, the court should proceed without a party whose absence from the litigation is compelled. Each of these interests must, in this case, be viewed entirely from an appellate perspective since the matter of joinder was not considered in the trial court. * * *

> Had the Court of Appeals applied Rule 19's criteria to the facts of the present case, it could hardly have reached the conclusion it did. We

begin with the plaintiffs' viewpoint. It is difficult to decide at this stage whether they would have had an "adequate" remedy had the action been dismissed before trial for non-joinder: We cannot here determine whether the plaintiffs could have brought the same action, against the same parties plus Dutcher, in a state court. After trial, however, the "adequacy" of this hypothetical alternative, from the plaintiffs' point of view, was obviously greatly diminished. Their interest in preserving a fully litigated judgment should be overborne only by rather greater opposing considerations than would be required at an earlier stage when the plaintiffs' only concern was for a federal rather than a state forum.

Opposing considerations in this case are hard to find. The defendants had no stake, either asserted or real, in the joinder of Dutcher. They showed no interest in joinder until the Court of Appeals took the matter into its own hands. This properly forecloses any interest of theirs, but for purposes of clarity we note that the insurance company, whose liability was limited to $100,000, had or will have full opportunity to litigate each claim on that fund against the claimant involved. Its only concern with the absence of Dutcher was and is to obtain a windfall escape from its defeat at trial.

The interest of the outsider, Dutcher, is more difficult to reckon. * * * Dutcher had an "adverse" interest[*] * * * because he would have been benefited by a ruling in favor of the insurance company; the question before the Court of Appeals, however, was whether Dutcher was harmed by the judgment against the insurance company.

The two questions are not the same. If the three plaintiffs had lost to the insurance company on the permission issue, that loss would have ended the matter favorably to Dutcher. If, as has happened, the three plaintiffs obtain a judgment against the insurance company on the permission issue, Dutcher may still claim that as a nonparty he is not estopped by that judgment from relitigating the issue. * * *

If Dutcher is not foreclosed by his failure to intervene below, then he is not "bound" by the judgment against the insurance company and, in theory, he has not been harmed. There remains, however, the practical question whether Dutcher is likely to have any need, and if so will have any opportunity, to relitigate. The only possible threat to him is that if the fund is used to pay judgments against Cionci the money may in fact have disappeared before Dutcher has an opportunity to assert his interest. Upon examination, we find this supposed threat neither large nor unavoidable.

The Court noted that the odds of recovery against Dutcher on vicarious liability grounds were slim to none, and that in any event, he would likely not be precluded from relitigating the issue of "permission" in later proceedings. Also, it noted that payment of the Cionci judgment by Lumbermens could await any

---

[*] Under the applicable state's "Dead Man" statute, Dutcher's "adverse" interest with the estate of Lynch forbad his being able to testify.

further litigation, as the district court seemed to have determined, and there was also some indication that the parties might be willing not to look beyond the policy of insurance for their recovery. Possible (but uncertain) efficiency concerns respecting potential relitigation by Dutcher that might have factored into the analysis at the trial stage had, at the appeals stage, "entirely disappeared: there was no reason then to throw away a valid judgment just because it did not theoretically settle the whole controversy."

5. Is the decision in *Helzberg* faithful to the ruling in *Provident Tradesmens Bank*? The appeals court suggests that even if Valley West might be subjected to inconsistent obligations (e.g., a judgment in the suit brought by Helzberg forbidding Valley West from honoring its lease to Lord's, and a judgment against it in a suit later brought by Lord's requiring Valley West to honor its lease to Lord's), the predicament is of Valley West's own making. Should that be a reason *not* to find Lord's indispensable? In the event of conflicting orders, and assuming that you are Valley West's lawyer, which of the two conflicting orders do you obey?

6. Rule 19(b) is a "soft" rule committed to the discretion of the Court to determine whether "in equity and good conscience" the suit may proceed in the absence of a party who should be joined, but cannot be. Can you see a way in which relief could be fashioned in the *Helzberg* lawsuit so as to avoid the potential for conflicting injunctive relief? Note that when a party makes a motion seeking to have the court determine that a nonjoined party who cannot be joined, is indispensable to the litigation, he is not asking the court to order the joinder of that party. He is seeking to have the action dismissed altogether.

7. Consider the Court's latest treatment of Rule 19(b) in REPUBLIC OF THE PHILIPPINES v. PIMENTEL, 553 U.S. 851, 128 S.Ct. 2180, 171 L.Ed.2d 131 (2008). Merrill Lynch filed an interpleader action in federal court when it was faced with conflicting claims to property in its possession formerly owned by Ferdinand Marcos, President of the Philippines. (Interpleader is discussed later in this Chapter, in Section II.) Among the named interpleader defendants (i.e., the claimants) were the Republic of the Philippines and a Philippine commission set up to recover property of Marcos, both of whom claimed that the property was stolen. Another claimant consisted of a class of approximately 10,000 persons who had obtained a large money judgment against Marcos for violations of their human rights. In the lower courts, the Commission and the Republic moved for dismissal of the proceedings under Rule 19(b), on the ground that they were required parties under Rule 19(a), but their joinder was not feasible because they were entitled to sovereign immunity. Although the Republic and the Commission were dismissed as parties, the trial court ultimately allowed the interpleader action to proceed against the remaining claimants. The district court then ruled that the disputed property be awarded to the class of human rights victims. The Ninth Circuit eventually affirmed the district court's decision to go forward with the interpleader proceedings without the Republic and the Commission. It concluded that, under Rule 19(b), the action could properly proceed in their absence, primarily based on its conclusion that the Republic and the Commission had little chance of recovery on the merits, owing to statute of limitations problems. The Supreme Court reversed. In the course of its opinion, it stated:

> Subdivision (a) of Rule 19 states the principles that determine when persons or entities must be joined in a suit. The Rule instructs that nonjoinder even of a required person does not always result in dismissal. Subdivision (a) opens by noting that it addresses joinder "if Feasible." Where joinder is not feasible, the question whether the action should proceed turns on the factors outlined in subdivision (b). The considerations set forth in subdivision (b) are nonexclusive, as made clear by the introductory statement that "[t]he factors for the court to consider include." Fed. Rule Civ. Proc. 19(b). The general direction is whether "in equity and good conscience, the action should proceed among the existing parties or should be dismissed." *Id.* The design of the Rule, then, indicates that the determination whether to proceed will turn upon factors that are case specific, which is consistent with a Rule based on equitable considerations. This is also consistent with the fact that the determination of who may, or must, be parties to a suit has consequences for the persons and entities affected by the judgment; for the judicial system and its interest in the integrity of its processes and the respect accorded to its decrees; and for society and its concern for the fair and prompt resolution of disputes. See, *e.g., Illinois Brick Co.* v. *Illinois*, 431 U.S. 720, 737-739 (1977). For these reasons, the issue of joinder can be complex, and determinations are case specific. See, *e.g., Provident Bank*, *supra*, at 118-119. * * *

The Court went on to conclude that the Court of Appeals had given too little weight to the sovereignty interests that would be prejudiced in the absence of the Republic and the Commission, whose claims were nonfrivolous. In addition. there was no possible way to avoid the prejudice to those sovereign interests. Nor would a judgment in their absence have been "adequate" because that consideration focuses not on the satisfaction of the claims of the victims of human rights violations, but on the "public stake in settling disputes by wholes, whenever possible." On the question whether the plaintiff would have an adequate alternative forum if the interpleader proceeding was dismissed, the Court indicated that the focus should not be solely on the "defendant" human rights claimants, but also on the "plaintiff" Merrill Lynch, who might be prejudiced in the absence of a judgment involving all potential claimants.

8. Finally, note that Rule 19 objections are not waived in the district court, even if not raised in a Rule 12 motion (assuming one is made), or in the answer to the complaint. What distinguishes such questions from, for example, objections to personal jurisdiction? Or venue?

ALTERNATIVES TO MANDATORY JOINDER:
MULTIDISTRICT LITIGATION AND CONSOLIDATION

The Multiparty, Multiforum Trial Jurisdiction Act of 2002, took effect in January, 2003. The Act, codified at 28 U.S.C. §1369(a) et seq., provides for federal court jurisdiction over "any civil action" involving a "single accident" where at least 75 persons have died from the accident, so long as there is "minimal diversity" between adverse parties — i.e., any one plaintiff and any one defendant are citizens of different states. Id. at §1369(c)(1). But if the "majority of all plaintiffs" are citizens of a single state of which the "primary defendants" are also citizens, and the claims asserted will be governed by that state's law, the federal court "shall abstain" from hearing the case. Id. at §1369(b). The idea of this limitation seems to be that the tail of minimal diversity should not wag the dog of what is essentially an intrastate controversy.[*] The statute elsewhere defines "accident" as a "sudden accident" or "a natural event culminating in an accident" with deaths occurring "at a discrete location." Id. at §1369(c)(4).

The new statute is awkwardly worded, but some of its effects on existing joinder rules and jurisdiction are clear. Imagine, for example, that multiple passengers and/or their families wish to sue a single defendant airline company over injuries and fatalities arising from a plane crash. Imagine further that suits are eventually filed by various plaintiffs in different state and federal courts. In a single incident tort action such as this, if one diverse plaintiff sued the defendant in a federal court, it is unlikely that the plaintiff or defendant could compel all other potential plaintiffs to join in that action. As indicated by *Temple v. Synthes, supra*, they would not be parties who would be required to be joined within the meaning of Rule 19. And although such parties would be persons who could be joined permissibly under Rule 20 as plaintiffs, the decision to join as a plaintiff under that Rule is typically left to the prospective plaintiffs. (Also, as noted below, damages class actions under Rule 23(b)(3) would permit any class member the right to opt out.)

The act, however, has the potential to effect a kind of mandatory joinder, largely at the defendant's option. By also amending the removal statutes, the new statute permits a defendant, sued by at least one diverse plaintiff in a federal court (either originally, or by removal under current 28 U.S.C. §1441), to remove *all other* suits filed against it in a state court that arise out of the same accident. See 28 U.S.C. §1441(e)(1). Such removable actions could even include state court actions filed solely between co-citizens, so long as the

---

[*] There are three triggering mechanisms, one of which must be met for the statute to apply: (1) the accident took place in state A and the defendant "resides" in a different state, even if it also resides in state A (residence is defined elsewhere in the statute for corporations as, inter alia, "doing business" — see §1369(c)(2)); or (2) there are multiple defendants and any two of them reside in the same state; or (3) "substantial parts of the accident took place in different states." 28 U.S.C. §1369(a)(1)-(3). What is the purpose of having to meet one of these three triggering devices, if minimal diversity otherwise exists?

defendant is already a defendant in a federal court action covered by the new statute. See id. at §1441(e)(1)(B). The theory, apparently, is that any such transactionally related state law claims between nondiverse parties can be viewed as pendent to the diversity claim arising out of the same accident, within the meaning of Article III (although not within the language of the supplemental jurisdiction statute, 28 U.S.C. §1367). Moreover, removal of state court lawsuits may be had from *any* state court to the federal court in which the §1369 action is pending — i.e., removal need not be limited to the federal district that encompasses the state court in which the state court action was brought. And the defendant may seek consolidation of any other federal actions brought against it by moving for transfer of venue to the preferred federal forum. Thus, the defendant can, if it chooses, effectively demand that all litigation that is proceeding against it in various forums, state or federal, diverse or nondiverse, be consolidated against it for trial in a single federal forum in which it has been sued (or to which it has first removed). Note also that the supplemental jurisdiction can be "springing" here, since the state court litigation might have been filed long before any federal action was ever filed, and thus might only become removable after the passage of time. See §1441(e)(1)(b).

Although phrased in terms of the death of 75 or more persons, the statute does not require that there be at least 75 plaintiffs; only that 75 persons die. As noted above, §1369 can be invoked upon the filing of a single suit by a single plaintiff. Of course, a diverse plaintiff might file suit in federal court over the accident under §1369, and join with him, under Rule 20, as many or as few willing co-plaintiffs as choose to join, whether or not those other plaintiffs are diverse from the defendant. But nothing in the statute gives plaintiffs in such a federal action an ability similar to that possessed by defendants (either on removal, or when sued in federal court as an original matter), to *compel* other plaintiffs' cases to brought into a single federal forum. The joinder of other plaintiffs from the plaintiffs' perspective is still subject to their willingness to do so under Rule 20, and the limitations on Rule 19 in tort cases. On the other hand, according to the new statute, any potential plaintiff may intervene in such an action, without regard to diversity with the defendant. This also arguably acts as a modification of the current supplemental jurisdiction statute, 28 U.S.C. §1367, which on its face would disallow supplemental jurisdiction in diversity actions over plaintiff intervenors who are nondiverse from defendants. We discuss intervention below in the section that follows.

Even if the federal court plaintiff does not purport to proceed under §1369, defendant can still invoke the statute. Also, the defendant can effectively "bring" such an action into federal court even if all actions arising from the accident have been filed in state court, so long as there is one diverse plaintiff in at least one of those actions. In other words, because the new statute states that federal courts shall have original jurisdiction over such single accident cases provided there is minimal diversity, a defendant who is sued in state court only, by plaintiffs who are incompletely diverse from him, can probably remove that action under the exiting removal statutes, 28 U.S.C. §1441(a)-(b), since it would now be an action over which the federal courts would have original jurisdiction under the new statute. Thus, even if no action as described by the statute is filed in federal court by a diverse plaintiff, the defendant can create such a suit by removing any lawsuit filed against it that arises out of the kind of accident described in the statute, provided there is minimal diversity in the state-court lawsuit.

Structurally, the Act builds upon the existing pre-trial multidistrict litigation statute, 28 U.S.C. §1407. The latter statute permits consolidated pre-trial proceedings of transactionally related lawsuits pending in different federal courts, to a single federal district. Application for such consolidation is made to a multidistrict judicial panel, which may assign to a single district judge — often a federal judge before whom a number of such cases are already pending — related pretrial proceedings (such as Rule 12 motions, discovery, and summary judgment). At their conclusion, all cases are remanded to the district whence they came. See Lexecon, Inc. v. Milberg Weiss, 523 U.S. 26, 118 S.Ct. 956, 140 L.Ed.2d 62 (1998) (refusing to read § 1407 as allowing pretrial transferee court to hear trial of cases transferred to it). By contrast, new §1369 seems to contemplate consolidation for trial, and (unlike pretrial proceedings under §1407) is designed largely to track existing venue choices by providing that a suit under §1369 may be brought in "any district in which any defendant resides or in which a substantial part of the accident giving rise to the action took place." See 28 U.S.C. §1391(g).

Finally, it is important to see that §1369 does something that other multiparty joinder provisions cannot do, or cannot always reliably do — although full appreciation of this point will have to await later materials in this Chapter. For example, the class action device (Section I, below) could not be counted on to effect joinder in such single-accident settings, because class-actions are plaintiff-triggered, and plaintiffs often want to bring their own actions independently, rather than bring a class action. Moreover, even if the hurdles of class certification under Fed. R. Civ. P. Rule 23 can be surmounted, members of the class in a damages class action will typically be able to opt out, and sue on their own. Indeed, §1369 seems to be directed to that very possibility and allows the defendant to override the plaintiffs' choices to sue in state court, or to proceed in another federal court. Also, interpleader under 28 U.S.C. §1335 (Section H, below) cannot generally serve the function of consolidating all related tort litigation, even when a limited fund (such as an insurance policy of one of the defendants) is in the picture. See State Farm Fire & Cas. Co. v. Tashire, 386 U.S. 523, 87 S.Ct. 1199, 18 L.Ed.2d 270 (1967).

SECTION G. INTERVENTION

It is helpful to consider the joinder devices discussed so far as an introduction to intervention. Rule 20 gives plaintiff the ability to join multiple parties as defendants, and Rule 13 and Rule 20 give the defendant the ability to join additional parties as defendants if a counterclaim is filed. Rule 19 gives a defendant the ability to seek mandatory joinder of a person who is not a party to the action. By contrast, intervention under Rule 24 offers a nonparty the opportunity to get into the lawsuit, even though none of the existing parties want her there.

Try to think about this issue from your own experience. You read about a lawsuit in the paper, hear about it on television or radio (or the Internet), or you hear about it from a friend and neighbor. Maybe the lawsuit involves a subject that you are concerned about. Or, more directly, you think that if plaintiff wins (or loses) the lawsuit, it will affect you in some way. Potential effects are endless — from the social or political to the financial. For example, a lawsuit to change the requirements for governmental benefits or admission to law school may affect you indirectly (i.e., you think the changes are desirable) or directly (you are applying to law school). A common instance of such impacts comes in litigation regarding the use of land, such as zoning disputes. Obviously, if you live in a residential neighborhood and your neighbor seeks approval to put a gas station next to your house, there is a direct impact. But even if you live down the block or two blocks away, there may be an effect.

Most of us who learn of a pending lawsuit that involves a subject we are concerned with or that may affect our interests are content to watch from the sidelines. Normally, we do not want to spend the time, effort and money to become involved, and don't believe the nature of our interest warrants participation. But sometimes we do, and that is when the ability to intervene becomes critical.

Keep in mind that if courts permitted even a small fraction of the people that had a social or economic concern with litigation to become involved, lawsuits could easily become unmanageable. Indeed, one can contrast the lawsuit with the political process, where almost anyone who wants to make the effort and to participate is allowed to do so. But the political process is necessarily unfocused in the sense of issues and decisions; lawsuits, by contrast, must decide concrete disputes between actual people.

Coalition of Arizona/New Mexico Counties for Stable Economic Growth v. Department of the Interior

United States Court of Appeals, Tenth Circuit, 1996.
100 F.3d 837.

HENRY, CIRCUIT JUDGE.

Dr. Robin Silver appeals from the order of the United States District Court for the District of New Mexico denying his application to intervene in plaintiff-appellee Coalition of Arizona/New Mexico Counties for Stable Economic Growth's ("Coalition") suit against the Department of the Interior ("DOI"), the United States Fish and Wildlife Service ("FWS") and various government officials. The Coalition challenges FWS's decision to protect the Mexican Spotted Owl ("the Owl") under the Endangered Species Act ("the Act"), alleging that FWS failed to follow proper procedures and lacked data sufficient to list the Owl as threatened. Dr. Silver sought to intervene pursuant to the Rule 24 of the Federal Rule of Civil Procedure. Dr. Silver grounded his application upon two facts: (1) he had photographed and studied the Owl in the wild; and (2) he was instrumental in FWS's initial decision to protect the Owl under the Act, see, e.g., 58 Fed. Reg. 14,248, 14,252 (1993) (citing Dr. Silver's petition as instigating FWS's decision to list the Owl as an endangered species).

An order denying intervention is final and subject to immediate review if it prevents the applicant from becoming a party to an action. Stringfellow v. Concerned Neighbors in Action, 480 U.S. 370, 377, 94 L. Ed. 2d 389, 107 S. Ct. 1177 (1987); Arney v. Finney, 967 F.2d 418, 421 (10th Cir. 1992). Accordingly, we accept jurisdiction pursuant to 28 U.S.C. §1291 and mindful that "the interest test is primarily a practical guide to disposing of lawsuits by involving as many apparently concerned persons as is compatible with efficiency and due process," see, e.g., Nuesse v. Camp, 128 U.S. App. D.C. 172, 385 F.2d 694, 700 (D.C. Cir. 1967), we reverse the decision of the district court and remand the case for further proceedings.

I. BACKGROUND

Dr. Silver is a commercial wildlife photographer, an amateur biologist, and a naturalist, specializing in photographing creatures in the American Southwest. Dr. Silver has sought out and photographed the Owl in its natural habitat — old-growth forests in the Southwest. For the past five years, he has been active in the effort to protect the Owl and its habitat. In December 1989, Dr. Silver petitioned FWS to list the Owl as a threatened or endangered species. See 16 U.S.C. §1533(b)(3)(A) (an "interested person" may petition FWS to add a species to the threatened and endangered species list). When FWS failed to act on his petition within the statutory time limit, see 16 U.S.C. §1533(b)(3)(B), Dr. Silver wrote a letter dated November 9, 1992, to the Secretary of the Interior threatening suit under the Act's citizen lawsuit provision, see 16 U.S.C. §1540(g)(2)(C).

In April 1993, FWS listed the Owl as a threatened species. See 58 Fed. Reg. 14,248 (1993). However, FWS failed to designate critical habitat for the Owl, stating that "designation of critical habitat is prudent, but is not determinable at this time." Id.; see 16 U.S.C. §1533(b)(6)(C). On November 11, 1993, Dr. Silver wrote the Secretary of Interior and the Director of FWS, threatening suit. In December 1993, Dr. Silver and other environmentalists filed suit in the United States District Court for the District of Arizona to force the designation of critical habitat for the Owl. * * * In October 1994, the court ordered FWS to designate critical habitat for the Owl, but FWS continued to delay. Dr. Silver moved to have FWS held in contempt of court, and the court ordered FWS to submit daily progress reports to Dr. Silver to insure that FWS would comply with the court's order. FWS designated critical habitat for the Owl on May 30, 1995. * * *

In September 1994, the Coalition filed the present lawsuit in the United States District Court for the District of New Mexico challenging the listing of the Owl as an endangered and threatened species under the Act. The Coalition alleges that FWS failed to follow proper procedures and lacked data sufficient to list the Owl as threatened. In May 1995, Dr. Silver filed an application to intervene as of right, or in the alternative, permissively, pursuant to Fed. R. Civ.

P. 24. Both the Coalition and the DOI opposed his application, and in July 1995 the district court denied it. The district court did, however, permit Dr. Silver to submit a brief as amicus curiae.

On appeal, Dr. Silver argues that it was error for the court to deny his petition to intervene as of right for the following reasons: he filed his petition in a timely fashion; he has a direct, substantial and legally protectable interest in the subject matter of the action; his interest might be impaired absent his intervention; and the DOI will not adequately represent his interest. See Fed. R. Civ. P. 24(a)(2); Alameda Water & Sanitation Dist. v. Browner, 9 F.3d 88, 90 (10th Cir. 1993). Alternatively, Dr. Silver contends that the district court erred by not allowing him to intervene permissively. The Coalition[1] argues that the district court's denial of Dr. Silver's application to intervene was proper because: his interest in the subject matter of the action is not direct, substantial and legally enforceable; his interest is not impaired; and the DOI will adequately represent his interest.

II. DISCUSSION

Fed. R. Civ. P. 24(a)(2) provides, in relevant part, as follows:

> Upon timely application anyone shall be permitted to intervene in an action * * * when the applicant claims an interest relating to the property or transaction which is the subject of the action and the applicant is so situated that the disposition of the action may as a practical matter impair or impede the applicant's ability to protect that interest, unless the applicant's interest is adequately represented by existing parties.

[The Rule has since been slightly reworded. — eds.]. Accordingly, an applicant may intervene as of right if: (1) the application is "timely"; (2) "the applicant claims an interest relating to the property or transaction which is the subject of the action"; (3) the applicant's interest "may as a practical matter" be "impaired or impeded"; and (4) "the applicant's interest is [not] adequately represented by existing parties." Id. We review for an abuse of discretion a district court's rulings on the timeliness of an application for intervention as of right, but we review de novo a district court's rulings on the three remaining requirements under Rule 24(a)(2). The parties agree that Dr. Silver's application was timely. We now address de novo whether Dr. Silver's application met the remaining three requirements under Rule 24(a)(2).

A.   Dr. Silver has a direct, substantial and legally protectable interest in the listing of the Owl.

Dr. Silver must first show that he has "an interest relating to the property or transaction which is the subject of the action." Fed. R. Civ. P. 24(a)(2). The contours of the interest requirement have not been clearly defined. See 7C C. Wright, A. Miller, & M. Kane, Federal Practice and Procedure §1908 at 263 (2d ed. 1986 & Supp. 1996). Dr. Silver cites Idaho Farm Bureau Fed'n v. Babbitt, 58 F.3d 1392 (9th Cir. 1995), for the proposition that he "is entitled as a matter of right to intervene in an action challenging the legality of a measure [he] has

---

[1]   The DOI did not submit a brief on appeal and therefore waived its opportunity to argue against Dr. Silver's intervention at oral argument. See Fed. R. App. P. 31(c).

supported." Id. at 1397; see also Yniguez v. Arizona, 939 F.2d 727 (9th Cir. 1991)[.] * * *

Our circuit and the Fifth Circuit require that "[the] interest in the proceedings be 'direct, substantial, and legally protectable.'" Vermejo Park Corp. v. Kaiser Coal Corp. (In re Kaiser Steel Corp.), 998 F.2d 783, 791 (10th Cir. 1993) (quoting United States v. Perry County Bd. of Educ., 567 F.2d 277, 279 (5th Cir. 1978)). "Whether an applicant has an interest sufficient to warrant intervention as a matter of right is a highly fact-specific determination," Security Ins. Co. v. Schipporeit, Inc., 69 F.3d 1377, 1381 (7th Cir. 1995), and "the 'interest' test is primarily a practical guide to disposing of lawsuits by involving as many apparently concerned persons as is compatible with efficiency and due process," Nuesse, 385 F.2d at 700; accord Sierra Club v. Espy, 18 F.3d 1202, 1207 (5th Cir. 1994)[.] * * * We now address the question of whether Dr. Silver's interest in the Owl, as a photographer, an amateur biologist, and a naturalist who has been at the forefront of efforts to protect the Owl under the Act, is "direct, substantial, and legally protectable" for the purposes of intervention under Rule 24(a)(2).

Dr. Silver initiated the process to protect the Owl by submitting a petition for its protection * * *. He pressed DOI and FWS in two letters to take action on his petition, and sued FWS when it failed to designate critical habitat for the Owl[.] * * * When FWS failed to comply with the court order to designate a critical habitat for the Owl, Dr. Silver twice moved for an order of contempt, resulting in a court order that FWS maintain a daily diary and inform Dr. Silver of its progress toward the designation of critical habitat[.]

We are not faced, as the Coalition suggests, with an applicant who has no interest in the present litigation other than prior litigation involving the same subject matter. Instead, Dr. Silver has been directly involved with the Owl as a wildlife photographer, an amateur biologist, and a naturalist who has photographed and studied the Owl in its natural environment. Dr. Silver's counsel admitted at oral argument that Dr. Silver had little economic interest in the Owl; however, economic interest is not the sine qua non of the interest analysis for intervention as of right. To limit intervention to situations where the applicant can show an economic interest would impermissibly narrow the broad right of intervention enacted by Congress and recognized by the courts. See Nuesse, 385 F.2d at 700; Sierra Club v. Espy, 18 F.3d at 1207[.] In sum, we hold that Dr. Silver's involvement with the Owl in the wild and his persistent record of advocacy for its protection amounts to a direct and substantial interest in the listing of the Owl for the purpose of intervention as of right, even though Dr. Silver has little economic interest in the Owl itself.

Additionally, Dr. Silver's interest in the Owl is legally protectable as evidenced by his successful effort to have the Owl protected as an endangered species under the Act. Section 1533(b)(3) of the Act requires the Secretary of the Interior to respond within twelve months to a petition submitted by an "interested person" requesting that the Secretary list a species as threatened or endangered, and if listing is warranted, to publish a proposed regulation for comment. 16 U.S.C. §1533(b)(3). Dr. Silver first threatened suit and later exercised his right under section 1540(g)(1)(C) to commence a civil suit against the DOI for failure to perform its non-discretionary duty under section 1533(b)(3). Thus, the Act provided Dr. Silver with the legal right to protect his interest in the Owl. Additionally, section 1540(g)(1)(A) of the Act gives a private citizen the right to "commence a civil suit on his own behalf . . . to enjoin any person, including the United States and any other governmental instrumentality or agency . . . , who is alleged to be in violation of [the Act]." 16 U.S.C. §1540(g)(1)(A). Language from the Supreme Court in *Lujan v. Defenders of Wildlife* further bolsters our conclusion that Dr. Silver's interest is legally protectable: "The desire to use or observe an animal species, even for purely esthetic purposes, is undeniably a cognizable interest for purpose of standing." 504 U.S. 555, 562-63, 112 S.Ct. 2130, 119 L.Ed. 2d 351 (1992) (citing Sierra Club v. Morton, 405 U.S. 727, 734, 31 L.Ed. 2d 636, 92 S.Ct. 1361 (1972)); see *Yniguez*, 939 F.2d at 735 (reasoning that "because the Article III standing requirements are morc stringent than those for intervention under rule 24(a), [the] determination that [the applicants] have standing under Article III compels the conclusion that they have an adequate interest under the rule").

Because Dr. Silver's interest in the litigation between the Coalition and the DOI is direct, substantial, and legally protectable, it sufficiently "relates to the property or transaction which is the subject of the action" and thereby satisfies the first element under Rule 24(a)(2). * * *

We recently discussed the interest requirement of Rule 24(a)(2) in City of Stilwell v. Ozarks Rural Elec. Coop., 79 F.3d 1038, 1042 (10th Cir. 1996). In *Ozarks*, KAMO Electric Cooperative sought to intervene in a condemnation proceeding brought by the City of Stilwell, Oklahoma, against Ozarks Rural Electric Cooperative. If Stilwell had prevailed, Ozarks would have lost the right to sell power to certain customers. KAMO's interest in the condemnation proceeding was "contingent;" that is, "KAMO, as Ozarks' supplier of electric power, [would have] benefited financially if Ozarks [was] allowed to continue to service its customers in Stilwell." Id. at 1042. We held that such a contingent interest is not sufficiently "direct and substantial" to satisfy the interest requirement of Rule 24(a)(2). Id.

The decision in *Ozarks* echoes that of an earlier Tenth Circuit case, Allard v. Frizzell, 536 F.2d 1332 (10th Cir. 1976) (per curiam). In *Allard*, we held that two public interest groups had an insufficient interest to intervene in a case in which several owners of native American artifacts made of eagle feathers challenged the Migratory Bird Act and the Eagle Protection Act. Id. at 1333. The subject of the suit was whether these federal laws infringed upon the plaintiffs' rights to the feathered artifacts. Id. The public interest groups sought to intervene to protect living birds and the environment. We held that the public interest groups were not entitled to intervene as of right because their interest in living birds and the environment was not sufficiently related to the plaintiffs' right to the already existing artifacts. Id.

The nature of the litigation between the Coalition and the DOI is different from that in *Ozarks Rural Electric Coop.* and *Allard*. Both of those cases involved what has been called traditional intervention. See United States v. Hooker Chemicals & Plastics Corp., 749 F.2d 968, 983 (2d Cir. 1984) ("'Rule [24(a)(2)] was designed with . . . traditional private actions in mind, and its adaptation to other contexts requires a flexible reading of its provisions.'") (quoting Note, Intervention in Government Enforcement Actions, 89 Harv. L. Rev. 1174, 1177 (1976) and citing *Nuesse v. Camp*, 385 F.2d at 700). *Ozarks* involved a condemnation dispute, and *Allard* involved private property interests in native American artifacts. The present litigation involves a challenge to FWS's decision to list the Owl, an administrative action not analogous to the litigation in *Ozarks* and *Allard*. Thus, the analysis of the interest requirement here is not analogous to the analyses of the interest requirements in those cases.

* * *

B. *Dr. Silver's Interest May Be Impaired*

To satisfy the second element under Rule 24(a)(2), Dr. Silver must show that the disposition of the Coalition's suit against the DOI "may as a practical matter impair or impede his ability to protect [his] interest." Fed. R. Civ. P. 24(a)(2). Such impairment or impediment need not be "of a strictly legal nature." Natural Resources Defense Council, Inc. v. United States Nuclear Regulatory Comm'n, 578 F.2d 1341, 1345 (10th Cir. 1978). "[We] may consider any significant legal effect in the applicant's interest and [we are] not restricted to a rigid res judicata test." Id. Thus, the stare decisis effect of the district court's judgment is sufficient impairment for intervention under Rule 24(a)(2). See *Sierra Club v. Espy*, 18 F.3d at 1207.

In its complaint against the DOI, the Coalition contends that the DOI "failed to use the best available data," misapplied the data, used unfounded assumptions and jeopardized the Southwestern forest ecosystem. As part of its remedy, the Coalition seeks "[a] permanent injunction enjoining [the DOI] from taking any actions pursuant to the listing of the [Owl]." Id. at 25. If the district court were to rule in favor of these contentions and to mandate that the DOI delist the Owl, Dr. Silver's interest in the protection of the Owl would be impaired. Dr. Silver could submit a new petition to FWS to protect the Owl; however, he would, "as a practical matter," be impaired by the stare decisis effect of the district court's decision, not to mention the direct effect of a possible permanent injunction. Furthermore, the Owl and its habitat would not be protected under the Act while Dr. Silver tried to lift such a permanent injunction and FWS considered Dr. Silver's new petition.

C. *The Existing Parties Do Not Adequately Represent Dr. Silver's Interest*

The burden is on the applicant in intervention to show that the representation by the existing parties may be inadequate, but this burden is "minimal." National Farm Lines v. I.C.C., 564 F.2d 381, 383 (10th Cir. 1977) (citing Trbovich v. United Mine Workers, 404 U.S. 528, 538 n. 10, 30 L. Ed. 2d 686, 92 S. Ct. 630 (1972)). "An applicant may fulfill this burden by showing collusion between the representative and an opposing party, that the representative has an interest adverse to the applicant, or that the representative failed in fulfilling his duty to represent the applicant's interest." Sanguine, Ltd. v. Dept. of Interior, 736 F.2d 1416, 1419 (10th Cir. 1984). "The possibility of divergence of interest need not be great in order to satisfy the burden of the applicants . . . ." *Natural Resources Defense Council*, 578 F.2d at 1346. However, "representation is adequate 'when the objective of the applicant for intervention is identical to that of one of the parties.'" *Ozarks Rural Elec. Coop.*, 79 F.3d at 1042 (quoting Bottoms v. Dresser Indus., Inc., 797 F.2d 869, 872 (10th Cir. 1986)); see also Northwest Forest Resource Council v. Glickman, 82 F.3d 825, 838 (9th Cir. 1996) ("Where an applicant for intervention and an existing party 'have the same ultimate objective, a presumption of adequacy of representation arises.'") (quoting Oregon Envtl. Council v. Oregon Dep't of Envtl. Quality, 775 F. Supp. 353, 359 (D. Ore. 1991) (citing American Nat'l Bank and Trust Co. v. City of Chicago, 865 F.2d 144, 148 n. 3 (7th Cir. 1989))). Dr. Silver argues that his interest and that of DOI are divergent and that DOI's failure to move to transfer venue to the district court in Arizona, where litigation over the protection of the Owl under the Act is pending, * * * evidences DOI's failure to protect his interest.

Our decision in *National Farm Lines*, [*supra*], is on point. There, several groups that represented motor carriers and that were registered with the Interstate Commerce Commission ("ICC") sought to intervene in a suit brought against ICC challenging the constitutionality of federal laws and regulations which protected the registered motor carriers against competition from unregistered motor carriers. The plaintiff, who was an unregistered motor carrier, argued that the applicants' interests were adequately represented by ICC, which promulgated the regulations. We disagreed and reversed the lower court's denial of the applicants' motion to intervene as of right, reasoning as follows:

> "We have here . . . the familiar situation in which the governmental agency is seeking to protect not only the interest of the public but also the private interest of the petitioners in intervention, a task which is on its face impossible. The cases correctly hold that this kind of a conflict satisfies the minimal burden of showing inadequacy of representation."

Id. at 384.

Like ICC in *National Farm Lines*, DOI must represent the public interest, which may differ from Dr. Silver's particular interest in the protection of the Owl in the habitat where he has photographed and studied the Owl. Cf. *Trbovich*, 404 U.S. at 538-39 (holding that a union member's interest was not adequately represented by the Secretary of Labor because the Secretary had a "duty to serve two distinct interests, which are related, but not identical:" that of the individual union member and that of the general public); *Sierra Club v. Espy*, 18 F.3d at 1207-08 (holding that timber industry representatives were not adequately represented by the government because "the government must represent the broad public interest, not just the economic concerns of the timber industry"), accord Mille Lacs Band of Chippewa Indians v. Minnesota, 989 F.2d 994, 1000-01 (8th Cir. 1993) (holding that counties and landowners could intervene as of right because their local and individual interests were not adequately represented by the State of Minnesota)[.] DOI's ability to adequately represent Dr. Silver despite its obligation to represent the public interest is made all the more suspect by its reluctance in protecting the Owl, doing so only after Dr. Silver threatened, and eventually brought, a law suit to force compliance with the Act. * * * Under these circumstances, we conclude that Dr. Silver has made the minimal showing necessary to suggest that the government's representation may be inadequate.

IV. CONCLUSION

We hold that Dr. Silver has a right to intervene in the action pursuant to Fed. R. Civ. P. 24(a)(2) because: Dr. Silver has a direct, substantial and legally protectable interest in the subject of the action between the Coalition and DOI; this interest may be impaired by the determination of the action; and neither DOI nor the Coalition will adequately represent Dr. Silver's interest. Because Dr. Silver may intervene as of right under Rule 24(a)(2), it is unnecessary to consider the question of intervention as a matter of discretion under Rule 24(b)(2). We therefore reverse the order denying Dr. Silver's motion to intervene under Rule 24(a)(2) and remand the case to the District Court for the District of New Mexico with the direction that Dr. Silver's application to intervene be granted.

NOTES AND PROBLEMS FOR DISCUSSION

1. Why did Dr. Silver want to intervene?

2. The Court says that Dr. Silver must meet four requirements: timeliness; interest in the subject matter; possible impairment or impeding of that interest; and inadequate representation.

(a) Focus on Dr. Silver's interest in the subject matter. Is his interest different (or stronger) than that of KAMO Electric Cooperative in the *City of Stilwell* case?

(b) How would Dr. Silver's interest — however it is described — be impaired had he been unable to intervene?

(c) Assuming that the Court ruled for the Coalition, why couldn't Dr. Silver bring a separate action to compel the DOI to protect the spotted owl?

(d) Why didn't the DOI adequately represent Silver?

3. Now, apply these concepts to the following potential intervenors:

(a) Mary Ann Sears, well known environmentalist and bird watcher.

(b) The Sierra Club.

(c) Owlie Hawk, owner of property in the habitat of the owl.

(d) The Chamber of Commerce of Pottstown, Arizona, which strongly supports local development and believes such protection limits growth and prevents development.

4. The *Coalition of Arizona* court cites the *Trbovich* decision and other cases for the proposition that the burden of showing inadequate representation is "minimal," and that this is especially true when one of the parties is the government. (In *Trbovich*, the Secretary of Labor had a "duty to serve two distinct interests, which are related, but not identical": the union member and the general public.) Do you see a problem with this reasoning in terms of the scope of intervention?

5. Turn Key Gaming Corporation contracted to build and manage a casino on land of the Oglala Sioux Tribe. To obtain funds, Turn Key borrowed $5 million from First Bank, and First Bank obtained a security interest (like a mortgage) from Turn Key in all of the property that Turn Key used to build and furnish the casino, and the revenues from managing the completed casino. The construction project experienced delays and cost overruns, the contract was cancelled, and the Oglala Tribe indicated it would operate the casino on its own. Turn Key brought an action against the Oglala Tribe for breach of contract, and the Tribe counterclaimed. First Bank moved to intervene. What arguments could Turn Key make that it satisfied each of the requirements of Rule 24, and how should the Court decide? See Turn Key Gaming, Inc. v. Oglala Sioux Tribe, 164 F.3d 1080 (8th Cir. 1999).

6. Apply Rule 24 in a simple tort situation, similar to *Temple v. Synthes Corp.* Patient is injured during an operation to insert a brace in her back. She sues Manufacturer on the theory that the brace was defective, and has threatened suit against Surgeon for negligence but does not actually join Surgeon in the lawsuit. Should Surgeon be permitted to intervene under Rule 24(a) to establish that he was not negligent?

7. Note also that intervention of right under Rule 24(a), is not mandatory, but is voluntary with the intervenor — unlike Rule 19(a). In MARTIN v. WILKS, 490 U.S. 755, 109 S.Ct. 2180, 104 L.Ed.2d 835 (1989), a district court entered a consent decree in an employment discrimination suit under Title VII of the 1964 Civil Rights Act, brought by African-American plaintiffs against the City of Birmingham and the County Personnel Board. The suit alleged racial discrimination in the hiring and promotion of Birmingham firefighters. In the decree, the City and Board agreed to engage in various forms of affirmative action to redress past discrimination in the hiring and promotion of black firefighters. White firefighters who were adversely affected by the order later sought to "undo" the decree when they subsequently sued the City and Board for reverse discrimination because of actions taken adverse to them pursuant to the implementation of the earlier decree. Although the particular plaintiffs had not attempted to intervene in the prior action, the Supreme Court observed that there was no necessity that they do so. The Court reiterated the traditional rule that nonparties to proceedings ordinarily cannot be adversely bound by them:

> Joinder as a party, rather than knowledge of a lawsuit and an opportunity to intervene, is the method by which potential parties are subjected to the jurisdiction of the court and bound by a judgment or decree. . . . It makes sense, therefore, to place on [the parties to a lawsuit] the burden of bringing in additional parties where such a step is indicated, rather than placing on potential additional parties a duty to intervene when they acquire knowledge of a lawsuit.

Consequently, the white firefighters were permitted to mount what looked like a collateral attack on the consent decree, even though they had been aware of the pending entry of the prior decree. Does the result make sense? What could or should the original plaintiffs have done in the original suit to obtain a judgment or decree that would have bound the white firefighters in the second lawsuit?

Congress later stepped in and seemed to make intervention quasi-mandatory in Title VII suits such as the one underlying *Martin v. Wilks*. In the Civil Rights Act of 1991, Congress amended section 703 of Title VII to provide than an employment practice "that implements and is within the scope of a litigated or consent judgment . . . may not be challenged" by a person who had "actual notice of the proposed judgment or order sufficient to apprise such person that such judgment or order might adversely affect the interests and legal rights of such person and that an opportunity was available to present objections to such judgment or order." Even without such notice, a third party would be barred from attacking a decree if his "interests were adequately represented by another person who had previously challenged the judgment or order on the same legal grounds and with a similar factual situation, unless there was an intervening change of law or fact." Are either of these provisions problematic? Although the statute deals with the collateral consequences of employment-related judgments and consent decrees, wouldn't Rule 19 still require joinder of parties such as the white firefighters in the first lawsuit in the first instance?

8. If a potential intervenor loses under Rule 24(a), it can always seek permissive intervention under Rule 24(b). Assuming Dr. Silver had been denied intervention as of right, what arguments would he make for satisfying Rule 24(b)? Most courts hold that permissive intervention is almost entirely discretionary and a decision will not be reversed on appeal.

9. *Coalition of Arizona* was a federal question suit. Subject matter jurisdiction over the claim of intervention was therefore unproblematic under 28 U.S.C. §1367(a). *Temple*, however, was a diversity case. Suppose that the surgeon wanted to intervene as a defendant in Temple's suit against Synthes, the manufacturer of the medical device, and suppose further (as was not the case in *Temple*) that the surgeon was nondiverse from the plaintiff. Will supplemental jurisdiction attach to the surgeon's claim in intervention as a defendant? See §1367(b).

10. Finally, note that personal jurisdiction over the intervenor and venue are nonissues, because the intervenor is voluntarily injecting himself into the suit and the district in which it has been brought.

SECTION H. INTERPLEADER

Consider John v. Sotheby's Inc., 141 F.R.D. 29 (S.D.N.Y. 1992). Ms. John had a painting by Rembrandt which she consigned to Sotheby's for auction. Dr. Nava contacted Sotheby's and told them that he owned the painting, having purchased it from John's husband some years earlier. What is Sotheby's to do? If it sells the painting, and gives the proceeds to John, it may be liable in conversion to Dr. Nava. If it refuses to sell, it may be liable for breach of its agreement with John to sell the painting. What Sotheby's needs is some way to get both John and Dr. Nava in the same court at the same time to fight it out, while it sits on the sidelines.

Or consider cases of disputes over insurance proceeds. Commonly litigated issues arise from situations where a person buys insurance and makes some form of general beneficiary designation, and the persons who fit that designation change before the policyholder's death. For example, the beneficiary is "my wife" and the policyholder has since divorced and remarried, or the beneficiary is "my children" and the policyholder with two children has another after purchasing the policy.

There probably was no problem in such cases if all the claimants were citizens of the same state. For example, if the policy designated "my wife," and Fran was the decedent's wife when the policy was purchased and Susan was his wife when he died, both Fran and Susan might be citizens of the same state and thus subject to personal jurisdiction in the same state. In such a situation, available procedural devices probably were sufficient to force them to litigate in the same lawsuit. But what if things weren't so neat? What if, for example, Fran was a citizen of Texas, and Susan a citizen of Montana. In essentially this kind of case, the Supreme Court held that each beneficiary could sue separately, notwithstanding the risk of double pay-out or liability. New York Life Insurance Co. v. Dunlevy, 241 U.S. 518, 36 S.Ct. 613, 60 L. Ed. 1140 (1916).

At equity, there was a procedural device to deal with these problems called a bill of interpleader. However, not only did the equitable device have severe restrictions on its availability but, perhaps more importantly, it didn't deal with jurisdictional problems created by the federal system (England being essentially one jurisdiction). Congress responded to *Dunlevy*, or perhaps more accurately, to lobbying by the life insurance industry, and passed the Interpleader Act, now codified in 28 U.S.C. §§1335, 1397, and 2361. In 1938, a provision for interpleader was incorporated in Rule 22 of the Rules. These are sometimes referred to respectively as Statutory Interpleader and Rule Interpleader.

Every interpleader case, by definition, starts with a "stakeholder" and at least two potential claimants. (There is no need for this kind of specialized device if there are only two parties to the dispute — the normal procedural rules can apply.) In addition, the issues we shall talk about assume that at least one of the three or more parties is a citizen of a state which is different than the others. This is because if the stakeholder and all the claimants are citizens of the same state, that state will ordinarily have jurisdiction to resolve any dispute among them.

The basic difference between statutory interpleader and Rule interpleader lies in their different jurisdictional provisions.[1] Consider, first, subject matter jurisdiction. For statutory interpleader, §1335 only requires diversity of citizenship between any two adverse claimants. Thus, if the insurance company in our example is a citizen of Texas as is Fran, and Susan is a citizen of Montana, there is diversity between two claimants Susan and Fran. By contrast, for Rule interpleader, the normal rules of diversity have long been thought to apply — i.e., complete diversity between all plaintiffs and all defendants. But

---

[1] Most interpleader actions arise under state law, and thus depend on diversity jurisdiction, and we focus on these. There are, however, some cases where there may be a basis for federal question jurisdiction.

the supplemental jurisdiction statute, 28 U.S.C. §1367(b), does not purport to deny supplemental jurisdiction in cases of Rule 22 interpleader. Most courts, however, have simply ignored this aspect of §1367(b). But even assuming that complete diversity is still called for, the requirement would be satisfied if the insurance company is a citizen of New Mexico and Susan and Fran are both citizens of Arizona (or, if Fran were a citizen of Texas, and Susan of Arizona). Of course, if the insurance company, Susan, and Fran are each citizens of a different state, the case would satisfy the subject matter jurisdiction requirements for both statutory and Rule interpleader.

Personal jurisdiction also may be an issue. For statutory interpleader, §2361 authorizes so-called nationwide service of process over claimants — i.e., the stakeholder can obtain jurisdiction over claimants from any state (subject to venue limitations discussed below). For Rule 22 interpleader, each defendant must be subject to personal jurisdiction in the same manner as in any other case — e.g., personal service on individual defendants within the particular state in which the interpleader proceeding is filed, or, satisfying the state's long-arm and having the requisite "minimum contacts" with the state. Finally, proper venue is also required. For statutory interpleader, §1397 permits venue in any judicial district in which any claimant resides. For Rule 22 interpleader, the general venue requirements of §1391 apply.

Given a choice, would a stakeholder ever prefer Rule interpleader to statutory interpleader? Can you think of any occasions when Rule interpleader would be available to the exclusion of statutory interpleader?

New Jersey Sports Productions, Inc. v. Don King Productions, Inc.

United States District Court, District of New Jersey, 1998.

15 F. Supp. 2d 534.

WILLIAM G. BASSLER DISTRICT JUDGE.

Plaintiff, New Jersey Sports Productions, Inc, d/b/a Main Events ("Main Events") moves for an Order: (1) permitting Main Events to pay into the Court registry the sum of $3,003,923.04 together with accrued interest, in connection with an interpleader action brought by Main Events; (2) restraining any other actions affecting the funds involved in this interpleader (except a disciplinary action brought by the Nevada Athletic Commission ("NAC") against the Defendant, Oliver McCall ("McCall")); and (3) directing that claims on the alleged fund be filed. Main Events asserts jurisdiction pursuant to 28 U.S.C. §1332 (diversity of citizenship). For the reasons set forth below, the Court grants Main Events' motions seeking an Order: (1) permitting Main Events to pay into the Court registry the sum of $3,003,923.04 together with accrued interest, in connection with an interpleader action brought by Main Events; (2) directing that claims on the alleged fund be filed; and (3) restraining any other actions affecting the funds involved in this interpleader (except a disciplinary action brought by the NAC against McCall).

I. BACKGROUND

The central events of this lawsuit concern a heavyweight title bout between McCall and Lennox Lewis that took place on February 7, 1997. McCall's purse for the fight was agreed to be $3,075,500.00.

Main Events, the promoter of the bout, entered into two contracts with McCall and his manager, Defendant Jimmy Adams ("Adams"). Under the first of these contracts, the World Boxing Council Official Championship Bout Contract ("WBC Contract"), McCall agreed to, among other things, refrain from the use of drugs. According to Main Events' Complaint, McCall thereafter was arrested on drug charges. Furthermore, McCall agreed to cooperate and assist Main Events in promoting the bout. According to the Complaint, McCall breached this obligation by refusing to cooperate with Main Events in promoting the bout.[3]

McCall and Main Events entered into a second contract titled, "Official Boxing Contract, Nevada Athletic Commission" (the "NAC Contract"), which provided that McCall would not be entitled to the purse if the NAC determined that McCall did not engage in honest competition or give an honest exhibition of his skills.

Paragraph 3 of the NAC Contract provides, in part:

> [The parties agree] that the contest shall be conducted in all respects in conformity with the laws of the State of Nevada, and the rules and regulations adopted by the Nevada Athletic Commission, which are hereby made a part of this agreement. . . . If the referee or the Nevada Athletic Commission shall decide that the Boxer and Manager, or either of them, did not enter into the contract in good faith; or the Boxer and Manager, or either of them, had any collusive understanding or agreement regarding the termination of the match other that the same should be an honest exhibition of skill on the part of the contestants, or that the Boxer is not honestly competing or did not give an honest exhibition of his skill, or is guilty of an act detrimental to the interest of boxing; it is agreed in any of such events that the Boxer shall not be entitled to the compensation above named, or any part thereof, unless so ordered by the Nevada Athletic Commission.

> It is further agreed that the Promoter [Main Events] shall pay said compensation to the said Commission in the event the Commission shall so order upon any of the above-mentioned grounds. The Commission shall thereupon, in its discretion, make such disposition of said purse as it deems to the best interest of legitimate sport and may forfeit to the Nevada Athletic Commission all or any part of the compensation or order the same or any portion thereof paid to the Boxer. All parties

---

[3] It appears from the allegations in the Complaint that McCall viewed Don King Productions, Inc. ("DKP") as McCall's exclusive promoter, and requested that all inquiries from Main Events regarding promotional activities in connection with the bout be directed through DKP.

hereto agree to accept and be bound by the decision of the said Commission and such decision shall be final and conclusive of the rights of the parties hereto.

According to the Complaint, DKP, purportedly on behalf of McCall, demanded that a letter of credit be provided to DKP in McCall's name. The Complaint further alleges that Main Events procured a letter of credit in the amount of $2,983,997, which was provided to DKP in McCall's name.[5] The letter of credit expired, by its terms, on March 7, 1997. No parties have drawn against the letter of credit; the funds representing McCall's disputed purse are kept in a segregated, interest-bearing account in Bergen Commercial Bank under Main Events's control.

According to the Complaint, McCall simply stopped fighting after the third round of the bout. As a result, the referee stopped the bout fifty-five seconds into the fifth round. Main Events alleges that McCall's actions breached both the NAC Contract and WBC Contract.

On February 7, 1997, shortly after the bout was stopped, the Nevada Athletic Commission notified Main Events that McCall breached the terms of his agreements and that he should not be paid the approximately $3 million provided for in the contracts between the parties. On February 18, 1997, the Nevada Attorney General's Office initiated a disciplinary action before the Nevada Athletic Commission seeking the imposition of fines totaling ten percent of McCall's purse and the revocation of McCall's Nevada boxing license.

On April 1, 1997, approximately 20 days after the Complaint in this action had been filed, McCall and the Nevada Attorney General's Office entered into a settlement agreement (the "Settlement"). According to the terms of the Settlement, McCall admitted that the manner and method in which he conducted himself was detrimental to boxing. McCall further agreed to pay a $250,000 fine to the State of Nevada and to suffer a one-year suspension from boxing in Nevada to commence nunc pro tunc February 7, 1997.

The Settlement must be approved by the NAC before it becomes final. (Settlement at p.9). The Settlement provides that the parties' agreement will be placed on the agenda of the next scheduled meeting of the NAC, which had been scheduled for April 26, 1997. The Attorney General agreed to recommend that the NAC approve the Settlement. The Attorney General also agreed to recommend that the NAC order that McCall receive the remaining monies due him, less and except the $250,000 fine, as per the WBC and NAC contracts.

Main Events indicates, in its reply brief, that, while it was aware of the pendency of the NAC hearings, Main Events was not a party to the settlement negotiations and in no way participated in them. Nor, it would appear, were any parties other than McCall and the NAC privy to the proposed settlement terms.

According to the Complaint, possible claimants to the disputed purse include:

---

[5] According to the Complaint, the difference between the amount of the letter of credit and the full purse of $3,075,550 represents sanction fees owed by McCall and paid to the WBC by Main Events on McCall's behalf.

(A)   McCall, who allegedly claims that he is due the entire purse;

(B)   DKP, which has also raised a claim to part of McCall's purse[8];

(C)   Time Warner Entertainment, Co., L.P. ("Time Warner"), which, through its broadcast division, Home Box Office, Inc., broadcast the bout[9];

(D)   Adams, McCall's manager;

(E)   The NAC, which has the power to fine McCall[10]; and

(F)   Main Events, which claims that the amount on deposit is not due because of various contract breaches.

Both DKP and McCall oppose Main Events's application to place the funds on deposit with the Court, to enjoin any other actions affecting the funds (except the pending disciplinary action), and to direct that claims against the fund be filed. They argue: (1) that this Court lacks subject matter jurisdiction over Main Events's interpleader claim; (2) that the interpleader claim is improperly venued in this district; (3) that this Court should abstain from exercising its interpleader jurisdiction in favor of the action pending before the NAC; (4) that the Court lacks personal jurisdiction over McCall; and (5) that the NAC Contract, by its terms, designates the NAC as the exclusive forum to hear these claims.

II. DISCUSSION

Interpleader is an equitable device that enables a party holding a fund to compel persons asserting conflicting claims to that fund to adjudicate their rights to the fund in a single action. The classic interpleader scenario involves a neutral stakeholder, such as an insurance company, faced with completing claims over the rights of the res — e.g., the proceeds of a life insurance policy where the beneficiaries dispute their relative distributions. Thus, as originally conceived, interpleader actions were limited to a relatively narrow range of cases.

Subsequent revisions to the United States Code and the Federal Rules of Civil Procedure have liberalized use of the interpleader device. The key prerequisite to maintaining an action in interpleader presently is that there be two or more claimants to the fund who are "adverse" to each other. 7 Wright & Miller, Federal Practice and Procedure §1705 at 507-509 (1986 & 1996 supp.). "This requirement is not met where one of the claims clearly is devoid of

---

[8]   Neither the Complaint nor Main Events's moving papers elaborate on the nature of the possible actions DKP might pursue against the res.

[9]   Time Warner filed its Counterclaim and Crossclaim in Interpleader on April 22, 1997 alleging that Time Warner advanced the funds at issue to Main Events through a letter of credit in favor of Main Events issued by Societe Generale, a New York bank. Time Warner alleges that, pursuant to a contract entered into between Time Warner and Main Events, Main Events promised to provide a competitive bout between Lennox Lewis and Oliver McCall. Time Warner further alleges that McCall's alleged breach of his obligations to Main Events to give an honest demonstration of his skills excused Time Warner from satisfying the letter of credit it had previously obtained in favor of Main Events. Time Warner further alleges that the Societe Generale letter of credit was cashed over Time Warner's objection. Time Warner thus claims a superior right to the funds at issue.

[10]   The Nevada Athletic Commission was dropped from the case on April 2, 1997 apparently on the understanding that the NAC did not intend to make a claim on McCall's purse.

substance, or one of the claimants is under the control of the stakeholder or has dropped his claim and the fear of multiple litigation or liability is groundless, or the claims are not asserted against the same fund, or the stakeholder may be liable to both claimants." Id. at 508-509; see also CNA Companies v. Waters, 926 F.2d 247, 251 (3d Cir. 1991) (only if stakeholder has a "bona fide" fear of adverse claims arising with respect to the res does a claim for interpleader arise).

Similarly, to properly invoke the interpleader jurisdiction of the Court, there must exist a limited fund or some specific, identifiable property as to which the claimants and stakeholder need the protection of one lawsuit.

An interpleader action may be brought in federal court pursuant to two different, yet overlapping, procedural devices. "Rule interpleader" is governed by Fed. R. Civ. P. 22, which states, in pertinent part:

> (1) Persons having claims against the plaintiff may be joined as defendants and required to interplead when their claims are such that the plaintiff is or may be exposed to double or multiple liability. It is not ground for objection to the joinder that the claims of the several claimants or the titles on which their claims depend do not have a common origin or are not identical but are adverse to and independent of one another, or that the plaintiff avers that the plaintiff is not liable in whole or in part to any or all of the claimants . . . .

> (2) The remedy herein provided is in addition to and in no way supersedes or limits the remedy provided by Title 28, U.S.C. §§1335, 1397 and 2361 . . . .

"Statutory interpleader" is governed by 28 U.S.C. §§1335, 1397 and 2361. 28 U.S.C. §1335 provides, in pertinent part:

> (a) The district courts shall have original jurisdiction of any civil action of interpleader or in the nature of interpleader filed by any person, firm, or corporation, association, or society having in his or its custody or possession money or property of the value of $500 or more . . . if

> (1) Two or more adverse claimants, of diverse citizenship as defined in section 1332 of this title, are claiming or may claim to be entitled to such money or property . . . .

Subject matter jurisdiction under statutory and rule interpleader differs. Under statutory interpleader, the value of the stake need only be $500 and diversity of citizenship need exist only between any two of the adverse claimants. In rule interpleader, on the other hand, jurisdiction must be based on the general statutes governing federal court jurisdiction — i.e., federal question (28 U.S.C. §1331) or diversity of citizenship (28 U.S.C. §1332). Thus, if a rule interpleader claimant asserts jurisdiction pursuant to 28 U.S.C. §1332, complete diversity must exist between the plaintiff stakeholder and the defendant claimants, and the amount in controversy must exceed $75,000. Id.

Similarly, the venue rules differ as between rule and statutory interpleader. Statutory interpleader restricts venue to any district in which one or more of the claimants resides. Under rule interpleader, on the other hand, venue is [governed by the basic venue statute, 28 U.S.C. §1391.]

A. DKP's Argument That Venue is Improper in This District

DKP argues that venue is improper in this district. This argument is misplaced. DKP points out that none of the named defendant-claimants in to the interpleader action reside in this district. DKP argues, therefore, that venue is not proper in this district. The Court concludes that * * * the District of New Jersey is a proper venue for Main Events's interpleader action. [The court first upheld venue under §1391 because New Jersey was the district of residence of the stakeholder—Main Events. Was it right to do so? — eds.]

Venue for statutory interpleader claims is governed by 28 U.S.C. §1397, which provides that "any civil action of interpleader or in the nature of interpleader under Section 1335 of this title may be brought in the judicial district in which one or more of the claimants reside."

Because none of the defendant-claimants reside in New Jersey, the question arises whether a plaintiff-stakeholder-claimant qualifies as a "claimant" within the meaning of Section 1397. Neither the parties' nor the Court's research has located a case discussing this issue.

The Court concludes that "claimant" as used in Section 1397 includes plaintiff-stakeholders who assert a claim on the stake. The Court's conclusion is based on a plain textual reading of the statute, which provides for venue in the district where any "claimant" resides. 28 U.S.C. §1397. This conclusion follows from the fact that plaintiff-stakeholders may, under Section 1335, assert a claim on the stake. State Farm Fire and Casualty Co. v. Tashire, 386 U.S. 523, 18 L.Ed. 2d 270, 87 S.Ct. 1199 (1967). A natural reading of Section 1397 compels the conclusion that where, as here, a plaintiff-stakeholder asserts a claim against the fund, its residence is relevant for determining whether venue is proper under Section 1397.

B. DKP's Argument That Interpleader is Improper Because There Exist No Adverse Claims to the Fund.

As stated above, the existence of two or more adverse claims to the fund at issue is a prerequisite to the maintenance of an interpleader action. Main Events has made an adequate showing on this motion that it has a "bona fide" fear of adverse claims relating to McCall's purse.

The Complaint in this action does not specify any theory pursuant to which DKP, who does not appear to be a party to either the WBC or the NAC contracts, could legitimately claim any part of the purse. See Gaines v. Sunray Oil Co., 539 F.2d 1136, 1141-42 (8th Cir. 1976) (denying interpleader; "Here, Amtel has not interpleaded a sum represented to be a reasonable commission owing to only one of several competing brokers, or to be divided among them. Rather, it has interpleaded a specific sum arising under a particular agreement to which only Amtel and Sunray were parties.").

Furthermore, there does not appear to be the requisite adversity between the possible claims of McCall and Adams. From a preliminary examination of the contracts at issue, it would appear that Adams's recovery from the purse, if any, would be dependent on McCall's recovery. (WBC Contract P 4 ("Promoter [Main Events] shall pay the Manager [Adams] of the Boxer [McCall] his share of Boxer's compensation, by separate check, in the amount agreed to by Boxer and his manager"). While both McCall and Adams would appear to be adverse to Main Events's position, on the record before the Court it is a stretch to conclude that they have the requisite adversity between themselves for the maintenance of an interpleader action.

Main Events, however, has submitted sufficient evidence that it has a legitimate fear of double liability stemming from dual obligations owing to McCall and Time Warner. Time Warner has asserted a claim against the res by way of counterclaim and crossclaim in interpleader. The Counterclaim and Crossclaim alleges that Time Warner advanced the funds at issue to Main Events through a letter of credit in favor of Main Events issued by Societe Generale, a New York bank. Time Warner alleges that, pursuant to a contract entered into between Time Warner and Main Events, that Main Events promised to provide a competitive bout between Lennox Lewis and Oliver McCall. Time Warner further alleges that McCall's breaches of his obligation to Main Events to give an honest demonstration of his skills excused Time Warner from satisfying the letter of credit it had previously obtained in favor of Main Events. Time Warner further alleges that the Societe Generale letter of credit was cashed over Time Warner's objection. Time Warner thus claims a superior right to the funds at issue.

This claim, together with McCall's, satisfies the adversity requirement. Significantly, should McCall be found to be entitled to all or part of the purse, as McCall's counsel alleges is the likely outcome of the NAC proceeding, and this or another court determines that Main Events is liable to Time Warner, Main Events could face double liability arising from the same transaction. Under these circumstances, Main Events has a bona fide fear of adverse claims arising with regard to the contract amounts in dispute.[15] Interpleader, therefore, is the appropriate remedy to allay those fears.

* * *

D. *DKP's Argument That This Court Lacks Personal Jurisdiction Over McCall*

McCall argues that this Court lacks jurisdiction over his person. The Court disagrees.

---

[15] DKP argues that Main Events's obligation to McCall is wholly separate and apart from its obligation to Time Warner and therefore that interpleader is inappropriate. DKP's position has conceptual appeal: there are separate contracts at issue and the "stake" in this case is a fungible good — money. Hence, DKP's oft-repeated assertion during oral argument that McCall does not care whether his purse money comes from the account maintained in the Bergen Commercial Bank or from Main Events's general accounts. DKP's argument, in the Court's view, proves too much. Because money is a fungible commodity, no claimant on a money stake cares about the origin of the money. What really matters is whether a party fears double liability on what amounts to one obligation. Here, though there are, as DKP points out, two contractual relationships (one between Main Events and McCall, and the other between Time Warner and Main Events), both contractual relationships involve the same transactional set of facts. That is, Time Warner's claim against Main Events is based on the same set of operative facts — whether McCall engaged in an honest exhibition — as is Main Events's claim against McCall. Based on this crucial circumstance, the Court concludes that Main Events has a bona fide fear of double liability and inconsistent verdicts justifying the invocation of this Court's interpleader jurisdiction.

Main Events first argues that personal jurisdiction over McCall is proper pursuant to 28 U.S.C. §2361 which provides for nationwide service of process in actions brought pursuant to 28 U.S.C. §1335. See NY Life Distributors, Inc. v. Adherence Group, Inc., 72 F.3d 371, 375 (3d Cir. 1995). The Court agrees that it may exercise personal jurisdiction over McCall pursuant to section 2361, at least with respect to Main Events's statutory interpleader claim.

It is unclear from Main Events's pleading, however, whether it is proceeding pursuant to Rule 22, in which case the action cannot be maintained unless the claimants can be served with process as in any other civil action within the territorial limits prescribed by Fed. R. Civ. P. 4.

The Court concludes, at least preliminarily, that the Court has personal jurisdiction over McCall with respect to Main Events's rule interpleader claim under the line of cases initiated by *International Shoe*. Thus, even if the proposed interpleader action is pursuant to Fed. R. Civ. P. 22, the Court has personal jurisdiction over McCall.[18]

* * *

E. *Main Events's Application to Enjoin Other State Proceedings*

Main Events also seeks an injunction restraining any other actions affecting the funds involved in this interpleader. Under either rule or statutory interpleader, an injunction is appropriate. Accordingly, the Court *grants* Main Events's motion seeking to restrain other actions affecting the funds involved in this interpleader.

28 U.S.C. §2361 acts as a statutory exception to the Anti-Injunction Act. Section 2361 authorizes a district court to enter an order restraining all claimants from instituting a proceeding in any state or federal court affecting the interpleaded res. Provident Mut. Life Ins. Co. of Philadelphia v. Ehrlich, 508 F.2d 129 (3d Cir. 1975). Because statutory interpleader allows for nationwide service of process, 28 U.S.C. §2361, an injunction issued under Section 2361 halts any proceedings deemed to be inconsistent with the statutory interpleader proceeding.

The Court may also enjoin parallel proceedings when the action is pursuant to Rule 22; the scope of the injunction, however, is narrower than under statutory interpleader. Under rule interpleader, the Court retains the discretion to restrain the litigants before the Court from litigating claims in derogation of the Court's exercise of jurisdiction. 7 Wright & Miller, Federal Practice and Procedure §1717 at 615 (". . . the mere fact that a nationwide injunction under Section 2361 is not available in a rule interpleader case does not mean that the court does not have discretion in the latter context to issue an order against those claimants that have been subjected to the court's jurisdiction in accordance with the more traditional rules of process applicable in cases under Rule 22.

---

[18] McCall dedicates only one page of his opposition brief to his argument that this Court lacks personal jurisdiction over McCall. For the reasons set forth above, the Court preliminarily determines, on the facts before it, that the Court may, consistent with "traditional notions of fair play and substantial justice," International Shoe v. State of Washington, 326 U.S. 310, 90 L. Ed. 95, 66 S. Ct. 154 (1945), exercise personal jurisdiction over McCall. * * *

Certainly if the court can assert personal jurisdiction over a claimant it has the power to issue an order designed to effectuate the exercise of jurisdiction.").

The Court, accordingly, grants Main Events's motion to restrain any other actions affecting the funds involved in this interpleader. Moreover, because the Court has determined that the case may proceed as a statutory interpleader, the injunction applies to any proceeding nationwide that the Court deems inconsistent with this interpleader proceeding.

* * *

III. CONCLUSION

For the foregoing reasons, Main Events's motion for an Order: (1) permitting Main Events to pay into the Court registry the sum of $3,003,923.04 together with accrued interest, in connection with an interpleader action brought by Main Events; (2) directing that claims on the alleged fund be filed; and (3) restraining any other actions affecting the funds involved in this interpleader (except a disciplinary action brought by the Nevada Athletic Commission against the Defendant, Oliver McCall) is granted.

NOTES AND PROBLEMS FOR DISCUSSION

1. Interpleader cases tend to be complicated because of the number of parties involved, and this one is certainly no exception. Focus on (a) the provision of §1335 that was at issue, and (b) why Main Events thought interpleader proper and McCall thought it wasn't.

2. Missing from the *New Jersey Sports* opinion is a discussion of subject matter jurisdiction. One must therefore conclude that the plaintiff/stakeholder, Main Events, was diverse from all of the defendant/claimants for Rule interpleader, or that at least two of the claimants were of diverse citizenship for statutory interpleader. Note that one of the claimants, Time Warner is a partnership and that its citizenship would therefore reflect the citizenship of each of its partners. How might this impact Rule and statutory interpleader?

3. Assume a partnership is formed to buy and sell antiques consisting of Able, Baker and Caine. Able is the managing partner; Baker and Caine put up money, but have nothing to do with the actual business. In January, Able purchased a golden calf from a private party for $100,000. In March, Baker brought a lawsuit against Able claiming that Able was negligent in overpaying and had a conflict of interest because the seller was his brother-in-law. In September, while the suit was still pending, Able sold the calf for $100,000. Caine brought suit claiming that Able was negligent in selling for such a low price and had a conflict of interest because the buyer was his wife's cousin. Able brings an interpleader action under both the interpleader statute and Rule 22 (assume jurisdiction and venue are proper). Is interpleader proper? See Bradley v. Kochenash, 44 F.3d 166 (2d Cir. 1995).

4. In many cases, a defendant may attempt to use interpleader to solve Rule 19 problems. Thus, in *John v. Sotheby's*, discussed at the start of this section, John sued Sotheby's for the Rembrandt painting, and Sotheby's moved to dismiss the action under Rule 19 or, in the alternative, to interplead Dr. Nava (the other claimant). What provision in Rule 19 might apply to deny a dismissal under these circumstances?

5. It is common in interpleader situations that, before the interpleader claim is asserted, one of the claimants has sued the stakeholder. This was true in both *New Jersey Sports* and *Sotheby's*. For the interpleader device to work, it is often critical that the stakeholder be able to get an injunction against the continuation of the other action. Do you see the risks that the stakeholder runs if it doesn't get an injunction? Note that 28 U.S.C. §2361 authorizes such an injunction in a statutory interpleader case (as well as nationwide service of process). In Rule 22 cases, an injunction may be somewhat more difficult to obtain, given limitations on the power of federal courts to enjoin already pending state court litigation. See 28 U.S.C. §2283.

6. Finally, note what interpleader generally cannot do. It cannot serve as a vehicle to consolidate all litigation arising out of a common accident, at least when there is no possibility that plaintiffs will be unable fully to recover against defendants in the litigation.

In STATE FARM FIRE & CASUALTY CO. v. TASHIRE, 386 U.S. 523, 87 S.Ct. 1199, 18 L.Ed.2d 270 (1967), a Greyhound bus collided with a pickup truck in California, resulting in injuries to 33 of the bus passengers and the deaths of two passengers. The truck driver, his passenger and the bus driver also died. The truck driver had an insurance policy issued by State Farm, but it was only for $20,000 and would be unable to satisfy the claims of all injured parties. The injured parties brought lawsuits in various state and federal courts, and sued Greyhound, the truck driver, its owner and the bus driver. Greyhound was a citizen of California and each of the individual defendants was a citizen of Oregon, and plaintiffs were from various states and Canada. State Farm then sought statutory interpleader in an Oregon federal court. The interpleader sought by State Farm would have compelled all litigation against their client to be consolidated in a single forum — a desirable result from State Farm's perspective because it was obliged under its insurance contract to defend their insured. (Greyhound also eventually sought consolidation of all litigation.) Interpleader would also insure that no one plaintiff would be able to walk off with the lion's share of the insurance proceeds.

The Supreme Court recognized the need for orderly distribution of the limited insurance fund, but also noted that it was a minor slice of the total potential liability. It therefore did not require the plaintiffs all to pursue their cases in the interpleader forum, noting that the function of interpleader was not to serve as a "bill of peace" that would compel all litigation to proceed under one roof. Instead, interpleader was available for equitable distribution of the proceeds after plaintiffs had prevailed in their lawsuits in the forum in which they had initially filed them. Did this result mean that State Farm won the battle but effectively lost the war? In the course of its decision, the Court upheld the constitutionality of the minimal diversity provisions of the interpleader statute that required only that any two claimants be diverse from one another.

SECTION I.   CLASS ACTIONS

1. INTRODUCTION

Given the numbers of people that they affect and their current popularity, class action lawsuits may be one of the most visible aspects of modern civil litigation. But a class action is not your ordinary lawsuit. With origins deep in the history of equity, class actions are suits brought by an individual or individuals, not only on behalf of themselves, but on behalf of others who are similarly situated. Those who bring the lawsuit are sometimes referred to as the named plaintiffs, or the class representatives. The others on whose behalf the lawsuit is brought are not joined individually as parties — at least not in the same way that party joinder might be made under Rule 19 or 20. Nevertheless, they will be bound by the outcome of the litigation as if they were formally made parties, assuming that the suit is one that may properly proceed as a class action. Because of the potential of the class action to affect the interests of persons who have not individually been made parties, it risks compromising the traditional notion that each party should have his or her day in court before their legal rights will be determined. Consequently, the procedures surrounding the authorization (or "certification") of a class action and the prerequisites for successfully maintaining one are stringent. Any scheme in which one private party purports to represent the interests of another — especially a stranger — and potentially preclude that party from litigating his own rights at a later date, requires close attention to the congruity of interests between the named representative and those he purports to represent, as well as appropriate notice to those affected in order that they may exercise control over their litigational destiny. In many cases, there may also be a need to justify why a class action is to be preferred to more ordinary means of litigation which would formally bind only those individuals who bring suit and defend it.

The latter point raises an important question. Why would anyone ever consider bringing suit not only for himself, but also for others? As the materials below will show, and as Rule 23 may suppose, some class actions are more necessary than others. For example, imagine a scenario in which many persons have been injured by a company's product, and the company's ability to pay out fully on all potential judgments might be limited in some way. The limit might exist either by law (e.g., the liability of some parties in connection with certain socially desirable activities may be capped to encourage the activity) or because a particular insurance policy may be the only available asset against which to enforce any judgments. If each injured party were permitted to sue on their own, the available assets might be depleted, leaving nothing for the remaining claimants. To be sure, the device of interpleader (discussed above) is addressed to similar concerns; but interpleader is triggered by the stakeholder, not the potential claimant or claimants, and in many settings the stakeholder may be indifferent as to who might recover. The necessity of equal treatment in such a limited fund case suggests the need for some kind of collective treatment even if interpleader is not sought by the stakeholder. The impetus for bringing the suit as a class action might therefore be the interest of those who fear they will not be able to recover later, and the incentive of class counsel would lie in being able to recover her fees out of the available fund if she is successful.

Another setting in which some might consider a class action to be critical is one in which the many would-be claimants have suffered similar injuries, but ones that would produce only modest recovery at any individual trial. For example, a defendant may have overcharged millions of customers a few dollars each in violation of a governmentally imposed price ceiling. It might be prohibitively expensive for an individual to bring such a suit, because the cost of hiring an attorney may greatly exceed the amount of individual recovery. Nor would an attorney have incentives to bring a claim for a percentage of an individual recovery in such a case. A fee-shifting statute enabling the successful plaintiff to recover her lawyer's fees in addition to damages might provide an incentive to bring a suit for a modest recovery. But in the American judicial system, fee shifting is not the norm and it generally exists only by statutory exception. On the other hand, a successful class action by many such persons similarly situated would have the potential effect of producing a large monetary recovery approximating the extent to which the defendant illegally profited. And from that recovery, class counsel could recover a reasonable fee, thus creating an incentive to bring suit. Indeed, absent the availability of a class action on behalf of such small claimants, their claims might never be brought, and the defendant's illegal behavior might go substantially unredressed.

Other kinds of class actions may be less necessary in the senses described above, but they might be able to add a measure of convenience in litigation. As a result of an airplane crash, for example, the hundreds of persons injured or killed might sue individually, or one or more of them might seek to represent others like themselves in a class proceeding. It is possible that if the proceeding were to take place under one roof rather than in various forums, a considerable amount of duplication of effort and waste of judicial time could be avoided. But the personal injury or wrongful death suits such as might arise out of a plane crash are precisely the sort of individual suits that parties have exercised the freedom to bring individually and in a proper forum of their own choosing. Moreover, there is no risk that such independently viable suits would not otherwise be brought absent class action treatment. Nor is there the same necessity for collective treatment as there is with a limited fund, at least so long as the defendant is solvent. While judicial efficiency is a value — and in such a suit there may be many common questions that could be adjudicated once and for all (such as the airline's negligence) — there is also value in allowing litigants to pursue such litigation on their own. Consequently, where efficiency rather than fairness is all that is at issue, class treatment may be less compelling. This is not to say that class treatment might never be available in such circumstances, but only that it may be harder to secure, and that values of litigant autonomy will play a competing role.

To a considerable extent, Rule 23 as currently designed reflects many of these basic concerns regarding necessity, efficiency, and litigant autonomy. As you work through the Rule, note that there are some requirements that are common to all class actions, while other requirements are unique to the type of class action that is involved. The latter essentially break down into three groupings: Rule 23(b)(1), which is addressed to settings in which there is a need for unitary treatment of the claimants (as, for example, in the limited fund context noted above); Rule 23(b)(2), which is addressed to class actions for injunctive relief; and Rule 23(b)(3), which is addressed to damages class actions not implicating the sort of concerns addressed by (b)(1). In this Part, we first address the due process issues associated with class action litigation, we then explore the certification process and the types of available class actions, and thereafter we treat issues of personal jurisdiction, choice of law, and settlement.

2. CLASS ACTIONS AND DUE PROCESS

The Due Process Clause limits the ability of a state to enter a binding judgment determining the rights of persons who have not been made parties to a proceeding in a court with personal jurisdiction. Cases as far back as *Pennoyer* suggest as much. The *Hansberry* case, which follows, deals directly with those concerns as they are implicated in the representative suit or class action. In addition, although *Hansberry* itself was not a federal court class action brought under Rule 23, the shape of the current rule is designed in large measure to address the sorts of due process issues that *Hansberry* identifies as inhering in class action litigation. Concerns for representational adequacy and commonality of interest between the class representative and those unnamed class members whom he represents are critical not only for purposes of due process but for purposes of Rule 23 as well. Indeed, many of the prerequisites for any class action under Rule 23(a), such as the requirement that the representative's claims be "typical" of those of the class members, that he be an "adequate" representative, and that the claims share "common questions" of law or fact are designed to insure the requisite commonality of interest to meet the concerns of due process. The Supreme Court has made clear that if the interests and claims of the unnamed members of the class are not sufficiently congruent with those of the class representative, then even a vigorous advocate will not be able to maintain a class suit because their fates may not be sufficiently linked, thus presenting an unacceptable risk that the class might be shortchanged. See General Tel. Co. of Southwest v. Falcon, 457 U.S. 147, 161, 102 S.Ct. 2364, 72 L.Ed.2d 740 (1982) (concluding that Hispanic class representative's promotion-related discrimination claim was insufficiently "typical" of claims of Hispanic class members denied employment).

Hansberry v. Lee

Supreme Court of the United States, 1940.

311 U.S. 32, 61 S.Ct. 115, 85 L.Ed. 22.

MR. JUSTICE STONE delivered the opinion of the Court.

The question is whether the Supreme Court of Illinois, by its adjudication that petitioners in this case are bound by a judgment rendered in an earlier litigation to which they were not parties, has deprived them of the due process of law guaranteed by the Fourteenth Amendment.

Respondents brought this suit in the Circuit Court of Cook County, Illinois, to enjoin the breach by petitioners of an agreement restricting the use of land within a described area of the City of Chicago, which was alleged to have been entered into by some five hundred of the land owners. The agreement stipulated that for a specified period no part of the land should be "sold, leased to or permitted to be occupied by any person of the colored race," and provided that it should not be effective unless signed by the "owners of 95 per centum of the frontage" within the described area. The bill of complaint set up that the owners of 95 per cent of the frontage had signed; that respondents are owners of land within the restricted area who have either signed the agreement or acquired their land from others who did sign and that petitioners Hansberry, who are Negroes, have, with the alleged aid of the other petitioners and with knowledge of the agreement, acquired and are occupying land in the restricted area formerly belonging to an owner who had signed the agreement.

To the defense that the agreement had never become effective because owners of 95 per cent of the frontage had not signed it, respondents pleaded that that issue was res judicata by the decree in an earlier suit. Burke v. Kleiman, 277 Ill.App. 519. To this petitioners pleaded, by way of rejoinder, that they were not parties to that suit or bound by its decree, and that denial of their right to litigate, in the present suit, the issue of performance of the condition precedent to the validity of the agreement would be a denial of due process of law guaranteed by the Fourteenth Amendment. It does not appear, nor is it contended that any of petitioners is the successor in interest to or in privity with any of the parties in the earlier suit.

The circuit court, after a trial on the merits, found that owners of only about 54 per cent of the frontage had signed the agreement, and that the only support of the judgment in the *Burke* case was a false and fraudulent stipulation of the parties that 95 per cent had signed. But it ruled that the issue of performance of the condition precedent to the validity of the agreement was res judicata as alleged and entered a decree for respondents. The Supreme Court of Illinois affirmed. We granted certiorari to resolve the constitutional question.

The Supreme Court of Illinois, upon an examination of the record in *Burke v. Kleiman, supra,* found that that suit, in the Superior Court of Cook County, was brought by a landowner in the restricted area to enforce the agreement which had been signed by her predecessor in title, in behalf of herself and other property owners in like situation, against four named individuals who had acquired or asserted an interest in a plot of land formerly owned by another signer of the agreement; that upon stipulation of the parties in that suit that the agreement had been signed by owners of 95 per cent of all the frontage, the court had adjudged that the agreement was in force, that it was a covenant running with the land and binding all the land within the described area in the hands of the parties to the agreement and those claiming under them including defendants, and had entered its decree restraining the breach of the agreement by the defendants and those claiming under them, and that the appellate court had affirmed the decree. It found that the stipulation was untrue but held, contrary to the trial court, that it was not fraudulent or collusive. It also appears from the record in *Burke v. Kleiman* that the case was tried on an agreed statement of facts which raised only a single issue, whether by reason of changes in the restricted area, the agreement had ceased to be enforceable in equity.

From this the Supreme Court of Illinois concluded in the present case that *Burke v. Kleiman* was a "class" or "representative" suit and that in such a suit "where the remedy is pursued by a plaintiff who has the right to represent the class to which he belongs, other members of the class are bound by the results in the case unless it is reversed or set aside on direct proceedings"; that petitioners in the present suit were members of the class represented by the plaintiffs in the earlier suit and consequently were bound by its decree which had rendered the issue of performance of the condition precedent to the restrictive agreement res judicata, so far as petitioners are concerned. The court thought that the circumstance that the stipulation in the earlier suit that owners of 95 per cent of the frontage had signed the agreement was contrary to the fact as found in the present suit did not militate against this conclusion since the court in the earlier suit had jurisdiction to determine the fact as between the parties before it and that its determination, because of the representative character of the suit, even though erroneous, was binding on petitioners until set aside by a direct attack on the first judgment.

State courts are free to attach such descriptive labels to litigations before them as they may choose and to attribute to them such consequences as they think appropriate under state constitutions and laws, subject only to the requirements of the Constitution of the United States. But when the judgment of a state court, ascribing to the judgment of another court the binding force and effect of res judicata, is challenged for want of due process it becomes the duty of this Court to examine the course of procedure in both litigations to ascertain whether the litigant whose rights have thus been adjudicated has been afforded such notice and opportunity to be heard as are requisite to the due process which the Constitution prescribes. Western Life Indemnity Co. v. Rupp, 235 U.S. 261, 273.

It is a principle of general application in Anglo-American jurisprudence that one is not bound by a judgment in personam in a litigation in which he is not designated as a party or to which he has not been made a party by service of process. Pennoyer v. Neff, 95 U.S. 714. * * * A judgment rendered in such circumstances is not entitled to the full faith and credit which the Constitution and statute of the United States, * * * prescribe, * * * and judicial action enforcing it against the person or property of the absent party is not that due process which the Fifth and Fourteenth Amendments requires.

To these general rules there is a recognized exception that, to an extent not precisely defined by judicial opinion, the judgment in a "class" or "representative" suit, to which some members of the class are parties, may bind members of the class or those represented who were not made parties to it.

The class suit was an invention of equity to enable it to proceed to a decree in suits where the number of those interested in the subject of the litigation is so great that their joinder as parties in conformity to the usual rules of procedure is impracticable. Courts are not infrequently called upon to proceed with causes in which the number of those interested in the litigation is so great as to make difficult or impossible the joinder of all because some are not within the jurisdiction or because their whereabouts is unknown or where if all were made parties to the suit its continued abatement by the death of some would prevent or unduly delay a decree. In such cases where the interests of those not joined are of the same class as the interests of those who are, and where it is considered that the latter fairly represent the former in the prosecution of the litigation of the issues in which all have a common interest, the court will proceed to a decree. * * *

It is evident that the considerations which may induce a court thus to proceed, despite a technical defect of parties, may differ from those which must be taken into account in determining whether the absent parties are bound by the decree or, if it is adjudged that they are, in ascertaining whether such an adjudication satisfies the requirements of due process and of full faith and credit. Nevertheless there is scope within the framework of the Constitution for holding in appropriate cases that a judgment rendered in a class suit is res judicata as to members of the class who are not formal parties to the suit. Here, as elsewhere, the Fourteenth Amendment does not compel state courts or legislatures to adopt any particular rule for establishing the conclusiveness of judgments in class suits; * * * nor does it compel the adoption of the particular rules thought by this court to be appropriate for the federal courts. With a proper regard for divergent local institutions and interests, cf. Jackson County v. United States, 308 U.S. 343, 351, this Court is justified in saying that there has been a failure of due process only in those cases where it cannot be said that the procedure adopted, fairly insures the protection of the interests of absent parties who are to be bound by it. Chicago, B. & Q.R. Co. v. Chicago, 166 U.S. 226, 235.

It is familiar doctrine of the federal courts that members of a class not present as parties to the litigation may be bound by the judgment where they are in fact adequately represented by parties who are present, or where they actually participate in the conduct of the litigation in which members of the class are present as parties, * * * or where the interest of the members of the class, some of whom are present as parties, is joint, or where for any other reason the relationship between the parties present and those who are absent is such as legally to entitle the former to stand in judgment for the latter.

In all such cases, so far as it can be said that the members of the class who are present are, by generally recognized rules of law, entitled to stand in judgment for those who are not, we may assume for present purposes that such procedure affords a protection to the parties who are represented though absent, which would satisfy the requirements of due process and full faith and credit. * * * Nor do we find it necessary for the decision of this case to say that, when the only circumstance defining the class is that the determination of the rights of its members turns upon a single issue of fact or law, a state could not constitutionally adopt a procedure whereby some of the members of the class could stand in judgment for all, provided that the procedure were so devised and applied as to insure that those present are of the same class as those absent and that the litigation is so conducted as to insure the full and fair consideration of the common issue. Compare New England Divisions Case, 261 U.S. 184, 197; Taggart v. Bremner, 7 Cir., 236 F. 544. We decide only that the procedure and the course of litigation sustained here by the plea of res judicata do not satisfy these requirements.

The restrictive agreement did not purport to create a joint obligation or liability. If valid and effective its promises were the several obligations of the signers and those claiming under them. The promises ran severally to every other signer. It is plain that in such circumstances all those alleged to be bound by the agreement would not constitute a single class in any litigation brought to enforce it. Those who sought to secure its benefits by enforcing it could not be said to be in the same class with or represent those whose interest was in resisting performance, for the agreement by its terms imposes obligations and confers rights on the owner of each plot of land who signs it. If those who thus seek to secure the benefits of the agreement were rightly regarded by the state Supreme Court as constituting a class, it is evident that those signers or their successors who are interested in challenging the validity of the agreement and resisting its performance are not of the same class in the sense that their interests are identical so that any group who had elected to enforce rights conferred by the agreement could be said to be acting in the interest of any others who were free to deny its obligation.

Because of the dual and potentially conflicting interests of those who are putative parties to the agreement in compelling or resisting its performance, it is impossible to say, solely because they are parties to it, that any two of them are of the same class. Nor without more, and with the due regard for the protection of the rights of absent parties which due process exacts, can some be permitted to stand in judgment for all.

It is one thing to say that some members of a class may represent other members in a litigation where the sole and common interest of the class in the litigation, is either to assert a common right or to challenge an asserted obligation. It is quite another to hold that all those who are free alternatively either to assert rights or to challenge them are of a single class, so that any group merely because it is of the class so constituted, may be deemed adequately to represent any others of the class in litigating their interests in either alternative. Such a selection of representatives for purposes of litigation, whose substantial interests are not necessarily or even probably the same as those whom they are deemed to represent, does not afford that protection to absent parties which due process requires. The doctrine of representation of absent parties in a class suit has not hitherto been thought to go so far. * * *

The plaintiffs in the *Burke* case sought to compel performance of the agreement in behalf of themselves and all others similarly situated. They did not designate the defendants in the suit as a class or seek any injunction or other relief against others than the named defendants, and the decree which was entered did not purport to bind others. In seeking to enforce the agreement the plaintiffs in that suit were not representing the petitioners here whose substantial interest is in resisting performance. The defendants in the first suit were not treated by the pleadings or decree as representing others or as foreclosing by their defense the rights of others, and even though nominal defendants, it does not appear that their interest in defeating the contract outweighed their interest in establishing its validity. For a court in this situation to ascribe to either the plaintiffs or defendants the performance of such functions on behalf of petitioners here, is to attribute to them a power that it cannot be said that they had assumed to exercise, and a responsibility which, in view of their dual interests it does not appear that they could rightly discharge.

Reversed.

MR. JUSTICE ROBERTS, MR. JUSTICE MCREYNOLDS, and MR. JUSTICE REED concur in the result.

NOTES AND PROBLEMS FOR DISCUSSION

1.   Consider the first of the two class actions discussed in *Hansberry*. Who brought the lawsuit, what right did they seek to vindicate, and against whom?

2.   How did the Illinois courts conclude in the second of the two actions that the Hansberrys had been members of the class in the first suit?

3.   Focus on the issue that the Hansberrys sought to relitigate in the second proceeding. What is the theory that would bind the Hansberrys if they *had* been held by the Supreme Court to be class members in the initial Illinois proceeding?

4.   The Court points out that the defendants in the first suit (persons presumably opposed to the enforcement of the racially restrictive covenant) were not themselves named or certified as a class. Assume that they had been. Would the Hansberrys have been bound then?

5.   Note what is not at issue from the perspective of the Constitution: the Fourteenth Amendment's Equal Protection Clause. State court enforcement of racially restrictive covenants would not be declared violative of equal protection until the decision in Shelley v. Kraemer, 334 U.S. 1, 68 S.Ct. 836, 92 L.Ed. 1161 (1948).

6.   *Hansberry*'s discussion of due process relates to the limits on the scope of class action litigation, and when such actions may properly bind others who have not been formally joined as parties to the proceeding. Other aspects of due process in the class action setting, including notice and personal jurisdiction, are taken up below, in connection with the decision in *Phillips Petroleum v. Shutts*.

3. THE STRUCTURE OF RULE 23

Read Rule 23. Then, in reading the following case, consider which of the provisions in Rule 23 might be compelled by due process and which of them impose safeguards above and beyond due process. (Note that the Rule's current wording is somewhat changed from that quoted in the opinion below.) Are there any constitutional infirmities in the occasional silences of Rule 23? Consider as well the structure of the requirements of Rule 23, some of which are applicable to all class actions, and others which are applicable only to certain class actions.

Hubler Chevrolet, Inc. v. General Motors Corp.

United States District Court, Southern District of Indiana, 2000.
193 F.R.D. 574.

SARAH EVANS BARKER, CHIEF JUDGE.

Plaintiffs, a group of Indiana automobile dealers who sell vehicles manufactured by General Motors (GM), a Delaware corporation, brought this action against GM on behalf of all Indiana dealers alleging that GM's marketing scheme violates the Indiana Deceptive Franchise Practices Act (IDFPA, Ind. Code 23-2-2.7-2(1)) and constitutes criminal conversion and unjust enrichment.[1] Plaintiffs claim that GM unlawfully altered its marketing program, under which it collects from dealers an extra one (1) percent of the Manufacturer's Suggested Retail Price (MSRP) of new cars sold. Formerly, the dealers authorized GM's collection of the one percent charge because GM redistributed the money to regional dealer marketing groups (DMGs) for use in local advertising campaigns. In April of 1999, GM began to retain the monies previously earmarked for local marketing efforts, announcing that it would now spend this money on national advertising. Plaintiffs' Complaint seeks to enjoin GM from assessing the alleged marketing charge against Indiana GM dealers, a declaration that the marketing funds in question belong to the dealers, disgorgement of illegal benefits that GM has derived from its marketing program since April of 1999, treble damages for conversion, and attorney fees under the IDFPA and Ind. Code 9-23-6-9. Pursuant to Federal Rule of Civil Procedure 23, Plaintiffs moved for certification of a class defined as all GM dealers located in Indiana.
* * *

DISCUSSION

1. Rule 23(a)

As a preliminary issue, we note that courts do not examine the merits of a dispute in considering whether to certify a class. Federal Rule of Civil Procedure 23 establishes a two-step procedure for determining whether a class can be certified. The first step is to satisfy the prerequisites of Rule 23(a), which provides that:

> One or more members of a class may sue or be sued as representative parties on behalf of all only if (1) the class is so numerous that joinder of all members is impracticable, (2) there are questions of law or fact common to the class, (3) the claims or defenses of the representative parties are typical of the claims or defenses of the class, and (4) the representative parties will fairly and adequately protect the interests of the class.

Fed. R. Civ. P. 23(a). The party seeking class certification bears the burden of proving that these prerequisites have been met and that class certification is appropriate. See General Tel. Co. of Southwest v. Falcon, 457 U.S. 147, 161, 72 L.Ed.2d 740, 102 S.Ct. 2364 (1982); Retired Chicago Police Ass'n v. City of

---

[1]   Jurisdiction is proper under 28 U.S.C. § 1332.

Chicago, 7 F.3d 584, 596 (7th Cir. 1993); Hurd v. Monsanto Co., 164 F.R.D. 234, 238 (S.D. Ind. 1995).   Because each element is a prerequisite to certification, failure to meet any one of them precludes certification as a class.

a.   Numerosity

As discussed above, Plaintiffs must show that the putative class is so numerous that "joinder of all [class] members is *impracticable*." Fed. R. Civ. P. 23(a)(1) (emphasis added).   While there is no magic number held to satisfy this requirement, classes of forty or more members have generally been found to be sufficiently numerous. By GM's own account, there are 258 current GM dealers in the state of Indiana. General Motors argues that joinder is not impracticable because all proposed class members' identities and addresses are readily ascertainable.   The authority it cites in support of its position represents a minority view; we rely instead on the established principle that "a showing of strong litigational hardship or inconvenience should be sufficient" to establish numerosity. See Herbert Newberg & Alba Conte, Newberg on Class Actions § 3.04 (3d ed. 1992).   In light of the circumstances of this action, including the geographic dispersion of the dealers and the difficulties of administering a case involving over 200 plaintiffs, we believe that joinder is impracticable and that Plaintiffs have satisfied the numerosity requirement.

b.   Commonality and Typicality

Rule 23(a)(2) requires that "there are questions of law or fact common to the class," and Rule 23(a)(3) requires that the plaintiff's claim be typical of those of the class. Fed. R. Civ. P. 23(a)(2), (3).   These two requirements are "closely related."   Rosario v. Livaditis, 963 F.2d 1013, 1018 (7th Cir. 1992). Commonality does not require that all questions of fact or law be identical. See Johns v. DeLeonardis, 145 F.R.D. 480, 483 (N.D. Ill. 1992). Factual variation among class grievances does not defeat a finding of commonality. Rather, this requirement is satisfied as long as "the class claims arise out of the same legal or remedial theory," *Johns*, 145 F.R.D. at 483. It is enough to satisfy commonality that there be a "common question . . . at the heart of the case . . .." *Rosario*, 963 F.2d at 1018.

GM's argument that Plaintiffs' claims are based on a variety of differing oral and written communications cannot defeat commonality and typicality, though it may be relevant in determining whether common issues predominate. Plaintiffs readily fulfill the element of commonality in this case. All members of the proposed class share an identical legal claim: that the one percent charge collected by GM, formerly distributed to the DMGs, belongs to them. The legality in Indiana of General Motors' marketing practices, namely its retention of the assessment against all new cars sold by its dealers, forms the common basis of the suit.

Similarly, typicality is shown if the named plaintiff's claim "arises from the same . . . practice or course of conduct that gives rise to the claims of other class members and his or her claims are based on the same legal theory." De La Fuente v. Stokely-Van Camp, Inc., 713 F.2d 225, 232 (7th Cir. 1983). Plaintiffs have alleged that General Motors requires dealers to pay a marketing fee of one percent of the sales price for all new cars sold, without regard to the brand of

GM vehicles purchased by the dealer, the dealer's marketing strategy, the size or geographic location of the dealership, or the local economic conditions in the dealership's area. This is easily characterized as a "single practice or course of conduct." *De La Fuente*, 713 F.2d at 232. As we have previously noted, all of the class members' claims are based on the same legal theory regarding the marketing charge and Rule 23(a)(3) is satisfied.

c. Adequacy of Representation

Rule 23(a)(4) requires that the representative parties fairly and adequately protect the interests of the class. This element reflects concerns about the competency of class counsel and potential conflicts of interest: "(a) the plaintiffs' attorney must be qualified, experienced, and generally able to conduct the proposed litigation; and (b) the plaintiffs must not have interests antagonistic to those of the class." *Rosario*, 963 F.2d at 1018; see General Tel. Co. v. Falcon, 457 U.S. at 157, n.13. Courts generally presume competency of class counsel at the outset of the litigation "in the absence of specific proof to the contrary by the defendant." See Newberg & Conte, Newberg on Class Actions at §3.42. General Motors provides no evidence that Plaintiffs' counsel is inadequate and we believe the briefs filed in this Court by class counsel support a presumption of competency. General Motor's allegation that a conflict of interest arises from counsel's representation of a local association of automobile dealers lacks merit as GM does not demonstrate that an actual conflict exists, nor does it cogently explain how the alleged conflict might harm class interests.

Similarly unavailing are GM's suggestions that the named plaintiffs are not adequate representatives of the class. General Motors presents deposition testimony excerpts of proposed class representatives to establish that the named plaintiffs have differing goals in the litigation. While the named plaintiffs may prefer different marketing strategies, it is clear that they share a common view that GM has unlawfully appropriated the one percent marketing charge at issue in this case for use in national advertising efforts. General Motors further alleges that some of the named plaintiffs provided "no input" in drafting the Complaint and are not willing to personally finance this litigation in its entirety. We think GM's arguments overstate the responsibilities of class representatives; the proposed representatives are not lawyers expected to understand intimately the legal nuances of the case. They may not comprehend perfectly their legal obligations as class representatives, but their testimony reveals genuine interest in the outcome of this litigation: one dealer expressed willingness to bear the entire costs of the action, while the others said they would pay their fair share. The fact that these businessmen made time to appear for scheduled depositions (one individual cut short a trip to attend his) also indicates commitment to this lawsuit and an understanding of the importance of their role. Furthermore, the plaintiffs' willingness to represent the class against GM, potentially damaging their franchise relationships with GM, demonstrates keen desire to pursue this cause. We disagree with GM's contention that these putative class representatives have "so little involvement in the class action that they would be unable or unwilling to protect the interests of the class against the possibly competing interests of the attorneys." They appear willing and able to preserve class interests against any adverse concerns.

Despite GM's speculative-but-thorough description of the ways in which the interests of Indiana GM dealers could vary, we reject GM's argument that these differences constitute antagonistic interests that should prevent class certification. The interests of the class members need not be identical; the only conflicts relevant to our inquiry are those that relate materially to Plaintiffs' claims. In addition, as will be addressed in our discussion of (b)(3) certification, if members of the putative class believe that the named plaintiffs do not adequately represent their interests, they may choose to opt out of the suit. We find that Plaintiffs have met the requirement of adequacy of representation. Plaintiffs have established that they meet all of Rule 23(a)'s prerequisites; thus, we turn to consideration of 23(b).

2. *Rule 23(b)*

It is not enough that the threshold requirements of Rule 23(a) are met; the action must also be maintainable under one of Rule 23(b)'s subparts. See Fed. R. Civ. P. 23(b); * * *.

a. *Rule 23(b)(1)*

Class certification under Rule 23(b)(1) is typically appropriate in cases where there exists either a common fund that may limit recovery to individual plaintiffs or a risk of establishing inconsistent standards of conduct for the defendant. See Jefferson v. Ingersoll Int'l Inc., 195 F.3d 894, 897 (7th Cir. 1999) (commenting that "domain of Rule 23(b)(1)" is "limited fund that must be distributed ratably," citing Ortiz v. Fibreboard Corp., 527 U.S. 815, 119 S. Ct. 2295, 144 L. Ed. 2d 715 (1999)). We discern no allegation of a limited fund that would demonstrate why this type of certification should apply in the instant case. Plaintiffs note that "the prosecution of separate actions will create the risk of varying adjudications with respect to individual dealers" that could "be dispositive of the interests of other GM dealers in the State of Indiana who are not parties to this action or will substantially impair or impede their ability to protect their interests." Pls.' Mem. Supp. Mot. Class Cert. at 17. However, "that some plaintiffs may ultimately be successful against a defendant while others may not is simply not a ground for invoking Rule 23(b)(1)(A)." *Hurd*, 164 F.R.D. at 239 (citations omitted).

b. *Rule 23(b)(2)*

Under Rule 23(b)(2), a class may be certified when "the party opposing the class has acted or refused to act on grounds generally applicable to the class," and the representatives are seeking "final injunctive relief or corresponding declaratory relief." Fed. R. Civ. P. 23(b)(2). The primary limitation imposed by this subsection is that injunctive or declaratory relief must predominate as the remedy being sought on behalf of the class. The subsection is not fulfilled where the plaintiffs are seeking predominantly money damages.

Plaintiffs have alleged conduct by General Motors clearly applicable to all members of the class: illegal conversion of one percent of the price of new vehicles, an amount formerly contributed to local advertising funds, for use in its own national marketing efforts. Thus, any obstacle to Plaintiffs' attempt to certify this class action under Rule 23(b)(2) would come from the type of relief they are seeking, that is, whether it is a form of final injunctive or corresponding declaratory relief. To determine whether the relief sought is primarily equitable or money damages, "the plaintiffs' specific request for relief must be closely scrutinized and consideration must be given to whether the 'crux of the action is for money damages.'"

Deciding whether Plaintiffs' case fits the (b)(2) paradigm presents a close issue because Plaintiffs want to prevent future economic harm and would be entitled to equitable recovery of the amounts paid under an unjust enrichment theory, but they also pursue treble damages on the conversion count and an award of attorney fees as provided for by Indiana statute. In one sense Plaintiffs seek a declaration that the one percent is their money, and relief would seem to flow directly from that proposition. Declaratory relief only "correspond[s]" to final injunctive relief when "as a practical purpose it affords injunctive relief or serves as a basis for later injunctive relief." 1966 Advisory Committee Note to Rule 23, 28 U.S.C.A. Rule 23 at 298. Declaratory relief is not to be used simply to "lay the basis for a later damage award." Sarafin v. Sears, Roebuck and Co., 446 F. Supp. 611, 615 (N.D. Ill. 1978)[.] "The use of a declaratory judgment in a class action where the real goal is a damage award undermines the purpose of Rule 23(b)(2)." *Sarafin*, 446 F. Supp. at 615. We do not think that Plaintiffs' prayer for declaratory relief is presented only to lay the basis for an award of treble damages and attorneys fees, but we cannot ignore the large amount of money involved in the potential recovery to class members.

In *Jefferson v. Ingersoll International*, Judge Easterbrook offered guidance to district courts deciding between 23(b)(2) and (b)(3) class certification. 195 F.3d 894, 898 (7th Cir. 1999). Questioning whether Rule 23(b)(2) may ever be used to certify a no-notice, no-opt-out class when compensatory or punitive damages are at issue, he pointed out that Rule 23

> does not say that the class must be certified under the first matching subsection. A court should endeavor to select the most appropriate one in the list. When substantial damages have been sought, the most appropriate approach is that of Rule 23(b)(3), because it allows notice and an opportunity to opt out.

Jefferson, 195 F.3d at 898. Plaintiffs' argument (regarding (b)(1) certification) recognizing that a decision that could "be dispositive of the interests of other GM dealers in the State of Indiana" who did not participate in that action might "substantially impair or impede their ability to protect their interests" reflects the disadvantage of (b)(2) certification: that Indiana GM dealers would be bound to a judgment or settlement in this case without notice or the opportunity to opt out. Because of the importance of money damages to Plaintiffs' claims, we believe that class members should have the opportunity to receive notice and opt out. We therefore decline to certify a (b)(2) class, though we recognize that any grant of injunctive relief may affect those who choose not to participate in the suit.

c.   Rule 23(b)(3)

A class action is maintainable under Rule 23(b)(3) if we find that "the questions of law or fact common to the members of the class predominate over any questions affecting only individual members, and that a class action is superior to other available methods for the fair and efficient adjudication of the controversy." Fed. R. Civ. P. 23(b)(3). The underlying purpose of Rule 23(b)(3)'s requirements is to assure that a class action has "practical utility" in the suit. Rule 23(b)(3) lays out four factors which we consider in analyzing these issues:

> (A) the interest of members of the class in individually controlling the prosecution . . . of separate actions; (B) the extent and nature of any litigation concerning the controversy already commenced by . . . members of the class; (C) the desirability or undesirability of concentrating the litigation of the claims in the particular forum; (D) the difficulties likely to be encountered in the management of a class action.

Fed. R. Civ. P. 23(b)(3).

i. *Predominance*

Predominance is met when "'one or more of the central issues in the action are common to the class and can be said to predominate. . .'." John Does 1-100 v. Boyd, 613 F. Supp. 1514, 1530 (D. Minn. 1985). Satisfying this criterion "normally turns on the answer to one basic question: is there an essential factual link between all class members and the defendant for which the law provides a remedy?" *Johns*, 145 F.R.D. at 484-85. We have determined that putative class members share a common basis for their suit: the issue of whether GM's marketing practices violate Indiana law. Each of the plaintiffs involved herein alleges that a one percent charge that he or she formerly agreed to pay for use in local advertising has been diverted to GM's national marketing without his or her consent. The legality of this alleged marketing assessment program under Indiana law is the "dominant, central focus" of the proposed class action. While their objections to General Motors' various marketing initiatives may differ, every member of the proposed class shares the desire to reassert control over what it believes is its marketing money and a common belief that General Motors has in essence stolen its money by exerting exclusive control over the marketing funds.

The essence of Defendant's claim that this class cannot be maintained under Rule 23(b)(3) is that the common issue of the legality of the one percent charge will require individual determination of many unique fact issues as well as legal issues arising from oral representations made to some but not all putative class members. In addition, GM maintains that the plaintiffs want different kinds of relief and that their damages must be individually calculated, thus overshadowing any common issues: "In this action, plaintiffs' goals and remedies are as varied and diverse as the named plaintiffs themselves and, indeed, as diverse as every putative class member."

Rule 23(b)(3) class actions commonly involve numerous levels of damages and injury for different class members. In *Johns*, *supra*, the court certified a class action despite dissimilar damage amounts because "the extent of damages is not an issue" when certifying the class, rather it is a question for the merits of the lawsuit. * * * Finally, determining damages in this case will not necessitate mini-trials because damages can be calculated easily from General Motors computer records tracking the number of vehicles sold by dealers.

The only possibility that Plaintiffs will need to present individualized proof lies in their IDFPA claim, an element of which is "coercion." Assuming that actual coercion must be shown to establish the IDFPA violation, Plaintiffs need not present individualized proof if coercion can be proven on a class-wide basis, for example through contracts, agreements and promotional materials uniformly applicable to all members of the proposed class. Other courts addressing this issue under similar fact patterns have held that the need to find coercion will not defeat class certification where it is based upon conduct applicable to the class as a whole. See Larry James Oldsmobile-Pontiac-GMC Truck Co. v. General Motors Corp., 164 F.R.D. 428, 439 (N.D. Miss. 1996) ("coercion may be implied on a class-wide basis when the defendant's challenged conduct constitutes a uniform agreement common to class members."); * * * .

We conclude that the common legal questions affecting General Motors' liability predominate over any individualized factual and legal questions involved in this case; however, we note that a class could be decertified if it became evident that Plaintiffs must rely upon facts unique to each dealer to show GM forced dealers to participate in the marketing scheme. To the extent the relevant communications differed according to GM division (e.g., different contracts or letters sent to Oldsmobile versus Pontiac dealers) we can create subclasses if material differences prevent their consideration as a single group, with the exception of Buick dealers unless the communications received by them resemble those sent to another type of dealer. (None of the named plaintiffs is a Buick dealer.)

ii. Superiority

Rule 23(b)(3) also requires Plaintiffs to establish that a class action would be the "superior" manner in which to resolve the controversy. It does not appear that individual class members have any particular interest in pursuing separate actions, and we are unaware of any other litigation surrounding this issue already commenced by class members. Thus, the two most relevant issues regarding the superiority of the class action form highlighted by Rule 23(b)(3) are the desirability of concentrating the actions in this forum and the difficulty that management of such a class action would impose upon us. See Fed. R. Civ. P. 23(b)(3)(C), (D).

One reason to favor a class action is to avoid duplicative lawsuits, which would thereby waste the parties' and the courts' time and resources. It is without question that allowing this case to proceed as a class action would allow economies of scale to operate and ultimately reduce the overall burden on the courts associated with pursuing the claims versus maintaining individual actions. Assuming for the moment that all of the potential plaintiffs filed suit individually, the federal courts would be open to an avalanche of suits involving duplicitous [sic] discovery and a repetition of legal determinations.

A class action allows discovery to proceed on all of the potential claims jointly. A class action also eliminates the potential that the defendants will be subject to contradictory resolutions of the ultimate legal issue; to wit, the validity of the marketing program, because the issue is resolved vis-à-vis all class members at once. A class action simplifies discovery because the defendants and the court will have to deal with only one plaintiffs' counsel, rather than a separate attorney for each individual plaintiff. Discovery disputes can be resolved and legal determinations made with respect to all of the parties at once instead of one plaintiff at a time.

While class actions may present undue pressure upon defendants to settle cases, this factor alone does not outweigh the advantages we have discussed. For these reasons, we hold that Plaintiffs' putative class action is superior to alternative methods of adjudicating the claims and thus this class action may be maintained under Rule 23(b)(3).

CONCLUSION

Plaintiffs' proposed class satisfies the demands of Rule 23(a) and is maintainable under Rule 23(b)(3). Plaintiffs' motion for class certification is therefore GRANTED.

NOTES AND PROBLEMS FOR DISCUSSION

1. The plaintiffs perceive an advantage in being able to have the lawsuit proceed as a class and the defendant GM perceives a disadvantage. Why? Would it be an advantage to be in federal court if Indiana did not allow suits like the one brought by plaintiffs in *Hubler* to be brought as class actions in state court? Or should Indiana's limitation on class actions govern the federal courts as well? See Shady Grove Orthopedic Assoc. v. Allstate Ins. Co., 559 U.S. 393, 130 S.Ct. 1431, 176 L.Ed. 2d 311 (2010) (concluding that Rule 23 controls in federal courts, state law to the contrary notwithstanding). *Shady Grove* is discussed above in Chapter 5.

2. The Rule 23(a) requirements are not particularly problematic in this case. Numerosity is rarely a problem and the class members' claims in *Hubler* are virtually identical, thus insuring that both the common question and typicality requirements will be satisfied by the named plaintiff(s). But consider how a court assesses at the beginning of a lawsuit whether the named representative will prove to be an adequate representative. It might look to the plaintiff and to his enthusiasm, as well as his resources to conduct the case, and/or it might look to the abilities and experience of the lawyer for the class. If these are relevant inquiries, why worry about typicality and commonality?

3. Also relatively unproblematic in *Hubler* is the Court's quick rejection of certification under Rule 23(b)(1). *Hubler* notes that a no-opt-out ("mandatory") class action under (b)(1) is available, for example, when there are multiple claims to a limited fund. The fund might be an identifiable "res" (such as an insurance policy), or it might be somewhat more fluid, where, for example, it can be shown that the available assets of a defendant could not meet the likely total of individual recoveries of compensatory damages. Compare In re Bendectin Prods. Liability Litigation, 749 F.2d 300 (6th Cir. 1984) (calling for strict scrutiny of question whether assets will be exhausted in product liability action) with Coburn v. 4-R Corp., 77 F.R.D. 43 (E.D. Ky. 1977) (applying arguably more lenient test in single incident disaster). See also Ortiz v. Fiberboard, 527 U.S. 815, 119 S.Ct. 2295, 144 L.Ed.2d 715 (1999) (invalidating a limited fund settlement class action in part because the parties' agreement created the limited fund).

4. Under the Anti-Injunction Act, 28 U.S.C. §2283, federal courts are barred from issuing injunctions of already ongoing state court proceedings except where expressly provided by Congress, to protect or effectuate the judgments a federal court has entered, or "in aid of" the federal court's jurisdiction. If an injunction of a go-it-alone class member is not considered to be in aid of preserving the (b)(1) court's "jurisdiction," is the "mandatory" Rule 23(b)(1) action really mandatory?

5. As for Rule 23(b)(2), clearly the class in *Hubler* could have been certified as such, if injunctive relief was all that the plaintiff class was seeking. Why do the parties care whether it is certified under (b)(2) only or under (b)(3) as well?

6. Note that the (b)(3) class action must jump through a number of hoops for certification that other class actions need not. Class members, as noted below, must receive individual notice, and they have a right to opt out so that they may file their own lawsuit. Often the most formidable requirement is that of "predominance" of common questions over individual questions (and that class treatment be "superior" to individual litigation). Given the possibility of different individual oral representations by G.M. to the various class members, how does the *Hubler* court conclude that common questions will actually predominate? Note that the predominance problem looms large when plaintiffs would have to prove individual reliance on a given misrepresentation. Cf. Perrone v. G.M.A.C., 232 F.3d 433 (5th Cir. 2000) (refusing to certify class in which individual reliance would have to be shown as lacking in commonality under Rule 23(a)). But sometimes, if reliance can be presumed or taken out of the plaintiffs' burden of proof, predominance concerns can be overcome. See Blackie v. Barrack, 524 F.2d 891 (9th Cir. 1975) (shifting to defendant the issue of plaintiffs' reliance on defendant's representations in securities action based on fraud-on-the-market theory).

7. Consider the reason for having extra requirements for a class to be certified under (b)(3), as opposed to under (b)(1) or (b)(2). At one point, before the 1966 revisions of the Federal Rules, class action damages suits that were little more than an aggregation of separable claims that individuals might file on their own were referred to as "spurious" class actions. What was spurious about them, do you suppose? It was probably the case that a (b)(3) action was considered as something of a step child in the class action family, partly because of the perceived lesser need for such suits to proceed as class actions and because of the traditional value placed on litigant autonomy. And historically speaking, class actions in equity (where they got their start) were probably closer in form to the sorts of actions associated now with (b)(1) and (b)(2).

8. Because of these extra hurdles in the damages class action — particularly the predominance requirement — federal courts were long reluctant to use Rule 23(b)(3) to certify classes in mass tort cases. That reluctance has not altogether disappeared. The Advisory Committee Note to the 1966 Amendments to Rule 23 indicated that "mass accident cases" were "not appropriate" for class treatment "because of the likelihood that significant questions, not only of damages but of liability and defenses to liability would be present, affecting individuals in different ways." Accordingly, the Note indicated that separate lawsuits would be the likely result even if class treatment were attempted.

Nevertheless, beginning in the 1980s, some courts began to warm to the idea of class treatment in at least some such cases — at first those involving single incident disasters, such as a train wreck or an oil spill. See, e.g., Sala v. Amtrak, 120 F.R.D. 494 (E.D. Pa. 1988) (certifying class of passengers injured in train wreck, and discussing trend in favor of certification in single incident disaster cases). Product liability claims have proved more problematic. See, e.g., Castano v. American Tobacco Co., 84 F.3d 734 (5th Cir. 1996) (decertifying, on predominance and superiority grounds, a nationwide class of "all nicotine-dependent persons" who smoked defendants' cigarettes); In re School Asbestos Litigation, 789 F.2d 996 (3d Cir.) (noting developments in receptivity to use of class actions in mass tort litigation generally), cert. denied, 479 U.S. 852, 107 S.Ct. 182, 93 L.Ed.2d 117 (1986). Of course, it might be possible to say that the common issues in such cases could be treated collectively and thus permit class certification on those issues alone. But would that comport with the language of Rule 23(b)(3) which requires not just that there be common issues, but that they somehow predominate over any individual questions in the case before certification can occur?

See also In re Bridgestone/Firestone Tires Products Liability Litigation, 288 F.3d 1012 (7th Cir. 2002) (reversing certification of nationwide product liability class action brought by consumers against tire manufacturer who supplied tires for Ford Explorers which allegedly experienced numerous accidents from tire blowouts). After the Seventh Circuit had determined that a nationwide class could not be certified, it ruled that an injunction should issue to prevent the refiling in state courts of similar nationwide product liability class actions. In re Bridgestone/Firestone Tires Products Liability Litigation, 333 F.3d 763 (7th Cir. 2003). In so ruling, the appeals court concluded that the injunction met an exception under 28 U.S.C. §2283 — the Anti-Injunction Act — to protect or effectuate prior judgments (here, the prior judgment of the court of appeals). On the other hand, no injunction was proper for subsequently filed class action lawsuits in state courts that were not nationwide in scope, but only statewide.

9. The presence or absence of common questions of law or fact for purposes of Rule 23(a)(2), did not pose much of a problem for the *Hubler* court. Consider the Supreme Court's treatment of that same requirement in the following high-profile nationwide class action recently decided by the Supreme Court:

Wal-Mart Stores, Inc. v. Dukes

Supreme Court of the United States, 2011.
564 U.S. 338, 131 S.Ct. 2541, 180 L.Ed. 2d 374.

JUSTICE SCALIA delivered the opinion of the Court.

We are presented with one of the most expansive class actions ever. The District Court and the Court of Appeals approved the certification of a class comprising about one and a half million plaintiffs, current and former female employees of petitioner Wal-Mart who allege that the discretion exercised by their local supervisors over pay and promotion matters violates Title VII by discriminating against women. In addition to injunctive and declaratory relief, the plaintiffs seek an award of backpay. We consider whether the certification of the plaintiff class was consistent with Federal Rules of Civil Procedure 23(a) and (b)(2).

I

A

Petitioner Wal-Mart is the Nation's largest private employer. It operates four types of retail stores throughout the country: Discount Stores, Supercenters, Neighborhood Markets, and Sam's Clubs. Those stores are divided into seven nationwide divisions, which in turn comprise 41 regions of 80 to 85 stores apiece. Each store has between 40 and 53 separate departments and 80 to 500 staff positions. In all, Wal-Mart operates approximately 3,400 stores and employs more than one million people.

Pay and promotion decisions at Wal-Mart are generally committed to local managers' broad discretion, which is exercised "in a largely subjective manner." * * * Local store managers may increase the wages of hourly employees (within limits) with only limited corporate oversight. As for salaried employees, such as store managers and their deputies, higher corporate authorities have discretion to set their pay within preestablished ranges.

Promotions work in a similar fashion. Wal-Mart permits store managers to apply their own subjective criteria when selecting candidates as "support managers," which is the first step on the path to management. Admission to Wal-Mart's management training program, however, does require that a candidate meet certain objective criteria, including an above-average performance rating, at least one year's tenure in the applicant's current position, and a willingness to relocate. But except for those requirements, regional and district managers have discretion to use their own judgment when selecting candidates for management training. Promotion to higher office—e.g., assistant manager, co-manager, or store manager—is similarly at the discretion of the employee's superiors after prescribed objective factors are satisfied.

B

The named plaintiffs in this lawsuit, representing the 1.5 million members of the certified class, are three current or former Wal-Mart employees who allege that the company discriminated against them on the basis of their sex by denying them equal pay or promotions, in violation of Title VII of the Civil Rights Act of 1964.

Betty Dukes began working at a Pittsburgh, California, Wal-Mart in 1994. She started as a cashier, but later sought and received a promotion to customer service manager. After a series of disciplinary violations, however, Dukes was demoted back to cashier and then to greeter. Dukes concedes she violated company policy, but contends that the disciplinary actions were in fact retaliation for invoking internal complaint procedures and that male employees have not been disciplined for similar infractions. Dukes also claims two male greeters in the Pittsburgh store are paid more than she is.

Christine Kwapnoski has worked at Sam's Club stores in Missouri and California for most of her adult life. She has held a number of positions, including a supervisory position. She claims that a male manager yelled at her frequently and screamed at female employees, but not at men. The manager in question "told her to 'doll up,' to wear some makeup, and to dress a little better."

The final named plaintiff, Edith Arana, worked at a Wal-Mart store in Duarte, California, from 1995 to 2001. In 2000, she approached the store manager on more than one occasion about management training, but was brushed off. Arana concluded she was being denied opportunity for advancement because of her sex. She initiated internal complaint procedures, whereupon she was told to apply directly to the district manager if she thought her store manager was being unfair. Arana, however, decided against that and never applied for management training again. In 2001, she was fired for failure to comply with Wal-Mart's timekeeping policy.

These plaintiffs, respondents here, do not allege that Wal-Mart has any express corporate policy against the advancement of women. Rather, they claim that their local managers' discretion over pay and promotions is exercised disproportionately in favor of men, leading to an unlawful disparate impact on female employees, see 42 U.S.C. § 2000e–2(k). And, respondents say, because Wal-Mart is aware of this effect, its refusal to cabin its managers' authority amounts to disparate treatment, see § 2000e–2(a). Their complaint seeks injunctive and declaratory relief, punitive damages, and backpay. It does not ask for compensatory damages.

Importantly for our purposes, respondents claim that the discrimination to which they have been subjected is common to *all* Wal-Mart's female employees. The basic theory of their case is that a strong and uniform "corporate culture" permits bias against women to infect, perhaps subconsciously, the discretionary decisionmaking of each one of Wal-Mart's thousands of managers—thereby making every woman at the company the victim of one common discriminatory practice. Respondents therefore wish to litigate the Title VII claims of all female employees at Wal-Mart's stores in a nationwide class action.

C

Class certification is governed by Federal Rule of Civil Procedure 23. Under Rule 23(a), the party seeking certification must demonstrate, first, that:

> (1) the class is so numerous that joinder of all members is impracticable,
>
> (2) there are questions of law or fact common to the class,
>
> (3) the claims or defenses of the representative parties are typical of the claims or defenses of the class, and
>
> (4) the representative parties will fairly and adequately protect the interests of the class".

Second, the proposed class must satisfy at least one of the three requirements listed in Rule 23(b). Respondents rely on Rule 23(b)(2), which applies when "the party opposing the class has acted or refused to act on grounds that apply generally to the class, so that final injunctive relief or corresponding declaratory relief is appropriate respecting the class as a whole."

Invoking these provisions, respondents moved the District Court to certify a plaintiff class consisting of "[a]ll women employed at any Wal-Mart domestic retail store at any time since December 26, 1998, who have been or may be subjected to Wal-Mart's challenged pay and management track promotions policies and practices." As evidence that there were indeed "questions of law or fact common to" all the women of Wal-Mart, as Rule 23(a)(2) requires, respondents relied chiefly on three forms of proof: statistical evidence about pay and promotion disparities between men and women at the company, anecdotal reports of discrimination from about 120 of Wal-Mart's female employees, and the testimony of a sociologist, Dr. William Bielby, who conducted a "social framework analysis" of Wal-Mart's "culture" and personnel practices, and concluded that the company was "vulnerable" to gender discrimination. 603 F.3d 571, 601 (CA9 2010) (en banc).

Wal-Mart unsuccessfully moved to strike much of this evidence. It also offered its own countervailing statistical and other proof in an effort to defeat Rule 23(a)'s requirements of commonality, typicality, and adequate representation. Wal-Mart further contended that respondents' monetary claims for backpay could not be certified under Rule 23(b)(2), first because that Rule refers only to injunctive and declaratory relief, and second because the backpay claims could not be manageably tried as a class without depriving Wal-Mart of its right to present certain statutory defenses. With one limitation not relevant here, the District Court granted respondents' motion and certified their proposed class. [A divided en banc Court of Appeals affirmed.] * * * We granted certiorari.

II

The class action is "an exception to the usual rule that litigation is conducted by and on behalf of the individual named parties only." * * * In order to justify a departure from that rule, "a class representative must be part of the class and 'possess the same interest and suffer the same injury' as the class members." * * * Rule 23(a) ensures that the named plaintiffs are appropriate representatives of the class whose claims they wish to litigate. The Rule's four requirements— numerosity, commonality, typicality, and adequate representation—"effectively 'limit the class claims to those fairly encompassed by the named plaintiff's claims.'" General Telephone Co. of Southwest v. Falcon, 457 U.S. 147, 156 (1982) (quoting General Telephone Co. of Northwest v. EEOC, 446 U.S. 318, 330 (1980)).

A

The crux of this case is commonality—the rule requiring a plaintiff to show that "there are questions of law or fact common to the class." Rule 23(a)(2).[5] That language is easy to misread, since "[a]ny competently crafted class complaint literally raises common 'questions.'" Nagareda, *Class Certification in the Age of Aggregate Proof*, 84 N.Y.U. L. Rev. 97, 131–132 (2009). For example: Do all of us plaintiffs indeed work for Wal-Mart? Do our managers have discretion over pay? Is that an unlawful employment practice? What remedies should we get? Reciting these questions is not sufficient to obtain class certification. Commonality requires the plaintiff to demonstrate that the class members "have suffered the same injury," *Falcon, supra*, at 157. This does not mean merely that they have all suffered a violation of the same provision of law. Title VII, for example, can be violated in many ways—by intentional discrimination, or by hiring and promotion criteria that result in disparate impact, and by the use of these practices on the part of many different superiors in a single company. Quite obviously, the mere claim by employees of the same company that they have suffered a Title VII injury, or even a disparate-impact Title VII injury, gives no cause to believe that all their claims can productively be litigated at once. Their claims must depend upon a common contention—for example, the assertion of discriminatory bias on the part of the same supervisor. That common contention, moreover, must be of such a nature that it is capable of classwide resolution—which means that determination of its truth or falsity will resolve an issue that is central to the validity of each one of the claims in one stroke.

> What matters to class certification . . . is not the raising of common "questions"—even in droves—but, rather the capacity of a classwide proceeding to generate common *answers* apt to drive the resolution of the litigation. Dissimilarities within the proposed class are what have the potential to impede the generation of common answers. Nagareda, *supra*, at 132.

Rule 23 does not set forth a mere pleading standard. A party seeking class certification must affirmatively demonstrate his compliance with the Rule—that is, he must be prepared to prove that there are *in fact* sufficiently numerous parties, common questions of law or fact, etc. We recognized in *Falcon* that "sometimes it may be necessary for the court to probe behind the pleadings before coming to rest on the certification question," 457 U.S., at 160, and that certification is proper only if "the trial court is satisfied, after a rigorous analysis,

---

[5] We have previously stated in this context that "[t]he commonality and typicality requirements of Rule 23(a) tend to merge. Both serve as guideposts for determining whether under the particular circumstances maintenance of a class action is economical and whether the named plaintiff's claim and the class claims are so interrelated that the interests of the class members will be fairly and adequately protected in their absence. Those requirements therefore also tend to merge with the adequacy-of-representation requirement, although the latter requirement also raises concerns about the competency of class counsel and conflicts of interest." [*Falcon*, 457 U.S. at 157–158, n.13.] In light of our disposition of the commonality question, however, it is unnecessary to resolve whether respondents have satisfied the typicality and adequate-representation requirements of Rule 23(a).

that the prerequisites of Rule 23(a) have been satisfied," *id.,* at 161; see *id.,* at 160 ("[A]ctual, not presumed, conformance with Rule 23(a) remain . . . indispensable"). Frequently that "rigorous analysis" will entail some overlap with the merits of the plaintiff's underlying claim. That cannot be helped. "'[T]he class determination generally involves considerations that are enmeshed in the factual and legal issues comprising the plaintiff's cause of action.'" [*Falcon*]. Nor is there anything unusual about that consequence: The necessity of touching aspects of the merits in order to resolve preliminary matters, *e.g.,* jurisdiction and venue, is a familiar feature of litigation. See Szabo v. Bridgeport Machines, Inc., 249 F.3d 672, 676–677 (7th Cir. 2001) (Easterbrook, J.).

In this case, proof of commonality necessarily overlaps with respondents' merits contention that Wal-Mart engages in a pattern or practice of discrimination. That is so because, in resolving an individual's Title VII claim, the crux of the inquiry is "the reason for a particular employment decision," Cooper v. Federal Reserve Bank of Richmond, 467 U.S. 867, 876 (1984). Here respondents wish to sue about literally millions of employment decisions at once. Without some glue holding the alleged *reasons* for all those decisions together, it will be impossible to say that examination of all the class members' claims for relief will produce a common answer to the crucial question *why was I disfavored.*

B

This Court's opinion in *Falcon* describes how the commonality issue must be approached. There an employee who claimed that he was deliberately denied a promotion on account of race obtained certification of a class comprising all employees wrongfully denied promotions and all applicants wrongfully denied jobs. 457 U.S., at 152. We rejected that composite class for lack of commonality and typicality, explaining:

> Conceptually, there is a wide gap between (a) an individual's claim that he has been denied a promotion [or higher pay] on discriminatory grounds, and his otherwise unsupported allegation that the company has a policy of discrimination, and (b) the existence of a class of persons who have suffered the same injury as that individual, such that the individual's claim and the class claim will share common questions of law or fact and that the individual's claim will be typical of the class claims. *Id.,* at 157–158.

Falcon suggested two ways in which that conceptual gap might be bridged. First, if the employer "used a biased testing procedure to evaluate both applicants for employment and incumbent employees, a class action on behalf of every applicant or employee who might have been prejudiced by the test clearly would satisfy the commonality and typicality requirements of Rule 23(a)." Second, "[s]ignificant proof that an employer operated under a general policy of discrimination conceivably could justify a class of both applicants and employees if the discrimination manifested itself in hiring and promotion practices in the same general fashion, such as through entirely subjective decisionmaking processes." We think that statement precisely describes respondents' burden in this case. The first manner of bridging the gap obviously has no application here; Wal-Mart has no testing procedure or other companywide evaluation method that can be charged with bias. The whole point of permitting discretionary decisionmaking is to avoid evaluating employees under a common standard.

The second manner of bridging the gap requires "significant proof" that Wal-Mart "operated under a general policy of discrimination." That is entirely absent here. Wal-Mart's announced policy forbids sex discrimination, and as the District Court recognized the company imposes penalties for denials of equal employment opportunity. The only evidence of a "general policy of discrimination" respondents produced was the testimony of Dr. William Bielby, their sociological expert. Relying on "social framework" analysis, Bielby testified that Wal-Mart has a "strong corporate culture," that makes it "vulnerable" to "gender bias." He could not, however, "determine with any specificity how regularly stereotypes play a meaningful role in employment decisions at Wal-Mart. At his deposition . . . Dr. Bielby conceded that he could not calculate whether 0.5 percent or 95 percent of the employment decisions at Wal-Mart might be determined by stereotyped thinking." * * * Bielby's testimony does nothing to advance respondents' case. "[W]hether 0.5 percent or 95 percent of the employment decisions at Wal-Mart might be determined by stereotyped thinking" is the essential question on which respondents' theory of commonality depends. If Bielby admittedly has no answer to that question, we can safely disregard what he has to say. It is worlds away from "significant proof" that Wal-Mart "operated under a general policy of discrimination."

C

The only corporate policy that the plaintiffs' evidence convincingly establishes is Wal-Mart's "policy" of *allowing discretion* by local supervisors over employment matters. On its face, of course, that is just the opposite of a uniform employment practice that would provide the commonality needed for a class action; it is a policy *against having* uniform employment practices. It is also a very common and presumptively reasonable way of doing business—one that we have said "should itself raise no inference of discriminatory conduct," Watson v. Fort Worth Bank & Trust, 487 U.S. 977, 990 (1988).

To be sure, we have recognized that, "in appropriate cases," giving discretion to lower-level supervisors can be the basis of Title VII liability under a disparate-impact theory—since "an employer's undisciplined system of subjective decisionmaking [can have] precisely the same effects as a system pervaded by impermissible intentional discrimination." *Id.,* at 990–991. But the recognition that this type of Title VII claim "can" exist does not lead to the conclusion that every employee in a company using a system of discretion has such a claim in common. To the contrary, left to their own devices most managers in any corporation—and surely most managers in a corporation that forbids sex discrimination—would select sex-neutral, performance-based criteria for hiring and promotion that produce no actionable disparity at all. Others may choose to reward various attributes that produce disparate impact—such as scores on general aptitude tests or educational achievements, see Griggs v. Duke Power Co., 401 U.S. 424, 431–432 (1971). And still other managers may be guilty of intentional discrimination that produces a sex-based disparity. In such a company, demonstrating the invalidity of one manager's use of discretion will do nothing to demonstrate the invalidity of another's. A party seeking to certify a nationwide class will be unable to show that all the employees' Title VII claims will in fact depend on the answers to common questions.

Respondents have not identified a common mode of exercising discretion that pervades the entire company—aside from their reliance on Dr. Bielby's social frameworks analysis that we have rejected. In a company of Wal-Mart's size and geographical scope, it is quite unbelievable that all managers would exercise their discretion in a common way without some common direction. Respondents attempt to make that showing by means of statistical and anecdotal evidence, but their evidence falls well short.

The statistical evidence consists primarily of regression analyses performed by Dr. Richard Drogin, a statistician, and Dr. Marc Bendick, a labor economist. Drogin conducted his analysis region-by-region, comparing the number of women promoted into management positions with the percentage of women in the available pool of hourly workers. After considering regional and national data, Drogin concluded that "there are statistically significant disparities between men and women at Wal-Mart . . . [and] these disparities . . . can be explained only by gender discrimination." * * * Bendick compared work-force data from Wal-Mart and competitive retailers and concluded that Wal-Mart "promotes a lower percentage of women than its competitors."

Even if they are taken at face value, these studies are insufficient to establish that respondents' theory can be proved on a classwide basis. In *Falcon*, we held that one named plaintiff's experience of discrimination was insufficient to infer that "discriminatory treatment is typical of [the employer's employment] practices." 457 U.S., at 158. A similar failure of inference arises here. As Judge Ikuta observed in her dissent, "[i]nformation about disparities at the regional and national level does not establish the existence of disparities at individual stores, let alone raise the inference that a company-wide policy of discrimination is implemented by discretionary decisions at the store and district level." A regional pay disparity, for example, may be attributable to only a small set of Wal-Mart stores, and cannot by itself establish the uniform, store-by-store disparity upon which the plaintiffs' theory of commonality depends.

There is another, more fundamental, respect in which respondents' statistical proof fails. Even if it established (as it does not) a pay or promotion pattern that differs from the nationwide figures or the regional figures in *all* of Wal-Mart's 3,400 stores, that would still not demonstrate that commonality of issue exists. Some managers will claim that the availability of women, or qualified women, or interested women, in their stores' area does not mirror the national or regional statistics. And almost all of them will claim to have been applying some sex-neutral, performance-based criteria—whose nature and effects will differ from store to store. In the landmark case of ours which held that giving discretion to lower-level supervisors can be the basis of Title VII liability under a disparate-impact theory, the plurality opinion *conditioned* that holding on the corollary that merely proving that the discretionary system has produced a racial or sexual disparity *is not enough*. "[T]he plaintiff must begin by identifying the specific employment practice that is challenged." *Watson*, 487 U.S., at 994 * * * . That is all the more necessary when a class of plaintiffs is sought to be certified. Other than the bare existence of delegated discretion, respondents have identified no "specific employment practice"—much less one that ties all their 1.5 million claims together. Merely showing that Wal-Mart's policy of discretion has produced an overall sex-based disparity does not suffice.

Respondents' anecdotal evidence suffers from the same defects, and in addition is too weak to raise any inference that all the individual, discretionary personnel decisions are discriminatory. [R]espondents filed some 120 affidavits reporting experiences of discrimination—about 1 for every 12,500 class members—relating to only some 235 out of Wal-Mart's 3,400 stores. 603 F.3d, at 634 (Ikuta, J., dissenting). More than half of these reports are concentrated in only six States (Alabama, California, Florida, Missouri, Texas, and Wisconsin); half of all States have only one or two anecdotes; and 14 States have no anecdotes about Wal-Mart's operations at all. *Id.,* at 634–635, and n.10. Even if every single one of these accounts is true, that would not demonstrate that the entire company "operate[s] under a general policy of discrimination," *Falcon, supra*, at 159, n.15, which is what respondents must show to certify a companywide class.

The dissent misunderstands the nature of the foregoing analysis. It criticizes our focus on the dissimilarities between the putative class members on the ground that we have "blend[ed]" Rule 23(a)(2)'s commonality requirement with Rule 23(b)(3)'s inquiry into whether common questions "predominate" over individual ones. That is not so. We quite agree that for purposes of Rule 23(a)(2) "'[e]ven a single [common] question'" will do (quoting Nagareda, *The Preexistence Principle and the Structure of the Class Action*, 103 Colum. L. Rev. 149, 176, n.110 (2003)). We consider dissimilarities not in order to determine (as Rule 23(b)(3) requires) whether common questions *predominate*, but in order to determine (as Rule 23(a)(2) requires) whether there *is* "[e]ven a single [common] question." And there is not here. Because respondents provide no convincing proof of a companywide discriminatory pay and promotion policy, we have concluded that they have not established the existence of any common question.

In sum, we agree with Chief Judge Kozinski that the members of the class:

> [H]eld a multitude of different jobs, at different levels of Wal-Mart's hierarchy, for variable lengths of time, in 3,400 stores, sprinkled across 50 states, with a kaleidoscope of supervisors (male and female), subject to a variety of regional policies that all differed... . Some thrived while others did poorly. They have little in common but their sex and this lawsuit. 603 F.3d, at 652 (dissenting opinion).

III

We also conclude that respondents' claims for backpay were improperly certified under Federal Rule of Civil Procedure 23(b)(2). Our opinion in Ticor Title Ins. Co. v. Brown, 511 U.S. 117, 121 (1994) *(per curiam)* expressed serious doubt about whether claims for monetary relief may be certified under that provision. We now hold that they may not, at least where (as here) the monetary relief is not incidental to the injunctive or declaratory relief. * * *

[*Reversed.*]

Justice Ginsburg, with whom Justice Breyer, Justice Sotomayor, and Justice Kagan join, concurring in part and dissenting in part.

The class in this case, I agree with the Court, should not have been certified under Federal Rule of Civil Procedure 23(b)(2). * * *

Whether the class the plaintiffs describe meets the specific requirements of Rule 23(b)(3) is not before the Court, and I would reserve that matter for consideration and decision on remand. The Court, however, disqualifies the class at the starting gate, holding that the plaintiffs cannot cross the "commonality" line set by Rule 23(a)(2). In so ruling, the Court imports into the Rule 23(a) determination concerns properly addressed in a Rule 23(b)(3) assessment.

I

A

Rule 23(a)(2) establishes a preliminary requirement for maintaining a class action: "[T]here are questions of law or fact common to the class." The Rule "does not require that all questions of law or fact raised in the litigation be common," 1 H. Newberg & A. Conte, Newberg on Class Actions § 3.10, pp. 3–48 to 3–49 (3d ed. 1992); indeed, "[e]ven a single question of law or fact common to the members of the class will satisfy the commonality requirement," Nagareda, *The Preexistence Principle and the Structure of the Class Action*, 103 Colum. L. Rev. 149, 176, n.110 (2003). See Advisory Committee's 1937 Notes on Fed. Rule Civ. Proc. 23, 28 U.S.C. App., p. 138 (citing with approval cases in which "there was only a question of law or fact common to" the class members).

B

The District Court, recognizing that "one significant issue common to the class may be sufficient to warrant certification," found that the plaintiffs easily met that test. Absent an error of law or an abuse of discretion, an appellate tribunal has no warrant to upset the District Court's finding of commonality. * * *

The District Court certified a class of "[a]ll women employed at any Wal-Mart domestic retail store at any time since December 26, 1998." The named plaintiffs, led by Betty Dukes, propose to litigate, on behalf of the class, allegations that Wal-Mart discriminates on the basis of gender in pay and promotions. They allege that the company "[r]eli[es] on gender stereotypes in making employment decisions such as . . . promotion[s] [and] pay." Wal-Mart permits those prejudices to infect personnel decisions, the plaintiffs contend, by leaving pay and promotions in the hands of "a nearly all male managerial workforce" using "arbitrary and subjective criteria." Further alleged barriers to the advancement of female employees include the company's requirement, "as a condition of promotion to management jobs, that employees be willing to relocate." Absent instruction otherwise, there is a risk that managers will act on the familiar assumption that women, because of their services to husband and children, are less mobile than men. * * *

Women fill 70 percent of the hourly jobs in the retailer's stores but make up only "33 percent of management employees." "[T]he higher one looks in the organization the lower the percentage of women." The plaintiffs' "largely uncontested descriptive statistics" also show that women working in the company's stores "are paid less than men in every region" and "that the salary gap widens over time even for men and women hired into the same jobs at the same time." * * *

The District Court identified "systems for . . . promoting in-store employees" that were "sufficiently similar across regions and stores" to conclude that "the manner in which these systems affect the class raises issues that are common to all class members." The selection of employees for promotion to in-store management "is fairly characterized as a 'tap on the shoulder' process," in which managers have discretion about whose shoulders to tap. Vacancies are not regularly posted; from among those employees satisfying minimum qualifications, managers choose whom to promote on the basis of their own subjective impressions.

Wal-Mart's compensation policies also operate uniformly across stores, the District Court found. The retailer leaves open a $2 band for every position's hourly pay rate. Wal-Mart provides no standards or criteria for setting wages within that band, and thus does nothing to counter unconscious bias on the part of supervisors. Wal-Mart's supervisors do not make their discretionary decisions in a vacuum. The District Court reviewed means Wal-Mart used to maintain a "carefully constructed . . . corporate culture," such as frequent meetings to reinforce the common way of thinking, regular transfers of managers between stores to ensure uniformity throughout the company, monitoring of stores "on a close and constant basis," and "Wal-Mart TV," "broadcas[t] . . . into all stores."

The plaintiffs' evidence, including class members' tales of their own experiences, suggests that gender bias suffused Wal-Mart's company culture. Among illustrations, senior management often refer to female associates as "little Janie Qs." One manager told an employee that "[m]en are here to make a career and women aren't." A committee of female Wal-Mart executives concluded that "[s]tereotypes limit the opportunities offered to women."

Finally, the plaintiffs presented an expert's appraisal to show that the pay and promotions disparities at Wal-Mart "can be explained only by gender discrimination and not by . . . neutral variables." Using regression analyses, their expert, Richard Drogin, controlled for factors including, *inter alia,* job performance, length of time with the company, and the store where an employee worked. The results, the District Court found, were sufficient to raise an "inference of discrimination."

C

The District Court's identification of a common question, whether Wal-Mart's pay and promotions policies gave rise to unlawful discrimination, was hardly infirm. The practice of delegating to supervisors large discretion to make personnel decisions, uncontrolled by formal standards, has long been known to have the potential to produce disparate effects. Managers, like all humankind, may be prey to biases of which they are unaware. The risk of discrimination is heightened when those managers are predominantly of one sex, and are steeped in a corporate culture that perpetuates gender stereotypes. * * *

The plaintiffs' allegations state claims of gender discrimination in the form of biased decisionmaking in both pay and promotions. The evidence reviewed by the District Court adequately demonstrated that resolving those claims would necessitate examination of particular policies and practices alleged to affect, adversely and globally, women employed at Wal-Mart's stores. Rule 23(a)(2), setting a necessary but not a sufficient criterion for class-action certification, demands nothing further.

II

A

The Court gives no credence to the key dispute common to the class: whether Wal-Mart's discretionary pay and promotion policies are discriminatory. "What matters," the Court asserts, "is not the raising of common 'questions,'" but whether there are "[d]issimilarities within the proposed class" that "have the potential to impede the generation of common answers."

The Court blends Rule 23(a)(2)'s threshold criterion with the more demanding criteria of Rule 23(b)(3), and thereby elevates the (a)(2) inquiry so that it is no longer "easily satisfied," 5 J. Moore et al., Moore's Federal Practice § 23.23[2], p. 23–72 (3d ed. 2011). Rule 23(b)(3) certification requires, in addition to the four 23(a) findings, determinations that "questions of law or fact common to class members predominate over any questions affecting only individual members" and that "a class action is superior to other available methods for . . . adjudicating the controversy."

The Court's emphasis on differences between class members mimics the Rule 23(b)(3) inquiry into whether common questions "predominate" over individual issues. And by asking whether the individual differences "impede" common adjudication, * * * the Court duplicates 23(b)(3)'s question whether "a class action is superior" to other modes of adjudication. Indeed, Professor Nagareda, whose "dissimilarities" inquiry the Court endorses, developed his position in the context of Rule 23(b)(3). See 84 N.Y.U. L. Rev., at 131 (Rule 23(b)(3) requires "some decisive degree of similarity across the proposed class" because it "speaks of common 'questions' that 'predominate' over individual ones"). "The Rule 23(b)(3) predominance inquiry" is meant to "tes[t] whether proposed classes are sufficiently cohesive to warrant adjudication by representation." Amchem Products, Inc. v. Windsor, 521 U.S. 591, 623 (1997). If courts must conduct a "dissimilarities" analysis at the Rule 23(a)(2) stage, no mission remains for Rule 23(b)(3).

Because Rule 23(a) is also a prerequisite for Rule 23(b)(1) and Rule 23(b)(2) classes, the Court's "dissimilarities" position is far reaching. Individual differences should not bar a Rule 23(b)(1) or Rule 23(b)(2) class, so long as the Rule 23(a) threshold is met. See *Amchem Products*, 521 U.S., at 623, n.19 (Rule 23(b)(1)(B) "does not have a predominance requirement"); Califano v. Yamasaki, 442 U.S. 682, 701 (1979) (Rule 23(b)(2) action in which the Court noted that "[i]t is unlikely that differences in the factual background of each claim will affect the outcome of the legal issue"). For example, in Franks v. Bowman Transp. Co., 424 U.S. 747 (1976), a Rule 23(b)(2) class of African-American truckdrivers complained that the defendant had discriminatorily refused to hire black applicants. We recognized that the "qualification[s] and performance" of individual class members might vary." *Id.,* at 772 (internal quotation marks omitted). "Generalizations concerning such individually applicable evidence," we cautioned, "cannot serve as a justification for the denial of [injunctive] relief to the entire class." *Ibid.*

B

The "dissimilarities" approach leads the Court to train its attention on what distinguishes individual class members, rather than on what unites them. Given the lack of standards for pay and promotions, the majority says, "demonstrating the invalidity of one manager's use of discretion will do nothing to demonstrate the invalidity of another's."

Wal-Mart's delegation of discretion over pay and promotions is a policy uniform throughout all stores. The very nature of discretion is that people will exercise it in various ways. A system of delegated discretion, *Watson* held, is a practice actionable under Title VII when it produces discriminatory outcomes. A finding that Wal-Mart's pay and promotions practices in fact violate the law would be the first step in the usual order of proof for plaintiffs seeking individual remedies for company-wide discrimination. * * * That each individual employee's unique circumstances will ultimately determine whether she is entitled to backpay or damages, § 2000e–5(g)(2)(A) (barring backpay if a plaintiff "was refused ... advancement . . . for any reason other than discrimination"), should not factor into the Rule 23(a)(2) determination.

NOTES AND PROBLEMS FOR DISCUSSION

1. The Court concludes that there was no evidence of commonality—i.e., "questions of law or fact common to the class" for purposes of Rule 23(a)(2). Why wasn't the question whether Wal-Mart's policy of allowing for localized supervisory discretion contributed to an overall discriminatory policy, a sufficient common question? The Court stated that "Wal-Mart's 'policy' of *allowing discretion* by local supervisors over employment matters" was "a policy *against having* uniform employment practices," and it could generate common questions of law or fact only with "'significant proof' that Wal-Mart 'operated under a general policy of discrimination.'" How was that proof lacking in Wal-Mart?

2. The Court looks closely at the merits allegations in determining whether Rule 23(a)(2)'s commonality requirement is met. Recall that in the *Eisen* decision (Casebook at 696) the Court suggested that there was to be no "preliminary inquiry into the merits" to resolve questions of who would pay for notice under Rule 23 at the certification stage. *Id.* at 699. In a footnote in *Wal-Mart*, the Court stated "To the extent the quoted statement [in *Eisen*] goes beyond the permissibility of a merits inquiry for any other pretrial purpose, it is the purest dictum and is contradicted by our other cases."

3. Even if the dissent had prevailed on the question of commonality under Rule 23(a)(2), the plaintiff's would still face the substantial hurdle of showing "predominance" under Rule 23(b)(3)—i.e., that common questions predominated over individual ones. Could they have prevailed on such a showing? If not, isn't the dissent merely seeking to postpone the inevitable day of reckoning?

4. What do the Wal-Mart plaintiffs do now? The Court hardly rejected the possibility that there was a Title VII violation. In fact, the majority and the dissent largely agree as to what sorts of acts might violate Title VII. Rather, the Court just rejects nationwide class-action treatment of the particular case. Perhaps there is insufficient financial incentive for individual victims to bring individual cases over relatively small Title VII claims (although fee-shifting would ordinarily be available as an incentive to counsel in such cases). But can't the plaintiffs now try to bring state-wide or possibly region-wide actions against Wal-Mart? If they can, why didn't they do so in the first place?

5. Problems of commonality and predominance also surface in securities fraud damages litigation brought as class actions under federal securities laws. To succeed on the merits in an individual case (i.e., a non-class action), a plaintiff typically has to show that the defendant made a materially false and misleading statement upon which plaintiff relied to his financial detriment. If each plaintiff in a securities fraud class action were required to show their own reliance on particular misrep-resentations, however, common questions would likely not predominate, and certification would therefore have to be denied under Rule 23(b)(3). Largely in response to this difficulty, the Supreme Court in 1988 embraced a "fraud on the market" theory, which basically presumes that plaintiffs in a well-functioning securities market will rely to their detriment on such misrepresentations. Basic, Inc. v. Levinson, 485 U.S. 224, 108 S.Ct. 978, 99 L.Ed.2d 194 (1988). *Basic* created an evidentiary presumption that the market had incorporated such statements into the stock's price and that the investor bought or sold in reliance on the integrity of the market price as reflecting the stock's underlying value. As a result of *Basic*, the predominance requirement of Rule 23(b)(3) would not create a barrier to certification; instead, the lack of reliance by a particular class member might be shown (and the presumption overcome) by the defendant, if at all, only *after* certification. In addition, after *Basic*, a defendant might be able to show, post-certification, that the misrepresentation did not impact the price of the stock.

In HALLIBURTON CO. v. ERICA P. JOHN FUND, INC., 573 U.S. ___, 134 S.Ct. 2398, 189 L.Ed.2d 339 (2014), the Court refused—largely on *stare decisis* grounds—to overturn *Basic*, despite criticism that the fraud-on-the-market theory was flawed—both in its assumption that a stock's market price generally reflected its underlying value, and the assumption that investors categorically rely on the integrity of the market price. Nevertheless, in the same decision, the Court permitted defendants to show that the alleged false statement(s) did not, in fact, affect the price of the stock, and to do so at the *pre-certification* stage. Although the Court indicated, consistent with *Basic*, that there was still a presumption that misrepresentation(s) would have a price impact, it also noted that defendants should to be allowed to put on evidence that might satisfy the district court to the contrary, and to have the case dismissed outright. Three dissenters would have overruled *Basic* and would have required plaintiffs to show actual reliance, without the aid of a presumption based on a fraud-on-the-market theory.

6. With the treatment of statistical evidence in *Wal-Mart* regarding certification, compare TYSON FOODS, INC. v. BOUAPHAKEO, 577 U.S. ___, 136 S.Ct. 1036, 194 L.Ed.2d 124 (2016). Plaintiff class members (more than 3,300 employees in defendant Tyson's pork processing plant in Iowa), claimed that they should have been compensated for the amount of time they spent putting on and removing certain protective gear required for their jobs ("donning and doffing"). They brought suit under the federal Fair Labor Standards Act, and under Iowa law as a class action under Rule 23(b)(3). (The FLSA suit was brought as a "collective action" as provided for in the statute, but the Court treated the certification questions similarly under the two provisions.) Because Tyson did not keep records for the amount of time spent donning and doffing, plaintiffs sought to rely on the study of an expert (Dr. Mericle) who observed that, on average, the time spent by employees in the "cut and retrim" departments was 18 minutes per day, and 21 minutes per day in the "kill department." Another expert study, aided by the first, concluded that over 90% of the plaintiffs were entitled to overtime pay for working more than 40 hours per week, once the average donning and doffing time was taken into account. Tyson resisted certification, arguing that questions common to the class did not "predominate" over individual issues regarding how much time each plaintiff actually took changing into and out of their gear. The "central dispute" before the Court on the question of certification, therefore, was whether it could be permissibly inferred from the Mericle study that each plaintiff spent the average times donning and doffing as observed in the study. If so, then the problem of individualized determinations would be minimized, and common questions would predominate, thus allowing for certification.

The Court agreed with the plaintiffs and upheld certification, although it purported not to "establish general rules governing the use of statistical evidence . . . in all class action cases," and it cautioned that propriety of its use would depend on the "facts and circumstances peculiar to" the case. Perhaps most significantly, it noted that if the suit had involved an individual rather than a class (or collective) action, the individual plaintiff would have been able to introduce statistical evidence such as that in the Mericle report, at least when the employer had failed to keep proper records as required by law. That was because such evidence would be sufficient for a rational factfinder to infer that the time spent by the particular employee conformed to the average for all employees; and it would then be up to the defendant-employer to show that the precise amount of time spent by the plaintiff was different. That much had effectively been decided by the Court some 70 years earlier, in a non-class suit, under the FLSA. There, the Court concluded that if an employee produced sufficient evidence from which a rational factfinder could find the "amount and extent" of uncompensated work through "reasonable inference," the then the employer would have to produce "evidence of the precise amount of work performed," or other evidence "to negative the reasonableness of the inference to be drawn" from the plaintiff's evidence.

In fact, it was on this very score that the Court distinguished *Wal-Mart*: "[*Wal-Mart*] held that the employees were not similarly situated, [and thus] none of them could have prevailed in an individual suit by relying on depositions detailing the ways in which other employees were discriminated against by their particular [i.e., different] store managers." That was largely because of the plaintiffs' failure to sufficiently show a common policy to which each employee was subject.

In addition, the Court observed that the expert evidence would have to meet the rigorous standards of Rule 702, Fed. R. Evid. And it also observed that allowance of the statistical evidence would "not deprive [Tyson Foods] of its ability to litigate individual defenses" (e.g., by offering individualized proof with respect to any particular plaintiff). The Court also dismissed a separate argument that certification had been improper because of the alleged absence of any mechanism to insure that only those plaintiffs who were actually injured would be compensated.

NOTICE FOR CLASS ACTIONS UNDER RULE 23

The *Hubler* court noted that damages actions under Rule 23(b)(3) call for notice and the right to opt out. The controlling language is that of Rule 23(c)(2)(B) which states that in Rule 23(b)(3) class actions "the court must direct to class members the best notice that is practicable under the circumstances, including individualized notice to all members who can be identified through reasonable effort."

In EISEN v. CARLISLE & JACQUELIN, 417 U.S. 156, 94 S.Ct. 2140, 40 L.Ed.2d 732 (1974), the Supreme Court addressed the requirements for notice in the (b)(3) class action. Eisen had brought suit on behalf of all buyers of odd lots (trades of less than 100 shares) on the New York Stock Exchange during a four-year period. His claim was based on the excessive differentials (or spreads) charged by respondents who controlled 99% of the odd-lot market on the exchange, and alleged violations of the Sherman Antitrust Act and violations by the New York Stock Exchange of the Securities Exchange Act of 1934. Petitioner's individual stake in damages was only $70. The Court recognized that the economic realities of small claims "dictated that petitioner's suit proceed as a class action or not at all." Respondents engaged in extensive legal battles over the requirements of Rule 23 in order to block Eisen's claims from progressing, resulting in complex and lengthy opinions by the lower courts.

The district court initially denied class certification under Rule 23. In making its determination the district court determined that Eisen had failed to satisfy the requirements of Rule 23(a)(4) (that the class representative would fairly and adequately represent the class interests). That decision was appealed to the Second Circuit, along with the district court's holding that the notice requirement of Rule 23(c)(2) and the Due Process Clause of the Fifth Amendment called for individual notice to all identifiable class members. [Note that the Rule has been modified somewhat since the *Eisen* decision, and the Court's references are to subsections as they were numbered at the time. The Rule's requirement of individualized notice in (b)(3) actions, however, remains unchanged.] The appeals court held that Eisen's suit satisfied the requirements of Rule 23, despite raising concerns over the manageability of the class under Rule 23(b)(3)(D). It declined to address the issue of notice and remanded the case to the district court to address the issues of manageability and notice.

On remand, the district court held that the case was maintainable as a class action. In addressing manageability, the district court focused on the concern of the appellate court that if class members were unlikely to share in any final judgment, class certification should be denied. The district court suggested the establishment of a fund for "fluid" class recovery that would be used to lower commissions for future odd-lot traders. Upon determining that individual notice and publication would cost $315,000, the district court concluded that neither Rule 23(c)(2) nor the Due Process Clause of the Fifth Amendment imposed such a costly outlay at the outset of litigation. The court therefore established a four-prong notification scheme: (1) individual notice to all member firms of the Exchange and to commercial banks with large trust departments; (2) individual notice to the approximately 2,000 identifiable class members with 10 or more odd-lot transactions during the relevant period; (3) individual notice to an additional 5,000 class members selected at random; and (4) prominent publication notice in the Wall Street Journal and in other newspapers in New York and California. It further held that, defendants should bear 90% of the cost of notice (over $20,000) because it appeared, after a preliminary hearing into the merits of the case, that Eisen was likely to prevail. Defendants appealed to the Second Circuit, which held that Rule 23(c)(2) required individual notice to all identifiable class members and that the entire cost of notice fell on Eisen as representative plaintiff. (The appeals court also held that the fluid-class recovery adopted was unmanageable, and ordered the suit dismissed as a class action.)

The Supreme Court granted certiorari to address the difficulties of applying Rule 23 to small claim class actions. The Court first concluded that the district court's order that respondents pay 90% of the notice costs was immediately appealable. As the defendant's right not to pay was a right immediately appealable or forever lost, and bore no ultimate relation on the determination of the case itself, the court of appeals was within its jurisdiction to hear the appeal.

The Court next addressed the issue of notice under Rule 23(c)(2) with respect to a (b)(3) class action:

> Rule 23(c)(2) provides that, in any class action maintained under subdivision (b)(3), each class member shall be advised that he has the right to exclude himself from the action on request or to enter an appearance through counsel, and further that the judgment, whether favorable or not, will bind all class members not requesting exclusion. To this end, the court is required to direct to class members "*the best*

notice practicable under the circumstances, including individual notice to all members who can be identified through reasonable effort." We think the import of this language is unmistakable. Individual notice must be sent to all class members whose names and addresses may be ascertained through reasonable effort.

The Advisory Committee's Note to Rule 23 reinforces this conclusion. The Advisory Committee described subdivision (c)(2) as "not merely discretionary" and added that the "mandatory notice pursuant to subdivision (c)(2) . . . is designed to fulfill requirements of due process to which the class action procedure is of course subject." The Committee explicated its incorporation of due process standards by citation of Mullane v. Central Hanover Bank & Trust Co., 339 U.S. 306 (1950), and like cases.

In *Mullane* the Court addressed the constitutional sufficiency of publication notice rather than mailed individual notice to known beneficiaries of a common trust fund as part of a judicial settlement of accounts. The Court observed that notice and an opportunity to be heard were fundamental requisites of the constitutional guarantee of procedural due process. It further stated that notice must be "reasonably calculated, under all the circumstances, to apprise interested parties of the pendency of the action and afford them an opportunity to present their objections." The Court then held that publication notice could not satisfy due process where the names and addresses of the beneficiaries were known. In such cases, "the reasons disappear for resort to means less likely than the mails to apprise them of [an action's] pendency." * * *

Viewed in this context, the express language and intent of Rule 23(c)(2) leave no doubt that individual notice must be provided to those class members who are identifiable through reasonable effort. In the present case, the names and addresses of 2,250,000 class members are easily ascertainable, and there is nothing to show that individual notice cannot be mailed to each. For these class members, individual notice is clearly the "best notice practicable" within the meaning of Rule 23(c)(2) and our prior decisions.

Petitioner contends, however, that we should dispense with the requirement of individual notice in this case, and he advances two reasons for our doing so. First, the prohibitively high cost of providing individual notice to 2,250,000 class members would end this suit as a class action and effectively frustrate petitioner's attempt to vindicate the policies underlying the antitrust and securities laws. Second, petitioner contends that individual notice is unnecessary in this case, because no prospective class member has a large enough stake in the matter to justify separate litigation of his individual claim. Hence, class members lack any incentive to opt out of the class action even if notified.

The short answer to these arguments is that individual notice to identifiable class members is not a discretionary consideration to be waived in a particular case. It is, rather, an unambiguous requirement of Rule 23. As the Advisory Committee's Note explained, the Rule was intended to insure that the judgment, whether favorable or not, would bind all class members who did not request exclusion from the suit. Accordingly, each class member who can be identified through reasonable effort must be notified that he may request exclusion from the action and thereby preserve his opportunity to press his claim separately or that he may remain in the class and perhaps participate in the management of the action. There is nothing in Rule 23 to suggest that the notice requirements can be tailored to fit the pocketbooks of particular plaintiffs.

Petitioner further contends that adequate representation, rather than notice, is the touchstone of due process in a class action and therefore satisfies Rule 23. We think this view has little to commend it. To begin with, Rule 23 speaks to notice as well as to adequacy of representation and requires that both be provided. Moreover, petitioner's argument proves too much, for it quickly leads to the conclusion that no notice at all, published or otherwise, would be required in the present case. This cannot be so, for quite apart from what due process may require, the command of Rule 23 is clearly to the contrary. We therefore conclude that Rule 23(c)(2) requires that individual notice be sent to all class members who can be identified with reasonable effort.

Last, the Court held that Rule 23 did not authorize the plaintiff to impose the costs of his suit on an adversarial defendant, and that the district court could not conduct a preliminary inquiry into the merits to assess who should pay costs. Because the plaintiff indicated he would not bear the costs of his class, the Court remanded the case to the lower courts with an order to dismiss the class.

NOTES AND PROBLEMS FOR DISCUSSION

1. The ruling in *Eisen* arguably enforced the procedural rights of unnamed members of the class to a particular form of notice, at the price of nonvindication of their underlying substantive rights. Is that something called for by due process, or Rule 23(c)?

2. At the time of *Eisen*, Rule 23 said nothing about the actual content of the notice to be sent to class members in (b)(3) actions. Current Rule 23(c)(2)(B) requires that notice must (among other things) define the class certified, identify the claims, indicate the binding consequences of a class-wide judgment, and provide information about how to opt out of an action.

3. At the time of *Eisen*, Rule 23(c)'s notice provision addressed only actions under Rule 23(b)(3), and the *Eisen* Court expressly refused to reach the question of what kind of notice is required in actions under (b)(1) or (b)(2). Rule 23(c) now states, however, that district courts "may direct appropriate notice to the class" in (b)(1) and (b)(2) actions.

4. In theory, at least, the class members in a (b)(1) action are persons so closely aligned in interest with the class representatives that opt out is counterproductive, so notice in such cases cannot be for the purposes of enabling dissatisfied class members to pursue their own lawsuits. For this reason perhaps, *Eisen*-type individualized notice might not be called for, as opposed, perhaps, to some form of more generalized notice.

5. Injunctive relief actions under (b)(2) present similar sorts of issues but not as starkly as in (b)(1) cases, and the ability of a class member to opt out of such cases is less than clear. In a class action seeking injunctive relief (and certain monetary damages afforded under Title VII) and certified under Rule 23(b)(2) against the Library of Congress for racially motivated employment practices, the court held district courts have discretion to allow would-be class members to opt-out. The court stated that Rule 23 is "sufficiently flexible" to allow district courts to allow opt-out in (b)(2) class actions, but only if in doing so the policy motives lying behind such class actions are not thwarted. Eubanks v. Billington, 110 F.3d 87, 94-95 (D.C. Cir. 1997).

6. Although the current Rule merely empowers courts to provide notice in (b)(1) and (b)(2) actions, due process may still require reasonable notice, even if it might not be for the purpose of allowing unnamed class members the right to pursue their own lawsuits (i.e., to opt out), as opposed to alerting them to the lawsuit, and to take whatever steps they may think appropriate to have a greater voice in the proceedings, whether by formal intervention, or securing of separate counsel, or by challenging the adequacy of the existing representative. Where injunctive and declaratory relief are sought, courts have suggested that no requirement of individualized notice or opportunity to opt out of the class is necessary. And, although notice is required in hybrid class actions under Rule 23(b)(2) where damages are also sought, that requirement may not demand individualized notice. Fontana v. Elrod, 826 F.2d 729, 731 (7th Cir. 1987).

4. CHOICE OF LAW AND JURISDICTION

Phillips Petroleum Co. v. Shutts

Supreme Court of the United States, 1985.
472 U.S. 797, 105 S.Ct. 2965, 86 L.Ed.2d 628.

JUSTICE REHNQUIST delivered the opinion of the Court.

Petitioner is a Delaware corporation which has its principal place of business in Oklahoma. During the 1970's it produced or purchased natural gas from leased land located in 11 different States, and sold most of the gas in interstate commerce. Respondents are some 28,000 of the royalty owners possessing rights to the leases from which petitioner produced the gas; they reside in all 50 States, the District of Columbia, and several foreign countries. Respondents brought a class action against petitioner in the Kansas state court, seeking to recover interest on royalty payments which had been delayed by petitioner. They recovered judgment in the trial court, and the Supreme Court of Kansas affirmed the judgment over petitioner's contentions that the Due Process Clause of the Fourteenth Amendment prevented Kansas from adjudicating the claims of all the respondents, and that the Due Process Clause and the Full Faith and Credit Clause of Article IV of the Constitution prohibited the application of Kansas law to all of the transactions between petitioner and respondents. We granted certiorari to consider these claims. We reject petitioner's jurisdictional claim, but sustain its claim regarding the choice of law.

Because petitioner sold the gas to its customers in interstate commerce, it was required to secure approval for price increases from what was then the Federal Power Commission, and is now the Federal Energy Regulatory Commission. Under its regulations the Federal Power Commission permitted petitioner to propose and collect tentative higher gas prices, subject to final approval by the Commission. If the Commission eventually denied petitioner's proposed price increase or reduced the proposed increase, petitioner would have to refund to its customers the difference between the approved price and the higher price charged, plus interest at a rate set by statute.

Although petitioner received higher gas prices pending review by the Commission, petitioner suspended any increase in royalties paid to the royalty owners because the higher price could be subject to recoupment by petitioner's customers. Petitioner agreed to pay the higher royalty only if the royalty owners would provide petitioner with a bond or indemnity for the increase, plus interest, in case the price increase was not ultimately approved and a refund was due to the customers. Petitioner set the interest rate on the indemnity agreements at the same interest rate the Commission would have required petitioner to refund to its customers. A small percentage of the royalty owners provided this indemnity and received royalties immediately from the interim price increases; these royalty owners are unimportant to this case.

The remaining royalty owners received no royalty on the unapproved portion of the prices until the Federal Power Commission approval of those prices became final. Royalties on the unapproved portion of the gas price were suspended three times by petitioner, corresponding to its three proposed price increases in the mid-1970's. In three written opinions the Commission approved all of petitioner's tentative price increases, so petitioner paid to its royalty owners the suspended royalties of $3.7 million in 1976, $4.7 million in 1977, and $2.9 million in 1978. Petitioner paid no interest to the royalty owners although it had the use of the suspended royalty money for a number of years.

Respondents Irl Shutts, Robert Anderson, and Betty Anderson filed suit against petitioner in Kansas state court, seeking interest payments on their suspended royalties which petitioner had possessed pending the Commission's approval of the price increases. Shutts is a resident of Kansas, and the Andersons live in Oklahoma. Shutts and the Andersons own gas leases in Oklahoma and Texas. Over petitioner's objection the Kansas trial court granted respondents' motion to certify the suit as a class action under Kansas law. Kan.Stat.Ann. §60-223 et seq. (1983). The class as certified was comprised of 33,000 royalty owners who had royalties suspended by petitioner. The average claim of each royalty owner for interest on the suspended royalties was $100.

After the class was certified respondents provided each class member with notice through first-class mail. The notice described the action and informed each class member that he could appear in person or by counsel; otherwise each member would be represented by Shutts and the Andersons, the named plaintiffs. The notices also stated that class members would be included in the class and bound by the judgment unless they "opted out" of the lawsuit by executing and returning a "request for exclusion" that was included with the notice. The final class as certified contained 28,100 members; 3,400 had "opted out" of the class by returning the request for exclusion, and notice could not be delivered to another 1,500 members, who were also excluded. Less than 1,000 of the class members resided in Kansas. Only a minuscule amount, approximately one quarter of one percent, of the gas leases involved in the lawsuit were on Kansas land.

After petitioner's mandamus petition to decertify the class was denied, the case was tried to the court. The court found petitioner liable under Kansas law for interest on the suspended royalties to all class members. The trial court relied heavily on an earlier, unrelated class action involving the same nominal plaintiff and the same defendant, Shutts, Executor v. Phillips Petroleum Co., 222 Kan. 527, 567 P.2d 1292 (1977), cert. denied, 434 U.S. 1068 (1978). The Kansas Supreme Court had held in *Shutts, Executor* that a gas company owed interest to royalty owners for royalties suspended pending final Commission approval of a price increase. No federal statutes touched on the liability for suspended royalties, and the court in *Shutts, Executor* held as a matter of Kansas equity law that the applicable interest rates for computation of interest on suspended royalties were the interest rates at which the gas company would have had to reimburse its customers had its interim price increase been rejected by the Commission. The court in *Shutts, Executor* viewed these as the fairest interest rates because they were also the rates that petitioner required the royalty owners to meet in their indemnity agreements in order to avoid suspended royalties.

The trial court in the present case applied the rule from *Shutts, Executor,* and held petitioner liable for prejudgment and postjudgment interest on the suspended royalties, computed at the Commission rates governing petitioner's three price increases. The applicable interest rates were: 7% for royalties retained until October 1974; 9% for royalties retained between October 1974 and September 1979; and thereafter at the average prime rate. The trial court did not determine whether any difference existed between the laws of Kansas and other States, or whether another State's laws should be applied to non-Kansas plaintiffs or to royalties from leases in States other than Kansas.

Petitioner raised two principal claims in its appeal to the Supreme Court of Kansas. It first asserted that the Kansas trial court did not possess personal jurisdiction over absent plaintiff class members as required by International Shoe Co. v. Washington, 326 U.S. 310 (1945), and similar cases. Related to this first claim was petitioner's contention that the "opt-out" notice to absent class members, which forced them to return the request for exclusion in order to avoid the suit, was insufficient to bind class members who were not residents of Kansas or who did not possess "minimum contacts" with Kansas. Second, petitioner claimed that Kansas courts could not apply Kansas law to every claim in the dispute. The trial court should have looked to the laws of each State where the leases were located to determine, on the basis of conflict of laws principles, whether interest on the suspended royalties was recoverable, and at what rate.

The Supreme Court of Kansas held that the entire cause of action was maintainable under the Kansas class-action statute, and the court rejected both of petitioner's claims. First, it held that the absent class members were plaintiffs, not defendants, and thus the traditional minimum contacts test of *International Shoe* did not apply. The court held that nonresident class-action plaintiffs were only entitled to adequate notice, an opportunity to be heard, an opportunity to opt out of the case, and adequate representation by the named plaintiffs. If these procedural due process minima were met, according to the court, Kansas could assert jurisdiction over the plaintiff class and bind each class member with a judgment on his claim. The court surveyed the course of the litigation and concluded that all of these minima had been met.

The court also rejected petitioner's contention that Kansas law could not be applied to plaintiffs and royalty arrangements having no connection with Kansas. The court stated that generally the law of the forum controlled all claims unless "compelling reasons" existed to apply a different law. The court found no compelling reasons, and noted that "[t]he plaintiff class members have indicated their desire to have this action determined under the laws of Kansas." The court affirmed as a matter of Kansas equity law the award of interest on the suspended royalties, at the rates imposed by the trial court. The court set the postjudgment interest rate on all claims at the Kansas statutory rate of 15%.

I

As a threshold matter we must determine whether petitioner has standing to assert the claim that Kansas did not possess proper jurisdiction over the many plaintiffs in the class who were not Kansas residents and had no connection to Kansas. * * *

Respondents claim that petitioner is barred by the rule requiring that a party assert only his own rights; they point out that respondents and petitioner are adversaries and do not have allied interests such that petitioner would be a good proponent of class members' interests. They further urge that petitioner's interference is unneeded because the class members have had opportunity to complain about Kansas' assertion of jurisdiction over their claim, but none have done so.

Respondents may be correct that petitioner does not possess standing *jus tertii*, but this is not the issue. Petitioner seeks to vindicate its own interests. As a class-action defendant petitioner is in a unique predicament. If Kansas does not possess jurisdiction over this plaintiff class, petitioner will be bound to 28,100 judgment holders scattered across the globe, but none of these will be bound by the Kansas decree. Petitioner could be subject to numerous later individual suits by these class members because a judgment issued without proper personal jurisdiction over an absent party is not entitled to full faith and credit elsewhere and thus has no res judicata effect as to that party. Whether it wins or loses on the merits, petitioner has a distinct and personal interest in seeing the entire plaintiff class bound by res judicata just as petitioner is bound. The only way a class-action defendant like petitioner can assure itself of this binding effect of the judgment is to ascertain that the forum court has jurisdiction over every plaintiff whose claim it seeks to adjudicate, sufficient to support a defense of res judicata in a later suit for damages by class members.

While it is true that a court adjudicating a dispute may not be able to predetermine the res judicata effect of its own judgment, petitioner has alleged that it would be obviously and immediately injured if this class-action judgment against it became final without binding the plaintiff class. We think that such an injury is sufficient to give petitioner standing on its own right to raise the jurisdiction claim in this Court.

* * *

II

Reduced to its essentials, petitioner's argument is that unless out-of-state plaintiffs affirmatively consent, the Kansas courts may not exert jurisdiction over their claims. Petitioner claims that failure to execute and return the "request for exclusion" provided with the class notice cannot constitute consent of the out-of-state plaintiffs; thus Kansas courts may exercise jurisdiction over these plaintiffs only if the plaintiffs possess the sufficient "minimum contacts" with Kansas as that term is used in cases involving personal jurisdiction over out-of-state defendants. *E.g.,* International Shoe Co. v. Washington, 326 U.S. 310 (1945); Shaffer v. Heitner, 433 U.S. 186 (1977); World-Wide Volkswagen Corp. v. Woodson, 444 U.S. 286 (1980). Since Kansas had no prelitigation contact with many of the plaintiffs and leases involved, petitioner claims that Kansas has exceeded its jurisdictional reach and thereby violated the due process rights of the absent plaintiffs.

In *International Shoe* we were faced with an out-of-state corporation which sought to avoid the exercise of personal jurisdiction over it as a defendant by a Washington state court. We held that the extent of the defendant's due process protection would depend "upon the quality and nature of the activity in relation to the fair and orderly administration of the laws. . . ."

We noted that the Due Process Clause did not permit a State to make a binding judgment against a person with whom the State had no contacts, ties, or relations. If the defendant possessed certain minimum contacts with the State, so that it was "reasonable and just, according to our traditional conception of fair play and substantial justice" for a State to exercise personal jurisdiction, the State could force the defendant to defend himself in the forum, upon pain of default, and could bind him to a judgment.

The purpose of this test, of course, is to protect a defendant from the travail of defending in a distant forum, unless the defendant's contacts with the forum make it just to force him to defend there. As we explained in *Woodson, supra,* the defendant's contacts should be such that "he should reasonably anticipate being haled" into the forum. 444 U.S., at 297 In Insurance Corp. of Ireland v. Compagnie des Bauxites de Guinee, 456 U.S. 694, 702-703, and n.10 (1982), we explained that the requirement that a court have personal jurisdiction comes from the Due Process Clause's protection of the defendant's personal liberty interest, and said that the requirement "represents a restriction on judicial power not as a matter of sovereignty, but as a matter of individual liberty."

Although the cases like *Shaffer* and *Woodson* which petitioner relies on for a minimum contacts requirement all dealt with out-of-state defendants or parties in the procedural posture of a defendant, petitioner claims that the same analysis must apply to absent class-action plaintiffs. In this regard petitioner correctly points out that a chose in action is a constitutionally recognized property interest possessed by each of the plaintiffs. Mullane v. Central Hanover Bank & Trust Co., 339 U.S. 306 (1950). An adverse judgment by Kansas courts in this case may extinguish the chose in action forever through res judicata. Such an adverse judgment, petitioner claims, would be every bit as onerous to an absent plaintiff as an adverse judgment on the merits would be to a defendant. Thus, the same due process protections should apply to absent plaintiffs: Kansas should not be able to exert jurisdiction over the plaintiffs claims unless the plaintiffs have sufficient minimum contacts with Kansas.

We think petitioner's premise is in error. The burdens placed by a State upon an absent class-action plaintiff are not of the same order or magnitude as those it places upon an absent defendant. An out-of-state defendant summoned by a plaintiff is faced with the full powers of the forum State to render judgment *against* it. The defendant must generally hire counsel and travel to the forum to defend itself from the plaintiffs claim, or suffer a default judgment. The defendant may be forced to participate in extended and often costly discovery, and will be forced to respond in damages or to comply with some other form of remedy imposed by the court should it lose the suit. The defendant may also face liability for court costs and attorney's fees. These burdens are substantial, and the minimum contacts requirement of the Due Process Clause prevents the forum State from unfairly imposing them upon the defendant.

A class-action plaintiff, however, is in quite a different posture. The Court noted this difference in Hansberry v. Lee, 311 U.S. 32, 40-41 (1940), which explained that a "class" or "representative" suit was an exception to the rule that one could not be bound by judgment *in personam* unless one was made fully a party in the traditional sense. Ibid., citing Pennoyer v. Neff, 95 U.S. (5 Otto) 714 (1878). As the Court pointed out in *Hansberry,* the class action was an invention of equity to enable it to proceed to a decree in suits where the number of those interested in the litigation was too great to permit joinder. The absent parties would be bound by the decree so long as the named parties adequately represented the absent class and the prosecution of the litigation was within the common interest.

Modern plaintiff class actions follow the same goals, permitting litigation of a suit involving common questions when there are too many plaintiffs for proper joinder. Class actions also may permit the plaintiffs to pool claims which would be uneconomical to litigate individually. For example, this lawsuit involves claims averaging about $100 per plaintiff; most of the plaintiffs would have no realistic day in court if a class action were not available.

In sharp contrast to the predicament of a defendant haled into an out-of-state forum, the plaintiffs in this suit were not haled anywhere to defend themselves upon pain of a default judgment. As commentators have noted, from the plaintiffs' point of view a class action resembles a "quasi-administrative proceeding, conducted by the judge." 3B J. Moore & J. Kennedy, Moore's Federal Practice ¶ 23.45[4.-5] (1984).

A plaintiff class in Kansas and numerous other jurisdictions cannot first be certified unless the judge, with the aid of the named plaintiffs and defendant, conducts an inquiry into the common nature of the named plaintiffs' and the absent plaintiffs' claims, the adequacy of representation, the jurisdiction possessed over the class, and any other matters that will bear upon proper representation of the absent plaintiffs' interest. See, e.g., Kan.Stat.Ann. §60-223 (1983); Fed. Rule Civ. Proc. 23. Unlike a defendant in a civil suit, a class-action plaintiff is not required to fend for himself. See Kan.Stat.Ann. §60-223(d) (1983). The court and named plaintiffs protect his interests. Indeed, the class-action defendant itself has a great interest in ensuring that the absent plaintiffs claims are properly before the forum. In this case, for example, the defendant sought to avoid class certification by alleging that the absent plaintiffs would not be adequately represented and were not amenable to jurisdiction.

The concern of the typical class-action rules for the absent plaintiffs is manifested in other ways. Most jurisdictions, including Kansas, require that a class action, once certified, may not be dismissed or compromised without the approval of the court. In many jurisdictions such as Kansas the court may amend the pleadings to ensure that all sections of the class are represented adequately. Kan.Stat.Ann. §60-223(d) (1983); see also, e.g., Fed. Rule Civ. Proc. 23(d).

Besides this continuing solicitude for their rights, absent plaintiff class members are not subject to other burdens imposed upon defendants. They need not hire counsel or appear. They are almost never subject to counterclaims or cross-claims, or liability for fees or costs.[2] Absent plaintiff class members are not subject to coercive or punitive remedies. Nor will an adverse judgment typically bind an absent plaintiff for any damages, although a valid adverse judgment may extinguish any of the plaintiffs claims which were litigated.

Unlike a defendant in a normal civil suit, an absent class-action plaintiff is not required to do anything. He may sit back and allow the litigation to run its course, content in knowing that there are safeguards provided for his protection. In most class actions an absent plaintiff is provided at least with an opportunity to "opt out" of the class, and if he takes advantage of that opportunity he is removed from the litigation entirely. This was true of the Kansas proceedings in this case. The Kansas procedure provided for the mailing of a notice to each class member by first-class mail. The notice, as we have previously indicated, described the action and informed the class member that he could appear in person or by counsel, in default of which he would be represented by the named plaintiffs and their attorneys. The notice further stated that class members would be included in the class and bound by the judgment unless they "opted

---

[2] Petitioner places emphasis on the fact that absent class members might be subject to discovery, counterclaims, cross-claims, or court costs. Petitioner cites no cases involving any such imposition upon plaintiffs, however. We are convinced that such burdens are rarely imposed upon plaintiff class members, and that the disposition of these issues is best left to a case which presents them in a more concrete way.

out" by executing and returning a "request for exclusion" that was included in the notice.

Petitioner contends, however, that the "opt out" procedure provided by Kansas is not good enough, and that an "opt in" procedure is required to satisfy the Due Process Clause of the Fourteenth Amendment. Insofar as plaintiffs who have no minimum contacts with the forum State are concerned, an "opt in" provision would require that each class member affirmatively consent to his inclusion within the class.

Because States place fewer burdens upon absent class plaintiffs than they do upon absent defendants in nonclass suits, the Due Process Clause need not and does not afford the former as much protection from state-court jurisdiction as it does the latter. The Fourteenth Amendment does protect "persons," not "defendants," however, so absent plaintiffs as well as absent defendants are entitled to some protection from the jurisdiction of a forum State which seeks to adjudicate their claims. In this case we hold that a forum State may exercise jurisdiction over the claim of an absent class-action plaintiff, even though that plaintiff may not possess the minimum contacts with the forum which would support personal jurisdiction over a defendant. If the forum State wishes to bind an absent plaintiff concerning a claim for money damages or similar relief at law,[3] it must provide minimal procedural due process protection. The plaintiff must receive notice plus an opportunity to be heard and participate in the litigation, whether in person or through counsel. The notice must be the best practicable, "reasonably calculated, under all the circumstances, to apprise interested parties of the pendency of the action and afford them an opportunity to present their objections." *Mullane,* 339 U.S., at 314-315; cf. Eisen v. Carlisle & Jacquelin, 417 U.S. 156, 174-175 (1974). The notice should describe the action and the plaintiffs' rights in it. Additionally, we hold that due process requires at a minimum that an absent plaintiff be provided with an opportunity to remove himself from the class by executing and returning an "opt out" or "request for exclusion" form to the court. Finally, the Due Process Clause of course requires that the named plaintiff at all times adequately represent the interests of the absent class members. *Hansberry,* 311 U.S., at 42-43, 45.

We reject petitioner's contention that the Due Process Clause of the Fourteenth Amendment requires that absent plaintiffs affirmatively "opt in" to the class, rather than be deemed members of the class if they do not "opt out." We think that such a contention is supported by little, if any precedent, and that it ignores the differences between class-action plaintiffs, on the one hand, and defendants in nonclass civil suits on the other. Any plaintiff may consent to jurisdiction. The essential question, then, is how stringent the requirement for a showing of consent will be.

---

[3] Our holding today is limited to those class actions which seek to bind known plaintiffs concerning claims wholly or predominately for money judgments. We intimate no view concerning other types of class actions, such as those seeking equitable relief. Nor, of course, does our discussion of personal jurisdiction address class actions where the jurisdiction is asserted against a *defendant* class.

We think that the procedure followed by Kansas, where a fully descriptive notice is sent first-class mail to each class member, with an explanation of the right to "opt out," satisfies due process. Requiring a plaintiff to affirmatively request inclusion would probably impede the prosecution of those class actions involving an aggregation of small individual claims, where a large number of claims are required to make it economical to bring suit. See, *e.g., Eisen, supra,* 417 U.S., at 161. The plaintiffs' claim may be so small, or the plaintiff so unfamiliar with the law, that he would not file suit individually, nor would he affirmatively request inclusion in the class if such a request were required by the Constitution.[4] If, on the other hand, the plaintiffs' claim is sufficiently large or important that he wishes to litigate it on his own, he will likely have retained an attorney or have thought about filing suit, and should be fully capable of exercising his right to "opt out."

In this case over 3,400 members of the potential class did "opt out," which belies the contention that "opt out" procedures result in guaranteed jurisdiction by inertia. Another 1,500 were excluded because the notice and "opt out" form was undeliverable. We think that such results show that the "opt out" procedure provided by Kansas is by no means *pro forma,* and that the Constitution does not require more to protect what must be the somewhat rare species of class member who is unwilling to execute an "opt out" form, but whose claim is nonetheless so important that he cannot be presumed to consent to being a member of the class by his failure to do so. Petitioner's "opt in" requirement would require the invalidation of scores of state statutes and of the class-action provision of the Federal Rules of Civil Procedure, and for the reasons stated we do not think that the Constitution requires the State to sacrifice the obvious advantages in judicial efficiency resulting from the "opt out" approach for the protection of the *rara avis* portrayed by petitioner.

We therefore hold that the protection afforded the plaintiff class members by the Kansas statute satisfies the Due Process Clause. The interests of the absent plaintiffs are sufficiently protected by the forum State when those plaintiffs are provided with a request for exclusion that can be returned within a reasonable time to the court. Both the Kansas trial court and the Supreme Court of Kansas held that the class received adequate representation, and no party disputes that conclusion here. We conclude that the Kansas court properly asserted personal jurisdiction over the absent plaintiffs and their claims against petitioner.

III

The Kansas courts applied Kansas contract and Kansas equity law to every claim in this case, notwithstanding that over 99% of the gas leases and some

---

[4] In this regard the Reporter for the 1966 amendments to the Federal Rules of Civil Procedure stated:

> "[R]equiring the individuals affirmatively to request inclusion in the lawsuit would result in freezing out the claims of people — especially small claims held by small people — who for one reason or another, ignorance, timidity, unfamiliarity with business or legal matters, will simply not take the affirmative step."

Kaplan, Continuing Work of the Civil Committee: 1966 Amendments of the Federal Rules of Civil Procedure (I), 81 Harv.L.Rev. 356, 397-398 (1967).

97% of the plaintiffs in the case had no apparent connection to the State of Kansas except for this lawsuit. * * *

* * *

Petitioner contends that total application of Kansas substantive law violated the constitutional limitations on choice of law mandated by the Due Process Clause of the Fourteenth Amendment and the Full Faith and Credit Clause of Article IV, §1. We must first determine whether Kansas law conflicts in any material way with any other law which could apply. There can be no injury in applying Kansas law if it is not in conflict with that of any other jurisdiction connected to this suit.

[The Court found that Kansas law conflicted with other states' laws concerning the amount of interest to be paid for suspended royalties, and that Texas law excused interest liability altogether once the gas company offers to take an indemnity from the royalty owner and pay him the suspended royalty while the price increase is still tentative. The Court referred to the plurality and other opinions in Allstate Ins. Co. v. Hague, 449 U.S. 302 (1981), to the effect "that for a State's substantive law to be selected in a constitutionally permissible manner, that State must have a significant contact or significant aggregation of contacts, creating state interests, such that choice of its law is neither arbitrary nor fundamentally unfair." While acknowledging that Kansas had some contacts with the underlying litigation (i.e., a few hundred Kansas claimants and some Kansas leases), contacts were lacking with respect to non-Kansas leases or not involving Kansas citizens. The Court rejected the idea that by failing to opt out the unnamed class members "consented" to have Kansas law apply. It also rejected the argument that choice of law could be affected by the presence of personal jurisdiction or "by the fact that it may be more difficult or more burdensome to comply with the constitutional limitations [on choice of law] because of the large number of transactions which the State proposes to adjudicate and which have little connection with the forum."

Given Kansas's lack of "interest" in claims unrelated to that State, and the substantive conflict with jurisdictions such as Texas, the Court concluded that "application of Kansas law to every claim in this case is sufficiently arbitrary and unfair as to exceed constitutional limits." The Court remanded the case for the Kansas courts to rework the choice of law analysis.]

It is so ordered.

JUSTICE POWELL took no part in the decision of this case.

[The opinion of JUSTICE STEVENS, concurring in part and dissenting in part, is omitted.]

NOTES AND PROBLEMS FOR DISCUSSION

1. *Shutts* presents two major holdings — one on personal jurisdiction, and one on choice of law. Focus on the first of the two.

(a) Who raised the personal jurisdiction objection on behalf of the unnamed members of the class, and what was their interest in doing so?

(b) The Court concludes that personal jurisdiction is an irrelevant question when it comes to unnamed plaintiffs in a class action. Why should that be the case? Remember, in the *Mullane* decision, discussed in *Shutts*, the Court considered the issue of personal jurisdiction over certain would-be claimants against a trustee, along with the issue of notice for which the case is better remembered. All that the claimants stood to lose was their ability to sue on a claim, like the unnamed members of the plaintiff class in *Shutts*. In what respects was their position different from that of the unnamed plaintiffs in *Shutts*?

(c) Although personal jurisdiction may not be a relevant inquiry when it comes to unnamed plaintiff class members, due process obviously still matters in other respects. Is the opt out right under Rule 23(b)(3) and analogous state rules like that at issue in *Shutts* one that is constitutionally compelled (at least when it comes to geographically remotely situated class members)?

2. Now, focus on the choice of law question. As with personal jurisdiction, due process requires that there be a sufficient nexus between the litigation and the state whose law is applied. (Full faith and credit requires something roughly similar.) But *Shutts* makes clear that a forum may have a sufficient nexus with a dispute and the parties for purposes of exercising personal jurisdiction over the defendant consistent with the Constitution, and yet have an insufficient nexus with the underlying transaction for purposes of applying its own law.

(a) Was there any one state's law that could have applied to all of the transactions in question in *Shutts*?

(b) Suppose the state court decided on remand to apply the law of multiple states to the relevant underlying transactions. If the state court had a class action provision similar to Rule 23(b)(3) requiring that common questions predominate over individual questions, what impact would the application of multiple states' laws have on the question of predominance? At least one decision has rejected the possibility that the federal courts might concoct a uniform, "Esperanto" version of what state law "generally" holds. See In re Rhone-Poulenc Rohrer, Inc., 51 F.3d 1293 (7th Cir. 1995).

SUBJECT MATTER JURISDICTION IN CLASS ACTIONS

Shutts was filed in state court. Consequently, subject matter jurisdiction was not really an issue. In federal court, however, subject matter jurisdiction over class actions can be problematic. If the action is based on a violation of federal law, of course, the case will come within the federal courts' federal question jurisdiction, without regard to the amount in controversy or citizenship of the parties to the suit. But class actions based on state law must confront the requirements of the diversity statute (and venue — 28 U.S.C. §1391).

Some time ago, in an equitable proceeding, the Supreme Court concluded that for purposes of citizenship, only the named representative's state of domicile had to be considered. If he was (or if all of the named representatives were) diverse from the defendant, that was sufficient, even if the unnamed class members might be nondiverse from the defendant. Supreme Tribe of Ben-Hur v. Cauble, 255 U.S. 356, 41 S.Ct. 338, 65 L.Ed. 673 (1921). How did this square with the complete diversity rule? Was it significant that in *Ben-Hur* the plaintiffs' claims would not have been considered "several" but were instead "joint" (as would be the case in many (b)(1) actions today)?

Nevertheless, as discussed in Chapter 3, the Court later held in an action under 23(b)(3) that each plaintiff had to have the requisite amount in controversy with the defendant. Zahn v. International Paper Co., 414 U.S. 291, 94 S.Ct. 505, 38 L.Ed.2d 511 (1973). The effect of the ruling was to eliminate from the federal courts many small claimant class actions grounded in state law. Of course, such cases could go to state court, although when *Zahn* was combined with *Shutts*, even state courts might have difficulty maintaining a nationwide class if divergent state laws will have to be applied.

Zahn notwithstanding, however, some lower courts concluded that the 1990 supplemental jurisdiction statute, 28 U.S.C. §1367, had overruled *Zahn* to the extent that the statute purported to allow for supplemental jurisdiction over transactionally related claims — including claims by additional parties — in any federal case in which there is an anchor claim that satisfies the requirements of federal diversity jurisdiction. See, e.g., In re Abbott Laboratories, 51 F.3d 524 (5th Cir. 1995). The basic rationale was that, although there are a number of exceptions under paragraph (b) of §1367 for diversity cases, there is no express mention that suits brought under Rule 23 are to be exempted from the supplemental jurisdiction provisions of paragraph (a) of §1367. For a time, the Supreme Court was unable to reach a decision on the question when it was presented for its review. See Free v. Abbott Laboratories, Inc., 529 U.S. 333, 120 S.Ct. 1578, 146 L.Ed.2d 306 (2000) (affirming without opinion, by an equally divided vote, the Fifth Circuit's decision in *Abbott Laboratories, supra*).

Then, in 2005, the Supreme Court held (5-4) that the supplemental jurisdiction statute did indeed overrule *Zahn*, at least with respect to the question of whether all class members had to have the requisite amount in controversy. See Exxon Mobil Corp. Inc. v. Allapattah Services, 545 U.S. 546, 125 S.Ct. 2621, 162 L.Ed.2d 502 (2005). The Court read §1367 as allowing supplemental jurisdiction over claims of unnamed class members in federal court class actions based on state law, without regard to the amount of their particular claim, so long as one diverse class member had the requisite amount in controversy. Note that the Class Action Fairness Act of 2005 (Section 5, below) accomplished something similar, at least as to certain kinds of class actions in which the claims in the aggregate exceed $5 million (but with no amount in controversy requirement for individual class members).[*] The *Exxon Mobil* Court seemed to assume, without saying, that the unnamed class members also did not have to be diverse from the defendant (which, since *Ben-Hur, supra,* they do not have to be). But some of the reasoning of the majority opinion in *Exxon Mobil* suggests that its logic should allow for supplemental jurisdiction only for class members'

---

[*] The Act, however, applies only to class actions filed after CAFA's enactment. See Pritchett v. Office Depot, 420 F.3d 1090 (10th Cir. 2005) (denying removal to class action filed before effective date of CAFA).

claims that were wanting in amount in controversy, as opposed to those that destroyed complete diversity. If the latter were true, of course, *Zahn* would be doubly reversed — class members need not all have the requisite amount in controversy, but they must be diverse. But it is unlikely that that is what the Court meant to do.

5. THE CLASS ACTION FAIRNESS ACT OF 2005

The 2005 Class Action Fairness Act (CAFA) substantially altered state-law based class action litigation brought in federal courts either originally or on removal from state court. The major features of the act, which are scattered throughout a number of federal jurisdictional provisions, are summarized here.

Most significantly, CAFA amends the diversity statute, 28 U.S.C. §1332, to allow federal courts to hear a state-law class action in which any plaintiff is diverse from any defendant, and the amount in controversy, in the aggregate, exceeds $5 million and involves 100 or more class members. See §1332(d)(2) and (d)(5)(B). (Recall that class actions based on *federal* law do not require any diversity whatsoever, or any amount in controversy.) Previously, all named plaintiff class representatives had to be diverse from the defendant, while the citizenship of unnamed class members was not taken into account. After CAFA, minimal diversity can be established if any class member or representative is diverse from any defendant. Courts had also been divided on the amount in controversy question. The last Supreme Court pronouncement prior to the passage of CAFA required that each plaintiff, including each class member, have the requisite amount in controversy (i.e., in excess of $75,000) — a conclusion that was soon rejected in *Exxon Mobil, supra*. Although much of the 2005 Act supercedes *Exxon Mobil* in many cases, the decision remains applicable to nonfederal law based class suits brought in federal court that do not otherwise fit within the parameters of CAFA.

The statute expressly does not apply to certain kinds of securities claims or suits involving corporate governance or breaches of fiduciary duty. §1332(d)(9). Also excluded from coverage are class actions in which "two-thirds or more" of the class members and the "primary defendants" are citizens of the state in which the action was originally filed. §1332(d)(4)(B). In addition, class actions are excluded in which "greater than two-thirds" of the class members are citizens of the state in which the action was brought and there is at least one defendant from that state from whom the class seeks "significant relief" and the injuries result from each defendant's conduct in that state (provided, however, that no class action alleging similar facts has been alleged against any of the defendants in the previous three years). §1332(d)(4)(A). If the number of in-state plaintiffs is "greater than one-third but less than two-thirds" of the class members, the district court *may* ("in the interests of justice and looking to the totality of the circumstances") decline to exercise jurisdiction based on a handful of factors. §1332(d)(3). Those factors include whether the action is based on the law of the state in which the suit was filed; whether the action was brought in a state with a "distinct nexus" with the plaintiffs, defendants or the alleged harm; and whether the suit involves a matter of national or interstate interest. See

§1332(d)(3)(A)-(F). Where one-third or fewer of the class members are citizens of the same state as the primary defendants (or any diverse defendant), CAFA is apparently fully applicable.

Also covered by CAFA are so-called "mass actions" — actions not filed as class actions, but in which there are claims of "100 or more" persons that "are proposed to be tried jointly" seeking monetary relief and raising common questions of law or fact. §1332(d)(11)(B). At the time of CAFA's enactment, these actions still required that each plaintiff meet the amount in controversy requirement independently, and, under CAFA, are likely to be brought in federal court only upon removal (see below). But now, after *Exxon Mobil*, each class member's meeting of the amount in controversy is presumably no longer required as a matter of the supplemental jurisdiction statute. Included among the cases *excepted* from this "mass action" category are claims that "arise from an event or occurrence in the State in which the action was filed" and that resulted in injuries in that state or in contiguous states. Also excepted from the "mass action" provision are claims asserted pursuant to a state statute expressly authorizing suit on behalf of the general public, or claims that have been joined by the defendant. See §1332(d)(11)(B)(ii)(I)-(IV).

Removal of cases fitting these requirements of CAFA is also possible. See 28 U.S.C. §1453 ("Removal of Class Actions"). That provision provides broadly that "A class action [under the meanings provided in §1332(d)(1)] may be removed to a district court of the United States in accordance with §1446[.]" Interestingly, the "home state" limitation on removal of nonfederal question cases when a defendant is sued in a state court in the state of its citizenship is lifted; not all defendants need join in the effort to remove; and the usual one-year removal limit from commencement of suit in diversity cases is made inapplicable in such cases. §1453(b). Provision for immediate appeal is also available of any ruling on a motion to remand, which the court of appeals "may accept." §1453(c)(2).

CAFA also includes provisions (28 U.S.C. §§1711-1715) that purport to protect the interests of class members by ratcheting up judicial scrutiny of and limiting attorney's fees for settlements that result in noncash awards, such as coupons, or in a settlement that results in a net assessment against class members.

NOTES AND PROBLEMS FOR DISCUSSION

1. What do you suppose were the purposes behind CAFA? In a wordy statutory introduction ("Findings and Purposes") Congress offered a number of reasons. Among the recited findings is that class action "abuses" have harmed both plaintiffs and defendants, adversely affected interstate commerce, and undermined respect for the judicial system. Congress also found that awards, especially nonmonetary awards, were often unfair and resulted in disproportionately large fees to prevailing plaintiffs' counsel. Congress also stated that the current system prevented federal courts from hearing cases of national importance, promoted bias against out of state defendants, and allowed for impermissible application of state laws to out of state transactions and parties. The purpose of the statute was said to be to encourage innovation and to lower consumer prices, as well as to "restore the intent of the framers of the United States Constitution by providing for Federal court consideration of interstate cases of national importance under diversity jurisdiction."

2. Suppose that a defendant removes a class suit otherwise fitting CAFA, but the federal court then determines that the prerequisites of Rule 23 are not met. What happens next? Is the case dismissed? If so, is it on jurisdictional grounds because the case is one to which CAFA does not extend? Perhaps if the class is not certified, the individual representative's action remains. But if that claim independently cannot satisfy federal subject matter jurisdiction, it will have to be remanded to state court, will it not? If the individual case is remanded to state court (or if the class claim is dismissed outright) might the state court then choose to certify the class under its own version of Rule 23? Or would the federal court's prior resolution preclude state court's subsequent resolution of class certification under its own class action rule? If the action can still be maintained as a class suit in state court, isn't that precisely the problem to which CAFA was directed?

3. New §1332(d)(8) provides that CAFA is applicable to "any class action before or after the entry of a class certification order." Does this mean that post-dismissal certification in state court would allow for re-removal? And perhaps re-dismissal? Ad infinitum? If the statute means to put an end to certain minimal diversity, state-law class actions in state court that meet the definition of CAFA but do not meet the requirements of Rule 23, is that a proper use of the diversity jurisdiction?

4. If a class representative wishes to avoid removal to federal court under CAFA, may she stipulate in her complaint that she seeks less than the $5 million threshold on behalf of the class under 28 U.S.C. §§ 1332(d)(2) & (5)? In STANDARD FIRE INS. CO. v. KNOWLES, 568 U.S. ___, 133 S.Ct. 1345, 185 L.Ed.2d 439 (2013), the Court concluded that such a pre-certification stipulation would not be binding on other members of the class, and that therefore it could not defeat federal jurisdiction over the class action, assuming the aggregate amount is met among those non-stipulating class members.

5. In MISSISSIPPI EX REL. HOOD v. AU OPTRONICS CORP., 571 U.S. ___, 134 S.Ct. 736, 187 L.Ed.2d 654 (2014), the Supreme Court held that for the purpose of CAFA, only named plaintiffs are counted towards the 100-plaintiff threshold for removing a "mass action" to federal court. The State of Mississippi sued respondents (LCD manufacturers) in state court alleging that they had violated a state anti-trust statute and a state consumer protection statute. Among other relief, the State sought recovery on its own behalf and on behalf of Mississippi purchasers. Respondents then removed the case to the Southern District of Mississippi federal court under CAFA, as either a class action or a mass action.

The District Court held that the case was not a class action, as it was not brought pursuant to Rule 23 or a similar state statute. But it ruled that the case was a mass action insofar as at least 100 Mississippi consumers could qualify as parties in interest by virtue of their having purchased the products in question. The District Court remanded the case, however, under the "general public exception" (28 U.S.C. §1332(d)(11)(B)(ii)(III)), which states that an action brought "on behalf of the general public (and not on behalf of individual claimants or members of a purported class) pursuant to a State statute purportedly authorizing such action," does not qualify as a mass action under §1332(d)(11)(B)(i). The Fifth Circuit reversed, concluding that the action was indeed a mass action and that it did not come under the "general public" exception given the existence of discrete Mississippi consumers as real parties in interest.

On appeal, the Supreme Court held that the suit was not removable as a mass action because unnamed parties (i.e., the consumers) did not count towards the 100-plaintiff threshold. The Court reasoned that, had Congress intended to include named as well as unnamed real parties in interest, it "easily could have drafted language to that effect," especially in light of the fact that such a distinction was made in other sections of the statute. Furthermore, the Court found that the term "persons," when used in similar contexts in other statutes and rules, did not refer to other unnamed parties in interest. Finally, the Court determined that the "stretch[ing]" of the term "plaintiff" to include all unnamed individuals with an interest in the suit would create "an administrative nightmare that Congress could not possibly have intended." Because Mississippi was the only named plaintiff, the case failed to meet the requirements for diversity jurisdiction, and it should have been remanded to state court.

6. SETTLEMENT OF CLASS ACTIONS

Rule 23(e) provides that class actions may be settled, but only with court approval. The approval requirement applies to any "proposed settlement, voluntary dismissal or compromise" of the claims, issues or defenses of a certified class. Id. That differs from ordinary practice whereby parties in nonclass suits may freely decide whether they will privately settle their dispute with each other, generally without interference by or scrutiny from the court. The obvious reason for the difference is that settlements of class suits do not settle merely the claims of the formal parties to the litigation; they also settle the claims of the unnamed class members as well. That is because, if a class has been properly certified, the settlement is binding. The enhanced judicial scrutiny of the settlement process therefore exists to safeguard the interests of these absentees.

If suit has already been filed and a class has been certified, and the parties thereafter come to an agreement after negotiations, the settlement will be proposed to the court, and a second round of "reasonable" notice is required. See Rule 23(e)(1). A fairness hearing will then be held to ascertain whether the settlement is fair and equitable to the class as a whole. Rule 23(e)(2) (requiring a finding that the settlement is "fair, reasonable, and adequate" to class members who would be bound). Typically, while objectors to the proposed settlement may be heard at the hearing, the trial court will not insist that the plaintiff class be awarded all that they might have won at trial. Rather, the court will look to see how the relief proposed compares to the potential recovery and discount it by the risk of nonrecovery. See In re Corrugated Container Antitrust Litigation, 643 F.2d 195 (5th Cir. 1981). Of course, in some cases seeking large monetary recovery on behalf of a populous class, even a marginal suit (i.e., one with a 5-10% chance of prevailing) may still carry a high settlement price tag — sometimes one that is less than the cost to the defendant of litigating the suit to conclusion. See In re Rhone-Poulenc Rorer, 51 F.3d 1293 (7th Cir. 1995) (refusing to permit class certification in such a setting and referring to the fact that defendants may be compelled to settle unmeritorious class suits).

Over the years, a practice developed whereby putative class representatives and defendants, eager to settle a potential lawsuit, would seek simultaneously to file, certify, and settle a class action. In such settings, all of the negotiation would take place without a lawsuit having been filed, or notice having been given to the would-be class. This fast track process meant, in damages actions under Rule 23(b)(3), that there would likely be only a single round of notice, describing not only the definition of the class and the nature of the suit, but the settlement as well, and giving unnamed class members the right to opt out of the settlement. Courts upheld the validity of the practice, but acknowledged that the risks for compromise of the interests of the plaintiff class were heightened in comparison to the ordinary route of filing, certification, negotiation, and then settlement. Indeed, some courts were willing, in the interests of avoiding protracted litigation, to certify such settlement classes even if they did not really meet all of the requirements of 23(b)(3), such as the predominance of common questions. In such cases courts might conclude that the supposedly common interest in settlement predominated over any individual issues that might arise were the case to go to trial.

In AMCHEM PRODUCTS, INC. v. WINDSOR, 521 U.S. 591, 117 S.Ct. 2231, 138 L.Ed.2d 689 (1997), the Court addressed the predominance requirement of Rule 23(b)(3) in the context of the settlement of a mass tort class action. In the face of extensive asbestos litigation, the Judicial Panel on Multidistrict Litigation (MDL Panel) consolidated in the Eastern District of Pennsylvania all pending federal asbestos complaints. (The MDL lacked authority to consolidate claims not yet filed or claims filed in state courts.)

In response to the consolidation, plaintiff and defense steering committees were established to commence settlement negotiations. Defendants' Steering Committee offered to settle *all pending and future* litigation over asbestos claims by providing a fund, to be administered by plaintiffs' counsel, for distribution among those exposed. Plaintiffs' Steering Committee rejected the proposal and negotiations collapsed.

Counsel for the Center for Claims Resolution (CCR), a consortium of 20 former asbestos manufacturers and member of the Defendants' Steering Committee, continued to seek a consolidated settlement. CCR approached the lead lawyers from the Plaintiffs' Steering Committee who represented thousands of existing claimants (the "inventory plaintiffs"). A second round of negotiations commenced, with CCR demanding as part of any settlement with existing claimants "some kind of protection for the future" — i.e., from future claimants. Settlement talks concentrated on "devising an administrative scheme for disposition of asbestos claims not yet in litigation."

These negotiations resulted in a mass settlement agreement whereby CCR settled the inventory plaintiffs' claims for $200 million. Following settlement of the inventory claims, CCR and inventory plaintiffs' counsel filed a class action on behalf of individuals not a part of the MDL proceeding (including future claimants). *Amchem* concerned this class action and its settlement. In fact, the class action was instituted not in order to litigate, but to settle. On January 15, 1993, CCR and the representatives of the plaintiff class "presented to the District Court a complaint, an answer, a proposed settlement agreement, and a joint motion for conditional class certification."

The complaint invoked the district court's diversity jurisdiction, consisted of various state law claims and was filed in the name of nine lead plaintiffs representing a class comprising all persons who had not filed an asbestos-related lawsuit against a CCR defendant as of the date of the complaint. The plaintiff class consisted of persons who had been exposed to asbestos or whose spouse or family members had been exposed.

Accompanying the pleadings was a stipulation of settlement that proposed to settle and "to preclude nearly all class members from litigating against CCR companies, all claims not filed before [the date of the complaint], involving compensation for present and future asbestos related personal injury or death." The stipulation also established a sliding damage award scale, based on the claimant's current injury or future prospect of suffering latent injuries; and it also precluded recovery for certain injuries even where allowable under state law.

The district court conditionally certified an opt-out class under Rule 23(b)(3) consisting of all persons exposed to asbestos and their families, who had not filed claims as of the date of the complaint. Members of the proposed class settlement (the "Objectors") raised numerous objections to the settlement, and challenged the fairness of the compensation scheme, and the notice provisions. They also argued that common issues of law or fact did not predominate, thus making the class inappropriate for certification. The district court found no collusion in negotiation of the settlement and rejected the Objectors' challenges. Addressing the issue of commonality and predominance, the district court held that:

> [t]he members of the class have all been exposed to asbestos products supplied by the defendants and all share an interest in receiving prompt and fair compensation for their claims while minimizing the risks and transaction costs inherent in the asbestos litigation process as it occurs presently in the tort system. Whether the proposed settlement satisfies this interest and is otherwise a fair, reasonable and adequate compromise of the claims of the class is a predominant issue for purposes of Rule 23(b)(3).

The district court also held that the claims of the class representatives were "typical" of the entire class, in compliance with Rule 23(a)(3) and that class settlement was "superior" to other methods of adjudication of the claims, in accord with Rule 23(b)(3).

Challenging the adequacy of representation and the composition of the class, the Objectors appealed. The United States Court of Appeals for the Third Circuit vacated the certification, holding that the requirements of Rule 23 had not been satisfied. The Supreme Court granted certiorari "to decide the role settlement may play, under existing Rule 23, in determining the propriety of class certification."

The Court made clear that the settlement provisions of Rules 23(e) did not make compliance with the provisions of Rule 23(a) and (b) unnecessary.

> Rule 23(e), on settlement class actions * * * was designed to function as an additional requirement, not a superseding direction, for the "class action." * * * Subdivisions (a) and (b) focus court attention on whether a proposed class has sufficient unity so that absent members can fairly be bound by decisions of class representatives. That dominant concern persists when settlement, rather than trial, is proposed.

Rule 23(e), said the Court, if allowed to eclipse the requirements of Rules 23(a) and (b), would disarm class counsel from bargaining with a credible threat of trial. In addition, the case would lack the normal adversarial investigation that could illuminate the fairness of any settlement. Moreover, simple fairness of a settlement standing alone does not make for proper class certification, as fairness itself is not one of the criteria for certification as set out in Rule 23.

The Court then turned to the concerns raised by the Objectors that common questions of law and fact must predominate as a precondition to certification under Rule 23(b)(3). The district court had determined that the predominance issue was satisfied for two reasons: (1) the class members had a common experience by their exposure to asbestos, and (2) they had a common interest in reaching a fair resolution of their claims with minimum transaction costs. The Court disagreed with the finding that predominance was satisfied. It concluded that the predominance question is one that tests "whether proposed classes are sufficiently cohesive to warrant adjudication by representation." And it added that the fairness requirement of 23(e) does not replace "class cohesion that legitimizes representative action."

Referring to the "predominance" requirement as far more "demanding" than the question of commonality under Rule 23(a), the Court concluded: "Given the greater number of questions peculiar to the several categories of class members, and to individuals within each category, and the significance of those uncommon questions, any overarching dispute about the health consequences of asbestos exposure cannot satisfy the Rule 23(b)(3) predominance standard." The Court found the particular settlement class to be "sprawling" in its nature because the class members were exposed to different products, in different quantities, at different times, and because each class member had a different history of behavior and health.

> Predominance is a test readily met in certain cases alleging consumer or securities fraud or violations of the antitrust law. * * * Even mass tort cases arising from a common cause or disaster may, depending upon the

circumstances, satisfy the predominance requirement. * * * [Though] the text of the rule does not categorically exclude mass tort cases from class certification [the Advisory Committee's warning that such cases are usually not appropriate for class treatment] continues to call for caution when individual stakes are high and disparities among class members great.

The Court held that the district court's certification could not be upheld, "for it rests on a conception of Rule 23(b)(3)'s predominance requirement irreconcilable with the rule's design." The Court also concluded that the class could not satisfy Rule 23(a)(4)'s requirement of representational adequacy because of conflicts within the class. For example, some had suffered exposure only and others had already manifested symptoms; for the latter, the goal was immediate compensation; for the former, the preservation of any overall settlement award. Because the Court determined class certification should fail on the issues of preponderance and inadequacy of representation, it declined to rule on the notice concerns raised by the respondents.

NOTES AND PROBLEMS FOR DISCUSSION

1. Why *not* look at the requirements of Rule 23 from the standpoint of settlement rather than litigation when the case is being settled and not litigated? Note that the Court distinguished the Rule 23(b)(3) requirements of predominance and superiority from that of manageability, which — according to *Amchem* — *can* be looked at from the standpoint of settlement rather than litigation.

2. The *Amchem* class plaintiffs included those who had existing medical conditions as well as those who had only been exposed to defendants' products. Given this fact, is adequacy of representation problematic, and if so, is the problem curable? Since the decision in *Amchem*, new provisions have been added to Rule 23 that bear specifically on how a court is to assess the adequacy of class counsel. See Rule 23(g).

3. The *Amchem* Court was troubled by the absence of a remedy in the proposed settlement for mere exposure, the lack of punitive damages, and the absence of a remedy for loss of consortium. Was inclusion of these remedies necessary for a fair settlement?

4. The bottom-line of the decision in *Amchem* is that global settlement of mass torts grounded in product liability will be difficult. Problems of predominance and the conflict of interest between present and future claimants will frequently be present. The ball appears to now be in Congress's court (or perhaps in the hands of the Rules' drafters). What, if anything, should they do?

5. *Amchem* dealt with settlement of a certified class, although certification was effectively simultaneous with settlement. What happens if the defendant offers a settlement *before* certification, or even before a motion for certification? At the pre-certification stage, Rule 23(e)'s requirement of judicial scrutiny of any settlement is less clear, and perhaps inapplicable. Could a defendant make a pre-certification motion "offer of judgment" under Rule 68 for the entire amount claimed by the named class representative — the result of which might arguably be to moot the class action? Compare Deposit Guaranty Nat'l Bank v. Roper, 445 U.S. 326, 100 S.Ct. 1166, 63 L.Ed.2d 427 (1980) (offer of settlement below amount claimed and refused by named plaintiffs, did not moot plaintiffs' case or ability to appeal class certification denial; "To deny the right of appeal simply because the defendant has sought to 'buy off' the individual private claims of the named plaintiffs would be contrary to sound judicial administration."). Note, however, that statutes of limitations are tolled for the putative class from the time of the filing of the complaint if certification should later be denied or overturned on appeal. Crown, Cork & Seal Co. v. Parker, 462 U.S. 345, 103 S.Ct. 2392, 76 L.Ed.2d 628 (1983). The Court recently addressed the question and concluded that refusal of a settlement offer made to the class representative at the pre-certification stage (and which would have provided them with complete relief on their individual claim), did not moot the plaintiff's individual claim or the class action. CAMPBELL-EWALD CO. v. GOMEZ, 577 U.S. ___, 136 S.Ct. 663, 193 L.Ed.2d 571 (2016). The Court relied on contract principles and Rule 68, Fed. R. Civ. P., to conclude that, once rejected, the offer "had no continuing efficacy."

6. *After* certification and after a settlement, who may appeal a settlement of a class action with which they are dissatisfied? Any member of the class? Many courts of appeals had concluded that, apart from the named representatives of the class (who might have little incentive to do so in the context of a settlement), only those class members who actually intervened in the lawsuit under Rule 24, and were thus conferred formal party status, could appeal. In Devlin v. Scardelletti, 536 U.S. 1, 122 S.Ct. 2005, 153 L.Ed.2d 27 (2002), however, the Supreme Court concluded that a non-named class member who had timely objected to the settlement at a fairness hearing, was sufficiently a "party" to appeal approval of the settlement, without the necessity of formal intervention.

CHAPTER 11

Trials

A distinctive feature of civil trials in the American judicial system is the decisionmaking role played by juries. Although the American jury system was derived from English practice, civil juries are generally no longer available in England except for certain actions such as defamation. And in civil law countries (i.e., non common law systems), the institution of the civil jury never really had a foothold. Once perceived as a bulwark against governmental overreaching, the jury system — according to some — has outlived its usefulness in civil litigation. Nevertheless, jury trials in civil cases in the federal courts have a constitutional foundation. In addition, civil jury trials have long co-existed with an important role for the trial judge to insure jury rationality and guarantee that judgments are made in accordance with law. In the first section of this Chapter, we address the scope of the right to trial by jury, and in the second, we address judicial control of jury decisionmaking.

SECTION A. THE RIGHT TO TRIAL BY JURY

Article III of the Constitution expressly provides that "all" criminal trials "shall be by jury." But no similar guarantee existed in the original Constitution of 1787 for civil suits. The Seventh Amendment to the U.S. Constitution (which, as part of the ten Amendments that made up the Bill of Rights, was ratified in 1791) provides:

> In suits at common law, where the value in controversy shall exceed twenty dollars, the right of trial by jury shall be preserved, and no fact tried by a jury shall be otherwise re-examined in any Court of the United States, than according to the rules of the common law.

This guarantee, being in the Bill of Rights, was a limitation on federal courts only, not state courts. But most states had and continue to have their own jury trial guarantees in civil actions. Interestingly, although many of the rights protected under the Bill of Rights have since been "incorporated" through the Due Process Clause of the Fourteenth Amendment (ratified after the Civil War) and made applicable against the states, the right to trial by jury in civil actions has not been. Consequently, state courts are not compelled by the Seventh Amendment to provide jury trials in common law actions.

The language of the Amendment is noteworthy. Why, for example, does the Amendment speak in terms of "preserving" the right to trial by jury in civil suits at common law, rather than guaranteeing it outright? Article III of the

Constitution states that the "trial of all *crimes* . . . shall be by jury." But jury trial rights are merely "preserved" in civil matters. Does the distinction matter?

Also, consider what it means to say that the jury trial right is preserved in civil actions "at common law." It is impossible to understand the scope of the civil jury trial right in suits at common law, without recognizing that the phrase was used to contrast suits in equity and suits in admiralty. As the Supreme Court put it early on: "The phrase 'common law,' found in this clause, is used in contradistinction to equity, and admiralty, and maritime jurisprudence." Parsons v. Bedford, 28 U.S. (3 Pet.) 433, 446-447, 7 L.Ed. 732 (1830). In turn, however, it is not possible to understand the distinction between law and equity (or admiralty) without having some sense of the English legal tradition in which those notions were originally developed, and which were, to a considerable extent, transplanted into the American court system during the eighteenth century. The story of equity jurisdiction and its relationship with common law courts is discussed in Chapter 7, and should be reviewed here.

While there were disputes over the proper sphere of law versus equity and admiralty, the basic lines of demarcation as well as the rules for dealing with overlapping cases were hammered out early on. Thus, once it was determined where the dispute was properly to be decided, the availability of jury trial followed automatically. Or, as some have said: jury trial was simply "the tail of the dog under a system in which you had to take the whole dog." FLEMING JAMES, JR., ET AL., CIVIL PROCEDURE 499 (5th ed. 2001). There were, of course, cases which were not so clear. For these, the Court generally looked at the language of "preserving" jury trial rights in suits at common law, and eventually held that these called for an historical test — one which made some effort to determine how the jury trial question would have been resolved if it had arisen at the time of the Seventh Amendment in 1791.

Our discussion of the present day jury trial rights focuses on three separate matters. First, the Seventh Amendment was based on the existence of separate courts of law and equity. Today, under the Federal Rules of Civil Procedure, there is no such separation and procedures have been "merged." The impact of the rules-based merger of law and equity might have resulted in no alteration of jury trial rights, but that proved not to be the case. Second, while suits at common law were generally actions arising under various common law writs (for example, an action in trespass, or for assumpsit), today many suits arise under statutes that create rights that bear little or no resemblance to suits at common law. Consider, for example, a lawsuit for damages under the Americans with Disabilities Act or the many statutes forbidding employment discrimination — statutes involving rights that were unheard of in 1791. Should a jury trial right extend to these new statutory actions if Congress has not provided for it? Third, the determination that trial should be by jury does not resolve the further question of the allocation of decisionmaking functions between judge and jury. While their roles generally align themselves with the resolution of questions of law (judges) and questions of fact (juries), the division of decisionmaking authority is not always so clear.

1. The Merger of Law and Equity

Prior to 1938, the federal courts were sometimes said to have different "sides" — consisting of law, equity, and admiralty. Each side had its own docket and its own rules of procedure, and a party always knew what side its case was before. If one was on the law side, there was a right to jury trial, and if on the equity said, there was no such right. The Federal Rules of Civil Procedure, adopted in 1938, abolished the distinction and said that henceforth there would only be one "civil action." As part of this process, legal and equitable claims and defenses could be brought in the same proceeding. Whereas before one could easily tell whether there was a right to jury trial by virtue of which side the federal court was sitting, this was no longer true.

Typical of the pre-merger practice was the Supreme Court's unanimous decision in AMERICAN LIFE INSURANCE CO. v. STEWART, 300 U.S. 203, 57 S.Ct. 377, 81 L.Ed. 605 (1937). Suit was over a life insurance policy, on the application for which the insured allegedly gave incorrect information. The policy contained an incontestability provision, which meant that after a given period of time, the insurance company lost the right to rescind the policy based on incorrect information given at the time of the application. The insured died before the incontestability period expired, and American Life brought an action in equity against the beneficiaries to rescind the policy on the ground of fraud. Historically, rescission was an equitable action. The basis for invoking equity was that if the insurance company didn't act, the beneficiaries might wait to bring suit only after the policy was no longer contestable. As an equitable action, the rescission claim would be tried to before the judge. After American Life filed its equitable action in federal court, the beneficiaries brought a suit in the same federal court to recover on the policy and sought a jury trial in that suit on the ground that the action was one at common law. Because there were facts common to both lawsuits, the first suit to be resolved would have generated preclusive consequences for the other. Hoping to avoid a jury trial of the relevant facts, American Life sought an injunction of the action at law pending the outcome of its earlier filed equity action. The beneficiaries, however, moved to dismiss the equitable action arguing that a court of equity should not act, because there was an adequate remedy at law — i.e., American Life could now raise the issue of fraud as a defense to the beneficiaries' suit to recover on the policy. The district court denied the motion to dismiss the equity action and tried it first, ahead of the action at law. The district court found that there had been fraudulent misrepresentations as claimed by American Life and ordered the policy cancelled. The court of appeals reversed, concluding that once the beneficiaries' claim to recover on the policy had been filed, there was an adequate remedy at law, and thus, the equitable action should not have proceeded.

The Supreme Court reversed the court of appeals. Through Justice Cardozo, the Court said that (a) the insurance company's equitable action was justified because of the incontestability provision, and (b) equity would not have "lost" jurisdiction because Stewart later sued to recover on the policy, even though fraudulent misrepresentation would have been a defense to liability in the suit on the policy (the principle being that equity does not lose jurisdiction because a later legal remedy becomes available). The issue of which suit would have priority in terms of sequencing then became discretionary, and, according to *Stewart*, the district court had properly exercised its discretion to try the equity action first and to proceed without a jury.

> The argument is made that the suits in equity should have been dismissed when it appeared upon the trial that after the filing of the bills, * * *, the beneficiaries of the policies had sued on them at law. But the settled rule is that equitable jurisdiction existing at the filing of a bill is not destroyed because an adequate legal remedy may have become available thereafter. * * * A court has control over its own docket. * * * In the exercise of a sound discretion it may hold one lawsuit in abeyance to abide the outcome of another, especially where the parties and the issues are the same. If request had been made by the respondents to suspend the suits in equity till the other causes were disposed of, the District Court could have considered whether justice would not be done by pursuing such a course, the remedy in equity being exceptional and the outcome of necessity. * * * There would be many circumstances to be weighed, as, for instance, the condition of the court calendar, whether the insurer had been precipitate or its adversaries dilatory, as well as other factors. In the end, benefit and hardship would have to be set off, the one against the other, and a balance ascertained. * * *

300 U.S. at 215-26, 57 S.Ct. at 380-81.

With the merger of law and equity, however, legal and equitable actions would not be filed in separate sides of the federal court, but would appear in the same action. Thus, Stewart's claim would have been a counterclaim — see Rule 13(a) — to the action brought by the insurance company, and it would be filed in the same suit. Consider how the fact that historically legal claims would be in the same lawsuit as historically equitable claims should affect the discretion of the court to proceed with the legal or the equitable claim in the first instance. Note that merger issues can come up in many guises, but here are some straightforward examples:

- The plaintiff joins legal and equitable claims. See Rule 18. For example, the plaintiff sues for specific performance of a contract to sell land, and damages caused by the defendant's breach of the contract.

- The plaintiff has a legal (or equitable) claim, and the defendant has an equitable or (legal) defense or counterclaim. This is the fact pattern presented by *Stewart*, albeit post-merger. Or, merger issues could arise on facts such as those in *Stewart* if Stewart sued first on the policy and the insurance company only thereafter sought rescission on the basis of fraud in a counterclaim.

- The plaintiff has a legal claim but uses a procedural mechanism only available in equity. To use a modern example, the plaintiff brings a class action for damages for securities fraud — the claim for securities fraud is a claim at law with a right to jury trial, but class actions could only be brought in equity.

The font of modern jurisprudence in this area is *Beacon Theatres, Inc. v. Westover*, which follows. This is a complex case made even more complex because it arises in the context of a suit for a declaratory judgment. A declaratory judgment is an action by a party for a declaration of rights arising out of a dispute that has not necessarily ripened into a suit for damages. Declaratory judgments were once frowned upon, based partly on concerns over whether a suit seeking no "coercive" relief (i.e., monetary damages or an injunction) satisfied the "case or controversy" requirement of Article III of the Constitution, and based partly on the fear that parties would waste the courts' time getting decisions on matters before disputes had actually arisen or just to satisfy an idle curiosity. Congress sought to overcome those fears by enacting the declaratory judgment statute, 28 U.S.C. §§2201, 2202, in 1934.

To understand *Beacon Theatres*, start with the following warm-up questions. Imagine that two parties are in a dispute over whether one of them is acting in restraint of trade in violation of federal antitrust laws — laws not in existence at the time of the Seventh Amendment's ratification. One of them, Beacon, believes that the other, Fox, has engaged in illegal behavior that has injured Beacon's business, in violation of federal law.

(a) Assume that Beacon sues Fox for damages for violating the antitrust laws. Would Beacon have had a right to a jury trial?

(b) Assume instead that Fox sues Beacon seeking a declaratory judgment that Fox had not violated the antitrust laws. Would Beacon have a right to a jury trial?

(c) Same as "b" except that when Fox sues, Beacon asserts an antitrust counterclaim for damages under Rule 13(a). Would Beacon have had a right to a jury trial?

(d) Assume Fox sues Beacon and seeks an injunction against harassment by Beacon because of its having threatened to sue those who have dealt with Fox and claiming Fox had violated the antitrust laws. Would Beacon have had a right to a jury trial?

(e) Now, you are ready for *Beacon Theatres* itself, which is to some extent a combination of "c" and "d."

Beacon Theatres, Inc. v. Westover

Supreme Court of the United States, 1959.

359 U.S. 500, 79 S.Ct. 948, 3 L.Ed.2d 988.

MR. JUSTICE BLACK delivered the opinion of the Court.

Petitioner, Beacon Theatres, Inc., sought by mandamus to require a district judge in the Southern District of California to vacate certain orders alleged to deprive it of a jury trial of issues arising in a suit brought against it by Fox West Coast Theatres, Inc. The Court of Appeals for the Ninth Circuit refused the writ, holding that the trial judge had acted within his proper discretion in denying petitioner's request for a jury. 252 F.2d 864. We granted certiorari, 356 U.S. 956, because "maintenance of the jury as a fact-finding body is of such importance and occupies so firm a place in our history and jurisprudence that any seeming curtailment of the right to a jury trial should be scrutinized with the utmost care." Dimick v. Schiedt, 293 U.S. 474, 486.

Fox had asked for declaratory relief against Beacon alleging a controversy arising under the Sherman Antitrust Act, 26 Stat. 209, as amended, 15 U.S.C. §1, 2, and under the Clayton Act, 38 Stat. 731, 15 U.S.C. §15, which authorizes suits for treble damages against Sherman Act violators. According to the complaint Fox operates a movie theatre in San Bernardino, California, and has long been exhibiting films under contracts with movie distributors. These contracts grant it the exclusive right to show "first run" pictures in the "San Bernardino competitive area" and provide for "clearance" — a period of time during which no other theatre can exhibit the same pictures. After building a drive-in theatre about 11 miles from San Bernardino, Beacon notified Fox that it considered contracts barring simultaneous exhibitions of first-run films in the two theatres to be overt acts in violation of the antitrust laws. Fox's complaint alleged that this notification, together with threats of treble damage suits against Fox and its distributors, gave rise to "duress and coercion" which deprived Fox of a valuable property right, the right to negotiate for exclusive first-run contracts. Unless Beacon was restrained, the complaint continued, irreparable harm would result. Accordingly, while its pleading was styled a "Complaint for Declaratory Relief," Fox prayed both for a declaration that a grant of clearance between the Fox and Beacon theatres is reasonable and not in violation of the antitrust laws, and for an injunction, pending final resolution of the litigation, to prevent Beacon from instituting any action under the antitrust laws against Fox and its distributors arising out of the controversy alleged in the complaint. Beacon filed an answer, a counterclaim against Fox, and a cross-claim against an exhibitor who had intervened. These denied the threats and asserted that there was no substantial competition between the two theatres, that the clearances granted were therefore unreasonable, and that a conspiracy existed between Fox and its distributors to manipulate contracts and clearances so as to restrain trade and monopolize first-run pictures in violation of the antitrust laws. Treble damages were asked.

Beacon demanded a jury trial of the factual issues in the case as provided by Federal Rule of Civil Procedure 38(b). The District Court, however, viewed the issues raised by the "Complaint for Declaratory Relief," including the question of competition between the two theatres, as essentially equitable. Acting under the purported authority of Rules 42(b) and 57, it directed that these issues be tried to the court before jury determination of the validity of the charges of antitrust violations made in the counterclaim and cross-claim. A common issue of the "Complaint for Declaratory Relief," the counterclaim, and the cross-claim was the reasonableness of the clearances granted to Fox, which depended, in part, on the existence of competition between the two theatres. Thus the effect of the action of the District Court could be, as the Court of Appeals believed, "to limit the petitioner's opportunity fully to try to a jury every issue which has a bearing upon its treble damage suit," for determination of the issue of clearances by the judge might "operate either by way of res judicata or collateral estoppel so as to conclude both parties with respect thereto at the subsequent trial of the treble damage claim."

The District Court's finding that the Complaint for Declaratory Relief presented basically equitable issues draws no support from the Declaratory Judgment Act, 28 U.S.C. §§2201, 2202; Fed. Rules Civ. Proc., 57. See also 48 Stat. 955, 28 U.S.C. (1940 ed.) §400. That statute, while allowing prospective defendants to sue to establish their nonliability, specifically preserves the right to jury trial for both parties. It follows that if Beacon would have been entitled to a jury trial in a treble damage suit against Fox it cannot be deprived of that right merely because Fox took advantage of the availability of declaratory relief to sue Beacon first. Since the right to trial by jury applies to treble damage suits under the antitrust laws, and is, in fact, an essential part of the congressional plan for making competition rather than monopoly the rule of trade, see Fleitmann v. Welsbach Street Lighting Co., 240 U.S. 27, 29, the Sherman and Clayton Act issues on which Fox sought a declaration were essentially jury questions.

Nevertheless the Court of Appeals refused to upset the order of the district judge. It held that the question of whether a right to jury trial existed was to be judged by Fox's complaint read as a whole. In addition to seeking a declaratory judgment, the court said, Fox's complaint can be read as making out a valid plea for injunctive relief, thus stating a claim traditionally cognizable in equity. A party who is entitled to maintain a suit in equity for an injunction, said the court, may have all the issues in his suit determined by the judge without a jury regardless of whether legal rights are involved. The court then rejected the argument that equitable relief, traditionally available only when legal remedies are inadequate, was rendered unnecessary in this case by the filing of the counterclaim and cross-claim which presented all the issues necessary to a determination of the right to injunctive relief. Relying on American Life Ins. Co. v. Stewart, 300 U.S. 203, 215, decided before the enactment of the Federal Rules of Civil Procedure, it invoked the principle that a court sitting in equity could retain jurisdiction even though later a legal remedy became available. In such instances the equity court had discretion to enjoin the later lawsuit in order to allow the whole dispute to be determined in one case in one court. Reasoning by analogy, the Court of Appeals held it was not an abuse of discretion for the district judge, acting under Federal Rule of Civil Procedure 42(b), to try the equitable cause first even though this might, through collateral estoppel, prevent a full jury trial of the counterclaim and cross-claim which were as effectively stopped as by an equity injunction.[6]

Beacon takes issue with the holding of the Court of Appeals that the complaint stated a claim upon which equitable relief could be granted. As initially filed the complaint alleged that threats of lawsuits by petitioner against Fox and its distributors were causing irreparable harm to Fox's business

---

[6] 252 F.2d at 874. In Ettelson v. Metropolitan Life Ins. Co., 317 U.S. 188, 192, this Court recognized that orders enabling equitable causes to be tried before legal ones had the same effect as injunctions. * * *

relationships. The prayer for relief, however, made no mention of the threats but asked only that pending litigation of the claim for declaratory judgment, Beacon be enjoined from beginning any lawsuits under the antitrust laws against Fox and its distributors arising out of the controversy alleged in the complaint. Evidently of the opinion that this prayer did not state a good claim for equitable relief, the Court of Appeals construed it to include a request for an injunction against threats of lawsuits. This liberal construction of a pleading is in line with Rule 8 of the Federal Rules of Civil Procedure. See Conley v. Gibson, 355 U.S. 41, 47-48. But this fact does not solve our problem. Assuming that the pleadings can be construed to support such a request and assuming additionally that the complaint can be read as alleging the kind of harassment by a multiplicity of lawsuits which would traditionally have justified equity to take jurisdiction and settle the case in one suit, we are nevertheless of the opinion that, under the Declaratory Judgment Act and the Federal Rules of Civil Procedure, neither claim can justify denying Beacon a trial by jury of all the issues in the antitrust controversy.

The basis of injunctive relief in the federal courts has always been irreparable harm and inadequacy of legal remedies. At least as much is required to justify a trial court in using its discretion under the Federal Rules to allow claims of equitable origins to be tried ahead of legal ones, since this has the same effect as an equitable injunction of the legal claims. And it is immaterial, in judging if that discretion is properly employed, that before the Federal Rules and the Declaratory Judgment Act were passed, courts of equity, exercising a jurisdiction separate from courts of law, were, in some cases, allowed to enjoin subsequent legal actions between the same parties involving the same controversy. This was because the subsequent legal action, though providing an opportunity to try the case to a jury, might not protect the right of the equity plaintiff to a fair and orderly adjudication of the controversy. See, e.g., New York Life Ins. Co. v. Seymour, 45 F.2d 47. Under such circumstances the legal remedy could quite naturally be deemed inadequate. Inadequacy of remedy and irreparable harm are practical terms, however. As such their existence today must be determined, not by precedents decided under discarded procedures, but in the light of the remedies now made available by the Declaratory Judgment Act and the Federal Rules.

Viewed in this manner, the use of discretion by the trial court under Rule 42(b) to deprive Beacon of a full jury trial on its counterclaim and cross-claim, as well as on Fox's plea for declaratory relief, cannot be justified. Under the Federal Rules the same court may try both legal and equitable causes in the same action. Fed. Rules Civ. Proc., 1, 2, 18. Thus any defenses, equitable or legal, Fox may have to charges of antitrust violations can be raised either in its suit for declaratory relief or in answer to Beacon's counterclaim. On proper showing, harassment by threats of other suits, or other suits actually brought, involving the issues being tried in this case, could be temporarily enjoined pending the outcome of this litigation. Whatever permanent injunctive relief Fox might be entitled to on the basis of the decision in this case could, of course, be given by the court after the jury renders its verdict. In this way the issues between these parties could be settled in one suit giving Beacon a full jury trial of every antitrust issue. By contrast, the holding of the court below while granting Fox no additional protection unless the avoidance of jury trial be considered as such, would compel Beacon to split his antitrust case, trying part to a judge and part to a jury.[10] Such a result, which involves the postponement and subordination of Fox's own legal claim for declaratory relief as well as of the counterclaim which Beacon was compelled by the Federal Rules to bring, is not permissible.

Our decision is consistent with the plan of the Federal Rules and the Declaratory Judgment Act to effect substantial procedural reform while retaining a distinction between jury and nonjury issues and leaving substantive rights unchanged. Since in the federal courts equity has always acted only when legal remedies were inadequate, the expansion of adequate legal remedies provided by the Declaratory Judgment Act and the Federal Rules necessarily affects the scope of equity. Thus, the justification for equity's deciding legal issues once it obtains jurisdiction, and refusing to dismiss a case, merely because subsequently a legal remedy becomes available, must be re-evaluated in the light of the liberal joinder provisions of the Federal Rules which allow legal and equitable causes to be brought and resolved in one civil action. Similarly the need for, and therefore, the availability of such equitable remedies as Bills of Peace, Quia Timet and Injunction must be reconsidered in view of the existence of the Declaratory Judgment Act as well as the liberal joinder provision of the Rules. This is not only in accord with the spirit of the Rules and the Act but is required by the provision in the Rules that "[t]he right to trial by jury as declared by the Seventh Amendment to the Constitution or as given by a statute of the United States shall be preserved . . . inviolate."[16]

If there should be cases where the availability of declaratory judgment or joinder in one suit of legal and equitable causes would not in all respects protect the plaintiff seeking equitable relief from irreparable harm while affording a jury trial in the legal cause, the trial court will necessarily have to use its discretion in deciding whether the legal or equitable cause should be tried first. Since the right to jury trial is a constitutional one, however while no similar requirement protects trials by the court, that discretion is very narrowly limited and must, wherever possible, be exercised to preserve jury trial. As this Court said in Scott v. Neely, 140 U.S. 106, 109-110: "In the Federal courts this [jury] right cannot be dispensed with, except by the assent of the parties entitled to it, nor can it be impaired by any blending with a claim, properly cognizable at law, of a demand for equitable relief in aid of the legal action or during its pendency." This longstanding principle of equity dictates that only under the most imperative circumstances, circumstances which in view of the flexible procedures of the Federal Rules we cannot now anticipate, can the right to a jury trial of legal

---

[10] Since the issue of violation of the antitrust laws often turns on the reasonableness of a restraint on trade in the light of all the facts, see, e.g., Standard Oil Co. v. United States, 221 U.S. 1, 60, it is particularly undesirable to have some of the relevant considerations tried by one fact finder and some by another.

[16] Fed. Rules Civ. Proc. 38(a). In delegating to the Supreme Court responsibility for drawing up rules, Congress declared that: "Such rules shall not abridge, enlarge or modify any substantive right and shall preserve the right of trial by jury as at common law and as declared by the Seventh Amendment to the Constitution." 28 U.S.C. §2072. * * *

issues be lost through prior determination of equitable claims. As we have shown, this is far from being such a case.

* * *

The judgment of the Court of Appeals is *Reversed.*

MR. JUSTICE FRANKFURTER took no part in the consideration or decision of this case.

MR. JUSTICE STEWART, with whom MR. JUSTICE HARLAN and MR. JUSTICE WHITTAKER concur, dissenting.

There can be no doubt that a litigant is entitled to a writ of mandamus to protect a clear constitutional or statutory right to a jury trial. But there was no denial of such a right here. The district judge simply exercised his inherent discretion, now explicitly confirmed by the Federal Rules of Civil Procedure, to schedule the trial of an equitable claim in advance of an action at law.

The complaint filed by Fox stated a claim traditionally cognizable in equity. That claim, in brief, was that Beacon had wrongfully interfered with the right of Fox to compete freely with Beacon and other distributors for the licensing of films for first-run exhibition in the San Bernardino area. The complaint alleged that the plaintiff was without an adequate remedy at law and would be irreparably harmed unless the defendant were restrained from continuing to interfere — by coercion and threats of litigation — with the plaintiff's lawful business relationships.

The Court of Appeals found that the complaint, although inartistically drawn, contained allegations entitling the petitioner to equitable relief. That finding is accepted in the prevailing opinion today. If the complaint had been answered simply by a general denial, therefore, the issues would under traditional principles have been triable as a proceeding in equity. Instead of just putting in issue the allegations of the complaint, however, Beacon filed pleadings which affirmatively alleged the existence of a broad conspiracy among the plaintiff and other theatre owners to monopolize the first-run exhibition of films in the San Bernardino area, to refrain from competing among themselves, and to discriminate against Beacon in granting film licenses. Based upon these allegations, Beacon asked damages in the amount of $300,000. Clearly these conspiracy allegations stated a cause of action triable as of right by a jury. What was demanded by Beacon, however, was a jury trial not only of this cause of action, but also of the issues presented by the original complaint.

Upon motion of Fox the trial judge ordered the original action for declaratory and equitable relief to be tried separately to the court and in advance of the trial of the defendant's counterclaim and cross-claim for damages. The court's order, which carefully preserved the right to trial by jury upon the conspiracy and damage issues raised by the counterclaim and cross-claim, was in conformity with the specific provisions of the Federal Rules of Civil Procedure. Yet it is decided today that the Court of Appeals must compel the district judge to rescind it.

Assuming the existence of a factual issue common both to the plaintiff's original action and the defendant's counterclaim for damages, I cannot agree that the District Court must be compelled to try the counterclaim first. It is, of course, a matter of no great moment in what order the issues between the parties in the present litigation are tried. What is disturbing is the process by which the Court arrives at its decision — a process which appears to disregard the historic relationship between equity and law.

I

The Court suggests that "the expansion of adequate legal remedies provided by the Declaratory Judgment Act . . . necessarily affects the scope of equity." Does the Court mean to say that the mere availability of an action for a declaratory judgment operates to furnish "an adequate remedy at law" so as to deprive a court of equity of the power to act? That novel line of reasoning is at least implied in the Court's opinion. But the Declaratory Judgment Act did not "expand" the substantive law. That Act merely provided a new statutory remedy, neither legal nor equitable, but available in the areas of both equity and law. When declaratory relief is sought, the right to trial by jury depends upon the basic context in which the issues are presented. If the basic issues in an action for declaratory relief are of a kind traditionally cognizable in equity, e.g., a suit for cancellation of a written instrument, the declaratory judgment is not a "remedy at law." If, on the other hand, the issues arise in a context traditionally cognizable at common law, the right to a jury trial of course remains unimpaired, even though the only relief demanded is a declaratory judgment.

Thus, if in this case the complaint had asked merely for a judgment declaring that the plaintiff's specified manner of business dealings with distributors and other exhibitors did not render it liable to Beacon under the antitrust laws, this would have been simply a "juxtaposition of parties" case in which Beacon could have demanded a jury trial.[7] But the complaint in the present case, as the Court recognizes, presented issues of exclusively equitable cognizance, going well beyond a mere defense to any subsequent action at law. Fox sought from the court protection against Beacon's allegedly unlawful interference with its business relationships — protection which this Court seems to recognize might not have been afforded by a declaratory judgment, unsupplemented by equitable relief. The availability of a declaratory judgment did not, therefore, operate to confer upon Beacon the right to trial by jury with respect to the issues raised by the complaint.

II

The Court's opinion does not, of course, hold or even suggest that a court of equity may never determine "legal rights." For indeed it is precisely such rights which the Chancellor, when his jurisdiction has been properly invoked, has often been called upon to decide. Issues of fact are rarely either "legal" or "equitable." All depends upon the context in which they arise. The examples

---

[7] Moore's Federal Practice (2d ed.) ¶57.31 2. "Transposition of parties" would perhaps be a more accurate description. A typical such case is one in which a plaintiff uses the declaratory judgment procedure to seek a determination of nonliability to a legal claim asserted by the defendant. The defendant in such a case is, of course, entitled to a jury trial.

cited by Chief Judge Pope in his thorough opinion in the Court of Appeals in this case are illustrative: ". . . [I]n a suit by one in possession of real property to quiet title, or to remove a cloud on title, the court of equity may determine the legal title. In a suit for specific performance of a contract, the court may determine the making, validity and the terms of the contract involved. In a suit for an injunction against trespass to real property the court may determine the legal right of the plaintiff to the possession of that property."

Though apparently not disputing these principles, the Court holds, quite apart from its reliance upon the Declaratory Judgment Act, that Beacon by filing its counterclaim and cross-claim acquired a right to trial by jury of issues which otherwise would have been properly triable to the court. Support for this position is found in the principle that, "in the federal courts equity has always acted only when legal remedies were inadequate. . . ." Yet that principle is not employed in its traditional sense as a limitation upon the exercise of power by a court of equity. This is apparent in the Court's recognition that the allegations of the complaint entitled Fox to equitable relief — relief to which Fox would not have been entitled if it had had an adequate remedy at law. Instead, the principle is employed today to mean that because it is possible under the counterclaim to have a jury trial of the factual issue of substantial competition, that issue must be tried by a jury, even though the issue was primarily presented in the original claim for equitable relief. This is a marked departure from long-settled principles.

It has been an established rule "that equitable jurisdiction existing at the filing of a bill is not destroyed because an adequate legal remedy may have become available thereafter."[8] American Life Ins. Co. v. Stewart, 300 U.S. 203, 215. See Dawson v. Kentucky Distilleries Co., 255 U.S. 288, 296. It has also been long settled that the District Court in its discretion may order the trial of a suit in equity in advance of an action at law between the same parties, even if there is a factual issue common to both. [The dissent then quoted the language excerpted earlier in this chapter, in *American Life Ins. Co. v. Stewart, supra.*]

III

The Court today sweeps away these basic principles as "precedents decided under discarded procedures." It suggests that the Federal Rules of Civil Procedure have somehow worked an "expansion of adequate legal remedies" so as to oust the District Courts of equitable jurisdiction, as well as to deprive them of their traditional power to control their own dockets. But obviously the Federal Rules could not and did not "expand" the substantive law one whit.

Like the Declaratory Judgment Act, the Federal Rules preserve inviolate the right to trial by jury in actions historically cognizable at common law, as under the Constitution they must. They do not create a right of trial by jury where that right "does not exist under the Constitution or statutes of the United States."

---

[8] The suggestion by the Court that "This was because the subsequent legal action, though providing an opportunity to try the case to a jury, might not protect the right of the equity plaintiff to a fair and orderly adjudication of the controversy" is plainly inconsistent with many of the cases in which the rule has been applied. See, e.g., Beedle v. Bennett, 122 U.S. 71; Clark v. Wooster, 119 U.S. 322.

Rule 39 (a). Since Beacon's counterclaim was compulsory under the Rules, see Rule 13 (a), it is apparent that by filing it Beacon could not be held to have waived its jury rights. Compare American Mills Co. v. American Surety Co., 260 U.S. 360. But neither can the counterclaim be held to have transformed Fox's original complaint into an action at law.[13]

The Rules make possible the trial of legal and equitable claims in the same proceeding, but they expressly affirm the power of a trial judge to determine the order in which claims shall be heard. Rule 42 (b). Certainly the Federal Rules were not intended to undermine the basic structure of equity jurisprudence, developed over the centuries and explicitly recognized in the United States Constitution.

For these reasons I think the petition for a writ of mandamus should have been dismissed.

NOTES AND PROBLEMS FOR DISCUSSION

1. Who is Westover, and what does he have to do with this case?

2. The Court in *Beacon Theatres* does not make altogether clear how declaratory judgments should be treated on the law-equity spectrum. Shouldn't the declaratory judgment usually take on the flavor of the claim that it is anticipating?

3. The Court holds that when factual issues overlap in cases presenting legal and equitable claims, a jury will ordinarily resolve the legal claims first and preclusively (vis-à-vis the equitable claims). Note that this allows a very small slice of the lawsuit potentially to control a very large pie. Under the earlier regime of *American Life Ins. v. Stewart, supra*, considerably greater flexibility was permitted to the district judge. And there clearly was no preclusion problem with the equity court's deciding first (and preclusively), vis-à-vis a factually overlapping action at law. Why, after enactment of the Rules, does the Seventh Amendment prohibit something it didn't prohibit before the Rules?

4. Assume a simple case where plaintiff sues for specific performance of a contract to purchase real property and seeks contractual damages as an alternative remedy. After *Beacon Theatres*, does the plaintiff have a right to jury trial?

5. Prior to *Beacon Theatres*, jury trial issues tended to come up (as in *Stewart*) in disputes over the jurisdiction of a court of equity and questions of possible deference to a pending legal action (and one factor in the analysis might be a right to a jury trial which was allegedly being overridden). But once the court determined that it had jurisdiction, the jury trial issue was perforce decided. The

---

[13] Determination of whether a claim stated by the complaint is triable by the court or by a jury will normally not be dependent upon the "legal" or "equitable" character of the counterclaim. See Borchard, Declaratory Judgments (2d ed.), p. 404. There are situations, however, such as a case in which the plaintiff seeks a declaration of invalidity or noninfringement of a patent, in which the relief sought by the counterclaim will determine the nature of the entire case. See Moore's Federal Practice (2d ed.) ¶38.29.

essence of *Beacon Theatres* is to move from an historical test to something else, without being entirely clear on what that something else is.

6. Two years after *Beacon Theatres*, the Court considered DAIRY QUEEN, INC. v. WOOD, 369 U.S. 469, 82 S.Ct. 894, 8 L.Ed.2d 44 (1962), a case arising from a dispute between a franchisor and a franchisee. The franchisor and owner of the "Dairy Queen" trademark, claimed that the franchise had terminated and sought an injunction prohibiting the franchisee's use of its trademark and prohibiting collection from other Dairy Queen stores in the relevant territory. The franchisor also sought an accounting for past profits (under the franchise agreement, the franchisee was to pay certain amounts which the franchisor claimed had not been properly calculated and paid). The franchisee demanded a jury trial, which was denied by the district court on the ground that the issues were solely equitable or, alternatively, the legal issues were incidental. The Court of Appeals affirmed. The Supreme Court reversed, and strongly reaffirmed the principles of *Beacon Theatres*:

> The most natural construction of the respondents' claim for a money judgment would seem to be that it is a claim that they are entitled to recover whatever was owed them under the contract as of the date of its purported termination plus damages for infringement of their trademark since that date. Alternatively, the complaint could be construed to set forth a full claim based upon both of these theories — that is, a claim that the respondents were entitled to recover both the debt due under the contract and damages for trademark infringement for the entire period of the alleged breach including that before the termination of the contract. Or it might possibly be construed to set forth a claim for recovery based completely on either one of these two theories — that is, a claim based solely upon the contract for the entire period both before and after the attempted termination on the theory that the termination, having been ignored, was of no consequence, or a claim based solely upon the charge of infringement on the theory that the contract, having been breached, could not be used as a defense to an infringement action even for the period prior to its termination. We find it unnecessary to resolve this ambiguity in the respondents' complaint because we think it plain that their claim for a money judgment is a claim wholly legal in its nature however the complaint is construed. As an action on a debt allegedly due under a contract, it would be difficult to conceive of an action of a more traditional legal character. And as an action for damages based upon a charge of trademark infringement it would be no less subject to cognizance by a court of law.
>
> The respondents' contention that this money claim is "purely equitable" is based primarily upon the fact that their complaint is cast in terms of an "accounting," rather than in terms of an action for "debt" or "damages." But the constitutional right to trial by jury cannot be made to depend upon the choice of words used in the pleadings. The necessary prerequisite to the right to maintain a suit for an equitable accounting, like all other equitable remedies, is, as we pointed out in *Beacon Theatres,* the absence of an adequate remedy at law.

Consequently, in order to maintain such a suit on a cause of action cognizable at law, as this one is, the plaintiff must be able to show that "accounts between the parties" are of such a "complicated nature" that only a court of equity can satisfactorily unravel them. In view of the powers given to District Courts by Federal Rule of Civil Procedure 53(b) to appoint masters to assist the jury in those exceptional cases where the legal issues are too complicated for the jury adequately to handle alone, the burden of such a showing is considerably increased and it will indeed be a rare case in which it can be met. Be that as it may, this is certainly not such a case. A jury, under proper instructions from the court, could readily determine the recovery, if any, to be had here, whether the theory finally settled upon is that of breach of contract, that of trademark infringement, or any combination of the two. The legal remedy cannot be characterized as inadequate merely because the measure of damages may necessitate a look into petitioner's business records.

Nor is the legal claim here rendered "purely equitable" by the nature of the defenses interposed by petitioner. Petitioner's primary defense to the charge of breach of contract — that is, that the contract was modified by a subsequent oral agreement — presents a purely legal question having nothing whatever to do either with novation, as the district judge suggested, or reformation, as suggested by the respondents here. Such a defense goes to the question of just what, under the law, the contract between the respondents and petitioner is and, in an action to collect a debt for breach of a contract between these parties, petitioner has a right to have the jury determine not only whether the contract has been breached and the extent of the damages if any but also just what the contract is.

369 U.S. at 470, 82 S.Ct. at 896. In reaching its decision, *Dairy Queen* gave short shrift to the traditional "clean-up" doctrine pursuant to which equity courts were allowed to resolve "incidental" issues of damages — issues that were ancillary to what was, at bottom, a largely equitable dispute. Some states, however, still adhere to the older practice. Does the logic of *Beacon Theatres* compel the demise in federal court of the clean up doctrine in cases like *Dairy Queen*?

7. A variation of the *Beacon Theatres* problem arises in situations where, for historical reasons, the plaintiff brings a type of action that can only be brought in equity regardless of the nature of the underlying claim. In ROSS v. BERNHARD, 396 U.S. 531, 90 S.Ct. 733, 24 L.Ed.2d 729 (1970), the plaintiff brought a stockholders' derivative suit against various officers and directors of Lehman Corporation, an investment company, and the corporation's brokers, Lehman Brothers, claiming various breaches of duty. A stockholders' derivative suit is an action brought on behalf of the corporation, and is based on the assumption that corporate wrongdoers cannot be expected to sue themselves. Historically, such suits could be brought only in a court of equity. See Rule 23.1. Plaintiff's demand for a jury trial under Rule 38 was denied by the lower courts, but reversed by the Supreme Court. According to the Court, a derivative suit had two components: the question of the plaintiff's right to sue (which was equitable and decided by the judge), and the underlying claim (which might be legal or equitable). Here, the claim for conversion of corporate assets and gross abuse of trust and other misconduct was considered by the Court to be legal. Thus, the case involved a combination of legal and equitable issues and, under *Beacon Theatres*, a jury trial was required.

> [L]egal claims are not magically converted into equitable issues by their presentation to a court of equity in a derivative suit. The claim pressed by the stockholder against directors or third parties "is not his own but the corporation's." Koster v. Lumbermens Mut. Cas. Co., 330 U.S. 518, 522 (1947). The corporation is a necessary party to the action; without it the case cannot proceed. Although named a defendant, it is the real party in interest, the stockholder being at best the nominal plaintiff. The proceeds of the action belong to the corporation and it is bound by the result of the suit. The heart of the action is the corporate claim. If it presents a legal issue, one entitling the corporation to a jury trial under the Seventh Amendment, the right to a jury is not forfeited merely because the stockholder's right to sue must first be adjudicated as an equitable issue triable to the court. *Beacon* and *Dairy Queen* require no less.
>
> In the instant case we have no doubt that the corporation's claim is, at least in part, a legal one. The relief sought is money damages. There are allegations in the complaint of a breach of fiduciary duty, but there are also allegations of ordinary breach of contract and gross negligence. The corporation, had it sued on its own behalf, would have been entitled to a jury's determination, at a minimum, of its damages against its broker under the brokerage contract and of its rights against its own directors because of their negligence. Under these circumstances it is unnecessary to decide whether the corporation's other claims are also properly triable to a jury. *Dairy Queen*[.]

The Court added a somewhat perplexing footnote, the third part of which has largely ignored since, that the "'legal' nature of an issue is determined by considering, first, the pre-merger custom with reference to such questions; second, the remedy sought; and third, the practical abilities and limitations of juries." *Bernhard*, 396 U.S. at 538 n.10.

2. NEW STATUTORY RIGHTS

In 1791, and for a long time thereafter, most civil lawsuits were based on common law rights — e.g., causes of action developed by judges at common law. The historical test of the Seventh Amendment was fairly easy to apply to such common law actions. And it still is with respect to present-day lawsuits based on familiar common-law causes of action.

Beginning in the late Nineteenth Century, and continuing on an accelerating basis through the Twentieth Century, Congress and state legislatures passed numerous statutes which either provide for or have been interpreted to provide for private rights of action by aggrieved parties. Examples include well known laws regarding such things as environmental pollution, labor law, discrimination in employment, antitrust, housing, rights to public benefits, and securities regulation. Questions soon arose whether there was a right to a jury trial in actions brought under such statutes. Sometimes the answer was easy because the statute itself either provided for a jury trial or was interpreted to provide for jury trial. But other times it wasn't so easy, and the matter was left to the courts.

For example, in CURTIS v. LOETHER, 415 U.S. 189, 94 S.Ct. 1005, 39 L.Ed.2d 260 (1974), the Court found a right to jury trial in an action for damages under a federal statute forbidding racial discrimination in housing on the ground that "the statute sounds basically in tort — the statute merely defines a new legal duty, and authorizes the courts to compensate a plaintiff for the injury caused by the defendant's breach. As the Court of Appeals noted, this cause of action is analogous to a number of tort actions recognized at common law. More important, the relief sought here — actual and punitive damages — is the traditional form of relief offered in the courts of law." 415 U.S. at 195-96. In a somewhat unusual twist, it was the defendant landlord who demanded a jury trial, and the plaintiff — an African-American woman — had argued that to permit jury trials could permit local juries to undermine the statutory remedy. The Court rejected such arguments on the basis of the "clear command" of the Seventh Amendment.

Later cases tended to discuss the right to jury trial in terms of the two factors referred to in *Curtis* — analogizing the action to a common law action, and looking at the remedy provided by the statute. The case below tries to deal with these factors in a labor law setting. Note, however, that unless one of the parties demands a jury trial under Rule 38, and does so in a timely manner, there won't be one.

Chauffeurs, Teamsters & Helpers Local No. 391 v. Terry

Supreme Court of the United States, 1990.

494 U.S. 558, 110 S.Ct. 1339, 108 L.Ed.2d 519.

JUSTICE MARSHALL delivered the opinion of the Court except as to III-A.

This case presents the question whether an employee who seeks relief in the form of backpay for a union's alleged breach of its duty of fair representation has a right to trial by jury. We hold that the Seventh Amendment entitles such a plaintiff to a jury trial.

I

McLean Trucking Company and the Chauffeurs, Teamsters, and Helpers Local Union No. 391 were parties to a collective-bargaining agreement that governed the terms and conditions of employment at McLean's terminals. The 27 respondents were employed by McLean as truckdrivers in bargaining units covered by the agreement, and all were members of the Union. In 1982 McLean implemented a change in operations that resulted in the elimination of some of its terminals and the reorganization of others. As part of that change, McLean transferred respondents to the terminal located in Winston-Salem and agreed to give them special seniority rights in relation to "inactive" employees in Winston-Salem who had been laid off temporarily.

[Respondents were then laid off and later called back to work several times at Winston-Salem. As a consequence, their seniority rights were adversely affected, and they filed a grievance with their Union which the Union pursued on their behalf. The grievance committee ordered McLean to change its practices. After the respondents' seniority rights were impaired on later occasions, additional grievances were filed. On the third such occasion, the Union refused to pursue the grievance asserting that the prior grievances had resolved the issues.]

In July 1983, respondents filed an action in District Court, alleging that McLean had breached the collective-bargaining agreement in violation of §301 of the Labor Management Relations Act, 1947, and that the Union had violated its duty of fair representation. Respondents requested a permanent injunction requiring the defendants to cease their illegal acts and to reinstate them to their proper seniority status; in addition, they sought, *inter alia,* compensatory damages for lost wages and health benefits. In 1986 McLean filed for bankruptcy; subsequently, the action against it was voluntarily dismissed, along with all claims for injunctive relief.

Respondents had requested a jury trial in their pleadings. The Union moved to strike the jury demand on the ground that no right to a jury trial exists in a duty of fair representation suit. The District Court denied the motion to strike. After an interlocutory appeal, the Fourth Circuit affirmed the trial court, holding that the Seventh Amendment entitled respondents to a jury trial of their claim for monetary relief. We granted the petition for certiorari * * *.

II

The duty of fair representation is inferred from unions' exclusive authority under the National Labor Relations Act, to represent all employees in a bargaining unit. The duty requires a union "to serve the interests of all members without hostility or discrimination toward any, to exercise its discretion with complete good faith and honesty, and to avoid arbitrary conduct." A union must discharge its duty both in bargaining with the employer and in its enforcement of the resulting collective bargaining agreement. Thus, the Union here was required to pursue respondents' grievances in a manner consistent with the principles of fair representation.

Because most collective-bargaining agreements accord finality to grievance or arbitration procedures established by the collective-bargaining agreement, an employee normally cannot bring a §301 action against an employer unless he can show that the union breached its duty of fair representation in its handling of his grievance. Whether the employee sues both the labor union and the employer or only one of those entities, he must prove the same two facts to recover money damages: that the employer's action violated the terms of the collective-bargaining agreement and that the union breached its duty of fair representation.

III

We turn now to the constitutional issue presented in this case — whether respondents are entitled to a jury trial.

To determine whether a particular action will resolve legal rights, we examine both the nature of the issues involved and the remedy sought. "First, we compare the statutory action to 18th-century actions brought in the courts of England prior to the merger of the courts of law and equity. Second, we examine the remedy sought and determine whether it is legal or equitable in nature." Tull v. United States, 481 U.S. 412, 107 S.Ct. 1831, 95 L.Ed.2d 365 (1987). The second inquiry is the more important in our analysis. Granfinanciera, SA. v. Nordberg, 492 U.S. 33, 109 S.Ct. 2782, 106 L.Ed.2d 26 (1989).[4]

A

An action for breach of a union's duty of fair representation was unknown in 18th-century England; in fact, collective-bargaining was unlawful. We must therefore look for an analogous cause of action that existed in the 18th century to determine whether the nature of this duty of fair representation suit is legal or equitable.

The Union contends that this duty of fair representation action resembles a suit brought to vacate an arbitration award because respondents seek to set aside the result of the grievance process. In the 18th Century, an action to set aside an arbitration award was considered equitable. * * *

The arbitration analogy is inapposite, however, to the Seventh Amendment question posed in this case. No grievance committee has considered respondents' claim that the Union violated its duty of fair representation; the grievance process was concerned only with the employer's alleged breach of the collective-bargaining agreement. Thus, respondents' claim against the Union cannot be characterized as an action to vacate an arbitration award * * *.

The Union next argues that respondents' duty of fair representation action is comparable to an action by a trust beneficiary against a trustee for breach of fiduciary duty. Such actions were within the exclusive jurisdiction of courts of equity. This analogy is far more persuasive than the arbitration analogy. Just as a trustee must act in the best interests of the beneficiaries, a union, as the exclusive representative of the workers, must exercise its power to act on behalf of the employees in good faith. Moreover, just as a beneficiary does not directly control the actions of a trustee, an individual employee lacks direct control over a union's actions taken on his behalf.

The trust analogy extends to a union's handling of grievances. In most cases, a trustee has the exclusive authority to sue third parties who injure the beneficiaries' interest in the trust, including any legal claim the trustee holds in trust for the beneficiaries. The trustee then has the sole responsibility for

---

[4] Justice Stevens' analysis emphasizes a third consideration, namely whether "the issues [presented by the claim] are typical grist for the jury's judgment." This Court, however, has never relied on this consideration "as an independent basis for extending the right to a jury trial under the Seventh Amendment." *Tull.* * * *

determining whether to settle, arbitrate, or otherwise dispose of the claim. Similarly, the union typically has broad discretion in its decision whether and how to pursue an employee's grievance against an employer. Just as a trust beneficiary can sue to enforce a contract entered into on his behalf by the trustee only if the trustee "improperly refuses or neglects to bring an action against the third person," Restatement (Second) of Trusts, §282(2), so an employee can sue his employer for a breach of the collective-bargaining agreement only if he shows that the union breached its duty of fair representation in its handling of the grievance.

Respondents contend that their duty of fair representation suit is less like a trust action than an attorney malpractice action which was historically an action at law. * * * We find that, in the context of the Seventh Amendment inquiry, the attorney malpractice analogy does not capture the relationship between the union and the represented employees as fully as the trust analogy does.

The attorney malpractice analogy is inadequate in several respects. Although an attorney malpractice suit is in some ways similar to a suit alleging a union's breach of its fiduciary duty, the two actions are fundamentally different. The nature of an action is in large part controlled by the nature of the underlying relationship between the parties. Unlike employees represented by a union, a client controls the significant decisions concerning his representation. Moreover, a client can fire his attorney if he is dissatisfied with his attorney's performance. This option is not available to an individual employee who is unhappy with a union's representation, unless a majority of the members of the bargaining unit share his dissatisfaction. Thus, we find the malpractice analogy less convincing than the trust analogy.

Nevertheless, the trust analogy does not persuade us to characterize respondents' claim as wholly equitable. The Union's argument mischaracterizes the nature of our comparison of the action before us to 18th-century forms of action. As we observed in Ross v. Bernhard, "The Seventh Amendment question depends on the nature of the *issue* to be tried rather than the character of the overall action." * * * [T]o recover from the Union here, respondents must prove both that McLean violated §301 by breaching the collective-bargaining agreement and that the Union breached its duty of fair representation.[6] When viewed in isolation, the duty of fair representation issue is analogous to a claim against a trustee for breach of fiduciary duty. The §301 issue, however, is comparable to a breach of contract claim — a legal issue.

Respondents' action against the Union thus encompasses both equitable and legal issues. The first part of our Seventh Amendment inquiry, then, leaves us in equipoise as to whether respondents are entitled to a jury trial.

---

[6] The dissent characterizes this opinion as "pars[ing] legal elements out of equitable claims." The question whether the Seventh Amendment analysis requires an examination of the nature of each element of a typical claim is not presented by this case. The claim we confront here is not typical; instead, it is a claim consisting of discrete issues that would normally be brought as two claims, one against the employer and one against the union. * * *

B

Our determination under the first part of the Seventh Amendment analysis is only preliminary. In this case, the only remedy sought is a request for compensatory damages representing backpay and benefits. Generally, an action for money damages was "the traditional form of relief offered in the courts of law." Curtis v. Loether, 415 U.S. 189, 196 (1974). This Court has not, however, held that "any award of monetary relief must *necessarily* be 'legal' relief." *Ibid.* (emphasis added). Nonetheless, because we conclude that the remedy respondents seek has none of the attributes that must be present before we will find an exception to the general rule and characterize damages as equitable, we find that the remedy sought by respondents is legal.

First, we have characterized damages as equitable where they are restitutionary, such as in "action[s] for disgorgement of improper profits," *Tull* [*supra*]. The backpay sought by respondents is not money wrongfully held by the Union, but wages and benefits they would have received from McLean had the Union processed the employees' grievances properly. Such relief is not restitutionary.

Second, a monetary award "incidental to or intertwined with injunctive relief" may be equitable. *Tull, supra*, 481 U.S., at 424. Because respondents seek only money damages, this characteristic is clearly absent from the case.[8]

The Union argues that the backpay relief sought here must nonetheless be considered equitable because this Court has labeled backpay awarded under Title VII, 42 U.S.C. §2000e et seq. (1982 ed.), as equitable. * * *

The Court has never held that a plaintiff seeking backpay under Title VII has a right to a jury trial. Assuming, without deciding, that such a Title VII plaintiff has no right to a jury trial, the Union's argument does not persuade us that respondents are not entitled to a jury trial here. Congress specifically characterized backpay under Title VII as a form of "equitable relief." 42 U.S.C. §2000e-5(g) (1982 ed.) * * *. See also Curtis v. Loether (distinguishing backpay under Title VII from damages under Title VIII, the fair housing provision of the Civil Rights Act, which the Court characterized as "legal" for Seventh Amendment purposes). Congress made no similar pronouncement regarding the duty of fair representation. Furthermore, the Court has noted that backpay sought from an employer under Title VII would generally be restitutionary in

---

[8] Both the Union and the dissent argue that the backpay award sought here is equitable because it is closely analogous to damages awarded to beneficiaries for a trustee's breach of trust. Such damages were available only in courts of equity because those courts had exclusive jurisdiction over actions involving a trustee's breach of his fiduciary duties.

The Union's argument, however, conflates the two parts of our Seventh Amendment inquiry. Under the dissent's approach, if the action at issue were analogous to an 18th-century action within the exclusive jurisdiction of the courts of equity, we would necessarily conclude that the remedy sought was also equitable because it would have been unavailable in a court of law. This view would, in effect, make the first part of our inquiry dispositive. We have clearly held, however, that the second part of the inquiry — the nature of the relief — is more important to the Seventh Amendment determination. The second part of the analysis, therefore, should not replicate the "abstruse historical" inquiry of the first part, *Ross*, 396 U.S., at 538, n.10, but requires consideration of the general types of relief provided by courts of law and equity.

nature, in contrast to the damages sought here from the Union. Thus, the remedy sought in this duty of fair representation case is clearly different from backpay sought for violations of Title VII.

* * *

We hold, then, that the remedy of backpay sought in this duty of fair representation action is legal in nature. Considering both parts of the Seventh Amendment inquiry, we find that respondents are entitled to a jury trial on all issues presented in their suit.

[Affirmed.]

JUSTICE BRENNAN, concurring in part and concurring in the judgment.

I agree with the Court that respondents seek a remedy that is legal in nature and that the Seventh Amendment entitles respondents to a jury trial on their duty of fair representation claims. I therefore join Parts I, II, III-B, and IV of the Court's opinion. I do not join that part of the opinion which reprises the particular historical analysis this Court has employed to determine whether a claim is a "Suit at common law" under the Seventh Amendment, because I believe the historical test can and should be simplified.

The current test, first expounded in *Curtis v. Loether,* requires a court to compare the right at issue to 18th-century English forms of action to determine whether the historically analogous right was vindicated in an action at law or in equity, and to examine whether the remedy sought is legal or equitable in nature. However, this Court, in expounding the test, has repeatedly discounted the significance of the analogous form of action for deciding where the Seventh Amendment applies. I think it is time we dispense with it altogether.[1] I would decide Seventh Amendment questions on the basis of the relief sought. If the relief is legal in nature, i.e., if it is the kind of relief that historically was available from courts of law, I would hold that the parties have a constitutional right to a trial by jury — unless Congress has permissibly delegated the particular dispute to a non-Article III decisionmaker and jury trials would frustrate Congress' purposes in enacting a particular statutory scheme.

I believe that our insistence that the jury trial right hinges in part on a comparison of the substantive right at issue to forms of action used in English courts 200 years ago needlessly convolutes our Seventh Amendment jurisprudence. For the past decade and a half, this Court has explained that the two parts of the historical test are not equal in weight, that the nature of the remedy is more important than the nature of the right. Since the existence of a right to jury trial therefore turns on the nature of the remedy, absent congressional delegation to a specialized decisionmaker, there remains little purpose to our rattling through dusty attics of ancient writs. The time has come to borrow William of Occam's razor and sever this portion of our analysis.

We have long acknowledged that, of the factors relevant to the jury trial right, comparison of the claim to ancient forms of action, "requiring extensive

---

[1] I therefore also do not join Part III-A of the Court opinion because it considers which 18th-century actions are comparable to the modern-day statutory claim brought here.

and possibly abstruse historical inquiry, is obviously the most difficult to apply." Ross v. Bernhard, 396 U.S. 531, 538, n. 10 (1970). Requiring judges, with neither the training nor time necessary for reputable historical scholarship, to root through the tangle of primary and secondary sources to determine which of a hundred or so writs is analogous to the right at issue has embroiled courts in recondite controversies better left to legal historians. * * *

* * *

To rest the historical test required by the Seventh Amendment solely on the nature of the relief sought would not, of course, offer the federal courts a rule that is in all cases self-executing. Courts will still be required to ask which remedies were traditionally available at law and which only in equity. But this inquiry involves fewer variables and simpler choices, on the whole, and is far more manageable than the scholasticist debates in which we have been engaged. Moreover, the rule I propose would remain true to the Seventh Amendment, as it is undisputed that, historically, "[j]urisdictional lines [between law and equity] were primarily a matter of remedy." McCoid, Procedural Reform and the Right to Jury Trial: A Study of Beacon Theatres, Inc. v. Westover, 116 U.Pa.L.Rev. 1 (1967). * * * [7]

This is not to say that the resulting division between claims entitled to jury trials and claims not so entitled would exactly mirror the division between law and equity in England in 1791. But it is too late in the day for this Court to profess that the Seventh Amendment preserves the right to jury trial only in cases that would have been heard in the British law courts of the 18th century.

Indeed, given this Court's repeated insistence that the nature of the remedy is always to be given more weight than the nature of the historically analogous right, it is unlikely that the simplified Seventh Amendment analysis I propose will result in different decisions than the analysis in current use. In the unusual circumstance that the nature of the remedy could be characterized equally as legal or equitable, I submit that the comparison of a contemporary statutory action unheard of in the 18th century to some ill-fitting ancient writ is too shaky a basis for the resolution of an issue as significant as the availability of a trial by jury. If, in the rare case, a tie-breaker is needed, let us break the tie in favor of jury trial.

---

[7] There are, to be sure, some who advocate abolishing the historical test altogether. See, e.g., Wolfram, The Constitutional History of the Seventh Amendment, 57 Minn.L.Rev. 639, 742-747 (1973). Contrary to the intimations in JUSTICE KENNEDY's dissent, I am not among them. I believe that it is imperative to retain a historical test, for determining when parties have a right to jury trial, for precisely the same reasons JUSTICE KENNEDY, does. It is mandated by the language of the Seventh Amendment and it is a bulwark against those who would restrict a right our forefathers held indispensable. Like JUSTICE KENNEDY, I have no doubt that courts can and do look to legal history for the answers to constitutional questions, and therefore the Seventh Amendment test I propose today obligates courts to do exactly that.

Where JUSTICE KENNEDY and I differ is in our evaluations of which historical test provides the more reliable results. My concern is that all too often the first prong of the current test requires courts to measure modern statutory actions against 18th-century English actions so remote in form and concept that there is no firm basis for comparison. * * * Thus, the historical test I propose, focusing on the nature of the relief sought, is not only more manageable than the current test, it is more reliably grounded in history.

JUSTICE STEVENS, concurring in part and concurring in the judgment.

* * *

As I have suggested in the past, I believe the duty of fair representation action resembles a common law action against an attorney for malpractice more closely than it does any other form of action. Of course, this action is not an exact counterpart to a malpractice suit. Indeed, by definition, no recently recognized form of action — whether the product of express congressional enactment or of judicial interpretation — can have a precise analogue in 17th or 18th century English law. Were it otherwise the form of action would not in fact be "recently recognized."

But the Court surely overstates this action's similarity to an action against a trustee. Collective bargaining involves no settlor, no trust corpus, and no trust instrument executed to convey property to beneficiaries chosen at the settlor's pleasure. * * *[2]

* * *

In my view, the evolution of this doctrine through suits tried to juries, the useful analogy to common-law malpractice cases, and the well-recognized duty to scrutinize any proposed curtailment of the right to a jury trial "with the utmost care," provide a plainly sufficient basis for the Court's holding today. I therefore join its judgment and all of its opinion except for Part III-A.

JUSTICE KENNEDY, with whom JUSTICE O'CONNOR and JUSTICE SCALIA join, dissenting.

This case asks whether the Seventh Amendment guarantees the respondent union members a jury trial in a duty of fair representation action against their labor union. The Court is quite correct, in my view, in its formulation of the initial premises that must govern the case. Under *Curtis v. Loether*, the right to a jury trial in a statutory action depends on the presence of "legal rights and remedies." To determine whether rights and remedies in a duty of fair representation action are legal in character, we must compare the action to the 18th-century cases permitted in the law courts of England, and we must examine the nature of the relief sought. I agree also with those Members of the Court who find that the duty of fair representation action resembles an equitable trust action more than a suit for malpractice.

I disagree with the analytic innovation of the Court that identification of the trust action as a model for modern duty of fair representation actions is insufficient to decide the case. The Seventh Amendment requires us to determine whether the duty of fair representation action "is more similar to cases that were tried in courts of law than to suits tried in courts of equity." *Tull* [*supra*]. Having made this decision in favor of an equitable action, our inquiry should end. Because the Court disagrees with this proposition, I dissent.

---

[2] Indeed, to make sense of the trust analogy, the majority must apparently be willing to assume that the union members, considered collectively, are both beneficiary and settlor, and that the settlor retains considerable power over the corpus, including the power to revoke the trust. That is an odd sort of trust.

* * *

II

The Court relies on two lines of precedents to overcome the conclusion that the trust action should serve as the controlling model. The first consists of cases in which the Court has considered simplifications in litigation resulting from modern procedural reforms in the federal courts. Justice Marshall asserts that these cases show that the Court must look at the character of individual issues rather than claims as a whole. The second line addresses the significance of the remedy in determining the equitable or legal nature of an action for the purpose of choosing the most appropriate analogy. Under these cases, the Court decides that the respondents have a right to a jury because they seek money damages. These authorities do not support the Court's holding.

A

In three cases [*Beacon Theatres, Dairy Queen,* and *Ross*] we have found a right to trial by jury where there are legal claims that, for procedural reasons, a plaintiff could have or must have raised in the courts of equity before the systems merged. * * *

These three cases responded to the difficulties created by a merged court system. They stand for the proposition that, because distinct courts of equity no longer exist, the possibility or necessity of using former equitable procedures to press a legal claim no longer will determine the right to a jury. Justice Marshall reads these cases to require a jury trial whenever a cause of action contains legal issues and would require a jury trial in this case because the respondents must prove a breach of the collective-bargaining agreement as one element of their claim.

I disagree. The respondents, as shown above, are asserting an equitable claim. Having reached this conclusion, the *Beacon, Dairy Queen,* and *Ross* cases are inapplicable. Although we have divided self-standing legal claims from equitable declaratory, accounting, and derivative procedures, we have never parsed legal elements out of equitable claims absent specific procedural justifications. Actions which, beyond all question, are equitable in nature may involve some predicate inquiry that would be submitted to a jury in other contexts. For example, just as the plaintiff in a duty of fair representation action against his union must show breach of the collective-bargaining agreement as an initial matter, in an action against a trustee for failing to pursue a claim the beneficiary must show that the claim had some merit. But the question of the claim's validity, even if the claim raises contract issues, would not bring the jury right into play in a suit against a trustee.

Our own writing confirms the consistency of this view with respect to the action before us. We have not deemed the elements of a duty of fair representation action to be independent of each other. Proving breach of the collective-bargaining agreement is but a preliminary and indispensable step to obtaining relief in a duty of fair representation action. * * * The absence of distinct equitable courts provides no procedural reason for wresting one of these elements from the other.

B

The Court also rules that, despite the appropriateness of the trust analogy as a whole, the respondents have a right to a jury trial because they seek money damages. The nature of the remedy remains a factor of considerable importance in determining whether a statutory action had a legal or equitable analog in 1791, but we have not adopted a rule that a statutory action permitting damages is by definition more analogous to a legal action than to any equitable suit. In each case, we look to the remedy to determine whether, taken with other factors, it places an action within the definition of "suits at common law."

In *Curtis,* for example, we ruled that the availability of actual and punitive damages made a statutory anti-discrimination action resemble a legal tort action more than any equitable action. We made explicit that we did not "go so far as to say that any award of monetary relief must necessarily be 'legal' relief." Although monetary damages might cause some statutory actions to resemble tort suits, the presence of monetary damages in this duty of fair representation action does not make it more analogous to a legal action than to an equitable action. Indeed, as shown above, the injunctive and monetary remedies available make the duty of fair representation suit less analogous to a malpractice action than to a suit against a trustee. * * *

III

The Court must adhere to the historical test in determining the right to a jury because the language of the Constitution requires it. The Seventh Amendment "preserves" the right to jury trial in civil cases. We cannot preserve a right existing in 1791 unless we look to history to identify it. Our precedents are in full agreement with this reasoning and insist on adherence to the historical test. No alternatives short of rewriting the Constitution exist. * * * If we abandon the plain language of the Constitution to expand the jury right, we may expect Courts with opposing views to curtail it in the future.

It is true that a historical inquiry into the distinction between law and equity may require us to enter into a domain becoming less familiar with time. Two centuries have passed since the Seventh Amendment's ratification and the incompleteness of our historical records makes it difficult to know the nature of certain actions in 1791. The historical test, nonetheless, has received more criticism than it deserves. Although our application of the analysis in some cases may seem biased in favor of jury trials, the test has not become a nullity. We do not require juries in all statutory actions. * * *

I would hesitate to abandon or curtail the historical test out of concern for the competence of the Court to understand legal history. We do look to history for the answers to constitutional questions. Although opinions will differ on what this history shows, the approach has no less validity in the Seventh Amendment context than elsewhere. * * *

NOTES AND PROBLEMS FOR DISCUSSION

1. Terry perceives an advantage in having a jury trial while the Union perceives a disadvantage. Why?

2. After *Terry*, if what looks like a "legal" remedy — such as compensatory damages — will be considered the "more important" factor in the jury trial analysis (and will readily trump the characterization of a claim seemingly analogous to one tried by the courts of equity in 1791), what is the function of the historical inquiry with respect to discovering an analogous eighteenth century cause of action?

3. Consider how helpful it is to subdivide the underlying claim in *Terry* and to call breach of contract a "legal" issue. There is scarcely any traditionally equitable claim in which a legal issue of this kind does not lurk. For example, in a classic equitable action involving specific performance of a contract, there lurks the "legal" question (per *Terry*) of breach. Does this mean that this most ancient of equitable actions should be recast as one at law, because the "legal" issue of breach of contract may have to be tried? If not, what is the argument for distinguishing a case like *Terry*?

4. At the time of *Terry*, Title VII of the Civil Rights Act of 1964, which forbids discrimination in employment, had no provision for compensatory or punitive damages as a remedy. The statute provided that "[T]he court may order such affirmative action as may be appropriate, which may include, but is not limited to, reinstatement or hiring of employees, with or without back pay . . . , or any other equitable relief as the court deems appropriate." On several occasions, the Supreme Court declined to decide whether there was a constitutional right to jury trial in back pay actions under Title VII. Lower courts had generally given a negative answer, however, based largely on the language in the statute governing available remedies. See, e.g., Keller v. Prince George's County, 827 F.2d 952 (4th Cir. 1987); Johnson v. Georgia Highway Express, Inc., 417 F.2d 1122 (5th Cir. 1969). Was there a contrary argument to be made? Should statutory language characterizing a particular remedy as equitable be relevant (or controlling) on the Seventh Amendment question? Note that under §102 of the Civil Rights Act of 1991, Title VII now includes provisions, with limits, for compensatory and punitive damages as well as a trial by jury when such damages are sought. But it says nothing about jury trials when only back pay is sought.

5. There are a number of other Supreme Court decisions deciding whether there is a right to jury trial under various federal statutes. For example, in TULL v. UNITED STATES, 481 U.S. 412, 107 S.Ct. 1831, 95 L.Ed.2d 365 (1987), the federal government brought proceedings against Tull for violation of the Clean Water Act, 33 U.S.C. §§1311; 1344; 1362. The government sought a civil penalty for each day that Tull had violated the Act and an injunction to cease the violation. The lower courts rejected Tull's demand for a jury trial and upheld a hefty fine. In the Supreme Court, Tull argued that the suit for a civil penalty was a "species of an action in debt that was within the jurisdiction of the courts of law" while the U.S. argued that "the closer historical analogue is an action to abate a public nuisance." The Court stated:

> Whether, as the Government argues, a public nuisance action is a better analogy than an action in debt is debatable. But we need not decide the question. * * * It suffices that we conclude that both the public nuisance action and the action in debt are appropriate analogies to

the instant statutory action. * * *

We reiterate our previously expressed view that characterizing the relief sought is "[m]ore important" than finding a precisely analogous common law cause of action in determining whether the Seventh Amendment guarantees a jury trial. *Curtis v. Loether, supra.*

A civil penalty was a type of remedy at common law that could only be enforced in courts of law. Remedies intended to punish culpable individuals, as opposed to those intended simply to extract compensation or restore the status quo, were issued by courts of law, not courts of equity. [This] action * * * is of this character. * * * [The Act's] authorization of punishment to further retribution and deterrence clearly evidences that this subsection reflects more than a concern to provide equitable relief. * * * Because the nature of the relief authorized by [the Act] was traditionally available only in a court of law, the petitioner in this present action is entitled to a jury trial on demand.

Interestingly, however, the Court in *Tull* also held that the judge could, as preferred by the Act, decide the *amount* of the civil penalty, without running afoul of the Seventh Amendment, even though the jury had to decide the question of liability. "Nothing in the Amendment's language suggests that the right to a jury trial extends to the remedy phase of a civil trial," said the Court. And "[s]ince Congress itself may fix the civil penalties, it may delegate that determination to trial judges."

In addition, the Court has concluded that patent infringement actions are to be tried by juries (although particular issues within such trials, such as the construction of a "patent claim," would be an issue of law for the judge, not an issue of fact for the jury). Markman v. Westview Instruments, Inc., 517 U.S. 370, 116 S.Ct. 1384, 134 L.Ed.2d 577 (1996) (discussed below); see also Wilson v. Quadramed Corp., 225 F.3d 350 (3d Cir. 2000) (concluding that whether language in letter sent to collect debt violated Fair Debt Collection Practices Act was a question of law, not fact); cf. Feltner v. Columbia Pictures Television, Inc., 523 U.S. 340, 118 S.Ct. 1279, 140 L.Ed.2d 438 (1998) (upholding Seventh Amendment right to jury trial in actions for statutory damages under §504(c) of the federal Copyright Act). And, in City of Monterey v. Del Monte Dunes, 526 U.S. 687, 119 S.Ct. 1624, 143 L.Ed.2d 882 (1999), the Court held that suits seeking just compensation for regulatory takings of property by local governments brought under 42 U.S.C. §1983 would be triable by jury as a matter of the Seventh Amendment, despite the arguable historical analogy of such actions to inverse condemnation proceedings, which were tried without a jury.

6. A somewhat different situation occurs if Congress takes a cause of action which either gave rise to a right to jury trial at common law, or is similar to a cause of action which gave rise to a right to jury trial at common law, and assigns the case to an administrative agency or specialized tribunal in which there is no jury trial. While the case law is far from consistent, many of the decisions can be reconciled by looking to whether or not the underlying claim originates from within a comprehensive regulatory scheme: if so, no jury trial is required. Compare, e.g., Atlas Roofing Co. v. Occupational Safety and Health

Review Commission, 430 U.S. 442, 97 S.Ct. 1261, 51 L.Ed.2d 464 (1977) (no jury trial for remedies regarding "public rights" created under OSHA's detailed scheme for regulating health and safety concerns in the workplace) with Granfinanciera, S.A. v. Nordberg, 492 U.S. 33, 109 S.Ct. 2782, 106 L.Ed.2d 26 (1989) (upholding right to jury trial in action to set aside fraudulent transfer brought in bankruptcy court by bankruptcy trustee against party who had not submitted any claim to the bankruptcy court; claim was not integral with administration of affairs in bankruptcy but, instead, involved attempt to enforce a "private" right). Thus, even when the Seventh Amendment might require a jury trial if a "public rights" matter were heard originally in a federal court, the same matter need not have a jury trial when lodged in an agency. *Atlas Roofing*, *supra*.

7. In TELLABS v. MAKOR ISSUES & RIGHTS, LTD., 551 U.S. 308, 127 S.Ct. 2499, 168 L.Ed.2d 179 (2007), the Court concluded that it would not run afoul of the Seventh Amendment for Congress to insist — as a matter of pleading — that the plaintiff must establish a "strong inference" of scienter in a federal action brought under federal securities statutes, and that as part of that requirement, the allegations must create an inference that was at least as likely as innocent explanations. The Court explained that such a requirement would not force the plaintiff "to plead more than she would be required to prove at trial."

> Congress, as creator of federal statutory claims, has power to prescribe what must be pleaded to state the claim, just as it has power to determine what must be proved to prevail on the merits. It is the federal lawmaker's prerogative, therefore, to allow, disallow, or shape the contours of — including the pleading and proof requirements for — private actions [under federal securities laws]. No decision of this Court questions that authority in general, or suggests, in particular, that the Seventh Amendment inhibits Congress from establishing whatever pleading requirements it finds appropriate for federal statutory claims. Cf. *Swierkiewicz* v. *Sorema N.A.*, 534 U.S. 506, 512-513 (2002); *Leatherman*, 507 U.S., at 168 (both recognizing that heightened pleading requirements can be established by Federal Rule, citing Fed. Rule Civ. Proc. 9(b), which requires that fraud or mistake be pleaded with particularity).

3. The Jury's Role

Even when trial is by jury, that does not mean that all matters in dispute will be resolved by the jury. There is another decisionmaker who has a role to play and that is the judge. Indeed, until the evidence has been fully presented to the jury, the judge's role is paramount, and the jury's is a comparatively passive one. At the risk of overgeneralization, the judge's role in the final decisionmaking process is to resolve disputed questions of law and for the jury to resolve disputed questions of fact. Of course, the jury will also decide how it will apply the relevant law — as given to them by the judge in her "instructions" or "charge" to the jury after all of the evidence has been presented (see below at Section B.2) — to the facts as they happen to find them. Perhaps this ability to apply the law to the facts in a given case and to render a general verdict of liability or no liability is all that is meant by some of the older statements that, at common law (and at the time of the framing of the Seventh Amendment), the jury in civil cases was the judge of both the law and the fact. See, e.g., Georgia v. Brailsford, 3 U.S. (3 Dall.) 1, 4, 1 L.Ed. 483 (1794). The jury could be expected to follow the judge's instructions as to the law, and if they did not, the court would simply order a new trial. This implicit law-fact division is born out in the Seventh Amendment itself which insists only that a jury's finding of "fact" should be largely immune from review, and its recognition that some review could be had of jury factfinding in accordance with the common law, which included new trials for verdicts that were contrary to the evidence (or the law). See below at Section B.4.

Sometimes the divide between law and fact will be clear, with questions of fact relating to those simpler matters "which catch the eye and ear." JAMES BRADLEY THAYER, A PRELIMINARY TREATISE ON EVIDENCE AT COMMON LAW 184 (1898). But other times, it will be less so, as the following case reveals. And the line between the two has not always been constant. Indeed, at the earliest stages of the jury's development, when jurors were themselves the witnesses rather than a more disinterested body of decisionmakers from the community who heard and evaluated witnesses and the evidence, the jury's function probably included a larger measure of what today would clearly be called "law."

Markman v. Westview Instruments, Inc.

Supreme Court of the United States, 1996.

517 U.S. 370, 116 S.Ct. 1384, 134 L.Ed.2d 577.

JUSTICE SOUTER delivered the opinion of the Court.

The question here is whether the interpretation of a so-called patent claim, the portion of the patent document that defines the scope of the patentee's rights, is a matter of law reserved entirely for the court, or subject to a Seventh Amendment guarantee that a jury will determine the meaning of any disputed term of art about which expert testimony is offered. We hold that the construction of a patent, including terms of art within its claim, is exclusively within the province of the court.

[Markman was the owner of a patent that described a system that could monitor and report the status, location, and movement of clothing in dry-cleaning establishments. Markman filed a patent infringement suit against Westview, alleging that Westview was the maker of an infringing product. Westview denied any infringement. The patent statute requires that a patentee not only provide a detailed description of his invention, but also make a "claim" or "claims" setting out what the applicant regards as the subject matter of the invention. One of Markman's claims stated that its product could "maintain an inventory total" and "detect and localize spurious additions to inventory." At trial, the dispute hinged in part upon the meaning of the word "inventory" in

Markman's claim. Westview argued that its allegedly infringing device could only maintain an inventory of receivables (monies owed by customers) by tracking transaction totals, while Markman's product could keep track of clothing and spurious additions to the inventory of clothing. Following a jury trial, the jury found infringement. The district court, however, granted Westview's post-verdict motion for judgment as a matter of law because under the court's own interpretation of the term "inventory," Westview's system did not infringe Markman's patent. The court of appeals affirmed the district court.]

* * *

II

The Seventh Amendment provides that "[i]n Suits at common law, where the value in controversy shall exceed twenty dollars, the right of trial by jury shall be preserved. . . ." U.S. Const., Amdt. 7. Since Justice Story's day, United States v. Wonson, 28 F. Cas. 745, 750 (No. 16,750) (CC Mass. 1812), we have understood that "[t]he right of trial by jury thus preserved is the right which existed under the English common law when the Amendment was adopted." Baltimore & Carolina Line, Inc. v. Redman, 295 U.S. 654, 657 (1935). In keeping with our long-standing adherence to this "historical test," * * * we ask, first, whether we are dealing with a cause of action that either was tried at law at the time of the Founding or is at least analogous to one that was, see, e.g., Tull v. United States, 481 U.S. 412, 417 (1987). If the action in question belongs in the law category, we then ask whether the particular trial decision must fall to the jury in order to preserve the substance of the common-law right as it existed in 1791.[3]

A

[The Court first concluded that patent infringement action "must be tried to a jury, as their predecessors were more than two centuries ago."]

B

This conclusion raises the second question, whether a particular issue occurring within a jury trial (here the construction of a patent claim) is itself necessarily a jury issue, the guarantee being essential to preserve the right to a jury's resolution of the ultimate dispute. In some instances the answer to this second question may be easy because of clear historical evidence that the very subsidiary question was so regarded under the English practice of leaving the issue for a jury. But when, as here, the old practice provides no clear answer, we are forced to make a judgment about the scope of the Seventh Amendment guarantee without the benefit of any foolproof test.

The Court has repeatedly said that the answer to the second question "must depend on whether the jury must shoulder this responsibility as *necessary to preserve the 'substance of the common-law right of trial by jury.'*" Tull v. United States, supra, at 426, (emphasis added) (quoting Colgrove v. Battin, 413 U.S. 149, 156 (1973)). * * *

---

[3] Our formulations of the historical test do not deal with the possibility of conflict between actual English common-law practice and American assumptions about what that practice was, or between English and American practices at the relevant time. No such complications arise in this case.

The "substance of the common-law right" is, however, a pretty blunt instrument for drawing distinctions. * * * We have tried to sharpen it, to be sure, by reference to the distinction between substance and procedure. * * * We have also spoken of the line as one between issues of fact and law.

But the sounder course, when available, is to classify a mongrel practice (like construing a term of art following receipt of evidence) by using the historical method, much as we do in characterizing the suits and actions within which they arise. Where there is no exact antecedent, the best hope lies in comparing the modern practice to earlier ones whose allocation to court or jury we do know, * * * seeking the best analogy we can draw between an old and the new * * *

C

"Prior to 1790 nothing in the nature of a claim had appeared either in British patent practice or in that of the American states," Lutz, Evolution of the Claims of U.S. Patents, 20 J. Pat. Off. Soc. 134 (1938), and we have accordingly found no direct antecedent of modern claim construction in the historical sources. * * *

Markman seeks to supply what the early case reports lack in so many words * * * to argue that the 18th-century juries must have acted as definers of patent terms just to reach the verdicts we know they rendered in patent cases turning on enablement or novelty. But the conclusion simply does not follow. There is no more reason to infer that juries supplied plenary interpretation of written instruments in patent litigation than in other cases implicating the meaning of documentary terms, and we do know that in other kinds of cases during this period judges, not juries, ordinarily construed written documents.[7]

III

Since evidence of common-law practice at the time of the Framing does not entail application of the Seventh Amendment's jury guarantee to the construction of the claim document, we must look elsewhere to characterize this determination of meaning in order to allocate it as between court or jury. We accordingly consult existing precedent and consider both the relative interpretive skills of judges and juries and the statutory policies that ought to be furthered by the allocation. * * *

A

The two elements of a simple patent case, construing the patent and determining whether infringement occurred, were characterized by the former

---

[7] See, *e.g.*, Devlin, Jury Trial of Complex Cases: English Practice at the Time of the Seventh Amendment, 80 Colum L. Rev. 43, 75 (1980); Weiner, The Civil Jury Trial and the Law-Fact Distinction, 54 Calif. L. Rev. 1867, 1932 (1966). For example, one historian observed that it was generally the practice of judges in the late 18th century "to keep the construction of writings *out of the jury's hands* and reserve it for themselves," a "safeguard" designed to prevent a jury from "constru[ing] or refin[ing] it at pleasure." 9 J. Wigmore, Evidence §2461, p. 194 (J. Chadbourn rev. ed. 1981) (emphasis in original; internal quotation marks omitted). The absence of any established practice supporting Markman's view is also shown by the disagreement between Justices Willis and Buller, reported in Macbeath v. Haldimand, 1 T. R. 173, 180-182, 99 Eng. Rep. 1036, 1040-1041 (K. B. 1786), as to whether juries could ever construe written documents when their meaning was disputed.

patent practitioner, Justice Curtis. "The first is a question of law, to be determined by the court, construing the letters-patent, and the description of the invention and specification of claim annexed to them. The second is a question of fact, to be submitted to a jury." Winans v. Denmead, 15 How. at 338[.]

In arguing for a different allocation of responsibility for the first question, Markman relies primarily on two cases, Bischoff v. Wethered, 9 Wall. 812 (1870), and Tucker v. Spalding, 13 Wall. 453 (1872). These are said to show that evidence of the meaning of patent terms was offered to 19th-century juries, and thus to imply that the meaning of a documentary term was a jury issue whenever it was subject to evidentiary proof. That is not what Markman's cases show, however.

In order to resolve the *Bischoff* suit implicating the construction of rival patents, we considered "whether the court below was bound to compare the two specifications, and to instruct the jury, as a matter of law, whether the inventions therein described were, or were not, identical." 9 Wall., at 813 (statement of the case). We said it was not bound to do that, on the ground that investing the court with so dispositive a role would improperly eliminate the jury's function in answering the ultimate question of infringement. On that ultimate issue, expert testimony had been admitted on "the nature of the various mechanisms or manufactures described in the different patents produced, and as to the identity or diversity between them." Id., at 814. Although the jury's consideration of that expert testimony in resolving the question of infringement was said to impinge upon the well-established principle "that it is the province of the court, and not the jury, to construe the meaning of documentary evidence," we decided that it was not so. We said that

> "the specifications . . . profess to describe mechanisms and complicated machinery, chemical compositions and other manufactured products, which have their existence in pais, outside of the documents themselves; and which are commonly described by terms of the art or mystery to which they respectively belong; and these descriptions and terms of art often require peculiar knowledge and education to understand them aright . . . . Indeed, the whole subject-matter of a patent is an embodied conception outside of the patent itself. . . . This outward embodiment of the terms contained in the patent is the thing invented, and is to be properly sought, like the explanation of all latent ambiguities arising from the description of external things, by evidence in pais." Ibid.

Bischoff does not then, as Markman contends, hold that the use of expert testimony about the meaning of terms of art requires the judge to submit the question of their construction to the jury. It is instead a case in which the Court drew a line between issues of document interpretation and product identification, and held that expert testimony was properly presented to the jury on the latter, ultimate issue, whether the physical objects produced by the patent were identical. The Court did not see the decision as bearing upon the appropriate treatment of disputed terms. As the opinion emphasized, the Court's "view of the case is not intended to, and does not, trench upon the doctrine that the construction of written instruments is the province of the court alone. It is not the construction of the instrument, but the character of the thing invented, which is sought in questions of identity and diversity of inventions." *Tucker*, the second case proffered by Markman, is to the same effect. Its reasoning rested expressly on *Bischoff*, and it just as clearly noted that in addressing the ultimate issue of mixed fact and law, it was for the court to "lay down to the jury the law which should govern them." *Tucker, supra*, at 455.

If the line drawn in these two opinions is a fine one, it is one that the Court has drawn repeatedly in explaining the respective roles of the jury and judge in patent cases, and one understood by commentators writing in the aftermath of the cases Markman cites. * * *

In sum, neither *Bischoff* nor *Tucker* indicates that juries resolved the meaning of terms of art in construing a patent, and neither case undercuts Justice Curtis's authority.

B

Where history and precedent provide no clear answers, functional considerations also play their part in the choice between judge and jury to define terms of art. We said in Miller v. Fenton, 474 U.S. 104, 114 (1985), that when an issue "falls somewhere between a pristine legal standard and a simple historical fact, the fact/law distinction at times has turned on a determination that, as a matter of the sound administration of justice, one judicial actor is better positioned than another to decide the issue in question." So it turns out here, for judges, not juries, are the better suited to find the acquired meaning of patent terms.

The construction of written instruments is one of those things that judges often do and are likely to do better than jurors unburdened by training in exegesis. Patent construction in particular "is a special occupation, requiring, like all others, special training and practice. The judge, from his training and discipline, is more likely to give a proper interpretation to such instruments than a jury; and he is, therefore, more likely to be right, in performing such a duty, than a jury can be expected to be." Parker v. Hulme, 18 F. Cas., at 1140. Such was the understanding nearly a century and a half ago, and there is no reason to weigh the respective strengths of judge and jury differently in relation to the modern claim; quite the contrary, for "the claims of patents have become highly technical in many respects as the result of special doctrines relating to the proper form and scope of claims that have been developed by the courts and the Patent Office." Woodward, Definiteness and Particularity in Patent Claims, 46 Mich. L. Rev. 755, 765 (1948).

Markman would trump these considerations with his argument that a jury should decide a question of meaning peculiar to a trade or profession simply because the question is a subject of testimony requiring credibility determinations, which are the jury's forte. It is, of course, true that credibility judgments have to be made about the experts who testify in patent cases, and in theory there could be a case in which a simple credibility judgment would suffice to choose between experts whose testimony was equally consistent with a patent's internal logic. But our own experience with document construction leaves us doubtful that trial courts will run into many cases like that. In the main, we expect, any credibility determinations will be subsumed within the necessarily sophisticated analysis of the whole document, required by the standard construction rule that a term can be defined only in a way that comports with the instrument as a whole. Thus, in these cases a jury's capabilities to evaluate demeanor, to sense the "mainsprings of human conduct," Commissioner of Internal Revenue v. Duberstein, 363 U.S. 278, 289 (1960), or to reflect community standards, United States v. McConney, 728 F.2d 1195, 1204 (9th Cir. 1984) (en banc), are much less significant than a trained ability to evaluate the testimony in relation to the overall structure of the patent. The decisionmaker vested with the task of construing the patent is in the better position to ascertain whether an expert's proposed definition fully comports with the specification and claims and so will preserve the patent's internal coherence. We accordingly think there is sufficient reason to treat construction of terms of art like many other responsibilities that we cede to a judge in the normal course of trial, notwithstanding its evidentiary underpinnings.

C

Finally, we see the importance of uniformity in the treatment of a given patent as an independent reason to allocate all issue of construction to the court. As we noted in General Elec. Co. v. Wabash Appliance Corp., 304 U.S. 364, 369 (1938), "[t]he limits of a patent must be known for the protection of the patentee, the encouragement of the inventive genius of others and the assurance that the subject of the patent will be dedicated ultimately to the public." Otherwise, a "zone of uncertainty which enterprise and experimentation may enter only at the risk of infringement claims would discourage invention only a little less than unequivocal foreclosure of the field." United Carbon Co. v. Binney & Smith Co., 317 U.S. 228, 236 (1942), and "[t]he public [would] be deprived of rights supposed to belong to it, without being clearly told what it is that limits these rights." Merrill v. Yeomans, 94 U.S. 568, 573 (1876). It was just for the sake of such desirable uniformity that Congress created the Court of Appeals for the Federal Circuit as an exclusive appellate court for patent cases, H.R. Rep. No. 97-312, pp. 20-23 (1981), observing that increased uniformity would "strengthen the United States patent system in such a way as to foster technological growth and industrial innovation."

Uniformity would, however, be ill served by submitting issues of document construction to juries. Making them jury issues would not, to be sure, necessarily leave evidentiary questions of meaning wide open in every new court in which a patent might be litigated, for principles of issue preclusion would ordinarily foster uniformity. Cf. Blonder-Tongue Laboratories, Inc. v. University of Ill. Foundation, 402 U.S. 313 (1971). But whereas issue preclusion could not be asserted against new and independent infringement defendants even within a given jurisdiction, treating interpretive issues as purely legal will promote (though it will not guarantee) intrajurisdictional certainty through the application of *stare decisis* on those questions not yet subject to interjurisdictional uniformity under the authority of the single appeals court.

* * *

Accordingly, we hold that the interpretation of the word "inventory" in this case is an issue for the judge, not the jury[.] [Affirmed.]

NOTES AND PROBLEMS FOR DISCUSSION

1. In *Markman*, the Court relies heavily on what it sees as the traditional view — namely, that terms in documents are appropriate for resolution by the judge rather than the jury. In a contract dispute, what happens if two parties disagree over their understanding of the meaning of a contractual provision? State of mind is a classic question of fact, and fact questions are for the jury. Does the answer depend on whether the underlying substantive contract law is "objective" versus "subjective" in its focus on the parties' intent?

2. The Court in *Markman* rests its analysis in part on functional considerations of who is better fitted institutionally — the judge or the jury — to resolve the question at hand and the impact that jury decisions might have on uniformity in patent litigation. Yet the Court also assumes that the question of infringement is for the jury to resolve after being properly instructed by the judge as to the meaning of infringement under the federal patent laws. Why the difference in treatment?

3. Is the court saying that interpretation of patents is too complex for the jury? Compare footnote 10 of *Bernhard, supra*.

4. When a contract is oral, and there is a dispute over what was said or what was agreed to, jury participation is typically required (even if the court may have to decide whether a binding contract exists). But what happens if the parties do not dispute the terms of their oral agreement? In DOBSON v. MASONITE, 359 F.2d 921 (5th Cir. 1966), the parties disagreed whether an oral contract to cut timber was a contract for services or a contract for the sale of land (i.e., the sale of standing timber); if it was the latter, it had to be in writing under the relevant state's statute of frauds to be enforceable. There was no disagreement over the terms of the contract or that one party had failed to perform. The court concluded that the question whether the contract was one for services or the sale of land was a factual question for the jury:

> [The case] calls for an interpretation of the agreement between the parties to determine what they meant by the terms of that agreement. Interpretation is always a question of fact. * * * As a question of fact, this issue was properly presented to, and determined by, the jury; and unless there was no evidence which, if believed, would authorize the jury's conclusions, they must stand. * * *

> Plainly what the parties meant by the language of the contract was uncertain and at the heart of this controversy[.]* * * On the record before us, there is certainly ample evidence from which the jury could conclude that the contract between Dobson and Masonite was for the rendition of services, rather than for the sale of standing timber. In drawing the ultimate conclusion as to the meaning of the parties, we believe the jury was fulfilling its traditional function as the finder of the facts. * * *

> The district court, apparently because there was no dispute regarding the existence of the oral contract or its terms, felt that only a legal question, what was the legal effect of the contract, was involved. But "legal effect" is the result of applying rules of law to the facts;

necessarily this determination must await a determination of all the facts. And, as we have stated, deciding what is the meaning of the contract is a question of fact. * * *

Is *Dobson* consistent with *Markman*? With *Dobson,* compare Modern Equipment Co. v. Continental Western Ins. Co., 355 F.3d 1125 (8th Cir. 2004), indicating that summary judgment is "particularly" appropriate in insurance disputes "because the proper construction of an insurance contract is always an issue of law for the court." Id. at 1128.

5. It is easy to confuse the law-fact distinction presented by *Markman* with the law-equity distinction presented by *Terry*. Simply because one has a "fact" issue in a case that is of the sort that juries would resolve in a jury trial does not mean that a jury will always resolve it. It will only do so if the suit is also one to which the jury trial guarantee adheres (or which is statutorily made jury triable). As discussed below, judges are the factfinders when there is no right to a jury trial, as in equity and admiralty cases.

6. Of course, not every question of fact in an action at law is decided by the jury. Some fact-laden questions, such as whether a party was served with process, will obviously be resolved by the court, pre-trial. In PAVEY v. CONLEY, 528 F.3d 494 (7th Cir. 2008), a prisoner brought a claim under 42 U.S.C. § 1983 claiming that his constitutional rights were violated when defendant prison guards used excessive force on him. Defendants alleged by way of defense that the prisoner failed to exhaust his administrative remedies as called for by federal statutes. In an affidavit, the prisoner stated that he could not exhaust his remedies because of the injuries he alleged he received at the hands of the guards and because, after the events in question, he had been sent to a different prison. There was a factual dispute over whether the matters stated in the affidavit were true or not. The trial court ruled that the question should go to the jury. The court of appeals reversed. Judge Posner wrote:

> [N]ot every factual issue that arises in the course of a litigation is triable to a jury as a matter of right, even if it is a suit at law (rather than in equity) within the meaning of the Seventh Amendment. The clearest example is subject-matter jurisdiction; often it turns on factual issues that may be genuinely debatable, but even if so the issues are resolved by the judge. * * * The same is true of factual issues relating to the defense of lack of personal jurisdiction or venue, * * * though these defenses are not jurisdictional in the sense of requiring the judge to decide them even if the parties do not make an issue of them — and to motions to abstain in favor of another court, or an agency. * * * A decision to relinquish supplemental jurisdiction to the state courts, see 28 U.S.C. § 1367, is likewise made by the judge even if there are contestable factual questions bearing on the decision.

> The generalization that emerges from these examples and others that might be given is that juries do not decide what forum a dispute is to be resolved in. Juries decide cases, not issues of judicial traffic control. Until the issue of exhaustion is resolved, the court cannot know whether it is to decide the case or the prison authorities are to. * * *

A peculiarity of this case is a possible overlap between the factual issues relating to exhaustion and those relating to the merits of the excessive-force claim. The broken arm is of course germane to both, and while the fact that it was broken is conceded, the severity of the break could well be an issue common to both the allegedly inexcusable failure to exhaust and the excessiveness of the force that caused the break. By analogy to the cases that require that claims at law be decided before equitable claims when both types of claim are presented, so that the judge's decision on the latter does not preclude or otherwise affect the jury's determination of the former, * * * we think that any finding that the judge makes, relating to exhaustion, that might affect the merits may be reexamined by the jury if — and only after — the prisoner overcomes the exhaustion defense and the case proceeds to the merits. The alternative of trying the merits before exhaustion, as under the *Beacon Theatres* line of cases, is unsatisfactory in the present setting because it would thwart Congress's effort to bar trials of prisoner cases in which the prisoner has failed to exhaust his administrative remedies. * * * A jury might decide the merits of a case that should never have gotten to the merits stage because the judge should have found that the prisoner had failed to exhaust his administrative remedies.

528 F.3d at 497. The court concluded that the case would proceed to trial only if and when the court found that the prisoner had properly exhausted his remedies. In addition, it noted that the court might allow some pre-trial discovery on the issue of exhaustion, prior to any discovery on the merits.

7. Finally, note that some questions that might at first blush appear to be questions of law — such as "Was the defendant negligent?" — are regularly treated as proper questions for the jury, even when there is no dispute about the underlying historical facts. For example, in RAILROAD COMPANY v. STOUT, 84 U.S. 657, 21 L.Ed. 745 (1873), the question was whether the judge or the jury would decide whether particular acts of the defendant amounted to negligence when the only dispute was about the inferences to be drawn from undisputed facts:

It is true, in many cases, that where the facts are undisputed the effect of them is for the judgment of the court, and not for the decision of the jury. * * * In some cases, * * * *the necessary* inference from the proof is so certain that it may be ruled as a question of law.

But these are extreme cases. The range between them is almost infinite in variety and extent. It is in relation to these intermediate cases that the opposite rule prevails. Upon the facts proven in such cases, it is a matter of judgment and discretion, of sound inference, what is the deduction to be drawn from the undisputed facts. Certain facts we may suppose to be clearly established from which one sensible, impartial man would infer that proper care had not been used, and that negligence existed; another man equally sensible and equally impartial would infer that proper care had been used, and that there was no negligence. It is this class of cases and those akin to it that the law commits to the decision of a jury. Twelve men of the average of the community, comprising men of education and men of little education, men of learning and men whose learning consists only in what they have themselves seen and heard, the merchant, the mechanic, the farmer, the laborer; these sit together, consult, apply their separate experience of the affairs of life to the facts proven, and draw a unanimous conclusion. This average judgment thus given it is the great effort of the law to obtain. It is assumed that twelve men know more of the common affairs of life than does one man, that they can draw wiser and safer conclusions from admitted facts thus occurring than can a single judge.

Stout does not mean that every negligence case will go to the jury, however. As noted below in Section B, and as hinted at in *Stout* itself, the court will be able to intervene in those cases in which it is able to conclude, as a matter of law, that reasonable jurors could not disagree as to the existence or nonexistence of negligence based on the evidence at trial.

4. SELECTING THE JURY

Some of you may be familiar with or have a rough idea of the mechanics of jury selection, so we will only briefly outline the process here.

Initially, it is necessary to identify and assemble prospective jurors. States and the federal government differ on methods for identifying jurors. Some use lists of registered voters or holders of drivers' licenses, although each of these obviously excludes persons not on such lists. Others use various combinations of methods. Once names are selected, potential jurors usually are sent a questionnaire to determine general availability. On the basis of answers to the questions, some persons will be excluded, such as persons with serious illness or who are out of the country.

In the questionnaire, prospective jurors will be asked about their occupations, and in some states persons with certain occupations may be automatically excluded. Although the tendency for many years was to exclude a broad range of occupations (including lawyers), automatic exclusion on the basis of occupations has narrowed considerably in recent years. Examples of automatic disqualification often include law enforcement officers, doctors, and teachers, but not many others. More than fifty years ago in Thiel v. Southern Pac. Co., 328 U.S. 217, 66 S.Ct. 984, 90 L.Ed. 1181 (1946), the Supreme Court held that the regular exclusion of persons who worked for a daily wage was improper and, for this reason, few groups are excluded automatically even if experience suggests that a substantial number of persons in the group will be excluded on an individual basis. Once called, other persons may be required to convince an administrator or judge that service would be an undue hardship — e.g., caregivers, persons with low incomes, students. Discrimination in selection on the basis of race, national origin, sex, or certain other bases is forbidden.

The group of potential jurors assembled is called the "venire." Parties may challenge the venire on the ground that it was not properly constituted or that certain groups were improperly excluded or that the jurors are not representative of the community. However, such challenges often require extensive proof regarding the composition of the venire; they are time consuming and expensive; and they are infrequently mounted (also, even if you win, you just get a new venire — you still have to win your case on the merits). The applicable federal statutes governing such challenges are codified at 28 U.S.C. §1863 et seq.

Once the venire is selected, then the process of selecting individual jurors begins. Generally, a group of jurors is seated, and there is a process for determining which individuals should serve. This process is called "voir dire" and generally begins with a general description of the case and certain issues, as well as an identification of the parties (and perhaps witnesses). Jurors who have a connection with a party, or who could not render a fair verdict are excluded. For example, in an accident case, any person who recently was in an accident will normally be excluded. If the case is long and complex, judges normally exclude persons who for one reason or another cannot serve for a long period — e.g., the mother of a small child might not be excused from a three day trial, but is likely to be excluded from a three month trial. Then, there is an opportunity to question individual jurors to find out a bit about their background and attitudes. In the federal courts, the general description and questioning of jurors is done by the judge, although the lawyers for parties can request the judge to ask certain questions and/or question the jurors themselves.

The parties have the power to challenge individual jurors, and challenges are of two types. Challenges for "cause" may be made if there are reasons to suspect that a juror cannot be fair and impartial. For example, if the defendant is a large corporation, persons who say they think all corporations are dishonest will be excluded, and in a discrimination lawsuit, persons who say that there is nothing wrong with discrimination will be excluded. Persons who work in the same industry may be excluded, such as those who work for a bank being excluded from a case where a bank is a party. The decision to allow exclusion for cause is highly discretionary.

There are also "peremptory" challenges which (subject to the discussion below) can be exercised without any explanation or reason. In federal court civil litigation, each side has three peremptory challenges. 28 U.S.C. §1870. Lawyers frequently use these to exclude persons whom they sought unsuccessfully to challenge for cause, as well as persons who are not likely to be sympathetic to their case. For example, in accident cases the conventional wisdom is that the young and old, and the less well educated are likely to be sympathetic to plaintiff, while those who work for large institutions such as banks and insurance companies are likely to be sympathetic to defendant. But it's as much a matter of intuition and instinct and even personalities, so all generalities are suspect.

Recent innovations have included various forms of social science research designed to identify traits of favorable jurors, the use of focus groups, and even the use of mock trials with "representative" jurors in which the deliberations are recorded. The latter not only enables the party to identify the types of jurors likely to be favorable, but also to gauge the effectiveness of various lines of argument, evidence and witnesses and to predict the likely outcome. All of these are very expensive, and are used only when the stakes justify the cost. While there is little systematic evidence as to whether they are reliable, there is certainly some anecdotal evidence which suggests high reliability. Also, one purpose of these devices is to identify cases that may be heading to disaster. An unfavorable result with a mock jury (and even more so with two mock juries) may convince a party to change its settlement strategy.

Until recently, a peremptory challenge could be made on any basis, and without any explanation. However, beginning in the 1970s, courts began questioning this practice, at least where there was some basis to think that the challenge was on racial grounds. Initially, the issue came to the forefront in criminal cases, see, e.g., Batson v. Kentucky, 476 U.S. 79, 106 S.Ct. 1712, 90 L.Ed.2d 69 (1986) (preventing race-based prosecutorial strikes of jurors), but later, it was extended (at least somewhat) to civil cases as well. See also Johnson v. California, 543 U.S. 449, 125 S.Ct. 2410, 162 L.Ed.2d 129 (2005) (observing, in criminal case, that burden of showing racial bias under *Batson* is that of: "more likely than not").

In Edmonson v. Leesville Concrete Co., 500 U.S. 614, 111 S.Ct. 2077, 114 L.Ed.2d 660 (1991), for example, the Court concluded that private litigants in civil cases could not use peremptory challenges to exclude potential jurors on the basis of race. It held that the sanctioning of such a practice would violate equal protection of the laws. Peremptory strikes based on gender, at least when exercised by the state as a civil litigant, were also struck down in J.E.B. v. Alabama, 511 U.S. 127, 114 S.Ct. 1419, 128 L.Ed.2d 89 (1994), as violative of equal protection. If race-based peremptory challenges by private litigants is forbidden, is there any rationale for failing to extend a similar prohibition to peremptory challenges made by a private litigant on any constitutionally impermissible basis, such as gender, national origin, or religion?

Although the Supreme Court has never made clear how far it is willing to go in applying anti-discrimination norms to peremptory challenges in civil cases, lower courts have had to deal with such issues, as in the following case.

Hidalgo v. Fagen, Inc.

United States Court of Appeals, Tenth Circuit, 2000.
206 F.3d 1013.

KELLY, CIRCUIT JUDGE.

Plaintiff-Appellant, Mr. Sabino Hidalgo, suffered grievous injuries to his arm while cleaning a screw conveyor at the Excel meat packing plant in Fort Morgan, Colorado. His arm ultimately required amputation. He brought suit against KWS Manufacturing, Inc. ("KWS"), the company that manufactured the component parts of the screw conveyor; Fagen, Inc. ("Fagen"), the contractor hired to construct the conveyor system; and two individuals, David Kaminski, who oversaw the construction of the conveyor, and Daryl Gillund, Fagen's chief financial officer. The district court granted summary judgment in favor of KWS, Mr. Kaminski and Mr. Gillund. The district court granted partial summary judgment in favor of Fagen on the claims that it was strictly liable for injuries caused by the conveyor, and it had breached express and implied warranties concerning the screw conveyor. The matter went to trial on Mr. Hildago's negligence claims against Fagen and the jury returned a verdict in favor of Fagen.

* * *

Mr. Hidalgo seeks a new trial on several grounds. He argues that the district court improperly denied his *Batson* challenge to Fagen's peremptory strikes, thereby permitting Fagen to exclude all Hispanics from the jury. Next, he challenges various evidentiary rulings. * * *

* * *

C. *Batson* Challenges

During voir dire, Fagen exercised two peremptory strikes against two apparent Hispanic women, Ms. Martinez and Ms. Gonzales (in that order). Upon Fagan's striking Ms. Gonzales, Mr. Hidalgo objected that the peremptory strike was racially motivated, reminding the court that she was one of two Hispanics on the jury. When Fagen struck Ms. Martinez earlier, Mr. Hidalgo did not object. The district court inquired as to Fagan's justification for exercising a peremptory strike on Ms. Gonzales. Counsel for Fagen responded:

> Your honor, when I approached this jury and this jury selection, one of the fundamental principles I was looking for is I prefer older people, rather than younger people. I would prefer men, rather than women. And when it came down to the third choice, I saw — I had a choice between two, and I chose the older — to keep the older and strike the younger because I think older people who have had trauma in their lives understand about getting on with it and I think Mr. Hidalgo has not. And therefore, that's why I prefer age over youth.

Aplt. App. at 655-56. The trial court further questioned whether or not Ms. Gonzales' Hispanic background motivated the strike. Counsel for Fagen answered:

> No. Quite frankly, I had some concerns about it; but I think she's intelligent. And quite frankly, I want an intelligent jury. . . .

Id. The trial court was satisfied that these responses were sufficiently race neutral, and rejected Mr. Hidalgo's challenge. Mr. Hidalgo made no further challenge, either based on race or gender discrimination. See Aplt. App. at 656.

On appeal, Mr. Hidalgo argues that the court should have (1) further pursued Fagen's remarks regarding Ms. Gonzales' intellect vis-a-vis her Hispanic background; (2) made independent inquiries into Fagen's justification for striking Ms. Martinez; (3) required Fagen to justify its exclusion of all Hispanics from the jury; and (4) raised, sua sponte, a *Batson* challenge against Fagen for its gender discriminatory justification for striking Ms. Gonzales. We deal with each argument in turn.

The *Batson* analytic is well settled. Once the party raising the *Batson* challenge establishes a prima facie case of racial discrimination, the proponent of the peremptory strike must submit a racially neutral explanation. The party raising the challenge must then be given the opportunity to show pretext. See Davis v. Baltimore Gas & Electric Co., 160 F.3d 1023, 1028 (4th Cir. 1998).

Subsequently, the trial court must decide whether the party raising the *Batson* claim has proven purposeful discrimination. See Purkett v. Elem, 514 U.S. 765, 767-68, 131 L.Ed.2d 834, 115 S.Ct. 1769 (1995). The party bringing the *Batson* challenge always carries the ultimate burden of persuasion. See Hurd v. Pittsburgh State Univ., 109 F.3d 1540, 1546 (10th Cir. 1997) (quoting *Elem*, 514 U.S. at 768). In our review of the district court's disposition of the *Batson* claim, we analyze Fagen's proffered racially neutral explanation as a legal issue, de novo. See United States v. Johnson, 941 F.2d 1102, 1108 (10th Cir. 1991). We review the trial court's ultimate finding that there was no intentional discrimination for clear error. See id.

We are satisfied that Fagen's explanation was race-neutral. A neutral explanation means an explanation based on something besides the race of the juror. See Hernandez v. New York, 500 U.S. 352, 360, 114 L.Ed.2d 395, 111 S.Ct. 1859 (1991). We look specifically at the facial validity of the explanation. Unless discriminatory intent is inherent in the justification, the reason offered will be deemed race neutral. See id.

A fair reading of the explanation for the strike is that Fagen's counsel struck Ms. Gonzales because of her youth. We have held this to be an acceptable race-neutral justification for exercising a peremptory strike. See United States v. Joe, 8 F.3d 1488, 1499 (10th Cir. 1993). Counsel's comment in response to the court's follow up does not evince an inherent discriminatory intent. As the Supreme Court made clear in *Hernandez*, discriminatory purpose in this context has a fixed meaning in the constellation of equal protection jurisprudence. That is, "discriminatory intent" implies that the decisionmaker chose a course of action "'because of,'" not merely "'in spite of,'" its adverse effects upon an identifiable group. *Hernandez*, 500 U.S. at 360 (quoting Personnel Administrator of Mass. v. Feeney, 442 U.S. 256, 279, 60 L.Ed.2d 870, 99 S.Ct. 2282 (1979)). When the trial court asked Fagen whether Ms. Gonzales' Hispanic background influenced his decision to strike her, he responded unequivocally that it did not. The district court's finding on this aspect of the *Batson* claim is not clearly erroneous.

We are unpersuaded by the remainder of Mr. Hidalgo's *Batson* arguments. The essence of these arguments is that the court should have independently required Fagen's counsel to justify the striking of all the Hispanics from the venire and should have raised *Batson* claims based upon the strike of Ms. Martinez and the remark by Fagen's counsel that he "preferred men to women."

Implicit in Mr. Hidalgo's *Batson* challenge to the striking of Ms. Gonzales, was the argument that the result was the removal of all Hispanics from the venire:

> Your Honor, there has been a challenge to Juror No. 1, Ms. Gonzales, who is one of two Hispanics on the jury, the only Spanish-speaking individual. Under Batsen v. Kentucky [sic], I would challenge that challenge.

Aplt. App. at 655. The district court then followed the proper procedure.

Finally, Mr. Hidalgo argues that he is entitled to relief because the trial court failed to raise, sua sponte, a *Batson* claim when Fagen stated, in reference to his striking Ms. Gonzales, that one of his organizing principles of jury selection in the instant case was that he preferred male jurors to female ones. See J.E.B. v. Alabama Ex Rel. T.B., 511 U.S. 127, 143, 128 L.Ed.2d 89, 114 S.Ct. 1419 (1994). Mr. Hidalgo failed to raise this objection at any point below. Thus, we review this claim for plain error only. See United States v. Bedonie, 913 F.2d 782, 794 (10th Cir. 1990). In the civil context, we will reverse only if the error is one that "seriously affects 'the fairness, integrity or public reputation of judicial proceedings.'" Glenn v. Cessna Aircraft Co., 32 F.3d 1462, 1464 (10th Cir. 1994). We are not persuaded that the trial court's failure to raise a *J.E.B.* claim in the instant case rises to this level. Thus, Mr. Hidalgo's claim for relief on this issue fails. * * *

AFFIRMED.

NOTES AND PROBLEMS FOR DISCUSSION

1. First focus on the process involved:

(a) Why didn't the plaintiff object to the challenge to Ms. Martinez?

(b) What was the process of objecting to the challenge of Ms. Gonzales and for resolving the objection?

2. Now focus on the explanation for the challenge to Ms. Gonzales. Is there a flaw in the entire process for determining whether challenges are on improper grounds, and if so, is there any way to remedy it? See Barnes v. Anderson, 202 F.3d 150 (2d Cir. 1999) (remanding case in which trial court failed to address the credibility of the defendant's race-neutral explanations with sufficient detail as required by *Batson*).

3. Assume now that the defendant's counsel challenged a third juror, Ms. Sanchez and, in response to a similar objection, says that the basis of the challenge is exactly the same. How should the court rule?

4. Suppose, instead of the explanation he gave, the defendant's lawyer had said: "I challenged Ms. Gonzales because she gave off bad vibes; you know, she just looked at me in a funny way. I rely heavily on my instincts in picking a jury." How should the court rule on an objection to the challenge? Cf. Heno v. Sprint/United Management Co., 208 F.3d 874 (10th Cir. 2000) (concluding, in employment discrimination lawsuit, that juror's support for affirmative action was a race-neutral reason for peremptory challenge).

5. Assume that the Court in #4 sustained the challenge. Can the plaintiff now go back and require an explanation of the challenge to Ms. Martinez?

SECTION B. CONTROL OF THE DECISIONMAKING PROCESS

A very basic premise of the legal system, and of due process, is that decisions will be made in accordance with the substantive rules of law. That is, if the substantive law requires the plaintiff to prove A, B and C to recover, then the plaintiff will be required to prove A, B and C. Conversely, if the substantive law requires the plaintiff to recover unless the defendant proves defense D or E, then the defendant will be required to prove D or E or the plaintiff will recover. There are really two elements of this process: first, correctly identifying the substantive law requirements of a claim or defense, and second, deciding whether such requirements have been established. The substantive law itself is the subject of courses in torts, contracts, etc. and we take it pretty much as a given. Here, we are concerned with assuring (1) whatever the requirements of substantive law, that they are properly conveyed to or considered by the decisionmaker, and (2) with respect to the decision itself, that such requirements have been established.

In dealing with (2) one could say that once the requirements of substantive law are properly conveyed to or considered by the decisionmaker, we will simply accept the decision, whatever it is. For good reasons, associated with minimal due process concerns for rational decisionmaking, this view has not prevailed in civil litigation.[*] Instead, courts have said that the very notion of a legal system and legal rules to govern conduct and create rights and liabilities implies that the decisions concerning legal rights and liabilities will be made according to the law. In other words, there must be some rational basis for a particular decision and for assuring that it is consistent with the substantive law. And while jury rationality is governed primarily by procedural rules, they are underpinned by due process.

This subchapter is concerned with the multitude of devices both to assure that the requirements of substantive law are properly conveyed to or considered by the decisionmaker, and for assuring that the decision is consistent with the substantive law. Our major focus is on cases in which the jury is the decisionmaker.

1. THE PHASES OF A TRIAL

As in the case of jury selection, many students will be at least vaguely familiar with the trial process, so our overview will be brief. We will examine some of the procedures for conveying the substantive law and assuring decisions which are consistent with the substantive law in later sections. We also assume a common case where the plaintiff has the burden of proof on most issues, although the defendant may have such a burden on one or more affirmative defenses.

Once the jury is selected, the trial begins. The plaintiff and defendant each make opening statements generally describing the issues and what each intends to prove (sometimes, the defendant will wait to make its opening statement until the plaintiff completes its evidence). Then the plaintiff offers evidence in the form of testimony or documents. Each witness is examined by the plaintiff, and cross examined by the defendant. The plaintiff then is permitted a rebuttal, although this is theoretically limited to new matters raised in cross examination.

---

[*]   Nevertheless, such a view *has* prevailed insofar as judgments of acquittal in criminal cases are concerned. Because of competing constitutional concerns, including the prohibition against double jeopardy, judgments of acquittal are basically immune from review — although judgments of conviction are not.

Although some additional examination may be permitted in the case of surprise or special circumstances, this is unusual. When the plaintiff's evidence is complete, the plaintiff rests.

At this point, if the defendant believes that the plaintiff has not proved her case — i.e., has not presented sufficient evidence from which a reasonable factfinder could find in her favor — the defendant can move for a judgment as a matter of law (formerly, and still commonly, called a directed verdict). See Rule 50(a); see also discussion below. Unless such a motion is granted, the defendant then proceeds with his case by introducing evidence in the form of testimony and documents, and the witnesses are subject to examination and cross examination as described above. At the conclusion of his case, the defendant may move again for a judgment as a matter of law, and, occasionally, the plaintiff may make such a motion as well.

Thereafter, the plaintiff will be permitted to reply which, again, is theoretically limited to responding to "new" matters introduced by the defendant. This tends to end the testimony phase of the trial although, again, the defendant may be permitted a brief response to "new" matters introduced in the plaintiff's reply, etc. But don't get carried away with the notion that the process is endless — courts expect the major evidence to be introduced as part of the main case, and any party who withholds key evidence to make a big splash right at the end runs a considerable risk that the judge will not permit it to be introduced.

After both sides rest, there may be another round of motions for judgment as a matter of law and, if there has been some problem with the trial, a motion for a new trial. Thereafter, each side has a summation (typically the plaintiff first, then the defendant, and then possibly a short reply by the plaintiff). At the conclusion, the judge conveys both the substantive rules and the standards for decision to the jury in the "charge"; the jury deliberates and hopefully reaches a verdict; and the verdict is announced in open court. The trial is now over, although each party may have a variety of post-trial procedural options which are discussed elsewhere in this chapter.

2. PROCEDURAL CONTROLS

We discuss here, in somewhat more detail, various devices to assure both that the jury gets an accurate view of the law and reaches a rational verdict.

a. *Trial Process/Law of Evidence.* One of the major devices to assure a rational decisionmaking process is the trial process and the law of evidence. During the trial, the lawyers generally will not be permitted to describe or state the requirements of the law itself (except, to a limited extent, in the opening and closing statements) and, if they stray, the judge is likely to admonish the jury not to consider what they have said. The judge will also control the demeanor of witnesses and the decorum in the courtroom, and seek to avoid actions which are likely to prejudice the jury for or against one party. In addition, the law of evidence with its rules on relevancy, and its limits on evidence that may be unreliable, helps to assure the rationality of the process.

b. *Charge to the Jury.* The charge to the jury is critical to convey what issues the jury must decide and what standards (burden of proof) should guide their decision — i.e., what the relevant law is and how the jury should go about applying it, depending on how they resolve the factual disputes in the case. There is a rather elaborate process relating to the charge. See Rule 51. Basically, the parties will submit proposed charges (at least on substantive law matters), with appropriate citations to case law supporting the charge. In many states, there are form or pattern instructions for common issues such as negligence and proximate cause in accident cases, or consideration in contract cases. The judge may then submit the proposed charge to the parties for comment and possible additions. Once the judge gives the charge, the parties must immediately raise any objections and/or request additional charges. It is well established that appellate courts will generally not review charges given or not given, if there has been no objection. To be sure, there is a supposed exception for cases where the judge has failed to give an accurate charge in areas that are well established, but appellate courts rarely reverse on this ground.

c. *Comment on the Evidence.* At common law the trial judge not only summed up the evidence and told the jury what legal consequences should follow upon their resolution of factual issues; he also had the power to comment on the evidence — i.e., to suggest who was and was not telling the truth, and even, who should win. To avoid invading the jury's province the judge was required to make it clear that the ultimate decision was for the jury. Cf. Quercia v. United States, 289 U.S. 466, 53 S.Ct. 698, 77 L.Ed. 1321 (1933). But, even with that caution, a comment from the judge often had strong persuasive force. As the Court put it long ago:

> [I]t is the right and duty of the court to aid [the jury] by recalling the testimony to their recollection, by collating its details, by suggesting grounds of preference where there is contradiction, by directing their attention to the most important facts. * * * There is none more important [duty] resting upon those who preside at jury trials. Constituted as juries are, it is frequently impossible for them to discharge their function wisely and well without this aid. In such cases, chance, mistake, or caprice, may determine the result.

NUDD v. BURROWS, 91 U.S. 246, 23 L.Ed. 318 (1875). Today, the federal courts and a few state courts still recognize this power to comment on the evidence subject to the proper caveats. But the practice which was once robust, is now a shadow of its former self.

d. *Verdicts.* The most common form of verdict is a so-called general verdict — the jury decides which side wins. There are two other alternatives, as described in Rule 49.

One is the so-called special verdict in which the court propounds a number of key questions to the jury, and molds the verdict to their answers. The other is a general verdict with interrogatories in which the jury renders a general verdict and also answers certain key questions. The theory of these devices is that the jury is more likely to focus on the key issues and the relevant evidence, and less likely to be swayed by passion and prejudice based on the premise that jurors will find it easier to disregard the specific issues and evidence in rendering a general verdict than in answering specific questions. In the federal courts, use of either of these devices is discretionary, while in some states, including California, a party has an absolute right to seek interrogatory answers in connection with a general verdict.

In theory, these devices should promote rational decisionmaking by making the jury focus on the precise questions before it, and provide a check on jury irrationality by forcing the decisionmaker to reveal (to some extent) its reasoning process. In practice, however, there are often difficulties in framing questions clearly (in some states there are "form" questions for common cases), including all the necessary questions, in getting unanimity or the necessary majority for answers to questions as compared with a general verdict, and in reconciling cases where the general verdict and answers don't agree.

3. TAKING A CASE FROM THE JURY

As previously noted, a basic premise of the judicial system is that jury verdicts will be supported by evidence. The corollary is that the jury will not be permitted to decide a case where the evidence is insufficient or, alternatively, that a jury verdict based on insufficient evidence will be reversed. The major procedural device to test the sufficiency of the evidence is the motion for judgment as a matter of law ("JMOL").

Rule 50(a)(1) directs the court to grant such a motion if "a reasonable jury would not have a legally sufficient evidentiary basis to find for the [non-moving] party on [an] issue." The motion may be made at any time before submission of the case to the factfinder, and is routinely made by the defendant at the close of the plaintiff's case, and also at the close of all of the evidence. Provided the motion was made at (or before) the close of all of the evidence, it may now be renewed after the jury's verdict under Rule 50(b), within 28 days after entry of judgment. (For many years, the limit was 10 days after entry of judgment.) Don't be confused over nomenclature. When made during trial, such motions were once called (and continue to be called), motions for a "directed verdict." The more traditional label for the post-verdict JMOL was "judgment n.o.v." (n.o.v. being an abbreviation for "non obstante veredicto," i.e., notwithstanding the verdict), or simply "JNOV."

While some courts phrase the Rule 50(a) issue in terms of whether the nonmoving party has satisfied its "burden of production" on an issue, and other courts in terms of whether "reasonable persons can differ," the formulae are not self defining. What the courts are groping for is a threshold concept of evidentiary sufficiency, to be decided on a case by case basis, and whether a given decision would or would not be rational. An experienced lawyer who has read scores of these cases has an intuitive feel for the concept. As a novice, the law student is reduced to reading close cases and considering factual variations. It is important to recognize, however, that cases are almost never identical, and each case is to some extent sui generis.

Finally, note that the standard for granting a judgment as a matter of law under Rule 50(a) is similar to the standard for the granting of summary judgment under Rule 56 (also now known as judgment as a matter of law). The goal of the Rule 50 and Rule 56 motions is the same: to take from the jury cases that reasonable factfinders could only resolve one way. The only difference is that of timing (Rule 56 motions obviously being pre-trial).

The case below has been a staple of civil procedure courses for over three-quarters of a century and discusses the problems of evidentiary sufficiency and jury rationality.

Pennsylvania Railroad Co. v. Chamberlain

Supreme Court of the United States, 1933.
288 U.S. 333, 53 S.Ct. 391, 77 L.Ed. 819.

MR. JUSTICE SUTHERLAND delivered the opinion of the Court.

This is an action brought by respondent against petitioner to recover for the death of a brakeman, alleged to have been caused by petitioner's negligence. The complaint alleges that the deceased, at the time of the accident resulting in his death, was assisting in the yard work of breaking up and making up trains and in the classifying and assorting of cars operating in interstate commerce; that in pursuance of such work, while riding a cut of cars, other cars ridden by fellow employees were negligently caused to be brought into violent contact with those upon which deceased was riding, with the result that he was thrown therefrom to the railroad track and run over by a car or cars, inflicting injuries from which he died.

At the conclusion of the evidence, the trial court directed the jury to find a verdict in favor of petitioner. Judgment upon a verdict so found was reversed by the court of appeals, Judge Swan dissenting. 59 F.2d 986.

That part of the yard in which the accident occurred contained a lead track and a large number of switching tracks branching therefrom. The lead track crossed a "hump," and the work of car distribution consisted of pushing a train of cars by means of a locomotive to the top of the "hump," and then allowing the cars, in separate strings, to descend by gravity, under the control of hand brakes, to their respective destinations in the various branch tracks. Deceased had charge of a string of two gondola cars, which he was piloting to track 14. Immediately ahead of him was a string of seven cars, and behind him a string of nine cars, both also destined for track 14. Soon after the cars ridden by deceased had passed to track 14, his body was found on that track some distance beyond the switch. He had evidently fallen onto the track and been run over by a car or cars.

The case for respondent rests wholly upon the claim that the fall of deceased was caused by a violent collision of the string of nine cars with the string ridden by deceased. Three employees, riding the nine-car string, testified positively that no such collision occurred. They were corroborated by every other employee in a position to see, all testifying that there was no contact between the nine-car string and that of the deceased. The testimony of these witnesses, if believed, establishes beyond doubt that there was no collision between these two strings of cars, and that the nine-car string contributed in no way to the accident. The only witness who testified for the respondent was one Bainbridge; and it is upon his testimony alone that respondent's right to recover is sought to be upheld. His testimony is concisely stated, in its most favorable light for respondent, in the prevailing opinion below by Judge Learned Hand, as follows:

> "The plaintiff's only witness to the event, one Bainbridge, then employed by the road, stood close to the yardmaster's office, near the 'hump.' He professed to have paid little attention to what went on, but he did see the deceased riding at the rear of his cars, whose speed when they passed him he took to be about eight or ten miles. Shortly thereafter a second string passed which was shunted into another track and this was followed by the nine, which, according to the plaintiff's theory, collided with the deceased's. After the nine cars had passed at a somewhat greater speed than the deceased's, Bainbridge paid no more attention to either string for a while, but looked again when the deceased, who was still standing in his place, had passed the switch and onto the assorting track where he was bound. At that time his speed had been checked to about three miles, but the speed of the following nine cars had increased. They were just passing the switch, about four or five cars behind the deceased. Bainbridge looked away again and soon heard what he described as a 'loud crash,' not however an unusual event in a switching yard. Apparently this did not cause him at once to turn, but he did so shortly thereafter, and saw the two strings together, still moving, and the deceased no longer in sight. Later still his attention was attracted by shouts and he went to the spot and saw the deceased between the rails. Until he left to go to the accident, he had stood fifty feet to the north of the track where the accident happened, and about nine hundred feet from where the body was found."

The court, although regarding Bainbridge's testimony as not only "somewhat suspicious in itself, but it's contradiction . . . so manifold as to leave little doubt," held, nevertheless, that the question was one of fact depending upon the credibility of the witnesses, and that it was for the jury to determine, as between the one witness and the many, where the truth lay. The dissenting opinion of Judge Swan proceeds upon the theory that Bainbridge did not testify that in fact a collision had taken place, but inferred it because he heard a crash, and because thereafter the two strings of cars appeared to him to be moving together. It is correctly pointed out in that opinion, however, that the crash might have come from elsewhere in the busy yard and that Bainbridge was in no position to see whether the two strings of cars were actually together; that Bainbridge repeatedly said he was paying no particular attention; and that his position was such, being 900 feet from the place where the body was found and less than 50 feet from the side of the track in question, that he necessarily saw the strings of cars at such an acute angle that it would be physically impossible even for an attentive observer to tell whether the forward end of the nine-car cut was actually in contact with the rear end of the two-car cut. The dissenting opinion further points out that all the witnesses who were in a position to see testified that there was no collision; that respondent's evidence was wholly circumstantial, and the inferences which might otherwise be drawn from it were shown to be utterly erroneous unless all of petitioner's witnesses were willful perjurers. "This is not a case," the opinion proceeds, "where direct testimony to an essential fact is contradicted by direct testimony of other witnesses, though even there it is conceded a directed verdict might be proper in some circumstances. Here, when all the testimony was in, the circumstantial evidence in support of negligence was thought by the trial judge to be so insubstantial and insufficient that it did not justify submission to the jury."

We thus summarize and quote from the prevailing and dissenting opinions, because they present the divergent views to be considered in reaching a correct determination of the question involved.

It, of course, is true, generally, that where there is a direct conflict of testimony upon a matter of fact, the question must be left to the jury to determine, without regard to the number of witnesses upon either side. But here there really is no conflict in the testimony as to the *facts*. The witnesses for petitioner flatly testified that there was no collision between the nine-car and the two-car strings. Bainbridge did not say there was such a collision. What he said was that he heard a "loud crash," which did not cause him at once to turn, but that shortly thereafter he did turn and saw the two strings of cars moving together with the deceased no longer in sight; that there was nothing unusual about the crash of cars — it happened every day; that there was nothing about this crash to attract his attention except that it was extra loud; that he paid no attention to it; that it was not sufficient to attract his attention. The record shows that there was a continuous movement of cars over and down the "hump," which were distributed among a large number of branch tracks within the yard, and that any two strings of these cars moving upon the same track might have come together and caused the crash which Bainbridge heard. There is no direct evidence that *in fact* the crash was occasioned by a collision of the two strings in question; and it is perfectly clear that no such fact was brought to Bainbridge's attention as a perception of the physical sense of sight or of hearing. At most there was an inference to that effect drawn from observed facts which gave equal support to the opposite inference that the crash was occasioned by the coming together of other strings of cars entirely away from the scene of the accident, or of the two-car string ridden by deceased and the seven-car string immediately ahead of it.

We, therefore, have a case belonging to that class of cases where proven facts give equal support to each of two inconsistent inferences; in which event, neither of them being established, judgment, as a matter of law, must go against the party upon whom rests the necessity of sustaining one of these inferences as against the other, before he is entitled to recover. United States F. & G. Co. v. Des Moines Nat. Bank, 145 Fed. 273, 279-280

The rule is succinctly stated in Smith v. First National Bank in Westfield, 99 Mass. 605, 611-612, quoted in the *Des Moines National Bank* case, *supra*:

"There being several inferences deducible from the facts which appear, and equally consistent with all those facts, the plaintiff has not maintained the proposition upon which alone he would be entitled to recover. There is strictly no evidence to warrant a jury in finding that the loss was occasioned by negligence and not by theft. When the evidence tends equally to sustain either of two inconsistent propositions, neither of them can be said to have been established by legitimate proof. A verdict in favor of the party bound to maintain one of those propositions against the other is necessarily wrong."

That Bainbridge concluded from what he himself observed that the crash was due to a collision between the two strings of cars in question is sufficiently indicated by his statements. But this, of course, proves nothing, since it is not allowable for a witness to resolve the doubt as to which of two equally justifiable inferences shall be adopted by drawing a conclusion, which, if accepted, will result in a purely gratuitous award in favor of the party who has failed to sustain the burden of proof cast upon him by the law.

And the desired inference is precluded for the further reason that respondent's right of recovery depends upon the existence of a particular fact which must be inferred from proven facts, and this is not permissible in the face of the positive and otherwise uncontradicted testimony of unimpeached witnesses consistent with the facts actually proved, from which testimony it affirmatively appears that the fact sought to be inferred did not exist. A rebuttable inference of fact, as said by the court in the *Wabash Railroad* case, "must necessarily yield to credible evidence of the actual occurrence." And, as stated by the court in *George* v. *Missouri Pac. R. Co., supra*, "It is well settled that where plaintiff's case is based upon an inference or inferences, that the case must fail upon proof of undisputed facts inconsistent with such inferences." Compare Fresh v. Gilson, 16 Pet. 327, 330-331. In *Southern Ry. Co.* v. *Walters, supra*, the negligence charged was failure to stop a train and flag a crossing before proceeding over it. The court concluded that the only support for the charge was an inference sought to be drawn from certain facts proved. In rejecting the inference, this court said:

> "It is argued that it may be inferred from the speed of the train when some of the witnesses observed it crossing other streets as well as Bond Avenue, and from a guess of the engineer as to the time required to get up such speed after a full stop, that none could have been made at Bond Avenue. But the argument amounts to mere speculation in view of the limited scope of the witnesses' observation, the down grade of the railway tracks at the point, and the time element involved. (Compare Chicago, M. & St. P.R. Co. v. Coogan, 271 U.S. 472.) Five witnesses for defendant [employees] testified that a full stop was made and the crossing flagged, and that no one was hit by the rear of the tender, which was the front of the train.

> "An examination of the record requires the conclusion that the evidence on the issue whether the train was stopped before crossing Bond Avenue was so insubstantial and insufficient that it did not justify a submission of that issue to the jury."

Not only is Bainbridge's testimony considered as a whole suspicious, insubstantial and insufficient, but his statement that when he turned shortly after hearing the crash the two strings were moving together is simply incredible, if he meant thereby to be understood as saying that he saw the two in contact; and if he meant by the words "moving together" simply that they were moving at the same time in the same direction but not in contact, the statement becomes immaterial. As we have already seen he was paying slight and only occasional attention to what was going on. The cars were eight or nine hundred feet from where he stood and moving almost directly away from him, his angle of vision being only 3 degrees 33 minutes from a straight line. At that sharp angle and from that distance, near dusk of a misty evening (as the proof shows), the practical impossibility of the witness being able to see whether the front of the nine-car string was in contact with the back of the two-car string is apparent. And, certainly, in the light of these conditions, no verdict based upon a statement so unbelievable reasonably could be sustained as against the positive testimony to the contrary of unimpeached witnesses, all in a position to see, as this witness was not, the precise relation of the cars to one another. The fact that these witnesses were employees of the petitioner, under the circumstances here disclosed, does not impair this conclusion. Chesapeake & Ohio Ry. v. Martin, 283 U.S. 209, 216-220.

We think, therefore, that the trial court was right in withdrawing the case from the jury. It repeatedly has been held by this court that before evidence may be left to the jury, "there is a preliminary question for the judge, not whether there is literally no evidence, but whether there is any upon which a jury can properly proceed to find a verdict for the party producing it, upon whom the *onus* of proof is imposed." Pleasants v. Fant, 22 Wall. 116, 120-121. And where the evidence is "so overwhelmingly on one side as to leave no room to doubt what the fact is, the court should give a peremptory instruction to the jury." Gunning v. Cooley, 281 U.S. 90, 94; Patton v. Texas & Pacific Ry. Co., 179 U.S. 658, 660. The rule is settled for the federal courts, and for many of the state courts, that whenever in the trial of a civil case the evidence is clearly such that if a verdict were rendered for one of the parties the other would be entitled to a new trial, it is the duty of the judge to direct the jury to find according to the views of the court. Such a practice, this court has said, not only saves time and expense, but "gives scientific certainty to the law in its application to the facts and promotes the ends of justice." Bowditch v. Boston, 101 U.S. 16, 18; Barrett v. Virginian Ry. Co., 250 U.S. 473, 476, and cases cited; Herbert v. Butler, 97 U.S. 319, 320. The scintilla rule has been definitely and repeatedly rejected so far as the federal courts are concerned. * * *

Leaving out of consideration, then, the inference relied upon, the case for respondent is left without any substantial support in the evidence, and a verdict in her favor would have rested upon mere speculation and conjecture. This, of course, is inadmissible. * * *

[Reversed. District Court Judgment Affirmed.]

MR. JUSTICE STONE and MR. JUSTICE CARDOZO concur in the result.

NOTES AND PROBLEMS FOR DISCUSSION

1. Would the result be different if Bainbridge had been standing 30 feet away instead of 900 feet, or if there were no employees riding on the second string of cars to testify as they did?

2. The Supreme Court states that Bainbridge's testimony is "suspicious" and that it is "unbelievable." Isn't witness credibility precisely the sort of factual question that the Seventh Amendment leaves to the jury?

3. Consider whether the Court articulated the strongest argument for the plaintiff. The motion for a directed verdict in this case was made at the close of all of the evidence. Assume that the defendant moved for a directed verdict at the close of the plaintiff's evidence (i.e., before defendant's evidence had been put on). Would defendant's motion for a directed verdict be granted at that point? With Bainbridge's testimony, the plaintiff endeavored to provide evidence of events leading up to the alleged collision. From this evidence, plaintiff would have the factfinder infer that a collision occurred. In other words, the events to which Bainbridge testified — that he saw the trailing string of cars' speed was increasing and gaining on the string of cars ahead of it, whose speed was decreasing, and on top of which Bainbridge saw the plaintiff's decedent, and that he soon heard the sound of a crash, turned, and no longer saw the decedent — were all circumstantial evidence of a collision. Looking only at the plaintiff's evidence in *Chamberlain*, and drawing all reasonable favorable inferences from it, could a reasonable factfinder conclude that there had been a collision involving the two strings of cars? As plaintiff's attorney, make the argument against dismissal at that stage.

4. *Chamberlain* seems unwilling to permit the jury to reason inferentially from what it considers weak circumstantial evidence, particularly when the direct evidence points in the opposite direction. Does direct evidence necessarily trump circumstantial evidence? After all, an eyewitness could be lying, and the circumstantial evidence could be strong (e.g., decedent's blood on the second string of cars). But in the language of the Court, where a party's circumstantial evidence gives rise to two "equal" inferences, the jury has no job to perform. Of course, the drawing of one particular inference from among many (so long as it is a reasonable inference) is a question of fact, as much as is determining the credibility of a witness. Why should the Court get to decide whether one inference is equal to another?

Suppose that one eyewitness testifies to a particular version of events that would, if believed, allow for the plaintiff to recover under the applicable law. Assume also, however, that the eyewitness is contradicted by a videotape whose accuracy is not otherwise challenged. Assuming no other evidence, should such a case go to the jury? That may depend on whether a court can conclude that a reasonable jury would be permitted to believe the witness, and to disbelieve the videotape. In Scott v. Harris, 550 U.S. 372, 127 S.Ct. 1769, 167 L.Ed.2d 686 (2007), the Supreme Court faced a somewhat similar question in a slightly different setting, and refused to let the case go to trial. A fuller description of the problem is presented above in connection with Summary Judgment (Chapter 9).

5. Alternatively, is the Court saying that it would be unreasonable to draw the plaintiff's desired inference in this case? See Galloway v. United States, 319 U.S. 372, 63 S.Ct. 1077, 87 L.Ed. 1458 (1943) (concluding, in the face of an evidentiary gap for eight years during supposedly "continuous" mental disability, that "inference is capable of bridging many gaps [b]ut not, in these circumstances, one so wide and deep as this").

6. Suppose that a rancher sues a railroad for the death of one of his cows. All agree that the cow was killed by one of the railroad's trains, and the cow was found alongside of the tracks. Under the applicable law, the railroad is liable for the death of the cow if the reason the cow strayed onto the tracks was because of the disrepair of the fences along the tracks (which the railroad is obligated to maintain). But the railroad is not liable if the reason the cow got onto the tracks is because a gate in the fence was open (for which the rancher has responsibility). Suppose the only facts in the case are that, near where the cow was hit by the railroad, a gate was open *and* the fence was down because it was is disrepair. In short, the cow might have wandered onto the tracks by either means. Assuming no more evidence (and assuming that the cow was equidistant from the downed fence and the open gate), would the case be one that should go to the jury? Is the problem that the inferences that might be drawn respecting how the cow got onto the tracks are "equal"? Or is the problem that no factfinder could rationally choose one inference over the other, based on these facts? (The facts have been liberally adapted from Reid v. San Pedro, L.A. & S.L.R.R., 39 Utah 627, 118 P. 1009 (1911).)

The Supreme Court more recently toyed with a similar hypothetical. Would it raise a "strong inference" that B took a jade falcon from a room if the evidence showed that only A and B had access to the room and the falcon went missing? Justice Ginsburg, writing for the majority in Tellabs v. Makor Issues & Rights, Ltd., 551 U.S. 308, 127 S.Ct. 2499, 168 L.Ed.2d 179 (2007) — seemed to say yes. Justice Scalia, in a concurring opinion, said no: "'Inference' connotes 'belief' in what is inferred, and it would be impossible to form a strong belief that it was B and not A, or A and not B." Does either the cow or the falcon hypothetical help explain what it was that concerned the Court in *Chamberlain*?

7. Compare the language of "scientific certainty" and the rejection of "mere speculation and conjecture" in *Chamberlain* with that in LAVENDER v. KURN, 327 U.S. 645, 66 S.Ct. 740, 90 L.Ed. 916 (1946) (discussed in Chapter 1). There, in another case under the Federal Employers' Liability Act with very weak (and mostly circumstantial) evidence for the plaintiff, the Supreme Court reversed a lower court's overturning of a jury verdict in favor of the plaintiff. With respect to the inferential gaps that the jury's reasoning would have to bridge, the Court declared, "Whenever facts are in dispute, or the evidence is such that fair-minded men may draw different inferences, *a measure of speculation and conjecture is required* on the part of those whose duty it is to settle the dispute . . . ." (emphasis supplied). Is *Lavender* more tolerant of the kind of conjecture that *Chamberlain* seems to condemn, and if so, why?

8. Even after the jury's verdict, on motion of the losing party, a court may also enter judgment and set aside the verdict. A motion for judgment notwithstanding the verdict (or post-verdict JMOL), is governed by the same standard for entering one at any of the other stages at which a rule 50(a) motion may be considered — whether a "reasonable jury" could decide as it did. In Unitherm Food Systems, Inc. v. Swift-Eckrich, Inc., 546 U.S. 394, 126 S.Ct. 980, 163 L.Ed.2d 974 (2006), the Court held that the defendant's failure to move under Rule 50(b) for a JMOL after the jury verdict, even though the defendant had made a Rule 50(a) motion at the close of all the evidence, precluded the appeals court from considering whether a JMOL should have been entered. Compare Note 11, below.

9. Why would a district judge who was willing to grant a post-verdict JMOL (JNOV) not simply grant the motion at the close of the evidence? Is there some advantage in waiting to see what the jury does?

10. The constitutionality of entry of judgment notwithstanding the verdict was upheld against a Seventh Amendment challenge, at least when a motion for a directed verdict had been made at the close of the evidence. Baltimore & Carolina Line, Inc. v. Redman, 295 U.S. 654, 55 S.Ct. 890, 79 L.Ed. 1636 (1935). The theory was that the post-verdict motion was merely a renewal of the earlier motion, and therefore did not amount to review of the jury's factfinding. Convincing? Justice Black once objected mightily on Seventh Amendment grounds to any power in the federal courts to prevent a case from going to a jury by means of a directed verdict and objected to what he considered to be a requirement that there be "substantial evidence" to uphold a jury's verdict. GALLOWAY v. UNITED STATES, 319 U.S. 372, 319 U.S. 372, 63 S.Ct. 1077, 87 L.Ed. 1458 (1943). He argued that such a practice "mark[ed] a continuation of the gradual process of judicial erosion which in one hundred fifty years has slowly worn away a major portion of the essential guarantee of the Seventh Amendment." Justice Black argued that at common law, courts could do no more than instruct a jury as to the dearth of evidence in favor of a particular party, and could remedy a jury's error only by the mechanism of a new trial. The only mechanisms at common law by which the judge could withdraw a case from the jury (such as the "demurrer to the evidence" at the close of plaintiff's case), required the defendant to waive his own right to a jury trial and consideration of his own evidence as the price for securing peremptory dismissal. Other mechanisms allowed the plaintiff to try again (such as the "compulsory nonsuit" at the close of all of the evidence).

The majority's response was to observe that the Seventh Amendment "did not bind the federal courts to the exact procedural incidents or details of jury trial according to the common law in 1791, any more than it tied them to the common-law system of pleading or the specific rules of evidence then prevailing." Moreover, they added, neither forcing the defendant to the all-or-nothing gamble of the common law demurrer, nor giving the plaintiff a perpetual option to start over once the defendant's evidence is in, was "essential" to the right protected by the Amendment. Even if Justice Black is right as an historical matter, given the once (but no longer) robust use of new trials, is it clear that the jury's power has really diminished over time?

11. As indicated in the discussion above, a party traditionally had to move for a JMOL at the close of all of the evidence as a precondition to seeking a post-verdict JMOL. The latest version of Rule 50(b), however, appears to dispense with that requirement. Instead, although it still permits post-verdict "renewing" of an earlier Rule 50(a) motion, it eliminates the long-standing qualifier that the renewed motion be a renewal of a Rule 50(a) motion made "at the close of all the evidence." Because a Rule 50(a) motion may be made "at any time" before the case is submitted to the jury — for example, at the close of the plaintiff's evidence — current Rule 50(b) suggests that a party now need not make a similar motion at the close of all of the evidence in order to preserve the ability to make a post-verdict motion.

Are any constitutional problems presented by this change in the wording of Rule 50? Even though the Rule may have changed, a party is still well advised to raise a Rule 50(a) motion at the close of all of the evidence, even if one has been raised earlier. But consider what happens if a party fails to re-raise the motion at the close of all of the evidence (assuming one has been made earlier). If the later post-verdict motion is a renewal of a Rule 50(a) motion made before all of the evidence was in, how is a court supposed to evaluate the propriety of such a motion? New evidence may have been introduced after the earlier motion which suggests that a JMOL is now indeed appropriate (even if it was not, at the time of the earlier Rule 50(a) motion). In such a setting, does the judge grant the post-verdict motion? The Advisory Committee Note states that "[b]ecause a Rule 50(b) motion is only a renewal of the pre-verdict motion, it can be granted only on grounds advanced in the preverdict motion." Does that help answer the question?

For additional practice in assessing the limits of rational inference, consider the following decision:

Howard v. Wal-Mart Stores, Inc.

United States Court of Appeals, Seventh Circuit, 1998.
160 F.3d 358.

POSNER, CHIEF JUDGE.

We have before us a charming miniature of a case. In 1993 Delores Howard, age 65, slipped and fell in a puddle of liquid soap that someone — no one knows who — had spilled on the floor of the aisle in a Wal-Mart store in Cahokia Illinois. She was injured, and brought suit against Wal-Mart in an Illinois state court; the defendant removed the case to federal district court. At the time the suit was brought and removed, there was enough possibility that Howard's injury was severe (the injured leg had become infected) to lift the case just over the then-$50,000 threshold for a diversity suit. But later she recovered and at trial asked for only $25,000 in damages. The jury awarded her $18,750. Wal-Mart has appealed out of fear (its lawyer explained to us at argument) of the precedential effect in future slip-and-fall cases of the judge's refusal to grant judgment for Wal-Mart as a matter of law. We don't tell people whether to exercise their rights of appeal, but we feel impelled to remind Wal-Mart and its lawyer that a district court's decision does not have precedential authority, *e.g.,* Old Republic Ins. Co. v. Chukah & Tecson, P.C., 84 F.3d 998, 1003-04 (7th Cir. 1996); Anderson v. Romero, 72 F.3d 518, 525 (7th Cir. 1995) — let alone a jury verdict or an unreported order by a magistrate judge (by any judicial officer, for that matter) refusing on unstated grounds to throw out a jury's verdict.

The issue on appeal is whether there was enough evidence of liability to allow the case to go to a jury, and, specifically, whether there was enough evidence that an employee rather than a customer spilled the soap. * * * Even if a customer spilled it, Wal-Mart could be liable if it failed to notice the spill and clean it up within a reasonable time. * * * It has a legal duty to make its premises reasonably safe for its customers. But there is no evidence with regard to how much time elapsed between the spill and the fall; it may have been minutes. Wal-Mart is not required to patrol the aisles continuously, but only at reasonable intervals. See Culli v. Marathon Petroleum Co., 862 F.2d 119 (7th Cir. 1988) (collecting Illinois cases). So Howard could prevail only if there was enough evidence that an employee spilled the soap to satisfy the requirement of proving causation by a preponderance of the evidence.

The accident occurred in the morning, and morning is also when the employees stock the shelves. The defendant presented evidence that the puddle of liquid soap on which Howard slipped was about the diameter of a softball and was in the middle of the aisle. Howard testified that it was a large puddle on the right side of the aisle and "when I got up, I had it all over me, my coat, my pants, my shoes, my socks." An employee could have dropped one of the plastic containers of liquid soap on the floor while trying to shelve it and the container could have broken and leaked. Or the cap on one of the containers might have come loose. Or the containers might have been packed improperly in the box from which they were loaded onto the shelves and one of them might have sprung a leak. Alternatively, as Wal-Mart points out, a customer, or a customer's child, might have knocked a container off the shelf. A curious feature of the case, however, is that the container that leaked and caused the spill was never found. Howard argues, not implausibly, that a customer who had come across a damaged container or had damaged it would be unlikely to purchase it, having lost part of its contents — a large part, if Howard's testimony was believed; and the jury was entitled to believe it — or indeed to put it in her shopping cart and risk smearing her other purchases with liquid soap. In light of this consideration, we cannot say that the jury was irrational in finding that the balance of probabilities tipped in favor of the plaintiff, though surely only by a hair's breadth.

Is a hair's breadth enough, though? Judges, and commentators on the law of evidence, have been troubled by cases in which the plaintiff has established a probability that only minutely exceeds 50 percent that his version of what happened is correct. The concern is illuminated by the much-discussed bus hypothetical. Suppose that the plaintiff is hit by a bus, and it is known that 51 percent of the buses on the road where the plaintiff was hit are owned by Bus Company A and 49 percent by Company B. The plaintiff sues A and asks for judgment on the basis of this statistic alone (we can ignore the other elements of liability besides causation by assuming they have all been satisfied, as in this case); he tenders no other evidence. If the defendant also puts in no evidence, should a jury be allowed to award judgment to the plaintiff? The law's answer is "no." See Richard W. Wright, "Causation, Responsibility, Risk, Probability, Naked Statistics, and Proof: Pruning the Bramble Bush by Clarifying the Concepts," 73 Ia. L. Rev. 1001, 1050-1051 (1988), and cases cited there. Our hypothetical case is a variant of Smith v. Rapid Transit, Inc., 317 Mass. 469, 58 N.E.2d 754 (Mass. 1945), where the court held that it "was not enough" "that perhaps the mathematical chances somewhat favor the proposition that a bus of the defendant caused the accident." 58 N.E.2d at 755. Kaminsky v. Hertz Corp., 94 Mich. App. 356, 288 N.W.2d 426 (Mich. App. 1979), is sometimes cited as being contrary to *Smith*, but this is not an accurate reading. Besides the fact that the corresponding percentages were 90 percent and 10 percent, there was nonstatistical evidence pointing to the defendant's ownership of the truck that had caused the accident.

Smith and *Kaminsky* involve explicitly probabilistic evidence. But as all evidence is probabilistic in the sense of lacking absolute certainty, all evidence can be expressed in probabilistic terms, and so the problem or dilemma presented by those cases is general. The eyewitness might say that he was "99 percent sure" that he had seen the defendant, and jurors appraising his testimony might reckon some different probability that he was correct. What powers the intuition that the plaintiff should lose the bus case is not the explicitly probabilistic nature of the evidence, but the evidentiary significance of missing evidence. If the 51/49 statistic is the plaintiff's only evidence, the inference to be drawn is not that there is a 51 percent probability that it was a bus owned by A that hit the plaintiff. It is that the plaintiff either investigated and discovered that the bus was actually owned by B (and B might not have been negligent and so not liable even if a cause of the accident, or might be judgment proof and so not worth suing), or that he simply has not bothered to conduct an investigation. If the first alternative is true, he should of course lose; and since it may be true, the probability that the plaintiff was hit by a bus owned by A is less than 51 percent and the plaintiff has failed to carry his burden of proof. If the second alternative is true — the plaintiff just hasn't conducted an investigation — he still should lose. A court shouldn't be required to expend its scarce resources of time and effort on a case until the plaintiff has conducted a sufficient investigation to make reasonably clear that an expenditure of public resources is likely to yield a significant social benefit. This principle is implicit in the law's decision to place the burden of producing evidence on the plaintiff rather than on the defendant. Suppose it would cost the court system $10,000 to try even a barebones case. This expenditure would be worthless from the standpoint of deterring accidents should it turn out that the bus was owned by B. It makes sense for the court to require some advance investigation by the plaintiff in order to increase the probability that a commitment of judicial resources would be worthwhile.

These objections to basing a decision on thin evidence do not apply to the present case. Not only is there no reason to suspect that the plaintiff is holding back unfavorable evidence; it would have been unreasonable, given the stakes, to expect her to conduct a more thorough investigation. This is a tiny case; not so tiny that it can be expelled from the federal court system without a decision, but so tiny that it would make no sense to try to coerce the parties to produce more evidence, when, as we have said, no inference can be drawn from the paucity of evidence that the plaintiff was afraid to look harder for fear that she would discover that a customer and not an employee of Wal-Mart had spilled the soap.

We conclude, therefore, that the jury verdict must stand. And, Wal-Mart, this decision, a reported appellate decision, unlike the decision of the district court, will have precedential authority!

NOTES AND PROBLEMS FOR DISCUSSION

1. Note that under Illinois law, the plaintiff cannot recover on a strict liability theory; rather, she must prove negligence on the part of an employee of Wal-Mart's, and that the employee's negligence caused her injury. Was the evidence of employee negligence in *Wal-Mart* any better than the evidence of negligence in *Chamberlain*?

2. Focus on the bus hypothetical posed by Judge Posner: Are you persuaded by his reasoning as to why the proof of a 51/49 statistical probability alone would not be enough to take a case to the jury?

3. The bus hypothetical appears to be geared to the evidence sufficient to survive a motion for judgment as a matter of law at the close of the plaintiff's case. When a court is considering a JMOL motion and has before it all of the evidence — either before the case is submitted to the jury (as in *Chamberlain*), or post-verdict (as in *Wal-Mart*) — through what sort of lens should the trial judge assess whether rational factfinders could disagree, or, instead, could only come out one way? The standard in the federal courts had not always been clear until the decision in REEVES v. SANDERSON PLUMBING PRODS., INC., 530 U.S. 133, 120 S.Ct. 2097, 147 L.Ed.2d 105 (2000). *Reeves* was an age discrimination case brought by an employee under the ADEA (Age Discrimination in Employment Act of 1967). To prevail under the statute, the employee had to prove that when he had been discharged, his employer was "actually motivated" by the plaintiff's age. Because "there will seldom be 'eyewitness' testimony as to the employer's mental processes," the Court had previously allowed victims of alleged employment discrimination to raise a presumption of intentional discrimination by putting on a "prima facie" case of such discrimination through indirect or circumstantial evidence.

In *Reeves*, the plaintiff's prima facie case consisted of proof that he was fired; that he was 57 years old (and thus covered by the ADEA which applied to workers at least 40 years old); that he was "otherwise qualified" for the job; and that persons in their thirties filled his position. Proof of a prima facie case enables employment discrimination plaintiffs to avoid a directed verdict at the close of their evidence, and it shifts the "burden of production" to the defendant to come forward with evidence of a nondiscriminatory reason for its actions. But it does not shift the "burden of persuasion," which remains with the plaintiff. In *Reeves*, the defendant proffered evidence that the plaintiff was fired for his "shoddy record keeping" and for his failure to discipline other employees as required by his job. The employee then put on evidence to the effect that his record keeping was not shoddy and that he was not responsible for the supposed failure to discipline. The Court had previously stated that a jury which disbelieved the employer's proffered nondiscriminatory reason for its action based on the plaintiff's rebuttal evidence would permit, but would not compel the jury to find in favor of the plaintiff. The ultimate question was whether the jury was persuaded by a preponderance of the evidence that the employer intentionally discriminated against the plaintiff.

The appellate court in *Reeves* concluded that proof of a prima facie case plus evidence from which a reasonable factfinder could (but did not have to) find that the employer's proffered nondiscriminatory reason was untrue, was not enough to sustain a jury verdict in plaintiff's favor, without additional evidence of discrimination. It therefore reversed the trial court's denial of the employer's post-verdict JMOL. The Supreme Court disagreed, finding that a prima facie case plus evidence from which a factfinder could find the employer's proffered nondiscriminatory reason was pretextual, permitted the trier of fact to conclude that the employer intentionally discriminated. At the same time, the Court was careful not to suggest that judgment as a matter of law would never be proper in such settings, if, for example, "the record conclusively revealed some other nondiscriminatory reason for the employer's decision, or if the plaintiff created only a weak issue of fact as to whether the employer's reason was untrue, and there was abundant and uncontroverted evidence that no discrimination had occurred." In such a case no rational finder of fact could conclude that the employer's action was discriminatory. The Court then applied its reasoning to the case before it:

> The remaining question is whether, despite the Court of Appeals' misconception of petitioner's evidentiary burden, respondent was nonetheless entitled to judgment as a matter of law. Under Rule 50, a court should render judgment as a matter of law when "a party has been fully heard on an issue and there is no legally sufficient evidentiary basis for a reasonable jury to find for that party on that issue." Fed. Rule Civ. Proc. 50(a). The Courts of Appeals have articulated differing formulations as to what evidence a court is to consider in ruling on a Rule 50 motion. Some decisions have stated that review is limited to that evidence favorable to the non-moving party, while most have held that review extends to the entire record, drawing all reasonable inferences in favor of the nonmovant. * * *

> On closer examination, this conflict seems more semantic than real. Those decisions holding that review under Rule 50 should be limited to evidence favorable to the nonmovant appear to have their genesis in Wilkerson v. McCarthy, 336 U.S. 53, 93 L.Ed. 497, 69 S.Ct. 413 (1949). * * * In *Wilkerson*, we stated that "in passing upon whether there is sufficient evidence to submit an issue to the jury we need look only to the evidence and reasonable inferences which tend to support the case of" the nonmoving party. But subsequent decisions have clarified that this passage was referring to the evidence to which the trial court should

give credence, not the evidence that the court should review. In the analogous context of summary judgment under Rule 56, we have stated that the court must review the record "taken as a whole." Matsushita Elec. Industrial Co. v. Zenith Radio Corp., 475 U.S. 574, 587, 89 L.Ed.2d 538, 106 S.Ct. 1348 (1986). And the standard for granting summary judgment "mirrors" the standard for judgment as a matter of law, such that "the inquiry under each is the same." Anderson v. Liberty Lobby, Inc., 477 U.S. 242, 250-251, 91 L.Ed.2d 202, 106 S.Ct. 2505 (1986). It therefore follows that, in entertaining a motion for judgment as a matter of law, the court should review all of the evidence in the record.

In doing so, however, the court must draw all reasonable inferences in favor of the nonmoving party, and it may not make credibility determinations or weigh the evidence. * * * Thus, although the court should review the record as a whole, it must disregard all evidence favorable to the moving party that the jury is not required to believe. See Wright & Miller 299. That is, the court should give credence to the evidence favoring the nonmovant as well as that "evidence supporting the moving party that is uncontradicted and unimpeached, at least to the extent that that evidence comes from disinterested witnesses." Id. at 300.

Applying this standard here, it is apparent that respondent was not entitled to judgment as a matter of law. In this case, in addition to establishing a prima facie case of discrimination and creating a jury issue as to the falsity of the employer's explanation, petitioner introduced additional evidence that Chesnut [plaintiff's boss] was motivated by age-based animus and was principally responsible for petitioner's firing. Petitioner testified that Chesnut had told him that he "was so old [he] must have come over on the Mayflower" and, on one occasion when petitioner was having difficulty starting a machine, that he "was too damn old to do [his] job." According to petitioner, Chesnut would regularly "cuss at me and shake his finger in my face." Oswalt, roughly 24 years younger than petitioner, corroborated that there was an "obvious difference" in how Chesnut treated them. He stated that, although he and Chesnut "had [their] differences," "it was nothing compared to the way [Chesnut] treated Roger." Oswalt explained that Chesnut "tolerated quite a bit" from him even though he "defied" Chesnut "quite often," but that Chesnut treated petitioner "in a manner, as you would . . . treat . . . a child when . . . you're angry with [him]." Petitioner also demonstrated that, according to company records, he and Oswalt had nearly identical rates of productivity in 1993. Yet respondent conducted an efficiency study of only the regular line, supervised by petitioner, and placed only petitioner on probation. Chesnut conducted that efficiency study and, after having testified to the contrary on direct examination, acknowledged on cross-examination that he had recommended that petitioner be placed on probation following the study. * * *

The ultimate question in every employment discrimination case involving a claim of disparate treatment is whether the plaintiff was the victim of intentional discrimination. Given the evidence in the record supporting petitioner, we see no reason to subject the parties to an additional round of litigation before the Court of Appeals rather than to resolve the matter here. The District Court plainly informed the jury that petitioner was required to show "by a preponderance of the evidence that his age was a determining and motivating factor in the decision of [respondent] to terminate him." The court instructed the jury that, to show that respondent's explanation was a pretext for discrimination, petitioner had to demonstrate "1, that the stated reasons were not the real reasons for [petitioner's] discharge; and 2, that age discrimination was the real reason for [petitioner's] discharge." Given that petitioner established a prima facie case of discrimination, introduced enough evidence for the jury to reject respondent's explanation, and produced additional evidence of age-based animus, there was sufficient evidence for the jury to find that respondent had intentionally discriminated. The District Court was therefore correct to submit the case to the jury, and the Court of Appeals erred in overturning its verdict.

The *Reeves* Court's conclusion that, when all of the evidence is in, a JMOL must be viewed in light of all of the evidence, while drawing all reasonable inferences in favor of the party against whom the motion is made, had been the practice of most federal courts, although some perceived that a somewhat more plaintiff-friendly standard applied in FELA cases. See Boeing v. Shipman, 411 F.2d 365 (5th Cir. 1969). Does Rule 50 permit application of a different standard depending on the substance of the underlying litigation?

4. NEW TRIALS

Another available post-verdict motion is the motion for a new trial. Read Rule 59 to get a sense of the procedures.

The motion for a new trial can be made on numerous grounds, but they can be usefully (although somewhat imperfectly) grouped into four categories. The first category arises when there has been an error of law during the course of the trial. Even though an error of law can be corrected on appeal, it can also be corrected by the trial judge on his own (or a party's) motion. Examples include an error in the admission or exclusion of evidence, improperly granting or denying permission to amend a pleading or pretrial order, or an incorrect charge to the jury. Note here that there is an additional consideration, since the trial judge will usually not grant a new trial simply because of a mistake, unless she also finds that the mistake prejudiced the substantial rights of the parties (e.g., it was material, it was not corrected pre-verdict, and it was on an important matter). Obviously, the system would quickly break down if every mistake no matter how trivial led to a new trial.

The second category involves even more discretionary types of rulings. Examples might include permitting or not permitting a witness to testify out of order, granting or refusing to grant a continuance, granting or refusing a juror's mid-trial request to be excused, improper conduct of a witness or argument of counsel that prejudiced the rights of a party, or admitting evidence whose prejudicial effect outweighed its probative value.

It should be noted that neither of these two categories of grounds for a new trial directly implicates questions relating to the strength of the evidence supporting the verdict — i.e., new trials on these grounds may be granted even if the evidence supporting the verdict is clearly sufficient and even quite strong. Nevertheless, as noted above, judges must also consider whether, if there has been a mistake, it was prejudicial — and that can only be determined in light of the strength of the verdict winner's case.

The third category speaks directly to the evidence considered by the jury in making its findings and permits a judge to grant a new trial if the verdict is against the weight of the evidence — or as it is sometimes formulated: against the "great" or "clear" weight of the evidence. Again, this is a somewhat vague standard that, if taken too literally, could seriously undermine the right to jury trial. The next case focuses on this issue. A related set of issues involves the grant of a new trial for excessiveness of the jury's verdict. We take up the problem of excessive damages in Section 5, below.

Finally, the fourth category involves misconduct of various kinds, including by jurors, counsel, parties and perhaps other participants.

Latino v. Kaizer

United States Court of Appeals, Seventh Circuit, 1995.

58 F.3d 310.

SHARP, CHIEF DISTRICT JUDGE.[*]

The defendants-appellants, police officer Edward Kaizer and the City of Chicago, appeal a jury award of damages against them in favor of plaintiffs-appellees Daniel Latino and Robert Slawinski for arrest without probable cause and false imprisonment. The plaintiffs' jury award came after the second trial in this case; the first jury trial found in favor of the defendants, but that verdict was vacated by the district judge on a post-trial motion under Federal Rule of Civil Procedure 59. The second jury awarded the plaintiffs $5500.00 each, and the district judge then awarded plaintiffs $120,113.50 in attorney fees and $1,019.34 in expenses under 42 U.S.C. §1988.

Latino and Slawinski sued Chicago and two officers, Kaizer and William Gordon, under the state common law tort of false imprisonment and 42 U.S.C. §1983 for alleged violations of their Fourth and Fourteenth Amendment rights. The plaintiffs were arrested by Officer Kaizer and an undetermined second officer on June 2, 1991 for ticket scalping at the first Bulls-Lakers game in the final round of the NBA playoffs. All agree that the arrest occurred the night of

---

[*] Chief District Judge Allen Sharp, Northern District of Indiana, sitting by designation.

June 2, 1991 outside the Chicago Stadium, but there ends the similarities between the parties' stories.

The jury in the first civil trial found against the plaintiffs in favor of defendants, but the district judge granted the plaintiffs' post-trial motion and vacated the jury's verdict. In so doing he found that the officers' version of events was perjury, and absent that testimony, the jury's verdict for the defendants was against the weight of the evidence. Because this court finds that the first jury verdict should not have been vacated, it reinstates that verdict in favor of the defendants.

Police Officers' Testimony

This case boils down to a swearing contest between the police officers and the plaintiffs. Officers Kaizer and Scornavacco testified that they were undercover at the Stadium, assigned to patrol on foot before the game to apprehend pickpockets and ticket scalpers. The officers spotted Latino and Slawinski on the north side of Madison Street walking west toward Gate 1 of the Stadium building, each holding something in his hand. The officers separated and crossed the street after the plaintiffs. Kaizer stated that he saw Latino and Slawinski stopped by a couple of people in front of Gate 1, and he walked over and joined the group. Latino and Slawinski were standing side-by-side, and each was holding a pair of tickets.

While Officer Scornavacco walked about 10 to 15 feet behind the plaintiffs, Kaizer heard someone in the crowd ask, "Well, what kind of seats are they?" Both plaintiffs replied that they were good seats. Kaizer then heard someone ask, "How much are they?" He did not hear the reply, but did hear someone comment "I don't want to pay that." Officer Kaizer repeated the question himself, asking Latino and Slawinski "How much are they?" Latino responded "$150." Officer Kaizer then looked at Slawinski and asked, "And yours?" Slawinski responded "$150" as well.

Officer Kaizer then announced that he was a police officer and that he was arresting them for ticket speculation, showed his badge, and placed a handcuff on Latino's right wrist. Officer Scornavacco walked up and placed the other half of the handcuffs around Slawinski's left wrist, handcuffing the plaintiffs together. Officer Kaizer then asked them for their tickets. Kaizer took two tickets from Latino, and Scornavacco took two from Slawinski. Kaizer then asked for their identification, and both produced wallets and drivers' licenses with their free hands. Kaizer and Scornavacco then walked the plaintiffs south across Madison Street into the parking lot and turned them over to a sergeant.

After the game started around 2:30 p.m., the officers left the stadium for the Thirteenth District police station. While Officer Kaizer processed the arrestees, he removed the confiscated tickets from his pocket and separated them from the identification cards, and placed them in individual inventory envelopes assigned to each arrestee. Latino and Slawinski were then locked up and were later released on recognizance bonds.

Plaintiffs' Testimony

The plaintiffs' version of events was strikingly different. At the time of his arrest, Latino was Director of Alcoholic Beverages for the Phar-Mor Drug

Company. He testified that as of the morning of June 2, 1991, he had received two tickets for the game from a Phar-Mor supplier. Latino invited Slawinski (his tennis partner and an area sales manager for an alcoholic beverage distributor) to attend the game with him. They met Latino's boss, Phar-Mor CEO Mickey Monus, and approximately eight other people associated with Phar-Mor for lunch at Pizzeria Uno near downtown Chicago.

Monus took the tickets from the people at the luncheon and redistributed them. Monus took Latino's two tickets, but gave him back four. He informed Latino that the extra two tickets should be given to buyers from Phar-Mor or others in the industry.

Latino and Slawinski drove in Latino's car to the stadium, arriving at approximately 1:00 p.m. Latino testified that he left his wallet and identification in his car. Slawinski testified that he had no wallet or identification. As the plaintiffs walked toward the stadium, they looked for but did not see anyone from Phar-Mor or Slawinski's company. Latino then spotted an acquaintance, Richard Scrima, in a parking lot on the south side of Madison Street. They crossed to the south side of the street and Latino went up to Scrima; Slawinski stopped about ten or twenty feet before Latino did.

Latino informed Scrima that he had extra tickets to the game, and asked him whether he had seen anyone from the industry, or for any suggestions about what to do with his extra tickets. Scrima testified that he offered to buy the tickets, but Latino refused.

Latino testified that Scrima asked him if he could help out Scrima's acquaintance who was standing there. The man pulled out two tickets, and asked whether Latino would "trade up" tickets. Latino refused, turned, and walked away.   Interestingly, Scrima testified that he did not remember introducing anyone to Latino, or the encounter about which Latino testified.

Just after Latino walked away from Scrima he was tapped on the shoulder by Officer Kaizer, who told him he was under arrest for scalping and cuffed his right wrist. Kaizer led Latino toward Slawinski (who then was standing not more than ten feet away). At this point Scrima noticed that Latino had been arrested, and stated that this had all occurred in about 25 or 30 seconds. Slawinski walked towards Latino, and was asked by another plainclothes officer (either Gordon or Scornavacco) if he knew Latino. When Slawinski said that Latino was a friend of his, the second officer cuffed Slawinski's left wrist to the other end of the cuff on Latino's right wrist.

Officer Kaizer asked Latino for identification and Latino told him it was in his car. Kaizer asked how many tickets he had, and Latino replied four. Kaizer did not request the tickets. Kaizer led Latino and Slawinski to the parking lot where they were turned over to another officer.

Slawinski testified that Kaizer did not ask for the tickets until they were at the station. When asked for them, Latino gave Kaizer all four. Slawinski said he had no tickets. Officer Kaizer paperclipped two tickets at random to Latino's form and two to Slawinski's.

Post-Trial Motions

The jury in the first trial found in favor of the defendants, Officers Kaizer and Gordon and the City of Chicago. The plaintiffs filed post-trial motions under Rules 50 and 59 with the district judge, requesting a new trial. The district judge denied the Rule 50 motion for judgment as a matter of law. He acknowledged that the admissible evidence presented by the defense, if believed by the jury, supported the defendants' verdict. However, Judge Shadur granted a new trial under Rule 59, finding that the police officers' testimony was perjury, and when the perjurious testimony was stricken, the verdict was against the weight of the remaining evidence. The district judge also vaguely referred to defense counsel's closing as improper, saying that added "some further weight" to the decision to grant the new trial.

Discussion

The plaintiffs-appellees attempt to reargue the facts before this court and show that their version of events was more believable. Such is not our role. We must decide only whether the district judge properly vacated the first jury verdict. Judge Shadur has provided a clear, straightforward, and precise statement of his reasons for finding perjury and vacating the first jury verdict. This court must determine whether such action was appropriate.

The defendants did not appeal the district judge's grant of a new trial, but rather proceeded with the second trial. An order granting a new trial is not a final order within the meaning of 28 U.S.C. §1291 and is therefore generally not immediately appealable. Nevertheless, after a new trial and entry of final judgment an appellate court entertaining an appeal from the final judgment may review the decision to grant a new trial and, where appropriate, reinstate the original verdict. *Juneau Square Corp. v. First Wisconsin Nat. Bank of Milwaukee,* 624 F.2d 798, 806 (7th Cir. 1980), cert. den., 449 U.S. 1013, 101 S.Ct. 571, 66 L.Ed.2d 472 (1980).

Judge Shadur was firm in his belief that the two different versions of events in this case were not merely a "swearing contest" between the parties. He believed that the officers' account of events was objectively and inherently improbable, and was therefore perjury. Judge Shadur believed that Officer Kaizer's testimony could lead only to the inference that Slawinski and Latino were attempting to sell all four of their tickets, and the judge could not believe that two men would make a special trip to the stadium to sell their seats to such "an extraordinary occasion" (despite the $600 profit at stake). Judge Shadur also believed that the mismatched pairs of tickets (Latino supposedly was offering seats 16 and 17, and Slawinski had 15 and 18) "directly puts the lie to Officer Kaizer's version." Judge Shadur found that the objective evidence "put the lie" to the officers' testimony, and it was therefore perjury. Excluding the officers' testimony, the verdict for the defendants was of course against the weight of the evidence. This court must determine whether Judge Shadur correctly applied the law in deciding to exclude the officers' testimony as perjury.

Appellate review of a district court's order for a new trial is limited. Because the trial judge is uniquely situated to rule on such a motion, the district court has great discretion in determining whether to grant a new trial. Forrester

v. White, 846 F.2d 29, 31 (7th Cir. 1988); see also Fort Howard Paper Co. v. Standard Havens, Inc., 901 F.2d 1373, 1377 (7th Cir. 1990); *Juneau*, 624 F.2d at 806. Therefore, in reviewing the new trial order, we do not seek to substitute our judgment for the trial judge's decision that a new trial was appropriate; "We seek only to determine whether he abused his discretion." *Fort Howard Paper*, 901 F.2d at 1377, *quoting Juneau*, 624 F.2d at 806.

When the trial judge disagrees with a jury verdict, the Seventh Amendment's limitations on the judge's power to reexamine the jury's verdict is implicated and a more exacting standard of review applies. Matter of Innovative Const. Systems, Inc., 793 F.2d 875, 888 (7th Cir. 1986). Nonetheless, the district judge's determination still warrants substantial deference. *Id.* In cases involving simple issues but highly disputed facts (an apt description of this case), greater deference should be afforded the jury's verdict than in cases involving complex issues with facts not highly disputed. Williams v. City of Valdosta, 689 F.2d 964, 974 (11th Cir. 1982); see also Williamson v. Consolidated Rail Corp., 926 F.2d 1344, 1352 (3rd Cir. 1991) ("Where the subject matter of the litigation is simple and within a layman's understanding, the district court is given less freedom to scrutinize the jury's verdict than in a case that deals with complex factual determinations."). *Williams v. Valdosta* also notes that the *grant* of a motion for a new trial begs more stringent review than a denial, and a still more rigorous review when the basis of the motion was the weight of the evidence. 689 F.2d at 974.

Despite the deference to be accorded a district court's decision to grant a new trial, new trials granted because the verdict is against the weight of the evidence are proper only when the record shows that the jury's verdict resulted in a miscarriage of justice or where the verdict, on the record, cries out to be overturned or shocks our conscience. *Williamson v. Consolidated Rail Corp.*, 926 F.2d at 1353.

In his oral ruling on November 16, 1993, Judge Shadur invoked the memory of a giant of the federal judiciary in a bygone era, Chief Judge John Barnes of the United States District Court in Chicago during the 1930s, '40s, and '50s. Chief Judge Barnes was a dynamic not-so-benevolent tyrant who ruled the district court in Chicago with an iron fist, sometimes but not always covered with a velvet glove. He was sometimes called "Old Iron Pants," which was not always a term of endearment. Judge Shadur noted that in a case in which the jury found against then attorney Shadur's client, Chief Judge Barnes said essentially, "In these cases I sit as the 13th juror. As I listened to the evidence I was convinced that there was major perjury presented to the jury. Unfortunately, the jury didn't recognize it, but I grant a new trial because the jury verdict was against the manifest weight of the evidence." The existence or not of the "13th juror rule" is a debate which need not be decided here. It is unlikely that even Chief Judge Barnes would have argued that a United States district judge has an absolute veto to set aside any civil jury verdict which that judge finds distasteful.

There are statements in the cases that, in ruling on the motion, the trial judge acts as a 13th juror. Properly understood and applied, no fault can be found with them for the judge does act to evaluate and weigh the evidence. But while he has a responsibility for the result no less than the jury, he should not set the verdict aside as against the weight of the evidence merely because, if he had acted as trier of the fact, he would have reached a different result; and in that sense he does not act as a 13th juror in approving or disapproving the verdict. And since the credibility of witnesses is peculiarly for the jury, it is an invasion of the jury's province to grant a new trial merely because the evidence was sharply in conflict. *Williams v. City of Valdosta,* 689 F.2d at 973 fn.7, citing Moore's Federal Practice, ¶59.08(5), at 59-158-59. See also Foster v. Continental Can Corp., 101 F.R.D. 710, 714 (N.D. Ind. 1984), *aff'd*, 783 F.2d 731 (7th Cir. 1986).

The district judge can take away from the jury testimony that reasonable persons could not believe. United States v. Kuzniar, 881 F.2d 466, 471 (7th Cir. 1989). However, that exception is a narrow one, and can be invoked only where the testimony contradicts indisputable physical facts or laws. Id.; see also id. at 471 fn.1 ("Testimony which does not contradict the physical laws of nature cannot be shielded from the jury."). Judge Shadur stated quite clearly his belief that the officers' testimony in the case now before us fell within that narrow exception. With all deference, we can not agree.

On three separate occasions Judge Shadur very carefully set forth his reasoning for vacating the verdict in the first jury trial. His transcribed oral statements of reasons for granting a new trial were fully and carefully crafted with the ring of candor and intellectual honesty. It is precisely because of their excellence that we have full insight into the precise reasons for granting a new trial. It is more than a matter of semantics.

The district judge found that the officers' testimony was perjury and therefore should not have provided a basis for the jury's decision. Once he decided to exclude the officers' testimony, then of course the jury verdict for the defendants was against the weight of the evidence.

Judge Shadur's finding that the police officers' testimony was perjury was not based on their demeanor. He very carefully and precisely set forth the basis of his finding, which was that the officers' story was inconsistent with his view of the physical evidence and was "at war with common sense." Judge Shadur believed the officers' testimony was objectively and inherently improbable to the extent that they must be lying. This court is fully capable of reviewing that basis, and finds that Judge Shadur's decision was an abuse of discretion.

The jury's verdict could only be disturbed under the narrowest of circumstances, which simply do not exist in this case. It does not contradict the laws of nature to believe that two men would rather receive $600 than attend a Bulls-Lakers game, and the district judge was not at liberty to effectively take that testimony away from the jury in deciding that the verdict was against the weight of the evidence. The court appreciates Judge Shadur's frustration at a jury verdict which he believed was based on a perjured account of events. However, it was the jury which had the duty to weigh the evidence, and we do not agree that the officers' testimony was so physically impossible or contrary to the evidence as to provide a legitimate basis for in effect excluding it from the jury's consideration.

Judge Shadur believed that there was no rational predicate for believing that Slawinski and Latino would go to the Chicago Stadium to sell all four tickets; he believed it to be inherently incredible. This court can not agree. That scenario is at worst improbable, and the jury was justified in crediting it. Preferring to sell all of one's tickets for a steep profit rather than to actually attend a Bulls-Lakers game might seem inherently incredible to a diehard fan, but legally it is not so.

It must be remembered that Latino and Slawinski had lunched together with Latino's boss in downtown Chicago before the game. It was there that they were given the four tickets at issue. Judge Shadur believed Kaizer's account of Slawinski's and Latino's actions could only support the inference that all four tickets were for sale. Perhaps so. Perhaps at first they planned to go to the game, but later decided to sell all of the tickets when they realized how much money they could get for them. Such is not a metaphysical impossibility; in fact there are many likely reasons to decide to sell all four tickets. Unlike cases involving complicated legal concepts, many jurors would have personal experience with identical situations. The jurors were in the best position to decide the rationality or reasonableness of the scalping charge. Such a scenario can not be considered to be outside the realm of possibility, and Judge Shadur should not have overridden the jury verdict on that basis.

Notwithstanding, this court believes that Officer Kaizer's testimony could support the inference that the plaintiffs were only selling their extra two tickets, or that perhaps they had planned to sell only two but were toying with the idea of selling all four when faced with quick, easy money. Regardless, even if Judge Shadur was correct that the only permissible inference from Kaizer's testimony was that there were four tickets for sale, that simply does not create a manifestly unbelievable scenario. For $300 per pair, whether the men would choose to sell both pairs and watch the game in a bar or sell one pair and watch it in person, either scenario is well within the range of reasonable human behavior, and likewise within the experience and understanding of the jury.

As physical proof of his belief that the officers' story was contrived, Judge Shadur pointed out that the tickets each plaintiff purportedly held were not in sequential pairs — Kaizer had placed tickets 16 and 17 in Latino's file, and 15 and 18 in Slawinski's. Judge Shadur considered that to be physical evidence completely and objectively at odds with Officer Kaizer's depiction of the plaintiffs' actions. Judge Shadur believed that Officer Kaizer *must* have taken all four tickets from Latino, as Latino testified, but when he booked them he attached two tickets to Latino's form and two to Slawinski's, inadvertently dividing them into unmatched pairs. The judge refused to believe that Slawinski and Latino could have each been holding mismatched pairs at the time of their arrest. Judge Shadur had already decided, upon seeing the exhibit before it was even entered into evidence, that the mismatched tickets alone "utterly destroyed the credibility of Officer Kaizer's depiction."

The jury would not have been unreasonable in deciding that Latino or Slawinski might have mismatched the tickets inadvertently when they divvied them up between themselves, or that the tickets were mixed up while Officer Kaizer took them from the plaintiffs and put them in his pocket before taking the plaintiffs to jail. Both sides put forth evidence on this issue and argued at length the inferences which could be derived from it. Defense counsel did a good job at presenting reasonable inferences based on the evidence which would explain the mismatched tickets without the necessity of contrivance on the part of the officers. Apparently, the jury may have agreed that the mismatched tickets did not destroy the officers' story or credibility.

Judge Shadur also points out his belief that two men handcuffed together physically could not have retrieved their wallets and identification as Officer Kaizer testified. Again, such may be improbable, but certainly not physically impossible. Detainees have performed far more surprisingly deft acrobatics while shackled much more constrictedly. These men each had a free hand, and the other was only restrained in its range of motion, not its ability to grasp. Most men pull their wallets out with one hand then hold it still with the other while extracting their identification. There is nothing about Latino's or Slawinski's condition that would have necessarily prevented that.

Judge Shadur also pointed out that Richard Scrima corroborated the plaintiffs' version rather than the police officers'. Scrima is a truck driver in the liquor industry known to Mr. Latino. There are various reasons why Mr. Scrima might have lied in favor of Mr. Latino, none of them material here. The fact is the jury apparently disbelieved Scrima, and that decision was their function. Disbelieving Scrima certainly does not challenge the laws of nature.

The plaintiffs' closing argument well encompassed their evidence and theory of the case. However, the jury believed the defendants. With the greatest deference to Judge Shadur, there was nothing demonstrably untrue about the defendants' evidence. It did not, for example, require a realignment of the laws of nature. This was a credibility-based decision — a swearing contest. The evidence for each side was essentially equal; it was merely a matter of whom to believe. "And since the credibility of witnesses is peculiarly for the jury, it is an invasion of the jury's province to grant a new trial merely because the evidence was sharply in conflict." *Williams v. City of Valdosta*, 689 F.2d at 973 fn.7. The jury spoke its verdict, and the Seventh Amendment affords it very considerable deference.

Judge Shadur usurped the jury's role in deciding the most reasonable inferences from the evidence. That flies in the face of the Seventh Amendment, and goes beyond the power of the district judge under Rule 59. With all deference, the grant of a new trial in this case was an abuse of discretion. It must most respectfully be decided here that with all good intentions the district judge did indeed cross the boundaries when he determined that the jury should not have been permitted to credit the officers' testimony. The officers' testimony was not objectively false, and excluding it after the fact second-guesses the jury in a way that strikes at the very heart of the Seventh Amendment. Judge Shadur certainly must be commended for his intellectual honesty and candor, but this court must be equally intellectually honest and candid in saying that the boundary was indeed crossed. The grant of a new trial based on Judge Shadur's reasoning was a clear abuse of discretion, and cannot be upheld.

Therefore, the verdict in the first trial must stand, which obviates the necessity of dealing with the other issues which are here presented. On these bases, the decision to grant a new trial in the first trial is reversed, and this case is remanded with instructions to reinstate the jury's verdict for the defendants in the first trial.

NOTES AND PROBLEMS FOR DISCUSSION

1. The defendants won the first jury verdict, and the Court granted the plaintiff, Latino, a new trial. Why didn't the defendants appeal after the first ruling, before going through the second trial? See 28 U.S.C. §1291.

2. *Latino* presents three separate issues: (a) the standard that the trial court should apply in granting a new trial; (b) the manner in which that standard should be applied to the facts; and (c) the standard that the appellate court should apply in reviewing the trial court's ruling whether or not to grant a new trial. What standard did the appellate court apply in *Latino*, and where did it find that Judge Shadur went awry?

3. Compare (and contrast) the standard for granting a new trial in the first instance under Rule 59 on the ground that the verdict is against the weight of the evidence, and the standard for a JMOL under Rule 50 for evidentiary insufficiency. Now, try to imagine a case in which there is sufficient evidence for a rational factfinder to come out the way it did, but at the same time the verdict is nevertheless against the great weight of the evidence. Is *Latino* such a case?

4. Consider why the Court in *Latino*, after articulating the new trial standard as whether the verdict is "against the weight of the evidence" (or "against the manifest weight of the evidence"), asserts that the jury's verdict should only be thrown out under such a standard to prevent "a miscarriage of justice" or when the verdict "shocks [the] conscience." The new trial weight-of-the-evidence standard is typically a somewhat *easier* standard for a moving party to meet than the standard for a JNOV or post-verdict JMOL. (Do you see why that should be?) Doesn't the court's gloss on "against the weight of the evidence" arguably make it almost as difficult (if not more difficult) to get a new trial as outright dismissal? Or is the court's rather stringent test for new trial motions good only in cases that amount to "he said; [s]he said" disputes that turn entirely on credibility determinations, as in *Latino* itself?

5. Don't be misled by *Latino*. Reversals of new trial rulings by district judges are infrequent, largely because of the broad discretion accorded district judges as reflected in the deferential standard of appellate review of such rulings (i.e., Did the district court abuse its discretion in ruling on the new trial?). Nevertheless, it may be true that somewhat greater appellate scrutiny is applied to *grants* of new trials, because they throw out a jury's verdict, as opposed to denials of new trials.

6. If the point of judicial intervention is to ensure rational decisionmaking in civil cases, why should a district judge be allowed to upset a jury verdict with a new trial on weight-of-the-evidence grounds when she is not prepared to grant a

JMOL — i.e., when she has decided that a rational factfinder could come out the way it did?

7. Does Rule 59 require the judge to state her reasons for granting a new trial? Cf. Rule 59(d). Ask yourself whether the plaintiffs in *Latino* would have been better off if, instead of giving the reasons he did, Judge Shadur simply had said "I think that the verdict is against the weight of the evidence and constitutes a miscarriage of justice."

8. Suppose that the jury comes in with its verdict. Suppose also that there was sufficient evidence for its verdict under Rule 50, and that it is also not against the weight of the evidence under Rule 59. Suppose further that upon listening to the jurors talk about their deliberations, it becomes clear to the trial judge that the jury reached its decision in an improper manner. Perhaps they considered material not presented to them at trial in reaching their verdict, or that there was other misconduct on their part. When will Rule 59 permit a remedy by way of a new trial?

In PETERSON v. WILSON, 141 F.3d 573 (5th Cir. 1998), the district court ordered a new trial based on "comments the jurors made to the court after returning the verdict [and outside the presence of the parties and their respective counsel], that the jury completely disregarded the Court's instructions." The district court further concluded that "it appears that the jury considered improper factors in reaching its verdict." Following a verdict in the second case, the loser of that case appealed, arguing that the award of a new trial after the first trial (which he had won) had been improperly granted. The Fifth Circuit agreed, and reinstated the earlier verdict. Judge Weiner wrote for the court:

> "It is a well-settled rule in this circuit that 'a verdict can be against the "great weight of the evidence," and thus justify a new trial, even if there is substantial evidence to support it.'" What courts cannot do — and what the district court here never purported to do — is to grant a new trial "simply because [the court] would have come to a different conclusion than the jury did."

> The district court's succinct but cryptic, three-sentence explanation for granting a new trial demonstrates beyond question that, following the verdict, the court impermissibly met with and interrogated the jurors *outside the presence of the parties and their respective counsel,* and then proceeded to act in direct reliance on the jurors' comments as though they constituted newly discovered evidence of a kind that the court could properly consider. It was not. The conclusion is inescapable that, in impeaching the jury's verdict in this case, the district court relied on information obtained from the jurors in the court's post-verdict, *ex parte* meeting with them and that, by definition, any information thus obtained had to come directly from their internal deliberations qua jurors.

> Rule 606(b) of the Federal Rules of Evidence (F.R.E.) tightly controls impeachment of jury verdicts. This rule [prior to a recent stylistic revision — eds.] states, in pertinent part:

>> Upon an inquiry into the validity of a verdict . . ., a juror may not testify as to any matter or statement occurring during the course

of the jury's deliberations or to the effect of anything upon that or any other juror's mind or emotions as influencing the juror to assent to or dissent from the verdict . . . or concerning the juror's mental processes in connection therewith, except that a juror may testify on the question whether extraneous prejudicial information was improperly brought to the jury's attention or whether any outside influence was improperly brought to the jury's attention or whether any outside influence was improperly brought to bear upon any juror. Nor may a juror's affidavit or evidence of any statement by the juror concerning a matter about which the juror would be precluded from testifying be received for these purposes. . . .

The landmark Supreme Court case on this issue is Tanner v. United States [483 U.S. 107, 107 S.Ct. 2739, 97 L.Ed.2d 90 (1987)]. After acknowledging that "by the beginning of this century, if not earlier, the near-universal and firmly established common-law rule in the United States flatly prohibited the admission of juror testimony to impeach a jury verdict," the Court observed that "Federal Rule of Evidence 606(b) is grounded in the common-law rule against admission of jury testimony to impeach a verdict and the exception for juror testimony relating to extraneous influences." Following *Tanner,* and more closely on point, we held in Robles v. Exxon Corp., 862 F.2d 1201 (5th Cir. 1989), that receiving testimony from the jurors after they have returned their verdict, for the purpose of ascertaining that the jury misunderstood its instructions, is absolutely prohibited by F.R.E. 606(b). We underscored that holding by noting that "the legislative history of the rule unmistakably points to the conclusion that Congress made a conscious decision to disallow juror testimony as to the jurors' mental processes or fidelity to the court's instructions." What is pellucid here, from the court's own unequivocal and unambiguous words, is that the jurors' statements to the court related directly to matters that transpired in the jury room, that these matters comprehended the mental processes of the jurors in their deliberations on the case, and that the jurors' statements formed the foundation of the court's impeachment of the verdict grounded in the jury's lack of "fidelity to the court's instructions." We cannot conceive of an example more explicitly violative of *Robles.*

9. Why are the mental processes of the jury not supposed to be subject to scrutiny, and why is it wrong to grant a new trial when it is clear that jurors have misunderstood or completely ignored the court's instructions? In answering this question consider the interests that are served in allowing the verdict to stand, and the policies underlying F.R.E. 606. At least one practical reason for the rule is that, without it, jury verdicts would regularly be subject to attack that they otherwise could not be, and litigation would seldom be final. How could the verdict loser resist the temptation to have a second jury trial on the decisionmaking processes in the first jury trial? And, if again unsuccessful, a third trial on the second trial, and so on?

Note, however, that Rule 606 does *not* prohibit a verdict's being impeached because of some improper "outside influence" on the jury, for example bribery, or threats to a juror by a third party, or the consideration of evidence not presented at trial. In the *Tanner* decision, discussed in *Peterson*, jurors in a criminal case had consumed alcohol, marijuana and cocaine during the trial, and even engaged in drug dealing with one another while "deliberating." The Supreme Court, however, held that these were not the sort of "outside influence[s]" that would allow a successful challenge to their verdict, either as a matter of Rule 606, or due process. Do you find the result troubling?

5. PROCEDURES GOVERNING POST-VERDICT MOTIONS

In *Latino*, the plaintiff moved for both a post-verdict judgment as a matter of law (JMOL) and a new trial. A fairly complex and somewhat controversial set of practices has emerged for handling post-verdict motions. You can get a flavor for them by reading Rule 50(b)-(e), and keeping in mind the general restriction against interlocutory appeals. Consider a simple case where A sues B, there is a verdict for A, and B moves for a JMOL and a new trial.

Assume first that the trial court grants the JMOL in favor of B:

a. The case is over and B has won. Must the court rule on the motion for a new trial? Why or why not?

b. Assume that there are three issues in the case, and the court has ruled in favor of B on each of them. In ruling on a new trial, what must the trial court determine with respect to the coming appeal?

c. Turn to the plaintiff A. He thought he won but the trial judge took away his verdict. Is there any procedural move available to him now in the trial court? See Rule 50(d).

Now, assume that the appellate court reverses the grant of a JMOL.

d. If the trial court granted a new trial, what happens?

e. If the trial court denied a new trial, what happens?

Flip the situation around, and assume that the trial court denies the JMOL:

f. If the trial court grants the new trial, can the defendant still appeal the denial of the JMOL? Can the plaintiff appeal the grant of the new trial? What happens next?

g. When can the plaintiff appeal the grant of the new trial?

h. If the trial court denies the new trial, can B appeal this denial?

Now, assume that the court of appeals reverses the denial of the JMOL. Think of the plight of A. A won in the trial court, and the trial judge denied B's motion for a new trial, as well as B's motion for a JMOL. All of a sudden, A has gone from winner to loser. Go back to your answer to question "c." If the plaintiff's verdict had been taken away in the trial court, at least he could have moved for a new trial there. But now, he's no longer in the trial court but the court of appeals. Can he move for a new trial in the appellate court? Can he go back to the trial court? In the following case, the Supreme Court deals with some of these issues.

Weisgram v. Marley Co.

Supreme Court of the United States, 2000.

528 U.S. 440, 120 S.Ct. 1011, 145 L.Ed.2d 958.

JUSTICE GINSBURG delivered the opinion for a unanimous Court.

This case concerns the respective authority of federal trial and appellate courts to decide whether, as a matter of law, judgment should be entered in favor of a verdict loser. The pattern we confront is this. Plaintiff in a product liability action gains a jury verdict. Defendant urges, unsuccessfully before the federal district court but successfully on appeal, that expert testimony plaintiff introduced was unreliable, and therefore inadmissible, under the analysis required by Daubert v. Merrell Dow Pharmaceuticals, Inc., 509 U.S. 579, 125 L.Ed.2d 469, 113 S.Ct. 2786 (1993). Shorn of the erroneously admitted expert testimony, the record evidence is insufficient to justify a plaintiff's verdict. May the court of appeals then instruct the entry of judgment as a matter of law for defendant, or must that tribunal remand the case, leaving to the district court's discretion the choice between final judgment for defendant or a new trial of plaintiff's case?

Our decision is guided by Federal Rule of Civil Procedure 50, which governs the entry of judgment as a matter of law, and by the Court's pathmarking opinion in Neely v. Martin K. Eby Construction Co., 386 U.S. 317, 18 L.Ed.2d 75, 87 S.Ct. 1072 (1967). As *Neely* teaches, courts of appeals should "be constantly alert" to "the trial judge's first-hand knowledge of witnesses, testimony, and issues"; in other words, appellate courts should give due consideration to the first-instance decisionmaker's "'feel' for the overall case." Id., at 325. But the court of appeals has authority to render the final decision. If, in the particular case, the appellate tribunal determines that the district court is better positioned to decide whether a new trial, rather than judgment for defendant, should be ordered, the court of appeals should return the case to the trial court for such an assessment. But if, as in the instant case, the court of appeals concludes that further proceedings are unwarranted because the loser on appeal has had a full and fair opportunity to present the case, including arguments for a new trial, the appellate court may appropriately instruct the district court to enter judgment against the jury-verdict winner. Appellate authority to make this determination is no less when the evidence is rendered insufficient by the removal of erroneously admitted testimony than it is when the evidence, without any deletion, is insufficient.

I

Firefighters arrived at the home of Bonnie Weisgram on December 30, 1993, to discover flames around the front entrance. Upon entering the home, they found Weisgram in an upstairs bathroom, dead of carbon monoxide poisoning. Her son, petitioner Chad Weisgram, individually and on behalf of Bonnie Weisgram's heirs, brought a diversity action in the United States District Court for the District of North Dakota seeking wrongful death damages. He alleged that a defect in an electric baseboard heater, manufactured by defendant (now respondent) Marley Company and located inside the door to Bonnie Weisgram's home, caused both the fire and his mother's death.[1]

At trial, Weisgram introduced the testimony of three witnesses, proffered as experts, in an endeavor to prove the alleged defect in the heater and its causal connection to the fire. The District Court overruled defendant Marley's objections, lodged both before and during the trial, that this testimony was unreliable and therefore inadmissible under Federal Rule of Evidence 702 as elucidated by *Daubert*. At the close of Weisgram's evidence, and again at the close of all the evidence, Marley unsuccessfully moved under Federal Rule of Civil Procedure 50(a) for judgment as a matter of law on the ground that plaintiffs had failed to meet their burden of proof on the issues of defect and causation. The jury returned a verdict for Weisgram. Marley again requested judgment as a matter of law, and additionally requested, in the alternative, a new trial, pursuant to Rules 50 and 59; among arguments in support of its post-trial motions, Marley reasserted that the expert testimony essential to prove Weisgram's case was unreliable and therefore inadmissible. The District Court denied the motions and entered judgment for Weisgram. Marley appealed.

The Court of Appeals for the Eighth Circuit held that Marley's motion for judgment as a matter of law should have been granted. 169 F.3d 514, 517 (1999). Writing for the panel majority, Chief Judge Bowman first examined the testimony of Weisgram's expert witnesses, the sole evidence supporting plaintiffs' product defect charge. Concluding that the testimony was speculative and not shown to be scientifically sound, the majority held the expert evidence incompetent to prove Weisgram's case. Ibid. The court then considered the remaining evidence in the light most favorable to Weisgram, found it insufficient to support the jury verdict, and directed judgment as a matter of law for Marley. In a footnote, the majority "rejected any contention that [it was] required to remand for a new trial." It recognized its discretion to do so under Rule 50(d), but stated: "We can discern no reason to give the plaintiffs a second chance to make out a case of strict liability. . . . This is not a close case. The plaintiffs had a fair opportunity to prove their claim and they failed to do so." Ibid. (internal citations omitted). The dissenting judge disagreed on both points, concluding that the expert evidence was properly admitted and that the appropriate remedy for improper admission of expert testimony is the award of a new trial, not judgment as a matter of law. Id., at 522, 525 (citing Midcontinent Broadcasting Co. v. North Central Airlines, Inc., 471 F.2d 357 (CA8 1973)).

Courts of appeals have divided on the question whether Federal Rule of Civil Procedure 50 permits an appellate court to direct the entry of judgment as a matter of law when it determines that evidence was erroneously admitted at trial and that the remaining, properly admitted evidence is insufficient to constitute a

---

[1] At trial and on appeal, the suit of the Weisgram heirs was consolidated with an action brought against Marley Company by State Farm Fire and Casualty Company, insurer of the Weisgram home, to recover benefits State Farm paid for the damage to the Weisgram townhouse and an adjoining townhouse. State Farm was dismissed from the appeal after certiorari was granted. For purposes of this opinion, we generally refer to the plaintiffs below, and to the petitioners before us, simply as "Weisgram."

submissible case. We granted certiorari to resolve the conflict, 527 U.S. 1069 (1999),[3] and we now affirm the Eighth Circuit's judgment.

II

Federal Rule of Civil Procedure 50, reproduced below, governs motions for judgment as a matter of law in jury trials. It allows the trial court to remove cases or issues from the jury's consideration "when the facts are sufficiently clear that the law requires a particular result." 9A C. Wright & A. Miller, Federal Practice and Procedure §2521, p. 240 (2d ed. 1995) (hereinafter Wright & Miller). Subdivision (d) [now, subdivision 50(e) — eds.] controls when, as here, the verdict loser appeals from the trial court's denial of a motion for judgment as a matter of law:

> "The party who prevailed on that motion may, as appellee, assert grounds entitling the party to a new trial in the event the appellate court concludes that the trial court erred in denying the motion for judgment. If the appellate court reverses the judgment, nothing in this rule precludes it from determining that the appellee is entitled to a new trial, or from directing the trial court to determine whether a new trial shall be granted."

Under this Rule, Weisgram urges, when a court of appeals determines that a jury verdict cannot be sustained due to an error in the admission of evidence, the appellate court may not order the entry of judgment for the verdict loser, but must instead remand the case to the trial court for a new trial determination. Nothing in Rule 50 expressly addresses this question.

In a series of pre-1967 decisions, this Court refrained from deciding the question, while emphasizing the importance of giving the party deprived of a verdict the opportunity to invoke the discretion of the trial judge to grant a new trial. [citations omitted]; see also 9A Wright & Miller, §2540, at 370. Then, in *Neely*, the Court reviewed its prior jurisprudence and ruled definitively that if a motion for judgment as a matter of law is erroneously denied by the district court, the appellate court does have the power to order the entry of judgment for the moving party. * * *

Neely first addressed the compatibility of appellate direction of judgment as a matter of law (then styled "judgment n.o.v.") with the Seventh Amendment's jury trial guarantee. It was settled, the Court pointed out, that a trial court, pursuant to Rule 50(b), could enter judgment for the verdict loser without offense to the Seventh Amendment. "As far as the Seventh Amendment's right to jury trial is concerned," the Court reasoned, "there is no greater restriction on the province of the jury when an appellate court enters judgment n.o.v. than when a trial court does"; accordingly, the Court concluded, "there is no

---

[3] We agreed to decide only the issue of the authority of a court of appeals to direct the entry of judgment as a matter of law, and accordingly accept as final the decision of the Eighth Circuit holding the testimony of Weisgram's experts unreliable, and therefore inadmissible under Federal Rule of Evidence 702, as explicated in Daubert v. Merrell Dow Pharmaceuticals, Inc., 509 U.S. 579, 125 L.Ed.2d 469, 113 S.Ct. 2786 (1993). We also accept as final the Eighth Circuit's determination that the remaining, properly admitted, evidence was insufficient to make a submissible case under state law.

constitutional bar to an appellate court granting judgment n.o.v." 311 U.S. at 322 (citing Baltimore & Carolina Line, Inc. v. Redman, 295 U.S. 654, 79 L.Ed. 1636, 55 S.Ct. 890 (1935)). The Court next turned to "the statutory grant of appellate jurisdiction to the courts of appeals [in 28 U.S.C. §2106],"[6] which it found "certainly broad enough to include the power to direct entry of judgment n.o.v. on appeal." 311 U.S. at 322. The remainder of the *Neely* opinion effectively complements Rules 50(c) and 50(d), providing guidance on the appropriate exercise of the appellate court's discretion when it reverses the trial court's denial of a defendant's Rule 50(b) motion for judgment as a matter of law. 311 U.S. at 322-330; cf. supra, note 5 (1963 observation of Advisory Committee that, as of that year, "problems [concerning motions for judgment coupled with new trial motions] had not been fully canvassed").

Neely represents no volte-face in the Court's understanding of the respective competences of trial and appellate forums. Immediately after declaring that appellate courts have the power to order the entry of judgment for a verdict loser, the Court cautioned:

> "Part of the Court's concern has been to protect the rights of the party whose jury verdict has been set aside on appeal and who may have valid grounds for a new trial, some or all of which should be passed upon by the district court, rather than the court of appeals, because of the trial judge's first-hand knowledge of witnesses, testimony, and issues — because of his 'feel' for the overall case. These are very valid concerns to which the court of appeals should be constantly alert." 311 U.S. at 325.

Nevertheless, the Court in *Neely* continued, due consideration of the rights of the verdict winner and the closeness of the trial court to the case "does not justify an ironclad rule that the court of appeals should never order dismissal or judgment for the defendant when the plaintiff's verdict has been set aside on appeal." 311 U.S. at 326. "Such a rule," the Court concluded, "would not serve the purpose of Rule 50 to speed litigation and to avoid unnecessary retrials." Ibid. *Neely* ultimately clarified that if a court of appeals determines that the district court erroneously denied a motion for judgment as a matter of law, the appellate court may (1) order a new trial at the verdict winner's request or on its own motion, (2) remand the case for the trial court to decide whether a new trial or entry of judgment for the defendant is warranted, or (3) direct the entry of judgment as a matter of law for the defendant. 311 U.S. 327-330; see also 9A Wright & Miller §2540, at 371-372.

III

The parties before us — and court of appeals opinions — diverge regarding *Neely*'s scope. Weisgram, in line with some appellate decisions, posits a

---

[6] Section 2106 reads:

"The Supreme Court or any other court of appellate jurisdiction may affirm, modify, vacate, set aside or reverse any judgment, decree, or order of a court lawfully brought before it for review, and may remand the cause and direct the entry of such appropriate judgment, decree, or order, or require such further proceedings to be had as may be just under the circumstances."

distinction between cases in which judgment as a matter of law is requested based on plaintiff's failure to produce enough evidence to warrant a jury verdict, as in *Neely*, and cases in which the proof introduced becomes insufficient because the court of appeals determines that certain evidence should not have been admitted, as in the instant case. Insufficiency caused by deletion of evidence, Weisgram contends, requires an "automatic remand" to the district court for consideration whether a new trial is warranted.

Weisgram relies on cases holding that, in fairness to a verdict winner who may have relied on erroneously admitted evidence, courts confronting questions of judgment as a matter of law should rule on the record as it went to the jury, without excising evidence inadmissible under Federal Rule of Evidence 702 [citations omitted]. These decisions are of questionable consistency with Rule 50(a)(1), which states that in ruling on a motion for judgment as a matter of law, the court is to inquire whether there is any "legally sufficient evidentiary basis for a reasonable jury to find for [the opponent of the motion]." Inadmissible evidence contributes nothing to a "legally sufficient evidentiary basis." See Brooke Group Ltd. v. Brown & Williamson Tobacco Corp., 509 U.S. 209, 242, 125 L.Ed.2d 168, 113 S.Ct. 2578 (1993) ("When an expert opinion is not supported by sufficient facts to validate it in the eyes of the law, or when indisputable record facts contradict or otherwise render the opinion unreasonable, it cannot support a jury's verdict.").[10]

As *Neely* recognized, appellate rulings on post-trial pleas for judgment as a matter of law call for the exercise of "informed discretion," 386 U.S. at 329, and fairness to the parties is surely key to the exercise of that discretion. But fairness concerns should loom as large when the verdict winner, in the appellate court's judgment, failed to present sufficient evidence as when the appellate court declares inadmissible record evidence essential to the verdict winner's case. In both situations, the party whose verdict is set aside on appeal will have had notice, before the close of evidence, of the alleged evidentiary deficiency. See Fed. Rule Civ. Proc. 50(a)(2) (motion for judgment as a matter of law "shall specify ... the law and facts on which the moving party is entitled to the judgment"). On appeal, both will have the opportunity to argue in support of the jury's verdict or, alternatively, for a new trial. And if judgment is instructed for the verdict loser, both will have a further chance to urge a new trial in a rehearing petition.[11]

---

[10] Weisgram additionally urges that the Seventh Amendment prohibits a court of appeals from directing judgment as a matter of law on a record different from the one considered by the jury. *Neely* made clear that a court of appeals may order entry of judgment as a matter of law on sufficiency-of-the-evidence grounds without violating the Seventh Amendment. 386 U.S. at 321-322. Entering judgment for the verdict loser when all of the evidence was properly before the jury is scarcely less destructive of the jury's verdict than is entry of such a judgment based on a record made insufficient by the removal of evidence the jury should not have had before it.

[11] We recognize that it is awkward for an appellee, who is wholeheartedly urging the correctness of the verdict, to point out, in the alternative, grounds for a new trial. * * * A petition for rehearing in the court of appeals, however, involves no conflicting tugs. We are not persuaded by Weisgram's objection that the 14 days allowed for the filing of a petition for rehearing is insufficient time to formulate compelling grounds for a new trial. Reply Brief 15-16.

Since *Daubert*, moreover, parties relying on expert evidence have had notice of the exacting standards of reliability such evidence must meet. * * * It is implausible to suggest, post-*Daubert*, that parties will initially present less than their best expert evidence in the expectation of a second chance should their first try fail. We therefore find unconvincing Weisgram's fears that allowing courts of appeals to direct the entry of judgment for defendants will punish plaintiffs who could have shored up their cases by other means had they known their expert testimony would be found inadmissible. In this case, for example, although Weisgram was on notice every step of the way that Marley was challenging his experts, he made no attempt to add or substitute other evidence.

After holding Weisgram's expert testimony inadmissible, the Court of Appeals evaluated the evidence presented at trial, viewing it in the light most favorable to Weisgram, and found the properly admitted evidence insufficient to support the verdict. Weisgram offered no specific grounds for a new trial to the Eighth Circuit. Even in the petition for rehearing, Weisgram argued only that the appellate court had misapplied state law, did not have the authority to direct judgment, and had failed to give adequate deference to the trial court's evidentiary rulings. The Eighth Circuit concluded that this was "not a close case." In these circumstances, the Eighth Circuit did not abuse its discretion by directing entry of judgment for Marley, instead of returning the case to the District Court for further proceedings.

Neely recognized that there are myriad situations in which the determination whether a new trial is in order is best made by the trial judge. 386 U.S. at 325-326. *Neely* held, however, that there are also cases in which a court of appeals may appropriately instruct the district court to enter judgment as a matter of law against the jury-verdict winner. Id., at 326. We adhere to *Neely*'s holding and rationale, and today hold that the authority of courts of appeals to direct the entry of judgment as a matter of law extends to cases in which, on excision of testimony erroneously admitted, there remains insufficient evidence to support the jury's verdict. [Affirmed.]

NOTES AND PROBLEMS FOR DISCUSSION

1. The Court of Appeals said that this was not a "close case," and the Supreme Court seems to share that view. Why?

2. *Weisgram* involved the questions whether certain evidence was admissible, and if not, whether a JMOL should have been granted. The *Neely* case (discussed in *Weisgram*) involved a question of sufficiency of the evidence pure

---

This time period is longer than the [then-applicable—eds.] ten days allowed a verdict winner to move for a new trial after a trial court grants judgment as a matter of law. See Fed. Rule Civ. Proc. 50(c)(2). Nor do we foreclose the possibility that a court of appeals might properly deny a petition for rehearing because it pressed an argument that plainly could have been formulated in a party's brief. See Louis, Post-Verdict Rulings on the Sufficiency of the Evidence: Neely v. Martin K. Eby Construction Co. Revisited, 1975 Wis. L. Rev. 503, 519-520, n.90 ("It is often difficult to argue that a gap in one's proof can be filled before a court has held that the gap exists . . . ." On the other hand, "the brief or oral argument will suffice . . . when the area of the alleged evidentiary insufficiency has previously been clearly identified.") (internal citation omitted).

IV

It does not appear that the District Court checked the jury's verdict against the relevant New York decisions demanding more than "industry standard" testimony to support an award of the size the jury returned in this case. As the Court of Appeals recognized, the uniqueness of the photographs and the plaintiff's earnings as photographer — past and reasonably projected — are factors relevant to appraisal of the award. * * * Accordingly, we vacate the judgment of the Court of Appeals and instruct that court to remand the case to the District Court so that the trial judge, revisiting his ruling on the new trial motion, may test the jury's verdict against CLPR §5501(c)'s "deviates materially" standard.

It is so ordered.

JUSTICE STEVENS, dissenting. [Omitted.]

JUSTICE SCALIA with whom the CHIEF JUSTICE and JUSTICE THOMAS join, dissenting.

Today the Court overrules a longstanding and well-reasoned line of precedent that has for years prohibited federal appellate courts from reviewing refusals by district courts to set aside civil jury awards as contrary to the weight of the evidence. One reason is given for overruling these cases: that the courts of appeals have, for some time now, decided to ignore them. Such unreasoned capitulation to the nullification of what was long regarded as a core component of the Bill of Rights — the Seventh Amendment's prohibition on appellate re-examination of civil jury awards — is wrong. It is not for us, much less for the courts of appeals, to decide that the Seventh Amendment's restriction on federal-court review of jury findings has outlived its usefulness.

The Court also holds today that a state practice that relates to the division of duties between state judges and juries must be followed by federal courts in diversity cases. On this issue, too, our prior cases are directly to the contrary. As I would reverse the judgment of the Court of Appeals, I respectfully dissent.

I

Because the Court and I disagree as to the character of the review that is before us, I recount briefly the nature of the New York practice rule at issue. Section 5501(c) of the N. Y. Civ. Prac. Law and Rules * * * directs New York intermediate appellate courts faced with a claim "that the award is excessive or inadequate and that a new trial should have been granted" to determine whether the jury's award "deviates materially from what would be reasonable compensation." In granting respondent a new trial under this standard, the Court of Appeals necessarily engaged in a two-step process. As it has explained the application of §5501(c), that provision "requires the reviewing court to determine the range it regards as reasonable, and to determine whether the particular jury award deviates materially from that range." Consorti v. Armstrong World Industries, Inc., 72 F.3d 1003, 1013 (1995). The first of these two steps — the determination as to "reasonable" damages — plainly requires the reviewing court to re-examine a factual matter tried by the jury: the appropriate measure of damages, on the evidence presented, under New York law. The second step — the determination as to the degree of difference between "reasonable" damages and the damages found by the jury (whether the latter "deviates materially" from the former) — establishes the degree of judicial tolerance for awards found not to be reasonable, whether at the trial-level or by the appellate court. No part of this exercise is appropriate for a federal court of appeals, whether or not it is sitting in a diversity case.

A

Granting appellate courts authority to decide whether an award is "excessive or inadequate" in the manner of CPLR §5501(c) may reflect a sound understanding of the capacities of modern juries and trial judges. That is to say, the people of the State of New York may well be correct that such a rule contributes to a more just legal system. But the practice of federal appellate re-examination of facts found by a jury is precisely what the People of the several States considered not to be good legal policy in 1791. Indeed, so fearful were they of such a practice that they constitutionally prohibited it by means of the Seventh Amendment.

* * *

The second clause of the Amendment responded to that concern by providing that "[i]n [s]uits at common law . . . no fact tried by a jury, shall be otherwise re-examined in any Court of the United States, than according to the rules of the common law." U.S. Const., Amdt. 7. The Re-examination Clause put to rest "apprehensions" of "new trials by the appellate courts," by adopting, in broad fashion, "the rules of the common law" to govern federal-court interference with jury determinations. The content of that law was familiar and fixed. See, e.g., * * * Dimick v. Schiedt, 293 U.S. 474, 487 (1935) (Seventh Amendment "in effect adopted the rules of the common law, in respect of trial by jury, as these rules existed in 1791"). It quite plainly barred reviewing courts from entertaining claims that the jury's verdict was contrary to the evidence.

C

The Court, as is its wont of late, all but ignores the relevant history. It acknowledges that federal appellate review of district-court refusals to set aside jury awards as against the weight of the evidence was "once deemed inconsonant with the Seventh Amendment's re-examination clause," but gives no indication of why ever we held that view; and its citation of only one of our cases subscribing to that proposition fails to convey how long and how clearly it was a fixture of federal practice, * * *. That our earlier cases are so poorly recounted is not surprising, however, given the scant analysis devoted to the conclusion that "appellate review for abuse of discretion is reconcilable with the Seventh Amendment."

No precedent of this Court affirmatively supports that proposition. * * *

II

The Court's holding that federal courts of appeals may review district court denials of motions for new trials for error of fact is not the only novel aspect of today's decision. The Court also directs that the case be remanded to the District

Court, so that it may "test the jury's verdict against CPLR §5501(c)'s 'deviates materially' standard[.]" This disposition contradicts the principle that "[t]he proper role of the trial and appellate courts in the federal system in reviewing the size of jury verdicts is . . . a matter of federal law." Donovan v. Penn Shipping Co., 429 U.S. 648, 649 (1977).

The Court acknowledges that state procedural rules cannot, as a general matter, be permitted to interfere with the allocation of functions in the federal court system. Indeed, it is at least partly for this reason that the Court rejects direct application of §5501(c) at the appellate level as inconsistent with an "'essential characteristic'" of the federal court system — by which the Court presumably means abuse-of-discretion review of denials of motions for new trials. But the scope of the Court's concern is oddly circumscribed. The "essential characteristic" of the federal jury, and, more specifically, the role of the federal trial court in reviewing jury judgments, apparently counts for little. The Court approves the "accommodat[ion]" achieved by having district courts review jury verdicts under the "deviates materially" standard, because it regards that as a means of giving effect to the State's purposes "without disrupting the federal system." But changing the standard by which trial judges review jury verdicts does disrupt the federal system, and is plainly inconsistent with "the strong federal policy against allowing state rules to disrupt the judge-jury relationship in federal court." Byrd. The Court's opinion does not even acknowledge, let alone address, this dislocation. * * *

* * *

The Court commits the classic Erie mistake of regarding whatever changes the outcome as substantive. That is not the only factor to be considered. See Byrd, 356 U.S., at 537 ("[W]ere 'outcome' the only consideration, a strong case might appear for saying that the federal court should follow the state practice. But there are affirmative countervailing considerations at work here"). Outcome-determination "was never intended to serve as a talisman," Hanna v. Plumer, 380 U.S. 460, 466-467 (1965), and does not have the power to convert the most classic elements of the process of assuring that the law is observed into the substantive law itself. * * *

* * *

The foregoing describes why I think the Court's Erie analysis is flawed. But in my view, one does not even reach the Erie question in this case. The standard to be applied by a district court in ruling on a motion for a new trial is set forth in Rule 59 of the Federal Rules of Civil Procedure, which provides that "[a] new trial may be granted . . . for any of the reasons for which new trials have heretofore been granted in actions at law in the courts of the United States" (emphasis added). That is undeniably a federal standard. Federal district courts in the Second Circuit have interpreted that standard to permit the granting of new trials where "'it is quite clear that the jury has reached a seriously erroneous result'" and letting the verdict stand would result in a "'miscarriage of justice.'" Assuming (as we have no reason to question) that this is a correct interpretation of what Rule 59 requires, it is undeniable that the federal rule is "'sufficiently broad' to cause a 'direct collision' with the state law or, implicitly, to 'control the issue' before the court, thereby leaving no room for the operation of that law." Burlington Northern R. Co. v. Woods, 480 U.S. 1, 4-5 (1987). It is simply not possible to give controlling effect both to the federal standard and the state standard in reviewing the jury's award. That being so, the court has no choice but to apply the Federal Rule, which is an exercise of what we have called Congress's "power to regulate matters which, though falling within the uncertain area between substance and procedure, are rationally capable of classification as either," *Hanna*, 380 U.S., at 472.

There is no small irony in the Court's declaration today that appellate review of refusals to grant new trials for error of fact is "a control necessary and proper to the fair administration of justice." It is objection to precisely that sort of "control" by federal appellate judges that gave birth to the Re-examination Clause of the Seventh Amendment. Alas, those who drew the Amendment, and the citizens who approved it, did not envision an age in which the Constitution means whatever this Court thinks it ought to mean — or indeed, whatever the courts of appeals have recently thought it ought to mean.

When there is added to the revision of the Seventh Amendment the Court's precedent-setting disregard of Congress's instructions in Rule 59, one must conclude that this is a bad day for the Constitution's distinctive Article III courts in general, and for the role of the jury in those courts in particular. I respectfully dissent.

NOTES AND PROBLEMS FOR DISCUSSION

1. Be sure you understand (a) the standard of review applied by trial judges in New York under New York law, and (b) the standard of review ordinarily applied by federal trial court judges, in assessing whether a new trial for excessive damages should be awarded. How are they different, and why does the Court conclude that a federal trial court *must* follow state law here?

2. Now consider (a) the standard of review applied by appellate court judges in New York under New York law, and (b) the standard of review ordinarily applied by federal appellate court judges, in assessing the propriety of a new trial for excessive damages. How are they different, and why does the Court conclude that a federal appeals court *must not* follow state law here?

3. Given the Seventh Amendment, does it makes sense that New York law should control the one (new trial motions for excessive damages) but not the other (appellate review) in federal court? To be sure, new trials ordered by federal trial courts were known to the common law as a way to review jury factfinding and thus escape Seventh Amendment difficulties. And no similar power inhered in federal appellate courts. Even so, does that mean that the Seventh Amendment is indifferent to the standard applied by a federal trial court in granting a new trial — particularly when that standard may have been unknown to the common law?

4. A properly promulgated Rule of Civil Procedure is capable of trumping state law. Why doesn't Rule 59, which governs the grant or denial of new trials in federal district courts, constitute such a rule? Read footnote 22 of the majority opinion. Is it convincing?

5. The *Gasperini* majority provides an extensive *Erie* analysis to determine whether state law or federal practice should apply in federal appellate courts reviewing federal trial court rulings on new trials for excessive damages. It also seems to conclude (in footnote 22) that Rule 59 does not speak to the question of whose standard of excessiveness should apply to the granting of new trials in federal trial courts in the first instance. If so, shouldn't the Court have offered an *Erie* analysis before concluding that state law should apply in federal trial courts? Or did the Court read Rule 59 as itself incorporating state law and thus as speaking to the question?

6. Federal courts, like almost all state courts, recognize the possibility that a new trial for excessive damages might be conditioned on the prevailing party's acceptance of a lesser (nonexcessive) sum. As noted above, the remittitur practice has deep roots within the American judicial system. Nevertheless, the constitutionality of the practice was once questioned by the Supreme Court in DIMICK v. SCHIEDT, 293 U.S. 474, 55 S.Ct. 296, 79 L.Ed. 603 (1935). But *Dimick* only held unconstitutional and violative of the Seventh Amendment right to trial by jury, the opposite practice of "additur" — i.e., in which the court set a higher figure to which the parties would consent as a means of avoiding a new trial in a case in which damages were grossly *in*adequate. Unlike remittitur, additur put the court in a position of allowing for an award of damages that no jury had found, whereas remittitur allowed the court to award damages that had been authorized by the jury, only less than what they found. Despite the constitutional doubts about the practice of remittitur expressed in *Dimick*, however, courts have not lately expressed similar sentiments, and the practice seems secure for now.

7. In the remittitur context, a number of questions are raised in connection with how the judge should determine the appropriate sum upon rejection of which a new trial would be ordered. One place to look might be the highest dollar amount that the court believes would be nonexcessive. A "fair" award in light of the judge's assessment of the evidence might be another. Which approach is preferable?

8. In the setting of compensatory damages, the federal district court does not enter an appropriate award itself if it believes the award is excessive under the applicable standard. Rather, it determines what it considers to be an appropriate award, and then indicates that it will award a new trial unless the verdict winner is prepared to accept the remitted award that the court has settled upon. If the verdict winner is unwilling to do so, there will be a new trial (although perhaps on damages alone). See Hetzel v. Prince William Cty., 523 U.S. 208 118 S.Ct. 1210, 140 L.Ed.2d 336 (1998) (concluding that, under the Seventh Amendment, a verdict winner must be given a choice to accept a remitted award of compensatory damages or a new trial).

9. In the punitive damages setting, excessiveness is governed by due process considerations. See Chapter 6, Section A.2. If a court believes that a particular award exceeds what due process would permit, may the court enter an appropriately reduced punitive damages award itself? Or must it order remittitur as in the compensatory damages setting, thus effectively requiring the verdict winner's consent to the amount of the reduced award? See Johansen v. Combustion Engineering Inc., 170 F.3d 1320 (11th Cir. 1999) (holding that remittitur was not required in the punitive damages setting because the due process/excessiveness issue presented a pure question of law); see also McClain v. Metabolife Int'l, Inc., 259 F. Supp. 2d 1225 (N.D. Ala. 2003) (applying *Johansen*); cf. Cooper Industries v. Leatherman Tool Group, Inc., 532 U.S. 424, 121 S.Ct. 1678, 149 L.Ed.2d 674 (2001) (making clear that appellate court review of the excessiveness of a punitive damages award on due process grounds was de novo).

7. A Detour: Review of Judicial Factfinding

In theory, at least, there is no judicial review of factfinding, outside of the context of the trial court's decision to grant a new trial for a verdict's being against the weight of the evidence. Judgments as a matter of law based on evidentiary insufficiency, although they require an assessment of the evidence at trial to determine whether rational factfinders could come out in a particular way, are treated as questions of law. Consequently, decisions with respect to the grant or denial of judgments as a matter of law are reviewable de novo, as in *Reeves, supra*, with no deference given to the court below. By contrast, as in *Latino, supra*, the grant or denial of a new trial on is reviewable for an abuse of discretion. But the factual findings of the jury are not otherwise subject to review.

What happens when the judge and not the jury is the factfinder? For example, the suit may be one in equity or admiralty, to which the Seventh Amendment does not apply. Or the trial might be one to which the jury trial guarantee attaches, but no one demanded a trial by jury. See Rule 38(d) (stating that jury trial rights are waived unless asserted in the manner required by Rule 38). No Seventh Amendment limit exists on the review of factfinding by nonjury decisionmakers, yet there would not be much point in having a trial if factfindings (as well as findings of law) could be reviewed de novo by an appellate court, just like questions of law. On the other hand, if the factfinder is the district judge, asking the district judge for a new trial because her verdict was against the weight of the evidence seems futile. And unless we are willing to give the judge the same kind of insulation that we give juries, some appellate review of judicial factfinding would seem to make sense. But how much? Read Rule 52(a)(6) (providing for reversal of judge-made factfindings only when they are "clearly erroneous"). We treat this standard of review in greater detail in Chapter 12.

Proponents of a less restrictive appeal process point to the importance of many interlocutory orders, their impact on the ongoing case, the fact that some orders simply can't be undone, and the further fact that a reversal after trial cannot restore the appealing party to its original position. For example, a wrong decision on issues of jurisdiction, venue, or party joinder often will mean that the whole litigation process must start over again. A wrong decision requiring certain discovery may, as a practical matter, be impossible to correct. Moreover, while a court reviewing an interlocutory order immediately after decision is likely to ask whether the order was right or wrong, a court reviewing an interlocutory order after a final decision is more likely to ask whether there is any basis on which the order can be sustained to avoid a retrial.

There clearly is no right or wrong answer to these arguments. However, as you go through these materials, you will see how frequently they arise in the course of decisions. Our focus for the remainder of this chapter will be on the Federal approach.

Finally, note that there is another dimension to the timing of appeals. Assuming there is a final decision in a federal civil suit, the time to appeal is "within 30 days after entry of the judgment or order appealed from." Rule 4(1)(A), Fed. R. App. P. The notice of appeal is filed in the district court (not the appeals court — see Rule 3, Fed. R. App. P.). And if there is a timely post-trial motion (such as a post-verdict motion for judgment as a matter of law or a motion for a new trial), the time for appeal begins to run from the disposition of the last such motion, not from the prior entry (or announcement) of judgment. But a prematurely filed notice of appeal (e.g., one filed after entry of judgment but before the filing of a timely post-trial motion), need not be refiled in the event of an intervening post-trial motion; the initial notice will suffice. (Prior practice was otherwise, and often caused confusion for counsel.) Of course, if a party wishes to appeal from a ruling of the district court in connection with any post-trial motion, a new notice of appeal (or an amended notice of appeal) is required. There is also a provision for extending a party's time within which to file an appeal. See Rule 4(a)(5)-(6), Fed. R App. P. In Bowles v. Russell, 551 U.S. 205, 127 S.Ct. 2360, 168 L.Ed.2d 96 (2007), the Supreme Court concluded that this particular limitation was "jurisdictional," and thus disallowed an appeal in a case in which counsel had relied on the district court's granting of greater time (than that allowed by the Rule) within which to file his appeal.

1. THE FINAL DECISION RULE AND ITS EXCEPTIONS

(a) The Final Decision Rule. Read 28 U.S.C. §1291 which states that the Courts of Appeals have jurisdiction over "final decisions." What is a final decision? For simplicity, assume it is one that decides the case for one party or the other — e.g., an order granting a motion to dismiss under Rule 12, granting summary judgment, granting a judgment as a matter of law before verdict, or entering judgment on a jury verdict.

(b) Statutory Exceptions. 28 U.S.C. §1292 sets forth several statutory exceptions in which immediate appeal of an interlocutory order is permitted. One important statutory exception is for interlocutory orders granting,

CHAPTER 12

Appeals

If you consider the typical media account of a high profile decision in a civil case, it is usually not too persnickety about procedural details. Instead, the account tends to describe the decision in terms of winning and losing. One thing you can be relatively sure of is that the loser or its counsel will be quoted as saying something along these lines: "We believe the court's decision was clearly wrong and unjust, and we plan to appeal. We are confident the appellate court will sustain our position."

Start with the proposition that most court systems have provisions for an appeal, and then consider a number of questions: Can every ruling be appealed? When can it be appealed? What standard will the appellate court apply in deciding the appeal? How long will it take and how much will it cost? What happens in between? And what are the chances of winning? If the loser wins on appeal, what happens next?

Before turning to these questions, a brief note. Notwithstanding the enthusiasm of losing parties for an appeal (after all, what else is there to be enthusiastic about?), the chances of winning on appeal are not great. In the federal courts, for example, nearly 90% of all appealed decisions in civil actions are affirmed (and others that are nominally reversed may be reversed on an insignificant matter such as a minor modification of a damage award). See RICHARD POSNER THE FEDERAL COURTS — CHALLENGE AND REFORM 70-71 (1996). Even the reported decisions are misleading. Many appellate courts write opinions only in the hard cases (which include reversals). The easier cases are affirmed without opinion or in unpublished opinions.

Several important policies are at work. For one, there is a public interest in repose — in putting an end to litigation. For another, litigation involves actions by parties, witnesses, lawyers, judges and juries in an unfamiliar (to some) and rigid setting, requiring numerous decisions in high pressure situations where legal and factual issues are sharply disputed. Mistakes at trial are frequent and inevitable. Appellate courts often articulate this reality by saying that the losing party is entitled to a fair trial, not a perfect trial. Still another factor affecting the scope and availability of appeals is the cost to the parties and the taxpayers that would be involved in repeated appeals and reversals. And, one could ask, would one really get more "justice" in the system in such a process?

For these and other reasons, the law governing appeals has built-in provisions that tend to uphold trial court decisions, and that both discourage appeals and make reversals unlikely (these being really different sides of the same coin). As you go through these materials, consider how the various rules governing appeals accomplish these goals. And also, consider the effect that these rules have on trial strategy and the decision to settle.

SECTION A.   THE TIMING OF APPEALS

In most cases, there are a number of rulings and decisions prior to the ultimate decision of who wins and loses. Most commonly, there will be rulings on motions concerning pleadings, joinder of claims and parties, amendments to pleadings, discovery, summary judgment and pretrial matters; but there are numerous other possibilities as well. In an actively litigated case, it is not uncommon that there will be 10-20 such rulings, and perhaps even more. Litigation would rapidly grind to a halt if each ruling could be appealed one at a time and further proceedings delayed during the appeal. There are essentially two approaches to the problem.

Under the approach in the federal courts (and many states as well), it is only final orders that can be appealed. A rough definition of a final order is one that decides the case (usually, a decision regarding who wins and who loses). Generally, any rulings or orders before the final order (called interlocutory orders) cannot be appealed until there is a final order. But, once there is a final order, the losing party can appeal not only the final order but all interlocutory orders as well; the winning party can cross appeal any interlocutory orders (in case the final order is reversed). For example, if A sues B for negligence and A obtains a judgment based on a jury verdict, B can appeal not only the judgment, but interlocutory orders such as refusing to change venue, to disallow certain discovery by B, or permitting A to amend the pretrial order; conversely, A can cross appeal the court's refusal to permit A to do certain testing on B's land.

Under the other approach, followed in New York, California, and some other states, some important interlocutory orders can be appealed immediately. Sometimes the types of orders that can be appealed are set forth by statute; sometimes the losing party can appeal any interlocutory order but the appellate court first has discretion to consider the question (and there is usually precedent establishing the types of orders which are likely to be considered); and sometimes front-end permission must be obtained from either the trial court or the appellate court.

Proponents of the federal approach argue that efficiency dictates one appeal per case. They point to the delays, interruptions, and uncertainties created by appeals, and the incentive for wealthier parties to increase the cost of litigation by taking appeals. In addition, they note that many things can happen in the case so that the interlocutory order is never appealed. For example, later rulings in the case may obviate the problem that led to the interlocutory order, and besides, most cases are settled so that there will be no need for an appeal. Finally, proponents argue that this approach maximizes the ability of the trial judge to control the case, and also reflects a basic confidence in trial judges.

modifying, refusing to grant or refusing to modify, injunctions under §1292(a)(1). Another statutory exception (under 28 U.S.C. §1292(b)), permits interlocutory review of certain decisions if the district court is able to certify that there is a controlling question of law; that there is a substantial ground for difference of opinion; and that an immediate appeal may advance the ultimate termination of the litigation. But under §1292(b), not only must the district court make such findings, the court of appeals must also agree to permit the appeal in its discretion.

(c) Rules-Based Exceptions. Rule 54(b) of the Federal Rules of Civil Procedure also provides for immediate appeal of a final decision on one part of a case that is separable from other remaining parts of the case, at least in multi-party or multi-claim litigation. See Sears, Roebuck & Co. v. Mackey, 351 U.S. 427, 76 S.Ct. 895, 100 L.Ed 1297 (1956) (concluding that Rule 54(b) was consistent with §1291's final decision rule and thus did not run afoul of the Rules Enabling Act, 28 U.S.C. §2072). And Rule 23(f) now permits discretionary appeals of orders granting or denying class action certification.

Note that if a judgment is indeed final under §1291, no permission to appeal or exercise of judicial discretion is required; appeal is automatic ("of right"). Exceptions to the final judgment rule may require the permission of only the district court (e.g., Rule 54(b)), or only the appellate court (e.g., Rule 23(f)), or both (e.g., §1292(b)).

(d) Judge-Made Glosses on the Final Decision Rule. Interlocutory appeals also may be entertained under two largely judge-made doctrines: the "collateral order doctrine," and a liberal approach to the writ of mandamus. It is possible that these two exceptions could also be considered statutorily-based as well, since the former is arguably an interpretation of the final decision rule under §1291, and the latter is provided for generally under the All Writs Act, 28 U.S.C. §1651(a).

(i) The collateral order doctrine. The collateral order doctrine is said to apply to an order which is unrelated to the merits of the action which cannot be effectively reviewed after the case is completely over. The rule is said to originate in COHEN v. BENEFICIAL INDUSTRIAL LOAN CORP., 337 U.S. 541, 69 S.Ct. 1221, 93 L.Ed. 1528, (1949). *Cohen* involved a shareholder derivative suit — an action by shareholders on behalf of a corporation against its officers and directors for wrongdoing. The case was brought in the federal court in New Jersey and, under a New Jersey statute, a plaintiff could not prosecute such an action unless he first posted security (in the amount of $125,000) for certain costs and expenses in the action, in case the plaintiff lost. The district court held that the New Jersey statute did not apply in the federal courts under the *Erie* doctrine. See Chapter 5. The defendants immediately appealed from the ruling arguing that the New Jersey statute was applicable in the federal courts, and the court of appeals agreed. On appeal to the Supreme Court, the Court first addressed whether the court of appeals had jurisdiction to hear an interlocutory appeal of the order denying the defendants' motion for the posting of security. It concluded that jurisdiction existed:

In ordinary civil litigation, a case
"final decisio[n]," 28 U.S.C. §1
disassociates itself from a case,'
514 U. S. 35, 42 (1995). A par
from that final decision. Th
"[p]ermitting piecemeal, prejudg
judicial administration' and encr
court judges, who play a 'specia
Mohawk Industries, Inc. v. C
(quoting Firestone Tire & Rub
(1981)).

The rules are different in l
"an aggregation of individual co
as stand-alone lawsuits but f
[Citation omitted.] According
orders in bankruptcy cases may
dispose of discrete disputes w
Service, Inc. v. Zurich Amer
(2006) (internal quotation ma
bankruptcy appeals statute ref
as of right not only from fi
judgments, orders, and decrees

The *Bullard* Court ultimately
confirmation of a particular bankruptc
was not a final decision. "An order
specific arrangement of relief embodi
not make the denial final any more th
sticker price is viewed as a "final" p
seller. 'It ain't over till it's over.'"

5. Sidney (passenger) and Sallie (dr
automobile accident with Ravens.
Ravens, and Ravens interposes a d
Sallie (there is no basis for such a d
verdict for Sidney, but is hung (i.e.,
Ravens lawsuit. Can Ravens appeal?

6. To have a case certified for
"controlling question" requires positi
appellate court. Some appellate cou
too readily. In Ahrenholz v. Board
Judge Posner suggested that too m
might be "useful to remind the di
careful application of the statutory
university for terminating his emplo
of free speech. The district court
on the ground that the plaintiff had
and certified the summary judgmen

The purpose [of §1291] is to combine in one review all stages of the proceeding that effectively may be reviewed and corrected if and when final judgment results. But this order of the District Court did not make any step toward final disposition of the merits of the case and will not be merged in final judgment. When that time comes, it will be too late effectively to review the present order, and the rights conferred by the [state] statute, if it is applicable, will have been lost, probably irreparably. We conclude that the matters embraced in the decision appealed from are not of such an interlocutory nature as to affect, or be affected by, decision of the merits of the case.

This decision appears to fall into that small class which finally determine claims of right separable from, and collateral to, rights asserted in the action, too important to be denied review and too independent of the cause itself to require that appellate consideration be deferred until the whole case is adjudicated. This Court has long given this provision of the statute a practical rather than a technical construction.

The Court then went on to uphold the court of appeals' conclusion that the New Jersey statute applied and that plaintiff was therefore obliged to post security before the class action could proceed. (Do you see why review of this issue after, rather than before trial would have been too little, too late?) The *Cohen* collateral order doctrine is discussed in greater detail in Part 2, below.

(ii) Mandamus as an "Appellate" Mechanism. Mandamus was originally a common law writ that permitted a court to direct a government official to perform some nondiscretionary duty according to law. As applied to the judicial setting, a losing party might request the appellate court to grant a writ of mandamus directing the lower court properly to follow the law and rule in favor of the losing party. But if such a writ were available any time a lower court erred, mandamus would operate as an end run around the final judgment rule. In federal courts, the use of the writ of mandamus has therefore been limited to allowing appellate courts to keep lower courts within their jurisdiction (or to command them to exercise that jurisdiction), rather than for the purpose of correcting "mere error" on the part of lower courts.

The federal courts traditionally have used the writ only "to confine an inferior court to a lawful exercise of its prescribed jurisdiction or to compel it to exercise its authority when it is its duty to do so." * * * In accord with this historic practice, we have held that only "exceptional circumstances amounting to a judicial 'usurpation of power'" will justify issuance of the writ. * * * Moreover, we have held that the party seeking mandamus has the "burden of showing that its right to issuance of the writ is 'clear and indisputable.'"

Gulfstream Aerospace Corp. v. Mayacamas Corp., 485 U.S. 271, 289, 108 S.Ct. 1133, 99 L.Ed.2d 296 (1988); cf. La Buy v. Howe's Leather Co., 352

First, certain questions, such as pure questions of law, are generally reviewed "de novo." This means that the appellate court decides whether the district court's ruling on the point of law is right or wrong. For example, if the district court rules that the statute of limitations is three years in certain contract actions, the appellate court will decide whether this is correct.

Second, certain questions (as discussed in the case that follows) will be reviewed on the basis of a "clearly erroneous" or "clear error" standard. This means that the appellate court will not reverse simply because it thinks the ruling wrong or would itself rule otherwise; the appellate court must decide that the question is not especially close and that the lower court's ruling was wrong to a heightened degree. This standard is applied, for example, to factual rulings of a trial court — e.g., in cases tried without a jury, or in factual rulings on motions (e.g., of which state is plaintiff a citizen).

Third, certain questions will be reviewed on the basis of a standard of "abuse of discretion." This standard potentially gives the district judge the broadest range of decisionmaking freedom (de novo review providing the narrowest).[*] See Harman v. Apfel, 211 F.3d 1172, 1174-75 (9th Cir. 2000) ("Normally, the decision of a trial court is reversed under the abuse of discretion standard only when the appellate court is firmly convinced that the reviewed decision lies beyond the pale of reasonable justification under the circumstances.") For example, most matters involving the running and supervision of the trial process are committed to the trial judge's discretion, which means she can rule either way as long as there is a reasonable basis for the ruling. A judge will have abused her discretion only if the ruling is without any rational basis. For example, rulings on such matters as amendments to pleadings, most discovery issues, and trial procedure will be reviewed by an abuse of discretion standard. As with the discussion of the clearly erroneous standard, the essence of a discretionary ruling is that the judge can decide either way, and the appellate court will not reverse her decision unless it decides that the ruling was altogether unjustified or had no legal basis.

It should be obvious that the chances of getting a reversal when the standard is "clearly erroneous" or "abuse of discretion" are not that great. Now consider the following case:

---

[*] Of course, many rulings that are ultimately subject to an abuse of discretion standard may implicate underlying findings of fact that might be somewhat more strictly scrutinized under the "clear error" standard of Rule 52(a), as discussed in the case that follows. In addition, appellate courts will also want to satisfy themselves that the district judge applied the proper legal standard — something that would be subject to de novo review — even in connection with a matter that ultimately rests within her discretion.

Anderson v. Bessemer City

Supreme Court of the United States, 1985.
470 U.S. 564, 105 S.Ct. 1504, 84 L.Ed.2d 518.

JUSTICE WHITE delivered the opinion of the Court.

In Pullman-Standard v. Swint, 456 U.S. 273 (1982), we held that a District Court's finding of discriminatory intent in an action brought under Title VII of the Civil Rights Act of 1964, 78 Stat. 253, as amended, 42 U.S.C. 2000e et seq., is a factual finding that may be overturned on appeal only if it is clearly erroneous. In this case, the Court of Appeals for the Fourth Circuit concluded that there was clear error in a District Court's finding of discrimination and reversed. Because our reading of the record convinces us that the Court of Appeals misapprehended and misapplied the clearly-erroneous standard, we reverse.

I

Early in 1975, officials of respondent Bessemer City, North Carolina, set about to hire a new Recreation Director for the city. * * * A five-member committee selected by the Mayor was responsible for choosing the Recreation Director. Of the five members, four were men; the one woman on the committee, Mrs. Auddie Boone, served as the chairperson.

Eight persons applied for the position of Recreation Director. Petitioner, at the time a 39-year-old schoolteacher with college degrees in social studies and education, was the only woman among the eight. The selection committee reviewed the resumes submitted by the applicants and briefly interviewed each of the jobseekers. Following the interviews, the committee offered the position to Mr. Donald Kincaid, a 24-year-old who had recently graduated from college with a degree in physical education. All four men on the committee voted to offer the job to Mr. Kincaid; Mrs. Boone voted for petitioner.

Believing that the committee had passed over her in favor of a less qualified candidate solely because she was a woman * * * .

Petitioner then filed this Title VII action in the United States District Court for the Western District of North Carolina. After a 2-day trial during which the court heard testimony from petitioner, Mr. Kincaid, and the five members of the selection committee, the court issued a brief memorandum of decision setting forth its finding that petitioner was entitled to judgment because she had been denied the position of Recreation Director on account of her sex. In addition to laying out the rationale for this finding, the memorandum requested that petitioner's counsel submit proposed findings of fact and conclusions of law expanding upon those set forth in the memorandum. Petitioner's counsel complied with this request by submitting a lengthy set of proposed findings; the court then requested and received a response setting forth in detail respondent's objections to the proposed findings — objections that were, in turn, answered by petitioner's counsel in a somewhat less lengthy reply. After receiving these submissions, the court issued its own findings of fact and conclusions of law.

As set forth in the formal findings of fact and conclusions of law, the court's finding that petitioner had been denied employment by respondent because of her sex rested on a number of subsidiary findings. First, the court found that at the time the selection committee made its choice, petitioner had been better qualified than Mr. Kincaid to perform the range of duties demanded by the position. The court based this finding on petitioner's experience as a classroom teacher responsible for supervising schoolchildren in recreational and athletic activities, her employment as a hospital recreation director in the late 1950's, her extensive involvement in a variety of civic organizations, her knowledge of sports acquired both as a high school athlete and as a mother of children involved in organized athletics, her skills as a public speaker, her experience in handling money (gained in the course of her community activities and in her work as a book-keeper for a group of physicians), and her knowledge of music, dance, and crafts. The court found that Mr. Kincaid's principal qualifications were his experience as a student teacher and as a coach in a local youth basketball league, his extensive knowledge of team and individual sports, acquired as a result of his lifelong involvement in athletics, and his formal training as a physical education major in college. Noting that the position of Recreation Director involved more than the management of athletic programs, the court concluded that petitioner's greater breadth of experience made her better qualified for the position.

Second, the court found that the male committee members had in fact been biased against petitioner because she was a woman. The court based this finding in part on the testimony of one of the committee members that he believed it would have been "real hard" for a woman to handle the job and that he would not want his wife to have to perform the duties of the Recreation Director. The finding of bias found additional support in evidence that another male committee member had told Mr. Kincaid, the successful applicant, of the vacancy and had also solicited applications from three other men, but had not attempted to recruit any women for the job.

Also critical to the court's inference of bias was its finding that petitioner, alone among the applicants for the job, had been asked whether she realized the job would involve night work and travel and whether her husband approved of her applying for the job. The court's finding that the committee had pursued this line of inquiry only with petitioner was based on the testimony of petitioner that these questions had been asked of her and the testimony of Mrs. Boone that similar questions had not been asked of the other applicants. Although Mrs. Boone also testified that during Mr. Kincaid's interview, she had made a "comment" to him regarding the reaction of his new bride to his taking the position of Recreation Director, the court concluded that this comment was not a serious inquiry, but merely a "facetious" remark prompted by Mrs. Boone's annoyance that only petitioner had been questioned about her spouse's reaction. The court also declined to credit the testimony of one of the male committee members that Mr. Kincaid had been asked about his wife's feelings "in a way" and the testimony of another committeeman that all applicants had been questioned regarding their willingness to work at night and their families' reaction to night work. The court concluded that the finding that only petitioner had been seriously questioned about her family's reaction suggested that the male committee members believed women had special family responsibilities that made certain forms of employment inappropriate.

Finally, the court found that the reasons offered by the male committee members for their choice of Mr. Kincaid were pretextual. The court rejected the proposition that Mr. Kincaid's degree in physical education justified his choice, as the evidence suggested that where male candidates were concerned, the committee valued experience more highly than formal training in physical education.[1] The court also rejected the claim of one of the committeemen that Mr. Kincaid had been hired because of the superiority of the recreational programs he planned to implement if selected for the job. The court credited the testimony of one of the other committeemen who had voted for Mr. Kincaid that the programs outlined by petitioner and Mr. Kincaid were substantially identical.

On the basis of its findings that petitioner was the most qualified candidate, that the committee had been biased against hiring a woman, and that the committee's explanations for its choice of Mr. Kincaid were pretextual, the court concluded that petitioner had met her burden of establishing that she had been denied the position of Recreation Director because of her sex. Petitioner having conceded that ordering the city to hire her would be an inappropriate remedy under the circumstances, the court awarded petitioner backpay in the amount of $30,397 and attorney's fees of $16,971.59.

The Fourth Circuit reversed the District Court's finding of discrimination. In the view of the Court of Appeals, three of the District Court's crucial findings were clearly erroneous: the finding that petitioner was the most qualified candidate, the finding that petitioner had been asked questions that other applicants were spared, and the finding that the male committee members were biased against hiring a woman. Having rejected these findings, the Court of Appeals concluded that the District Court had erred in finding that petitioner had been discriminated against on account of her sex.

II

We must deal at the outset with the Fourth Circuit's suggestion that "close scrutiny of the record in this case [was] justified by the manner in which the opinion was prepared," id., at 156 — that is, by the District Court's adoption of petitioner's proposed findings of fact and conclusions of law. The court recalled that the Fourth Circuit had on many occasions condemned the practice of announcing a decision and leaving it to the prevailing party to write the findings of fact and conclusions of law. * * * The court rejected petitioner's contention that the procedure followed by the trial judge in this case was proper because the judge had given respondent an opportunity to object to the proposed findings and had not adopted petitioner's findings verbatim. According to the court, the vice of the procedure lay in the trial court's solicitation of findings after it had

---

[1] The evidence established that the committee members had initially favored a third candidate, Bert Broadway, and had decided not to hire him only because he stated that he was unwilling to move to Bessemer City. Mr. Broadway had two years of experience as a community recreation director; but like petitioner, he lacked a college degree in physical education.

already announced its decision and in the court's adoption of the "substance" of petitioner's proposed findings.

We, too, have criticized courts for their verbatim adoption of findings of fact prepared by prevailing parties, particularly when those findings have taken the form of conclusory statements unsupported by citation to the record. We are also aware of the potential for overreaching and exaggeration on the part of attorneys preparing findings of fact when they have already been informed that the judge has decided in their favor. Nonetheless, our previous discussions of the subject suggest that even when the trial judge adopts proposed findings verbatim, the findings are those of the court and may be reversed only if clearly erroneous.

In any event, the District Court in this case does not appear to have uncritically accepted findings prepared without judicial guidance by the prevailing party. The court itself provided the framework for the proposed findings when it issued its preliminary memorandum, which set forth its essential findings and directed petitioner's counsel to submit a more detailed set of findings consistent with them. Further, respondent was provided and availed itself of the opportunity to respond at length to the proposed findings. Nor did the District Court simply adopt petitioner's proposed findings: the findings it ultimately issued — and particularly the crucial findings regarding petitioner's qualifications, the questioning to which petitioner was subjected, and bias on the part of the committeemen — vary considerably in organization and content from those submitted by petitioner's counsel. Under these circumstances, we see no reason to doubt that the findings issued by the District Court represent the judge's own considered conclusions. There is no reason to subject those findings to a more stringent appellate review than is called for by the applicable rules.

III

Because a finding of intentional discrimination is a finding of fact, the standard governing appellate review of a district court's finding of discrimination is that set forth in Federal Rule of Civil Procedure 52(a): "Findings of fact shall not be set aside unless clearly erroneous, and due regard shall be given to the opportunity of the trial court to judge of the credibility of the witnesses."[*] The question before us, then, is whether the Court of Appeals erred in holding the District Court's finding of discrimination to be clearly erroneous.

Although the meaning of the phrase "clearly erroneous" is not immediately apparent, certain general principles governing the exercise of the appellate court's power to overturn findings of a district court may be derived from our cases. The foremost of these principles, as the Fourth Circuit itself recognized, is that "[a] finding is 'clearly erroneous' when although there is evidence to support it, the reviewing court on the entire evidence is left with the definite and firm conviction that a mistake has been committed." United States v. United

---

[*] [The current version of the Rule (Rule 52(a)(6)), is slightly reworded — eds. See Note 6, below.]

States Gypsum Co., 333 U.S. 364, 395 (1948). This standard plainly does not entitle a reviewing court to reverse the finding of the trier of fact simply because it is convinced that it would have decided the case differently. The reviewing court oversteps the bounds of its duty under Rule 52(a) if it undertakes to duplicate the role of the lower court. "In applying the clearly erroneous standard to the findings of a district court sitting without a jury, appellate courts must constantly have in mind that their function is not to decide factual issues de novo." If the district court's account of the evidence is plausible in light of the record viewed in its entirety, the court of appeals may not reverse it even though convinced that had it been sitting as the trier of fact, it would have weighed the evidence differently. Where there are two permissible views of the evidence, the factfinder's choice between them cannot be clearly erroneous.

This is so even when the district court's findings do not rest on credibility determinations, but are based instead on physical or documentary evidence or inferences from other facts. To be sure, various Courts of Appeals have on occasion asserted the theory that an appellate court may exercise de novo review over findings not based on credibility determinations. * * * This theory has an impressive genealogy, having first been articulated in an opinion written by Judge Frank and subscribed to by Judge Augustus Hand, * * * but it is impossible to trace the theory's lineage back to the text of Rule 52(a), which states straightforwardly that "findings of fact shall not be set aside unless clearly erroneous." That the Rule goes on to emphasize the special deference to be paid credibility determinations does not alter its clear command: Rule 52(a) "does not make exceptions or purport to exclude certain categories of factual findings from the obligation of a court of appeals to accept a district court's findings unless clearly erroneous." *Pullman-Standard v. Swint*, 456 U.S., at 287.

The rationale for deference to the original finder of fact is not limited to the superiority of the trial judge's position to make determinations of credibility. The trial judge's major role is the determination of fact, and with experience in fulfilling that role comes expertise. Duplication of the trial judge's efforts in the court of appeals would very likely contribute only negligibly to the accuracy of fact determination at a huge cost in diversion of judicial resources. In addition, the parties to a case on appeal have already been forced to concentrate their energies and resources on persuading the trial judge that their account of the facts is the correct one; requiring them to persuade three more judges at the appellate level is requiring too much. As the Court has stated in a different context, the trial on the merits should be "the 'main event' . . . rather than a 'tryout on the road.'" Wainwright v. Sykes, 433 U.S. 72, 90 (1977). For these reasons, review of factual findings under the clearly-erroneous standard — with its deference to the trier of fact — is the rule, not the exception.

When findings are based on determinations regarding the credibility of witnesses, Rule 52(a) demands even greater deference to the trial court's findings; for only the trial judge can be aware of the variations in demeanor and tone of voice that bear so heavily on the listener's understanding of and belief in what is said. This is not to suggest that the trial judge may insulate his findings from review by denominating them credibility determinations, for factors other than demeanor and inflection go into the decision whether or not to believe a witness. Documents or objective evidence may contradict the witness' story; or the story itself may be so internally inconsistent or implausible on its face that a reasonable factfinder would not credit it. Where such factors are present, the court of appeals may well find clear error even in a finding purportedly based on a credibility determination. But when a trial judge's finding is based on his decision to credit the testimony of one of two or more witnesses, each of whom has told a coherent and facially plausible story that is not contradicted by extrinsic evidence, that finding, if not internally inconsistent, can virtually never be clear error.

IV

Application of the foregoing principles to the facts of the case lays bare the errors committed by the Fourth Circuit in its employment of the clearly-erroneous standard. In detecting clear error in the District Court's finding that petitioner was better qualified than Mr. Kincaid, the Fourth Circuit improperly conducted what amounted to a de novo weighing of the evidence in the record. The District Court's finding was based on essentially undisputed evidence regarding the respective backgrounds of petitioner and Mr. Kincaid and the duties that went with the position of Recreation Director. The District Court, after considering the evidence, concluded that the position of Recreation Director in Bessemer City carried with it broad responsibilities for creating and managing a recreation program involving not only athletics, but also other activities for citizens of all ages and interests. The court determined that petitioner's more varied educational and employment background and her extensive involvement in a variety of civic activities left her better qualified to implement such a rounded program than Mr. Kincaid, whose background was more narrowly focused on athletics.

The Fourth Circuit, reading the same record, concluded that the basic duty of the Recreation Director was to implement an athletic program, and that the essential qualification for a successful applicant would be either education or experience specifically related to athletics.[2] Accordingly, it seemed evident to the Court of Appeals that Mr. Kincaid was in fact better qualified than petitioner.

Based on our own reading of the record, we cannot say that either interpretation of the facts is illogical or implausible. Each has support in inferences that may be drawn from the facts in the record; and if either interpretation had been drawn by a district court on the record before us, we would not be inclined to find it clearly erroneous. The question we must answer, however, is not whether the Fourth Circuit's interpretation of the facts was clearly erroneous, but whether the District Court's finding was clearly erroneous. The District Court determined that petitioner was better qualified, and, as we have stated above, such a finding is entitled to deference

---

[2] The Fourth Circuit thus saw no inconsistency between the statement of the male committee members that they preferred Bert Broadway because of his experience and their claim that they had selected Mr. Kincaid over petitioner because of his formal training. See n.1, supra. In the view of the Court of Appeals, this demonstrated only that Mr. Broadway had relevant experience and Mr. Kincaid had relevant education, while petitioner had neither.

notwithstanding that it is not based on credibility determinations. When the record is examined in light of the appropriately deferential standard, it is apparent that it contains nothing that mandates a finding that the District Court's conclusion was clearly erroneous.

Somewhat different concerns are raised by the Fourth Circuit's treatment of the District Court's finding that petitioner, alone among the applicants for the position of Recreation Director, was asked questions regarding her spouse's feelings about her application for the position. Here the error of the Court of Appeals was its failure to give due regard to the ability of the District Court to interpret and discern the credibility of oral testimony. The Court of Appeals rested its rejection of the District Court's finding of differential treatment on its own interpretation of testimony by Mrs. Boone — the very witness whose testimony, in the view of the District Court, supported the finding. In the eyes of the Fourth Circuit, Mrs. Boone's testimony that she had made a "comment" to Mr. Kincaid about the feelings of his wife (a comment judged "facetious" by the District Court) conclusively established that Mr. Kincaid, and perhaps other male applicants as well, had been questioned about the feelings of his spouse.

Mrs. Boone's testimony on this point, which is set forth in the margin,[3] is certainly not free from ambiguity. But Mrs. Boone several times stated that other candidates had not been questioned about the reaction of their wives — at least, "not in the same context" as had petitioner. And even after recalling and calling to the attention of the court that she had made a comment on the subject to Mr. Kincaid, Mrs. Boone denied that she had "asked" Mr. Kincaid about his wife's reaction. Mrs. Boone's testimony on these matters is not inconsistent with the theory that her remark was not a serious inquiry into whether Mr. Kincaid's wife approved of his applying for the position. Whether the judge's interpretation is actually correct is impossible to tell from the paper record, but it

---

[3] "Q: Did the committee members ask that same kind of question of the other applicants?
"A: Not that I recall. . . .
"Q: Do you deny that the other applicants, aside from the plaintiff, were asked about the prospect of working at night in that position?
"A: Not to my knowledge.
"Q: Are you saying they were not asked that?
"A: They were not asked, not in the context that they were asked of Phyllis. I don't know whether they were worried because Jim wasn't going to get his supper or what. You know, that goes both ways.
"Q: Did you tell Phyllis Anderson that Donnie Kincaid was not asked about night work?
"A: He wasn't asked about night work.
"Q: That answers one question. Now, let's answer the other one. Did you tell Phyllis Anderson that, that Donnie Kincaid was not asked about night work?
"A: Yes, after the interviews — I think the next day or sometime, and I know — may I answer something?
"Q: If it's a question that has been asked; otherwise, no. It's up to the Judge to say.
"A: You asked if there was any question asked about — I think Donnie was just married, and I think I made the comment to him personally — and your new bride won't mind.
"Q: So, you asked him yourself about his own wife's reaction?
"A: No, no.
"Q: That is what you just said.
"Mr. Gibson: Objection, Your Honor.
"[The] Court: Sustained. You don't have to rephrase the answer."

is easy to imagine that the tone of voice in which the witness related her comment, coupled with her immediate denial that she had questioned Mr. Kincaid on the subject, might have conclusively established that the remark was a facetious one. We therefore cannot agree that the judge's conclusion that the remark was facetious was clearly erroneous.

Once the trial court's characterization of Mrs. Boone's remark is accepted, it is apparent that the finding that the male candidates were not seriously questioned about the feelings of their wives cannot be deemed clearly erroneous. The trial judge was faced with the testimony of three witnesses, one of whom (Mrs. Boone) stated that none of the other candidates had been so questioned, one of whom (a male committee member) testified that Mr. Kincaid had been asked such a question "in a way," and one of whom (another committeeman) testified that all the candidates had been subjected to similar questioning. None of these accounts is implausible on its face, and none is contradicted by any reliable extrinsic evidence. Under these circumstances, the trial court's decision to credit Mrs. Boone was not clearly erroneous.

The Fourth Circuit's refusal to accept the District Court's finding that the committee members were biased against hiring a woman was based to a large extent on its rejection of the finding that petitioner had been subjected to questioning that the other applicants were spared. Given that that finding was not clearly erroneous, the finding of bias cannot be termed erroneous: it finds support not only in the treatment of petitioner in her interview, but also in the testimony of one committee member that he believed it would have been difficult for a woman to perform the job and in the evidence that another member solicited applications for the position only from men.[4]

Our determination that the findings of the District Court regarding petitioner's qualifications, the conduct of her interview, and the bias of the male committee members were not clearly erroneous leads us to conclude that the court's finding that petitioner was discriminated against on account of her sex was also not clearly erroneous. The District Court's findings regarding petitioner's superior qualifications and the bias of the selection committee are sufficient to support the inference that petitioner was denied the position of Recreation Director on account of her sex. Accordingly, we hold that the Fourth Circuit erred in denying petitioner relief under Title VII.

In so holding, we do not assert that our knowledge of what happened 10 years ago in Bessemer City is superior to that of the Court of Appeals; nor do we claim to have greater insight than the Court of Appeals into the state of mind of the men on the selection committee who rejected petitioner for the position of Recreation Director. Even the trial judge, who has heard the witnesses directly

---

[4]	The Fourth Circuit's suggestion that any inference of bias was dispelled by the fact that each of the male committee members was married to a woman who had worked at some point in the marriage is insufficient to establish that the finding of bias was clearly erroneous. Although we decline to hold that a man's attitude toward his wife's employment is irrelevant to the question whether he may be found to have a bias against working women, any relevance the factor may have in a particular case is a matter for the district court to weigh in its consideration of bias, not the court of appeals.

and who is more closely in touch than the appeals court with the milieu out of which the controversy before him arises, cannot always be confident that he "knows" what happened. Often, he can only determine whether the plaintiff has succeeded in presenting an account of the facts that is more likely to be true than not. Our task — and the task of appellate tribunals generally — is more limited still: we must determine whether the trial judge's conclusions are clearly erroneous. On the record before us, we cannot say that they are. Accordingly, the judgment of the Court of Appeals is

Reversed.

[JUSTICE POWELL's concurring opinion, and JUSTICE BLACKMUN's opinion concurring in the judgment are omitted.]

NOTES AND PROBLEMS FOR DISCUSSION

1. Sort out the relevant inquiries and standards of review.

(a) What is the standard that the district judge applies in making a factfinding?

(b) What is the standard that the court of appeals applies in reviewing that factfinding?

(c) What is the standard that the Supreme Court applies in reviewing the court of appeals?

2. Does *Bessemer City* give you a good sense as to when a factfinding will be "clearly" erroneous? The fact that the appeals court may think a particular finding is wrong is presumably not enough. But how erroneous such a finding will have to be before it will be clearly, and not "merely," erroneous is another question.

3. If the appeals court states that it is "left with a firm conviction that a mistake has been made," should the Supreme Court second guess the appeals court if the Supreme Court is not left with a similar conviction?

4. The factfinder in *Bessemer City* was the district judge, because, at the time, jury trials were unavailable in Title VII cases. If, after proper instructions, a jury rather than a judge had found intentional discrimination, what would have been the standard of review in connection with that factfinding? Although the district judge cannot ordinarily review jury factfindings (as opposed to the legal question of sufficiency of the evidence to support a jury's factfinding), the device of granting a new trial is one way for the district judge to police jury factfinding if she believes that the jury's decision is against the great weight of the evidence. See Rule 59.

5. Juries generally don't have to explain their verdicts, or the factfinding that led to their verdict, so it is often hard to know if they have acted rationally in the particular case (as opposed to their having had a rational basis for their decision per Rule 50). Judges have to explain their own factfinding, however, per Rule 52(a)(6). Apart from the lack of any Seventh Amendment problem when judges decide facts in cases not warranting a jury trial, does this explain why there can be somewhat greater scrutiny of judicial factfinding (as opposed to jury factfinding)?

6. Credibility was partly at issue in *Bessemer City*. But as the opinion points out, there had been a tradition in some federal appeals courts of providing more searching review of judicial factfinding that was made upon documentary and other evidence not raising credibility questions. Why should the district judge be given any factfinding deference in cases not implicating issues of witness credibility? Note that *Bessemer* arose prior to the 1985 amendment and later stylistic revision of Rule 52, which now includes the language "whether based on oral or other evidence." Rule 52(a)(6). Does this resolve the problem of some courts giving less deference to factual findings based on documentary evidence?

7. Rule 52(a) governs factfinding by district judges in a wide variety of settings, including suits for equitable relief, admiralty and maritime cases, and in other settings in which matters are not submitted to juries, such as factfindings associated with rulings on personal or subject matter jurisdiction. In *Bessemer City*, the district court tracked verbatim some of the proposed findings of fact submitted by one of the parties. Even if those findings are otherwise reasonable, doesn't such a practice suggest that the decisionmaking process might itself be flawed?

8. By contrast to a judge's factfinding errors (and as noted above), errors of law can ordinarily be reviewed de novo by each court next up the ladder in the judicial hierarchy. In other words, errors of law will be policed rigorously on appeal, and if the appellate court believes that the lower court was wrong on a question of law that matters to the outcome, it will reverse. This is true even when the underlying issues are ones of state law in a diversity action and where it might be said that the local district judge has some greater "expertise" in deciphering state law. See Salve Regina College v. Russell, 499 U.S. 225, 111 S.Ct. 1217, 113 L.Ed.2d 190 (1991) (discussed in Chapter 5).

9. In TEVA PHARMACEUTICALS USA, INC. v. SANDOZ, INC., 574 U.S. ___, 135 S.Ct. 831, 190 L.Ed.2d 719 (2015), the Court concluded that Rule 52(a) applied to a trial court's factual determinations made in the context of the construction of a patent claim. A majority stated: "In our view, this rule and the standard it sets forth must apply when a court of appeals reviews a district court's resolution of subsidiary factual matters made in the course of its construction of a patent claim." Is the decision consistent with Markman v. Westfall Instruments, 517 U.S. 379 (1996) (discussed in Chapter 11), which concluded that questions regarding the construction of patent claims were essentially questions of law for the court, and not for a jury.

10. Consider now the standard of review of a case that the parties have agreed to arbitrate. (We discuss arbitration at greater length in Chapter 14.) The Seventh Circuit addressed the question in HILL v. NORFOLK & WESTERN RAILWAY CO., 814 F.2d 1192 (7th Cir. 1987), in which a railroad employee sought arbitration over a claim he had against his employer:

> Hill, a brakeman fired by the Norfolk and Western railroad, took the matter to arbitration before [an arbitration board chosen pursuant to procedures agreed to by Hill's union and his employer] which

unanimously rejected his claim that he had been fired in violation of the collective bargaining agreement between the railroad and his union. He then brought this suit * * * to set aside the board's decision, lost in the district court, and appeals to us. The appeal has no merit; indeed, it reveals a serious misunderstanding of the scope of federal judicial review of the arbitration decisions.

    As we have said too many times to want to repeat again, the question for decision by a federal court asked to set aside an arbitration award — whether the award is made under the Railway Labor Act, the Taft-Hartley Act, or the United States Arbitration Act — is not whether the arbitrator or arbitrators erred in interpreting the contract; it is not whether they clearly erred in interpreting the contract; it is not whether they grossly erred in interpreting the contract; *it is whether they interpreted the contract.* * * * If they did, their interpretation is *conclusive.* By making a contract with an arbitration clause the parties agreed to be bound by the arbitrators' interpretation of the contract. A party can complain if the arbitrators didn't interpret the contract – that is, if they disregard the contract and implement their own notions of what is reasonable or fair. A party can complain if an arbitrator's decision is infected by fraud or other corruption, or if it orders [a party to commit] an illegal act. But a party will not be heard to complain merely because the arbitrators' interpretation is a misinterpretation. Granted, the grosser the apparent misinterpretation, the likelier it is that the arbitrators weren't interpreting the contract at all. But once the court is satisfied that they were interpreting the contract, judicial review is at an end, provided there is no fraud or corruption and the arbitrators haven't ordered anyone to do an illegal act.

Id. at 1194-1195 (emphasis added). The Court went on to impose sanctions on Hill's counsel for the filing of an appeal based on frivolous grounds.

11. In addition to limitations on review effected by the standards for review, there are other doctrines which as a practical matter limit review. Two of them are briefly described here.

    (a) The Contemporaneous Objection Rule. A losing party generally cannot raise an issue on appeal unless she has raised the issue in the trial court and properly preserved the question for appeal. For example, evidence improperly admitted or excluded, or an improper jury instruction will generally not be considered as grounds for reversal on appeal unless there has been a timely objection. See Rule 51. In the case of erroneous instructions, a party also may be required to offer a substitute instruction. In this connection, failure to make a timely post-verdict motion for judgment as a matter of law has traditionally barred raising the question on appeal, as does failure to move for a new trial. See Rules 50(b), 59.

    (b) The Harmless Error Rule. Appellate courts will not review rulings that are errors, but which are determined to be harmless. Rule 61 suggests that any such ruling will be disregarded unless "inconsistent with substantial justice," and sometimes courts phrase the test as: a ruling which affected the "substantial

rights of the parties." This doctrine frequently is applied with respect to rulings on discovery issues before trial and evidence rulings during the trial (on evidence rulings, courts may also say, in somewhat the same vein, that excluded evidence was "cumulative"). See Rule 103, Fed. R. Evid. Of course, to the party who suffered the erroneous ruling, the error may seem as though it is anything but harmless, and no one can really tell what would (or would not) have made a difference. Nevertheless, the harmless error rule gives appellate courts considerable power to disregard errors — often with the statement, noted above, that the appellant is entitled to a fair trial and not a perfect trial. Should error that cannot be clearly shown to be outcome determinative ever be considered harmful, or should it be enough that a particular error might possibly have affected the outcome of the litigation

SECTION C. RELIEF FROM JUDGMENT — RULE 60(b)

Once appeals have been exhausted, or the time for seeking an appeal has come and gone, a judgment becomes final and enforceable. Final judgments entered by a court with good jurisdiction are ordinarily to be given preclusive effect, even if the decision might have been erroneous in some respect. See generally Chapter 13. Nevertheless, in the federal court system (and under analogous provisions in the states) there still exists a limited ability to return to the court that rendered the judgment to seek relief from judgment. See Rule 60(b). The Rule is not, strictly speaking, an "appellate" mechanism. Indeed, courts go out of their way to say that Rule 60(b) was not designed to provide relief for legal error or to take the place of an appeal. See Title v. United States, 263 F.2d 28, 31 (9th Cir. 1959) ("Rule 60(b) was not intended to provide relief for error on the part of the trial court or to affect a substitute for appeal."). Nevertheless, it enables the disappointed party to try, try again, even though the judgment of which he is complaining has become final. Rule 60(b) is quite limited however. And as the following case shows, mere error of law may not provide much of an avenue for relief from judgment.

DeWeerth v. Baldinger

United States Court of Appeals, Second Circuit, 1994.
38 F.3d 1266, cert. denied, 513 U.S. 1001, 115 S.Ct. 512, 130 L.Ed.2d 419.

WALKER, CIRCUIT JUDGE.

This appeal is the latest episode in a decade-long dispute over the ownership of an oil painting entitled "Champs de Blé à Vétheuil" by Claude Monet. The work by the celebrated French Impressionist was previously owned by plaintiff Gerda Dorothea DeWeerth, a German citizen. It was discovered missing from DeWeerth's family castle after World War II, and was subsequently purchased by defendant Edith Marks Baldinger, a New York resident, from third-party-defendant Wildenstein & Co., a New York art gallery. Baldinger and Wildenstein & Co. (referred to collectively as "defendants") appeal from a judgment entered in the United States District Court for the Southern District of New York (Vincent L. Broderick, Judge) that granted DeWeerth's motion pursuant to Fed. R. Civ. P.60(b) for relief from the final judgment entered in favor of defendants in accordance with our decision in DeWeerth v. Baldinger, 836 F.2d 103 (2d Cir. 1987), cert. denied, 486 U.S. 1056 (1988), and entered a new judgment in plaintiffs favor. We conclude that the district court * * * abused its discretion in ordering relief from the final judgment based on Rule 60(b).

I. Background

* * *

DeWeerth claims that her father purchased the Monet from a Berlin gallery in 1908 and that she inherited the painting after her father's death in 1922. She had the painting in her possession until 1943 when she transferred it to her sister's castle in southern Germany for safekeeping during World War II. DeWeerth's sister discovered that the painting was missing in 1945, after the departure of American soldiers who had been quartered in her home. The Monet resurfaced in 1956, at which time Wildenstein & Co. acquired it from a Swiss art dealer. Baldinger subsequently purchased the painting from Wildenstein in 1957 in undisputed good faith.

In 1982, DeWeerth discovered that Baldinger was in possession of the Monet and demanded its return. When Baldinger refused, DeWeerth promptly commenced a diversity action to recover it. Baldinger in turn brought a third-party action against Wildenstein & Co. * * * In April 1987, after a bench trial, Judge Broderick found that DeWeerth had established a superior right to possession of the Monet and issued a ruling in her favor. The district court specifically rejected Baldinger's two principal defenses of [statute of] limitations and laches. The district court concluded that the three-year statute of limitations applicable to [actions of replevin], see N.Y. Civ. Prac. L. & R. §214(3) (McKinney 1990), did not begin to run until Baldinger refused DeWeerth's demand for the painting [and ruled that the suit was therefore timely]. The district court ordered Baldinger to deliver the painting to DeWeerth.

In December 1987, a panel of this court *reversed* the district court's judgment on the ground that New York limitations law required a showing of reasonable diligence in locating stolen property and that DeWeerth had failed to make such a showing. * * * On June 13, 1988, the Supreme Court denied DeWeerth's petition for a writ of certiorari.

* * *

On September 27, 1991, DeWeerth moved in the district court for relief pursuant to Fed. R. Civ. P. 60(b)(5) and (6). [Plaintiff argued that the intervening decision from New York's highest court in Guggenheim v. Lubell, 77 N.Y.2d 311 (1991), had concluded that, in cases such as the plaintiff's involving stolen art in the hands of a good faith purchaser, New York limitations law did not require a showing of reasonable diligence in locating the stolen property prior to making demand on the property's current possessor (i.e., the purchaser), provided the owner made demand on the possessor within a reasonable time after actually learning the identity of the possessor. Rather, the statute of limitations began to run only after demand upon the party currently in possession of the property and their refusal to return it.] By Order dated October 16, 1992, Judge Broderick [therefore] granted DeWeerth's motion and once again ordered Baldinger to surrender the Monet to DeWeerth. Judgment was entered on February 2, 1993, and this appeal followed. * * *

* * *

II. Did the District Court Abuse its Discretion in Granting DeWeerth's Rule 60(b) Motion?

The district court granted DeWeerth's motion for relief from the final judgment under Rule 60(b)(6) and, alternatively, under Rule 60(b)(5). A "district court's grant or denial of relief under Rule 60(b), unless rooted in an error of law, may be reversed only for abuse of discretion." Twelve John Does v. District of Columbia, 268 U.S. App. D.C. 308, 841 F.2d 1133, 1138 (D.C. Cir. 1988).

A. The Rule 60(b)(6) Determination

Rule 60(b) provides that the district court may relieve a party or a party's legal representative from a final judgment, order, or proceeding in five enumerated circumstances and, according to the sixth subpart, for "any other reason justifying relief from the operation of the judgment." Fed. R. Civ. P. 60(b)(6). We have held that subpart (6) is "properly invoked where there are extraordinary circumstances or where the judgment may work an extreme and undue hardship."

Judge Broderick determined that the *Guggenheim* decision, and its import for this case, constituted an "extraordinary circumstance" justifying relief under Rule 60(b)(6). Like *DeWeerth*, *Guggenheim* involved a suit by the owner of an allegedly stolen art object against the subsequent good faith purchaser for return of the stolen item. In the first appeal in *DeWeerth*, we held that New York's applicable statute of limitations required the previous owner to demonstrate that she had acted with reasonable diligence in attempting to locate the stolen object, and that absent such a showing, the owner's otherwise timely suit would be barred. In *Guggenheim*, the New York Court of Appeals not only applied a contrary rule, but also expressly stated that the conception of New York law that we reached three years earlier in *DeWeerth* was wrong. In a unanimous decision, the Court of Appeals held that New York had a clearly established rule that the statute of limitations does not start to run until a bona fide purchaser refuses an owner's demand for return of a stolen art object, and that the Second Circuit should not have modified this rule by imposing a duty of reasonable diligence. It reasoned that the Second Circuit's decision contravened New York's longstanding policy of favoring owners over bona fide purchasers so that New York would not become a haven for stolen art.

Based on the New York Court of Appeals' opinion, the district court determined that DeWeerth would have prevailed in this case had she originally brought her suit in the New York state courts. It then held that Erie Railroad Co. v. Tompkins, 304 U.S. 64 (1938), and its progeny entitled plaintiff to a modification of the final judgment in this case to avoid this inconsistency. It determined that the countervailing interest of both the parties and the courts in the finality of litigation was outweighed by the need "to prevent the working of an extreme and undue hardship upon plaintiff, to accomplish substantial justice and to act with appropriate regard for the principles of federalism which underlie our dual judicial system."

We have carefully considered the circumstances analyzed by the district court and conclude that they do not warrant relief under Rule 60(b)(6). While acknowledging that Judge Broderick engaged in a scholarly and thorough discussion of the issues, we think that his decision inappropriately disturbed a final judgment in a case that had been fully litigated and was long since closed. In our view, *Erie* simply does not stand for the proposition that a plaintiff is entitled to reopen a federal court case that has been closed for several years in order to gain the benefit of a newly-announced decision of a state court. The limited holding of *Erie* is that federal courts sitting in diversity are bound to follow state law on any matter of substantive law not "governed by the Federal Constitution or by Acts of Congress." 304 U.S. at 78. However, the fact that federal courts must follow state law when deciding a diversity case does not mean that a subsequent change in the law of the state will provide grounds for relief under Rule 60(b)(6). See Brown v. Clark Equip. Co., 96 F.R.D. 166, 173 (D. Me. 1982) ("mere change in decisional law does not constitute an 'extraordinary circumstance'" under Rule 60(b)(6), especially where "plaintiffs elected to proceed in the federal forum, thereby voluntarily depriving themselves of the opportunity to attempt to persuade the [state court]"); Atwell v. Equifax, Inc., 86 F.R.D. 686, 688 (D. Md. 1980) (change in the state decisional law upon which appellate court based decision held "insufficient to warrant reopening a final judgment"). This principle also applies in federal cases where the Supreme Court has changed the applicable rule of law. See Picco v. Global Marine Drilling Co., 900 F.2d 846, 851 (5th Cir. 1989); Travelers Indem. Co. v. Sarkisian, 794 F.2d 754, 757 (2d Cir.), cert. denied, 479 U.S. 885 (1986).

DeWeerth argues that this case is distinguishable because the state court did not announce a "change in the law," but rather clarified that New York law is — and always was — contrary to what the federal court held it to be. While we agree that *Guggenheim* did not involve a "change in the law" in the sense that it adopted a rule different from one that previously existed, we do not agree that *Guggenheim* stated that the question decided by the *DeWeerth* panel had long been settled in New York. The *Guggenheim* court stated only that New York's demand and refusal rule was well established; it did not state that the question of whether a due diligence requirement should be added to this rule was clearly settled. In fact, no earlier New York case had addressed this issue. The earlier *DeWeerth* panel noted that this question was an open one; although it could have certified the question to the New York Court of Appeals, it chose to decide the issue itself since it did not think the issue would "recur with sufficient frequency to warrant use of the certification procedure."

When confronted with an unsettled issue of state law, a federal court sitting in diversity must make its best effort to predict how the state courts would decide the issue. Stafford v. International Harvester Co., 668 F.2d 142, 148 (2d Cir. 1981). The comprehensive opinion by now Chief Judge Jon O. Newman in *DeWeerth* accordingly surveyed New York caselaw and determined that a New

York court called upon to decide the issue would be likely to impose a requirement of due diligence. The decision was based in part on the fact that plaintiffs argument would create an incongruity in the treatment of bona fide purchasers and thieves. In New York, the three-year statute of limitations starts running against thieves once the owner discovers that the art object has been stolen, while under plaintiff's theory, it would not start running against a good faith purchaser until he refused the owner's request to return the art object. The court determined in *DeWeerth* that this rule conflicted with a policy inherent in certain New York cases of protecting bona fide purchasers of stolen objects from stale claims by alleged owners. Based on this incongruity, New York's policy of discouraging stale claims in other settings, and the fact that in most other states the limitations period begins to run when a good faith purchaser acquires stolen property thereby prompting due diligence on the part of the previous owner, we determined that New York courts would adopt a due diligence requirement for owners attempting to locate stolen property.

It turned out that the *DeWeerth* panel's prediction was wrong. However, by bringing this suit, DeWeerth exposed herself to the possibility that her adversaries would argue for a change in the applicable rules of law. By filing her state law claim in a federal forum, she knew that any open question of state law would be decided by a federal as opposed to a New York state court. The subsequent outcome of the *Guggenheim* decision does not impugn the integrity of the *DeWeerth* decision or the fairness of the process that was accorded DeWeerth. The result in this case would be no different if DeWeerth had filed her claim in state court and Baldinger had removed the action to federal court. The very nature of diversity jurisdiction leaves open the possibility that a state court will subsequently disagree with a federal court's interpretation of state law. However, this aspect of our dual justice system does not mean that all diversity judgments are subject to revision once a state court later addresses the litigated issues. Such a rule would be tantamount to holding that the doctrine of finality does not apply to diversity judgments, a theory that has no basis in *Erie* or its progeny.

We believe that the prior *DeWeerth* panel made a reasonable ruling on the due diligence question given the information presented to it. In fact, a key reason for the *Guggenheim* court's contrary conclusion was not even presented to the *DeWeerth* panel as part of the parties' original briefing. In deciding not to adopt a due diligence requirement, the *Guggenheim* decision placed considerable weight on the fact that efforts to modify the demand and refusal rule by the New York State Legislature were unsuccessful. Specifically, in July 1986 Governor Mario Cuomo vetoed a bill passed by both houses of the State Legislature that would have caused the statute of limitations to start running from the time an art owner discovered or reasonably should have discovered the whereabouts of a work of art when bringing suit against certain not-for-profit institutions. As part of his veto message, Governor Cuomo stated that if the bill became law, it would have caused New York to become "a haven for cultural property stolen abroad." See *Guggenheim*, 77 N.Y.2d at 319. The *Guggenheim* court concluded that "the history of this bill and the concerns expressed by the Governor in vetoing it, when considered together with the abundant case law spelling out the demand

and refusal rule, convince us that that rule remains the law in New York and that there is no reason to obscure its straightforward protection of true owners by creating a duty of reasonable diligence." Id. The existence of this bill was not discussed in the *DeWeerth* opinion and was not brought to the attention of the court until DeWeerth filed a petition for rehearing. It is well established in this circuit that arguments raised for the first time on a petition for rehearing are deemed abandoned unless manifest injustice would otherwise result. It is thus likely that the prior *DeWeerth* panel deemed DeWeerth to have waived a key component of the argument that was ultimately successful before the New York Court of Appeals.

We conclude that the prior *DeWeerth* panel conscientiously satisfied its duty to predict how New York courts would decide the due diligence question, and that *Erie* and its progeny require no more than this. The fact that the New York Court of Appeals subsequently reached a contrary conclusion in *Guggenheim* does not constitute an "extraordinary circumstance" that would justify reopening this case in order to achieve a similar result. There is nothing in *Erie* that suggests that consistency must be achieved at the expense of finality, or that federal cases finally disposed of must be revisited anytime an unrelated state case clarifies the applicable rules of law. Attempting to obtain such a result through Rule 60(b)(6) is simply an improvident course that would encourage countless attacks on federal judgments long since closed. While our conclusion relies in part on our belief that the prior *DeWeerth* decision fully comported with *Erie* and did not, as plaintiff suggests, mistakenly apply settled state law and reach a clearly wrong result, we note that even if those were the circumstances, the doctrine of finality would still pose a considerable hurdle to reopening the final judgment in this case. Whether, in such circumstances, the result would be different if the issue were raised within one year pursuant to Rule 60(b)(1) is an issue we need not decide.

The caselaw relied on by the district court as support for its decision is distinguishable from the present case. In Pierce v. Cook & Co., 518 F.2d 720 (10th Cir. 1975), cert. denied, 423 U.S. 1079 (1976), the Tenth Circuit granted Rule 60(b)(6) relief based on an Oklahoma Supreme Court decision that undermined the basis for the Tenth Circuit's three-year-old dismissal of plaintiffs action. However, a major factor in the *Pierce* decision was that the change in state law would have caused federal and state tort actions arising out of the same accident and involving the same parties to have opposite results. See id. at 723. Whatever the merits of this rationale, as to which we express no opinion, it cannot justify the district court's decision in this case since *DeWeerth* and *Guggenheim* do not arise out of the same facts.

In American Iron & Steel Institute v. EPA, 560 F.2d 589 (3d Cir. 1977), cert. denied, 435 U.S. 914 (1978), the Third Circuit recalled its mandate because a subsequent Supreme Court case called into question the reasoning of the Third Circuit's decision issued one year and four months earlier. However, the court expressly stated that the mandate was recalled in part because the original panel decision placed on the defendant "continuing" obligations the validity of which was now suspect. See id. at 599. As discussed more fully below, the judgment in *DeWeerth* was finite in nature and did not have ongoing consequences for the parties involved. The other cases cited by the district court have fewer factual similarities to the instant case and provide even less persuasive authority for its holding.

We believe that the district court abused its discretion in ruling that the important interest in the finality of the judgment in this case, which was more than four years old at the time of that ruling, was outweighed by any injustice DeWeerth believes she has suffered by litigating her case in the federal as opposed to the state forum. Accordingly, we reverse the district court's decision granting her motion under Rule 60(b)(6).

B. The Rule 60(b)(5) Determination

Rule 60(b)(5) provides that a court may relieve a party from a final judgment where "the judgment has been satisfied, released, or discharged, or a prior judgment upon which it is based has been reversed or otherwise vacated, or it is no longer equitable that the judgment should have prospective application." Fed. R. Civ. P. 60(b)(5). The district court ruled that DeWeerth was entitled to relief under the prospective application clause of this Rule. Defendants contend that the final judgment in this case does not have prospective application and therefore is not subject to being reopened under this clause.

Since this circuit has never attempted to define the term "prospective application" as utilized in Rule 60(b)(5), we turn to a decision on this issue by the District of Columbia Court of Appeals. In *Twelve John Does* [*supra*], the court analyzed the two Supreme Court cases that led to the promulgation of the prospective application clause, United States v. Swift & Co., 286 U.S. 106 (1932), and Pennsylvania v. Wheeling & Belmont Bridge Co., 59 U.S. (18 How.) 421 (1856), and concluded that the standard to be applied "in determining whether an order or judgment has prospective application within the meaning of Rule 60(b)(5) is whether it is 'executory' or involves 'the supervision of changing conduct or conditions,' within the meaning of *Wheeling* and *Swift*." 841 F.2d at 1139. In *Wheeling*, the Court determined that the part of its former decree that directed the abatement of the construction of a bridge spanning the Ohio River was "executory" in nature since it required not only the removal of the bridge, but enjoined defendants against any reconstruction or continuance, and, as a "continuing decree," could be modified in light of a subsequent congressional act declaring the bridge lawful. In *Swift*, the Court rejected a request to modify a previously-issued injunction in light of changed circumstances, but nonetheless observed that a "continuing decree of injunction directed to events to come," which involves "the supervision of changing conduct or conditions," is always subject "to adaptation as events may shape the need."

In practical terms, these standards mean that judgments involving injunctions have "prospective application," while money judgments do not. The district court recognized this dichotomy and determined that the final judgment in this case was more similar to an injunction than a money judgment. It reasoned that the relief DeWeerth sought in bringing this suit would require Baldinger to perform the future act of physically returning the Monet and that the judgment rendered would have a continuing effect on future custody of the painting. It therefore concluded that the final judgment in this case had "prospective application" under Rule 60(b)(5).

We think this conclusion was erroneous as a matter of law. The nature of the judgment sought in this case was a declaration of rights regarding title to personal property. The fact that physical transfer of the Monet would have been required to comport with the judgment if DeWeerth had prevailed does not render the judgment "executory." A similar transfer of assets is also required where the court enters a money judgment. Even if the district court in this case were involved in enforcing an ordered transfer, its involvement would not constitute "supervision of changing conduct or conditions."

* * *

As such, the only prospective effect of the court's judgment is its bar to future relitigation of custody to the painting. * * * Accordingly, we conclude that the final judgment in this case did not have prospective application as this term is utilized in Rule 60(b)(5) and that the district court's holding to the contrary was an error of law requiring reversal.

Because of our decision that it was inappropriate for the district court to grant relief under either Rule 60(b)(6) or 60(b)(5), it is unnecessary for us to consider defendants' further arguments that the district court wrongly decided the merits of their laches defense and the question of superior title.

[Reversed.]

Owen, District Judge.

I respectfully dissent.

The majority recognizes that in dismissing Mrs. DeWeerth's action on New York statute of limitations grounds, the prior "*DeWeerth* panel's prediction was wrong." It was wrong in adding to New York's well-established demand and refusal rule a due diligence requirement, which the panel then found had not been met. Nevertheless, the majority leaves the dismissal standing, asserting first, that the prior panel was confronted with "an unsettled issue of state law," and second, that the doctrine of finality of judgments outweighs "any injustice DeWeerth believes she has suffered by litigating her case in the federal as opposed to the state forum."

I am unable to accept either of these conclusions. As to the majority's view that the pre-*DeWeerth* New York law was "unsettled", no prior New York statute of limitations ruling had any suggestion of a pre-demand due diligence requirement, or that the issue was ever raised, or even could have been considered. The New York Court of Appeals in Gillet v. Roberts, 57 N.Y. 28 in 1874, stated at 34.

> The rule is a reasonable and just one, that an innocent purchaser of personal property from a wrongdoer shall first be informed of the defect in his title, and have an opportunity to deliver the property to the true owner, before he shall be made liable as a tort feasor for a wrongful conversion. * * *

Thereafter, Menzel v. List, 22 A.D.2d 647, 253 N.Y.S.2d 43, 44 (1st Dep't.

1964), * * * again held that "a demand by the rightful owner is a substantive, rather than a procedural, prerequisite to the bringing of an action for conversion by the owner[,]" and therefore, "the statute of limitations did not begin to run until demand and refusal."

This well-established New York law, as I view it, was further confirmed prior to our 1987 *DeWeerth* opinion by the fact that in 1986 a bill passed the New York legislature proposing to institute a "discovery rule" providing that as to certain not-for-profit institutions, the statute of limitations would run from the time those institutions gave notice, as specified in the bill, that they were in possession of a particular object. The bill was vetoed by Governor Cuomo. The majority recognizes the fact, as do I, that the fate of this bill is wholly consistent with the complete absence in any pre-*Guggenheim* authorities of any such requirement.

* * *

New York case law has long protected the right of the owner whose property has been stolen to recover that property, even if it is in the possession of a good faith purchaser for value (see, Saltus & Saltus v. Everett, 20 Wend. 267, 282). There is a three-year Statute of Limitations for recovery of a chattel (CPLR 214 [3]). The rule in this State is that a cause of action for replevin against the good-faith purchaser of a stolen chattel accrues when the true owner makes demand for return of the chattel and the person in possession of the chattel refuses to return it. Until demand is made and refused, possession of the stolen property by the good-faith purchaser for value is not considered wrongful. [Because *Guggenheim* concluded expressly that "the Second circuit [in *DeWeerth*] should not have imposed a duty of reasonable diligence"] in my view, this case is a most compelling one for relief under Fed R. Civ. P. 60(b)(6). * * *

NOTES AND PROBLEMS FOR DISCUSSION

1. The decision in the first *DeWeerth* appeal got New York law flat wrong. The second *DeWeerth* appeal admits as much. What policy justifies letting Baldinger keep the painting?

2. Under Erie R. Co. v. Tompkins, 304 U.S. 64, 58 S.Ct. 817, 82 L.Ed. 1188 (1938), federal courts are obliged to follow state substantive law in a diversity case such as *DeWeerth*, and to follow the state's statute of limitations. See Chapter 5. Should it matter whether the error of law made by the federal court was a reasonable one, as hinted by the majority?

3. Ms. DeWeerth would likely have won her case had she filed in state court. She filed in federal court instead, for whatever reason. Would she have had a stronger case for relief from judgment if she had filed in state court and the defendant had removed (assuming defendant could do so)?

4. The decision in *DeWeerth* may argue for not having federal courts decide unclear questions of state law. But recall that the supposed purpose of diversity is to provide a neutral forum for noncitizens and to free them from the possible bias, or the perception of bias, of state courts. If so, perhaps federal courts *should* maintain a role in "guessing" or "predicting" the meaning of state law in diversity cases lest that role be subverted, even though such a practice may step on the toes of the state courts in their *Erie*-recognized power as "lawmakers." Note also that it may never be possible to predict with complete certainty how a state court would answer a question of state law, even when it appears to be an easy question, based on previous precedent. State courts can and do reinterpret their own laws, and one never can be sure when that will happen. See Kansas Pub. Employees Ret. Sys. v. Reimer & Kroger Assoc., 194 F.3d 922 (8th Cir. 1999) (concluding that *Erie* does not require changes to final judgments just because there has been an intervening change in law).

5. In PIERCE v. COOK & CO., 518 F.2d 720 (10th Cir. 1975) — distinguished in *DeWeerth* — there had been parallel litigation in the federal and state courts arising out of a common vehicular accident in the State of Oklahoma. Two plaintiffs went forward against the defendant in federal court; a third went forward in state court against the same defendant. The federal court held that, under a venerable 34-year old Oklahoma precedent, a shipper was not liable for the torts of an independent contractor; it therefore granted summary judgment in the two cases before it because the injury had been caused by the negligence of an independent contractor of the defendant's. Six months after the federal judgments became final, however, the state supreme court, in deciding the third of the three cases, reversed its older precedent, and held for the first time that the shipper had to exercise reasonable care in the selection of a competent carrier. The federal plaintiffs then sought and obtained post-judgment relief which the Tenth Circuit upheld. The court of appeals narrowly circumscribed its holding to take care of the "unusual combination of events" that made "the situation extraordinary." Id. at 723. The court was of the view that in "diversity cases the results in federal court should be substantially the same as those in state court litigation arising out of the same transaction or occurrence." Id. The court distinguished its own earlier precedent in which the decisional change had come in unrelated litigation. See Collins v. City of Wichita, Kansas, 254 F.2d 837, 839 (10th Cir. 1958). The Tenth Circuit also noted that, in *Pierce*, the federal plaintiffs had been forced to litigate in federal court because of the removal statute.

6. As *DeWeerth* indicates, Rule 60(b)(5) has a somewhat easier time being satisfied when a party seeks modification of, or an end to, continued injunctive relief. Why should that be? As with an award of damages, injunctive relief may have been entered in a case based on the law as then understood, but the law may have changed in the interim. The issue often arises in public law litigation where a defendant public body argues that changes in the legal landscape ought to relieve it of some or all of its continuing obligations under a federal court's order to restructure its institutions. For example, in RUFO v. INMATES OF SUFFOLK CTY. JAIL, 502 U.S. 367, 112 S.Ct. 748, 116 L.Ed.2d 867 (1992) — a case involving prison reform litigation — the Court held that while intervening changes in the law might not be enough standing alone to permit relief under Rule 60(b)(5), a court should have the flexibility to allow for relief when there has been a significant change in the law. In *Rufo*, the county jail was under an injunction that required it to avoid practices that were once (but no longer) thought to be unconstitutional. See also Agostini v. Felton, 521 U.S. 203, 105

S.Ct. 3232, 87 L.Ed.2d 290 (1997) (allowing, under Rule 60(b)(5), for reopening of 12 year old injunction forbidding public school teachers from providing remedial education at religious schools, given intervening developments in Supreme Court's Establishment Clause jurisprudence). Are the continuing effects of a damages judgment entered on possibly erroneous grounds (even at the time) easier to tolerate than the continuing effects of an injunction — especially one against a public body — whose legal basis has eroded over time?

In connection with *Rufo*, consider the problem of state officials who might be inclined to settle previously filed lawsuits on terms very favorable to the plaintiffs. Should state officials of one administration be able to bind future administrations in perpetuity? Should Rule 60(b) be given a liberal reading to avoid such a possibility? See also Horne v. Flores, 557 U.S. 433, 129 S.Ct. 1694, 173 L.Ed.2d 1054 (2009) (noting federalism concerns in the area of institutional reform litigation and reaffirming *Rufo*'s "flexible approach" to Rule 60(b)(5) in such litigation).

In Frew v. Hawkins, 540 U.S. 431, 124 S.Ct. 899, 157 L.Ed.2d 855 (2004), the Supreme Court stated that injunctive actions against state officials to enforce a consent decree previously entered into by earlier state officials did not run afoul of principles of sovereign immunity. It added, however, that if the terms of a given consent decree were too onerous, the way to address the problem was through relief from judgment Rule 60(b).

7. Note that under Rule 60(b), some errors must be brought up within a one year period following a final judgment. For example, a showing of "newly discovered evidence," "fraud . . . misrepresentation, or misconduct of the adverse party," or "mistake, inadvertence, surprise, or excusable neglect" would provide a basis for reopening a judgment within a year, but not thereafter. Would any of these have provided a basis for relief from judgment on the facts of *DeWeerth* if the motion had been made within a year? By having moved "more than one year after the judgment" Ms. DeWeerth was forced to try to squeeze her claim into one of the harder-to-fit categories — in her case, Rule 60(b)(5) or 60(b)(6). The latter motions need only be made "within a reasonable time."

8. Finally, Rule 60(d) specifically allows for the possibility that a court might entertain "an independent action to relieve a party from a judgment, order, or proceeding." What grounds should entitle a party to relief in such an action? Note that if such an "independent action" could be based on considerations that Rule 60(b) already contemplates (some of them under severe time constraints), there might not be much point to having Rule 60(b). In UNITED STATES v. BEGGERLY, 524 U.S. 38, 118 S.Ct. 1862, 141 L.Ed.2d 32 (1988), the Supreme Court upheld the availability of an independent action and refused to require an independent subject matter jurisdictional showing for such suits, so long as there had been good subject matter jurisdiction in the underlying suit that the action sought to reopen. But the Court cautioned: "If relief may be obtained through an independent action in a case such as this, [which would have implicated, at most, a claim of misrepresentation by the adverse party], the strict 1-year time limit on such motions would be set at naught. Independent actions must, if Rule

60(b) is to be interpreted as a coherent whole, be reserved for those cases of 'injustices which, in certain instances, are deemed sufficiently gross to demand a departure' from rigid adherence to the doctrine of res judicata."

Section D. Collateral Attack (vs. Appeal)

Suppose that a judgment from a state court has become final. All avenues of direct appeal (up the judicial hierarchy) have proved unsuccessful. At this point (if not before), one could expect that the victor would want to have his judgment enforced. If enforcement takes place in another state, recall from Chapter 2 that a jurisdictionally valid judgment will ordinarily be given full faith and credit in the enforcing state — as called for by Article IV of the Constitution and the Full Faith and Credit Act, 28 U.S.C.A. §1738. In the chapter that follows (Chapter 13), we will explore the scope of the preclusive consequences that a judicial system might choose to give its own judgments. Here, we consider what it means to give full faith and credit to another state's judgment.

Keep in mind a number of questions as you read the materials below. May the enforcing state choose to deny full faith and credit because of errors of law — perhaps gross errors of law — made in the proceedings that led to the judgment that a party is seeking to enforce? What if the judgment runs counter to the public policy of the state in which enforcement is sought, such as a judgment on a contract that carries with it an interest rate that the enforcing court (but not the judgment rendering court) would consider usurious? In addition, although you know that jurisdictionally valid judgments will ordinarily be recognized and enforced, consider what happens when the parties actually litigate the question of jurisdiction in the court that renders the judgment, but the court incorrectly found jurisdiction. Will those findings themselves be preclusive against the party who litigated and lost on the jurisdictional question? Even if the court lacked jurisdiction "in fact"?

Fauntleroy v. Lum

Supreme Court of the United States, 1908.
210 U.S. 230, 28 S.Ct. 641, 52 L.Ed. 1039.

Mr. Justice Holmes delivered the opinion of the Court.

This is an action upon a Missouri judgment, brought in a court of Mississippi. The declaration set forth the record of the judgment. The defendant [Lum] pleaded that the original cause of action arose in Mississippi out of a gambling transaction in cotton futures; that he declined to pay the loss; * * * [that] thereafter, finding the defendant temporarily in Missouri, the plaintiff brought suit there * * *; that * * * a verdict was rendered and the judgment in suit entered upon the same. [In the Mississippi action] [t]he [defendant's] plea was demurred to on constitutional grounds, and the demurrer was overruled, subject to exception. * * * The supreme court of Mississippi held the plea good * * * and judgment was entered for the defendant.

Thereupon the case was brought here. The main argument urged by the defendant to sustain the judgment below is addressed to the jurisdiction of the Mississippi courts. The laws of Mississippi make dealing in futures a misdemeanor, and provide that contracts of that sort, made without intent to deliver the commodity or to pay the price, "shall not be enforced by any court." Annotated Code of 1892, 1120, 1121, 2117. * * *

* * * The statute now before us seems to us only to lay down a rule of decision. The Mississippi court in which this action was brought is a court of general jurisdiction and would have to decide upon the validity of the bar, if the suit * * * upon the original cause of action had been [originally] brought [in Mississippi]. The words 'shall not be enforced by any court' are simply another, possibly less emphatic, way of saying that an action shall not be brought to enforce such contracts. * * * [Therefore,] we proceed at once to the further question, whether the illegality of the original cause of action in Mississippi can be relied upon there as a ground for denying a recovery upon a judgment of another state.

The doctrine laid down by Chief Justice Marshall was "that the judgment of a state court should have the same credit, validity, and effect in every other court in the United States which it had in the state where it was pronounced, and that whatever pleas would be good to a suit thereon in such state, and none others, could be pleaded in any other court in the United States." Hampton v. M'Connel, 3 Wheat. 234. There is no doubt that this quotation was supposed to be an accurate statement of the law as late as Christmas v. Russell, 5 Wall. 290, where an attempt of Mississippi, by statute, to go behind judgments recovered in other states, was declared void, and it was held that such judgments could not be impeached even for fraud.

We assume that the statement of Chief Justice Marshall is correct. It is confirmed by the act of May 26, 1790, chap. 11, 1 Stat. 122 (Rev. Stat. 905, U. S. Comp. Stat. 1901), providing that the said records and judicial proceedings "shall have such faith and credit given to them in every court within the United States as they have by law or usage in the courts of the state from whence the said records are or shall be taken." See further Tilt v. Kelsey, 207 U.S. 43, 57, ante. Whether . . . the ruling of the Missouri court upon th[e] matter was right or wrong, there can be no question that the judgment was conclusive in Missouri on the validity of the cause of action. * * * A judgment is conclusive as to all the media concludendi * * * and it needs no authority to show that it cannot be impeached either in or out of the state by showing that it was based upon a mistake of law. Of course, a want of jurisdiction over either the person or the subject-matter might be shown. Andrews v. Andrews, 188 U.S. 14; Clarke v. Clarke, 178 U.S. 186. But, as the jurisdiction of the Missouri court is not open to dispute, the judgment cannot be impeached in Mississippi even if it went upon a misapprehension of the Mississippi law. * * *

We feel no apprehensions that painful or humiliating consequences will follow upon our decision. No court would give judgment for a plaintiff unless it believed that the facts were a cause of action by the law determining their effect. Mistakes will be rare. In this case the Missouri court no doubt supposed that the [debt] was binding by the law of Mississippi. If it was mistaken, it made a natural mistake. The validity of its judgment, even in Mississippi, is, as we believe, the result of the Constitution as it always has been understood, and is not a matter to arouse the susceptibilities of the states, all of which are equally concerned in the question and equally on both sides.

Judgment reversed.

MR. JUSTICE WHITE, with whom concurred MR. JUSTICE HARLAN, MR. JUSTICE MCKENNA, and MR. JUSTICE DAY, dissenting:

Admonished that the considerations which control me are presumptively faulty, as the court holds them to be without merit, yet so strong is my belief that the decision now made unduly expands the due faith and credit clause of the Constitution, I state the reasons for my dissent.

By law the state of Mississippi prohibited certain forms of gambling in futures, and inhibited its courts from giving effect to any contract or dealing made in violation of the prohibitive statute. In addition, it was made criminal to do any of the forbidden acts. With the statutes in force, two citizens and residents of Mississippi made contracts in that state which were performed therein, and which were in violation of both the civil and criminal statutes referred to. One of the parties asserting that the other was indebted to him because of the contracts, * * * succeeded in getting personal service [in Missouri] upon the other citizen of Mississippi, the latter being temporarily in the state of Missouri. * * * A verdict and judgment went in favor of the plaintiff. [The victor in the Missouri proceedings then sought to enforce the judgment in Mississippi.] Ultimately the case went to the supreme court of the state of Mississippi, where it was decided that the Missouri judgment was not required, under the full faith and credit clause, to be enforced in Mississippi, as it concerned transactions which had taken place exclusively in Mississippi, between residents of that state, which were in violation of laws embodying the public policy of that state, and to give effect to which would be enforcing transactions which the courts of Mississippi had no authority to enforce.

The court now reverses on the ground that the full faith and credit clause obliged the courts of Mississippi, in consequence of the action of the Missouri court, to give efficacy to transactions in Mississippi which were criminal, and which were against the public policy of that state. Although not wishing in the slightest degree to weaken the operation of the full faith and credit clause as interpreted and applied from the beginning, it to me seems that this ruling so enlarges that clause as to cause it to obliterate all state lines, since the effect will be to endow each state with authority to overthrow the public policy and criminal statutes of the others, thereby depriving all of their lawful authority.

NOTES AND PROBLEMS FOR DISCUSSION

1. *Fauntleroy* requires Mississippi to enforce a Missouri judgment that was likely erroneous on the merits. Moreover, it requires Mississippi to enforce a judgment that Mississippi concludes erroneously construed Mississippi law. Are the benefits of finality and of deference to sister state judgments worth the cost of having to live with mistaken judgments such as this?[*]

2. *Fauntleroy* also refuses to permit Mississippi to raise a "public policy" objection to enforcement of the Missouri judgment. Why shouldn't such an objection be an exception to full faith and credit to judgments?

3. Note that, as between independent nations, and in the absence of a treaty, judgment recognition is governed not by full faith and credit, but by notions of "comity" — a term that suggests general respect for the workings of other judicial systems. It is a notion that typically gives the forum in which enforcement is sought considerably more latitude to decline recognition to foreign judgments than would be the case under full faith and credit. Moreover, unlike in *Fauntleroy*, "public policy" may be raised as an objection to enforcement of a foreign country's judgment. One effect of full faith and credit is therefore to require states not to treat sister state judgments as if they came from foreign countries.

4. Prior to the decision in Obergefell v. Hodges, 576 U.S. ___, 135 S.Ct. 2584, 192 L.Ed.2d 609 (2015)—which recognized a constitutional right to same sex marriage—there had been concerns that same-sex marriages from sister-states might have to be given full faith and credit by states in which such marriages were (then) unlawful. In response to those concerns, Congress enacted the Defense of Marriage Act (DOMA), 28 U.S.C. §1738C. The Act purported to give states the discretion not to recognize such marriages from other states, even though valid where entered into. There was debate, however, whether Congress needed to enact such legislation to accomplish this result, at least as a matter of full faith and credit. *Fauntleroy* was concerned only about full faith and credit to judicial judgments. Historically, and perhaps despite the language of the Full Faith and Credit Clause and the current statute, recognition and enforcement of matters other than judicial judgments have always been less rigorously policed. (The question, of course has been largely mooted by *Obergefell*, which legalized such marriages nationally.)

5. As suggested in Note 1, above, *Fauntleroy* shows that mere errors of law will not be easily revisited once all appeals (i.e., up the ladder of direct review within a judicial system) have been exhausted or bypassed and there is a final judgment. Under the full faith and credit statute, a state court's judgments will generally be given the same preclusive effect by another court in the U.S. as they would have in the state in which they were rendered — no more, no less. Do you see why there would not be a doctrine of full faith and credit if only "correct" judgments were required to be enforced?

6. Note also that, on direct review from a trial court, errors of law can ordinarily be reviewed *de novo* by each court next up in the judicial hierarchy.

---

[*] A complication in *Fauntleroy* was that the Missouri court was actually being asked to enforce an earlier arbitration award that had itself overlooked the question of the contract's illegality. The Missouri court disallowed Lum from attempting to show the underlying contract's illegality in its own proceedings as well, even though illegality would likely have been a defense to enforcement of the arbitration award under Mississippi law.

In other words, errors of law will typically be policed rigorously on appeal, and if the appellate court believes that the lower court was wrong on a question of law that matters to the outcome, it will reverse the judgment below. But after vertical appeals are over in civil litigation, principles of finality will kick in.

7. The obvious exception to all of this is collateral attack upon *criminal* judgments through the mechanism of habeas corpus. Although you do not need to know all of the details, habeas corpus now allows for some degree of relitigation (in a second or "collateral" proceeding) of certain errors of law made in the criminal proceeding in which the habeas applicant was convicted. But even in the habeas context, do you think a prisoner should be able to relitigate an issue of law on which he has previously litigated and lost? I.e., again and again until a later court concludes that the convicting courts were wrong (i.e., until the criminal defendant "wins")? Or should "finality" never be a principle that trumps a claim of constitutional error that would result in a new trial or freedom?

8. Lastly, note that *factual* error is much harder to police on direct review (post-trial) than is an error of law. Factual decisionmaking by juries will generally only be overturned if the trial court (or an appellate court) believes that there was an insufficient evidentiary basis for a rational jury to come to the conclusion that it did. See Rule 50, Fed. R. Civ. P. (governing directed verdicts and judgments notwithstanding the verdict in federal courts ("judgment as a matter of law")); see generally Chapter 11. A court therefore will not substitute its own factfinding for a jury's simply because it disagrees with its conclusion, or even because it believes that the decision was strongly against the weight of the evidence. Reasonable juries can often come to opposite results reasonably, on the same set of facts. On the other hand, the device of granting a new trial is a way for a district (trial) judge to force a retrial if she believes that the jury's decision is against the weight (or, as some courts phrase it, the "clear" or "great" weight) of the evidence. See Rule 59. This device, however, does not result in the substitution of the trial court's view of the facts for the jury's; it only means that a new jury will decide the facts again, in a second proceeding.

Baldwin v. Iowa-State Travelling Men's Ass'n

Supreme Court of the United States, 1931.

283 U.S. 522, 51 S.Ct. 517, 75 L.Ed. 1244.

MR. JUSTICE ROBERTS delivered the opinion of the Court.

A writ of certiorari was granted herein to review the affirmance by the Circuit Court of Appeals of a judgment for respondent rendered by the District Court for Southern Iowa. The action was upon the record of a judgment rendered in favor of the petitioner against the respondent in the United States District Court for Western Missouri.

The defense was lack of jurisdiction of the person of the respondent in the court which entered the judgment. After hearing, in which a jury was waived, this defense was sustained and the action dismissed. The first suit was begun in a Missouri state court and removed to the District Court. Respondent appeared specially and * * * moved to set aside the service, quash the return, and dismiss the case for want of jurisdiction of its person. After a hearing on affidavits and briefs, the motion was overruled, with leave to plead within thirty days. No plea having been filed within that period, the cause proceeded, and judgment was entered for the amount claimed. Respondent did not move to set aside the judgment nor sue out a writ of error.

The ground of the motion made in the first suit is the same as that relied on as a defense to this one, namely, that the respondent is an Iowa corporation, that it never was present in Missouri, and that the person served with process in the latter state was not such an agent that service on him constituted a service on the corporation. The petitioner objected to proof of these matters, asserting that the defense constituted a collateral attack and a retrial of an issue settled in the first suit. The overruling of this objection and the resulting judgment for respondent are assigned as error.

The petitioner suggests that article 4, section 1, of the Constitution, forbade the retrial of the question determined on respondent's motion in the Missouri District Court; but the full faith and credit required by that clause is not involved, since neither of the courts concerned was a state court. Compare Cooper v. Newell, 173 U.S. 555, 567; Supreme Lodge, Knights of Pythias v. Meyer, 265 U.S. 30, 33. The respondent, on the other hand, insists that to deprive it of the defense which it made in the court below, of lack of jurisdiction over it by the Missouri District Court, would be to deny the due process guaranteed by the Fourteenth Amendment; but there is involved in that doctrine no right to litigate the same question twice. Chicago Life Ins. Co. v. Cherry, 244 U.S. 25; compare York v. Texas, 137 U.S. 15.

The substantial matter for determination is whether the judgment amounts to res judicata on the question of the jurisdiction of the court which rendered it over the person of the respondent. It is of no moment that the appearance was a special one expressly saving any submission to such jurisdiction. That fact would be important upon appeal from the judgment, and would save the question of the propriety of the court's decision on the matter, even though, after the motion had been overruled, the respondent had proceeded, subject to a reserved objection and exception, to a trial on the merits. Harkness v. Hyde, 98 U.S. 476. The special appearance gives point to the fact that the respondent entered the Missouri court for the very purpose of litigating the question of jurisdiction over its person. It had the election not to appear at all. If, in the absence of appearance, the court had proceeded to judgment, and the present suit had been brought thereon, respondent could have raised and tried out the issue in the present action, because it would never have had its day in court with respect to jurisdiction. Thompson v. Whitman, 18 Wall. (85 U.S.) 457; Pennoyer v. Neff, 95 U.S. 714. It had also the right to appeal from the decision of the Missouri District Court, as is shown by *Harkness v. Hyde, supra*, and the other authorities cited. It elected to follow neither of those courses, but, after having been defeated upon full hearing in its contention as to jurisdiction, it took no further steps, and the judgment in question resulted.

Public policy dictates that there be an end of litigation; that those who have contested an issue shall be bound by the result of the contest; and that matters once tried shall be considered forever settled between the parties. We see no reason why this doctrine should not apply in every case where one voluntarily appears, presents his case and is fully heard, and why he should not, in the absence of fraud, be thereafter concluded by the judgment of the tribunal to which he has submitted his cause. * * * The judgment is reversed and the cause remanded for further proceedings in conformity with this opinion.

NOTES AND PROBLEMS FOR DISCUSSION

1. Entertain the possibility that the Missouri federal court was wrong on the question of its jurisdiction over the Iowa State Travelling Men's Association (TMA). If so, how can a court that lacks personal jurisdiction issue a binding judgment as to its own jurisdiction (or anything else)?

2. TMA chose to enter the Missouri proceedings for the purpose of challenging jurisdiction. As the Court notes, it had the option not to appear at all, and had it chosen that option, it could have raised the jurisdictional objection in the Iowa enforcement proceeding for the first time, free of res judicata. Could it be argued that, once the defendant made that initial choice, it was consenting to that court's (and to the relevant appellate court's) decision on the question of jurisdiction? If so, what should the defendant have done after losing its motion to dismiss for lack of jurisdiction?

3. A court that lacks jurisdiction presumably has the power to make a ruling that so finds. If a court therefore has jurisdiction to decide whether it has jurisdiction, doesn't it have the power to decide that question either way? See Durfee v. Duke, 375 U.S. 106, 84 S.Ct. 242, 11 L.Ed.2d 186 (1963) (requiring Missouri to give full faith and credit to Nebraska state court judgment in a quiet title action, which resolved that disputed land was located within Nebraska, despite objection in subsequent quiet title action between same parties that land was, in fact, located in Missouri).

4. If TMA had appealed the Missouri federal court's ruling, where would the appeal have gone? Federal court appeals are generally to a regional circuit court that geographically encompasses the state in which the federal trial court sits. Missouri and Iowa are in the same circuit. Do we have a sense as to how TMA would have fared had it appealed the Missouri court's decision?

5. All states have some mechanism that allows for what has traditionally been called a "special appearance" — a device that permits a party to appear for the sole purpose of objecting to jurisdiction over him without thereby making a general appearance. Under the Restatement Second of the Conflict of Laws, § 81: "A state will not exercise judicial jurisdiction over an individual who appears in the action for the sole purpose of objecting that there is no jurisdiction over him."

6. The Restatement Second of Judgments § 10, Comment b says something similar:

While all states now provide at least for a special appearance, most go further in liberalizing the opportunity to make preliminary objection to notice and territorial jurisdiction. The most widely adopted procedural scheme is that prescribed in Federal Rules of Civil Procedure Rule 12(b). Under this procedure, a defendant may make an objection to process in a preliminary motion before asserting any other objections or defenses. Such a motion is in effect a special appearance, although it need not be designated as such in order to avoid submission to the court's jurisdiction. However, the scheme of Rule 12(b) is broader, for it permits a defendant to make an objection to process in a motion that also raises other objections such as improper venue, lack of subject matter jurisdiction, or failure of the complaint to state a claim. He may also assert the objection in his answer. The only requirement is that the motion or answer be his first appearance in the action.

7. Different jurisdictions have different mechanisms for appellate review of jurisdictional rulings in trial courts. Obviously, if a motion to dismiss on jurisdictional grounds is granted, the case is over and is appealable. The problem arises when the motion to dismiss on jurisdictional grounds is denied. Historically, jurisdictions have followed three different approaches, although only the first two are much in current use.

- Some have required immediate appeal (interlocutory review) of the jurisdictional ruling if a party wishes to have any appellate review. In those jurisdictions, litigation on the merits is treated as a waiver of the objection. Litigation on the merits will therefore typically have to wait until the appellate process is exhausted.

- Others have required that litigation go forward on the merits first, but that the properly preserved jurisdictional objection may be raised on appeal after a final judgment, along with any other appealable issues. This is the practice in the federal courts.

- Finally, some jurisdictions have required that a party suffer a default judgment as a precondition to securing appellate review.

8. Why would a state (and why did Congress, in requiring a final judgment before federal trial court errors could be appealed under 28 U.S.C. §1291) choose to structure its system such that appellate review of rejected jurisdictional objections would be postponed? Immediate appeal can obviously avoid what could turn out to be an unnecessary trial, thus saving the trial court's and litigants' time. But if interlocutory review is available, it is likely that the party who lost on a nonfrivolous motion to dismiss on jurisdictional grounds would immediately appeal the issue in nearly every case, thus adding substantial costs at the appellate level, as well as delay at the trial level. Plus, most of those appeals will turn out to be fruitless, assuming that trial courts are right more often than wrong in their jurisdictional rulings. A final judgment rule thus considers the systemic costs of greater individualized treatment associated with interlocutory review to outweigh the occasional benefits of the latter.

CHAPTER 13

The Preclusive Effect of Adjudication on Subsequent Litigation

SECTION A. GENERAL INTRODUCTION

Throughout this book we have explored a series of issues by reading and analyzing opinions by trial and appellate court judges. Sometimes these courts were called upon to construe a federal statute; sometimes they interpreted the meaning of a Federal Rule of Civil Procedure. On other occasions the courts created common law doctrines to resolve the disputes before them. But regardless of the methodology employed, the importance of all of these cases transcended the individual interests of the parties to each controversy. Without having expressly articulated the concept, it is nevertheless true that we read each of these cases because they tell us something about how the deciding court, and others, will resolve that same issue when it reappears in another case. We simply take for granted the idea that once a particular issue has been authoritatively resolved, the interests in continuity, predictability, consistency and stability in the law demand that, within limits, an issue be accorded the same interpretation in future cases. In fact, no less an eminence than Justice Louis Brandeis once declared that "[s]tare decisis is usually the wise policy, because in most matters it is more important that the applicable rule of law be settled than that it be settled right."[*]

The notion that a court is expected to adhere to a settled ruling on an issue of law by that court or a hierarchically superior court is a cornerstone of common law legal systems as well as the most obvious example of the binding or preclusive effect of one adjudication on subsequent litigation. This doctrine is known by two names — precedent and *stare decisis*. However, it is but one of four distinct doctrines that regulate the extent to which a decision in one proceeding should or must have some preclusive impact on all or part of another case or of a separate proceeding in that same case. The other three doctrines are: (1) the law of the case; (2) claim preclusion (*res judicata*); and (3) issue preclusion (collateral estoppel). Each of these doctrines arises under a distinct set of circumstances and serves disparate interests and objectives. Nevertheless, many courts frequently ignore the distinction between claim and issue preclusion and sloppily refer to both preclusion concepts as "res judicata." As you read the cases presented in the subsequent sections of this Chapter, scrutinize each of

---

[*] Burnet v. Coronado Oil & Gas Co., 285 U.S. 393, 406, 52 S.Ct. 443, 447, 76 L.Ed.2d 815 (1932) (Brandeis, J., dissenting).

these opinions to determine which of these preclusion doctrines should be and are discussed by the courts.

SECTION B. *STARE DECISIS* AND THE LAW OF THE CASE

Society of Separationists, Inc. v. Herman

United States Court of Appeals, Fifth Circuit, 1991, aff'd and rev'd in part on other grounds, 959 F.2d 1283 (1992), cert. denied, 506 U.S. 866, 113 S.Ct. 191, 121 L.Ed.2d 135 (1992).

939 F.2d 1207.

GOLDBERG, CIRCUIT JUDGE:

An atheist, summoned for jury duty in a Texas court, declined to take the required pre-voir dire oath because it included a reference to God. Offered an affirmation containing a reference to God, she continued to refuse. When she was offered the opportunity to raise her hand and be affirmed without such reference, she still declined, explaining that she considered an affirmation just as religious as an oath. The judge disagreed with her belief that such an affirmation was religious, and jailed her for contempt. Released after posting bond, the woman sued under [42 U.S.C.] §1983, alleging violation of the Free Exercise Clause, and seeking damages and injunctive and declaratory relief.

We hold that the judge's actions violated the potential juror's right to Free Exercise guaranteed by the First and Fourteenth Amendments. * * * We also consider matters of stare decisis, claim and issue preclusion, [and law of the case] * * *.

I. Background

On December 15, 1987, Robin Murray-O'Hair, an American Atheist, appeared for jury duty at the Travis County Courthouse, located in Austin, Texas. She refused to take the oath required of venire members before voir dire questioning, stating that she was an atheist and could not take an oath which included a reference to God. The presiding judge, Guy Herman, offered to allow Murray-O'Hair to affirm, but the affirmation still included a reference to God, and Murray-O'Hair refused. Murray-O'Hair was told to be seated and the other jurors were sworn in.

Murray-O'Hair was told to proceed to Herman's regular courtroom, where the judge again requested that she take the oath. Now accompanied by her attorney, Murray-O'Hair restated her objections and Herman offered to allow her to raise her hand and make an affirmation without any reference to "God or anything of that nature." Murray-O'Hair declined, stating that she could not affirm because an affirmation "is just as religious as an oath." Herman warned her that if she refused to take an oath or make an affirmation, he would hold her in civil contempt. Murray-O'Hair responded that she was not trying to evade her jury duty, but sought to avoid "participating in a religious statement." The judge never inquired as to what form of assurance of truthfulness would meet

Murray-O'Hair's objections. Herman and Murray-O'Hair then debated the nature of affirmations. Herman * * * concluded that "affirmances are for atheists and other folks that do not wish to take oaths." In his view, an affirmation was not a "religious statement"; it was merely a pledge that one would give true answers to the voir dire questions and met the qualifications for jury service. * * *

Murray-O'Hair continued to refuse and * * * Herman ordered her jailed on the spot for a term of three days "and thereafter until you purge yourself of the contempt by taking the affirmation." She was jailed, but was released on bond approximately six hours later. She did not, or was not permitted to, resume her place in the jury pool.

* * * [O]n August 11, 1987, Murray-O'Hair and other individual plaintiffs brought suit in federal district court against the Travis County District Court and the Texas Attorney General, alleging a continuing pattern whereby they (1) respond as requested for jury service in the Travis County District Court, (2) refuse to take a "God" oath, and (3) are excluded by the presiding Judge from jury service. The district court dismissed for failure to state a claim. We affirmed, holding that there is no constitutionally protected right to serve on a jury and adding that "[m]oreover, . . . jurors are not required to swear an oath to a deity . . . an affirmation [is not] the same as an oath to a deity." Neither opinion fleshes out the factual context of the plaintiffs' claims; the district court simply notes that "[t]he manner of excluding the Plaintiffs from jury service varies from incident to incident," adding without explanation that "the differences are not material." Neither opinion mentions Judge Herman or refers to anyone being jailed for their refusal to swear or affirm.

* * * [O]n November 16, 1989, Murray-O'Hair and the Society of Separationists filed this §1983 action seeking damages and declaratory and injunctive relief against Herman, Travis County Judge Bill Aleshire, Travis County, the "Travis County court system," and the clerk, sheriff and court bailiffs of Travis County. The suit * * * claimed that Murray-O'Hair's First and Fourteenth Amendment rights had been violated because she was imprisoned for refusing to take a religious oath.

The district court * * * held that the earlier Murray decision was res judicata * * *. The plaintiffs appealed * * *.

We hold that the previous suit does not bar this action; * * * [and] that Herman did violate Murray-O'Hair's Free Exercise rights * * *.

II. Discussion

A. Stare Decisis and Preclusion

The government argues, and the district court held, that Murray-O'Hair's constitutional claim is barred by the res judicata effect of the earlier Murray decision. We disagree. We analyze the relation between Murray and the instant case according to principles not just of res judicata, but also stare decisis, collateral estoppel, and law of the case. From any of these perspectives, however, Murray is without preclusive effect.

As an initial matter, we set out our rules on stare decisis, specifically, the law on the binding effect of prior panel decisions. In this circuit, one panel may not overrule the decision, right or wrong, of a prior panel in the absence of an intervening contrary or superseding decision by the court en banc or the Supreme Court. Where two previous holdings or lines of precedent conflict, "the earlier opinion controls and is the binding precedent in the circuit." Even a decision not necessary to support the ultimate ruling, such as an alternative holding, is binding. Dicta, however, is persuasive authority only, and is not binding.

In the earlier Murray case, Murray-O'Hair and other plaintiffs argued that they had a right to serve on juries, and that they were subjected to a continuing pattern of exclusion in violation of their rights; as the district court framed the question, "Does the practice of a State trial court in excluding from jury service persons who refuse to make an oath deny a vested interest . . . [or] violate the Constitutional provision of separation of church and state?" The district court found no violation, holding without citation of authority that "Plaintiffs have no Constitutionally protected interest in sitting on a jury" and that "[a] jury oath which refers to a deity does not violate" the Establishment Clause; the court analyzed the juror oath using the Lemon test factors (purpose, effect, and entanglement). We affirmed in an unpublished decision, holding without citation that:

> [T]he district court dismissed the case because the plaintiffs failed to state a claim upon which relief can be granted. Specifically, the district court determined that because the right to serve on a jury is not a constitutionally protected one, the plaintiffs' cause of action had failed to state a claim. We agree. The occasion to serve on a jury is undeniably a duty, a privilege, and an opportunity for many citizens to actively and personally serve their government. Indeed, the opportunity for many citizens to serve on a jury might be the only opportunity they have to serve their government. Even so, jury service has not been construed as a constitutionally protected right.
>
> Moreover, as the plaintiffs concede, jurors are not required to swear an oath to a deity; rather, jurors are free to simply make an affirmation that the testimony which they are about to present will be the truth. An affirmation is no more than a solemn declaration made under the penalties of perjury. We do not consider, as plaintiffs would have us do, an affirmation to be the same as an oath to a deity.[12]

Thus, the "Moreover" language in Murray suggests that, for Establishment Clause purposes, an affirmation is not to be considered to have a religious nature and its use in the courtroom therefore constitutes no violation of that clause.

A year later, in Ferguson v. Commissioner, 921 F.2d 588 (5th Cir.1991), we held that the tax court violated the Free Exercise Clause * * * by requiring a witness to take an oath or affirmation, where the witness felt that an affirmation had a religious nature inconsistent with her own faith. We explained that "the

---

[12] Murray v. Travis County Dist. Court, 898 F.2d 150 (5th Cir.) (unpublished opinion), cert. denied, 498 U.S. 824, 111 S.Ct. 75, 112 L.Ed.2d 49 (1990).

protection of the free exercise clause extends to all sincere religious beliefs; courts may not evaluate religious truth." That is, the plaintiff's sincere belief that an affirmation has a religious nature is sufficient to implicate free exercise concerns. Ferguson 's discussion is plenary and replete with citations.

In light of the law on prior panel decisions, we must decide whether Murray's comment on the jury oath casts doubt on Ferguson or otherwise serves as binding precedent in the instant case. We hold that it does not. For one thing, this language, bare of citation and argument, is of no decisional value;[16] it is simply obiter dicta.

More significantly, Murray was an Establishment Clause case; our case, and Ferguson, are Free Exercise challenges. The two kinds of cases are governed by altogether different legal standards. Even the question of the religious nature of an affirmation is distinct under these two clauses; as Murray and Ferguson suggest, our inquiry in Establishment Clause cases is whether a "reasonable observer" might construe the affirmation as religious, whereas the Free Exercise query is whether this particular plaintiff holds a sincere belief that the affirmation is religious. These inquiries are distinct, as the Free Exercise Clause protects even an unreasonable belief that an affirmation is religious, so long as the belief is not so bizarre, so clearly nonreligious in motivation. Accordingly, Ferguson is the applicable precedent.

As to claim preclusion (res judicata), our rule is that the earlier suit is res judicata if, inter alia, the parties are identical in both suits.[21] This condition is not met here: Herman was not a defendant in the first suit, nor was he in privity with one: the institutional defendant in the first case was the Travis County District Court, but Herman serves on the Travis County Probate Court, which is a redesignated Travis County Court at Law. The Probate Court and the County Courts at Law are altogether separate courts from the District Courts. Hence, Murray is not res judicata.

As to issue preclusion (collateral estoppel), we note that "for a prior judgment to have preclusive effect as to a particular issue, the doctrine of collateral estoppel requires that: (1) the issue at stake be identical to the one involved in the prior litigation; (2) that the issue has been actually litigated in the prior litigation; and (3) that the determination of the issue in the prior litigation has been a critical and necessary part of the judgment in that earlier action." None of these conditions are met here: as discussed above, a Free Exercise claim is altogether different from an Establishment Clause claim, and Murray's discussion of the jury oath is not a "critical and necessary part" of the decision.[25]

Further, the Murray district court's reduction of the facts to a skeletal "fact

---

[16] Indeed, since the Murray decision is unpublished, the entire opinion is considered to have "no precedential value," although it is "precedent." 5th Cir.R. 47.5.1, 47.5.3.

[21] * * * The other requisites are that the same cause of action was involved in both cases, the prior judgment was rendered by a court of competent jurisdiction and that it was a final judgment on the merits.

[25] Cf. Hicks v. Quaker Oats Co., 662 F.2d 1158, 1168-73 (5th Cir. Unit A 1981) (unappealed alternate grounds of decision do not have offensive collateral estoppel effect; rejecting in part the "alternative ground" rule that "if a court decides a case on two grounds, each is a good estoppel," and adopting position of Restatement of Judgments).

pattern," coupled with the differences in parties and causes of action, makes evident that the "issue" here is a pure question of law, not one of fact or of rights between parties. In this circuit, pure questions of law are subject to collateral estoppel, but only where there is no change in controlling legal principles between the two decisions. Here, if Ferguson and Murray are considered to be in conflict, then Ferguson represents a drastic change in applicable law. Accordingly, Murray does not provide a basis for collateral estoppel of Murray-O'Hair's claims.

Finally, for the sake of completeness, we mention law of the case. This doctrine is applicable only "during the pendency of . . . a single proceeding, and operates to foreclose re-examination of decided issues either on remand or on a subsequent appeal."[28] Murray and the case before us are altogether separate proceedings, so law of the case is inapplicable.[29]

[On the merits, the court ruled that all of the defendants other than the trial judge were immune from liability. As for the trial judge, the court found that his attempt to coerce the plaintiff to take an affirmation in the face of her sincere religious objections violated her rights under the Free Exercise Clause of the First Amendment of the U.S. Constitution. But since the judge's action was taken as part of his normal judicial function, the court found that he was immune from a suit for damages. Nevertheless, as this immunity did not extend to the issuance of equitable relief, the court issued a declaratory judgment requiring trial judges hereafter to allow an individual in these circumstances either to withdraw from jury duty without penalty or to make a public commitment to answer truthfully that does not transgress that individual's sincerely held religious beliefs.]

NOTES AND PROBLEMS FOR DISCUSSION

1. At the outset of its opinion, the circuit panel indicated that its opinion would address matters of *stare decisis*, claim and issue preclusion, and law of the case. How do these four doctrines compare with respect to:

   (a) the circumstances in which they apply?

   (b) the result they produce when applied?

   (c) the interests or objectives they are designed to serve?

2. In what way was each of these four principles arguably applicable in *Herman* and what was the appellate court's decision with respect to law of the case, claim preclusion and issue preclusion?

---

[28] Schexnider v. McDermott Int'l, Inc., 868 F.2d 717, 718 (5th Cir.1989) ("The decision of a legal issue by an appellate court establishes the 'law of the case' and must be followed in all subsequent proceedings in the same case at both the trial and appellate levels" subject to certain exceptions), cert. denied, [493 U.S. 851,] 110 S.Ct. 150, 107 L.Ed.2d 108.

[29] In addition, we provide an exception to law of the case where "the controlling authority has since made a contrary decision of law applicable to such issues, or the decision was clearly erroneous and would work a manifest injustice." Ferguson would trigger this exception, since it is contrary to the Murray dicta.

3. Did the court in the principal case accord *stare decisis* effect to any of its prior rulings?

(a) The court concluded that the statement in the first of the plaintiffs' two actions about the non-religious nature of an affirmation was "of no decisional value" because it was "simply obiter dicta." On what basis did it make that judgment?

(b) In assessing the precedential value of its ruling in the first of the plaintiffs' two lawsuits, the Fifth Circuit mentioned that its opinion in that case was unpublished. The decision whether or not to publish a federal circuit court opinion is typically controlled by a local rule of procedure adopted by each circuit court of appeals. In footnote 16, the court cites a Fifth Circuit Local Rule providing that an unpublished opinion enjoys "no precedential value" although it is "precedent." What is the distinction between these two terms?

(c) What other reason did the circuit court in the principal case give for not adhering to its ruling in the first of the plaintiffs' two cases?

4. Suppose that the issue in *Herman* had been whether the requirement of taking an affirmation violated the plaintiff's rights under a federal statute and that the Fifth Circuit had interpreted that statute thirty years earlier to forbid the imposition of any oath or affirmation that was viewed by the objector as religious in nature. Would or should the *stare decisis* question be treated any differently under these circumstances?

In HILTON v. SOUTH CAROLINA PUBLIC RAILWAYS COMMISSION, 502 U.S. 197, 112 S.Ct. 560, 116 L.Ed.2d 560 (1991), a railroad worker brought an action under the Federal Employers' Liability Act (FELA) in state court to recover damages from injuries allegedly caused by the defendant railroad's negligence. The FELA provides such a right of action for employees of "[e]very common carrier by railroad." However, since the defendant railroad was owned by South Carolina, the issue was whether the FELA was intended to include state-owned railroads. Twenty-eight years earlier, the Supreme Court had held that Congress intended the FELA to include state-owned railroads. The defendant/respondent urged the Supreme Court to reject the invocation of *stare decisis* and to overrule that prior case. The Court refused to do so and offered this explanation for its decision:

> "Considerations of stare decisis have special force in the area of statutory interpretation, for here, unlike in the context of constitutional interpretation, the legislative power is implicated, and Congress remains free to alter what we have done. Congress has had almost 30 years in which it could have corrected our decision * * * if it disagreed with it, and has not chosen to do so. We should accord weight to this continued acceptance of our earlier holding. Stare decisis has added force when the legislature, in the public sphere, and citizens, in the private realm, have acted in reliance on a previous decision, for in this instance overruling the decision would dislodge settled rights and expectations or require an extensive legislative response. This is so in the case before us."

502 U.S. at 202, 112 S.Ct. at 564.

Do you agree with the Court's assessment of the significance of Congress' failure to amend the FELA in response to the Court's original interpretation of that statute? Is agreement with or acquiescence to the court's construction of a statute the only, or at least the most reasonable explanation for subsequent legislative inaction?

5. In addition to distinguishing the prior case or characterizing the rule articulated in that case as *dictum* rather than holding, there are two other grounds for avoiding the binding effect of precedent. First, *stare decisis* does not apply to a prior ruling by a court outside of the subject court's judicial hierarchy. Thus, just as a federal district court is not compelled to adhere to an apposite ruling by circuit courts of appeals other than the one with appellate jurisdiction over it, a state court is not bound by rulings of courts of other states. Such decisions, however, can be considered and relied upon to the extent of their inherent persuasive force. Second, instead of following precedent, a court can decide to overrule it, as the Supreme Court did in *Erie* when it repudiated its ruling in *Swift*. But since overruling or repudiating otherwise apposite precedent creates precisely the instability, unpredictability and frustration of expectations that adherence to precedent is designed to avoid, courts do not lightly decide either to overrule their prior decisions or to refuse to abide by apposite rulings of a higher tribunal. Rather, a court typically will overturn or ignore precedent only when it determines that the prior decision is seriously out of step with contemporary developments in the law or has become impractical or unworkable in light of intervening jurisprudential or other developments.

6. Whereas the doctrine of *stare decisis* defines the binding impact of the holding in one case on the resolution of a similarly situated pending or subsequently filed action, the doctrine of law of the case operates only within the confines of a single case. A decision of law at one stage of a lawsuit precludes reconsideration of that issue in any subsequent proceeding in that same case. For example, a decision of an appellate court on an issue of law establishes the law of the case and precludes reconsideration of that issue if the case is remanded for further proceedings. Similarly, when a trial court's ruling on a question of law is the subject of an interlocutory appeal, the appellate court's decision establishes the law of the case and thus is binding in subsequent proceedings in that action, including the appeal from the trial court's final judgment. The doctrine of law of the case is, however, also subject to exceptions. Most obviously, it does not preclude appellate review of a lower court's ruling. Nor will a prior ruling by a trial or appellate court be binding at a later stage in that same case if there has been a contrary intervening decision on that issue by a higher court. The law of the case rule is designed to promote both finality of judgments and litigative efficiency by avoiding the squandering of resources on duplicative litigation. Finally, as with *stare decisis*, the doctrine of law of the case only applies to holdings and not to *dictum*.

SECTION C. CLAIM PRECLUSION (*RES JUDICATA*)

In addition to their potential precedential value, judgments in one case can also have a more direct and lethal impact on subsequent lawsuits. We would expect that a party that is dissatisfied with the result of an adjudication would be precluded, other than through a direct appeal, from seeking another, more favorable outcome in another lawsuit. Assuming that the interest in avoiding duplicative litigation and promoting the finality of judgments (other than through the appellate process) means that parties should be limited to only one bite at the apple, is there a workable standard for determining when a second lawsuit is unacceptably duplicative of a prior adjudication? For example, should a plaintiff be permitted to file another lawsuit if she changes the legal theory upon which she claims relief? Alternatively, if the plaintiff seeks a different form of remedy (e.g., an injunction as opposed to money damages) for the same injury, would that render the second suit sufficiently distinguishable from the original judgment to avoid its preclusive effect? Or what if the first lawsuit seeks damages for an injury caused by the defendant's negligence and, years later, the plaintiff develops additional and unanticipated injuries arising out of that same tortious conduct? The circumstances under which a judgment in one civil action precludes the parties to that action from attempting to relitigate part or all of that claim are addressed by the common law doctrine of claim preclusion. Although "claim preclusion" is a more accurate designation for this concept, it continues also to be referred to by its traditional, though less descriptive name, *res judicata*.

Sopha v. Owens-Corning Fiberglas Corporation

Supreme Court of Wisconsin, 1999.
230 Wis.2d 212, 601 N.W.2d 627.

ABRAHAMSON, CHIEF JUSTICE:

* * *

I

* * * Robert Sopha worked as an insulator from 1951 until his retirement in 1995. He was regularly exposed to insulation products containing asbestos during his employment. Sometime prior to 1987 Robert Sopha was apparently diagnosed with non-malignant pleural thickening. Pleural thickening is a non-malignant physical condition involving the lining surrounding each lung and the lining inside the chest cavity and is often indicative of exposure to asbestos.

In March 1987, Robert Sopha and his wife filed a complaint in the Circuit Court for Milwaukee County seeking damages for injuries to his lungs, namely, "asbestosis, pulmonary fibrosis and other pathology of the lungs plus the risk of cancer," allegedly caused by exposure to asbestos. After the defendants moved to dismiss the lawsuit on the basis of the three-year statute of limitations, the plaintiffs moved to voluntarily dismiss the action. The action was dismissed "on the merits and with prejudice" by order dated October 23, 1989. The circuit court made no findings of fact.

In December 1996 Robert Sopha was diagnosed for the first time with mesothelioma, a malignant condition of the pleural lining allegedly caused by exposure to asbestos. The plaintiffs brought an action to recover damages for mesothelioma in March 1997. * * *

* * *

Robert Sopha died in November 1997 of mesothelioma, and the complaint was amended to include a claim for wrongful death. On November 26, 1997, the defendants moved to dismiss the action on the grounds that the action was barred by the statute of limitations and by the doctrine of claim preclusion. Relying on information outside the pleadings, the circuit court treated the motion to dismiss as one for summary judgment.

* * *

[The circuit court ruled that (1) the statute of limitations barred the 1997 action, but (2) claim preclusion did not apply because the plaintiff could not have recovered for mesothelioma in the original action. The state court of appeals certified the appeal to the Wisconsin Supreme Court.]

III

* * *

The statute of limitations applicable to the present case provides that an action to recover damages for injuries to the person shall be commenced within three years from the time the cause of action accrues. The question thus becomes: When did the plaintiffs' cause of action to recover damages for mesothelioma accrue?

* * *

The defendants argue that the plaintiffs' cause of action accrued when Robert Sopha was diagnosed with pleural thickening or asbestosis in the late 1970s or early 1980s. * * *

* * *

The defendants contend that the determinative rule in the present case is the "single cause of action" rule, sometimes referred to as the "single injury rule" or the "rule against claim splitting." The single cause of action rule determines what constitutes a cause of action. According to the single cause of action rule, all injuries caused by a single transaction or series of transactions by a tortfeasor are part of a single cause of action so that a later injury from the same tortious act does not restart the running of the statute of limitations.

* * *

The plaintiffs rely on the discovery rule * * *. The discovery rule established that a tort claim accrues for the purposes of the statute of limitations on the date the injury is discovered or with reasonable diligence should be discovered, whichever occurs first. * * * [I]t is manifestly unjust for the statute of limitations to begin to run before a claimant could reasonably become aware of the injury.

The plaintiffs argue that they had no way of discovering Robert Sopha's mesothelioma until he was diagnosed with the condition in 1996 and that pursuant to the discovery rule their cause of action for mesothelioma accrued at that time.

The defendants contend that the discovery rule does not apply in the present case because in the 1980s the plaintiffs knew that they had an injury allegedly attributable to the defendants' conduct, even though they did not know the full extent of the injury. Therefore, according to the defendants, even if we were to apply the discovery rule, all the elements of the plaintiffs' cause of action based on exposure to asbestos were present in the 1980s and the statute of limitations began to run. They conclude that the 1997 action is therefore barred by the statute of limitations.

The defendants make a valid point. Several Wisconsin cases support the proposition that the appearance of the first compensable injury starts the statute of limitations running for all claims based on the tortfeasor's single course of conduct, even for future injuries that may be difficult to predict.

The defendants' argument leads to discussion of the third rule that demarcates the damages recoverable in an action and therefore affects what constitutes a cause of action and the date of accrual. The third rule declares that recovery for damages may be had for reasonably certain injurious consequences of the tortfeasor's negligent conduct, not for merely possible injurious consequences. In Wisconsin a claimant cannot recover for speculative or conjectural damages.

* * * [F]or purposes of this appeal we assume that the plaintiffs could not have recovered damages for mesothelioma before 1996, because it was not reasonably certain before that year that Robert Sopha would develop mesothelioma. According to the defendants' reasoning, the plaintiffs' claim for mesothelioma was therefore, on the one hand, barred by the statute of limitations if brought in 1997 because the cause of action accrued in the 1980s under the single cause of action and discovery rules. On the other hand, according to the defendants' reasoning, the plaintiffs' claim for mesothelioma would have been premature if brought in the 1980s because recovery of damages was limited to reasonably certain injuries. If the court adopts the defendants' position, the plaintiffs will have no opportunity, at any time, to recover for the most severe injuries allegedly caused by defendants' conduct. The defendants' argument imparts * * * ultimate meaning to the phrase "catch 22".

These three rules, delineating for purposes of the statute of limitations what constitutes a cause of action, when a cause of action accrues and what damages are recoverable in an action, are not ironclad. The question of what constitutes a cause of action and the concept of a statute of limitation is basically a question of public policy

* * *

The single cause of action rule * * * seeks to deter stale claims and to allow repose for alleged tortfeasors, thus enabling them to plan for the future with certainty about liability. The single cause of action rule also seeks to deter vexatious and multiple lawsuits arising out of the same tortious incident.

The discovery rule, by comparison, is grounded in considerations of justice, reasonableness and fundamental fairness. The discovery rule allows a cause of action to go forward when an injured person has had no opportunity to litigate a claim. Allowing such a meritorious claim to proceed outweighs the threat of stale or fraudulent actions. Although the * * * single cause of action rule * * * [is] designed to deny a forum to claimants who do not diligently pursue their claims, the plaintiffs in the present case did not "sleep" on their claim for mesothelioma. They brought the 1997 action promptly after the diagnosis. In this case the discovery rule militates in favor of splitting the actions and starting the statute of limitations anew upon the diagnosis of mesothelioma.

* * *

Although the objectives of the single cause of action rule are finality and judicial economy, allowing a separate cause of action for an asbestos-related malignancy if and when it occurs promotes judicial economy.

As the plaintiffs argue, and as other jurisdictions have recognized, a holding that bars the plaintiffs' cause of action for an asbestos-related malignancy creates incentives for claimants to rush to the courthouse to initiate anticipatory litigation. Those who are diagnosed with pleural thickening or other non-malignant asbestos-related injuries will be encouraged to file lawsuits immediately upon diagnosis, even if they are asymptomatic and would otherwise be reluctant to sue. To protect themselves they will be forced to initiate litigation based on the possibility that they will develop more serious asbestos-related conditions in the future.

The court must also take into account the objective of tort law that meritorious claimants recover adequate compensation from tortfeasors. Unless the plaintiffs' 1997 action is allowed to proceed the plaintiffs may never recover for serious injuries allegedly caused by the defendants.

* * *

We therefore hold that the statute of limitations does not bar the plaintiffs' 1997 action. * * *

* * *

IV

Even if we were to hold for the plaintiffs on the statute of limitations issue, the defendants argue that the doctrine of claim preclusion requires dismissal of the plaintiffs' action.[25]

The doctrine of claim preclusion provides that a final judgment on the merits bars parties from relitigating any claim that arises out of the same relevant facts, transactions or occurrences.[26] Ordinarily a final judgment is conclusive in all subsequent actions as to all matters which were litigated or which might have been litigated in the former proceedings. Claim preclusion focuses on judgments and their preclusive effect.

Under the doctrine of claim preclusion, a subsequent action is barred when the following three factors are present: (1) identity between the parties or their

---

[25] The term claim preclusion replaces res judicata; the term issue preclusion replaces collateral estoppel.

[26] * * * See DePratt v. West Bend Mutual Ins. Co., 113 Wis.2d 306, 311-12, 334 N.W.2d 883 (1983)(adopting the transactional approach set forth in the Restatement (Second) of Judgments §24 (1982) to determine whether two suits involve the same cause of action).

privies in the prior and present suits;[28] (2) prior litigation resulted in a final judgment on the merits by a court with jurisdiction;[29] and (3) identity of the causes of action in the two suits.

We address the question whether the 1987 and 1997 actions are based on the same cause of action so that claim preclusion applies. Our analysis is similar to our earlier discussion of when a cause of action accrues for the purposes of the statute of limitations. The policies underlying claim preclusion and the single cause of action rule, which we discussed earlier in addressing the statute of limitations, are closely related.

The plaintiffs argue that claim preclusion does not apply because they could not have recovered for mesothelioma in 1987, when there was no "reasonable certainty" that Robert Sopha would develop this condition. This argument would not generally bar the defense of claim preclusion. Ordinarily, a subsequent injury resulting from a tortfeasor's conduct does not give rise to a new cause of action for the purposes of claim preclusion. The Restatement (Second) of Judgments explains: "It is immaterial that in trying the first action he [the claimant] was not in possession of enough information about the damages, past or prospective, or that the damages turned out to be unexpectedly large and in excess of the judgment."[31]

In contrast to the rule stated in the Restatement, some courts would allow claim splitting when the claimant does not know the full dimensions of the claim at the time of the first action.

Claim preclusion rests on the policy that justice is better served by ensuring finality of judgments and furthering repose, rather than by allowing a claimant the opportunity to obtain improved justice in a second action. * * * [T]he doctrine of claim preclusion provides an effective and useful means to relieve parties of the cost and vexation of multiple lawsuits, conserve judicial resources, and, by preventing inconsistent decisions, encourage reliance on adjudication.

Although the purposes underlying claim preclusion are important, this court does not blindly apply the doctrine of claim preclusion. * * *

Exceptions to the doctrine of claim preclusion, confined within proper

---

[28] The parties to the 1987 and 1997 actions are, for the most part, identical. In the 1987 action both Margaret and Robert Sopha were named plaintiffs. In the 1997 action Margaret Sopha is suing in her own right and on behalf of Robert Sopha's estate.

Ten of the thirteen defendants named in the present action were also named in the 1987 action. One of the new defendants, Rapid American Corp., was sued in part for assuming the asbestos-related liabilities of a defendant in the first action, Celotex. Two defendants (Amchem Products Inc. and All Temp Insulation Inc.) were not parties to the first action. The defendants assert that because the plaintiffs have not disputed claim preclusion as to these new defendants on the grounds that they were not sued in the first action, the plaintiffs have waived such an argument. Because we hold that the plaintiffs' action is not barred by claim preclusion, we do not address the merits of this argument relating to these three defendants.

[29] The plaintiffs' 1987 action was dismissed on the merits and with prejudice. We do not address the plaintiffs' contention that when an earlier judgment does not contain any factual findings it does not bind the parties on any issue which might arise in a subsequent case involving a different cause of action.

[31] Restatement (Second) of Judgments §25, cmt. c (1982).

limits, are "central to the fair administration of the doctrine of res judicata." Restatement (Second) of Judgments §26, cmt. i (1982). Claim preclusion may be disregarded in appropriate circumstances when the policies favoring preclusion of a second action are trumped by other significant policies. Claim preclusion, like the single cause of action rule and the discovery rule, is a principle of public policy applied to render justice, not to deny it. Any exception to claim preclusion, however, must be limited to special circumstances or the exceptions will weaken the values of repose and reliance.

We conclude that this case presents a special circumstance in which claim preclusion should not apply. A holding that claim preclusion bars a second action would force claimants to choose between seeking recovery for non-malignant asbestos-related injuries, such as pleural thickening, or waiting for the development of more serious malignant injuries. Those claimants who wait and do not develop malignant conditions would likely lose their claim for non-malignant injuries because the statute of limitations will have run. Those claimants, like the plaintiffs, who bring an action immediately for damages for their non-malignant injuries would be forced to seek damages for the fear of developing cancer; they would not be permitted to recover for the malignant condition they might later develop.

Exposure to asbestos can result in several injuries that have long latency periods. A claimant in an asbestos case cannot know all the injuries when the early manifested harms appear and consequently cannot sue for all damages at one time. Although latent conditions may occur as a result of any tortious conduct, we can reasonably expect latent conditions to materialize in asbestos cases. That factor distinguishes asbestos cases from most other tort cases. Under these special circumstances relating to exposure to asbestos, the interest in finality of judgments is outweighed by the needs of claimants who, through no fault of their own, cannot discover all possible injuries when the first injury appears.

This court continues to recognize the important values inherent in the doctrine of claim preclusion. Today's decision carves out what we view as a narrow exception to that doctrine. Allowing the plaintiffs' 1997 action to proceed permits a meritorious claim to be litigated and at the same time does not open the courts to vexatious, repetitious or needless claims.

In sum, the court concludes that because the development of mesothelioma could not have been reasonably predicted when the 1987 action was brought, an exception to claim preclusion is justified in this case. As the Restatement of Judgments declares, claim preclusion shall not be enforced if it "is clearly and convincingly shown that the policies favoring preclusion of a second action are overcome for an extraordinary reason. . . ." Restatement (Second) of Judgments §26(f) (1982). The overwhelming interest in justice served by allowing the plaintiffs' 1997 cause of action to proceed outweighs the policies favoring claim preclusion. To bar plaintiffs' cause of action in this case would be to deny justice.

V

* * *

C.

* * *

The defendants further contend that allowing multiple actions for different injuries caused by the same course of tortious conduct creates a slippery slope down which our jurisprudence relating to statute of limitations and claim preclusion would slide. The defendants misconstrue the nature of our holding. We do not overrule any of our prior cases. Our decision today carves out a limited exception to the single cause of action rule and the claim preclusion doctrine. Although unforeseen injuries with long latency periods may occur in any tort case, asbestos cases are different. We know that exposure to asbestos can involve both long latency periods before the appearance of physical changes and the progression of distinct physical diseases. These aspects of exposure to asbestos are what differentiate asbestos cases from the run of the mill personal injury case and are central to our holding. We recognize that claims based on exposure to other toxic substances may have patterns of disease progression similar to claims based on exposure to asbestos. The court will consider those cases when they are presented.

* * *

E.

The defendants propose alternative options for claimants who are diagnosed with pleural thickening or minor asbestos-related injuries that will allow the claimants to file litigation if serious injuries develop in the future. First, the defendants suggest that a claimant can seek in a lawsuit or in a negotiated settlement the right to file subsequent litigation if and when cancer or other more serious asbestos-related injuries arise.[38] Second, the defendants suggest that a claimant can sign up on the "pleural registry." The registry, as we understand it, was created by members of the plaintiffs' and defendants' bars and allows those exposed to asbestos to "sign up" upon discovering that they have pleural thickening or other non-malignant asbestos-related conditions. Those who sign up may bring future claims if and when they develop more serious asbestos-related injuries, and the signatory entities agree not to assert the defense of the statute of limitations.

While these may be good solutions to an admittedly difficult situation for both claimants and alleged tortfeasors, this court cannot rely on voluntary private arrangements to dictate our jurisprudence for those who cannot or do not avail themselves of these alternatives.

Indeed, if we were to hold today that the plaintiffs' 1997 action was barred by the statute of limitations or the doctrine of claim preclusion, alleged tortfeasors may have little reason to enter any such agreements or maintain a registry. In any event, these alternatives do not help the plaintiffs in the present

---

[38] Restatement (Second) of Judgments §26(1)(b) and cmt b. (1982) explain that a court in a first action may expressly reserve a claimant's right to maintain a second action.

case.

* * *

* * * The order of the circuit court is reversed and the cause is remanded for further proceedings not inconsistent with this holding.

NOTES AND PROBLEMS FOR DISCUSSION

1. As the opinion in *Sopha* reflects, in order for the doctrine of claim preclusion to apply, three requirements must be met: (1) the two lawsuits must involve the same parties (or their privies); (2) the original case must have produced a final, jurisdictionally valid judgment on the merits; and (3) both actions must involve the same cause of action. Each of these requirements raises its own set of issues. Consider the following:

(a) **Identity of Parties**. In *Sopha*, the court mentioned that the "same parties" requirement is satisfied if the second suit involves those in privity with the parties to the earlier action. While any extended discussion of the doctrine of privity is more appropriately left to a course in commercial or property law, it is sufficient to note that in the claim preclusion context (as well as in the issue preclusion context, see Note 4 after *Parklane* in Section D 2. of this Chapter, *infra*), "privity" is used to describe a range of legal relationships between the party and the nominal nonparty that justify binding the nonparty to a judgment issued against the original party. The most obvious examples of privies are successors in interest, trustees, organizational affiliates and assignors and assignees.

Not infrequently, an attempt at creating a privity relationship is made for the purpose of either evading or exploiting the doctrine of claim preclusion. For example, in PERRY v. GLOBE AUTO RECYCLING, INC., 227 F.3d 950 (7th Cir.2000), a vocal critic brought a series of challenges to a municipal ordinance that permitted the seizure of abandoned vehicles without prior notice to the owner of record. The first of these suits involved a claim against a municipal employee and the towing company used to impound the vehicles, alleging that the municipality's impoundment procedure violated his federal constitutional due process rights. The trial court granted partial summary judgment that the policy was unconstitutional, but when the plaintiff failed to comply with some discovery requests in connection with the damages phase of the case, the court sanctioned him by dismissing the case. Subsequently, Mr. Perry brought several other suits against these defendants under the federal Racketeer Influenced and Corrupt Organizations Act (commonly known as RICO), alleging that they had engaged in an unlawful conspiracy to violate the constitutional rights of individuals whose cars were impounded. After all of these RICO suits were dismissed, Mr. Perry paid one Mr. Lahucik $100 for the assignment of all of Lahucik's rights and claims arising out of the impounding of his car. Perry then filed another RICO action challenging the seizure of Lahucik's car. The trial court dismissed the action on the ground of claim preclusion, stating that "the assignment of the claim does not preclude privity." After noting that the plaintiff conceded that the claims in the two actions were identical, the appeals court addressed the only remaining issue, i.e., whether there was identity of parties:

"The question thus becomes whether Lahucik's decision to assign his claim to Perry transforms the claim from one that could be brought to one that is barred by Perry's earlier unsuccessful efforts. We see no reason why this should be so. Indeed, it is routine for institutions like banks or insurance companies to take assignments of large numbers of claims arising out of a single transaction or occurrence, and given the vagaries of litigation they undoubtedly win some and lose some. The more common problem arises when the assignor tries to evade claim preclusion by selling the claim to another party; in that situation, the district court's statement that assignment does not prevent a finding of privity is certainly true. As the Supreme Court put it long ago in Postal Telegraph Cable Co. v. City of Newport, 247 U.S. 464, 474-75, 38 S.Ct. 566, 62 L.Ed. 1215 (1918), '[t]he ground upon which, and upon which alone, a judgment against a prior owner is held conclusive against his successor in interest, is that the estoppel runs with the property, that the grantor can transfer no better right or title than he himself has.'

But we have the opposite situation here. The applicable rule is therefore the one holding that the assignee stands in the shoes of the assignor and assumes the same rights, title and interest possessed by the assignor. So, even though Perry could receive no more than Lahucik had, it is also true that he received no less. Since Lahucik had the right to bring his own claim, that is what he conveyed to Perry in the assignment.

Globe [the defendant towing company] also argues that Perry could have brought Lahucik's claim as part of his earlier litigation, but that is also not correct. Ordinarily, of course, people have no standing to assert the rights of third parties. None of the exceptions to that rule that permit jus tertii litigation would have permitted Perry, without a hint of consent from Lahucik, to litigate Lahucik's claims. And there is definitely no rule (and never will be one, as far as we are concerned) under which strangers to a lawsuit might be precluded in a later action just because the first litigant hypothetically could have tried to persuade a court to certify a class.

Thus, the specific ground on which the district court dismissed Perry's action in his capacity as Lahucik's assignee was not correct. That does not mean, however, that district courts are powerless to prevent this genre of abuse. Even as an assignee, Perry was subject to the normal strictures of Rule 11 of the Federal Rules of Civil Procedure, under which both parties and their lawyers can be sanctioned for bringing frivolous lawsuits. The string of defeats Perry knew that he had suffered in his own suits gave him a very good idea of the likelihood of success another person would have on precisely the same question. * * *

We therefore REVERSE and REMAND this case to the district court for further proceedings consistent with this opinion. Costs on appeal will be taxed against Perry."

227 F.3d at 953-54.

How did the court in *Sopha* resolve the identity of parties issue?

The "privity" exception to the general rule — that one is not bound by a judgment in a lawsuit in which that individual was not a party — is but one of a group of exceptions to the rule against nonparty preclusion. A nonparty who agrees to be bound by a judgment in an action between others is bound in accord with that agreement; in limited circumstances (typically consisting of class actions or suits by a fiduciary), a nonparty is bound where she is deemed to have been adequately represented by someone with the same interests who was a party to the suit; a nonparty will be bound to a judgment in a lawsuit in which that nonparty assumed control; a nonparty who is deemed to be acting as an agent for a party in the original action will be bound by that judgment; and a nonparty will be bound in cases involving a special statutory scheme that expressly forecloses successive litigation by nonlitigants such as bankruptcy and probate proceedings. In addition to these traditionally recognized exceptions (applicable in both claim and issue preclusion contexts), some federal circuit courts, in varying forms, recognized a "virtual representation" exception to nonparty preclusion in cases that would not fit within any of the established exceptions. Under this theory, a nonparty could be bound by a judgment if he was "virtually represented" by a party to that litigation, i.e., where, based on a consideration of factors that differed from circuit to circuit, the court determined that the relationship between the party sought to be bound and the party to the judgment was close enough to justify invoking preclusion doctrine. To make that determination, the trial court was required to find that the party sought to be bound shared an identity of interests with a party to the judgment and, depending upon the circuit, also was instructed to consider a collection of other indicators.

Invoking the authority it had declared in Semtek v. Lockheed Martin, 531 U.S. 497, 121 S.Ct. 1021, 149 L.Ed.2d 32 (2001) (discussed below), to provide uniform federal common law rules of preclusion for judgments of federal courts in federal question cases, the Supreme Court in TAYLOR v. STURGELL, 553 U.S. 880, 128 S.Ct. 2161, 171 L.Ed.2d 155 (2008), unanimously renounced the "virtual representation" exception to nonparty preclusion. The Court concluded that this non-uniform set of considerations created a vague and amorphous balancing test that was at odds with its preference for a set of discrete, clear-cut, and limited exceptions to nonparty preclusion. Such a "diffuse balancing approach," the Court reasoned, would only complicate the task of district judges in dealing with assertions of preclusion — a doctrine that was intended to reduce the burden of litigation on courts and parties. Consequently, it ruled, the preclusive effects of a claim or issue adjudged in a federal question case by a federal judge should be determined according only to the previously recognized grounds for nonparty preclusion (such as those noted above). But because, in the Court's judgment, it was conceivable that nonparty preclusion in the instant case could be justified under the exception for cases where the nonparty is deemed to be an agent or representative of a party to the prior adjudication, it remanded for a determination of whether the plaintiff had acted as an agent of a party to the prior adjudication. The Court also noted that it never had defined the showing required to establish that sort of agency relationship. Nevertheless, since that issue had not been briefed in sufficient detail, the Court reserved judgment on that matter as well. Yet it went so far as to advise the courts below to be "cautious" about finding preclusion on this basis. "A mere whiff of tactical maneuvering will not suffice", it cautioned. Rather, principles of agency law "are suggestive" and would justify preclusion only if the putative agent's conduct of the subsequent suit was subject to the control of the party to the prior adjudication. And finally, because preclusion is an affirmative defense, the Court reaffirmed that the defendant bears the burden of persuasion on establishing the justification for imposing nonparty preclusion.

(b) **Valid and Final Judgment on the Merits**. As the terminology of this requirement makes manifest, the initial ruling on the subject cause of action must be part of a (1) final judgment, (2) on the merits, (3) by a court of competent jurisdiction.

1. Throughout our discussion of personal jurisdiction in Chapter 2, we presumed that if a trial court dismissed the plaintiff's complaint for lack of personal jurisdiction or for improper venue, the plaintiff could simply attempt to refile that same lawsuit against the defendant in a state where either jurisdiction could attach or venue would lie, and where the statute of limitations had not expired. Why isn't that second action precluded by doctrine of claim preclusion?

2. Suppose the parties to a commercial dispute reached a settlement of all claims prior to trial. A month later, the original plaintiff determined that the settlement was not satisfactory and reasserted his claims against the defendant in a new lawsuit. How should the court rule on the defendant's motion to dismiss the second action on the grounds of claim preclusion? Is there anything the attorney for the defendant could have done to ensure that the settlement would preclude further litigation on the matter?

3. Should claim preclusion apply when the earlier action ended as the result of:

(a) a plaintiff's voluntarily dismissal of the complaint?

(b) a default judgment?

(c) dismissal for failure to state a cause of action?

(d) dismissal for failure to file the complaint within the governing limitations period?

(e) dismissal for failure to comply with the court's discovery order? See Federal Rule of Civil Procedure 41(a)-(b); Restatement (Second) of Judgments §§19, 20 (1982).

In KREMER v. CHEMICAL CONSTRUCTION CORP., 456 U.S. 461, 102 S.Ct. 1883, 72 L.Ed.2d 262 (1982), after bringing an unsuccessful claim in state court under the state antidiscrimination law, the plaintiff filed a separate action against his employer in federal court under the federal Civil Rights Act of 1964. In ruling that the state judgment was entitled to full faith and credit and, therefore, precluded the refiling of a parallel federal claim in federal court, the Court noted that claim preclusion required that the plaintiff have a "full and fair opportunity" to litigate its claim. This "full and fair opportunity" standard (which was a traditional requirement for collateral estoppel and which the *Kremer* Court explicitly transplanted from that doctrine to claim preclusion) is sometimes asserted as an independent requirement for claim preclusion and sometimes melded into the determination of whether the original adjudication was a valid and final judgment on the merits. The *Kremer* Court added that this standard would be met as long as the proceedings that led to the original judgment met the minimum procedural requirements of the due process clause of the U.S. Constitution.

4. Is a judgment that is pending appeal entitled to preclusive effect or is the "final judgment" rule satisfied only when all appeals have been exhausted? See Restatement (Second) of Judgments §13 cmt. f (1982).

(c) **Same Cause of Action**. Of the three requirements for claim preclusion, this is typically the most nettlesome because it turns on the meaning of the elusive concept of a claim or cause of action. In *Sopha*, the court adopted the widely, though not universally, adopted transactional approach that is codified in the Restatement and is reflected in the "single cause of action" rule. Pursuant to that doctrine, one looks to see whether the two claims share a common factual underpinning, rather than whether the plaintiffs are asserting the same substantive legal theory or are seeking the same form or type of damages. In what its comment "b" admits is not a "mathematically precise definition," Section 24 of the Restatement (Second) of Judgments offers this demarcation of the boundaries of a single cause of action:

> "What factual grouping constitutes a 'transaction', and what groupings constitute a 'series' are to be determined pragmatically, giving weight to such considerations as whether the facts are related in time, space, origin or motivation, whether they form a convenient trial unit, and whether their treatment as a unit conforms to the parties' expectations or business understanding or usage."

By focusing on the transactional foundations of a claim, this modern formulation of the meaning of cause of action — which has been adopted by the overwhelming majority of jurisdictions — is consistent with the liberal joinder and amendment provisions of the federal and most state rules of procedure. By way of contrast, when the more rigid pleading requirements of the common law writ regime were in vogue, the courts took a less expansive view of the scope of claim preclusion since the plaintiff's opportunity to join multiple claims in the original action was severely circumscribed. But now that plaintiffs have an unbridled opportunity to assert multiple claims against individual defendants, see Rule 18 of the Federal Rules, the courts are more willing to invoke preclusion for failure to join such claims in the suit that resulted in the first filed judgment.

Under this prevailing standard, how should a court handle the following situations?

1. A plaintiff brought a tort claim against the manufacturer of a defective computer anti-virus program seeking an award of compensatory damages for losses suffered from the ensuing harm to her computer and the

loss of data contained on its hard drive. Some months after obtaining a judgment in her favor, the plaintiff brought a separate civil action against the same software company seeking damages for the emotional pain and suffering she experienced as a result of the damage to her computer and data. The defendant moved to dismiss the second complaint on the grounds of claim preclusion.

2. A plaintiff brought a tort claim for damages sounding in strict liability against the manufacturer of a defective product. After the jury rendered a verdict in favor of the defendant, that plaintiff brought a separate action against the same manufacturer alleging a contract claim for breach of implied warranty of merchantability and a claim under the federal Magnuson-Moss Warranty Act also alleging a breach of the manufacturer's implied warranty of merchantability. The defendant moved to dismiss the second suit on the grounds of claim preclusion.

3. In a New York plaintiff's breach of contract action against a California defendant, the New York state trial court denied the defendant's motion to dismiss for lack of personal jurisdiction. The only other defense contained in the defendant's answer was an allegation that the contract was unenforceable as a matter of public policy. After a trial, the jury rendered a verdict in favor of the plaintiff in the amount of $1 million. Although the defendant had sufficient contacts with New York to subject herself to the exercise of personal jurisdiction, all of her assets were in California. Consequently, the plaintiff subsequently filed an action in California to enforce the New York judgment. The defendant's answer alleged that the New York judgment was unenforceable because that action was barred by the expiration of the governing New York statute of limitations.

As previously mentioned, however, not every jurisdiction has adopted this transactional definition of cause of action. Instead of focusing on the event that gave rise to the claims, a minority of jurisdictions looks either to the elements of each claim or to whether the claims alleges an infringement of the same "primary right" in order to determine whether they form part of a single cause of action for preclusion purposes. Thus, for example, if a plaintiff seeks to recover for a violation of her right to be free from discrimination, she will not be permitted to assert that right in separate actions based on different legal theories or requests for different forms of damages. Alternatively, if the elements of the two claims, i.e., the facts needed to prove the two claims, are coincident, these claims will be viewed as part of a single cause of action. Since these "primary right" and "same evidence" doctrines define a cause of action more narrowly than the transactional approach, they are less likely to result in preclusion than application of the transactional standard.

2. One of the distinguishing features of claim preclusion is the fact that a final and valid adjudication on the merits of a single cause of action bars the parties from subsequently litigating any and every component of that cause of action, both with respect to the affirmative claim and any defenses to that claim. Thus, claim preclusion bars assertion of both matters that were and were not litigated in the prior action, as long as those matters could have been asserted as part of

appealed to the Court of Appeals for the Ninth Circuit, which affirmed the District Court's order. Petitioner also brought suit against respondent in the State Circuit Court for Baltimore City, Maryland, alleging the same causes of action, which were not time barred under Maryland's 3-year statute of limitations. Respondent * * * removed the action to the United States District Court for the District of Maryland on federal-question grounds (diversity grounds were not available because Lockheed is a Maryland citizen). The * * * Maryland federal court remanded the case to state court because the federal question arose only by way of defense. Following a hearing, the Maryland state court granted respondent's motion to dismiss on the ground of res judicata. * * * Petitioner * * * appealed the Maryland trial court's order of dismissal to the Maryland Court of Special Appeals. The Court of Special Appeals affirmed, holding that, regardless of whether California would have accorded claim-preclusive effect to a statute-of-limitations dismissal by one of its own courts, the dismissal by the California federal court barred the complaint filed in Maryland, since the res judicata effect of federal diversity judgments is prescribed by federal law, under which the earlier dismissal was on the merits and claim preclusive. After the Maryland Court of Appeals declined to review the case, we granted certiorari.

Petitioner contends that the outcome of this case is controlled by Dupasseur v. Rochereau, 21 Wall. 130, 135, 22 L.Ed. 588 (1875), which held that the res judicata effect of a federal diversity judgment "is such as would belong to judgments of the State courts rendered under similar circumstances," and may not be accorded any "higher sanctity or effect." Since, petitioner argues, the dismissal of an action on statute-of-limitations grounds by a California state court would not be claim preclusive, it follows that the similar dismissal of this diversity action by the California federal court cannot be claim preclusive. While we agree that this would be the result demanded by Dupasseur, the case is not dispositive because it was decided under the Conformity Act of 1872, 17 Stat. 196, which required federal courts to apply the procedural law of the forum State in nonequity cases. That arguably affected the outcome of the case.

Respondent, for its part, contends that the outcome of this case is controlled by Federal Rule of Civil Procedure 41(b), which provides as follows:

> "Involuntary Dismissal: Effect Thereof. For failure of the plaintiff to prosecute or to comply with these rules or any order of court, a defendant may move for dismissal of an action or of any claim against the defendant. Unless the court in its order for dismissal otherwise specifies, a dismissal under this subdivision and any dismissal not provided for in this rule, other than a dismissal for lack of jurisdiction, for improper venue, or for failure to join a party under Rule 19, operates as an adjudication upon the merits."

Since the dismissal here did not "otherwise specif[y]" (indeed, it specifically stated that it was "on the merits"), and did not pertain to the excepted subjects of jurisdiction, venue, or joinder, it follows, respondent contends, that the dismissal is entitled to claim preclusive effect.

Implicit in this reasoning is the unstated minor premise that all judgments denominated "on the merits" are entitled to claim-preclusive effect. That premise is not necessarily valid. The original connotation of an "on the merits" adjudication is one that actually "pass[es] directly on the substance of [a particular] claim" before the court. Restatement §19, Comment a, at 161. That connotation remains common to every jurisdiction of which we are aware. And it is, we think, the meaning intended in those many statements to the effect that a judgment "on the merits" triggers the doctrine of res judicata or claim preclusion.

But over the years the meaning of the term "judgment on the merits" * * * has come to be applied to some judgments (such as the one involved here) that do not pass upon the substantive merits of a claim and hence do not (in many jurisdictions) entail claim-preclusive effect. That is why the Restatement of Judgments has abandoned the use of the term — "because of its possibly misleading connotations," Restatement §19, Comment a, at 161.

In short, it is no longer true that a judgment "on the merits" is necessarily a judgment entitled to claim-preclusive effect; and there are a number of reasons for believing that the phrase "adjudication upon the merits" does not bear that meaning in Rule 41(b). To begin with, Rule 41(b) sets forth nothing more than a default rule for determining the import of a dismissal (a dismissal is "upon the merits," with the three stated exceptions, unless the court "otherwise specifies"). This would be a highly peculiar context in which to announce a federally prescribed rule on the complex question of claim preclusion, saying in effect, "All federal dismissals (with three specified exceptions) preclude suit elsewhere, unless the court otherwise specifies."

And even apart from the purely default character of Rule 41(b), it would be peculiar to find a rule governing the effect that must be accorded federal judgments by other courts ensconced in rules governing the internal procedures of the rendering court itself. Indeed, such a rule would arguably violate the jurisdictional limitation of the Rules Enabling Act: that the Rules "shall not abridge, enlarge or modify any substantive right," 28 U.S.C. §2072(b). In the present case, for example, if California law left petitioner free to sue on this claim in Maryland even after the California statute of limitations had expired, the federal court's extinguishment of that right (through Rule 41(b)'s mandated claim-preclusive effect of its judgment) would seem to violate this limitation.

Moreover, as so interpreted, the Rule would in many cases violate the federalism principle of Erie R. Co. by engendering "'substantial' variations [in outcomes] between state and federal litigation" which would "[l]ikely . . . influence the choice of a forum." Hanna v. Plumer. With regard to the claim-preclusion issue involved in the present case, for example, the traditional rule is that expiration of the applicable statute of limitations merely bars the remedy and does not extinguish the substantive right, so that dismissal on that ground does not have claim-preclusive effect in other jurisdictions with longer, unexpired limitation periods. See Restatement (Second) of Conflict of Laws §§142(2), 143 (1969); Restatement of Judgments §49, Comment a (1942). Out-of-state defendants sued on stale claims in California and in other States adhering to this traditional rule would systematically remove state-law suits brought against them to federal court — where, unless otherwise specified, a statute-of-limitations dismissal would bar suit everywhere.[1]

Finally, if Rule 41(b) did mean what respondent suggests, we would surely have relied upon it in our cases recognizing the claim-preclusive effect of federal judgments in federal-question cases. Yet for over half a century since the promulgation of Rule 41(b), we have not once done so. See, e.g., Heck v. Humphrey, 512 U.S. 477, 488-489n.9, 114 S.Ct. 2364, 129 L.Ed.2d 383 (1994).

We think the key to a more reasonable interpretation of the meaning of "operates as an adjudication upon the merits" in Rule 41(b) is to be found in Rule 41(a), which, in discussing the effect of voluntary dismissal by the plaintiff, makes clear that an "adjudication upon the merits" is the opposite of a "dismissal without prejudice".

The primary meaning of "dismissal without prejudice," we think, is dismissal without barring the defendant from returning later, to the same court, with the same underlying claim. That will also ordinarily (though not always) have the consequence of not barring the claim from other courts, but its primary meaning relates to the dismissing court itself. * * *

We think, then, that the effect of the "adjudication upon the merits" default provision of Rule 41(b) — and, presumably, of the explicit order in the present case that used the language of that default provision — is simply that, unlike a dismissal "without prejudice," the dismissal in the present case barred refiling of the same claim in the United States District Court for the Central District of California. That is undoubtedly a necessary condition, but it is not a sufficient one, for claim-preclusive effect in other courts.[2]

III

Having concluded that the claim-preclusive effect, in Maryland, of this California federal diversity judgment is dictated neither by Dupasseur v. Rochereau, as petitioner contends, nor by Rule 41(b), as respondent contends, we turn to consideration of what determines the issue. Neither the Full Faith and Credit Clause nor the full faith and credit statute addresses the question. By their terms they govern the effects to be given only to state-court judgments (and, in the case of the statute, to judgments by courts of territories and possessions). And no other federal textual provision, neither of the Constitution nor of any statute, addresses the claim-preclusive effect of a judgment in a federal diversity action.

---

[1] Rule 41(b), interpreted as a preclusion-establishing rule, would not have the two effects described in the preceding paragraphs — arguable violation of the Rules Enabling Act and incompatibility with *Erie* — if the court's failure to specify an other-than-on-the-merits dismissal were subject to reversal on appeal whenever it would alter the rule of claim preclusion applied by the State in which the federal court sits. No one suggests that this is the rule, and we are aware of no case that applies it.

[2] We do not decide whether, in a diversity case, a federal court's "dismissal upon the merits" (in the sense we have described), under circumstances where a state court would decree only a "dismissal without prejudice," abridges a "substantive right" and thus exceeds the authorization of the Rules Enabling Act. We think the situation will present itself more rarely than would the arguable violation of the Act that would ensue from interpreting Rule 41(b) as a rule of claim preclusion; and if it is a violation, can be more easily dealt with on direct appeal.

It is also true, however, that no federal textual provision addresses the claim-preclusive effect of a federal-court judgment in a federal-question case, yet we have long held that States cannot give those judgments merely whatever effect they would give their own judgments, but must accord them the effect that this Court prescribes. The reasoning of that line of cases suggests, moreover, that even when States are allowed to give federal judgments (notably, judgments in diversity cases) no more than the effect accorded to state judgments, that disposition is by direction of this Court, which has the last word on the claim-preclusive effect of all federal judgments.

In other words, in Dupasseur the State was allowed (indeed, required) to give a federal diversity judgment no more effect than it would accord one of its own judgments only because reference to state law was the federal rule that this Court deemed appropriate. In short, federal common law governs the claim-preclusive effect of a dismissal by a federal court sitting in diversity.

It is left to us, then, to determine the appropriate federal rule. And despite the sea change that has occurred in the background law since Dupasseur was decided — not only repeal of the Conformity Act but also the watershed decision of this Court in Erie — we think the result decreed by Dupasseur continues to be correct for diversity cases. Since state, rather than federal, substantive law is at issue there is no need for a uniform federal rule. And indeed, nationwide uniformity in the substance of the matter is better served by having the same claim-preclusive rule (the state rule) apply whether the dismissal has been ordered by a state or a federal court. This is, it seems to us, a classic case for adopting, as the federally prescribed rule of decision, the law that would be applied by state courts in the State in which the federal diversity court sits. See Gasperini v. Center for Humanities, Inc. As we have alluded to above, any other rule would produce the sort of forum-shopping and inequitable administration of the laws that Erie seeks to avoid, since filing in, or removing to, federal court would be encouraged by the divergent effects that the litigants would anticipate from likely grounds of dismissal. See Guaranty Trust Co. v. York.

This federal reference to state law will not obtain, of course, in situations in which the state law is incompatible with federal interests. If, for example, state law did not accord claim-preclusive effect to dismissals for willful violation of discovery orders, federal courts' interest in the integrity of their own processes might justify a contrary federal rule. No such conflict with potential federal interests exists in the present case. Dismissal of this state cause of action was decreed by the California federal court only because the California statute of limitations so required; and there is no conceivable federal interest in giving that time bar more effect in other courts than the California courts themselves would impose.

Because the claim-preclusive effect of the California federal court's dismissal "upon the merits" of petitioner's action on statute-of-limitations grounds is governed by a federal rule that in turn incorporates California's law of claim preclusion (the content of which we do not pass upon today), the Maryland Court of Special Appeals erred in holding that the dismissal necessarily precluded the bringing of this action in the Maryland courts. The action but fails to do so is precluded, after the rendition of judgment in that action, from maintaining an action on the claim if:

(a) The counterclaim is required to be interposed by a compulsory counterclaim statute or rule of court, or

(b) The relationship between the counterclaim and the plaintiff's claim is such that successful prosecution of the second action would nullify the initial judgment or would impair rights established in the initial action."

SECTION D.   ISSUE PRECLUSION (COLLATERAL ESTOPPEL)

The desire to avoid redundant use of the judicial system and to prevent inconsistent adjudications can also arise in situations that do not fit within the requirements of the doctrine of claim preclusion, i.e., where either the cause of action is not the same or the parties are not identical in both lawsuits. For example, when the passenger and driver of one automobile are injured in a collision with another car and each wants to bring a negligence claim against the driver of that other vehicle, the two suits will not involve the same parties. Alternatively, where the driver of one car sues the driver of the other car for his injuries and then brings a separate action against that same driver in connection with a failed business deal, although the two suits involve the same parties, the cause of action is not the same in each action. In either of these cases, the requirements for invoking claim preclusion would not be satisfied. Nevertheless, it is possible that the resolution of each of the actions in these two situations will require the adjudication of one, if not more, common factual and/or legal issues. Should the interests in promoting the finality and consistency of judgments and avoiding wasteful duplication of litigative resources preclude the relitigation of the same issue in two separate lawsuits?

This is the focus of the doctrine of collateral estoppel, a concept that is now generally referred to by its more expressive title — issue preclusion. In fact, this more descriptive term by its very name highlights the crucial difference between it and claim preclusion. Issue preclusion applies only to the attempt to relitigate an issue of law or fact that has actually been the subject of a prior adjudication. It is a comparatively more precise instrument than claim preclusion in that it excises only a specific issue, rather than an entire cause of action, from judicial consideration. Consequently, issue preclusion can only occur when the claim containing the subject issue was not barred by claim preclusion. Moreover, in contrast to claim preclusion, issue preclusion does not bar litigation of a matter that was not, but could or should have been, adjudicated.

As you read each of the cases in this section, to reinforce your understanding of the preceding materials on claim preclusion, ask yourself not only why the court did or did not invoke issue preclusion, but why it also did not rely on claim preclusion to dismiss the action.

1. The Essential Elements

a) Identicality

In re the Termination of Parental Rights to Greg H. L., a Person Under the Age of 18: Gail M. and Roger M. v. Jerome E. M.

Court of Appeals of Wisconsin, 2001.

243 Wis.2d 117, 627 N.W.2d 549.

Appeal from an order of the circuit court for Rock County: John H. Lussow, Judge. Affirmed.

Roggensack, J.

Jerome E.M. appeals the termination of his parental rights to his son, Greg H.L. He ascribes the following error to the circuit court: * * * it should have applied claim preclusion or issue preclusion to bar this action * * *. Because we conclude there is no merit to * * * Jerome's contentions, we affirm the judgment of the circuit court.

BACKGROUND

Gail M. and Jerome are the parents of Greg, who was born June 28, 1991, in Wisconsin. Jerome and Gail have never been married, and Jerome, who maintains residences in both Wisconsin and Hawaii, contributed nothing to the costs of Gail's pregnancy or Greg's birth. Additionally, he has paid no child support, nor has he provided any other financial support, such as health insurance, school fees, or clothing allowance.

When Greg was almost three years old, Jerome petitioned Milwaukee County Circuit Court to be adjudicated his father. That adjudication occurred in the circuit court on June 24, 1997.[2] Subsequent to the determination of paternity, Jerome still did not make child support payments, cover health insurance costs, clothing costs, or school fees costs, or in any other way provide financial support to Greg. He has also provided no emotional support for his child. Jerome has never seen or visited Greg, nor has he communicated with or attempted to communicate with him or anyone else who could have provided information about Greg, except for a conversation in 1995 with the then-guardian ad litem, Kevin Dunn.

Since Greg was one year old, he has resided with Roger M. in addition to Gail. Gail and Roger filed a petition to terminate Jerome's parental rights on July 19, 1999, in Rock County Circuit Court, and Roger has petitioned to adopt Greg if Jerome's parental rights are terminated.

On October 5, 1999, the circuit court held a fact-finding hearing on the termination petition. Testimony was adduced showing past threats and violent conduct by Jerome, both in regard to his wife and children during his first

---

[2] Gail appealed the judgment of paternity, which appeal was pending when the petition to terminate Jerome's parental rights was filed.

marriage and in regard to Gail. * * * Based on the testimony at the October 5 hearing, the court found that Jerome had abandoned Greg and had failed to assume parental responsibility pursuant to Wis. Stat. §48.415(1) and (6). The court then found that Jerome was unfit pursuant to Wis. Stat. §48.424(4).

A dispositional hearing was held on May 18 and 19, 2000, wherein the court evaluated whether the standard for the termination of parental rights, "the best interests of the child", had been met. After a full evidentiary hearing, the circuit court concluded that it was in Greg's best interests to terminate Jerome's parental rights, and it so ordered. Jerome appeals.

DISCUSSION

* * *

Claim Preclusion/Issue Preclusion.

* * *

Jerome * * * argues that the prior paternity determination, which concluded that he is Greg's biological father and ordered periods of physical placement of Greg with Jerome contingent upon Jerome meeting certain conditions, prevents the termination of his parental rights. In his brief, he labels the argument "res judicata," and he also asserts that Gail should be collaterally estopped by the paternity proceeding from petitioning to terminate his parental rights. The Wisconsin Supreme Court has chosen different words to describe res judicata and collateral estoppel. Res judicata is now known as claim preclusion, and collateral estoppel is now known as issue preclusion. Sopha v. Owens-Corning Fiberglas Corp., 230 Wis.2d 212, 232n.25, 601 N.W.2d 627,636n.25 (1999). However, notwithstanding the label applied to these doctrines, the tenets underlying them remain the same. Claim preclusion establishes that a final judgment between the same parties or their privies is conclusive for all subsequent actions between those same parties, as to all matters which were or which could have been litigated in the proceeding from which the judgment arose. To be applied, claim preclusion requires: (1) identity of parties or their privies in both actions; (2) a prior final judgment on the merits by a court with jurisdiction; and (3) identity of causes of action in the two suits. Sopha, 601 N.W.2d at 637.

In the paternity proceeding, Jerome claimed that he was Greg's father. The petition to terminate Jerome's parental rights is not a collateral attack on the judgment that Jerome is Greg's biological father, but rather a claim that it is in Greg's best interests to have Jerome's parental rights terminated. No determination was made on this later claim during the paternity proceeding. Additionally, Gail was not required to raise her claim as a counterclaim in the paternity action. Claim preclusion does not bar this proceeding to terminate Jerome's parental rights.

Issue preclusion "has the dual purpose of protecting litigants from the burden of relitigating an identical issue with the same party or his privy and of promoting judicial economy by preventing needless litigation." Parklane Hosiery Co. v. Shore, 439 U.S. 322,326 (1979). As a threshold matter, issue preclusion, unlike claim preclusion, requires more than a judgment on the merits. For issue preclusion to be applied, there must have been actual litigation of the same issue that was necessary to the outcome of the first action. While issue preclusion can prevent re-litigation of issues actually litigated and determined in a prior lawsuit, even if the cause of action in the second lawsuit is different from the first, its ultimate application is a discretionary decision of the circuit court whether it should be applied.

Here, the circuit court determined that Greg's best interests would be furthered by terminating Jerome's parental rights. Jerome asserts that the court could not have determined him to be the biological father of Greg without making a contrary finding. We disagree. The court did not determine whether it was in Greg's best interests to adjudicate Jerome as his father. And, even if it had, the paternity action did not address whether Jerome had abandoned Greg or failed to assume parental responsibility for him, but rather, whether he had the legal right to parent him. Therefore, we conclude that the circuit court did not err in refusing to apply issue preclusion to bar this action.

CONCLUSION

* * * [W]e conclude that * * * [the trial court's] determination to terminate Jerome's parental rights to Greg was not erroneous. Accordingly, we affirm the order of the circuit court.

NOTES AND PROBLEMS FOR DISCUSSION

1. Which preclusion doctrines were discussed in the principal case?

2. How and why did the court rule on each of these doctrines?

3. Consider the following situations that raise different aspects of the general question of whether two cases involve adjudication of the identical issue:

(a) Melinda Shaw, an Ohio citizen, brought a breach of contract action against Lemuel Koffee in federal district court in Ohio on the basis of diversity of citizenship jurisdiction. The trial court granted the defendant's motion to dismiss for lack of subject matter jurisdiction, finding that Koffee was a citizen of Ohio. Six months later, Shaw was involved in an automobile accident with Koffee and brought a diversity-based tort claim against Koffee in that same federal district court, offering evidence of Koffee's non-Ohio citizenship that was not tendered in the first action. Koffee again filed a Rule 12(b)(1) motion, claiming that the plaintiff was precluded from relitigating the issue of his citizenship. How should the court resolve the preclusion issue? See Du Page Forklift Service, Inc. v. Material Handling Services, Inc., 195 Ill.2d 71 (Ill.Sup.Ct.2001).

(b) In 1990, Robin Axelrod successfully sued her employer in a case alleging sexual harassment. In that case, the trial court granted the defense motion to strike the plaintiff's request for compensatory damages on the ground that such damages were not awardable under Title VII. Ten years later, Axelrod brought another sexual harassment claim against that same employer and again sought damages for her emotional pain and suffering. In 1991, Congress passed a law amending Title VII to permit the recovery of compensatory damages in sexual harassment cases. Can the defendant preclude the relitigation of the availability of compensatory damages in this second lawsuit? See

Commissioner v. Sunnen, 333 U.S. 591, 68 S.Ct. 715, 92 L.Ed. 898 (1949); Montana v. U.S., 440 U.S. 147, 99 S.Ct. 970, 59 L.Ed.2d 210 (1979).

(c) Edward Chase was found not guilty of drug trafficking in a criminal action filed against him by the federal government. Subsequently, the federal government brought a civil action against Chase seeking forfeiture of the boat that the government claimed was used in the drug trafficking operation. How should the trial court rule on Mr. Chase's motion to preclude relitigation of the issue of whether or not he was engaged in drug trafficking? See One Lot Emerald Cut Stones v. United States, 409 U.S. 232, 93 S.Ct. 489, 34 L.Ed.2d 438 (1972).

(d) Would the result in "(c)" be the same if the government had obtained a conviction in the criminal proceeding?

(e) The plaintiff alleges that the defendant failed to make a payment pursuant to an installment contract. The defendant maintains that the contract is unenforceable because it was a contract of adhesion. The court enters judgment in favor of the plaintiff. One year later, the plaintiff files another action alleging a subsequent default by the defendant. Can the plaintiff preclude the defendant from claiming that the same contract is unenforceable under the statute of frauds?

(f) Joe Franks filed a tort claim against Ashley Davies alleging that Ashley's negligence in driving her car in excess of the posted speed limit caused the accident that left Joe with a broken neck. The jury rendered a verdict for Ashley based on its finding that she was not speeding at the time of the accident. Five years later, Joe developed paralysis that he claimed was caused by the accident with Ashley. In a second suit against Ashley (assume it is not subject to claim preclusion), Joe alleged that his injury was directly caused by Ashley's negligent failure to obey a stop sign at the intersection where the collision occurred. Should the trial court preclude Joe from litigating the issue of Ashley's negligence?

4. The court in the principal case stated that issue preclusion occurs if there was (1) actual litigation (2) of the same issue (3) that was necessary to the outcome of the first action. To put it another way, a court will preclude relitigation of an issue if (1) that identical issue (2) was actually litigated and determined in (3) a separate suit in which resolution of that issue was necessary or essential to the judgment. The first of these three components was addressed in *Gail M*. The following cases and their accompanying notes and problems examine the other two requirements for issue preclusion.

b) Actually Litigated and Unambiguously Determined

Herrera v. Reicher

Missouri Court of Appeals, Western District, 1980.

608 S.W.2d 539

FLANIGAN, SPECIAL JUDGE:

In 1976 plaintiff John Herrera was struck by an automobile owned by Paul A. Reicher, Sr. ("Reicher") and driven by his son, Paul Reicher, Jr. ("Paul, Jr."). Reicher carried a policy of liability insurance with American Family Mutual Insurance Company ("American Family"). Herrera brought a tort action against Paul, Jr. and Reicher. A jury awarded plaintiff $8,000 on his claim against Paul, Jr. but denied him recovery on his claim against Reicher. Judgment was entered on the verdict.

Later the instant action was filed by plaintiff Herrera against defendants Reicher[1] and American Family. The petition sought payment under the American Family policy of the $8,000 judgment, then final, which plaintiff had obtained against Paul, Jr. in the tort action. * * *

Prior to filing a responsive pleading, defendants Reicher and American Family filed a motion for summary judgment. * * * The trial court sustained the motion and entered summary judgment in favor of Reicher and American Family. Plaintiff appeals.

* * *

On this appeal plaintiff claims that the trial court's ruling was based on the doctrine of collateral estoppel. Defendants' brief seeks to uphold the ruling solely on that ground. The trial briefs of the parties, and the trial court's order sustaining the motion, lend support to plaintiff's assertion that the trial court's order was based on collateral estoppel and no other basis is apparent from the record. Accordingly this opinion is confined to the question of whether the trial court's ruling is supported by that doctrine.

* * *

* * * It is certain that collateral estoppel forecloses a party from litigating an issue only if that exact issue was unambiguously decided in the earlier case.

It was, and is, plaintiff's position that the issue of whether Paul, Jr. had the permission, express or implied, of Reicher to drive the Dodge at the time of the accident was not decided in the tort action and that the trial court erred in invoking collateral estoppel.

Relying upon collateral estoppel, defendants Reicher and American Family take this position: (a) The judgment in favor of defendant Reicher in the tort

---

[1] The petition sought no relief against Reicher. Plaintiff's basis for including Reicher as a defendant in the instant action is not clear. In addition to the motion for summary judgment, Reicher filed "in the alternative" a motion to dismiss for failure to state a claim upon which relief can be granted. The trial court made no ruling on that motion and, on remand, it remains pending. This court expresses no opinion on its merits.

action constituted a determination that Reicher did not know or have reason to know that Paul, Jr. used the car; (b) thus, Reicher did not and, in fact, could not give express or implied permission (to Paul, Jr. to operate the car) within the meaning of the policy's omnibus clause; and (c) accordingly plaintiff may not, in the instant action, attempt to bring Paul, Jr. within the category of "persons insured" under the American Family policy by showing that at the time of the accident Paul, Jr. was operating the Dodge with the permission of Reicher.

In support of their contention defendants rely primarily upon two things: (a) the contents of instruction 7,[4] plaintiff's verdict-directing instruction against Reicher in the tort action, and (b) the fact that the jury verdict in the tort action was in favor of Reicher and judgment was entered thereon.

The parties agree that plaintiff's theory in the tort action, so far as his claim against Reicher was concerned, was based on "negligent entrustment." Instruction 7 sought to submit that theory to the jury. This opinion neither deals with nor rules on the correctness or incorrectness of instruction 7. The wording of the instruction does, however, affect the issue of the propriety of the trial court's application of collateral estoppel.

Under instruction 7 the jury was required to believe all of the seven propositions enumerated in it before they could return a verdict for plaintiff against Reicher. In their briefs and in their oral arguments before this court the parties agree that the propositions set forth in paragraphs Second, Third, Fifth and Sixth were not in serious dispute or, in view of the verdict against Paul, Jr., were resolved by the jury in favor of the plaintiff.

As plaintiff points out, the verdict in favor of Reicher was a general verdict and it does not show which element or elements of instruction 7 the jury failed to believe. Although the jury's disbelief of the proposition set forth in paragraph First might be one explanation for the verdict, plaintiff argues that is not the only possible explanation. Plaintiff says that it is also possible that the jury did believe the proposition of paragraph First and also believed that portion of paragraph Fourth which required the jury to find that Reicher made the Dodge available to Paul, Jr. Nevertheless, in spite of the foregoing beliefs, plaintiff says the jury might have returned the verdict in favor of Reicher for either of the

---

[4] "INSTRUCTION NO. 7
Your verdict must be for Plaintiff and against Defendant Paul A. Reicher, Sr., if you believe:
First, Defendant Paul A. Reicher, Sr., either knew or had reason to know that Paul A. Reicher, Jr., was using the 1966 Dodge automobile, and
Second, Paul A. Reicher, Jr., was under the age of sixteen years at the time of this occurrence, and
Third, at the time Defendant Paul A. Reicher, Sr., either knew or had reason to know that Paul A. Reicher, Jr., was under the age of sixteen years, and
Fourth, that in making the 1966 Dodge automobile available to Paul A. Reicher, Jr., Defendant Paul A. Reicher, Sr., was thereby negligent, and
Fifth, that Paul A. Reicher, Jr., thereafter started the 1966 Dodge automobile from a stop at a time when such movement could not have been made with reasonable safety, and
Sixth, Paul A. Reicher, Jr., was thereby negligent, and
Seventh, such negligence of Paul A. Reicher, Jr., directly combined with the negligence of Defendant Paul A. Reicher, Sr., to cause damage to plaintiff . . . ."

following reasons: (a) a disbelief that Reicher was negligent as required by paragraph Fourth; (b) a disbelief that Reicher's negligence, if negligent he was, directly combined with the negligence of Paul, Jr. to cause plaintiff's damage as required by paragraph Seventh.

Defendants' brief says: "Under Missouri law, it is well settled that a person who knowingly permits another under sixteen years of age to operate a motor vehicle is negligent as a matter of law. Thus, it would be impossible as a matter of law for the jury to find that Reicher, Sr. entrusted the car to Reicher, Jr., without being negligent." In effect defendants argue that instruction 7, which plaintiff himself submitted, placed upon plaintiff the burden of proving certain propositions which plaintiff did not have to prove and which the jury was not free to disbelieve.

Defendants also argue that it is "self-evidently frivolous" for plaintiff to say that the jury could have found that Reicher was negligent in making the car available to Paul, Jr. but that such negligence did not combine with that of Paul, Jr. to cause plaintiff's damage. If Reicher was negligent in that respect, say defendants, it is obvious that Reicher's negligence combined with that of Paul, Jr. to cause plaintiff's injury.

Defendants then argue that the only explanation for the verdict in favor of Reicher under instruction 7 is that the jury failed to believe the proposition set forth in paragraph First. Thus, defendants say, the jury found that Reicher did not know or have reason to know that Paul, Jr. was using the car on the occasion in question and, absent such knowledge, there could be no permission, express or implied, emanating from Reicher to Paul, Jr.

Defendants' argument is unsound. If it is assumed that instruction 7 was a correct statement of the law, the jury could have believed all of the propositions contained in that instruction except that portion of paragraph Fourth which required a belief that Reicher was negligent in making the car available to Paul, Jr. If the jury believed that he made the car so available, but in doing so was not negligent, they were required to return a verdict for Reicher. If, on the other hand, instruction 7 was an incorrect statement of the law, the verdict could be explained on the same basis.

It is no answer for defendants to say that it would be improper, "as a matter of law," for the jury to find that Reicher entrusted the car to Paul, Jr. without being negligent. Whether the instruction was proper or improper, it was the duty of the jury, in the tort action, to follow it in arriving at their verdict. Right or wrong, it was the law of that case so far as that jury was concerned. Indeed any reversal which is based on an instruction error rests on the theory that the jury was influenced, and the verdict thereby tainted, by the error.

The doctrine of collateral estoppel does not come into play unless the issue presented in the second action is identical to the issue which was "unambiguously decided" * * * in the first action. If, as here, the prior adjudication, by reason of its ambiguity, fails to meet that requirement, the doctrine may not be invoked. No matter what its genesis, ambiguity exists. Ambiguity is the flaw and the mere fact that the flaw may stem from another flaw, consisting of an erroneous instruction, is of no moment.

The judgment is reversed and the cause remanded.

NOTES AND PROBLEMS FOR DISCUSSION

1. (a) Why did the appellate court reject the issue preclusion defense?

(b) Without changing any of the operative facts, could the defendant have done anything differently in the first lawsuit to change the result in the subsequent proceeding?

2. Why didn't Mr. Reicher move to dismiss the plaintiff's second action against him on claim preclusion grounds?

3. On January 1, 1996, Lisa Loring agreed to purchase a 1994 Mustang convertible from her friend, Matt Daring, for $15,000. After receiving the car, Lisa had it checked by a mechanic who determined that the brakes were defective and needed to be replaced at a cost of $2,000. When Lisa told Matt about the problem and asked for a reduction in the purchase price, Matt insisted that they had already finalized the deal and demanded payment in full. Lisa rejected this demand and sent Matt payment in the amount of $13,000, even though she did not have the brakes fixed. On March 16, 2001, Matt filed a breach of contract suit against Lisa seeking the $2,000 remaining on the original purchase price. In her answer, Lisa alleged that the defective condition of the car breached the implied warranty of merchantability and relieved her of her obligation to pay the amount claimed in the complaint. She also asserted that Matt's suit should be dismissed for failure to file it within the five year statute of limitations governing breach of contract actions. After a trial on the merits, the jury returned a general verdict for Lisa. Shortly thereafter, Lisa and Matt were involved in an automobile accident, which led to an action by Matt against Lisa in which he alleged that the accident was the result of the faulty braking system in Lisa's Mustang. Matt filed a motion with the trial court asking that Lisa be estopped from litigating the issue of her non-negligence on the ground that the faulty condition of the brakes had been adjudicated in the prior action. Lisa admits that she never had the brakes repaired. How should the court rule on Matt's motion?

4. (a) In a breach of contract action brought by a retailer alleging that a purchaser defaulted on an installment payment, the parties stipulated that the installment contract was enforceable because it was not a contract of adhesion. When the purchaser subsequently defaulted on a subsequent installment payment under the same contract, the retailer filed another breach of contract action. How should the trial court rule on the plaintiff's motion to strike the defendant's contract of adhesion defense?

(b) Would your answer to "(a)", *supra*, change if instead of entering into a stipulation, the parties consented to a judgment that the purchaser was not in default because the contract was unenforceable as a contract of adhesion? See *Arizona v. California*, 530 U.S. 392, 120 S.Ct. 2304, 147 L.Ed.2d 374 (2000).

(c) If the court had issued a default judgment in favor of the plaintiff retailer in the initial action because of the defendant's failure to appear, could the purchaser be precluded from challenging the enforceability of the installment contract in a second action brought by the retailer upon the purchaser's failure to make a subsequent installment payment?

c) Necessarily Decided

Rudow v. Fogel

Supreme Judicial Court of Massachusetts, 1978.

376 Mass. 587, 382 N.E.2d 1046

KAPLAN, JUSTICE.

* * *

William Rudow, a minor, by his father Marvin, in 1973 commenced the present action in the Superior Court, Essex County, against his uncle Albert Fogel to obtain a judgment that Fogel holds certain real property in Rockport on a trust for him, William. The complaint alleged, in substance, that Marvin purchased the property in 1958, taking it in his name and that of his wife Florence (William's mother) as tenants by the entirety; that Marvin in March, 1962, quitclaimed his interest to Florence on the understanding and agreement that she would hold the property in trust for their son William; and that Florence in July, 1962, conveyed the property without consideration to Fogel (her brother), the latter knowing of the understanding with respect to William and agreeing to hold the property on the same trust. The complaint went on to charge that Fogel was repudiating his trust obligation, wherefore relief was sought.

Fogel, answering, alleged by way of defense that in a prior action there had been an adjudication against the existence of the trust which should carry over as res judicata to the present action. Fogel then moved for summary judgment, and from his supporting papers we learn that the prior action was one of ejectment by Fogel against Marvin in the District Court of Eastern Essex. Fogel claimed a right to the possession and asserted that Marvin was in wrongful possession. Marvin attacked Fogel's claimed right by pointing to the supposed trust, and justified his own possession by right of curtesy [a common law right enjoyed by a surviving husband to a life estate in land owned by the wife during the marriage — eds.], as he had survived Florence who received the fee during the marriage. Proof was taken and the judge found, first, a trust was not made out on the facts; second, Marvin was entitled to curtesy and was thus, in effect, a common tenant for his lifetime with Fogel, and could not be ejected at Fogel's suit. Judgment entered for Marvin.

The judge of the Superior Court in the present action allowed Fogel's motion for summary judgment, evidently believing that the defense of res judicata had been established. This was held by the Appeals Court to be error.

The determination against Marvin in the ejectment action on the issue of the existence of the trust cannot be used preclusively against William in the current action for the reason that there is no sufficient legal identity between the defendant in the first action and the plaintiff in the second. Argument to the contrary has a superficial attractiveness because of the parent-child relationship, but considerations of policy forbid assimilation in this context of an individual litigating on his own behalf (Marvin being sued personally in the first action) with that individual litigating as representative of another (Marvin acting for William in the present action). * * *

If that question could be overcome and the same persona could be conceived to have litigated in both actions, it would still be wrong to apply in the later action the determination in the earlier that a trust had not been raised. For it is a condition of such "issue preclusion" (terminology now favored over "collateral estoppel") that the determination to be carried over shall not only have been litigated in the first action, but shall have been essential to the judgment in that action. This was the nub of Cambria v. Jeffery, 307 Mass. 49, 29 N.E.2d 555 (1940), where in a collision case the court found the plaintiff negligent and the defendant also negligent, with judgment for the defendant: the finding of defendant's negligence being unnecessary to the judgment indeed, taken of itself, repugnant to the judgment could not be transported to, and given preclusive effect in a later action by the defendant against the plaintiff based on the same collision.[5] The reason for this requirement of essentiality partakes of the reason why a dictum is usually given less weight as a precedent in our law than a holding; in addition we have in the Cambria case the important consideration that the defendant, as the winner in the first action had no occasion or right to take an appeal to challenge the finding that he was negligent. So, in our situation, Marvin for all that appears had neither cause nor opportunity to take to a higher court for possible review and reversal the finding of the District Court that negated the existence of the trust.

* * *

Thus we agree that the judgment of the Superior Court should be reversed.

NOTES AND PROBLEMS FOR DISCUSSION

1. (a) On what grounds did the court in the principal case reverse the trial court's grant of summary judgment?

(b) Which, if any, of those rulings would be entitled to *stare decisis* effect in subsequent cases that raise either of these two general questions?

2. How does the ruling in *Rudow* compare to the holding in *Herrera*?

3. Do you agree with the court's conclusion in *Rudow* that the parties should be permitted to relitigate an issue that clearly was adjudicated and unambiguously decided in the initial action?

---

[5]   Under the rules of procedure in force at the time of Cambria, the defendant was not obliged to assert his claim against the plaintiff in the first action by way of compulsory counterclaim.

York Ford, Inc. v. Building Inspector and Zoning Administrator of Saugus

Appeals Court of Massachusetts, 1995.

38 Mass.App.Ct. 938, 647 N.E.2d 85.

Couchow, Judge:

The question before us is whether York Ford, Inc. (York), is barred by principles of issue preclusion from challenging the validity of a zoning enforcement order of the building inspector. The order demanded that York cease parking "business related" cars on a residentially zoned lot in violation of the town's "use regulations." Four months prior to the issuance of the order, the board of zoning and building appeals (board), had denied York's application for a special permit to extend what York claimed was a preexisting nonconforming use. One of the two grounds on which the board had based its decision was that York's present use was illegal, that is, it was not a valid preexisting nonconforming use.

York had been parking cars on Lot A-112, a residentially zoned lot for over thirty years * * *. In its application for a special permit, York proposed to extend parking further into Lot A-112 and to replace an existing auto-body building with a more modern one. After a hearing on September 2, 1992, the board, on October 30, 1992, denied the special permit on two grounds: * * * [1] that the * * * [existing] use is * * * illegal and [2] the expansion would be substantially more detrimental to the neighborhood [than the *status quo*]. York did not take an appeal from the decision of the board * * *.

On February 23, 1993, the building inspector ordered York to remove "all business related vehicles from Lot A-112" as "you are currently in violation of the Town of Saugus Zoning Bylaw." York appealed the building inspector's order to the board. Although a public hearing was initially scheduled, on motion of one of the board's members, the matter was struck from the agenda on the ground that York's appeal "was an identical petition [to the one] presented at the September 2, 1992" board meeting. The decision of the board [was] dated May 10, 1993 * * *.

In June, York filed an appeal from the May 10 decision of the board and, on the same date, filed a complaint for a declaratory judgment, seeking, inter alia, a declaration that the appeal to the board was not repetitive of the September, 1992 hearing. * * *

* * * [T]he judge dismissed * * * [the declaratory judgment action] on the ground that York, having failed to seek judicial review of the October 30, 1992 decision of the board within the required time, could not now challenge the building inspector's order which was based on the board's determination that York's present parking on lot A-112 was illegal. * * * This is an appeal by York from [that] * * * judgment.

* * *

The question * * * [is] whether York, as urged by the board and the building inspector, is barred on principles of issue preclusion from relitigating the prior determination of the board that York's present parking is illegal. The general rule is that stated in §27 of the Restatement (Second) of Judgments (1982):

> "When an issue of fact or law is actually litigated and determined by a valid and final judgment, and the determination is essential to the judgment, the determination is conclusive in a subsequent action between the parties, whether on the same or a different claim."

Where there are alternative determinations by the court of first instance (or administrative tribunal), the authorities are divided.[6] The Restatement analogizes the case to that of a nonessential determination and opts, "in the interest of predictability and simplicity," for a uniform rule of nonpreclusion. Thus the Restatement (Second), §27 comment i provides:

> "If a judgment of a court of first instance [or of an administrative tribunal] is based on determinations of two issues, either of which standing independently would be sufficient to support the result, the judgment [or administrative adjudication] is not conclusive with respect to either issue standing alone."[7]

While there is authority that when any one of two or more findings of fact have formed the basis for a prior determination each may be given preclusive effect, a view taken by the first Restatement of Judgments §68 comment n (1942), there are sound policy reasons underlying the position of the second Restatement. First, when there are two bases for the decision, an appellant in York's position would have little motivation to appeal from the allegedly erroneous finding as to illegal use since, even if its claim were sustained, a court could easily uphold the denial of the permit on the basis of the board's finding that the expansion was substantially more detrimental to the neighborhood. More important, to require York to take an appeal

> "to protect issues in future collateral suits would not serve one important purpose of the doctrine of collateral estoppel, to minimize litigation and bring it to an end. Such a requirement would, in effect, require cautionary appeals litigating issues on appeal for their possible effect on future indeterminate collateral litigation, which neither party can be sure will occur. The rule at best would preclude some future trial litigation at the expense of currently creating extra appellate litigation."

In addition, in this case, had York appealed the October, 1992 order and admitted that it no longer sought the special permit, the reviewing court might well have considered frivolous and dismissed the appeal which asserted error only in the finding that York's present use was illegal. The availability of

---

[6] Justice Scalia, in *Dozier v. Ford Motor Co.,* 702 F.2d 1189, 1194 (D.C.Cir.1983), noting the division, commented that "a real dilemma is presented. A rule declining to accord *res judicata* effect to an alternate ground must of course apply to both grounds, which would mean that a case which is doubly inadequate can be refiled whereas a case inadequate in only one respect cannot. On the other hand, a rule which gives *res judicata* effect to both grounds leaves the losing party who concedes the adequacy of one no appellate remedy for the patent invalidity of the other except a frivolous appeal."

[7] If, however, there is an appeal and the appellate court upholds both determinations, the judgment is conclusive as to both. §27 comment o.

appellate review of the October, 1992 board decision, a most important factor in the application of the principles of issue preclusion, see Restatement (Second) §28(1) and comment a, is in this case by no means clear.

The trend appears in favor of adopting the position of the second Restatement. Some authorities [nevertheless] take an intermediate position. See, e.g., *Eagle Properties Ltd. v. Scharbauer,* 807 S.W.2d 714, 722 (Tex.1991) (where one issue rigorously considered, alternative "finding" did not preclude defensive use of issue preclusion); 18 Wright, Miller & Cooper, Federal Practice & Procedure §4421, at 208 (1981 and 1994 Supp.) ("tempting to suggest that preclusion should arise from independently sufficient alternative findings only if a second court can determine without extended inquiry that a particular finding reflects a careful process of decision.").

We need not decide whether to adopt comment i of the Restatement in all circumstances. In the present case, we conclude that York is not barred from relitigating the finding of illegality by reason of two interrelated policy considerations. First, and of critical importance, is the uncertain status of York's right to obtain judicial review of the 1992 finding by the board. York might have been dissuaded from appealing because of the likelihood that the board's alternate finding (that the expansion would be substantially more detrimental to the neighborhood) would be upheld, and the finding crucial to York not even reached. Moreover, in the circumstances, an appellate court might well have deemed such an appeal frivolous.

Second, York had no reason to foresee that seeking a special permit to extend its present parking use which had continued without interference for more than thirty years * * * would endanger that use without an opportunity to obtain a full adjudication of that issue. See Restatement (Second) §28(5).[10] This is particularly true where, as here, the building inspector did not act until the time for an appeal had expired. Had its present use been threatened, York would have had more incentive to raise additional defenses, such as a claim * * * that its present use was protected by a prior building permit.

Accordingly, the judgment * * * is vacated and a new judgment is to enter remanding the matter to the board, to hear York's appeal from the February 23, 1993, order of the building inspector.

---

[10] Two of the exceptions to the general rule of issue preclusion provided in §28 of the Restatement are relevant. That section provides in part:

"§28. Exceptions to the General Rule of Issue Preclusion: Although an issue is actually litigated and determined by a valid and final judgment, and the determination is essential to the judgment, relitigation of the issue in a subsequent action between the parties is not precluded in the following circumstances:

(1) The party against whom preclusion is sought could not, as a matter of law, have obtained review of the judgment in the initial action; or * * *

(5) There is a clear and convincing need for a new determination of the issue ... (b) because it was not sufficiently foreseeable at the time of the initial action that the issue would arise in the context of a subsequent action, or (c) because the party sought to be precluded, as a result of the conduct of his adversary or other special circumstances, did not have an adequate opportunity or incentive to obtain a full and fair adjudication in the initial action."

NOTES AND PROBLEMS FOR DISCUSSION

1.   How does the ruling in *York Ford* differ from the holding in *Rudow*?

2.   Paul Banyon bought a television from Ace Equipment, Inc. He sued Ace on a breach of contract claim to recover the purchase price, alleging that the television was defective in that it constantly lost its picture because of faulty wiring in the picture tube. In its answer, Ace denied the defect and also claimed that its purchase agreement contained an explicit disclaimer of warranties. The case was tried without a jury and in her written findings, the trial judge ruled that the television did not contain faulty wiring in the picture tube and that the contractual disclaimer was enforceable against the consumer. Two days later, Banyon was injured when the picture tube in the television shattered and thrust glass projectiles into his face and hands. He brought a tort claim against the Ace alleging that the defective wiring in the picture tube caused his injury. Ace filed a motion asking the court to dismiss Banyon's allegation that the television had defective wiring in the picture tube. How should the court rule on this motion?

3.   Although the ruling in *York Ford* (and the dictum in *Rudow*) to the effect that a judgment resting upon alternative, independently sufficient bases will not preclude relitigation of either determination represents the "modern" rule adopted by the Restatement as well as the overwhelming majority of states, a majority of federal circuit courts accord issue preclusion to each alternate, independently sustainable finding. Compare Jean Alexander Cosmetics, Inc. v. L'Oreal USA, Inc., 458 F.3d 244 (3d Cir.2006) (according preclusive effect to independently sufficient alternative findings and noting it ws joining First, Second, Seventh, Ninth and Eleventh Circuits) with Turney v. O'Toole 898 F.2d 1470 (10th Cir. 1990) (citing Restatement and denying preclusive effect to either such ruling). Which view is more persuasive to you?

4.   (a) Lorne Dune's application for a position as a power tool operator was rejected by Power, Inc., a company with offices across the United States. Lorne filed suit in federal district court in New York alleging that her rejection by the New York office of Power was based on his disability in violation of the federal Americans with Disabilities Act (ADA). In its answer, Power asserted the statutory affirmative defense that Dune's employment posed a risk to the health and safety of others since he suffered from epilepsy. The case was tried without a jury and the court entered judgment in favor of the defendant. The trial judge ruled that while Dune did not pose a threat to others in that job, she did pose a serious risk of danger to herself and since the U.S. Second Circuit had ruled that the defense applies to individuals who posed a risk either to others or to themselves, the defendant had established this affirmative defense. Two months later, Dune moved to Los Angeles, applied for the same position with Power's L.A. office and was again rejected. He filed another ADA suit, this time in the federal district court in Los Angeles. Along with its answer asserting that same affirmative defense, Power filed a Rule 12(c) motion for judgment on the pleadings on the ground that it was entitled to judgment as a matter of law on its affirmative defense since Dune was precluded from relitigating the issue. In response, Dune argued that since the Ninth Circuit had consistently ruled that this defense applies only to an individual who poses a risk to the safety or health of others, issue preclusion should not apply. How should the court rule?

(b) Would your analysis of the preceding hypothetical change if Lorne had filed that initial lawsuit in New York state court alleging a violation of the New York Disabilities Rights Act and everything else remained the same?

5. Take care not to confuse the *issue* preclusion requirement that a previously decided issue be "essential" to the judgment rendered in that case with the *claim* preclusion requirement that the previously issued judgment constitute an adjudication on the merits. This confusion is most likely to occur when a court dismisses a case on jurisdictional grounds. As we mentioned in connection with Note 1(b)(1) following *Sopha* in Section C of this Chapter, *supra*, a dismissal for lack of jurisdiction or venue does not constitute an adjudication on the merits and, therefore, does not preclude the plaintiff from refiling that identical claim against the same defendant(s) in a jurisdictionally appropriate court. However, any issue whose decision was essential to that dismissal would be precluded from relitigation in the subsequently filed action. For example, suppose after the trial court denied its motion to dismiss for lack of personal jurisdiction, the defendant defaulted and the court issued a default judgment. When the plaintiff seeks to enforce that default judgment in another jurisdiction, the defendant will be precluded from collaterally challenging the judgment-issuing court's exercise of personal jurisdiction over him. On the other hand, when preclusion is sought in the refiled case over an issue decided as part of the previous dismissal, since both proceedings in this scenario involve the same cause of action, the relevant doctrine is often referred to as direct, rather than collateral, estoppel.

6. The context under which the issue preclusion question arose in *York Ford* differs markedly from that present in every other case we have considered in this Chapter. In *York Ford*, the court was asked to give preclusive effect to a decision rendered by an administrative agency. This same issue arises when the initial adjudication is a product of arbitration or some other extra-judicial dispute resolution mechanism. The generally applied rule is that the traditional rules of issue preclusion apply as long as the initial proceeding provided the parties with a full and fair opportunity to litigate the issue. This latter requirement is added to ensure (a) that the parties had an incentive to vigorously litigate the issue during the first proceeding, and (b) that the procedures afforded the parties in the first proceeding (e.g., evidentiary rules, availability of a written record, or extent of available discovery tools) did not deprive them of the opportunity to vigorously litigate the issue when compared to the procedures available in the subsequent proceeding.

In determining whether to give collateral estoppel effect to a state administrative agency's findings in a subsequent action brought in federal court, the federal courts will also examine whether Congress expressed its intention in the federal claim-creating statute to preclude such "administrative" issue preclusion. This intent is most frequently divined in civil rights statutes. For example, in UNIVERSITY of TENNESSEE v. ELLIOTT, 478 U.S. 788, 106 L.Ed.2d 3220, 92 L.Ed.2d 635 (1986), the Supreme Court held that Congress intended that unreviewed (i.e., unappealed to state court) findings by state administrative agencies not be accorded preclusive effect on claims litigated in federal court under Title VII of the 1964 Civil Rights Act. In that same case, however, the Court also found no statement of Congressional intent to prevent agency fact-findings resulting from proceedings that are "judicial in nature" from having preclusive effect on claims brought under a nineteenth century civil rights act codified at 42 U.S.C. §1983. Subsequently, in ASTORIA FEDERAL SAVINGS and LOAN ASS'N v. SOLIMINO, 501 U.S. 104, 111 S.Ct. 2166, 115 L.Ed.2d 96 (1991), the Court embellished a bit on the standard to be applied in gauging Congress' views about the preclusive effect of state and federal administrative decisions on courts adjudicating federal statutory claims. The Court rejected the view that preclusion should be imposed only in the presence of a "clear statement" of Congressional intent because "[r]ules of plain statement and strict construction prevail only to the protection of weighty and constant values, be they constitutional or otherwise." And administrative preclusion, in the Court's view, did not "represent independent values of such magnitude and constancy." Instead, the Court erected a rebuttable presumption in favor of "administrative preclusion" on the theory that "Congress is understood to legislate against a background of common-law adjudicatory principles" such as the rules of preclusion. This presumption, the Court added, could be rebutted by a judicial determination (even in the absence of supporting legislative language) that invoking preclusion would be inconsistent with the objectives underlying the passage of that statute.

The Court reexamined the issue of administrative issue preclusion nearly twenty-five years later in the context of trademark law in B&B HARDWARE, INC. v. HARGIS INDUSTRIES, INC., 575 U.S. ___, 135 S.Ct. 1293, 191 L.Ed.2d 222 (2015). Here, the adverse parties used similar trademarks. The plaintiff, Hargis, attempted to register the mark with the U.S. Patent and Trademark Office pursuant to the terms of the Lanham Act. The defendant, B&B, opposed registration and the federal administrative agency tasked with adjudicating such matters, the Trademark Trial and Appeal Board (TTAB), decided in favor of B&B and did not permit the mark to be registered. While the trademark registration matter was proceeding, B&B sued Hargis in federal court for trademark infringement with respect to these same two trademarks. Both the infringement suit and the registration proceeding involved an adjudication of the question of whether a likelihood of confusion existed between the two marks. The issue before the Supreme Court was whether the district court in the infringement action should have applied issue preclusion to the TTAB's decision (in the registration proceeding) that the likelihood of such confusion existed. In a 7-2 opinion, the Court, citing *Astoria Federal Savings*, applied the presumption in favor of administrative issue preclusion. It expressly rejected the plaintiff's suggestion that it jettison administrative preclusion in whole or in part to avoid potential conflict with either the Seventh Amendment right to a jury trial or Article III. The Court noted that it previously had ruled that there was no Seventh Amendment denial of the right to a jury trial when an administrative decision has preclusive effect on a subsequent federal court action that involved a jury trial. Similarly, it ruled that precedent required it to reject the plaintiff's claim that issue preclusion should not apply to the TTAB decision because federal administrative agencies did not exist at common law. Finally, the Court found equally unpersuasive the plaintiff's claim that the Lanham Act should be read narrowly to avoid Article III concerns. The Court stated that invoking administrative preclusion in a subsequent proceeding in federal court did not violate Article III because—citing *Astoria Federal Savings* and *University of Tennessee*—Congress was presumed to have intended that a federal or state agency's determination has preclusive effect. And, the Court concluded, there was nothing in the Lanham Act to suggest that Congress did not intend for that presumption to apply in the trademark context.

Unlike the other principal cases that we read in this section, the two proceedings examined in *Rudow* did not involve identical parties. Should the requirement of identity of parties, which is an essential requirement for the use of claim preclusion, also be a prerequisite to invoke issue preclusion? For example, suppose you and your friend are injured in an automobile accident when the car in which both of you are seated falls into a huge sinkhole on a city street. As you read the materials in the next section of this Chapter, consider the following scenarios:

(a) If you sue the City for your damages and the City is found non-negligent, should the City be allowed to preclude your friend from relitigating the issue of its negligence in the friend's lawsuit against the City?

(b) If each of you chooses to file a separate negligence action against the City, and the first litigated case results in a finding that the City was negligent, should your friend be able to preclude the City from relitigating the issue of its non-negligence?

(c) If in your action against the City, the jury finds that you were negligent, if you subsequently file an action against the manufacturer of your car, can the manufacturer preclude you from relitigating the issue of your non-negligence?

---

2. PARTIES SUBJECT TO ISSUE PRECLUSION: THE DEATH OF MUTUALITY

Parklane Hosiery Company, Inc. v. Shore

Supreme Court of the United States, 1979.

439 U.S. 322, 99 S.Ct. 645, 58 L.Ed.2d 552.

MR. JUSTICE STEWART delivered the opinion of the Court.

This case presents the question whether a party who has had issues of fact adjudicated adversely to it in an equitable action may be collaterally estopped from relitigating the same issues before a jury in a subsequent legal action brought against it by a new party.

The respondent brought this stockholder's class action against the petitioners in a Federal District Court. The complaint alleged that the petitioners, Parklane

Hosiery Co., Inc. (Parklane), and 13 of its officers, directors, and stockholders, had issued a materially false and misleading proxy statement in connection with a merger. The proxy statement, according to the complaint, had violated §§14(a), 10(b), and 20(a) of the Securities Exchange Act of 1934, as well as various rules and regulations promulgated by the Securities and Exchange Commission (SEC). The complaint sought damages, rescission of the merger, and recovery of costs.

Before this action came to trial, the SEC filed suit against the same defendants in the Federal District Court, alleging that the proxy statement that had been issued by Parklane was materially false and misleading in essentially the same respects as those that had been alleged in the respondent's complaint. Injunctive relief was requested. After a 4-day trial, the District Court found that the proxy statement was materially false and misleading in the respects alleged, and entered a declaratory judgment to that effect. The Court of Appeals for the Second Circuit affirmed this judgment.

The respondent in the present case then moved for partial summary judgment against the petitioners, asserting that the petitioners were collaterally estopped from relitigating the issues that had been resolved against them in the action brought by the SEC.[2] The District Court denied the motion on the ground that such an application of collateral estoppel would deny the petitioners their Seventh Amendment right to a jury trial. The * * * Second Circuit reversed, holding that a party who has had issues of fact determined against him after a full and fair opportunity to litigate in a nonjury trial is collaterally estopped from obtaining a subsequent jury trial of these same issues of fact. * * *

I

The threshold question to be considered is whether, quite apart from the right to a jury trial under the Seventh Amendment, the petitioners can be precluded from relitigating facts resolved adversely to them in a prior equitable proceeding with another party under the general law of collateral estoppel. Specifically, we must determine whether a litigant who was not a party to a prior judgment may nevertheless use that judgment "offensively" to prevent a defendant from relitigating issues resolved in the earlier proceeding.[4]

A

Collateral estoppel, like the related doctrine of res judicata, has the dual purpose of protecting litigants from the burden of relitigating an identical issue with the same party or his privy and of promoting judicial economy by

---

[2] A private plaintiff in an action under the proxy rules is not entitled to relief simply by demonstrating that the proxy solicitation was materially false and misleading. The plaintiff must also show that he was injured and prove damages. Since the SEC action was limited to a determination of whether the proxy statement contained materially false and misleading information, the respondent conceded that he would still have to prove these other elements of his prima facie case in the private action. The petitioners' right to a jury trial on those remaining issues is not contested.

[4] In this context, offensive use of collateral estoppel occurs when the plaintiff seeks to foreclose the defendant from litigating an issue the defendant has previously litigated unsuccessfully in an action with another party. Defensive use occurs when a defendant seeks to prevent a plaintiff from asserting a claim the plaintiff has previously litigated and lost against another defendant.

preventing needless litigation. Until relatively recently, however, the scope of collateral estoppel was limited by the doctrine of mutuality of parties. Under this mutuality doctrine, neither party could use a prior judgment as an estoppel against the other unless both parties were bound by the judgment. Based on the premise that it is somehow unfair to allow a party to use a prior judgment when he himself would not be so bound,[7] the mutuality requirement provided a party who had litigated and lost in a previous action an opportunity to relitigate identical issues with new parties.

By failing to recognize the obvious difference in position between a party who has never litigated an issue and one who has fully litigated and lost, the mutuality requirement was criticized almost from its inception. Recognizing the validity of this criticism, the Court in Blonder-Tongue Laboratories, *supra*, abandoned the mutuality requirement, at least in cases where a patentee seeks to relitigate the validity of a patent after a federal court in a previous lawsuit has already declared it invalid. The "broader question" before the Court, however, was "whether it is any longer tenable to afford a litigant more than one full and fair opportunity for judicial resolution of the same issue." 402 U.S., at 328, 91 S.Ct., at 1442. The Court strongly suggested a negative answer to that question:

> "In any lawsuit where a defendant, because of the mutuality principle, is forced to present a complete defense on the merits to a claim which the plaintiff has fully litigated and lost in a prior action, there is an arguable misallocation of resources. To the extent the defendant in the second suit may not win by asserting, without contradiction, that the plaintiff had fully and fairly, but unsuccessfully, litigated the same claim in the prior suit, the defendant's time and money are diverted from alternative uses — productive or otherwise — to relitigation of a decided issue. And, still assuming that the issue was resolved correctly in the first suit, there is reason to be concerned about the plaintiff's allocation of resources. Permitting repeated litigation of the same issue as long as the supply of unrelated defendants holds out reflects * * * the aura of the gaming table * * *. Although neither judges, the parties, nor the adversary system performs perfectly in all cases, the requirement of determining whether the party against whom an estoppel is asserted had a full and fair opportunity to litigate is a most significant safeguard."

B

The *Blonder-Tongue* case involved defensive use of collateral estoppel — a plaintiff was estopped from asserting a claim that the plaintiff had previously litigated and lost against another defendant. The present case, by contrast, involves offensive use of collateral estoppel — a plaintiff is seeking to estop a defendant from relitigating the issues which the defendant previously litigated and lost against another plaintiff. In both the offensive and defensive use situations, the party against whom estoppel is asserted has litigated and lost in an earlier action. Nevertheless, several reasons have been advanced why the two

---

[7] It is a violation of due process for a judgment to be binding on a litigant who was not a party or a privy and therefore has never had an opportunity to be heard. Blonder-Tongue Laboratories, Inc. v. University of Illinois Foundation, 402 U.S. 313, 91 S.Ct. 1434, 28 L.Ed.2d 788 (1971).

situations should be treated differently.

First, offensive use of collateral estoppel does not promote judicial economy in the same manner as defensive use does. Defensive use of collateral estoppel precludes a plaintiff from relitigating identical issues by merely switching adversaries. Thus defensive collateral estoppel gives a plaintiff a strong incentive to join all potential defendants in the first action if possible. Offensive use of collateral estoppel, on the other hand, creates precisely the opposite incentive. Since a plaintiff will be able to rely on a previous judgment against a defendant but will not be bound by that judgment if the defendant wins, the plaintiff has every incentive to adopt a "wait and see" attitude, in the hope that the first action by another plaintiff will result in a favorable judgment. Thus offensive use of collateral estoppel will likely increase rather than decrease the total amount of litigation, since potential plaintiffs will have everything to gain and nothing to lose by not intervening in the first action.

A second argument against offensive use of collateral estoppel is that it may be unfair to a defendant. If a defendant in the first action is sued for small or nominal damages, he may have little incentive to defend vigorously, particularly if future suits are not foreseeable. Allowing offensive collateral estoppel may also be unfair to a defendant if the judgment relied upon as a basis for the estoppel is itself inconsistent with one or more previous judgments in favor of the defendant.[14] Still another situation where it might be unfair to apply offensive estoppel is where the second action affords the defendant procedural opportunities unavailable in the first action that could readily cause a different result.[15]

C

We have concluded that the preferable approach for dealing with these problems in the federal courts is not to preclude the use of offensive collateral estoppel, but to grant trial courts broad discretion to determine when it should be applied.[16] The general rule should be that in cases where a plaintiff could easily

---

[14] In Professor Currie's familiar example, a railroad collision injures 50 passengers all of whom bring separate actions against the railroad. After the railroad wins the first 25 suits, a plaintiff wins in suit 26. Professor Currie argues that offensive use of collateral estoppel should not be applied so as to allow plaintiffs 27 through 50 automatically to recover. Currie, Mutuality of Estoppel: Limits of the *Bernhard* Doctrine, 9 Stan.L.Rev. 281,304 (1957). See Restatement (Second) of Judgments §88(4).

[15] If, for example, the defendant in the first action was forced to defend in an inconvenient forum and therefore was unable to engage in full scale discovery or call witnesses, application of offensive collateral estoppel may be unwarranted. Indeed, differences in available procedures may sometimes justify not allowing a prior judgment to have estoppel effect in a subsequent action even between the same parties, or where defensive estoppel is asserted against a plaintiff who has litigated and lost. The problem of unfairness is particularly acute in cases of offensive estoppel, however, because the defendant against whom estoppel is asserted typically will not have chosen the forum in the first action.

[16] This is essentially the approach of [The Restatement (Second) of Judgments] §88, which recognizes that "the distinct trend if not the clear weight of recent authority is to the effect that there is no intrinsic difference between 'offensive' as distinct from 'defensive' issue preclusion, although a stronger showing that the prior opportunity to litigate was adequate may be required in the former situation than the latter." Reporter's Note, at 99.

have joined in the earlier action or where, either for the reasons discussed above or for other reasons, the application of offensive estoppel would be unfair to a defendant, a trial judge should not allow the use of offensive collateral estoppel.

In the present case, however, none of the circumstances that might justify reluctance to allow the offensive use of collateral estoppel is present. The application of offensive collateral estoppel will not here reward a private plaintiff who could have joined in the previous action, since the respondent probably could not have joined in the injunctive action brought by the SEC even had he so desired.[17] Similarly, there is no unfairness to the petitioners in applying offensive collateral estoppel in this case. First, in light of the serious allegations made in the SEC's complaint against the petitioners, as well as the foreseeability of subsequent private suits that typically follow a successful Government judgment, the petitioners had every incentive to litigate the SEC lawsuit fully and vigorously.[18] Second, the judgment in the SEC action was not inconsistent with any previous decision. Finally, there will in the respondent's action be no procedural opportunities available to the petitioners that were unavailable in the first action of a kind that might be likely to cause a different result.[19]

We conclude, therefore, that none of the considerations that would justify a refusal to allow the use of offensive collateral estoppel is present in this case. Since the petitioners received a "full and fair" opportunity to litigate their claims in the SEC action, the contemporary law of collateral estoppel leads inescapably to the conclusion that the petitioners are collaterally estopped from relitigating the question of whether the proxy statement was materially false and misleading.

II

The question that remains is whether, notwithstanding the law of collateral estoppel, the use of offensive collateral estoppel in this case would violate the petitioners' Seventh Amendment right to a jury trial.

A

"[T]he thrust of the [Seventh] Amendment was to preserve the right to jury trial as it existed in 1791." Curtis v. Loether, 415 U.S. 189, 193, 94 S.Ct. 1005, 1007, 39 L.Ed.2d 260. At common law, a litigant was not entitled to have a jury determine issues that had been previously adjudicated by a chancellor in equity.

* * *

* * * [I]n Katchen v. Landy, 382 U.S. 323, 86 S.Ct. 467, 15 L.Ed.2d 391 * * * the Court * * * recognized that an equitable determination can have collateral-estoppel effect in a subsequent legal action and that this estoppel does

---

[17] * * * [C]onsolidation of a private action with one brought by the SEC without its consent is prohibited by statute.

[18] * * * [T]he petitioners were already aware of the action brought by the respondent, since it had commenced before the filing of the SEC action.

[19] It is true, of course, that the petitioners in the present action would be entitled to a jury trial of the issues bearing on whether the proxy statement was materially false and misleading had the SEC action never been brought * * *. But the presence or absence of a jury as factfinder is basically neutral, quite unlike, for example, the necessity of defending the first lawsuit in an inconvenient forum.

968 CHAPTER 13: THE PRECLUSIVE EFFECT OF ADJUDICATION ON SUBSEQUENT LITIGATION

not violate the Seventh Amendment.

B

Despite the strong support to be found both in history and in the recent decisional law of this Court for the proposition that an equitable determination can have collateral-estoppel effect in a subsequent legal action, the petitioners argue that application of collateral estoppel in this case would nevertheless violate their Seventh Amendment right to a jury trial. The petitioners contend that since the scope of the Amendment must be determined by reference to the common law as it existed in 1791, and since the common law permitted collateral estoppel only where there was mutuality of parties, collateral estoppel cannot constitutionally be applied when such mutuality is absent.

The petitioners have advanced no persuasive reason, however, why the meaning of the Seventh Amendment should depend on whether or not mutuality of parties is present. A litigant who has lost because of adverse factual findings in an equity action is equally deprived of a jury trial whether he is estopped from relitigating the factual issues against the same party or a new party. In either case, the party against whom estoppel is asserted has litigated questions of fact, and has had the facts determined against him in an earlier proceeding. In either case there is no further factfinding function for the jury to perform, since the common factual issues have been resolved in the previous action.

The Seventh Amendment has never been interpreted in the rigid manner advocated by the petitioners. On the contrary, many procedural devices developed since 1791 that have diminished the civil jury's historic domain have been found not to be inconsistent with the Seventh Amendment. See Galloway v. United States, 319 U.S. 372, 388-393, 63 S.Ct. 1077, 1086-1088, 87 L.Ed. 1458 (directed verdict does not violate the Seventh Amendment); Gasoline Products Co. v. Champlin Refining Co., 283 U.S. 494, 497-498, 51 S.Ct. 513-514, 75 L.Ed. 1188 (retrial limited to question of damages does not violate the Seventh Amendment even though there was no practice at common law for setting aside a verdict in part); Fidelity & Deposit Co. v. United States, 187 U.S. 315, 319-321, 23 S.Ct. 120, 121-122, 47 L.Ed. 194 (summary judgment does not violate the Seventh Amendment).

* * *

The law of collateral estoppel, like the law in other procedural areas defining the scope of the jury's function, has evolved since 1791. * * * [T]hese developments are not repugnant to the Seventh Amendment simply for the reason that they did not exist in 1791. Thus if, as we have held, the law of collateral estoppel forecloses the petitioners from relitigating the factual issues determined against them in the SEC action, nothing in the Seventh Amendment dictates a different result, even though because of lack of mutuality there would have been no collateral estoppel in 1791.

The judgment of the Court of Appeals is affirmed.

MR. JUSTICE REHNQUIST, dissenting.

* * *

The right of trial by jury in civil cases at common law is fundamental to our history and jurisprudence. Today, however, the Court reduces this valued right, which Blackstone praised as "the glory of the English law," to a mere "neutral" factor and in the name of procedural reform denies the right of jury trial to defendants in a vast number of cases in which defendants, heretofore, have enjoyed jury trials.[1] * * *

I

* * *

* * * [T]he decision of this case turns on the scope and effect of the Seventh Amendment, which, perhaps more than with any other provision of the Constitution, are determined by reference to the historical setting in which the Amendment was adopted. * * *

A

* * *

* * * Responding to the pressures for a civil jury guarantee generated during the ratification debates, the first Congress under the new Constitution at its first session in 1789 proposed to amend the Constitution by adding the following language: "In suits at common law, between man and man, the trial by jury, as one of the best securities to the rights of the people, ought to remain inviolate." 1 Annals of Cong. 435 (1789). That provision, altered in language to what became the Seventh Amendment, was proposed by the Congress in 1789 to the legislatures of the several States and became effective with its ratification by Virginia on December 15, 1791.

* * * The founders of our Nation considered the right of trial by jury in civil cases an important bulwark against tyranny and corruption, a safeguard too precious to be left to the whim of the sovereign, or, it might be added, to that of the judiciary. Those who passionately advocated the right to a civil jury trial did not do so because they considered the jury a familiar procedural device that should be continued; the concerns for the institution of jury trial that led to the passages of the Declaration of Independence and to the Seventh Amendment were not animated by a belief that use of juries would lead to more efficient judicial administration. Trial by a jury of laymen rather than by the sovereign's judges was important to the founders because juries represent the layman's common sense, the "passional elements in our nature," and thus keep the administration of law in accord with the wishes and feelings of the community. O. Holmes, Collected Legal Papers 237 (1920). Those who favored juries believed that a jury would reach a result that a judge either could not or would not reach. It is with these values that underlie the Seventh Amendment in mind that the Court should, but obviously does not, approach the decision of this case.

B

The Seventh Amendment requires that the right of trial by jury be "preserved." Because the Seventh Amendment demands preservation of the jury

---

[1] Because I believe that the use of offensive collateral estoppel in this particular case was improper, it is not necessary for me to decide whether I would approve its use in circumstances where the defendant's right to a jury trial was not impaired.

trial right, our cases have uniformly held that the content of the right must be judged by historical standards. Thus, in Baltimore & Carolina Line v. Redman, 295 U.S. 654, 657, 55 S.Ct. 890, 891, 79 L.Ed. 1636 (1935), the Court stated that "[t]he right of trial by jury thus preserved is the right which existed under the English common law when the amendment was adopted." * * * If a jury would have been impaneled in a particular kind of case in 1791, then the Seventh Amendment requires a jury trial today, if either party so desires.

* * *

To say that the Seventh Amendment does not tie federal courts to the exact procedure of the common law in 1791 does not imply, however, that any nominally "procedural" change can be implemented, regardless of its impact on the functions of the jury. For to sanction creation of procedural devices which limit the province of the jury to a greater degree than permitted at common law in 1791 is in direct contravention of the Seventh Amendment. And since we deal here not with the common law *qua* common law but with the Constitution, no amount of argument that the device provides for more efficiency or more accuracy or is fairer will save it if the degree of invasion of the jury's province is greater than allowed in 1791. To rule otherwise would effectively permit judicial repeal of the Seventh Amendment because nearly any change in the province of the jury, no matter how drastic the diminution of its functions, can always be denominated "procedural reform."

* * *

C

Judged by the foregoing principles, I think it is clear that petitioners were denied their Seventh Amendment right to a jury trial in this case. Neither respondent nor the Court doubts that at common law as it existed in 1791, petitioners would have been entitled in the private action to have a jury determine whether the proxy statement was false and misleading in the respects alleged. The reason is that at common law in 1791, collateral estoppel was permitted only where the parties in the first action were identical to, or in privity with, the parties to the subsequent action. It was not until 1971 that the doctrine of mutuality was abrogated by this Court in certain limited circumstances. But developments in the judge-made doctrine of collateral estoppel, however salutary, cannot, consistent with the Seventh Amendment, contract in any material fashion the right to a jury trial that a defendant would have enjoyed in 1791. In the instant case, resort to the doctrine of collateral estoppel does more than merely contract the right to a jury trial: It eliminates the right entirely and therefore contravenes the Seventh Amendment.

The Court responds, however, that at common law "a litigant was not entitled to have a jury [in a subsequent action at law between the same parties] determine issues that had been previously adjudicated by a chancellor in equity," and that "petitioners have advanced no persuasive reason . . . why the meaning of the Seventh Amendment should depend on whether or not mutuality of parties is present." But that is tantamount to saying that since a party would not be entitled to a jury trial if he brought an equitable action, there is no persuasive reason why he should receive a jury trial on virtually the same issues if instead he chooses to bring his lawsuit in the nature of a legal action. The persuasive reason is that the Seventh Amendment requires that a party's right to jury trial which existed at common law be "preserved" from incursions by the government or the judiciary. Whether this Court believes that use of a jury trial in a particular instance is necessary, or fair or repetitive is simply irrelevant. If that view is "rigid," it is the Constitution which commands that rigidity. To hold otherwise is to rewrite the Seventh Amendment so that a party is guaranteed a jury trial in civil cases unless this Court thinks that a jury trial would be inappropriate.

No doubt parallel "procedural reforms" could be instituted in the area of criminal jurisprudence, which would accomplish much the same sort of expedition of court calendars and conservation of judicial resources as would the extension of collateral estoppel in civil litigation. Government motions for summary judgment, or for a directed verdict in favor of the prosecution at the close of the evidence, would presumably save countless hours of judges' and jurors' time. It can scarcely be doubted, though, that such "procedural reforms" would not survive constitutional scrutiny under the jury trial guarantee of the Sixth Amendment. Just as the principle of separation of powers was not incorporated by the Framers into the Constitution in order to promote efficiency or dispatch in the business of government, the right to a jury trial was not guaranteed in order to facilitate prompt and accurate decision of lawsuits. The essence of that right lies in its insistence that a body of laymen not permanently attached to the sovereign participate along with the judge in the factfinding necessitated by a lawsuit. And that essence is as much a part of the Seventh Amendment's guarantee in civil cases as it is of the Sixth Amendment's guarantee in criminal prosecutions.

* * * [T]he Court's actions today constitute a far greater infringement of the defendant's rights than it ever before has sanctioned. In *Galloway*, the Court upheld the modern form of directed verdict against a Seventh Amendment challenge, but it is clear that a similar form of directed verdict existed at common law in 1791. The modern form did not materially alter the function of the jury. Similarly, the modern device of summary judgment was found not to violate the Seventh Amendment because in 1791 a demurrer to the evidence, a procedural device substantially similar to summary judgment was a common practice. The procedural devices of summary judgment and directed verdict are direct descendants of their common-law antecedents. They accomplish nothing more than could have been done at common law, albeit by a more cumbersome procedure. * * *

By contrast, the development of nonmutual estoppel is a substantial departure from the common law and its use in this case completely deprives petitioners of their right to have a jury determine contested issues of fact. I am simply unwilling to accept the Court's presumption that the complete extinguishment of petitioners' right to trial by jury can be justified as a mere change in "procedural incident or detail." * * *

II

Even accepting, *arguendo*, the majority's position that there is no violation of the Seventh Amendment here, I nonetheless would not sanction the use of collateral estoppel in this case. * * *

* * *

* * * [T]he use of offensive collateral estoppel in this case runs counter to the strong federal policy favoring jury trials, even if it does not, as the majority holds, violate the Seventh Amendment. * * * Today's decision will mean that in a large number of private cases defendants will no longer enjoy the right to jury trial.[20] Neither the Court nor respondent has adverted or cited to any unmanageable problems that have resulted from according defendants jury trials in such cases. I simply see no "imperative circumstances" requiring this wholesale abrogation of jury trials.

* * * I believe that the opportunity for a jury trial in the second action could easily lead to a different result from that obtained in the first action before the court and therefore that it is unfair to estop petitioners from relitigating the issues before a jury. This is the position adopted in the Restatement (Second) of Judgments, which disapproves of the application of offensive collateral estoppel where the defendant has an opportunity for a jury trial in the second lawsuit that was not available in the first action. The Court accepts the proposition that it is unfair to apply offensive collateral estoppel "where the second action affords the defendant procedural opportunities unavailable in the first action that could readily cause a different result." Differences in discovery opportunities between the two actions are cited as examples of situations where it would be unfair to permit offensive collateral estoppel. But in the Court's view, the fact that petitioners would have been entitled to a jury trial in the present action is not such a "procedural opportunit[y]" because "the presence or absence of a jury as factfinder is basically neutral, quite unlike, for example, the necessity of defending the first lawsuit in an inconvenient forum."

As is evident from the prior brief discussion of the development of the civil jury trial guarantee in this country, those who drafted the Declaration of Independence and debated so passionately the proposed Constitution during the ratification period, would indeed be astounded to learn that the presence or absence of a jury is merely "neutral," whereas the availability of discovery, a device unmentioned in the Constitution, may be controlling. It is precisely because the Framers believed that they might receive a different result at the hands of a jury of their peers than at the mercy of the sovereign's judges, that the Seventh Amendment was adopted. And I suspect that anyone who litigates cases before juries in the 1970's would be equally amazed to hear of the supposed lack of distinction between trial by court and trial by jury. The Court can cite no authority in support of this curious proposition. The merits of civil juries have been long debated, but I suspect that juries have never been accused of being merely "neutral" factors.

* * *

_____

[20] The Court's decision today may well extend to other areas, such as antitrust, labor, employment discrimination, consumer protection, and the like, where a private plaintiff may sue for damages based on the same or similar violations that are the subject of government actions.

The ultimate irony of today's decision is that its potential for significantly conserving the resources of either the litigants or the judiciary is doubtful at best. That being the case, I see absolutely no reason to frustrate so cavalierly the important federal policy favoring jury decisions of disputed fact questions. The instant case is an apt example of the minimal savings that will be accomplished by the Court's decision. As the Court admits, even if petitioners are collaterally estopped from relitigating whether the proxy was materially false and misleading, they are still entitled to have a jury determine whether respondent was injured by the alleged misstatements and the amount of damages, if any, sustained by respondent. Thus, a jury must be impaneled in this case in any event. The time saved by not trying the issue of whether the proxy was materially false and misleading before the jury is likely to be insubstantial. It is just as probable that today's decision will have the result of coercing defendants to agree to consent orders or settlements in agency enforcement actions in order to preserve their right to jury trial in the private actions. In that event, the Court, for no compelling reason, will have simply added a powerful club to the administrative agencies' arsenals that even Congress was unwilling to provide them.

NOTES AND PROBLEMS FOR DISCUSSION

1. What were the two preeminent issues decided by the Supreme Court in *Parklane*?

2. Other than for purposes of doctrinal symmetry, why was the claim preclusion requirement of identity of parties also, prior to the Court's rulings in *Blonder-Tongue* and *Parklane*, applied to issue preclusion?

3. The *Parklane* Court makes repeated references to the offensive and defensive uses of collateral estoppel/issue preclusion.

(a) What characterizes the offensive and defensive uses of nonmutual issue preclusion?

(b) Under what circumstances did the *Parklane* Court conditionally approve the use of either offensive or defensive nonmutual issue preclusion?

4. Quite aside from the question of whether nonparties can invoke issue preclusion, the Court in *Parklane* noted that the common law requirement of mutuality of parties always was deemed satisfied by the presence of either the identical parties or their privies. (The same rule also applies to claim preclusion.) The recognition of a "privity" exception to the due process rule underlying mutuality of parties (i.e., that a litigant cannot be bound to an adverse decision in a case in which it did not participate) is justified on the ground that the privity relationship provides assurance that the interests of the unnamed party were adequately represented by the actions of its privy in the first proceeding. Or, to put it simply, the stranger to the first proceeding did have its "day in court." Thus, in its most conclusory terms, privity connotes that relationship between a named and unnamed party to a proceeding that justifies binding the nonparty to a decision rendered against the privy. But the courts have not been able to agree upon a more exacting definition of this term. In fact, the Restatement (Second) of Judgments does not even refer to "privity," but, rather, lists discrete categories of nonparties subject to claim and issue preclusion. Nevertheless, courts have found the existence of a privity relationship when the named and unnamed parties share the same legal rights in some relevant sense. This sharing of rights, in turn, is generally found when either (a) the named party assigned or transferred its interest in property to the unnamed party, or (b) the unnamed party authorized the named party to litigate on its behalf and ceded control over that litigation to the named party. Examples of privity relationships falling into these categories include, respectively, (a) successors in interest, and (b) trustees, guardians, executors, or membership organizations such as labor unions.

On the other hand, privity is not established merely by demonstrating that persons are interested in the same question or in proving or disproving the same factor set of facts. Cf. Taylor v. Sturgell, 553 U.S. 880, 128 S.Ct. 2161, 171 L.Ed.2d 155 (2008) (discussed above in Section C) (renouncing a "virtual representation" exception to nonparty preclusion in federal question cases). For example, in MAZZIOTTI v. ALLSTATE INSURANCE CO., 240 Conn. 799, 695 A.2d 1010 (1997), an insured who obtained judgment against an underinsured tortfeasor and then sued his (the plaintiff's) insurer to recover underinsured motorist benefits was not permitted to invoke issue preclusion against the insurer with respect to the liability and damages determinations in the initial suit. The Connecticut Supreme Court held that the plaintiff's insurer was not in privity with the tortfeasor. As the court explained, even though the tortfeasor and the insurance company shared a common interest with respect to the issues of the tortfeasor's negligence and the extent of the insured's damages, they did not share the same legal rights because the insured's suit to recover under the insurance policy against the insurer was an action in contract while his claim for damages against the tortfeasor was an action in tort. The court also found an absence of privity on the ground that since the tortfeasor had limited exposure under his own insurance policy, he had little incentive to litigate against a recovery in excess of that amount, and that the plaintiff's insurer, with five times the risk, had such a significantly greater incentive to litigate that its interests were not sufficiently represented by the tortfeasor in the prior action.

5. (a) Should the ruling in *Parklane* equally apply when offensive nonmutual issue preclusion is asserted against the federal government rather than against private defendants? In U.S. v. MENDOZA, 464 U.S. 154, 104 S.Ct. 568, 78 L.Ed.2d 379 (1984), a Filipino national petitioned for naturalization based on his service in the American army during World War II. Although the federal statute providing for naturalization under these circumstances had expired prior to his filing of the naturalization petition, he claimed that the government's manner of enforcement of that statute during its effective period violated his rights to due process of law under the U.S. Constitution. He also maintained that the government was estopped from relitigating this issue by a prior ruling against the government on this issue in an unappealed federal district court decision in a separate action brought by other Filipino nationals.

The Supreme Court rejected the plaintiff's argument. It unanimously ruled that in light of the breadth of cases involving the federal government that address issues of national significance warranting relitigation (particularly cases involving constitutional questions where, because of the state action requirement, the government is always a party), offensive nonmutual issue preclusion could not be asserted against the federal government. Since the government was more likely than any private litigant to be involved in suits against different parties raising common issues, the Court concluded that the interest in conserving judicial resources was trumped by the need to promote a considered development of legal doctrine that is achieved by permitting the different circuit courts to independently explore difficult issues. As the Court explained, it was more important in this context to obtain "a second opinion" than to "freeze the first final decision" rendered on an issue. It also stated that the repeated application of offensive nonmutual preclusion against the government would so impair the opportunity for different circuits to consider the same legal issue that it might have to revise its policy of tying the granting of petitions for certiorari to the presence of a conflict between the circuits. Similarly, it explained, to avoid the consequences of a widespread availability of offensive nonmutual issue preclusion, the Solicitor General (who, unlike private litigants, considers factors other than the likelihood of success in determining which cases to appeal) would likely be compelled to appeal every adverse ruling. And the Court also acknowledged that the application of nonmutual issue preclusion against the government would also severely constrict the opportunity for successive presidential administrations to change the government's position on legal issues of national importance.

Although the Court stated in *Mendoza* that it would not permit the use of offensive nonmutual issue preclusion against the federal government with respect to issues "such as those involved in this case," it did not offer an example of a situation in which preclusion would be permitted. Nor did it articulate any standard by which it defined "issues such as this". However, the Court did emphasize that its ruling was limited to cases involving offensive nonmutual issue preclusion against the federal government, by noting that in U.S. v. Stauffer Chemical Co., 464 U.S. 165, 104 S.Ct. 575, 78 L.Ed.2d 388 (1984), a companion case decided on the same day as *Mendoza*, it reaffirmed that both claim preclusion and issue preclusion are available against the government when the parties to both lawsuits are the same.

(b) Should the ruling in *Mendoza* be extended to cases involving state government defendants? See Chambers v. Ohio Dep't of Human Services, 145 F.3d 793 (6th Cir.), cert. denied, 525 U.S. 964, 119 S.Ct. 408, 142 L.Ed.2d 331 (1998) (extending *Mendoza* rule to claim against state agency).

6. (a) In mass tort cases (such as an airplane crash or environmental disaster) or mass products liability actions (such as asbestosis or smoking), the various claimants frequently choose to file separate actions against their common opponent. Assume that the defendant is found non-negligent in each of the first round of such cases. Clearly, the defendant would be constitutionally barred from invoking nonmutual collateral estoppel against future plaintiffs because its non-negligence was determined in lawsuits to which these plaintiffs were not a party. But also suppose that in one of those subsequently filed cases, the defendant is found negligent. Does footnote 14 of *Parklane* offer guidance into whether plaintiffs thereafter can bind the defendant to that adverse determination?

(b) On the other hand, suppose the plaintiff in the first of these many anticipated lawsuits obtains a favorable result. Should this single ruling be accorded preclusive effect on all of the succeeding actions simply because of the fortuity that the defendant lost the first filed case?

7. Should issue preclusion be applied in the following situations?

(a) A professional basketball player is driving in a car with his high school coach when they are involved in a collision with another car. The player breaks both of his legs, while the coach walks away with a few scratches and minor medical bills. In the coach's personal injury action against the driver of the other car, the jury finds that the defendant was negligent and awards the plaintiff the entire $5,000 sought in his complaint. When the player files his action against the driver, can he preclude the driver from relitigating the issue of the driver's negligence?

(b) In a tort action brought in state court against the driver of a car, the jury finds that the plaintiff was negligent. Subsequently, the plaintiff brings another tort claim against the owner of that same car in connection with the same collision. But this second suit is filed in federal court based on diversity of jurisdiction. Can the defendant preclude the plaintiff from relitigating the issue of the plaintiff's negligence in the second action when the state preclusion law of the state in which the first case was adjudicated requires mutuality of estoppel?

(c) Assume all the facts set forth in "(b)," *supra*, except that the first action was filed in federal court and the second in state court. Can the defendant successfully invoke issue preclusion in the second case?

CHAPTER 14

Alternatives to Litigation — ADR

Section A. General Overview

The preceding thirteen chapters of this book have focused exclusively on issues arising out of the use of civil litigation as *the* method by which legal disputes are resolved. But litigation is neither the sole method nor even the primary vehicle for settling disputes. To the contrary, only a tiny fraction of conflicts are resolved via adjudication in a lawsuit. In the overwhelming majority of instances, the denouement is the product of private negotiation, mediation, arbitration, ombudspersons, mini-trials, special masters, private judges or hybrid combinations of any of these alternative mechanisms. And while the subject of alternative (to litigation) dispute resolution (ADR) is, quite properly, the subject of an entirely separate course, it is essential for any student of civil procedure to have a basic familiarity with the nature of these alternative approaches, their comparative advantages and disadvantages and the most pressing legal issues associated with their use. The following materials are provided to that end.

ADR mechanisms come in a variety of flavors; some exist as adjuncts to the judicial system and others are free standing and invoked by private agreement. And while some share common features, all, of course, share the ultimate objective of resolving legal disputes.

These various techniques fall along a continuum of third party interventionism from purely advisory processes such as mediation and neutral fact finding to fully adjudicatory mechanisms like arbitration. They also vary widely with respect to their level of procedural formality. The following is a brief description of the most commonly employed ADR processes.

Negotiation: a process by which the parties, with or without counsel, exchange proposals and counterproposals in the absence of a third party in the hope of achieving a voluntary settlement of the dispute.

Neutral Fact Finding: the parties agree to submit a particular factual issue or issues to a neutral third party who can hold a hearing, receive submissions, and/ or conduct an independent investigation. The neutral reports his findings to the parties who are free then to accept or ignore them. If settlement is not achieved, this report can be introduced into evidence at trial.

Ombudsman: a neutral third-party fact finder selected to investigate complaints from an organization's employees or clients. She makes nonbinding advisory recommendations to the organization about how to resolve the dispute, but typically does not have decision-making authority. The ombudsman is compensated by the organization and is frequently a salaried employee. Nevertheless, he is not expected to act as an agent of the organization but, rather, to fairly evaluate each claim on its merits.

Mediation: a confidential, purely advisory procedure whereby parties retain the services of a neutral third party to act as a facilitator and sounding board with the express purpose of aiding the parties to achieve a voluntary, negotiated settlement of their dispute. The third party does not possess any authority to resolve the dispute, and typically refrains from assessing the strengths and weaknesses of each party's positions. This non-evaluative approach is pursued in order to maintain trust and credibility and to encourage the parties to focus on their needs or interests instead of their respective legal rights or obligations in order to fashion a "win-win" result. The parties can appear with or without counsel, and although participants in mediation are never required to agree to a settlement, participation in the process itself can be either voluntary or compulsory. Resort to mediation is increasingly contained in commercial and employment contracts as a prerequisite to suit and, in what is referred to as court-annexed mediation, some state and federal courts are requiring resort to mediation as a prerequisite to trial.

Early Neutral Evaluation (ENE): a court-annexed, confidential, non-adjudicative technique designed either to produce voluntary settlements at an early stage of the pre-trial process or to improve case management efficiency. The parties make a factual presentation and legal argument to a third party neutral at an early stage in the litigation. This neutral is chosen, by consent or by the court, because of her expertise in the underlying subject matter. After the parties' presentations, she identifies the strengths and weaknesses of each side's position, estimates the cost and duration of litigation, and offers her expert assessment of the merits, all in an attempt either to effectuate a settlement or, at least, to expedite the pace of subsequent proceedings.

Contractual Arbitration: an adjudicative process in which the parties to a contract agree to submit designated classes of disputes to a neutral third party or panel that is empowered to issue a final and binding decision on the merits. The decision is rendered after a full hearing with counsel given the opportunity to present evidence and to engage in examination and cross-examination of witnesses, although generally not subject to the formal rules of evidence that govern judicial trials. This process results in a quicker and less costly resolution of the dispute than a trial. The arbitrator issues a written opinion, although he is often not required to supply any explanation or reasoning to justify the decision.

Certain variations on the general arbitral scheme also exist. In **final offer arbitration,** the parties agree to limit the role of the arbitrator to choosing between each side's final proposal. This is the procedure used in the arbitration of certain contractual disputes involving professional baseball players. In **med-arb**, a hybrid of mediation and arbitration, the neutral initially acts as a mediator, but if settlement is not achieved through this process, the neutral is authorized by the parties to conduct an arbitration hearing and issue a decision that can be either final and binding or merely advisory.

Court-Annexed Arbitration: as prescribed either by court rule or statute, certain categories of cases must go through the arbitration process. Beyond being compulsory, the major difference between court-annexed and contractual arbitration is that arbitral decisions rendered in court-administered arbitration are nonbinding. The arbitrator's ruling is intended to provide the parties with an assessment of their case for settlement purposes. The parties are provided with a specified time frame after the arbitrator's decision is issued within which to decide whether to undertake a trial *de novo* or not. If a party chooses to go to trial, it is usually subject to the imposition of some penalty when the resulting judgment did not place that party in a better position than the arbitrator's proposed award. On the other hand, if the parties agree to accept the arbitrator's decision, it is transformed into a final judgment of the court.

Mini-Trial: a form of advisory arbitration where the parties engage in limited discovery and appear, with counsel, in a confidential proceeding tailored to their particular needs and requirements although usually subject to the evidentiary and procedural rules governing a trial. After this abbreviated form of private trial, the neutral offers her assessment of the merits to the parties. Lawyers often choose this modality in order to expose their clients to the realities of litigation without being subject to all of its expense and time commitment.

Summary Jury Trial: after the trial has begun, each side makes a presentation, with witnesses and other testimony, to a jury within a set time period and subject to the governing rules of evidence and procedure. A judge presides over the proceeding, although usually not the trial judge. This process is designed to enhance the chances of settlement by providing the clients with a "day in court" as well as an assessment of their presentation from the jurors both in the form of a formal, though nonbinding, verdict and in post-event debriefings. If the parties are unable or unwilling to settle the case, it is set for trial *de novo*. Occasionally, the parties agree in advance to be bound by the jury's decision, and in a **hi-low summary jury trial**, the parties set a maximum and minimum limit on recovery. This provides the plaintiff with protection against a defense verdict and caps the defendant's liability.

Rent-A-Judge: the real life version of Judges Wapner, Judy and Jerry, in which the parties try the case before a privately retained "judge" or referee under somewhat more liberal rules of evidence and procedure that those that would apply at trial. The judge renders a decision that is final and binding.

Developments in the Law, The Paths of Civil Litigation

113 Harv.L.Rev. 1752,1851-1862 (2000).

* * *

Any discussion of recent developments in civil litigation must address the virtual revolution that has taken place regarding alternative dispute resolution (ADR). Attorneys have witnessed a steady growth in their clients' recourse to ADR in place of lawsuits, and ADR is increasingly incorporated into the litigation process itself--in the form of court-annexed arbitration, mediation, summary jury trials, early neutral evaluation, and judicial settlement conferences. "Alternative" models of dispute resolution have inarguably penetrated the mainstream; the relevant question now is how they will change it.

* * *

The oft-cited statistic that fewer than ten percent of all cases filed result in a judicially adjudicated decision reflects the salience of settlement negotiation as the primary vehicle of private dispute resolution. More formal mechanisms of private dispute resolution are also longstanding; arbitration in commercial settings and mediation by community leaders have provided effective means of conflict management for centuries. During the first half of the twentieth century, large-scale collective bargaining disputes encouraged the development of professional mediation, and some courts began experimenting with mediation in the 1950s to resolve minor criminal and family disputes. In the 1960s, local communities established neighborhood justice centers to provide facilitative dispute resolution services for neighbors, families, tenants, and consumers.

The Birth of the Modern ADR Movement

In the 1970s, jurists began to voice concerns about the rising costs and increasing delays associated with litigation, and some envisioned cheaper, faster, less formal, and more effective dispute resolution in such alternatives as arbitration and mediation. As the use of ADR mechanisms grew, proponents viewed them as promising vehicles for an array of agendas. Jurists hoped ADR would relieve docket congestion, while litigators — especially repeat players in the insurance and securities industries — were attracted to its promise of cheaper, faster resolution of claims that raised no new issues of law. Community development advocates hoped ADR would provide broader access to dispute resolution for those unable to afford traditional litigation. In the 1980s, social scientists, game theorists, and other scholars showed how ADR mechanisms could facilitate settlement by dealing proactively with heuristic biases through the strategic imposition of a neutral third party. Meanwhile, process-oriented ADR advocates emphasized that problem-solving approaches would yield remedies better tailored to parties' unique needs and that the more direct involvement of disputants would encourage greater compliance with outcomes and help rebuild ruptured relationships. Some supporters lauded ADR for its potential to restore a culture of civility to the legal system.

As ADR gained prominence in judicial, academic, and private circles, it also attracted the attention of critics. In the first serious attack on ADR, Professor Owen Fiss exhorted the legal community not to subordinate what he considered the primary function of the judiciary — the articulation of public values through the application of legal principles — to its ancillary role of resolving private disputes. Subsequent critical scholarship has continued to press the concern that ADR falls too far on the private law side of the public/private quandary, threatening rights-based jurisprudence and the rule of law, public accountability, and even the judiciary itself. Some proceduralist critics fear that ADR's negotiation-based approach may disempower vulnerable parties with limited bargaining strength, particularly civil rights and family law disputants.

Furthermore, critics argue that ADR fails to address real problems of the legal system. Skeptics challenge the notion that ADR is more efficient than litigation, questioning whether it really saves time or money and disputing the asserted judicial overload itself. Others worry that ADR creates ethical problems for practitioners. At least one scholar suggests that many benefits of ADR have already been diminished over the course of its institutionalization, which has gradually rendered ADR more like the system it sought to transform.

ADR at the Turn of the Century

Even as jurists debated the merits of the budding ADR movement, contractual arbitration and, later, mediation developed as preferred methods of dispute resolution in major areas of law practice, especially commercial and employment law, as well as in the administration of mass insurance claims and class action torts. ADR mechanisms nurtured in the neighborhood justice centers of the 1960s emerged by the late 1990s as the darlings of the business world for their cost efficiency and facilitation of continuing business relationships. In a 1997 Price Waterhouse survey of the "Fortune 1000" companies, nearly all of the 530 respondents had used some form of ADR, and ninety percent classified ADR as a "critical cost control technique." Private ADR vendors and law firms' ADR practice groups began to market their services more widely.

Today, contractual ADR use continues to expand in the construction, health care, entertainment, telecommunications, intellectual property, and technology industries. ADR is proving significant in the resolution of environmental and other public policy disputes, and mediation techniques are increasingly used in community fora addressing juvenile justice and violence in schools. ADR is also apt for disputes involving online commerce between geographically disparate parties, and a rapidly developing area of ADR is on the Internet itself, where an array of dispute resolution services are available online. Finally, increased international exchange has led to the widespread adoption of ADR in international arenas that lack a uniform set of legal and cultural expectations regarding the management of disputes. * * *

* * * The practice of ADR has coalesced into two realms: the private (or "contractual") sphere, in which parties agree to submit disputes to nonjudicial fora of resolution, and the judicial (or "court-annexed") sphere, in which litigants engage in ADR through the court system, sometimes at their option and sometimes as mandated by statute or local rule. Private ADR receives only limited judicial review, as courts presume that participation in arbitration is consensual and as mediated settlements are consensual by definition. In contrast, the results of court-annexed arbitration are rarely binding, and though good-faith participation in court-annexed mediation may be compelled, parties are not required to reach agreement.

Mediation

According to a 1996 study of the federal courts by the Federal Judicial Center and the Center for Public Resources, mediation is the most prevalent form of court-annexed ADR. In 1996, over half of all federal district courts provided mediation services, generally in-house or in cooperation with an external ADR provider. Although outcomes in court-annexed mediation remain consensual, courts often compel participation by certain claimants. * * *

Arbitration

As of 1999, statute or local rule provided for court-annexed arbitration in thirty-three states and twenty-two federal district courts. Federal courts generally do not compel participation in court-annexed arbitration, but the same is not true of state courts. Although judicial arbitration is rarely binding, courts may impose disincentives for rejecting the arbitrator's decision — for example, requiring that respondents who achieve results in subsequent trials as or less favorable to the arbitration award pay fines or fees.

Other Forms of ADR

Mediation and arbitration remain the most widespread forms of ADR, but practitioners continue to develop additional problem-solving means of resolving disputes. Summary jury trial, a mock trial settlement device, involves the truncated presentation of evidence and argument before a judge and a jury, which renders a nonbinding decision; afterward, the parties engage in better-informed settlement negotiations. Similarly, in early neutral evaluation, a knowledgeable third-party neutral meets with the parties before litigation begins and evaluates their positions on the merits, facilitating more realistic settlement negotiation. Courts are also experimenting with the use of minitrials and special settlement masters. Finally, judicially mandated settlement conferences, in which judges attempt to mediate settlement negotiations during the pre-trial phase, are now routine in many courts.

* * *

Statutory Developments

Overturning the traditional common law doctrine declining enforcement of arbitration agreements, Congress first declared a national policy favoring arbitration in 1925 with passage of the Federal Arbitration Act (FAA), which rendered contracts to arbitrate binding and provided federal recognition of arbitration awards. In 1990, Congress passed the Administrative Dispute Resolution Act, which authorized federal agencies to use a full range of ADR mechanisms and required them to explore how use of ADR could advance their missions. In 1996, Congress significantly extended the scope of the Act by authorizing true binding arbitration for federal agencies, simplifying the procedural requirements for negotiated rulemaking, and enhancing confidentiality protections.

At the same time, the judiciary fostered the paradigm shift toward pre-trial settlement through Rule 16 of the Federal Rules of Civil Procedure, which facilitated settlements by granting trial courts discretion to convene pre-trial settlement conferences. Amendments to Rule 16 in 1983 required judges to address the possibility of using extrajudicial procedures to resolve disputes, and further amendments in 1993 specified these procedures as ADR. The promotion of settlement by the evolving Federal Rules has, as powerfully as any legislative action, laid the foundation for our modern culture of settlement.

The 1990 passage of the Civil Justice Reform Act (CJRA), which authorized the federal judiciary to implement pilot court-annexed ADR programs, closed the divide between legislative and judicial postures toward ADR. In 1993 and 1994, based on the success of such programs, legislators proposed mandating the provision of court-annexed arbitration in federal district courts, but the judiciary insisted that such provision be optional. The compromise plan continued authorization of the twenty districts with existing ADR programs — ten of which could provide only voluntary, nonbinding arbitration and ten of which could, at their option, require participation in arbitration programs.

The most important statutory development to date, the Alternative Dispute Resolution Act (ADRA) of 1998, mandates that every federal district court implement an ADR program * * *. The Act requires federal civil litigants to consider ADR at appropriate stages in litigation and instructs each district court to offer at least one ADR alternative. Significantly, the Act authorizes courts to compel participation in mediation or early neutral evaluation processes but requires consent for court-annexed arbitration. Although the judicialization of ADR may itself raise threshold questions, the most troubling aspect of the statute is the lack of procedural guidelines provided for courts required to implement ADR programs. * * * The discretion afforded individual courts to determine the nature and extent of annexed ADR programs may encourage helpful evolution of ADR, but it may also lead to undesirable variety in procedure and practice. Furthermore, the Act appropriates no funding to implement programs, rendering impotent hopes of significant innovations in courts already struggling to cover basic expenses. * * *

SECTION B. A COMPARATIVE ASSESSMENT OF ADR AND LITIGATION: BOUQUETS, BATS AND STATS

Compare the two perspectives on the virtues and vices of ADR mechanisms reflected in the following two excerpted publications:

Jethro K. Lieberman & James F. Henry, Lessons from the Alternative Dispute Resolution Movement

53 U.Chi.L.Rev. 424, 425-435 (1986).

* * *

What often prevents disputes from being resolved is a failure to communicate stemming from a lack of trust between the parties. ADR is premised on the hypothesis that if the parties could overcome this distrust, they could voluntarily reach a settlement as just as the result a court would impose.

The adversary process — the engine of the adjudicatory system — operates on a theory of fundamental distrust: Never put faith in the adversary. Litigation thus becomes formal, tricky, divisive, time-consuming, and distorting. These characteristics are reflected in the common image of discovery in large-scale commercial cases that takes years to conduct, in the careful coaching and preparation of witnesses, and in the skillful impeachment of sound witnesses during cross-examination. In contrast, the creation of trust is central to the design of many ADR processes.

* * *

One lesson that ADR teaches * * * is that processes designed to restore and build trust can overcome the suspicion and mutual hostility fostered by the adversary system and can lead the parties to settle their differences. When the substantive outcome is compared to the likely result in court — and the costs of continued litigation are weighed in the balance — both parties generally benefit from ADR.

* * * [T]he results of ADR are often superior to court judgments — and even more clearly superior to conventional settlements.

First, adjudication is characterized by a "winner-take-all" outcome. This cannot be wholly true, for jury damage awards can work compromises, and the parties can shape consent decrees through bargaining. Nevertheless, in many cases, the fundamental issue of liability can be resolved only by holding for the plaintiff or the defendant. ADR, by contrast, is not bound by the zero-sum game of adjudication. While we have defined ADR as concerned with "legal disputes," participants in ADR are free to go beyond the legal definition of the scope of their dispute. They can search for creative solutions to the problem that gave rise to the dispute, and those solutions may be far more novel than any remedy a court has the power to provide.

Second, in classes of cases involving complex institutions, negotiations conducted by executives are likely to yield results superior to those conducted by the lawyers. The executives are far more familiar than their lawyers with the nuances of their business and can respond more quickly and creatively to proposals raised by their counterparts. We do not mean to diminish the role or responsibilities of lawyers in the negotiations; their legal knowledge will often be crucial to successful settlements and good lawyer-negotiators may be more skillful than poorly trained executive-negotiators. Nevertheless, the business executive may be presumed to be less distracted by the shadow the law casts over the dispute; the executive will look at the complete business picture, unconstrained by the narrow parameters imposed by legal doctrine.

Third, direct involvement by the client can obviate or minimize difficulties arising from the self-interest of lawyers. This point may be particularly instructive for judges. By requiring clients to attend pretrial conferences, judges can be sure that the clients know and approve of the propositions their lawyers will assert in court on their behalf.

Fourth, ADR techniques and processes can be far more systematic than the horsetrading of conventional settlement negotiations. Settlement negotiations are often perceived as consisting of sharp tactics and bluff. "Unprincipled" negotiations occur in large part because the parties lack a means of communicating with each other. ADR processes permit realistic assessments of whether offers and counteroffers are in good faith.

Fifth, properly designed ADR processes make it more likely that settlement decisions will be based on the merits of disputes. * * * [V]arious factors may contribute more or less to settlement. Delay in the judicial system tends to increase the likelihood of settlement by reducing the stakes in the case, in part because delay diminishes the present value of the ultimate award. Other factors include rules governing prejudgment interest and the availability of pretrial discovery. This analysis could lead the courts to advocate policies that would increase delay (or other costs of litigation) in order to prompt settlement. The resulting settlements would not necessarily be just, however, because they would not have taken account of power disparities. The party with the more meritorious claim might not prevail because he is too poor to amass the requisite evidence through the discovery process. Society may have the power to foster higher settlement rates by manipulating the factors that induce people to stay out of court, but many proponents of ADR would not view such policies as consonant with the ADR philosophy. A dispute should not merely be settled; it should be settled justly.

As a simple example of this difficulty, the divorce mediation model has lately come under attack from feminists and others precisely because in that model — where husband and wife are in a room with a mediator attempting to resolve their financial affairs and custody arrangements — neither participant has an attorney, and the spouse with superior knowledge and staying power will be able to force a better and possibly unjust settlement. Responsible proponents of ADR do not advocate settlement at any cost. The ADR processes now being implemented are designed to reflect the dual notion that settlements should be both just and efficient.

Finally, a sixth reason to think that ADR leads to "better" outcomes is that the use of private neutrals permits the parties to submit their dispute to one with greater expertise in their particular subject than does the luck of the draw in the courtroom. Many complex disputes involve data and concepts that lie beyond the knowledge of generalist judges (and of all juries). The ADR neutral can be selected for a particular expertise, thus saving the parties the cost of educating the fact-finder (and the risk of failing to do so). Moreover, if the parties have personally participated in selecting the neutral, they may be psychologically disposed to accept his statement of the case, whether it is a binding decision (as in arbitration) or an advisory opinion (as in a mini-trial).

Proponents of ADR suggest that its value lies in reducing the burden on courts and disputants. Alarmed at the ever-increasing numbers of cases filed, * * * [they] see arbitration and other practices as ways of removing large individual cases and even large classes of cases from the courts, thus removing a burden from the shoulders of judges (while shifting it to someone else). To the delight of their critics, they have occasionally forgotten that whether this change is beneficial depends on the relative justice and expense of dispositions through formal in-court adjudication and through less formal out-of-court methods of dispute resolution.

Critics of ADR, like Owen Fiss, suggest that ADR proponents mistake the function of courts as "mere" dispute resolvers. By diverting cases from courts, society loses the benefit of court-sanctioned judgments:

> The advocates of ADR are led . . . to exalt the idea of settlement more generally because they view adjudication as a process to resolve disputes. They act as though courts arose to resolve quarrels between

neighbors who had reached an impasse and turned to a stranger for help. Courts are seen as an institutionalization of the stranger and adjudication is viewed as the process by which the stranger exercises power . . . . The dispute-resolution story makes settlement appear as a perfect substitute for judgment . . . by trivializing the remedial dimensions of a lawsuit, and also by reducing the social function of the lawsuit to one of resolving private disputes: In that story, settlement appears to achieve exactly the same purpose as judgment--peace between the parties — but at considerably less expense to society.[36]

Fiss also argues that advocates of ADR have an unstated political agenda: to keep the activist state from meddling with powerful private economic interests. Finally, Fiss suggests that settlements lack the legitimacy of cases fully adjudicated to judgment.

Four responses to this critique are in order. One short answer to Fiss is that most ADR proponents make no claim for shunting all, or even most, litigation into alternative forums. The ADR movement of the 1980s does not suppose that every legal dispute has a non-judicial solution. Indeed, the ADR literature recognizes that some types of cases are not suited to resolution outside the courtroom, including particularly cases in which the plaintiff seeks a declaration of law by the court. Fiss overlooks this accepted limitation of ADR because he assumes, at least implicitly, that all cases resemble Brown v. Board of Education. But, of course, they do not. It seems obvious that large classes of cases are not so consequential, and do not call for the definitive ruling of a judge or the imprimatur of an official organ of the state. Automobile accidents, uncontested divorces, breaches of contract, and other common types of suits do not cry out to be memorialized in the official reports, and, in any event, most are settled far short of trial.

A second response to Fiss's critique is that his "conspiracy theory" of ADR is dubious. Many people who seek to use ADR are scarcely "powerful"' economic interests — ADR is not limited to adoption by Fortune 500 companies. Moreover, ADR does not dispense with community norms. All dispute resolution takes place with an eye toward existing alternatives — including litigation. Finally, the choice to employ ADR is made by parties who have determined that the injustice resulting from delay and the prohibitive costs of pursuing a case through the courts (direct expenditures for lawyers and expenses, as well as significant indirect expenditures, like lost opportunity costs) far outweigh any putative injustice stemming from the decision to forgo judgment by the court.

A third response to Fiss is that not all questions need to be answered. An open society needs the tension of open questions; parties who settle do not thereby foreclose answers at some later time when matters of principle are truly at stake and the issues cannot be compromised. Fiss agrees that avoidance has a value to society * * *. He questions, however, whether settlement will result in too much avoidance. But we know of no way to measure the appropriateness of

---

[36] Owen Fiss, Against Settlement, 93 YALE L.J. 1073, 1075, 1085 (1984).

avoidance. Furthermore, Fiss's concern is one sided. We should be equally concerned to prevent courts from rendering judgment when settlement is more appropriate.

Finally, Fiss's position is seriously weakened by his failure to offer proof that court judgments are more just. He says, for example, that "[a]djudication is more likely to do justice than conversation, mediation, arbitration, settlement, rent-a-judge, mini-trials, community moots or any other contrivance of ADR, precisely because it vests the power of the state in officials who act as trustees for the public, who are highly visible, and who are committed to reason."

Does ADR reach a just result or merely an expedient one? How can one measure the justice of a private settlement? The question is important, but it has not been well discussed in the ADR literature — no doubt because it is so difficult a proposition to test. Whatever the answer, it seems fair to ask the same questions of courts. In theory, courts are committed to reason, but in practice much stands in their way. Some judges are dispassionate and disinterested seekers after justice, but not all are. And all judges are busy; it is a fair assumption that they do not have sufficient time to devote to any single case. Moreover, the maneuvering of partisan lawyers alone is often enough to ensure that justice will not be done.

A perhaps more controversial response to Fiss's argument about the quality of outcomes is that in certain important classes of cases — cases involving public institutions like schools, hospitals, and prisons (the very cases that particularly interest Fiss) — courts themselves invoke processes that are firmly lodged in the ADR arsenal. Stories that describe litigation over unconstitutional prison conditions, inhumane mental hospital conditions, and segregated schools frequently depict the judge acting as mediator, helping the parties to negotiate the remedy the court will impose by consent decree. If the courts themselves find these processes useful or even necessary, chances are good that the same processes can be as beneficial when invoked outside the courts.

* * *

Harry T. Edwards, Alternative Dispute Resolution: Panacea or Anathema?[*]

99 Harv.L.Rev. 668, 676–682 (1986).

* * *

* * * In strictly private disputes, ADR mechanisms such as arbitration often are superior to adjudication. Disputes can be resolved by neutrals with substantive expertise, preferably chosen by the parties, and the substance of disputes can be examined without issue-obscuring procedural rules. Tens of thousands of cases are resolved this way each year by labor and commercial arbitration, and even more private disputes undoubtedly could be better resolved through ADR than by adjudication.

---

[*] Judge Edwards sits on the U.S. Court of Appeals for the District of Columbia Circuit and is a former distinguished law professor.

However, if ADR is extended to resolve difficult issues of constitutional or public law — making use of nonlegal values to resolve important social issues or allowing those the law seeks to regulate to delimit public rights and duties — there is real reason for concern. An oft-forgotten virtue of adjudication is that it ensures the proper resolution and application of public values. In our rush to embrace alternatives to litigation, we must be careful not to endanger what law has accomplished or to destroy this important function of formal adjudication. As Professor Fiss notes:

> Adjudication uses public resources, and employs not strangers chosen by the parties but public officials chosen by a process in which the public participates. These officials, liek members of the legislative and executive branches, possess a power that has been defined and conferred by public law, not by private agreement. Their job is not to maximize the ends of private parties, not simply to secure the peace, but to explicate and give force to the values embodied in authoritative texts such as the Constitution and statutes: to interpret those values and to bring reality in accord with them.[29]

The concern here is that ADR will replace the rule of law with nonlegal values. * * * [O]ften our nation's most basic values — such as equal justice under the law — conflict with local nonlegal mores. This was true in Boston during the school desegregation battle, and it was true in the South during the civil rights battles of the sixties. This conflict, however, between national public values reflected in rules of law and nonlegal values that might be embraced in alternative dispute resolution, exists in even more mundane public issues.

For example, many environmental disputes are now settled by negotiation and mediation instead of adjudication. * * * Yet, as necessary as environmental negotiation may be, it is still troubling. When Congress or a government agency has enacted strict environmental protection standards, negotiations that compromise these strict standards with weaker standards result in the application of values that are simply inconsistent with the rule of law. Furthermore, environmental mediation and negotiation present the danger that environmental standards will be set by private groups without the democratic checks of governmental institutions. * * *

* * * [T]he mere resolution of a dispute is not proof that the public interest has been served. This is not to say that private settlements can never produce results that are consistent with the public interest; rather, it is to say that private settlements are troubling when we have no assurance that the legislative- or agency-mandated standards have been followed, and when we have no satisfactory explanation as to why there may have been a variance from the rule of law.

* * * [For] example, we should be concerned if private negotiators settled * * * [an] environmental dispute without any meaningful input or participation from government regulators, or if the private parties negotiated a settlement at variance with the environmental standard that had been established by

---

[29] Fiss, Against Settlement, 93 YALE L.J. 1073, 1085 (1984).

government agencies. If, however, government agencies promulgated the governing environmental standards pursuant to legislatively established rulemaking procedures (which, of course, involve public participation), and if the private parties negotiated a settlement in accordance with these agency standards and subject to agency approval, then the ADR process may be seen to have worked well in conjunction with the rule of law. Indeed, the environmental negotiators may have facilitated the implementation of the rule of law by doing what agency regulators had been unable to achieve for seventeen years.

A subtle variation on this problem of private application of public standards is the acceptance by many ADR advocates of the "broken-telephone" theory of dispute resolution that suggests that disputes are simply "failures to communicate" and will therefore yield to repair service by the expert facilitator. * * *

* * * [M]utual understanding and good feeling among disputants obviously facilitates intelligent dispute resolution, but there are some disputes that cannot be resolved simply by mutual agreement and good faith. It is a fact of political life that many disputes reflect sharply contrasting views about fundamental public values that can never be eliminated by techniques that encourage disputants to 'understand' each other. Indeed, many disputants understand their opponents all too well. Those who view tobacco as an unacceptable health risk, for example, can never fully reconcile their differences with the tobacco industry, and we should not assume otherwise. One essential function of law is to reflect the public resolution of such irreconcilable differences; lawmakers are forced to choose among these differing visions of the public good. A potential danger of ADR is that disputants who seek only understanding and reconciliation may treat as irrelevant the choices made by our lawmakers and may, as a result, ignore public values reflected in rules of law.

We must also be concerned lest ADR becomes a tool for diminishing the judicial development of legal rights for the disadvantaged. * * * ADR may result in the reduction of possibilities for legal redress of wrongs suffered by the poor and underprivileged, in the name of increased access to justice and judicial efficiency. Inexpensive, expeditious, and informal adjudication is not always synonymous with fair and just adjudication. The decisionmakers may not understand the values at stake and parties to disputes do not always possess equal power and resources. Sometimes because of this inequality and sometimes because of deficiencies in informal processes lacking procedural protections, the use of alternative mechanisms will produce nothing more than inexpensive and ill-informed decisions. And these decisions may merely legitimate decisions made by the existing power structure within society. Additionally, by diverting particular types of cases away from adjudication, we may stifle the development of law in certain disfavored areas of law. Imagine, for example, the impoverished nature of civil rights law that would have resulted had all race discrimination cases in the sixties and seventies been mediated rather than adjudicated. The wholesale diversion of cases involving the legal rights of the poor may result in the definition of these rights by the powerful in our society rather than by the application of fundamental societal values reflected in the rule of law.

Family law offers one example of this concern that ADR will lead to "second-class justice." In the last ten years, women have belatedly gained many new rights, including new laws to protect battered women and new mechanisms to ensure the enforcement of child-support awards. There is a real danger, however, that these new rights will become simply a mirage if all "family law" disputes are blindly pushed into mediation. The issues presented extend beyond questions of unequal bargaining power. For example, battered women often need the batter ordered out of the home or arrested — goals fundamentally inconsistent with mediation.

Some forms of mediation, however, would protect the public values at stake. * * * [D]ivorce settlements can be mediated successfully despite disparities in bargaining power by requiring court review of settlements that deviate from a predefined norm. Additionally, some disputes that are not otherwise subject to court review also might be well suited for mediation. Many cases, however, may require nothing less than judicial resolution. At the very least we must carefully evaluate the appropriateness of ADR in the resolution of particular disputes.

Even with these concerns, however, there are a number of promising areas in which we might employ ADR in lieu of traditional litigation. Once a body of law is well developed, arbitration and other ADR mechanisms can be structured in such a way that public rights and duties would not be defined and delimited by private groups. The recent experience of labor arbitrators in the federal sector, who are required to police compliance with laws, rules, and regulations, suggests that the interpretation and application of law may not lie outside the competence of arbitrators. So long as we restrict arbitrators to the application of clearly defined rules of law, and strictly confine the articulation of public law to our courts, ADR can be an effective means of reducing mushrooming caseloads. Employment discrimination cases offer a promising example. Many employment discrimination cases are highly fact-bound and can be resolved by applying established principles of law. Others, however, present novel questions that should be resolved by a court. If the more routine cases could be certified to an effective alternative dispute resolution system that would have the authority to make some final determinations, the courts could devote greater attention to novel legal questions, and the overall efficiency of an anti-discrimination law might be enhanced.

In other areas, we could capitalize on the substantive expertise and standards developed by well-established ADR mechanisms. For example, * * * the qualities of labor arbitration that make it so successful in the context of collective bargaining are readily transferable to other fields of law. The presence of a skilled neutral with substantive expertise, the avoidance of issue-obscuring procedural rules, the arbitrator's freedom to exercise common sense, the selection of arbitrators by the parties, and the tradition of limited judicial review of arbitral decisions — factors that make arbitration superior to litigation in labor cases — would make arbitration superior to litigation in other contexts as well. * * * Perhaps arbitration could prove useful in moderating disagreements between citizens, in resolving grievances of citizens against social service agencies, and in resolving complaints of prisoners over conditions of confinement.

Finally, there are some disputes in which community values — coupled with the rule of law — may be a rich source of justice. Mediation of disputes between parents and schools about special education programs for handicapped children has been very successful. A majority of disputes have been settled by mediation, and parents are generally positive about both the outcome and the process. At issue in these mediations is the appropriate education for a child, a matter best resolved by parents and educators — not courts. Similarly, many landlord-tenant disputes can ultimately be resolved only by negotiation. Most tenant "rights" are merely procedural rather than substantive. Yet tenants desire substantive improvement in housing conditions or assurances that they will not be evicted. Mediation of landlord-tenant disputes, therefore, can be very successful — often more successful than adjudication — because both parties have much to gain by agreement.

In both of these examples, however, the option of ultimate resort to adjudication is essential. It is only because handicapped children have a statutory right to education that parent-school mediation is successful. It is only because tenants have procedural rights that landlords will bargain at all.

ADR can thus play a vital role in constructing a judicial system that is both more manageable and more responsive to the needs of our citizens. It is essential * * * that this role of ADR be strictly limited to prevent the resolution of important constitutional and public law issues by ADR mechanisms that are independent of our courts. * * *

NOTES AND PROBLEMS FOR DISCUSSION

1. Although the preceding two articles reflect differing evaluations of the overall efficacy of ADR devices, the authors of both of these publications recognize that the various non-litigative approaches to conflict resolution do provide advantages to claimants with, at least, certain categories of disputes. How would you balance the interests in efficiency and enhanced access against the desire to define, proclaim and respect legal and nonlegal public values?

2. Notwithstanding the concern articulated by Judge Edwards and others with respect to the use of ADR mechanisms for the resolution of disputes involving public values, employers are increasingly requiring their employees to agree to arbitrate disputes that raise both contractual and statutory issues. This is especially prevalent in the employment context, where disputes frequently involve claims that the employer has violated both the substantive terms of the employment contract as well as the provisions of a federal antidiscrimination statute. For example, suppose an employee alleges that she was denied a promotion because of her gender. Since most employers have implemented policies guaranteeing equal employment opportunity to all employees and job applicants, this individual could assert both a breach of contract claim and a cause of action under the Title VII of the federal Civil Rights Act of 1964. If, however, the employee is subject to either an individually or collectively bargained agreement requiring all employment disputes, whether contractual or statutory in origin, to be submitted to final and binding arbitration, should the individual be found to have forfeited her right to judicial resolution of her statutory claim?

Over the past decade, employers seeking to reap the benefits of speed and reduced expense associated with arbitration, as well as to avoid the impact of a judicial decision maker, have sought to funnel all employment-related disputes, including both contractual and statutory claims, to the arbitral forum. Ultimately, the courts had to confront the difficult question of whether an employee covered by such an arbitration agreement should be required to submit a statutory dispute to arbitration, thereby foregoing judicial resolution of that claim. Again, the question is not whether the employee has waived her statutory rights but, rather, whether the enforcement of those rights should be in the hands of a judge or an arbitrator.

In 1925, Congress passed The Federal Arbitration Act (FAA), which reversed the common law rule against the enforcement of arbitration agreements that American courts had inherited from their English forbearers and placed arbitration agreements upon the same footing as other contracts. The statute provides that written arbitration agreements in any maritime transaction or contract evidencing a transaction involving commerce shall be enforceable, subject to legal or equitable grounds for the revocation of that contract. It also created an exemption for employment contracts applicable to workers engaged in foreign or interstate commerce. Does the FAA mandate the enforcement of arbitration clauses, including those that cover statutory claims?

In ALEXANDER v. GARDNER-DENVER CO., 415 U.S. 36, 94 S.Ct. 1011, 39 L.Ed.2d 147 (1974), the Court held that an employee who had arbitrated a grievance pursuant to an arbitration clause contained in a collectively bargained agreement was not precluded from subsequently bringing a Title VII action based on the conduct that was the subject of the grievance. The court noted that the employee's contractual rights under the collective bargaining agreement were distinct from his statutory Title VII rights and that the arbitrator's role was to effectuate the intent of the parties as expressed in the collective bargaining agreement, and not to enforce public laws. The Court also determined that there was no suggestion in the statutory scheme that a prior arbitral decision either foreclosed an individual's right to sue or divested federal courts of jurisdiction.

Seventeen years later, the Supreme Court addressed the enforceability of an arbitration agreement in the non-union context. In GILMER v. INTERSTATE/JOHNSON LANE CORP., 500 U.S. 20, 111 S.Ct. 1647, 114 L.Ed.2d 26 (1991), the plaintiff stockbroker was required as part of his employment to register with several stock exchanges. A rule of one of the exchanges required the arbitration of any controversy between the employee and his employer arising out of termination of employment. After his discharge, the plaintiff filed an ADEA charge with the EEOC and subsequently brought suit against his former employer. The employer, relying on the arbitration agreement and upon the FAA, moved to compel arbitration of the ADEA claim. The district court denied the motion on the ground that Congress had intended in the ADEA to protect claimants from the waiver of a judicial forum. The Supreme Court disagreed.

The Supreme Court held that the FAA was applicable to statutory discrimination claims and that plaintiff had failed to demonstrate that Congress intended to preclude arbitration of claims made under the ADEA. Nothing in the text or legislative history of the Act precluded arbitration, the Court reasoned, and arbitration was not inherently inconsistent with the statutory framework and purposes of the ADEA. The Court also emphasized that by agreeing to to arbitrate statutory claims, the employee did not waive his substantive rights, he only agreed to submit their resolution to an arbitrator rather than a judge. And, it continued, "so long as the prospective litigant effectively may vindicate his statutory cause of action in the arbitral forum, the statute will continue to serve both its remedial and deterrent function." 500 U.S. at 28, 111 S.Ct. at 1653. *Gardner-Denver* was distinguished on several grounds. First, the arbitration agreement in that case was intended to cover only contractual claims. Second, in *Gardner-Denver* the agreement was contained in a collectively bargained agreement that also provided that employees would be represented in the arbitration by their union. Finally, *Gardner-Denver* was not decided under the FAA, a statute designed to encourage federal enforcement of arbitration agreements.

Following the decision in *Gilmer*, the lower federal courts reconciled its ruling with that of *Garnder-Denver* by holding that arbitration clauses in *individual* employment contracts are at least presumptively enforceable under the FAA and, therefore, operate to foreclose the assertion of statutory claims. See, e.g., Cole v. Burns Int'l Sec. Services, 105 F.3d 1465 (D.C. Cir. 1997)(Title VII and §1981); Mattews v. Rollins Hudig Hall Co., 72 F.3d 50 (7th Cir. 1995)(ADEA and fraudulent inducement claims); and Willis v. Dean Witter Reynolds, Inc., 948 F.2d 305 (6th Cir. 1991)(Title VII). However, the fact that general arbitration clauses are presumptively enforceable does not mean that they will be enforced in every case. The courts have voided arbitration clauses where the terms are so one-sided that the agreement is deemed a contract of adhesion. Examples include where the employer retained complete discretion over arbitration rules, including an unlimited right to modify its procedures, Floss v. Ryan's Family Steak Houses, 211 F.3d 306 (6th Cir. 2000), and where the employer was not required to pay the full cost of the proceeding, including the arbitrator's fee, Shankle v. B-G Maint. Mgmt. of Colo., Inc., 163 F.3d 1230 (10th Cir. 1999).

The Court sidestepped its most recent opportunity to definitively rule on the enforceability of *collectively bargained* arbitration clauses intended to apply to statutory claims. In WRIGHT v. UNIVERSAL MARINE SERVICE CORP., 525 U.S. 70, 119 S.Ct. 391, 142 L.Ed.2d 361 (1998), the Supreme Court distinguished arbitration clauses in collective bargaining agreements from those contained in individual employment contracts but avoided the central question of whether a union can bargain away the rights of members to judicial resolution of statutory claims. Writing for a unanimous Court, Justice Scalia recognized the "tension" between *Gardner-Denver* and *Gilmer*, but concluded that it was unnecessary to decide whether *Gilmer* had so undermined *Gardner-Denver* that a union could waive employees' right to a judicial forum on statutory causes of action through a bargained-for arbitration clause. Instead, he focused exclusively on the preliminary question of whether the instant arbitration clause was, in fact, designed to cover statutory claims. He explained that the previously recognized general presumption of in favor of arbitration of labor disputes was intended to extend only to issues of contract interpretation. On the other hand, any contractual intention to extend arbitrability to statutory claims would have to be "clear and unmistakable." And since the language of the instant contract was highly ambiguous on this question (providing for arbitration of "matters under dispute"), the Court concluded that this standard had not been satisfied. Accordingly, having construed the arbitration provision in the collective agreement not to cover statutory claims, the Court did not have to reach the question of whether the FAA mandated the enforcement of that arbitration promise.

Subsequently, in CIRCUIT CITY STORES v. ADAMS, 532 U.S. 105, 121 S.Ct. 1302, 149 L.Ed.2d 234 (2001), the Court, by a 5-4 vote, construed the FAA exemption for employment contracts of employees "engaged in foreign or interstate commerce" only to exempt contracts of employment of transportation industry workers.

3. One of the basic concepts of contractual arbitration is that the arbitrator's decision — both as to facts and law — is final and binding upon the parties, even when the claimant asserts a statutory right. But while judicial review of arbitration awards is exceedingly circumscribed, it is not entirely nonexistent. The generally applied rule is that the arbitrator must act in "manifest disregard" of the applicable law in order for an award to be set aside. In DIRUSSA v. DEAN WITTER REYNOLDS, INC., 121 F.3d 818 (2d Cir. 1997), cert. denied, 522 U.S. 1049, 118 S.Ct. 695, 139 L.Ed.2d 639 (1998), the Second Circuit explained that to modify or vacate an award, a court must find both that the arbitrator refused to apply, or ignored, a governing principle of which it was aware, and which was well defined, explicit, and clearly applicable. Such an error, the court continued, must have been obvious and capable of being readily and instantly perceived by the average person qualified to serve as an arbitrator. Some courts, such as the Fifth Circuit apply an even more deferential version of the "manifest disregard" standard. See Williams v. Cigna Financial Advisors, Inc., 197 F.3d 752 (5th Cir. 1999), cert. denied, 529 U.S. 1099, 120 S.Ct. 1833 (2000)(arbitration award should be upheld unless it is manifest to the court that the arbitrator acted contrary to applicable law and when enforcing such an award would result in "significant injustice"). On the other hand, the D.C. Circuit has adopted a more aggressive approach towards protecting employee rights. It interprets the ruling in *Gilmer* as reflective of the Supreme Court's assumption that arbitration awards are subject to judicial review sufficiently rigorous to ensure compliance with statutory law. See Cole v. Burns Int'l Sec. Services, 105 F.3d 1465 (D.C. Cir. 1997).

4. Because arbitrators are perceived as generally not well equipped to decide public law issues, and because they are often tempted to decide cases by "splitting the difference" rather than purely on the merits, do you agree with the underlying notion in *Gilmer* that an employees can "vindicate his statutory cause of action in the arbitral forum"?

5. Consider how the following empirical evidence influences your assessment of the overall value of ADR.

Susan K. Gauvey, ADR's Integration in the Federal Court System[*]

34-APR Md. B.J. 36, 39-43 (2001).

* * *

In 1992, the Federal Judicial Center conducted a survey of United States district court judges that demonstrated their acceptance of ADR as an integral part of the federal judicial system. Eighty-six percent disagreed with the proposition that ADR should never be used in federal courts; 66 percent of judges disagreed with the proposition that courts should only resolve litigation through traditional procedures; and 56 percent said ADR should be used in federal courts because it produces a fairer outcome in some cases than traditional litigation.

* * *

In 1998, the Congress passed the Alternative Dispute Resolution Act of 1998 * * *. * * * The Act defines the ADR process as "any process or procedure, other than adjudication by a presiding judge in which a neutral third party participates to assist in the resolution of issues in controversy through processes such as early neutral evaluation, mediation, minitrial and arbitration." The Act requires that each district court authorize use of ADR in all civil actions and devise its own program to encourage and promote use of ADR. Each district court must provide at least one ADR modality, which may include mediation by magistrate judges. Arbitration is only voluntary and its use prohibited in cases involving constitutional rights brought under Section 1343 (civil rights jurisdiction), or where money damages are greater than $150,000.

* * *

Based on 1996 data, in the 94 districts in the United States judicial system, the most commonly used form of ADR is the judge-hosted settlement conference. See Elizabeth Plapinger & Donna Stienstra, ADR and Settlement in the Federal District Courts, a Sourcebook for Judges & Lawyers 100 (Federal Judicial Center 1996). Almost all ninety-four districts use judicial settlement conferences, approximately one third of which employ magistrate judges. Mediation has emerged as the second most dominant ADR technique in federal district courts, with 51 districts offering mediation. Most courts administer their own mediation programs while a few delegate the administration to bar groups or private ADR providers. In the vast majority of courts, parties must bear expenses of mediation. Twenty-two district courts offer arbitration, most of which are voluntary; 14 districts offer early neutral evaluation; three districts employ settlement weeks; and 48 districts offer summary jury trial. There is no data yet on the frequency of use of these types of ADR.

---

[*] Judge Gauvey is a Magistrate for the District Court for the District of Maryland.

* * *

* * * [S]tatistics demonstrate that an attempt at resolution through ADR prior to trial is more likely to occur now than in years past. If you compare the cases which went to trial in the months of September, October, and November of 1995 with the cases that went to trial in the same months in 1999, only 19 percent of the 1995 cases had settlement conferences while 42 percent of the 1999 cases had settlement conferences.

Use of ADR likewise has increased in the private sector. The American Arbitration Association, the oldest private ADR organization, has experienced steady growth in its arbitration and mediation services.

Year	Total AAA Caseloads
1956	2,817
1966	12,957
1976	35,156
1986	46,683
1994	59,424
1996	70,516

JAMS, another private ADR association, processed over 20,000 ADR cases in 1996.

* * *

As use of ADR in the private and judicial fora has increased, the rate of civil trials has fallen. Administrative Office of the United States Courts statistics show the civil trial rate is already low and has been steadily declining. The following chart shows the percentage of civil cases * * * resolved by trial.

Year	Civil Trial Rate
1970	7.5%
1975	8.4%
1980	6.5%
1985	4.7%
1990	4.2%
1991	3.7%
1992	3.5%
1993	3.4%
1994	3.5%
1995	3.2%
1996	3.0%
1997	3.0%
1998	2.6%
1999	2.3%
2000	2.3%

* * *

Several studies have assessed the effectiveness of different ADR techniques to see whether the goals of ADR of lower cost, quicker resolution and more satisfying resolution have been met.

The Federal Judicial Center examined the demonstration districts under the 1990 Civil Justice Reform Act. The Federal Judicial Center, Report to the Judicial Conference Committee on Court Administration and Case Management: A Study of the Five Demonstration Programs Established Under the Civil Justice Reform Act of 1990 16-24 (Donna Stienstra, Molly Johnson and Patricia Lombard eds. 1997). The Northern District of California used arbitration, mediation and early neutral evaluation. The Western District of Missouri had an early assessment program with random assignment of parties — one third of the parties to mandatory ADR, one third to voluntary ADR, and the final third of parties were ineligible for any ADR program. The Northern District of West Virginia used a settlement week program.

As to the pace of litigation, the findings of the survey showed that a greater percentage of attorneys rated ADR as moving litigation along than slowing litigation down by factor of at least three. As to costs, the survey revealed that a greater percentage of attorneys generally thought ADR decreased, rather than increased, costs by less than a factor of two, except in the Western District of Missouri. In most cases, the mean savings per case was thought to be between $12,000 and $43,000. The disposition time in those cases required to participate in ADR in the Western District of Missouri decreased by more than two months; the median age of a case at termination was seven months as opposed to 9.7 months where there was no ADR participation. In the other two demonstration districts, there was no evidence of an increase in disposition time, and a high percentage of attorneys (60 percent) perceived a decrease in disposition time in their cases. As to fairness, the findings showed that over 80% of the attorneys thought that ADR was very fair, fair or somewhat fair. Across these three ADR demonstration districts, attorneys identified four factors — the timing of the ADR session, client attendance, the quality of the neutral, and whether the case settled — as central to the effectiveness of the ADR.

Research surrounding court annexed non-binding arbitration has revealed that cases referred to arbitration typically settle before trial. In the Northern District of California, 94 percent of eligible cases were terminated without returning to the trial calendar, and 99 percent of eligible cases terminated short of trial. See B. Meierhoefer & C. Seron, Court-Annexed Arbitration in the Northern District of California 12 (Federal Judicial Center 1988). In the Eastern District of Pennsylvania, 90 percent of eligible cases were terminated without returning to the trial calendar, and 97 percent of eligible cases terminated short of trial. In the Western District of Oklahoma, 91 percent of eligible cases were terminated without returning to the trial calendar, and 98 percent of eligible cases terminated short of trial.

The RAND Institute for Civil Justice investigated mediation and early neutral evaluation in six pilot federal district courts and six comparison federal district courts. See James S. Kakalik et al., An Evaluation of Mediation and Early Neutral Evaluation Under the Civil Justice Reform Act, (1996) (hereinafter the "RAND Report"). The RAND Report concluded that there was no strong statistical evidence as to time to disposition or costs of litigation. Attorneys' views of fairness or satisfaction were not significantly affected, either positively or negatively. There was too small of a response from litigants to draw conclusions based on their views. The study did find that ADR programs appear to increase the fraction of cases with monetary settlement and that the participants in ADR programs were supportive of ADR in general and in their cases in particular.

In another RAND study, the focus was on the attitudes and perceptions of individual plaintiffs and defendants in relatively small personal injury tort claims in three state courts: the 19th Circuit Court in Fairfax County, VA; the Court of Common Pleas in Bucks County, PA; and the 7th Circuit Court in Prince George's County, MD. See E. Allan Lind et al., The Perception of Justice, Tort Litigants' Views of Trial, Court-Annexed Arbitration, and Judicial Settlement Conferences 29 (1989). Specifically, the study focused on tort litigants' perceptions of the civil justice system. The study compared trial, court-annexed arbitration, and judicial settlement conferences. By and large, arbitration hearings and trials were viewed more favorably than were settlement conferences. The settlement conferences studied, however, did not include participation of the parties. In particular, fairness judgments were strongly correlated with perceptions that procedures are unbiased and with the perceived dignity of the procedure, the perceived carefulness of the process, evaluations of counsel, comfort with the procedure, and perceived control over case events and outcomes. System satisfaction was strongly correlated with evaluations of counsel, the perceived dignity of the procedure, comfort with the procedure, perceptions that procedures are unbiased, perceived control, and the perceived carefulness of the process. Perceptions of fairness and satisfaction were not strongly related to the personal characteristics of the litigants. The data suggest that tort litigants do not view trials as lessening their involvement in the legal process, but rather as increasing their involvement.

The tort litigants studied appeared to want a dignified, careful, and unbiased hearing of their cases, and wanted to exercise some control over the handling of their cases and over the ultimate outcome of these cases. They wanted procedures with which they could feel comfortable, but this does not mean that they wanted less formal procedures. Informality did not make litigants either more or less comfortable. Surprisingly, there was little relation between litigants' judgments of fairness and satisfaction and the cost of the case or length of time to disposition.

* * *

SECTION C. THE FUTURE — CYBER-ADR?

Henry H. Perritt, Jr., Dispute Resolution in Cyberspace: Demand for New Forms of ADR

15 Ohio State Journal on Dispute Resolution 675,676,684-92,694,702 (2000).

The Internet has heightened interest in alternative dispute resolution (ADR). Three characteristics of the Internet make traditional dispute resolution through administrative agency and judicial procedures unsatisfactory for many controversies that arise in Internet-based commerce and political interaction. The Internet's low economic barriers to entry invite participation in commerce and politics by small entities and individuals who cannot afford direct participation in many traditional markets and political arenas. These low barriers to entry, and greater participation by individuals and small entities, also mean a greater incidence of small transactions. When dispute resolution costs are high, as they are for traditional administrative and judicial procedures, the transaction costs of dispute resolution threaten to swamp the value of the underlying transaction, meaning on the one hand that victims are less likely to seek vindication of their rights and, on the other hand, that actors and alleged wrongdoers may face litigation costs that outweigh the advantages of their offering goods and services in the new electronic markets. To realize the potential of participation by small entities and individuals and of small transactions, it is necessary to reduce the costs of dispute resolution.

Second, the geographic openness of electronic commerce makes stranger-to-stranger transactions more likely. The absence of informal means of developing trust, as when one shops regularly at the local bookstore, means that both merchants and consumers will be inhibited in engaging in commerce unless they have some recourse if the deal goes sour.

Third, the Internet is inherently global. Offering to sell goods on a web page published on a server physically located in Kansas is as visible to consumers in Kosovo as in Kansas. In other words, it is difficult to localize injury-producing conduct or the injury itself in Internet-based markets or political arenas. Traditional dispute resolution machinery depends upon localization to determine jurisdiction. Impediments to localization create uncertainty and controversy over assertions of jurisdiction. That uncertainty has two results. It may frustrate communities that resent being unable to reach through their legal machinery to protect local victims against conduct occurring in a far-off country. It also subjects anyone using the Internet to jurisdiction by any of nearly 200 countries in the world and, in many cases, to their subordinate political units.

Alternative dispute resolution, including not only arbitration and mediation but also a wider range of alternatives such as credit card chargebacks, escrow arrangements, complaint bulletin boards, and complaint aggregation services culminating in official enforcement activity, helps respond to these challenges in two ways. First, ADR can be designed to be much cheaper than traditional procedures. It also is inherently transnational when those agreeing to participate in the ADR process are in different countries.

Appropriately designed ADR mechanisms offer lower costs, reassure participants, and solve the jurisdictional problem because use of them manifests consent. As important, many forms of ADR involve a readily available fund (usually the payment for the disputed transaction) as a way of satisfying a decision for either disputant. The availability of a fund * * * may explain why intermediary-provided dispute resolution, such as credit card chargebacks and escrow arrangements, prove more attractive in practice than independent third-party mechanisms such as arbitration or mediation. The successful party to an arbitration still must be concerned about the enforceability of an arbitration award against a reluctant loser.

* * *

The Virtual Magistrate [VMAG] is an online arbitration system initially implemented in the fall of 1996. VMAG resulted from discussions organized * * * [by a group of individuals] concerned about the dilemma confronting online service providers such as America Online when they were accused of allowing access to illegal material, such as postings or e-mail messages that infringed copyright, invaded privacy, represented consumer fraud, or were defamatory. In such circumstances, the service provider could choose to remove the accused material, potentially exposing the service provider to liability in favor of the author or sponsor, or the provider could allow it to remain, resulting in potential liability to the accuser. Now, the Online Copyright Infringement Liability Limitation Act provides a safe harbor for service providers that implement detailed procedures for removing material. In 1996, however, no such statutory safe harbor existed. The designers of VMAG sought to provide a mechanism for a quick and inexpensive interlocutory dispute resolution mechanism to decide whether accused material should be removed immediately or should be allowed to remain.

While the design of VMAG may not have met all the requirements of the New York Convention or the Federal Arbitration Act, and thus * * * may not have the same preclusive effect as arbitration awards, VMAG designers nevertheless thought that the existence of an interlocutory decision by a third party would show that the service provider acted in good faith in dealing with accused material and that the decision would be given some weight by a court ultimately deciding the dispute on the merits, or that, at the least, it would avoid damages linked to bad faith or indifference

From the beginning, VMAG was implemented entirely through the World Wide Web, with e-mail communication as a backup. No aspect of the procedure involved paper submissions or reports or face-to-face contact. Disputes were handled pursuant to procedural rules posted on the VMAG website. A complainant could initiate a VMAG case by clicking on an e-mail button on the website to post a complaint. Complaints thus posted initially were screened by an AAA [American Arbitration Association] staff member who determined whether the complaint facially was within the jurisdiction of VMAG. An affirmative determination resulted in the AAA staff member selecting a virtual magistrate from a roster maintained by the AAA. One could be listed on the roster by qualifying under general AAA rules to be an arbitrator and also demonstrating familiarity with Internet technology.

Once a virtual magistrate was selected, the magistrate would forward the complaint to the respondent and any affected third parties, such as an online service provider or the originator of the accused material. Respondents were given several hours to respond through the website. The virtual magistrate then was obligated to make a decision within seventy-two hours. Until a decision was made, the record of the proceedings was not open to the public, but a decision triggered an automatic routine that moved the complaint, the response, the decision, and other pertinent materials to a part of the website open to the public. In the first two years of VMAG's existence, only one case was decided. Several dozen other complaints were submitted, however, and a few of these resulted in settlements. Most of the others were determined to be outside the scope of VMAG jurisdiction.

* * *

The features of VMAG represent a logical use of the Internet and the Web for alternative dispute resolution involving relatively simple disputes. The initial rules confine the dispute resolution system to a very narrow set of cases, resulting in the rejection of a number of complaints in the early years of the system's operation. Even after the rules were modified to expand the scope of VMAG jurisdiction, however, few complaints were filed and no additional disputes were decided.

* * *

One reason for VMAG's limited popularity is that initial predictions that online service providers would refer large numbers of cases to VMAG proved to be wrong. America Online in particular, which was a strong original proponent of developing the VMAG system, found that its own internal terms-of-service complaint mechanisms resolved most controversies successfully and that the feared exposure to conflicting liability before outside fora did not materialize. Keeping complaints within the internal system gave AOL and other service providers complete control over the outcome of the complaint process. Referring the complaints to VMAG would result in loss of control. Also, the failure of significant numbers of complainants to submit disputes to VMAG is likely due to the fact they did not know about VMAG — at least they had no easy way to file a complaint with VMAG, as contrasted with filing complaints with service providers directly or in other fora.

Two conclusions can be drawn from the VMAG experience, both applicable to online dispute resolution systems in general. First, proponents of online ADR must recognize that whoever has superior economic power in a dispute is unlikely to be eager to surrender that power to a third party decisionmaker. Nonunion employers have not embraced arbitration of employment disputes even though arbitration might protect them from lawsuits in regular judicial fora. * * * The fact is, most complaints about online services are resolved through complaint mechanisms such as AOL's term-of-service procedure or credit card chargeback mechanisms. One may be skeptical of the fairness of such mechanisms, either because decisionmakers have an economic interest in particular outcomes or because the process does not result in a binding resolution of the dispute. Nevertheless, complainants stop with these procedures in the vast majority of cases rather than going on to file lawsuits or complaints with administrative agencies. Thus, the purported benefit of online arbitration is modest.

Second, online dispute resolution procedures must be easy to find and easy to access, preferably by a link directly on the site where the controversy arises. For example, one wishing to submit a complaint about noncompliance with voluntarily adopted privacy policies is far less likely to submit that complaint to an unfamiliar online dispute resolution process that is not linked directly to the offending site. The complainant must look for and find the dispute resolution procedure and then cannot have any confidence that the dispute resolution forum will have jurisdiction over the complaint, in the sense that any meaningful relief can be obtained. On the other hand, if the site at which the controversy arises has a link to the dispute resolution site, and if the site in controversy represents that it will accept and be bound by a decision of the dispute resolution forum, complainants are more likely to make use of that dispute resolution machinery.

Shortly after VMAG was launched, * * * the University of Massachusetts launched a virtual mediation system * * * as a mechanism for resolving student complaints under University rules * * *.

* * *

The University of Massachusetts's virtual mediation project was much more active than VMAG. Some of this is attributable to its association with an institution that referred large numbers of complaints. Some of it is attributable to more effective marketing. Some of it may be attributable to the superiority of mediation to arbitration as an online dispute resolution process, although this conclusion is hard to justify given the absence of any real experience with disputants who made it as far as arbitration and somehow found that procedure unsatisfactory.

The most common form of alternative dispute resolution for consumer disputes is a credit card chargeback. Under the Fair Credit Billing Act, credit card issuers must investigate cardholder claims of billing errors. * * * When cardholders allege * * * nonacceptance or nondelivery, the card issuer may not insist on the charge without determining "that such goods were actually delivered, mailed, or otherwise sent to the obligor and provid[ing] the obligor with a statement of such determination."

* * *

Card issuers typically retain only limited authority — defined by the merchant and cardholder agreements — actually to adjudicate the dispute * * *. In most cases, the cardholder protests the charge, a chargeback results, the merchant substantiates the charge, informal negotiation directly between merchant and cardholder may ensue, and the charge is reinstated.

Although good empirical data is lacking, it appears that the system satisfies both consumers and merchants. Almost no reported cases in the regular courts exist, suggesting that consumers rarely are motivated to go beyond the chargeback process to more formal forms of dispute resolution. * * * Several hypotheses can be offered as to why it works so well. Chargebacks give customers leverage with merchants against whom they have claims, thus equalizing to some extent otherwise disparate bargaining power. Psychological satisfaction results from triggering a chargeback even if the customer eventually has to pay the full price. In at least some cases, triggering a chargeback gets the merchant's attention, allowing the merchant and the consumer to work out a compromise. And, in extreme cases, there is the possibility that the consumer will not have to pay or that the merchant will be excluded from the credit card network, ending a pattern of consumer abuse. Moreover, the system is cheap, easily accessible, and quick. A consumer need not search for and find a lawyer or a third-party dispute resolution forum. All that is necessary upon receiving a monthly credit card statement is to call or write the card issuer and protest the charge. The card issuer and the merchant handle the rest. No dispute resolution fees are involved.

* * *

EBay is a Web-based auction service popular with individuals and small businesses wishing to buy and sell merchandise and services. Apparently because eBay fears that people will stop using its service because of threats of fraud and nonperformance of agreements, it offers several mechanisms for avoiding or resolving disputes. One mechanism is iEscrow, which allows purchasers to escrow their payments until they accept delivered merchandise. * * * EBay also offers a complaint mechanism and feedback and evaluation of buyers and sellers. The combination of these services permits an unsophisticated user to assess, in advance, whether it wishes to deal with another unsophisticated user based on that user's reputation in the eBay community. Then, if a complaint arises, the victim can enlist eBay in attempting to resolve the dispute. Ultimately, eBay commits only to refer serious complaints to public authorities. This is an obvious example of traditional law backing up a private dispute resolution mechanism.

* * *

"Build it and they will come" is an aphorism clearly unwarranted for online dispute resolution. There is no empirical support for the proposition that persons or institutions involved in cyberspace disputes or other disputes readily embrace unfamiliar forms of dispute resolution. Rather, the growing use of alternative dispute resolution almost always is associated with explicit linkage of ADR to or by one of the disputing parties, as through arbitration or mediation provisions in terms-of-service or sales contracts, or by the annexation of ADR procedures to well-known court systems, as in the case of court-annexed arbitration or family court mediation and conciliation procedures.

* * *

INDEX

References are to Pages